Advanced AutoCAD 2023
A Problem-Solving Approach
(3D and Advanced)

26th Edition

CADCIM Technologies
525 St. Andrews Drive
Schererville, IN 46375, USA
(www.cadcim.com)

Contributing Author
Sham Tickoo
Professor
Department of Mechanical Engineering Technology
Purdue University Northwest
Hammond, Indiana, USA

CADCIM Technologies

Advanced AutoCAD 2023: A Problem-Solving Approach, 3D and Advanced, 26th Edition
Sham Tickoo

CADCIM Technologies
525 St Andrews Drive
Schererville, Indiana 46375, USA
www.cadcim.com

ISBN 978-1-64057-156-3

www.cadcim.com

DEDICATION

*To teachers, who make it possible to disseminate knowledge
to enlighten the young and curious minds
of our future generations*

*To students, who are dedicated to learning new technologies
and making the world a better place to live in*

SPECIAL RECOGNITION

*A special thanks to Mr. Denis Cadu and the ADN team of Autodesk Inc.
for their valuable support and professional guidance to
procure the software for writing this textbook*

THANKS

*To the faculty and students of the MET department of
Purdue University Northwest for their cooperation*

To employees of CADCIM Technologies for their valuable help

Online Training Program Offered by CADCIM Technologies

CADCIM Technologies provides effective and affordable virtual online training on various software packages including Computer Aided Design, Manufacturing and Engineering (CAD/CAM/CAE), computer programming languages, animation, architecture, and GIS. The training is delivered 'live' via Internet at any time, any place, and at any pace to individuals as well as the students of colleges, universities, and CAD/CAM/CAE training centers. The main features of this program are:

Training for Students and Companies in a Classroom Setting

Highly experienced instructors and qualified engineers at CADCIM Technologies conduct the classes under the guidance of Prof. Sham Tickoo of Purdue University Northwest, USA. This team has authored several textbooks that are rated "one of the best" in their categories and are used in various colleges, universities, and training centers in North America, Europe, and in other parts of the world.

Training for Individuals

CADCIM Technologies with its cost effective and time saving initiative strives to deliver the training in the comfort of your home or work place, thereby relieving you from the hassles of traveling to training centers.

Training Offered on Software Packages

CADCIM provides basic and advanced training on the following software packages:

***CAD/CAM/CAE**: CATIA, Pro/ENGINEER Wildfire, PTC Creo Parametric, Creo Direct, SOLIDWORKS, Autodesk Inventor, Solid Edge, NX, AutoCAD, AutoCAD LT, AutoCAD Plant 3D, Customizing AutoCAD, EdgeCAM, and ANSYS*

***Architecture and GIS**: Autodesk Revit (Architecture/Structure/MEP), AutoCAD Civil 3D, AutoCAD Map 3D, Navisworks, Primavera, and Bentley STAAD Pro*

***Animation and Styling**: Autodesk 3ds Max, Autodesk 3ds Max Design, Autodesk Maya, Autodesk Alias, The Foundry NukeX, MAXON CINEMA 4D, Adobe Flash, and Adobe Premiere*

***Computer Programming**: C++, VB.NET, Oracle, AJAX, and Java*

For more information, please visit the following link: ***https://www.cadcim.com***

Note

If you are a faculty member, you can register by clicking on the following link to access the teaching resources: ***https://www.cadcim.com/Registration.aspx***. The student resources are available at ***https://www.cadcim.com***. We also provide **Live Virtual Online Training** on various software packages. For more information, write us at ***sales@cadcim.com***.

Table of Contents

Chapter 5: Working with Data Exchange & Object Linking and Embedding

Chapter 6: The User Coordinate System

Chapter 7: Getting Started with 3D

Chapter 8: Creating Solid Models

Chapter 9: Editing 3D Objects-I

Chapter 11: Surface Modeling

Chapter 12: Mesh Modeling

Chapter 13: Rendering and Animating Designs

Chapter 14: Hyperlinks and 3D Printing

Chapter 15: Script Files and Slide Shows

Chapter 16: Creating Linetypes and Hatch Patterns

Chapter 17: Customizing the acad.pgp File

Chapter 18: Conventional Dimensioning and Projection Theory Using AutoCAD

Chapter 19: Isometric Drawings

PROJECT AVAILABLE FOR FREE DOWNLOAD

In this textbook, two projects have been given for free download. You can download these projects from our website ***www.cadcim.com***. To download these projects, follow the given path: *Textbooks > CAD/CAM > AutoCAD Advanced > Advanced AutoCAD 2023: A Problem-Solving Approach, 3D and Advanced > Projects for Free Download* and then click on required file.

Preface

AutoCAD 2023

AutoCAD, developed by Autodesk Inc., is the most popular PC-CAD system available in the market. Today, over 7 million people use AutoCAD and other AutoCAD-based design products. 100% of the Fortune 100 firms and 98% of the Fortune 500 firms are Autodesk customers. AutoCAD's open architecture allows third-party developers to write application software that has significantly added to its popularity. For example, the author of this book has developed a software package "**SMLayout**" for sheet metal products that generates a flat layout of various geometrical shapes such as transitions, intersections, cones, elbows, tank heads, and so on. Several companies in Canada and United States are using this software package with AutoCAD to design and manufacture various products. AutoCAD also facilitates customization that enables the users to increase their efficiency and improve their productivity.

The **Advanced AutoCAD 2023: A Problem-Solving Approach, 3D and Advanced** textbook contains detailed explanation of AutoCAD commands and their applications to solve design problems. Every AutoCAD command is thoroughly explained with the help of examples and illustrations. This makes it easy for the users to understand the functions and applications of the tools and commands.

After reading this textbook, you will be able to create 3D objects, apply materials to objects, generate drafting views of a model, create surface or mesh objects, and render and animate designs.

The book covers designing concepts in detail as well as provides elaborative description of technical drawing in AutoCAD including orthographic projections, dimensioning principles, sectioning, auxiliary views, and assembly drawings. While going through this textbook, you will discover some new unique applications of AutoCAD that will have a significant effect on your drawings and designs. In addition, you will be able to understand why AutoCAD has become such a popular software package and an international standard in PC-CAD.

Symbols Used in the Textbook

Note

The author has provided additional information to the users about the topic being discussed in the form of notes.

Tip

Special information and techniques are provided in the form of tips that will increase the efficiency of the users.

New

This symbol indicates that the command or tool being discussed is new.

Enhanced

This symbol indicates that the command or tool being discussed has been enhanced in AutoCAD 2023.

Formatting Conventions Used in the Textbook

Refer to the following list for the formatting conventions used in this textbook.

- Command names are capitalized and written in boldface letters.

  Example: The **MOVE** command

- A key icon appears when you have to respond by pressing the Enter or the Return key.

- Command sequences are indented. The responses are indicated in boldface. The directions are indicated in italics and the comments are enclosed in parentheses.

  Command: **MOVE**
  Select object: **G**
  Enter group name: *Enter a group name (the group name is group1)*

- The methods of invoking a tool/option from the **Ribbon**, **Menu Bar**, **Quick Access Toolbar**, **Tool Palettes**, **Application menu**, toolbars, Status Bar, and Command prompt are enclosed in a shaded box.

Ribbon:	Draw > Line
Menu Bar:	Draw > Line
Tool Palettes:	Draw > Line
Toolbar:	Draw > Line
Command:	LINE or L

Naming Conventions Used in the Textbook

Tool

If you click on an item in a toolbar or a panel of the **Ribbon** and a command is invoked to create/edit an object or perform some action, then that item is termed as **tool**, refer to Figure 1.

For example:
To Create: **Line** tool, **Circle** tool, **Extrude** tool
To Edit: **Fillet** tool, **Array** tool, **Stretch** tool
Action: **Zoom** tool, **Move** tool, **Copy** tool

If you click on an item in a toolbar or a panel of the **Ribbon** and a dialog box is invoked wherein you can set the properties to create/edit an object, then that item is also termed as **tool**, refer to Figure 1.

For example:
To Create: **Define Attributes** tool, **Create** tool, **Insert** tool
To Edit: **Edit Attributes** tool, **Block Editor** tool

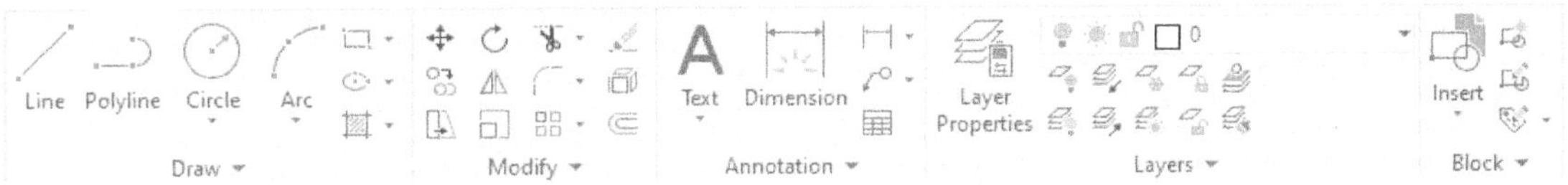

Figure 1** Various tools in the **Ribbon

Button

If you click on an item in a toolbar or a panel of the **Ribbon** and the display of the corresponding object is toggled on/off, then that item is termed as **Button**. For example, **Grid** button, **Snap** button, **Ortho** button, **Properties** button, **Tool Palettes** button, and so on; refer to Figure 2.

Figure 2** Various buttons displayed in the **Status Bar** and **Ribbon

The item in a dialog box that has a 3D shape like a button is also termed as **Button**. For example, **OK** button, **Cancel** button, **Apply** button, and so on.

Dialog Box

In this textbook, different terms are used for referring to the components of a dialog box. Refer to Figure 3 for the terminology used.

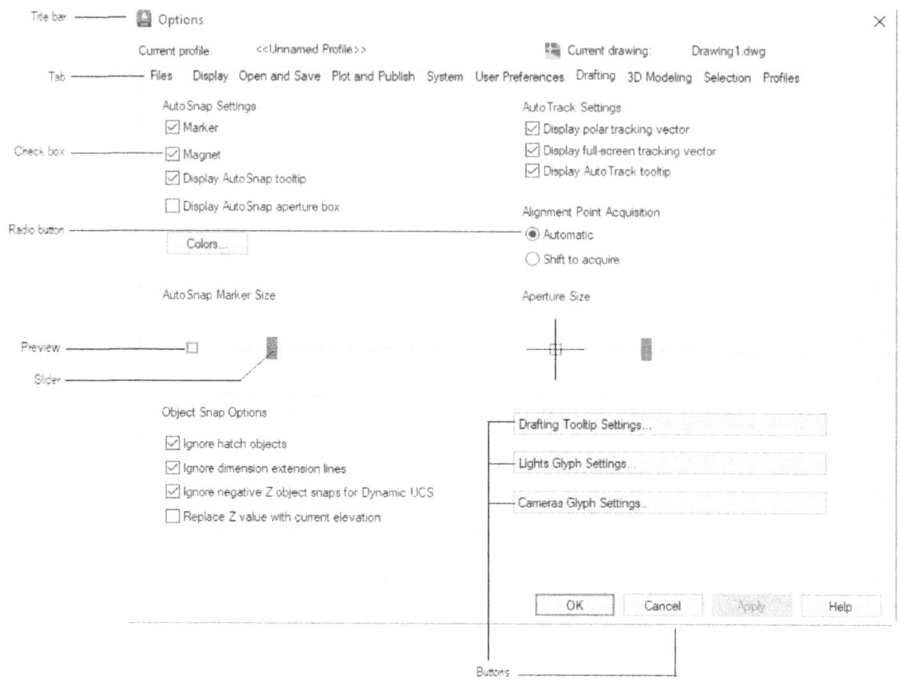

Figure 3 The components of a dialog box

Drop-down

A drop-down is the one in which a set of common tools are grouped together. You can identify a drop-down with a down arrow on it. These drop-downs are given a name based on the tools grouped in them. For example, **Circle** drop-down, **Fillet/Chamfer** drop-down, **Create Light** drop-down, and so on; refer to Figure 4.

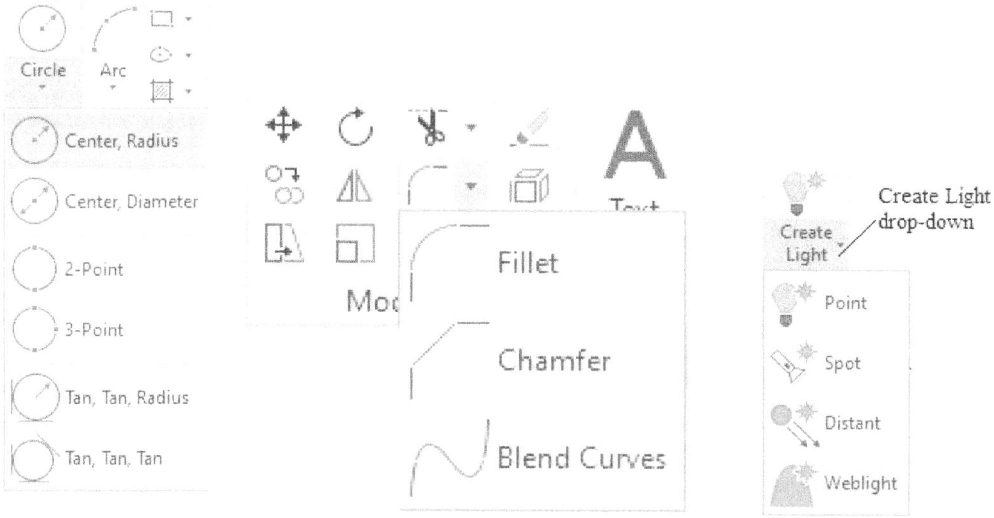

*Figure 4 The **Circle, Fillet/Chamfer**, and **Create Light** drop-downs*

Drop-down List

A drop-down list is the one in which a set of options are grouped together. You can set various parameters using these options. You can identify a drop-down list with a down arrow on it. To know the name of a drop-down list, move the cursor over it; its name will be displayed as a tool tip. For example, **Lineweight** drop-down list, **Linetype** drop-down list, **Object Color** drop-down list, **Visual Styles** drop-down list, and so on; refer to Figure 5.

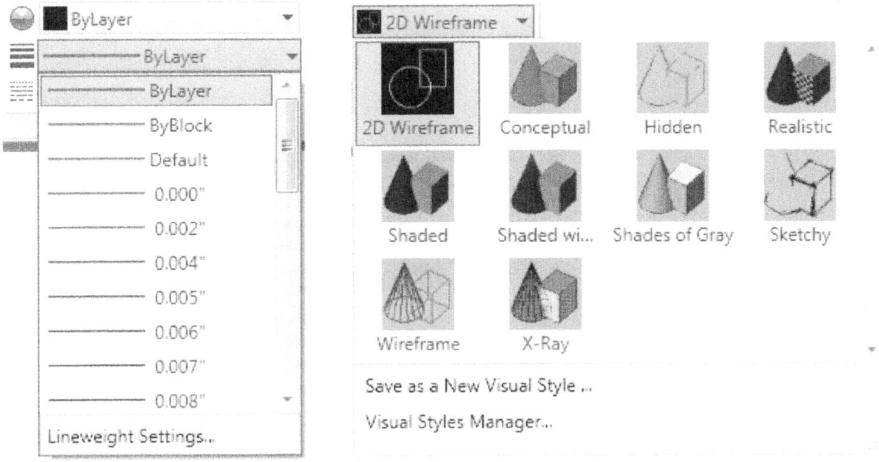

Figure 5 *The* ***Lineweight*** *and* ***Visual Styles*** *drop-down lists*

Options

Options are the items that are available in shortcut menu, drop-down list, Command prompt, **Properties** panel, and so on. For example, choose the **Properties** option from the shortcut menu displayed on right-clicking in the drawing area, refer to Figure 6.

Tools and Options in Menu Bar

A menu bar consists of both tools and options. As mentioned earlier, the term **tool** is used to create/edit something or to perform some action. For example, in Figure 7, the item Box has been used to create a box shaped surface, therefore it will be referred to as the **Box** tool.

Similarly, an option in the menu bar is the one that is used to set some parameters. For example, in Figure 7, the item Linetype has been used to set/load the linetype, therefore it will be referred to as an option.

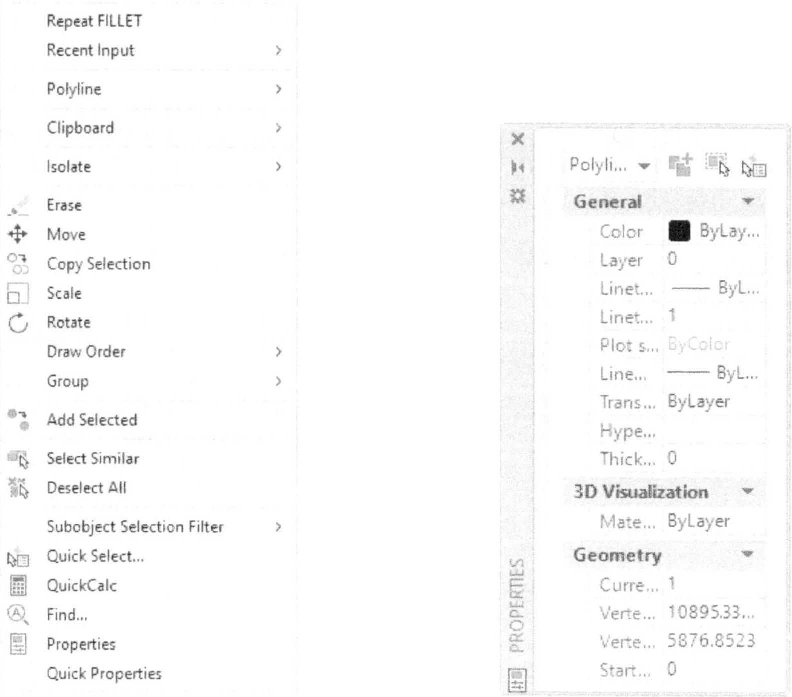

Figure 6 *Options in the shortcut menu and the* ***Properties*** *palette*

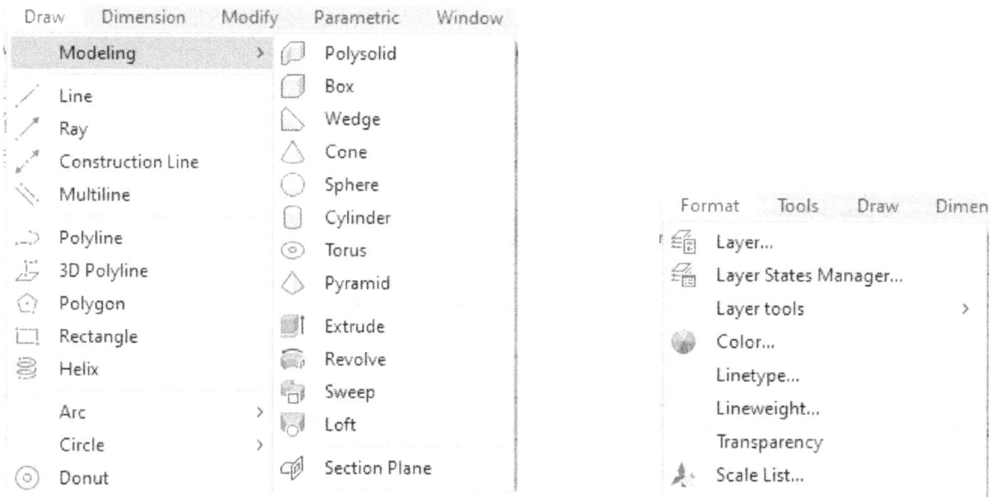

Figure 7 *Tools and options in the menu bar*

Free Companion Website

It has been our constant endeavor to provide you the best textbooks and services at affordable price. In this endeavor, we have come out with a Free Companion website that will facilitate the process of teaching and learning of AutoCAD 2023. If you purchase this textbook, you will get access to the files on the Companion website.

The following resources are available for the faculty and students in this website:

Faculty Resources

- **Technical Support**
  The faculty can get online technical support by contacting ***techsupport@cadcim.com***.

- **Instructor Guide**
  Solutions to all review questions and exercises in the textbook are provided in this guide to help the faculty members test the skills of the students.

- **Part Files**
  The part files used in illustrations, examples, and exercises are available for free download.

- **Drawing Files**
  The drawing files used in examples and exercises.

Student Resources

- **Technical Support**
  You can get online technical support by contacting ***techsupport@cadcim.com***.

- **Part Files**
  The part files used in illustrations and examples are available for free download.

You can access additional learning resources by visiting ***https://allaboutcadcam.blogspot.com***.

If you face any problem in accessing these files, please contact the publisher at ***sales@cadcim.com*** or the author at ***stickoo@pnw.edu*** or ***tickoo525@gmail.com***.

Video Courses

CADCIM offers video courses in CAD, CAE Simulation, BIM, Civil/GIS, and Animation domains on various e-Learning/Video platforms. To enroll for the video courses, please visit the CADCIM website using the following link: ***https://www.cadcim.com/video-courses***

Stay Connected

You can now stay connected with us through Facebook and Twitter to get the latest information about our textbooks, videos, and teaching/learning resources. To stay informed of such updates, follow us on Facebook (***www.facebook.com/cadcim***) and Twitter (***@cadcimtech***). You can also subscribe to our You Tube channel (***www.youtube.com/cadcimtech***) to get the information about our latest video tutorials.

This page is intentionally left blank

Chapter 1

Adding Constraints to Sketches

Learning Objectives

After completing this chapter, you will be able to:

- *Add geometric constraints to sketches*
- *Control the display of constraints*
- *Apply constraints automatically*
- *Apply dimensional constraints to sketches*
- *Convert a dimensional constraint into an annotational constraint*
- *Create expressions*

Key Terms

- *Horizontal*
- *Vertical*
- *Coincident*
- *Fix*
- *Collinear*
- *Parallel*
- *Concentric*
- *Tangent*
- *Symmetric*
- *Equal*
- *Smooth*
- *Infer Constraints*
- *Dimensional Constraints*
- *Annotational Constraints*
- *Dynamic Constraint Mode*
- *Annotational Constraint Mode*
- *Fully-Defined Sketch*
- *Under-Defined Sketch*
- *Over-Defined Sketch*
- *Parameters Manager*

INTRODUCTION

In AutoCAD, a wide set of tools are available that help you create parametric drawings. These tools are available in the **Parametric** tab of the **Ribbon** as well as in the **Parametric** toolbar. The parametric nature of a drawing implies that the shape and size of a geometry can be defined using standard properties or parameters. The main function of parametric property is to drive a new size or shape to the selected geometry without considering its original dimensions. Also, you can modify the shape and size of any entity of a sketch at any stage of the design process. This property makes the designing process very easy.

To make a drawing parametric, you need to apply constraints. When you apply constraints to sketches, it restricts their degrees of freedom, thereby making them stable. The stability ensures that the size, shape, and location of sketches do not change unexpectedly with respect to surroundings. You can apply two types of constraints to sketches, geometric and dimensional. Geometric constraints are applied between two entities in a sketch and they control the shape of a drawing, whereas dimensional constraints are applied to a single entity and they control the size of the object in a drawing. Remember that dimensions applied and dimensional constraints applied are two different things. You will learn about the difference in this chapter.

If you need to draw a sketch of parts such as bolt, nut, valves, and so on in which the size of one entity is driven by one basic dimension, then in AutoCAD, you can draw these parts quickly and easily using the **Parameters Manager**.

ADDING GEOMETRIC CONSTRAINTS

AutoCAD provides you with twelve types of geometric constraints. Usually, these constraints are applied between two entities in a sketch and control the shape of a drawing. However, there are constraints, such as Fix, that are applied to a single entity. Whenever you apply a geometric constraint between two entities, the entity that is selected last is affected. For example, if you apply the parallel constraint between two lines, the line selected second will orient toward the first line. It is recommended to first apply geometric constraints so that the shape of a sketched entity does not change on applying dimensional constraints. If the **Infer Constraints** button is chosen in the Status Bar, some of the geometric constraints are applied automatically while sketching or editing. For example, if you draw a horizontal line then the Horizontal constraint will be applied automatically and the corresponding constraint bar will be displayed above the line. In the following section, different geometric constraints and the procedure to apply them manually are discussed.

Applying the Horizontal Constraint

Ribbon: Parametric > Geometric > Horizontal **Command:** GEOMCONSTRAINT > H
Toolbar: Geometric Constraint >Horizontal or Parametric > Constraint drop-down > Horizontal
Menu Bar: Parametric > Geometric Constraints > Horizontal

The Horizontal constraint forces a selected line, polyline, or two points to become horizontal. To apply this constraint, choose the **Horizontal** tool from the **Geometric** panel of the **Parametric** tab of the **Ribbon**. The prompt sequence after choosing this tool is given next.

Select an object or [2Points] <2Points>: *Select a line or polyline.*

Remember that if you apply this constraint to a line on which no other constraint is applied, then the line will orient such that the endpoint nearer to the location you clicked on will become the fixed point and the other endpoint will become horizontal, thereby making the line horizontal.

If you need to make two points horizontal, press Enter when the **Select an object or [2Points] <2Points>** prompt is displayed. The following prompt sequence will be displayed:

Select an object or [2Points] <2Points>: Enter.
Select first point: *Select the first point.*
Select second point: *Select the second point.*

Note
*You can also apply constraints by entering **GEOMCONSTRAINT** at the command prompt.*

Applying the Vertical Constraint

Ribbon: Parametric > Geometric > Vertical **Command:** GEOMCONSTRAINT > V
Toolbar: Geometric Constraint > Vertical or Parametric > Constraint drop-down > Vertical
Menu Bar: Parametric > Geometric Constraints > Vertical

The Vertical constraint forces a selected line, polyline, or two points to become vertical. To apply this constraint, choose the **Vertical** tool from the **Geometric** panel of the **Parametric** tab. The prompt sequence after choosing this tool is given next.

Select an object or [2Points] <2Points>: *Select a line or polyline.*

Remember that if you apply this constraint to a line on which no other constraint is applied, then the line will orient such that the endpoint nearer to the location you clicked on will become the fixed point and the other endpoint will become vertical, thereby making the line vertical.

If you need to make two points vertical, press Enter when the **Select an object or [2Points] <2Points>** prompt is displayed. The following prompt sequence will be displayed:

Select an object or [2Points] <2Points>: Enter.
Select first point: *Select the first point.*
Select second point: *Select the second point.*

Note
On applying a constraint to an entity, the corresponding symbol is displayed near the entity, as shown in Figure 1-1. If you move the cursor over the symbol, the symbol will be highlighted and a cross mark (X) will be displayed. Click on the cross mark to hide the symbol. However, if you place the cursor on the entity on which a constraint has already been applied, a glyph will be displayed stating that a constraint is applied.

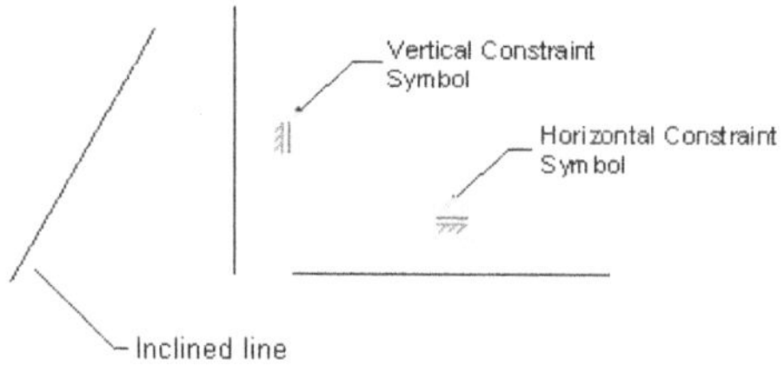

Figure 1-1 *The Vertical and Horizontal Constraint symbols*

Applying the Coincident Constraint

Ribbon: Parametric > Geometric > Coincident **Command:** GEOMCONSTRAINT > C
Toolbar: Geometric Constraint > Coincident or Parametric > Constraint drop-down > Coincident
Menu Bar: Parametric > Geometric Constraints > Coincident

The Coincident constraint forces a selected point or keypoint of an entity to be coincident with the point or keypoint of another entity. The entity selected can be a line, polyline, circle, an arc or ellipse. Similarly, the selected point can be a point, or keypoints such as an endpoint or midpoint of a line, an arc or a polyline, or the centerpoint of an arc, ellipse, or a circle. To apply this constraint, choose the **Coincident** tool from the **Geometric** panel of the **Parametric** tab; the cursor will be replaced by a selection box along with the coincident symbol. Also, you will be prompted to select first point. Move the cursor over an entity; the keypoint that is close to the cursor will be highlighted in red. Next, click to select it; you will be prompted to select the second point to be coincident with the first object. Select the keypoint of the second entity; the keypoint of the second entity will move and coincide with that of the first entity.

Even if you have drawn the complete sketch by snapping keypoints, the coincident constraint will not be applied automatically. To apply the coincident constraints at all intersections at the same time, invoke the **Coincident** tool. The command prompt sequence to apply the **Autoconstrain** is given next.

Select first point or [Object/Autoconstrain] <Object>: *A* Enter.
Select objects: *Select objects individually or by using the selection window:*
Select objects: *Select more objects or* Enter.

Note

The options to change the default settings for the ***Autoconstrain*** *option will be discussed later in this chapter.*

Applying the Fix Constraint

Ribbon: Parametric > Geometric > Fix **Command:** GEOMCONSTRAINT > F
Toolbar: Geometric Constraint > Fix or Parametric > Constraint drop-down > Fix
Menu Bar: Parametric > Geometric Constraints > Fix

The Fix constraint forces the selected entity to become fixed at a position. If you apply this constraint to a line or to an arc, its location will be fixed with respect to the selected keypoint. But you can change the size of the entity by dragging its endpoints. To apply the Fix constraint, choose the **Fix** tool from the **Geometric** panel of the **Parametric** tab; you will be prompted to select a point or an object. Next, move the cursor over the entity; the point closer to the cursor will be highlighted. Click to fix the highlighted keypoint. Now, you cannot move the fixed keypoint. However, you can drag and relocate other keypoints.

To fix all keypoints of an object, invoke the Fix constraint and press Enter when the **Select point or [Object] <Object>** command prompt is displayed; you will be prompted to select an object. Select the object; all its keypoints will be fixed.

Applying the Perpendicular Constraint

Ribbon: Parametric > Geometric > Perpendicular **Command:** GEOMCONSTRAINT > P
Toolbar: Geometric Constraint > Perpendicular or
Parametric > Constraint drop-down > Perpendicular
Menu Bar: Parametric > Geometric Constraints > Perpendicular

The Perpendicular constraint forces the selected lines to become perpendicular to each other. To apply this constraint, choose the **Perpendicular** tool from the **Geometric** panel; you will be prompted to select the first object. Select a line or a polyline; you will be prompted to select the second object. Select another line or a polyline. The object selected second will become perpendicular to the object selected first. Figure 1-2 shows two lines before and after applying the Perpendicular constraint.

Applying the Parallel Constraint

Ribbon: Parametric > Geometric > Parallel **Command:** GEOMCONSTRAINT > PA
Toolbar: Geometric Constraint > Parallel or Parametric > Constraint drop-down > Parallel
Menu Bar: Parametric > Geometric Constraints > Parallel

The Parallel constraint forces the selected lines to become parallel to each other. To apply this constraint, choose the **Parallel** tool from the **Geometric** panel; you will be prompted to select the first object. Select a line or a polyline; you will be prompted to select the second object. Select another line or a polyline; the object selected second will become parallel to the object selected first. Figure 1-3 shows two lines before and after applying the Parallel constraint.

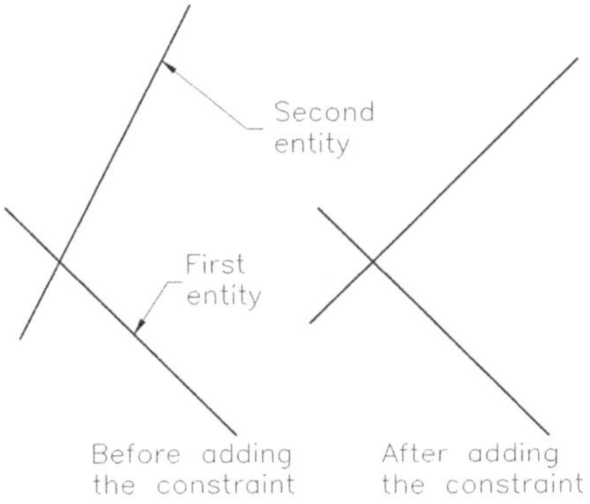

Figure 1-2 *Entities before and after applying the Perpendicular constraint*

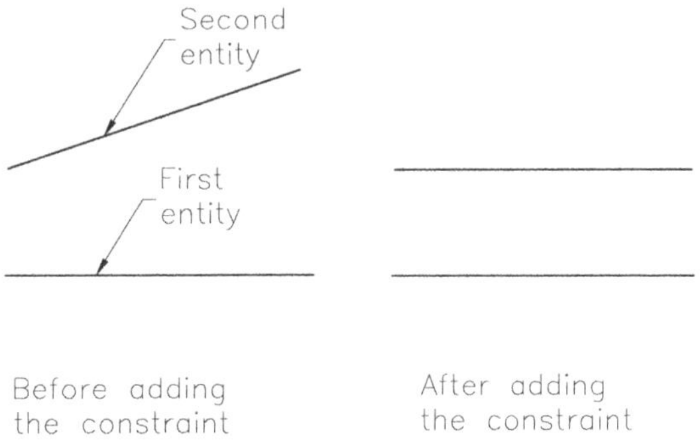

Figure 1-3 *Entities before and after applying the Parallel constraint*

Applying the Collinear Constraint

Ribbon: Parametric > Geometric > Collinear **Command:** GEOMCONSTRAINT > COL
Toolbar: Geometric Constraint > Collinear or Parametric > Constraint drop-down > Collinear
Menu Bar: Parametric > Geometric Constraints > Collinear

The Collinear constraint forces the selected lines to lie on the same infinite line. To apply this constraint, choose the **Collinear** tool from the **Geometric** panel; you will be prompted to select the first object. Select a line; you will be prompted to select the second object. Select another line; the line selected later will become collinear with the first line.

To apply the Collinear constraint to multiple lines, choose the **Collinear** tool; the **Select first object or [Multiple]** prompt will be displayed at the command prompt. Enter **M** and press Enter; you will be prompted to select the first object. Select a line; you will be prompted to select the second object. Select the lines that need to be made collinear with the line selected first and then press Enter; the selected lines will become collinear to the line selected first.

Applying the Concentric Constraint

Ribbon: Parametric > Geometric > Concentric **Command:** GEOMCONSTRAINT > CON
Toolbar: Geometric Constraint > Concentric or
Parametric > Constraint drop-down > Concentric
Menu Bar: Parametric > Geometric Constraints > Concentric

The Concentric constraint forces the selected arc or circle to share the center point of another arc, circle, or ellipse. To apply this constraint, choose the **Concentric** tool from the **Geometric** panel; you will be prompted to select the first object. Select an arc, ellipse, or a circle; you will be prompted to select the second object. Select another arc, ellipse, or circle; the object selected second will become concentric to the object selected first.

Applying the Tangent Constraint

Ribbon: Parametric > Geometric > Tangent **Command:** GEOMCONSTRAINT > T
Toolbar: Geometric Constraint > Tangent or Parametric > Constraint drop-down > Tangent
Menu Bar: Parametric > Geometric Constraints > Tangent

The Tangent constraint forces the selected arc, circle, spline, or ellipse to become tangent to another arc, circle, spline, ellipse, or line. To apply this constraint, choose the **Tangent** tool from the **Geometric** panel; you will be prompted to select the first object. Select an arc, circle, spline, line, or an ellipse; you will be prompted to select the second object. Select another arc, circle, spline, ellipse, or line; the object selected second will become tangent to the object selected first. Figure 1-4 shows a line and a circle before and after applying the Tangent constraint. Figure 1-5 shows two arcs before and after applying the Tangent constraint.

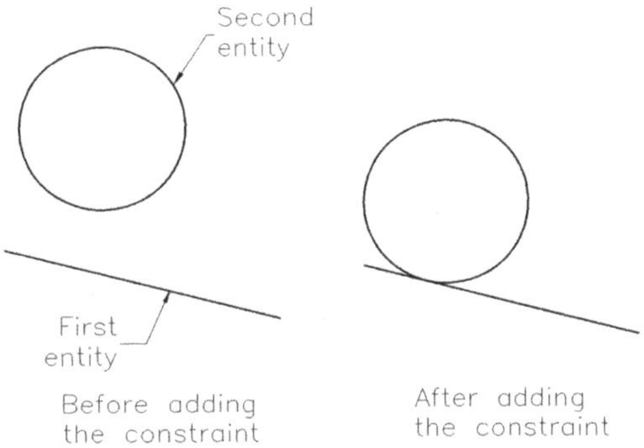

***Figure 1-4** A line and a circle before and after applying the Tangent constraint*

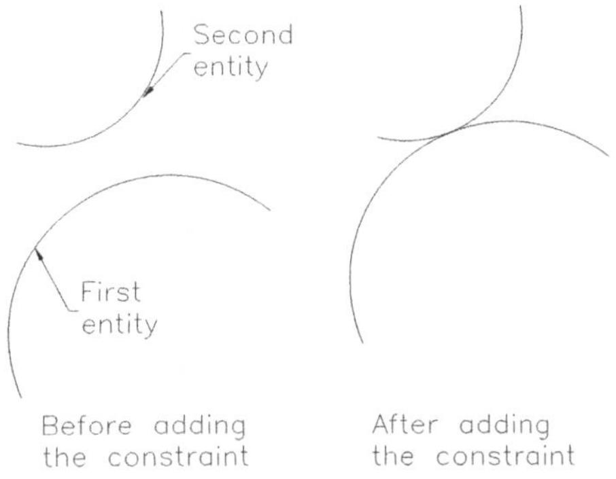

***Figure 1-5** Two arcs before and after applying the Tangent constraint*

Applying the Symmetric Constraint

Ribbon: Parametric > Geometric > Symmetric
Toolbar: Geometric Constraint > Symmetric or Parametric > Constraint drop-down > Symmetric
Menu Bar: Parametric > Geometric Constraints > Symmetric
Command: GEOMCONSTRAINT > S

The Symmetric constraint forces two selected lines, arcs, circles, or ellipses to remain equidistant from the centerline. To apply this constraint, choose the **Symmetric** tool from the **Geometric** panel; you will be prompted to select the first object or two points. Select an arc, an ellipse, a line, or a circle; you will be prompted to select the second object. Select another arc, ellipse, circle, or line; you will be prompted to select the symmetry line. Select a line; the selected objects will become symmetric with respect to the selected line. You can also make two points symmetric. To do so, press Enter at the **Select first object or (2 points)** command prompt. Next, select two points and the symmetric line; the selected points will become symmetric to the selected line.

Applying the Equal Constraint

Ribbon: Parametric > Geometric > Equal
Toolbar: Geometric Constraint > Equal or Parametric > Constraint drop-down > Equal
Menu Bar: Parametric > Geometric Constraints > Equal
Command: GEOMCONSTRAINT > E

The Equal constraint forces the selected lines or polylines to have equal length, or the selected circles, arcs, or an arc and a circle to have equal radii. To apply this constraint, choose the **Equal** tool from the **Geometric** panel; you will be prompted to select an object. Select the first object; you will be prompted to select the second object. Select another object; the size of the second object will become equal to that of the object selected first.

If you need to apply the equal constraint to multiple objects, choose the **Equal** tool from the **Geometric** panel; the Select first object or [Multiple] prompt will be displayed at the command prompt. Enter **M** and press Enter; you will be prompted to select the first object. Select an object; you will be prompted to select other objects. Select the other objects that need to be equal and press Enter; the size of the objects selected later will become equal to that of the object selected first.

Applying the Smooth Constraint

Ribbon: Parametric > Geometric > Smooth **Command:** GEOMCONSTRAINT > SM
Toolbar: Geometric Constraint > Smooth or Parametric > Constraint drop-down > Smooth
Menu Bar: Parametric > Geometric Constraints > Smooth

The Smooth constraint is used to apply curvature continuity between a spline and an entity connected together. The entities that can be connected to a spline include a line, spline, polyline, or an arc. To apply this constraint, choose the **Smooth** tool from the **Geometric** panel; you will be prompted to select the first object. Select a spline as the first object; you will be prompted to select the second object. Select another object; the smooth constraint will be applied between the selected objects.

CONTROLLING THE DISPLAY OF CONSTRAINTS

To control the display of the constraints, click on the inclined arrow in the **Geometric** panel of the **Parametric** tab; the **Constraint Settings** dialog box will be displayed, as shown in Figure 1-6. In this dialog box, the **Geometric** tab will be chosen and the check boxes of all constraints will be selected. Also, the **Show constraint bars after applying constraints to selected objects** check box will be selected by default. Therefore, on applying a constraint, a constraint bar will be displayed above the sketch and the symbol of that particular constraint will be displayed in the constraint bar by default. If you do not need any particular constraint symbol to be displayed then in the **Constraint bar display settings** area, clear the check box of the constraints that you do not want to be displayed. If you do not need the constraint bar to be displayed on applying the constraints, then clear the **Show constraint bars after applying constraints to selected objects** check box. However, if the **Show constraint bars when objects are selected** check box is selected, then the constraint bars will be displayed when you select an object. You can control the transparency of the constraint bars by setting the value in the **Constraint bar transparency** area of the **Constraint Settings** dialog box. In AutoCAD, you can apply the constraints while sketching or editing. To do so, select the **Infer geometric constraints** check box. You can also choose the **Infer Constraints** button from the Status Bar to apply constraints while sketching or editing. After specifying the parameters, choose the **OK** button to exit the dialog box.

On moving the cursor over a constraint bar, the constraint symbol and entities on which the constraint was applied will be highlighted. If multiple constraints are displayed in a sketch, it causes confusion. Therefore, you need to hide or display the constraint symbols. To hide a particular constraint, move the cursor over that constraint; the constraint bar will be highlighted and a cross-mark will be displayed on it. Click on the cross-mark to hide that constraint. To hide all constraints, choose the **Hide All** button in the **Geometric** panel. To display all hidden constraints, choose the **Show All** button from the **Geometric** panel. If you need to display constraints of a particular entity, choose the **Show/Hide** button from the **Geometric** panel; you will be prompted to select an entity. Select the entity from the drawing area and press Enter; a menu will be displayed and you will be prompted to select an option. Select the **Show** option; the constraints of that particular entity will be displayed. Remember that hiding a constraint does not delete that constraint. To delete a constraint, move the cursor over the constraint bar and press the Delete key. If you need to delete multiple applied constraints, choose the **Delete Constraints** button in the **Manage** panel of the **Parametric** tab of the **Ribbon**; you will be prompted to select entities. Select the entities individually or by using the selection box, and then press Enter; the constraints applied on the selected entities will be deleted.

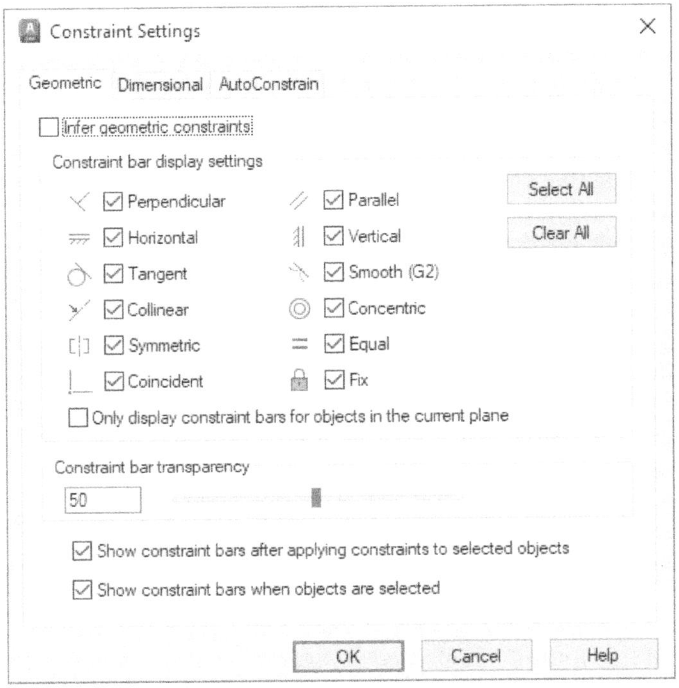

***Figure 1-6** The **Constraint Settings** dialog box with the **Geometric** tab chosen*

Tip

*If you move the cursor over a constraint bar and right-click, a shortcut menu will be displayed. Choose the corresponding option to delete or hide a constraint. Also, you can choose the **Constraint Bar Settings** option to display the **Constraint Settings** dialog box.*

Example 1

Draw the sketch shown in Figure 1-7 and apply appropriate constraints to it. Do not dimension the sketch.

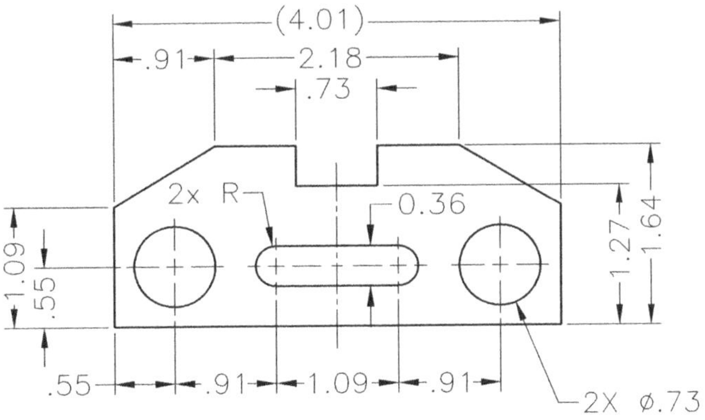

***Figure 1-7** Sketch for Example 1*

In this example, you will select the **Infer geometric constraints** check box and draw the sketch. Therefore, some of the constraints will be applied while sketching. Next, you will apply the constraints that are not applied automatically while sketching. First, you will create the outer loop of the sketch using the **Line** tool.

1. Start a new file with the *acad.dwt* template in the **Drafting & Annotation** workspace.

2. Ensure that the **Infer Constraints** button is chosen in the Status Bar. By using the **Line** tool, draw the outer profile similar to that shown in Figure 1-7. Make sure that the endpoints are snapped so that they form a closed sketch, as shown in Figure 1-8. Note that in your drawing, the constraints applied by default may be different from that shown in Figure 1-8, as it depends upon the start point and the procedure used to draw the lines.

   Next, you need to apply the constraints that are not applied by default. First, you will apply the Equal constraint.

3. Choose the **Equal** tool from the **Geometric** panel in the **Parametric** tab; the cursor changes to a selection box with the Equal constraint's symbol attached to it. Also, you are prompted to select the first object.

4. Select the vertical line on the left as the first object; you are prompted to select the second object.

5. Select the vertical line on the right as the second object; the equal constraint is applied and the constraint bar is displayed.

6. Similarly, apply the equal constraint between the two inclined lines, two small vertical lines, and two small horizontal lines. The sketch after applying all the constraints is shown in Figure 1-9.

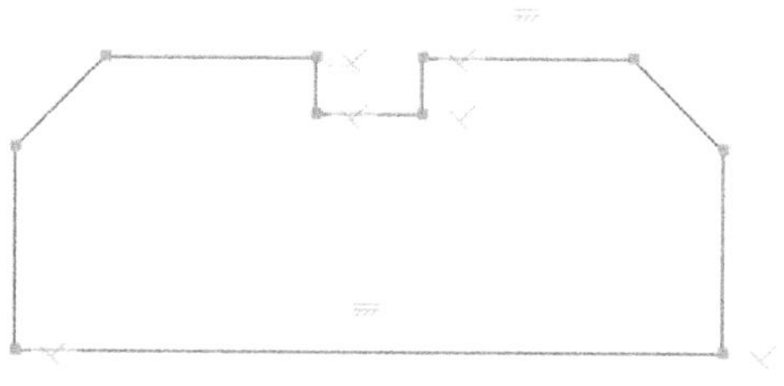

Figure 1-8 *Outer loop of the sketch*

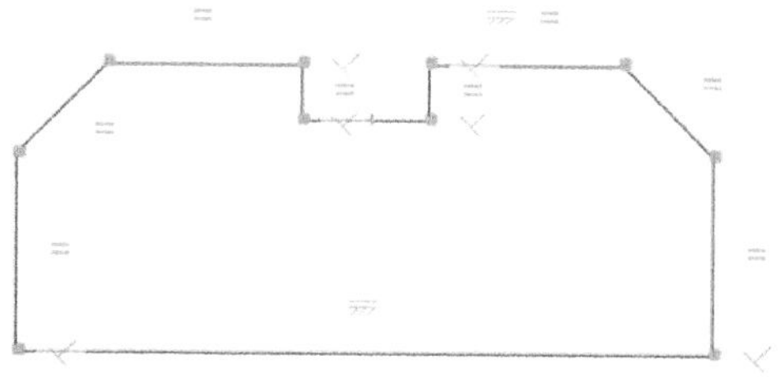

Figure 1-9 *Sketch after applying all constraints*

   Next, you need to apply the symmetric constraint between entities on either side of the centerline.

7. Choose the **Infer Constraints** button from the Status Bar to turn off the infer constraints.

8. Draw a vertical centerline that passes through the midpoint of the horizontal line at the bottom, as shown in Figure 1-10.

9. Choose the **Symmetric** tool from the **Geometric** panel; the cursor changes to a selection box with symmetric symbol attached to it. Also, you are prompted to select the first object.

10. Select the vertical line on the left as the first object; you are prompted to select the second object.

11. Select the vertical line on the right as the second object; you are prompted to select the symmetry line.

12. Select the centerline as the symmetry line; the vertical lines become symmetric to the centerline and the symmetric symbol is displayed, as shown in Figure 1-11. Note that in this figure, other constraints are hidden for clarity.

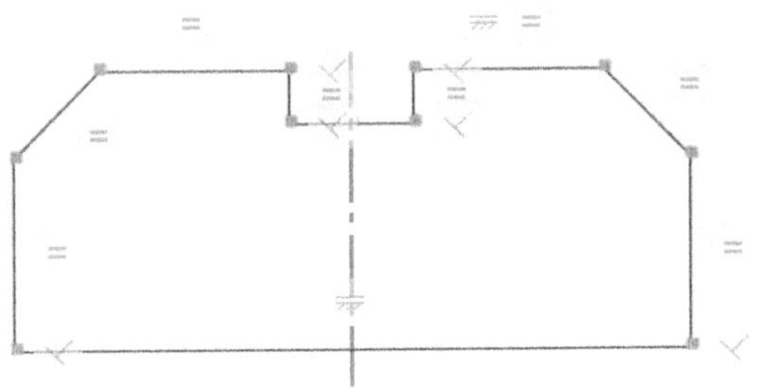

Figure 1-10 *Sketch after drawing the centerline*

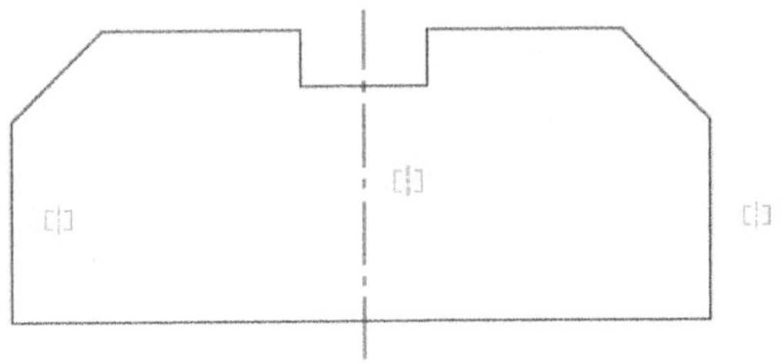

Figure 1-11 *The Symmetric constraint symbol*

13. Similarly, apply the symmetric constraints between the two inclined lines and then between the two small horizontal lines. The three symmetric constraints are applied as shown in Figure 1-12.

14. Choose the **Hide All** button from the **Parametric** tab of the **Geometric** panel to hide all constraint bars. Figure 1-13 shows the sketch after hiding all constraint bars.

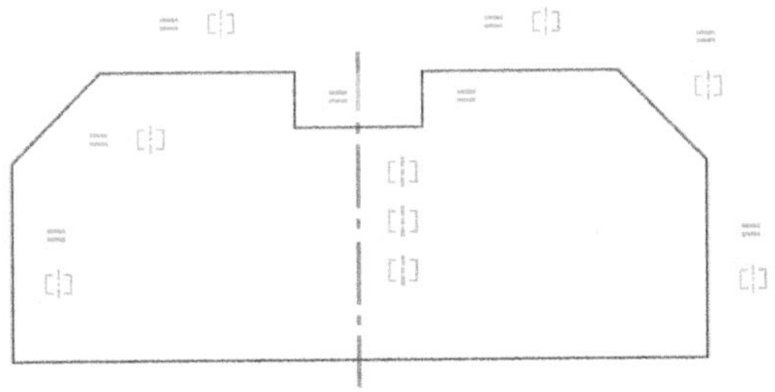

Figure 1-12 *Sketch with symmetric constraints*

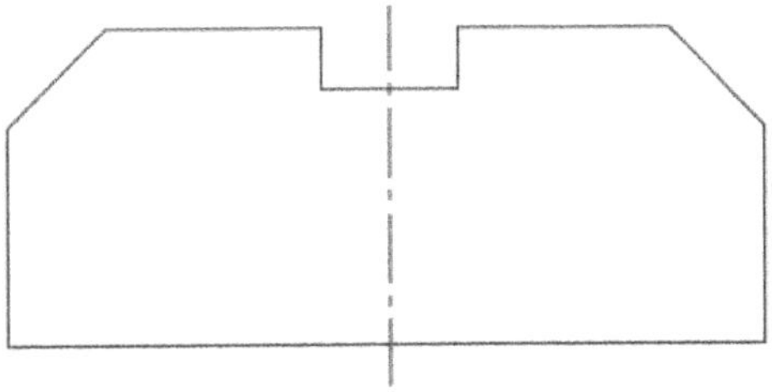

Figure 1-13 *Sketch after hiding all constraints*

Next, you need to create the inner loop using the **Arc**, **Circle**, and **Line** tools at an arbitrary location. But the profile should be similar to that given in Figure 1-7. Next, you need to apply the constraints.

15. Draw two circles of any radius inside the outer loop.

16. Choose the **Infer Constraints** button from the Status Bar to turn on the infer constraints.

17. Draw a slot using the **Center**, **Start**, **End** arc and **Line** tools. The sketch after drawing the circles and the slot is shown in Figure 1-14. You can also draw the profile of the slot using the **Polyline** tool. However, the sketch in this example has been drawn using the **Center**, **Start**, **End** arc and **Line** tools.

18. Apply the equal constraint first between two circles and then between two arcs.

19. Apply the symmetric constraint between the circles as well as between the arcs.

20. Choose the **Tangent** tool from the **Geometric** panel; the cursor changes to a selection box with the tangent symbol attached to it. Also, you are prompted to select the first object.

21. Select an arc; you are prompted to select the second object.

22. Select a line; the tangent constraint will be applied at one end of the line and the tangent symbol will be displayed.

23. Similarly, apply the tangent constraint at all other places in the slot, as shown in Figure 1-15. You need to choose the **Show/Hide** button to display all constraints.

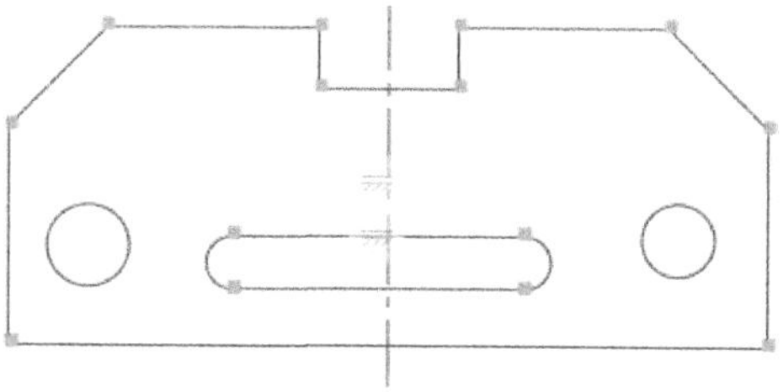

Figure 1-14 *Sketch after applying the Coincident constraint*

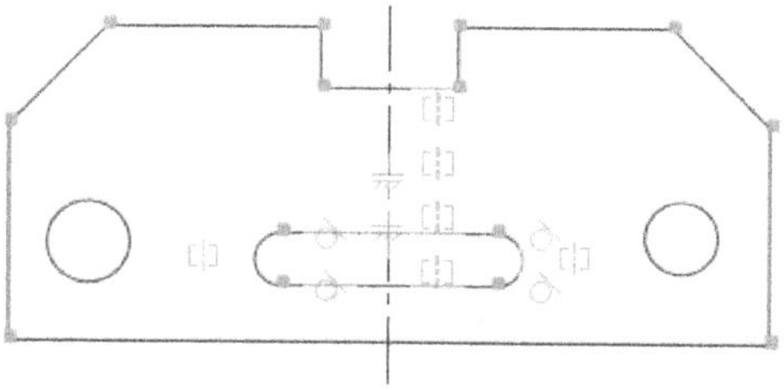

Figure 1-15 *Sketch after applying all Tangent constraints*

Next, you need to make the centerpoint of the circles and the slot to be in a straight line.

24. Choose the **Horizontal** tool from the **Geometric** panel; the prompt sequence that follows is given next.

Select an object or [2Points] <2Points>: Enter.
Select first point: *Select the circle on the left side* Enter.
Select second point: *cen* Enter.
of: *Select the center of the arc on the left side* Enter.

The sketch after applying the Horizontal constraint is shown in Figure 1-16.

25. Similarly, apply the Horizontal constraint to the circle and arc on the right side.

26. Choose the **Show/Hide** button from the **Parametric** tab and hide the display of all constraint bars and save the drawing. The sketch after applying and hiding all constraints is shown in Figure 1-17.

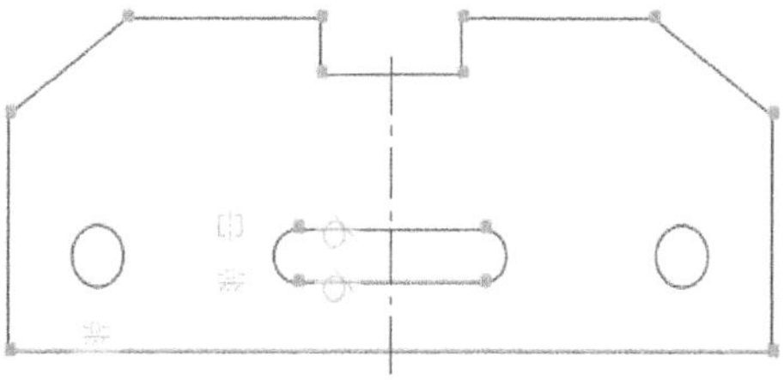

Figure 1-16 Sketch after applying the Horizontal constraint between a circle and an arc

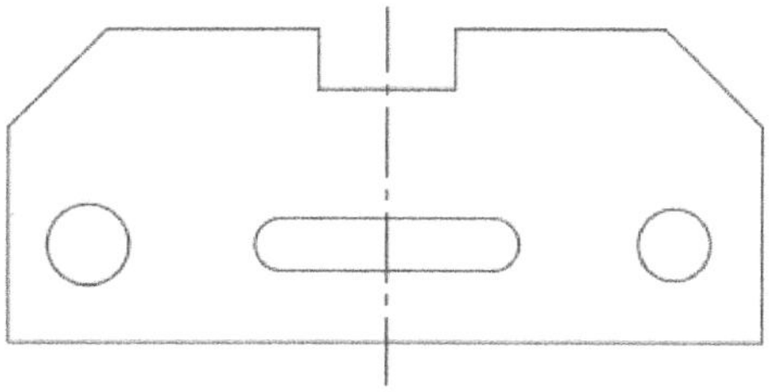

Figure 1-17 Sketch after applying and hiding all constraints

APPLYING CONSTRAINTS AUTOMATICALLY

In the previous section, twelve types of constraints are discussed. Nine of these constraints can be applied automatically, provided you have a closed sketch. To apply constraints automatically, choose the **AutoConstrain** tool in the **Geometric** panel of the **Parametric** tab of the **Ribbon**; you will be prompted to select an object. Select the entities individually or by using the selection box, and then press Enter; all possible constraints will be applied automatically.

You can also specify the settings of the constraints that need to be applied automatically. To do so, choose the **AutoConstrain** button; the **Select objects or [Settings]** prompt will be displayed at the command prompt. Enter **S** at the command prompt and press the Enter key; the **Constraint Settings** dialog box will be displayed, as shown in Figure 1-18.

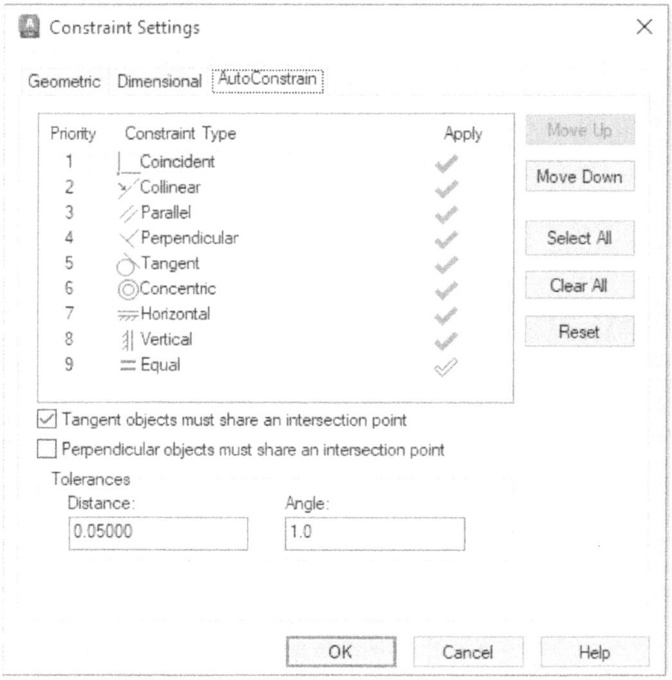

***Figure 1-18** The **Constraint Settings** dialog box with the **AutoConstrain** tab chosen*

In this dialog box, the **AutoConstrain** tab is chosen by default and the nine constraints that can be applied automatically are displayed. You can rearrange these constraints according to your priorities by choosing the **Move Up** or **Move Down** button. If you do not need a particular constraint to be applied automatically to the sketch, click on the green tick mark corresponding to the constraint; the tick mark will turn white indicating that the corresponding constraints will not be applied automatically. If the **Tangent objects must share an intersection point** check box is selected, the tangent constraint will be applied, only if the two entities intersect at a point. If you clear this check box, the tangent constraint will be applied, only if the distance between the endpoints satisfies the value specified in the **Tolerances** area. Similarly, if the **Perpendicular objects must share an intersection point** check box is selected, the Perpendicular constraint will be applied, only if the two entities intersect at a point. If you clear this check box, the Perpendicular constraint will be applied, only if the distance between the endpoints satisfies the tolerances value specified in the **Tolerances** area.

Exercise 1

Draw the sketch shown in Figure 1-19 and apply appropriate constraints to it. Do not dimension the sketch.

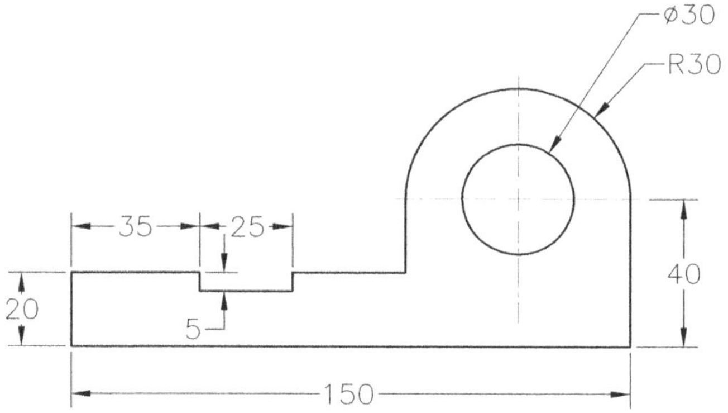

Figure 1-19 *Sketch for Exercise 1*

APPLYING DIMENSIONAL CONSTRAINTS

The older versions of AutoCAD were mainly used during the documentation stage of a design. However, the introduction of dimensional constraint has made AutoCAD a complete design package. In AutoCAD, you can apply dimensional constraint to an entity and change the size of the entity with ease. Therefore, now you can use AutoCAD at the initial design stage itself. Remember that the dimensions, which you apply using the tools in the **Dimensions** panel of the **Annotate** tab of the **Ribbon** do not change the size of the entity. However, because of their associative nature, if you change the size of an entity by dragging grips, the dimension will get changed.

You can apply the horizontal, vertical, aligned, angular, radius, and diameter dimensional constraint to a sketch. The procedure to apply a dimensional constraint to an entity is similar to that of applying dimension to an entity. For example, to apply the horizontal dimensional constraint, invoke the **Linear** tool from **Parametric > Dimensional > Dimensional Constraints** drop-down; you will be prompted to select the first constraint point. Move the cursor near one of the keypoints; it will be highlighted. Click to select the keypoint; you will be prompted to select the second constraint point. Move the cursor near the other keypoint and click, when it gets highlighted; the dimension will be attached to the cursor and you will be prompted to place the dimension. On placing the dimension, the dimension value will be displayed in a textbox. Press Enter to accept the value. If you need to change the value, enter a new value in the dimension box and press Enter. A lock symbol will be displayed next to the dimension value indicating that it is a dimensional constraint. In this way, you can apply other dimensional constraints as well.

Instead of selecting keypoints to apply the dimensional constraint, you can also select the entity to be dimensioned. To do so, invoke the **Linear** tool from **Parametric > Dimensional > Dimensional Constraints** drop-down and press Enter when the **Specify first constraint point or [Object] <Object>** prompt is displayed; you will be prompted to select an object. Select the object; the dimension will be attached to the cursor. Place it at the required position.

Tip
*You can also enter the arithmetic functions directly in the text box that is displayed on placing a dimensional constraint. For example, if you have an arithmetic function such as (22 *5.5)-30+5, which is equal to 96, you do not need to calculate this function. Just enter the function in the text box and press Enter; AutoCAD will automatically solve the mathematical expression. However, only the mathematical expression will be displayed in the text box and not the result.*

CONVERTING A DIMENSIONAL CONSTRAINT INTO AN ANNOTATIONAL CONSTRAINT

As discussed earlier, the dimensional constraint applied and the dimensions applied are different. The dimensional constraints are applied by using the tools available in the **Dimensional** panel of the **Parametric** tab. Whereas, dimensions are applied using the tools in the **Dimensions** panel of the **Annotate** tab. The dimensions that are applied using the tools from the **Dimensions** panel are called annotational constraints as they are used only for annotational purpose and cannot control the size of an entity.

If you have applied a dimension (annotational constraint) to an entity, you can convert it into a dimensional constraint. To do so, choose the **Convert** tool from the **Dimensional** panel of the **Parametric** tab; you will be prompted to select a dimension. Select the dimension and press Enter; the dimension (annotational constraint) will be converted into the dimensional constraint.

You can also convert a dimensional constraint into an annotational constraint. To do so, select a dimensional constraint and invoke the **PROPERTIES** palette. Select **Annotational** from the **Constraint Form** field in the **Constraint** rollout; the dimensional constraint will change to the annotational constraint and the options in the **Properties** rollout will change accordingly.

A dimensional constraint will not be plotted when you plot the drawing using the **Plot** tool. Therefore, you need to convert a dimensional constraint into an annotational constraint, as discussed above. You can also place the dimensional constraint in the annotational constraint mode. To do so, expand the **Dimensional** panel in the **Parametric** tab. You will notice that the **Dynamic Constraint Mode** is chosen by default. Choose the **Annotational Constraint Mode**. Now, if you place the dimensional constraint, you can plot them.

You can also make a dimensional constraint as a reference constraint. A reference constraint is displayed in brackets and is driven by a dimensional or annotational constraint. To make a dimensional constraint as reference, invoke the **PROPERTIES** palette of a dimensional constraint and select **Yes** in the **Reference** field of the **Constraint** rollout. If you have changed a dimensional constraint to an annotational constraint, you can make this annotational constraint as a reference constraint using the **PROPERTIES** palette.

CONCEPT OF A FULLY-DEFINED SKETCH

It is important for you to understand the concept of fully-defined sketches. If you have created a sketch in the design stage, you need to add the required geometrical and dimensional constraints to the sketch to constrain its degrees of freedom with respect to the surrounding. After applying the required constraints, the sketch may exist in any of the following three states:

1. Under-defined
2. Fully-defined
3. Over-defined

Under-defined

An under-defined sketch is the one in which some of the geometrical constraints or dimensional constraints are not defined. As a result, the degrees of freedom of the sketch are not fully constrained, and therefore, the entities may move or change their size unexpectedly. So, you need to add some geometrical constraints or dimensional constraints to it to make it fully-defined.

Fully-defined

A fully-defined sketch is the one in which all entities and their positions are fully-defined by geometrical constraints, dimensional constraints, or both. In a fully-defined sketch, all degrees of freedom of a sketch are constrained, and therefore, the sketched entities cannot move or change their size and location unexpectedly.

Over-defined

An over-defined sketch is the one in which some of the geometrical constraints, dimensional constraints, or both are conflicting. Also, if the geometrical constraints or the dimensional constraints in a sketch exceed the required number, the sketch will be over-defined. If you try to apply more geometrical constraints or dimensional constraints to a fully-defined entity, a message box will be displayed with the message that applying this constraint will over define the entity, as shown in Figure 1-20 and Figure 1-21.

Note

If you apply dimensional constraint to a fully-defined entity, the ***Dimensional Constraints*** *message box will be displayed, refer to Figure 1-21. Choose the* ***Create a reference dimension*** *option from the message box to convert that particular dimension into a reference dimension.*

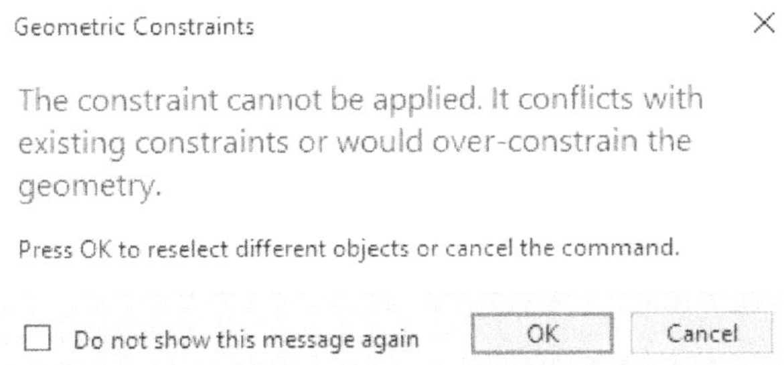

***Figure 1-20** The **Geometric Constraints** message box displayed on applying more than the required geometric constraints*

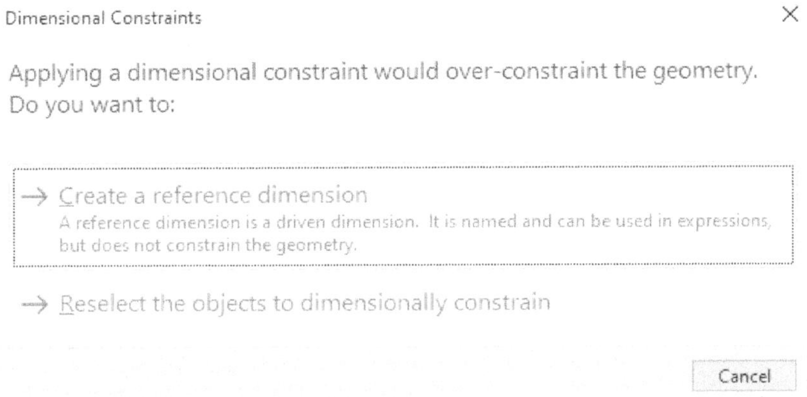

***Figure 1-21** The **Dimensional Constraints** message box displayed on applying more than the suggested dimensional constraints*

CONTROLLING THE DISPLAY OF THE DIMENSIONAL CONSTRAINT

On applying a dimensional constraint to an entity, a value will be displayed along with a name. If you have also applied annotational constraints to the sketch, then the sketch will be cluttered with dimensions. Therefore, you need to hide these constraints. To do so, choose the **Hide All** button from the **Dimensional** panel of the **Parametric** tab.

You can hide the selected dimensional constraints of an object by using the **Show/Hide** button. To do so, choose the **Show/Hide** button and select the respective constraint and press Enter. Next, right-click in the drawing area; a shortcut menu will be displayed. Choose the **Hide** option from it; the selected constraint will be hidden.

To display all dimensional constraints in the drawing, choose the **Show All** button from the **Dimensional** panel of the **Parametric** tab. To hide the annotational constraint, turn off the corresponding layer from the **LAYER PROPERTIES MANAGER**.

When you apply a dimensional constraint to an entity, a default name and a lock symbol will be displayed along with the value. If you need to display only the value, click on the inclined arrow on the **Dimensional** panel of the **Parametric** tab; the **Constraint Settings** dialog box will be displayed with the **Dimensional** tab chosen, as shown in Figure 1-22. Specify the format of the dimensional constraint to be displayed in the **Dimension name format** drop-down list available in the **Dimensional constraint format** area of this dialog box.

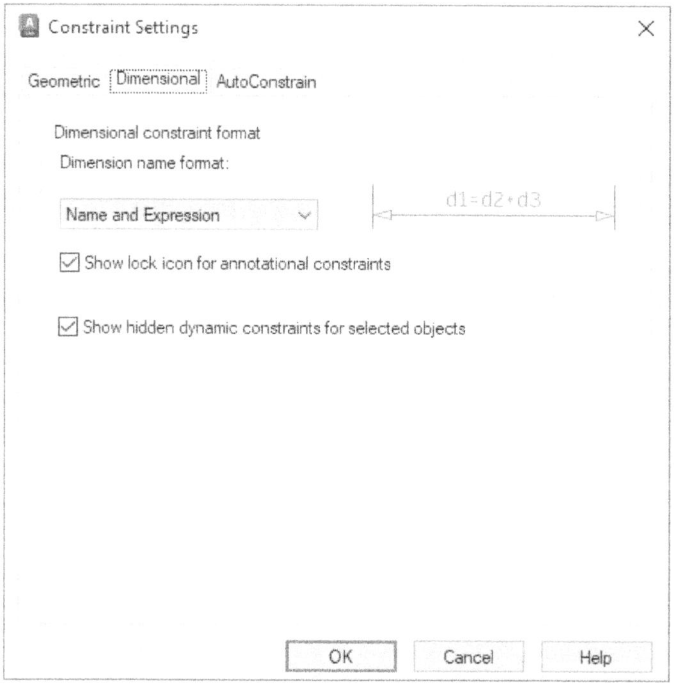

***Figure 1-22** The **Constraint Settings** dialog box with the **Dimensional** tab chosen*

If you convert a dimensional constraint into an annotational constraint, a lock symbol will be displayed. If you do not need the lock symbol to be displayed for an annotational constraint, clear the **Show lock icon for annotational constraints** check box from the **Constraint Settings** dialog box. In case, you want to view the dynamic constraints of an entity whose dimensional constraints are hidden by choosing the **Show lock icon for annotational constraints** button, select the **Show hidden dynamic constraints for selected objects** check box in the **Constraint Settings** dialog box. Now, if you select an entity whose dynamic constraints are hidden, the dynamic constraints will be displayed.

Example 2

In this example, you will draw the sketch shown in Figure 1-23, and then apply the geometric and dimensional constraints to it.

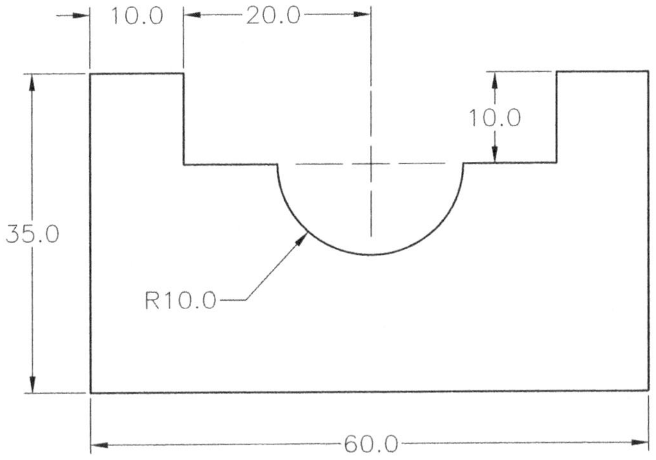

Figure 1-23 *Sketch for Example 2*

First, you will draw the profile and apply the geometrical constraints.

1. Start a new file with the *acad.dwt* template in the **Drafting & Annotation** workspace and draw the outer profile with dimensions close to that given in Figure 1-23. Make sure that the endpoints are snapped so that they form a closed sketch, as shown in Figure 1-24.

2. Choose the **AutoConstrain** button from the **Geometric** panel of the **Parametric** tab, enter **S** at the command prompt, and press Enter; the **Constraint Settings** dialog box is displayed.

3. Make sure that all constraints are selected. As there is no need to apply the concentric or tangent constraints in this sketch, select the **Concentric** and **Tangent** constraints individually and move them down using the **Move Down** button.

4. Choose the **OK** button; you are prompted to select objects. Select all entities of the sketch by dragging a selection box. Next, press Enter; all possible constraints are applied to the sketch, as shown in Figure 1-25.

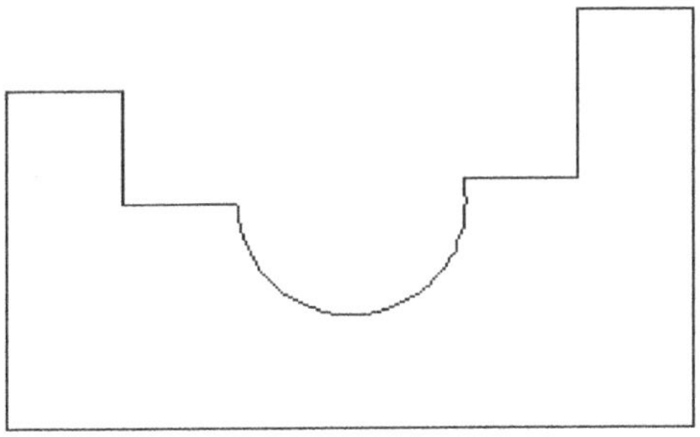

Figure 1-24 *Closed sketch drawn*

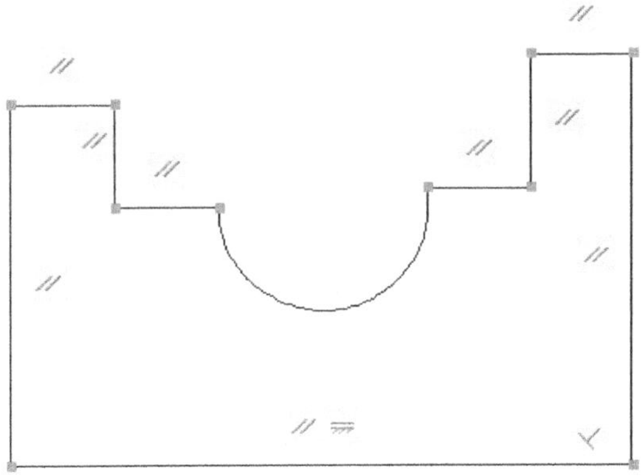

Figure 1-25 *Constraints applied automatically*

Note

*The constraints applied using the **AutoConstrain** tool may vary depending upon the profile. In your case, if the constraints are different from that shown in Figure 1-25, apply the missing constraints. Also, choose the **Show All** button from the **Geometric** panel if the constraints are not visible by default.*

5. Now, you need to apply the equal constraint. To do so, choose the **Equal** tool from the **Geometric** panel of the **Parametric** tab and apply the Equal constraint between the lines that are supposed to have equal dimensions. For dimensions, refer to Figure 1-23. The equal constraints need to be applied to the two pairs of horizontal and two pairs of vertical lines in the sketch. The sketch after applying the Equal constraint is shown in Figure 1-26.

Note

If you do not want to apply the Equal constraint to vertical lines, you need to apply the Collinear constraint to the two pairs of horizontal lines. But after applying the Equal constraint if you apply the Collinear constraint, a message box will be displayed stating that this constraint cannot be applied and conflicts the existing constraints or is over-constraining the geometry.

Next, you need to make the centerpoint of the circle and the horizontal line to be in a line.

6. Choose the **Horizontal** tool from the **Geometric** panel of the **Parametric** tab; the prompt sequence that will follow is given next.

Select an object or [2Points] <2Points>: Enter.
Select first point: *Move the cursor over the horizontal line and click when the endpoint near the arc is highlighted.*
Select second point: *cen* Enter *and select the arc on the left side.*

The sketch after applying the **Horizontal** constraint is shown in Figure 1-27.

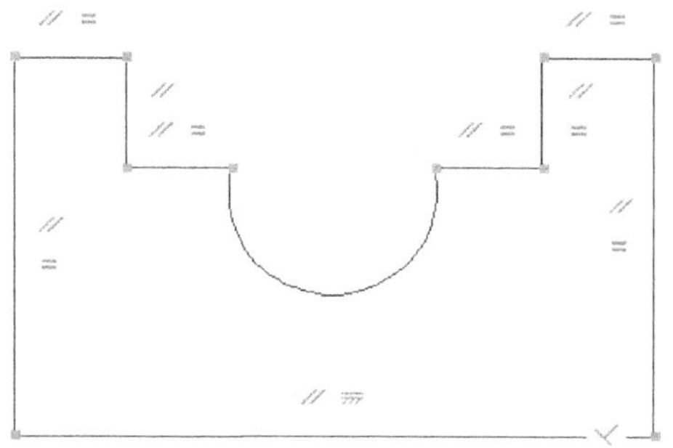

Figure 1-26 *Sketch after applying the Equal constraint*

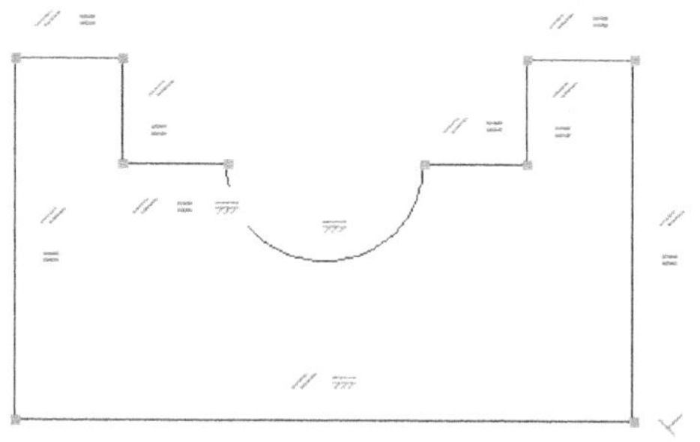

Figure 1-27 *Sketch after applying the Horizontal constraint*

7. Choose the **Hide All** button from the **Geometric** panel in the **Parametric** tab; all constraint bars disappear.

Now, you need to apply dimensional constraints. Before that, expand the **Dimensional** panel and ensure that the **Dynamic Constraint Mode** option is chosen.

8. Choose the **Linear** tool from **Parametric > Dimensional > Dimensional Constraint** drop-down and follow the prompt sequence given next.

   Specify first constraint point or [Object] <Object>: Enter.
   Select object: *Select the horizontal line at the bottom.*
   Specify dimension line location: *Move the cursor down and place the horizontal dimension at the required location. Enter **60** in the text box and press Enter.*

9. Press the Enter key again or choose the **Linear** tool from the **Dimensional** panel of the **Parametric** tab and follow the prompt sequence given next.

   Specify first constraint point or [Object] <Object>: Enter.
   Select object: *Select the vertical line on the left.*
   Specify dimension line location: *Move the cursor toward the left and place the vertical dimension at the required location. Enter **35** in the textbox.*

10. Similarly, apply the dimension to the horizontal and vertical lines, refer to Figure 1-28 and change the value to **10**.

11. Choose the **Radius** tool from the **Dimensional** panel of the **Parametric** tab; you are prompted to select the arc or the circle.

12. Select the arc and enter **10** as radius.

Now, you need to apply the dimension between the center of the arc and the vertical line on the left, refer to Figure 1-23.

13. Invoke the **Linear** tool from the **Parametric > Dimensional > Dimensional Constraints** drop-down and follow the prompt sequence given next.

    Specify first constraint point or [Object] <Object>: *Select the keypoint at the top of the smaller vertical line on the left.*
    Specify second constraint point: *cen* Enter *and select the arc.*
    Specify dimension line location: *Place the dimension at the required location and enter **20**; the **Dimensional Constraints** message box is displayed.*

14. Choose the **Create a reference dimension** option from the message box. The value **20** is displayed in parenthesis stating that it is a reference dimension. The sketch after applying all dimensional constraints is shown in Figure 1-28.

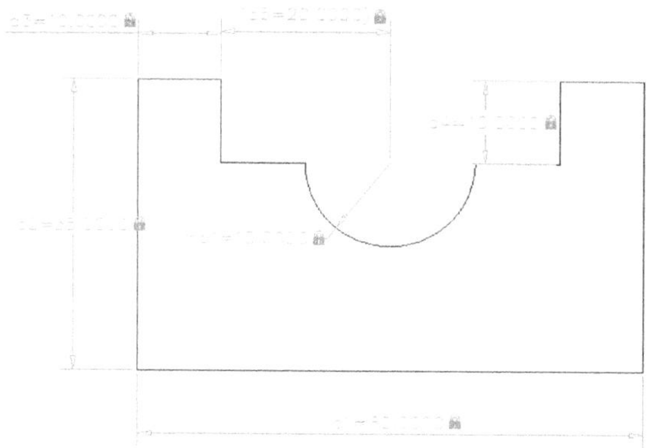

Figure 1-28 *Sketch with all dimensional constraints*

WORKING WITH EQUATIONS

Equations are mathematical relations between dimensions. Consider the sketch of a bolt. All the dimensions of a bolt are driven by the base diameter. In AutoCAD, if you need to draw the sketch of an object whose dimensions are driven by a base dimension, you can draw it easily by using equations in which all dimensions are equated with base dimensions. If you want to relate one or two dimensions with base dimension, you can do so by applying a dimensional constraint. But if most of the dimensions need to be represented as equations, then you need to use the **Parameters Manager**. Both these methods are discussed next.

Adding Equations while Applying Dimensional Constraints

When you apply the dimensional constraint using the tools from the **Dimensional** panel, the dimensions are displayed along with a default name. For the next dimensional constraint to be placed, you can represent it as an equation with the name of the first constraint. For example, to create a rectangle of length *l* units and width *w* units, which is half the length, you need to follow the steps given below.

1. Draw a rectangle and apply the required geometric constraints to it.
2. Choose the **Linear** tool from the **Dimensional** panel and select one of the lines representing the length and place the dimension; a text box will be displayed.
3. Enter **10** in the text box and press Enter; a new dimension will be displayed with the default name d1=10.0000.
4. Choose the **Linear** tool from the **Dimensional** panel and select one of the lines representing the width and place the dimension; a text box will be displayed.
5. Enter **0.5*d1** in the text box and press Enter; the rectangle will resize and a new dimension will be displayed with the default name fx: d2=0.5*d1.
6. Now, if you change the dimension of the length, the width will also change automatically.

Note that, if you change the default name, d1, the name in the expression d2 will also change.

Adding Equations Using the Parameters Manager

Adding equations to dimensions while applying constraints may look simpler, but in actual practice, when there are more dimensions, it is quite difficult. This problem can be solved by applying equations to dimensions using the **PARAMETERS MANAGER**. After applying dimensional constraints, choose the **Parameters Manager** button from the **Manage** panel of the **Parametric** tab; the **PARAMETERS MANAGER** palette will be displayed with all dimensions and expressions, as shown in Figure 1-29. The names of the dimensional constraints applied will be listed under the **Name** column in the **Dimensional Constraint Parameters** node. Also, the expression of the corresponding constraints will be listed in the **Expression** column.

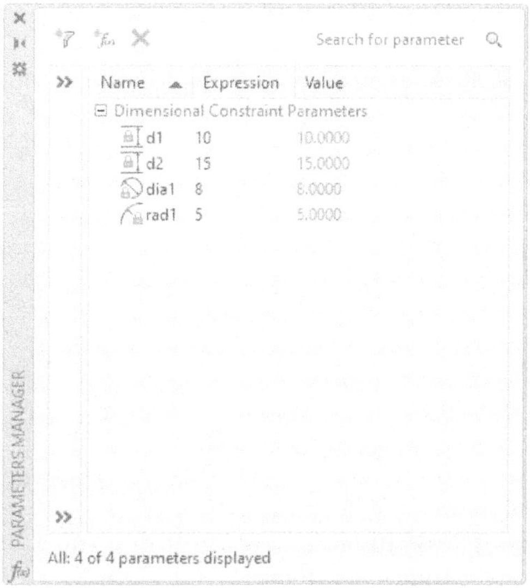

***Figure 1-29** The **PARAMETERS MANAGER** palette*

Now, you can change the existing expressions or add new expressions. To do so, double-click in the corresponding **Expression** field and add a new expression. If you want to add a list of new user-defined expressions, choose the **Creates a new user parameter** button from the **PARAMETERS MANAGER** palette; a new field will be added under the **User Parameters** node.

Example 3

In this example, you will open the sketch created in Exercise 1 of this chapter. You had applied geometrical constraints to this sketch. Now, you will apply dimensional constraints and then equate all the dimensions except the dimension 20 mm, with respect to the base length, 150 mm. For the dimension 20 mm, you will apply user-defined expressions as d150 = 20, d75 = 10, d300 = 40, and d100 = 13.3.

1. Choose the **Open** button from the **Quick Access Toolbar** and open the drawing created in Exercise 1 of this chapter.

2. Make sure that you have applied all the required geometrical constraints, as shown in Figure 1-30.

Note

If you have not applied all constraints to the sketch, it may get deformed while applying dimensional constraints.

3. Invoke the **Linear** tool from **Parametric > Dimensional > Dimensional Constraints** drop-down and follow the prompt sequence given next.

   Specify first constraint point or [Object] <Object>: Enter.
   Select object: *Select the horizontal line at the bottom.*
   Specify dimension line location: *Move the cursor down and place the horizontal dimension at the required location. Enter **150** in the text box and press Enter.*

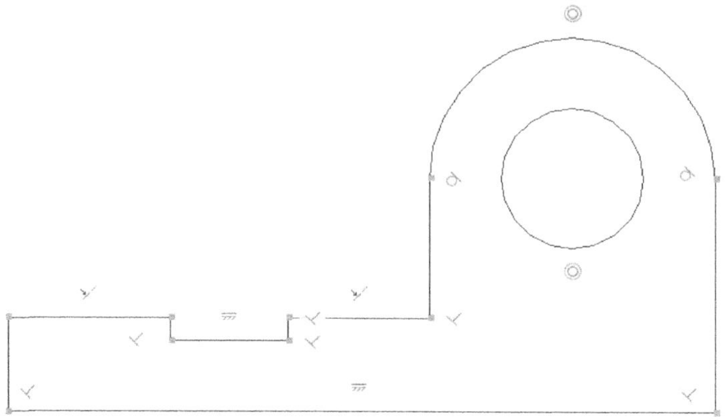

Figure 1-30 *Sketch with all constraints applied*

4. Press Enter again or choose the **Linear** tool from the **Dimensional** panel and follow the prompt sequence given next.

   Specify first constraint point or [Object] <Object>: Enter.
   Select object: *Select the vertical line on the left.*
   Specify dimension line location: *Move the cursor to left side and place the vertical dimension at the required location. Enter **20** in the text box and press Enter.*

5. Similarly, apply dimensions to other horizontal and vertical lines.

6. Choose the **Radius** tool from the **Dimensional** panel of the **Parametric** tab; you are prompted to select an arc or a circle.

7. Select the arc and enter **30** as the value of radius.

8. Choose the **Diameter** tool from the **Dimensional** panel of the **Parametric** tab; you are prompted to select the circle.

9. Select the circle and enter **30** as diameter.

10. Choose the **Parameters Manager** button from the **Manage** panel; the **PARAMETERS MANAGER** palette will be displayed with the names of dimensional constraints and their values, as shown in Figure 1-31.

11. Double-click on **40** in the **Expression** column of the **PARAMETERS MANAGER** palette and enter **d1/3.75**.

12. Resize the palette. Double-click in the **Description** column corresponding to the value **40** and enter **Hole Location**.

13. Similarly, add the expression and description to all dimensions, except the vertical dimension **20**, as given next.

Value to be selected from the Expression column	Expression to be added	Description to be added
35	d1/30*7	Slot Location
25	d1/6	Slot Width
5	d1/30	Slot Depth
30 (Diameter value)	d1/5	Hole Diameter
30 (Radius value)	d1/5	Radius

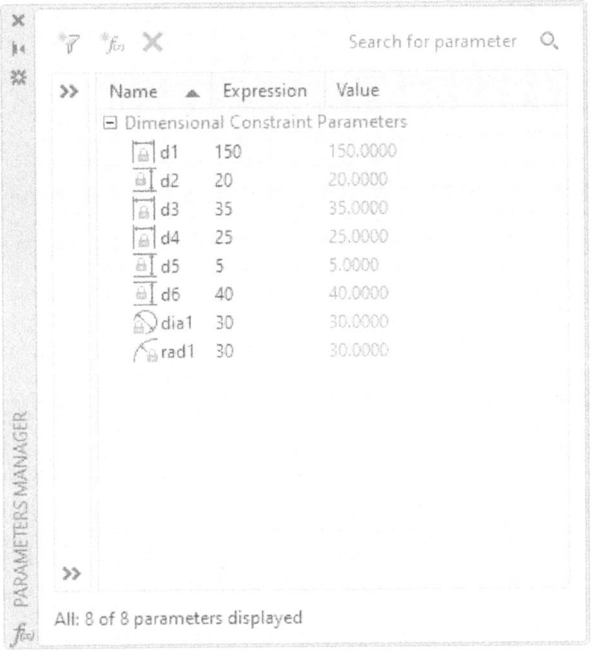

Figure 1-31 *The **PARAMETERS MANAGER** palette after applying all dimensions*

Note

*If the **Type** and **Description** columns are not added by default, right-click on the title of a column and choose appropriate options.*

The **PARAMETERS MANAGER** palette after you have changed all the expressions, is shown in Figure 1-32.

For the value 20, you need to create a user-defined expression as follows:

14. Choose the **Creates a new user parameter** button in the **PARAMETERS MANAGER** palette; the **User Parameters** node is added with the default name, **user1**.

15. Change the name user1 to **d150**, the corresponding expression to **20**, and the description to **If d1 = 150**.

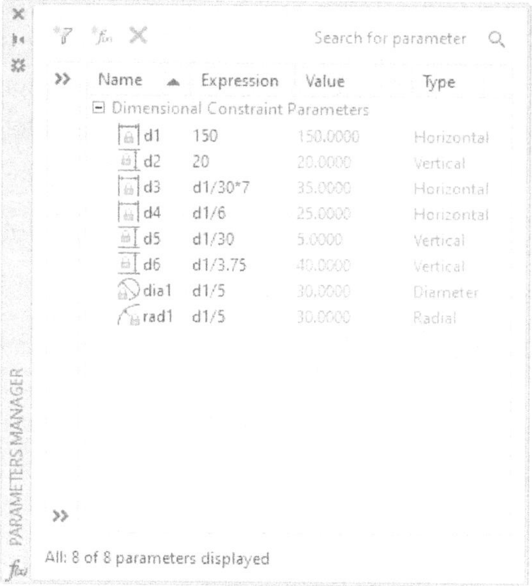

Figure 1-32 *The* ***PARAMETERS MANAGER*** *palette after adding all expressions*

16. Similarly, add three more user parameters and their corresponding expressions and descriptions as given below.

User parameter to be added	**Expression to be added**	**Description to be added**
d75	10	If d1 = 75
d300	40	If d1 = 300
d100	13.3	If d1 = 100

Note

You can also write a suitable expression for the dimension ***20*** *in the* ***Dimensional Constraints*** *node. For illustration, the expression for the dimension* ***20*** *is given as a user variable.*

17. If the dimensional constraints are displayed, choose the **Show/Hide** button from the **Dimensional** panel of the **Parametric** tab to hide the dimensional constraints.

18. Now, change the dimensional constraints **d1** and **d2**, as specified below in the **PARAMETERS MANAGER** palette. Observe the change in the sketch in the drawing area and the dimension value in the **Value** column of the **PARAMETERS MANAGER** palette.

d1 = 300, d2 = d300
d1 = 100, d2 = d100
d1 = 150, d2 = 20

Self-Evaluation Test

Answer the following questions and then compare them to those given at the end of this chapter:

1. Which of the following tools should be chosen in the **Dimensional** panel to apply both horizontal and linear dimensional constraints?

   (a) **Aligned** (b) **Linear**
   (c) **Lateral** (d) None of these

2. What will be the state of the sketch which does not have all its constraints defined?

   (a) Under-defined (b) Fully-defined
   (c) Over-defined (d) All of these

3. AutoCAD provides you __________ types of geometric constraints.

4. The __________ constraints are applied between two entities in a sketch and they control the shape of the drawing.

5. The __________ constraint forces the selected lines to lie on the same infinite line.

6. Invoke the __________ palette to add equations to dimensional constraints.

7. Whenever you apply a geometric constraint between two entities, the entity selected first will be affected. (T/F)

8. You cannot apply the coincident constraint to all the keypoints at a time. (T/F)

9. It is always recommended to first apply dimensional constraints so that the shape of the sketched entity does not change on applying geometric constraints. (T/F)

10. You can add equations while applying dimensional constraints. (T/F)

Review Questions

Answer the following questions:

1. How many geometric constraints can be applied automatically?

   (a) Nine (b) Ten
   (c) Eight (d) Twelve

2. Which of the following constraints forces two lines or polylines to have equal length and the selected circles, arcs, or an arc and circle to have equal radii?

   (a) **Concentric** (b) **Equal**
   (c) **Collinear** (d) **Lock**

3. The __________ makes you to change or modify the shape and size of an entity of a sketch at any stage of the design process.

4. The __________ constraint is used to apply curvature continuity between a spline and an entity connected together.

5. A __________ dimensional constraint is displayed in brackets and is driven by a dimensional or annotational constraint.

6. The dimensions that you apply using the tools in the __________ panel do not change the size of an entity.

7. The symmetric constraint forces two selected lines, arcs, circles, or splines to remain equidistant from the centerline. (T/F)

8. Using the fix constraint, you can only fix the points. (T/F)

9. You can also enter arithmetic symbols directly in the text box that is displayed on placing a dimensional constraint. (T/F)

10. If you hide the display of a constraint, the constraint applied gets deleted. (T/F)

Exercise 2

Draw the sketches shown in Figure 1-33 and Figure 1-34. Next, add geometric and dimensional constraints to them.

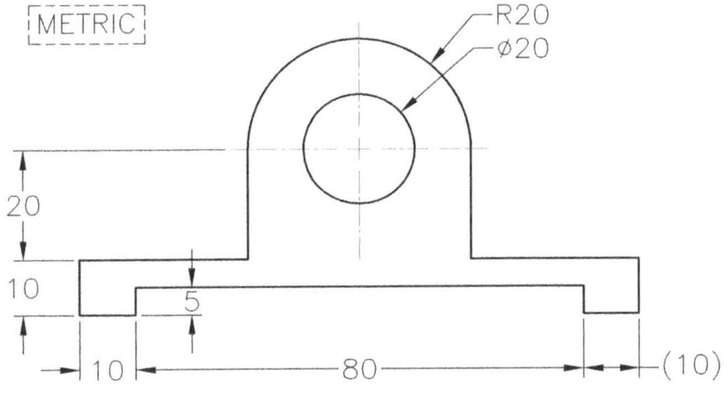

Figure 1-33 *Sketch for Exercise 2*

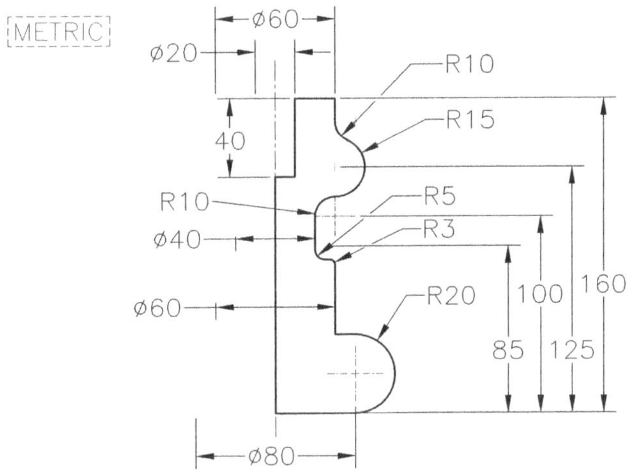

Figure 1-34 *Sketch for Exercise 2*

Answers to Self-Evaluation Test

1. b, **2.** a, **3.** twelve, **4. Geometric**, **5. Collinear**, **6. PARAMETERS MANAGER**, **7.** F, **8.** F, **9.** F, **10.** T

Chapter 2

Understanding External References

Learning Objectives

After completing this chapter, you will be able to:

- *Understand external references and their applications*
- *Understand dependent symbols*
- *Use the External References Palette*
- *Use the Attach, Unload, Reload, Detach, and Bind options*
- *Edit the path of an xref*
- *Understand the difference between the Overlay and Attachment options*
- *Use the Attach tool*
- *Work with Underlays*
- *Use the DesignCenter to attach a drawing as an xref*
- *Use the Bind tool to add dependent symbols*
- *Use the Clip tool to clip xref drawings*
- *Use the Edit Reference tool for in-place editing*

Key Terms

- *XRef*
- *Attach*
- *Reload*
- *Detach*
- *Unload*
- *Bind*
- *Overlay*
- *Underlay*
- *Frame*
- *Clip*

EXTERNAL REFERENCES

The external reference feature allows you to reference an external drawing without making that drawing a permanent part of the existing drawing. For example, assume that you have an assembly drawing ASSEM1 that consists of two parts, SHAFT and BEARING. The SHAFT and BEARING are separate drawings created by two CAD operators or provided by two different vendors. You want to create an assembly drawing from these two parts. One way to create an assembly drawing is to insert these two drawings as blocks by using the **Insert** tool in the **Block** panel. Now assume that the design of BEARING has changed due to customer or product requirements. To update the assembly drawing, you have to make sure that you insert the BEARING drawing after the changes have been made. If you forget to update the assembly drawing, then the assembly drawing will not reflect the changes made in the piece part drawing. In a production environment, this could have serious consequences.

You can solve this problem by using the external reference facility, which lets you link the piece part drawings with the assembly drawing. If the xref drawings (piece part) get updated, the changes are automatically reflected in the assembly drawing. This way the assembly drawing stays updated, no matter when the changes were made in the piece part drawings. There is no limit to the number of drawings that you can reference. You can also have nested references. For example, the piece part drawing BEARING could be referenced in the SHAFT drawing, and the SHAFT drawing could be referenced in the assembly drawing ASSEM1. When you open or plot the assembly drawing, AutoCAD automatically loads the referenced drawing SHAFT and the nested drawing BEARING. While using external references, several people working on the same project can reference the same drawing and all the changes made are displayed everywhere the particular drawing is being used.

If you use the **Insert** tool to insert the piece parts, the piece parts become a permanent part of the drawing, and therefore, the drawing file size increases. However, if you use the external reference feature to link the drawings, the piece part drawings are not saved with the assembly drawing. AutoCAD only saves the reference information with the assembly drawing; therefore, the size of the drawing is minimized. Like blocks, the xref drawings can be scaled, rotated, or positioned at any desired location, but they cannot be exploded. You can also use only a part of the xref by making clipped boundary of xrefs.

Tip

External referenced drawings are useful for creating parts or subassemblies and then putting them together in one drawing to create the main assembly. You can also use it for laying out the contents of a drawing with multiple views before plotting.

DEPENDENT SYMBOLS

When you use the **Insert** tool to insert a drawing, the information about the named objects is lost, if names are duplicated. However, if they are unique, they are imported. The named objects are entries such as blocks, text styles and layers. For example, if the assembly drawing has a layer Hidden of green color and HIDDEN linetype and the piece part Bearing has also a layer Hidden of blue color and HIDDEN2 linetype, the values set in the assembly drawing will override the values of the inserted drawing when the Bearing drawing is inserted in the assembly drawing, refer to Figure 2-1. As a result, in the assembly drawing, the layer Hidden will retain green color and HIDDEN linetype, ignoring the layer settings of the inserted drawing. Only those layers that have the same names are affected. The remaining layers that have different layer names are added to the current drawing.

Figure 2-1** Partial view of the layer settings of the current drawing in the **LAYER PROPERTIES MANAGER

In the xref drawings, the information about the named objects is not lost because AutoCAD will create additional named objects such as specified layer settings, as shown in Figure 2-2. For xref drawings, these named objects become dependent symbols (features such as layers, linetypes, object color, text style, and so on).

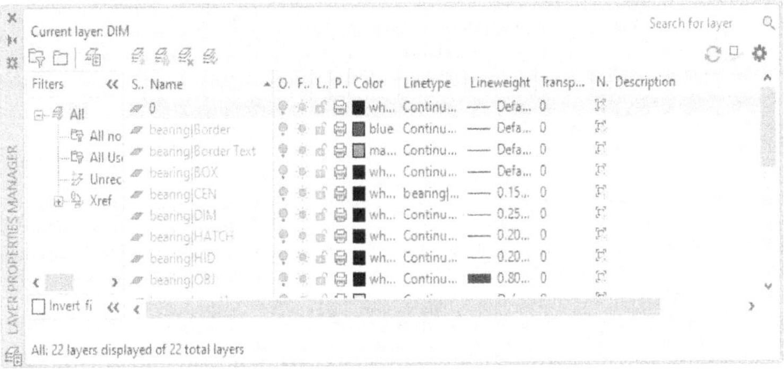

***Figure 2-2** Additional layers created by xref*

The layer Hidden of the xref drawing (Bearing) is appended with the name of the xref drawing Bearing, and the two are separated by the vertical bar symbol (|). The names of these layers appear in light gray color in the **LAYER PROPERTIES MANAGER** or **Layer** drop-down list of the **Layers** panel in the **Home** tab. These layers can neither be selected nor be made current. The layer name Object changes to Bearing|Object. Similarly, Center is renamed as Bearing|Center, refer to Figure 2-2. The information added to the current drawing is not permanent. It is added only when the xref drawing is loaded. If you detach the xref drawing, the dependent symbols are automatically erased from the current drawing.

When you xref a drawing, AutoCAD does not let you reference the symbols directly. For example, you cannot make the dependent layer, Bearing|Object, as current layer. Therefore, you cannot add any objects to that layer. However, you can change the color, linetype, lineweight, plotstyle, or visibility (on/off, freeze/thaw) of the layer in the current drawing.

Note

You cannot make the xref-dependent layers current in a drawing. When the xref drawing is bound to the current drawing by using the ***XBIND*** *command, only then you can make the xref-dependent layers a permanent part of the current drawing and use them. The* ***XBIND*** *command will be discussed later in this chapter.*

MANAGING EXTERNAL REFERENCES IN A DRAWING

Ribbon: View > Palettes > External References Palette
Toolbar: Reference > External References
Menu Bar: Insert > External References
Command: XREF

When you choose the **External References Palette** button from the **Palettes** panel of the **View** tab, refer to Figure 2-3, AutoCAD displays the **EXTERNAL REFERENCES** palette, as shown in Figure 2-4. The **EXTERNAL REFERENCES** palette displays the status of each Xref in the current drawing and the relation between various Xrefs. It allows you to attach a new xref and detach, unload, and load an existing one, change an attachment to an overlay, or an overlay to an attachment. You can also open a reference drawing for editing from this palette. Additionally, it allows you to edit an xref's path and bind the xref definition to the drawing.

Figure 2-3 *The* ***Palettes*** *panel*

Apart from the methods mentioned in the command box, you can also invoke the **EXTERNAL REFERENCES** palette by selecting an xref in the current drawing and then right-clicking in the drawing area to display a shortcut menu. Next, choose **External References** from the shortcut menu; the **EXTERNAL REFERENCES** palette will be displayed.

The upper right corner of the palette has two buttons: **List View** and **Tree View**.

List View

When you choose the **List View** button, the xrefs present in the drawing are displayed in alphabetical order. This is the default view. The list view displays information about xrefs in the current drawing under the following headings:

Reference Name

This column lists the name of all existing references in the current drawing.

Status

This column lists the current status of each xref in the drawing. It lists whether an xref is loaded, unloaded, unreferenced, not found, orphaned, unresolved, or marked to be reloaded. A loaded xref implies that the xref is attached to the current drawing. You can then unload it and then reload it using the options in the dialog box (this will be discussed later). An xref selected to be unloaded or reloaded displays **Unload** and **Needs reloading** respectively, under the **Status** column. If the xref has nested references that cannot be found, the status is **Unreferenced**, and if the parent of the nested reference gets unloaded, or cannot be found, its status is described as **Orphaned**. An unreferenced xref will not be displayed. If the xref is not found in the search paths defined, its status is **Not Found**. A missing xref or one that cannot be found is **Unresolved**.

*Figure 2-4 The **EXTERNAL REFERENCES** palette*

Size

The file size of each xref is listed here.

Type

This column lists whether the xref is an attachment or overlay.

Date

This column lists the date on which the xref drawing was last saved.

Saved Path

This column lists the path of the xref, that is, the route taken to locate the particular referenced drawing.

Choose any of these headings; AutoCAD sorts and lists the Xrefs in the current drawing according to that particular title. For example, on choosing **Reference Name**, the xrefs are sorted and listed as per the name. The column widths can be increased or decreased as per your requirements. When you place your cursor at the edge of a column title button, the cursor changes to a horizontal resizing cursor. Now, press the pick button of your mouse and drag the column edge to increase or decrease its width. After you increase the column widths, it is possible that the widths of the columns extend beyond the widths of list boxes. In such a case, a horizontal scroll bar appears at the bottom of the list box. You can use the scroll bar to view the columns that extend beyond the width of the list box.

Tree View

On choosing the **Tree View** button available in the right side of the **File References** title bar, the xrefs are displayed in a hierarchical tree view in the **EXTERNAL REFERENCES** palette. It displays information on nested xrefs and their relationship with one another. Xrefs are indicated by an icon of a paper with a paper clip. This icon appears with a cross mark when the xref gets unloaded, and if there is a missing xref, the "!" sign appears. Similarly, the arrow pointing downward indicates that the xref is unloaded. You can also choose **List View** and **Tree View** by pressing the F3 and F4 keys, respectively.

Attaching an Xref Drawing (Attach Option)

The **Attach** drop-down list is available at the upper left corner of the **EXTERNAL REFERENCES** palette. If you choose the down arrow on this button, a flyout will be displayed. Choose the **Attach DWG** option from the **Attach** drop-down list to attach an xref drawing to the current drawing. This option can also be invoked by right-clicking on the **File References** area. The following examples illustrate the process of attaching an xref to the current drawing. In this example, it is assumed that there are two drawings, SHAFT and BEARING. SHAFT is the current drawing that is loaded on the screen, as shown in Figure 2-5 and the BEARING drawing is saved on the disk. If you want to xref the BEARING drawing in the SHAFT drawing, you need to follow the steps given below:

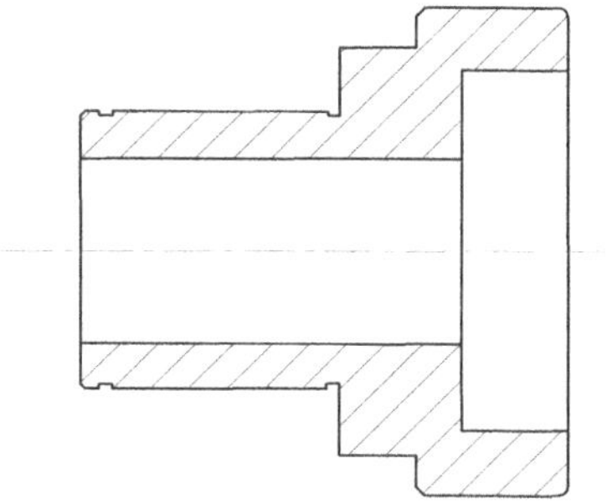

Figure 2-5 *Drawing of SHAFT*

1. The first step is to make sure that the SHAFT drawing is on the screen (draw the shaft drawing with assumed dimensions).

Tip

No drawing needs to be on the screen. You could attach both drawings, BEARING and SHAFT to an existing drawing, even if it is a blank drawing.

2. Choose the **External References Palette** button from the **Palettes** panel to display the **EXTERNAL REFERENCES** palette. In this palette, choose the **Attach DWG** option; the **Select Reference File** dialog box will be displayed.

   Select the drawing that you want to attach (BEARING) and then choose the **Open** button; the **Attach External Reference** dialog box will be displayed, as shown in Figure 2-6. In this dialog box, the name of the file that you have selected to be attached to the current drawing as an xref is displayed in the **Name** drop-down list. You can also specify the name of the file to be attached from the **Name** drop-down list.

Note

AutoCAD also searches for the xref file in the paths defined in the ***Project Files Search Path*** *folder in the* ***Files*** *tab of the* ***Options*** *dialog box. This folder does not have any path defined in it and displays* ***Empty*** *when the tree view is expanded. To define a search path, select* ***Empty*** *and choose the* ***Add*** *button in the dialog box. You can enter a project name here, if you want. Now, expand the tree view, select* ***Empty*** *again, and choose the* ***Browse*** *button; the* ***Browse for Folder*** *window is displayed. Select the folder that is to be searched for the file and choose the* ***OK*** *button. Then, choose the* ***Apply*** *button and the* ***OK*** *button from the* ***Options*** *dialog box to exit it.*

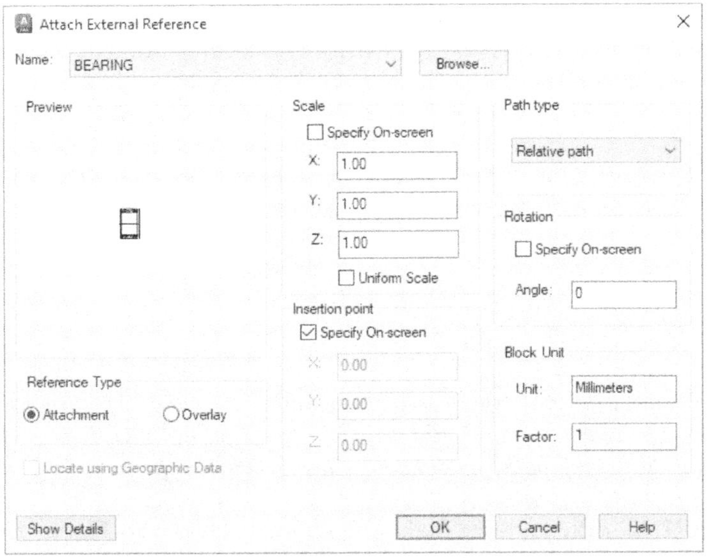

***Figure 2-6** The **Attach External Reference** dialog box*

In the **Reference Type** area, select the **Attachment** radio button, if it is not selected by default. The **Overlay** option is discussed later in this chapter. The **Path type** drop-down list is used to specify whether you want to attach a drawing with full path, relative path, or no path. If you select the **Full path** option, the precise location of the xreffed drawing is saved. If you select the **Relative path** option (if not selected by default), the position of the xreffed drawing with reference to the host drawing is saved. If you select the **No path** option, AutoCAD will search for the xreffed drawing in only that folder in which the host drawing is saved. You can also specify the insertion point, scale factors, and rotation angle in the respective **X**, **Y**, **Z**, and **Angle** edit boxes or select the **Specify On-screen** check boxes to use the pointing device to specify them on the screen. By default, the scale factors in **X**, **Y**, and **Z** edit boxes is 1 and the rotation angle is 0. The **Block Unit** area provides information regarding the units of the inserted block. The **Unit** edit box displays the unit of the block. The **Factor** edit box displays the scale factor, depending on the unit of the block and that of the current drawing. If you choose the **Show Details** button, the path of the file is displayed adjacent to **Found in**. Also, the saved path of the file is displayed adjacent to **Saved path**. Choose the **OK** button from the **Attach External Reference** dialog box to accept the default values and exit the dialog box. Specify the insertion point; the drawing is attached to the current drawing, but it appears faded. After attaching the BEARING drawing as an xref, save the current drawing with the file name SHAFT, as shown in Figure 2-7. You can control the fading intensity of the attached objects by using the options from the **Fade control** area of the **Display** tab in the **Options** dialog box. In this area, you can either use the slider bar

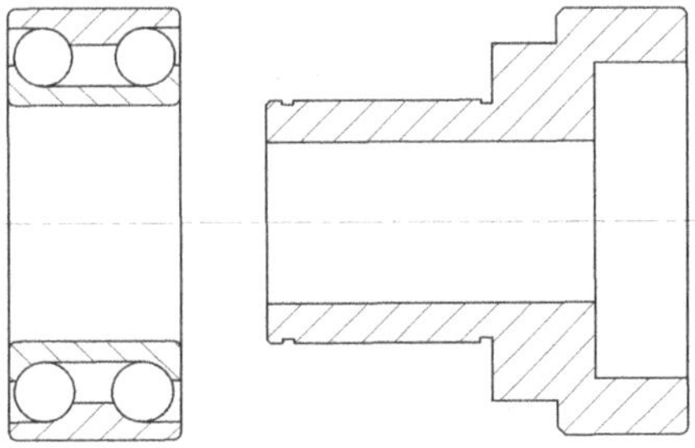

***Figure 2-7** Attaching the BEARING drawing as an xref*

to increase or decrease the fading intensity or you can enter a value in the edit box. You can also use the **XDWGFADECTL** variable to control the fading intensity of other objects while editing them. By default, the fading intensity value is set to 50.

Note

In AutoCAD, you can also control the Path type by using ***REFPATHTYPE*** *system variable. This system variable has three values which are given next:*

0=No path
1=Relative path (default value)
2=Full path

You can also change the Path type of an existing xreffed drawing by first invoking a shortcut menu by right-clicking on the name of xreffed drawing from ***EXTERNAL REFERENCES*** *palette and then choosing the desired path type from the* ***Change Path Type*** *cascading menu.*

3. Open the BEARING drawing and make the changes shown in Figure 2-8 (draw polylines on the sides). Now, save the drawing with the file name BEARING.

4. Open the SHAFT drawing. In the **EXTERNAL REFERENCES** palette, you will notice that the message Needs reloading displayed in the **Status** column of the BEARING drawing. Right-click on BEARING and choose **Reload**; the BEARING drawing is automatically updated, refer to Figure 2-9. This is the most useful feature of external reference. You can insert the drawing as a block also, but in that case any modification made in the drawing will not reflect automatically in the drawing in which it is inserted.

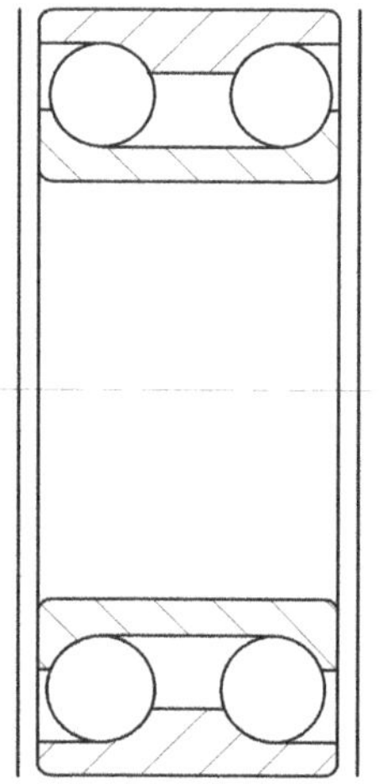

Figure 2-8 *The modified xref BEARING drawing*

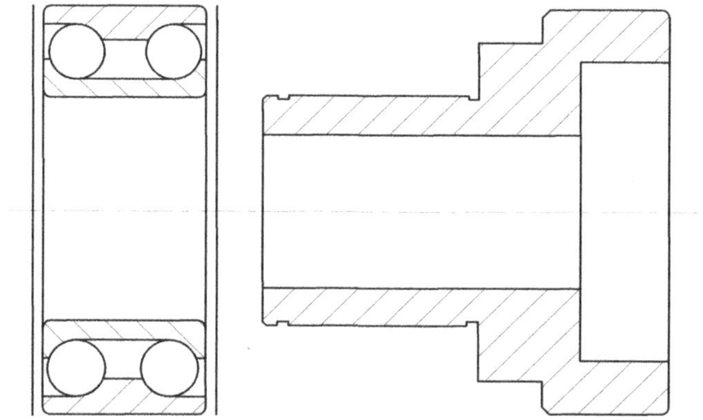

Figure 2-9 *BEARING drawing automatically updated after loading the SHAFT drawing*

However, when you make modifications in a large drawing file, it is not easy to find out where the modification were made. AutoCAD 2023 comes with **Xref Compare** bar that helps you detect the changes made in the xref drawings. Whenever you modify a drawing and click on the **Modify** option, the **Xref Compare** bar with modified drawing will be displayed, as shown in Figure 2-10.

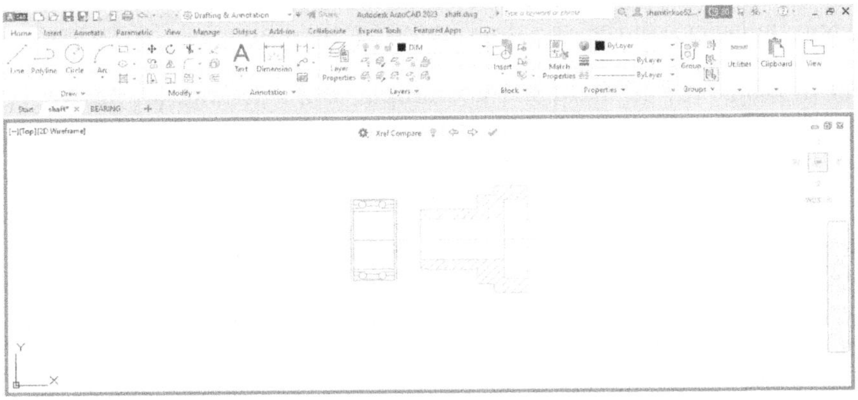

*Figure 2-10 The **Xref Compare** bar with modified drawing*

You will notice that the by default, the identical part between the two drawings is displayed in gray color. The elements which have been modified are displayed in green color.

In the **Xref Compare** bar, a number of parameters can be set to change the appearance of the modified elements using the tools in the **Settings** button. For example, if you want to change the color of the modified elements into blue, choose green color from color swatch in the **Difference** area; the **Select Color** dialog box will be displayed. In this dialog box, select blue color and choose the **OK** button; the color of the modified element will change into blue. You can also turn **On/Off** the visibility of the respective elements using the **Visibility toggle** button available on the left of the color swatch in the **Difference** area.

Now once you attach an xref drawing, AutoCAD remembers the name of the attached drawing If you xref the drawing again, AutoCAD displays a message as given next.
Xref "BEARING" has already been defined.
Using existing definition.
Specify insertion point or [Scale/X/Y/Z/Rotate/PScale/PX/PY/PZ/PRotate]: *Specify the location to place another copy of the xref.*

Note
*If the external reference drawing that you want to attach is currently being edited, AutoCAD will attach the drawing that was last saved through the **Save, Write Block,** or **Exit Autodesk AutoCAD 2023** buttons.*

Points to Remember about Xref

1. When you enter the name of the xref drawing, AutoCAD checks for block names and xref names. If a block exists with the same name as the name of the xref drawing in the current drawing, the **Attach** tool is terminated and an error message is displayed.

2. When you xref a drawing, the objects that are in the model space are attached. Any objects that are in the paper space are not attached to the current drawing.

3. The layer 0, DEFPOINTS, and the linetype CONTINUOUS are treated differently. The current drawing layers 0, DEFPOINTS, and linetype CONTINUOUS will override the layers and linetypes of the xref drawing. For example, if the layer 0 of the current drawing is white and the layer 0 of the xref drawing is red, the white color will override the red.

4. The xref drawings can be nested. For example, if the BEARING drawing contains the reference INRACE and you xref the BEARING drawing to the current drawing, the INRACE drawing is automatically attached to the current drawing. If you detach the BEARING drawing, the INRACE drawing gets detached automatically.

5. You can rename an xref under the **File References** column name in the list box of the **EXTERNAL REFERENCES** palette by double-clicking on the xref. You can now enter a new name. An AutoCAD warning is displayed: **Caution! "XXXX" is an externally referenced block. Renaming it will also rename its dependent symbols**.

6. When you xref a drawing, AutoCAD stores the name and path of the drawing by default. If the name of the xref drawing or the path where the drawing was originally stored has changed or you cannot find it in the path specified in the **Options** dialog box, AutoCAD cannot load the drawing, plot it, or use the **Reload** option of the **EXTERNAL REFERENCES** palette.

Detaching an Xref Drawing (Detach Option)

The **Detach** option can be used to detach or remove the xref drawings. If there are any nested xref drawings defined with the xref drawings, they are also detached. Once a drawing is detached, it is erased from the screen. To detach an xref drawing, select the file name in the **EXTERNAL REFERENCES** palette list box to highlight it and then right-click on it, a flyout will be displayed. Next, choose the **Detach** option from the flyout, the xref is completely removed from the current drawing.

Updating an Xref Drawing (Reload Option)

When you load a drawing, AutoCAD automatically loads the referenced drawings. The **Reload** option of the **EXTERNAL REFERENCES** palette lets you update the xref drawings and nested xref drawings at any time. You do not need to exit the drawing editor and then reload the drawing. To reload the xref drawings, invoke the **EXTERNAL REFERENCES** palette, select the xreffed drawing in the list box, and then right-click on it to choose the **Reload** option from the shortcut menu. AutoCAD will scan for the referenced drawings and the nested xref drawings and load the most recently saved version of the drawing.

You can reload all the attached xref drawings at one time by selecting **Reload All References** from the drop-down list of the **Refresh** button on the upper left corner of the **EXTERNAL REFERENCES** palette.

The **Reload** option is generally used when the xref drawings are currently being edited and you want to load the updated drawings. The xref drawings are updated based on what is saved on the disk. Therefore, before reloading an xref drawing, you should make sure that the xref drawings that are being edited have been saved. If AutoCAD encounters an error while loading the referenced drawings, the **External References** tool is terminated, and the entire reload operation is canceled.

Unloading an Xref Drawing (Unload Option)

The **Unload** option allows you to temporarily remove the definition of an xref drawing from the current drawing. However, AutoCAD retains the pointer to the xref drawings. When you unload the xref drawings, the drawings are not displayed on the screen. You can reload the xref drawings by using the **Reload** option.

> **Tip**
> *It is recommended that you unload the referenced drawings if they are not being used. After unloading the xref drawings, the drawings load much faster and need lesser memory.*

Adding an Xref Drawing (Bind Option)

The **Bind** option lets you convert the xref drawings to blocks in the current drawing. The bound drawings, including the nested xref drawings (that are no longer xrefs), become a permanent part of the current drawing. The bound drawing cannot be detached or reloaded. You can use this option when you want to send a copy of your drawing to a customer for review. Because the xref drawings are a part of the existing drawing, you do not need to include the xref drawings or the path information. You can also use this option to safeguard the master drawing from accidental editing of the piece parts. To bind the xref drawings, select the file names in the **EXTERNAL REFERENCES** palette and then right-click and choose the **Bind** option from the shortcut menu; the **Bind Xrefs/DGN underlays** dialog box is displayed, as shown in Figure 2-11. AutoCAD provides two methods to bind the xref drawing in the **Bind Type** area of the dialog box. These methods are discussed next.

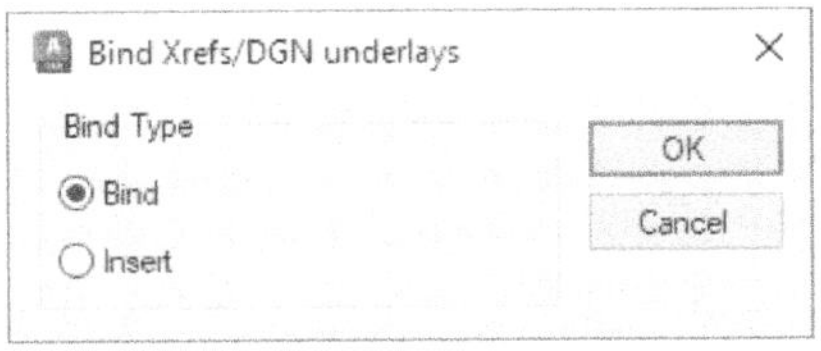

***Figure 2-11** The **Bind Xrefs/DGN underlays** dialog box*

Bind

When you use the **Bind** radio button, AutoCAD binds the selected xref definition to the current drawing. All the xrefs are converted to blocks and the named objects are renamed. For example, if you xref the drawing Bearing with a layer named Object, a new layer Bearing|Object is created in the current drawing. When you bind this drawing, the xref dependent layer Bearing|Object will become a locally defined layer Bearing0 Object, refer to Figure 2-12. If the Bearing0 Object layer already exits, AutoCAD will automatically increment the number, and the layer name becomes Bearing1Object.

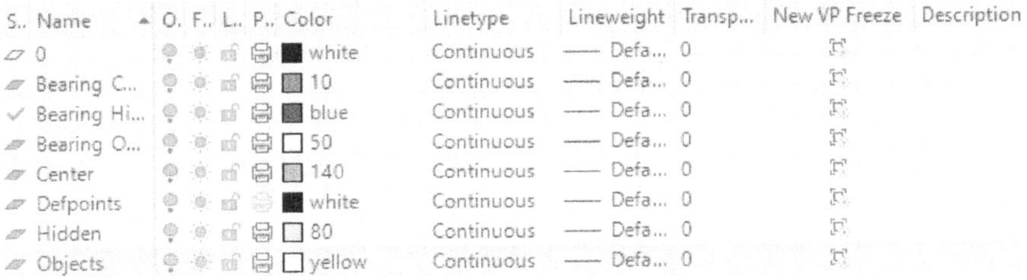

***Figure 2-12** Partial view of the LAYER PROPERTIES MANAGER*

Insert

When you use the **Insert** radio button, AutoCAD inserts the xref drawing. The xrefs get converted into blocks. For example, if you xref the drawing Shaft with a layer named Object, a new layer Shaft|Object is created in the current drawing. If you use the **Insert** option to bind the xref drawing, the layer name Shaft|Object is renamed as Object. If the object layer already exists, then the values set in the current drawing override the values of the inserted drawing.

Editing an XREF's Path

By default, AutoCAD saves the path of the referenced drawing and displays it in the **Saved Path** column of the **EXTERNAL REFERENCES** palette. As mentioned earlier, when AutoCAD loads the drawing containing a referenced file, and if it is not able to find the file at the location specified in the **Saved Path** column of the **EXTERNAL REFERENCES** palette, it searches for the file in the current directory, and in the **Support File Search Path** locations specified in the **Files** tab of the **Options** dialog box. If a file with the same name is found, it is loaded. Now, when you invoke the **EXTERNAL REFERENCES** palette, you will notice that if you select an xref name in the list box to highlight it, the path displayed in the **Found At** column for the xref file is different from the one displayed in the **Saved Path** edit box. To update the path of the xref file, choose the Browse button. The new path is saved and displayed in the **Found At** column.

If AutoCAD is unable to locate the specified file even in the directories specified in the **Files** tab of the **Options** dialog box, it will display an error message saying that it cannot find the specified file. The path of the file is displayed as a marker text in the current drawing. Now, when you invoke the **EXTERNAL REFERENCES** palette, the status of the drawing is shown as **Not Found**. To specify a new path for the xref file, click in the **Saved Path** field; the path will be highlighted and the Browse button will be displayed next to the path. Click on this button; the **Select new path** dialog box will be displayed. Using this dialog box, you can locate the drawing to be used as xref. Once you have found the file, choose the **Open** button to return to the **EXTERNAL REFERENCES** palette. The new path is displayed in the **Found At** column and the **Saved Path** edit box. The specified xref file is reloaded and replaces the marker text in the drawing, when you choose the **OK** button in the **EXTERNAL REFERENCES** palette. If you remember the new location of the xref file, you can also enter it in the **Saved Path** edit box. For example, if a drawing, which was originally in the C:\CAD\Proj1 subdirectory, has been moved to C:\Parts directory, the path must be edited so that AutoCAD is able to load the xref drawing.

In AutoCAD, you can assign new path to the xreffed file whose path is missing by choosing the **Select New Path** option from the shortcut menu invoked by right clicking on the name of xreffed drawing from **EXTERNAL REFERENCES** palette. You can also assign the same path to every file whose path is missing using this tool.

You can change the path of various xreffed drawings having same path by choosing the **Find and Replace** option from the shortcut menu invoked by right-clicking on the name of xreffed drawing from **EXTERNAL REFERENCES** palette and assign new path to all the drawings at once.

THE OVERLAY OPTION

As discussed earlier, when you attach an xref to a drawing, the **Attach External Reference** dialog box is displayed. The **Reference Type** area of this dialog box has two radio buttons, **Attachment** and **Overlay**. You can select any of these radio buttons to xref a drawing. The **Attachment** radio button is selected by default. The advantage of selecting the **Overlay** radio button is that you can access the desired drawing instead of the drawing along with its xreffed attachments. For example, consider three people working on three different drawings that are a part of the same project. The first designer is working on the layout of walls of a room, the second designer is working on the furniture layout of the room, and the third on the electrical layout of that room. The names of the drawings are WALLS, FURNITURE, and ELECTRICAL, respectively. Assume that the designer working on the walls layout selects the **Attachment** radio button to xref the FURNITURE drawing so that he or she can check the furniture layout according to the wall structure. After insertion, the WALLS drawing will comprise the wall structure (current drawing) along with the furniture layout (xreffed drawing). Now, if the designer working on the electrical layout xrefs the WALLS drawing to check the location of electrical fittings with respect to the walls, he/she will get the drawing that has the furniture layout as well as the wall layout. This is because the FURNITURE drawing was xreffed in the WALLS drawing by selecting the **Attachment** radio button.

In this example, the designer working on the ELECTRICAL drawing may not require the FURNITURE drawing. This is because at this stage, the designer will be more interested in checking the electrical fittings with respect to the wall structure. So the furniture layout that is xreffed with the wall structure needs to be avoided. This can be done by selecting the **Overlay** radio button while X-referencing the FURNITURE drawing in the WALLS drawing. This means that the designer working on the wall structure needs to xref the furniture layout by selecting the **Overlay** radio button. Now, if the wall structure is xreffed in some other drawing, the furniture layout will not appear.

One of the problems of using the **Attachment** option is that you cannot have a circular reference. For example, assume you are designing the plant layout of a manufacturing unit. One person is working on the floor plan, refer to Figure 2-13, and the second person is working on the furniture layout in the offices, refer to Figure 2-14. The names of the drawings are FLOORPLAN and OFFICES, respectively. The person working on the office layout uses the **Attachment** option to insert the FLOORPLN drawing so that he or she has the latest floor plan drawing. The person who is working on the floor plan wants to reference the OFFICES drawing.

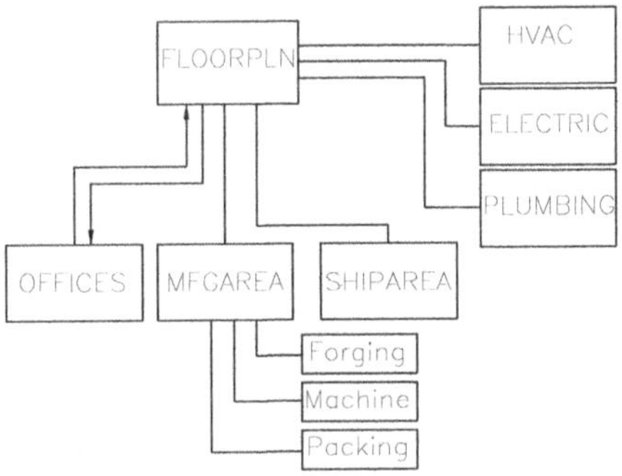

Figure 2-13 *Hierarchy of FLOORPLAN drawing*

Now, if the **Attachment** option is used to reference the drawings, AutoCAD displays an error message. This is because by attaching the OFFICES drawing, a circular reference is created. The AutoCAD message displayed is "**Circular references detected. Continue?**", as shown in Figure 2-15. If you choose the **No** button, the **External References Palette** tool is canceled and no drawing is referenced. But if you choose the **Yes** button, the following message **Breaking circular reference from "offices" to "current drawing"** is displayed at command line and the particular file you wanted to reference gets referenced.

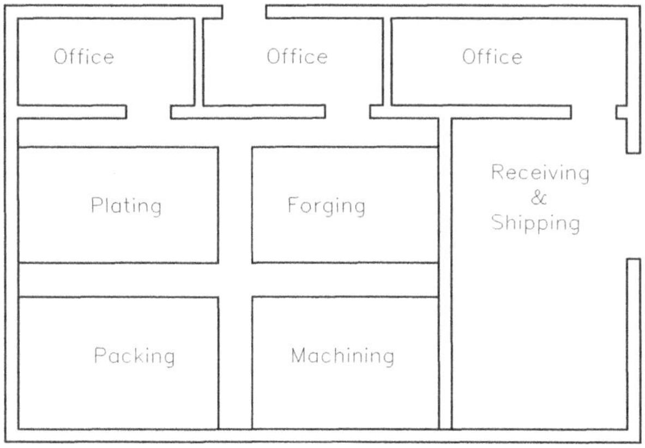

Figure 2-14 *Hierarchy of OFFICES drawing*

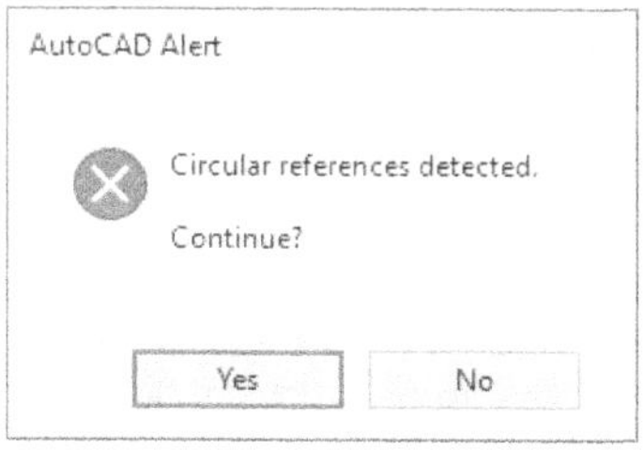

Figure 2-15 *The* ***AutoCAD Alert*** *message box*

However, to overcome this problem of circular reference, you can use the **Overlay** option to overlay the OFFICES drawing. This is a very useful option because the **Overlay** option allows different operators avoid circular reference and share the drawing data without affecting the drawing. Overlaying allows you to view a referenced drawing without having to attach it to the current drawing. This option can be invoked by selecting the **Overlay** radio button in the **Attach External Reference** dialog box, which is displayed after you have selected a drawing to reference. Also, when a drawing that has a nested overlay is overlaid, the nested overlay is not visible in the current drawing. This is another difference between attaching an xref and overlaying an xref to a drawing. This feature is especially useful when you want to reference a drawing that another user who is referencing your drawing does not need. Although the attachment will reference the nested reference too, the overlay option ignores nested references.

In AutoCAD, you can change an external referenced file from attachment to overlay and vice-versa. To do so, select the file from the **EXTERNAL REFERENCES** palette and right-click on it; a shortcut menu will be displayed, refer to Figure 2-16. Hover the cursor on the **Xref Type** option in the shortcut menu; two options are displayed, **Attach** and **Overlay**. Select the option as per requirement. The selected file will become attachment or overlay as per the option selected. You can change the type of multiple reference files by selecting all of them and then right-clicking on them.

Figure 2-16 *The shortcut menu*

Example 1 — Attachment and Overlay

In this example, you will use the **Attachment** and **Overlay** options to attach and reference the drawings. Two drawings, PLAN and PLANFORG are given. The PLAN drawing, refer to Figure 2-17, consists of the floor plan layout, and the PLANFORG drawing, refer to Figure 2-18 has the details of the forging section only. The CAD operator who is working on the PLANFORG drawing wants to xref the PLAN drawing for reference. Also, the CAD operator working on the PLAN drawing should be able to xref the PLANFORG drawing to complete the project. The following steps illustrate how to accomplish the defined task without creating a circular reference.

Download these files from https://www.cadcim.com. The path of the file is as follows: *Textbooks > CAD/CAM > AutoCAD Advanced > Advanced AutoCAD 2023: A Problem-Solving Approach, 3D and Advanced > Input Files.*

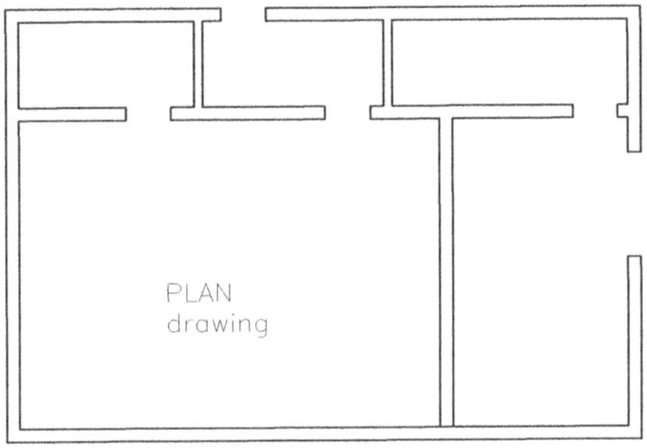

Figure 2-17 *The PLAN drawing*

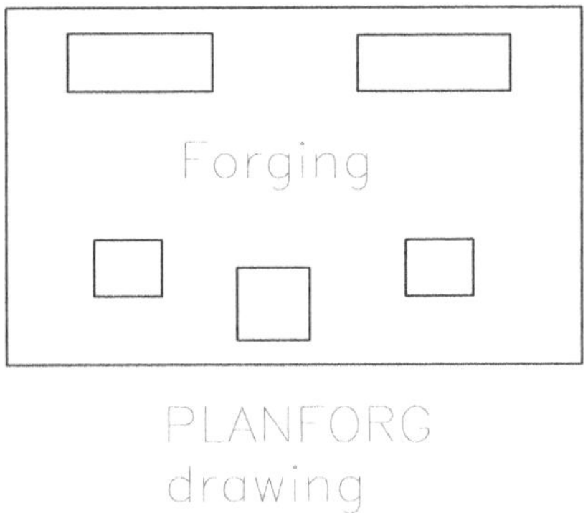

Figure 2-18 *The PLANFORG drawing*

How circular reference is caused?

1. Open the drawing PLANFORG and then choose the **External References Palette** button from the **Palettes** panel in the **View** tab. Next, choose the **Attach DWG** option from the **EXTERNAL REFERENCES** palette; the **Select Reference File** dialog box is displayed. Select the PLAN drawing from the list box of the **Select Reference File** dialog box and choose the **Open** button; the **Attach External Reference** dialog box is displayed. In this dialog box, the name of the PLAN drawing is displayed in the **Name** edit box, and the **Attachment** radio button is selected by default in the **Reference Type** area. Choose the **OK** button to exit the dialog box and specify an insertion point on the screen. Now, the drawing consists of the PLANFORG and PLAN. Save the drawing.

2. Open the drawing file PLAN. Next, choose the **External References Palette** button and attach the PLANFORG drawing to the PLAN drawing using the same steps as described in Step 1. AutoCAD will display the message that the circular reference has been detected and will ask you if you want to continue. If you choose **Yes** in the AutoCAD message box, the circular reference is broken and you are allowed to reference the specific drawing.

The possible solution for the operator working on the PLANFORG drawing is to detach the PLAN drawing. This way the PLANFORG drawing does not contain any reference to the PLAN drawing and would not cause any circular reference. The other solution is to use the **Overlay** option, as follows:

How to prevent circular reference?

3. Open the PLANFORG drawing, refer to Figure 2-19 and select the **Overlay** radio button in the **Attach External Reference** dialog box, which is displayed after you have selected the PLAN drawing to reference. The PLAN drawing is overlaid on the PLANFORG drawing, refer to Figure 2-20. Save the drawing.

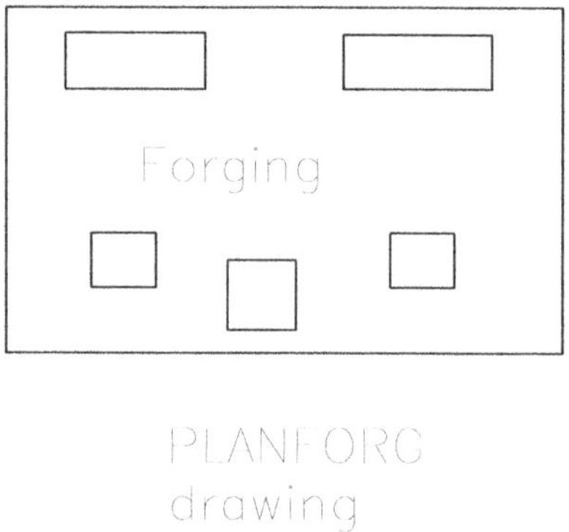

***Figure 2-19** The PLANFORG drawing*

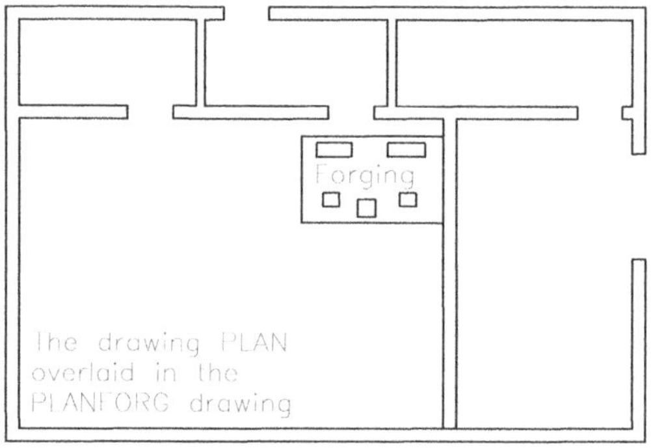

***Figure 2-20** The PLANFORG drawing after overlaying the PLAN drawing*

4. Open the drawing file PLAN, refer to Figure 2-21, and select the **Attachment** radio button in the **Attach External Reference** dialog box, which is displayed when you select the PLANFORG drawing in the **Select Reference File** dialog box to attach it as an xref to the PLAN drawing. You will notice that only the PLANFORG drawing is attached, refer to Figure 2-22. The drawing that was overlaid in the PLANFORG drawing (PLAN) does not appear in the current drawing. This way, the CAD operator working on the PLANFORG drawing can overlay the PLAN drawing, and the CAD operator working on the PLAN drawing can attach the PLANFORG drawing, without causing a circular reference.

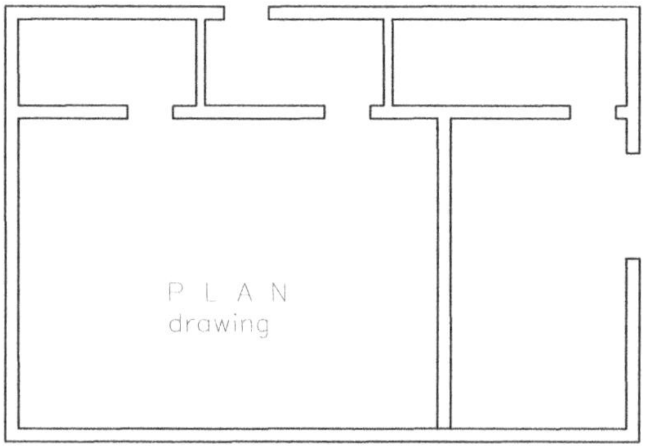

***Figure 2-21** The PLAN drawing*

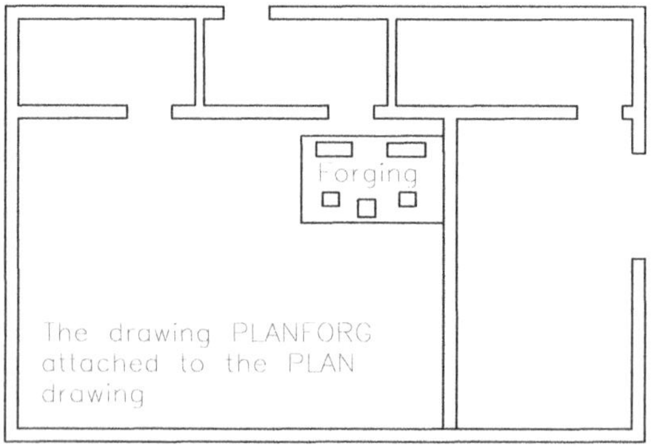

***Figure 2-22** The PLAN drawing after attaching the PLANFORG drawing*

ATTACHING FILES TO A DRAWING

Ribbon: Insert > Reference > Attach **Command:** ATTACH

You can use the **Attach** tool in the **Reference** panel, refer to Figure 2-23, to attach a DWG, DGN, DWF, PDF, Autodesk Point Cloud files, Navisworks files, or image file without invoking the **EXTERNAL REFERENCES** palette. Using this tool, you can attach a drawing file easily, since most of the xref operations involve simply attaching a drawing file. When you invoke this tool, AutoCAD displays the **Select Reference File** dialog box. To attach a *.dwg, .dgn, .dwf, .pdf, .rcp, rcs, .nwc, .nwd*, or image file, specify it in the **Files of type** drop-down list in the **Select Reference File** dialog box; the corresponding files will be listed in the dialog box. Select the drawing file to be attached and choose the **Open** button; the **Attach External Reference** dialog box is displayed. Select the **Attachment** radio button (if not selected by default) under the **Reference Type** area. You can specify the insertion point, scale, and rotation angle on screen or in the respective edit boxes.

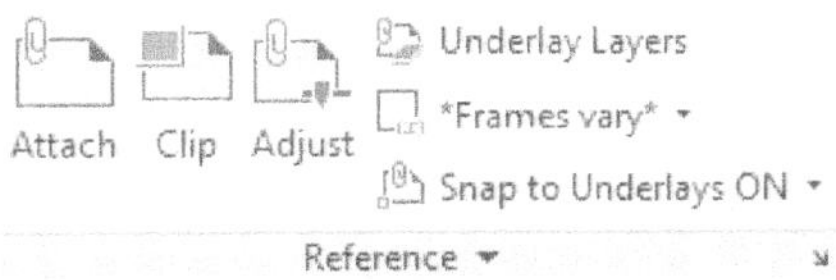

***Figure 2-23** The **Attach** tool in the **Reference** panel*

Note

*1. To select a .dgn, .dwf, .pdf, or image file, specify the file type in the **Files of type** drop-down list in the **Select Reference File** dialog box; the files will be attached as an underlay. Underlays are discussed in the next section.*

*2. AutoCAD maintains a log file (.xlg) for xref drawings if the **XREFCTL** system variable is set to 1. This file lists information about the date and time of loading and other xref operations to be completed. This .xlg file is saved in the current drawing with the same name as the current drawing and is updated each time the drawing is loaded or any xref operations are carried out.*

WORKING WITH UNDERLAYS

You can attach a DWF, DGN, or PDF file as an underlay to the current drawing file. The underlay files are not a part of original drawing files. Therefore, if you add a file as an underlay, it does not increase the file size of the current drawing. The procedure to add a file as an underlay is similar to attaching a drawing file using the **Attach** tool. After you select the file to attach, the **Attach <XXXX> Underlay** dialog box will be displayed, where <XXXX> is the file type. Figure 2-24 shows the **Attach PDF Underlay** dialog box that is displayed on selecting a pdf file from the **Select Reference File** dialog box.

If the selected *.pdf* file has multiple pages, all pages of the pdf file are listed in the **Select one or more pages from the PDF file** area. Select the pages to be attached from this area. If you have selected multiple pages as well as the **Specify on-screen** check box from the **Insertion point** area, then you are prompted to specify different insertion points for different pages.

The files attached as an underlay behave like blocks. The general modify commands like move, copy, rotate, mirror, and so on can be applied on them. However, you cannot bind a file that is attached as an underlay or modify the attached file in the current drawing file.

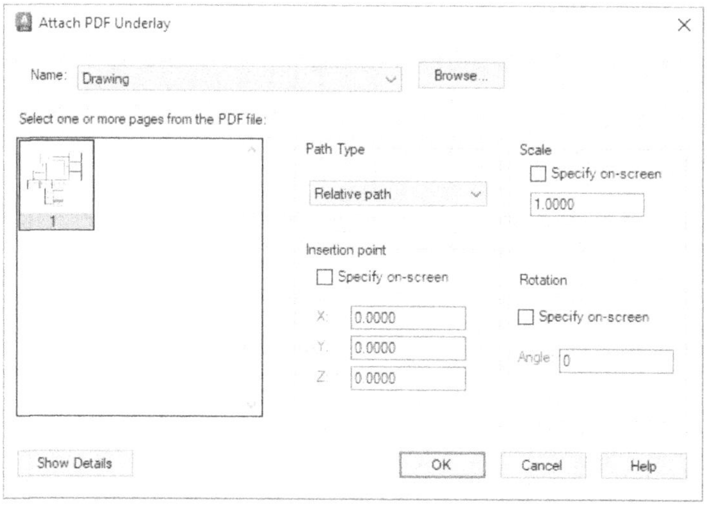

*Figure 2-24 The **Attach PDF Underlay** dialog box*

Editing an Underlay

As discussed earlier, you cannot edit a file that is attached as an underlay. However, you can control the appearance of the underlay by adjusting the contrast, fade, and monochrome display. To do so, select the attached object; a contextual tab will be displayed. Figure 2-25 shows the **PDF Underlay** tab that is displayed on selecting a PDF file.

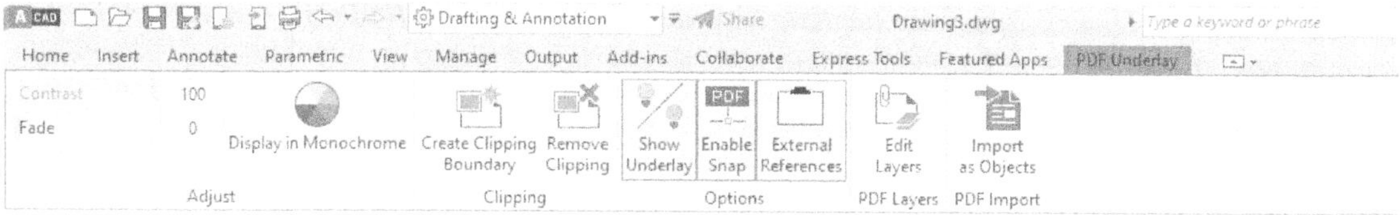

*Figure 2-25 The **PDF Underlay** tab*

You can use the options in this contextual tab to adjust the fade, contrast, and monochrome display of the underlay. You can create a new clipping boundary similar to that of an attached drawing. By default, the **Enable Snap** button is chosen in the **Options** panel. Therefore, you can snap entities in the underlaid object. If you deselect this button, you cannot snap entities in the underlaid objects. You can use the **Show Underlay** button from the **Options** panel to display/hide the underlaid objects. Both **Enable Snap** and **Show Underlay** are toggle buttons. If the attached underlay has layers, you can hide/display the selected layers. To do so, choose the **Edit Layers** button from the **PDF Layers** panel of the **PDF Underlay** contextual tab; the **Underlay Layers** dialog box will be displayed, as shown in Figure 2-26. If multiple drawings are attached as an underlay, all file names will be listed in the **Reference Name** drop-down list. Select the file from the **Reference Name** drop-down list for which you need to hide the layers; the corresponding layers will be listed in the list box. Click on the bulb icon of the layer to be hidden. Alternatively, select the layer from the list box and right-click; a shortcut menu will be displayed. Choose the **Layer(s) Off** option to hide the selected layer. To hide multiple layers, press the CTRL key and select the layers to be hidden. Next, choose **Layer(s) Off**. Then, choose the **OK** button to exit the **Underlay Layers** dialog box.

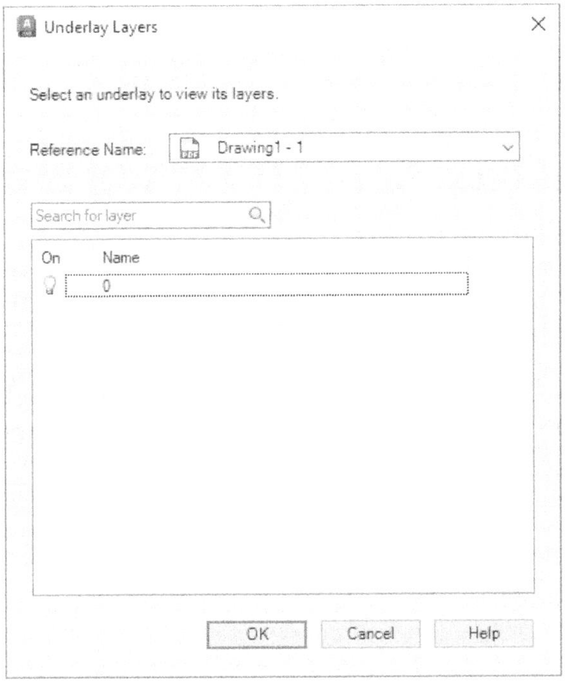

***Figure 2-26** The **Underlay Layers** dialog box*

If you have attached a file as an underlay, you can invoke the **Underlay Layers** dialog box without invoking the contextual tab by choosing the **Underlay Layers** tool from the **Reference** panel in the **Insert** tab. Similarly, you can switch on/off the OSNAP settings for the drawing that are underlaid by choosing the **Snap to Underlays ON / Snap to Underlays OFF** tool, respectively from the **Snap to Underlays** drop-down in the **Reference** panel. You can import the geometry, fills and hatches, raster images, and TrueType text objects from a specified PDF file by choosing the **Import as Objects** button from the **PDF Import** panel of the **PDF Underlay** contextual tab.

Note

*If there are more underlays of different file types and you have set different osnap setting for each file type, then the **Underlay Osnap's Vary** tool will be activated in the **Snap to Underlays** drop-down in the **Reference** panel. However, if you choose the **Snap to Underlays ON / Snap to Underlays OFF** tool, the corresponding osnap setting will be applied to all underlays.*

OPENING AN XREFFED OBJECT IN A SEPARATE WINDOW

If you are in the host drawing and you want to open a selected xreffed object in a separate window without using the **Select File** dialog box, you can use the **Open Reference** tool available in the **External Reference** contextual tab which is displayed on selecting an external reference. Select the xreffed object that you want to open in a separate window. When you select the desired xref, AutoCAD opens the DWG file of the xreffed object in a separate window. You can now make the desired changes in the DWG file of the xreffed object. Save the changes and then close the drawing. When you open the host drawing, you will notice that the **Manage xrefs** displays a message that the external reference file has changed and the xreffed drawing needs to be reloaded. Reload the xreffed drawing using the **EXTERNAL REFERENCES** palette and you will notice that the host drawing is updated.

USING THE DesignCenter TO ATTACH A DRAWING AS AN XREF

The **DESIGNCENTER** can also be used to attach an xref to a drawing. To do so, choose the **DesignCenter** button from the **Palettes** panel in the **View** tab; the **DESIGNCENTER** palette will be displayed. In the **DESIGNCENTER** palette, choose the **Tree View Toggle** button, if it is not chosen already, to display the tree pane. Expand the **Tree view** and double-click on the folder whose contents you want to view. The contents of the selected folder are displayed in the palette. From the thumbnails of drawings displayed on the right-side of the palette, right-click on the drawing to be attached as an xref; a shortcut menu is displayed, refer to Figure 2-27. Choose **Attach as Xref** from the shortcut menu; the **Attach External Reference** dialog box will be displayed. Alternatively, you can also use the right mouse button to drag and drop the drawing into the current drawing; a shortcut menu will be displayed. Choose the **Create Xref** option to insert the drawing as an xref.

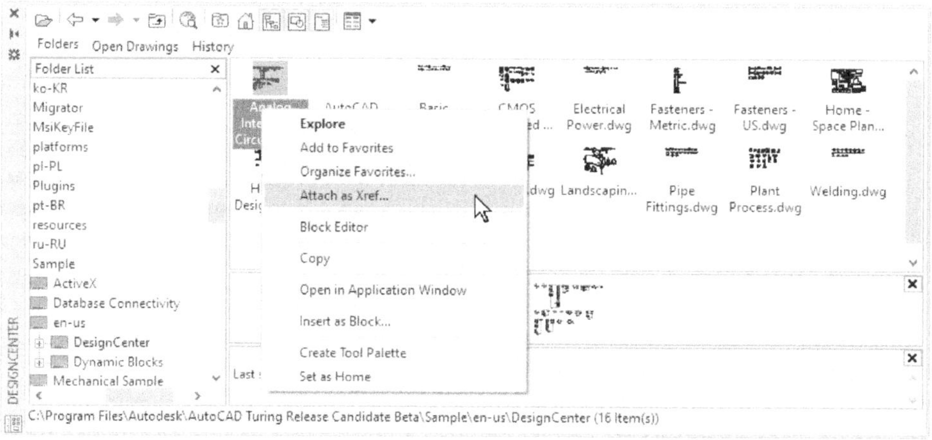

Figure 2-27 *The shortcut menu displayed*

In the **Attach External Reference** dialog box, the **Name** drop-down displays the name of the selected file to be inserted as an xref. Select the **Attachment** radio button in the **Reference Type** area, if not already selected. Specify the **Insertion point**, **Scale**, and **Rotation** in the respective edit boxes or select the **Specify On-screen** check boxes to specify this information on the screen. Choose the **OK** button to exit the dialog box; the selected object is attached as an xref to the current drawing.

ADDING XREF DEPENDENT NAMED OBJECTS

Menu Bar: Modify > Object > External Reference > Bind
Toolbar: Reference > Xbind **Command:** XB/XBIND

You can use the **Xbind** tool to add the selected named objects such as blocks, dimension styles, layers, line types, and text styles of the xref drawing to the current drawing. The following example describes the use of this command.

1. Load the drawing Bearing that was created earlier. Make sure the drawing has the following layer setup. Otherwise, create the following layers using the **LAYER PROPERTIES MANAGER**.

Layer Name	Color	Linetype
0	White	Continuous
Object	Red	Continuous
Hidden	Blue	Hidden2
Center	White	Center2
Hatch	Green	Continuous

2. Draw a circle and create it as a block with the name SIDE. Save the drawing as Bearing.

3. Start a new drawing with the following layer setup:

Layer Name	Color	Linetype
0	White	Continuous
Object	Red	Continuous
Hidden	Green	Hidden

4. Use the **Attach** tool in the **Reference** panel to attach the Bearing drawing to the current drawing. When you xref the drawing, the layers will be added to the current drawing, as discussed earlier in this chapter.

5. Now, invoke the **Xbind** tool; the **Xbind** dialog box is displayed. This dialog box has two areas with list boxes. They are **Xrefs** and **Definitions to Bind**. If you want to bind the blocks defined in the xref drawing Bearing, first click on the plus sign adjacent to the xref Bearing; the icons for the named objects in the drawing are displayed in a tree view, refer to Figure 2-28. Click on the plus sign next to the Block icon. AutoCAD lists the blocks defined in the xref drawing (Bearing). Select the block Bearing|SIDE and then choose the **Add** button. The block name will be added to the **Definitions to Bind** list box. Choose the **OK** button to exit the dialog box. AutoCAD will bind the block with the current drawing and a message is displayed at the command prompt: **1 Block(s) bound**. The name of the block will change to Bearing0SIDE. You can invoke the **Block Definition** dialog box by choosing the **Create Block** tool in the **Block Definition** panel and check the **Name** drop-down list to see if the block with the name Bearing0SIDE has been added to the drawing. If you

want to insert the block, you must enter the new block name (Bearing0SIDE). You can also rename the block to another name that is easier to use.

If the block contains a reference to another xref drawing, AutoCAD binds that xref drawing and all its dependent symbols to the current drawing also. Once you bind the dependent symbols, AutoCAD does not delete them, not even when the xref drawing is detached. For example, the block Bearing0SIDE will not be deleted even when you detach the xref drawing or end the drawing session.

Figure 2-28 *The named objects in the* ***Xbind*** *dialog box*

You can also use the **-XBIND** command to bind the selected dependent symbols of the xref drawing using the command prompt.

6. Similarly, you can bind the dependent symbols, Bearing|Standard (textstyle), Bearing|Hidden, and Bearing|Object layers of the xref drawing. Click on the plus signs adjacent to the respective icons to display the contents and then select the layer or textstyle you want to bind and choose the **Add** button. The selected named objects are displayed in the **Definitions to Bind** list box. If you have selected a named object that you do not want to bind, select it in the **Definitions to Bind** list box and choose the **Remove** button. Once you have finished selecting the named objects that you want to bind to the current drawing, choose the **OK** button. A message indicating the number of named objects that are bound to the current drawing is displayed at the command prompt.

Once bound, the layer names will change to Bearing0Hidden and Bearing0Object. If the layer name Bearing0Hidden was already there, the layer will be named Bearing1Hidden. These two layers become a permanent part of the current drawing. Even if the xref drawing is detached or the current drawing session is closed, the layers are not discarded.

CLIPPING EXTERNAL REFERENCES

Ribbon: Insert > Reference > Clip **Command:** CLIP

The **Clip** tool (Figure 2-29) is used to trim an xref after it has been attached to a drawing to display only a portion of the drawing, refer to Figure 2-30. After you have attached an xref to a drawing, you can trim it to display only a portion of the drawing by using the **Clip** tool. However, clipping xref does not modify the referenced drawing. On invoking the **Clip** tool, you are prompted to select an object to clip. Select a DWG, DGN, IMAGE, or PDF; the respective clipping options will be displayed.

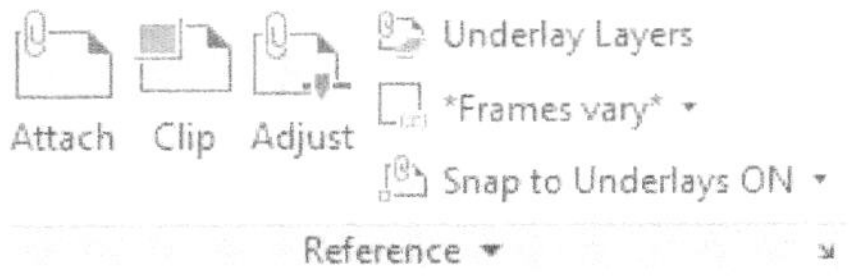

Figure 2-29 *The* ***Clip*** *tool in the* ***Reference*** *panel*

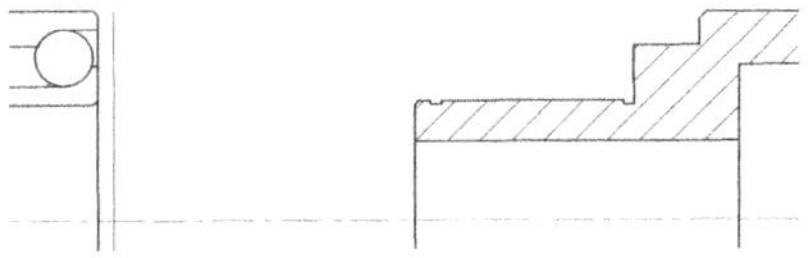

Figure 2-30 *Using the* ***Clip*** *tool to clip*

You can also invoke the **Clip** tool by selecting an xref and then right-clicking in the drawing area to display a shortcut menu. Next, choose the corresponding clip command from it. For example, to clip an attached *.dwg* file, select the attached *.dwg* file, right-click, and choose the **Clip Xref** option; the following prompt sequence will be displayed.

Enter clipping option [ON/OFF/Clipdepth/Delete/generate Polyline/New boundary] <New>: *Press Enter to specify a new clip boundary or enter an option.*
Specify clipping boundary or select invert option: [Select polyline/Polygonal/Rectangular/Invert clip] <Rectangular>: *Press Enter to select the* ***Rectangular*** *option, and then specify two corners of the rectangular boundary.*

You can also right-click in the drawing area at the enter clipping option prompt to display a shortcut menu. This shortcut menu displays all the options available at the command prompt that can be selected here. All the clipping options available are discussed next.

New boundary

The clipping boundary can be specified by using the **Rectangular**, **Polygonal**, or **Select polyline** option. The **Rectangular** option generates a rectangular boundary and the **Polygonal** option allows you to specify a boundary of any shape. You can draw a boundary using the **Polyline** tool or the **Polygon** tool and then, use the **Select polyline** option to select this polyline as the clipping boundary. The **Invert clip** option inverts the direction of the clipping. For example, if the objects outside the clipping boundary are hidden, by default, the **Invert clip** option will hide the objects inside the clipping boundary and display the objects outside the boundary. After selecting the **Invert clip** option, you need to redefine the clipping boundary using any one of the options discussed above. The **Invert clip** option can only be used with the 2D Wireframe visual style. If a boundary already exists, AutoCAD will ask you if the old boundary should be deleted. You can enter **YES** if you want to delete the old boundary and define a new one. If you enter **NO**, the old boundary is retained and the **Clip Xref** tool exits.

ON/OFF

The **ON/OFF** option allows you to specify whether to display the clipped portion or not. When the clipping boundary is off, you can see the complete xref drawing and when it is on, the drawing that is within the clipping polygon is displayed.

Delete

The **Delete** option completely deletes the predefined clipping boundary and the entire xref gets displayed. The **Erase** tool cannot be used to delete the clipping boundary.

generate Polyline

If you have a clipped boundary, select this option to create a polyline coinciding with the boundary of the clipped xref drawing. You can edit the polyline boundary without affecting the clipped drawing. For example, if you stretch the boundary, it does not affect the xref drawing. The edited boundary can be used later to specify a new clipping boundary.

Clipdepth

This option allows you to define the front and back clipping planes for 3D xref objects or blocks. The objects between the front and back planes will be displayed, refer to Figure 2-31 and Figure 2-32. In the figures that follow, the clipping boundary is defined aligned to the front face of the object, and therefore, the clipping planes will get defined parallel to it. The xref must contain a clip boundary before specifying a clip depth. If you use the **Clipdepth** option, it prompts you to specify a front clip point and a back clip point. Specifying these points, creates a clipping frame passing through them and parallel to the clipping boundary. If the front clipping plane is specified behind the back clipping plane, AutoCAD displays an error message and the clipdepth is also not applied. The **Distance** option for specifying the front or back clip points creates a clipping plane at a specified distance from the clipping boundary parallel to it. The **Remove** option removes both the front and back clipping planes and the entire object is visible.

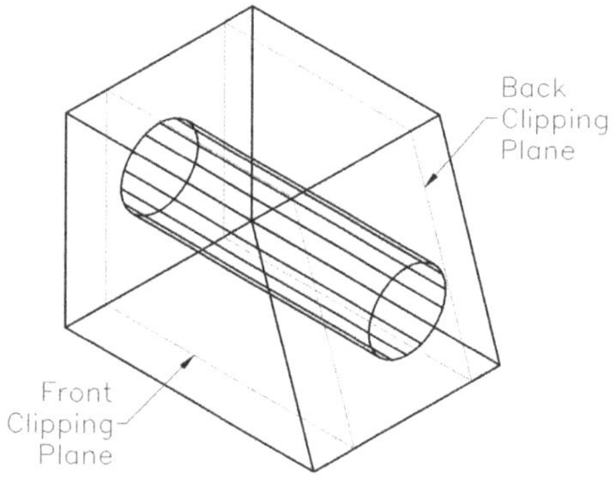

Figure 2-31 *3D xref object before clipping*

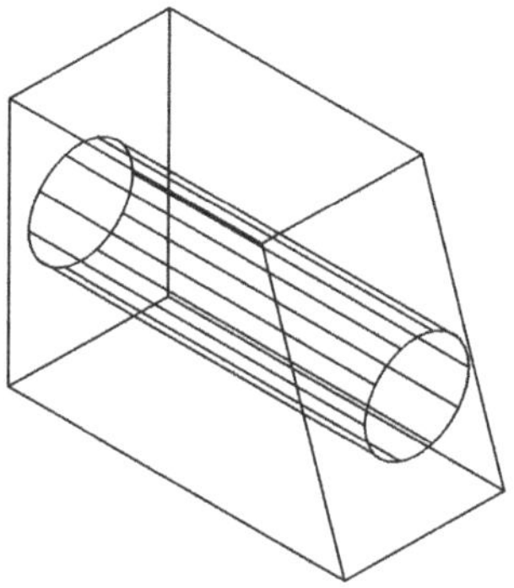

Figure 2-32 *3D xref object after clipping*

Similarly, you can clip the other underlaid xrefs. The options available for clipping the underlaid Xrefs are **ON**, **OFF**, **Delete**, and **New Boundary**. These options are the same as discussed above.

DISPLAYING CLIPPING FRAME

You can select the appropriate option from the **Frames** drop-down list in the **Reference** panel of the **Insert** tab, refer to Figure 2-33, to turn on or off the display of clipping boundary of all clipped Xrefs. If there are multiple underlays of different file types and you have set different frame settings for each file type, then the **Frames vary** button will be displayed in the **Reference** panel of the **Insert** tab. You can also use the **FRAME** system variable to turn on or off the display of clipping boundary of all clipped xrefs. When the value of **FRAME** system variable is 0, the clipping boundary will neither be displayed or plotted. When it is 1, the clipping boundary will be displayed and plotted. When it is 2, the clipping boundary will be displayed, but not plotted. When it is 3 (default), the settings vary for all the clipping boundaries. To control the display of frames of individual attached Xrefs, you need to invoke the individual system variables like **XCLIPFRAME**, **DGNFRAME**, **PDFFRAME**, and **IMAGEFRAME**.

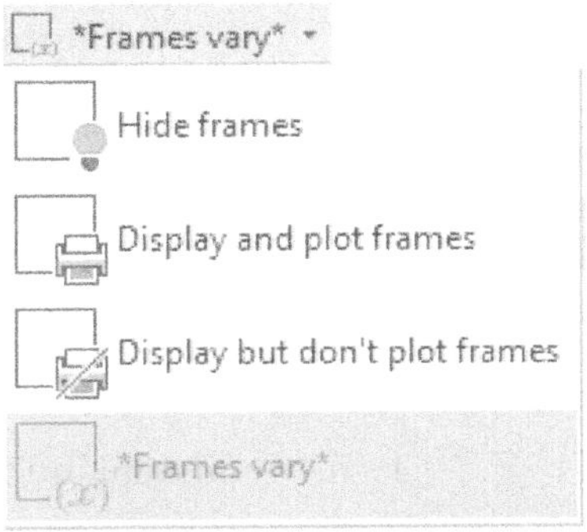

*Figure 2-33 Options in the **FRAME** drop-down list*

DEMAND LOADING

The demand loading feature loads only that part of the referenced drawing that is required in the existing drawing. For example, demand loading provides a mechanism by which objects on frozen layers are not loaded. Also, only the clipped portion of the referenced drawing can be loaded. This makes the xref operation more efficient since less disk space is used, especially when the drawing is reopened. Demand loading is enabled by default. You can modify its settings in the **External References (Xrefs)** area of the **Open and Save** tab of the **Options** dialog box, refer to Figure 2-34. You can select any of the three options available in the **Demand load Xrefs** drop-down list in this dialog box. These options are **Disabled**, **Enabled**, and **Enabled with copy**. These options correspond to a value of **0**, **1**, and **2** of the **XLOADCTL** system variable, respectively, and are discussed next.

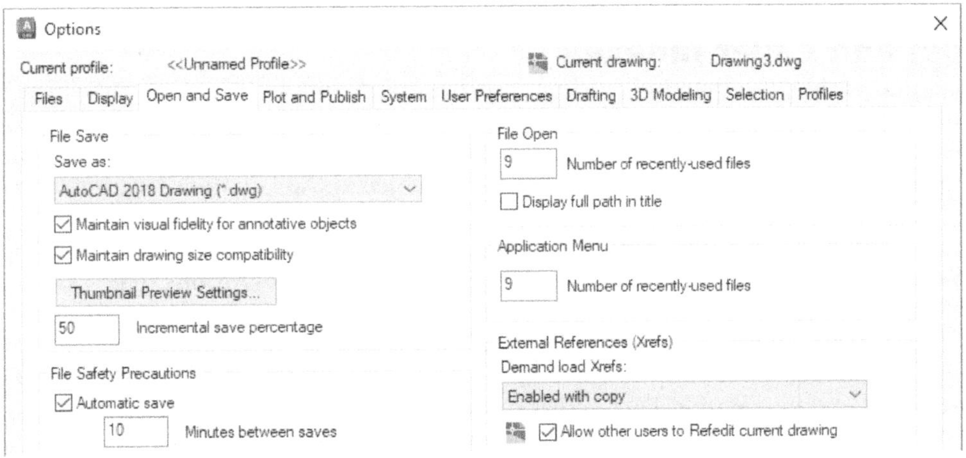

*Figure 2-34 Partial view of the **Options** dialog box with the **Open and Save** tab chosen*

Setting	Value of XLOADCTL	Features
Disabled	0	1. Turns off demand loading. 2. Loads entire xref drawing file. 3. The file is available on the server and other users can edit the xref drawing.
Enabled	1	1. Turns on demand loading. 2. The referenced file is kept open. 3. Makes the referenced file read-only for other users.
Enabled with copy	2	1. Turns on demand loading with the copy option. 2. A copy of a referenced drawing is opened. 3. Other users can access and edit the original referenced drawing file.

You can also set the value of **XLOADCTL** at the command prompt. When you are using the **Enabled with copy** option of demand loading, the temporary copies of the xref are saved in the AutoCAD temporary files directory (defined in the **Temporary External Reference File Location** folder in the **Files** tab of the **Options** dialog box) or in a user-specified directory. The **XLOADPATH** system variable creates a temporary path to store demand loaded Xrefs.

Spatial and Layer Indexes

As mentioned earlier, the demand loading improves performance when the drawing contains referenced files. To make it work effectively and to take full advantage of demand loading, you must store a drawing with Layer and Spatial indexes. The layer index maintains a list of objects in different layers and the spatial index contains lists of objects based on their location in 3D space.

Layer and spatial indexes are created using the **Save Drawing As** dialog box. Choose the **Options** option from the **Tools** drop-down to display the **Saveas Options** dialog box. Choose the **DWG Options** tab if it is not already chosen and select the type of index from the **Index type** drop-down list. **None** is the default option selected in the drop-down list. As a result, no indexes are created. The other options available are: **Layer**, **Spatial**, and **Layer & Spatial**. Once you have selected the type of index to create, choose the **OK** button to exit the dialog box and choose the **Save** button in the **Save Drawing As** dialog box to save the drawing with the indexes. The **INDEXCTL** variable also controls the creation of layer index and spatial index and its value can be set using the command prompt. The following are the settings of the **INDEXCTL** system variable, and they correspond to the **Index type** options available in the **DWG Options** tab of the **Save as Options** dialog box.

Setting	Features	Index Type option
0	No index created	None
1	Layer index created	Layer
2	Spatial index created	Spatial
3	Layer and spatial index created	Layer and Spatial

EDITING REFERENCES IN-PLACE

Ribbon: Insert > Reference > Edit Reference **Command:** REFEDIT
Toolbar: Refedit > Edit Reference In-Place

Often you have to make minor changes in the xref drawing if you want to save yourself from the trouble of going back and forth between drawings. In this situation, you can use in-place reference editing to select the xref, modify it, and then save it after modifications. The following steps explain the referencing editing process.

1. To edit in-place, select an external referenced object; the **External Reference** contextual tab will be added to the **Ribbon**, as shown in Figure 2-35. Choose the **Edit Reference In-Place** tool from the **Edit** panel; the **Reference Edit** dialog box will be displayed.

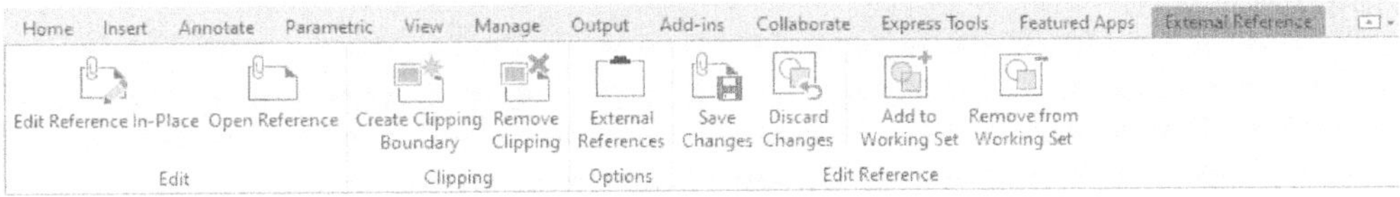

*Figure 2-35 The **External Reference** contextual tab added to the **Ribbon***

2. In the **Reference name** list box of the **Reference Edit** dialog box, the selected reference and its nested references are listed. Select the specific xref you wish to edit from the list.

3. In the **Settings** tab of the dialog box, select both the **Create unique layer**, **style**, **and block names** and the **Lock objects not in working set** check boxes. The **Display attribute definitions for editing** check box is disabled by default. In the **Identify Reference** tab of the dialog box, select the **Prompt to select nested objects** radio button. Choose the **OK** button to return to the current drawing. At the **Select nested objects:** prompt, select the objects you want to modify and press Enter. The objects that have not been selected for modifications will become faded. The fading is controlled by the **XFADECTL** system variable or by using the **Xref display** slider bar in the **Display** tab of the **Options** dialog box. You can add or remove objects to the working set by choosing the respective tools in the **Edit Reference** panel or by using the **REFSET** command. Once you have defined a working set, all the standard AutoCAD commands can be used to modify them.

4. When you choose the **Save Changes** tool in the **Edit Reference** panel, AutoCAD displays a message: **All references edits will be saved**. Choose the **OK** button to return to the drawing area. The modifications made are saved in the drawing as well as in the current drawing as a reference. On choosing the **Discard Changes** tool in the **Edit Reference** panel, the changes made will not be saved and the current drawing is redisplayed.

Note

*In the **External References (Xrefs)** area of the **Open and Save** tab of the **Options** dialog box, if you select the **Allow other users to Refedit current drawing** check box, the current drawing can be edited in-place by other users even when it is open and is being referenced by another file. This option is selected by default and can also be controlled by the **XEDIT** system variable. The default value of **XEDIT** is 1 and can be changed using the command prompt.*

Self-Evaluation Test

Answer the following questions and then compare them to those given at the end of this chapter:

1. The _________ are entries such as blocks, layers, and text styles.
2. If you use the **Insert** tool to insert a drawing, the information about the named objects is lost if the names are _________, and if the names are _________, the drawing will be imported.
3. The ___________ option from the **Attach** drop-down list of the **EXTERNAL REFERENCES** palette is used to attach an xref drawing to the current drawing.
4. The _________ feature loads only that part of the referenced drawing that is required in the existing drawing.
5. The _________ option can be used to overcome the problem of circular reference.
6. After selecting the _________ option, the xref is completely removed from the current drawing.
7. If an assembly drawing has been created by inserting a drawing, the drawing will be updated automatically if a change is made in the inserted drawing. (T/F)
8. The external reference facility helps you keep a drawing updated no matter when the changes were made in the piece part drawings. (T/F)
9. Objects can be added to a dependent layer. (T/F)
10. The **Overlay** option ignores the nested references. (T/F).

Review Questions

Answer the following questions:

1. Which of the following features is used to reference an external drawing without making this drawing a permanent part of the existing drawing?

   (a) demand loading (b) external reference
   (c) external clipping (d) insert drawing

2. If an xref has nested references that cannot be found, which of the following will be displayed under the status heading of the **List View** button in the **EXTERNAL REFERENCES** palette?

   (a) **Orphaned** (b) **Not found**
   (c) **Unreferenced** (d) **Unresolved**

3. Which of the following system variables, when set to 1, will allow AutoCAD to maintain a log file (*.xlg*) for xref drawings?

   (a) **XLOADCTL** (b) **XLOADPATH**
   (c) **XREFCTL** (d) **INDEXCTL**

4. Which of the following system variables, when set to 0, will not allow the clipping boundary to be displayed?

   (a) **XCLIPFRAME** (b) **XLOADCTL**
   (c) **INDEXCTL** (d) **XREFCTL**

5. In the __________ drawings, the information regarding dependent symbols is not lost.

6. AutoCAD maintains a log file for xref drawings, if the __________ variable is set to 1.

7. It is possible to edit xrefs in-place using the __________ tool.

8. You can use the __________ tool to add the selected dependent symbols from the xref drawing to the current drawing.

9. If the xref drawings get updated, changes are not automatically reflected in the assembly drawing when you open an assembly drawing. (T/F)

10. There is a limit to the number of drawings you can reference. (T/F)

11. It is not possible to have nested references. (T/F)

12. Like blocks, the xref drawings can be scaled, rotated, or positioned at any desired location. (T/F)

13. You can change the color, linetype, or visibility (on/off, freeze/thaw) of a dependent layer. (T/F)

Exercise 1 *Bind Xref*

In this exercise, you will start a new drawing and xref the drawings as Part-1 and Part-2, refer to Figure 2-36 and Figure 2-37. For assembly, refer to Figure 2-38. You will also edit one of the piece parts to correct the size and use the **Bind Xref** option to bind some of the dependent symbols to the current drawing. The parameters of layers for Part-1, Part-2 and ASSEM1 are as follows:

For Part-1, set up the following layers:

Layer Name	Color	Linetype
0	White	Continuous
Object	Red	Continuous
Hidden	Blue	Hidden2
Center	White	Center2
Dim-Part1	Green	Continuous

For Part-2, set up the following layers:

Layer Name	Color	Linetype
0	White	Continuous
Object	Red	Continuous
Hidden	Blue	Hidden
Center	White	Center
Dim-Part2	Green	Continuous
Hatch	Magenta	Continuous

For ASSEM1, set up the following layers:

Layer Name	Color	Linetype
0	White	Continuous
Object	Blue	Continuous
Hidden	Yellow	Hidden

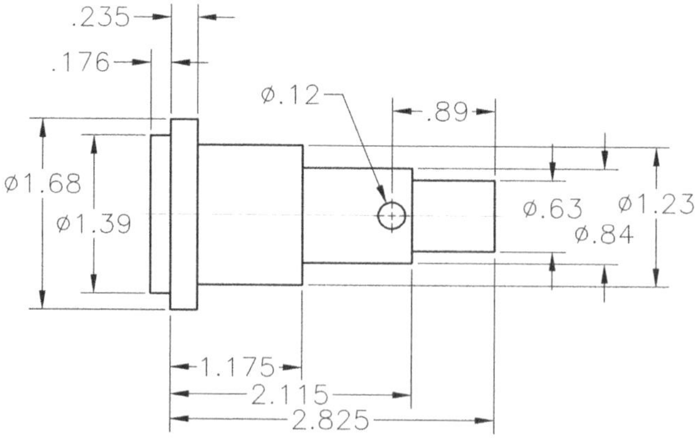

Figure 2-36 Drawing of Part-1

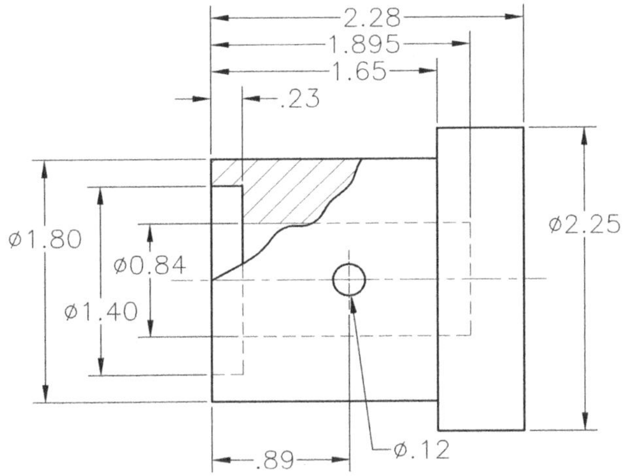

Figure 2-37 *Drawing of Part-2*

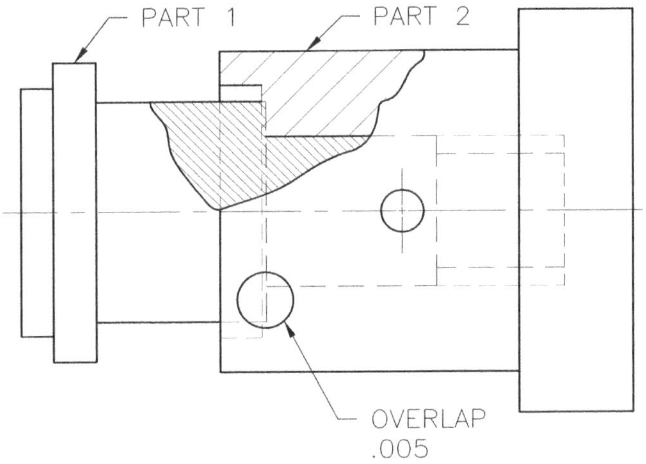

Figure 2-38 *Assembly drawing after attaching Part-1 and Part-2*

Answers to Self-Evaluation Test

1. named objects, **2.** duplicated, unique, **3. Attach DWG**, **4.** demand loading, **5. Overlay**, **6. Detach**, **7.** F, **8.** T, **9.** F, **10.** T

Chapter 3

Working with Advanced Drawing Options

Learning Objectives

After completing this chapter, you will be able to:

- *Define multiline style and specify the properties of multilines using the Multiline Style command*
- *Draw various types of multilines using the MLINE command*
- *Edit multilines using the MLEDIT command*
- *Draw NURBS splines using the Spline tool*
- *Edit NURBS splines using the Edit Spline tool*
- *Compare Drawings*

Key Terms

- *Multiline*
- *MLEDIT*
- *Revision Cloud*
- *Wipeout*
- *Spline*
- *Fit Points*
- *CV*
- *Knots*
- *Kink*
- *Weight*
- *DWG Compare*
- *Markup Import*

UNDERSTANDING THE USE OF MULTILINES

The Multiline feature allows you to draw composite lines that consist of multiple parallel lines. These parallel lines are called elements. You can draw these lines using the **MLINE** command. But before drawing multilines, you need to set multiline styles. This can be accomplished by using the **MLSTYLE** command. You can also edit multilines by using the **MLEDIT** command.

DEFINING A MULTILINE STYLE

Menu Bar: Format > Multiline Style **Command:** MLSTYLE

You can create a multiline style by using the **MLSTYLE** command. You can specify the number of elements in a multiline and the properties of each element. The style also controls the start and end caps, the start and end lines, and the color of multilines and fill. When you invoke the **Multiline Style** tool from the **Format** menu or by using the **MLSTYLE** command, AutoCAD displays the **Multiline Style** dialog box, as shown in Figure 3-1. Using this dialog box, you can set the spacing between parallel lines, specify linetype pattern, set colors, solid fill, and capping arrangements. By default, the multiline style (STANDARD) has two lines that are offset at 0.5 and -0.5.

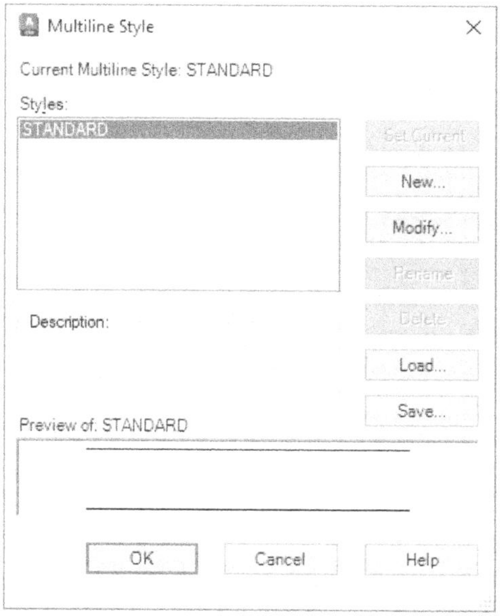

***Figure 3-1** The **Multiline Style** dialog box*

Note

You cannot modify a multiline style that is in use in the current drawing. To do so, you first need to delete the multiline from all the places where it is used and then you can modify its style.

Styles List Box

The **Styles** list box displays the names of the styles. By default, the **STANDARD** style is available in this list box. If several styles have been defined, all of them will be listed in this list box.

Set Current

If several styles have been defined, select a style from the **Styles** list box and choose the **Set Current** button to make the style as the current style. The current multiline style is saved in the **CMLSTYLE** system variable.

New

The **New** button is chosen to create a new multilinestyle. On choosing this button, the **Create New Multiline Style** dialog box will be displayed, as shown in Figure 3-2. The **New Style Name** edit box is used to specify the name of the new multiline style that you want to define. The **Start With** drop-down list will be available only if some styles have already been defined. You can select an existing style as a reference to create the new style. The new style will start with the properties associated with the style selected from the **Start With** drop-down list. As soon as you specify the name of the new style, the **Continue** button is highlighted. To create a new style, enter the name of the new style in the **New Style Name** edit box and then choose the **Continue** button; the **New Multiline Style** dialog box will be displayed, as shown in Figure 3-3.

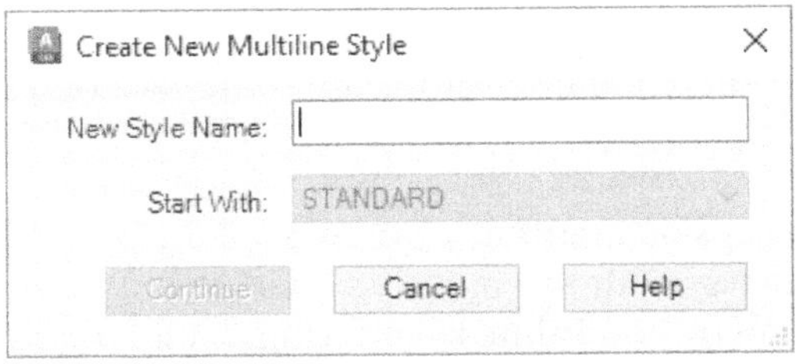

***Figure 3-2** The **Create New Multiline Style** dialog box*

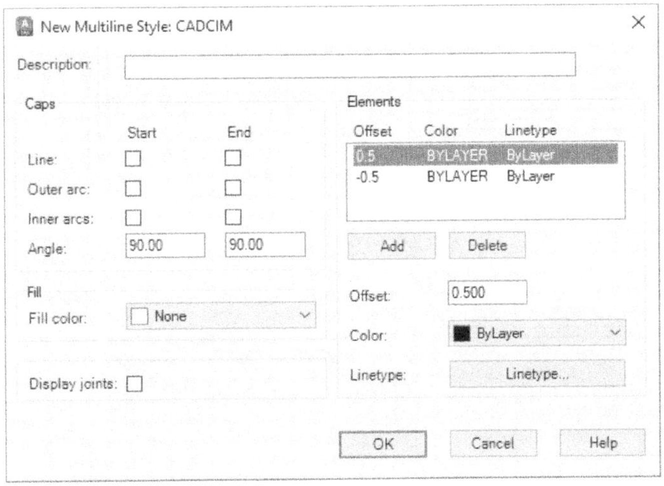

***Figure 3-3** The **New Multiline Style** dialog box*

The title bar of the **New Multiline Style** dialog box displays the name of the new style. By default, some properties in the dialog box are defined at some preset values. These values correspond to the selection made in the **Start With** drop-down list of the **Create New Multiline Style** dialog box.

Description

This edit box is used to specify the description of the new multiline style. Giving information in this edit box is optional, so you can leave it blank if you want.

Caps Area

The options under this area are used to set the type and location of the start and end caps of the multilines. These options are discussed next.

Line: Selecting the **Start** and **End** check boxes of this option caps the multiline with a line at the start point and the endpoint, refer to Figure 3-4.

Outer arc: Selecting the **Start** and **End** check boxes of this option draws a semicircular arc between the endpoints of the outermost lines, refer to Figure 3-4.

Inner arcs: This option is used to draw a semicircular arc between the two innermost lines at the start point and endpoint of a multiline. The arc is drawn between the even-numbered inner lines, refer to Figure 3-4. For example, if there are two inner lines, an arc will be drawn at their ends. On the other hand, if there are three inner lines, the two outer lines are capped with the arc and the middle line is not capped.

Angle: By default, the end caps of a multiline are drawn tangentially to the multiline elements, that is, the angle the cap makes with the multiline elements is 90 degree. You can control the cap angle at the start and end of a multiline by entering angles in the corresponding **Angle** edit boxes, refer to Figure 3-4. This angle can be between 10 degree and 170 degree.

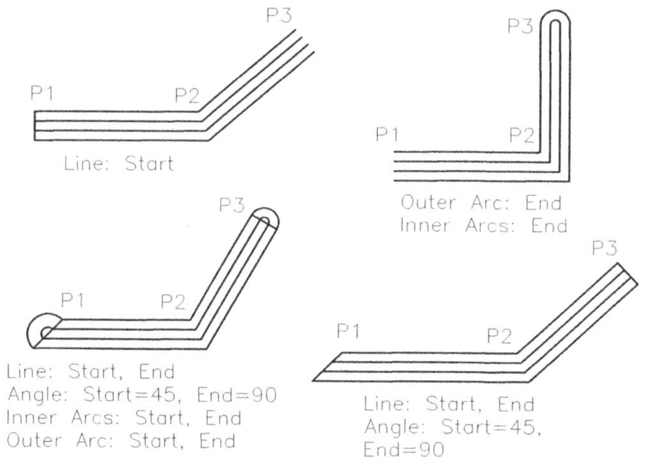

Figure 3-4 Drawing multilines with different end cap specifications

Fill Area

The options under this area are used to fill the multiline with a specified color. By default, **None** is selected in the **Fill color** drop-down list. As a result, there is no fill effect in the multiline. To specify a fill color, select it from this drop-down list. On selecting the **Select Color** option, the **Select Color** dialog box will be displayed which can be used to select additional colors.

Display joints

If you select the **Display joints** check box, AutoCAD will draw a line across all elements of the multiline at the vertex points, where the multiline changes direction. The joints of the multiline are also called miter joints. If you draw only one multiline segment, no line is drawn at the miter joint.

Elements Area

The options in this area modify the element properties of the multiline style. The element properties include the number of lines, color, and linetype of the lines comprising the multiline. The following options are available for setting the properties of the individual lines (elements) that constitute the multiline.

Offset, Color, and Linetype: This list box displays the offset, color, and linetype of each line that constitutes the current multiline style. The lines are always listed in the descending order, based on the offset distance. For example, a line with a 0.5 offset will be listed first and a line with a 0.25 offset will be listed next. You can select an element to be modified from the list box; the selected element is highlighted.

Add: This button allows you to add new lines to the current line style. When you choose the **Add** button, AutoCAD inserts a line with the **Offset** = 0.0, **Color** = BYLAYER, and **Linetype** = Bylayer. The new element gets added between two existing elements. After the line is added, you can change its offset distance, color, or linetype. The offset distance can be entered in the **Offset** edit box. Similarly, you can select the options in the **Color** drop-down list to specify a color for the selected element of the multiline. Also, you can choose the **Linetype** button to display the **Select Linetype** dialog box. You can use this dialog box and its options to load and select the linetype you want to apply to the selected element of a multiline.

Delete: This button allows you to delete a selected element from the multiline style. The highlighted element is removed from the **Elements** list box.

Offset: This edit box allows you to change the offset distance of the selected line in the **Elements** list box. The offset distance is defined with respect to the origin (0,0). The offset distance can be a positive or a negative value, which enables you to center the lines.

Color: This drop-down list allows you to assign a color to the selected line. When you select the **Select Color** option from this drop-down list, AutoCAD displays the **Select Color** dialog box. You can select a color from the dialog box or enter a color number or name in the **Color** edit box.

Linetype: This button allows you to assign a linetype to the selected line. When you choose this button, AutoCAD displays the **Select Linetype** dialog box. After selecting a linetype in this dialog box, choose the **OK** button to exit. You can also choose the **Load** button in the **Select Linetype** dialog box to display the **Load or Reload Linetypes** dialog box, where you can select the linetype that you want to use. The selected linetype is displayed in the **Loaded linetypes** list box of the **Select Linetype** dialog box. You can now select the specific linetype and apply it to a selected element of a multiline.

After you have added the elements to a multiline and set their properties, choose the **OK** button to exit the **New Multiline Style** dialog box. An image of the current multiline style is displayed in the **Preview of** area in the **Multiline Style** dialog box. The new style is now listed in the **Style** list box.

Load

Choose this button from the **Multiline Style** dialog box to load a multiline style from an external multiline library file (*acad.mln*). On choosing this button, the **Load Multiline Styles** dialog box will be displayed, as shown in Figure 3-5. This dialog box displays all multiline styles available in the current *mln* directory. If the style is saved in another directory or file, choose the **File** button to display the **Load Multiline Style From File** dialog box and then select the multiline file that you want to load. Once the file is loaded, all styles saved under it are displayed in the list box. You can select the style and then choose the **OK** button to make it current.

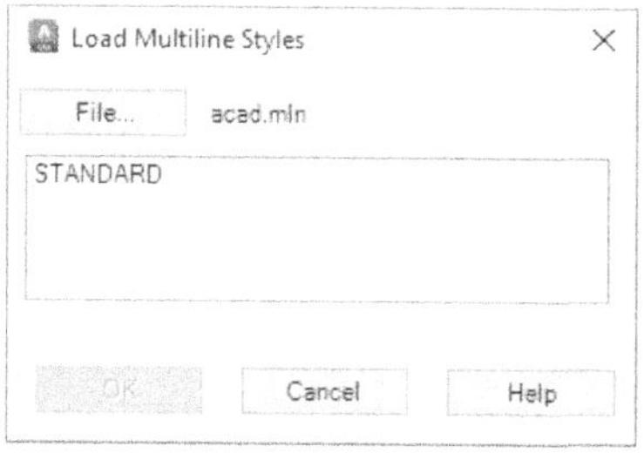

***Figure 3-5** The **Load Multiline Styles** dialog box*

Save

This button lets you save a multiline style to an external file (*.mln*). When you choose this button, AutoCAD displays the **Save Multiline Style** dialog box. This dialog box lists the names of the available predefined multiline style files (*.mln*). From the file listing, select or enter the name of the file where you want to save the current multiline style and choose the **Save** button. By default, the multiline styles get saved in the *acad.mln* file at the location *C:\Users\<user name>\AppData\Roaming\Autodesk\AutoCAD 2023\R24.2\enu\Support*.

Rename

This button allows you to rename the current multiline style. To do so, select the multiline style to be renamed and choose the **Rename** button; the text will be displayed in an edit box. Rename the text and click once on the list box. Note that you cannot rename the **STANDARD** multiline style.

Preview of Area

The **Multiline Style** dialog box also displays the current multiline configuration in the **Preview of** area. The panel will display the color, linetype, caps and relative spacing of the lines. As you select another multiline style, the image in the preview area also gets updated accordingly. The name of the multiline style whose preview is being shown is displayed above the **Preview of** area.

DRAWING MULTILINES

Menu Bar: Draw > Multiline	**Command:** MLINE/ML

The **MLINE** command is used to draw multilines. The following is the prompt sequence for the **MLINE** command:

Specify start point or [Justification/Scale/STyle]: *Select a start point or enter an option.*
Specify next point: *Select the second point.*

Specify next point or [Undo]: *Select the next point.*
Specify next point or [Close/Undo]: *Select the next point, enter **U**, or enter **C** for close.*

When you invoke the **MLINE** command, it always displays the current status of the multiline justification, scale, and style name. Remember that all line segments created in a single **MLINE** command are a single entity. The options provided under this command are discussed next.

Justification Option

The justification determines how a multiline is drawn between the specified points. Three justifications are available for the **MLINE** command. They are **Top**, **Zero**, and **Bottom**.

Top

This justification produces a multiline in which the top line coincides with the points you selected on the screen. Since the line offsets in a multiline are arranged in descending order, the line with the largest positive offset will coincide with the selected points. This is the default justification option, refer to Figure 3-6.

Zero

This option will produce a multiline in which the zero offset position of the multiline coincides with the selected points. Multilines will be centered if the positive and negative offsets are equal, refer to Figure 3-6.

Bottom

This option will produce a multiline in which the bottom line (the line with the least offset distance) coincides with the selected point when the line is drawn from left to right, refer to Figure 3-6.

Scale Option

The **Scale** option is used to change the scale of a multiline. For example, if the scale factor is 0.5, the distance between the lines (offset distance) will be reduced to half, as shown in Figure 3-7. Therefore, the width of the multiline will be half of what was defined in the multiline style. A negative scale factor will reverse the order of the offset lines. The multilines will now be drawn such that the line with the maximum negative offset distance is at the top and the line with the maximum positive offset distance is at the bottom. For example, if you enter a scale factor of -0.5, the order in which the lines are drawn will be reversed, and the offset distances will be reduced by half. Here it is assumed that the lines are drawn from left to right. If the lines are drawn from right to left, the offsets are reversed. Also, if the scale factor is 0, AutoCAD forces the multiline into a single line. However, the line will still possess the properties of a multiline. This scale factor does not affect the linetype scale factor (**LTSCALE**).

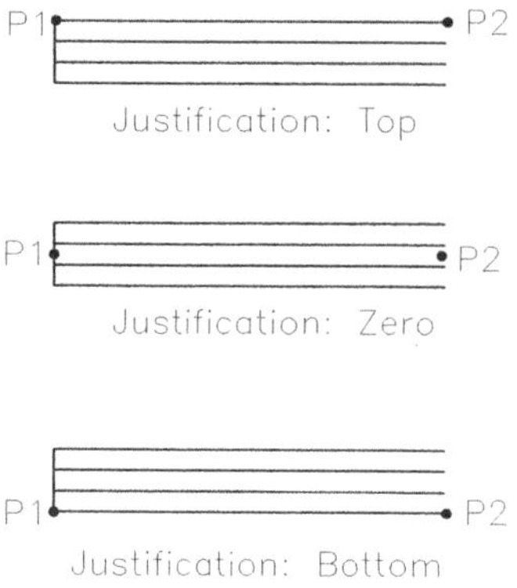

***Figure 3-6** Justifications in multilines*

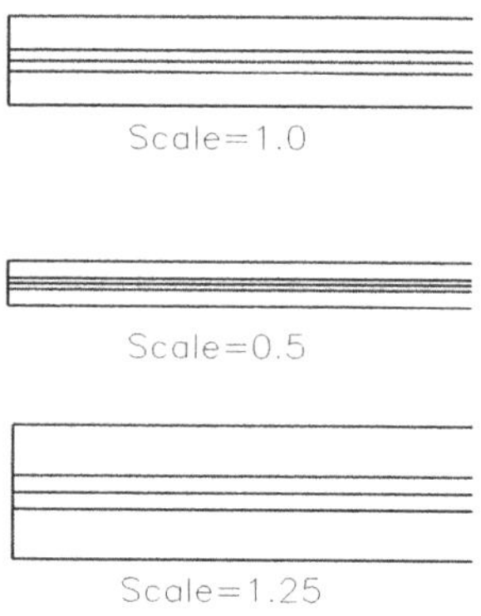

***Figure 3-7** Different multiline scales*

STyle Option

The **STyle** option allows you to change the current multiline style. The style must be defined before using the **STyle** option.

Note

All options explained above are available at the dynamic prompt. To access the options through dynamic prompt, press the down arrow key whenever dynamic prompting is available at the cursor. Now, select the option using the cursor.

EDITING MULTILINES BY USING GRIPS

Multilines can be easily edited using grips. When you select a multiline, the grips appear at the endpoints, based on the justification used while drawing multilines. For example, if the multilines are top-justified, the grips will be displayed at the endpoint of the first (top) line segment. Similarly, for zero and bottom-justified multilines, the grips are displayed on the centerline and bottom line, respectively.

Note

*Multilines do not support certain editing tools such as **Break**, **Chamfer**, and **Fillet**. However, tools such as **Copy**, **Move**, **Rotate**, **Mirror**, **Stretch**, **Scale**, and **Explode** as well as most object snap modes can be used with multilines.*

EDITING MULTILINES BY USING DIALOG BOX

Menu Bar: Modify > Object > Multiline **Command:** MLEDIT

When you invoke the **MLEDIT** command, AutoCAD displays the **Multilines Edit Tools** dialog box, as shown in Figure 3-8. This dialog box contains five basic editing tools. To edit a multiline, first select the editing operation you want to perform by clicking on the image tile. Once you have selected the editing option, AutoCAD will prompt you to select the first and second multilines. After editing one set of multilines, you will be prompted again to select the first multiline or undo the last editing. Press Enter to exit this command after you have finished the editing.

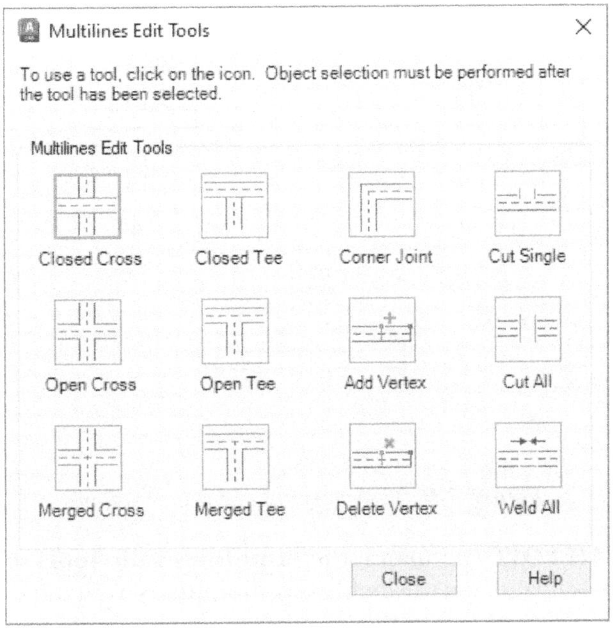

***Figure 3-8** The **Multilines Edit Tools** dialog box*

The following is the list of options for editing multilines:

Cross Intersection
Closed Cross (CC), Open Cross (OC), Merged Cross (MC)

Tee Intersection
Closed Tee (CT), Open Tee (OT), Merged Tee (MT)

Corner Joint (CJ)

Adding and Deleting Vertices
Add Vertex (AV), Delete Vertex (DV)

Cutting and Welding Multilines
Cut Single (CS), Cut All (CA), Weld All (WA)

Cross Intersection (CC/OC/MC)

Using options in the **Multilines Edit Tools** dialog box, you can create three types of cross intersections: closed, open, and merged. You must be careful about the order in which you select multilines for editing. The order in which multilines are selected determines the edited shape of a multiline, refer to Figure 3-9. The cross intersection can belong to a self-intersecting multiline or two different multilines.

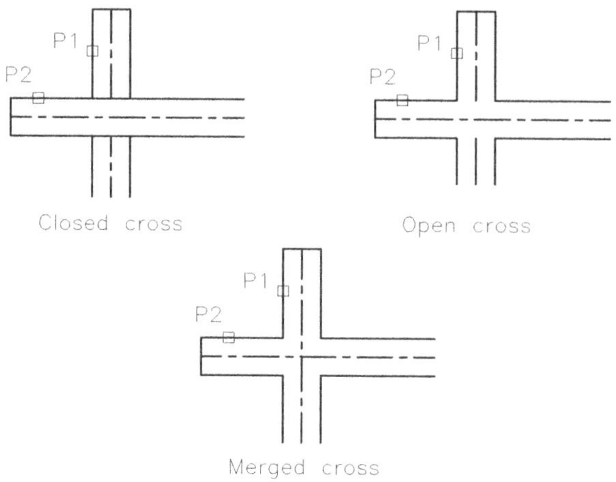

Figure 3-9 *Three types of cross intersections*

When you invoke the **MLEDIT** command, the **Multilines Edit Tools** dialog box is displayed. Choose the **Closed Cross** image tile; the dialog box disappears from the screen and the following prompts appear in the command prompt:

Select first mline: *Select the first multiline.*
Select second mline: *Select the second multiline.*
Select first mline or [Undo]: *Select another multiline, press Enter to end the command, or enter **U** to undo the last operation.*

If you enter **U**, AutoCAD will undo the last editing operation and prompt you to select the first multiline. However, if you do not enter **U** and select another multiline, AutoCAD will prompt you to select the second multiline.

Tee Intersection (CT/OT/MT)

Using options in the **Multilines Edit Tools** dialog box, you can create three types of tee-shaped intersections: closed, open, and merged. Similar to the cross intersection, in this type of intersection also, you have to be careful how you select the objects because the order in which you select them determines the edited shape of a multiline, refer to Figure 3-10. The prompt sequence for the tee intersection is the same as that for the cross intersection.

When you invoke the **MLEDIT** command, the **Multilines Edit Tools** dialog box will be displayed. Choose the **Closed Tee** image tile; the dialog box disappears from the screen and the following prompts appear in the command prompt.

Select first mline: *Select the first multiline.*
Select second mline: *Select the intersecting multiline.*
Select first mline or [Undo]: *Select another multiline, enter **U** to undo the last operation, or press Enter to end the command.*

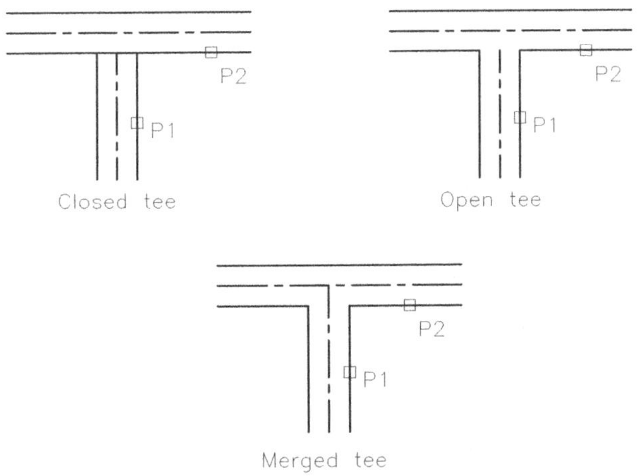

Figure 3-10 *Three types of tee intersections*

Corner Joint (CJ)

The **Corner Joint** option is used to create a corner joint between the two selected multilines. The multilines must be two separate objects (multilines) or self-intersecting multilines, refer to Figure 3-11. When you specify two multilines, AutoCAD trims or extends the first multiline to intersect with the second one. The prompt sequence that follows when you invoke this option is given next.

Select first mline: *Select the multiline to trim or extend.*
Select second mline: *Select the intersecting multiline.*
Select first mline or [Undo]: *Select another multiline, enter* ***U*** *to undo the last operation, or press Enter to end the command.*

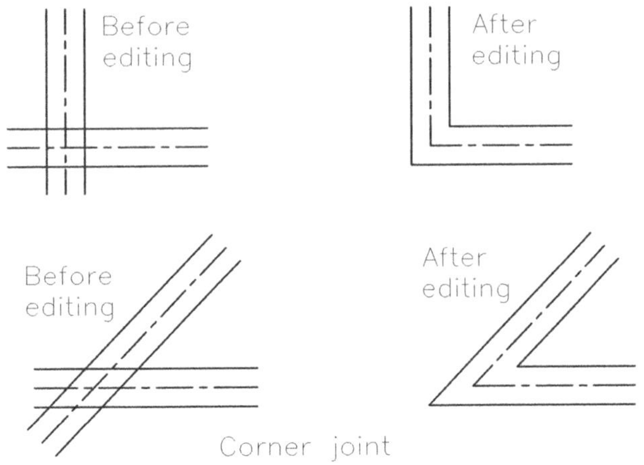

Figure 3-11 *Editing corner joints*

Adding and Deleting Vertices (AV/DV)

You can use the **MLEDIT** command to add or delete the vertices of a multiline, refer to Figure 3-12. When you select a multiline for adding a vertex, AutoCAD inserts a vertex point at the point where you clicked on the object while selecting it. Later, you can move the vertex by using grips. Similarly, you can also use the **MLEDIT** command to delete vertices by selecting the object whose vertex point you want to delete. AutoCAD removes the vertex that is nearest to the point where you click to select the multiline segment.

When you invoke the **MLEDIT** command, the **Multilines Edit Tools** dialog box is displayed. Choose the **Add Vertex** image tile; the dialog box is removed from the screen and the following prompts appear in the command prompt.

Select mline: *Select the multiline for adding vertex.*
Select mline or [Undo]: *Select another multiline for modifications; enter **U** to undo the last operation, or press Enter to exit the command.*

A same prompt sequence appears at the command prompt when you use the **Delete Vertex** option.

Cutting and Welding Multilines (CS/CA/WA)

You can also use the **MLEDIT** command to cut or weld multilines. When you cut a multiline, it does not create two separate multilines. They continue to be a part of the same object (multiline). You can cut away an area from any of the elements of a multiline or from the entire multiline. Also, the points selected for cutting the multiline do not have to be on the same element of the multiline, refer to Figure 3-13. You can select the two points that define the cut on different elements of the multiline. While cutting a single element of the multiline, if you select the two cut points on different elements, the element you selected first gets cut by the distance defined by the two points.

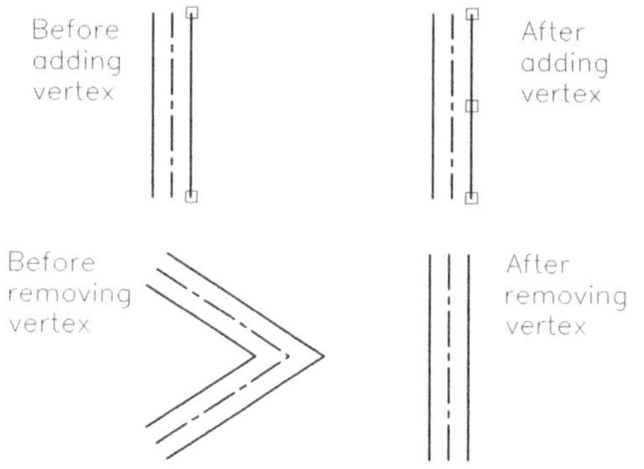

Figure 3-12 *Adding and deleting vertices*

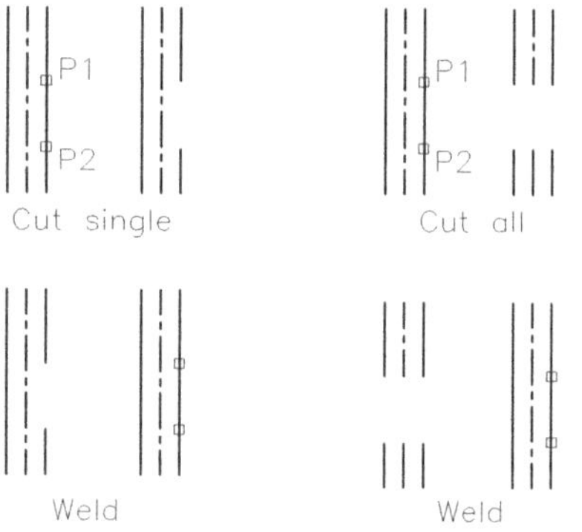

Figure 3-13 *Cutting and welding multilines*

In the **Multilines Edit Tools** dialog box, choose the **Cut Single** image tile; the dialog box is removed from the screen, and the following prompts appear at the command prompt.

Select mline: Select the multiline.
(The point where you select the multiline specifies the first cut point.)
Select second point: *Select the second cut point.*
Select mline or [Undo]: *Select another multiline to cut, enter **U** to undo the last operation, or press Enter to exit the command.*

The **Weld All** option reconnects the multilines that have been cut by using the **Cut Single** or **Cut All** option of the **MLEDIT** command (Figure 3-13). You cannot weld or join separate multilines.

In the **Multilines Edit Tools** dialog box, choose the **Weld All** image tile; the dialog box is removed from the screen, and the following prompts appear at the command prompt.

Select mline: *Select the multiline.*
Select second point: *Select a point on the other side of the cut.*
Select mline or [Undo]: *Select another multiline to modify, enter **U** to undo the last operation, or press Enter to exit the command.*

Note
*The following system variables store values for various aspects of multilines. The **CMLJUST** variable stores the justification of the current multiline (0-Top, 1-Middle, 2-Bottom). The **CMLSCALE** variable stores the scale of the current multiline (Default scale = 1.0000), and the **CMLSTYLE** variable stores the name of the current multiline style (Default style = STANDARD).*

Tip
*You can also edit multilines by entering the **-MLEDIT** command at the pointer input. On doing so, all the options are displayed at the dynamic prompt, refer to Figure 3-14.*

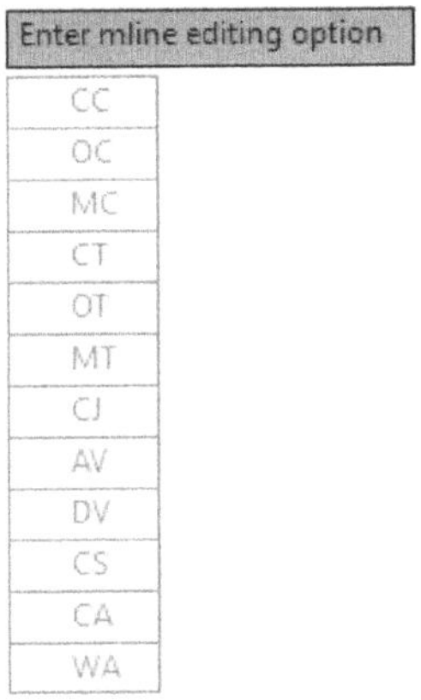

Figure 3-14 *Dynamic prompt for the **-MLEDIT** command*

Example 1 — Multiline

In this example, you will create a multiline style that represents a wood-frame wall system. The wall system consists of ½" wallboard, 4 X ½" wood stud, and ½" wallboard.

1. Enter **MLSTYLE** at the command prompt to display the **Multiline Style** dialog box. Also, the current style **STANDARD** is displayed in the **Styles** list box.

2. Choose the **New** button to invoke the **Create New Multiline Style** dialog box. Enter **MYSTYLE** in the **New Style Name** edit box and choose **Continue** to display the **New Multiline Style: MYSTYLE** dialog box.

3. Enter **Wood-frame Wall System** in the **Description** edit box.

4. Select the **0.5** line definition in the **Elements** list box. In the **Offset** edit box, replace **0.500** with **1.00**. This redefines the first line which will now be 1.00" above the centerline of the wall.

5. Select the **-0.5** line definition in the **Elements** list box. In the **Offset** edit box, replace **-0.500** with **-1.00**. This redefines the second line which will now be placed 1.00" below the centerline of the wall.

6. Choose the **Add** button; a new line is added with offset value of 0 and is highlighted in the **Elements** list box.

7. In the **Offset** edit box, replace **0.000** with **1.50**.

8. Select **Yellow** from the **Color** drop-down list.

9. Repeat steps 6 through 8, but this time use the value **-1.50** in place of **1.50** in step 7 to add another line to the current multiline style. The color of this line should be red.

10. Choose the **OK** button and return to the **Multiline Style** dialog box. The new multiline style is displayed in the **Preview of** area.

11. Choose the **Set Current** button to make the **MYSTYLE** as current style.

12. Choose the **OK** button from the **Multiline Style** dialog box to return to the drawing area. To test the new multiline style, use the **MLINE** command and draw a series of lines, refer to Figure 3-15.

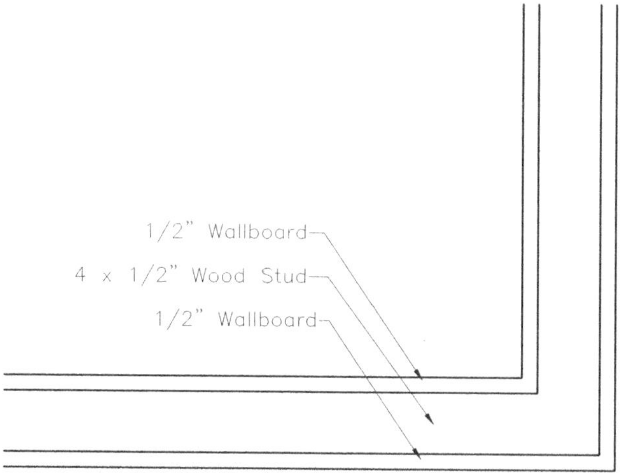

Figure 3-15 *Multiline style created for Example 1*

CREATING REVISION CLOUDS

Ribbon: Home > Draw > Revision Cloud drop-down or
Annotate > Markup > Revision Cloud drop-down
Tool Palettes: Draw > Revision Cloud **Toolbar:** Draw > Revision Cloud
Menu Bar: Draw > Revision Cloud **Command:** REVCLOUD

Revision cloud is the sequential arc of polylines and is used to create a cloud shaped object. Revision clouds can be used to highlight the details of a drawing. The tools to draw a revision cloud are grouped in the **Revision Cloud** drop-down of the **Draw** panel in the **Ribbon**, refer to Figure 3-16. Remember that the tool that was used last to create a revision cloud will be displayed in this drop-down. The different methods to draw a revision cloud are discussed next.

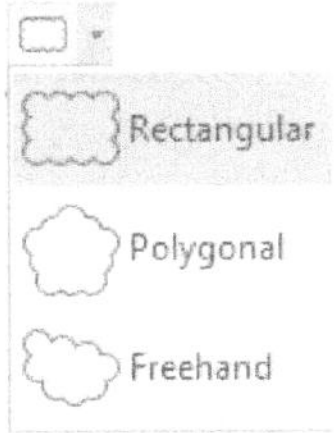

***Figure 3-16** The tools in the **Revision Cloud** drop-down*

Rectangular Revision Cloud

To draw a rectangular revision cloud, choose the **Rectangular Revision Cloud** tool from the **Revision Cloud** drop-down in the **Draw** panel; you will be prompted to specify the first point. Specify the first point or enter coordinates. Next, specify the opposite corner point of the rectangle. The prompt sequence that will follow when you choose this tool is as follows:

Specify first corner point or [Arc length/Object/Rectangular/Polygonal/Freehand/Style/Modify] <Object>: *Specify first corner point of rectangle.*
Specify opposite corner: *Specify opposite corner point of rectangle.*

Polygonal Revision Cloud

To draw a polygonal revision cloud, choose the **Polygonal Revision Cloud** tool from the **Draw** panel, refer to Figure 3-16. On doing so, you will be prompted to specify the first point. Specify the first point; you will be prompted to specify the next point. Keep specifying the points until the desired polygonal revision cloud is created. Press Enter to terminate the command. The prompt sequence that will follow when you choose this tool from the **Draw** panel is as follows:

Specify start point or [Arc length/Object/Rectangular/Polygonal/Freehand/Style/Modify] <Object>: *Specify the start point of the revision cloud.*
Specify next point: *Specify the next point of the revision cloud.*
Specify next point or [Undo]: *Specify the next point of the revision cloud.*
Specify next point or [Undo]: *Specify the next point of the revision cloud, or press Enter to exit the tool.*

Freehand Revision Cloud

To draw a freehand revision cloud, choose the **Freehand Revision Cloud** tool from the **Draw** panel, refer to Figure 3-16. On doing so, you will be prompted to specify the first point. Specify the first point. Now, as you move the cursor, different arcs of the cloud with varied radii are drawn. When the start point and endpoint meet, the revision cloud is completed and you get a message that the revision cloud has been created. The prompt sequence that will follow when you choose this tool from the **Draw** panel is as follows:

Specify first point or [Arc length/Object/Rectangular/Polygonal/Freehand/Style/Modify] <Object>: *Specify the start point of the revision cloud.*
Guide crosshairs along cloud path...
Revision cloud finished.

While making any type of the revision cloud, you can define the length of the arcs to be drawn using the **Arc length** option from the command prompt. The arcs drawn using this option will be of constant length. You can convert a closed loop into a revision cloud using the **Object** option. Note that the selected closed loop should be a single entity such as an ellipse, a circle, a rectangle, a polyline, and so on. The **Style** option is used to define the arc style for the revision cloud. The default style is **Normal** that creates a revision cloud similar to the one shown in Figure 3-17. You can change the style to **Calligraphy** to create a revision cloud similar to the one shown in Figure 3-18.

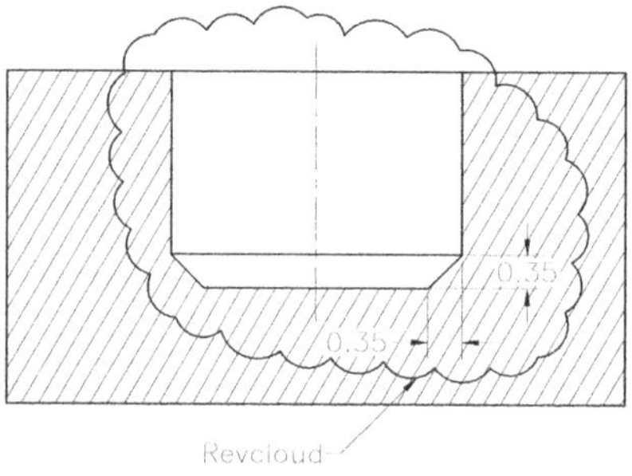

***Figure 3-17** Revcloud*

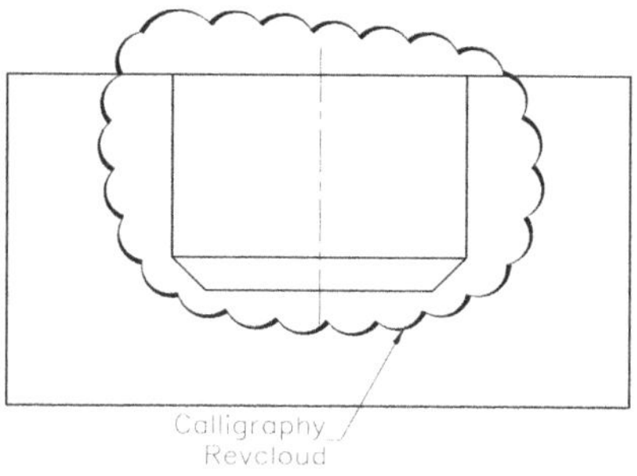

***Figure 3-18** Calligraphy revcloud*

Note

*The **REVCLOUD** stores the last used arc length in the system registry. This value is multiplied by the **DIMSCALE** value to provide consistency when the program is used with drawings that have different scale factors.*

CREATING WIPEOUTS

Ribbon: Home > Draw > Wipeout or Annotate > Markup > Wipeout
Command: WIPEOUT

The **Wipeout** tool is used to create a polygonal area to cover the existing objects with the current background color. The area defined by this tool is governed by the wipeout frame. The frame can be turned on and off for editing and plotting the drawings, respectively. This tool can be used to add notes and details to a drawing. The prompt sequence that will follow when you choose the **Wipeout** tool from the **Draw** panel is as follows:

Specify first point or [Frames/Polyline] <Polyline>: *Specify the start point of the wipeout.*
Specify next point: *Specify the next point of the wipeout.*
Specify next point or [Undo]: *Specify the next point of the wipeout.*
Specify next point or [Close/Undo]: *Specify the next point of the wipeout or press Enter.*

Figure 3-19 shows a drawing before creating a wipeout and Figure 3-20 shows a drawing after creating the wipeout.

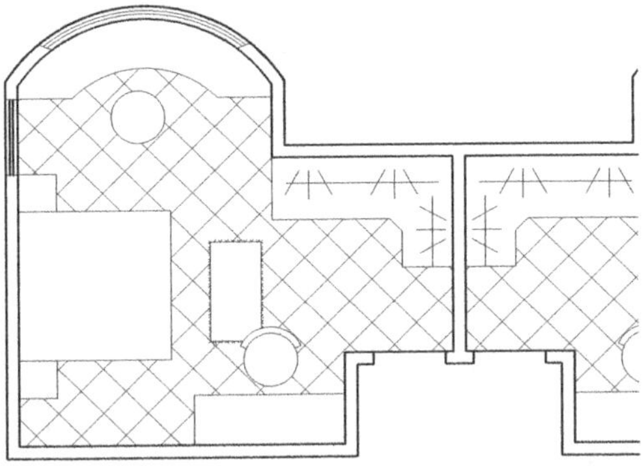

Figure 3-19 *Drawing before creating a wipeout*

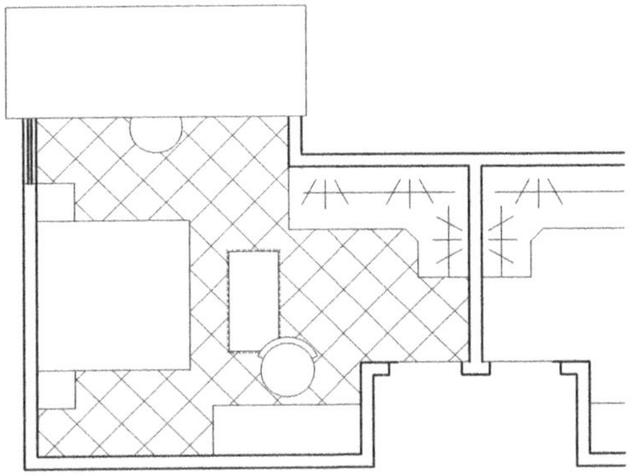

Figure 3-20 *Drawing after creating a wipeout*

If you do not want the frame of the wipeout to be displayed, enter **F** at the **Specify first point or [Frames/Polyline] <Polyline>** prompt and turn the frame off. The display of frames of all existing wipeouts will be turned off. Also, the display of frames of all new wipeouts will be turned off.

CREATING NURBS

Ribbon: Home > Draw > Spline Fit **Menu Bar:** Draw > Spline > Fit Points
Tool Palettes: Draw > Spline **Toolbar:** Draw > Spline **Command:** SPLINE/SPL

The NURBS is an acronym for **Non-Uniform Rational Bezier-Spline**. These splines are considered true splines. In AutoCAD, you can create NURBS using the **Spline** tool. The spline created with the **Spline** tool is different from the spline created using the **Polyline** tool. The non-uniform aspect of the spline enables the spline to have sharp corners because the spacing between the spline elements that constitute a spline can be irregular. Rational means that irregular geometry such as arcs, circles, and ellipses can be combined with free-form curves. The Bezier-spline (B-spline) is the core that enables accurate fitting of curves to input data with Bezier's curve-fitting interface. Not only are spline curves more accurate compared to smooth polyline curves, but they also use less disk space.

The prompt sequence to draw a spline with six fit points is given below.

*Choose the **Spline** tool.*
Specify first point or [Method/Knots/Object]: *Select point P1.*
Enter next point or [start Tangency/toLerance]: *Select point P2.*
Enter next point or [end Tangency/toLerance/Undo]: *Select point P3.*
Enter next point or [end Tangency/toLerance/Undo/Close]: *Select point P4.*
Enter next point or [end Tangency/toLerance/Undo/Close]: *Select point P5.*
Enter next point or [end Tangency/toLerance/Undo/Close]: *Select point P6 and press Enter to end the process of point specification.*

Options for Creating Splines

On invoking the **Spline** tool, the following options are displayed for creating the splines:

Object

This option allows you to change a 2D or 3D spline fitted polyline into a NURBS feature. The original splined polyline is deleted if the system variable **DELOBJ** is set to 1, which is the default value of the variable. You can change a polyline into a splined polyline using the **Spline** option of the **Edit Polyline** tool.

Method

In AutoCAD, you can create a spline by specifying fit points or control vertices. By default, a spline is created by specifying the fit points. Fit points are the points through which the spline will pass. Control vertices determine the shape of the curve. To set the method to create a spline, enter **M** at the **Specify first point or [Method/Knots/Object]** prompt. Then, you need to specify the method at the **Enter spline creation method [Fit/CV] <Fit>:** prompt. Figure 3-21 shows the spline created by using the **Fit** method. Figure 3-22 shows the spline created by using the **CV** method.

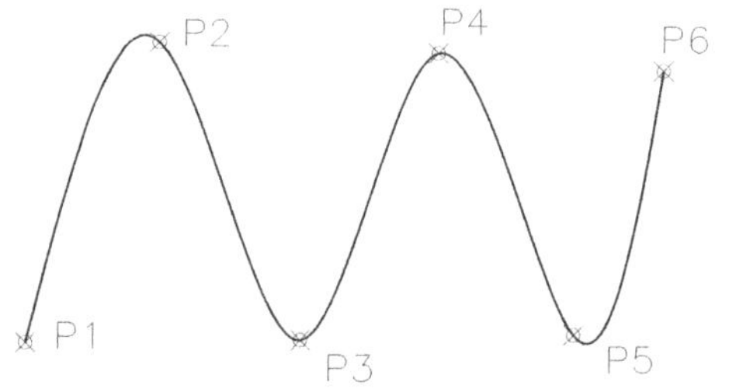

Figure 3-21 *Spline drawn by using the* ***Fit*** *method*

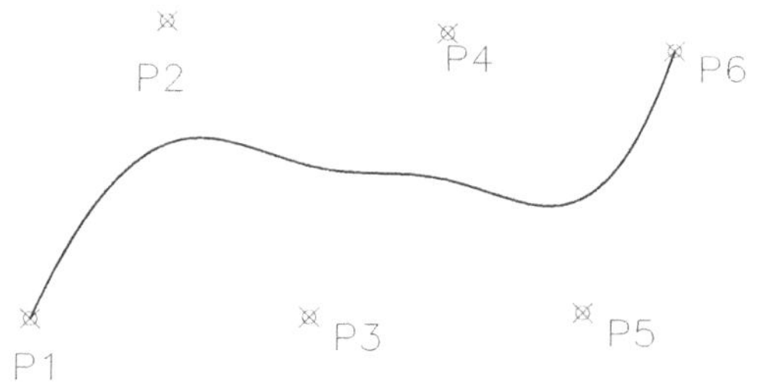

Figure 3-22 *Spline drawn by using the* ***CV*** *method*

Note

On selecting a spline, a grip will be displayed at the start point. Left-click on the grip; a shortcut menu will be displayed. Now, you can choose an appropriate option to display the fit points or the control vertices, as shown in Figure 3-23.

Knots

If you have selected the **Fit** method, the **Knots** option will be displayed at the command prompt, as given below.

Enter spline creation method [Fit/CV] <CV>: **FIT**
Current settings: Method=Fit Knots=Uniform
Specify first point or [Method/Knots/Object]:

You can specify three types of knots: **Chord**, **Square root**, and **Uniform**. Figure 3-24 shows the splines formed by using three different knot options.

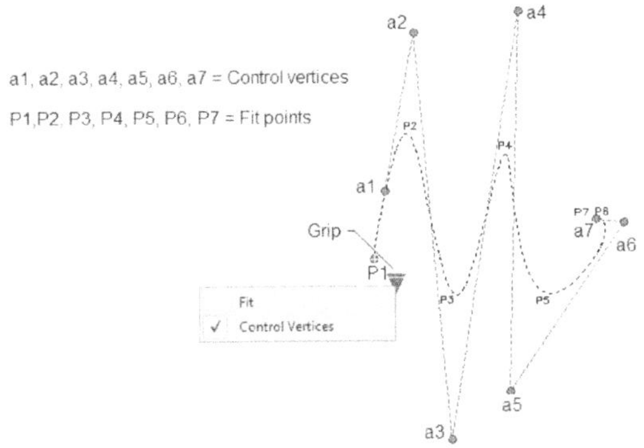

Figure 3-23 *Control vertices and fit points of a spline*

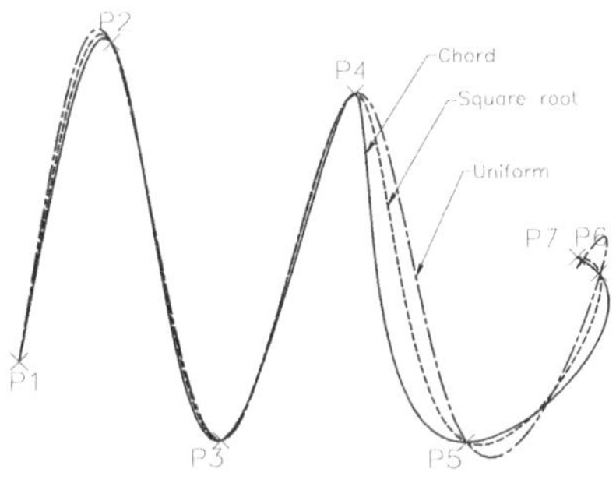

Figure 3-24 *Splines with different knot options*

Degree

If you have selected the **CV** method, then the **Specify first point or [Method/Degree/Object]** prompt will be displayed. Enter **D** at the command prompt and specify the degree.

Close

This option allows you to create closed NURBS. When you use this option, AutoCAD will automatically join the endpoint of the spline with the start point.

Tolerance

This option is used to control the fit of the spline between specified points. By default, this value is zero; as a result, the spline passes through the points by which it is created. Using this option, you can specify the tolerance values that will govern the spline creation, refer to Figure 3-25. The splines will be offset from the specified point by a distance equal to the tolerance value. The smaller the value of the tolerance, the closer the spline will be to the specified points.

Start and End Tangency

This option is used to control the tangency of a spline at its start point and the endpoint. On entering **T** at the **Enter next point or [start Tangency/toLerance]** or **Enter next point or [end Tangency/toLerance/Undo/Close]** prompt, you will be prompted to specify the tangent. Specify a point; the tangency will be determined by the slope of the spline at the specified point. Remember that after specifying the start point of the spline, you need to specify the start tangency. If you specify the second point, the default value will be used for the tangency. Similarly, you need to specify the end tangency after specifying the last point of the spline. Figure 3-26 shows a spline with start and end tangencies. The virtual tangent line is for reference.

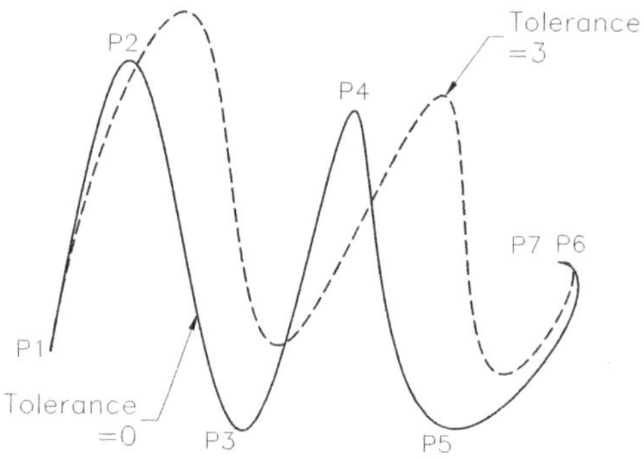

Figure 3-25 *Creating a spline with* ***Tolerance*** *of 0 and 3*

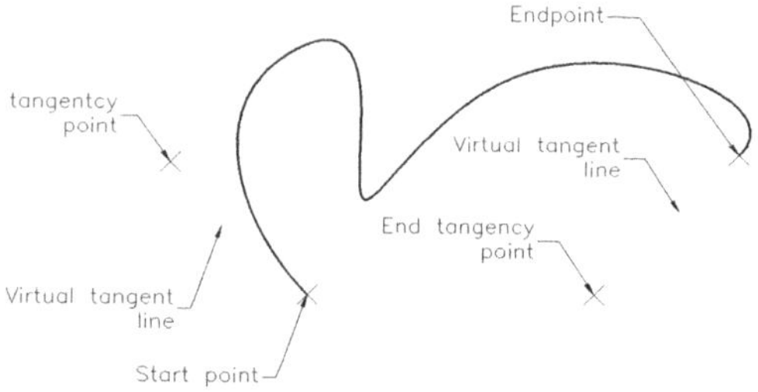

Figure 3-26 *Spline with start and end tangencies*

EDITING SPLINES

Ribbon: Home > Modify > Edit Spline
Tool Palettes: Modify > Edit spline
Command: SPLINEDIT /SPE
Menu Bar: Modify > Object > Spline
Toolbar: Modify II > Edit Spline

The NURBS can be edited using the **Edit Spline** tool. Using this tool, you can fit data in a selected spline, close or open a spline, move vertex points, and refine or reverse a spline. Apart from the ways mentioned in the preceding command box, you can choose the options available in the **Spline** cascading menu that will be displayed when you select a spline and right-click. The prompt sequence that will follow when you choose the **Edit Spline** tool in the **Modify** panel is given next.

Select spline: *Select the spline to be edited if not selected already using the above-mentioned shortcut menu.*
Enter an option [Close/Join/Fit data/Edit vertex/convert to Polyline/Reverse/Undo/eXit] <eXit>: *Select any one of the options.*

Options for Editing Splines

On invoking the **Edit Spline** tool, the following options are displayed for editing the splines:

Fit data

When you draw a spline, the spline fits as per the specified points (data points). The **Fit data** option allows you to edit these points. You can add, delete, or move the data points. These data points or control points are also referred to as fit points. For example, if you want to redefine the start and end tangents of a spline, select the **Fit data** option and then select the **Tangents** option. The prompt sequence that will follow when you invoke this option is given next.

Select spline: *Select the spline to be edited.*
Enter an option [Close/Join/Fit data/Edit vertex/convert to Polyline/Reverse/Undo/eXit] <eXit>: **F** Enter.
Enter a fit data option [Add/Close/Delete/Kink/Move/Purge/Tangents/toLerance/eXit] <eXit>: **T** Enter.

The start and end tangent points can be selected or their coordinates can be entered. The options available within the **Fit data** option are as follows:

Add: You can use this option to add new fit points to the spline. When you invoke this option, you will be prompted to specify the existing fit point on the spline. After selecting the existing fit point, you will be prompted to specify the location of the new control points. The fit point you select and the next fit point appear as selected grips. You can now add a fit point between these two selected fit points, as shown in Figure 3-27. If you select the start point or endpoint of the spline, only they get highlighted. When you select the start point of the spline, you are prompted to specify whether you want to add the new fit point before or after the start point of the spline. AutoCAD will continue prompting for the location of new control points until you press Enter at the **Specify new fit point to add <exit>** prompt.

Close/Open: This option is used to close an open spline or open a closed spline, refer to Figure 3-28. If the spline is open, the **Close** option is available and if the spline is closed, the **Open** option is displayed.

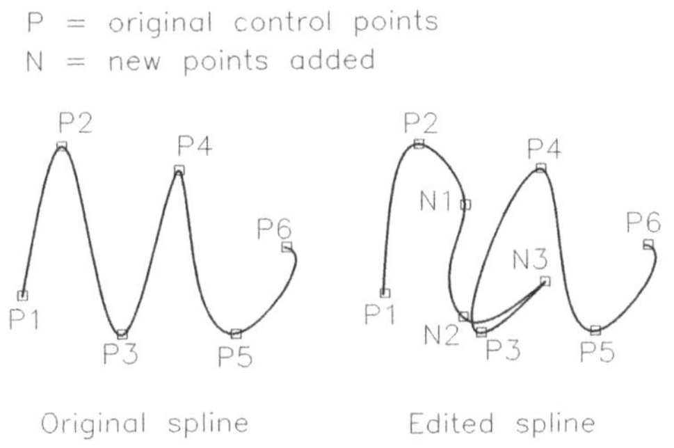

Figure 3-27 The original spline and the edited spline after adding fit points

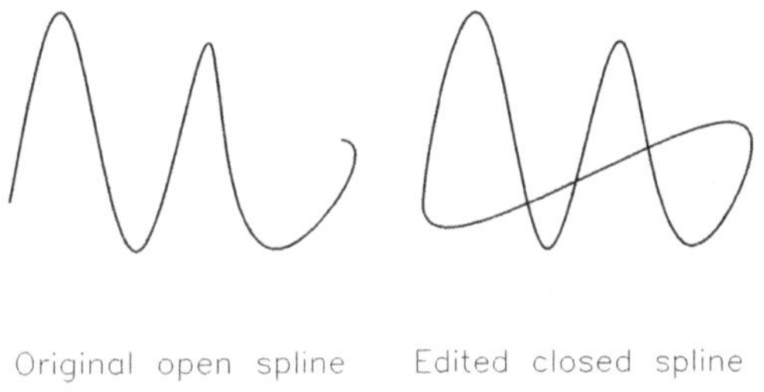

Figure 3-28 An open spline and a closed spline

Delete: This option is used to delete a selected fit point from a spline. You can continue deleting fit points from a spline until only two fit points are left in the spline.

Kink: This option is used to add a knot and a fit point to the selected point. On selecting this option, you will be prompted to specify a point on the spline. Select a point; a kink will be added.

Move: You can move fit points by using this option. When you select this option, the start point of the spline is selected and the following prompt sequence appears:

Specify new location or [Next/Previous/Select point/eXit] <N>: *Select a new location for the start point using the mouse pick button or enter any one of these options.*

You can enter **N** if you want to select the next point, **P** if you want to select a previous point, or **S** if you want to select any other point, and **X** if you want to exit the tool. Figure 3-29 shows the movement of data points in a spline. Remember that this option is used to move only the data points on the spline and not the control points on the Bezier control frame.

Purge: This option is used to remove fit point data from a spline. This reduces the file size, which is useful when a drawing, for example, a landscape contour map, contains large number of splines. Purging simplifies the spline definition and the drawing file size.

Tangents: This option is used to modify the tangents of the start and endpoints of a selected spline, refer to Figure 3-30. When you select this option, you will be prompted to specify the start and end tangents of the spline. You can specify the start and end tangents or use the systems default tangents.

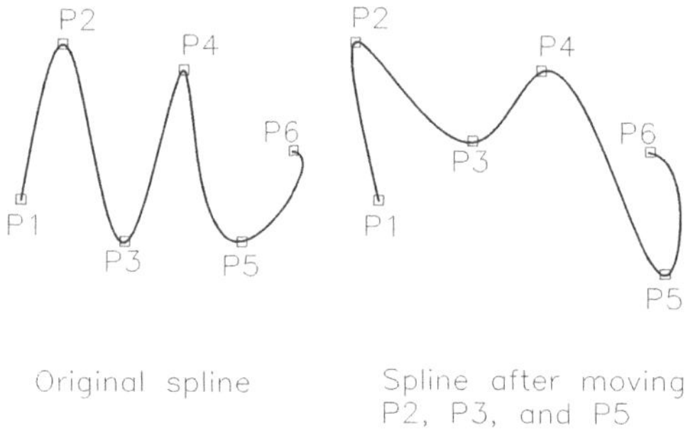

Figure 3-29 The original spline and the edited spline after moving the data points

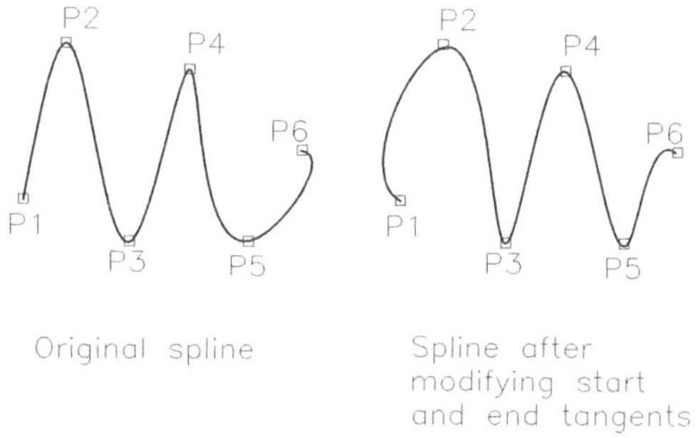

Figure 3-30 The original spline and the spline after modifying the start and end tangents

toLerance: This option is used to modify the fit tolerance values of a selected spline. As discussed, while creating the splines, different tolerance values produce different splines. A smaller tolerance value creates a spline that passes very closely through the definition points of a spline. When you invoke this option, you will be prompted to specify the tolerance value for the spline.

eXit: Choose this option to exit the **Fit data** option of editing splines.

Close/Open

This option is used to close an open spline or open a closed spline. When you select the **Close** option, AutoCAD lets you open, edit the vertex, convert spline to polyline, or reverse the spline.

Edit Vertex

This option is used to refine a spline by adding more control points in it, elevating the order, or adding weight to vertex points. The prompt sequence that will follow when you invoke this option is given next.

Enter an option [Open/Fit data/Edit vertex/convert to Polyline/Reverse/Undo/eXit] <eXit>: ***E*** Enter.

Enter a vertex editing option [Add/Delete/Elevate order/Move/Weight/eXit] <eXit>:

The options in this prompt are discussed next.

Add: This option is used to add more control points on the spline. When you invoke this option, you will be prompted to specify the location of the new point on the spline. You can directly specify the location of the new point using the left mouse button. A new control point will be added at the specified location.

Delete: This option is used to delete a selected fit point from a spline.

Elevate order: This option is used to increase the order of a spline curve. The order of a curve can be defined as the highest power of the algebraic expression that defines the spline plus 1. For example, the order of a cubic spline will be 3 + 1 = 4. Using the **Elevate order** option, you can increase this order for a selected spline. This results in more control points on the curve and a greater possibility of controlling the spline. The value of the spline order varies from 4 to 26. You can only increase the order and not decrease it. For example, if a spline order is 18, you can elevate its order to any value greater than 18, but not less than 18.

Move: When you draw a spline, it is associated with the Bezier control frame. The **Move** option allows you to move the vertices of the control frame. The **Move** option is similar to the **Move** option of **Fit data** for editing the splines. The prompt sequence that follows when you invoke this option is given next.

> Enter an option [Close/Join/Fit data/Edit vertex/convert to Polyline/Reverse/Undo/eXit] <eXit>: **E** Enter.
> Enter a vertex editing option [Add/Delete/Elevate order/Move/Weight/eXit] <eXit>: **M** Enter.
> Specify new location or [Next/Previous/Select point/eXit] <N>:

Weight: You can also add weight to any of the control vertices of a spline by using this option. When weight is added to a particular vertex, the spline gets pulled more towards it. Similarly, a lower value of weight of a particular spline vertex will result in the spline getting pulled less towards that particular vertex. In other words, adding weight to a particular point will force the selected point to maintain its tangency with the point. More weight added to the point, more is the distance through which the spline will remain tangent to the point. By default, the spline gets pulled equally towards the vertices of the spline. The default value of weight provided to each control point is 1.0 and can have only positive values. Once you have added the weight to a point, you can proceed to the next point. You can also directly select the point to which the weight has to be added. The prompt sequence for using this option is given next.

> Enter an option [Close/Join/Fit data/Edit vertex/convert to Polyline/Reverse/Undo/eXit] <eXit>: **E** Enter.
> Enter a vertex editing option [Add/Delete/Elevate order/Move/Weight/eXit] <eXit>: **W** Enter.
> Enter new weight (current = 1.0000) or [Next/Previous/Select point/eXit] <N>: **S** Enter.
> Specify existing fit point on spline <exit>: *Select a fit point.*
> Enter new weight (current = 1.0000) or [Next/Previous/Select point/eXit] <N>: **3** Enter.
> Enter new weight (current = 1.0000) or [Next/Previous/Select point/eXit] <N>: **Exit** Enter.

Join

If a spline, line, or an arc is joined to the spline that is being edited, then you can use this option to join those entities to the spline. On choosing this option, you will be prompted to select an open curve. Select the curves to be joined and press Enter; all the curves will be joined to the spline and knot and fit points will be added at the joining point. The prompt sequence for using this option is given next.

Enter an option [Close/Join/Fit data/Edit vertex/convert to Polyline/Reverse/Undo/eXit] <eXit>: **J**
Select any open curves to join to source: *Select an object. 1 found*
Select any open curves to join to source: *Select an object. 1 found, 2 total*
Select any open curves to join to source:
2 objects joined to source

Reverse

This option is used to reverse the spline direction. This implies that when you apply this option to a spline, its start point becomes its endpoint and vice versa.

convert to Polyline

This option is used to convert a spline into a polyline. On specifying this option, you will be prompted to specify a precision value. Specify a value between 0 and 99, and then press Enter; the spline will be converted into a polyline. The precision value determines the accuracy of the resulting polyline.

Undo

This option will undo the previous editing operation applied to a spline within the current session of the **Edit Spline** tool. You can continue to use this option till you reach the spline as it was when you started to edit it.

EDITING SPLINES USING 3D EDIT BAR

Command: 3DEDITBAR

The **3DEDITBAR** command is used to edit a spline by using the **Move** gizmo. To edit a spline using this command, select the spline and right click; a shortcut menu will be displayed. Choose the **Spline > 3D Edit Bar** option from the shortcut menu; you will be prompted to select a point on the curve. Select a point on the curve at the position where you want to modify the spline; the Move gizmo will be displayed with one extra arrow tangential to the curve at the selected point. This arrow can be used to change the tangent direction as well as the magnitude of tangency at the point. Using this arrow, you can dynamically edit the spline.

MARKUP IMPORT AND MARKUP ASSIST FEATURES

New

Ribbon: Collaborate > Traces > Markup Import **Command:** MARKUPIMPORT

In AutoCAD 2023 two new features, Markup Import and Markup Assist have been added. The Markup Import feature is used to import and place the marked version of a drawing file on the top of the original drawing. Using this feature, you can view and easily incorporate changes into your drawing. You can import PDF, PNG, or JPG type of files. In addition, you can even mark changes in the printed version of a drawing file, take its photograph and then import the same as a JPG or PNG file. On the other hand, the Markup Assist feature is used to identify markups as text, leaders, and revision clouds.

To import the marked version of a drawing file, choose the **Markup Import** tool from the **Traces** panel of the **Collaborate** tab; the **Welcome to the New Markup Experience** window appears. In this window, click on **I understand**; the **Select a markup file to import** dialog box appears, refer to Figure 3-31. Notice the types of files displayed in the **Files of type** drop-down list. Navigate and select the desired file from this dialog box and then choose the **Open** button; the **Import Markup** message box is displayed that shows the progress of the file being imported, refer to Figure 3-32. This message box disappears and the drawing area is modified with the trace of imported drawing overlapping the original drawing, as shown in Figure 3-33.

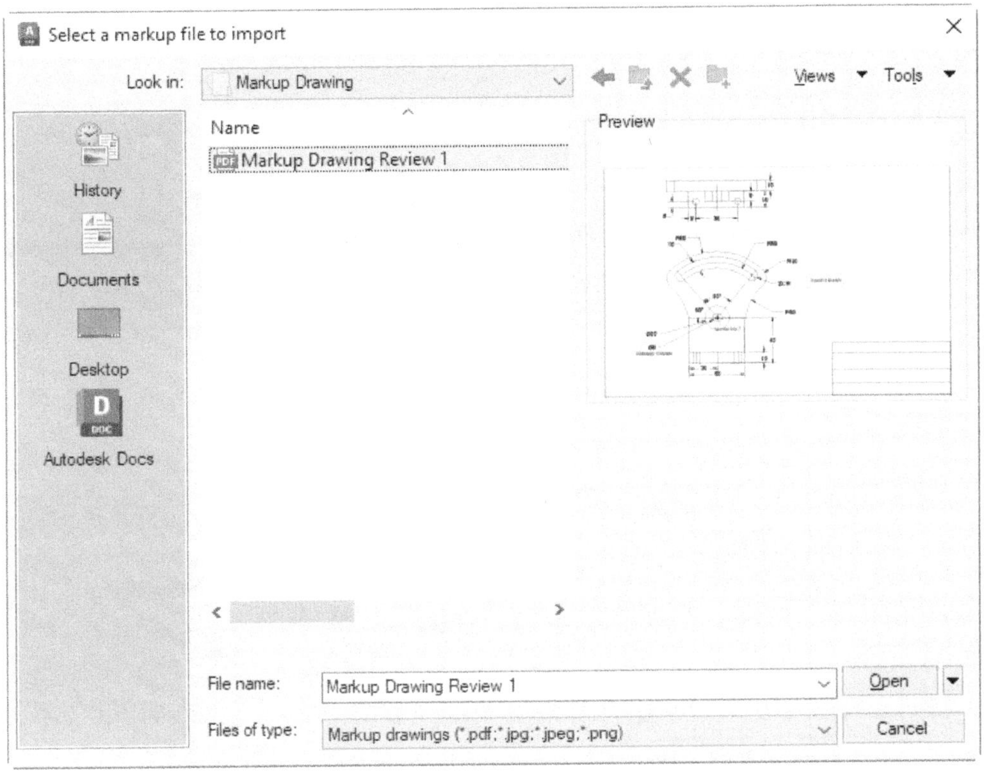

*Figure 3-31 The **Select a markup file to import** dialog box*

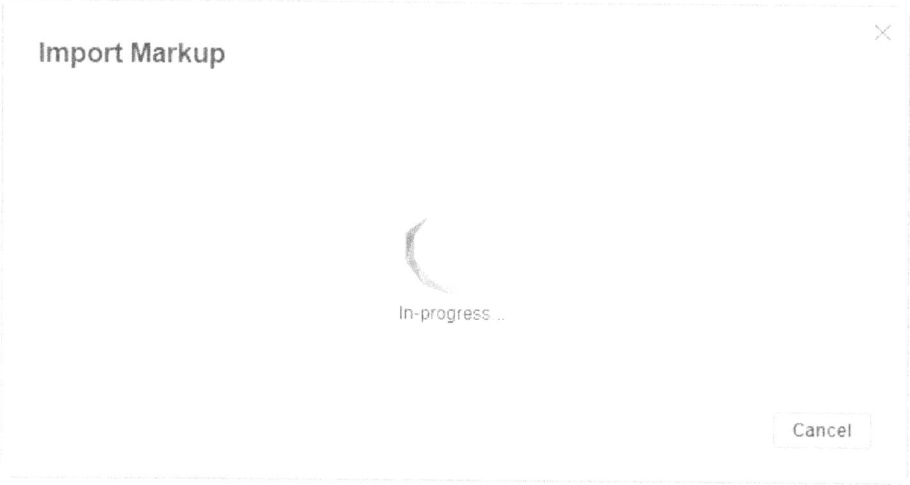

Figure 3-32 *The* ***Import Markup*** *message box*

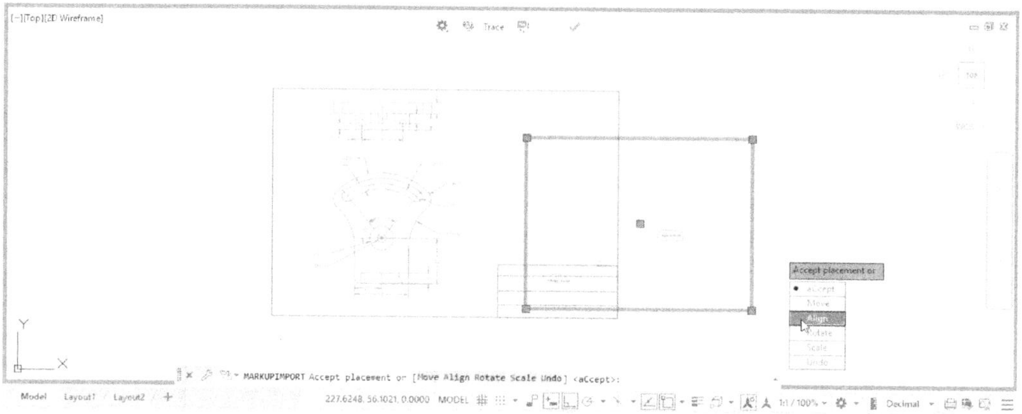

Figure 3-33 *Trace of drawing overlapping the original drawing*

You can notice from the above figure that the trace is not actually fit on the original drawing. To align it, you can use the **Move**, **Align**, **Rotate**, **Scale**, and **Undo** options displayed at the bottom of the drawing area. Once alignment of the trace is done, you need to choose the **aCcept** option to complete the alignment process. Figure 3-34 displays the trace of drawing aligned with the original drawing using the **Align** option.

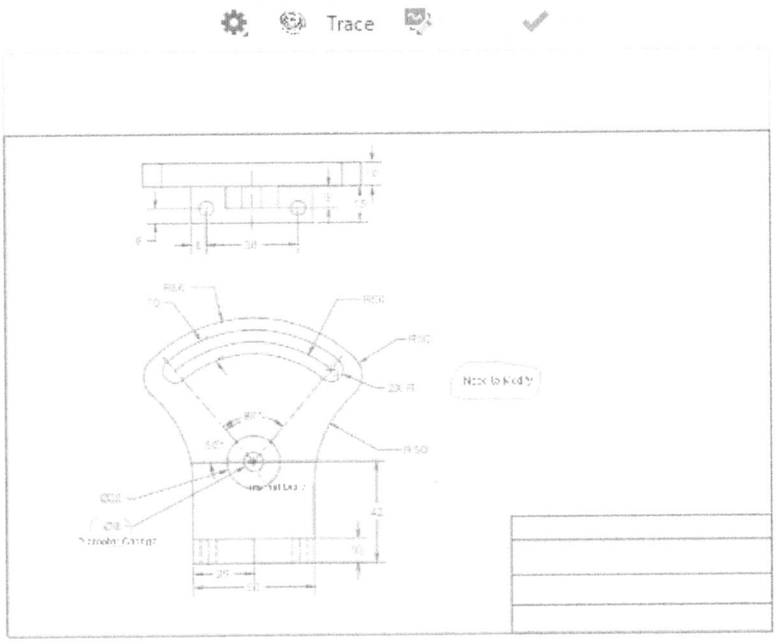

Figure 3-34 Trace of drawing aligned with the original drawing

There are three buttons at the center of the drawing area, namely: **Trace Settings**, **Edit Trace** or **View Trace**, and **Close Trace**. These buttons are discussed next.

The **Trace Settings** button is used to adjust the transparency settings of the trace and imported markups. When you choose this button, the **Markup** flyout will be displayed, as shown in Figure 3-35. In this box, you can adjust the transparency of the background of the trace using the **Drawing Background** slider.

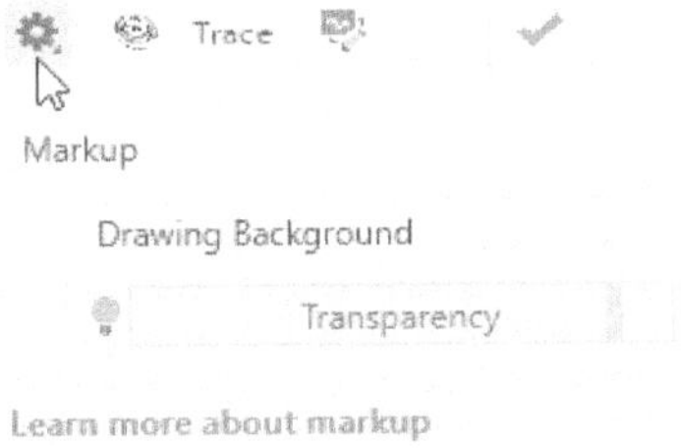

Figure 3-35 The ***Markup*** *flyout displayed*

The **Edit Trace or View Trace** button is used to toggle between the trace editing or drawing editing at the time of viewing the trace. When this button is activated, a dotted border will be displayed around the trace. Also, a dotted blue square will be displayed around the text annotations and markups in the drawing, refer to Figure 3-36.

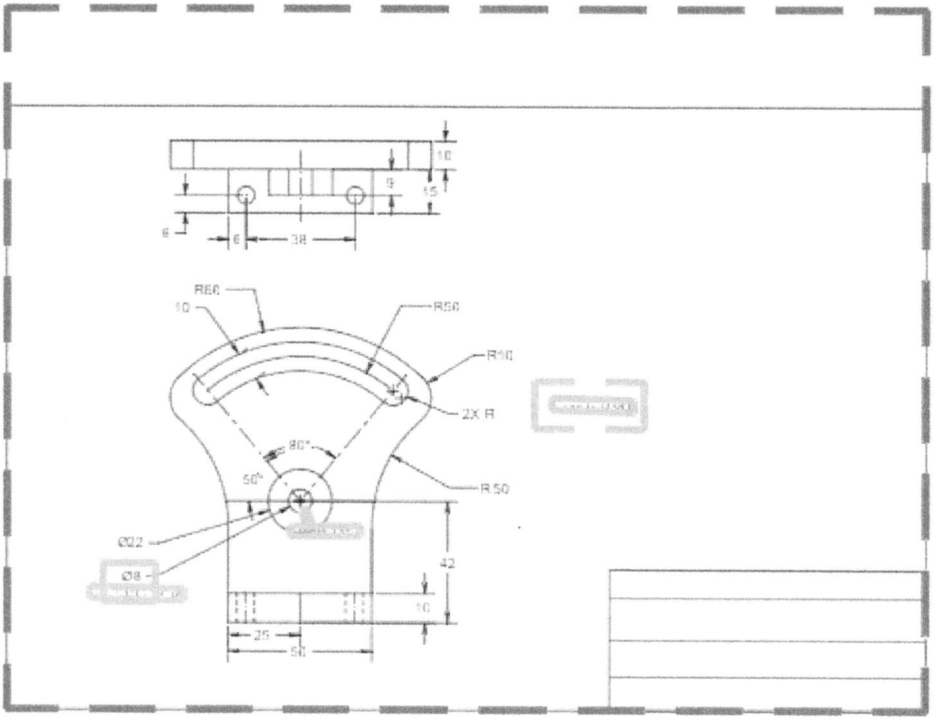

Figure 3-36 Dotted blue square displayed around the text annotations and markups

When you zoom in over a text annotation and hover the cursor around it, a message box will be displayed in which the text annotation will be referred to as a '**Markup Assist identified text**' and you will be prompted to click on it to explore more options, refer to Figure 3-37. When you click on the blue border, the **Markup Assist Text** dialog box will be displayed, as shown in Figure 3-38. Using the options in this dialog box, you can insert the marked text as Mleader, Mtext, or you can copy the text to clipboard.

The **Close Trace** button is used to close a trace.

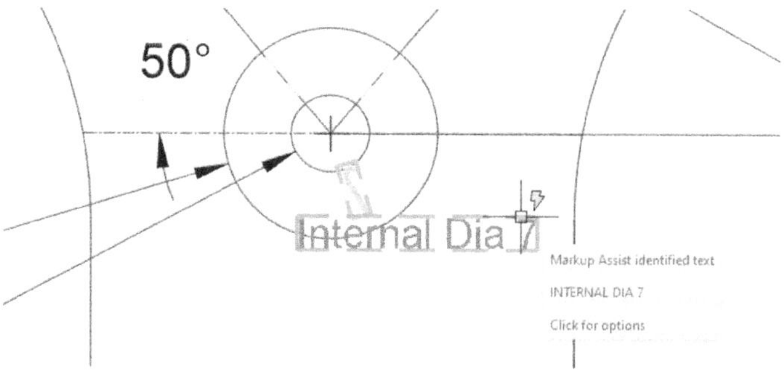

*Figure 3-37 The **Markup Assist identified text** message box displayed*

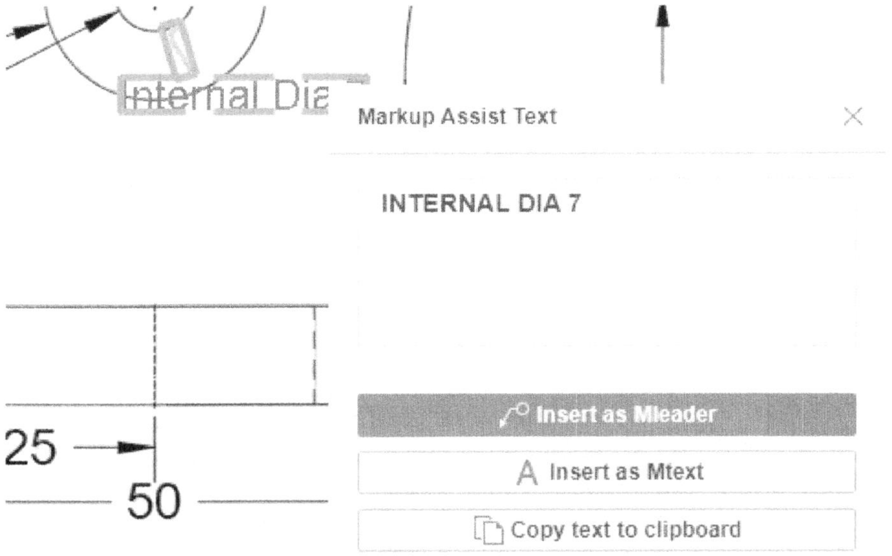

*Figure 3-38 The **Markup Assist Text** dialog box displayed*

DWG Compare

Ribbon: Collaborate > Compare > DWG Compare **Command:** COMPARE

The **DWG Compare** tool is used to compare two drawings with each other. It highlights the differences between two revisions of the same drawing or different drawings. First open a drawing, and then choose **DWG Compare** tool from the Application Menu, refer to Figure 3-39.

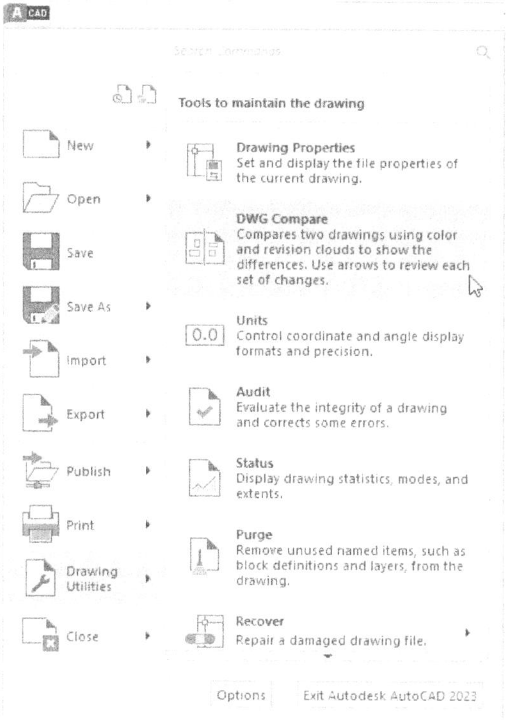

Figure 3-39** The **DWG Compare** tool in the **Application Menu

On choosing the **DWG Compare** tool from the **Application Menu**, the **Select a drawing to compare** dialog box will be displayed, as shown in Figure 3-40.

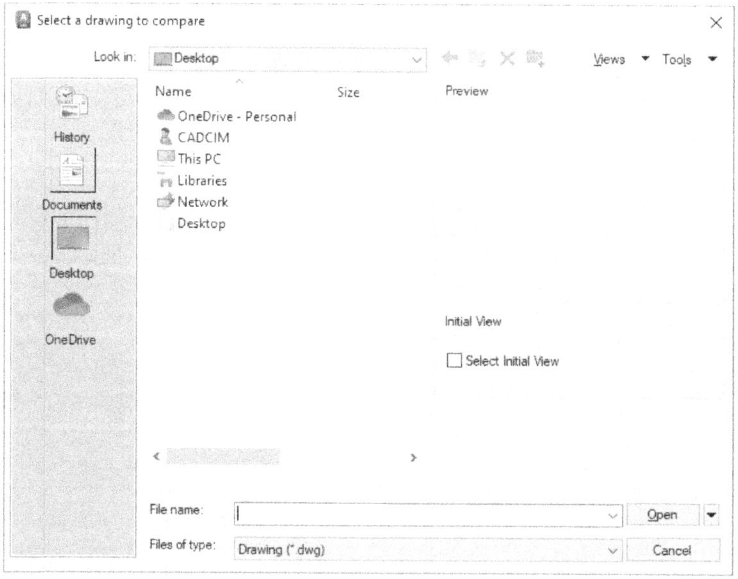

***Figure 3-40** The **Select a drawing to compare** dialog box*

Now, select the second drawing file and choose the **Open** button; a drawing window will be displayed showing the difference between the two drawings, as shown in Figure 3-41.

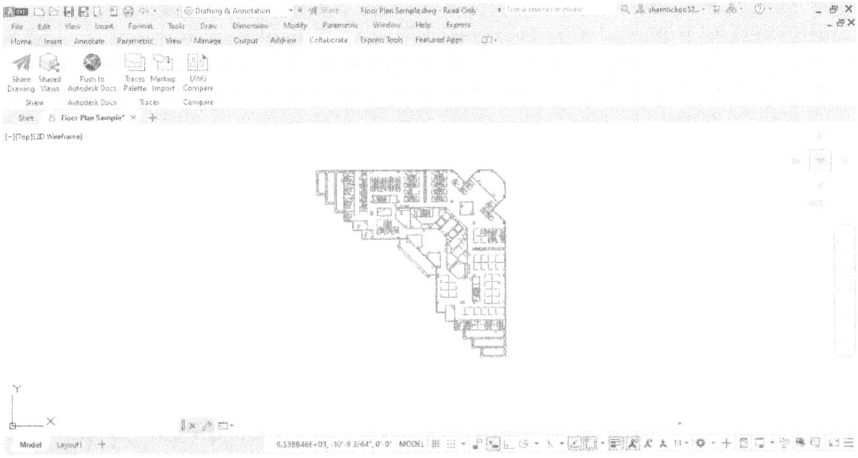

Figure 3-41 *Drawing window displaying the difference between two drawings*

Note

To get a better idea of the functioning of this tool, open or create a drawing file and save it with any name at a desired location. After saving the file, make some modifications in it and then save it with a new name. Next, compare the two files using the ***DWG Compare*** *tool; a drawing window will open displaying the difference between the two drawings.*

Figure 3-42 shows the zoomed view of the modified area which is highlighted after comparing the two drawing files.

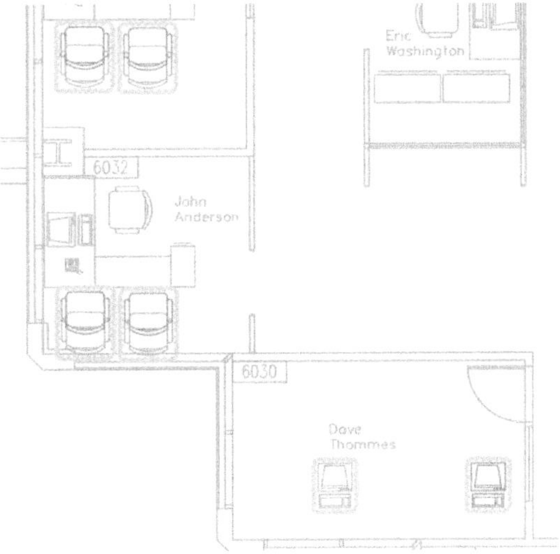

Figure 3-42 *Zoomed view of the compared area*

Notice that after comparing the drawing files, the resultant compared drawing file is displayed in different colors, refer to Figure 3-42. By default, the identical part between the two drawings is displayed in Grey color in this file. The elements which have been modified are displayed in Green color. Also, the original location of the modified elements is displayed in Green color. Red color displays the modified elements at their new location and also indicates the position of the new elements which have been added to the drawing file. The modified area in the two compared drawings can be easily identified as it is displayed in the Orange colored revision cloud in the resultant drawing file, refer to Figure 3-42.

As discussed earlier, as you choose the **Compare** button in the **DWG Compare** dialog box; a drawing window is displayed with a bar named **DWG Compare**, refer to Figure 3-43.

Figure 3-43 *The* ***DWG Compare*** *bar added to drawing area*

In the **DWG Compare** bar, click on the **Settings** button to access a number of options that can be set to change the appearance of the compared elements. For example, if you want to change the color of the modified elements to blue, choose green color from color swatch in the **Difference** area; the **Select Color** dialog box will be displayed. In this dialog box, select blue color and choose the **OK** button; the color of the modified element will be changed to blue. You can also turn the visibility of the respective elements **ON/OFF** using the Visibility toggle button available on the left of the color swatch in the **Difference** area, refer to Figure 3-44.

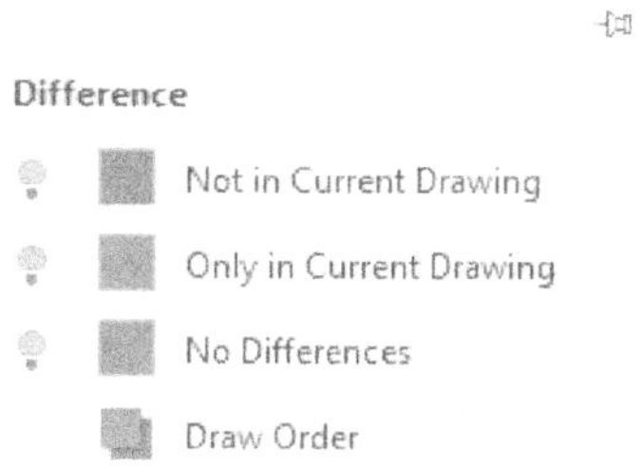

Figure 3-44 *The* ***Difference*** *area*

The **Text** and **Hatch** toggle buttons available in the **Filter** area control whether the texts and hatches are to be compared or not. If these buttons are turned on, then both the texts and hatches available in the drawings will be compared. If these buttons are turned off, then AutoCAD will exclude texts and hatches while comparing the drawings.

You can turn the visibility of revision clouds on/off using the visibility toggle button available in the **Revision Clouds** area. In this area, you can also change the shape and size of the revision clouds.

Note

When drawings to be compared are already open, then the ***DWG Compare*** *tool will be available in the* ***Drawing Utilities*** *flyout of the* ***Application Menu****. You can also access this tool from the* ***Compare*** *panel of the* ***Collaborate*** *tab. If you use this tool when drawings to be compared are already open; a third window will open displaying the compared file.*

Self-Evaluation Test

Answer the following questions and then compare them to those given at the end of this chapter:

1. When you use the **Inner arcs** option for multilines, a capping arc is drawn between the __________ numbered inner lines.

2. The **Multilines Edit tools** dialog box consists of __________ basic editing tools.

3. The __________ option of the **Fit data** option of the **Edit Spline** tool is used to reduce the file size by removing the fit data of the selected splines.

4. The __________ system variable stores the justification of the current multiline.

5. The name of the multiline style that you enter in the **New Style Name** edit box of the **Create New Multiline style** dialog box can have up to thirty-one characters including spaces. (T/F)

6. The **Zero** option is used to create a multiline so that the zero offset position of the multiline coincides with the selected points. (T/F)

7. Multilines cannot be edited using grips. (T/F)

8. While using the **Top** justification option to draw a multiline, the line with the largest positive offset coincides with the points selected on the screen. (T/F)

9. When a multiline is cut, two separate multilines are created. (T/F)

10. You cannot weld or join separate multilines. (T/F)

Review Questions

Answer the following questions:

1. In which file are the multiline styles saved by default?

   (a) *acad.mln* (b) *acad.pat*
   (c) *acad.mpr* (d) *acad.plt*

2. Which of the following is the default value of the start and end angles for multilines?

   (a) 90 (b) 180
   (c) 45 (d) 0

3. Which of the following tools does not work on multilines?

   (a) **Mirror** (b) **Fillet**
   (c) **Stretch** (d) **Explode**

4. Which of the following options can be used to reverse the direction of spline creation while editing a spline?

   (a) **Fit data** (b) **Refine**
   (c) **Reverse** (d) **Weight**

5. AutoCAD forces a multiline to turn into a single line if the scale factor of the multiline is_______.

6. The current multiline style is saved in the __________ system variable and the default value is **STANDARD**.

7. The three justifications that are available for the **MLINE** command are __________, __________, and __________.

8. Using options of the **MLEDIT** command, you can create three types of cross intersections: __________, __________, and __________.

9. If the value of **Fit tolerance** of a spline is __________, the spline passes exactly through the fit points of the spline.

10. You need to set the degree of a spline if you are drawing the spline by using the __________ method.

11. By default, the *.mln* files are saved at *C:\Users\<user name>\AppData\Roaming\Autodesk\AutoCAD 2023\R24.2\enu\Support*. (T/F)

12. Once the **Purge** option of **Fit data** is used on a spline, the **Fit data** option is no longer available for the particular spline. (T/F)

13. You can break or trim a multiline. (T/F)

14. You cannot change the lineweights of the lines that constitute a multiline. (T/F)

Exercise 1

Create the drawing shown in Figure 3-45.

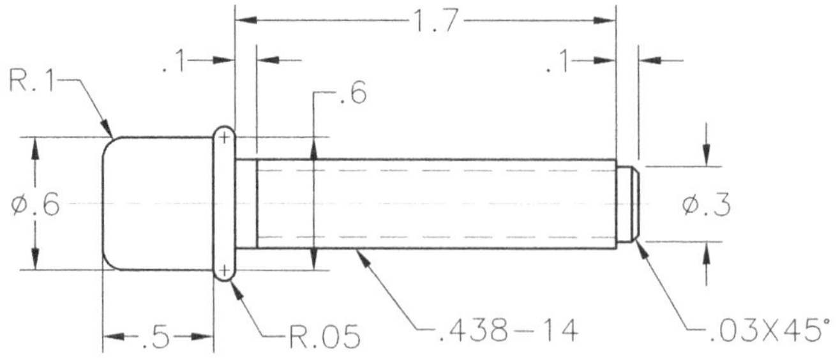

Figure 3-45 *Drawing for Exercise 1*

Exercise 2

Create the drawing shown in Figure 3-46. Use the **MLINE** command to draw the walls. The wall thickness is 12 inches. Assume the missing dimensions.

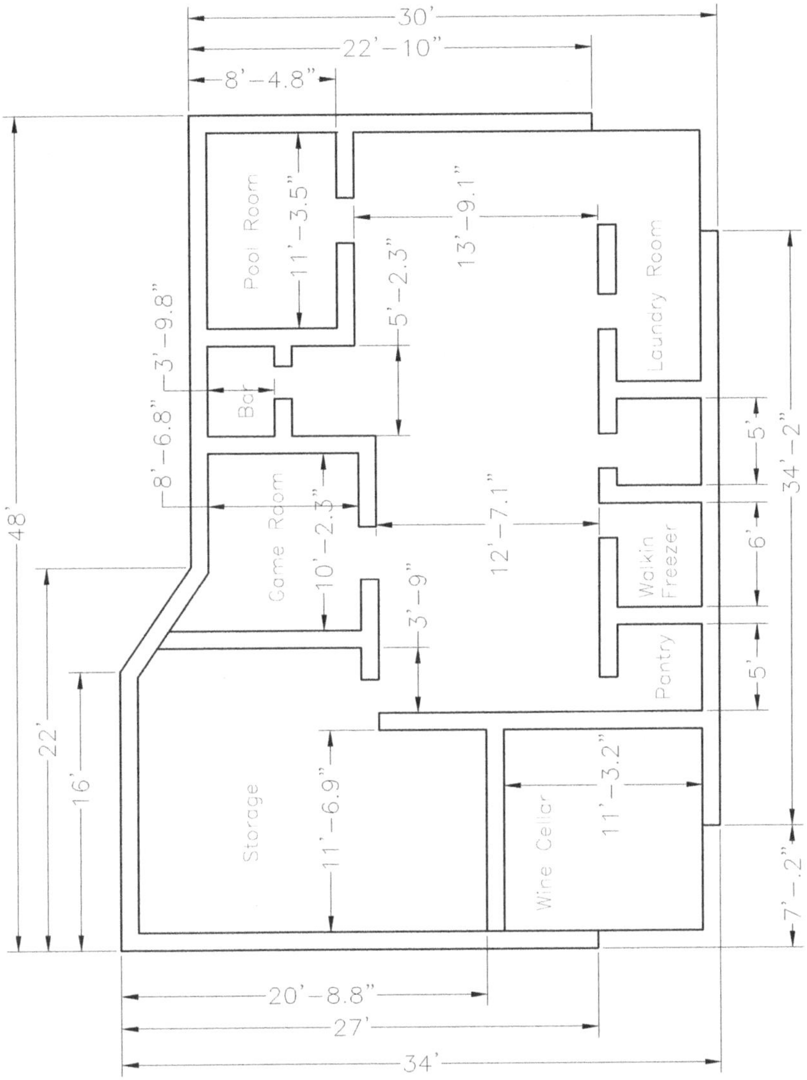

Figure 3-46 *Drawing for Exercise 2*

Problem-Solving Exercise 1

Create the orthographic view shown in Figure 3-47. The required dimensions are shown in the same view.

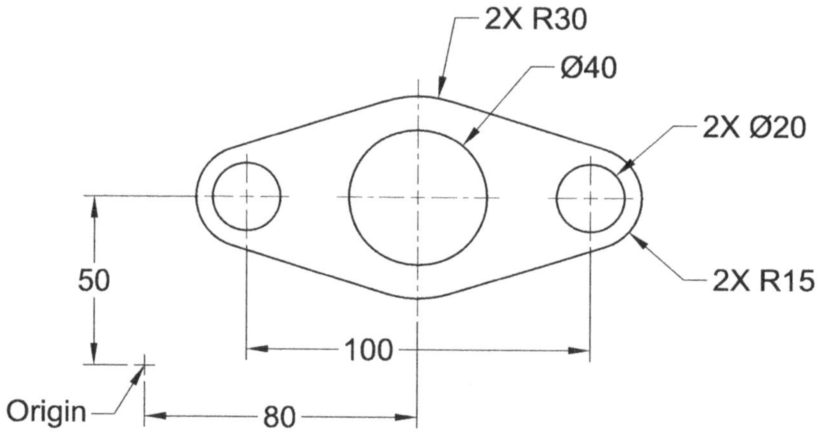

Figure 3-47 *Views and dimensions for Problem-Solving Exercise 1*

Problem-Solving Exercise 2

Create the orthographic view shown in Figure 3-48. The required dimensions are shown in the same view.

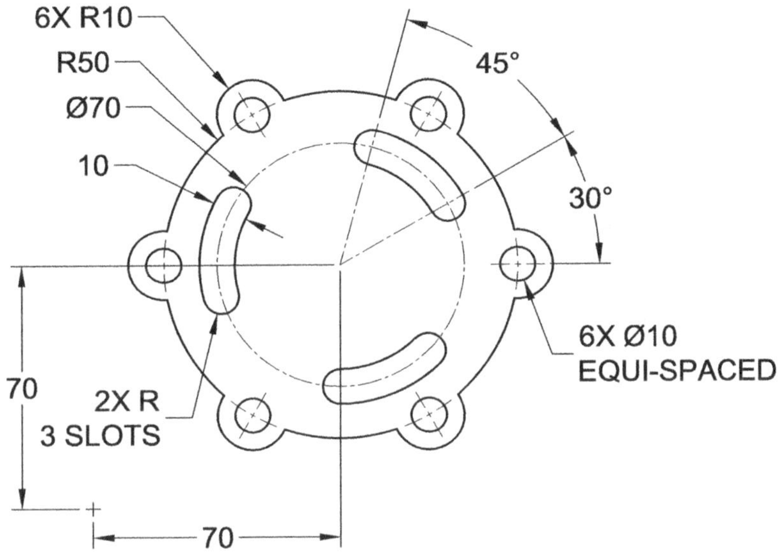

Figure 3-48 *Views and Dimensions for Problem-Solving Exercise 2*

Problem-Solving Exercise 3

Create the orthographic views shown in Figure 3-49. The required dimensions are shown in the same views.

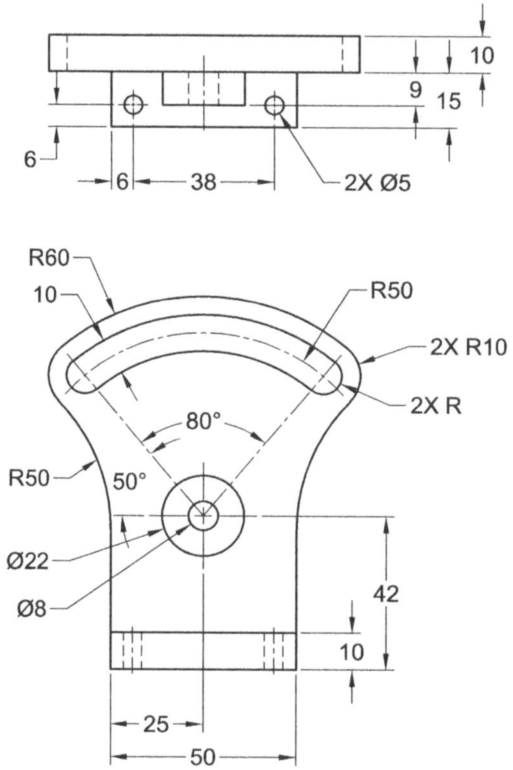

Figure 3-49 *Views and dimensions for Problem-Solving Exercise 3*

Problem-Solving Exercise 4

Create the drawing shown in Figure 3-50. Some of the reference dimensions are given in the drawing. Assume the missing dimensions.

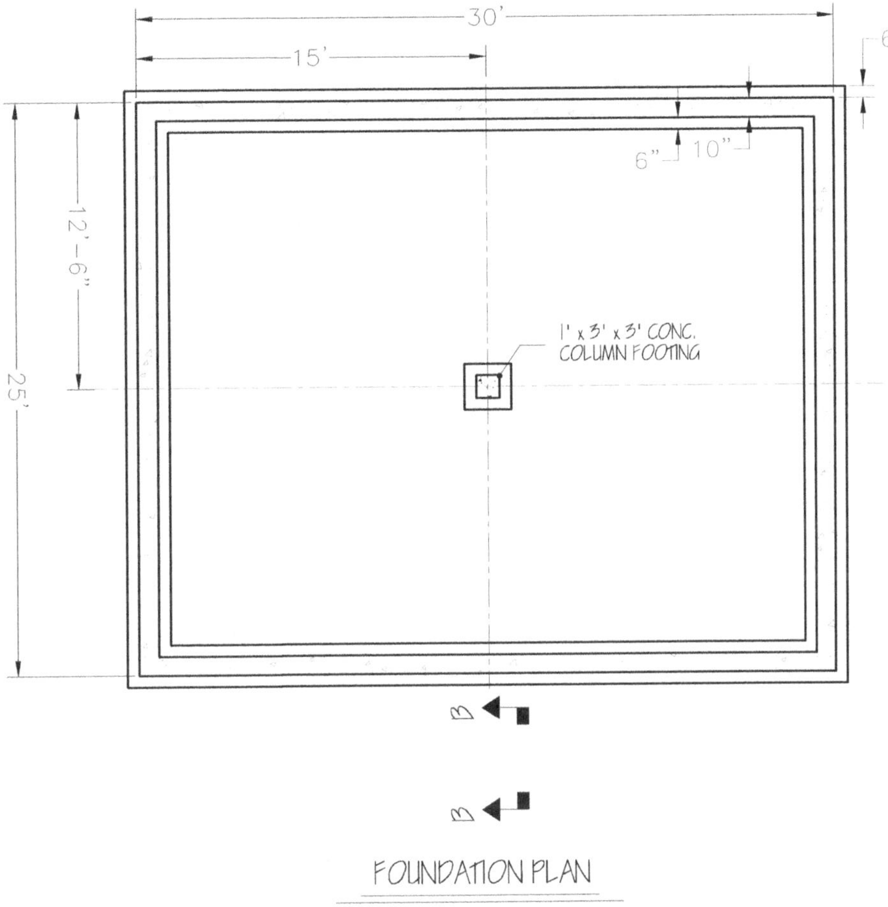

Figure 3-50 *Drawing for Problem-Solving Exercise 4*

Problem-Solving Exercise 5

Create the orthographic view shown in Figure 3-51. The required dimensions are shown in the same view.

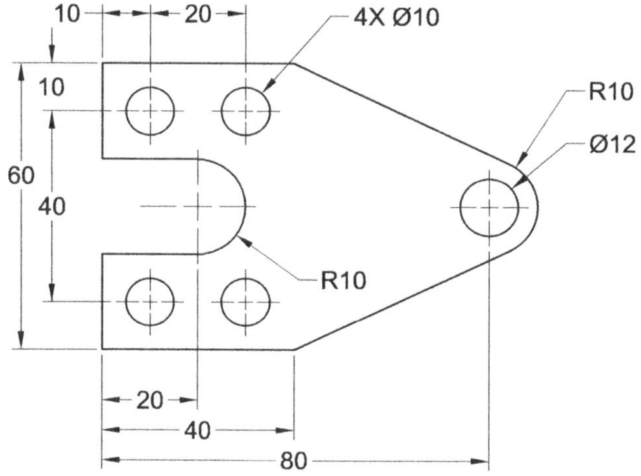

Figure 3-51 *Views and dimensions for Problem-Solving Exercise 5*

Problem-Solving Exercise 6

Create the drawing shown in Figure 3-52. Some of the reference dimensions are given in the drawing. Assume the missing dimensions.

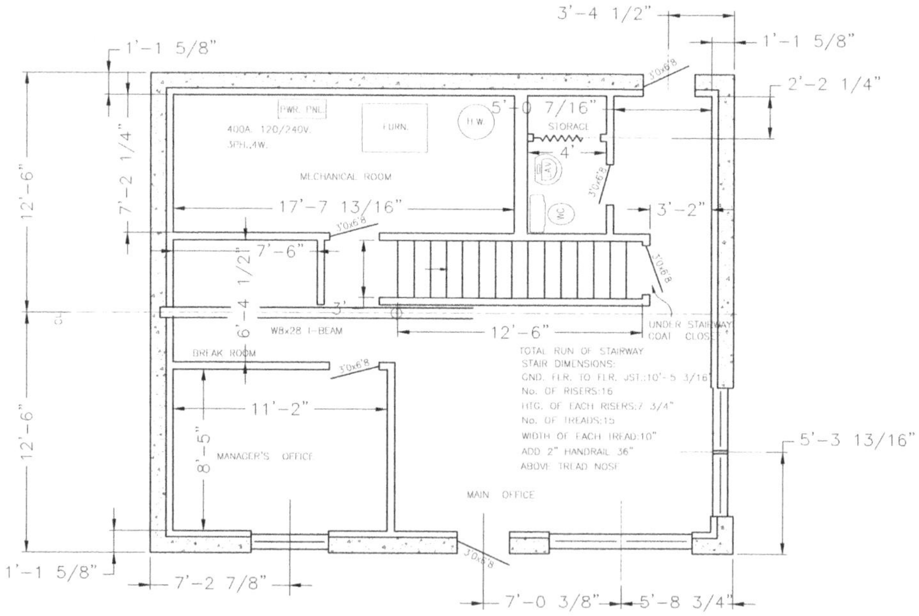

Figure 3-52 *Drawing for Problem-Solving Exercise 6*

Problem-Solving Exercise 7

Create the drawing shown in Figure 3-53. Some of the reference dimensions are given in the drawing. Assume the missing dimensions.

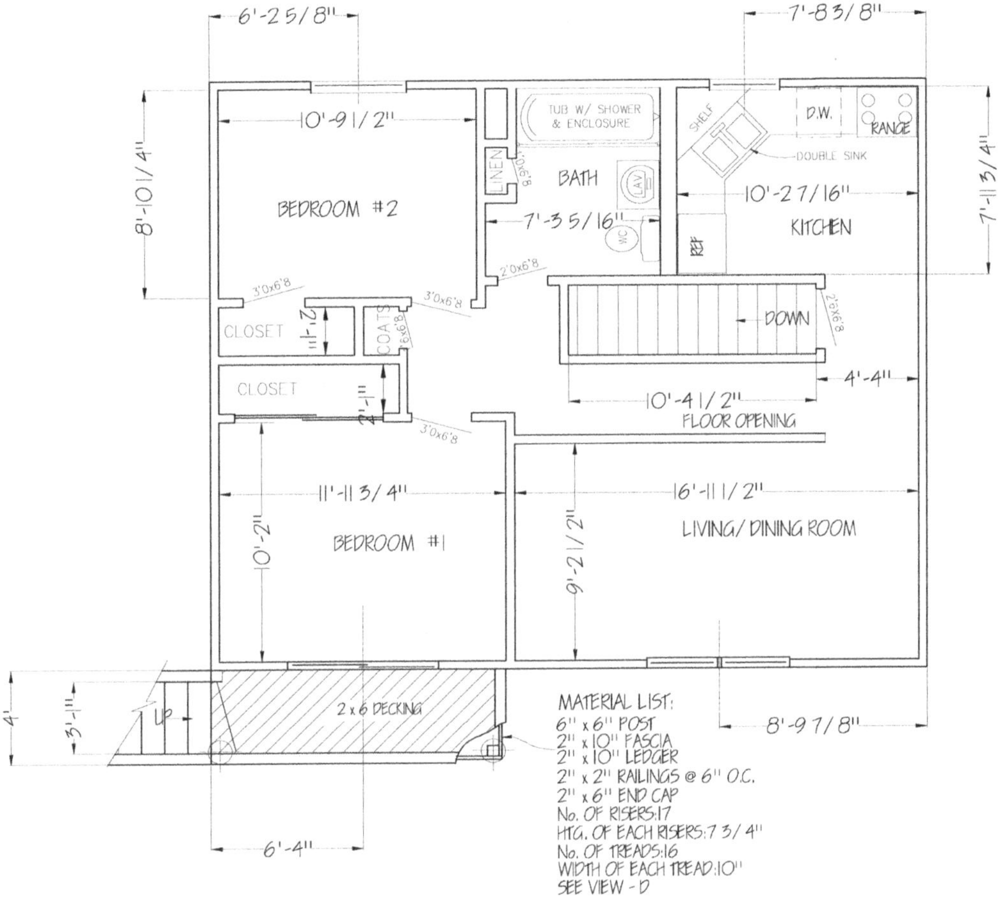

Figure 3-53 Drawing for Problem-Solving Exercise 7

Answers to Self-Evaluation Test

1. even, **2**. five, **3**. **Purge**, **4**. **CMLJUST**, **5.** T, **6**. T, **7**. F, **8**. T, **9**. F, **10**. T

Chapter 4

Grouping and Advanced Editing of Sketched Objects

Learning Objectives

After completing this chapter, you will be able to:

- *Group sketched objects*
- *Select and cycle through defined groups*
- *Change properties and location of sketched objects*
- *Perform editing operations on polylines*
- *Explode compound objects and undo previous commands*
- *Rename the named objects and remove unused named objects*

Key Terms

- *Group*
- *Explode*
- *Polyline Edit*
- *SPLINETYPE*
- *Undo*
- *Redo*
- *Rename*
- *Purge*

GROUPING SKETCHED OBJECTS USING THE OBJECT GROUPING DIALOG BOX

Ribbon: Home > Groups > Group Manager **Command:** CLASSICGROUP

In AutoCAD, you can group sketched objects using the **Object Grouping** dialog box, as shown in Figure 4-1. To invoke the **Object Grouping** dialog box, you need to choose the **Group Manager** tool from the **Groups** panel in the **Home** tab. You can use the **Object Grouping** dialog box to group AutoCAD objects and assign a name to the group. Once you have created groups, you can select the objects by the group name. The individual characteristics of an object are not affected by forming groups. Groups enable you to select all the objects in a group together for editing. It makes the object selection process easier and faster. Objects can be members of several groups. Also, a group can contain several smaller groups. This may be referred to as nested groups.

Although an object belongs to a group, you can still select an object as if it does not belong to any group. Groups can be selected by entering the group name or by selecting an object that belongs to the group. You can also highlight the objects in a group or sequentially highlight the groups to which an object belongs. The options in the **Object Grouping** dialog box are discussed next.

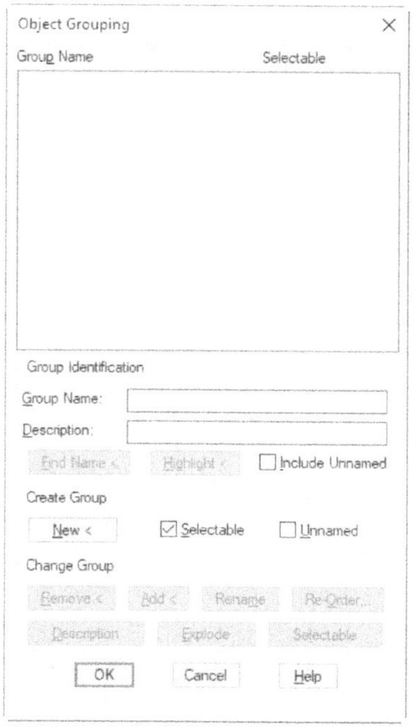

***Figure 4-1** The **Object Grouping** dialog box*

Group Name List Box

The **Group Name** list box in the **Object Grouping** dialog box displays the names of the existing groups. The list box also displays whether a group is selectable or not, under the **Selectable** column. A selectable group is the one in which all members of the group are selected on selecting a single member. However, the members that are in frozen or locked layers are not selected. You can also make a group non-selectable; which helps you to select the objects in the group individually.

Group Identification Area

The options under the **Group Identification** area are as follows:

Group Name

The **Group Name** edit box displays the name of the selected group. You can also use the **Group Name** edit box to enter the name of a new group. You can enter any name, but it is recommended that you use a name that reflects the type of objects in the group. For example, the group name WALLS can include all lines that form walls. Group names can be up to thirty-one characters long and can include letters, numbers, and special characters ($, _, and -). Group names cannot have spaces.

Description
The **Description** edit box displays the description of the selected group. It can be used to enter the description of a group.

Find Name
The **Find Name** button is used to find the group name or names associated with an object. When you choose this button, the dialog box temporarily disappears from the screen and AutoCAD prompts you to **Pick a member of a group**. Once you select the object, the **Group Member List** dialog box will be displayed, as shown in Figure 4-2, showing the group name(s) to which the selected object belongs.

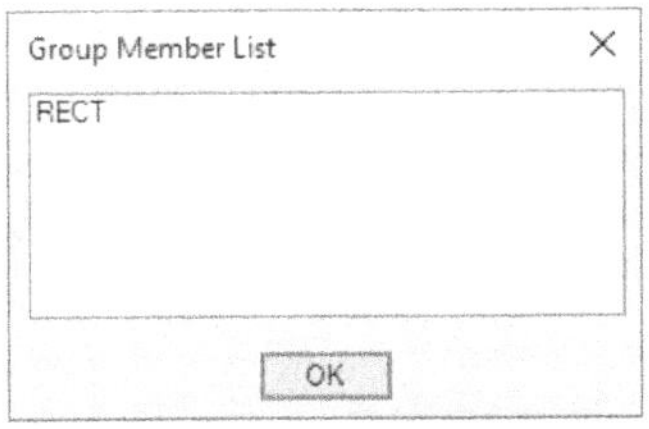

***Figure 4-2** The **Group Member List** dialog box*

Highlight
The **Highlight** button is used to highlight the objects in the selected group name. This button is available only when you select a group from the **Group Name** list box. When you choose the **Highlight** button, the objects that are members of the selected group are highlighted in the drawing and the **Object Grouping** message box is displayed, as shown in Figure 4-3. Choose the **Continue** button or press Enter to return to the **Object Grouping** dialog box.

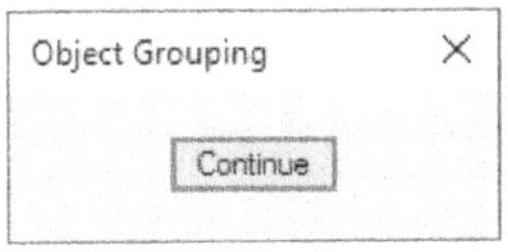

***Figure 4-3** The **Object Grouping** message box*

Include Unnamed
The **Include Unnamed** check box is used to display the names of the unnamed groups in the **Object Grouping** dialog box. The unnamed groups are created when you select the **Unnamed** check box in the **Create Group** area or when you copy the objects that belong to a group. AutoCAD automatically groups and assigns a name to the copied objects. The format of the name is A*n* (for example, *A1, *A2, *A3). If you select the **Include Unnamed** check box, the unnamed group names (*A1, *A2, *A3, ...) will also be displayed in the **Group Name** list box of the dialog box. The unnamed groups can also be created by not assigning a name to the group (refer to the **Unnamed** option in the next section, "**Create Group** Area").

Create Group Area
The options under this area are discussed next.

New
The **New** button is used to create a new group. To create a group, enter the name of the group in the **Group Name** edit box and then choose the **New** button; the **Object Grouping** dialog box will be temporarily closed and you will be prompted to select the objects to be included in the group. After selecting the objects, right-click; the dialog box will be displayed again and a new group will be created from the selected objects. The new group name is now displayed in the **Group Name** list box of the dialog box. The group names in the **Group Name** list box are listed alphabetically.

Selectable
The **Selectable** check box allows you to define a group as selectable. A selectable group has a property that if you select any one object in the group, the entire group will be selected. If you

clear this check box while defining a group, the new group created will not be selected at once. Therefore, you need to select all members of the group individually as the entire group will not be selected upon selecting the individual entities of the group.

Even if a group is defined as selectable, and the **PICKSTYLE** system variable is set to 0, you will not be able to select the entire group by selecting one of its members. You will be able to individually select members of the group. You can also turn the group selectability on or off by selecting or clearing the **Object grouping** check box in the **Selection modes** area of the **Selection** tab of the **Options** dialog box or by using the Shift+Ctrl+A toggle keys.

Unnamed

When you create a group, you can assign it a name or leave it unnamed. If you select the **Unnamed** check box, AutoCAD will automatically assign a group name to the selected objects and these unnamed groups will be listed in the **Group Name** list box. To view the name of the unnamed group, the **Include Unnamed** check box should be selected. The format used for assigning a name is A*n* (*A1, *A2, *A3 ...), where *n* is a number which increments by 1 with each newly added unnamed group.

Change Group Area

All the options under this area, other than the **Re-Order** button, will be available only when you highlight a group name by selecting it in the **Group Name** list box of the dialog box. The options in this area are used to modify the properties of the existing group. These options are as follows.

Remove

The **Remove** button is used to remove objects from the selected group. Once you select the group name from the **Group Name** list box and then choose the **Remove** button; the dialog box will be temporarily closed and AutoCAD will display the following prompts at the command prompt.

Select objects to remove from group...
Remove objects: *(Select the objects that you want to remove from the selected group.)*

Also, all objects belonging to the selected group will be highlighted. As you select the objects to be removed from the group, they no longer appear highlighted. Note that even if you remove all objects from the group, the group name will still exist, unless you use the **Explode** option to remove the group definition (discussed later in this section). If you remove objects and then add them later in the same drawing session, the objects retain their order in the group.

Add

The **Add** button is used to add objects to the selected group. When you select this option, AutoCAD will prompt you to select the objects you want to add to the selected group. The prompt sequence in this case will be similar to that of the **Remove** option. Similar to removing an object, all objects belonging to the selected group are highlighted and as soon as you select an object to be added to the group, it also gets highlighted.

Rename

The **Rename** button is used to rename the selected group. To rename a group, first select the group name from the **Group Name** list box, enter the new name in the **Group Name** edit box, and then choose the **Rename** button. AutoCAD will rename the specified group. You can use this option to rename unnamed groups that were discussed earlier.

Re-Order

The **Re-Order** button is used to change the order of the objects in the selected group. The objects are numbered in the order in which you select them when selecting objects for the group. Sometimes, while creating a tool path, you may want to change the order of these objects to get a continuous tool motion. You can do this using the **Re-Order** button. This option is also useful in some batch operations where one object needs to be on top of another object for display reasons. When you choose the **Re-Order** button, AutoCAD displays the **Order Group** dialog box, as shown in Figure 4-4, where you can change the order of the group members.

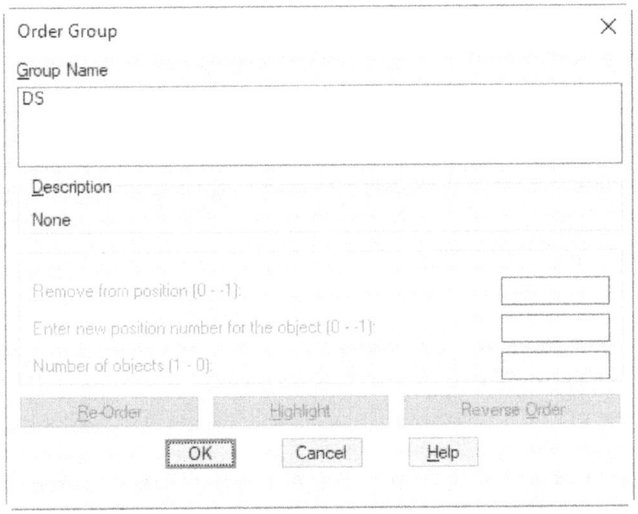

***Figure 4-4** The **Order Group** dialog box*

Description

The **Description** button is used to change the description of the selected group. To change the description of a group, first select the group name from the **Group Name** list box, enter the new description in the **Description** text box, and then choose the **Description** button. AutoCAD will update the description of the specified group.

Explode

The **Explode** option is used to delete group definition of the selected group. The objects that were in the group become regular objects without a group reference. If you had made copies of the group that was exploded in a drawing, they shall remain as unnamed groups in the drawing. You can select the **Include Unnamed** check box in the **Group Identification** area of the **Object Grouping** dialog box to view the names of the unnamed groups in the **Group Name** list box. You can then select them in the list box and explode them or rename them as required.

Selectable

The **Selectable** button is used to change the selectable status of the selected group. To change the selectable status of the group, first select the group name from the **Group Name** list box, and then choose the **Selectable** button. This button acts like a toggle key between the options of selectable and non-selectable. If the selectable status for a group is displayed as "**Yes**", you can choose the **Selectable** button to change it to "**No**". Selectable implies that the entire group gets selected when one object in the group is selected. If the selectable status is "**No**", you cannot select the entire group by selecting one object in the group.

Example 1 — Reorder Group

In this example, you will draw a rectangle representing a toolpath. The rectangle should comprise of four individual lines. Group all lines by selecting them in the order shown in Figure 4-5(a). Then, highlight the order, and re-order the group, as shown in Figure 4-5(b).

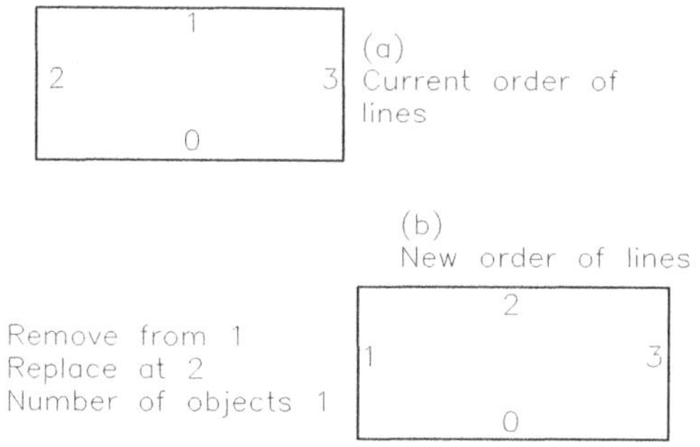

Figure 4-5 *Changing the order of group objects*

1. Draw four lines that are connected at the end points to form a rectangle.

2 Choose the **Group Manager** tool from the **Groups** panel; the **Object Grouping** dialog box is displayed.

3. Type **G1** in the **Group Name** edit box and choose the **New** button; the **Object Grouping** dialog box will disappear and you will be prompted to select the objects for grouping.

4. Select the lines in the order specified in Figure 4-5(a) and right-click; the **Object Grouping** dialog box is displayed again.

5. Make the group (G1) current by selecting it in the **Group Name** list box and choose the **Re-Order** button in the dialog box; the **Order Group** dialog box is displayed.

6. Select the group G1 in the **Group Name** list box, if not already selected, and choose the **Highlight** button; the **Object Grouping** dialog box is displayed, as shown in Figure 4-6. You can use the **Next** and **Previous** buttons to highlight the grouped objects in the order of selection.

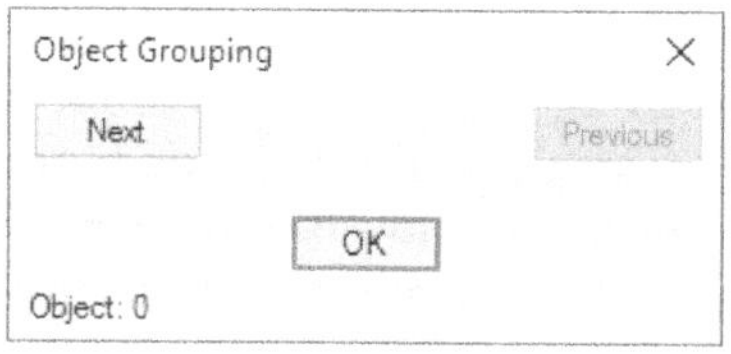

Figure 4-6 *The **Object Grouping** dialog box*

You will notice that the order of selection is not proper. As these lines represent a tool path, you need to reorder the objects, as shown in Figure 4-5(b).

7. To get a clockwise tool path, you must switch object numbers 1 and 2. You can do so by entering the necessary information in the **Order Group** dialog box. Enter **1** in the **Remove from position (0-3)** edit box and **2** in the **Enter new position number for the object (0-3)** edit box. Enter **1** in the **Number of objects (1-4)** edit box because there is only one object to be replaced.

8. After entering the information, choose the **Re-Order** button to define the new order of the objects. You can confirm the change by choosing the **Highlight** button again and cycling through the objects.

GROUPING SKETCHED OBJECTS USING THE GROUP BUTTON

Ribbon: Home > Groups > Group **Command:** GROUP/G
Toolbar: Group > Group

In AutoCAD, you can group objects by using the **Group** tool from the **Groups** panel of the **Home** tab. The prompt sequence to create a group is given next:

Choose the ***Group*** *tool.*
Select objects or [Name/Description]: **N** Enter.
Enter a group name or [?]: *Enter the group name* Enter.
Select objects or [Name/Description]: *Select the objects to be grouped.*
Select objects or [Name/Description]: Enter.
Group "*group name*" has been created.

You can also group the objects by using the shortcut menu. Select the objects to be grouped, and right-click in the drawing area; a shortcut menu will be displayed. Choose **Group > Group** from the shortcut menu; the selected objects will be grouped as *Unnamed group*.

Later on, you can ungroup them using **Ungroup** option from the same shortcut menu.

SELECTING GROUPS

You can select a group by name by entering **G** at the **Select objects** prompt. For example, if you have to move a particular group, choose the **Move** tool from the **Modify** panel in the **Home** tab and then enter the following prompt sequence:

Select objects: **G** Enter.
Enter group name: *Enter the group name.*
n found
Select objects: Enter.

Instead of entering **G** at the **Select Objects** prompt, if you select any member of a selectable group, all the group members get selected. Make sure that the **PICKSTYLE** system variable is set to 1 or 3. Also, the group selection can be turned on or off by pressing Shift+Ctrl+A. If the group selection is off and you want to erase a group from a drawing, choose the **Erase** tool from the **Modify** panel. The prompt sequence for erasing the group is given next.

Select objects: *Press Shift+Ctrl+A keys.*
<Groups on> *Select an object that belongs to a group. (If the group has been defined as selectable, all objects belonging to that group will be selected.)*

If the group has not been defined as selectable, you cannot select all objects in the group, even if you turn the group selection on by pressing the Shift+Ctrl+A keys. This setting can also be changed in the **Selection** tab of the **Options** dialog box. You can select or clear the **Object grouping** check box in the **Selection modes** area of the dialog box to turn group selectability on or off.

Tip
The keyboard shortcut Shift+Ctrl+A is used as a toggle key to turn the group selection on or off.

CHANGING PROPERTIES OF AN OBJECT

AutoCAD provides you different options for changing the properties of an object. These options are discussed next.

Using the PROPERTIES Palette

Ribbon: View > Palettes > Properties **Toolbar:** Standard > Properties
Quick Access Toolbar: Properties (*Customize to Add*)
Command: PROPERTIES/PR/CH/MO

The categories displayed in the **PROPERTIES** palette depend on the type of object selected. The **General** category displays the general properties of objects, such as color, layer, linetype, linetype scale, plot style, lineweight, hyperlink, and thickness. In this chapter, the **Geometry** category containing properties that control the geometry of an object will be discussed. Depending on the type of object selected, the **Geometry** category will contain a set of different properties. If you have selected many types of objects in a drawing, the drop-down list at the top of the **PROPERTIES** palette will display all the type of selected objects. If you select a type of object from the drop-down list, the corresponding categories of the object properties will be displayed in the palette. You can also invoke the **PROPERTIES** palette from the shortcut menu displayed on selecting the object.

Selecting a Line

If you have selected a line in the drawing, the **PROPERTIES** palette appears similar to what is shown in Figure 4-7, where you can change the properties of the selected object.

Start X/Start Y/Start Z: The **Start X/Start Y/Start Z** fields in the **Geometry** category display the start point coordinates of the selected line. You can enter new values in these fields or use the Pick Point button that appears in the field you click in. When you choose the Pick Point button, a rubber-band line gets attached to the cursor on its start point and the endpoint of the line is fixed. You can now move the cursor and specify a new start point for the line.

End X/End Y/End Z: Similar to the start point, you can also modify the location of the endpoint of a line by entering new coordinate values in the **End X**, **End Y**, **End Z** fields. You can also choose the Pick Point button in the respective fields and select a new location for the endpoint of the selected line. The Pick Point button appears in the fields when you click on them.

Note

*The **Delta X**, **Delta Y**, **Delta Z**, **Length**, and **Angle** fields are not available for change but the values in these fields get updated as the start and endpoints of the line are changed.*

Selecting a Circle

When you select a circle, the **Geometry** category displays the categories as shown in Figure 4-8. You can modify the values in these fields. The effects of modifying the values are discussed next.

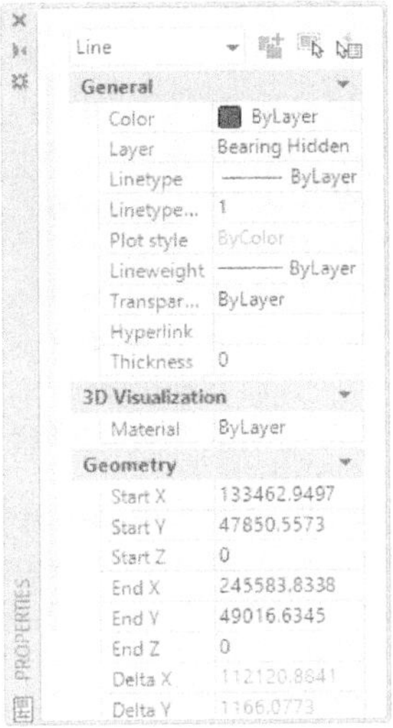

*Figure 4-7 The **PROPERTIES** palette for a line*

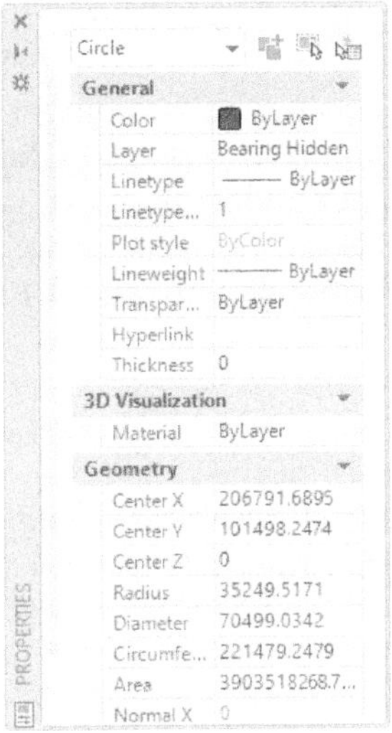

*Figure 4-8 The **PROPERTIES** palette for a circle*

Center X/Center Y/Center Z: Here, under the Center X/Center Y/Center Z fields of the Geometry category, you can specify a new location of the center point of the circle by entering new coordinate values in the Center X, Center Y, and Center Z fields. When you click in any of these fields; the **Pick Point** button is displayed. You can choose this button to locate a new location of the center point of the circle. The circle will be drawn at the new location with the same radius as specified before. It is as if the circle has moved from the old location to a new one.

Radius/Diameter: You can enter a new value for the radius or diameter of the circle in the **Radius** or **Diameter** fields respectively. The circle's radius or diameter is modified as per the new values you have entered. As you modify the values of the radius or the diameter, the values in the **Circumference** and **Area** fields get modified accordingly.

Note

*You can also enter new values of the circumference or area in the **Circumference** and **Area** fields, respectively, if you want to create a circle with a given value of circumference or area. You will notice that the radius and diameter values are modified accordingly. The **Normal X**, **Normal Y**, and **Normal Z** fields are not available for modifications.*

Selecting the Multiline Text

If you select multiline text written in a drawing and invoke the **PROPERTIES** palette, refer to Figure 4-9, apart from the **General** category, three more categories of properties are displayed: **Text**, **3D Visualization**, and **Geometry**. The properties in the **Text** and **Geometry** categories and how they can be modified are discussed next.

***Figure 4-9** The **Text** and **Geometry** categories of the **PROPERTIES** palette*

Contents: The current contents of the text are displayed in the **Contents** field under the **Text** category of the **PROPERTIES** palette. To modify the contents, click in the field and the button is displayed at the right-corner of the field. You can then choose this button to display the **Text Editor** where you can make the necessary modifications using the options in the dialog box. Once you have made the changes, choose the **Close Text Editor** button from the **Text Editor** contextual tab to exit the text editing and return to the **PROPERTIES** palette. The changes you made are reflected in the value of the **Contents** field of the **PROPERTIES** palette and in the drawing.

Style: When you click in the **Style** field in the **PROPERTIES** palette, a drop-down list of the defined text styles is displayed. By default, only the Standard style is displayed. If you had defined more text styles in the drawing, they can be selected from the drop-down list and applied to the current text in the drawing.

Annotative: You can convert the non-annotative text to annotative and vice-versa by selecting the **Yes** and **No** options respectively from the **Annotative** drop-down list.

Justify: All the text justification options are available in the **Justify** drop-down list. This drop-down list will be available when you click in the **Justify** field. By default, the Top left justification is applied to the text. You can select a text justification from the drop-down list to be applied to the selected text in the drawing.

Direction: This drop-down list displays the possible directions for the text. This option is generally available for the multiline text objects.

Text height: You can enter a new value for the height of the selected text in the drawing. The default text height is 0.2. But, you can make the text smaller or larger in the drawing by simply entering a new value in the **Text height** field of the **PROPERTIES** palette.

Rotation: This field displays the current angle of the selected text and is 0 degree by default. You can change the angle of rotation of the text by entering an angle by which you want to rotate the selected text in the **Rotation** field and then pressing Enter. The effect is immediately visible in the drawing.

Line space factor: The effect of changing the value of this field is more evident when you have selected a paragraph or multiline text. This value controls the spacing between the lines in a paragraph or multiline text. A scale factor of 1 is the default value. You can increase or decrease the spacing between the lines of the selected paragraph text by entering a new scale factor of your choice and pressing Enter. The result is immediately visible in the drawing.

Line space distance: This field is used to modify the distance between the spacing of each line of the multiline text. Click in this field and enter the new value in it.

Line space style: This field when selected displays two line spacing options in the corresponding drop-down list. They are **Exactly** and **At least**. **At least** is the default option.

Background mask: This field specifies whether or not any background mask is assigned to the multiline text.

Columns: Columns are of three types, None, Static, or Dynamic. To edit the column settings, choose the button; the **Column Settings** dialog box will be displayed. You can change the column settings through this dialog box.

Defined width/Defined height: These fields display the defined width/height of the text window in the **In-Place Text Editor**. These fields will be available, when you choose the **None** option from the **Columns** field. To change the values of these fields, click in the field and enter the new value in it.

Position X/Position Y/Position Z: You can change the location of the insertion point of the selected text by entering new *X/Y/Z* coordinates for the text in these fields. You can also use the Pick Points button that is displayed in these fields when you click in them. When you choose the Pick Points button, a rubber-band line is attached between the cursor and the selected text and you can move the cursor and specify a new location for the text on the screen. The values of the three fields get updated automatically.

Selecting the Annotative Block Reference

When you select a block in the drawing and invoke the **PROPERTIES** palette, apart from the **General** category, three more categories containing the properties of the block are available. They are **Geometry**, **3D Visualization**, and **Misc**. The properties under these categories are discussed next.

Position X/Position Y/Position Z: In the **Position X/Position Y/Position Z** fields of the **Geometry** category, you can enter new *X*, *Y*, and *Z* coordinates respectively for the selected block. The block reference shall move to the new location as you specify the coordinates. You can also click in any one of the fields to display the Pick Points button and choose it to specify a new location for the block on the screen.

Scale X/Scale Y/Scale Z: You can specify new X, Y, and Z scale factors for the selected block in the **Scale X**, **Scale Y**, and **Scale Z** fields, respectively. The current scale factors for the block are displayed in the **Scale X**, **Scale Y**, and **Scale Z** fields and as you change them, the modifications are reflected in the drawing.

Name: This field under the **Misc** category displays the name of the selected block reference and is not available for modifications.

Rotation: This field specifies the current rotation angle of the selected block. You can specify a new angle of rotation for the selected block in this field. After specifying an angle, when you press Enter, the selected block in the drawing is rotated through the specified angle.

Annotative: This field specifies whether the block is annotative or non-annotative. This information is read-only.

Annotative scale: This field displays the current annotation scale of the drawing. You can add more annotation scales to the drawing in the **Annotation Object Scale** dialog box that will be displayed when you choose the button from the **Annotative scale** field.

Match orientation to layout: This field displays whether or not the orientation of the text used in the block is forced to align with the orientation of the floating viewports. This information is read-only.

Block Unit: This field specifies the unit of the block.

Unit factor. This field specifies the conversion factor between the block unit and the drawing unit.

Selecting the Annotative Attribute

When you select an attribute before converting it into a block, apart from the **General** category, the other three categories under which the properties of an attribute are displayed are **Text**, **3D Visualization**, and **Misc**.

Tag: You can modify the text of the tag by entering a new value in the **Tag** field under the **Text** category. After you have modified the tag text and pressed Enter, the old attribute text in the drawing is replaced by the new text.

Annotative: This field specifies whether the attribute is annotative or non-annotative. Select the appropriate option from the **Annotative** drop-down list to change the annotative property of the attributes.

Annotative scale: This field displays the current annotation scale of the drawing. You can add more annotation scales to the drawing in the **Annotation Object Scale** dialog box that will be displayed when you choose the button from the **Annotative scale** field.

Prompt: You can also change the text of the prompt and enter a new prompt value in the **Prompt** field.

Value: This field displays the default value of the selected attribute. You can change this default value by entering a new value in the **Value** field.

Style: When you click in this field, the **Style** drop-down list is available. You can select a style for the attribute text from this drop-down list. Only the text styles that already have been defined are available in this drop-down list and can be selected.

Justify: You can select an attribute text justification from the **Justify** drop-down list.

Paper text height: This field displays the height of the annotative text that is to be maintained on the paper.

Model text height: This field displays the height of the text that is to be displayed in the model space. The **Model text height** value depends on the **Paper text height** value and the **Annotative scale**.

Height: You can change the height of the selected non-annotative attribute text by entering a new value in this field.

Rotation: You can rotate the selected attribute text by specifying an angle in the **Rotation** field.

Width factor: You can modify the width factor of the attribute text by entering a new value in the **Width factor** field of the **PROPERTIES** palette.

Obliquing: The attribute text can also be made slanting by entering an angle value in the **Obliquing** field of the **PROPERTIES** palette.

Direction: This field displays the flow direction of the attribute text.

Boundary Width: This field displays the width of the text window in the **In-Place Text Editor**. The value displayed here is the relative value, specifying a value less than **1** will decrease the boundary width and a value more than **1** will increase the boundary width. The value in the **Boundary Width** will be available only if the **Multiple lines** check box is selected in the **Mode** area of the **Attribute Definition** dialog box. You can also select the **Yes** option from the **Multiple lines** drop-down list in the **Misc** area of the **PROPERTIES** Palette.

Text alignment X/Text alignment Y/Text alignment Z: The **Text alignment X/Text alignment Y/Text alignment Z** fields of the **Text** category display the *X*, *Y*, and *Z* coordinates of the alignment point of the selected attribute. Note that these fields will be available only if you modify the properties such as the text alignment of the attributes, while defining them. If these fields are available and you click on them, the Pick Point button appears in the field. You can use this button to specify the new location of the attribute.

Note

*If you modify the text alignment of the first attribute and define the remaining attributes below this attribute, the remaining attributes will also have the **Text Alignment** fields active.*

Misc: As discussed earlier, under the **Misc** category, you can redefine the attribute modes that have been defined at the time of the attribute definition. You can also make the attribute text appear upside-down or backwards by selecting **Yes** from the **Upside down** drop-down list and the **Backward** drop-down list, respectively.

Note

*Choose the **QuickCalc** button from the respective fields to open the Quick Calculator. Using the Quick Calculator, you can enter the numerical values as mathematical equations. These equations may include scientific calculations. You can also perform units conversion using the Quick Calculator.*

Exercise 1 Properties

Draw a hexagon on OBJ layer in red color. Let the linetype be hidden. Now, use the **PROPERTIES** palette to change the layer of the hexagon to some other existing layer, the color to yellow, and the linetype to continuous. Also, in the **PROPERTIES** palette, under the **Geometry** category, specify a vertex in the **Vertex** field or select one using the arrow (Next or Previous) buttons and then relocate it. The values of the **Vertex X** and **Vertex Y** fields change as the coordinate values of the vertices change. Also, notice the change in the value in the **Area** field. You can also assign a start and end lineweight to each of the hexagon segments between the specified vertices. Use the **Tools > Inquiry > List** tool from the menu bar to verify that the changes have taken place.

EXPLODING COMPOUND OBJECTS

Ribbon: Home > Modify > Explode **Toolbar:** Modify > Explode
Menu Bar: Modify > Explode **Command:** EXPLODE/X

The **Explode** tool is used to split compound objects such as blocks, polylines, regions, polyface meshes, polygon meshes, multilines, 3D solids, 3D meshes, bodies, or dimensions into the basic objects that make them up, refer to Figure 4-10. For example, if you explode a polyline or a 3D polyline, the result will be ordinary lines or arcs (tangent specification and width are not considered). When a 3D polygon mesh is exploded, the result is 3D faces. Polyface meshes are turned into 3D faces, points, and lines. Upon exploding 3D solids, the planar surfaces of the 3D solid turn into regions, and non-planar surfaces turn into bodies, multilines are changed to lines. Regions turn into lines, ellipses, splines, or arcs. On exploding, 2D polylines lose their width and tangent specifications and 3D polylines explode into lines. When a body is exploded, it changes into single-surface bodies, curves, or regions. When a leader is exploded, the components are lines, splines, solids, block inserts, text or multiline text, tolerance objects, and so on. Multiline text explodes into a single line text. This tool is especially useful when you have inserted an entire drawing and you need to alter a small detail. After you invoke the **Explode** tool, you are prompted to select the objects you want to explode. After selecting the objects, press Enter or right-click to explode the selected objects and then end the command.

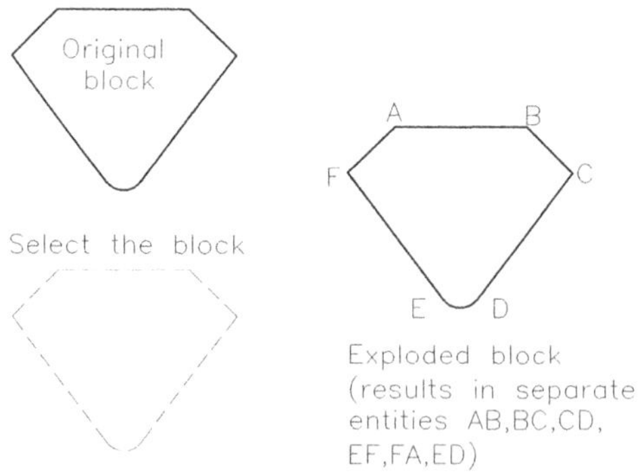

Figure 4-10 *Use of the **Explode** tool*

When a block or dimension is exploded, there is no visible change in the drawing. The drawing remains the same except that the color and linetype may have changed because of floating layers, colors, or linetypes. The exploded block is turned into a group of objects that can be modified separately. To check whether the explosion of the block has taken place, select any object that was a part of the block. If the block has been exploded, only that particular object will be highlighted. With the **Explode** tool, only one nesting level is exploded at a time. Hence, if there is a nested block or a polyline in a block and you explode it, the inner block or the polyline will not be exploded. Attribute values are deleted when a block is exploded, and the attribute definitions are redisplayed.

Note

*Remember that the blocks inserted using the **MINSERT** command and x-refs cannot be exploded.*

Tip

*If you want to insert a block in the form of its separate components while using the **INSERT** tool, select the **Explode** check box in the **Insert** dialog box. Also, if you are using the **-INSERT** command, type * prior to the block name at the **Enter block name or [?]:** prompt, the block will be inserted in the drawing as separate component object, and not as an entire block.*

EDITING POLYLINES

A polyline can assume various characteristics such as width, linetype, joined polyline, and closed polyline. You can edit polylines, polygons, or rectangles to attain the desired characteristics using the **Edit Polyline** tool. In this section, you will learn how to edit simple 2D polylines. The following are the editing operations that can be performed on an existing polyline using the **Edit Polyline** tool. These operations are discussed in detail later in this chapter.

1. A polyline of varying widths can be converted to a polyline of uniform width.
2. An open polyline can be closed and a closed one can be opened.
3. You can remove bends and curved segments between two vertices to make a straight polyline.
4. A polyline can be split up into two and individual polylines or polyarcs connected to one another can be joined into a single polyline.
5. After invoking the **Edit Polyline** tool, if you select an entity that is not a polyline, you are prompted to specify whether you want the entity to be converted into a polyline. You can avoid this prompt by setting the value of the **PEDITACCEPT** variable to 1.
6. Multiple polylines can be edited.
7. The appearance of a polyline can be changed by moving and adding vertices.
8. Curves of arcs and B-spline curves can be fitted to all vertices in a polyline, with the specification of the tangent of each vertex being optional.
9. The linetype generation at the vertices of a polyline can be controlled.
10. Multiple polylines can be joined together to form a single polyline.

Editing Single Polyline

Ribbon: Home > Modify > Edit Polyline	**Toolbar:** Modify II > Edit Polyline
Menu Bar: Modify > Object > Polyline	**Command:** PEDIT/PE

You can edit a single polyline by using the **Edit Polyline** tool. To invoke this tool, choose the **Edit Polyline** tool from the expanded **Modify** panel of the **Home** tab; the following prompt sequence is displayed:

Select polyline or [Multiple]:

If the selected entity is not a polyline, the following message will be displayed at the command prompt.

Object selected is not a polyline.
Do you want to turn it into one? <Y>:

If you want to turn the object into a polyline, respond by entering Y or by simply pressing Enter. To let the object be as it is, enter N. If you enter N, then AutoCAD will prompt you to select another polyline or object to edit. As mentioned earlier, you can avoid this prompt by setting the value of the **PEDITACCEPT** variable to **1**. The subsequent prompts and editing options depend on the type of polyline that has been selected. AutoCAD provides you the option of either selecting a single polyline or multiple polylines. In this case, a single 2D polyline is selected, and its prompt sequence is given next.

Enter an option [Close/Join/Width/Edit vertex/Fit/Spline/Decurve/Ltype gen/Reverse/Undo]: *Enter an option or press Enter to end command.*

Note

*Depending on the type of polyline selected, the options of the **Edit Polyline** tool get changed. In this chapter, the **2D polyline** options have been discussed.*

The options available in the **Single** polyline selection method are discussed next.

Close (C) Option

This option is used to close an open polyline. The **Close** option creates the segment that connects the last segment of the polyline to the first. You will get this option only if the polyline is not closed. Figure 4-11 illustrates this option.

Open (O) Option

If you close an open polyline, the **Close** option will be replaced by the **Open** option. Enter **O** for open; the closing segment will be removed, refer to Figure 4-11.

Join (J) Option

This option appends lines, polylines, or arcs whose endpoints meet a selected polyline at any of its endpoints and adds (joins) them to it, refer to Figure 4-12. This option can be used only if a polyline is open. After this option has been selected, AutoCAD prompts you to select objects. Once you have chosen the objects to be joined to the original polyline, AutoCAD examines them to determine whether any of them has an endpoint in common with the current polyline, and joins such an object with the original polyline. The search is then repeated using new endpoints. They will not join if the endpoint of the object does not exactly meet the polyline. The line touching a polyline at its endpoint to form a T will not be joined. If two lines meet a polyline in a Y shape, only one of them will be selected, and this selection depends upon the sequence of selecting the lines. If you select the two lines, the first selected line will get joined to the polyline.

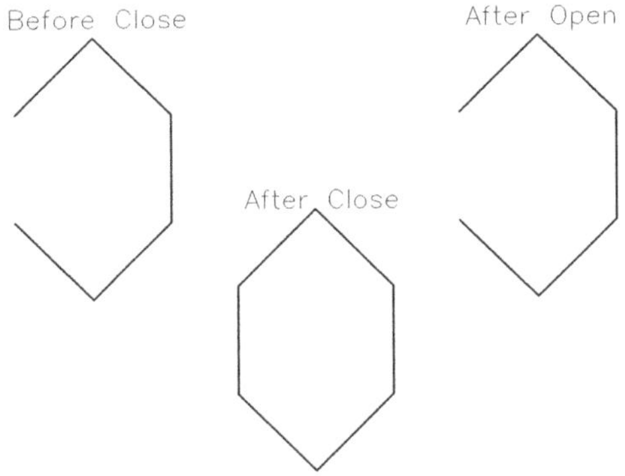

Figure 4-11 *The* ***Close*** *and* ***Open*** *options*

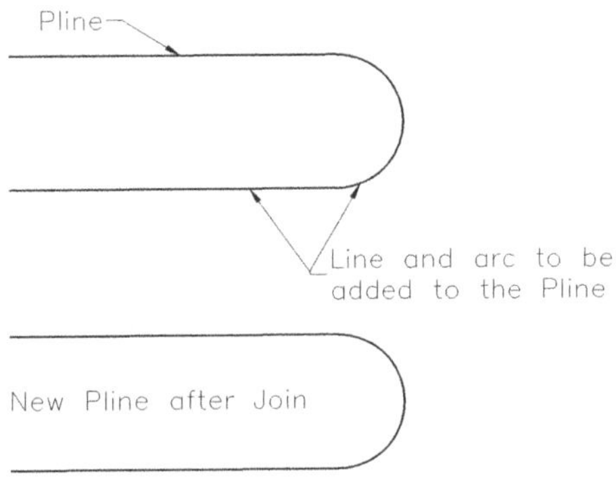

Figure 4-12 *Using the* ***Join*** *option*

Width (W) Option

The **W** option allows you to define a new, unvarying width for all segments of a polyline, refer to Figure 4-13. It changes the width of a polyline with a constant or a varying width. The desired new width can be specified either by entering the width using the keyboard or by specifying the width as the distance between the two specified points. Once the width has been specified, the polyline assumes it. Here, you will change the width of the given polyline in figure from 0.20 to 0.5, refer to Figure 4-14. On invoking the **Edit Polyline** tool, the following prompt is displayed:

Select polyline or [Multiple]: *Select a polyline.*
Enter an option [Close/Join/Width/Edit vertex/Fit/Spline/Decurve/Ltype gen/Reverse/Undo]: **W** Enter.
Specify new width for all segments: **0.5** Enter.

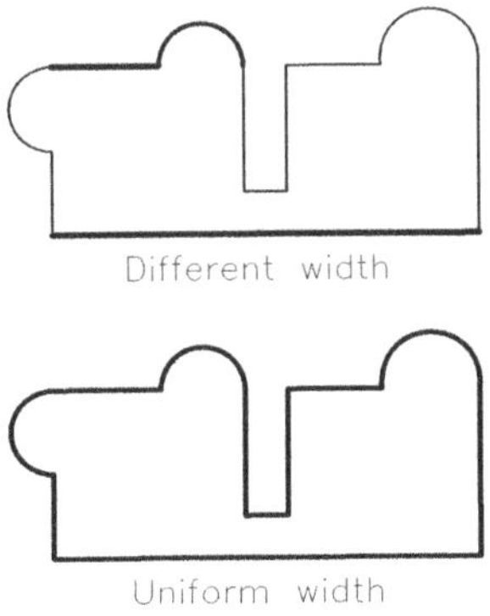

Figure 4-13 *Making the width of a polyline uniform*

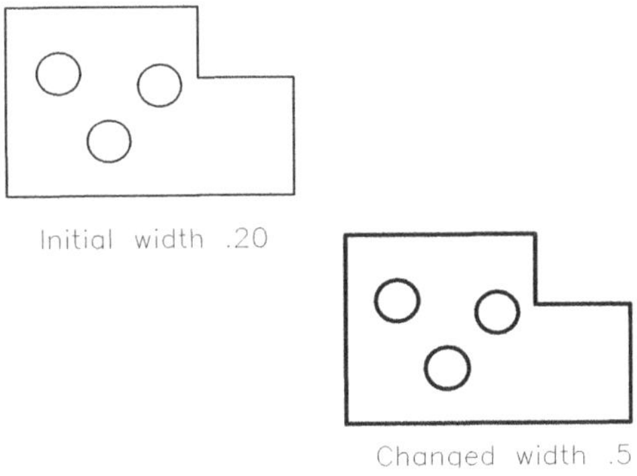

Figure 4-14 *Changing the width of all segments*

Note

*Circles drawn using the **Circle** tools cannot be changed to polylines. However, for polycircles drawn by using the **Arc** option of the **Polyline** tool (by drawing two semicircular polyarcs) or by using the **Donut** tool, you can modify the thickness using the **Width** option of the **Edit Polyline** tool.*

Edit vertex (E) Option

The **Edit vertex** option allows you select vertex of a polyline and perform different editing operations on the vertex and the segments following it. A polyline segment has two vertices. The first one is at the start point of the polyline segment; the other one is at the endpoint of the segment. When you invoke this option, an X marker appears on the screen at the first vertex of the selected polyline. If a tangent direction has been specified for this particular vertex, an arrow is generated in that direction. After this option has been selected, the next prompt appears with a list of options for this prompt. The prompt sequence, after you invoke the **Edit Polyline** tool, is given next.

Select polyline or [Multiple]: *Select the polyline to be edited.*
Enter an option [Close/Join/Width/Edit vertex/Fit/Spline/Decurve/Ltype gen/Reverse/Undo]: **E** Enter.
Enter a vertex editing option [Next/Previous/Break/Insert/Move/Regen/Straighten/Tangent/Width/eXit]<N>: *Enter an editing option or press **Enter** to accept default.*

All the options for the **Edit vertex** option are discussed next.

Next and Previous Options: These options move the X marker to the next or the previous vertex of a polyline. The default value in the **Edit vertex** option is one of these two options. The option selected as default is the one you chose last. In this manner, the **Next** and **Previous** options help you to move the X marker to any vertex of the polyline by selecting one of these two options, and then pressing Enter to reach the desired vertex. These options cycle back and forth between the first and last vertices, but cannot move past the first or last vertex, even if the polyline is closed, refer to Figure 4-15.

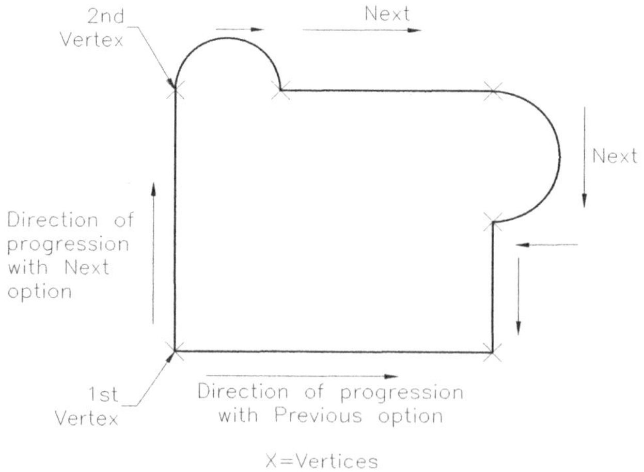

***Figure 4-15** The **Next** and **Previous** options*

The prompt sequence for using the **Edit vertex** option, after you invoke the **Edit Polyline** tool, is given next.

Select polyline or [Multiple]: *Select the polyline to be edited.*
Enter an option [Close/Join/Width/Edit vertex/Fit/Spline/Decurve/Ltype gen/Reverse/Undo]: **E** Enter.
Enter a vertex editing option [Next/Previous/Break/Insert/Move/Regen/Straighten/Tangent/Width/eXit] <N>: *Enter N or P to move to the next or previous vertices respectively.*

Break Option: With the **Break** option, you can remove a portion of the polyline, as shown in Figure 4-16 or break it at a single point. You can specify the vertices within which the polyline would be removed. By specifying two different vertices, all the polyline segments and vertices between the specified vertices are erased. If one of the selected vertices is at the endpoint of the polyline, the **Break** option will erase all the segments between the first vertex and the endpoint of the polyline. The exception to this is that AutoCAD does not erase the entire polyline, if you specify the first vertex at the start point (first vertex) of the polyline and the second vertex at the endpoint (last vertex) of the polyline. If both vertices are at the endpoint of the polyline, or only one vertex is specified and its location is at the endpoint of the polyline, no change is made to the polyline. The last two selections of vertices are treated as invalid by AutoCAD, which acknowledges this by displaying the message ***Invalid***.

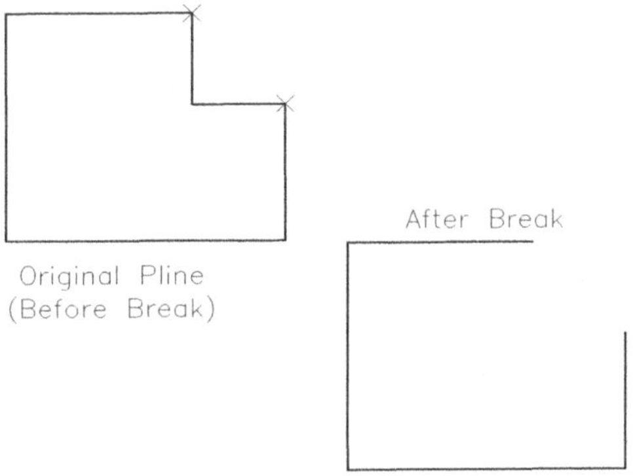

Figure 4-16 *Using the **Break** option*

To use the **Break** option, first you need to move the marker to the first vertex where you want the split to start. The placement of the marker can be achieved with the help of the **Next** and **Previous** options. Once you have selected the first vertex to be used in the **Break** operation, invoke the **Break** option by entering **B** at the command prompt. AutoCAD takes the vertex where the marker (X) is placed as the first point of the breakup. The next prompt asks you to specify the position of the next vertex for the breakup. You can enter **G** at this prompt if you want to split the polyline at one vertex only. Otherwise, use the **Next** or **Previous** option to specify the position of the next vertex and then enter **G**. On doing so, the polyline segments between the two selected vertices will be erased. The prompt sequence for using this option, after you have invoked the **Edit Polyline** tool, is given next.

Select polyline or [Multiple]: *Select the polyline to be edited.*
Enter an option [Close/Join/Width/Edit vertex/Fit/Spline/Decurve/Ltype gen/Reverse/Undo]: **E** Enter.

Enter a vertex editing option [Next/Previous/Break/Insert/Move/Regen/Straighten/Tangent/Width/eXit]<N>: *Enter N or P to locate the first vertex for the **Break** option.*
Enter a vertex editing option [Next/Previous/Break/Insert/Move/Regen/Straighten/Tangent/Width/eXit]<N>: **B** Enter.

Once you invoke the **Break** option, AutoCAD treats the vertex where the marker (X) is displayed as the first point for splitting the polyline. The next prompt issued is given next.

Enter an option [Next/Previous/Go/eXit] <N>: *Enter **G** if you want to split the polyline at one vertex only or move the X marker using the **Next** or **Previous** option to specify the position of the next vertex for breakup.*

After you have specified the next position of the X marker using the **Next** and **Previous** options, entering **GO** deletes the polyline segment between the two markers specified. Now, exit the enter a vertex editing option prompt using the **eXit** option.

Insert Option: The **Insert** option is used to define a new vertex and add it to the polyline, refer to Figure 4-17. You can invoke this option by entering I for Insert. You should invoke this option only after you have moved the marker (X) to the vertex after which the new vertex is to be added. The new vertex is inserted immediately after the vertex with the X mark. After you invoke the **Edit Polyline** tool, the prompt sequence for using the **Insert** option will be as follows:

Select polyline or [Multiple]: *Select the polyline to be edited.*
Enter an option [Close/Join/Width/Edit vertex/Fit/Spline/Decurve/Ltype gen/Reverse/Undo]: **E** Enter.
Enter a vertex editing option [Next/Previous/Break/Insert/Move/Regen/Straighten/Tangent/Width/eXit]<N>: *Move the marker to the vertex after which the new vertex is to be inserted.*
Enter a vertex editing option[Next/Previous/Break/Insert/Move/Regen/Straighten/Tangent/Width/eXit]<N>: **I** Enter.
Specify location for new vertex: *Move the cursor and click to specify the location of the new vertex or enter the coordinates of the new location.*

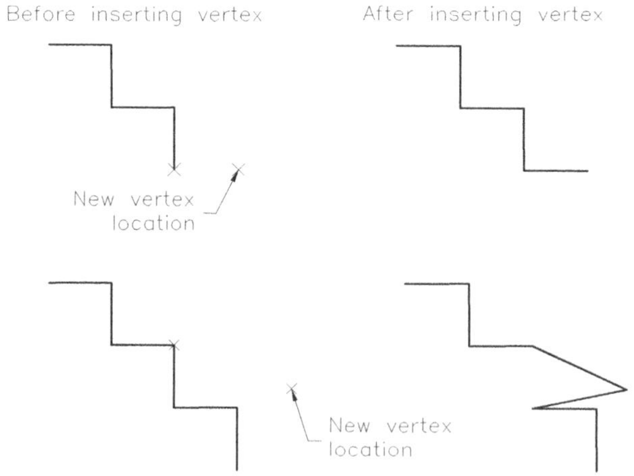

Figure 4-17 *Using the **Insert** option to define new vertex points*

Tip

*In AutoCAD, you can insert vertex by using the shortcut menu. To do so, select a polyline; the grips will be displayed. Hold the cursor on one of the grips; a shortcut menu will be displayed. Choose the **Add Vertex** option and click on the drawing area to add new vertex. You can also stretch the selected arc or convert the line to arc or vice versa by selecting appropriate option from the shortcut menu.*

Move option: This option is used to move the X-marked vertex to a new position, refer to Figure 4-18. Before invoking the **Move** option, you must move the X marker to the vertex you want to relocate by selecting the **Next** or **Previous** option. The prompt sequence for relocating a vertex after you invoke the **Edit Polyline** tool is given next.

Select polyline or [Multiple]: *Select the polyline to be edited.*
Enter an option [Close/Join/Width/Edit vertex/Fit/Spline/Decurve/Ltype gen/Reverse/Undo]: **E** Enter.
Enter a vertex editing option [Next/Previous/Break/Insert/Move/Regen/Straighten/Tangent/Width/eXit]<N>: *Enter **N** or **P** to move the X marker to the vertex you want to relocate.*
Enter a vertex editing option [Next/Previous/Break/Insert/Move/Regen/Straighten/Tangent/Width/eXit]<N>: **M** Enter.
Specify new location for marked vertex: *Specify the new location for the selected vertex by using the pick button of your pointing device or by entering its coordinate values.*
Enter a vertex editing option [Next/Previous/Break/Insert/Move/Regen/Straighten/Tangent/Width/eXit]<N>: *Enter an option or enter **X** to exit.*

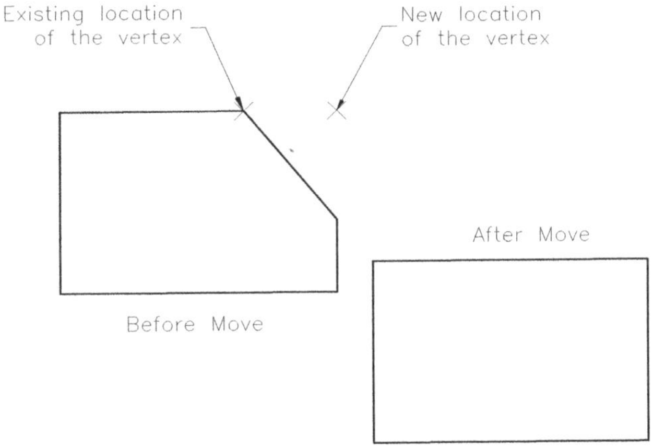

***Figure 4-18** The **Move** option*

Regen Option: The **Regen** option regenerates the polyline to display the effects of edits you have made, without having to exit the vertex mode editing. It is used most often with the **Width** option.

Straighten Option: The **Straighten** option is used to straighten polyline segments or arcs between specified vertices, refer to Figure 4-19. It deletes the arcs, line segments, or vertices between the two specified vertices and substitutes them with one polyline segment.

The prompt sequence to use this option after you invoke the **Edit Polyline** tool is given next.

Select polyline or [Multiple]: *Select the polyline to be edited.*
Enter an option [Close/Join/Width/Edit vertex/Fit/Spline/Decurve/Ltype gen/Reverse/Undo]: **E** Enter.
Enter a vertex editing option [Next/Previous/Break/Insert/Move/Regen/Straighten/Tangent/Width/eXit]<N>: *Move the marker to the desired vertex from where you want to start applying the **Straighten** option with the **Next** or **Previous** option.*
Enter a vertex editing option [Next/Previous/Break/Insert/Move/Regen/Straighten/Tangent/Width/eXit]<N>: **S** Enter.
Enter an option [Next/Previous/Go/eXit] <N>: *Move the marker to the next desired vertex, until you reach the vertex you want to straighten.* Enter an option [Next/Previous/Go/eXit] <N>: **G** Enter.

The polyline segments between two marker locations are replaced by a single straight line segment. If you specify a single vertex, the segment following the specified vertex is straightened, if it is curved.

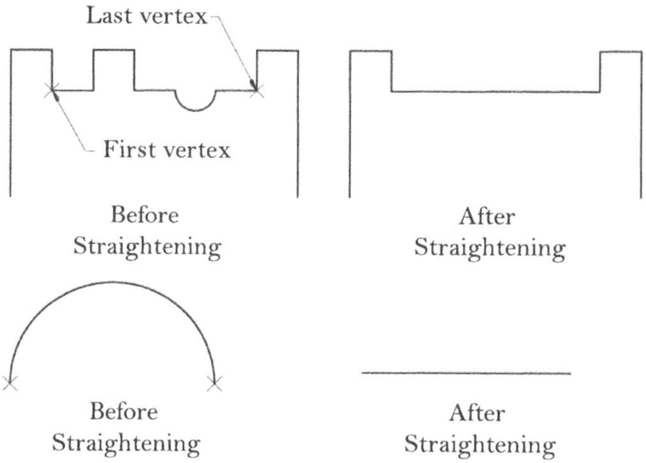

Figure 4-19 *Using the **Straighten** option to straighten polylines*

Tangent option: The **Tangent** option is used to associate a tangent direction to the current vertex (marked by X). The tangent direction is used in the curve fitting or the **Fit** option of the **Edit Polyline** tool. This option is discussed in detail in the subsequent section on curve fitting. The prompt issued on using the **Tangent** option is given next.

Specify direction of vertex tangent: *Specify a point or enter an angle.*

You can specify the direction of the vertex tangent by entering an angle at the previous prompt or by selecting a point to express the direction with respect to the current vertex. You can then move the marker to another vertex using the **Next** or **Previous** option and change its direction of tangent or enter X to exit the **Enter a vertex editing option** prompt.

Width option: The **Width** option allows you to change the width at the start and end points of a polyline segment that follows the current vertex, refer to Figure 4-20. By default, the ending width is equal to the starting width and hence, you can get a polyline segment of uniform width by pressing Enter at the **Specify ending width for next segment <starting width>** prompt. You can also specify different starting and ending widths to get a varying-width polyline. The prompt sequence is given next.

Enter an option [Close/Join/Width/Edit vertex/Fit/Spline/Decurve/Ltype gen/Reverse/Undo]: **E** Enter.
Enter a vertex editing option [Next/Previous/Break/Insert/Move/Regen/Straighten/Tangent/Width/eXit]<N>: *Move the marker to the starting vertex of the segment whose width is to be altered, using the **Next** or **Previous** option.*
Enter a vertex editing option [Next/Previous/Break/Insert/Move/Regen/Straighten/Tangent/Width/eXit]<N>: **W** Enter.
Specify starting width for next segment <current>: *Enter the revised starting width.*
Specify ending width for next segment <starting width>: *Enter the revised ending width or press Enter to accept the default option of keeping the ending width of the segment equal to the starting width.*

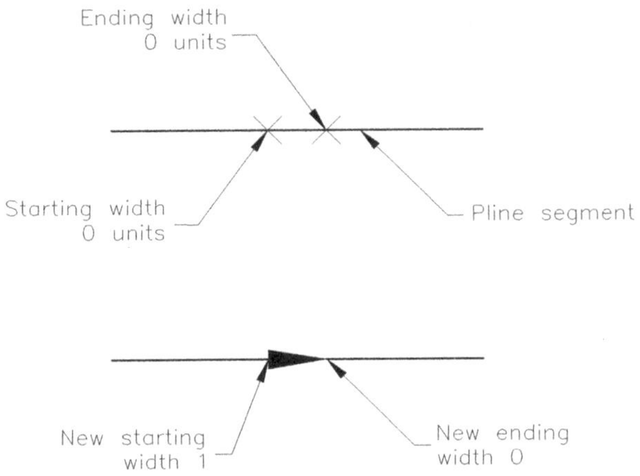

Figure 4-20 *Using the **Width** option to change the width of a polyline*

If no difference is noticed in the appearance of the polyline, you may need to use the **Regen** option. The segment with the revised widths is redrawn after invoking the **Regen** option or when you exit the vertex mode editing.

eXit Option. This option lets you exit the vertex mode editing and return to the **Edit Polyline** prompt.

Fit Option

The **Fit** or **Fit curve** option is used to generate a curve that passes through all the corners (vertices) of the polyline, using the tangent directions of the vertices, refer to Figure 4-21.

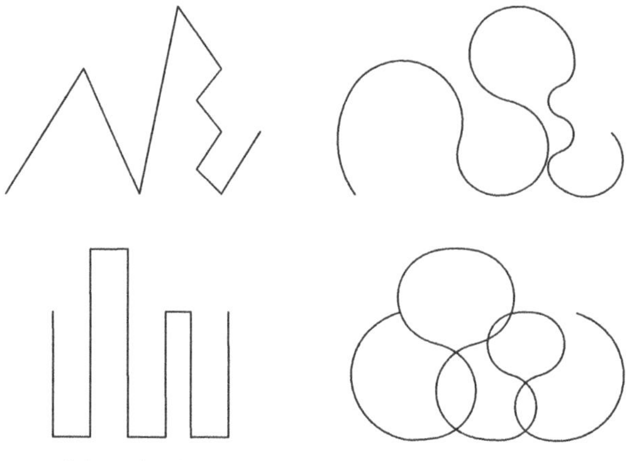

Figure 4-21 *Curves generated using the* ***Fit*** *option*

The curve is composed of a series of arcs passing through the corners (vertices) of the polyline. This option is used when you draw a polyline with sharp corners and you need to convert it into a series of smooth curves. An example of this is a graph. In a graph, we need to show a curve by joining a series of plotted points. The process involved is called curve fitting; therefore, this option is known as **Fit**. The vertices of the polyline are also known as the control points. The closer these control points are, the smoother is the curve. Therefore, if the **Fit** option does not give optimum results, insert more vertices into the polyline or edit the tangent directions of vertices and then use the **Fit** option on the polyline. Before using this option, you may give each vertex a tangent direction.

The curve is then constructed according to the tangent directions you have specified. The following prompt sequence illustrates the **Fit** option after you invoke the **Edit Polyline** tool.

Select polyline or [Multiple]: *Select the polyline to be edited.*
Enter an option [Close/Join/Width/Edit vertex/Fit/Spline/Decurve/Ltype gen/Reverse/Undo]: **F** Enter.

If the tangent directions need to be edited, use the **Edit vertex** option of the **Edit Polyline** tool. Move the X marker to each of the vertices that need to be changed. Now, you can invoke the **Tangent** option, and either enter the tangent direction in degrees or select points. The chosen direction is expressed by an arrow placed at the vertex. The prompt sequence to use the **Tangent** option of the **Edit Polyline** tool is given next.

Select polyline or [Multiple]: *Select the polyline to be edited.*
Enter an option [Close/Join/Width/Edit vertex/Fit/Spline/Decurve/Ltype gen/Reverse/Undo]: **E** Enter.
Enter a vertex editing option [Next/Previous/Break/Insert/Move/Regen/Straighten/Tangent/Width/eXit]<N>: **T** Enter.
Specify direction of vertex tangent: *Specify a direction in + or - degrees, or select a point in the desired direction. Press Enter.*

Once you specify the tangent direction, use the **eXit** option to return to the previous prompt and use its **Fit** option.

> **Tip**
> *In AutoCAD, after applying the **Fit** option to a polyline, you can change the tangent direction by using the tool tip. To do so, select a polyline; the grips will be displayed. Move the cursor near one of the grips; a tooltip will be displayed. Choose the **Tangent Direction** option and specify the new direction in the drawing area.*

Spline Option

The **Spline** option, refer to Figure 4-22, also smoothens the corners of a straight segment polyline, as does the **Fit** option, but the curve passes through only the first and the last control points (vertices), except in the case of a closed polyline. The spline curve is stretched toward the other control points (vertices) but does not pass through them, as in the case of the **Fit** option. The greater the number of control points, the greater the force with which the curve is stretched toward them. The prompt sequence on invoking the **Edit Polyline** tool is as follows:

Select polyline or [Multiple]: *Select the polyline.*
Enter an option [Close/Join/Width/Edit vertex/Fit/Spline/Decurve/Ltype gen/Reverse/Undo]: **S** Enter.

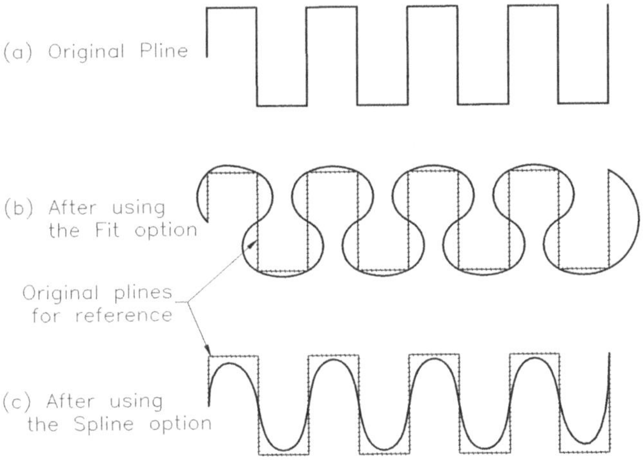

Figure 4-22 *Smoothening the corners using the **Spline** option*

The generated curve is a B-spline curve. The frame is the original polyline without any curves in it. If the original polyline has arc segments, these segments are straightened when the spline's frame is formed. A frame that has width produces a spline curve that tapers smoothly from the width of the first vertex to that of the last. Any other width specification between the first width specification and the last is neglected. When a spline is formed from a polyline, the frame is displayed as a polyline with a zero width and a continuous linetype. Also, AutoCAD saves its frame so that it may be restored to its original form. Tangent specifications on control point vertices do not affect spline construction.

By default, the spline frames are not shown on the screen, but you may want them displayed for reference. In this case, the system variable **SPLFRAME** needs to be manipulated. The default value for this variable is zero. If you want to see the spline frame as well, set it to 1.

Now, whenever the **Spline** option is used on a polyline, the frame will also be displayed. Most editing tools such as **Move**, **Erase**, **Copy**, **Mirror**, **Rotate**, and **Scale** work similarly for both the Fit curves and Spline curves. They work on both the curve and its frame, whether the frame is visible or not. The **Extend** tool changes the frame by adding a vertex at the point the last segment intersects with the boundary. If you use any of the previously mentioned tools and then use the **Decurve** option to decurve the spline curve and later use the **Spline** option again, the same spline curve is generated. The **Break**, **Trim**, and **Explode** tools delete the frame. The **Divide**, **Measure**, **Fillet**, **Chamfer**, **Area**, and **Hatch** tools recognize only the spline curve and do not consider the frame. The **Stretch** tool first stretches the frame and then fits the spline curve to it.

When you use the **Join** option of the **Edit Polyline** tool, the spline curve is decurved and the original spline information is lost. The **Next** and **Previous** options of the **Edit vertex** option of the **Edit Polyline** tool move the marker only to the points on the frame, whether visible or not. The **Break** option discards the spline curve. The **Insert**, **Move**, **Straighten**, and **Width** options refit the spline curve. Object Snaps consider the spline curve and not the frame; therefore, if you wish to snap to the frame control points, restore the original frame.

There are two types of spline curves: **Quadratic B-spline** and **Cubic B-spline**. These types of curves pass through the first and the last control points, which is the characteristic of the spline curve. Cubic curves are very smooth. A cubic curve passes through the first and last control points, and the curve is closer to the other control points. Quadratic curves are not as smooth as the cubic ones, but they are smoother than the curves produced by the **Fit curve** option. A quadratic curve passes through the first and last control points, and the rest of the curve is tangent to the polyline segments between the remaining control points, refer to Figure 4-23.

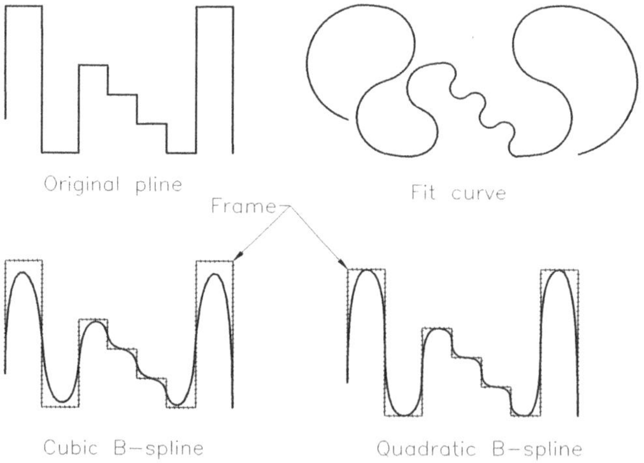

Figure 4-23 *Comparison of fit curve, quadratic B-spline, and cubic B-spline*

Generation of different types of spline curves: If you want to edit a polyline into a B-spline curve, you are first required to enter a relevant value in the **SPLINETYPE** system variable. A value of 5 produces the quadratic curve, whereas a value of 6 produces a cubic curve. The default value is 6, which implies that when we use the **Spline** option of the **Edit Polyline** tool, a cubic curve is produced by default. You can change the value of the **SPLINETYPE** variable using the command prompt.

In case you are editing 3D polygon meshes, the smoothness of the meshes is controlled by the **SURFTYPE** variable. The value of the variable can be set on the command prompt. You can select the type of polygon mesh you want when you are using the **Smooth Surface** option of the **Edit Polyline** tool.

SPLINESEGS. The system variable **SPLINESEGS** governs the number of line segments used to construct the spline curves, and therefore you can use this variable to control the smoothness of the curve. The default value for this variable is 8. With this value, a reasonably smooth curve that does not need much regeneration time is generated. The greater the value of this variable, the smoother will be the curve. But greater the regeneration time, the more space will be occupied by the drawing file.

Figure 4-24 shows cubic curves with different values for the **SPLINESEGS** variable.

Decurve Option

The **Decurve** option straightens the curves generated after using the **Fit** or **Spline** option on a polyline. On using this option, the curves return to their original shape, refer to Figure 4-25. The polyline segments are straightened using the **Decurve** option. The vertices inserted after using the **Fit** or **Spline** option are also removed. Information entered for the tangent reference is retained for use in future fit curve operations. You can also use this tool to straighten out any curve drawn with the help of the **Arc** option of the **Polyline** tool. Enter **D** at the **Enter an option [Close/Join/Width/Edit vertex/Fit/Spline/Decurve/Ltype gen/Reverse/Undo]** prompt to invoke the **Decurve** option of the **Edit Polyline** tool.

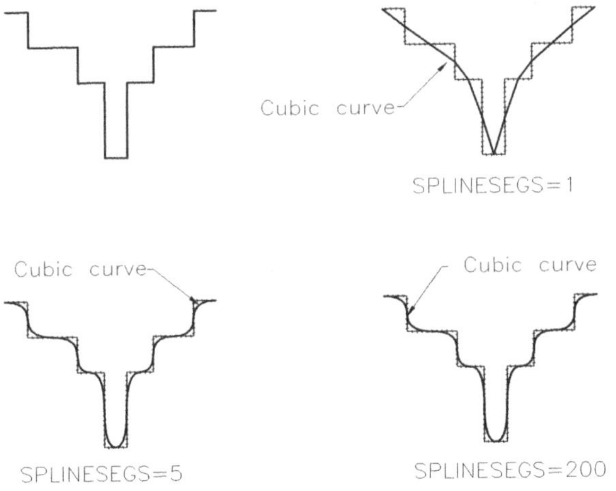

***Figure 4-24** Using the **SPLINESEGS** variable*

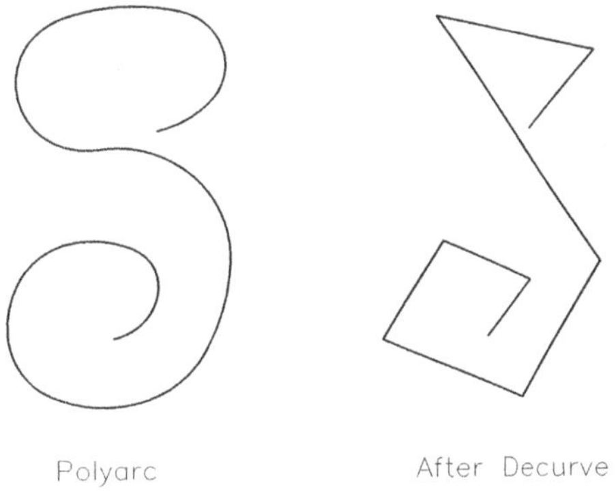

***Figure 4-25** Using the **Decurve** option*

Note

*If you use editing tools such as the **Break** or **Trim** on spline curves, the **Decurve** option cannot be used.*

Ltype gen Option

You can use this option to control the linetype pattern generation for linetypes other than Continuous with respect to the vertices of the polyline. This option has two modes: ON and OFF. If turned off, the break in the noncontinuous linetypes will be avoided at the vertices of the polyline and a continuous segment will be displayed at the vertices, refer to Figure 4-26. If turned on, this option generates the linetype in a continuous pattern such that the gaps may be displayed at the vertices. This option is not applicable to polylines with tapered segments.

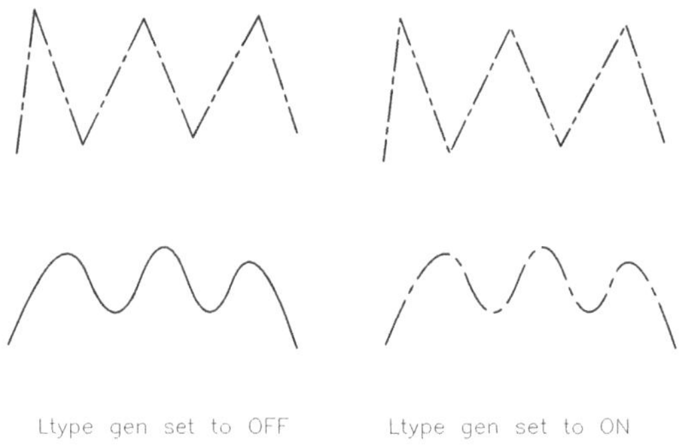

Figure 4-26 *Using the* ***Ltype gen*** *option*

The command prompt displayed when you select a polyline and invoke the **Ltype gen** option of the **Edit Polyline** tool is given next.

Enter polyline linetype generation option [ON/OFF] <Off>: *Enter* ***ON*** *or press Enter to accept the default value.*

The linetype generation for new polylines can also be controlled with the help of the **PLINEGEN** system variable, which acts as a toggle function. The default value of this variable is off. Entering the value **ON** turns on the **Ltype gen** option. Alternatively, select the appropriate option in the **Linetype generation** field in the **Misc** area of the **PROPERTIES** palette with the polyline selected.

Reverse Option

The **Reverse** option is used to change the start point of the polyline. On entering **R** and pressing Enter at the **Enter an option [Close/Join/Width/Edit vertex/Fit/Spline/Decurve/Ltype gen/Reverse/Undo]** command prompt, the start point of the polyline will be changed. This can be confirmed by using the **Edit vertex** option of the **Edit Polyline** tool before and after using the **Reverse** option.

Undo (U) Option

The **Undo** option negates the effect of the most recent polyline editing operation. You can go back as far as you need to in the current polyline editing session by using the **Undo** option repeatedly until you get the desired screen. If you started editing by converting an object into a polyline, and you want to change the polyline back to the object from which it was created, the **Undo** option of the **Edit Polyline** tool will not work. In this case, you will have to exit to the command prompt and use the **Undo** tool to undo the operation.

Editing Multiple Polylines

Selecting the **Multiple** option of the **Edit Polyline** tool allows you to select more than one polyline for editing. You can select the polylines using any of the objects selection techniques. After the objects to be edited are selected, press Enter or right-click to proceed with the command. The prompt sequence that will follow is given next.

Enter an option [Close/Open/Join/Width/Fit/Spline/Decurve/Ltype gen/Reverse/Undo]:

Join

This option is used to join more than one polylines that may or may not be in contact with each other. Even the polylines that are not coincident can be joined using this option. The polylines are joined using a specified distance value called the **Fuzz distance**. After you select the **Join** option, the sequence of prompt is as follows.

Enter fuzz distance or [Jointype] <current>: *Enter a distance or* ***J*** *for changing the* ***Jointype****.*

The prompt sequence to follow when you enter **J** at the above prompt is given next.

Enter join type [Extend/Add/Both] <Extend>:

Extend: This option is used to extend or trim the selected polylines at the endpoints that are nearest to each other, refer to Figure 4-27. Keep in mind that the segments of the selected polylines that are nearest to each other should not be parallel. This means that the segments that are nearest to each other should intersect at some point when extended.

Add: This option is used to join the selected polylines by drawing a straight line between the nearest endpoints, refer to Figure 4-28. The fuzz distance should be greater than the actual distance between the two endpoints to be joined.

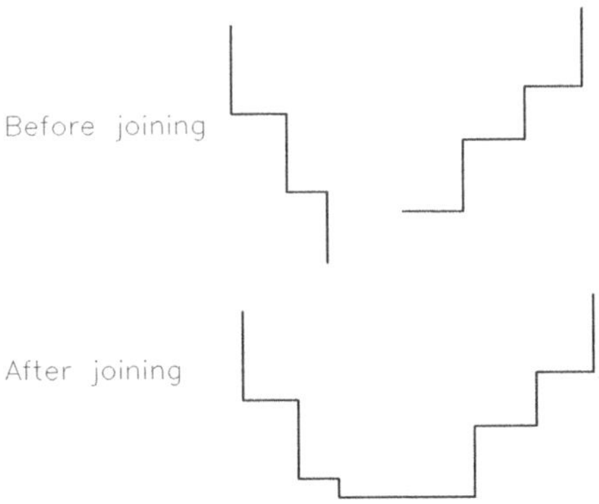

Figure 4-27 *Joining two polylines using the* ***Extend*** *option*

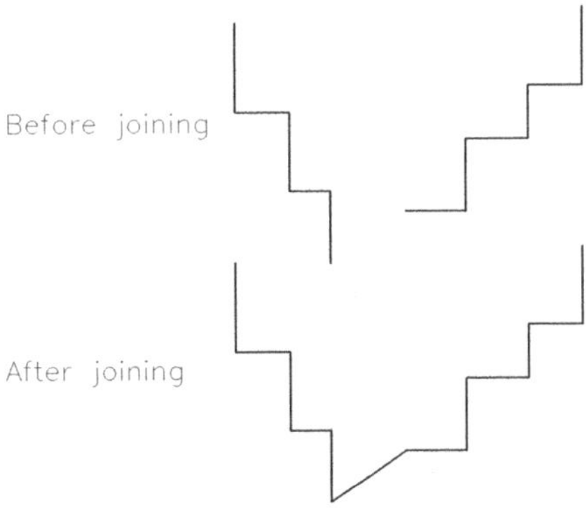

Figure 4-28 *Joining two polylines using the* ***Add*** *option*

Both: This option joins the endpoints by extending or trimming if possible; otherwise, it adds a line segment between the two endpoints.

Exercise 2 — *Edit Polyline*

a. Draw a line from point (0,0) to point (6,6). Convert the line into a polyline with a starting width 0.30 and an ending width 0.00.

b. Draw different polylines of varying width segments and then use the **Join** option to join all the segments into one polyline. After joining the segments, make their width uniform with the **Width** option.

Exercise 3 — *Edit Polyline*

a. Draw a staircase-shaped polyline and use the different options of the **Edit Polyline** tool to generate a fit curve, a quadratic B-spline, and a cubic B-spline, and then convert the curves back to the original polyline.

b. Draw square-wave-shaped polylines, and use different options of the **Edit vertex** option to navigate around the polyline, split the polyline into two at the third vertex, insert more vertices at different locations in the original polyline, and convert the square-wave-shaped polyline into a straight-line polyline.

UNDOING PREVIOUS COMMANDS

Quick Access Toolbar: Undo **Toolbar:** Standard > Undo **Command:** UNDO/U

In AutoCAD, there are many tools with the **Undo** option, which can be used to undo (nullify) the changes made within these commands. The **Undo** option is used to undo a previous command or to undo more than one command at a time. This command can be invoked by entering **UNDO** at the command prompt. **Undo** is also available in the **Quick Access Toolbar**, the **Edit** menu, and the **Standard** toolbar. The **Undo** tool in the **Quick Access Toolbar** can only undo the previous command and only one command at a time. If you right-click in the drawing area; a shortcut menu will be displayed. Choose **Undo**. It is equivalent to **UNDO > 1** or to enter **U** at the command prompt. The **U** command can undo only one operation at a time. You can use **U** as many times as you want until AutoCAD displays the message: **Nothing to undo**. When an operation cannot be undone, a message is displayed but no action takes place. External commands such as **PLOT** cannot be undone.

Undoing Previous Commands using the Quick Access Toolbar

Click the arrow on the **Undo** tool in the **Quick Access Toolbar**; the **Undo** list box will be displayed. All commands used recently will be listed in the **Undo** list box. Select the commands that you want to undo by placing the cursor in the list box and moving downward. The Commands selected are highlighted in blue color, as shown in Figure 4-29. The Status Bar below the **Undo** list box displays the number of commands selected. Click the left mouse button to confirm the selections.

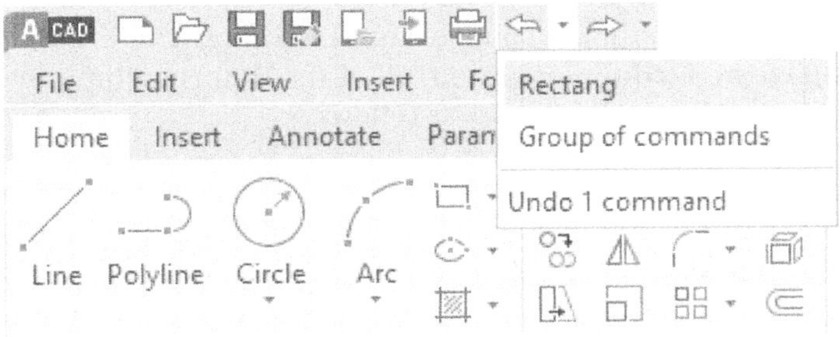

Figure 4-29 The ***Undo*** *list box*

Undoing Previous Commands using the Command Prompt

To Undo previous commands using the command Line, enter **UNDO** at the command prompt (if you are working in dynamic mode, the command will be entered at pointer input). The prompt sequence for the **UNDO** command is given next.

Command: **UNDO**
Enter the number of operations to undo or [Auto/Control/BEgin/End/Mark/Back] <1>:
Enter a positive number, an option, or press Enter to undo a single operation.

Various options of this command are discussed next.

Number (N) Option

This is the default option. This number represents the number of previous command sequences to be deleted. For example, if the number entered is 1, the previous command is undone; if the number entered is 4, the previous four commands are undone, and so on. This is identical to invoking the **U** command four times, except that only one regeneration takes place. AutoCAD allows you to know which commands were undone by displaying a message after you press Enter. The prompt sequence is given next.

Command: **UNDO**
Enter the number of operations to undo or [Auto/Control/BEgin/End/Mark/Back]<1>:3 Enter.
PLINE LINE CIRCLE

Control (C) Option

This option allows you to determine how many of the options are active for the **Undo** tool. You can disable the options you do not need. With this option, you can even disable the **Undo** tool. To access this option, type C. You will get the following prompt.

Enter an UNDO control option [ALL/None/One/Combine/Layer] <All>: *Enter an option or press Enter to accept the default option.*

ALL

The **All** option activates all the features (options) of the **Undo** tool.

None (N)

This option turns off the **Undo** tool. If you have used the **BEgin** and **End** options or the **Mark** and **Back** options to create **Undo** information, all of that information is undone. The prompt sequence for invoking the **Control** option is as follows.

> Command: **UNDO**
> Enter the number of operations to undo [Auto/Control/BEgin/End/Mark/Back] <1>: **C** Enter.
> Enter an UNDO control option [ALL/None/One/Combine/Layer] <All>: **N** Enter.

If you try to use the **Undo** tool now, AutoCAD gives you the following message.

> U command disabled. Use **UNDO** command to turn it on.

The prompt sequence for the **UNDO** command after issuing the **None** option is given next.

> Command: **UNDO**
> Enter an UNDO control option [All/None/One/Combine/Layer] <All>: *Enter O or press Enter to accept the default option.*

To enable the **UNDO** options again, you must enter the **All** or **One** (one mode) option.

One (O)

This option restrains the **UNDO** command to a single operation. All **UNDO** information saved earlier during editing is scrapped. The prompt sequence is as follows.

> Enter the number of operations to undo or [Auto/Control/BEgin/End/Mark/Back] <1>: **C** Enter.
> Enter an UNDO control option [All/None/One/Combine/Layer] <All>: **O** Enter.

If you then enter the **UNDO** command, you will get the prompt that is given next.

> Command: **UNDO**
> Enter an option [Control] <1>: *Press Enter to undo the last operation or enter **C** to select another control option.*

In response to this last prompt, you can now either press Enter to undo only the previous command, or go into the **Control** options by entering C. AutoCAD acknowledges undoing the previous command with messages given next.

> Command: **UNDO**
> Enter an option [Control] <1>: Enter.
> CIRCLE
> Everything has been undone

Tip

*AutoCAD stores all information about all the **UNDO** operations performed in a drawing session. When you use the **None** control option of the **UNDO** command, this information is removed and the disk space is made available. In case of limited disk space, it may be a good idea to use the **One** suboption of the **UNDO Control** command. Using **One** control option, you can **UNDO** commands and at the same time make the disk space available.*

Combine

This option allows you to combine all the consecutive **Zoom** and **Pan** operations as a single operation while using the **UNDO** and **REDO** commands.

Layer

This option allows you to combine layer property actions as a single action.

Auto (A) Option

Enter **A** to invoke this option. The following prompt is displayed:

Enter UNDO Auto mode [ON/OFF] <On>: *Select ON or OFF or press Enter to accept the default setting.*

This option is turned on by default and every menu item is a single operation. When you use the **Begin** and **End** options to group a series of commands as a single operation, entering **U** at the command prompt removes the objects individually and not as a group, if the **Auto** option is turned on. But if the **Auto** option is turned off, entering **U** at the command prompt will remove the entire group of objects you had grouped using the **Begin** and **End** options in one single operation.

Also, if you have put a marker in between the start and end operations and if **Auto** is On, the group of commands till the marker is undone altogether on using the **Back** option. This group of commands is considered to be a single group and is undone as a single command Although entering **U** at the command prompt removes the objects individually until the marker is encountered. But if the **Auto** option is turned off, entering **U** at the command prompt, or using the **Back** option of the **UNDO** command, undoes the entire group of operations irrespective of the marker being there.

BEgin (BE) and End (E) Options

A group of commands is treated as one command for the **U** and **UNDO** commands (provided the **Auto** option is turned off) by embedding the commands between the **BEgin** and **End** options of the **UNDO** command. If you anticipate the removal of a group of successive commands later in a drawing, you can use this option, since all of the commands after the **BEgin** option and before the **End** option are treated as a single command by the **U** command (if the **Auto** option is turned Off). For example, the following sequence illustrates the possibility of removal of two commands.

Command: **UNDO**
Enter the number of operations to undo or [Auto/Control/BEgin/End/Mark/Back] <1>: **BE** Enter.

Command: **CIRCLE**
Specify center point for circle or [3P/2P/Ttr (tan tan radius)]: *Specify the center.*
Specify radius of circle or [Diameter] <current>: *Specify the radius of the circle.*
Command: **PLINE**
Specify start point: *Select the first point.*
Specify next point or [Arc/Halfwidth/Length/Undo/Width]: *Select the next point.*
Specify next point or [Arc/Close/Halfwidth/Length/Undo/Width]: *Press Enter.*
Command: **UNDO**
Enter the number of operations to UNDO or [Auto/Control/BEgin/End/Mark/Back]: **E** Enter.
Command: **U**

To start the next group after having finished specifying the current group, use the **End** option to end the operation. Another method is to enter the **BEgin** option to start the next group while the current group is active. This is equivalent to issuing the **End** option followed by the **BEgin** option. The group is complete only when the **End** option is invoked to match a **BEgin** option. If **U** or the **UNDO** command is issued after the **BEgin** option has been invoked and before the **End** option has been issued, only one command is undone at a time until it reaches the juncture where the **BEgin** option has been entered. If you want to undo the commands issued before the **BEgin** option was invoked, you must enter the **End** option so that the group is complete.

Mark (M) and Back (B) Options

The **Mark** option installs a marker in the Undo file. The **Back** option allows you to undo all the operations until the mark. In other words, the **Back** option returns the drawing to the point where the previous mark was inserted. For example, if you have completed a portion of your drawing and do not want anything up to this point to be deleted, you can insert a marker and then proceed. Then, even if you use the **Back** option, it will work only until the marker. You can insert multiple markers, and with the help of the **Back** option, you can return to the successive mark points. The following prompt sequence is used to introduce a mark point:

Command: **UNDO**
Enter the number of operations to undo or [Auto/Control/BEgin/End/Mark/Back]: **M** Enter.

The prompt sequence for using the **Back** option is given next.

Command: **UNDO**
Enter the number of operations to undo or [Auto/Control/BEgin/End/Mark/Back]: **B** Enter.

Once all the marks have been exhausted with the successive **Back** options, any further invoking of the **Back** option displays the message: **This will undo everything. OK? <Y>**. If you enter Y (Yes) at this prompt, all operations carried out since you entered the current drawing session will be undone. If you enter N (No) at this prompt, the **Back** option will be disregarded.

You cannot undo certain commands and system variables, for example, **DIST**, **LIST**, **DELAY**, **NEW**, **OPEN**, **QUIT**, **AREA**, **HELP**, **PLOT**, **QSAVE** and **SAVE**, among many more. Actually, these commands have no effect that can be undone. Commands that change operating modes (**GRID**, **UNITS**, **SNAP**, **ORTHO**) can be undone, though the effect may not be apparent at first. This is the reason why AutoCAD displays the command names as they are undone.

REVERSING THE UNDO OPERATION

Quick Access Toolbar: Redo **Toolbar:** Standard > Redo **Command:** REDO

If you right-click in the drawing area, a shortcut menu is displayed with **Redo(x)** as one of the commands,where x represents the last used command. Choose the **Redo(x)** command to redo the undo operation. The **REDO** command brings back the process you removed previously using the **U** and **UNDO** commands. This command undoes the last **UNDO** command performed, provided it is entered immediately after the **UNDO** command. On using this command, the objects previously undone reappear on the screen. Click on the **Redo** button in the **Quick Access Toolbar**; the **Redo** drop-down is displayed, refer to Figure 4-30. It lists the commands that have been recently undone. Select the commands that you want to **Redo** and click the left mouse button to confirm the selection.

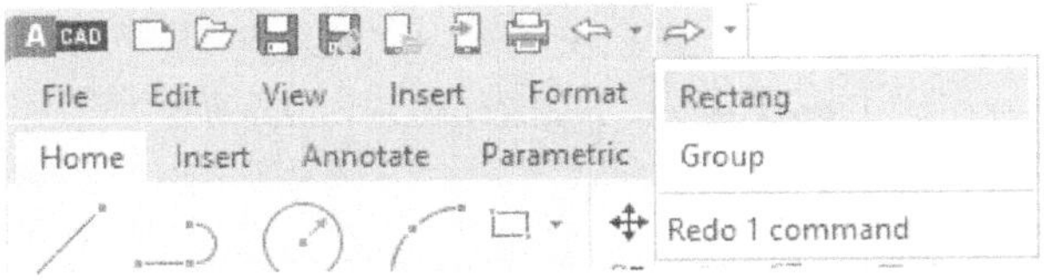

*Figure 4-30 The **Redo** drop-down*

Note

*Consecutive **Zoom** and **Pan** operations can be undone or redone by using the **Undo** or **Redo** command only once so that the drawing returns to the initial zoom state. To disable this feature, clear the **Combine zoom and pan commands** check box in the **Undo/Redo** area of the **User Preferences** tab of the **Options** dialog box.*

RENAMING NAMED OBJECTS

Menu Bar: Format > Rename **Command:** RENAME

You can edit the names of the named objects such as blocks, dimension styles, layers, linetypes, styles, UCS, views, and viewports using the **Rename** dialog box. You can select the named object from the list in the **Named Objects** area of the dialog box. The corresponding names of all the objects of the specified type that can be renamed are displayed in the **Items** area. For example, if you want to rename the layer named HID to HIDDEN, the process will be as follows:

1. Enter **RENAME** at the command prompt and then press Enter; the **Rename** dialog box will be displayed, as shown in Figure 4-31.

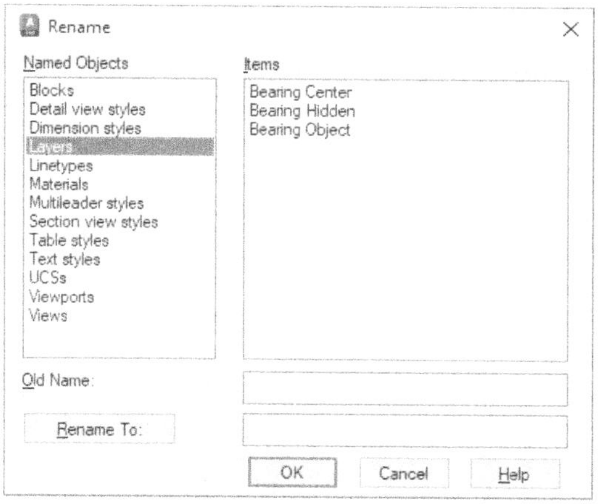

Figure 4-31 *The **Rename** dialog box*

2. Select **Layers** in the **Named Objects** list box, if not already selected. All the layer names in the current drawing that can be renamed are displayed in the **Items** list box.

3. Select **HID** in the **Items** list box to highlight it. HID will be displayed in the **Old Name** edit box.

4. Enter **HIDDEN** in the **Rename To** edit box, and choose the **OK** button.

Now, the layer named **HID** will be renamed to **HIDDEN**. You can view the change in the **Layer** drop-down list in the **Layers** panel of the **Home** tab or invoke the **LAYER PROPERTIES MANAGER** to notice this change. You can rename blocks, dimension styles, linetypes, styles, UCS, views, and viewports in the same way.

Note

*1. The **RENAME** command cannot be used to rename drawing files created using the **Insert > Block Definition > Create Block > Write Block** method. You can change the name of a drawing file by using the **Rename** option of your Operating System.*

*2. The Layer **0** and the **Continuous** linetype cannot be renamed and, therefore, do not appear in the **Items** list box of the **Rename** dialog box.*

REMOVING UNUSED NAMED OBJECTS

Application Menu: Drawing Utilities > Purge
Menu Bar: File > Drawing Utilities > Purge **Command:** PURGE

This is another editing operation used for deletion and it was discussed earlier in relation to blocks. You can delete unused named objects such as blocks, layers, dimension styles, linetypes, text styles, shapes, and so on with the help of the **PURGE** tool. When you create a new drawing or open an existing one, AutoCAD records the named objects in that drawing and notes other drawings that reference the named objects. Usually only a few of the named objects in the drawing (such as layers, linetypes, and blocks) are used. For example, when you create a new drawing, the prototype drawing settings may contain various text styles, blocks, and layers which you do not want to use. Also, you may want to delete particular unused named objects such as unused blocks in an existing drawing. Deleting inactive named objects is important and useful because doing so reduces the space occupied by the drawing. With the **PURGE** tool, you can select the named objects you want to delete. You can invoke this tool at any time in the drawing session. On invoking the **PURGE** command, the **Purge** dialog box is displayed, as shown in Figure 4-32. The options in this dialog box are discussed next.

Purgeable Items Tab

In this tab, AutoCAD displays the tree view of all the named items that are in the current drawing and can be purged. By default, this tab is chosen, and the **Named Item Not Used** and **Options** areas are displayed in the **Purge** dialog box, refer to Figure 4-32. The options in these areas are discussed next.

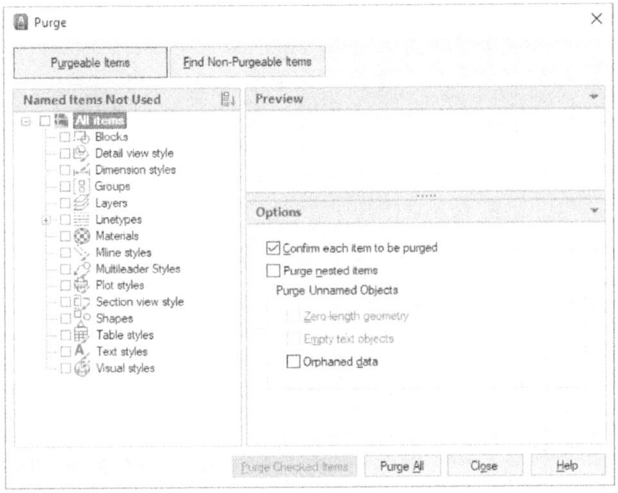

*Figure 4-32 The **Purge** dialog box with purgeable items*

Named Item Not Used

This area lists all the named objects that can be purged. You can list the items of any object type by choosing the plus (+) sign or by double-clicking on the named object in the tree view. Select the items to be purged. You can select more than one item by holding down the Shift or the Ctrl key.

Confirm each item to be purged

This check box is selected to confirm before purging the selected item. The **Confirm Purge** dialog box is displayed when items are selected to be purged and after the **Purge** or **Purge All** button is chosen. You can confirm or skip the items to be purged in this dialog box.

Purge nested items

This check box, when selected, removes all the nested items not in use. This removes the nested items only when you choose the **Purge All** button or select blocks.

Purge zero - length geometry and empty text objects

While drawing a line, arc, or polyline if the same point is selected as the start and the end point by mistake, then a zero length geometry will be created. Also, if there is only empty space created by mistake while creating a text, then the **Purge zero-length geometry and empty text objects** check box will be available. You can purge the zero length geometry or the empty spaces by selecting this check box.

Find Non-Purgeable Items Tab

In this tab, AutoCAD displays the tree view of all the named items that are in the current drawing and cannot be purged, refer to Figure 4-33. On choosing this tab, the items in the **Named Items in Use** area are displayed. When you select an item from this area, the information about why the selected item cannot be purged is displayed in the **Possible Reasons** area.

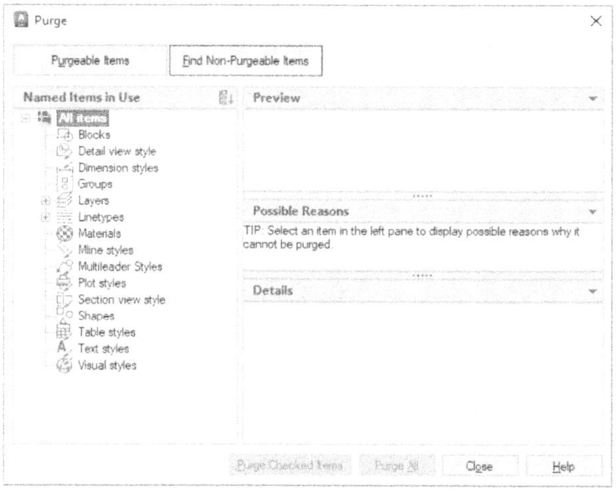

*Figure 4-33 The **Purge** dialog box with non-purgeable items*

Note

*1. The **Entire Drawing** option of the **Write Block** dialog box, which is invoked on using the **WBLOCK** command or the **-WBLOCK** option, has the same effect as the **PURGE All** command. The only difference is that in this case the unused named objects are removed automatically without any verification, though this method is much faster as compared to the previous one.*

*2. Standard objects created by AutoCAD (such as layer 0, STANDARD text style, Dimension style, and linetype CONTINUOUS) cannot be removed by the **PURGE** command, even if these objects are not used.*

SETTING SELECTION MODES USING THE OPTIONS DIALOG BOX

Application Menu: Options **Command:** OPTIONS/OP

When you select a number of objects, the selected objects form a selection set. You can specify the objects to be selected in the **Options** dialog box which is invoked by choosing the **Options** button from the **Application Menu**, as shown in Figure 4-34. Five selection modes are provided in the **Selection** tab of this dialog box. You can select any one of these modes or a combination of various modes.

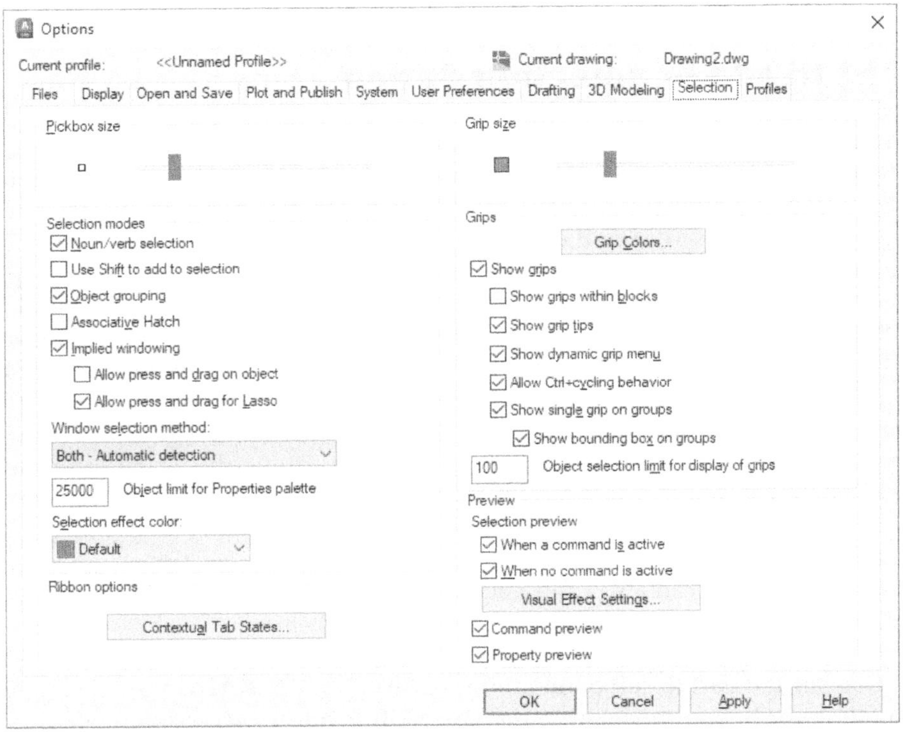

Figure 4-34 The ***Selection*** *tab of the* ***Options*** *dialog box*

Noun/verb selection

By selecting the **Noun/verb selection** check box, you can select the objects (noun) first and then specify the operation (verb) (command) to be performed on the selection set. This mode is active by default. For example, if you want to move some objects when the mode **Noun/verb selection** is enabled, first select the objects to be moved, and then invoke the **MOVE** command. The objects selected are highlighted automatically when the **MOVE** command is invoked and AutoCAD does not issue any **Select objects** prompt. The following are some of the commands that can be used on the selected objects when the **Noun/verb selection** mode is active.

ARRAY	**BLOCK**	**CHANGE**	**CHPROP**	**COPY**
DVIEW	**EXPLODE**	**ERASE**	**LIST**	**MIRROR**
MOVE	**PROPERTIES**	**ROTATE**	**SCALE**	**WBLOCK**

The following are some of the commands that are not affected by the **Noun/verb selection** mode. You are required to specify the objects (noun) on which an operation (command/verb) is to be performed, after specifying the command (verb).

BREAK	**CHAMFER**	**DIVIDE**	**EDGESURF**	**EXTEND**
FILLET	**MEASURE**	**OFFSET**	**REVSURF**	**RULESURF**
TABSURF	**TRIM**			

When the **Noun/verb selection** mode is active, the **PICKFIRST** system variable is set to 1 (On). In other words, you can also activate the **Noun/verb selection** mode by setting the **PICKFIRST** system variable to 1 (On).

Use Shift to add to selection Option

The next option in the **Selection modes** area of the **Selection** tab of the **Options** dialog box is **Use Shift to add to selection**. Selecting this option establishes the additive selection mode, which is the normal method of most Windows programs. In this mode, you have to hold down the **Shift** key when you want to add objects to the selection set. For example, suppose X, Y, and Z are three objects on the screen and you have selected the **Use Shift to add to selection** check box in the **Selection modes** area of the **Options** dialog box. Select object X. It is highlighted and put in the selection set. After selecting X, and while selecting object Y, if you do not hold down the **Shift** key, only object Y is highlighted and it replaces object X in the selection set. On the other hand, if you hold down the **Shift** key while selecting Y, it is added to the selection set (which contains X), and the resulting selection set contains both X and Y. Also, both X and Y are highlighted. To summarize the concept, objects are added to the selection set only when the **Shift** key is held down while objects are selected. Objects can be discarded from the selection set by reselecting these objects while the **Shift** key is held down.

If you want to clear an entire selection set quickly, draw a blank selection window anywhere in a blank drawing area. You can also right-click to display a shortcut menu and choose **Deselect All**. All selected objects in the selection set are discarded from it.

When the **Use Shift to add to selection** mode is active, the **PICKADD** system variable is set to 0 (Off). In other words, you can activate the **Use Shift to add to selection** mode by setting the **PICKADD** system variable to off.

Implied windowing

By selecting this option, you can automatically create a Window or Crossing selection when the **Select objects** prompt is issued. The selection window or crossing window, in this case, is created in the following manner: At the **Select objects** prompt, select a point in the empty space on the screen. This becomes the first corner point of the selection window. After this, AutoCAD prompts you to specify the other corner point of the selection window. If the first corner point is to the right of the second corner point, a Crossing selection is defined; and if the first corner point is to the left of the second corner point, a Window selection is defined. The **Implied windowing** check box is selected by default.

If this option is not active, or if you need to select the first corner in a crowded area where selecting would select an object, you need to specify Window or Crossing at the **Select objects** prompt, depending on your requirement.

When the **Implied windowing** mode is active, the **PICKAUTO** system variable is set to 1 (On). In other words, you can activate the **Implied windowing** mode by setting the value of the **PICKAUTO** system variable to 1 (On).

Press and drag

This selection mode is used to govern the way you can define a selection window or a crossing window. When you select this option, you can create the window by pressing the pick button to select one corner of the window and continuing to hold down the pick button and dragging the cursor to define the other diagonal point of the window. When you have the window you want, release the pick button. If the **Press and drag** mode is not active, you have to select twice to specify the two diagonal corners of the window to be defined. This mode is not active by default. This implies that to define a selection window or a crossing window, you have to select twice to define their two opposite corner points.

When the **Press and drag** mode is active, the **PICKDRAG** system variable is set to 1 (On). In other words, you can activate the **Press and drag** mode by setting **PICKDRAG** to On.

Object grouping

This turns the automatic group selection on and off. When this option is on and you select a member of a group, the whole group is selected. You can also activate this option by setting the value of the **PICKSTYLE** system variable to 1. (Groups were discussed earlier in this chapter.)

Tip

*You can clear the **Object grouping** check box in the **Selection Modes** area of the **Selection** tab of the **Options** dialog box to be able to select the objects of a group individually for editing without having to explode the group.*

Associative Hatch

If the **Associative Hatch** check box is selected in the **Selection modes** area of the **Selection** tab of the **Options** dialog box, the boundary object is also selected when an associative hatch is selected. You can also select this option by setting the value of the **PICKSTYLE** system variable to 2 or 3. It is recommended that you select the **Associative Hatch** check box for most drawings.

Pickbox Size

The **Pickbox** slider bar controls the size of the pickbox. The size ranges from 0 to 50. The default size is 3. You can also use the **PICKBOX** system variable.

Window selection method

This drop-down list can be used to control the selection method. During the window selection, you can control the window behavior in the following two ways:

Click and Click. Using this method, you can define the selection window by clicking in the screen to specify the start point and endpoint of the window.

Press and drag. Using this method, you can define the selection window by clicking on any position in the drawing screen and dragging the cursor according to requirement.

You can also use both options by selecting **Both - Automatic detection** from the **Window selection method** drop-down list.

Self-Evaluation Test

Answer the following questions and then compare them to those given at the end of this chapter:

1. A group of commands is treated as one command for the **U** and **UNDO** commands by embedding them between the __________ and __________ options of the **UNDO** command.

2. If the **Press and Drag** mode is not active, you have to select __________ to specify the two diagonal points of a selection window.

3. The _________ option in the prompt of the **Edit Polyline** tool can be used to change the starting and ending widths of a polyline separately to a desired value.

4. The __________ option of the **Edit Polyline** tool is used to select more than one polyline.

5. You can move the first and last vertices in a closed polyline by using either the ______ option or the __________ option.

6. While using the _______ tool, if you select a line or an arc, AutoCAD provides you with the option of converting them into a polyline first.

7. Even if a group is defined as selectable and the **PICKSTYLE** system variable is set to 0, you cannot select the entire group by selecting one of its members. (T/F)

8. The **PROPERTIES** palette is used to change the properties associated with an object. (T/F)

9. The **PROPERTIES** palette can be used to modify the geometry of objects apart from their general properties. (T/F)

10. The **RENAME** command can be used to change the name of a drawing file created by using the **Write Block** tool. (T/F)

Review Questions

Answer the following questions:

1. In which of the following notations will the name of a group be displayed in the **Group Name** list box if you make a copy of the group without naming it?

   (a) $A1 (b) @A1
   (c) %A1 (d) *A1

2. Which of the following options is used to delete a selected group from a drawing?

   (a) **Remove** (b) **Reorder**
   (c) **Explode** (d) **Rename**

3. Which of the following system variables controls the smoothness of a curve?

   (a) **SPLINETYPE** (b) **SPLINESEGS**
   (c) **PLINEGEN** (d) **PICKFIRST**

4. Which of the following options of the **Edit Polyline** tool can straighten a curve drawn with the help of the **Polyline** tool?

   (a) **Join** (b) **Close**
   (c) **Decurve** (d) None of these

5. Which of the following properties cannot be changed using the **CHANGE** command?

   (a) **Lineweight** (b) **Color**
   (c) **Plotstyle** (d) **Thickness**

6. The ________ command can be used to change the name of a block.

7. If the __________ option of the **UNDO** command is set to off, any group of commands grouped together using the **Begin** and **End** options of the **UNDO** command are undone together.

8. Circles drawn using the **Circle** tool can be changed to _________.

9. The __________ option in the **Group** tool is used to change the order of the objects in the selected group.

10. You can select a group by entering _________ at the command prompt.

11. The __________ option of the **UNDO** command disables the **UNDO** and **U** commands entirely.

12. When you use the **Group** tool to form object groups, AutoCAD allows you to sequentially highlight the groups of which the selected object is a member. (T/F)

13. The standard objects created by AutoCAD (such as layer 0, STANDARD text style, and linetype CONTINUOUS) cannot be removed by using the **PURGE** tool. (T/F)

14. If you explode an object, it remains identical to its original geometry; only the color and linetype may change because of floating layers, colors, or linetypes. (T/F)

15. The **PURGE** tool has the same effect as that of the **WBLOCK Entire drawing** or the **-WBLOCK** method. The only difference is that with the **PURGE** tool, deletion takes place automatically. (T/F)

Exercise 4 Properties and Edit Polyline

Draw part (a) in Figure 4-35 and then using the **Properties** and relevant **Edit Polyline** tool options, convert it into parts (b), (c), and (d). The linetype used in part (d) is HIDDEN.

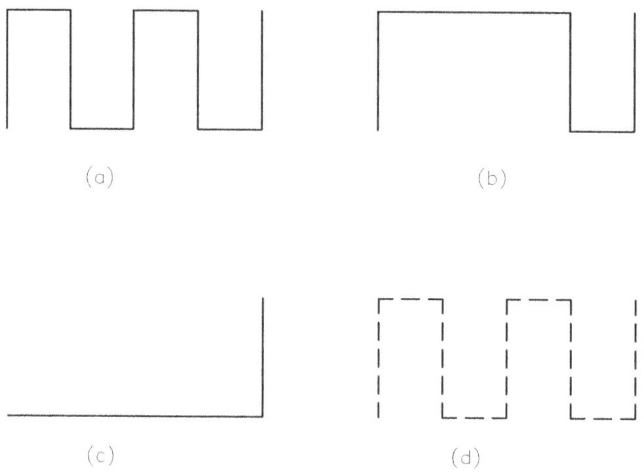

Figure 4-35 *Drawing for Exercise 4*

Exercise 5 Edit Polyline

Draw the sketch shown in Figure 4-36 using the **Line** tool. Change the object to a polyline with a width of 0.05.

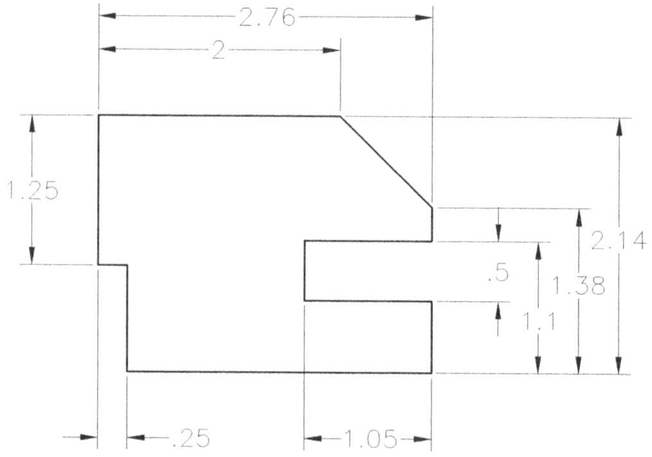

Figure 4-36 *Drawing for Exercise 5*

Exercise 6 *Edit Polyline*

Draw part (a) of Figure 4-37 and then using the relevant **Edit Polyline** tool options, convert it into drawing (b).

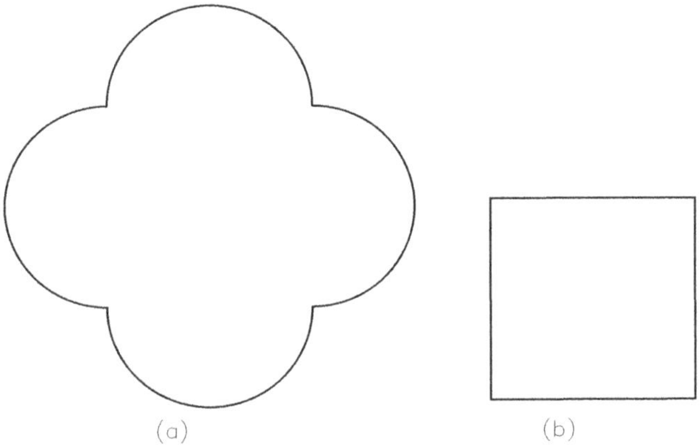

Figure 4-37 *Drawing for Exercise 6*

Exercise 7 *Edit Polyline*

Draw part (a) of Figure 4-38 and then using the relevant **Edit Polyline** tool options, convert it into drawings (b), (c), and (d). Identify the types of curves.

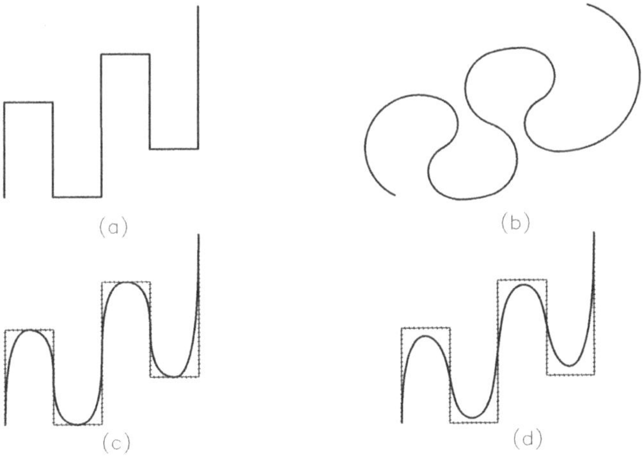

Figure 4-38 *Drawing for Exercise 7*

Exercise 8 — Edit Polyline

Draw part (a) of Figure 4-39 and then using the relevant **Edit Polyline** tool options, convert it into drawing (b).

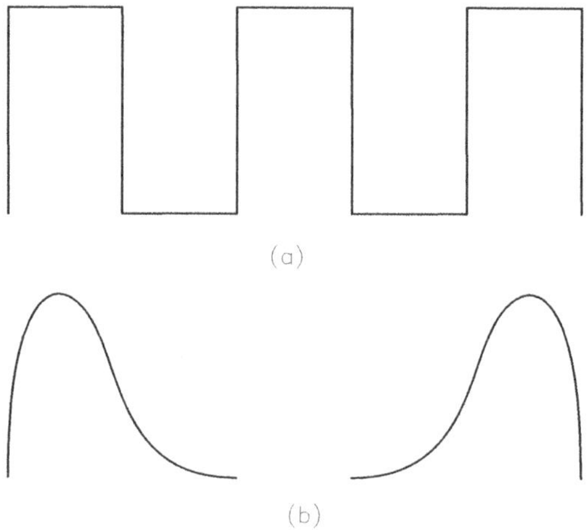

Figure 4-39 *Drawing for Exercise 8*

Exercise 9 — Edit Polyline

Draw the part (a) of Figure 4-40 and change it into the figure shown in part (b) by using the appropriate commands. You can also use grips to obtain this illustration.

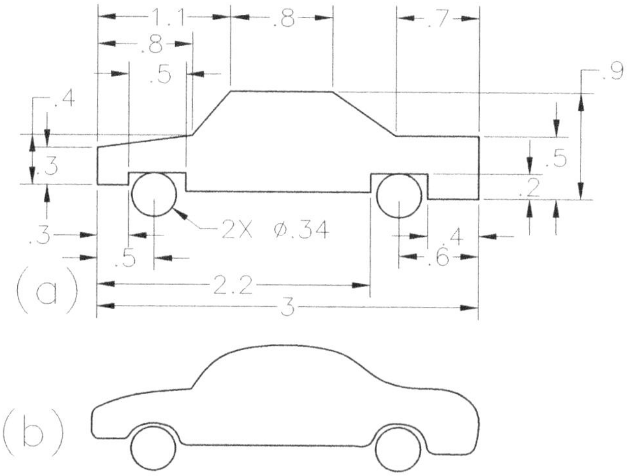

Figure 4-40 *Drawing for Exercise 9*

Exercise 10 — Edit Polyline

Create the drawing shown in Figure 4-41. Use the splined polylines to draw the break lines. Dimension the drawing as shown.

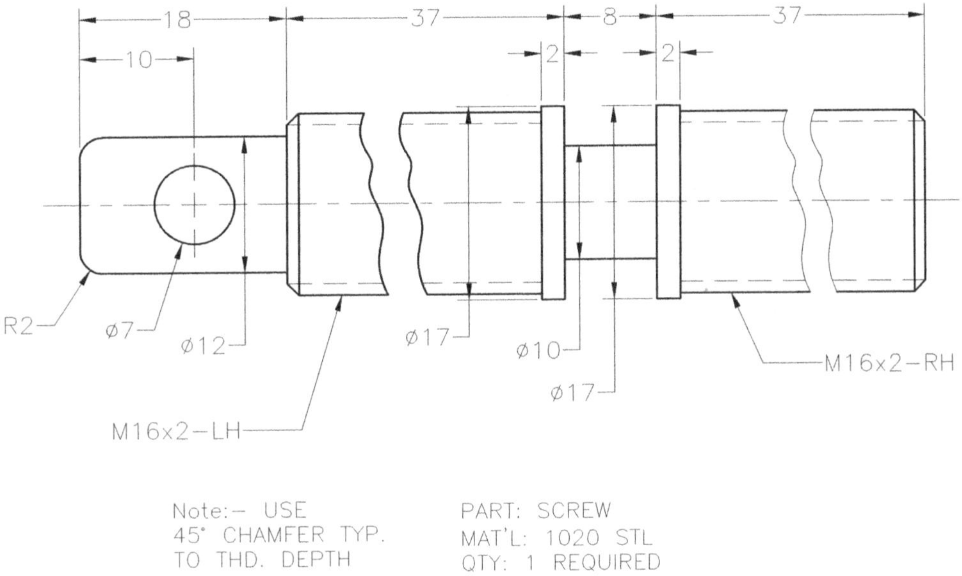

Figure 4-41 *Drawing for Exercise 10*

Answers to Self-Evaluation Test

1. Begin, **End**, **2.** Twice, **3.** Width, **4. Multiple**, **5. Next**, **Previous**, **6. Edit Polyline**, **7.** T, **8.** T, **9.** T, **10.** F

Chapter 5

Working with Data Exchange & Object Linking and Embedding

Learning Objectives

After completing this chapter, you will be able to:

- *Import and export .dxf files using the Save As and Open tools*
- *Import files*
- *Convert scanned drawings into the drawing editor using the DXB file format*
- *Attach the raster images to the current drawing*
- *Edit raster images*
- *Understand the embedding and linking functions of the OLE feature of Windows*
- *Use DWG Convert and CONTENT EXPLORER*

Key Terms

- *DXF Files*
- *DXB Files*
- *ACIS Files*
- *DWG Convert*
- *PDF Files*
- *3D Studio Files*
- *DGN Files*
- *BMP Files*
- *Attach Image*
- *EPS Files*
- *OLE Objects*
- *Draw Order*

UNDERSTANDING THE CONCEPT OF DATA EXCHANGE IN AutoCAD

Different companies have developed different softwares for applications such as CAD, desktop publishing, and rendering. This non-standardization of software has led to the development of various data exchange formats that enable the transfer (translation) of data from one data processing software to the other. This chapter will cover various data exchange formats provided in AutoCAD. AutoCAD uses the *.dwg* format to store drawing files. This format is not recognized by some other CAD softwares. To address this problem, AutoCAD provides various data exchange formats such as DXF (Data Interchange Format) and DXB (Drawing Interchange Binary).

CREATING DATA INTERCHANGE (DXF) FILES

The DXF file format generates a text file in ASCII code from the original drawing. This allows any computer system to manipulate (read/write) data in a DXF file. Usually, the DXF format is used for CAD packages based on microcomputers. For example, packages like SmartCAM use DXF files. Some desktop publishing packages, such as PageMaker and Ventura Publisher also use DXF files.

Creating a Data Interchange File

Using the **Save** or **Save As** tool, you can create an ASCII file with a *.dxf* extension from an AutoCAD drawing file. Once you invoke any of these tools, the **Save Drawing As** dialog box will be displayed. Next, choose the **Options** option from the **Tools** drop-down to display the **Saveas Options** dialog box, as shown in Figure 5-1. In this dialog box, the **DWG Options** tab is chosen by default. Select the required *.dxf file extension type from the **Save all drawings as** drop-down list. Next, choose the **DXF Options** tab and enter the degree of accuracy for the numeric values. The default value for the degree of accuracy is sixteen decimal places. You can enter a value between 0 and 16 decimal places.

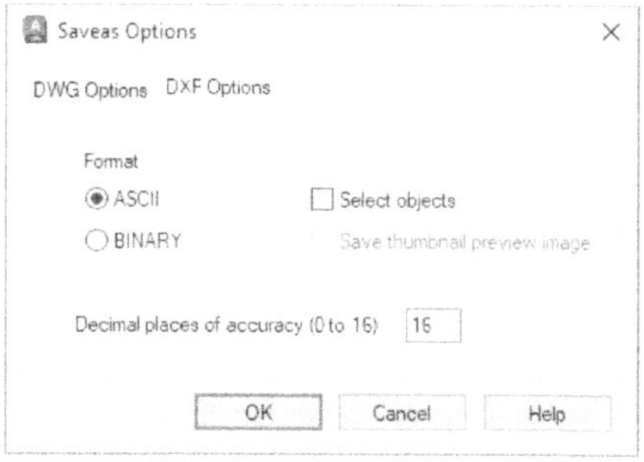

Figure 5-1 *The **Saveas Options** dialog box*

In the **DXF Options** tab, you can also select the **Select objects** check box which allows you to specify the objects to be included in the DXF file. In this case, the definitions of the named objects such as block definitions, text styles, and so on are not exported.

Select the **ASCII** radio button. Choose the **OK** button to return to the **Save Drawing As** dialog box. Choose the **Save** button here. Now, an ASCII file with a *.dxf* extension has been created and this file can be accessed by other CAD systems. This file contains data on the objects specified. By default, DXF files are created in the ASCII format. However, you can also create binary format files by selecting the **BINARY** radio button in the **Saveas Options** dialog box. Binary DXF files are more efficient and occupy only 75 percent of the ASCII DXF file. You can access a binary format file more quickly than an ASCII format file.

Note

*You can also create a DXF file by using the **-WBLOCK** command. When you execute this command, the **Create Drawing File** dialog box will be displayed, where you can enter the name of the file in the **File name** edit box and select any version of DXF [*dxf] from the **Files of type** drop-down list. By default, the DXF file to be created assumes the name of the drawing file from which it will be created.*

Information in a DXF File

The DXF file contains data of the objects which are specified using the **Select objects** check box in the **Saveas Options** dialog box. You can change the data in this file as per your requirement. To examine the data in this file, load the ASCII file in the word processing software. A DXF file is composed of the following parts:

Header

In this part of the drawing database, all variables in the drawing and their values are displayed.

Classes

This section deals with the internal database.

Tables

All named objects such as linetypes, layers, blocks, text styles, dimension styles, and views are listed in this part.

Blocks

The objects that define blocks and their respective values are displayed in this part.

Entities

All entities in the drawing, such as lines, circles, and so on are listed in this part.

Objects

Objects in the drawing are listed in this part.

Converting DXF Files into Drawing Files

You can import a DXF file into a new AutoCAD drawing file with the **Open** tool. After you invoke the **Open** tool, the **Select File** dialog box is displayed. From the **Files of type** drop-down list, select the **DXF (*.dxf)** option. In the **File name** edit box, enter the name of the file you want to import into AutoCAD or select the file from the list. Choose the **Open** button. Once this is done, the specified DXF file is converted into a standard DWG file, regeneration is carried out, and the file is inserted into the new drawing. Now, you can perform different operations on this file just as with the other drawing files.

Tip
A data interchange file (DXF) can also be inserted into the current drawing using the ***Insert*** *tool.*

Importing CAD Files

Ribbon: Insert > Import > Import drop-down > Import
Menu Bar: File > Import **Command:** IMPORT

You can import any surface, solid, 2D and 3D wire geometry from the supported file formats to AutoCAD. In AutoCAD, you can import IGES, CATIA, Rhino, Pro/ENGINEER and many other file formats. To import a CAD geometry to AutoCAD, choose the **Import** tool from the **Import** drop-down of the **Import** panel; the **Import File** dialog box will be displayed. From the **Files of type** drop-down list, select the required format. Next, browse to the required file and then choose the **Open** button from the dialog box; the **Import - Processing Background Job** message box will be displayed stating that the import job is processing in the background. Next, close the message box. The details of the progress can be seen on the bottom-right corner of the screen. After the processing gets completed, a link will be displayed as pop-up. Click on the link to import the CAD geometry into AutoCAD; the inserted part geometry will be placed as a block reference.

OTHER DATA EXCHANGE FORMATS

The other formats that can be used to exchange data from one data processing format to the other are discussed next.

DXB File Format

Menu Bar: Insert > Drawing Exchange Binary **Command:** DXBIN

AutoCAD offers another file format for data interchange, DXB. This format is much more compressed than the binary DXF format and is used when you want to translate a large amount of data from one CAD system to another. For example, when you scan a drawing, a DXB file is created. This file has a huge amount of data in it. To import a DXB file, enter the **DXBIN** command at the command prompt; the **Select DXB File** dialog box will be displayed. In the **File name** edit box, enter the name of the file (in DXB format) you want to import into AutoCAD. Choose the **Open** button. Once this is done, the specified DXB file will be converted into a standard DWG file and is inserted into the current drawing.

Note
Before importing a DXB file, you must create a new drawing file. No editing or drawing setup (limits, units, and so on) can be performed on this file. This is because if you import a DXB file to an old drawing, the settings (definitions) of layers, blocks, and so on, of the file being imported are overruled by the settings of the file to which you are importing the DXB file.

Creating and Using an ACIS File

Application Menu: Export > Other Formats **Command:** EXPORT, ACISOUT

Trimmed NURBS, regions, and solids can be exported to an ACIS file with an ASCII format. To do so, choose **Export > Other Formats** from the **Application Menu**; the **Export Data** dialog box will be displayed. Enter a file name in the **File name** edit box. From the **Files of type** drop-down list, select **ACIS (*.sat)** and then choose the **Save** button; you will be prompted to select the objects. Select the solids, regions, or ACIS bodies that you want to add to the file and press Enter. AutoCAD appends the file extension *.sat* to the file name. You can also use the **ACISOUT** command to perform this function. It prompts you to select objects before the **Create ACIS File** dialog box is displayed on the screen. Keep in mind that only solids, regions, or ACIS bodies can be selected to add to the *.sat* file.

To import an ACIS file, choose the **Import** tool from the **Import** drop-down of the **Import** panel in the **Insert** tab; the **Import File** dialog box will be displayed. In the **Files of type** drop-down list, select the *.sat* file format. Next, select a file to be imported and choose the **Open** button; the file will be inserted. Alternatively, enter **ACISIN** at the command prompt and import the file using the **Select ACIS File** dialog box.

Importing PDF Files

Ribbon: Insert > Import > Import drop-down > PDF Import **Command:** PDFIMPORT

You can import the geometry, raster images, fills, and true type text objects from a PDF file into the current drawing as AutoCAD objects. To do so, choose the **PDF Import** tool from the **Import** drop-down of the **Import** panel in the **Insert** tab; the **Select PDF File** dialog box will be displayed. Select a PDF file to import and choose the **Open** button; the **Import PDF** dialog box will be displayed, as shown in Figure 5-2.

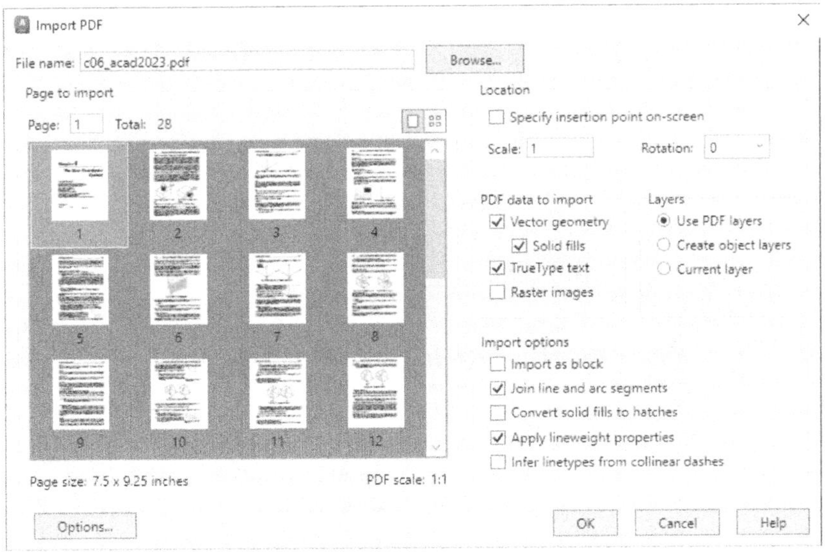

*Figure 5-2 The **Import PDF** dialog box*

Enter the page number in the **Page** edit box under the **Page to import** area of the **Import PDF** dialog box. To specify the scale, rotation and point of insertion of the imported geometry choose the respective options under the **Location** area. You can also choose the type of data to be imported using the options available in the **PDF data to import** area. To specify the layers in which the PDF data is to be imported, choose the options under the **Layers** area. The options under the **Import options** area are discussed next.

You can join 2D solids with the coincident edges and convert them to hatch objects by choosing the **Convert solid fills to hatches** check box. Choose the **Apply lineweight properties** check box to apply the lineweights of the PDF to the extracted geometry. You can choose the **Infer linetypes from collinear dashes** check box to collect collinear dash and dot segments and replace them with a single polyline. If you uncheck this box, each segment in a dashed line is imported as a separate polyline. Choose the **Options** button at the bottom of the **Import PDF** dialog box; the **Options** dialog box will be displayed. In the **Options** dialog box, you can specify the file location for image files that are extracted from the PDF and attached to the drawing.

Alternatively, you can import different objects from the previously attached PDF by entering the **PDFIMPORT** command at the command bar. On doing so, you will be prompted to select PDF underlay. Select an attached PDF from the drawing area; you will be prompted to specify a rectangular or polygonal boundary around the objects that you want to import or choose the **All** option from the command prompt to import all the objects in the overlay. Choose the **Settings** option from the command prompt to invoke the **PDF Import Settings** dialog box, as shown in Figure 5-3. The options in this dialog box are same as discussed for the **Import PDF** dialog box. After selecting the boundary you can choose the options in the command prompt to keep, detach, or unload the PDF underlay after the objects are imported into the current drawing.

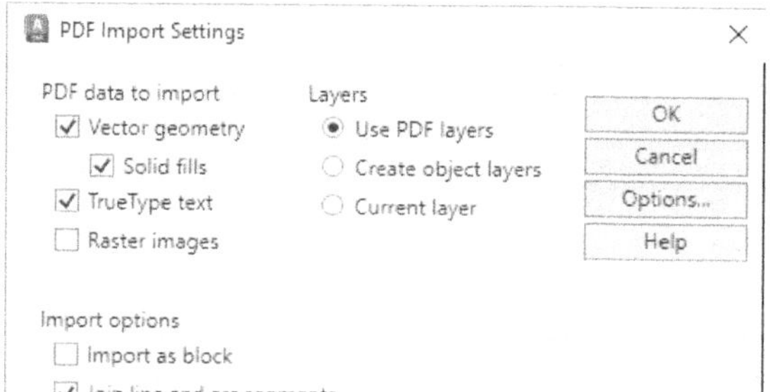

Figure 5-3 *The* ***PDF Import Settings*** *dialog box*

While importing a PDF file, it is possible that some of the text strings are not recognized by AutoCAD. To make this text recognized by AutoCAD, choose the **Recognize SHX Text** tool from the **Import** panel; you will be prompted to select the unrecognized text. Select the text stamps that were previously not recognized by AutoCAD; the selected text stamps will be recognized. This tool recognizes the text by comparing its geometry with some pre-defined text styles. You can also set the list of text styles by using the **PDF Text Recognition Settings** dialog box. To invoke this dialog box, choose the **Recognition Settings** tool from the **Import** panel; the **PDF Text Recognition Settings** dialog box will be displayed, as shown in Figure 5-4. You can select any text style and add or remove more text styles by choosing required options from the **SHX fonts to compare** area of this dialog box.

In the **Create text on** area, you can create the recognized text on the set layer or on the same layer by selecting the **Current layer** or **Same layer as geometry** radio buttons, respectively. Also, you can set the percentage for matching geometry to the defined text style from the **Recognition threshold** slider in the **Conversion settings** area.

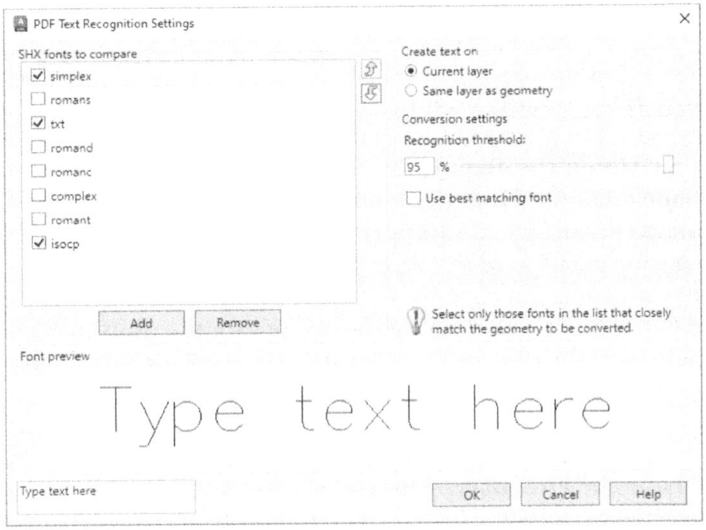

Figure 5-4 *The* ***PDF Text Recognition Settings*** *dialog box*

Tip
You can also access the PDF import options by choosing the ***Import as Objects*** *tool in the* ***PDF Import*** *panel of the* ***PDF Underlay*** *contextual tab which will be displayed on selecting the object.*

Importing 3D Studio Files

Menu Bar: Insert > 3D Studio **Command:** 3DSIN

You can import 3D geometry, views, lights, and objects with surface characteristics created in 3D Studio and saved in *.3ds* format. To do so, choose the **3D Studio** tool from the **Insert** menu; the **3D Studio File Import** dialog box will be displayed. Select the file you wish to import and choose the **Open** button. You can use the **3DSIN** command to import 3D Studio file.

Creating and Using a Windows Metafile

Application Menu: Export > Other Formats **Command:** EXPORT, WMFOUT

The Windows Metafile format (WMF) file contains screen vector and raster graphic formats. In the **Export Data** dialog box or in the **Create WMF File** dialog box, enter the file name. Select **Metafile (*.wmf)** from the **Files of type** drop-down list. The extension *.wmf* is appended to the file name. Next, save the settings and then select the objects you want to save in this file format.

The **WMFIN** command invokes the **Import WMF** dialog box. Select the *.wmf* file you want to import and choose the **Open** button. Specify an insertion point, rotation angle, and scale factor. Specify the scaling by entering a scale factor using the **Corner** option to specify an imaginary box whose dimensions correspond to the scale factor, or by using the **X**, **Y**, or **Z** option to specify 3D scale factors. You can also import a *.wmf* file by using the **Import File** dialog box that will be displayed on choosing the **Import** tool from the **Import** panel in the **Insert** tab.

Creating and Using a V8 DGN File

Application Menu: Export > DGN **Command:** EXPORT, DGNEXPORT

The **V8 DGN** (*.DGN*) file format is used by the Microstation software. A **.dwg* file created in AutoCAD can be exported to Microstation using this format. To do so, choose **Export > DGN** from the **Application Menu**; the **Export DGN File** dialog box will be displayed. Enter a file name in the **File name** edit box. From the **Files of type** drop-down list, select **V8 DGN (*.dgn)** and then choose the **Save** button; the **Export DGN Settings** dialog box will be displayed. In this dialog box, you can specify how the externally referenced files in the current drawing are taken care of while converting the current drawing into the DGN file. You can also specify the seed files (standard template files containing the settings for the units to be used for conversion, working units, resolution of the drawing, and so on) to be used for conversion in this dialog box.

To import a DGN file, choose **Open > DGN** from the **Application Menu**; the **Import DGN File** dialog box will be displayed. Alternatively, you can use the **DGNIMPORT** command to import a DGN file. From the **Files of type** drop-down list, select the **MicroStation DGN (*.dgn)** option, if it is not selected by default. Next, select or enter the name of the design file and choose the **Open** button; the **Import DGN Settings** dialog box will be invoked. You can exchange the data of the drawing files and design files using the **Export/Import DGN Settings** dialog box. For example, you can translate DGN elements to DWG objects, Levels to Layers, Line Styles to Linetypes, Cells to Blocks, Sheet Model to DWG Layouts, etc. You can save and reuse, modify, rename or delete the mapping translations using the **DGNMAPPING** command.

Creating a BMP File

Application Menu: Export > Other Formats **Command:** EXPORT, BMPOUT

This is used to create bitmap images of the objects in your drawing. In the **Export Data** dialog box, enter the name of the file, select **Bitmap (*.bmp)** from the **Files of type** drop-down list and then choose the **Save** button. Select the objects you wish to save as bitmap and press Enter. Entering **BMPOUT** displays the **Create Raster File** dialog box. Enter the file name and choose the **Save** button. Select the objects to be saved as bitmap. The file extension *.bmp* is appended to the file name.

RASTER IMAGES

A raster image consists of small square-shaped dots known as pixels. In a colored image, the color is determined by the color of pixels. The raster images can be moved, copied, or clipped. They will be used as a cutting edge with the **Trim** tool. They can also be modified by using grips. You can also control the image contrast, transparency, and quality of the image. AutoCAD stores images in a special temporary image swap file whose default location is the Windows Temp directory. You can change the location of this file by modifying it under **Temporary Drawing File Location** in the **Files** tab of the **Options** dialog box.

The images can be 8-bit gray, 8-bit color, 24-bit color, or bitonal. When the image transparency is set to On, the image file formats with transparent pixels is recognized by AutoCAD and transparency is allowed. The transparent images can be in color or grayscale. AutoCAD supports many formats and some of them are given next.

Image Type	File Extension	Description
BMP	*.bmp*	Windows and OS/2 Bitmap Format
JFIF or JPEG	*.jpg, jpeg*	Joint Photographics Expert group
PCX	*.pcx*	Picture PC Paintbrush Picture
PNG	*.png*	Portable Network Graphic
TARGA	*.tga*	True Vision Raster based Data format
TIFF/LZW	*.tif, .tiff*	Tagged Image File Format

When you store images as Tiled Images, that is, in the Tagged Image File Format (TIFF), you can edit or modify any portion of the image; only the modified portion is regenerated, thus saving time. Tiled images load much faster as compared to the untiled images.

Attaching Raster Images

Ribbon: Insert > Reference > Attach **Tool Palettes:** Draw > Attach Image
Toolbar: Reference > Attach Image or Insert > Attach Image **Command:** IMAGEATTACH

Attaching raster images to a drawing does not make them part of the drawing. To attach an image, choose the **Attach** tool from the **Reference** panel; the **Select Reference File** dialog box will be displayed, as shown in Figure 5-5. Select the image to be attached; a preview of the selected image will be displayed in the **Preview** area of the dialog box. Next, choose the **Open** button; the **Attach Image** dialog box will be displayed, as shown in Figure 5-6. The name of the selected image is displayed in the **Name** drop-down list. You can select another file by using the **Browse** button. The **Name** drop-down list displays the names of all the images in the current drawing. Select the **Specify on-screen** check boxes to specify the **Insertion point**, the **Scale**, and **Rotation** angle on the screen. Alternatively, you can clear these check boxes and enter values in the respective edit boxes. On choosing the **Show Details** button, the **Attach Image** dialog box is expanded and it provides the image information such as the Horizontal and Vertical resolution values, current AutoCAD unit, and Image size in pixels and units. Choose the **OK** button to return to the drawing screen.

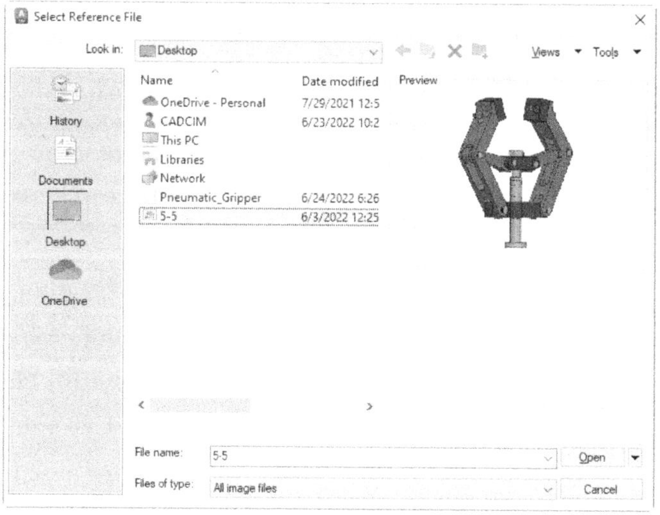

*Figure 5-5 The **Select Reference File** dialog box*

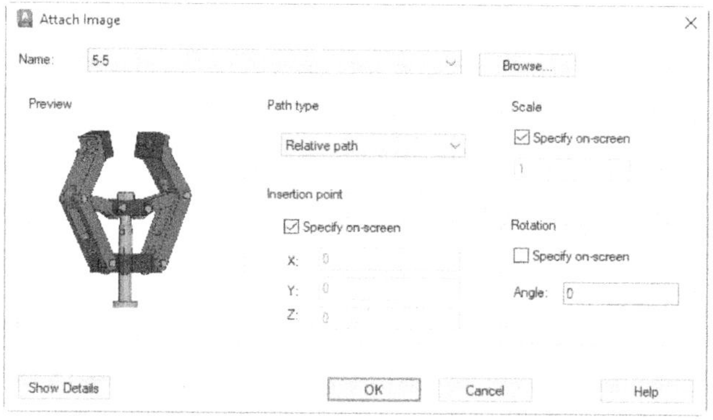

*Figure 5-6 The **Attach Image** dialog box*

You can also attach and scale an image from the Internet. In the **Select Reference File** dialog box, choose the **Search the Web** button. Once you have located the image file you wish to attach to the current drawing, enter the URL address in the **Look in** drop-down list and the image file name in the **Name or URL** edit box. Choose the **Open** button. Specify the insertion point, scale, and rotation angle in the **Attach Image** dialog box. You can also right-click on the image you wish to attach to the current drawing and choose **Properties** from the shortcut menu to display the **Properties** palette. From here, you can select, cut, and paste the URL address in the **File name** edit box of the **Select Reference File** dialog box.

Managing Raster Images

Ribbon: View > Palettes > External References Palette **Command:** IMAGE
Toolbar: Reference > External References **Menu Bar:** Insert > External References

Choose the **External References Palette** button from the **Palettes** panel; the **EXTERNAL REFERENCES** palette will be displayed, refer to Figure 5-7. If the image has not been inserted earlier, right-click in the **File References** area and choose the **Attach Image** option from the shortcut menu. You can view the image information either as a list or as a tree view by choosing the respective buttons located at the right corner of the **File References** head of the **EXTERNAL REFERENCES** palette. The **List View** displays the names, loading status, size, date last modified on, and search path of all images in the drawing. The **Tree View** displays images in hierarchal structure. These images show its nesting levels within blocks and Xrefs. The **Tree View** does not display the status, size, or any other information about an image file. You can rename an image file in this dialog box.

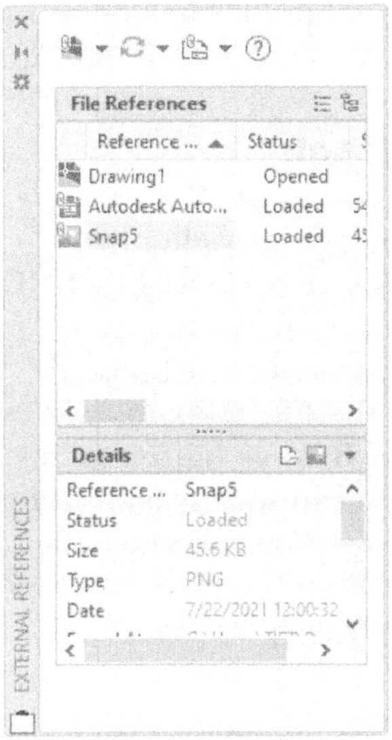

Figure 5-7 The ***EXTERNAL REFERENCES*** *palette*

Preview

To display the **Preview** area, choose the **Preview** button located at the right corner of the **Details** area. In this area, you can see the preview of the image. This area displays the preview of the image file attached to the current drawing and the file details of the attached image file. To get the file details, choose the **Details** button located adjacent to the **Preview** button. The information about the image file such as file name, saved path, and so on will be listed, as shown in Figure 5-8. Once you have referenced an image file to the current drawing, you can replace it with another image file by using the **Saved Path** edit box. To do so, choose the Browse [...] button in the corner of the edit box to display the **Select Image File** dialog box. Browse and select the image file and then choose the **Open** button. Now, the new path will be displayed in the **Found At** and **Saved Path** edit boxes.

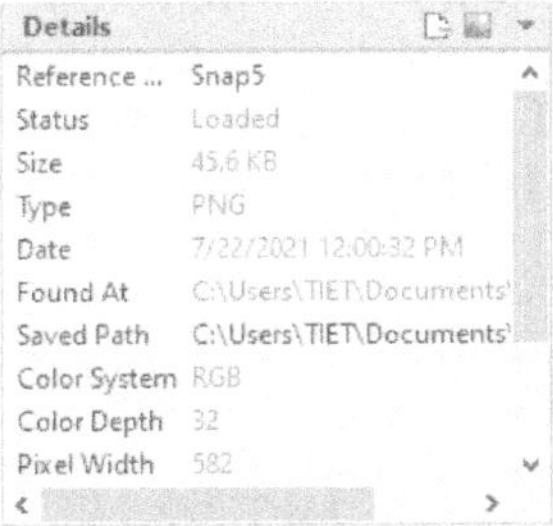

Figure 5-8 The ***Details*** *area of the* ***EXTERNAL REFERENCES*** *palette*

Tip

You can also use the command prompt for managing the image files using the ***-IMAGE*** *command. Except the* ***Open*** *option, all the other options of the* ***EXTERNAL REFERENCES*** *palette will be available in the command prompt.*

When you select the name of the attached image and right-click on it, a shortcut menu will be displayed. The options in this shortcut menu are discussed next.

Open

This option enables you to open the attached image in its default viewing software from its current location in the AutoCAD file.

Attach

This option allows you to attach an image file with the current drawing. You can also attach an image file by choosing the **Attach Image** option from the flyout on the upper left corner of the **EXTERNAL REFERENCES** palette; the **Select Reference File** dialog box will be displayed. Select the file that you want to attach to the drawing and the selected image is displayed in the **Preview** box. Choose the **Open** button; the **Attach Image** dialog box is displayed. The name of the file, its path, and extension are displayed in the **Attach Image** dialog box. You can use the **Browse** button to select another file. Choose the **OK** button in the **Attach Image** dialog box and specify a point to insert the image. Next, AutoCAD will prompt you to enter the scale factor. You can enter the scale factor or specify a point on the screen.

Detach

This option detaches the selected and all associated raster images from the current drawing. Once the image is detached, no information about the image is retained in the drawing.

Reload

The **Reload** option simply reloads an image. The changes made to the image since the last insert will be loaded on the screen.

Unload

The **Unload** option unloads an image. An image is unloaded when it is not needed in the current drawing session. When you unload an image, AutoCAD retains information about the location and size of the image in the database of the current file. Unloading a file does not unlink the file from the drawing and the image frame is displayed. If you reload the image, the image will appear at the same point and in the same size as the image was before unloading. Unloading the raster images enhances AutoCAD performance. Also, the unloaded images are not plotted. If multiple images are to be loaded and the memory is insufficient, AutoCAD automatically unloads them.

Change Path Type

The **Change Path Type** option is used to change the path type from where the image can be imported. You can set three types of paths by selecting the desired option from the **Change Path Type** cascading menu invoked by clicking on the **Change Path Type** option in the shortcut menu. The options in this cascading menu are discussed next.

Make Absolute: This option is used to set full path of the attached image which includes drive, url, or network server location.

Make Relative: This option is used to set most flexible path because it does not save drive name. Therefore, by using this option, you can easily move your file in different drawings with same folder structure without breaking the reference.

Remove path: This option is used when you do not want to set any path. On selecting this option, you can move your drawing wherever you want without facing any problem.

Select New Path

The **Select New Path** option is used to change the current path of the attached image whose referenced path has been changed. Also, you can attach a different image by using this option.

Find and Replace

This option is used to simultaneously change the path of all the attached images having same path from one location to another.

EDITING RASTER IMAGE FILES

Raster image files can be easily edited. The different methods to edit a raster image files are discussed next.

Clipping Raster Images

Ribbon: Insert > Reference > Clip	**Toolbar:** Reference > Clip Image
Menu Bar: Modify > Clip > Image	**Command:** IMAGECLIP

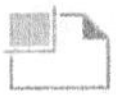

The **Clip** tool is used to clip the boundaries of images and to provide a desired shape to them. To invoke this tool, select the image to be clipped; the **Image** tab will be added to the **Ribbon**. Choose the **Create Clipping Boundary** tool; you will be prompted to specify the boundary. Specify a rectangular or polygonal boundary; the image will be clipped at the specified boundary. Also, an arrow will be displayed pointing inside the clipping boundary. Click on the arrow to flip the clipping direction.

You can also invoke this tool by selecting and right-clicking on an image to be clipped and choose **Image > Clip** from the shortcut menu displayed.

After choosing this tool, AutoCAD will prompt you to select the image to be clipped. Select the raster image by selecting the edge of the image. The image boundary must be visible to select it. The clipping boundary must be specified in the same plane as the image or a plane that is parallel to it. The following prompt sequence is displayed when you choose the **Clip** tool from the **Reference** panel.

Select object to clip: *Select the boundary of an image.*
Enter image clipping option [ON/OFF/Delete/New boundary] <New>:

New boundary

This option is used to define a boundary for clipping the image. When you invoke this option, you are prompted to specify whether or not you want to delete the old boundary, if a boundary already exists. If you enter **No** at the **Delete old boundary? [No/Yes] <Yes>** prompt, this command will end. You can enter **Yes** to specify the new clipping boundary. The boundary can be defined in a rectangular shape or a polygonal shape.

ON

This option is used to turn the image clipping on. The image will be clipped using the last boundary.

OFF

This option is used to turn the image clipping off. If you have a clipped image, you can redisplay the entire image.

Delete

This option is used to delete the existing clipping boundary.

One such clipping is shown in Figure 5-9 and Figure 5-10. Figure 5-9 shows the actual image and Figure 5-10 shows the clipped image where the clipping boundary is created by using the midpoints of all the four sides of the image.

Figure 5-9 *Image before clipping*

Figure 5-10 *Image after clipping*

Tip

*You can improve the performance by turning off the highlighting of an image. This can be done by clearing the **Highlight raster image frame only** check box in the **Display** tab of the **Options** dialog box. You can also use the **IMAGEHLT** system variable. By default, **IMAGEHLT** is set to 0, that is, only the raster image frame will be highlighted.*

Adjusting Raster Images

Ribbon: Insert > Reference > Adjust	**Menu Bar:** Modify > Object > Image > Adjust
Toolbar: Reference > Adjust Image	**Command:** IMAGEADJUST/ADJUST

The **Adjust** tool allows you to adjust the brightness, contrast, and fade of a raster image. On selecting an attached image, the **Image** tab will be added to the **Ribbon**. Adjust the brightness, contrast, and fade using the corresponding option in the **Adjust** panel of the **Image** tab.

Alternatively, choose the **Adjust Image** tool from the **Reference** toolbar; you will be prompted to select the image. Select the attached image; the **Image Adjust** dialog box will be displayed, as shown in Figure 5-11. This dialog box is used to adjust an image. As you adjust the brightness, contrast, or fade, the changes are dynamically made in the image. If you choose the **Reset** button, the values will be returned to the default values (Brightness= 50, Contrast= 50, and Fade= 0). You can also choose **Properties** in the shortcut menu to display the **PROPERTIES** palette. In this palette, you can enter new values of brightness, contrast, and fade. If you choose the **Adjust** tool from the **Reference** panel, you need to set the values in the command prompt.

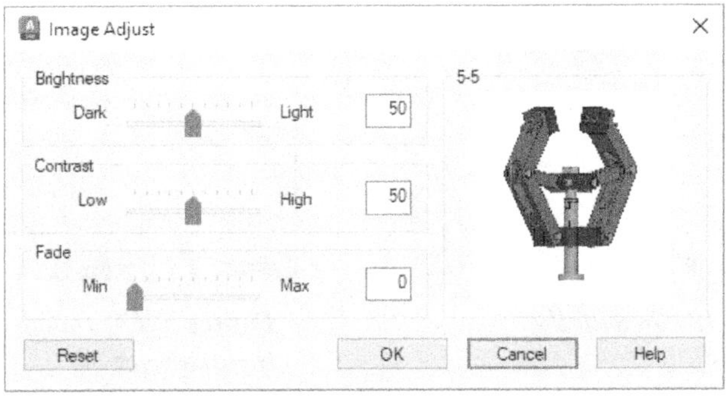

Figure 5-11 *The **Image Adjust** dialog box*

Modifying the Image Quality

Menu Bar: Modify > Object > Image > Quality **Command:** IMAGEQUALITY
Toolbar: Reference > Image Quality

The **Quality** tool allows you to control the quality of the image that affects the display performance. To control the quality, choose the **Quality** tool from **Modify > Object > Image** in the Menu bar; you will be prompted to specify the quality of image. A high-quality image takes a longer time to display. When you change the quality, the display changes immediately without causing a **REGEN**. The images are always plotted using a high-quality display. Although draft quality images appear grainier, they are displayed more quickly.

Modifying the Transparency of an Image

Toolbar: Reference > Image Transparency **Command:** TRANSPARENCY
Menu Bar: Modify > Object > Image > Transparency

When you attach an image with transparent background to a drawing, the transparent background turns opaque. To control the transparency of the attached image, select it; the **Image** tab will be added to the **Ribbon**. Choose the **Background Transparency** button from the **Image** tab to turn on the transparency of the image; the background of the image will become transparent. The **TRANSPARENCY** command can also be used to control the transparency of an image. Figure 5-12 shows two images one over the other with the transparency of the top image turned off. Figure 5-13 shows the figure with the transparency of the top image turned on. You can also right-click on an image and choose **Properties** from the shortcut menu displayed. In the **PROPERTIES** palette, select an option from the **Background transparency** drop-down list displayed under the **Misc** list.

Note

You have to choose images in such a way that they can give the effect of transparency. Dull and opaque images will not give the effect of transparency.

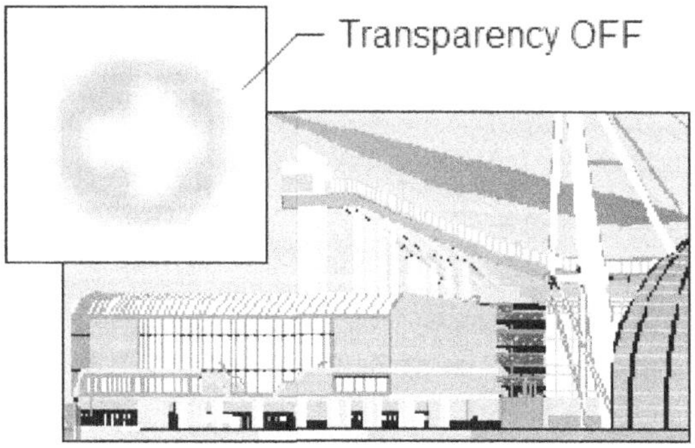

Figure 5-12 *Image with the transparency off*

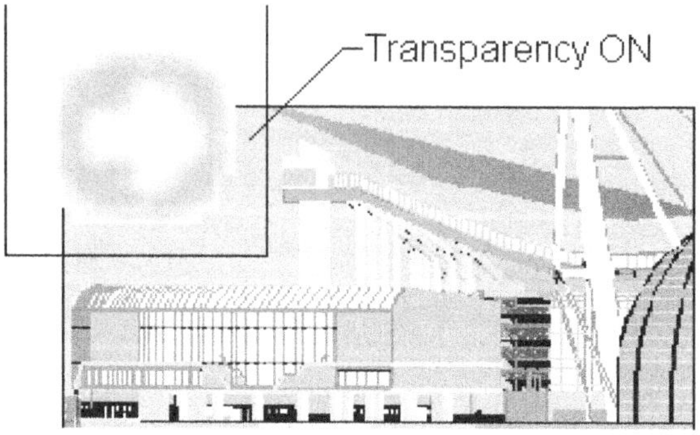

Figure 5-13 *Image after turning the transparency on*

Controlling the Display of Image Frames

Menu Bar: Modify > Object > Image > Frame **Command:** IMAGEFRAME
Toolbar: Reference > Image Frame

The **FRAME** tool is used to turn the image boundary on or off. This tool can be invoked from **Modify > Object > Image** menu. If the image boundary is off, the image cannot be selected with the pointing device and therefore cannot be accidentally moved or modified.

CHANGING THE DISPLAY ORDER

Ribbon: Home > Modify > Draw Order drop-down
Command: DRAWORDER/DR **Toolbar:** Draw Order

The tools in the **Draw Order** drop-down, refer to Figure 5-14, of the **Modify** panel are used to change the display order of the selected images and other objects.

If you choose the **Bring to Front** tool, the selected object will be moved to the front of all entities. If you choose the **Send to Back** tool, the selected object will be moved behind all entities. If you choose the **Bring Above Objects** tool, the selected object will be moved above the referenced objects. If you choose the **Send Under Objects** tool, the selected object will be moved under the referenced objects.

The **Bring Text to Front** tool can be used to bring entire text to the front of all entities. If you choose **Bring Dimensions to Front**, all dimensions will come to front of all the entities. The **Send Hatches to Back** tool is used to send all the hatches to the back of all entities.

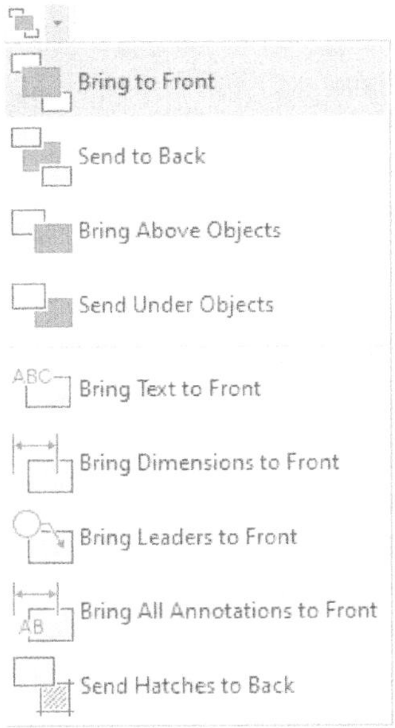

***Figure 5-14** Tools in the **Draw Order** drop-down*

Other Editing Operations

You can also perform other editing operations such as copy, move, and stretch to edit a raster image. Remember that you can also use the image as the trimming edge for trimming objects. However, you cannot trim an image. You can insert the raster image several times or make multiple copies of it. Each copy can have a different clipping boundary. You can also edit the image using grips. You can use the **Properties** palette to change the image layer, boundary linetype, and color, and perform other editing commands such as changing the scale, rotation, width, and height by entering new values in the respective edit boxes. You can also display an image or turn off the display by selecting options from the **Show image** drop-down list in the **Misc** field of the **Properties** palette. If you select **Yes**, the image is displayed and if you select **No**, the display of the image is turned off. You can turn off the display of the image when you do not need it, thus improving the performance.

Scaling Raster Images

The scale of the inserted image is determined by the actual size of the image and the unit of measurement (inches, feet, and so on). For example, if the image is 1" X 1.26" and you insert this image with a scale factor of 1, its size on the screen will be 1 by 1.26 AutoCAD units. If the scale factor is 5, the image will be five times larger. The image that you want to insert must contain the resolution information (DPI). If the image does not contain this information, AutoCAD treats the width of the image as one unit.

DWG CONVERT

Application Menu: Save As > DWG Convert **Command:** DWGCONVERT
Menu Bar: File > DWG Convert

The **DWG Convert** tool is used to convert a single or batch of the AutoCAD drawing files into any older version of AutoCAD drawing format. You can do the conversion by following the procedure given next.

Invoke the **DWG Convert** dialog box by choosing the **DWG Convert** tool from the **File** menu; the **DWG Convert** dialog box will be displayed, as shown in Figure 5-15. Choose the **Add file** button from the bottom of the **Files Tree** area; the **Select File** dialog box will be displayed. Next, browse to the required location, select the required file/files, and then choose the **Open** button; the selected files will be displayed in tree form in the **Files Tree** area of the **DWG Convert** dialog box. Also, a check box will be displayed on the left of each drawing file. By default, all the check boxes are selected. You can clear the check box corresponding to the files that are not to be converted. You can also view the selected files along with their details such as their path and location, version, size, date, and so on in the form of a table by choosing the **Files Table** tab. If you want to save the current file list, then choose the **Save list** button; the **Save Conversion List** dialog box will be displayed. Save the file list in the desired folder.

You can select the version of output file from the **Select a conversion setup** area; the description of the conversion setup will be displayed in the **Setup description** area. You can also specify the conversion settings, if required, by choosing the **Conversion Setups** button. This is discussed in the next head. Now, choose the **Convert** button located at the lower right corner of the dialog box; the **Conversion Package Creation is in Progress** window will be displayed and in a few moments the files will be converted. Exit the dialog box by choosing the **Close** button.

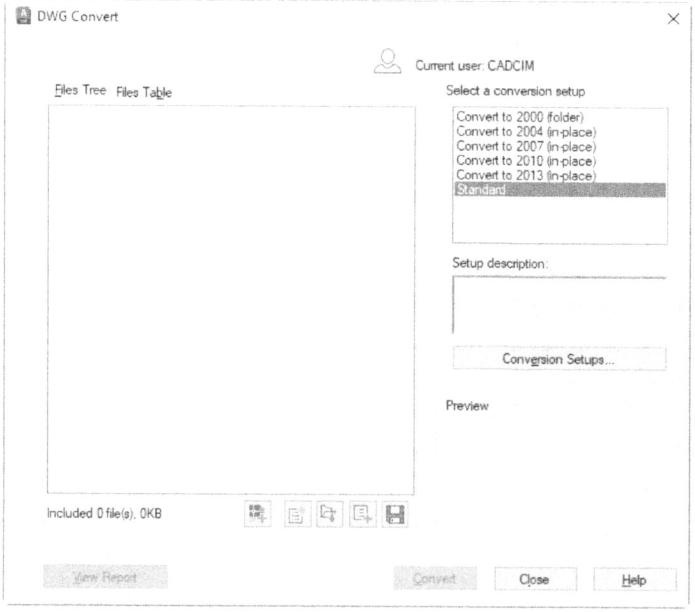

*Figure 5-15 The **DWG Convert** dialog box*

You can also open any previously saved file list by using the **Open list** button. If you choose this button, the **Open Conversion List** dialog box will be displayed. Browse to the required file and choose the **Open** button; all files in the conversion list will be imported in the **Files Tree** area of the **DWG Convert** dialog box. Later on, you can replace this list with a new list using the **Append list** button.

Conversion Setup Options

The **Conversion Setups** options are used to control the output of the files to be converted. To modify the conversion settings, choose the **Conversion Setups** button from the **DWG Convert** dialog box; the **Conversion Setups** dialog box will be displayed, as shown in Figure 5-16. The options in this dialog box are discussed next.

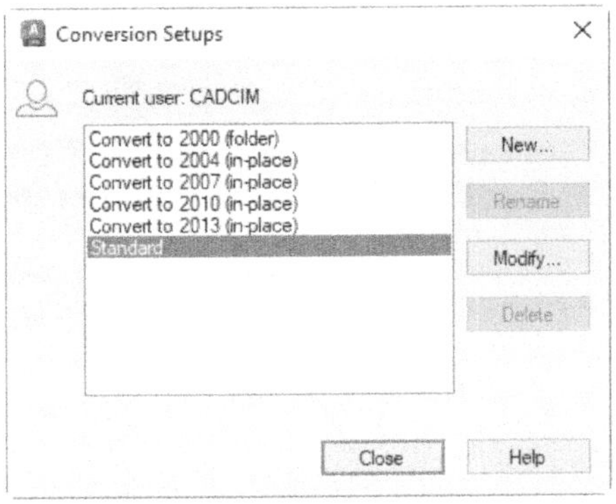

Figure 5-16 The ***Conversion Setups*** *dialog box*

New

This button is used to create a new conversion scheme. On choosing this button, the **New Conversion Setup** dialog box will be displayed, as shown in Figure 5-17. You can enter the name of new conversion setup in the **New Conversion setup name** edit box. Next, select an option from the **Based on** drop-down list. Finally, choose the **Continue** button; the **Modify Conversion Setup** dialog box will be displayed. This dialog box is discussed later in this chapter.

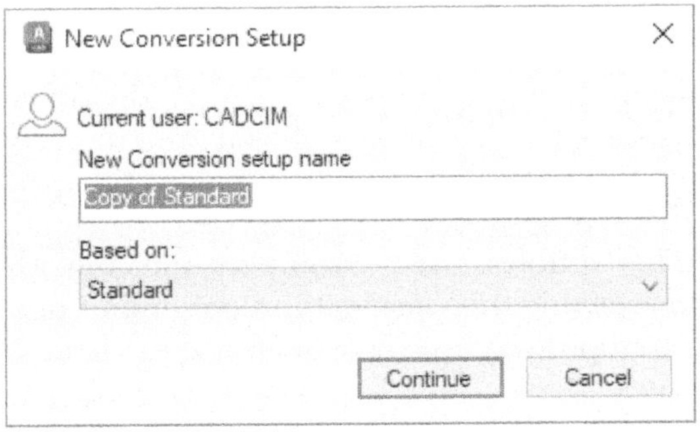

Figure 5-17 The ***New Conversion Setup*** *dialog box*

Rename

This button is used to rename the selected conversion setup.

Modify

This button is used to modify the existing conversion settings according to the desired output. On choosing the **Modify** button, the **Modify Conversion Setup** dialog box will be displayed, as shown in Figure 5-18. Using this dialog box, you can modify conversion settings. The options in this dialog box are discussed next.

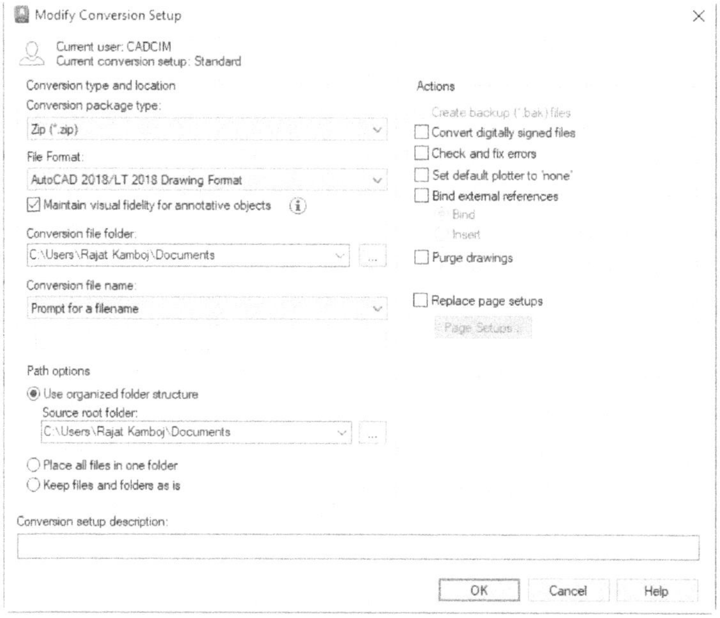

*Figure 5-18 The **Modify Conversion Setup** dialog box*

Conversion type and location Area

The options under the **Conversion package type** drop-down list in this area are discussed next.

In-place (overwrite files): This option is used if you want the converted files to be in the same directory, in which the source files are present. If you want to overwrite the existing files, this option also allows the software to overwrite the previous files with the converted new files.

Folder (set of files): This option is used if you want the converted files to be saved in the specified directory. On selecting this option, the **Conversion file folder** drop-down list will be activated. Using this drop-down list, you can browse to the desired folder where you want to save the converted files.

Zip (*.zip): This option is used to bind all converted drawing files into a zip file, which can be uncompressed to the specific location later.

Path options Area

The **Path options** area will be enabled when you select the **Folder (set of files)** or **Zip (*.zip)** option from the **Conversion package type** drop-down list. In the **Path options** area, there are three radio buttons that are explained next.

Use organized folder structure: On selecting this radio button, you can store the converted files in the specified folder in same organized way as they are present in the source folder (in **Source root folder** drop-down).

Place all files in one folder: On selecting this radio button, you can save all converted files in one folder which is specified as output folder.

Keep files and folder as is: On selecting this radio button, the files are saved in the way they were originally present. In other word, the hierarchy remains the same as of original file location.

Actions Area

In the **Actions** area, there are 8 check boxes. Description of these check boxes is given next.

Create backup(*.bak) files: This check box will be enabled only when the **In-place (overwrite files)** conversion package type is selected. If you select this check box, then the backup file will also be created with the converted file.

Convert digitally signed files: On selecting this check box, the digitally signed files will be included in the conversion list.

Check and fix errors: If you select this check box, the errors will automatically be fixed during the conversion.

Set default plotter to 'none': If you select this check box, the plotter for all converted files will be set to **None**.

Bind external references: You can bind the external referenced files with the converted drawing files using this check box. This option has two radio buttons, **Bind** and **Insert**. **Bind** is used to bind the external referenced file as external object. **Insert** is used to bind the external reference as internal object of the drawing.

Purge drawings: Select this check box if you want to purge the drawings.

Replace page setups: Select this check box if you want to replace the page setup of the converted drawing files with a pre-stored template. To get a pre-stored template, choose the **Page Setups** button after selecting the check box; the **Page Setups** dialog box will be displayed. Choose the **Browse** button, and then select a pre-stored template.

Conversion setup description Area

This area is located at the bottom of the dialog box. You can enter the description of the conversion setup in the **Conversion setup description** edit box in this area.

Delete

This button is used to delete any of the conversion setup in the list.

WORKING WITH POSTSCRIPT FILES

Application Menu: Export > Other Formats **Menu Bar:** File > Export
Command: EXPORT, PSOUT

PostScript is a page description language developed by Adobe Systems. It is mostly used in DTP (desktop publishing) applications. AutoCAD allows you to work with PostScript files. You can create and export PostScript files from AutoCAD, so that these files can be used for DTP applications. PostScript images have a higher resolution than raster images. The extension for these files is *.eps* (Encapsulated PostScript).

Creating PostScript Files

As just mentioned, any AutoCAD drawing file can be converted into a PostScript file. This can be accomplished by using the **PSOUT** command. When you invoke this command, the **Create PostScript File** dialog box is displayed, as shown in Figure 5-19. You can also use the **Export** tool to display the **Export Data** dialog box. The options are similar in both the dialog boxes.

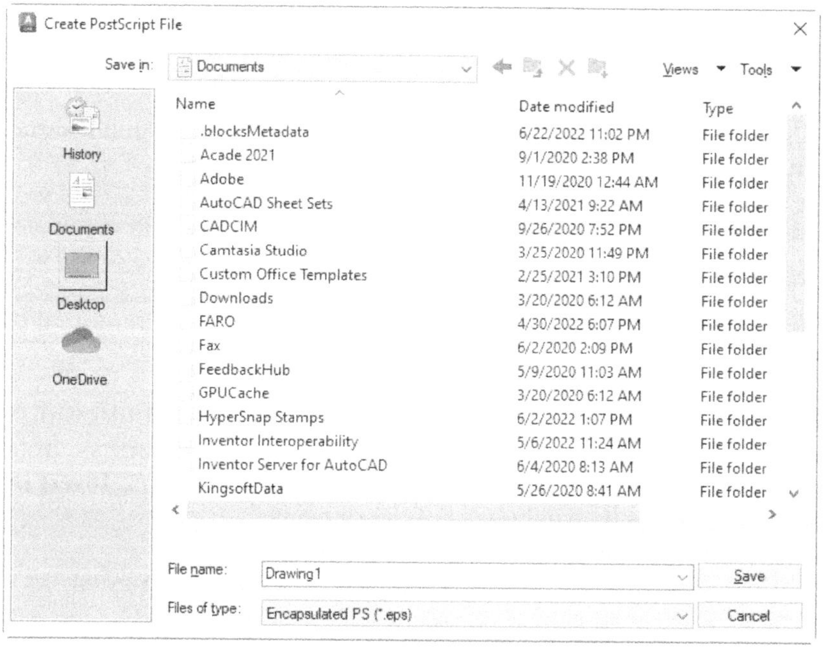

***Figure 5-19** The **Create PostScript File** dialog box*

In the **File name** edit box, enter the name of the PostScript (EPS) file you want to create. Select **Encapsulated PS (*.eps)** from the **Files of type** drop-down list. Next, choose the **Save** button to accept the default setting and create the PostScript file. You can also choose the **Options** option from the **Tools** flyout of the **Create PostScript File** dialog box to change the settings through the **PostScript Out Options** dialog box and then save the file. The **PostScript Out Options** dialog box, as shown in Figure 5-20, provides the options given next.

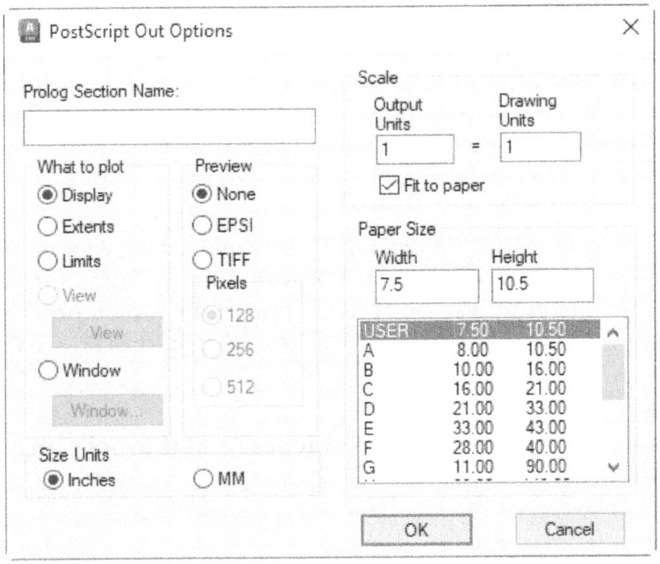

*Figure 5-20 The **PostScript Out Options** dialog box*

Prolog Section Name

In this edit box, you can assign a name for a prolog section to be read from the *acad.eps* file.

What to plot Area

The **What to plot** area of the dialog box has the following options:

Display: If you select this radio button when you are in the model space, the display in the current view is saved in the specified EPS file. Similarly, if you are in the layouts, the current viewport is saved in the specified EPS file.

Extents: If you use this option, the PostScript file will contain the section of the AutoCAD drawing that currently holds objects. In this way, this option is similar to the **Zoom Extents** option. If you add objects to the drawing, they are also included in the PostScript file to be created because the extents of the drawing are also altered. If you reduce the drawing extents by erasing, moving, or scaling objects, then you must use the **Zoom Extents** or **Zoom All** option. Only then does the **Extents** option of the **PSOUT** command calculate the extents of the drawing to be exported. If you are in the model space, the PostScript file is created in relation to the model space extents; if you are in the paper space, the PostScript file is created in relation to the paper space extents.

Limits: With this option, you can export the whole area specified by the drawing limits. If the current view is not the plan view [viewpoint (0,0,1)], the **Limits** option exports the area just as the **Extents** option would.

View: Any view created with the **VIEW** command can be exported with this radio button. This radio button will be available only when you have created a view using the **VIEW** command. Select the **View** radio button to invoke the **View Name** dialog box from where you can select the view.

Window: In this option, you need to specify the area to be exported with the help of a window. When this radio button is selected, the **Window** button is also available. Choose the **Window** button to display the **Window Selection** dialog box where you can choose the **Pick** button and then specify the two corners of the window on the screen. You can also enter the coordinates of the two corners in the **Window Selection** dialog box.

Preview Area

The **Preview** area of the dialog box has two types of formats to preview images: **EPSI** and **TIFF**. If you want a preview image with no format, select the **None** radio button. If you select **TIFF** or **EPSI**, you are required to enter the pixel resolution of the screen preview in the **Pixels** area. You can select a preview image size of 128 X 128, 256 X 256, or 512 X 512.

Size Units Area

In this area, you can set the paper size units to **Inches** or **MM** by selecting their corresponding radio buttons.

Scale Area

In this area, you can set an explicit scale by specifying how many drawing units are to be output per unit. You can select the **Fit to paper** check box so that the view to be exported is made as large as possible for the specified paper size.

Paper Size Area

You can select a size from the list or enter a new size in the **Width** and **Height** edit boxes to specify a paper size for the exported PostScript image.

OBJECT LINKING AND EMBEDDING (OLE)

With Windows, it is possible to work with different Windows-based applications by transferring information between them. You can edit and modify the information in the original Windows application, and then update this information in other applications. This is made possible by creating links between different applications and then updating those links, which in turn update or modify the information in the corresponding applications. This linking is a function of the OLE feature of Microsoft Windows. The OLE feature can also join together separate pieces of information from different applications into a single document. AutoCAD and other Windows-based applications such as Microsoft Word, Notepad, and Windows WordPad support the Windows OLE feature.

For the OLE feature, you should have a source document where the actual object is created in the form of a drawing or a document. This document is created in an application called a server application. AutoCAD for Windows and Paintbrush can be used as server applications. Now this source document is to be linked to (or embedded in) the compound (destination) document, which is created in a different application, known as the container application. AutoCAD for Windows, Microsoft Word, and Windows WordPad can be used as container applications.

Clipboard

The transfer of a drawing from one Windows application to another is performed by copying the drawing or the document from the server application to the Clipboard. The drawing or document is then pasted in the container application from the Clipboard. Hence, a Clipboard is used as a medium for storing the documents while transferring them from one Windows application to another. The drawing or the document on the Clipboard stays there until you copy a new drawing, which overwrites the previous one, or until you exit Windows. You can save the information present on the Clipboard with the *.clp* extension.

Object Embedding

You can use the embedding function of the OLE feature when you want to ensure that there is no effect on the source document even if the destination document has been changed through the server application. Once a document is embedded, it has no connection with the source. Although editing is always done in the server application, the source document remains unchanged. Embedding can be accomplished by means of the following steps. In this example, AutoCAD for Windows is the server application and MS Word is the container application.

1. Create a drawing in AutoCAD (the server application).

2. Open MS Word (container application).

3. It is preferable to arrange both the container and server windows so that both are visible, as shown in Figure 5-21.

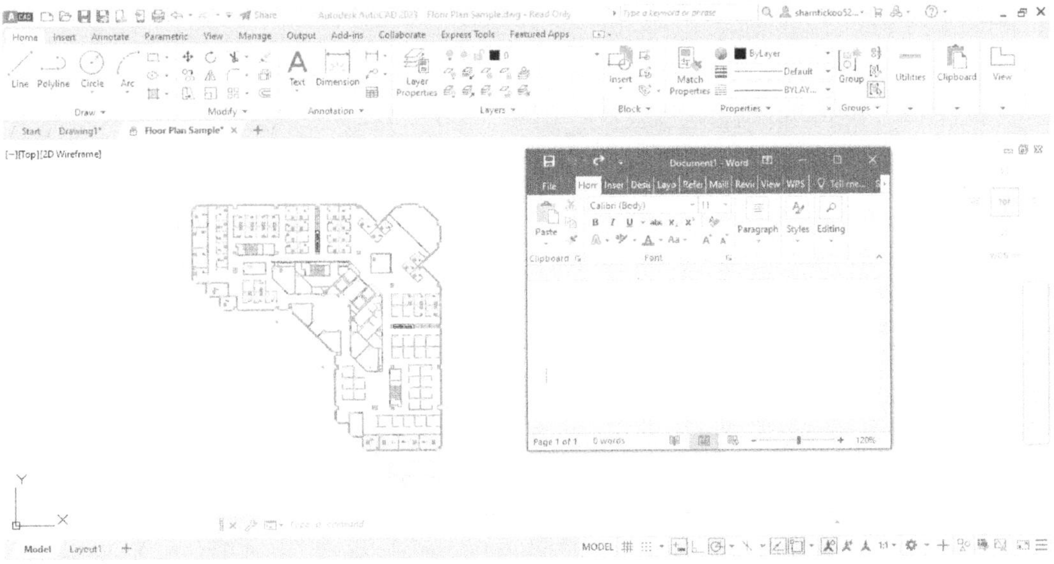

Figure 5-21 *AutoCAD graphics screen with the MS Word window*

4. In AutoCAD, copy the drawing using the Ctrl+C keys; the **copyclip** tool is invoked. This tool can be used to embed drawings. You can also invoke this tool from the **Edit** menu, or by entering **COPYCLIP** at the command prompt. The next prompt, **Select objects**, allows you to select the entities you want to transfer. You can either select the full drawing by entering

ALL or select some of the entities by selecting them. You can use any of the object selection methods for selecting objects. With this command, the selected objects are automatically copied to the Windows Clipboard.

5. After the objects are copied to the Clipboard, make the MS Word window active. To get the drawing from the Clipboard to the MS Word application (client), you need to paste it into the Word application. Choose the **Paste Special** tool from **Home > Clipboard > Paste** drop-down, refer to Figure 5-22; the **Paste Special** dialog box will be displayed, as shown in Figure 5-23. In this dialog box, select the **Paste** radio button (default) for embedding, and then choose the **OK** button. The drawing is now embedded in the MS Word window.

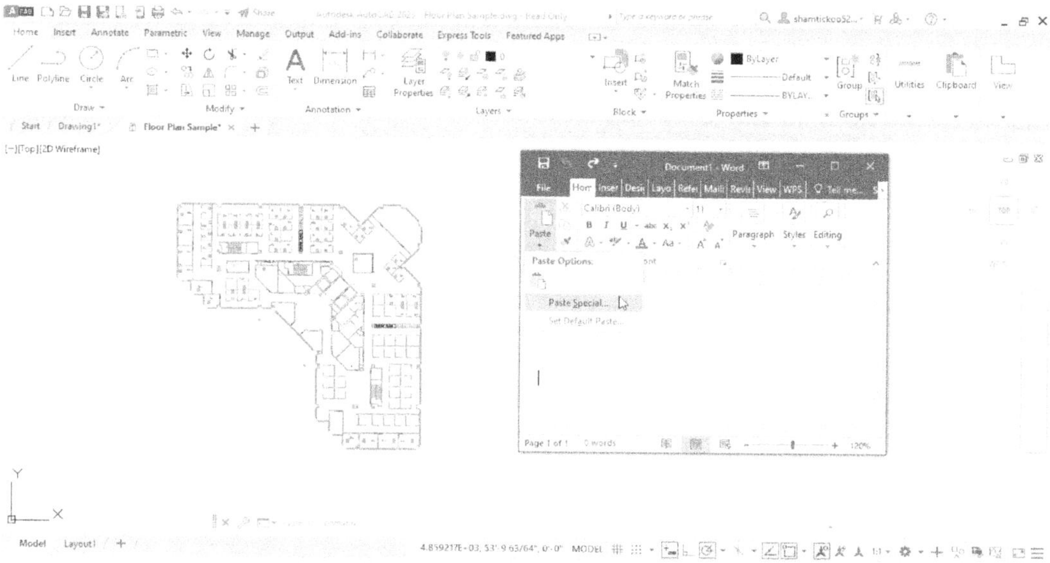

Figure 5-22 Pasting a drawing into the MS Word application

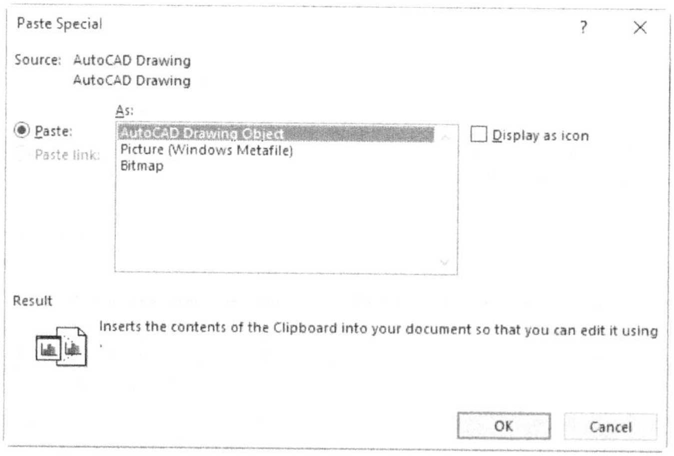

*Figure 5-23 The **Paste Special** dialog box*

6. Your drawing is now displayed in the MS Word window, but it may not be displayed at the proper position. You can get the drawing displayed in the current viewport by moving the scroll bar up or down in the MS Word window. You can also save your embedded drawing by choosing the **Save** button in MS Word. On doing so, the **Save As** dialog box is displayed where you can enter a file name. Save the file and then exit AutoCAD.

7. Now, you need to edit the embedded drawing. Editing is performed in the server application, which in this case is AutoCAD. You can get the embedded drawing into the server application (AutoCAD) directly from the container application (MS Word) by double-clicking on the drawing in MS Word. The other method of editing an embedded drawing is by right-clicking on it and then choosing **AutoCAD Drawing Object > Edit** from the shortcut menu.

8. Now, you are in AutoCAD, with your embedded drawing displayed on the screen, but as a temporary file with a file name such as [Drawing in Document]. Here, you can edit the drawing by changing the color and linetype or by adding and deleting the text, entities, and so on. In this example, the plate has been hatched.

9. After you have finished modifying your drawing, choose the **Update Microsoft Word** option from the **File** menu in the server (AutoCAD), refer to Figure 5-24. To display the menu bar, click on the down arrow in the **Quick Access Toolbar** and select **Show Menu Bar**. AutoCAD automatically updates the drawing in MS Word (container application). Now, you can exit this temporary file in AutoCAD.

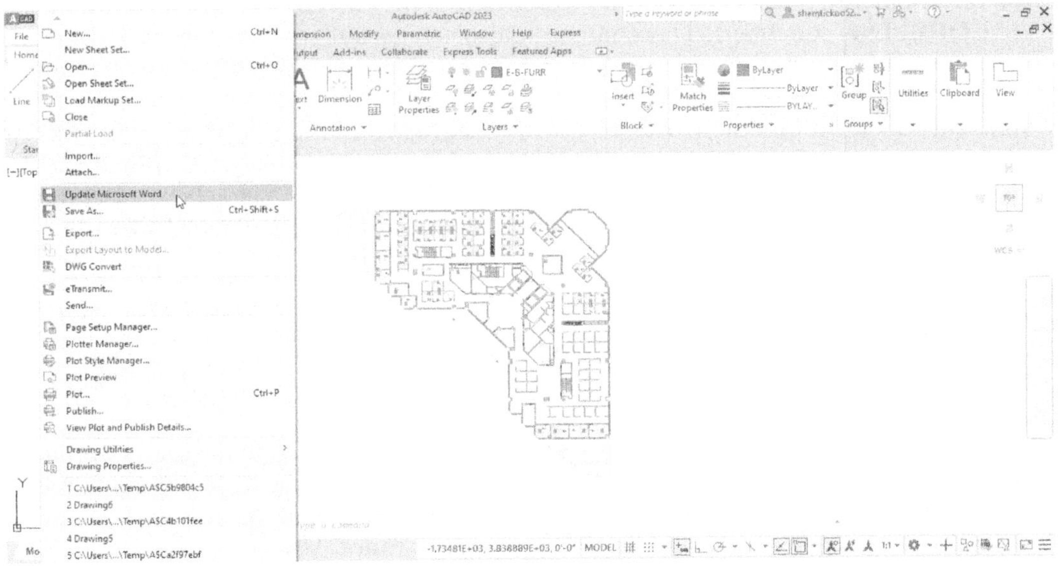

Figure 5-24 Updating the AutoCAD drawing in Microsoft Word

Note

Do not zoom or pan the drawing in the temporary file. If you do so, this will be included in the updating and the new file will display only that portion of the drawing that lies inside the original area.

10. This completes the embedding function. Now, you can exit the container application. While exiting it, a message box asking whether or not to save changes in MS Word is displayed.

Linking Objects

The linking function of OLE is similar to the embedding function. The only difference is that here a link is created between the source document and the destination document. If you edit the source, you can simply update the link, which automatically updates the client. This allows you to place the same document in a number of applications, and if you make a change in the source document, the clients will also change by simply updating the corresponding links. Consider AutoCAD for Windows to be the server application and MS Word to be the container application. Linking can be performed by means discussed next.

1. Open a drawing in the server application (AutoCAD). If you have created a new drawing, then you must save it before you can link it with the container application. Next, open MS Word (container application).

2. It is preferable to arrange both the container and the server windows so that both are visible.

3. In AutoCAD, choose the **Copy Link** option from the **Edit** menu of the menu bar to invoke the **COPYLINK** command. This command can be used for linking the drawing. This command copies all objects that are displayed in the current viewport directly to the Clipboard. Here, you cannot select objects for linking. If you want only a portion of the drawing to be linked, you can zoom into that view so that it is displayed in the current viewport prior to invoking the **COPYLINK** command. This command also creates a new view of the drawing having the name OLE1.

4. Make the MS Word window active. To get the drawing from the Clipboard to the MS Word (container) application, choose the **Paste Special** tool from **Home > Clipboard > Paste** drop-down; the **Paste Special** dialog box will be displayed. In this dialog box, select the **Paste link** radio button for linking. Choose the **OK** button. Note that the **Paste link** radio button in the **Paste Special** dialog box will not be available if you have not saved the drawing.

5. The drawing is now displayed in the MS Word window and is linked to the original drawing. You can also save your linked drawing by choosing the **Save** button from the **Quick Access Toolbar** in MS Word. It displays the **Save As** dialog box where you can enter a file name.

6. You can now edit your original drawing. Editing can be performed in the server application, which, in this case, is AutoCAD for Windows. You can edit the drawing by changing the color and linetype or by adding and deleting text, entities, and so on. Next, save your drawing in AutoCAD by using the **Save** tool. You can now exit AutoCAD.

7. You will notice that the drawing is automatically updated, and the changes made in the source drawing are present in the destination drawing also. If the drawing is not updated automatically, right-click on the drawing shown in MS word and then choose the **Update Link** option from the shortcut menu displayed. Automatic updating is possible if the **Automatic** radio button is selected in the **Links** dialog box, refer to Figure 5-25. The **Links** dialog box can be invoked by choosing **Linked AutoCAD Drawing Object > Links** from the shortcut menu displayed on right-clicking on the drawing in the Word application.

8. Exit the container application after saving the updated file.

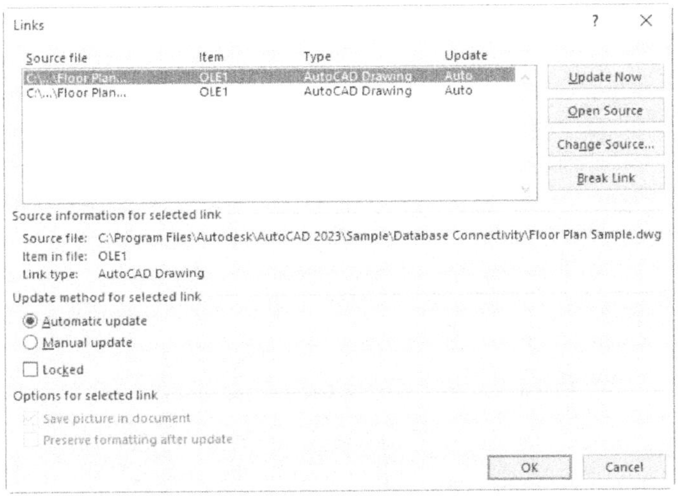

***Figure 5-25** The **Links** dialog box*

Note

The dialog box may be different in your case as it depends on the version of MS Word being used currently.

Linking Information to AutoCAD

You can also embed and link information from a server application into an AutoCAD drawing. You can also drag selected OLE objects from another application into AutoCAD, provided this application supports Microsoft ActiveX and the application is running and visible on the screen. Dragging and dropping is like cutting and pasting. If you press the Ctrl key while you drag the object, it is copied to AutoCAD. Dragging and dropping an OLE object into AutoCAD embeds it into AutoCAD.

Linking Objects to AutoCAD

Start any server application such as MS Word and open a document in it. Select the information you wish to use in AutoCAD with your pointing device and choose the **Copy** tool to copy this data to the Clipboard. Open the AutoCAD drawing to which you want to link this data. Choose the **Paste Special** tool from **Home > Clipboard > Paste** drop-down or use the **PASTESPEC** command; the **Paste Special** dialog box will be displayed, as shown in Figure 5-26. In the **As** list box, select the data format you wish to use. Select the **Paste Link** radio button to paste the contents of the Clipboard into the current drawing. If you select the **Paste** radio button, the data will be embedded and not linked. Choose the **OK** button to exit the dialog box. Specify the insertion point; the data will be displayed in the drawing.

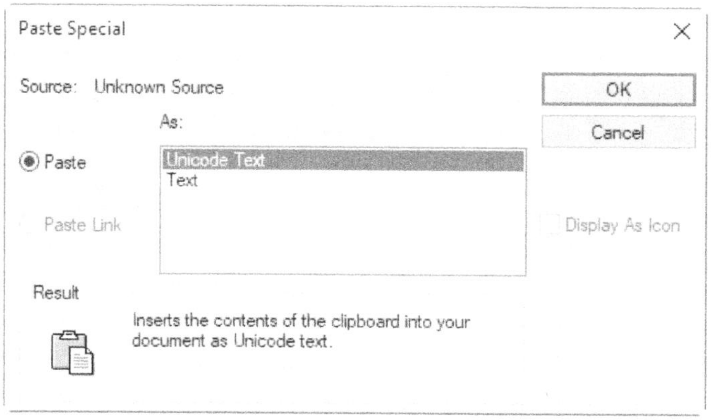

***Figure 5-26** The **Paste Special** dialog box*

You can insert objects in the drawing by choosing the **OLE Object** tool from the **Data** panel of the **Insert** tab, or by choosing the **OLE Object** tool in the **Insert** toolbar. This command links an entire file to a drawing from within AutoCAD. On invoking this command, the **Insert Object** dialog box is displayed, as shown in Figure 5-27.

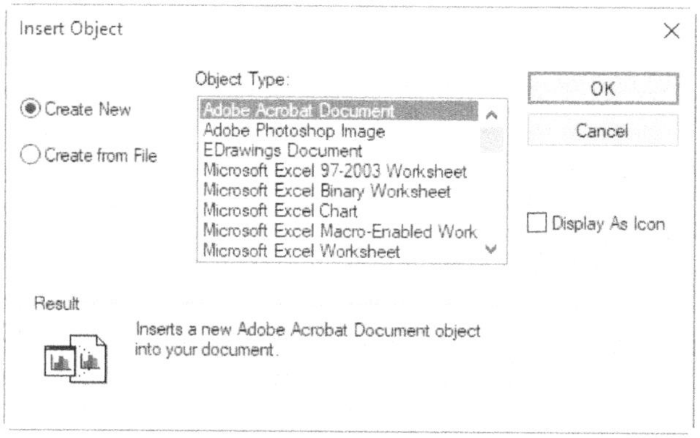

***Figure 5-27** The **Insert Object** dialog box*

Select the **Create from File** radio button. Also, select the **Link** check box. Choosing the **Browse** button displays the **Browse** dialog box. Select a file you want to link from the list box or enter a name in the **File name** edit box and choose the **Open** button. The path of the file is displayed in the **File** edit box of the **Insert Object** dialog box. If you select the **Display As Icon** check box, an icon is displayed in the dialog box as well as in the drawing. Choose the **OK** button to exit the dialog box; the selected file is linked to the AutoCAD drawing.

Whenever the server document changes, AutoCAD updates links automatically. But, you can use the **Links** dialog box to change these settings, refer to Figure 5-28. This dialog box can be displayed by choosing the **OLE Links** tool from the **Edit** menu. In the **Links** dialog box, select the link you want to update and then choose the **Update Now** button. Next, choose the **Close** button. If the server file location changes or if it is renamed, you can choose the **Change Source** button in the **Links** dialog box to display the **Change Source** dialog box. In this dialog box, locate the server file name and location and choose the **Open** button. You can also choose the **Break Link** button in the **Links** dialog box to disconnect the inserted information from the server application. This is done when the linking between the two is no longer required.

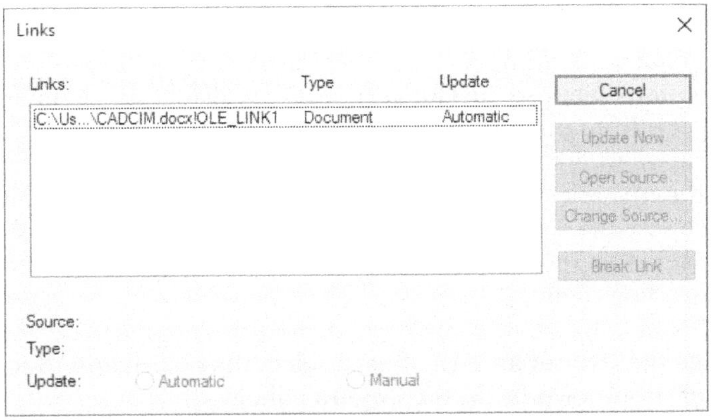

*Figure 5-28 The **Links** dialog box*

Embedding Objects into AutoCAD

Open the server application and select the data you want to embed into the AutoCAD drawing. Copy this data to the Clipboard by choosing the **Copy** tool in the toolbar or **Copy** from the **Edit** menu. Open the AutoCAD drawing and choose **Paste** from the AutoCAD **Edit** menu. You can also use the **PASTECLIP** command. Specify the insertion point; the selected information is embedded into the AutoCAD drawing.

You can also create and embed an object into an AutoCAD drawing. To do so, choose the **OLE Object** tool from the **Data** panel of the **Insert** tab; the **Insert Object** dialog box will be invoked. In this dialog box, select the **Create New** radio button and select the application you wish to use from the **Object Type** list box. Choose the **OK** button, the selected application opens. Now, you can create the information you wish to insert in the AutoCAD drawing and save it before closing the application. You can edit information embedded in the AutoCAD drawing by double-clicking on the inserted OLE object; the server application will open. The modifications made in the server application get automatically reflected in the AutoCAD drawing.

Working with OLE Objects

Select an OLE object and right-click to display a shortcut menu. Next, choose the **Properties** option from the shortcut menu; the **PROPERTIES** palette will be displayed. Specify a new height value and a new width value in the **Height** and **Width** edit boxes in the **Geometry** area. Enter a value in percentage of the current values in the **Scale height %** and **Scale width %** edit boxes. If you select the **Yes** option in the **Lock aspect** field, whenever you change the height or the width from the **Scale height %** and **Scale width %** edit boxes, the respective width or height changes automatically to maintain the aspect ratio. If you want to change only the height or the width, select **No** for this field.

The pointing device can be used to modify and scale an OLE object in the AutoCAD drawing. Selecting the object displays the object frame and handles. These handles allow you to move and stretch a frame. Stretching the object's frame does not scale objects proportionately.

Select an OLE object and right-click to display a shortcut menu. You can choose **Clipboard > Cut** to remove an object from a drawing and paste it on the Clipboard. The **Copy** option is used to place a copy of the selected object on the Clipboard. The **Erase** option is used to remove an object from a drawing but it does not place the object on the Clipboard. Choose the **OLE** option from the shortcut menu; a cascading menu will be displayed containing the **Open**, **Reset**, **Text Size**, and **Convert** options. Choose the **Convert** option to display the **Convert** dialog box where you can convert objects from one type to another. Choose the **Open** option to open an object in the Server application where you can edit and update it in the current drawing. Choose the **Reset** option to restore the selected OLE objects to their original size, that is, the size they were in when inserted. Choose the **Text Size** option to resize the text. You can set the draw order of the object by first invoking a shortcut menu and then choosing the corresponding option from the **Draw Order** cascading menu.

If you want to change the layer of an OLE object, select the object, and then select the required layer from the **Layer** drop-down list in the **Layers** panel.

The **OLEHIDE** system variable controls the display of OLE objects in AutoCAD. The default value is 0, which makes all OLE objects visible. The different values and their effects are as follows:

0	All OLE objects are visible
1	OLE objects are visible in paper space only
2	OLE objects are visible in model space only
3	No OLE objects are visible

The **OLEHIDE** system variable affects both screen display and printing.

SHARING DRAWING VIEWS

Ribbon: Collaborate > Share > Shared Views **Application Menu:** Publish > Share View
Command: SHAREDVIEWS

The **Shared Views** tool is used to share designs with internal and external stakeholders without releasing the original drawing files. With the introduction of this tool, it is no more required to publish DWF or PDF format files or email them whenever you need to share the data. Using this tool, you can extract views and data from the drawing and store them in the cloud, generate a link. You can share this link with others to view the design on a browser and leave comments from any web-enabled devices such as desktop, tablet, or mobile.

After the link is generated and shared, the recipients can view, review, measure, comment on, and mark up the design right from the Autodesk Viewer in their web browser, and can share their feedback. You can access that feedback from within AutoCAD. Note that, shared views automatically expire after 30 days, but you can extend or terminate the link at any time.

Choose the **Shared Views** tool from the **Share** panel of the **Collaborate** tab in the **Ribbon**; the **SHARED VIEWS** palette will be displayed, refer to Figure 5-29.

Figure 5-29 *The **SHARED VIEWS** palette*

Now, choose the **New Shared View** button from the **SHARED VIEWS** palette; the **Share View** dialog box will be displayed, refer to Figure 5-30.

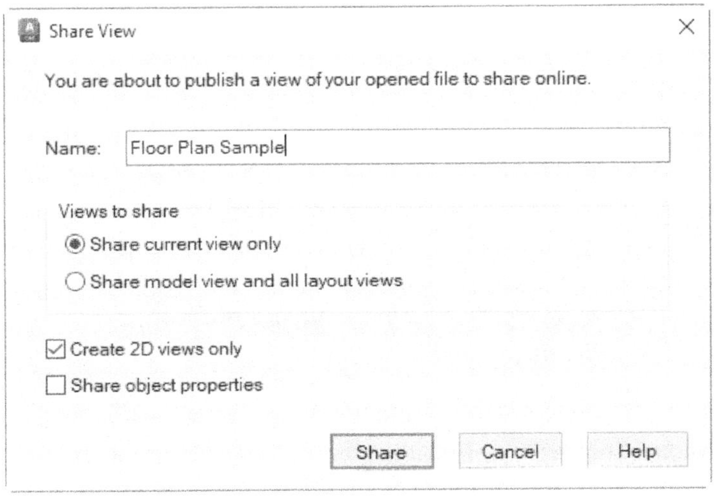

Figure 5-30 *The **Share View** dialog box*

The options in this dialog box are discussed next.

Name

This edit box is used to specify the name of the shared view. The name can have up to 255 characters and can include letters, numbers, blank spaces, and any special character which is not being used by the operating system or the program for other purposes.

Views to share

The options in this area allow you to publish a representation of the current space or the entire drawing for online viewing and sharing. This facilitates communication and collaboration with stakeholders without sharing the source DWG files. The options in this area are discussed next.

Share current view only

This radio button is selected by default and allows you to publish the unclipped extents of model space or the current layout.

Share model view and all layout views

If you select this radio button, the unclipped extents of model space and all layouts will be published.

Create 2D views only

This check box is selected by default and limits the view creation to 2D objects only.

Share object properties

If you select this check box, the object properties will also be extracted along with the view creation.

After selecting the required options in the **Share View** dialog box, choose the **Share** button; the **Share View - Processing Ready to Start** message box will be displayed, refer to Figure 5-31.

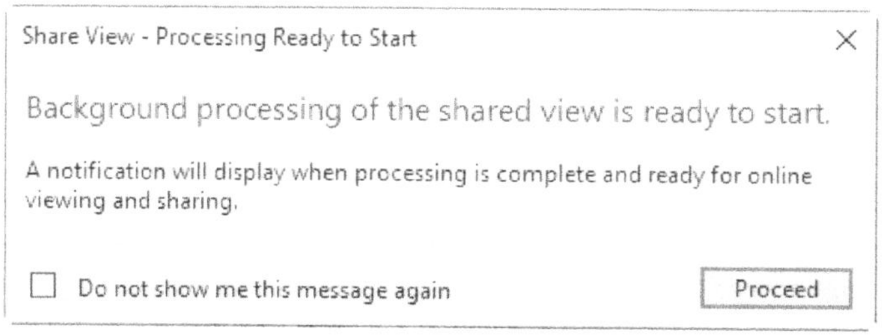

Figure 5-31 *The **Share View - Processing Ready to Start** message box*

Choose the **Proceed** button from this message box. Once the sharing process gets completed, the **Share View Upload Complete** notification bubble appears, refer to Figure 5-32.

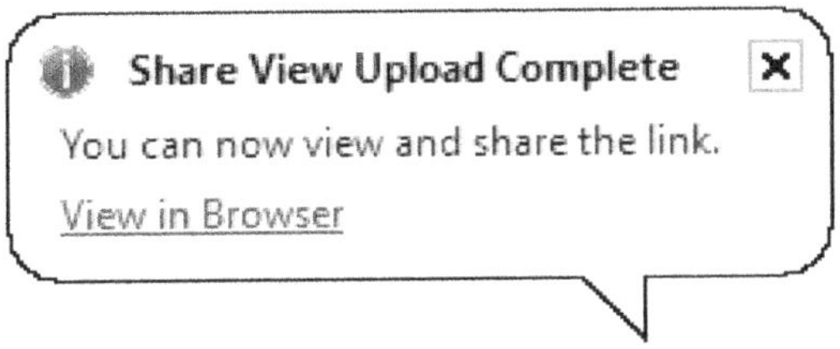

Figure 5-32 *The* ***Share View Upload Complete*** *notification bubble*

Click on the **View in Browser** link in this notification bubble; the **Autodesk Viewer** window will be displayed, refer to Figure 5-33.

Figure 5-33 *The* ***Autodesk Viewer*** *window*

Choose the **Share** button available at the right in this window; the **Sign in to share** palette will be displayed. Sign in to your Autodesk account; the **Share** palette will be displayed along with the shareable link of the file, refer to Figure 5-34.

Figure 5-34 *The* ***Share*** *palette along with the link*

Now, choose the **Copy** button from the **Share** palette; the link will be copied to the clipboard and can be shared with anyone. Once the sharing process gets completed, the shared file is displayed in the **SHARED VIEWS** palette. If the shared file is not displayed automatically, then choose the **Refresh** button available at the top in the **SHARED VIEWS** palette.

Self-Evaluation Test

Answer the following questions and then compare them to those given at the end of this chapter:

1. You can import a DXB file into an AutoCAD drawing file by using the __________ command.

2. The __________ system variable controls the display of OLE objects in AutoCAD.

3. If you import a DXB file into an old drawing, the settings of layers, blocks, and so on of the file being imported are __________ by the settings of the file into which you are importing the DXB file.

4. The __________ is used as a medium of storing documents while transferring them from one Windows application to the other.

5. You can get an embedded drawing into the Server application directly from the container application by __________ on the drawing.

6. The **Copy** tool copies a drawing from the __________ to the Clipboard.

7. The DXF file format generates a text file in ASCII code. (T/F)

8. You can directly open a DXF file in AutoCAD by using the **Open** tool. (T/F)

9. An image attached to AutoCAD cannot be detached. (T/F)

10. A file in the container application is automatically modified only when a link is maintained between the server application and the container application. (T/F)

Review Questions

Answer the following questions:

1. Which of the following tools can be used to open a DXF format file?

   (a) **Open** (b) **New**
   (c) **Save** (d) None of these

2. Which of the following tools is used to add an image to the drawing as an external reference?

   (a) **Attach** (b) **Insert**
   (c) **Adjust** (d) **Create Block**

3. In which of the following panels, the options are used to modify the brightness of an image?

   (a) **Options** (b) **Visual Styles**
   (c) **Clipping** (d) **Adjust**

4. The __________ tool is used to modify frames by retaining only the desired portion of the images.

5. The __________ tool is used to create an ASCII format file with the *.dxf* extension from the AutoCAD drawing files.

6. Binary DXF files are __________ efficient and occupy only 75 percent of the ASCII DXF file.

7. File access for files in binary format is __________ than for the same file in ASCII format.

8. If the **OLEHIDE** system variable value is __________, the OLE objects are visible in the paper space only.

9. When you select an image file to attach, the __________ dialog box is displayed where you can define the insertion point, scale factor, and rotation angle for the image.

10. The clipping boundary for the raster images can be of __________ or the __________ shape.

11. In AutoCAD, you can clip the boundary of an image and give it the desired shape. (T/F)

12. The scanned files can be imported into the current session of AutoCAD using the **Attach** tool. (T/F)

13. You can export an AutoCAD drawing into 3D Studio MAX. (T/F)

14. Raster images can be attached using the **Attach** tool. (T/F)

Exercise 1

In this exercise, you will create a cup and a plate, refer to Figure 5-35 for dimensions. Assume the missing dimensions. Below the cup and plate, enter the following text in MS Word: **These objects are drawn in AutoCAD**. Then using OLE, paste the text into the current drawing.

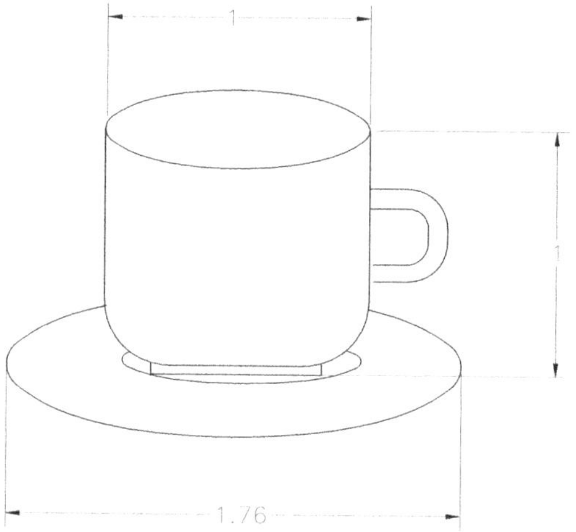

Figure 5-35 Dimensions for Exercise 1

Answers to Self-Evaluation Test

1. DXBIN, **2. OLEHIDE**, **3.** overruled, **4.** Clipboard, **5.** double-clicking, **6.** current display, **7.** T, **8.** T, **9.** F, **10.** T

Chapter 6

The User Coordinate System

Learning Objectives

After completing this chapter, you will be able to:

- *Understand the concept of World Coordinate System (WCS)*
- *Understand the concept of User Coordinate System*
- *Control the display of UCS icon*
- *Change the current UCS icon type*
- *Use the UCS command*
- *Dynamically move and align the UCS*
- *Understand different options for changing UCS using the UCS tool*
- *Change UCS using the Dynamic UCS button*
- *Manage UCS through the UCS dialog box*
- *Understand different system variables related to the UCS and the UCS icon*

Key Terms

- *UCS Icon*
- *UCS*
- *UCS Manager*

THE USER COORDINATE SYSTEM (UCS)

When you start a new drawing in AutoCAD, the world coordinate system (WCS) is applied by default. The objects you draw use the WCS to locate itself in the drawing space. In WCS, the *X*, *Y*, and *Z* coordinates of any point are measured with respect to the fixed origin (0,0,0). By default, this origin is located at the lower left corner of the screen, and by nature this coordinate system is fixed and can not be moved. Generally, 2D drawings, wireframe models, and surface models can be created in WCS but in the case of solid models it is not possible to keep the origin and the orientation of the *X*, *Y*, and *Z* axes at the same place every time. The reason for this is that in case you want to create a feature on the top face of an existing model you will need to shift the working plane to the top face of the model. This can be done by using the Elevation option of the **ELEV** command, refer to Figure 6-1. But, on using the **ELEV** command, it is not possible to create a feature on the faces other than the top and bottom faces of an existing model.

This problem can be solved by using the user coordinate system (UCS). Using the **UCS** command, you can relocate and reorient the origin and *X*, *Y*, and *Z* axes and establish your own coordinate system, depending on your requirement. The UCS is mostly used in 3D drawings, where you may need to specify points that vary from each other along the *X*, *Y*, and *Z* axes. It is also useful for relocating the origin or rotating the *X* and *Y* axes in 2D work, such as ordinate dimensioning, drawing auxiliary views, or controlling the hatch alignment. The UCS and its icon can be modified using the **UCSICON** and **UCS** commands. After reorienting the UCS, you can create a feature on any of the face of an existing model, refer to Figure 6-2.

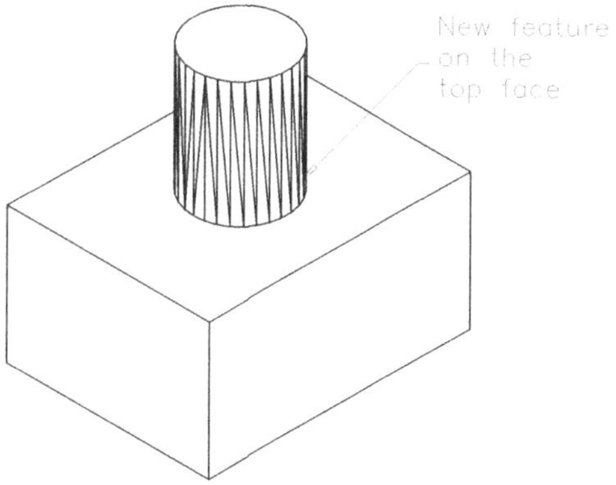

Figure 6-1 *Creating a new feature on the top face*

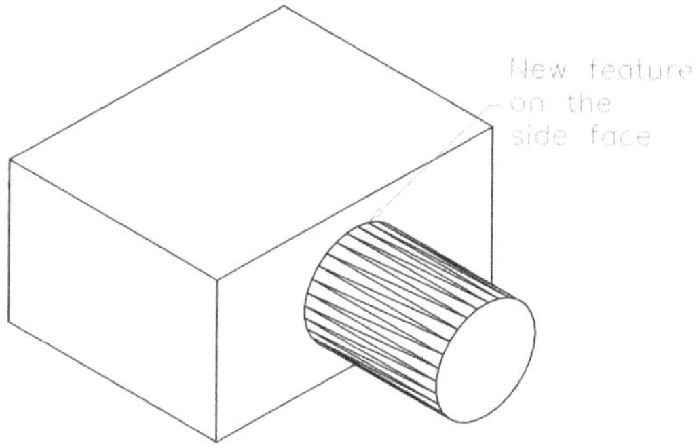

Figure 6-2 *Creating a new feature on the side face*

CONTROLLING THE VISIBILITY OF THE UCS ICON

Ribbon: View > Viewport Tools > UCS Icon
Menu Bar: View > Display > UCS Icon > On **Command:** UCSICON

The **UCS Icon** tool is used to control the visibility and location of the UCS icon, which is a geometric representation of the directions of the current *X*, *Y*, and *Z* axes. AutoCAD displays different UCS icons in model space and paper space, as shown in Figures 6-3 and 6-4. By default, the UCS icon is displayed near the bottom left corner of the drawing area. You can change the location and visibility of this icon using the **UCSICON** command. The prompt sequence for the **UCSICON** command is given next.

Enter an option [ON/OFF/All/Noorigin/ORigin/Selectable/Properties] <ON>: *You can specify any option or press Enter to accept the default option.*

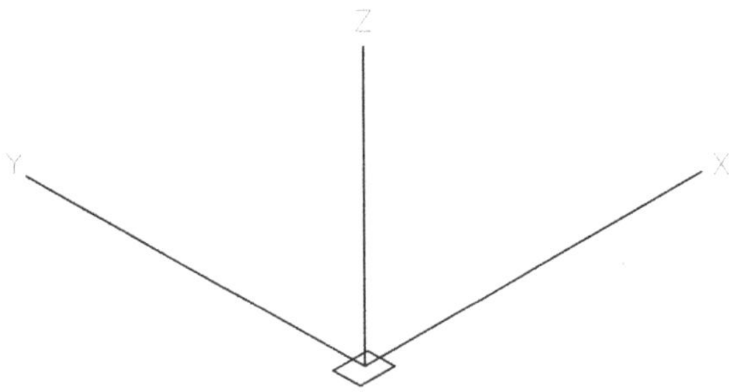

Figure 6-3 *The UCS icon in the Model space*

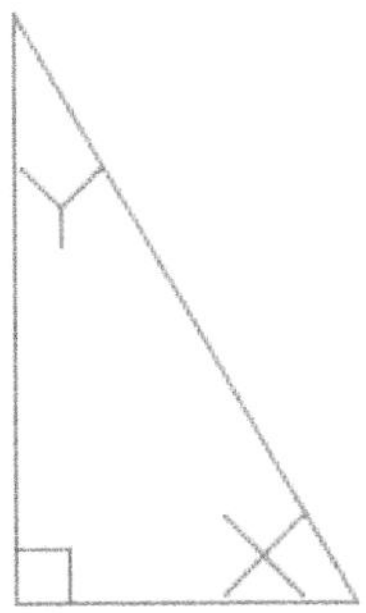

Figure 6-4 *The UCS icon in the Paper space*

ON

This option is used to display the UCS icon on the screen. You can also display the UCS icon by choosing the **Show UCS Icon** tool from the **Show UCS** drop-down list of **Coordinates** panel in the **Home** tab.

OFF

This option is used to make the UCS icon invisible from the screen. When you choose this option, the UCS icon will no longer be displayed on the screen. You can again turn on the display using the **ON** option of the **UCSICON** command. Alternatively, choose the **Hide UCS Icon** tool from the **Show UCS** drop-down list of **Coordinates** panel in the **Home** tab to make the UCS icon invisible.

All

This option is used to apply changes to the UCS icon in all active viewports. If this option is not used, the changes will be applied only to the current viewport.

Noorigin

This option is used to display the UCS icon at the lower left corner of the viewport, irrespective of the actual location of the origin of the current UCS.

ORigin

This option is used to place the UCS icon at the origin of the current UCS. You can also choose the **Show UCS Icon at Origin** tool from the **Show UCS** drop-down list of the **Coordinates** panel in the **Home** tab. Alternatively, type **UCSICON** at the command prompt and press enter. Next, select the **ORigin** option from the options displayed.

Note

You can switch into different workspaces using the ***Workspace Switching*** *drop-down list available at the right in the* ***Status Bar****.*

Selectable

This option allows you to control the selection of UCS. By default, UCS is selectable.

Properties

When you select this option, the **UCS Icon** dialog box will be displayed, as shown in Figure 6-5. You can also display this dialog box by choosing the **UCS Icon, Properties** tool from the **Coordinates** panel in the **Home** tab. Alternatively, place the cursor over the UCS Icon in the drawing area and right-click; a shortcut menu will be displayed. Choose **UCS Icon Settings > Properties** from the shortcut menu; the **UCS Icon** dialog box will be displayed. The options in this dialog box are discussed next.

UCS icon style Area

The options in this area are discussed next.

3D: This button is selected by default. As a result, the 3D UCS icon will be displayed in the model space.

2D: If this radio button is selected, the 2D UCS icon will be displayed instead of the 3D UCS icon, refer to Figure 6-6.

Line width. This drop-down list is used to specify the line width of the 3D UCS icon. The default value for the line width is 1. Note that this drop-down list will not be activated if the **2D** radio button is selected.

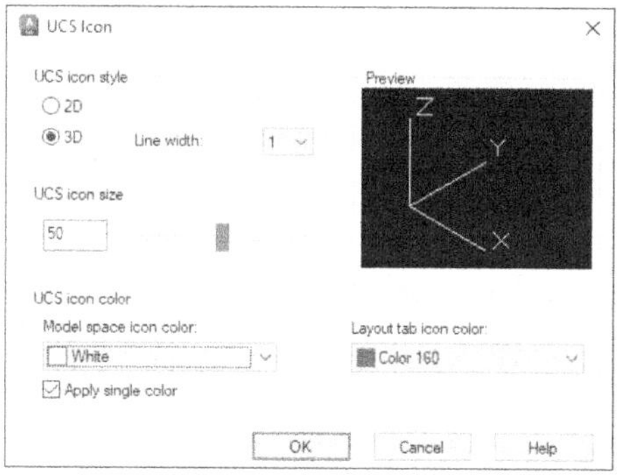

Figure 6-5 *The* ***UCS Icon*** *dialog box*

Figure 6-6 *2D UCS icon at the World position*

UCS icon size Area

The edit box and slider bar provided in this area are used to control the size of the UCS icon. You can specify values ranging from 5 to 95 either by entering values in the edit box or by adjusting the sliding bar. The size of the UCS icon is proportional to the viewport size as the value entered is the percentage of the viewport size.

UCS icon color Area

The **UCS icon color** area has two drop-down lists, **Model space icon color** and **Layout tab icon color**. The options in these drop-down lists are used to change the color of the UCS icon. By default, the color selected in the **Model space icon color** drop-down list is **White** and in the **Layout tab icon color** drop-down list is **Color 160**. You can assign any color to the UCS icon. By default, there are seven colors in first and eight colors in second drop-down list. However, you can also select a color from the **Select Color** dialog box which will be displayed after you select the **Select Color** option from the **Model space icon color** drop-down list or the **Layout tab icon color** drop-down list.

DEFINING THE NEW UCS

Ribbon: Visualize > Coordinates > UCS	**Toolbar:** UCS
Menu Bar: Tools > New UCS	**Command:** UCS

The **UCS** tool is used to set a new coordinate system by shifting the working plane (*XY* plane) to the desired location. For some views of the drawing, it is better to have the origin of measurements at some other point on or relative to your drawing objects. This makes locating the features and dimensioning the objects easier. The change in the UCS can be viewed by the change in the position and orientation of the UCS icon, which is placed by default at the lower left corner of the drawing window. The origin and orientation of a coordinate system can be redefined by using the **UCS** command. Alternatively, choose the **UCS** tool from the **Coordinates** panel of the **Visualize** tab. The prompt sequence after choosing this tool is given next:

Current ucs name: *WORLD*
Specify origin of UCS or [Face/NAmed/OBject/Previous/View/World/X/Y/Z/ZAxis] <World>: *Select an option.*

If the **UCSFOLLOW** system variable is set to 0, any change in the UCS will not affect the drawing view.

If you choose the default option of the **UCS** tool, you can establish a new coordinate system by specifying a new origin point, a point on the positive side of the new *X* axis, and a point on the positive side of the new *Y* axis. The direction of the *Z* axis is determined by applying the right-hand rule, about which you will learn in the next chapter. This option changes the orientation of the UCS to any angled surface. The prompt sequence that will follow is given next.

Specify origin of UCS or [Face/NAmed/OBject/Previous/View/World/X/Y/Z/ZAxis] <World>: *Specify the origin point of the new UCS.*
Specify point on X-axis or <accept>: *Specify a point on the positive portion of the X axis.*
Specify point on the XY plane or <accept>: *Specify a point on the positive portion of the Y axis to define the orientation of the UCS completely.*

In AutoCAD, you can directly manipulate the UCS as per your requirement. This implies that you can easily move the origin of UCS, align the UCS with objects, or rotate it around X, Y, and Z axis without invoking the UCS command.

You can also move the UCS and place it at the desired location without using any command. To do so, select the UCS; the grips are displayed on it. Place the cursor on the rectangular grip displayed at the intersection of three axes of UCS; a shortcut menu will be displayed, as shown in Figure 6-7.

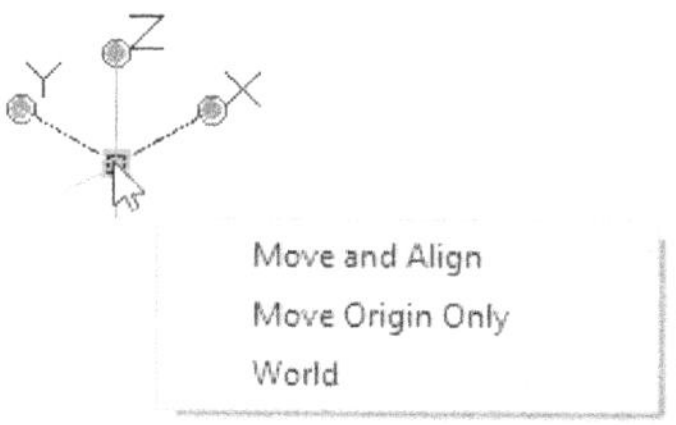

Figure 6-7 *UCS shortcut menu*

Choose the **Move and Align** option from the shortcut menu; the UCS will be displayed attached to the cursor. You can move the UCS to any point but you can align it only with the face of a 3D object, surface, or mesh. To align the UCS, move it to any point on the face of a 3D object, surface, or mesh; the face gets highlighted and the UCS automatically aligns with the orientation of that face, surface, or mesh, as shown in Figure 6-8.

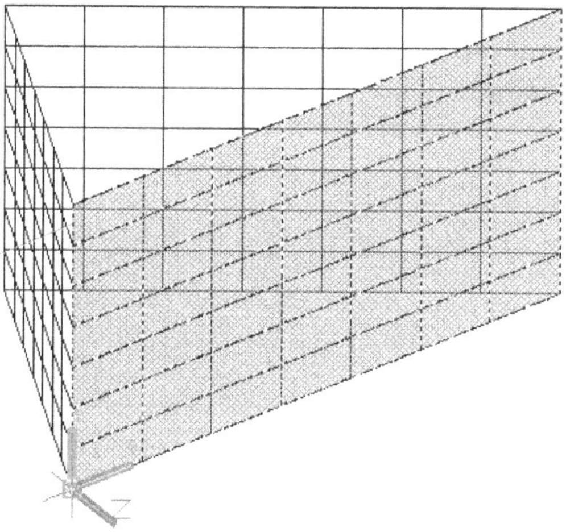

Figure 6-8 *UCS aligned to the highlighted face*

In case of a curved surface, the UCS will get aligned in such a way that the Z-axis becomes normal to the surface at the specified point. After aligning the UCS to the selected face, you can change the direction of X axis, Y axis, or Z axis dynamically. You can also use the shortcut menu displayed on placing the cursor on the X, Y, or Z grip.

If you choose **World** from the UCS shortcut menu, then the UCS will move and align to the World Coordinate System. The World Coordinate System is discussed next.

Note

Depending upon the type of UCS required, you can choose the corresponding tools from the ***Coordinates*** *panel of the* ***Home*** *tab.*

A null response to the point on the *X* or *Y* axis prompt will lead to a coordinate system, in which the *X* or *Y* axis of the new UCS is parallel to that of the previous UCS.

W (World) Option

Using this option, you can set the current UCS back to the WCS, which is the default coordinate system. When the UCS is placed at the world position, a small rectangle is displayed at the point where all the three axes meet in the UCS icon, refer to Figure 6-9 (a). If the UCS is moved from its default position, this rectangle is no longer displayed, indicating that the UCS is not at the world position, as shown in Figure 6-9(b).

Note

If 2D UCS icon is selected instead of 3D UCS icon and if the UCS is not at the world position; the W icon will not be displayed.

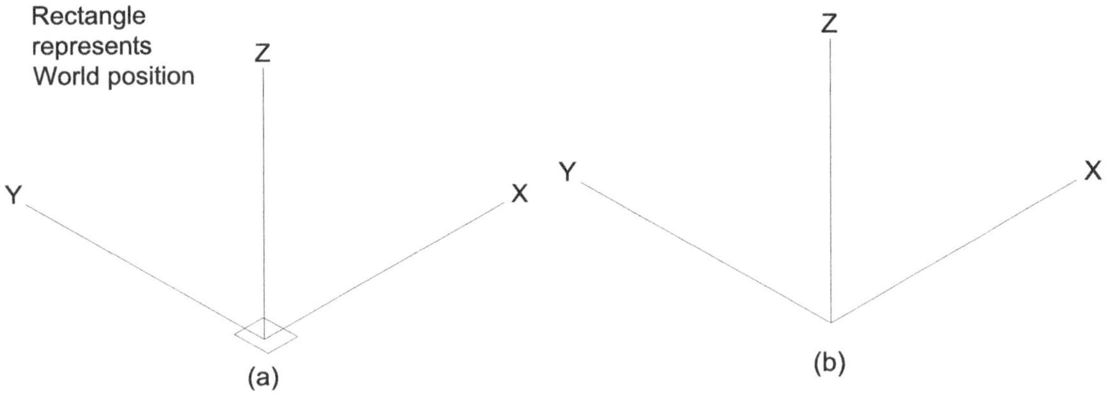

Figure 6-9 *UCS at the world position and UCS not at the world position*

F (Face) Option

This option is used to align a new UCS with the selected face of a solid object. You can invoke this option by choosing the **Face** tool from the Align UCS drop-down list in the **Coordinates** panel, as shown in Figure 6-10. The prompt sequence that will follow when you choose this tool is given next.

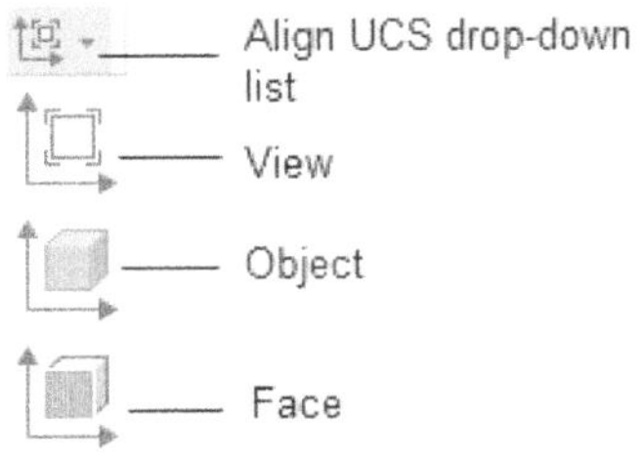

Figure 6-10 *The **Face** tool in the Align UCS drop-down list*

Select face of solid, surface, or mesh: *Select the face to align the UCS.*
Enter an option [Next/Xflip/Yflip] <accept>: *Select an option or accept the selected face to align.*

The **Next** option is used to locate the new UCS on the adjacent face or the back face of the selected edge. **Xflip** rotates the new UCS by 180 degrees about the *X* axis and **Yflip** rotates it about the *Y* axis. Pressing Enter at the **Enter an option [Next/Xflip/Yflip] <accept>** prompt accepts the location of the new UCS as specified.

OB (OBject) Option

With the **OB** (**OBject**) option of the **UCS** tool, you can establish a new coordinate system by selecting an object in the drawing. However, some of the objects such as 3D polyline,

3D mesh, viewport object, or xline cannot be used for defining a UCS. The positive *Z* axis of the new UCS is in the same direction as the positive *Z* axis of the object selected. If the *X* and *Z* axes are given, the new *Y* axis is determined by the right-hand rule. You can also invoke this option by choosing the **Object** tool from the Align UCS drop-down list in the **Coordinates** panel. The prompt sequence that will follow when you choose this tool is given next.

Select object to align UCS: *Select the object to align the UCS.*

In Figure 6-11, the UCS is relocated using the **OBject** option and is aligned to the circle. The origin and the *X* axis of the new UCS are determined by using the following rules:

Arc

When you select an arc, its center becomes the origin for the new UCS. The *X* axis passes through the endpoint of the arc that is closest to the point selected on the object.

Circle/Cylinder/Ellipse

When you select a circle, cylinder, or an ellipse, its center becomes the origin of the new UCS, and the *X* axis passes through the point selected on the object, refer to Figure 6-12.

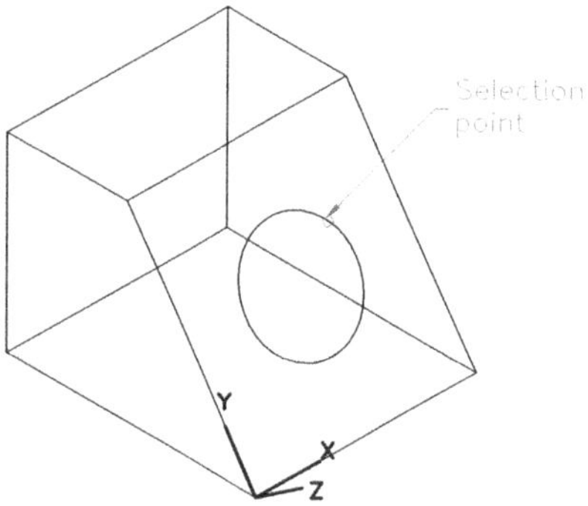

Figure 6-11 *Relocating the UCS using a circle*

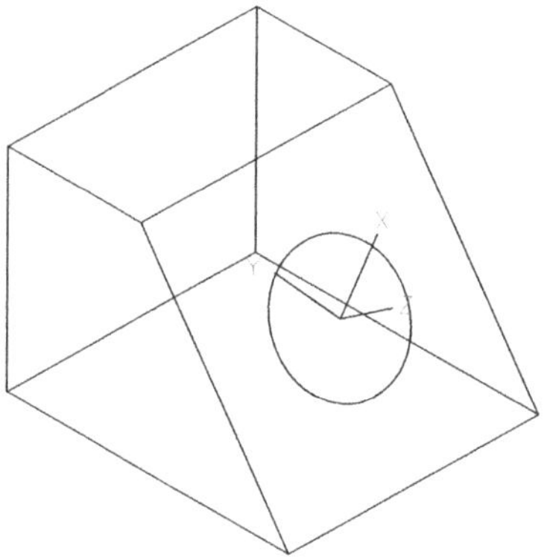

Figure 6-12 *UCS at a new location*

Line/Mline/Ray/Leader

When you select a line, mline, ray, or a leader, the endpoint nearest to the point selected on it becomes the origin of the new UCS. The *X* axis is defined so that the line lies on the *XY* plane of the new UCS. Therefore, in the new UCS, the *Y* coordinate of the second endpoint of the line is 0.

Note

The linear edges of solid models or regions are considered as individual lines when selected to align a UCS.

Spline

When you select a spline, the endpoint that is nearest to the point selected on the spline becomes the origin of the new UCS. An imaginary line will be drawn between the two endpoints of the spline and the *X* axis will be aligned along this imaginary line.

Dimension

When you select a dimension, the middle point of the dimension text becomes the origin of the new UCS. The *X* axis direction is identical to the direction of the *X* axis of the UCS that existed when the dimension was drawn.

Point

The position of the point is the origin of the new UCS. The directions of the *X*, *Y*, and *Z* axes will be same as those of the previous UCS.

Solid

When you select a solid, the first point selected on the solid becomes the origin of the new UCS. The *X* axis of the new UCS lies along the line between the first and second points of the solid.

2D Polyline

When you select a polyline, the end point nearest to the point selected on the polyline becomes the origin of the new UCS. The *X* axis extends from the start point to the next vertex.

3D Face

When you select a 3D face, its first point becomes the origin of the new UCS. The *X* axis is determined by using the first two points, and the positive side of the *Y* axis is determined by the first and fourth points for a flat rectangular face. For a flat planar face, the X axis will always be parallel to the edge through which the UCS is moved on the face. The *Z* axis is determined by applying the right-hand rule.

Shape/Text/Block/Attribute/Attribute Definition

When you select a shape, text, block, attribute, or an attribute definition, its insertion point becomes the origin of the new UCS. The new X axis is defined by the rotation of the object around its positive Z axis. Therefore, the object you select will have a rotation angle of zero in the new UCS.

Tip

Except for 3D faces, the XY plane of the new UCS will be parallel to the XY plane of the object when it was drawn. However, X and Y axes may be rotated.

V (View) Option

The **V (View)** option of the **UCS** tool is used to define a new UCS whose *XY* plane is parallel to the current viewing plane. The current viewing plane, in this case, is the screen of the monitor. Therefore, a new UCS is defined that is parallel to the screen of the monitor. The origin of the UCS defined in this option remains unaltered. This option is used mostly to view a drawing from an oblique viewing direction or to write text for the objects on the screen. You can also invoke this option by choosing the **View** tool from the **Align UCS** drop-down list in the **Coordinates** panel. As soon as you choose this tool, a new UCS is defined parallel to the screen of the monitor.

X/Y/Z

With these options, you can rotate the current UCS around the desired axis. You can specify the angle by entering the angle value at the required prompt or by selecting two points on the screen with the help of a pointing device. You can specify a positive or a negative angle. The new angle is taken relative to the *X* axis of the existing UCS. The **UCSAXISANG** system variable stores the default angle by which the UCS is rotated around the specified axis, by using the **X/ Y/ Z** options of the **UCS** tool. The right-hand thumb rule is used to determine the positive direction of rotation of the selected axis. You can also invoke the corresponding option by choosing the **X/Y/Z** button from the Rotate UCS drop-down in the **Coordinates** panel, as shown in Figure 6-13. However, in AutoCAD, you can rotate the UCS dynamically using the grips and shortcut menu.

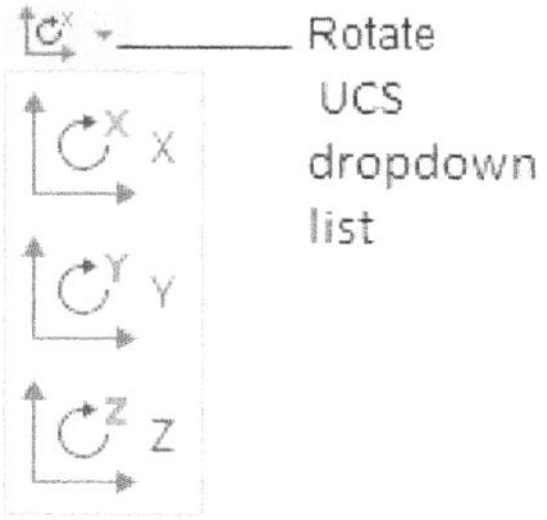

Figure 6-13 *Tools in the* ***Rotate UCS*** *drop-down list*

X

In Figure 6-14, the UCS is rotated using the X option by specifying an angle about the X axis at the command prompt. The first model shows the UCS before the UCS was relocated and the second model shows the relocated UCS.

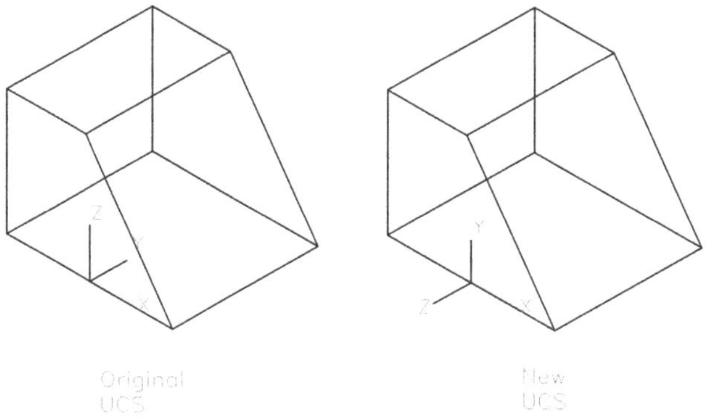

Figure 6-14 *Rotating the UCS about the X axis*

You can also choose the X tool from the Rotate UCS drop-down list in the **Coordinates** panel. The prompt sequence that will follow when you choose the **X** tool is given next.

Specify rotation angle about X axis <90>: *Specify the rotation angle.*

Alternatively, you can dynamically rotate the UCS about the X axis by following the steps given below:

1. Click on the UCS in the drawing area to select it.

2. Move the cursor to the grip of the Y or Z axis; a shortcut menu will be displayed, as shown in Figure 6-15.

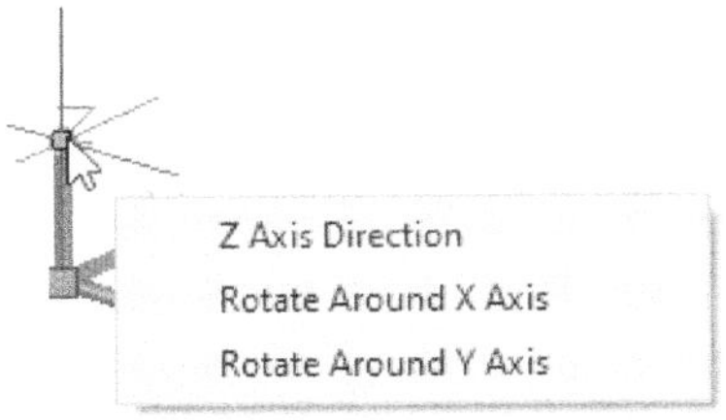

Figure 6-15 *Shortcut menu for UCS rotation*

3. Choose the **Rotate Around X Axis** option from the shortcut menu and then rotate the UCS dynamically. You can also enter the desired rotation angle in the edit box attached to the cursor.

Y

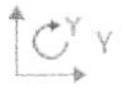

In Figure 6-16, the UCS is rotated using the **Y** option by specifying an angle about the Y axis. The first model shows the UCS setting before the UCS was relocated and the second model shows the relocated UCS. The prompt sequence that will follow when you choose the **Y** tool from the Rotate UCS drop-down list is given next.

Specify rotation angle about Y axis <90>: *Specify the angle.*

Alternatively, you can dynamically rotate the UCS about the Y axis by following the steps given below:

1. Click on the UCS in the drawing area to select it.
2. Move the cursor to the grip of the X or Z axis.
3. Choose the **Rotate Around Y Axis** option from the shortcut menu and rotate the UCS dynamically or specify the desired angle.

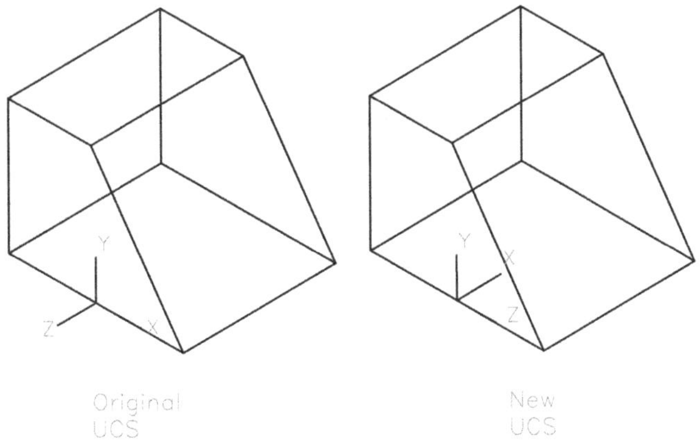

Figure 6-16 *Rotating the UCS about the Y axis*

Z

In Figure 6-17, the UCS is rotated using the **Z** option by specifying an angle about the *Z* axis. The first model shows the UCS setting before the UCS was rotated and the second model shows the rotated UCS. The prompt sequence that will follow when you choose the **Z** tool from the **Rotate UCS** drop-down is given next.

Specify rotation angle about Z axis <90>: *Specify the angle.*

Alternatively, you can dynamically rotate the UCS about the Z axis by following the steps given below:

1. Click on the UCS in the drawing area to select it.
2. Move the cursor to the grip of the X or Y axis.
3. Choose the **Rotate Around Z Axis** option from the shortcut menu and rotate the UCS dynamically or specify the desired rotation angle.

Note

You can rotate the UCS about any axis also by using the options in the shortcut menu displayed on right-clicking on the UCS. To do so, move the cursor on the ***Rotate Axis*** *sub-menu in the shortcut menu and then choose the required option.*

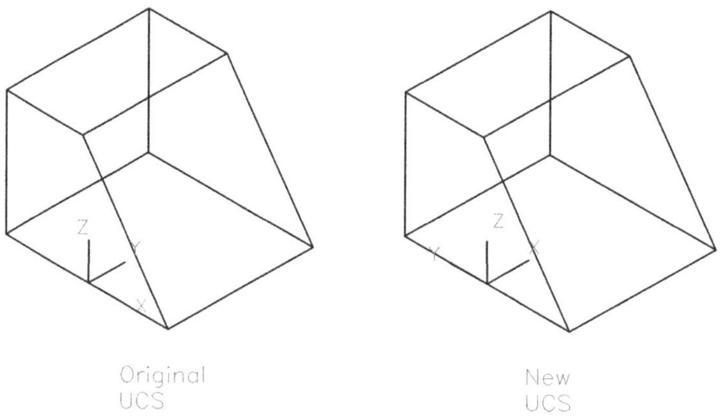

Figure 6-17 *Rotating the UCS about the Z axis*

ZA (ZAxis) Option

This option is used to change the coordinate system by selecting the origin point of the *XY* plane and a point on the positive *Z* axis. After you specify a point on the *Z* axis, AutoCAD determines the *X* and *Y* axes of the new coordinate system accordingly. The prompt sequence that will follow when you choose the **Z Axis Vector** tool from the **Coordinates** panel is given next.

Specify new origin point or [Object] <0,0,0>: *Specify the origin point, as shown in Figure 6-18.*
Specify point on positive portion of Z-axis <default>: **@0,-1,0**

Now, the front face of the model will become the new work plane, refer to Figure 6-19 and all the new objects are oriented accordingly. If you give a null response to the **Specify point on positive portion of Z-axis <current>** prompt, the *Z* axis of the new coordinate system will be parallel to (in the same direction as) the *Z* axis of the previous coordinate system. Null responses to the origin point and the point on the positive *Z* axis establish a new coordinate system in which the direction of the *Z* axis is identical to that of the previous coordinate system; however, the *X* and *Y* axes may be rotated around the *Z* axis. The positive *Z* axis direction is also known as the extrusion direction.

When the **Object** option is selected at the **Specify new origin point or [Object] <0,0,0>** prompt, then you are prompted to select an object. Select an open object and the UCS will be placed at the end point nearest to the point of the object selection, with its Z-axis along the tangent direction at that end point and pointing away from the object.

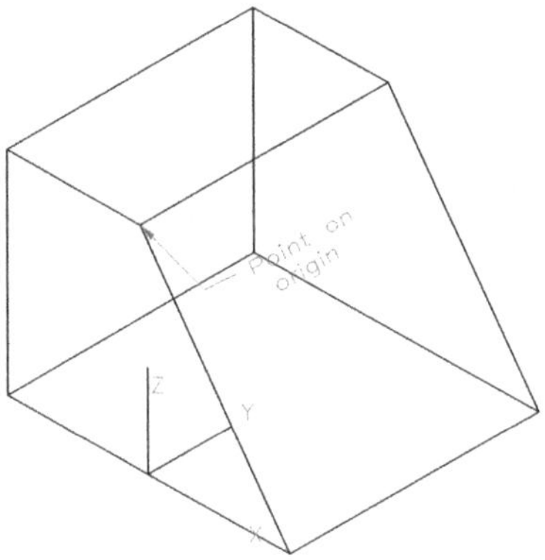

Figure 6-18 Specifying a point on the origin

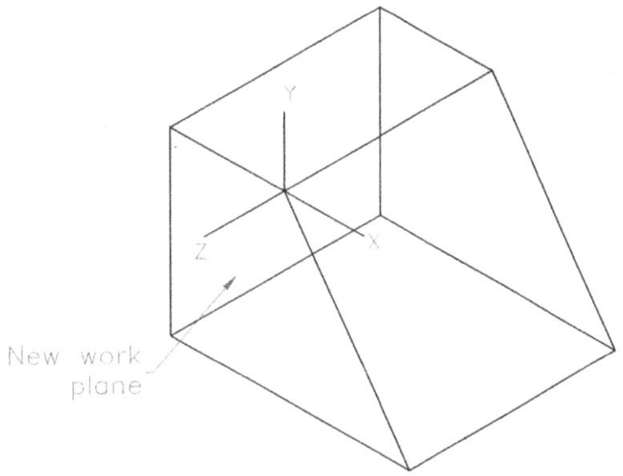

Figure 6-19 Relocating the UCS using the ***ZA*** *option*

Previous Option

The **Previous** option is used to restore the current UCS settings to the previous UCS settings. AutoCAD saves the last ten UCS settings. You can go back to the previous ten UCS settings in the current space using the **Previous** option. If the value of **TILEMODE** is 0, the last ten coordinate systems in paper space and in model space are saved. You can also invoke this option by choosing the **UCS, Previous** tool from the **Coordinates** panel. When you choose this tool, the previous UCS settings are automatically restored.

NAmed Option

This option is used to name and save the current UCS settings, restore a previously saved UCS setting, view a previously saved UCS list, and delete the saved UCS from the list. The prompt sequence for this option is given next.

Command: **UCS**
Current ucs name: *WORLD*
Specify origin of UCS or [Face/NAmed/OBject/Previous/View/World/X/Y/Z/ZAxis]

<World>: **NA**
Enter an option [Restore/Save/Delete/?]: *Enter an option.*

Depending on your requirement, you can select any one of the following options:

Restore Option

The **Restore** option of the **UCS** command is used to restore a previously saved named UCS. Once it is restored, it becomes the current UCS. However, the viewing direction of the saved UCS is not restored. You can also restore a named UCS by selecting it from the **UCS** dialog box that appears when you invoke the **UCS, Named UCS** tool from the **Coordinates** panel. As this option does not have a button to restore the Named UCS, you need to choose this option by using the **UCS** command at the command prompt. The prompt sequence that will follow when you invoke the **UCS** command is given next.

Enter an option [Restore/Save/Delete/?]: ***R***
Enter name of UCS to restore or [?]: *Specify the name of UCS.*

You can specify the name of the UCS to be restored or list the UCSs that can be restored by entering **?** at the previous prompt. The prompt sequence that will be followed is given next.

Enter UCS name(s) to list <*>: *Specify the name of the UCS to list or give a null response to list all available UCSs.*

If you give a null response at the previously mentioned prompt, then the AutoCAD text window will be opened listing all the available UCSs.

Save Option

With this option, you can name and save the current UCS settings. The following points should be kept in mind while naming the UCS:

1. The name can be up to 255 characters long.
2. The name can contain letters, digits, blank spaces and the special characters $ (dollar), - (hyphen), and _ (underscore).

As this option does not have a tool, you can invoke this option using the command prompt. The prompt sequence that will follow after entering the **UCS** command is given next.

Current ucs name: *WORLD*
Specify origin of UCS or [Face/NAmed/OBject/Previous/View/World/X/Y/Z/ZAxis]<WORLD>: **NA**
Enter an option [Restore/Save/Delete/?]: **S**
Enter name to save current UCS or [?]: *Specify a name to the UCS.*

Enter a valid name for the UCS at this prompt. AutoCAD saves it as a UCS. You can also list the previously saved UCSs by entering **?** at this prompt. The next prompt sequence is:

Enter UCS name(s) to list <*>:

Enter the name of the UCS to list or give a null response to list all the available UCSs.

Delete Option

The **Delete** option is used to delete the selected UCS from the list of saved coordinate systems. As this option does not have a button, you can invoke this option using the command prompt. The prompt sequence that will follow after entering the **UCS** command is given next.

Current ucs name: *WORLD*
Specify origin of UCS or [Face/NAmed/OBject/Previous/View/World/X/Y/Z/ZAxis]: **NA**
Enter an option [Restore/Save/Delete/?]: **D**
Enter UCS name(s) to delete <none>: *Specify the name of the UCS to delete.*

The UCS name you enter at this prompt is deleted. You can delete more than one UCS by entering the UCS names separated with commas.

? Option

By invoking this option, you can list the name of the specified UCS. This option gives you the name, origin, and *X*, *Y*, and *Z* axes of all the coordinate systems relative to the existing UCS. If the current UCS has no name, it is listed as WORLD or UNNAMED. The choice between these two names depends on whether the current UCS is the same as the WCS. The prompt sequence that will be displayed when you invoke this option using the command prompt is given next.

Current ucs name: *WORLD*
Specify origin of UCS or [Face/NAmed/OBject/Previous/View/World/X/Y/Z/ZAxis]
<WORLD>: **NA**
Enter an option [Restore/Save/Delete/?]: **?**
Enter UCS name(s) to list <*>:

Apply Option

The **Apply** option applies the current UCS settings to a specified viewport or to all the active viewports in a drawing session. If the **UCSVP** system variable is set to 1, each viewport saves its UCS settings. The **Apply** option is not displayed at the command prompt as an option for the **UCS** command. Therefore, you have to choose the **Apply** button from the **UCS** toolbar. The prompt sequence that will follow when you choose this button is given next.

Pick viewport to apply current UCS or [All]<current>: *Pick inside the viewport or enter **A** to apply the current UCS settings to all viewports.*

Origin Option

This option is used to define a new UCS by changing the origin of the current UCS, without changing the directions of the X, Y, Z axes, refer to Figures 6-20 and 6-21. The new point defined becomes the origin point (0,0,0) for all the coordinate entries, until the origin is changed again. You can specify the coordinates of the new origin or click on the screen using the pointing device. The **Origin** option is not displayed at the command prompt as an option for the **UCS** command. Therefore, you have to choose the **Origin** button from the **UCS** toolbar. Alternatively, choose the **Origin** tool from the **Coordinates** panel to specify the coordinates of the new origin.

The prompt sequence that will follow when you choose this tool is given next.

Specify new origin point <0,0,0>: *Specify the origin point, as shown in Figure 6-20.*

Tip
If you do not provide the Z coordinate for the origin, the current Z coordinate value will be assigned to the UCS.

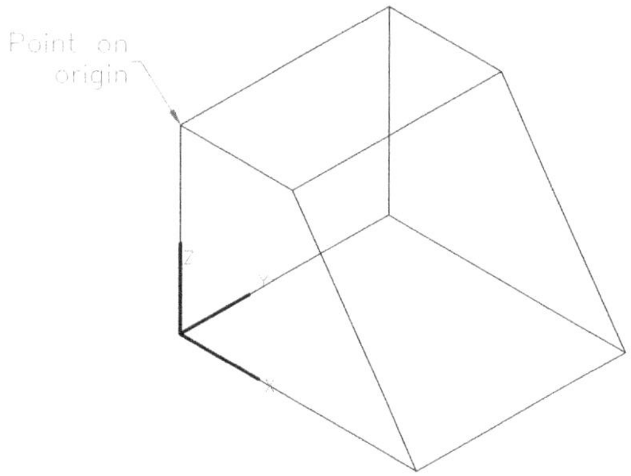

Figure 6-20 *Defining a new origin for the UCS*

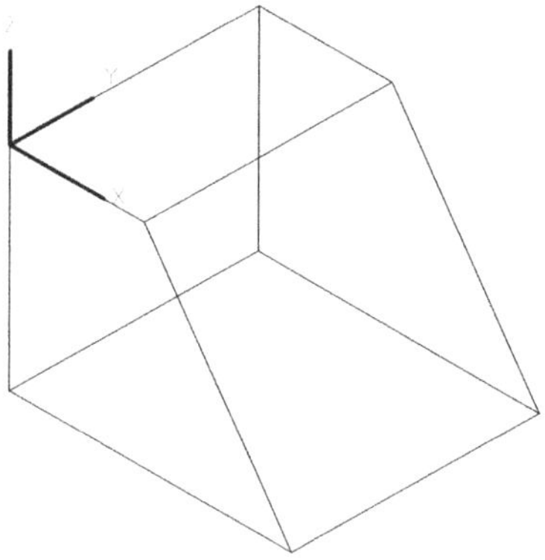

Figure 6-21 *Relocating the UCS for the new origin*

3-Point Option

The **3-Point** option is the default option of the **UCS** command. With this option, you can establish a new coordinate system by specifying a new origin point, a point on the positive side of the new *X* axis, and a point on the positive side of the new *Y* axis, refer to Figure 6-22. The direction of the *Z* axis is determined by applying the right-hand rule about which you will learn in the next chapter. This option can also be used to align the UCS at any angled surface. The prompt sequence that will follow when you choose the **3-Point** tool from the **Coordinates** panel is given next.

Specify new origin point <0,0,0>: *Specify the origin point of the new UCS.*
Specify point on positive portion of X-axis <default>: *Specify a point on the positive portion of the X axis.*
Specify point on positive-Y portion of the UCS XY plane<default>: *Specify a point on the positive portion of the Y axis.*

A null response to the **Specify new origin point <0,0,0>** prompt will lead to a coordinate system in which the origin of the new UCS is identical to that of the previous UCS. Similarly, null responses to the point on the *X* or *Y* axis prompt will lead to a coordinate system in which the *X* or *Y* axis of the new UCS is parallel to that of the previous UCS. In Figure 6-23, the UCS has been relocated by specifying three points (the origin point, a point on the positive portion of the *X* axis, and a point on the positive portion of the *Y* axis).

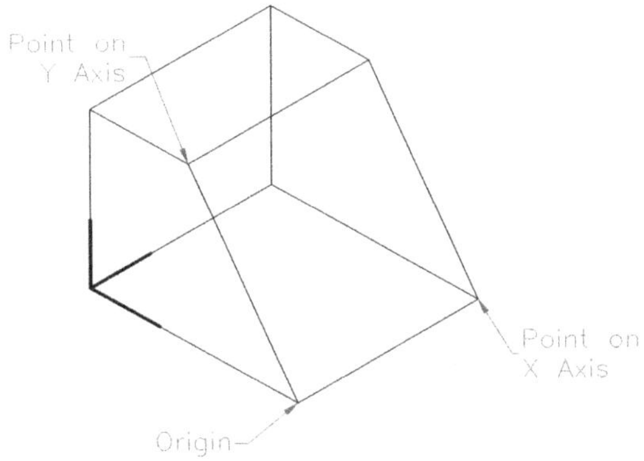

Figure 6-22 *Relocating the UCS using the **3-Point** option*

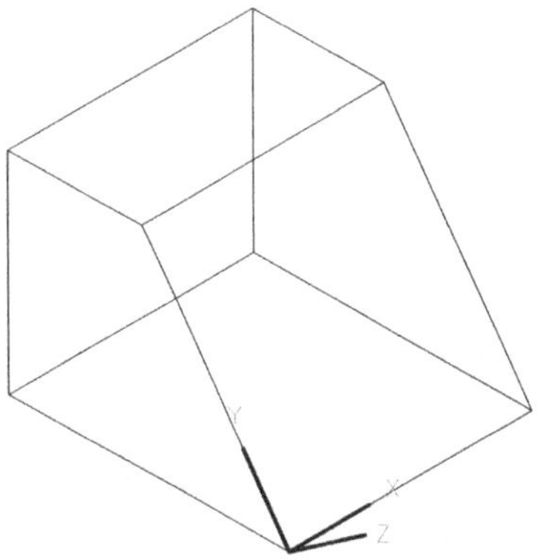

Figure 6-23 *UCS at a new position*

Example 1 — 3-Point

In this example, you will draw a tapered rectangular block. After drawing it, you will align the UCS with the inclined face of the block by using the dynamic alignment. Next, you will draw a circle on the inclined face. The dimensions for the block and the circle are shown in Figure 6-24.

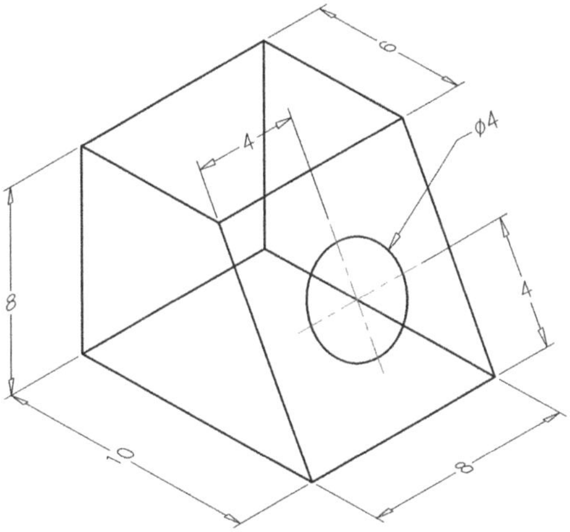

Figure 6-24 *Model for Example 1*

The steps to do this example are given next.

- Draw the edges of the bottom face of the tapered block.
- Specify a new origin.
- Draw the edges of the top face of the tapered block.
- Draw the remaining edges of the block.

- Align the UCS to the inclined face.
- Draw the circle on the inclined face.

These steps are discussed next.

1. Start a new drawing and choose the **Line** tool. The prompt sequence is given next.

   Specify first point: **1,1**
   Specify next point or [Undo]: **@10,0**
   Specify next point or [Undo]: **@0,8**
   Specify next point or [Close/Undo]: **@-10,0**
   Specify next point or [Close/Undo]: **C**

2. As the top face of the model is at a distance of 8 units from the bottom face in the positive *Z* direction, you need to define a UCS at a distance of 8 units to create the top face. To do so, select the UCS and then move the cursor to the rectangular grip displayed at the intersection of the three axes; a shortcut menu will be displayed. Choose the **Move Origin Only** option; AutoCAD will prompt you to specify a new origin point. The prompt sequence is as follows:

   Specify origin point : **0,0,8**

3. Choose the **Line** tool from the **Draw** panel. The prompt sequence is as follows:

   Specify first point: **1,1**
   Specify next point or [Undo]: **@6,0**
   Specify next point or [Undo]: **@0,8**
   Specify next point or [Close/Undo]: **@-6,0**
   Specify next point or [Close/Undo]: **C**

4. When you open a new drawing, you view the model from the top view by default. Therefore, when viewing from the top, the three edges of the top side overlap with the corresponding bottom edges. As a result, you will not be able to see all the edges. However, you can change the viewpoint to clearly view the model in 3D. Choose **SE Isometric** from the **View Controls** list in the **In-Canvas Viewport Controls** to orient the view to the SE isometric view. Now, you can see the 3D view of the objects, refer to Figure 6-25.

5. Join the remaining edges of the model using the **Line** tool.The model after joining all edges should look similar to the one shown in Figure 6-26.

Now, dynamic alignment of UCS can be done with a surface, a mesh, and a solid face but the inclined portion is a wire frame. So, you need to convert the wire frame into a surface by using the **Region** tool.

6. Invoke the **Region** tool from the **Draw** panel in the **Home** tab; AutoCAD will prompt you to select objects for generating a region. Next, select the four edges bounding the inclined face and press Enter; a region will be generated.

7. Next, select the UCS and place the cursor on the rectangular grip; a shortcut menu will be

displayed. Choose the **Move and Align** option from the shortcut menu; you will be prompted to select a face, surface, or mesh.

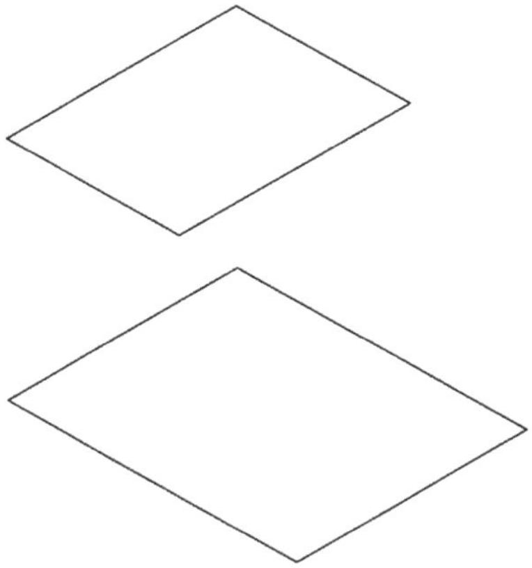

Figure 6-25 *3D view of the objects*

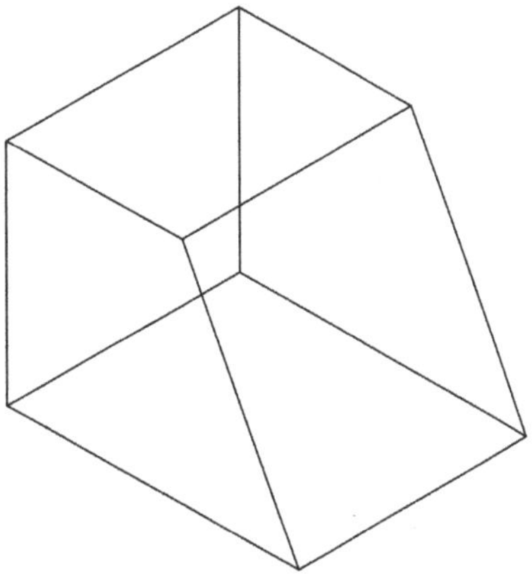

Figure 6-26 *Model after joining all the edges*

8. Select the inclined face by moving through the edge to which you want the X axis to be parallel or you can align the axes by dynamically rotating them. In this case, the X axis is parallel to P1P2 line, refer to Figure 6-27.

9. Choose the **Center, Radius** tool from the **Circle** drop-down in the **Draw** panel and draw the circle on the inclined face.

The final model should look similar to the one shown in Figure 6-28.

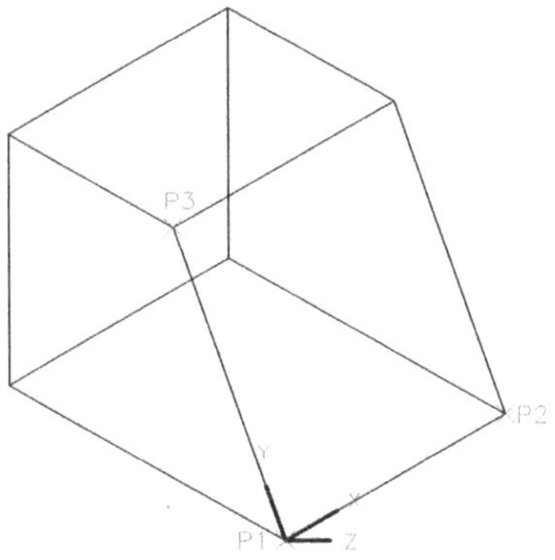

Figure 6-27 *Model after aligning the UCS on the inclined face*

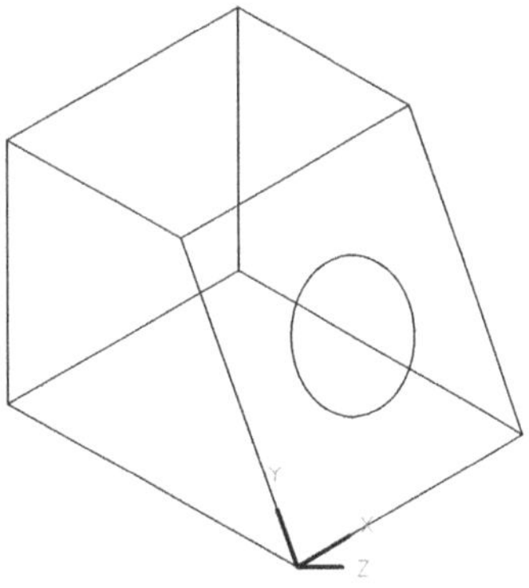

Figure 6-28 *Final model for Example 1*

MANAGING THE UCS THROUGH THE DIALOG BOX

Ribbon: Visualize > Coordinates > UCS, Named UCS **Command:** UCSMAN
Menu Bar: Tools > Named UCS

In AutoCAD, you can save and restore the UCS by using the **UCS, Named UCS** tool from the **Coordinates** panel. On choosing this tool, the **UCS** dialog box will be displayed, as shown in Figure 6-29. This dialog box is used to restore the saved and orthographic UCSs, specify the UCS icon settings, and rename UCSs. This dialog box has three tabs: **Named UCSs**, **Orthographic UCSs**, and **Settings**. These tabs are discussed next.

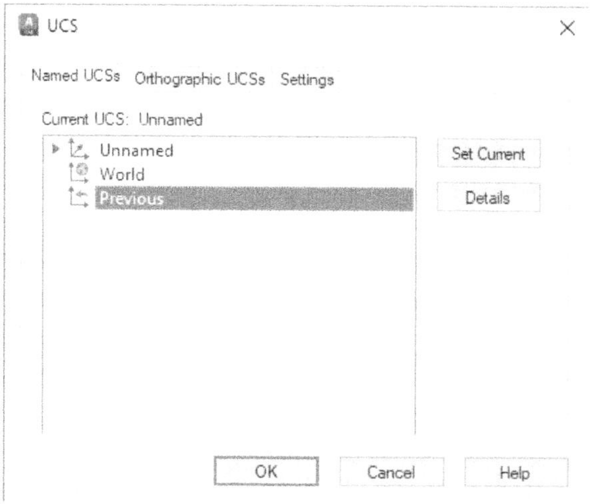

*Figure 6-29 The **Named UCSs** tab of the **UCS** dialog box*

Named UCSs Tab

The list of all coordinate systems defined (saved) on your system is displayed in the list box of the **Named UCSs** tab. The first entry in this list is **World**, which means WCS. The next entry will be **Previous**, if you have defined any other coordinate systems in the current editing session. Selecting the **Previous** entry and then choosing the **OK** button repeatedly allows you to go backward through the coordinate systems defined in the current editing session. If you have created a new UCS as the current coordinate system and not named it, then **Unnamed** will be the first entry in the list. Double-click on the name and rename it. Else, the unnamed UCS will disappear on selecting other UCS. If there are a number of viewports and unnamed settings, only the current viewport UCS name will be displayed in the list. The current coordinate system is indicated by a small pointer icon to the left of the coordinate system's name. The name of the current UCS is also displayed next to **Current UCS** on top of this list box. To make other coordinate system current, select its name in the list, choose the **Set Current** button, and choose the **OK** button. Alternatively, select the required UCS from the **Named UCS Combo Control** drop-down list available in the **Coordinates** panel of the **Visualize** tab. To delete a coordinate system created previously, select its name, and then right-click to display a shortcut menu. Choose the **Delete** option to delete the selected UCS name. To rename a coordinate system, select its name and then right-click to display a shortcut menu and choose **Rename**. Now, enter the new name. You can also double-click on the name you need to modify, and then change the name. The other options in the shortcut menu are **Set Current** and **Details**.

Tip

*All the changes and updating of the UCS information in the drawing are carried out only after you choose the **OK** button.*

If you want to check the current coordinate system's origin and *X*, *Y*, and *Z* axis values, select a UCS from the list and then choose the **Details** button; the **UCS Details** dialog box containing that information is displayed, refer to Figure 6-30. Alternatively, right-click on the name of the specific UCS in the list box and then choose the **Details** option from the shortcut menu.

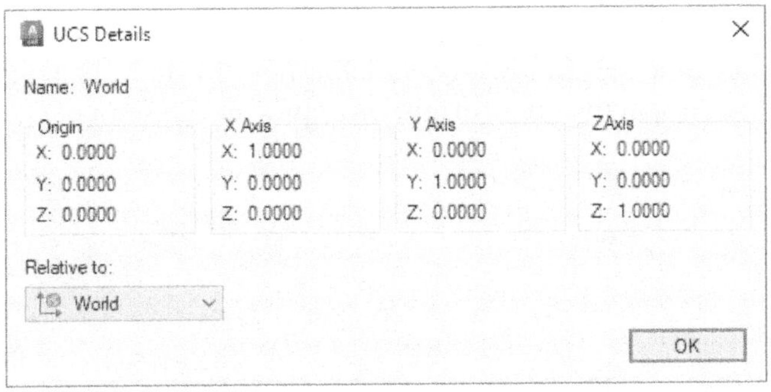

***Figure 6-30** The **UCS Details** dialog box*

Orthographic UCSs Tab

Different orthographic views are listed in the **Orthographic UCSs** tab, as shown in Figure 6-31. You can select any one of the six orthographic views of the WCS or the user defined coordinate system using the **UCS** dialog box. To define an orthographic coordinate system relative to a UCS, select it from the **Relative to** drop-down list. Next, select the orthographic view from the list of preset orthographic views, and then choose the **Set Current** button; the UCS icon is placed at the corresponding view. You can also right-click on the specific orthographic UCS name in the list and choose **Set Current** from the shortcut menu. The name of the current UCS is displayed above the list of orthographic view. If the current settings have not been saved and named, the **Current UCS** name displayed is **Unnamed**.

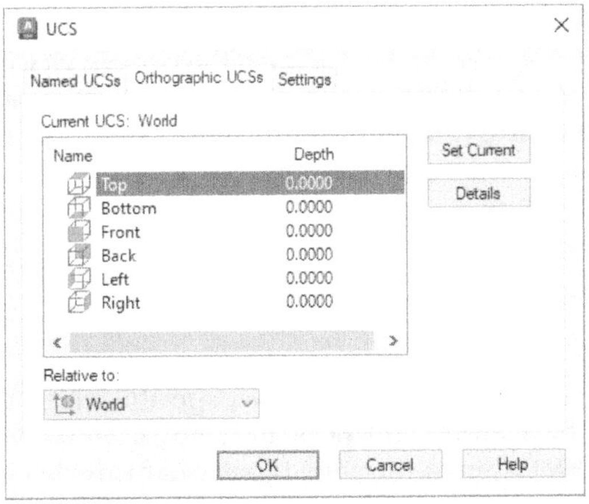

***Figure 6-31** The **Orthographic UCSs** tab of the **UCS** dialog box*

The **Depth** field in the list box of this dialog box displays the distance between the *XY* plane of the selected orthographic UCS setting and the parallel plane passing through the origin of the UCS base setting. The **UCSBASE** system variable stores the name of the UCS, which is considered as the base setting; that is, it defines the origin and orientation. You can enter or modify the values of depth by double-clicking on the depth value of the selected UCS in the list box. On doing so, the **Orthographic UCS depth** dialog box will be displayed, where you can enter new depth values, refer to Figure 6-32. You can also right-click on a specific orthographic UCS in the list box to display a shortcut menu. Choose **Depth** to display the **Orthographic UCS depth** dialog box. Enter a value in the edit box. If you need to pick a position from the drawing area, choose the **Select new origin** button available next to the edit box; the dialog box will disappear allowing you to specify a new origin or depth on the screen.

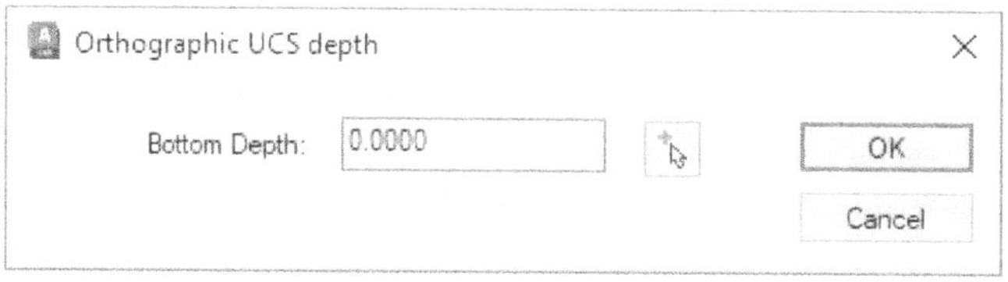

Figure 6-32 *The* ***Orthographic UCS depth*** *dialog box*

Choosing the **Details** button displays the **UCS Details** dialog box with the origin and the *X*, *Y*, *Z* coordinate values of the selected UCS. You can also choose **Details** from the shortcut menu that is displayed on right-clicking on a UCS in the list box. The shortcut menu also has the **Reset** option. Choosing **Reset** from the shortcut menu restores the selected UCS to its default settings. Also, the depth value, if assigned, becomes zero.

Settings Tab

The **Settings** tab of the **UCS** dialog box, refer to Figure 6-33, is used to display and modify the UCS and UCS icon settings of a specified viewport. If you choose the inclined arrow on the **Coordinates** panel, the **UCS** dialog box will be displayed with the **Settings** tab chosen. The options in this dialog box are discussed next.

UCS Icon settings Area

Selecting the **On** check box displays the UCS icon in the current viewport. This process is similar to using the **UCSICON** command and enables you to set the display of the UCS icon to on or off. If you select the **Display at UCS origin point** check box, the UCS icon is displayed at the origin point of the coordinate system in use in the current viewport. If the origin point is not visible in the current viewport, or if the check box is cleared, the UCS icon is displayed in the lower left corner of the viewport. Selecting the **Apply to all active viewports** check box applies the current UCS icon settings to all the active viewports in the current drawing.

UCS settings Area

This area of the **Settings** tab in the **UCS** dialog box specifies the UCS settings for the current viewport. Selecting the **Save UCS with viewport** check box saves the UCS with the viewport. This setting is stored in the **UCSVP** system variable. If you clear this check box, the **UCSVP** variable will be set to 0 and the UCS of the viewport will reflect the UCS of the current viewport. When you select the **Update view to Plan when UCS is changed** check box, the plan view is restored after the UCS in the viewport is changed. When the selected UCS is restored, the plan view is also restored. The value is stored in the **UCSFOLLOW** system variable.

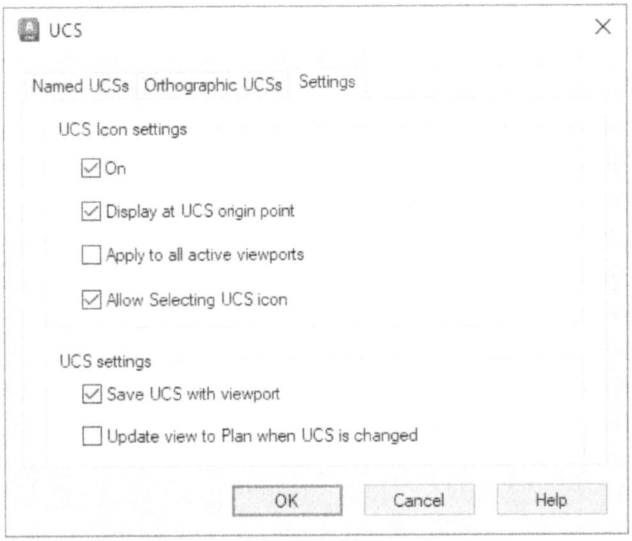

Figure 6-33 *The **Settings** tab of the **UCS** dialog box*

SYSTEM VARIABLES

The coordinate value of the origin of the current UCS is held in the **UCSORG** system variable. The *X* and *Y* axis directions of the current UCS are held in the **UCSXDIR** and **UCSYDIR** system variables, respectively. The name of the current UCS is held in the **UCSNAME** variable. All these variables are read-only. If the current UCS is identical to the WCS, the **WORLDUCS** system variable is set to 1; otherwise, it holds the value 0. The current UCS icon setting can be examined and manipulated with the help of the **UCSICON** command. This command defines the UCS icon setting of the current viewport. If more than one viewport is active, each one can have a different value for the **UCSICON** variable. If you are in paper space, the **UCSICON** variable will contain the setting for the UCS icon of the paper space. The **UCSFOLLOW** system variable controls the automatic display of a plan view when you switch from one UCS to another. If **UCSFOLLOW** is set to 1 and you switch from one UCS to another, a plan view is automatically displayed. The **UCSAXISANG** variable stores the default angle value for the *X*, *Y*, or *Z* axis around which the UCS is rotated using the ***X***, ***Y***, ***Z*** options of the **UCS** command. The **UCSBASE** variable stores the name of the UCS that acts as the base; that is, it defines the origin and orientation of the orthographic UCS setting. The **UCSVP** variable decides whether the UCS settings are stored with the viewport or not.

Self-Evaluation Test

Answer the following questions and then compare them to those given at the end of this chapter:

1. By default, the __________ is established as the coordinate system in the AutoCAD environment.

2. The __________ coordinate system can be moved to and rotated about any desired location.

3. Once a saved UCS is restored, it becomes the __________ UCS.

4. You can change the 3D UCS icon to a 2D UCS icon using the __________ radio button of the **UCS Icon** dialog box.

5. The __________ point of the 3D face defines the origin of the new UCS.

6. In dynamic alignment of UCS for a flat planar face, the __________ will always be parallel to the edge through which the UCS is moved on the face.

7. You can move the World Coordinate System from its original position. (T/F)

8. The **View** tool in the **Align UCS** drop-down of the **Coordinates** panel of the **Visualize** tab is used to define a new UCS whose *XY* plane is parallel to the current viewing plane. (T/F)

9. An ellipse cannot be used as an object for defining a new UCS. (T/F)

10. While moving the UCS, if you do not specify the *Z* coordinate of the new point, the previous *Z* coordinate will be taken for the new value. (T/F)

Review Questions

Answer the following questions:

1. Which of the following options is used to restore the previous UCS settings?

   (a) **ZAxis** (b) **Restore**
   (c) **Previous** (d) **Save**

2. Which of the following options is used to list names of all the saved UCSs?

   (a) **ZAxis** (b) **Restore**
   (c) **?** (d) **Save**

3. Which of the following system variables is used to control the automatic display of the plan view when you switch to the new UCS?

   (a) **UCSORG** (b) **UCSFOLLOW**
   (c) **UCS** (d) **UCSBASE**

4. Which of the following system variables is used to store the coordinates of the origin of the current UCS?

   (a) **UCSICON** (b) **UCSORG**
   (c) **UCSVP** (d) **UCSFOLLOW**

5. Which of the following tools is used to manage the UCS using a dialog box?

(a) **UCS Icon, Properties** (b) **UCS, Named UCS**
(c) **UCS** (d) **UCS, World**

6. The __________ variable is used to control the *X* axis direction of the current UCS.

7. The __________ direction is known as the extrusion direction.

8. The lineweight of the UCS icon can be changed using the __________ option of the **UCS Icon** dialog box.

9. The __________ option of the **UCS** command is used to change the origin of the current UCS.

10. The __________ variable is used to control the *Y* axis direction of the current UCS.

11. The __________ variable is used to store the default angle value by which the UCS will be rotated.

12. You can change the line width of the UCS icon. (T/F)

13. The size of the UCS icon can vary between 5 and 100. (T/F)

14. The name of the current UCS is stored in the **UCSNAME** variable. (T/F)

15. The selection of the UCS can be controlled by using the options in the **Settings** tab of the **UCS** dialog box. (T/F)

Exercises 1 through 4

Draw the objects shown in Figures 6-34 through 6-37. Use the **UCS** tools to align the UCS icon and then draw the objects.

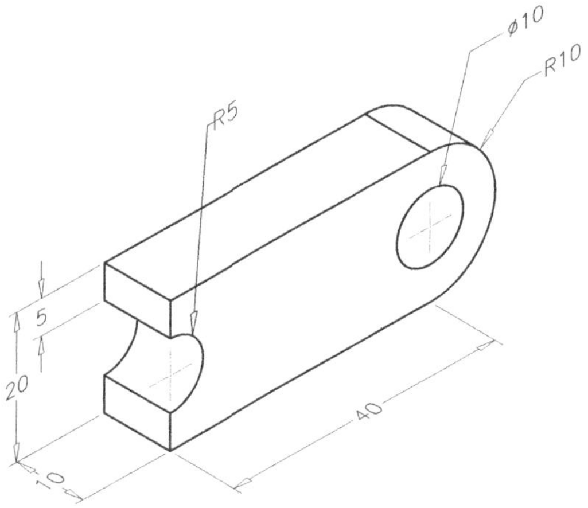

Figure 6-34 *Drawing for Exercise 1*

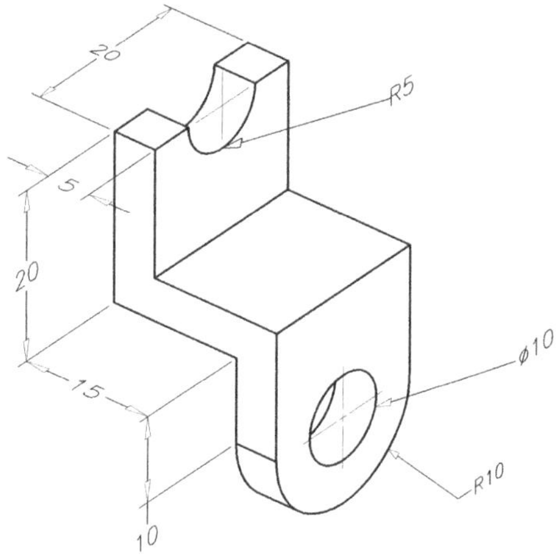

Figure 6-35 *Drawing for Exercise 2*

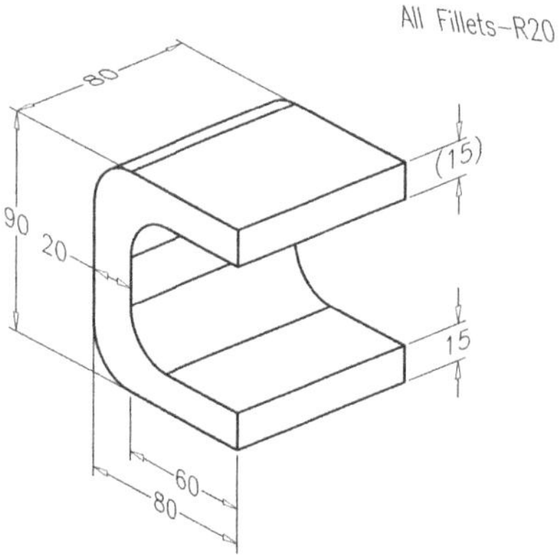

Figure 6-36 *Drawing for Exercise 3*

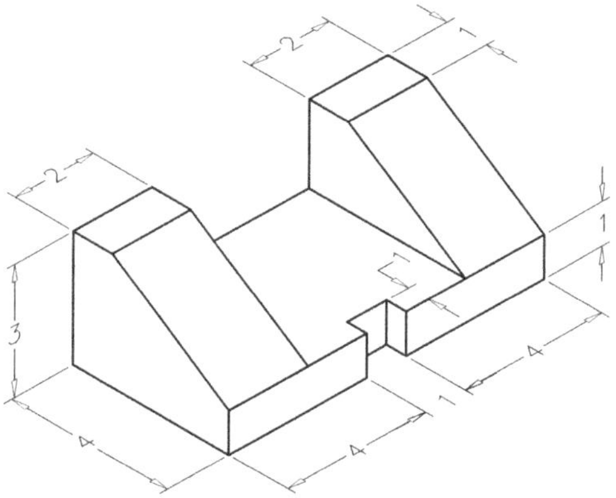

Figure 6-37 *Drawing for Exercise 4*

Exercise 5

Create the drawing shown in Figure 6-38. Align the UCS icon and then draw the objects. Note that in this drawing the left side of the transition should make a 90-degree angle with the bottom.

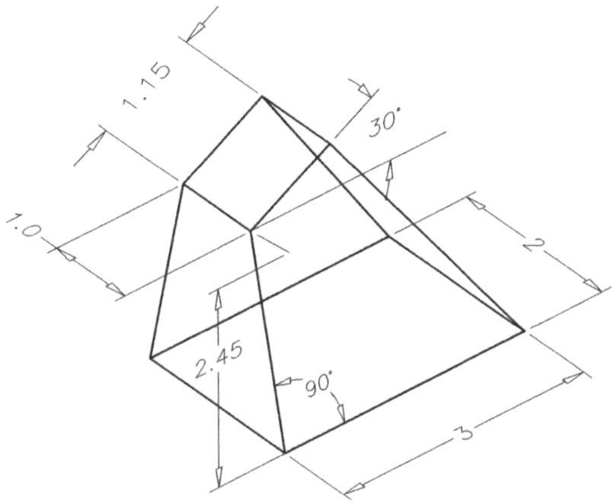

Figure 6-38 Model for Exercise 5

Exercise 6

Create the drawing shown in Figure 6-39. Position the UCS icon and then draw the objects. Note that in this drawing, the center of the top polygon is offset at 0.75 units from the center of the bottom polygon.

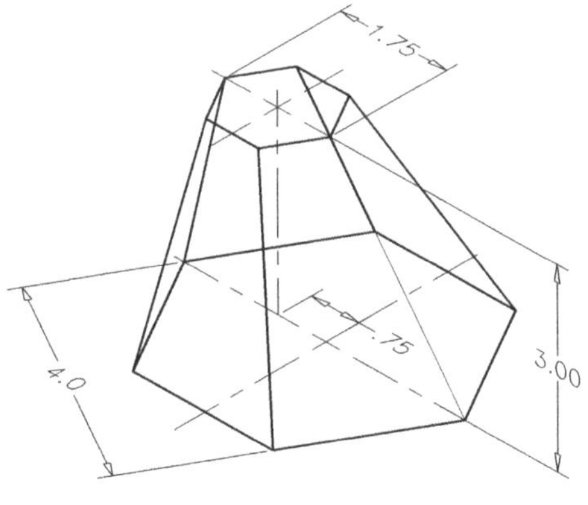

Figure 6-39 Model for Exercise 6

Exercises 7 and 8

In these exercises, you will create the drawing shown in Figures 6-40 and 6-41. Figure 6-42 shows the front view of the model for Exercise 8.

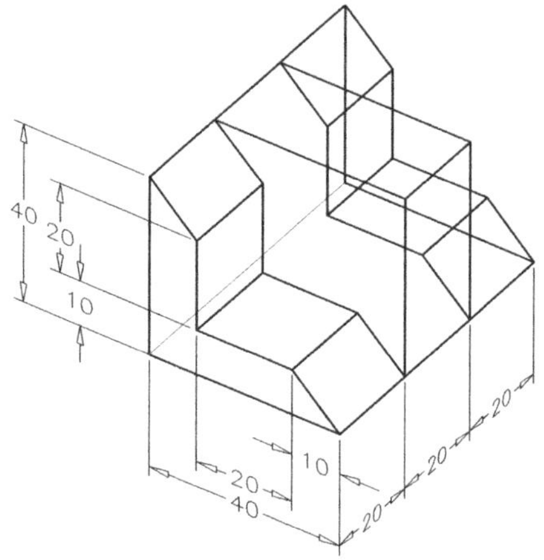

Figure 6-40 *Model for Exercise 7*

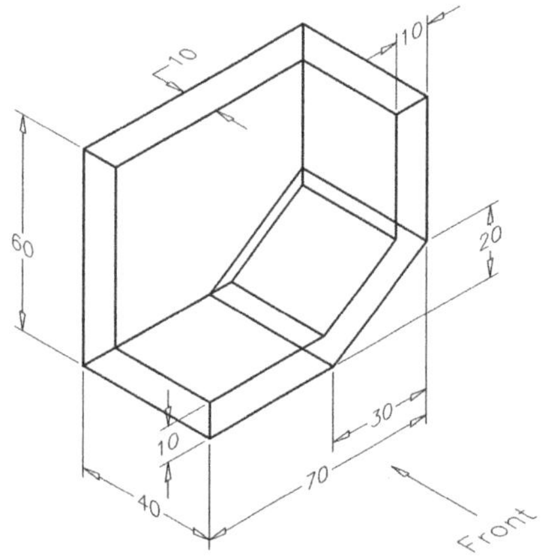

Figure 6-41 *Model for Exercise 8*

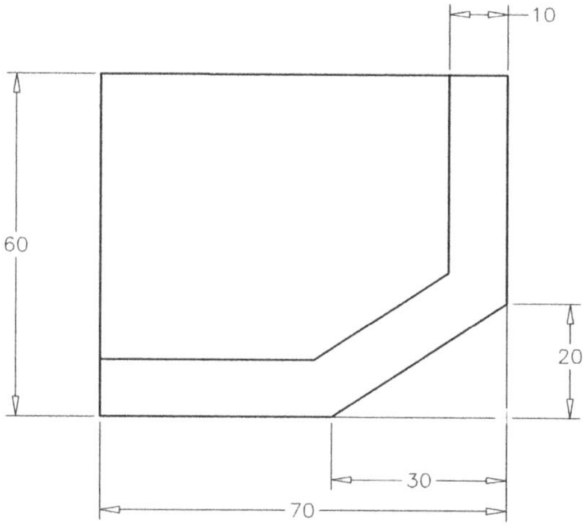

Figure 6-42 *Front view of the Model for exercise 8*

Answers to Self-Evaluation Test

1. World Coordinate System, **2.** user, **3.** current, **4.** 2D, **5.** first, **6.** X axis, **7.** F, **8.** T, **9.** F, **10.** T

Chapter 7

Getting Started with 3D

Learning Objectives

After completing this chapter, you will be able to:

- *Start 3D workspace in AutoCAD for creating models*
- *Use three-dimensional (3D) drawing*
- *Use various types of 3D models*
- *Know conventions used in AutoCAD*
- *Use the Viewpoint Presets tool to view objects in 3D space*
- *Use the ViewCube to view objects easily in 3D space*
- *Know various types of 3D coordinate systems*
- *Set thickness and elevation for objects*
- *Dynamically view 3D objects using the Orbit tool*
- *Use the SteeringWheel for viewing a model*

Key Terms

- *Wireframe*
- *Surface*
- *Solids*
- *ViewCube*
- *DDVPOINT*
- *3D Coordinate System*
- *ELEV*
- *Hide*
- *3D Polyline*
- *3D Face*
- *PFACE*
- *3DMESH*
- *Edit Polyline*
- *SteeringWheel*
- *Orbit*
- *3DCLIP*
- *Nudge*

STARTING THREE DIMENSIONAL (3D) MODELING IN AutoCAD

In AutoCAD, you can start the 3D Modeling in a separate workspace. All tools required to create the 3D design are displayed in this workspace by default. To start a new file in the 3D workspace, invoke the **Select template** dialog box and select the *acad3D.dwt* template. This template file supports the 3D environment. The other template files that support the 3D workspace are *acadiso3D.dwt*, *acad -Named Plot Styles3D.dwt*, and *acadISO -Named Plot Styles3D.dwt*. Next, select the **3D Modeling** option from the **Workspace** drop-down list available at the right in the **Status Bar**. Figure 7-1 shows the **3D Modeling** workspace of AutoCAD.

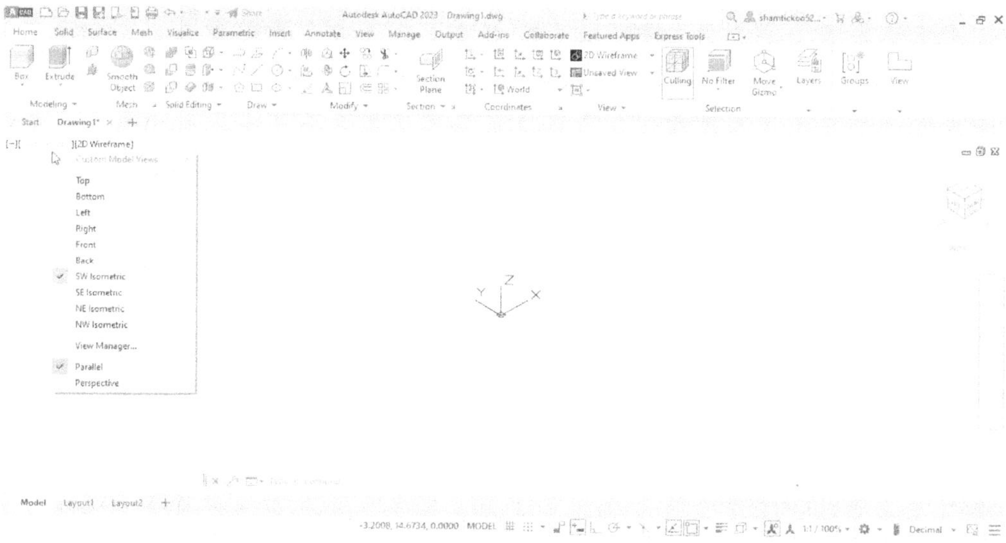

Figure 7-1 The ***3D Modeling*** *workspace of AutoCAD*

USE OF THREE-DIMENSIONAL DRAWING

The real world, and literally whatever you see around it, is three-dimensional (3D). Each and every design idea you think of is 3D. Before the development of 3D software packages, it was not possible to materialize these ideas in the design industry due to the lack of the third dimension. This is because the drawings were made on the drawing sheets, which are two dimensional objects with only *X* and *Y* coordinates. Therefore, it was not possible to draw the 3D objects. As prototyping is a very long and costly affair, therefore, the designers had to suppress their ideas and convert the 3D designs into 2D drawings.

The use of computers and the CADD (Computer Aided Design & Drafting) Technology has brought a significant improvement in materializing the design ideas and creating the engineering drawings. You can create a proper 3D object in the computer using the CADD Technology. This technology allows you to create models with the third coordinate called the *Z* coordinate, in addition to the *X* and *Y* coordinates. Apart from materializing the design ideas, the 3D models have the following advantages:

1. **Generate the drawing views:** Once you have created a 3D model, its 2D drawing views can be automatically generated.

2. **Provide realistic effects**: You can provide realistic effects to the 3D models by assigning a material and providing light effects to them. For example, an architectural drawing can be made more realistic and presentable by assigning the material to the walls and interiors and adding lights to it. You can also create its bitmap image and use it in presentations.

3. **Create the assemblies and check them for interference**: You can assemble various 3D models and create the assemblies. Once the components are assembled, you can check them for interference to reduce the errors and material loss during manufacturing. You can also generate the 2D drawing views of the assemblies.

4. **Create an animation of the assemblies**: You can animate the assemblies and view the animation to provide the clear display of the mating parts.

5. **Apply Boolean operations**: You can apply Boolean operations to the 3D models.

6. **Calculate the mass properties**: You can calculate the mass properties of the 3D models.

7. **Cut Sections**: You can cut sections through the solid models to view the shape at that cross-section.

8. **NC Programs**: You can generate an NC program with the help of 3D models by using a CAM software.

TYPES OF 3D MODELS

In AutoCAD, depending on their characteristics, the 3D models are divided into the following three categories:

Wireframe Models

Wireframe models are created using simple AutoCAD entities such as lines, polylines, rectangles, polygons, or some other entities such as 3D faces, and so on. To understand the wireframe models, consider a 3D model made up of match sticks or wires. These models consist of edges only, therefore you can see through them. You cannot apply the Boolean operations on these models and cannot calculate their mass properties. Wireframe models are generally used in frame building of vehicles. Figure 7-2 shows a wireframe model.

Surface Models

Surface models are made up of one or more surfaces. They have a negligible wall thickness and are hollow inside. To understand these models, consider a wireframe model with a cloth wrapped around it. You cannot see through it. These models are used in the plastic molding industry, such as shoe manufacturing, utensils manufacturing, and so on.

You can directly create a surface or a mesh. Alternatively, you can create wireframe model and then convert it into a mesh or surface model. Remember that you cannot perform the Boolean operations in surface models. Figure 7-3 shows a surface model created using a single surface or a mesh and Figure 7-4 shows a surface model created using a combination of surfaces.

Solid Models

Solid models are the solid filled models having mass properties. To understand a solid model, consider a model made up of metal or wood. You can perform Boolean operations on these models such as cutting a hole through them, or even cutting them into slices. Figure 7-5 shows a solid model.

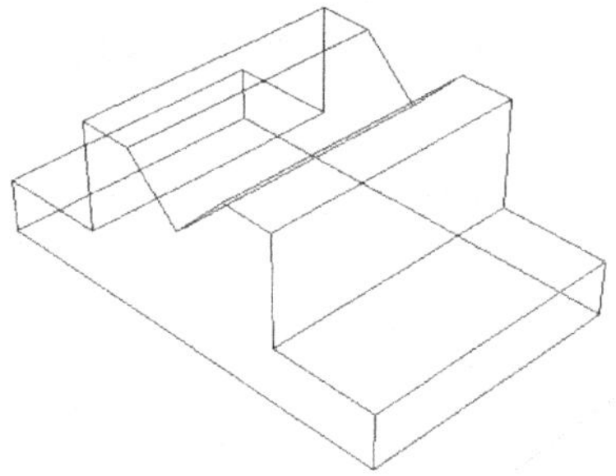

Figure 7-2 *A wireframe model*

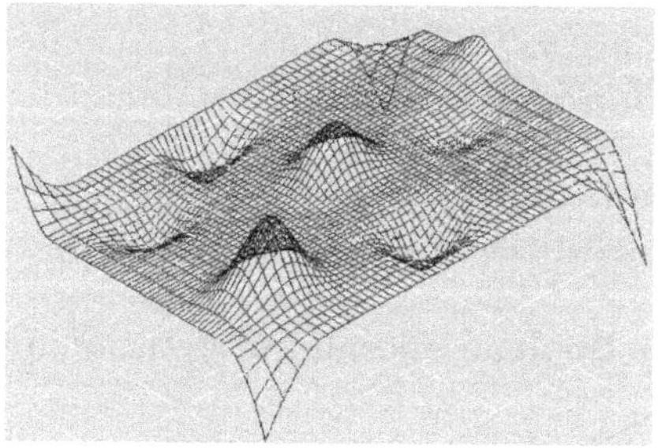

Figure 7-3 *A surface model created using a single surface*

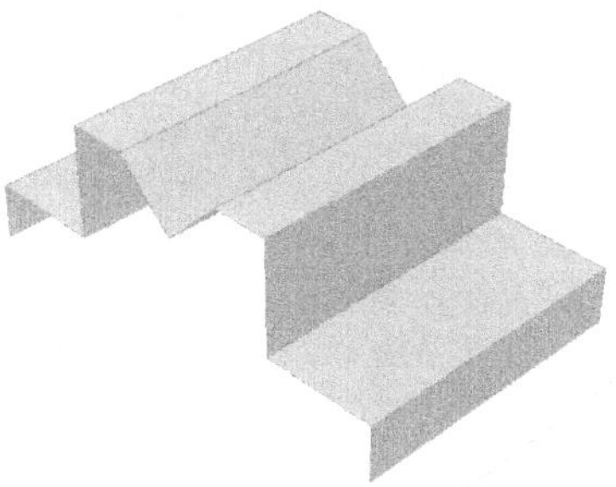

Figure 7-4 *A semi-finished surface model created using more than one surface*

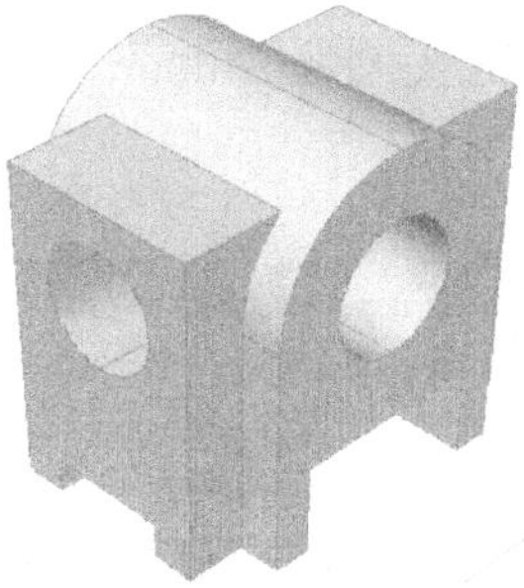

Figure 7-5 *A solid model*

CONVENTIONS FOLLOWED IN AutoCAD

It is important for you to know the conventions in AutoCAD before you proceed with 3D. AutoCAD follows these three conventions:

1. By default, any drawing you create in AutoCAD will be in the world XY plane.

2. The right-hand thumb rule is followed in AutoCAD to identify the *X*, *Y*, and *Z* axis directions. This rule states that if you keep the thumb, index finger, and middle finger of the right hand mutually perpendicular to each other, as shown in Figure 7-6(a), then the thumb of the right hand will represent the direction of the positive *X* axis, the index finger will represent the direction of the positive *Y* axis, and the middle finger of the right hand will represent the direction of the positive *Z* axis, refer to Figure 7-6(b).

3. The right-hand thumb rule is followed in AutoCAD to determine the direction of rotation or revolution in the 3D space. The right-hand thumb rule states that if the thumb of the right hand points in the direction of the axis of rotation, then the direction of the curled fingers will define the positive direction of rotation, refer to Figure 7-6(c).

This rule will be used during the rotation of 3D models or the UCS and also, during the creation of revolved surfaces and revolved solids.

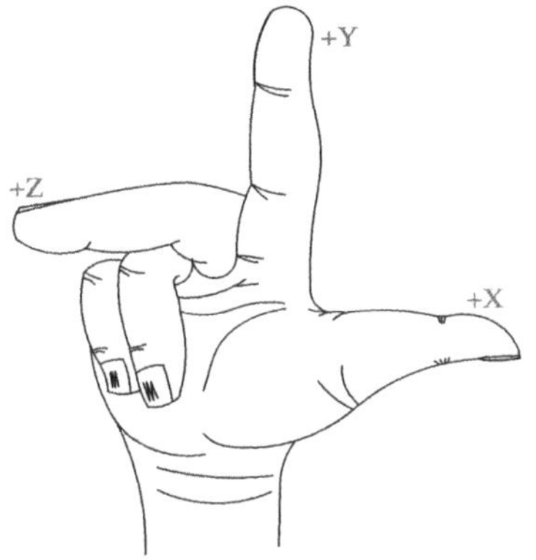

Figure 7-6(a) *The orientation of fingers as per the right-hand thumb rule*

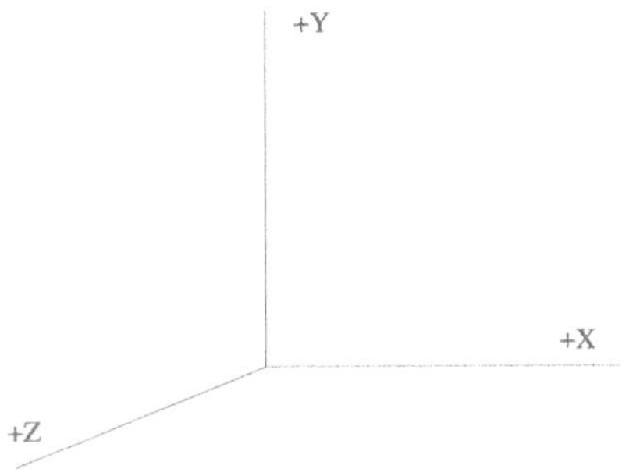

Figure 7-6(b) *Orientation of the X, Y, and Z axes*

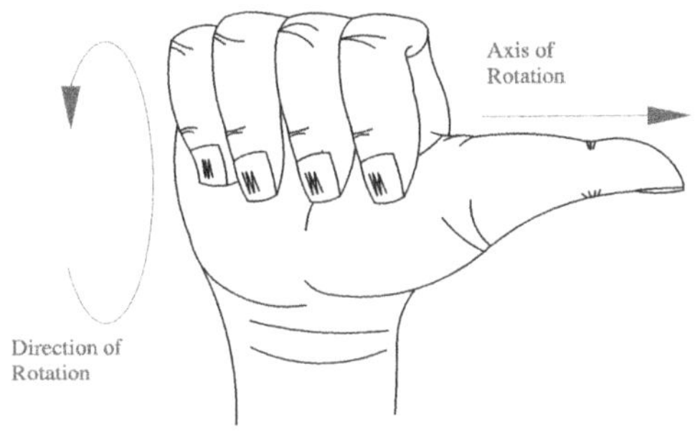

Figure 7-6(c) *Right-hand thumb rule showing the axis and direction of rotation*

CHANGING THE VIEWPOINT TO VIEW 3D MODELS

Until now, you have been drawing only the 2D entities in the *XY* plane and in the Plan view. But in the Plan view, it is very difficult to find out whether the object displayed is a 2D entity or a 3D model, refer to Figure 7-7. In this view, the cuboid displayed appears as a rectangle. The reason for this is that, by default, you view the objects in the Plan view from the direction of the positive *Z* axis. You can avoid this confusion by viewing the object from a direction that also displays the *Z* axis. In order to do that, you need to change the viewpoint so that the object is displayed in the space with all three axes, as shown in Figure 7-8. In this view, you can also see the *Z* axis of the model along with the *X* and *Y* axes. It will now be clear that the original object is not a rectangle but a 3D model. The viewpoint can be changed by using the ViewCube available in the drawing area or by using the options in the **View** panel.

Figure 7-7 *Cuboid looking like a rectangle in the Plan view*

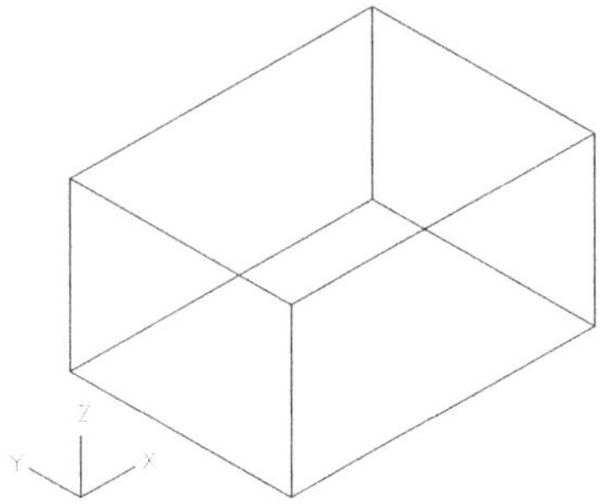

Figure 7-8 *Viewing the 3D model after changing the viewpoint*

Tip

Remember that changing the viewpoint does not affect the dimensions or the location of the model. When you change the viewpoint, the model is not moved from its original location. Changing the viewpoint only changes the direction from which you view the model.

Changing the Viewpoint Using the ViewCube

You can change the view of the models easily and quickly using the ViewCube. The ViewCube is displayed when the **3D Modeling** workspace is enabled and it allows you to switch between the standard and isometric views, roll the current view, or return to the **Home** view of a model. ViewCube consists of Cube, Home, Compass, and WCS menu. When you move the cursor over the ViewCube, it becomes active and the area at the pointer tip gets highlighted. The highlighted area can be a face, a corner, or an edge of the ViewCube. These highlighted areas are called hotspots. There are 6 faces, 12 edges, and 8 corners on a cube, refer to Figure 7-9. So, you can get 26 views by using the ViewCube. You can select the required hotspot to restore a view. You can also go back to the Home view by clicking on the Home icon of the ViewCube. You can set any existing view as the Home view by choosing the **Set Current View as Home** option from the shortcut menu that is displayed on right-clicking on the ViewCube. By default, a model is displayed in the perspective view. To display a model in parallel projection, right-click on the ViewCube and choose **Parallel** from the shortcut menu.

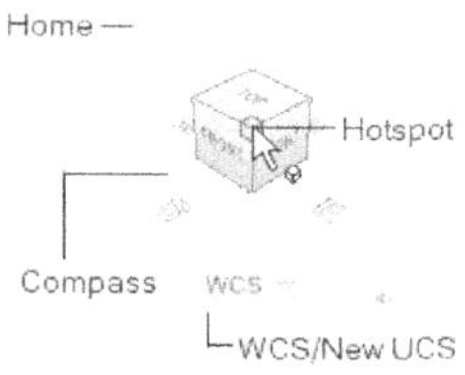

Figure 7-9 *The ViewCube*

The compass on the ViewCube indicates the geographic location of a model. The **N**, **E**, **S**, and **W** alphabets on the compass indicate the North, East, South, and West directions of a 3D model. You can pick and drag the compass ring to rotate the current view in the same plane. You can choose between the **UCS** and **WCS** from the WCS menu and even create a new UCS from the menu. When you right-click on the ViewCube, a shortcut menu will be displayed. Choose the **ViewCube Settings** option from it; the **ViewCube Settings** dialog box will be displayed, refer to Figure 7-10. This dialog box allows you to adjust the display of the compass ring and UCS menu, size, appearance, and location of the ViewCube.

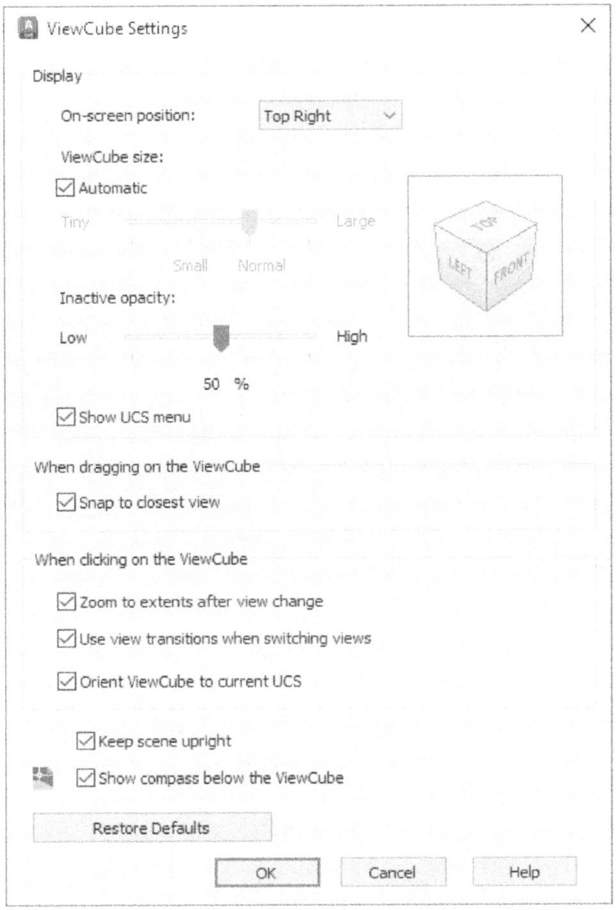

Figure 7-10 *The* ***ViewCube Settings*** *dialog box*

Note

In AutoCAD, you can change the current viewport by using the ***In-canvas Viewport controls****, displayed as* ***[-][Custom View][Realistic]****. It is available at the top left corner of the drawing area. When you choose the* ***[Custom View]*** *option, a flyout is displayed, refer to Figure 7-1. You can select the desired view from the flyout.*

Changing the Viewpoint Using the Ribbon or the Toolbar

You can also set the viewpoint either by using the **Named Views** panel in the **Visualize** tab of the **Ribbon** or by using the **View** toolbar.

The **Restore View** drop-down list in the **Named Views** panel consists of six preset orthographic views: **Top**, **Bottom**, **Left**, **Right**, **Front**, and **Back**; and four preset isometric views: **SW Isometric**, **SE Isometric**, **NE Isometric**, and **NW Isometric**, refer to Figure 7-11. This drop-down list also allows you to retrieve the previously set views or any previously created named views. All the above-mentioned controls are also available in the **View Manager** dialog box that is invoked on selecting the **View Manager** option from the **Restore View** drop-down list.

Choose the **New** button from the **View Manager** dialog box to create a new view; the **New View / Shot Properties** dialog box will be displayed, as shown in Figure 7-12.

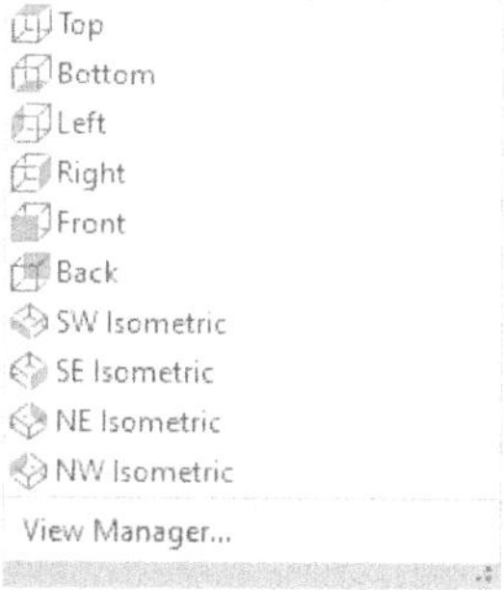

*Figure 7-11 The **Restore View** drop-down list*

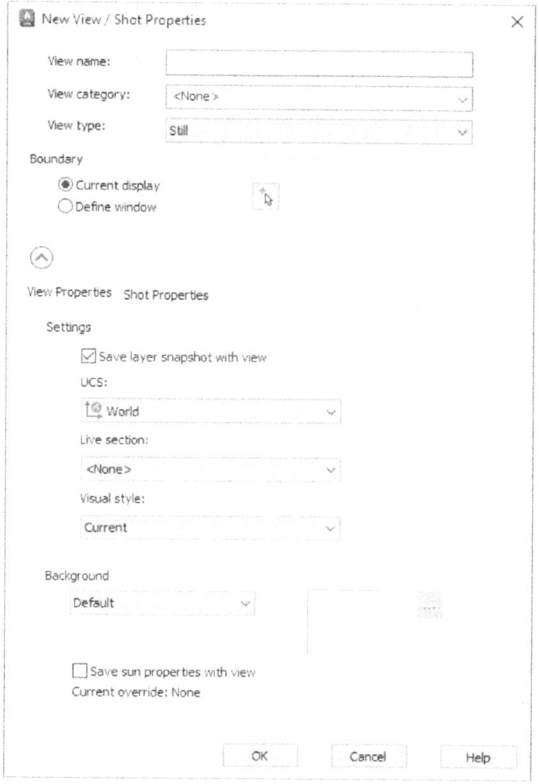

*Figure 7-12 The **New View / Shot Properties** dialog box*

Enter a name in the **View name** edit box to save the view. You can save different types of views into different categories using the options in this dialog box. The different types of views available in the **View type** drop-down list are **Still**, **Cinematic**, and **Recorded Walk**. But only **Still** is used for creating views and the other two are used for creating shots. The **View Properties** tab of this dialog box has three main areas: **Boundary**, **Settings,** and **Background**. The **Boundary** area allows you to save the current display or you can select an area of display by choosing the **Define window** radio button. In the **Settings** area, you can control the position of UCS to save the view, select the section of the view, and control the display of the model. The drop-down list in the **Background** area is used to select the type of background to save the view. The preview of the selected background is displayed in the preview area next to the drop-down list. You need to select the **Save sun properties with view** check box to save the view with the sun properties.

Tip

*When you select any of the preset orthographic views from the **View** drop-down list, the UCS is also aligned to that view.*

Changing the Viewpoint Using the Viewpoint Presets Dialog Box

Menu Bar: View > 3D Views > Viewpoint Presets **Command:** DDVPOINT (VPOINT)

You can invoke the **Viewpoint Presets** dialog box using the **VPOINT** command for setting the viewpoint to view 3D models. The viewpoint is set with respect to the angle from the X axis and the angle from the XY plane. Figure 7-13 shows different view direction parameters.

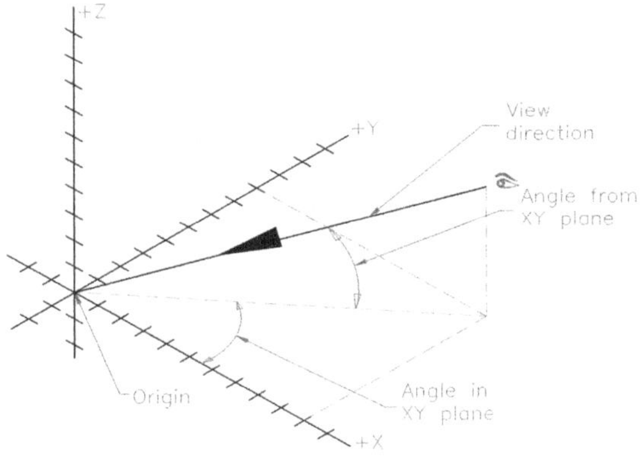

Figure 7-13 *View direction parameters*

Viewpoint Presets Dialog Box Options

The options in the **Viewpoint Presets** dialog box are discussed next, refer to Figure 7-14.

Absolute to WCS. This radio button is selected by default and used to set the viewpoint with respect to the world coordinate system (WCS).

Relative to UCS. This radio button is selected to set the viewpoint with respect to the current user coordinate system (UCS).

Note

The WCS and UCS have already been discussed in Chapter 6.

From: X Axis. This edit box is used to specify the angle in the *XY* plane from the *X* axis. You can directly enter the required angle in this edit box or select the desired angle from the image tile, refer to Figure 7-15. There are two arms in this image tile, and by default, they are placed one over the other. One arm displays current viewing angle and the other displays new viewing angle. On selecting a new angle from the image tile, it is automatically displayed in the **X Axis** edit box. This value can vary between **0** and **359.9**.

From: XY Plane. This edit box is used to specify the angle from the *XY* plane. You can directly enter the desired angle in it or select the angle from the image tile, as shown in Figure 7-16. This value can vary from -90 to +90.

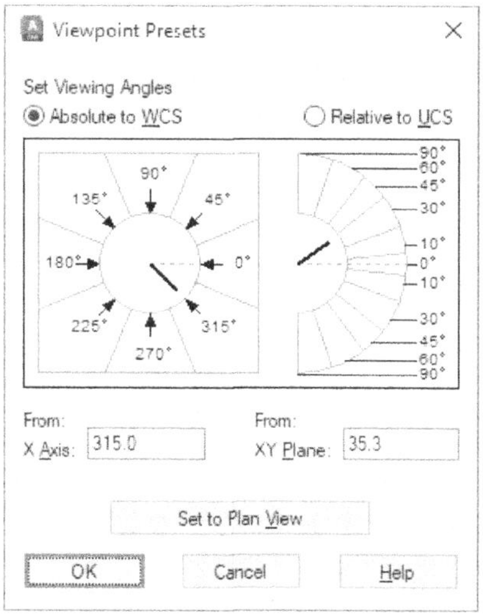

Figure 7-14 *The **Viewpoint Presets** dialog box*

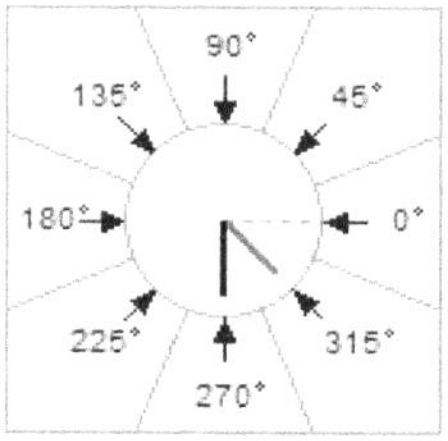

Figure 7-15 *The image tile for selecting the angle from X axis*

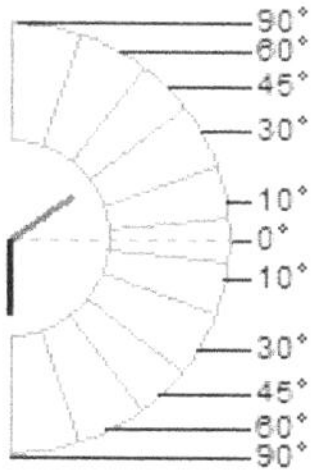

Figure 7-16 *The image tile for selecting the angle from the XY plane*

Set to Plan View. This button is chosen to set the viewpoint to the Plan view of the WCS or the UCS. If the **Absolute to WCS** radio button is selected, the viewpoint will be set to the Plan view of the WCS. If the **Relative to UCS** radio button is selected, the viewpoint will be set to the Plan view of the current UCS. Figures 7-17 and 7-18 show the 3D models from different viewing angles.

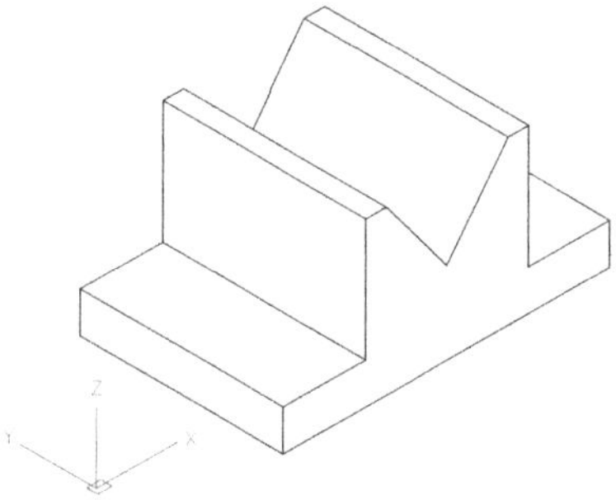

Figure 7-17 *Viewing the 3D model with the angle in the XY plane as **225** and the angle from the XY plane as **30***

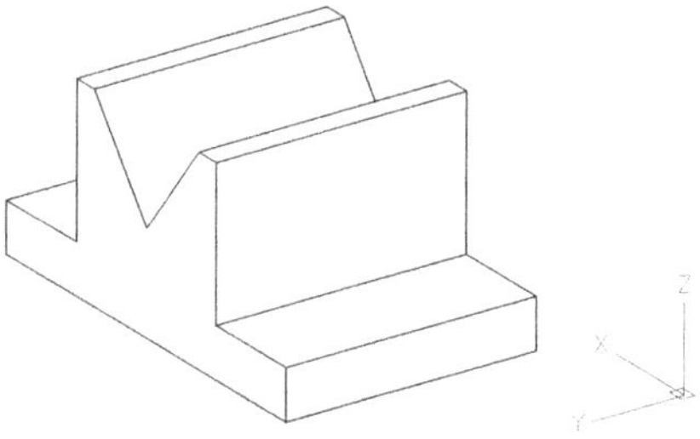

Figure 7-18 *Viewing the 3D model with the angle in the XY plane as **145** and the angle from the XY plane as **25***

Tip

1. If you set a negative angle from the XY plane, the Z axis will be displayed as a dotted line, indicating a negative Z direction, refer to Figures 7-19 and 7-20.

2. In case of confusion in identifying the direction of X, Y, and Z axes, use the right-hand thumb rule.

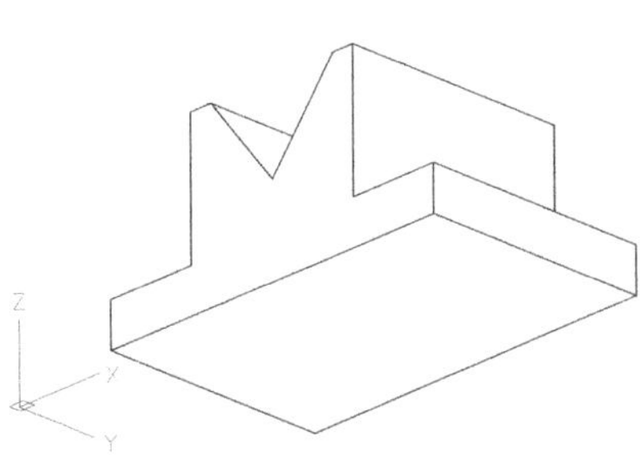

Figure 7-19 *Viewing the 3D model with the angle in the XY plane as* ***315*** *and the angle from the XY plane as* ***-25***

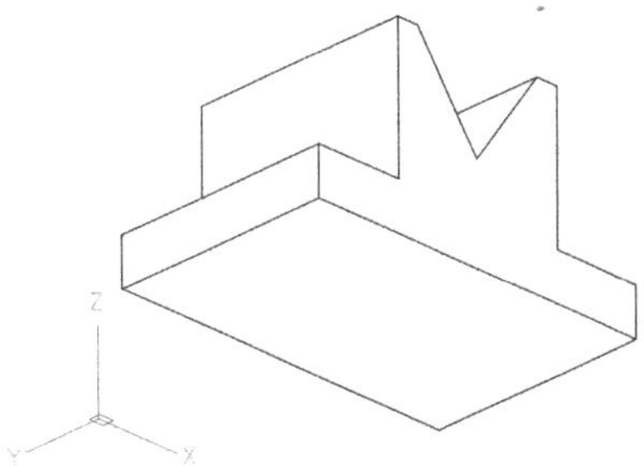

Figure 7-20 *Viewing the 3D model with the angle in the XY plane as* ***225*** *and the angle from the XY plane as* ***-25***

Changing the Viewpoint Using the -VPOINT Command

Menu Bar: View > 3D Views > Viewpoint **Command:** -VPOINT

The **-VPOINT** command is used to set the viewpoint for viewing the 3D models. Using this command, the users can specify a point in the 3D space that will act as the viewpoint.

Specifying a Viewpoint

This is the default option and is used to set a viewpoint by specifying its location (of viewer) using the *X*, *Y*, and *Z* coordinates of that particular point. AutoCAD follows a convention of the sides of the 3D model for specifying the viewpoint. The convention states that if the UCS is at the World position (default position), then

1. The side at the positive *X* axis direction will be taken as the right side of the model.
2. The side at the negative *X* axis direction will be taken as the left side of the model.
3. The side at the negative *Y* axis direction will be taken as the front side of the model.
4. The side at the positive *Y* axis direction will be taken as the back side of the model.
5. The side at the positive *Z* axis direction will be taken as the top side of the model.
6. The side at the negative *Z* axis direction will be taken as the bottom side of the model.

Some standard viewpoint coordinates and the view they display are given next.

Value	View	Value	View	Value	View
1,0,0	Right side	-1,0,0	Left side	0,1,0	Back
0,-1,0	Front	0,0,1	Top view	0,0,-1	Bottom view
1,1,1	NE Isometric	-1,1,1	NW Isometric	1,-1,1	SE Isometric
-1,-1,1	SW Isometric	1,1,-1	Right, Back, Bottom	-1,1,-1	Left, Back, Bottom
1,-1,-1	Right, Front, Bottom	-1,-1,-1	Left, Front, Bottom		

You can also enter the values in decimal, but the resultant views will not be the standard views. Figures 7-21 through 7-24 show a 3D model from different viewpoints.

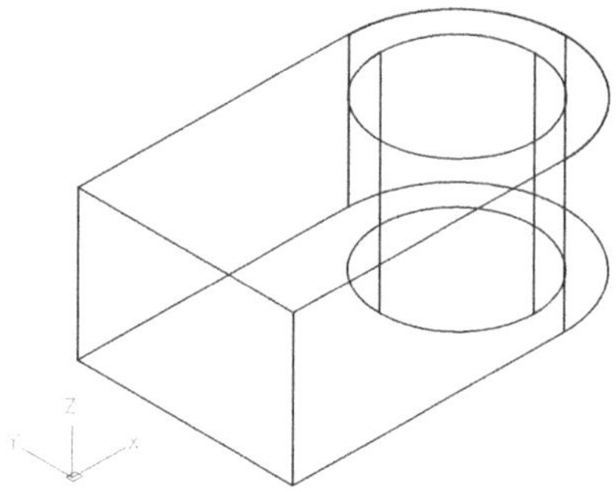

Figure 7-21 *Viewing the model from the viewpoint -1,-1,1*

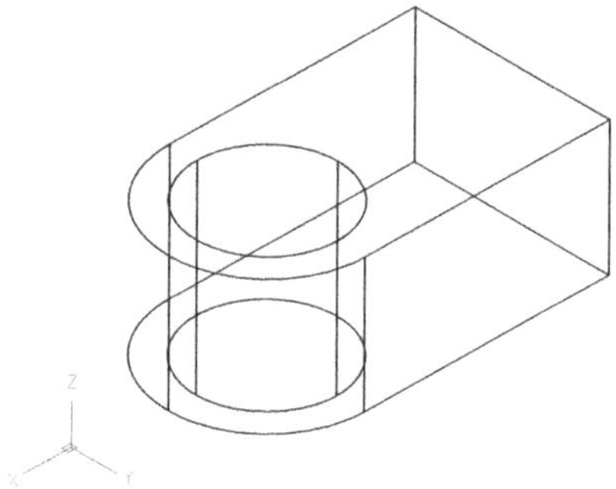

Figure 7-22 *Viewing the model from the viewpoint 1,1,1*

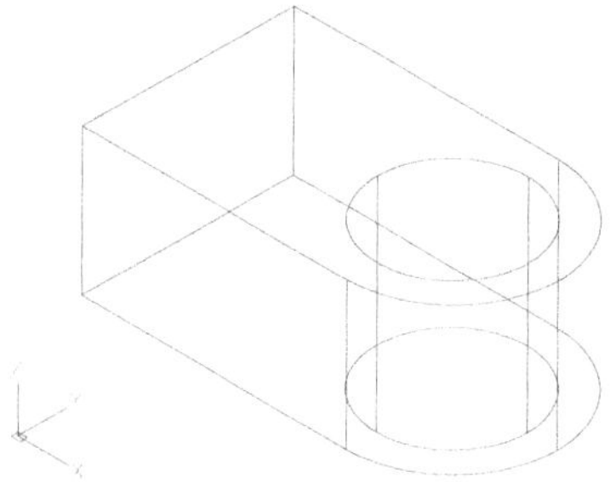

Figure 7-23 *Viewing the model from the viewpoint 1,-1,1*

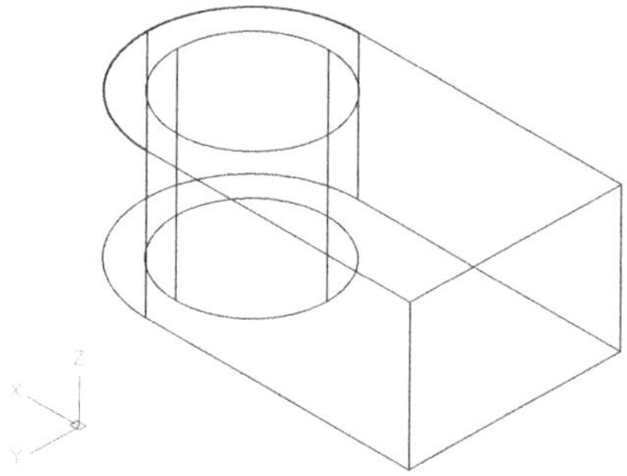

Figure 7-24 *Viewing the model from the viewpoint -1,1,1*

Compass and Tripod

When you choose **View > 3D Views > Viewpoint** from the menu bar, a compass and an axis tripod are displayed, as shown in Figure 7-25. You can directly set the viewpoint using this compass and can select any point on this compass to specify the viewpoint. The compass consists of two circles, a smaller circle and a bigger circle. Both these circles are divided into four quadrants: first, second, third, and fourth. The resultant view will depend upon the quadrant and the circle on which you select the point. In the first quadrant, both the X and Y axes are positive; in the second quadrant, the X axis is negative and the Y axis is positive; in the third quadrant, both the X and Y axes are negative; and in the fourth quadrant, the X axis is positive and the Y axis is negative. Now, if you select a point inside the inner circle, it will be in the positive Z axis direction. If you select the point outside the inner circle and inside the outer circle, it will be in the negative Z axis direction. Therefore, if the previously mentioned statements are added, the following is concluded.

1. If you select a point inside the smaller circle in the first quadrant, the resultant view will be the Right, Back, or Top view. If you select a point outside the smaller circle and inside the bigger circle in this quadrant, the resultant view will be the Right, Back, or Bottom view, refer to Figure 7-26.

2. If you select a point inside the smaller circle in the second quadrant, the resultant view will be the Left, Back, or Top view. If you select a point outside the smaller circle and inside

the bigger circle in this quadrant, the resultant view will be the Left, Back, or Bottom view, refer to Figure 7-26.

3. If you select a point inside the smaller circle in the third quadrant, the resultant view will be the Left, Front, or Top view. If you select a point outside the smaller circle and inside the bigger circle in this quadrant, the resultant view will be the Left, Front, or Bottom view, refer to Figure 7-26.

4. If you select a point inside the smaller circle in the fourth quadrant, the resultant view will be the Right, Front, or Top view. If you select a point outside the smaller circle and inside the bigger circle in this quadrant, the resultant view will be the Right, Front, or Bottom view, refer to Figure 7-26.

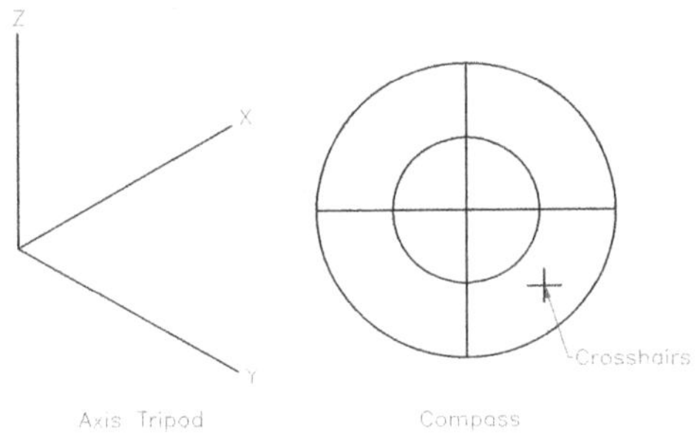

Figure 7-25 *The axis tripod and the compass*

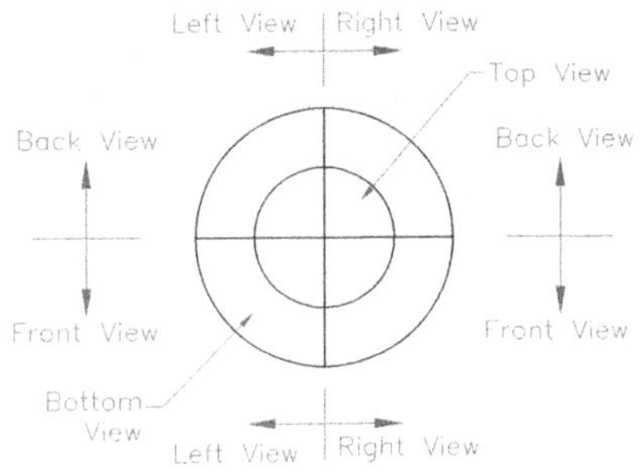

Figure 7-26 *The directions of the compass*

Rotate

This option is similar to setting the viewpoint in the **Viewpoint Presets** dialog box, which is displayed by invoking the **-VPOINT** command. When you select this option, you will be prompted to specify the angle in the *XY* plane and the angle from the *XY* plane. The angle in the *XY* plane will be taken from the *X* axis.

IN-CANVAS VIEWPORT CONTROL

The **In-canvas Viewport control** enables you to control the viewport as well as visual style. By default, the **In-canvas Viewport control** is displayed as **[-][Custom View][Realistic]** in the top left corner of the drawing area. The tools available in this viewport control are discussed next.

[-]

When you choose the **[-]** button in the **In-canvas Viewport control,** a flyout will be displayed, as shown in Figure 7-27. Options in this flyout are discussed next.

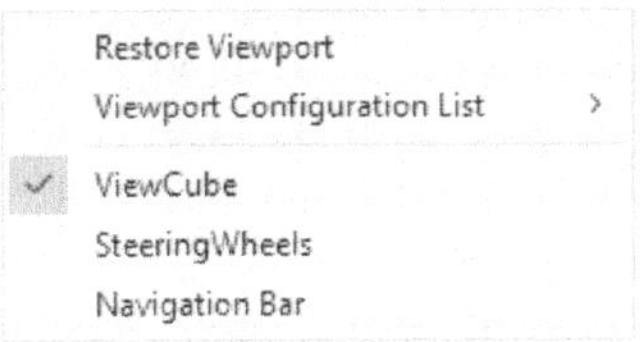

Figure 7-27 *Flyout displayed on choosing the [-] button*

Restore Viewport

When you choose this option, the drawing screen is displayed with four equal partitions. In each of these partitions, a **[+]** button is displayed in the upper left corner. When you click on the **[+]** button, a flyout will be displayed with the **Maximize Viewport** option. Using this option, you can maximize the partition window.

Viewport Configuration List

When you choose this option, a flyout will be displayed, as shown in the Figure 7-28. In this flyout, 12 options are available for viewport settings. Using these options, you can set as many partitions as needed to be created and their position in the drawing area.

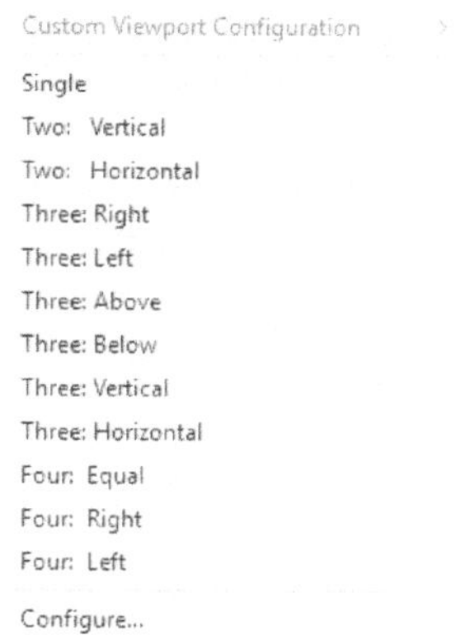

***Figure 7-28** The **Viewport Configuration List** flyout*

Viewcube, SteeringWheels, and Navigation Bar

ViewCube is used to minimize the time required in changing the view of the model, while the SteeringWheels and Navigation Bar are used to minimize the navigation time. Using the ViewCube from the Viewport Controls flyout, you can toggle the display of the ViewCube. As you choose the **SteeringWheels** option, SteeringWheels will get attached to the cursor. SteeringWheels will be discussed in detail later in this chapter. Using the **Navigation Bar** option, you can toggle the display of the Navigation Bar in the right of the drawing screen.

View Controls

The **View Controls** flyout contains various options to change your current view or to create a new view. This flyout is displayed on choosing the **Custom View** button from the **In-canvas Viewport controls**, refer to Figure 7-29. The options in this flyout are used for setting view controls and are discussed next.

***Figure 7-29** The **View Controls** flyout*

- **Custom Model Views:** This flyout consists of custom views created by using the **View Manager**.
- **Views:** There are 10 view options available in this flyout to set 10 different views. When you change the view, the UCS gets reoriented according to the view selected.
- **View Manager:** Using this option, you can create a new view or edit the view settings of an existing view.
- **Parallel and Perspective:** These options are used to control the projection. If you choose the **Parallel** option, the drawing will be displayed parallel to the screen. If you choose the **Perspective** option, the drawing will be displayed in a perspective view.

Visual Style Controls

The **Visual Style Controls** flyout is used to control the visual style of the model. This flyout is displayed when you select the **Realistic** button from the **Visual Style Controls**, as shown in Figure 7-30. The options in this flyout are used for setting visual styles and are discussed next.

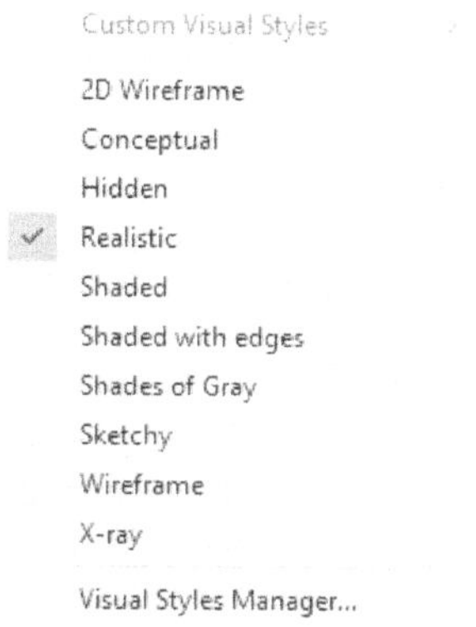

***Figure 7-30** The Visual **View Controls** flyout*

- **Custom Visual Styles**. When you click on this option, a flyout is displayed. This flyout displays the visual styles that you have created.
- **Visual Styles**. There are 10 options that enable you to select the required visual style.

- **Visual Styles Manager**. This option is used to create a new visual style as well as to change the settings of the current visual style.

3D COORDINATE SYSTEMS

Similar to 2D coordinate systems, there are two types of 3D coordinate systems. They are discussed next.

Absolute Coordinate System

This type of coordinate system is similar to the 2D absolute coordinate system in which the coordinates of the point are calculated from the origin (0,0). The only difference here is that, along with the *X* and *Y* coordinates, the *Z* coordinate is also included. For example, to draw a line in 3D space starting from the origin to a point say 10,6,6, the procedure to be followed is given next.

Command: *Choose the **Line** tool from the **Draw** panel.*
Specify first point: **0,0,0**
Specify next point or [Undo]: **10,6,6**
Specify next point or [Undo]: Enter.

Figure 7-31 shows the model drawn using the absolute coordinate system.

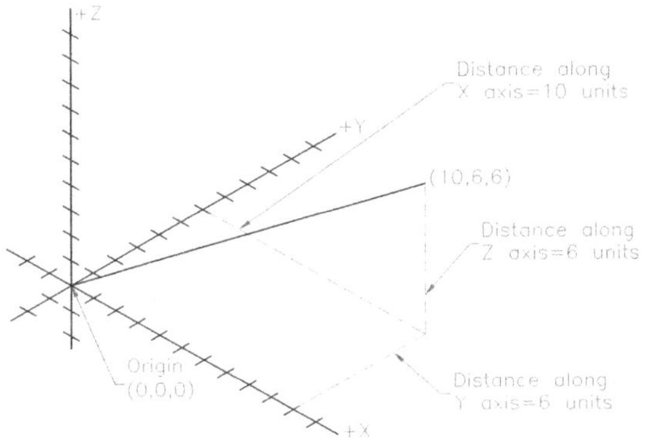

***Figure 7-31** Drawing a line from origin to 10,6,6*

Relative Coordinate System

The following are the three types of relative coordinate systems in 3D:

Relative Rectangular Coordinate System

This coordinate system is similar to the relative rectangular coordinate system of 2D, except that in 3D you also have to enter the *Z* coordinate along with the *X* and *Y* coordinates. The syntax of the relative rectangular system for the 3D is **@X coordinate, Y coordinate, Z coordinate**.

Relative Cylindrical Coordinate System

In this coordinate system, you can locate the point by specifying its distance from the reference point, the angle in the *XY* plane, and its distance from the *XY* plane. The syntax of the relative cylindrical coordinate system is **@Distance from the reference point in the XY plane < Angle in the XY plane from the X axis, Distance from the XY plane along the Z axis**. Figure 7-32 shows the components of the relative cylindrical coordinate system.

Relative Spherical Coordinate System

In this coordinate system, you can locate the point by specifying its distance from the reference point, the angle in the *XY* plane, and the angle from the *XY* plane. The syntax of the relative spherical coordinate system is **@Length of the line from the reference point < Angle in the XY plane from the X axis < Angle from the XY plane**. Figure 7-33 shows the components of the relative spherical coordinate system.

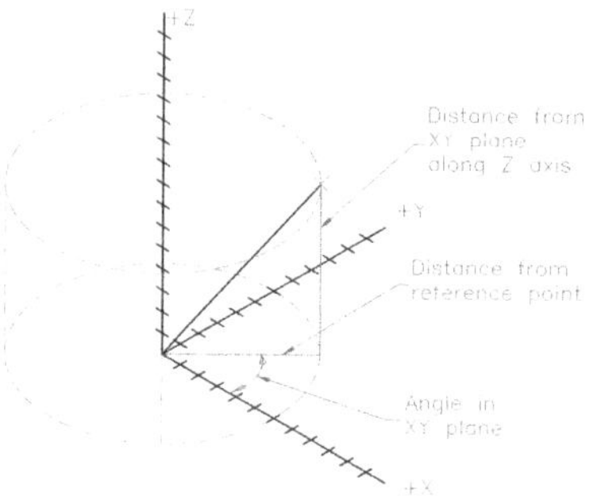

Figure 7-32 *Various components of the relative cylindrical coordinate system*

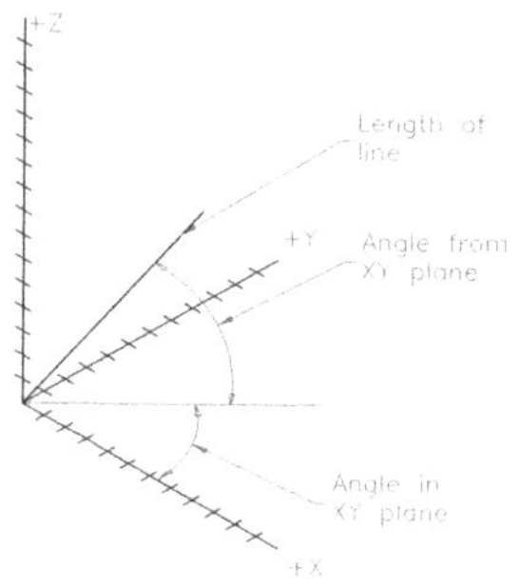

Figure 7-33 *Various components of the relative spherical coordinate system*

Tip

The major difference between the relative cylindrical and relative spherical coordinate systems is that in the relative cylindrical coordinate system, the specified distance is the distance from the reference point in the XY plane. On the other hand, in the relative spherical coordinate system, the specified distance is the total length of the line in the 3D space.

Example 1 Relative Coordinate System

In this example, you will draw the 3D wireframe model shown in Figure 7-34. Its dimensions are given in Figure 7-35.

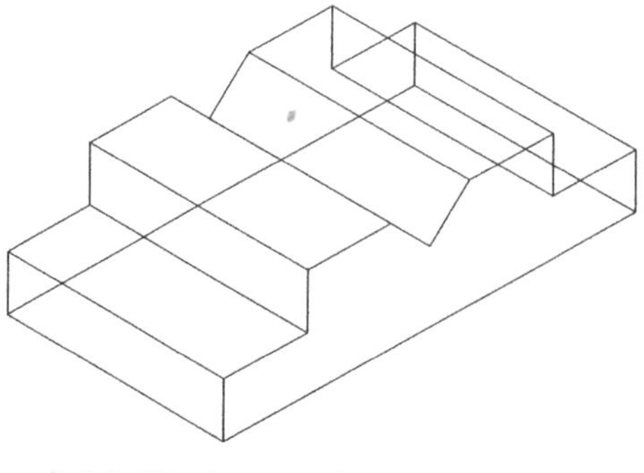

Figure 7-34 *The 3D Wireframe model for Example 1*

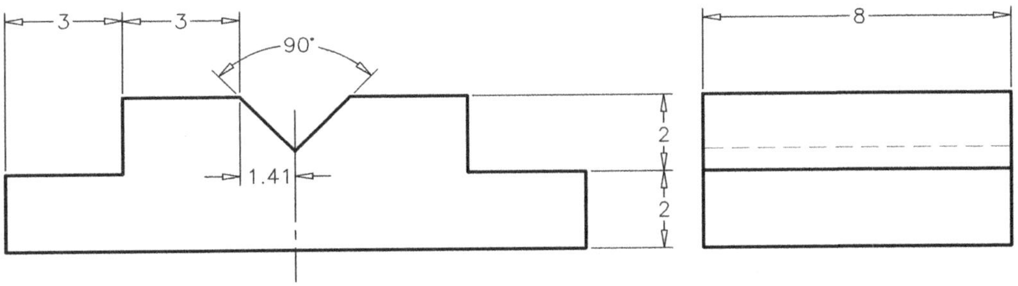

Figure 7-35 Orthographic views of the Wireframe model

1. Start a new *acad3D.dwt* file in the **3D Modeling** workspace and select the **SW Isometric** option from the **Restore View** drop-down list in the **View** panel of the **Home** tab. Alternatively, select the SouthWest top corner hotspot on the ViewCube, refer to the compass of the ViewCube to get the SouthWest view of the model.

2. As the start point of the model is not given, you can start the model from any point. Choose the **Line** tool from the **Draw** panel of the **Home** tab and follow the prompt sequence given next.

Specify first point: **4,2,0**
Specify next point or [Undo]: **@0,0,2**
Specify next point or [Undo]: **@3,0,0**
Specify next point or [Close/Undo]: **@0,0,2**
Specify next point or [Close/Undo]: **@3,0,0**
Specify next point or [Close/Undo]: **@2<0<315**
Specify next point or [Close/Undo]: **@2<0<45**
Specify next point or [Close/Undo]: **@3,0,0**
Specify next point or [Close/Undo]: **@0,0,-2**
Specify next point or [Close/Undo]: **@3,0,0**
Specify next point or [Close/Undo]: **@0,0,-2**
Specify next point or [Close/Undo]: **C**

3. Choose the **Line** tool again and follow the prompt sequence given next.

Specify first point: **4,2,0**
Specify next point or [Undo]: **@0,8,0**
Specify next point or [Undo]: **@0,0,2**
Specify next point or [Close/Undo]: **@3,0,0**
Specify next point or [Close/Undo]: **@0,0,2**
Specify next point or [Close/Undo]: **@3,0,0**
Specify next point or [Close/Undo]: **@2<0<315**
Specify next point or [Close/Undo]: **@2<0<45**
Specify next point or [Close/Undo]: **@3,0,0**
Specify next point or [Close/Undo]: **@0,0,-2**

Specify next point or [Close/Undo]: **@3,0,0**
Specify next point or [Close/Undo]: **@0,0,-2**
Specify next point or [Close/Undo]: **@0,-8,0**
Specify next point or [Close/Undo]: Enter.

4. Complete the model by joining the remaining edges using the **Line** tool.

5. The final 3D wireframe model should look similar to the one shown in Figure 7-36.

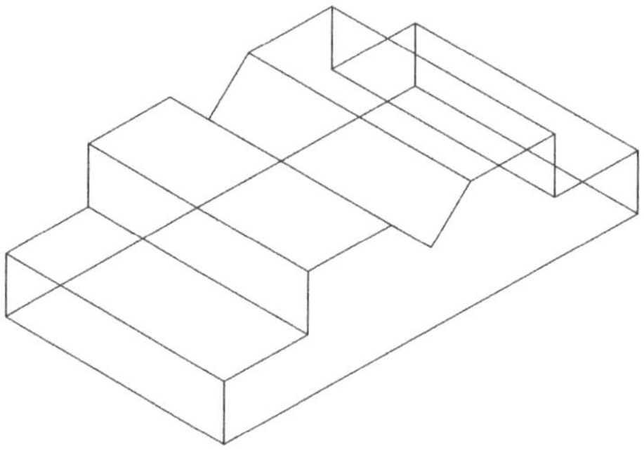

Figure 7-36 *The final 3D wireframe model for Example 1*

DIRECT DISTANCE ENTRY METHOD

In AutoCAD, you can directly create models in 3D space. This method is similar to that in 2D. The easiest way to draw a model by using the **Line** tool in 3D space of AutoCAD is by using the Direct Distance Entry method. Before drawing a model by using this method, ensure that the **Dynamic Input** button is chosen in the Status Bar. Next choose the **Line** tool; you will be prompted to specify the start point. Enter the coordinate values in the text box and press Enter; you will be prompted to specify the next point. Move the cursor along the direction in which you need to draw the line and enter the absolute length of the line and its angle in the corresponding text boxes, with respect to the previous point. Note that you can use the TAB key to toggle between the text boxes.

To draw a line along the Z axis, move the cursor along the Z axis; you will notice that the tool tip displays **Ortho: (current length) < +Z**, if the ortho mode is on. Type the absolute distance and the angle, and press Enter. If the ortho mode is not chosen, position the cursor at the desired angle, type the length at the Command prompt, and then press Enter. If necessary, change the UCS as discussed earlier.

Example 2 Direct Distance Entry

In this example, you will draw the 3D wireframe model shown in Figure 7-37.

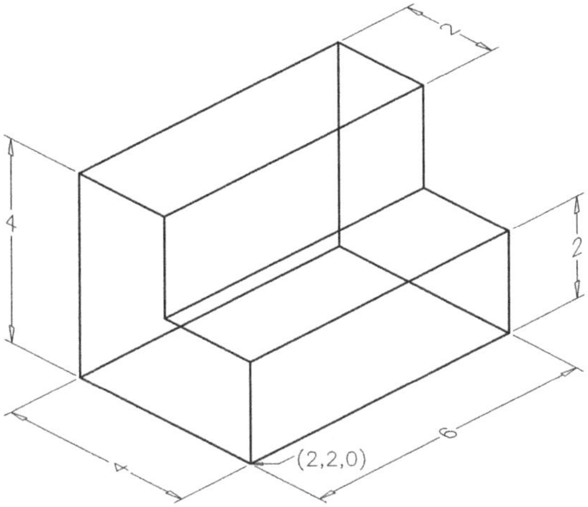

Figure 7-37 3D wireframe model for Example 2

1. Start a new *acad3D.dwt* file in the **3D Modeling** workspace and make sure the **Ortho Mode** and **Dynamic Input** buttons are chosen. Then, change the drawing view by using the ViewCube. The view needed is **SW Isometric**. The Southwest view of the ViewCube has three hotspots: bottom, edge, and top. You need to select the top hotspot to get the required view. Refer to Figure 7-38 for the SW Isometric hotspot. However, you can check different hotspots and view the model in different angles by using the ViewCube.

2. Choose the **Line** tool from the **Draw** panel and specify the start point at 2,2,0.

3. Move the cursor along the positive X axis. Then, type **6** and press Enter; a line of length 6 units is drawn along the X axis.

4. Move the cursor along the positive Y axis, type **4**, and press Enter; a line of length 4 units is drawn along the Y axis.

5. Draw the other two lines to create the closed profile at the bottom of the model.

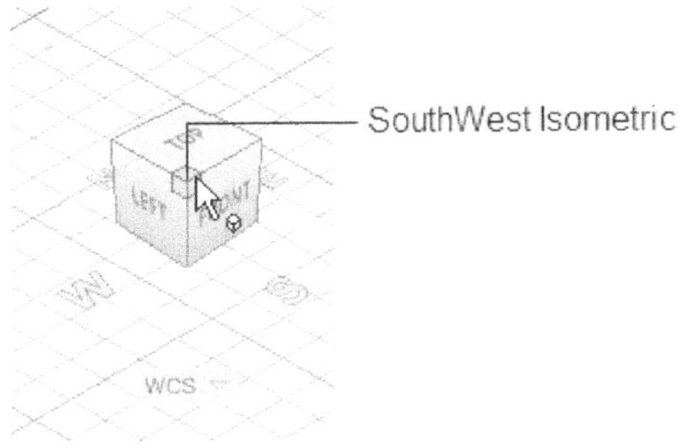

Figure 7-38 ViewCube showing the SW Isometric

6. From the start point of the model, move the cursor along the positive Z axis. You will notice that the tooltip displays **Ortho: (current length) < +Z**, as shown in Figure 7-39.

7. Type **2** at the Command prompt and press Enter; a line of length 2 units is drawn.

8. Move the cursor along the positive X axis, type **6**, and press Enter; a line of length 6 units is drawn.

9. Similarly, draw other lines to complete the model. The final model should look similar to the one shown in Figure 7-40.

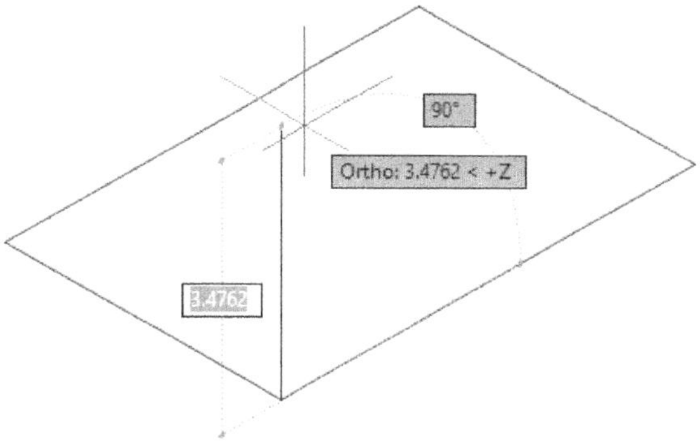

Figure 7-39 *Tooltip displayed on moving the cursor along the positive Z axis*

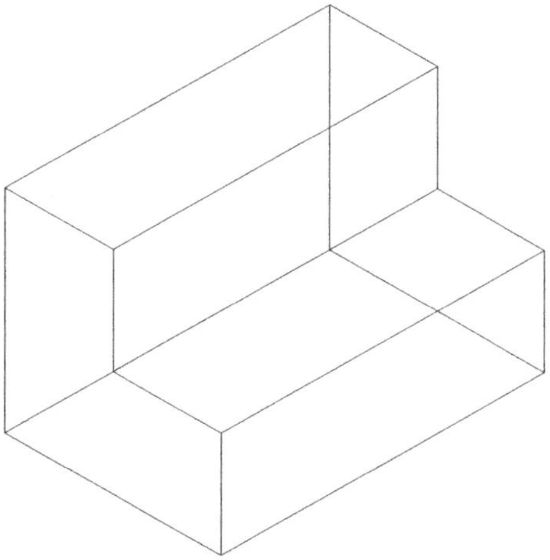

Figure 7-40 *Final 3D model for Example 2*

Exercise 1

In this exercise, you will draw the 3D wireframe model shown in Figure 7-41. Its dimensions are given in the same figure. You can start the model from any point.

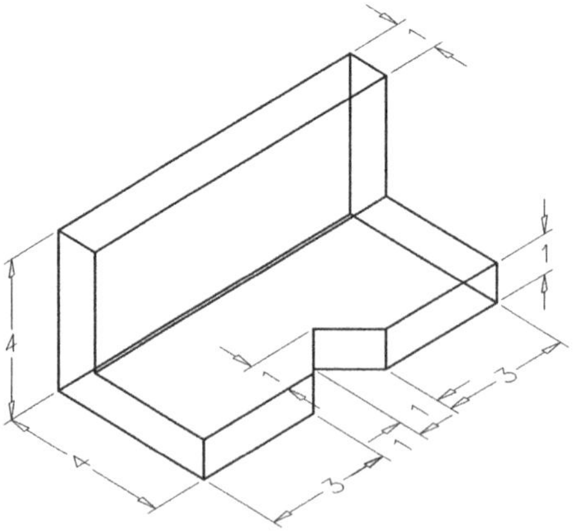

Figure 7-41 *Wireframe model for Exercise 1*

TRIM, EXTEND, AND FILLET TOOLS

In AutoCAD, you can use the trim, extend, and fillet tools in 3D workspace. You can also use the **PROJMODE** and **EDGEMODE** variables. The **PROJMODE** variable sets the projection mode for trimming and extending. The value of 0 implies **True 3D mode**, that is, no projection. In this case, the objects must intersect in 3D space to be trimmed or extended. It is similar to using the **None** option of the **Project** mode of the **Extend** and **Trim** tools. A value of 1 projects onto the *XY* plane of the current UCS and is similar to using the **UCS** option of the **Project** option of the **Trim** or **Extend** tools. A value of 2 projects onto the current view plane and is like using the **View** option of the **Project** option of the **Trim** or **Extend** tools. The value of the **EDGEMODE** system variable controls the cutting or trimming boundaries. A value of 0 considers the selected edge with no extension. You can also use the **No extend** option of the **Edge** option of the **Trim** or **Extend** tools. A value of 1 considers an imaginary extension of the selected edge. This is similar to using the **Extend** option of the **Edge** option of the **Trim** or **Extend** tools.

You can fillet coplanar objects whose extrusion directions are not parallel to the *Z* axis of the current UCS, by using the **Fillet** tool. The fillet arc exists on the same plane and has the same extrusion direction as the coplanar objects. If the coplanar objects to be filleted exist in opposite directions, the fillet arc will be on the same plane but will be inclined toward the positive *Z* axis.

SETTING THICKNESS AND ELEVATION FOR NEW OBJECTS

You can create the objects with a preset elevation or thickness using the **ELEV** command. This command is discussed next.

The ELEV Command

Command: ELEV

This is a transparent command and is used to set elevation and thickness for new objects. The following prompt sequence is displayed when you invoke this command:

Specify new default elevation <0.0000>: *Enter the new elevation value.*
Specify new default thickness <0.0000>: *Enter the new thickness value.*

Elevation

This option is used to specify the elevation value for new objects. Setting the elevation is nothing but moving the working plane from its default position. By default, the working plane is on the world *XY* plane. You can move this working plane by specifying the new value for elevation using the **ELEV** command. However, remember that the working plane can be moved only along the *Z* axis, refer to Figure 7-42. The default elevation value is 0.0 and you can set any positive or negative value. All objects that will be drawn hereafter will be with the specified elevation. The **ELEV** command sets the elevation only for the new objects and the existing objects are not modified using this option.

Thickness

This option is used to specify the thickness values for new objects. It can be considered as another method of creating surface models. Specifying the thickness creates extruded surface models. The thickness is always taken along the Z axis direction, refer to Figure 7-43. The 3D faces will be automatically applied on the vertical faces of the objects drawn with a thickness. The **Thickness** option sets the thickness only for the new objects and the existing objects are not modified.

Note

*By default, the model will be displayed in the **Realistic** visual style. To change it to wireframe, choose the **2D Wireframe** from the **Visual Style Controls** flyout in the **In-canvas Viewport Controls**. You can suppress the hidden edges in the model by using the **Hide** tool. The **Hide** tool is discussed in the next section.*

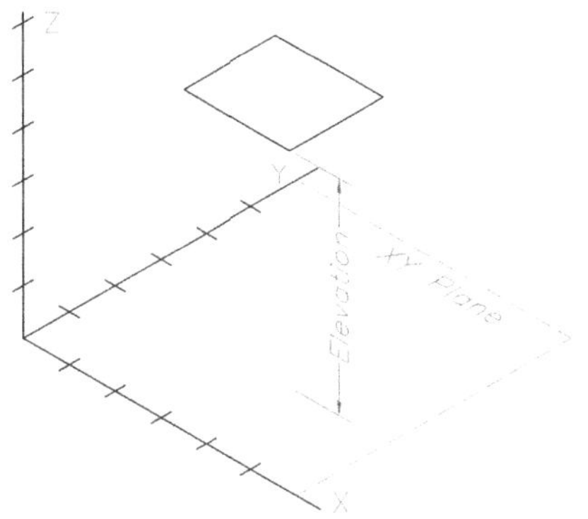

Figure 7-42 *Object drawn with elevation*

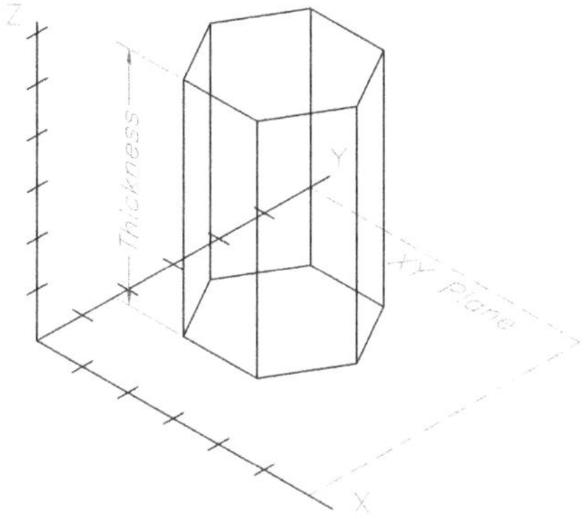

Figure 7-43 *Object drawn with thickness*

Tip

1. The elevation value will be reset to 0.0 when you change the coordinate system to WCS.

*2. The rectangles drawn using the **Rectangle** tool do not consider the thickness value set by using the **ELEV** command. To draw a rectangle with thickness, use the **Thickness** option of the **Rectangle** tool.*

3. Figure 7-44 shows a point, line, polygon, circle drawn with a thickness of 5 units.

4. To write text with thickness, first write a single line text and then change its thickness using any of the commands that modify its property, refer to Figure 7-45.

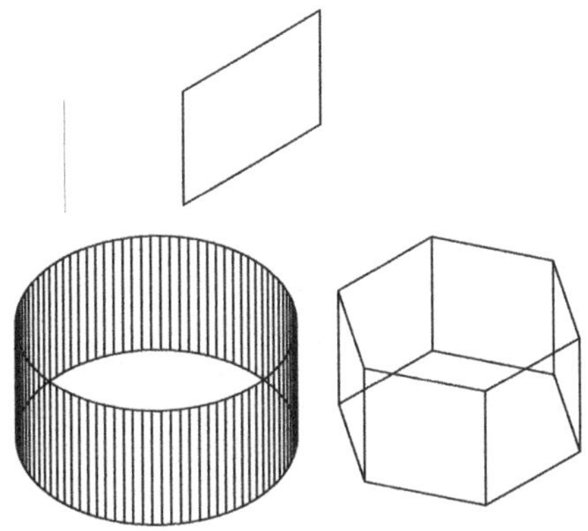

Figure 7-44 *A point, line, polygon, and circle drawn with a thickness of 5 units*

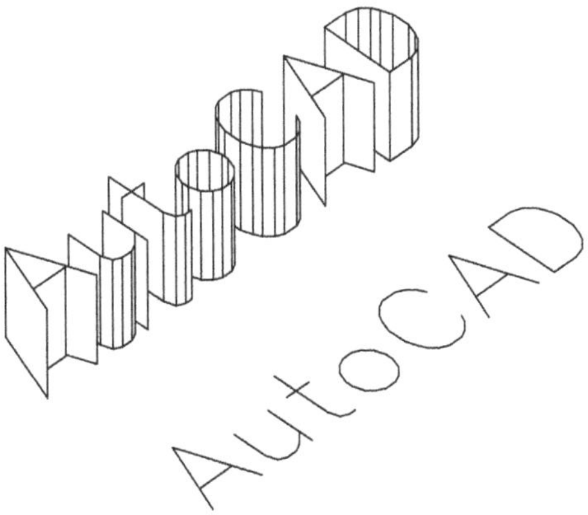

Figure 7-45 *Text with and without thickness*

SUPPRESSING THE HIDDEN EDGES

Menu Bar: View > Hide	Toolbar: Render > Hide	Command: HIDE

Whenever you create a surface or a solid model, the edges that lie at the back, called the hidden edges too, also become visible. As a result, the model appears like a wireframe model. You need to manually suppress the hidden lines in the 3D model using the **Hide** command. When you invoke this tool, all objects on the screen are regenerated. Also, the 3D models are displayed with the hidden edges suppressed. If the value of the **DISPSILH** system variable is set to **1**, the model is displayed only with the silhouette edges. The internal edges that have facets will not be displayed. The hidden lines are again included in the drawing when the next regeneration takes place. Figure 7-46 shows the surface models displaying the hidden edges. Figure 7-47 shows surface models without the hidden edges.

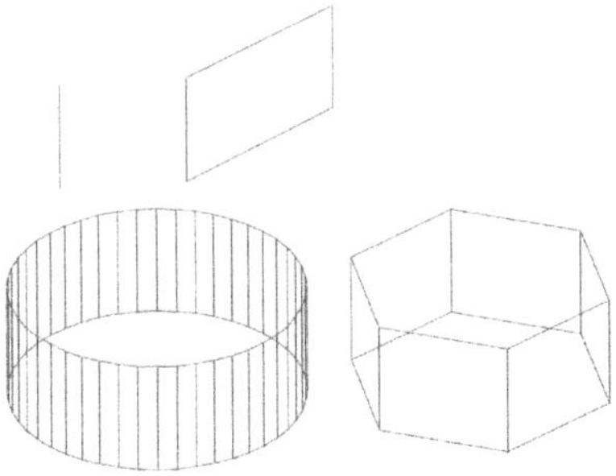

Figure 7-46 *3D models with hidden edges*

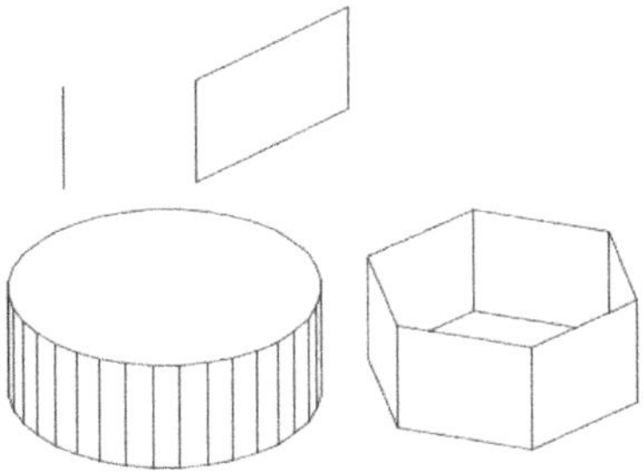

Figure 7-47 *Models without hidden edges*

Tip

*The **Hide** command considers Circles, Solids, Traces, Polylines with width, Regions, and 3D Faces as opaque surfaces that will hide objects.*

CREATING A 3D POLYLINE

Ribbon: Home > Draw > 3D Polyline **Menu Bar:** Draw > 3D Polyline
Command: 3DPOLY

The **3DPolyline** tool is used to draw straight polylines in a 2D plane or a 3D space. This tool is similar to the **Polyline** tool except the fact that you can draw polylines in a plane other than the *XY* plane also by using this tool. However, this tool does not provide the **Width** option or the **Arc** option; and therefore you cannot create a 3D polyline with a width or an arc. The **Close** and **Undo** options of this tool are similar to those of the **Polyline** tool.

Tip
You can fit a spline curve about the 3D polyline using the ***Edit Polyline*** *tool. Use the* ***Spline curve*** *option to fit the spline curve and the* ***Decurve*** *option to remove it.*

CONVERTING WIREFRAME MODELS INTO SURFACE MODELS

You can convert a wireframe model into a surface model using the **3DFACE** command and the **PFACE** command. These tools are discussed next.

Creating 3D Faces

Menu Bar: Draw > Modeling > Meshes > 3D Face **Command:** 3DFACE

The **3D Face** tool is used to create 3D faces in space. You can create three-sided or four-sided faces using this tool. You can specify the same or a different Z coordinate value for each point of the face. On invoking this tool, you will be prompted to specify the first, second, third, and fourth points of the 3D face. Once you have specified the first four points, it will again prompt you to specify the third and fourth points. In this case, it will take the previous third and fourth points as the first and second points, respectively. This process will continue until you press Enter at the **Specify third point or [Invisible] <exit>** prompt. Keep in mind that the points must be specified in the natural clockwise or the counterclockwise direction to create a proper 3D face. Figure 7-48 shows 3D faces created on the 3D wireframe model.

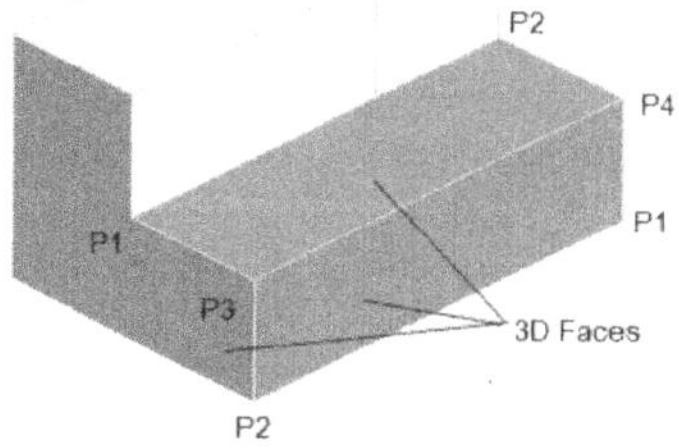

Figure 7-48 *3D faces created on the 3D wireframe model*

However, in case of complex wireframe models, refer to Figure 7-49, it is not easy to apply 3D faces. This is because when you apply a 3D face, it generates edges about all points that you specify. These edges will be displayed on the wireframe model, as shown in Figure 7-49. You can avoid these unwanted visible edges by applying the 3D faces with invisible edges using the **Invisible** option. It is very important to note here that the edge that will be created after you enter **I** at the **Specify next point or [Invisible] <exit>** prompt will not be the invisible edge. The edge that will be created after this edge will be the invisible edge. Therefore, to make the P3 edge and P4 edge invisible, specify P1 as the first point and P2 as the second point. Before specifying P3 as the third point, enter **I** at the **Specify third point or [Invisible] <exit>** prompt. Similarly, follow the same procedure for creating the other invisible edges, refer to Figure 7-50.

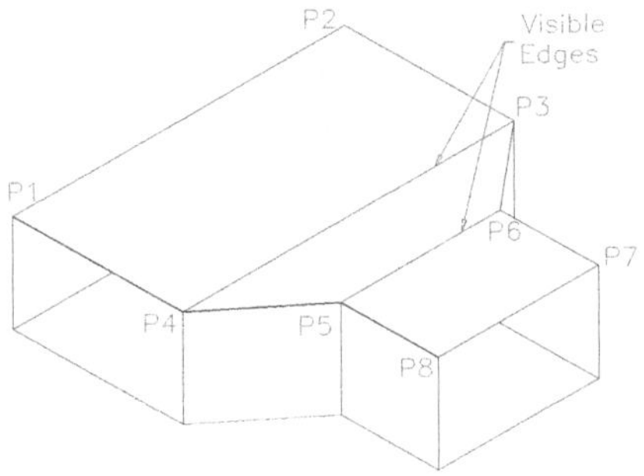

Figure 7-49 *Wireframe model with edges*

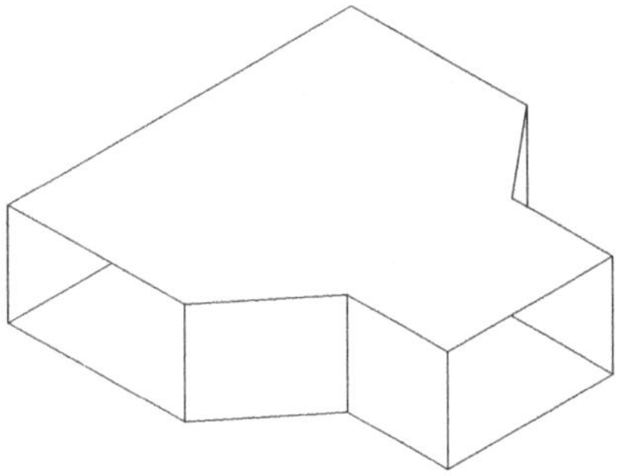

Figure 7-50 *Wireframe model without edges*

Creating Polyface Meshes

Command: PFACE

The **PFACE** command is similar to the **3D Face** tool. This command also allows you to create a mesh of any desired surface shape by specifying the coordinates of the vertices and assigning the vertices to the faces in the mesh. The difference between them is that on using the **3D Face** tool, you do not select the vertices that join another face twice. With the **PFACE** command, you need to select all the vertices of a face, even if they are coincident with the vertices of another face. In this way, you can avoid generating unrelated 3D faces that have coincident vertices. Also, with this command, there is no restriction on the number of faces and vertices the mesh can have.

Command: **PFACE**
Specify location for vertex 1: *Specify the location of the first vertex.*
Specify location for vertex 2 or <define faces>: *Specify the location of the second vertex.*
Specify location for vertex 3 or <define faces>: *Specify the location of the third vertex.*
Specify location for vertex 4 or <define faces>: *Specify the location of the fourth vertex.*
Specify location for vertex 5 or <define faces>: *Specify the location of the fifth vertex.*
Specify location for vertex 6 or <define faces>: *Specify the location of the sixth vertex.*
Specify location for vertex 7 or <define faces>: *Specify the location of the seventh vertex.*
Specify location for vertex 8 or <define faces>: *Specify the location of the eighth vertex.*
Specify location for vertex 9 or <define faces>: Enter.

After defining the locations of all the vertices, press Enter and assign vertices to the first face.
Face 1, vertex 1: *Specify the location of the first vertex.*

Enter a vertex number or [Color/Layer]: **1**
Face 1, vertex 2:
Enter a vertex number or [Color/Layer] <next face>: **2**
Face 1, vertex 3:
Enter a vertex number or [Color/Layer] <next face>: **3**
Face 1, vertex 4:
Enter a vertex number or [Color/Layer] <next face>: **4**

Once you have assigned the vertices to the first face, give a null response at the next prompt. Similarly, assign vertices to all faces, refer to Figure 7-51. To view the faces, select the **Realistic** option from the **Visual Styles** drop-down list in the **View** panel of the **Home** tab. To make an edge invisible, specify a negative number for its first vertex. The display of the invisible edges of 3D solid surfaces is governed by the **SPLFRAME** system variable. If **SPLFRAME** is set to 0, invisible edges are not displayed. If this variable is set to a number other than 0, all invisible edges are displayed after regeneration using the **REGENALL** command.

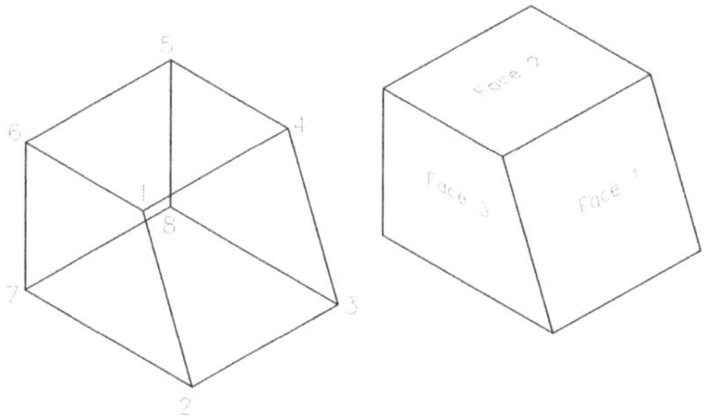

Figure 7-51 *Faces of block and assigned vertices*

Controlling the Visibility of the 3D Face Edges

Command: EDGE

The **EDGE** command is used to control the visibility of the edges created by using the **3D Face** tool. You can hide the edges of the 3D faces or display them using this command, refer to Figures 7-52 and 7-53. On invoking this command, you will be prompted to specify the 3D face edge to toggle its visibility or display. To hide an edge, select it. To display the edges, enter **D** at the **Specify edge of 3dface to toggle visibility or [Display]** prompt. You can display all invisible 3D face edges or the selected edges using this option.

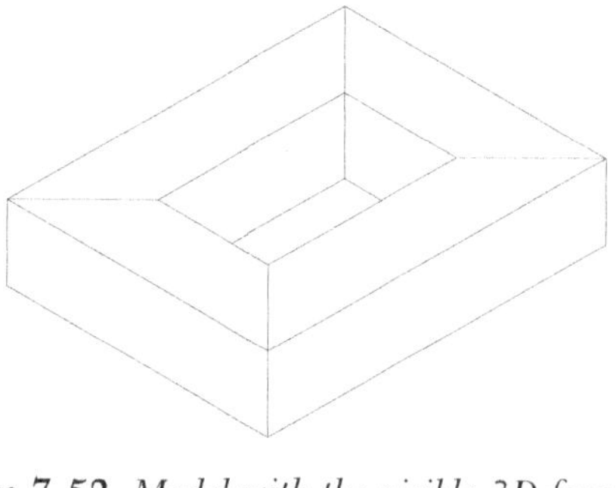

Figure 7-52 *Model with the visible 3D face edges*

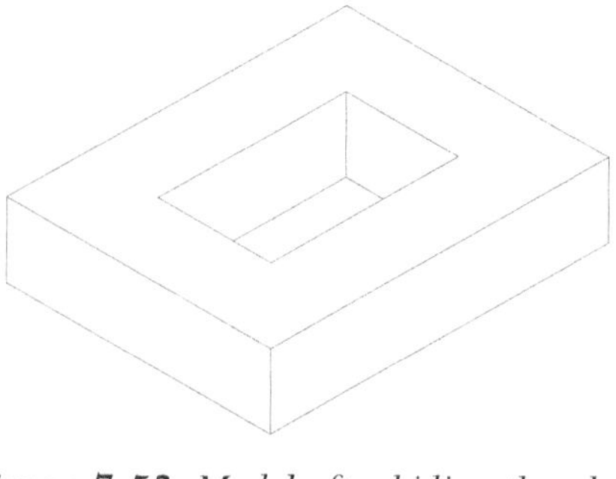

Figure 7-53 *Model after hiding the edges*

Exercise 2 3D Face

In this exercise, you will apply the 3D faces to the 3D wireframe model created in Example 2.

CREATING PLANAR SURFACES

Ribbon: Surface > Create > Planar **Toolbar:** Modeling > Planar Surface
Command: PLANESURF

The **Planar** tool is used to generate 2D surfaces on the working plane by specifying two diagonally opposite points. These two points specify the rectangular shape area to be covered by this planar surface, refer to Figure 7-54. The prompt sequence displayed on choosing the **Planar** tool from the **Create** panel in the **Surface** tab is discussed next.

Specify first corner or [Object] <Object>: *Specify the first corner point of the planar surface.*
Specify other corner: *Specify the diagonally opposite point of the planar surface.*

You can also convert an existing object to a surface by entering **O** at the **Specify first corner or [Object] <Object>** prompt. While selecting the object, you can directly select a closed boundary or a number of individual objects that result in a closed boundary, refer to Figure 7-55.

The number of lines displayed in the surface is controlled by the **SURFU** and **SURFV** system variables. The **SURFU** variable controls the number of lines to be displayed in the M direction and the **SURFV** variable controls the number of lines to be displayed in the N direction. These M and N directions are taken parallel to X and Y axis of the UCS respectively.

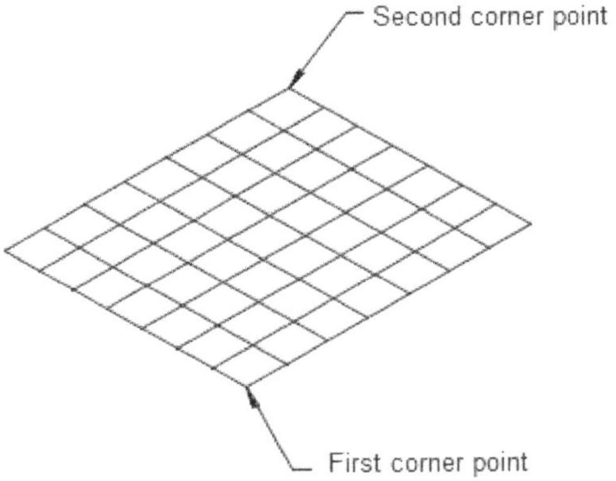

Figure 7-54 *Planar surface created by specifying corner points*

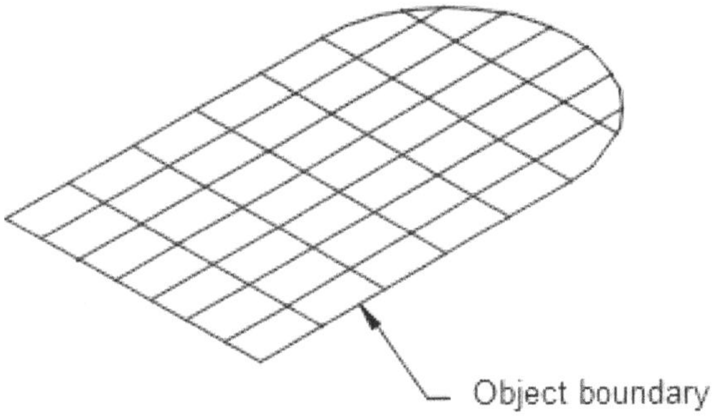

Figure 7-55 *Planar surface created by selecting an object*

THE 3DMESH COMMAND

Command: 3DMESH

The **3DMESH** command is used to create a free-form polygon mesh by using a matrix of M X N size. When you invoke this command, you will be prompted to specify the size of the mesh in the M direction and the N direction, where M X N is the total number of vertices in the mesh.

The values of M and N can be 2 to 256. Once you have specified the size, you need to specify the coordinates of each and every vertex individually. For example, if the size of the mesh in the M and N directions is 12 X 12, then you will have to specify the coordinates of all the 144 vertices. You can specify any 2D or 3D coordinates for the vertices. Figure 7-54 shows a freeform mesh. This command is mostly used for programming. The 3D polygon mesh is always open in the M and N directions. You can edit the mesh created using the **3DMESH** command with the help of the **Edit Polyline** tool.

EDITING THE SURFACE MESH

The polyface or polygon meshes can be edited using the **Edit Polyline** tool as discussed next.

The Edit Polyline Tool

Ribbon: Home > Modify > Edit Polyline	**Menu Bar:** Modify > Object > Polyline
Toolbar: Modify II > Edit Polyline	**Command:** PEDIT

To edit a polyface or polygon mesh, invoke the **Edit Polyline** tool from the **Modify** panel. You can also select the **Polyline Edit** option from the shortcut menu displayed on selecting the surface mesh and right-clicking on it, to edit a polyface or polygon face. The prompt sequence that will be followed on choosing the **Edit Polyline** tool and selecting the mesh is given next.

Select polyline or [Multiple]: *Select the 3D mesh.*
Enter an option [Edit vertex/Smooth surface/Desmooth/Mclose/Nclose/Undo]: *Select an option.*

Edit Vertex

This option is used for the individual editing of vertices of the mesh in the M direction or the N direction. On invoking this option, a cross will appear on the first point of the mesh and the following sub-options will be provided. Change the visual style to Wireframe by selecting the **Wireframe** option from the **Visual Styles** drop-down list in the **View** panel of the **Home** tab, so that you can view the vertices clearly.

Next. This sub-option is used to move the cross to the next vertex.

Previous. This sub-option is used to move the cross to the previous vertex.

Left. This sub-option is used to move the cross to the previous vertex in the N direction of the mesh.

Right. This sub-option is used to move the cross to the next vertex in the N direction of the mesh.

Up. This sub-option is used to move the cross to the next vertex in the M direction of the mesh.

Down. This sub-option is used to move the cross to the previous vertex in the M direction of the mesh.

Move. This sub-option is used to redefine the location of the current vertex. You can define a new location by using any of the coordinate systems or can directly select the location on the screen, refer to Figures 7-56 and 7-57.

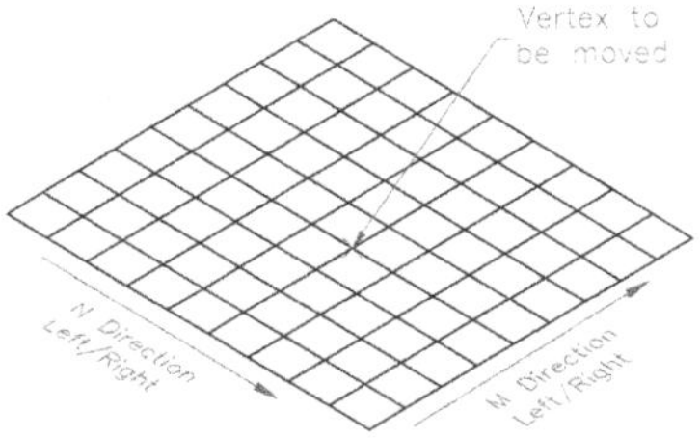

Figure 7-56 *Vertex before moving*

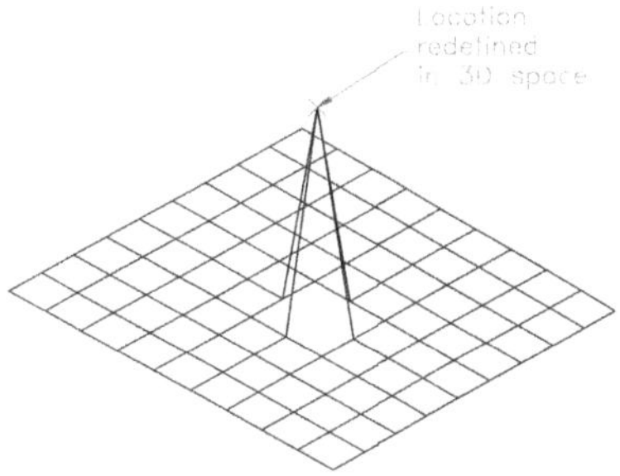

Figure 7-57 *Vertex after moving*

REgen. This sub-option is used to regenerate the 3D mesh.

eXit. This sub-option is used to exit the **Edit Vertex** option.

Smooth surface

This option is used to smoothen the surface of the 3D mesh by fitting a smooth surface, as shown in Figures 7-58 and 7-59. The smoothness of the surface will depend upon the **SURFU** and **SURFV** system variables. The value of these system variables can vary between 0 and 200.

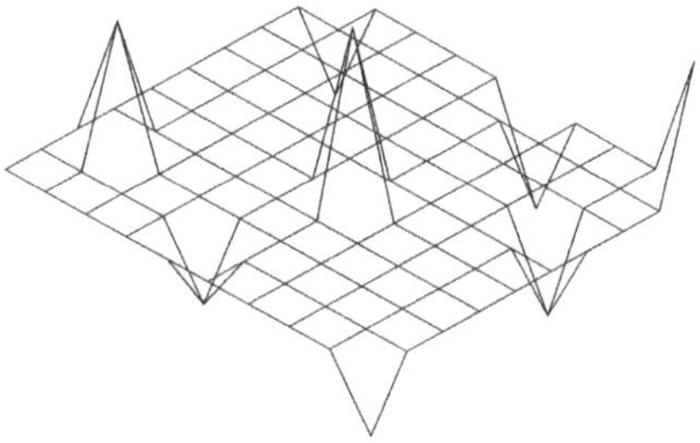

Figure 7-58 *3D mesh before fitting the smooth surface*

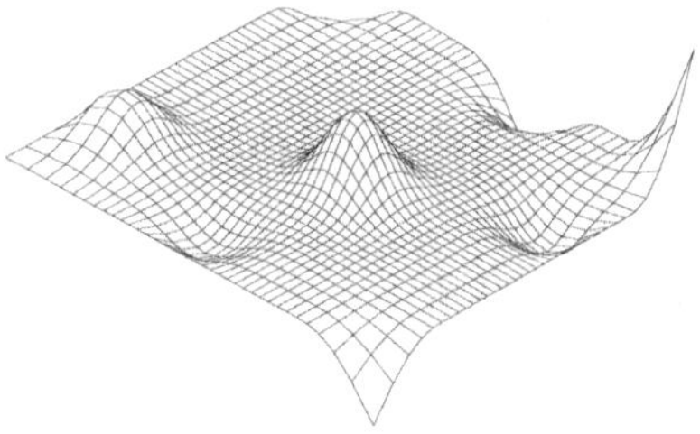

Figure 7-59 *3D mesh after fitting the smooth surface*

The type of the smooth surface to be fitted is controlled by the **SURFTYPE** system variable. If you set the value of the **SURFTYPE** system variable to 5, it will fit a Quadratic B-spline surface. If you set the value to 6, it will fit a Cubic B-spline surface. If you set the value to 8, it will fit a Bezier surface.

Desmooth

This option is used to remove the smooth surface that was fitted on the 3D mesh using the **Smooth surface** option and restore to the original mesh.

Mclose

This option is used to close the 3D mesh in the M direction, as shown in Figures 7-60 and 7-61.

Nclose
This option is used to close the 3D mesh in the N direction, as shown in Figures 7-60 and 7-61.

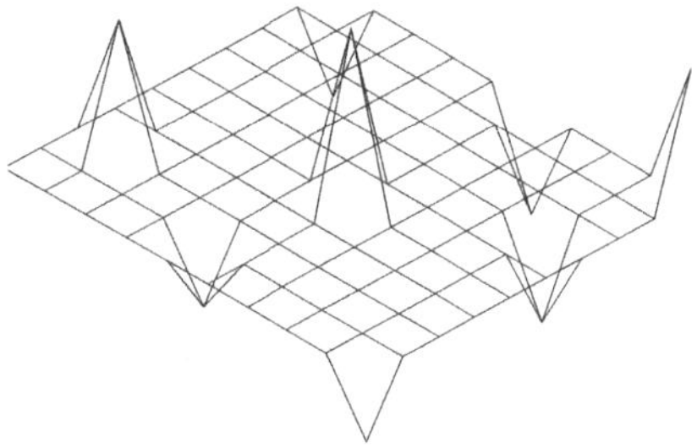

Figure 7-60 *3D mesh open in the M and N directions*

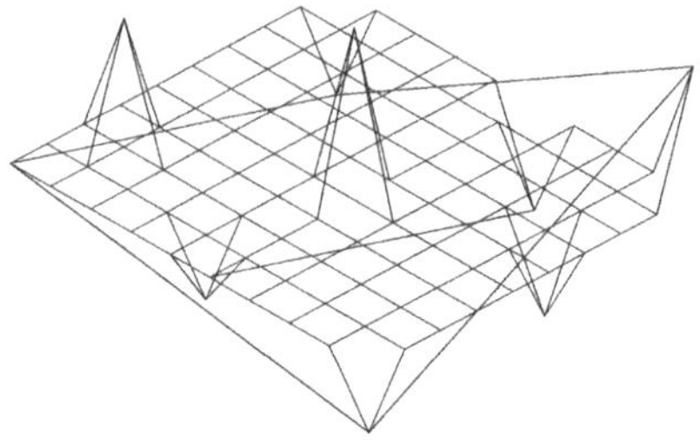

Figure 7-61 *3D mesh closed in the M and N directions*

Mopen
This option will be available if the 3D mesh is closed in the M direction. It is used to open the 3D mesh in the M direction, refer to Figures 7-60 and 7-61.

Nopen
This option will be available if the 3D mesh is closed in the N direction. It is used to open the 3D mesh in the N direction, refer to Figures 7-60 and 7-61.

Undo
This option is used to undo all the operations done by the **Edit Polyline** tool.

DYNAMIC VIEWING OF 3D OBJECTS

Ribbon: View > Navigate > SteeringWheels (Customize to add)
Navigator Bar: Full Navigation Wheel **Command:** NAVSWHEEL

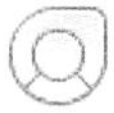

The options available in the **Full Navigation Wheel** make the entire process of the solid modeling very interesting. You can dynamically rotate the solid models on the screen to view them from different angles. You can also define clipping planes and then rotate the solid models such that whenever the models pass through the cutting planes, they are sectioned just to be viewed. The original model can be restored as soon as you exit these commands or tools. The tools and their options that are used to perform all these functions are discussed next.

Using the SteeringWheels
The SteeringWheels enables you to easily view and navigate through your 3D models. It is an ideal tool for navigating through your models. It includes not only the common navigating tools such as **Zoom**, **Pan**, and **Orbit** but also an option to move the user specified center of the model to the center of the display window. Using this tool, you can also rewind and get back your previous views. It is a time saving tool, since it combines many common navigation tools into a single tool.

The SteeringWheel is divided into different sections known as Wedges. Each wedge on a wheel represents a command. You can activate a particular navigation option by clicking on the respective wedges and then modify the view of the model by dragging the cursor, refer to Figure 7-62. The navigation tools available in the SteeringWheels are discussed next.

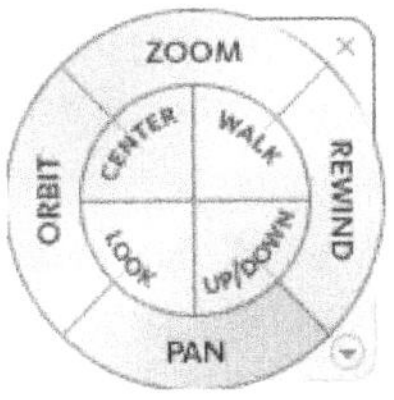

***Figure 7-62** The SteeringWheel*

ZOOM

This wedge is used in the same way as you use camera's zoom lens. It makes the object appear closer or far away, without changing the position of the camera. To invoke the **ZOOM** tool, move the cursor to the **ZOOM** wedge, press and hold left mouse button; a magnifier will be attached to the cursor that allows you to zoom in or out with reference to a base point. Now, drag to zoom in and zoom out. However, you can change the base point or pivot point to zoom in or zoom out of the model by choosing the **CENTER** wedge. You can even enable the incremental zoom of 25 percent on a single click from the **Zoom** area of the **SteeringWheels Settings** dialog box. To invoke this dialog box, right-click on the SteeringWheels; a shortcut menu will be displayed. Choose the **SteeringWheels Settings** option from the shortcut menu; the **SteeringWheels Settings** dialog box will be displayed. You can even choose the **Fit to Window** option from the shortcut menu of the SteeringWheels to view the entire drawing in the viewport.

REWIND

This wedge enables you to quickly restore the previous views. To invoke this tool, move the cursor to the **REWIND** wedge and click; a series of frames from the previous view orientation are displayed. You can now quickly pick the required view and control the thumbnail previews generated on changing various views using the **Rewind thumbnail** area of the **SteeringWheels Settings** dialog box.

PAN

This wedge allows you to drag the view to a new location in the drawing window. To invoke this tool, move the cursor to the **PAN** wedge, press and hold left mouse button; a plus arrow is attached to the cursor, enabling you to drag the view in any direction. Now, drag your mouse to pan in model space. You can choose the **Fit to Window** option from the shortcut menu of the SteeringWheels to view the entire drawing in the viewport.

ORBIT

This wedge allows you to visually maneuver around the 3D objects to obtain different views. When you move your cursor to the **ORBIT** wedge press and hold left mouse button; a circular arrow is attached to the cursor. Now, you can rotate the model with respect to a base point. Similar to the **ZOOM** option, in this case also, you can specify the required center point of the view and rotate the model using the **CENTER** wedge option. You can also set the viewpoint upside down using the options in the **SteeringWheels Settings** dialog box. Moreover, you can choose the **Fit to Window** option to view the full drawing view.

CENTER

This wedge helps you specify the pivot or center point of the view to orbit or zoom a model. When you move your cursor to this wedge and drag, a pivot ball is attached to the cursor. You can now adjust your center or target point by placing the cursor at the required point. However, you can restore the center of the viewport by choosing the **Restore Original Center** option from the shortcut menu of the SteeringWheels. You can also restore the home view of the model by choosing the **Go Home** option from the shortcut menu.

LOOK

This tool works similar to turning the camera on a tripod without changing the distance between the camera and the target. This means the source remains the same, but the target changes. To invoke this tool, move the cursor to the **LOOK** wedge; an arc is attached to the cursor which enables you to change your view direction. You can also invert the vertical direction of the **Look** tool by selecting the **Invert vertical axis for Look tool** check box from the **SteeringWheels Settings** dialog box. You can choose the **Fit to Window** option to view the entire drawing in the viewport.

WALK

This tool moves the camera around the model as if you are walking away or towards the focus direction of the camera. In the walk 3D navigation, the camera moves parallel to the XY plane and gives the effect as if you are walking. To invoke this tool, move the cursor to the **WALK** wedge. An arrow is attached to the cursor showing the direction of the camera. You can drag the cursor to move around the model and also control the walk speed using the options in the **Walk Tool** area of the **SteeringWheels Settings** dialog box. Using this dialog box, you can also constraint the walk angle to the ground plane.

UP/DOWN

This option slides the view along the Y-axis of the screen, which is like being in an elevator. When you move your cursor to the **UP/DOWN** wedge, a vertical slider is attached to the cursor. You can slide from up to down in the slider to view the model from up to down. Using the options in the shortcut menu of the SteeringWheels, you can go back to the original view, restore the original center, or fit the entire drawing in the viewport.

Modes of SteeringWheels

There are four working modes of SteeringWheels, refer to Figure 7-63. These working modes are discussed next.

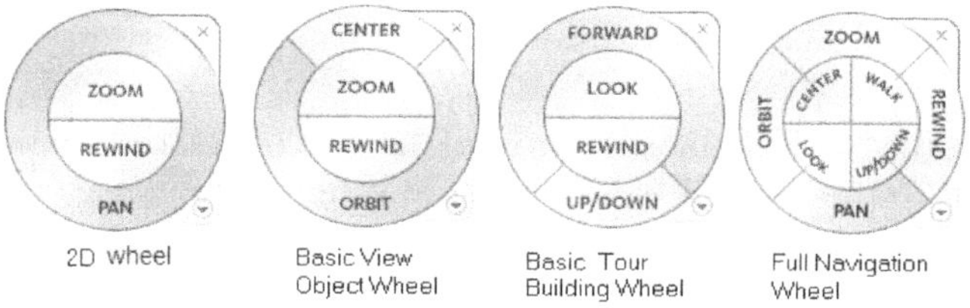

Figure 7-63 *Different modes of the SteeringWheels*

2D Wheel

You can invoke the SteeringWheel that has only the 2D navigation tools. To do so, choose the **2D** tool from **View > Navigate > SteeringWheels** drop-down; the 2D SteeringWheel with the **PAN**, **ZOOM**, and **REWIND** tools will be displayed.

Basic View Object Wheel

This mode contains only the viewing tools such as **CENTER**, **ZOOM**, **REWIND**, and **ORBIT**. You can invoke this mode by choosing **Basic Wheels > View Object Wheel** from the shortcut menu of the SteeringWheels or by choosing **Basic View Object Wheel** from the flyout that is displayed on clicking the down-arrow in the **SteeringWheels** group in the **Navigation bar**.

Basic Tour Building Wheel

This mode is ideal for navigating inside a building. It contains the **FORWARD**, **REWIND**, **LOOK**, and **UP/DOWN** tools. You can invoke this mode by choosing **Basic Wheels > Tour Building Wheel** from the shortcut menu of the SteeringWheels or by choosing **Mini Tour Building Wheel** from the flyout that is displayed on clicking on the down-arrow in the **SteeringWheels** group in the **Navigation bar**.

Full Navigation Wheel

This mode contains both the view and the navigating tools. It enables you to select a variety of tools from a single wheel. You can invoke this mode by choosing the **Full Navigation Wheel** option from the shortcut menu of the SteeringWheels or from the **Navigation bar**.

The SteeringWheels are of two types: Big Wheels and Mini Wheels. Both the wheels have the same functioning modes. The Big Wheels mode is displayed by default, whereas the Mini Wheels mode is invoked by choosing the **Mini View Object Wheel**, **Mini Tour Building Wheel**, or **Mini Full Navigation Wheel** option from the shortcut menu of the SteeringWheels or by choosing option from the **SteeringWheels** drop-down in the **Navigation bar** or by choosing option from the **SteeringWheels** drop-down in the **Navigate** panel of the **View** tab. You can customize the size, appearance, and behavior of the Steering Wheel using the **SteeringWheels Settings** dialog box, refer to Figure 7-64.

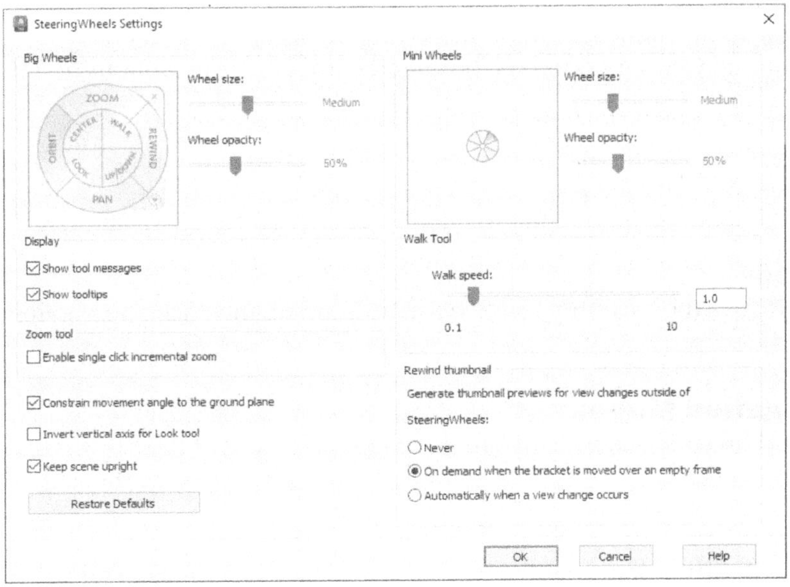

Figure 7-64 *The **SteeringWheels Settings** dialog box*

You can control the size and opacity of the Big Wheels and Mini Wheels with the help of a slider available next to the wheels. Also, using this dialog box you can control the tooltips and messages that are displayed when you move the cursor over any wedge.

Dynamically Rotating the View of a Model

Ribbon: View > Navigate > Orbit **Navigation Bar:** Orbit
Toolbar: 3D Navigation > Constrained Orbit **Command:** 3DO(3DORBIT)

The **Orbit** tool allows you to visually maneuver around 3D objects to obtain different views. This is one of the most important tools for the advanced 3D viewing options. All other advanced 3D viewing options can be invoked inside this tool or using the **3D Navigation** toolbar. This tool activates a 3D Orbit view in the current viewport. You can click and drag your pointing device to view the 3D object from different angles. In 3D orbit viewing, the target is considered stationary and the camera location is considered to be moving around it. The cursor looks like a sphere encircled by two arc shaped arrows. This is known as **Orbit mode** cursor, and clicking and dragging the pointing device allows you to rotate the view freely. You can move the **Orbit mode** cursor horizontally, vertically, and diagonally. If you drag the pointing device horizontally, the camera will move parallel to the XY plane of the WCS. If you move your pointing device vertically, then the camera will move along the Z axis. This tool is a transparent tool and can be invoked inside any other tool. You can select individual objects or the entire drawing to view before you invoke the **Orbit** tool.

Tip

Press and hold the Shift key and the middle mouse button to temporarily enter the constrained orbit mode.

You can invoke the other advanced viewing options using the shortcut menu that is displayed on right-clicking in the drawing window when you are inside the **Orbit** tool. The shortcut menu with other advanced viewing options is shown in Figure 7-65. The options of the shortcut menu are discussed next.

Exit

This option is used to exit the **Orbit** tool. You can also exit this tool by pressing Esc.

Current Mode

This option displays the currently active navigation mode in which you obtained this shortcut menu.

Other Navigation Modes

This option enables you to choose the other navigation modes of the **3D Navigation** toolbar. In this way, you can toggle between the navigation modes without exiting the tool. The sub-options provided by the **Other Navigation Modes** are as follows:

Free Orbit. This sub-option can be invoked by choosing the **Free Orbit** tool from **View > Navigate > Orbit** drop-down in the **View Tab** of the **Ribbon**, refer to Figure 7-66; 3D orbit view will be activated in the current viewport. When you invoke the **Free Orbit** tool, an arcball appears. This arcball is a circle with four smaller circles placed such that they divide the bigger circle into quadrants. The UCS icon is replaced by a shaded 3D UCS icon. In the 3D orbit viewing, the target is considered stationary and the camera location is considered to be moving around it. The target is the center of the arcball. The **Free Orbit** tool is a transparent tool and can be invoked inside any other tool.

The cursor icon changes as you move the cursor over the 3D Orbit view. The different icons indicate the different directions in which the view is being rotated. They are as follows.

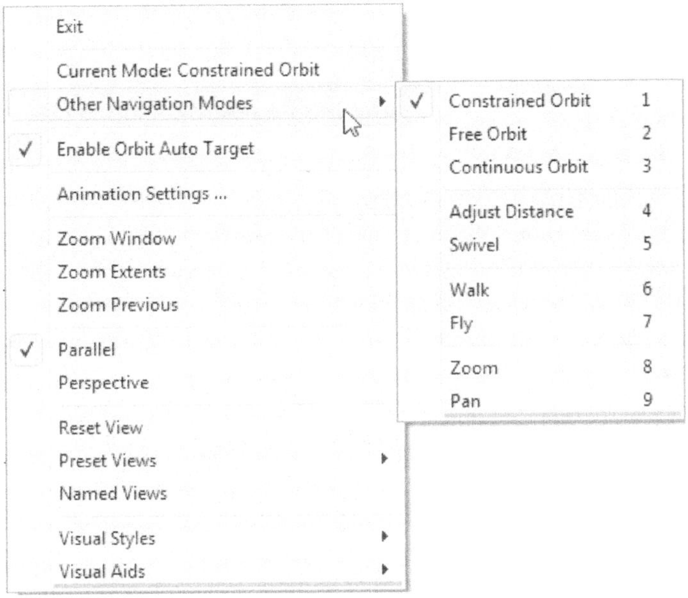

*Figure 7-65 The shortcut menu displayed when the **3DORBIT** command is active*

*Figure 7-66 The tools in the **Orbit** drop-down*

Orbit mode. When you move the cursor within the arcball, the cursor looks like a sphere encircled by two lines. This icon is the **Orbit mode** cursor, and clicking and dragging the pointing device allows you to rotate the view freely as if the cursor was grabbing a sphere surrounding the objects and moving it around the target point. You can move the **Orbit mode** cursor horizontally, vertically, and diagonally.

Roll mode. When you move the cursor outside the arcball, it changes to look like a sphere encircled by a circular arrow. When you click and drag, the view is rotated around an axis that extends through the center of the arcball, perpendicular to the screen.

Orbit Left-Right. When you move the cursor to the small circles placed on the left and right of the arcball, it changes into a sphere surrounded by a horizontal ellipse. When you click and drag, the view is rotated around the *Y* axis of the screen.

Orbit Up-down. When you move the cursor to the circles placed in the top or bottom of the arcball, it changes into a sphere surrounded by a vertical ellipse. Clicking and dragging the cursor rotates the view around the horizontal axis or the *X* axis of the screen, and passes it through the middle of the arcball.

Figure 7-67 shows a model being rotated using the **Free Orbit** tool.

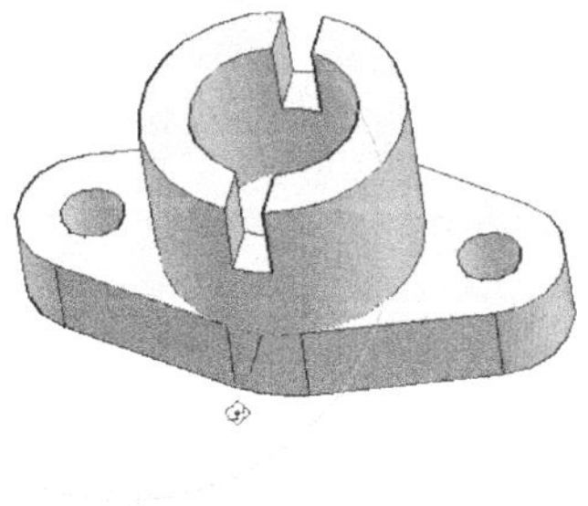

Figure 7-67 *Model being rotated using the* ***Free Orbit*** *tool*

Tip

1 . Press and hold the Shift+Ctrl keys and the middle button of the mouse to temporarily enter the ***Free Orbit*** *navigation mode.*

2 . If you are in the ***3D Orbit*** *navigation mode, press and hold the Shift key to temporarily enter the* ***Free Orbit*** *navigation mode.*

Continuous Orbit. This tool allows you to set the objects you select in a 3D view into continuous motion in a free-form orbit. You can invoke this tool by choosing the **Continuous Orbit** tool from **View > Navigate > Orbit** drop-down. While using this tool, the cursor icon changes to the continuous orbit cursor. Clicking in the drawing area and dragging the pointing device in any direction starts to move the object(s) in the direction you have dragged it. When you release the pointing device button, that is, stop clicking and dragging, the object continues to move in its orbit in the direction you specified. The speed at which the cursor is moved determines the speed at which the objects spin. You can click and drag again to specify another direction for rotation in the continuous orbit. While using this sub-option, you can right-click in the drawing area to display the shortcut menu and choose the other sub-options without exiting the tool. Choosing **Pan**, **Zoom**, **Orbit**, **Adjust Clipping Plane** ends the continuous orbit.

Adjust Distance. This sub-option can be invoked by choosing **Other Navigation Modes > Adjust Distance** from the shortcut menu displayed on right-clicking in the drawing area. Alternatively, choose **View > Camera > Adjust Distance** from the menu bar. This sub-option is similar to taking the camera closer to or farther away from the target object. Therefore, it makes the object appear closer or farther away. You can press the left button and drag the mouse to adjust the distance between the target and the camera. This option is used to reduce the distance between the camera and the object when the object rotates by a large angle.

Swivel Camera. This sub-option can be invoked by choosing **View > Camera > Swivel** from the menu bar. It works similar to turning the camera on a tripod without changing the distance between the camera and the target. You can press the left mouse button and drag the mouse to swivel the camera.

Walk. This sub-option can be invoked by choosing the **Walk** tool from **Visualize > Animations> Walk** drop-down after customizing. It is similar to the **Walk** option in the SteeringWheel. This sub-option is used to move the camera around a model with the help of the keyboard, as if you are walking away or toward the focus direction of the camera. In walk 3D navigation, the camera moves parallel to the XY plane and this seems as if you are walking. Choose the **Walk** button; the **POSITION LOCATOR** window, showing the top view of the model with the location of the camera indicated by a red spot, will be displayed. The **POSITION LOCATOR** window shows a dynamic preview of the location and movement of the camera with respect to the object, refer to Figure 7-68. The following keys are used to control the location of the camera with respect to the object.

Motion Type	Key
Move the camera in the forward direction	UP ARROW or W key
Move the camera in the backward direction	DOWN ARROW or S key
Move the camera in the left direction	LEFT ARROW or A key
Move the camera in the right direction	RIGHT ARROW or D key
Change the focus direction of the camera	Press and hold the left mouse button in the drawing area and drag the mouse in the desired direction
Change the orientation of the XY plane	Press and hold the middle mouse button in the drawing area and drag the mouse in the desired direction
Change the distance of the camera	Move the cursor to the green triangular area in the **POSITION LOCATOR** window and pan to the desired location
Change the coverage area of the camera	Move the cursor onto the camera in the **POSITION LOCATOR** window and pan the camera

Fly. This sub-option can be invoked by choosing the **Fly** tool from **Visualize > Anima> Walk** drop-down after customizing. This sub-option is used to move the camera through a model with the help of the keyboard as if you are flying away or toward the focus direction, refer to Figure 7-68 of the camera. In the fly 3D navigation, the camera can even move at an inclination with the XY plane and this seems as if you are flying around the object. The **POSITION LOCATOR** window will be displayed on the screen while using the **Fly** tool also. The position of the camera with respect to the object can be controlled by using the same procedure as discussed in the **Walk** tool.

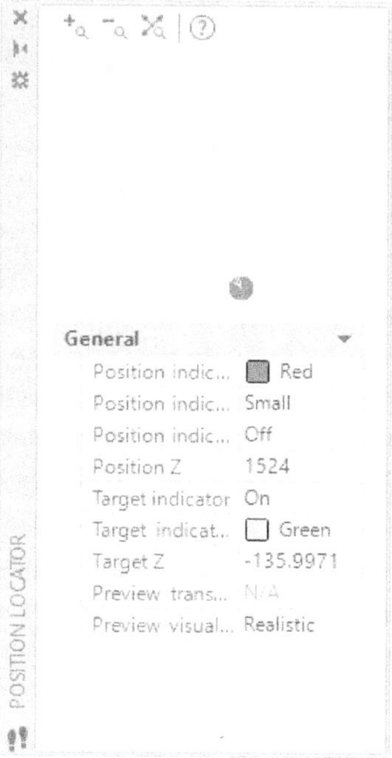

Figure 7-68 *The **POSITION LOCATOR** window*

Note

*1. To control the settings related to walk and fly, invoke the tool and right-click in the drawing area. Next, choose the **Walk and Fly Settings** option; the **Walk and Fly Settings** dialog box will be displayed. You can specify the settings in this dialog box.*

2. The Walk and Fly 3D navigation modes can be activated only in the perspective view. Activating the Walk or Fly 3D navigation mode in the parallel projection will display a warning window, as shown in Figure 7-69.

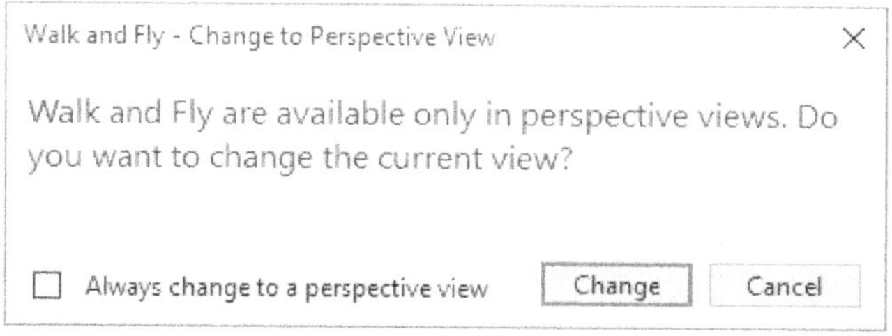

Figure 7-69 *Warning displayed on activating the Walk and Fly 3D navigation modes in the parallel projection*

Tip
You can toggle between the 3D navigation modes from the shortcut menu or by entering the number displayed in front of each option in the shortcut menu at the Command prompt.

Zoom. This sub-option can be invoked by choosing **View > Zoom** from the menu bar. It is similar to the **ZOOM** option in the SteeringWheel and functions like the camera's zoom lens. You can invoke the other options of the Zoom by entering **3DZOOM** at the Command prompt. Alternatively, the options can also be displayed by right-clicking in the drawing area when you are inside this tool.

Pan. The **Pan** sub-option is invoked by choosing **View > Pan** from the menu bar. It is similar to the **PAN** option in the SteeringWheel. This tool also starts the 3D interactive viewing. You can right-click in the drawing area, when you are inside this tool, to display a shortcut menu that displays all the 3D Orbit options.

Enable Orbit Auto Target

This option, if chosen, ensures that the target point is focused on the object while rotating the view. If this option is cleared, the target point is set at the center of the viewport, in which the **Orbit** tool is invoked.

Animation Settings

This option, if chosen, displays the **Animation Settings** dialog box, refer to Figure 7-70. Using this dialog box, you can change the settings for visual style, resolution, number of frames to be captured in one second, and the format in which you want to save the file while creating the animation of 3D navigation. Creating animations will be discussed in the next chapter.

Zoom Window/Extents/Previous

These options are used to zoom the solid model using a window, zoom the objects to the extents, or retrieve the previous zoomed views of the model.

Parallel

This option is chosen to display the selected model using the parallel projection method. It is the default method when a new AutoCAD file is started with 2D templates. In this method, no parallel lines in the model converge at any point.

Perspective

This option is chosen to use the one point perspective method to display a model. It is the default method when a new AutoCAD file is started with 3D templates. In this method, all parallel lines in the model converge at a single point, thus providing a realistic view of the model when viewed with the naked eye, refer to Figure 7-71.

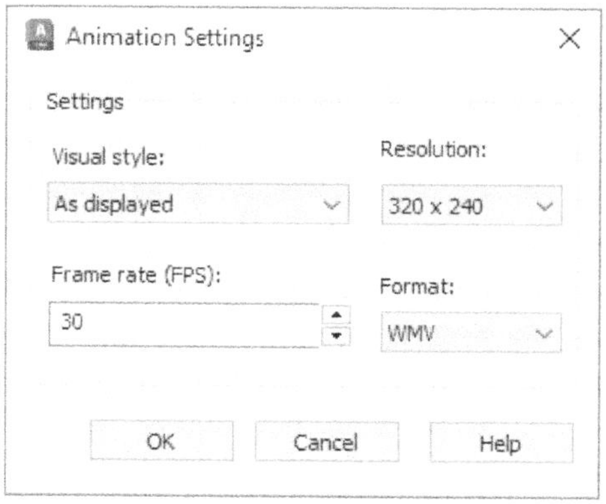

*Figure 7-70 The **Animation Settings** dialog box*

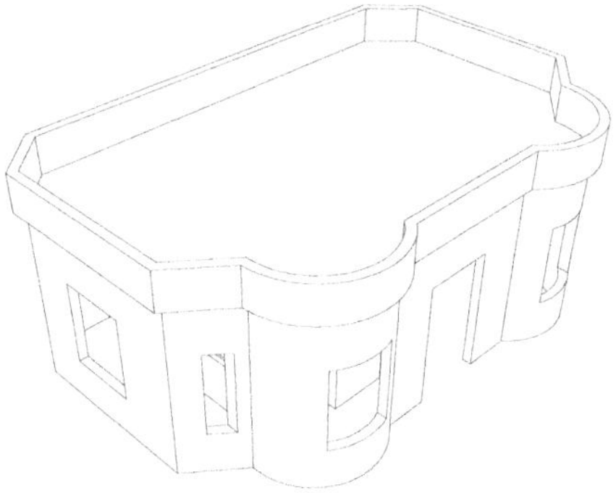

Figure 7-71 Viewing the model using the perspective projection

Reset View

This option, when chosen automatically, restores the view that was current when you started rotating the solid model in the 3D orbit. Note that you will not exit the **Orbit** tool if you choose this option.

Preset Views

This option is used to select any of the six standard orthogonal views or four isometric views.

Named Views

If you have created some views using the **VIEW** command, then the existing named views will be displayed as the sub-options under the **Named Views** option in the **3D Orbit** shortcut menu. Use this option to activate the saved view.

Visual Aids

The **Orbit** tool provides you with three visual aids for the ease of visualizing the solid model in the 3D orbit view. These visual aids are **Compass**, **Grid**, and **UCS Icon**. A check mark is displayed in front of the options you have selected. You can select none, one, two, or all three of the visual aids. Choosing **Compass** displays a sphere drawn within the arcball with three lines. These lines indicate the *X*, *Y*, and *Z* axis directions. Choosing the **Grid** displays a grid at the current *XY* plane. You can specify the height by using the **ELEVATION** system variable. The **GRID** system variable controls the display options of the **Grid** before using the **Orbit** tool. The size of the grid will depend upon the limits of the drawing. Choosing the **UCS Icon** displays the UCS icon. If this option is not selected, then AutoCAD turns off the display of the UCS icon. While using any of the 3D Orbit options, interactive 3D viewing is on and a shaded 3D view UCS icon is displayed. The *X* axis is red, the *Y* axis is green, and the *Z* axis is blue or cyan. Figure 7-72 shows a realistic shaded solid model displaying the compass, grid, and UCS icon.

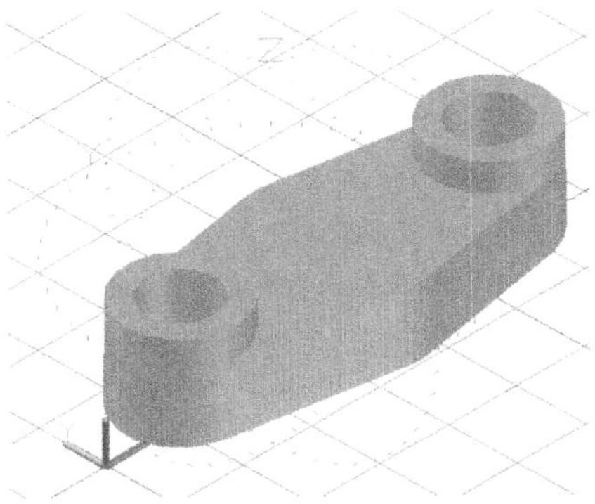

Figure 7-72 *Realistic shaded solid model showing the compass, grid, and UCS icon*

Clipping the View of a Model Dynamically

Command: 3DCLIP

The **3DCLIP** command is used to adjust the clipping planes for sectioning the selected solid model. Note that the actual solid model is not modified by this command. This command is used only for the purpose of viewing. The original solid model will be restored when you exit this command. With this option, you can adjust the location of the clipping planes. When you choose this option, the **Adjust Clipping Planes** window will be displayed, as shown in Figure 7-73. In this window, the object appears rotated at 90-degree to the top of the current view in the window. This facilitates the display of cutting planes. Setting the location of the front and back clipping planes in this window is reflected in the result in the current view. The various options of the **3DCLIP** command are displayed in the **Adjust Clipping Planes** toolbar in the window. There are seven buttons provided in this window. The functions of these buttons are discussed next.

Adjust Front Clipping. This button is chosen to locate the front clipping plane, which is defined by the line located in the lower end of the **Adjust Clipping Planes** window. You can see the result in the 3D Orbit view if the front clipping is on.

Adjust Back Clipping. This button is chosen to locate the back clipping plane, which is defined by the line located in the upper end of the **Adjust Clipping Planes** window. You can see the result in the 3D Orbit view if the back clipping is on.

Create Slice. Choosing this button causes both the front and back clipping planes to move together. The slice is created between the two clipping planes and is displayed in the current 3D view. You can first adjust the front and the back clipping planes individually by choosing the respective options. Next, by choosing the **Create Slice** button, activate both the clipping planes simultaneously and display the result in the current view.

Pan. Displays the pan cursor that you can use to pan the object in **Adjust Clipping Planes** window. Hold down the left mouse button and drag it in any direction. The pan cursor stays active until you click another button.

Zoom. Displays a magnifying-glass cursor that you can use to enlarge or reduce the clipping plane. To do so, choose the **Zoom** tool and hold the left mouse button and drag it in up or down direction.

Front Clipping On/Off. Turns on or off the sectioning of a solid model using the front clipping

plane, refer to Figure 7-74.

Back Clipping On/Off. Turns on or off the sectioning of the solid model using the back clipping

plane, refer to Figure 7-74.

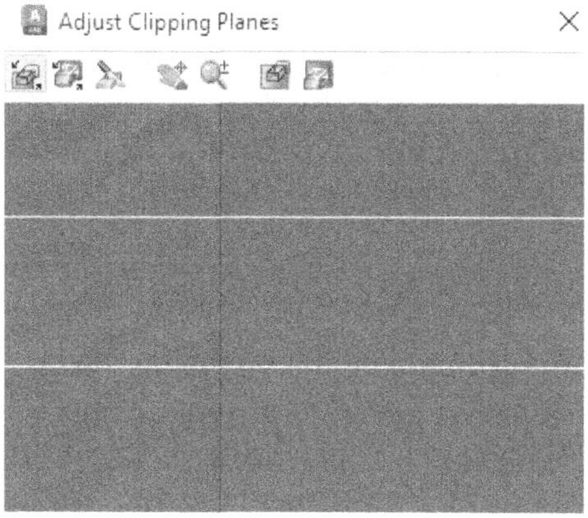

Figure 7-73 The ***Adjust Clipping Planes*** *window*

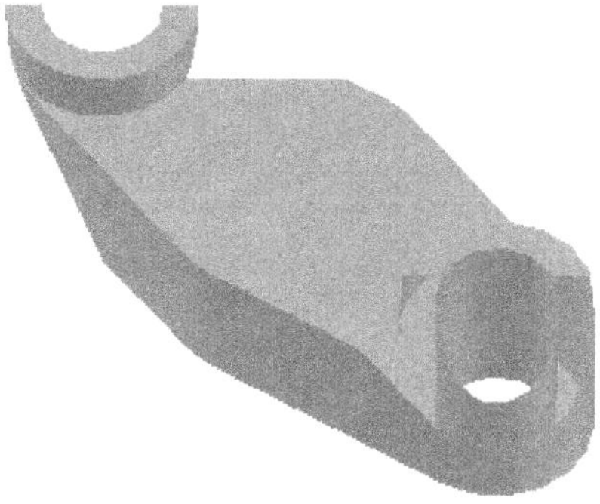

Figure 7-74 Model with the front and back clipping on

NUDGE FUNCTIONALITY

Nudge functionality gives you the freedom to move any kind of object by 2 pixels in any direction orthogonal to screen. When the snap mode is ON, the object moves to the distance specified in the **Snap spacing** edit box in the **Drafting Settings** dialog box. To nudge any object, select the object and press Ctrl + arrow key corresponding to the direction in which you want to move the object.

Self-Evaluation Test

Answer the following questions and then compare them to those given at the end of this chapter:

1. The __________ and __________ commands can be used to change the viewpoint for viewing models in the 3D space.

2. Using the **Viewpoint Presets** dialog box, you can set the viewpoint with respect to __________ and __________.

3. The two types of 3D coordinate systems are __________ and __________.

4. To view 3D clipping on an object, the __________ command is used.

5. The **VPOINT** command is used to change the viewpoint to view a solid model. (T/F)

6. The wireframe models can be converted into surface models as well as solid models. (T/F)

7. In AutoCAD, the right-hand thumb rule is followed to identify the direction of the X, Y, and Z axes. (T/F)

8. In AutoCAD, the right-hand thumb rule is followed to find the direction of rotation in the 3D space. (T/F)

9. Once you exit the 3DCLIP command, the original solid model is restored. (T/F)

10. When you change the viewpoint, the 3D model moves from its default position. (T/F)

Review Questions

Answer the following questions:

1. In which of the following views a model is displayed by default in 3D Modeling workspace?

   (a) **Perspective View** (b) **Parallel View**
   (c) **Top View** (d) None of these

2. Which of the following tools is used to create a 3D polyline?

   (a) **Polyline** (b) **3D Poly**
   (c) **3D Polyline** (d) **Polyline 3D**

3. Which of the following commands is used to set the elevation and thickness for new objects?

   (a) **ELEVATION** (b) **THICKNESS**
   (c) **ELEV** (d) **THICK**

4. Which of the following commands is used to suppress the hidden edges in a 3D model?

(a) **SUPPRESS** (b) **HIDE**
(c) **3DHIDE** (d) **EDGE**

5. Which of the following views is set by default when you open a new drawing?

(a) SE Isometric View (b) SW Isometric View
(c) Custom View (d) Bottom View

6. For the **Sphere** and **Torus** meshes if the **MESHTYPE** system variable is set to 0, the resulting surface will be a __________ mesh.

7. The highlighted area in a ViewCube that is used to change a view is called __________.

8. A 3D model can be rotated continuously using the **3D Orbit** tool. (T/F)

9. The **ELEV** command is a transparent command. (T/F)

10. You can directly write a text with thickness. (T/F)

Exercises 3 and 4

In these exercises, you will create the models shown in Figures 7-75 and 7-76. Assume the missing dimensions.

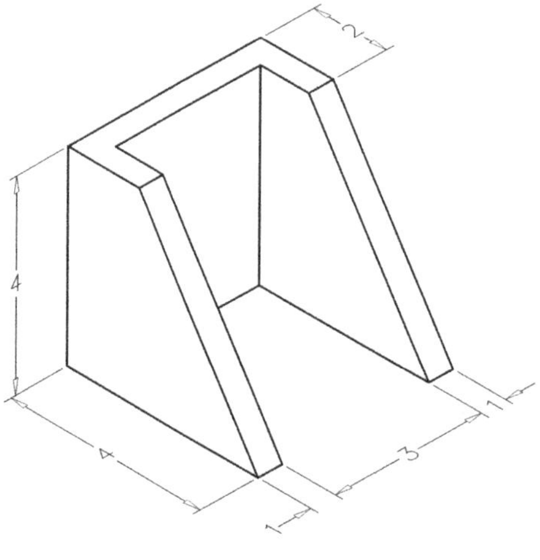

Figure 7-75 *Model for Exercise 3*

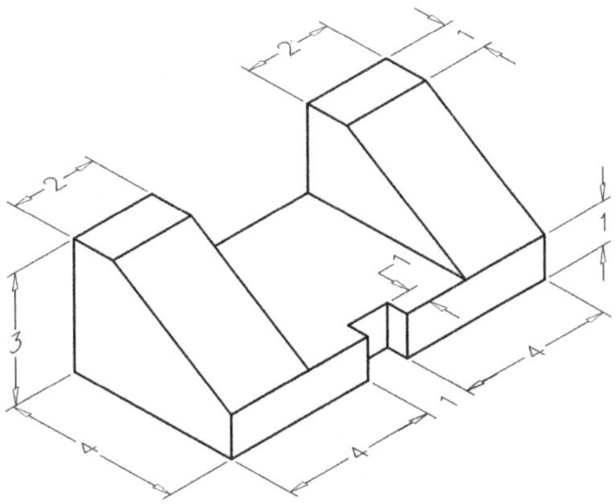

Figure 7-76 *Model for Exercise 4*

Answers to Self-Evaluation Test

1. **VPOINT, -VPOINT**, **2**. the angle in the *XY* plane from the *X* axis, angle from the *XY* plane, **3**. absolute, relative coordinate systems **4**. **3DCLIP**, **5**. T, **6**. F, **7**. T, **8**. T, **9**. T, **10**. F

Chapter 8

Creating Solid Models

Learning Objectives

After completing this chapter, you will be able to:

- *Create standard solid primitives and polysolids*
- *Create regions*
- *Use Boolean operations*
- *Modify the visual styles of solids*
- *Define new UCS using the Dynamic UCS, DDUCS, ViewCube, and Ribbon*
- *Use the Extrude and Revolve tools to create solid models*
- *Create complex solid models using the Sweep and Loft tools*
- *Use the Presspull tool*

Key Terms

- *Solid Primitives*
- *Box*
- *Cone*
- *Cylinder*
- *Sphere*
- *Torus*
- *Wedge*
- *Pyramid*
- *Polysolid*
- *Helix*
- *Visual Styles*
- *Region*
- *Union*
- *Intersect*
- *INTERFERE*
- *3D Snap*
- *Dynamic UCS*
- *Extrude*
- *Mode*
- *Revolve*
- *Sweep*
- *Loft*
- *Solid*
- *Surface*
- *Presspull*

WHAT IS SOLID MODELING?

Solid modeling is the process of building objects that have all the attributes of an actual solid object. For example, if you draw a wireframe or a surface model of a bushing, it is sufficient to define the shape and size of the object. However, in engineering, the shape and size alone are not enough to describe an object. For engineering analysis, you need more information such as volume, mass, moment of inertia, and material properties (density, Young's modulus, Poisson's ratio, thermal conductivity, and so on). When you know these physical attributes of an object, it can be subjected to various tests to make sure that it performs as required by the product specifications. It eliminates the need for building expensive prototypes and makes the product development cycle shorter. Solid models also make it easy to visualize the objects because you always think of and see the objects as solids. With computers getting faster and software getting more sophisticated and affordable, solid modeling has become the core of the manufacturing process. AutoCAD solid modeling is based on the ACIS solid modeler, which is a part of the core technology.

CREATING PREDEFINED SOLID PRIMITIVES

The Solid primitives form the basic building blocks for a complex solid. ACIS has seven predefined solid primitives that can be used to construct a solid model such as Box, Cylinder, Cone, Sphere, Pyramid, Wedge, and Torus. The number of lines in a solid primitive is controlled by the value assigned to the **ISOLINES** variable. These lines are called tessellation lines. The number of lines determine the number of computations needed to generate a solid. If the value is high, it will take significantly more time to generate a solid on the screen. Therefore, the value assigned to the **ISOLINES** variable should be realistic. When you invoke tools for creating solid primitives, AutoCAD Solids will prompt you to enter information about the part geometry. The height of the primitive is always along the positive Z axis and perpendicular to the construction plane. Similar to surface meshes, solids are also displayed as wireframe models unless you hide, render, or shade them. The **FACETRES** system variable controls the smoothness in the shaded and rendered objects and its value can go up to 10. The tools to create solid primitives are grouped in the **Solid Primitives** drop-down in the **Modeling** panel, as shown in Figure 8-1.

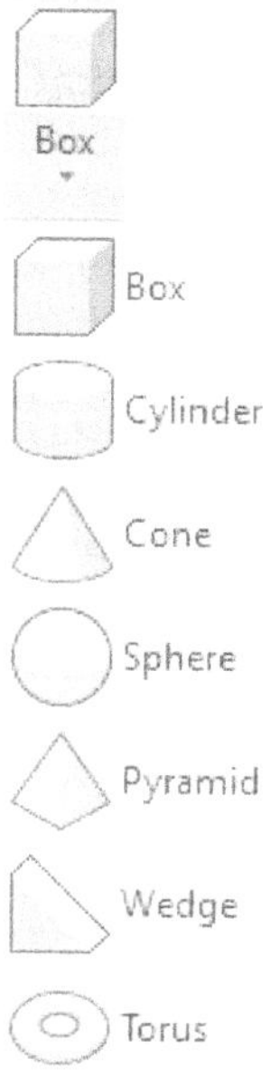

Figure 8-1 *Tools in the* ***Solid Primitives*** *drop-down*

Creating a Solid Box

Ribbon: Home > Modeling > Solid Primitives Drop-down > Box
Menu Bar: Draw > Modeling > Box **Toolbar:** Modeling > Box
Command: BOX

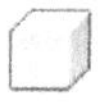

The **Box** tool is used to create a solid rectangular box or a cube. Start a new file using the *acad3D.dwt* template. In 3D drawing templates, you can dynamically preview the operations that you perform. The methods to create a solid box are discussed next.

Creating a Box Dynamically

To create a box dynamically, choose the **Box** tool from the **Modeling** panel. Specify the first corner point of the box and then specify the diagonally opposite corner point for defining the base of the box, refer to Figure 8-2. Now, specify the height of the box by moving the cursor away from the base. After getting the desired height, click in the drawing window to create the box or specify the height of the box in the dynamic input box, refer to Figure 8-2.

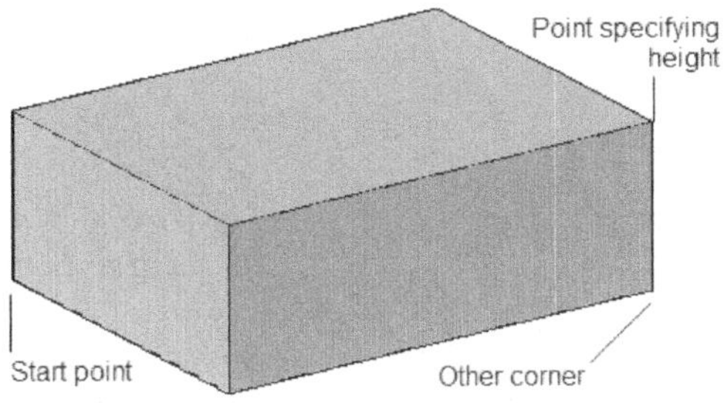

Figure 8-2 *Box created dynamically*

Two Corner Option

This option is selected by default. You can use this option to create a solid box by defining the first corner of the box and then its other corner, refer to Figure 8-3. Note that the length of the box will always be taken along the *X* axis, the width along the *Y* axis, and the height along the *Z* axis. Therefore, in this case, when you specify the other corner, the value along the *X* axis will be taken as the length of the box, the value along the *Y* axis will be taken as the width of the box, and the value along Z axis will be taken as height of the box. Given below is the prompt sequence to draw a box of length 5 units and height 4 units.

Specify first corner or [Center] : *Specify start point.*
Specify other corner or [Cube/Length]: *Drag the cursor in any one of the quadrants and type* ***5*** *(Planar face of length 5 units is displayed).*
Specify height or [2Point]: *4*

Center-Length Option

The center of the box is the point where the center of gravity of the box lies. This option is used to create a box by specifying the center of the box followed by the length, width, and height of the box, refer to Figure 8-4. The following prompt sequence is displayed when you choose the **Box** tool:

Specify first corner or [Center] : **C**
Specify center : **4,4**
Specify corner or [Cube/Length]: **L**
Specify length: **8** Enter.
Specify width: **6** Enter.
Specify height or [2point]: **3** Enter.

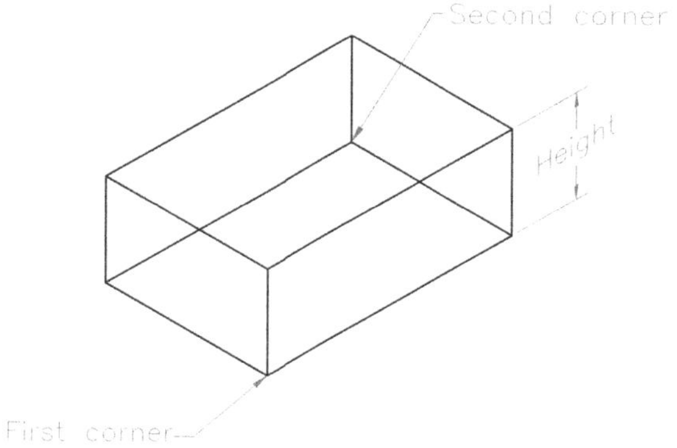

Figure 8-3 Creating a box using the ***Two Corner*** *option*

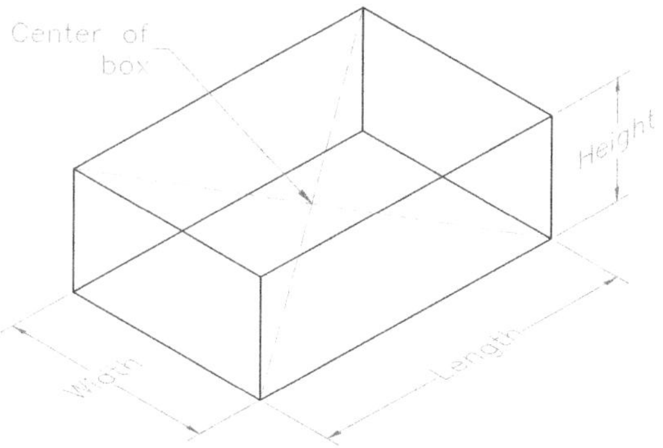

Figure 8-4 Creating a box using the ***Center-Length*** *option*

Note

1. The ***Corner-Length*** *option is similar to the* ***Center-Length*** *option with the only difference that in the* ***Corner-Length*** *option, you will define the first corner of the box and then the length, width, and height of the box.*

2. In the ***Two Corner*** *option, you need to specify the height of the box by specifying 2 points using the pointing device.*

Corner-Cube Option

This option is used to create a cube starting from a specified corner, as shown in Figure 8-5. As you are creating a cube, you will be prompted to enter the length of the cube that will also act as the width and height. The prompt sequence for creating the cube using the **Corner-Cube** option is given next.

Specify first corner or [Center] : **2,2**
Specify other corner or [Cube/Length]: **C**
Specify length: **5**

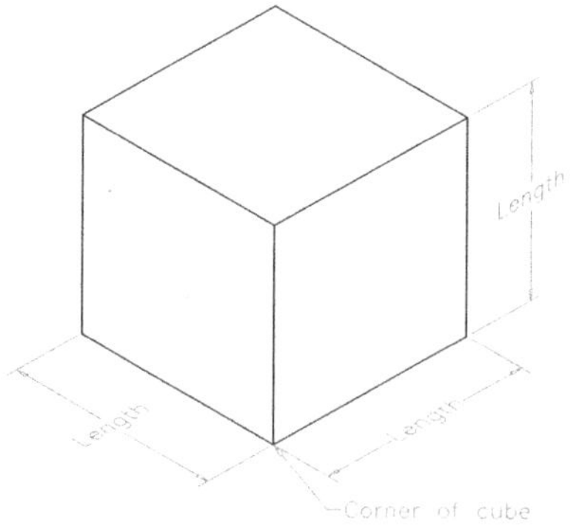

Figure 8-5 Creating a cube using the ***Corner-Cube*** *option*

Note

*The **Center-Cube** option is similar to the **Corner-Cube** option with the only difference that in the **Center-Cube** option you will have to define the center and the length of the cube.*

Creating a Solid Cone

Ribbon: Home > Modeling > Solid Primitives drop-down > Cone
Menu Bar: Draw > Modeling > Cone **Toolbar:** Modeling > Cone
Command: CONE

The **Cone** tool creates a solid cone with an elliptical or circular base. This tool provides you the option of defining the cone height or the location of the cone apex. Defining the location of the apex will also define the height of the cone and the orientation of the cone base from the *XY* plane.

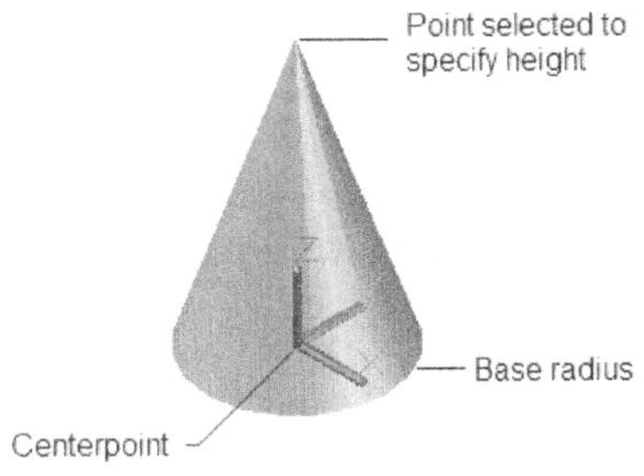

Figure 8-6 *Cone created dynamically*

To create a cone, start a new file using the *acad3D.dwt* template file and choose the **Cone** tool from the **Modeling** panel and specify the center point and the radius of the base, as shown in Figure 8-6. Next, specify the height of the cone by moving the cursor away from the base. After getting the desired height, click in the drawing window to create the cone. You can also enter all parameters defining the cone in the dynamic input box. Figure 8-6 shows a cone created dynamically.

Different methods to create a cone are discussed next.

Creating a Cone with Circular Base

The options for defining the circular base are Center Radius, Center Diameter, 3 Point, 2 Point, and Tangent tangent radius. The prompt sequence that will be displayed when you choose the **Cone** tool is given next.

Specify center point of base or [3P/2P/Ttr/Elliptical]: *Specify the center of the base.*

The default option to define a cone with circular base is Center Radius. In this option, after specifying the center point, enter the radius value and then the height of the cone. If you need to enter the diameter value, then enter **D** at the **Specify base radius or [Diameter]** prompt and specify the diameter value followed by the height. The prompt sequence for using this option is given below.

Specify center point of base or [3P/2P/Ttr/Elliptical]: *Specify the center of the base.*
Specify base radius or [Diameter] <default>: *Specify the radius or enter **D** to specify the diameter of the cone.*
Specify height or [2Point/Axis endpoint/Top radius]<default>: *Specify the height of the cone or enter an option or press the Enter key to accept the default value.*

If you want to create a cone by specifying two ends of the circular base, then type **2P** at the **Specify center point of base or [3P/2P/Ttr/Elliptical]** prompt and then specify the two ends of the diameter. Similarly, if the base of the cone is tangent to two circles, choose **Ttr** at the **Specify center point of base or [3P/2P/Ttr/Elliptical]** prompt, select the circles in succession, and then specify the radius.

Creating a Cone with Elliptical Base

To create a cone with elliptical base as shown in Figure 8-7, choose the **Elliptical** option at the **Specify center point of base of cone or [3P/2P/Ttr/Elliptical]** prompt. On selecting this option, the **Specify endpoint of first axis or [Center]** prompt will be displayed. Now, you can create the elliptical base by specifying the endpoints of axis, the location of the minor axis, and then the height. If you know the centerpoint of the ellipse, enter **C** at the **Specify endpoint of first axis or [Center]** prompt and specify the centerpoint, endpoint of the other two axes in succession, and finally the height; a cone with elliptical base will be created.

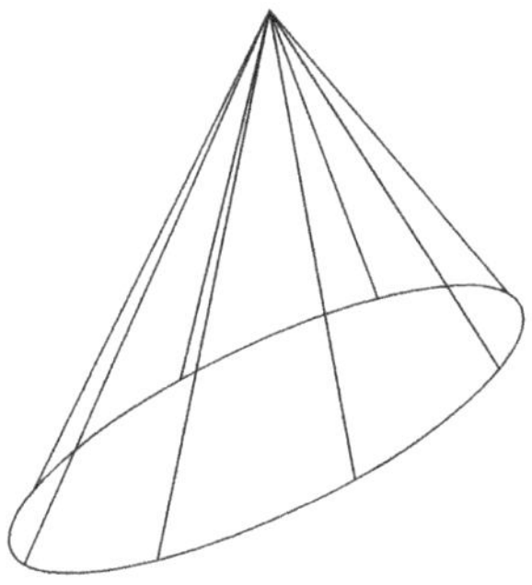

Figure 8-7 *An elliptical cone*

Creating a Cone with Apex

To create a cone with apex, first specify the base of the cone. Then, specify the height of the cone by choosing an option at the **Specify height or [2Point/Axis endpoint/Top radius]** prompt. By default, you will be prompted to specify the height of the cone. Enter the height of the cone or specify a location in the drawing area; the cone will be created.

To specify the height using the **2Point** option, enter **2P** at this prompt and specify two points in the drawing area. The distance between these two specified points will be considered as the height of the cone. The prompt sequence that will follow is given next.

Specify height or [2Point/Axis endpoint/Top radius] <current>: **2P**
Specify first point: *Specify the first point.*
Specify second point: *Specify the second point on the screen.*

To specify the height using the **Axis endpoint** option, choose the **Axis endpoint** option at the **Specify height or [2Point/Axis endpoint/Top radius]** prompt. On selecting this option, you can specify the endpoint of the axis, whose start point is the center of the base. Apart from fixing the height of the cone, this option is also used to specify the orientation of the cone in 3D space. This means you can also create an inclined cone, refer to Figure 8-8. The prompt sequence is as follows:

Specify axis endpoint: *Specify the location of the apex or axis endpoint of the right circular cone in 3D space.*

Creating the Frustum of a Cone

To create the frustum of a cone, choose the **Top radius** option at the **Specify height or [2Point/Axis endpoint/Top radius]** prompt; you will be prompted to specify the top radius. Specify the radius of the top of the frustum as the top radius; you will be prompted to specify the height.

Specify the height as discussed earlier; a frustum of a cone will be created, refer to Figure 8-9. The prompt to create a frustum of a cone is given next.

Specify top radius <default>: *Specify the radius for the top of the cone frustum.*
Specify height or [2Point/Axis endpoint] <default>: *Specify the height of the frustum or choose an option.*

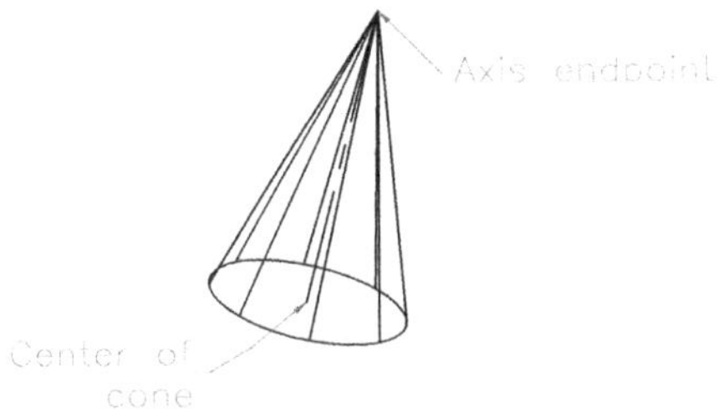

Figure 8-8 *Creating a cone using the* ***Axis endpoint*** *option*

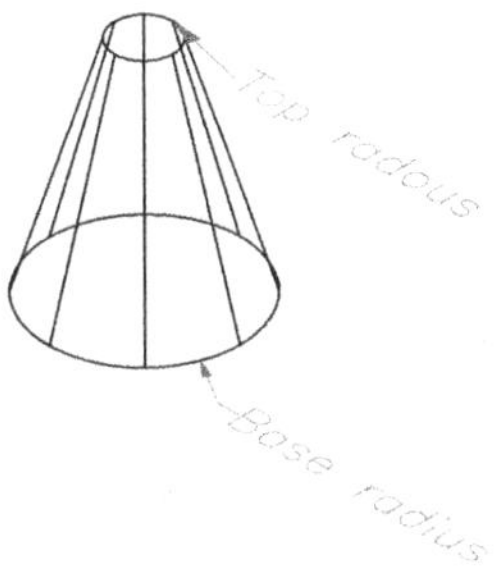

Figure 8-9 *Creating a cone using the* ***Top radius*** *option*

Tip
In AutoCAD, when you select a primitive shape, grips are displayed on it. You can modify the dimensions of the primitive by dragging these grips.

Creating a Solid Cylinder

Ribbon: Home > Modeling > Solid Primitives drop-down > Cylinder
Menu Bar: Draw > Modeling > Cylinder **Toolbar:** Modeling > Cylinder
Command: CYL (CYLINDER)

To create a cylinder, start a new drawing using the *acad3D.dwt* template file and choose the **Cylinder** tool from the **Solid Primitives** drop-down of the **Modeling** panel. Next, specify the center point of the base and then specify the radius of the base, as shown in Figure 8-10. Now, specify the height of the cylinder by moving the cursor away from the base. After getting the desired height, click in the drawing window to create the cylinder. You can also enter all parameters in the dynamic input box to define the cylinder.

Similar to the **Cone** tool, this tool provides you two options for creating the cylinder: circular cylinder and elliptical cylinder, refer to Figures 8-10 and 8-11. This tool also allows you to define the height of a cylinder dynamically or specify the height by using the **2Point** or **Axis endpoint** options. On selecting the **Axis endpoint** option, you can specify the endpoint of the axis, whose start point is the center of the base. Apart from fixing the height of the cylinder, this option is also used to specify the orientation of the cylinder in 3D space. This means you can also create an inclined cylinder, as shown in Figures 8-12 and 8-13.

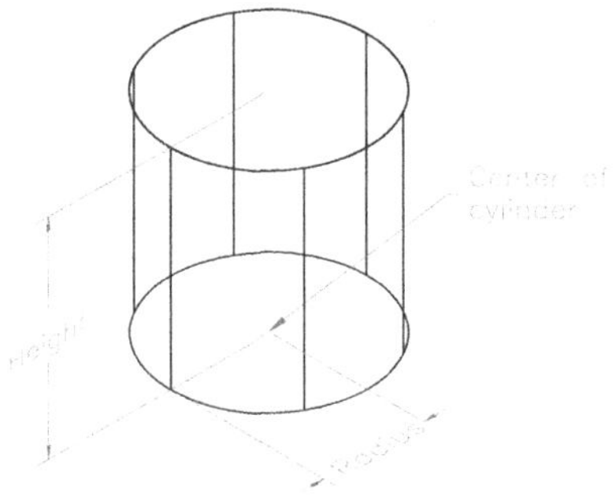

Figure 8-10 *Creating a circular cylinder*

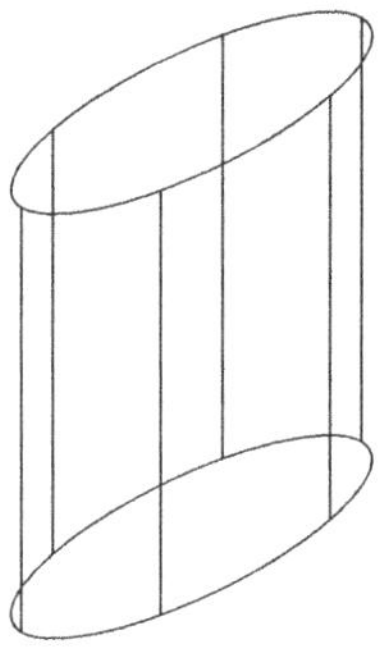

Figure 8-11 *Creating an elliptical cylinder*

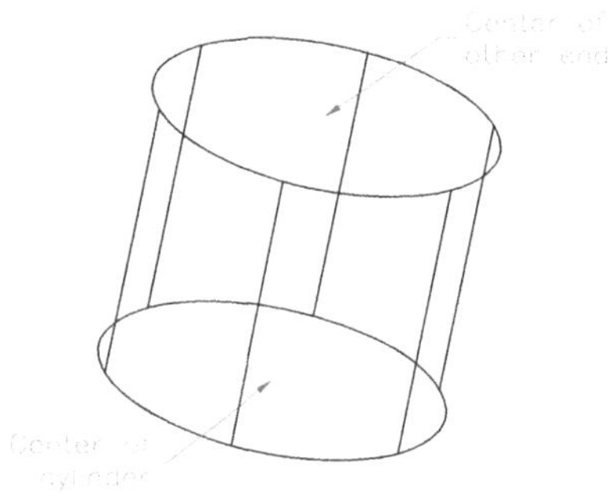

Figure 8-12 *Creating an inclined cylinder with circular base*

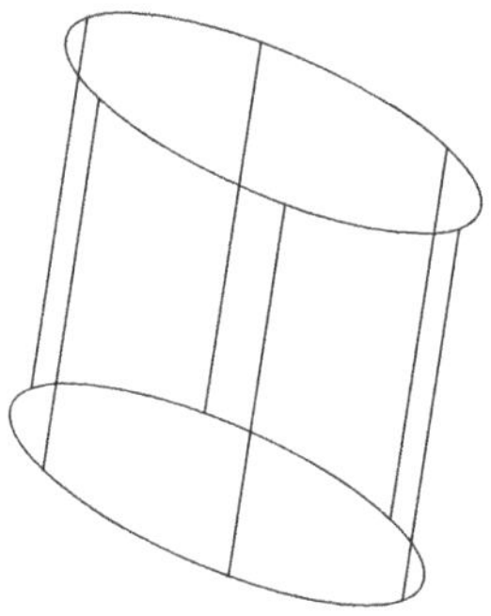

Figure 8-13 *Creating an inclined cylinder with elliptical base*

Creating a Solid Sphere

Ribbon: Home > Modeling > Solid Primitives drop-down > Sphere
Menu Bar: Draw > Modeling > Sphere **Toolbar:** Modeling > Sphere
Command: SPHERE

To create a sphere, choose the **Sphere** tool from the **Modeling** panel; you will be prompted to specify the center of the sphere. After specifying the center, you can create the sphere by defining its radius or diameter, as shown in Figure 8-14. Instead of specifying the center of the sphere, you can specify its circumference by choosing any one of the **3P/2P/Ttr** options as discussed earlier.

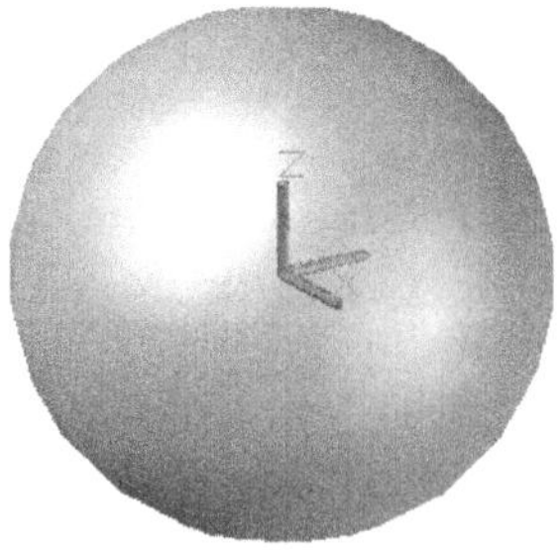

Figure 8-14 *Solid sphere created*

Creating a Solid Torus

Ribbon: Home > Modeling > Solid Primitives drop-down > Torus
Menu Bar: Draw > Modeling > Torus **Toolbar:** Modeling > Torus
Command: TOR (TORUS)

You can use the **Torus** tool to create a torus, refer to Figure 8-15. A torus is centered on the construction plane. The top half of the torus is above the construction plane and the other half is below it. To create a torus, choose the **Torus** tool from the **Modeling** panel; you will be prompted to enter the diameter or the radius of the torus and the diameter or the radius of tube, refer to Figure 8-16. The radius of torus is the distance from the center of the torus to the center-line of the tube. This radius can have a positive or a negative value. If the value is negative, the torus will have a rugby-ball like shape, refer to Figure 8-17. A torus can be self-intersecting. If both the radii of the tube and the torus are positive and the radius of the tube is greater than the radius of the torus, the resulting solid looks like an apple, refer to Figure 8-18. Instead of specifying the radius or diameter of the torus, you can specify the points through which the circumference of the torus will pass by choosing any one of the **3P**, **2P**, and **Ttr** options. These options are discussed earlier.

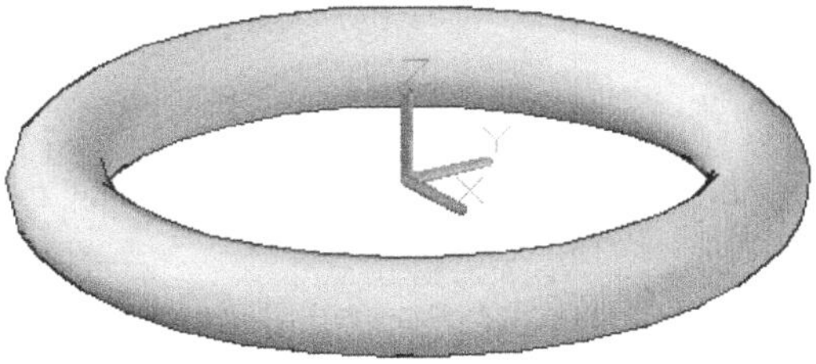

Figure 8-15 Torus created dynamically

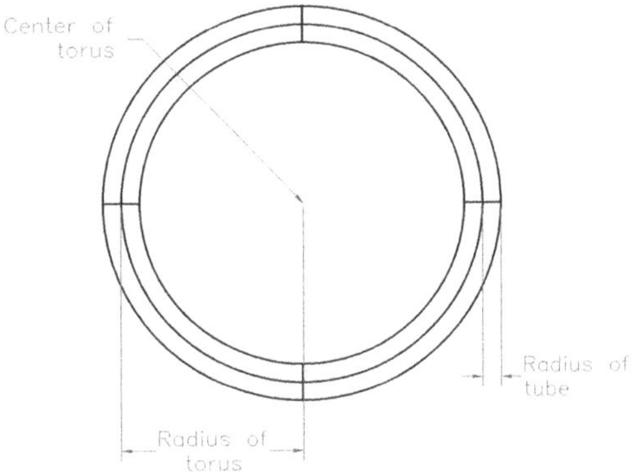

Figure 8-16 Parameters associated with a torus

Figure 8-17 Torus with a negative radius value

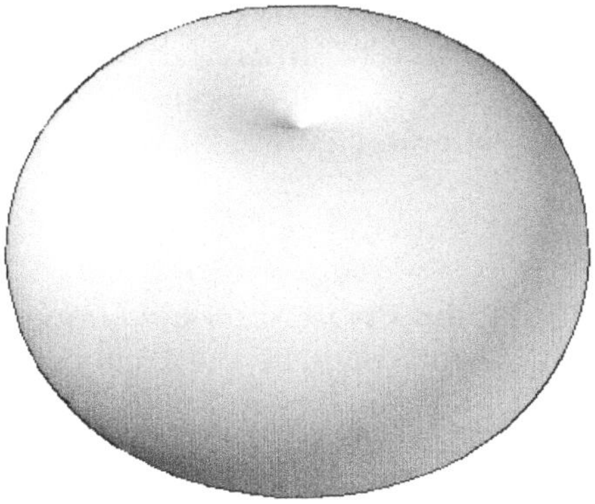

Figure 8-18 Torus with radius of tube more than the radius of torus

Creating a Solid Wedge

Ribbon: Home > Modeling > Solid Primitives drop-down > Wedge
Menu Bar: Draw > Modeling > Wedge **Toolbar:** Modeling > Wedge
Command: WEDGE

You can create a solid wedge by using the **Wedge** tool. To create a wedge by using this tool, you need to specify the start point, the diagonally opposite point, and the height of the wedge, refer to Figure 8-19. The other options to create a wedge are similar to those that are used to create a box.

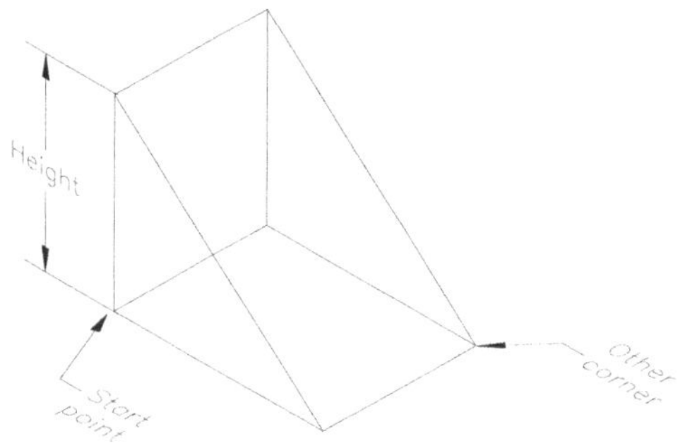

Figure 8-19 *Parameters of a wedge*

Creating a Pyramid

Ribbon: Home > Modeling > Solid Primitives drop-down > Pyramid
Menu Bar: Draw > Modeling > Pyramid **Toolbar:** Modeling > Pyramid
Command: PYR (PYRAMID)

The **Pyramid** tool is used to create a solid pyramid where all faces, other than the base, are triangular and converge at a point called apex, refer to Figure 8-20. The base of a pyramid can be any polygon but generally it is a square. To create a pyramid, choose the **Pyramid** tool from the **Modeling** panel and follow the prompt sequence given next.

Specify center point of base or [Edge/Sides]: *Specify the center point.*
Specify base radius or [Inscribed] <Current Value>: *Specify the base radius.*
Specify height or [2Point/Axis endpoint/Top radius] <Current Value>: *Specify the height to create the pyramid,* refer to Figure 8-20.

Different methods for creating a solid pyramid are discussed next.

On invoking the **Pyramid** tool, you need to specify the center point of the base polygon or the length of the edges, or the number of sides of the polygon. If you select the **Edge** option in the Command prompt, you will be prompted to pick two points from the drawing area that determine the length and orientation of the edge of the base polygon. If you select the **Sides** option, you will be prompted to specify the number of sides of the base polygon. Note that in AutoCAD, the number of sides of a pyramid can vary from 3 to 32.

Next, you need to specify the base radius of the circle in which the base polygon is created. The base polygon is either circumscribed around a circle or inscribed within a circle. By default, the base of the pyramid is circumscribed. After specifying the base radius, you need to specify the height of the pyramid or select an option.

The options to specify the height are same as for cone or cylinder.

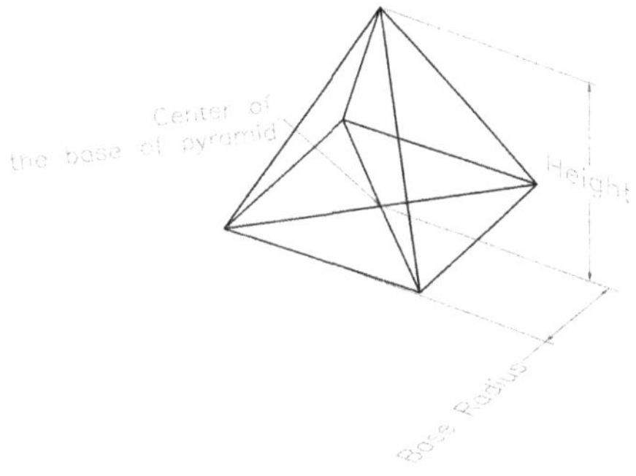

Figure 8-20 Parameters associated with a pyramid

You can also create the frustum of a pyramid by selecting the **Top radius** option at the **Specify height or [2Point/Axis endpoint/Top radius]** Command prompt. On selecting this option, you are prompted to specify the radius of the top of the pyramid frustum. Then, you need to specify the height of the frustum either dynamically or by selecting the **2Point** or the **Axis endpoint** option.

Creating a Polysolid

Ribbon: Home > Modeling > Polysolid **Menu Bar:** Draw > Modeling > Polysolid
Command: POLYSOLID or PSOLID

The **Polysolid** tool is similar to the **Polyline** tool with the only difference that this tool is used to create a solid with a rectangular cross-section of a specified width and height. This tool can also be used to convert existing lines, 2D polylines, arcs, and circles into a polysolid feature. To create a polysolid, choose the **Polysolid** tool from the **Modeling** panel and follow the prompt sequence given next.

Height = current, Width = current, Justification = current
Specify start point or [Object/Height/Width/Justify]<Object>: *Specify the start point for the profile of the polysolid. Else, press the Enter key to select an object to convert it into a polysolid or enter an option.*

The options available at the Command prompt are discussed next.

Next Point of Polysolid

When you specify the start point for the profile of the solid, this option is displayed. This option is used to specify the next point of the current polysolid segment. If additional polysolid segments are added to the first polysolid, AutoCAD automatically makes the endpoint of the previous polysolid, the start point of the next polysolid segment. The prompt sequence is given next.

Specify start point or [Object/Height/Width/Justify] <Object>: *Specify the start point.*
Specify next point or [Arc/Undo]: *Specify the endpoint of the first polysolid segment.*
Specify next point or [Arc/Close/Undo]: *Specify the endpoint of the second polysolid segment or press the Enter key to exit the tool.*

Arc. This option is used to switch from drawing linear polysolid segments to drawing curved polysolid segments. The prompt sequence that will follow is given next.

Specify next point or [Arc/Close/Undo]: **A** Enter.
Specify end point of the arc or [Close/Direction/Line/Second point/Undo]: *Specify the endpoint of the arc or choose an option to create the arc.*

The **Close** option closes the polysolid by creating an arc shaped trajectory from the most recent endpoint to the initial start point and exits the **Polysolid** tool. Usually, the arc drawn with the **Polysolid** tool is tangent to the previous polysolid segment. This means that the starting direction of the arc is the ending direction of the previous segment. The **Direction** option allows you to specify the tangent direction of your choice for the arc segment to be drawn. You can specify the direction by specifying a point. The **Line** option switches the command to the **Line** mode. The **Second point** option selects the second point of the arc in the **3P** arc option. The **Undo** option reverses the changes made in the previously drawn polysolid.

Close. This option is available when at least two segments of the polysolid are drawn. It closes the polysolid segment by creating a linear polysolid from the recent endpoint to the initial point.

Undo. This option is used to erase the most recently drawn polysolid segment. You can use this option repeatedly until you reach the start point of the first polysolid segment.

Object

This option is used to convert an existing 2D object into a polysolid. The 2D objects that can be converted into a polysolid include lines, 2D polylines, arcs, and circles. Figure 8-21 shows a polysolid object created by converting a 2D polyline. Note that the polysolid is displayed in the **Realistic** visual style by default, but for clarity, it has been displayed in the **Wireframe** visual style. The prompt sequence for using this option is given next.

Specify start point or [Object/Height/Width/Justify]<Object>: Enter.
Select object: *Select an object to convert it into a polysolid.*

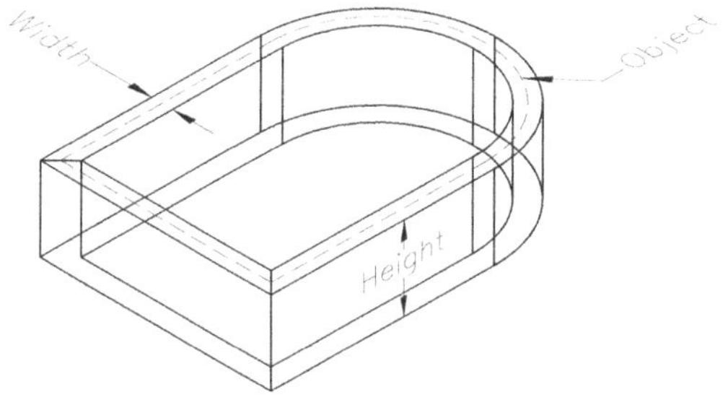

Figure 8-21 *Object converted to a polysolid by using the* ***Object*** *option*

Height

This option is used to specify the height of the rectangular cross-section of the polysolid. The value that you specify will be set as the default value for this tool. The prompt sequence for this option is given next.

> Specify start point or [Object/Height/Width/Justify]<Object>: **H** Enter.
> Specify height <current>: *Specify the value of the height or press the Enter key to accept the current value.*
> Specify start point [Object/Height/Width/Justify]<Object>: *Specify the start point of the polysolid or choose an option.*

Width

This option is used to specify the width of the rectangular cross-section of a polysolid. The prompt sequence for this option is given next.

> Specify start point [Object/Height/Width/Justify]<Object>: **W** Enter.
> Specify width <current>: *Specify the width or press the Enter key to accept the current value.*
> Specify start point [Object/Height/Width/Justify]<Object>: *Specify the start point of the polysolid or choose an option.*

Justify

The justification option determines the position of the created polysolid with respect to the starting point. The three justifications that are available for a **Polysolid** tool are **Left**, **Center**, and **Right**.

Left. This justification produces a polysolid with its left extent fixed at the start point and the width added to the right of the start point when the polysolid is viewed from the direction of its creation, refer to Figure 8-22.

Center. This justification produces a polysolid with its center fixed at the start point and the width added equally to both the sides of the start point when you view the polysolid from the direction of its creation, refer to Figure 8-22.

Right. This justification produces a polysolid with its right extent fixed at the start point and the width added to the left of the start point, when you view the polysolid from the direction of its creation, refer to Figure 8-22.

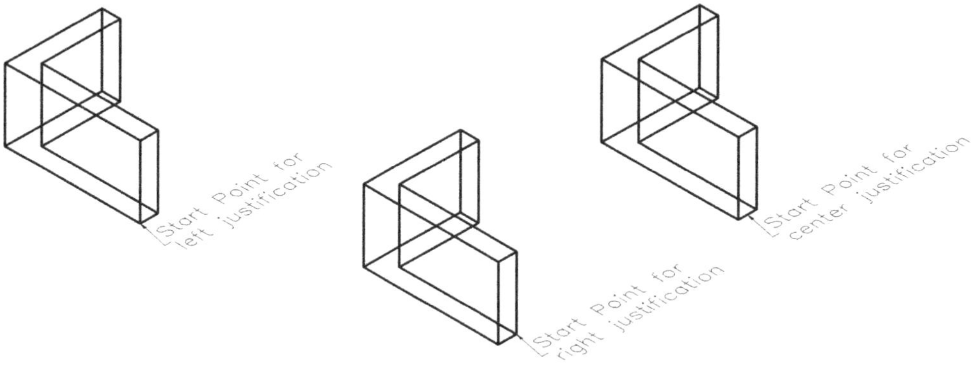

Figure 8-22 *Start point for the **Left**, **Right**, and **Center** justifications of a polysolid*

Creating a Helix

Ribbon: Home > Draw > Helix **Toolbar:** Modeling > Helix
Menu Bar: Draw > Helix **Command:** HELIX

The **Helix** tool is used to create a 3D helical curve. To generate a helical curve, you need to first specify the center for the base of the helix. Next, you need to specify the base radius, radius at the top of the helix, and height of the helix. A helix of converging or diverging shape can also be generated by specifying different values for the base and top radius. You can also control the number of turns in a helix and specify whether the twist will be in the clockwise direction or counter clockwise direction. Figure 8-23 shows a helix with the parameters to be defined.

The prompt sequence displayed on choosing the **Helix** tool is given next.

Specify center point of base: *Specify a point for the center of the helix base.*
Specify base radius or [Diameter] <default1.0000>: *Specify the value for the base radius, enter **D** to specify the diameter, or press the Enter key to select the default value for the radius.*
Specify top radius or [Diameter] <current>: *Specify the value for the top radius of the helix, enter **D** to specify the diameter, or press the Enter key to select the current value of the base radius.*
Specify helix height or [Axis endpoint/Turns/turn Height/tWist] <default>: *Specify the height of the helix and press the Enter key to select the default value or choose an option.*

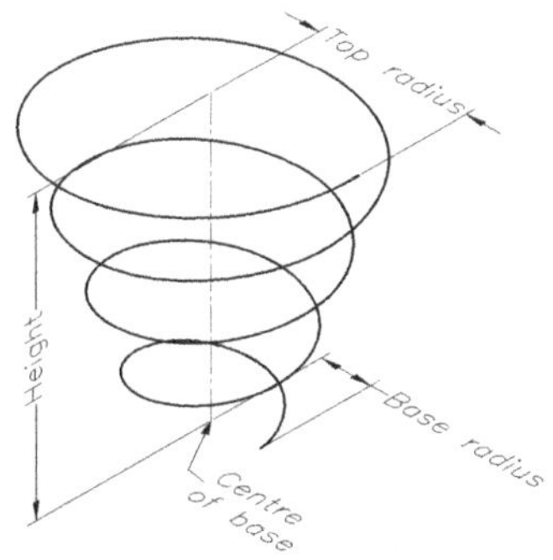

Figure 8-23 Helix with associated parameters

The options available at the Command prompt are discussed next.

Axis endpoint

To specify the height using the **Axis endpoint** option, choose the **Axis endpoint** option at the **Specify helix height or [Axis endpoint/Turns/turn Height/tWist]** prompt. Using this option, you can specify the endpoint of the axis, whose start point is assumed to be at the center of the base of the helix. Apart from specifying the height of the helix, this option is also used to specify the orientation of the helix in 3D space or in other words, you can also create an inclined helix, refer to Figure 8-24.

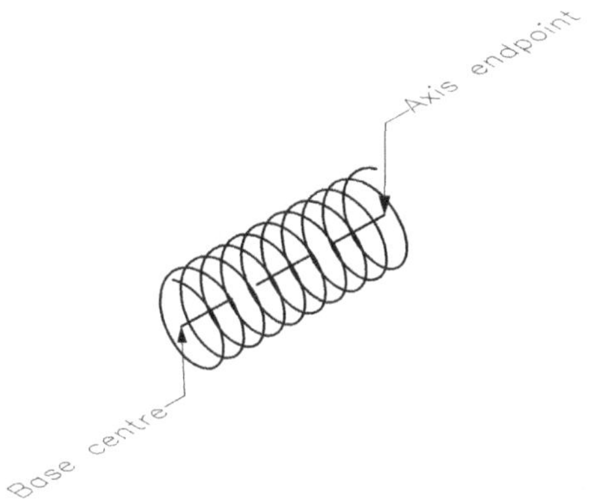

*Figure 8-24 Helix created using the **Axis endpoint** option*

Turns

To specify the number of turns in the helix, choose the **Turns** option at the **Specify helix height or [Axis endpoint/Turns/turn Height/tWist]** prompt. Using this option, you can change the number of turns in the helical curve. The default number of turns for the **Helix** tool is three.

Note

In a helical curve, the number of turns cannot be more than 500.

turn Height

To specify the pitch of the helix, choose the **turn Height** option at the **Specify helix height or [Axis endpoint/Turns/turn Height/tWist]** prompt. Using this option, instead of specifying the whole height of the helix, you can specify the height of one complete single turn of the helix. The helical curve will be generated with the total height equal to the turn height multiplied by the number of turns.

tWist

To specify the starting direction of the helical curve, choose the **tWist** option from the shortcut menu at the **Specify helix height or [Axis endpoint/Turns/turn Height/tWist]** prompt. By using this option, you can specify whether the curves will be generated in the clockwise or the counterclockwise direction. Figure 8-25 shows a helix with counterclockwise turns and Figure 8-26 shows a helix with clockwise turns. The default value for the starting direction of the helical curve is counterclockwise.

Figure 8-25 *Helix created using the **CCW** option*

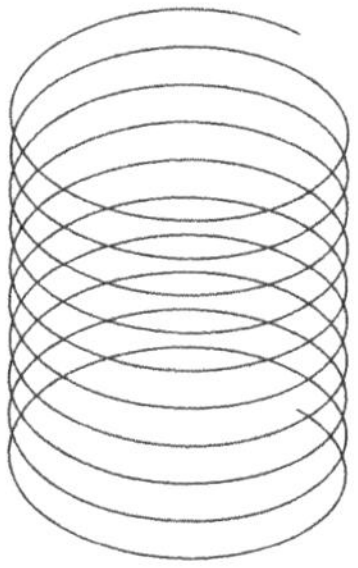

Figure 8-26 *Helix created using the **CW** option*

Tip

*You can use the generated helix as a trajectory for the **Sweep** tool. This tool will be discussed later in this chapter.*

MODIFYING THE VISUAL STYLES OF SOLIDS

Ribbon: Home > View > Visual Styles drop-down > Visual Styles Manager
Menu Bar: Tools > Palettes > Visual Styles **Command:** VISUALSTYLES

AutoCAD provides you with various predefined modes of visual styles. These visual styles are grouped together in the **Visual Styles Manager**, refer to Figure 8-27. To invoke the **VISUAL STYLES MANAGER**, select the **Visual Styles Manager** option from the **Visual Styles** drop-down list in the **View** panel. Alternatively, click on the inclined arrow at the bottom right of the **Visual Styles** panel in the **Visualize** tab. There are ten visual styles available in the **Available Visual Styles in Drawing** rollout of the **VISUAL STYLES MANAGER**. To apply a visual style, you need to double-click on it. Alternatively, select the desired visual style from the **Visual Styles** drop-down list in the **View** panel; the model will be updated automatically to the new visual style.

The properties of the selected visual style will be displayed below the **Available Visual Styles in Drawing** rollout. You can modify these properties depending upon your requirement. You can also create a user-defined visual style based on the current visual style applied to the model. To do so, choose the **Create New Visual Style** button from the tool strip at the bottom of the **Available Visual Styles in Drawing** rollout; the **Create New Visual Style** dialog box will be displayed. Enter a new name and description for the newly created visual style. Next, choose **OK**; a new visual style will be created. Set the properties of the new visual style by modifying the default properties. Alternatively, set the properties of the visual style and then select **Save as a New Visual Style** from the **Visual Styles** drop-down list in the **Visualize** tab; you will be prompted to specify a name to save the current visual style. Enter a name and press Enter; the new visual style will be saved.

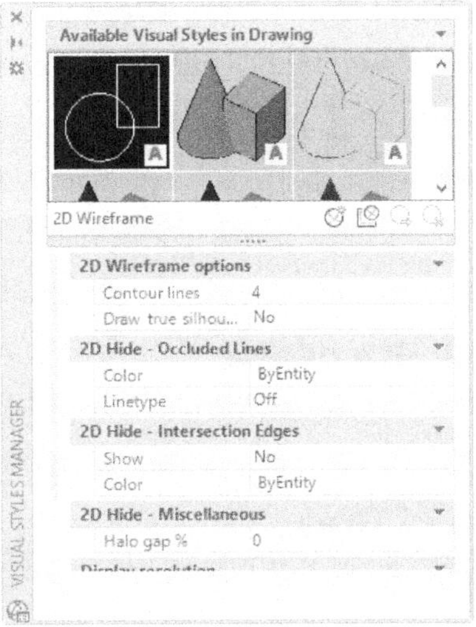

*Figure 8-27 The **VISUAL STYLES MANAGER***

> **Tip**
> *In AutoCAD, you can also use the **In-canvas Viewport controls** displayed on the top left corner of the drawing area for changing the visual style of a solid by simply clicking on the **Visual Style Controls** and selecting **Visual Styles Manager** which is the last option available in the flyout displayed.*

Available Visual Styles in Drawing

The options available in this rollout are discussed next.

2D Wireframe

On applying this visual style, all hidden lines will be displayed along with the visible lines in the model. Sometimes, it becomes difficult to recognize the visible lines and hidden lines if you set this visual style for complex models.

Conceptual

In this visual style, the model will be displayed as shaded and the edges of the visible faces of the model will also be displayed.

Hidden

On applying this visual style, the hidden lines in the model will not be displayed and only the edges of the faces that are visible in the current viewport will be displayed.

Realistic

This visual style is the same as **Conceptual** but with a more realistic appearance. Moreover, if materials are applied to a model, this visual style will display the model along with the materials applied.

Shaded

In this visual style, smooth shading is applied to the faces of a model. In this case, the edges of the visible faces are not visible.

Shaded with edges

In this visual style, smooth shading is applied to the faces of a model and the edges of the visible faces are visible.

Shades of Gray

In this visual style, a single shade (grey) is applied to all faces of a model.

Sketchy

In this visual style, a model appears as if it is hand sketched.

Wireframe

This visual style is used to display a solid model as a wireframe model. You can see through the solid model while the model is being rotated in the 3D orbit view.

X-Ray

This visual style is used to display the model with shading and mild transparency. In this case, the hidden lines will be visible.

2D Wireframe options

The options in this area are discussed next.

Contour Lines

The lines that are displayed on the curved surface of a solid are known as contour lines. The default value for the number of contours to be displayed on each curved surface is 4 and it is controlled by system variable **ISOLINES**. Figure 8-28 shows a cylinder with 4 contour lines and Figure 8-29 shows a cylinder with 8 contour lines.

Draw true silhouettes

This option is used to specify whether or not to display the true silhouette edges of a model when it is hidden by using the **Hide** tool. If you select **Yes** from this drop-down list, the silhouette edges will be displayed when you hide the model, refer to Figure 8-30. However, when you select **No** from this drop-down list, the silhouette edges will not be displayed when you hide the model, refer to Figure 8-31.

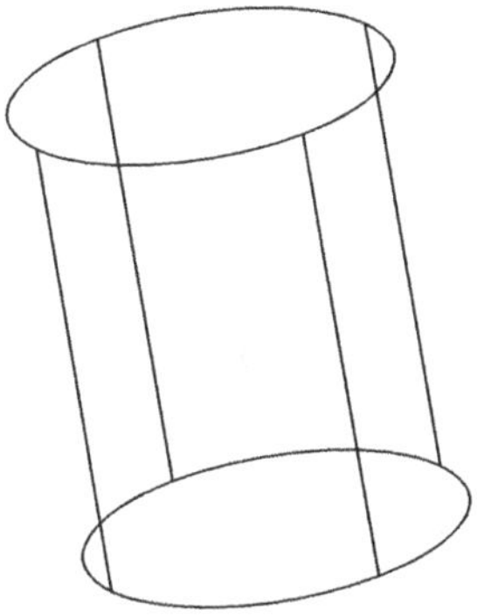

Figure 8-28 Cylinder with 4 contour lines

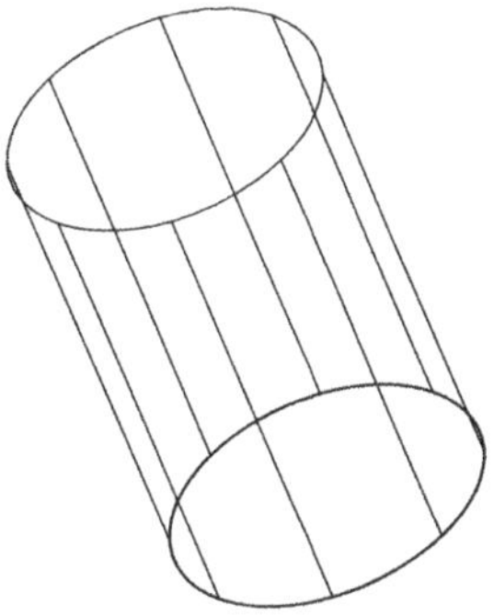

Figure 8-29 Cylinder with 8 contour lines

Figure 8-30 Model with the true silhouette edges on

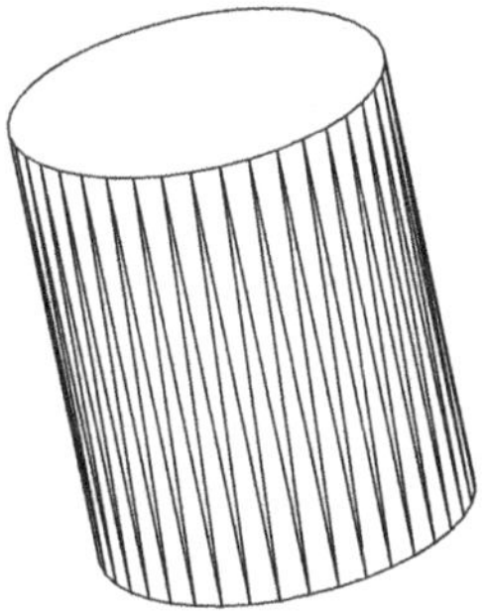

Figure 8-31 Model with the true silhouette edges off

2D Hide - Occluded Lines

The options in this area are used to set the linetype and color of the hidden lines (also called occluded lines).

Linetype

This drop-down list is used to set the linetype for the obscured lines. You can select the desired linetype from this drop-down list. The linetype of the hidden lines can also be modified using the **OBSCUREDLTYPE** system variable. The default value of this variable is 0. As a result, the hidden lines are suppressed when you invoke the **Hide** tool. You can set any value between 0 and 11 for this system variable. The following table gives the details of the different values of this system variable and the corresponding linetypes that will be assigned to the hidden lines:

Value	Linetype	Sample
0	Off	None
1	Solid	
2	Dashed	
3	Dotted	
4	Short Dash	
5	Medium Dash	
6	Long Dash	
7	Double Short Dash	
8	Double Medium Dash	
9	Double Long Dash	
10	Medium Long Dash	
11	Sparse Dot	

Figure 8-32 shows a model with a hidden linetype changed to dashed lines and Figure 8-33 shows the same model with hidden lines changed to dotted lines.

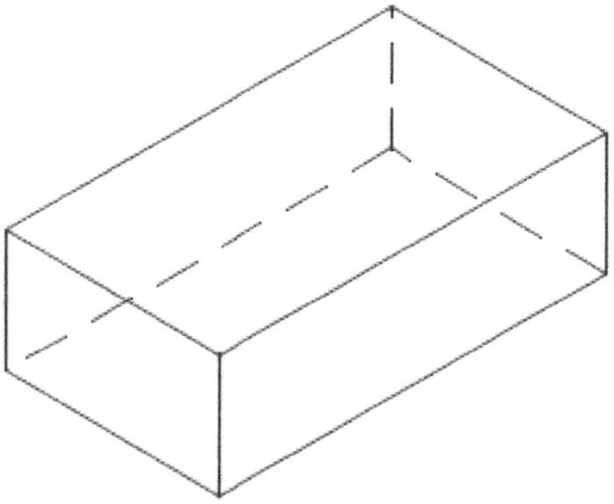

Figure 8-32 *Model with hidden lines changed to dashed lines*

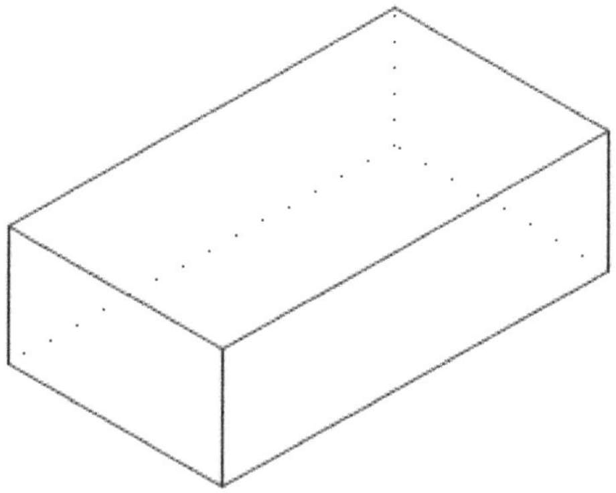

Figure 8-33 *Model with hidden lines changed to dotted lines*

Color

The **Color** drop-down list is used to define the color for the obscured lines. If you define a separate color, the hidden lines will be displayed with that color, when you invoke the **Hide** tool.

You can select the required color from this drop-down list. This can also be done by using the **OBSCUREDCOLOR** system variable. Using this variable, you can define the color to be assigned to the hidden lines. The default value is 257. This value corresponds to the **ByEntity** color. You can enter the number of any color at the sequence that will follow when you enter this system variable. For example, if you set the value of the **OBSCUREDLTYPE** variable to **2**, and that of the **OBSCUREDCOLOR** to **1**, the hidden lines will appear in red dashed lines when you invoke the **Hide** tool.

Note

The linetype and the color for the hidden lines defined using the previously mentioned variables are valid only when you invoke the ***Hide*** *tool. They do not work if the model is regenerated.*

2D Hide - Intersection Edges

The options in this area are used to display a 3D curve at the intersection of two surfaces. Note that the 3D curve is displayed only after invoking the **Hide** tool. These options are discussed next.

Show

If you select **Yes** from the **Show** drop-down list, a 3D curve will define the intersecting portion of the 3D surfaces or solid models.

Color

The **Color** drop-down list is used to specify the color of the 3D curve that is displayed at the intersection of the 3D surfaces or solid models.

2D Hide - Miscellaneous

This head in the **Visual Styles Manager** is used to set the percentage for halo gap.

Halo gap %

The **Halo gap %** area is used to specify the distance in terms of percentage of unit length by which the edges that are hidden by a surface or solid model will be shortened, refer to Figures 8-34 and 8-35.

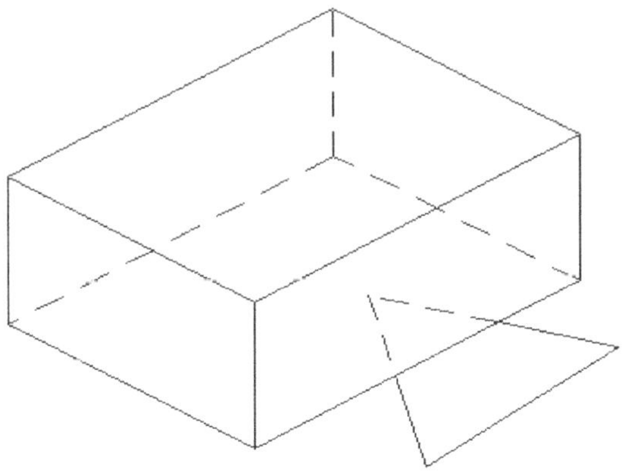

Figure 8-34 *Hiding lines with halo gap % as* ***0***

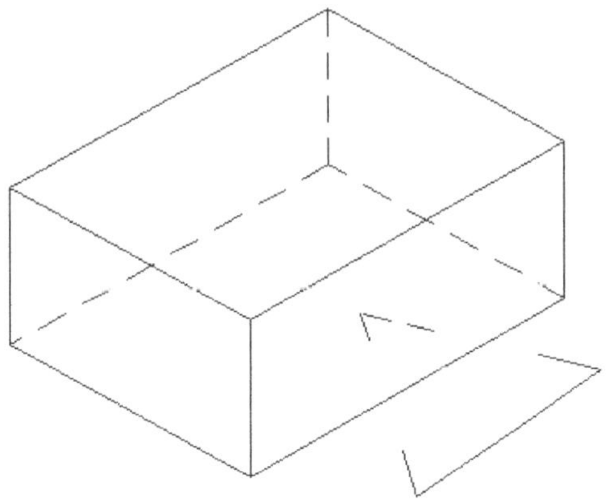

Figure 8-35 *Hiding lines with halo gap % as* ***40***

Note
The obscured linetype in Figures 8-34 and 8-35 has been changed to dashed.

Display resolution

The options in this area are used to set the resolutions for the curves, splines, and solids. These options are discussed next.

Arc/Circle Smoothing

This option is used to vary the smoothness of the curved surfaces of a 3D model. By default the value for smoothing of the curves or circles is 1000. You can change the value as per your requirement and this smoothness is controlled by the system variable **VIEWRES**.

Spline Segments

This option is used to set the number of segments in a polyline that can be fitted in the spline curve. By default, the number of segments that are displayed in a spline are 8. You can also set the number of segments by using the **SPLINESEGS** variable.

Solid Smoothness

The **Solid Smoothness** area is used to specify the smoothness of the surfaces of the 3D model. By default 0.5 is specified as the smoothness value for the surfaces and you can change this value from **0.1** to **10**. This solid smoothness can also be controlled by system variable **FACETRES**.

Similarly, you can specify the settings for faces, edges, and environment required for other visual styles. These settings are discussed next.

Controlling the Settings of Edges

You can control display settings of the edges by using the **Edge Settings** rollout in the **Available Visual Styles in Drawing** palette. Figure 8-36 shows different types of edge display. The **Show** field in this rollout has three options: **None**, **Isolines**, and **Facet Edges**. On selecting the **Isolines** option, the contour lines on the surface of the solid will be displayed. Also, the **Always on top** field will be available in the **Edge Settings** rollout. On selecting the **Yes** option in this field, all isolines in the model will be displayed. If you do not want the edges to be displayed, choose **None** in the **Show** field. On selecting the **Facet Edges** option in the **Show** field, the edges between the planar surfaces will be displayed. You can also set other options in the sub rollout. Note that some of the sub rollouts will not be available for the **Shaded** and **Realistic** visual styles.

The **Occluded Edges** sub rollout is used to control the display of hidden edges. Select the **Yes** option in the **Show** field to display the hidden edges. You can also set the color and the line type of the hidden edges in the **Color** and **Linetype** fields, respectively.

The options in the **Intersection Edges** sub rollout are used to control the display of the resulting curve when two surfaces intersect. Select the **Yes** option in the **Show** field to display the curve at the intersection. You can also set the color and the line type of the resulting curve in the **Color** and **Linetype** fields, respectively.

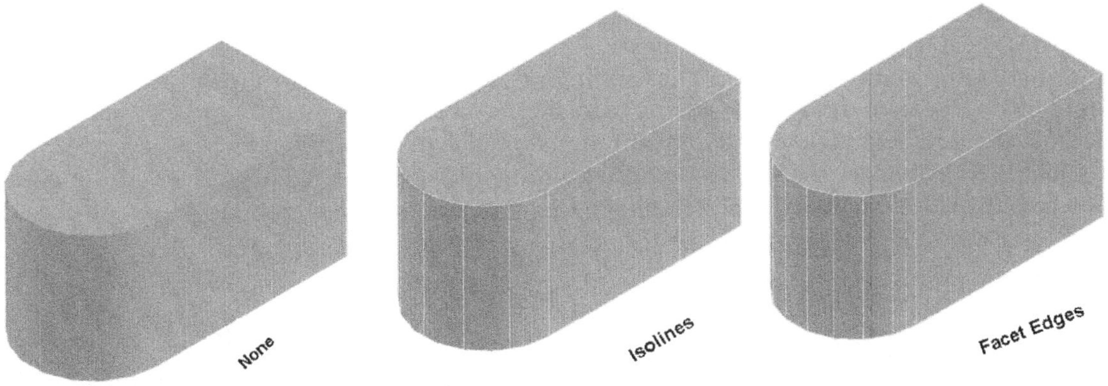

Figure 8-36 Different types of edge display

The **Silhouette Edges** sub rollout is used to control the display of the silhouette edges. Select the **Yes** option in the **Show** field to display the silhouette edges. You can set the width of the silhouette edges in the **Width** field. This value ranges from 1 to 25.

The **Edge Modifiers** sub rollout is used to assign special effects such as **Line Extensions** and **Jitter** to edges. Both the effects exhibit a hand-drawn effect with the only difference that the sketches drawn in **Line Extensions** extend beyond the model, whereas in **Jitter**, the edges look as if they were drawn using pencil and has multiple lines. Note that you need to choose the **Line Extension edges** and **Jitter edges** buttons from the title bar of the sub rollout to enable these options. You can set the value for the extension line from the vertices by using the **Line Extensions** spinner. Similarly, you can control the effect of jitter by using the options in the **Jitter** drop-down list. Figure 8-37 shows the effect of line extensions and jitter edges. The **Crease angle** field will be displayed only if you choose the **Facets Edges** option in the **Edge Settings** rollout. Note that the Facets edges will be displayed only if the angle between the facets is smaller than the specified crease angle.

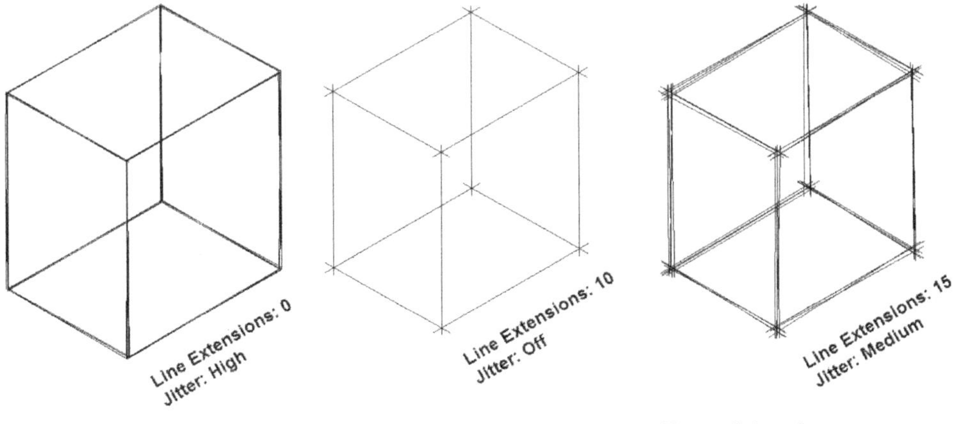

***Figure 8-37** The **Line Extensions** and **Jitter** effects of the edges*

Controlling the Face Display

AutoCAD enables you to control the display of faces by providing options to apply color effects and shading to solids or surfaces. The shading of models can be controlled by using the **Face style** field. The options in this field are **Realistic**, **Gooch**, and **None**, refer to Figure 8-38. By default, the **Realistic** option is chosen and therefore gives a real world effect to the model. The **Gooch** effect enhances the display by using light colors, instead of dark colors. If the **None** option is chosen, then no style will be applied to the model and only the edges will be displayed.

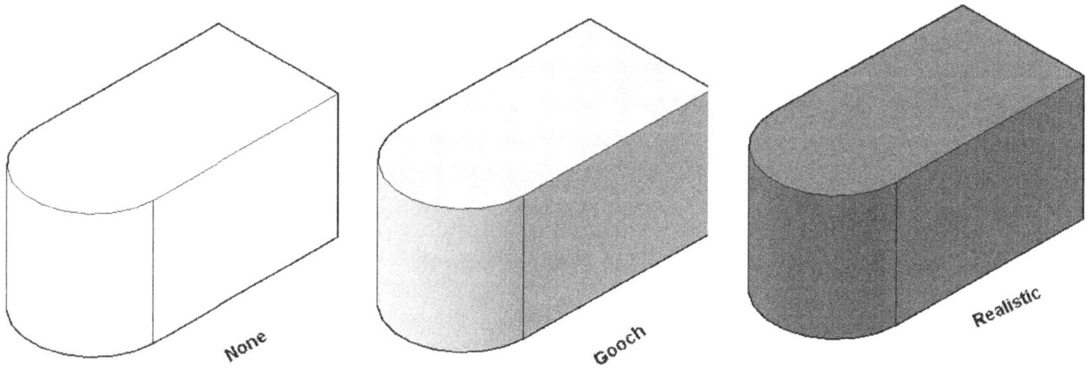

Figure 8-38 *Different face styles*

You can also control the appearance of faces in solids or surfaces using the **Lighting quality** field. The options available in this field are **Faceted**, **Smooth**, and **Smoothest**. On selecting the **Faceted** option, the color is applied to each face, thereby making the object to appear flat. On selecting the **Smooth** option, the color applied is the gradient between the two vertices of the face. This option is selected by default. On selecting the **Smoothest** option, the color is calculated for per pixel lighting.

You can apply different color settings to faces by selecting an option from the **Color** drop-down list in the **Face Settings** rollout. The options in this drop-down list are **Normal**, **Monochrome**, **Tint**, and **Desaturate**. No face color will be applied if the **Normal** option is selected. If you select the **Monochrome** option, all faces will be shaded with a single color. If you want to use the same color to shade all faces by changing the hue and saturation values of the color, then select the **Tint** option. The hue and saturation values can be changed by using the **Tint Color** drop-down list. Select the **Desaturate** option to soften the color by reducing the saturation by 30%.

You can also control the opacity of solid models by choosing the **Opacity** button in the title bar of the **Face Settings** rollout. On doing so, the **Opacity** field will be enabled. Specify the desired transparency level. Figure 8-39 shows an object with different opacity values.

The shininess of an object is set by using the options in the **Lighting** rollout. To set the shininess, choose the **Highlight intensity** button on the title bar of this rollout and set the required value in the **Highlight intensity** spinner. Note that you cannot set this value when a material is applied on it.

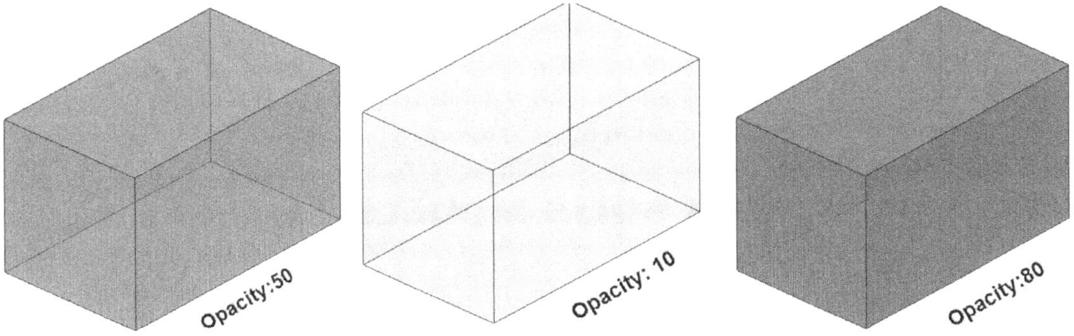

Figure 8-39 *An object with different opacity values*

Shadows provide a real effect at rendering. Shadows are generated when light is applied. Lights can be user-defined lights or the sunlight. The options in this drop-down list are **Off**, **Ground Shadow**, and **Mapped Object shadows**. The Ground Shadows are the shadows that an object casts on the ground. The Mapped Object shadows are the shadows cast by one object on other objects. Shadows appear darker when they overlap. Use of shadows can slow down the system performance. So, you need to turn off the shadows while working, and turn them on when you need shadows. You can set the display of the shadow by using the **Properties** palette. The shadows will be explained in detail in later chapters.

Controlling the Backgrounds

You can control the display of background by using the option in the **Environment Settings** rollout. You can turn on or off the background by using the **Backgrounds** drop-down list in this rollout. The background can be a single solid color, a gradient fill, an image, or the sun and the sky. This is explained in detail in the chapter. (Rendering and Animating Designs).

Note
*In AutoCAD, the default visual style applied to a model is **Realistic**. However, in this textbook, the **Wireframe** visual style is applied to models for clarity of printing.*

CREATING COMPLEX SOLID MODELS

Until now you have learned how to create simple solid models using the standard solid primitives. However, the real-time designs are not just the simple solid primitives but complex solid models. These complex solid models can be created by modifying the standard solid primitives with the boolean operations or directly by creating complex solid models by extruding or revolving the regions. All these options of creating complex solid models are discussed next.

Creating Regions

Ribbon: Home > Draw > Region **Menu Bar:** Draw > Region
Command: REG(REGION)

The **Region** tool is used to create regions from the selected loops or closed entities. Regions are the 2D entities with properties of 3D solids. You can apply the Boolean operation on the regions and you can also calculate their mass properties. Bear in mind that the 2D entity you want to convert into a region should be a closed loop. Once you have created regions, the original object is deleted automatically. However, if the value of the **DELOBJ** system variable is set to **0**, the original object is retained. The valid selection set for creating the regions are closed polylines, lines, arcs, splines, circles, or ellipses. The current color, layer, linetype, and lineweight will be applied to the regions.

CREATING COMPLEX SOLID MODELS BY APPLYING BOOLEAN OPERATIONS

You can create complex solid models by applying the Boolean operations on the standard solid primitives. The Boolean operations that can be performed are union, subtract, intersect, and interfere. The tools used to apply these Boolean operations are discussed next.

Combining Solid Models

Ribbon: Home > Boolean > Solid, Union
Menu Bar: Modify > Solid Editing > Union
Command: UNI(UNION)
Toolbar: Modeling / Solid Editing > Union

The **Solid, Union** tool is used to apply the Union Boolean operations on the selected set of solids or regions. You can create a composite solid or region by combining them using this tool. You can combine any number of solids or regions. When you invoke this tool, you will be prompted to select the solids or regions to be added. Figure 8-40 shows two solid models before union and Figure 8-41 shows the composite solid created after union.

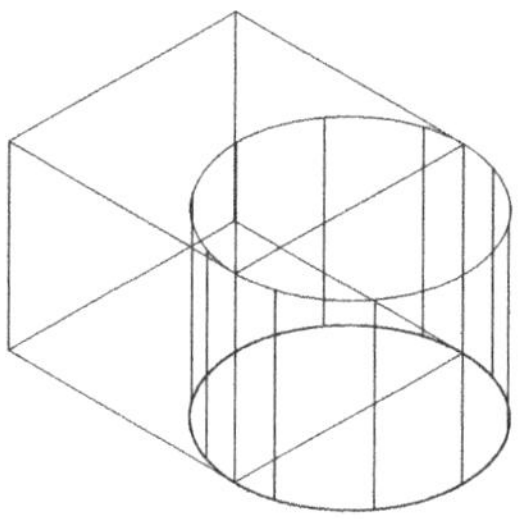

Figure 8-40 *Solid models before union*

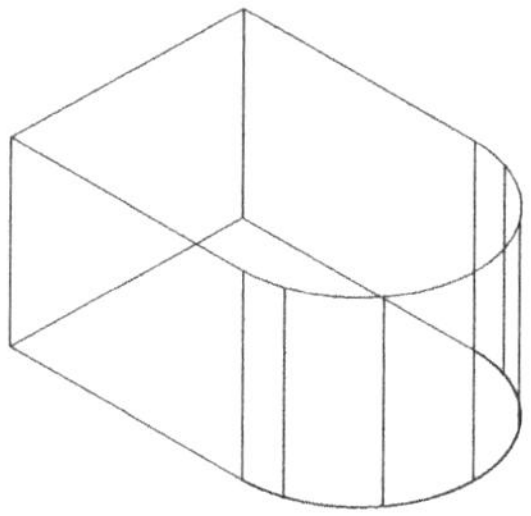

Figure 8-41 *Composite solid created after union*

Subtracting One Solid From the Other

Ribbon: Home > Boolean > Solid, Subtract
Menu Bar: Modify > Solid Editing > Subtract
Toolbar: Modeling / Solid Editing > Subtract
Command: SUBTRACT

The **Subtract** tool is used to create a composite solid by removing the material common to the selected set of solids or regions. On invoking this tool, you will be prompted to select the set of solids or regions to subtract from. After selecting it, press Enter; you will be prompted to select the solids or regions to subtract. After selecting it, press Enter again.

The material common to the first selection set and the second selection set is removed from the first selection set. The resultant object will be a single composite solid, refer to Figures 8-42 and 8-43.

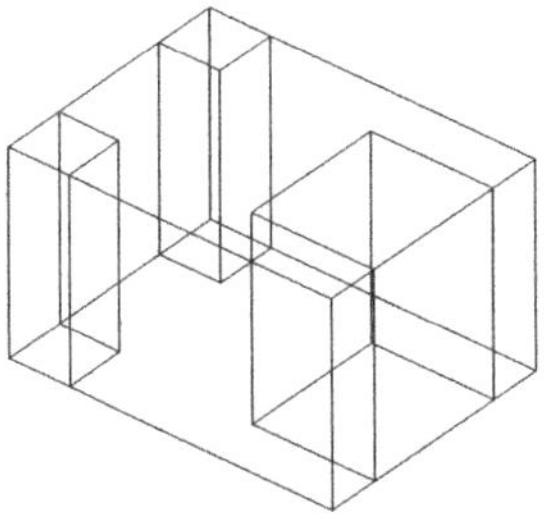

Figure 8-42 Solid models before subtracting

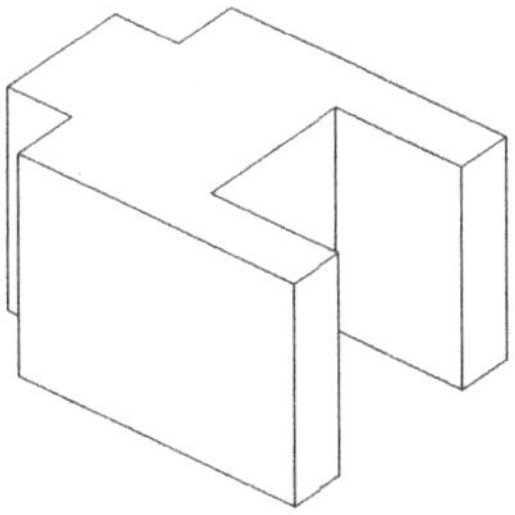

Figure 8-43 Composite solid created after subtracting

Intersecting Solid Models

Ribbon: Home > Boolean > Solid, Intersect
Menu Bar: Modify > Solid Editing > Intersect
Toolbar: Modeling / Solid Editing > Intersect **Command:** INTERSECT

The **Solid, Intersect** tool is used to create a composite solid or region by retaining the material common to the selected set of solids or regions. When you invoke this tool, you will be prompted to select the solids or regions to intersect. The material common to all the selected solids or regions will be retained to create a new composite solid, refer to Figures 8-44 and 8-45.

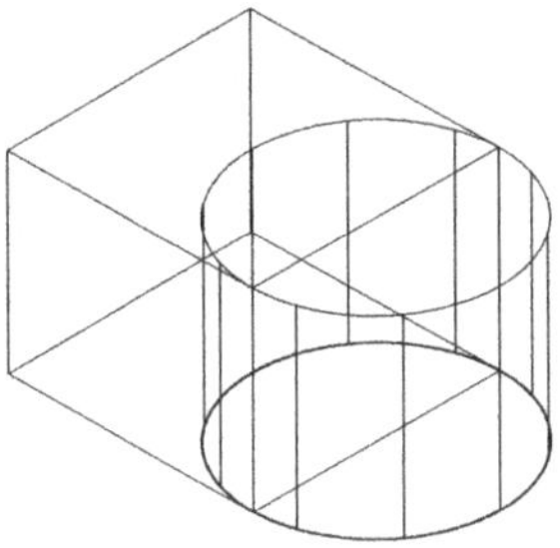

Figure 8-44 Solid models before intersecting

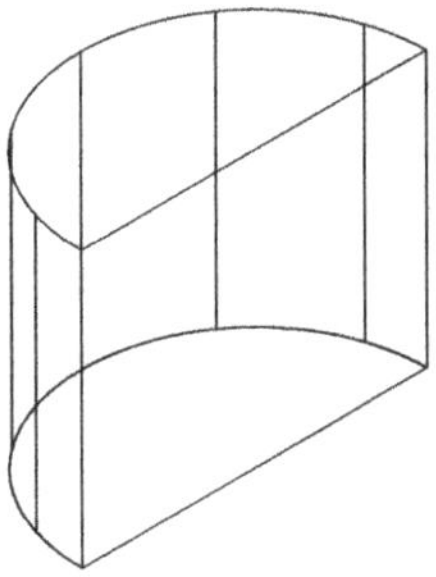

Figure 8-45 Solid model created after intersecting

Checking Interference in Solids

Ribbon: Home > Solid Editing > Interfere
Menu Bar: Modify > 3D Operations > Interference Checking **Command:** INTERFERE

The **Interfere** tool is used to create a composite solid model by retaining the material common to the selected sets of solids. This tool is generally used for analyzing interference between the mating parts of an assembly. On invoking this tool, you will be prompted to select the first set of objects. Once you have selected them, press Enter; you will be prompted to select the second set of objects. Select the second set of objects and press Enter; the **Interference Checking** dialog box will be displayed. Also, the interference will be highlighted in the drawing area. The **Interfering objects** area in this dialog box displays the number of objects selected in both the first and second sets and the number of interferences found between them. Choose the **Previous** or the **Next** button in the **Highlight** area to view the previous or next interferences. If the **Zoom to pair** check box is selected in this area, the interference is zoomed while cycling through the interference objects. You can also use the navigation tools in the **Interference Checking** dialog box to view the interfering area clearly. Clear the **Delete interference objects created on Close** check box, if you need to retain the interference objects after closing the dialog box. Close this dialog box by choosing the **Close** button.

If you clear the **Delete interference objects created on Close** check box and then close the **Interference Checking** dialog box, you can move the interfering objects by using the **Move** tool. Figure 8-46 shows two mating components of an assembly with interference between them and Figure 8-47 shows the interference solid created and moved out.

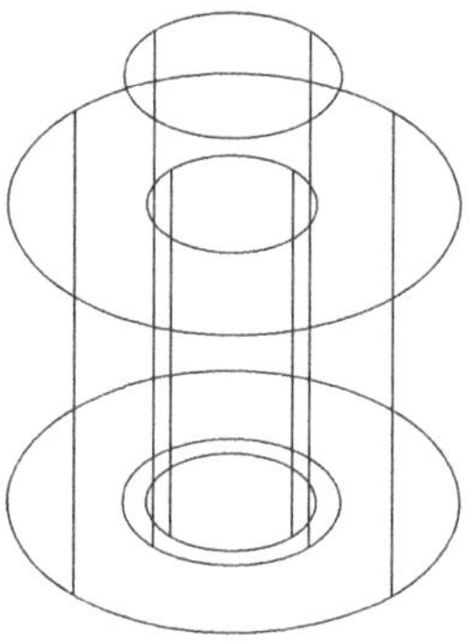

Figure 8-46 *Two mating components with interference*

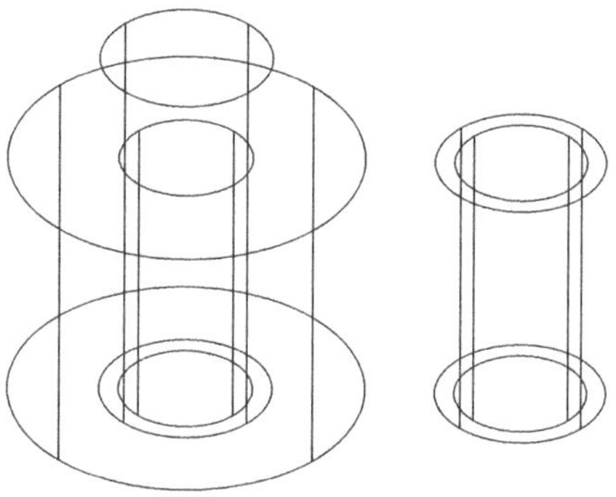

Figure 8-47 *Interference solid created using the* ***Interfere*** *tool*

You can also specify the visual style and color for the interfering objects. To do so, invoke the **Interfere** tool, type **S** at the **Select first set of Objects or [Nested selection/Settings]** prompt and press Enter; the **Interference Settings** dialog box will be displayed. In this dialog box, specify the required parameters.

Example 1

In this example, you will create the solid model shown in Figure 8-48.

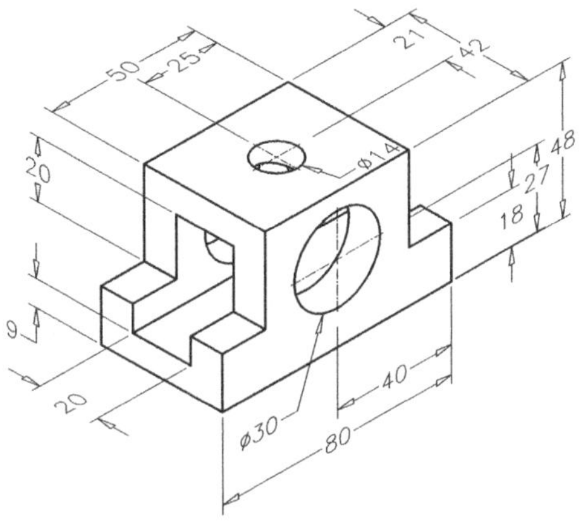

Figure 8-48 *Solid model for Example 1*

1. Increase the drawing limits to 100,100. Zoom to the limits of the drawing.

2. Enter **UCSICON** at the Command prompt. The following prompt sequence is displayed:

   Enter an option [ON/OFF/All/Noorigin/ORigin/Selectable/Properties] <ON>: **N**

3. Right-click on the ViewCube and then choose the **Parallel** option.

4. Invoke the ortho mode, if it is not turned on.

5. Choose **Wireframe** from **Home > View > Visual Styles** drop-down to set the visual style as Wireframe.

6. Choose the **Box** tool from **Home > Modeling > Solid Primitives** drop-down and follow the prompt sequence given next.

   Specify first corner or [Center] : **10, 10**
   Specify other corner or [Cube/Length]: **L**
   Specify length: *(Move the cursor along Y axis)* **80**
   Specify width: **42**
   Specify height: **48**

7. Again, invoke the **Box** tool and follow the prompt sequence given below.

   Specify first corner or [Center] : **10, 10, 18**
   Specify other corner or [Cube/Length]: **L**

Specify length: *(Move the cursor along X axis)* **42**
Specify width: **15**
Specify height: **30**

8. Right-click on the **3D Object Snap** button in the Status Bar and then choose the **Vertex** option. Clear the other options in this shortcut menu.

9. Turn **on** the **3D Object Snap** by choosing it, if it is not already turned **on**.

10. Move the new box inside the old box by snapping the midpoint on edge of both the boxes.

11. By using the **Copy** tool and the **Vertex** option of the **3D Object Snap**, copy the new box to the other side of the box, refer to Figure 8-49.

12. Choose the **Solid, Subtract** tool from the **Solid Editing** panel and follow the prompt sequence given next.

Select solids, surfaces, and regions to subtract from.
Select objects: *Select the bigger box.*
Select objects: Enter.
Select solids, surfaces, and regions to subtract from.
Select objects: *Select one of the smaller boxes.*
Select objects: *Select other smaller boxes.*
Select objects: Enter.

13. Change the visual style to **Hidden** from the **In-canvas Visual Style controls**. The model after subtracting the boxes should look similar to the one shown in Figure 8-50.

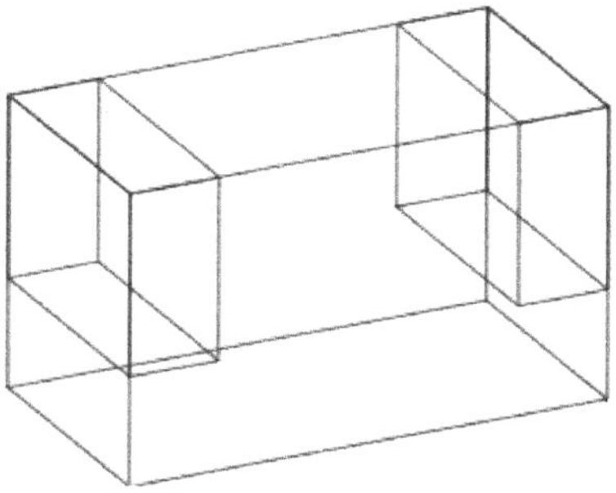

Figure 8-49 *Boxes moved inside the bigger box using midpoints*

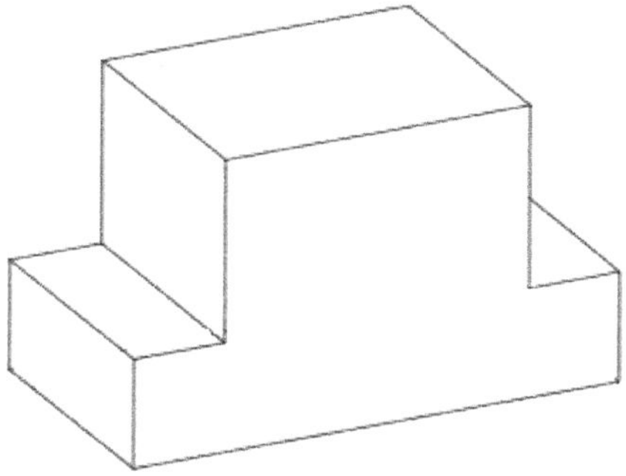

Figure 8-50 *Model after subtracting the smaller boxes*

14. Again, change the visual style to **Wireframe**. Then, choose the **Box** tool and follow the prompt sequence given next.

Specify first corner or [Center] : **21,10,9**
Specify other corner or [Cube/Length]: **L**

Specify length: *(Move the cursor along the X axis)* **20**
Specify width: **80**
Specify height: **29**
The box created is shown in Figure 8-51.

15. Invoke the **Move** tool and select the box created in the previous step.

16. Specify the midpoint of the lower edge as the base point; the **Specify second point or <use first point as displacement>** prompt is displayed.

17. Enter **From** and press Enter; you are prompted to specify the base point.

18. Specify the midpoint of the lower edge of the solid created by using the **Subtract** tool.

19. Move the cursor vertically upward. Enter **9** at the Command prompt and press Enter; the box is moved, as shown in Figure 8-51.

20. Choose the **Solid, Subtract** tool from the **Solid Editing** panel and follow the prompt sequence.

    Select solids and regions to subtract from.
    Select objects: *Select the model.*
    Select objects: Enter.
    Select solids, surfaces, and regions to subtract.
    Select objects: *Select the box.*
    Select objects: Enter.

    The model after changing the visual style to Hidden should look similar to the one shown in Figure 8-52.

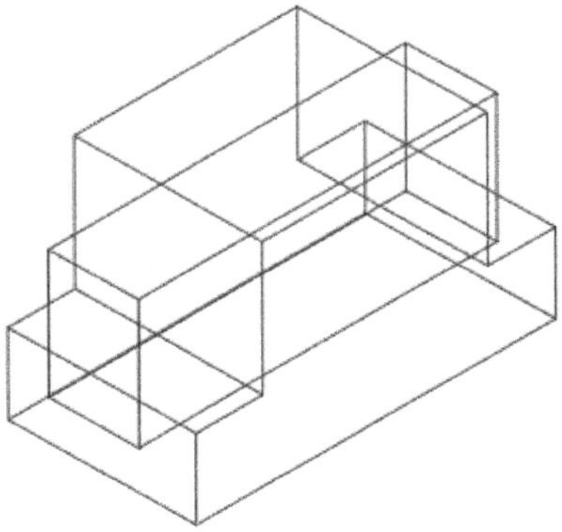

Figure 8-51 *Model before subtraction*

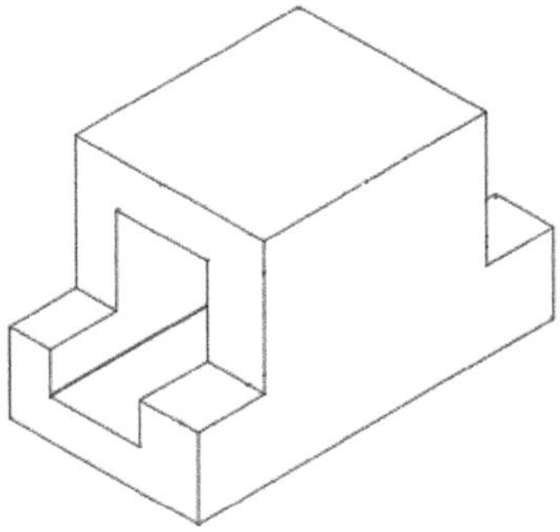

Figure 8-52 *Model after subtraction*

21. Right-click on the **3D Object Snap** button in the Status Bar and choose the **Center of face** option. Clear the other options in this shortcut menu.

22. Choose the **Cylinder** tool from **Home > Modeling > Solid Primitives** drop-down and follow the command sequence given next to create the cylinder, as shown in Figure 8-53.

    Specify center point of base or [3P / 2P / Ttr/ Elliptical]: *Move the cursor on top face of the model and snap the center of the top face.*
    Specify base radius or [Diameter]: **7**
    Specify height or [2Point / Axis endpoint]: *Move the cursor vertically downward and enter **10***

23. Subtract this cylinder from the existing model, refer to Figure 8-54.

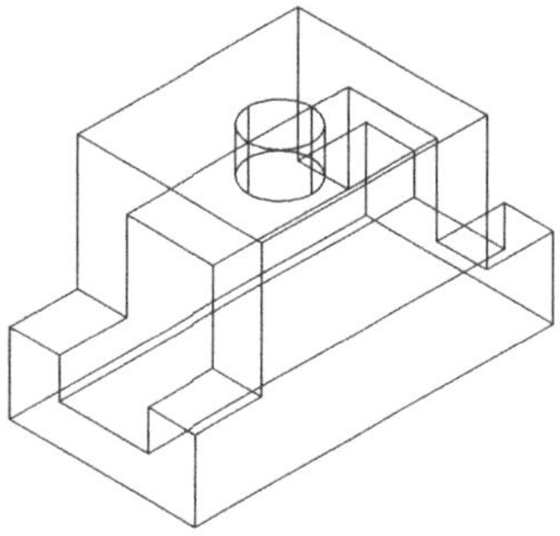

Figure 8-53 *Model before subtraction*

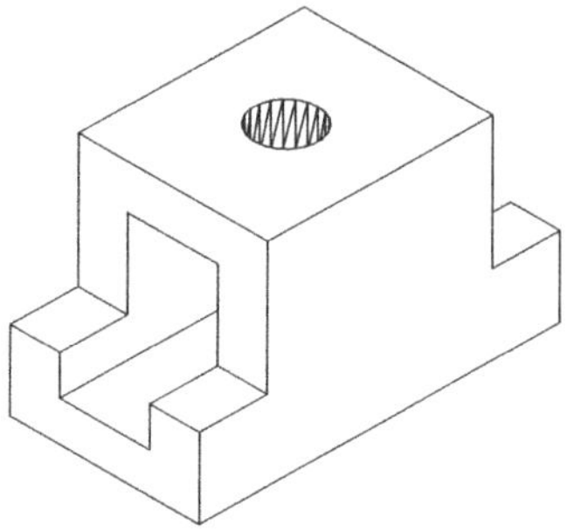

Figure 8-54 *Model after subtraction*

24. Create a new UCS on the left face of the model.

25. Choose **Cylinder** from **Home > Modeling > Solid Primitives** drop-down in the **Ribbon**. The following command sequence will be displayed:

    Specify center point of base or [3P / 2P / Ttr/ Elliptical]: *Use the **From** option to specify the center point of the cylinder at a distance of **27** units from the midpoint of the longer edge of the base.*
    Specify base radius or [Diameter]: **15**
    Specify height or [2Point / Axis endpoint]: **42**

26. Subtract this cylinder from the model and change the visual style to **Shades of Gray**. The final model should look similar to the one shown in Figure 8-55.

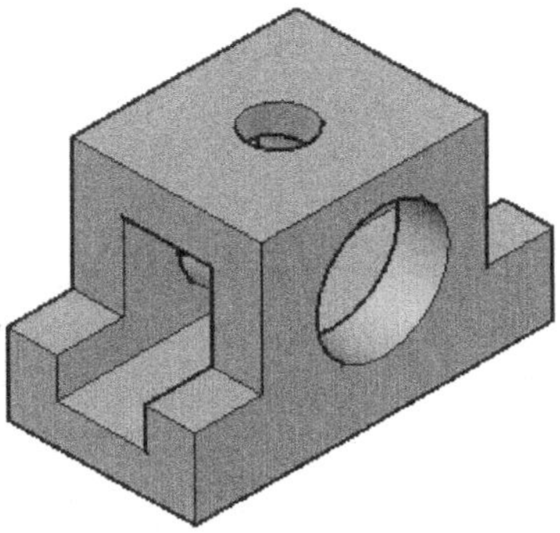

Figure 8-55 *Final solid model for Example 1*

Exercise 1

In this exercise, you will create the solid model shown in Figure 8-56. Save this drawing with the name *C-03_Exercise1.dwg*.

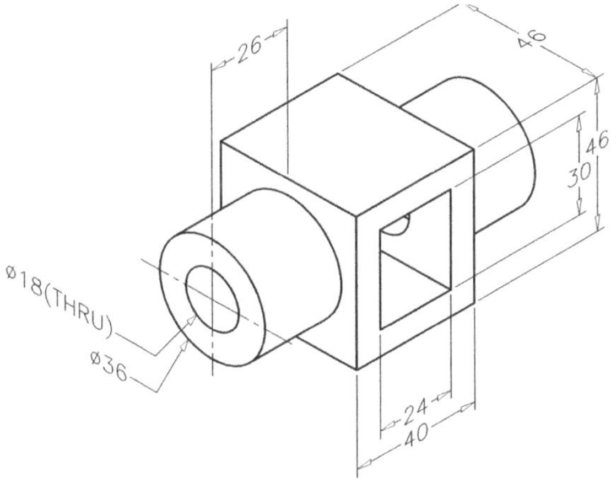

Figure 8-56 *Solid model for Exercise 1*

DYNAMIC UCS

This option is used to temporarily align the XY plane of the current UCS with the selected face of an existing solid. Choose the **Dynamic UCS** toggle button from the Status Bar to turn it on. Now, invoke a tool and move the cursor near the face on which you want to create the new sketch or solid; the face will be highlighted in dashed lines. Click the left mouse button on the desired face; the XY plane of the UCS will automatically be aligned with the selected face. Now, you can create the sketch or solid at the selected face. After the completion of the sketch or feature, the UCS will again move automatically to its original position.

For example, if you want to create a cylinder on the slant face of the model shown in Figure 8-57, choose the **Dynamic UCS** button from the Status Bar to turn it on. Then, choose the **Cylinder** tool from the **Solid Primitives** drop-down in the **Modeling** panel. Next, move the cursor near the slant face of the model; the slant face of the model will be highlighted. Next, left-click on that face and create the cylinder, as shown in Figure 8-58.

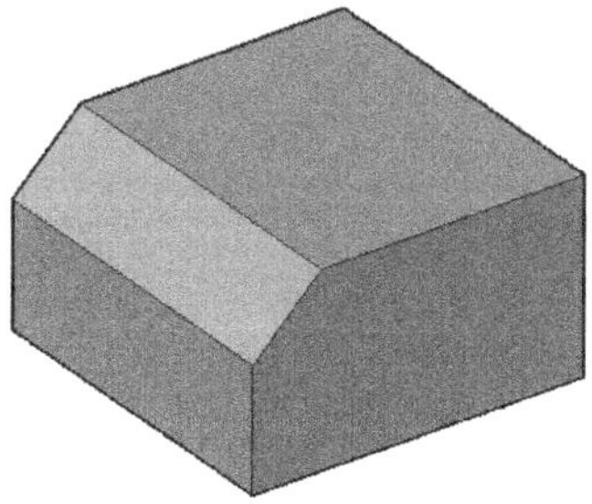

Figure 8-57 *Model with UCS at the origin*

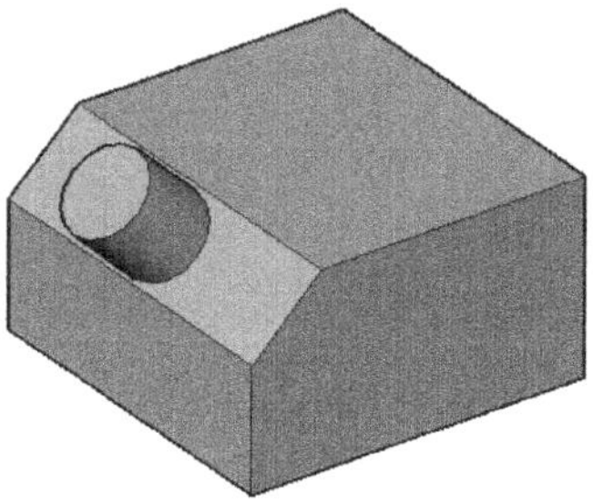

Figure 8-58 *UCS dynamically moved on the slant face of the model*

If you want a better visualization of how the X, Y, and Z axes of the UCS will be oriented, right-click in the drawing area and choose **Options** from the shortcut menu; the **Options** dialog box will be displayed. Choose the **3D Modeling** tab from the dialog box and select the **Show labels for dynamic UCS** check box in the **3D Crosshairs** area. This will enable you to see the X, Y and Z labels attached with the axes and they will keep on changing as you move the cursor to different faces.

Note

*The option of **DUCS** works only when any tool is active.*

Tip

*To toggle between the ON and OFF states of the **Dynamic UCS** button, use the F6 function key.*

DEFINING THE NEW UCS USING THE ViewCube AND THE RIBBON

In the earlier chapters, you learned how to create new UCS using the **UCS** tool. You can also define a new UCS whose XY plane is parallel to the current viewing plane by using the ViewCube and the **Ribbon**. To define a new UCS whose XY plane is parallel to the current viewing plane, click on a hotspot in the ViewCube; the view corresponding to the hotspot will become normal to the screen. Next, choose **WCS > New UCS** from the **WCS** flyout in the ViewCube; you will be prompted to specify the origin. Enter **V** at the Command prompt and press Enter; a new UCS will be created at the current viewing plane. Now, if you draw a sketch, it will be in the new UCS. To save the new UCS, choose the **UCS, Named UCS** tool from the **Coordinates** panel in the **Home** tab; the **UCS** dialog box will be displayed with the **Unnamed** option. Rename it and choose **OK**; the new name of the UCS will be saved and also displayed in the **WCS** flyout of the ViewCube.

To define a new UCS using the **Ribbon**, choose any one of the predefined orthographic views from the 3D Navigation drop-down list in the **View** panel of the **Home** tab; the model will orient to that view. Also, you will notice that the ViewCube is also oriented according to the selected view, but **Top** is displayed as the view and **Unnamed** is displayed at the **WCS** flyout. Now, if you draw a sketch, it will be in the new UCS. However, if there are different faces parallel to the new UCS, you can draw sketches on those faces.

CREATING EXTRUDED SOLIDS

Ribbon: Home > Modeling > Solid Creation drop-down > Extrude
Menu Bar: Draw > Modeling > Extrude **Toolbar:** Modeling > Extrude
Command: EXT (EXTRUDE)

Sometimes, the shape of a solid model is such that it cannot be created by just applying the Boolean operations on the standard solid primitives. In such cases, you can use the tools from the **Solid Creation** drop-down, as shown in Figure 8-59. These tools are also available in the **Solid** panel of the **Solid** tab. Using these tools, you can create solid models of any complex shape.

The **Extrude** tool is used to create a complex solid/surface model by extruding a 2D entity or a region along the *Z* axis or any specified direction or about a specified path. On invoking this tool, following prompt sequence will be displayed.

Select objects to extrude or [MOde]: _MO Closed profiles creation mode
[SOlid/SUrface] <Solid>: _SO
Select objects to extrude or [MOde]:

***Figure 8-59** Tools in the **Solid Creation** drop-down*

In AutoCAD, you can specify mode to extrude an object. There are two modes available: **Solid** and **Surface**. If you need to change the mode, enter **MO** at the **Select objects to extrude or [MOde]** prompt and specify the mode. Note that if the original entity is a closed loop or a region, you can extrude it as a solid/surface model. If the 2D entity is an open loop, then you can extrude it as a surface only. After specifying the mode, select the objects to be extruded and press Enter; the **Specify height of extrusion or [Direction/Path/Taper angle/Expression]** prompt will be displayed. Specify the depth of extrusion or select other options to specify the depth. Different methods to extrude an object by using the options at the Command prompt are discussed next.

Extruding along the Normal

This is the default option and is used to create a model by extruding a 2D entity or a region along the normal. Figure 8-60 shows the region to be converted into an extruded solid and Figure 8-61 shows the solid created on extruding the region. The prompt sequence that will be displayed when you choose the **Extrude** tool is given next.

Select objects to extrude: *Select the region.*
Select objects to extrude: Enter.
Specify height of extrusion or [Direction /Path /Taper angle/Expression]: *Specify the height.*

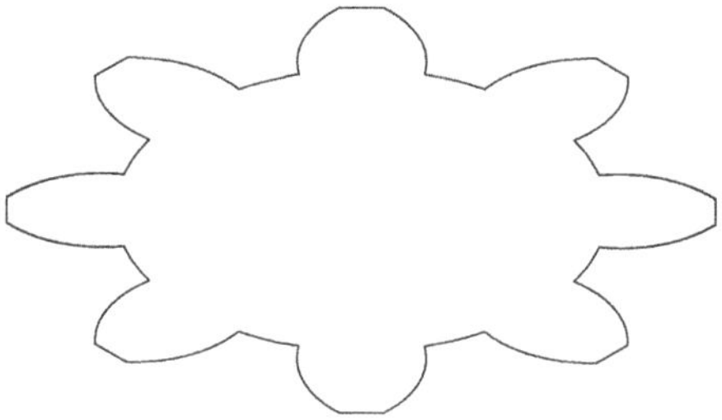

Figure 8-60 Region for extruding

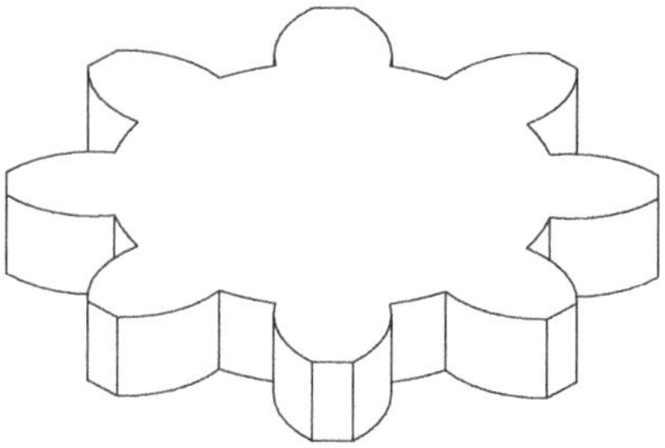

Figure 8-61 Solid created on extruding

Extruding with a Taper Angle

You can specify the taper angle for an extruded solid/surface by selecting the **Taper angle** option at the **Specify height of extrusion or [Direction/Path/Taper angle/Expression]** prompt. The positive value of the taper angle will taper in from the base object and the negative value will taper out of the base object, refer to Figure 8-62.

Extruding along a Direction

This option is used to create a solid by extruding a 2D entity or a region in any desired direction by specifying two points. You can create an inclined extruded object by selecting a start point and an endpoint. The distance between the start point and endpoint acts as the height of the extrusion. Figure 8-63 shows an object extruding along a direction.

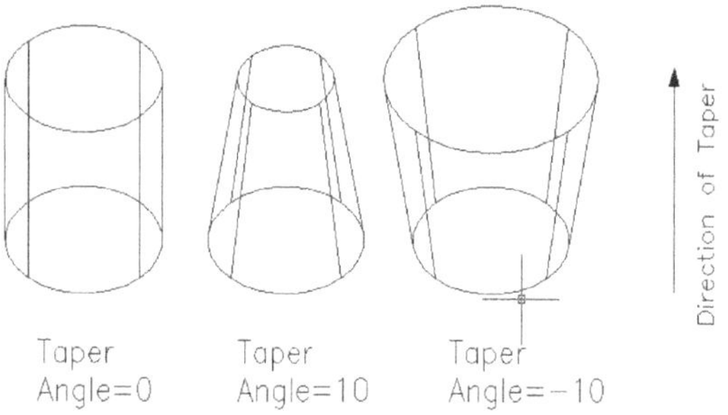

Figure 8-62 Results of various taper angles

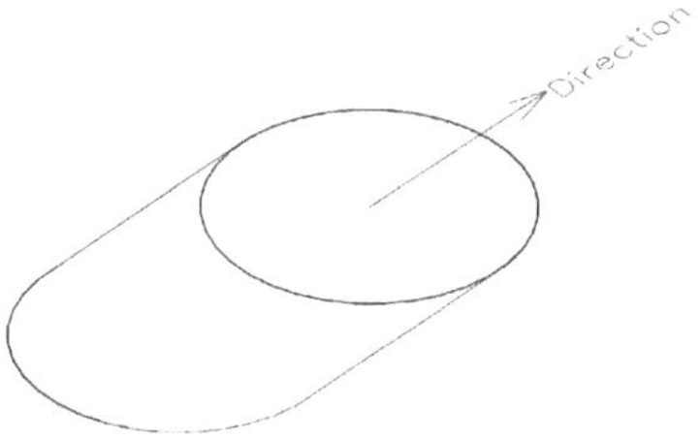

Figure 8-63 Object extruding along a direction

Extruding along a Path

This option is used to extrude a 2D entity or a region about a specified path. Bear in mind that the path of extrusion should be normal to the plane of the base object. If the path consists of more than one entity, all of them should be first joined using the **Edit Polyline** tool so that the path remains a single entity. This option is generally used for creating complex pipelines and also by architects and interior designers for creating beadings. The path used for extrusion can be a closed entity or an open entity and the valid entities that can be used as path are lines, circles, ellipses, polygons, arcs, polylines, or splines. You cannot specify the taper angle when you use a path. Figure 8-64 shows a base object and a path about which the base object has to be extruded and Figure 8-65 shows the solid created upon extruding the base entity about the specified path.

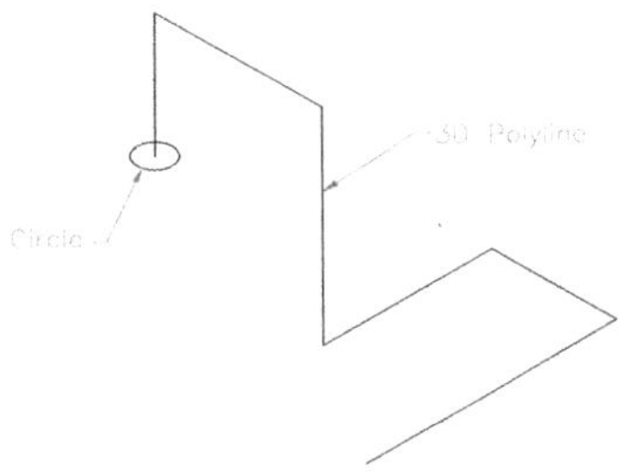

Figure 8-64 The base object and the path for extrusion

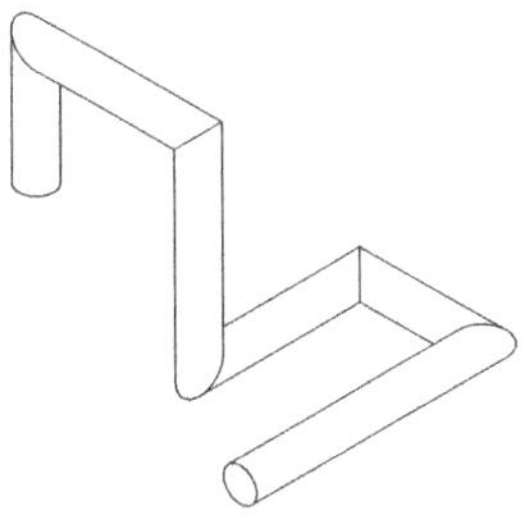

Figure 8-65 Solid model created on extruding the base entity about the specified path

Extruding using Expressions

This option is used to specify the extrusion depth in terms of formula or equations as you have created parametric drawings.

CREATING REVOLVED SOLIDS

Ribbon: Home > Modeling > Solid Creation drop-down > Revolve
Menu Bar: Draw > Modeling > Revolve **Toolbar:** Modeling > Revolve
Command: REV(REVOLVE)

The **Revolve** tool is used to create a complex model by revolving 2D entities or regions about a specified revolution axis. The entire 2D entity should be on one side of the revolution axis. Self-intersecting and crossed entities cannot be revolved using this tool. Remember that the direction of revolution is determined using the right-hand thumb rule. The axis of rotation is defined by specifying two points using the *X* or *Y* axis of the current UCS, or using an existing object. Similar to the **Extrude** tool, you can create a solid/surface model by specifying the mode after invoking the **Revolve** tool. On specifying the mode and selecting the object, the **Specify axis start point or define axis by [Object/X/Y/Z]** prompt will be displayed. Specify the axis of revolution. After setting the revolution axis option, you will be prompted to specify the angle of revolution. The default value is 360°. You can enter the required value at this prompt.

The options that are used to specify the axis are discussed next.

Start Point for the Axis of Revolution

This option is used to define the axis of revolution using two points: the start point and the endpoint of the axis of revolution. The positive direction of the axis will be from the start point to the endpoint and the direction of revolution will be defined using the right-hand thumb rule. Before revolving, make sure the complete 2D entity is on one side of the axis of revolution.

Object

This option is used to create a revolved model by revolving a selected 2D entity or a region about a specified object. The valid entities that can be used as an object for defining the axis of revolution can be a line or a single segment of a polyline. If the polyline selected as the object consists of more than one entity, then AutoCAD draws an imaginary line from the start point of the first segment to the endpoint of the last segment. This imaginary line is then taken as the object for revolution.

X

This option uses the positive direction of the *X* axis of the current UCS for revolving the selected entity. If the selected entity is not completely on one side of the *X* axis, it will give you an error message that it cannot revolve the selected object.

Y

This option uses the positive direction of the *Y* axis of the current UCS as the axis of revolution for creating the revolved solid.

Z

This option uses the positive direction of the *Z* axis of the current UCS as the axis of revolution for creating the revolved solid.

Figure 8-66 shows the entity to be revolved and the revolution axis along with the revolved solid. Figure 8-67 shows the same solid revolved through an angle of 270°.

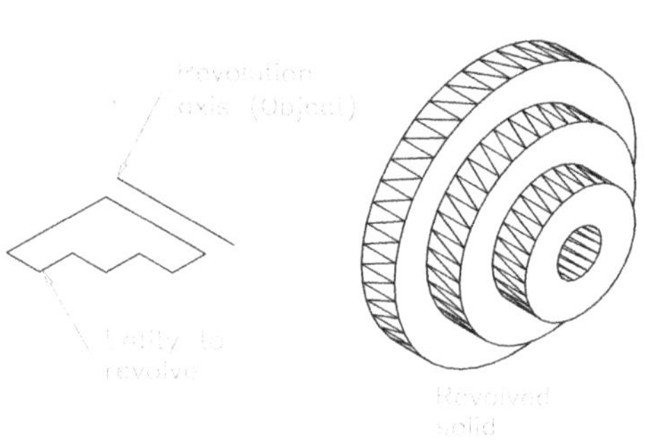

Figure 8-66 *Creating a revolved solid*

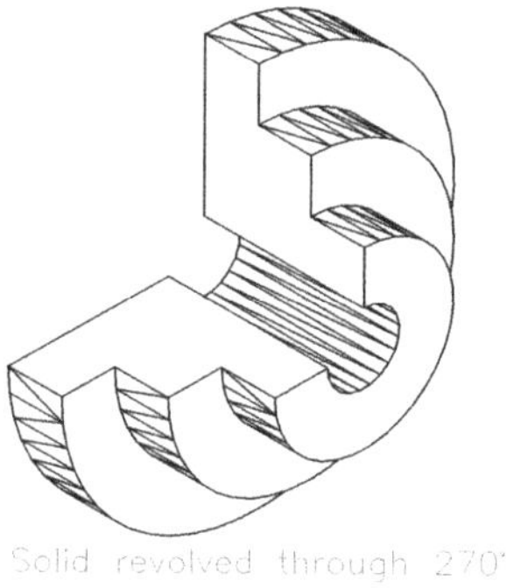

Figure 8-67 *Solid revolved to an angle*

CREATING SWEPT SOLIDS

Ribbon: Home > Modeling > Solid Creation drop-down > Sweep
Menu Bar: Draw > Modeling > Sweep **Toolbar:** Modeling > Sweep
Command: SWEEP

The **Sweep** tool is used to sweep an open or a closed profile along a path. This tool is also available in the **Solid** panel of the **Solid** tab. To create this model by using this tool, you need an object and a path. The object is a cross-section for the sweep feature and the path is the course taken by the object while creating the swept solid. Figure 8-68 shows the object to be swept and the path to be followed and Figure 8-69 shows the resulting sweep feature.

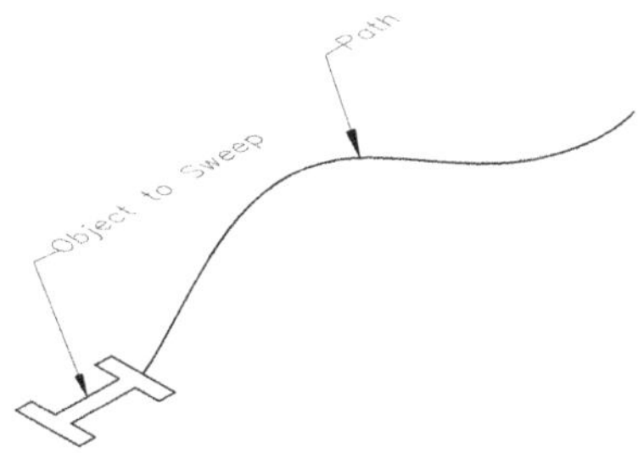

Figure 8-68 Object to be swept and the path

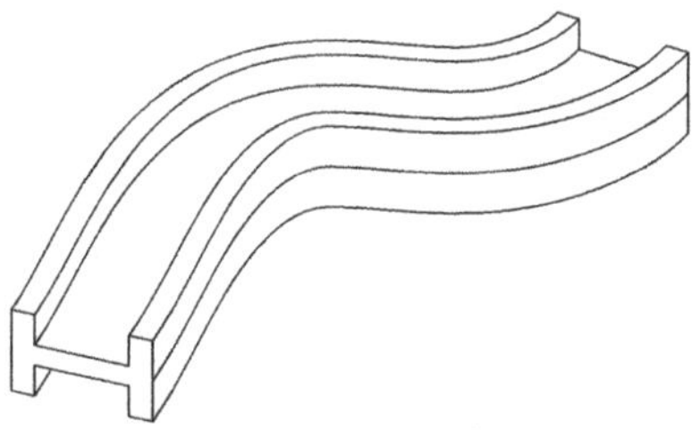

Figure 8-69 Resulting sweep feature

The path specified for the profile and the object for the cross-section of the swept model can be open or closed. If the object for the cross-section is open, or closed but not forming a single region, the generated feature will result in a surface sweep. If the object for the section is closed and it forms a single region, the generated feature will be a solid. Figure 8-70 shows the object and the closed path and Figure 8-71 shows the resulting sweep feature.

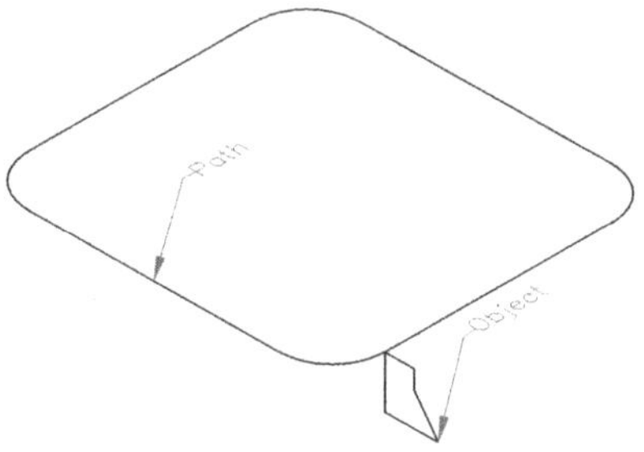

Figure 8-70 Object to be swept with a closed path

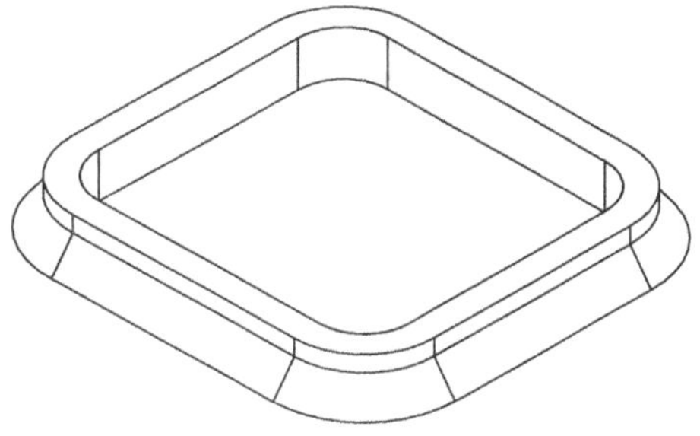

Figure 8-71 Resulting sweep feature

Note

The path selected for the ***Sweep*** *tool should not form a self-intersecting loop.*

You can select more than one section at a time to be swept along a path, but all these sections should be drawn on the same plane. To create a sweep, draw the cross section profile, path, and select the **Sweep** tool. Then, follow the prompt sequence given next.

Select objects to sweep or [MOde]: *Select the object to be swept.*
Select objects to sweep or [MOde]: *Select more objects to be swept or press Enter.*
Select sweep path or [Alignment/Base point/Scale/Twist]: *Select the path to be followed by the object or enter an option.*

Depending on your requirement, you can invoke the following options at the **Select sweep path or [Alignment/ Base point/Scale/Twist]** prompt:

Alignment

This option is used to specify whether the object will be oriented normal to the curve at the start point. By default, the sweep feature is created with a section normal to the path at the start point. To avoid this, choose **No** from the shortcut menu at the **Align sweep object perpendicular to path before sweep [Yes/No]** prompt. Figure 8-72 shows the object and the path for the sweep tool. Figure 8-73 shows the resulting sweep feature on choosing the aligned option **Yes** and Figure 8-74 shows the resulting sweep feature on choosing the aligned option **No**.

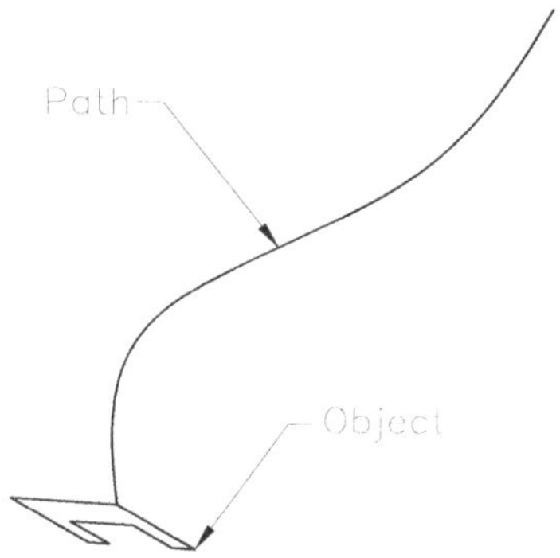

Figure 8-72 *Object and path for* ***Sweep*** *command*

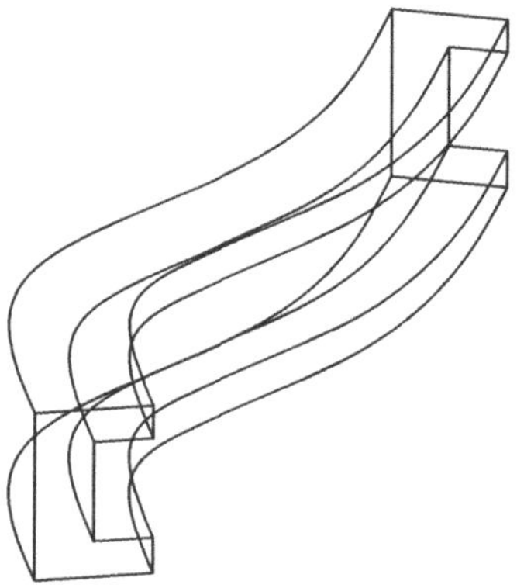

Figure 8-73 *Swept solid with the aligned option* ***Yes***

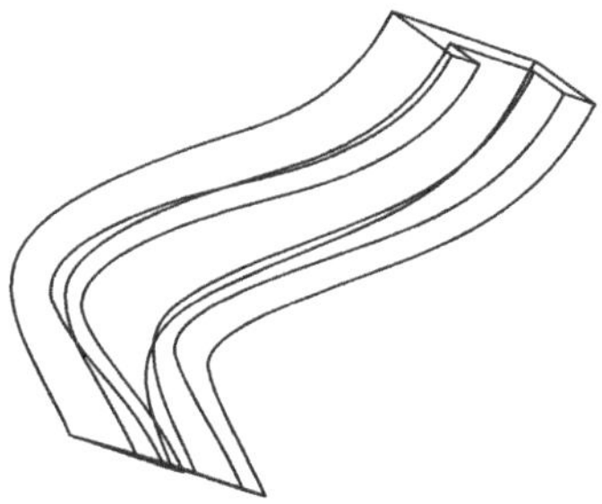

Figure 8-74 *Swept solid with the aligned option* ***No***

Base Point

This option is used to specify a point on the object that will be attached to the path while sweeping it. You can specify the location of the cross-section while sweeping it when prompted to specify the base point. Figure 8-75 shows the path and the cross-section with base points P1 and P2. Figure 8-76 shows the resulting sweep feature with P1 as the base point and Figure 8-77 shows the resulting sweep feature with P2 as the base point.

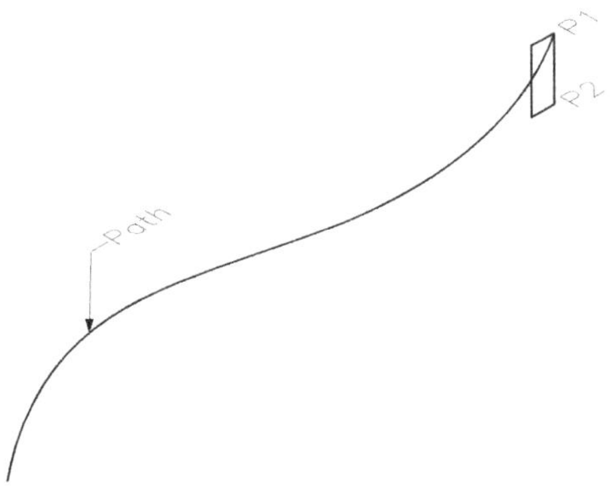

Figure 8-75 *Path with object and P1 and P2 as base points*

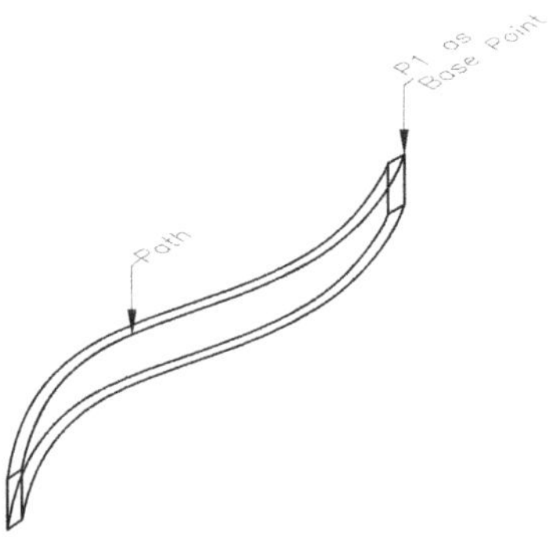

Figure 8-76 *Sweep with P1 as base point*

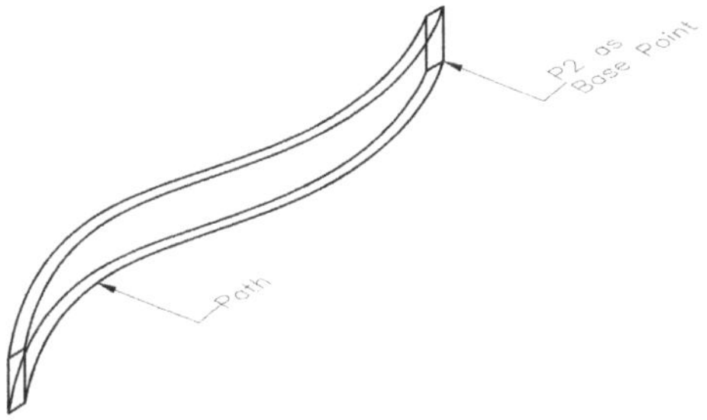

Figure 8-77 *Sweep with P2 as the base point*

Scale

This option is used to scale an object uniformly from the start of the path to the end of the path while sweeping it. Note that the size of the start section will remain the same and then end section will be scaled by the specified value. Also, the transition from the beginning to the end is smooth. Figure 8-78 shows a pentagon swept along a path with a scale factor of 0.25.

Twist

You can rotate an object about a path uniformly from the start to the end with a specified angle. The value of the twist should be less than 360 degrees. Figure 8-79 shows a sweep feature with 300 degrees of twist.

Note

A helix can also be used as the path for the ***Sweep*** *tool. Figure 8-80 shows the object and a helical path generated using the* ***Helix*** *tool and Figure 8-81 shows the resulting swept solid.*

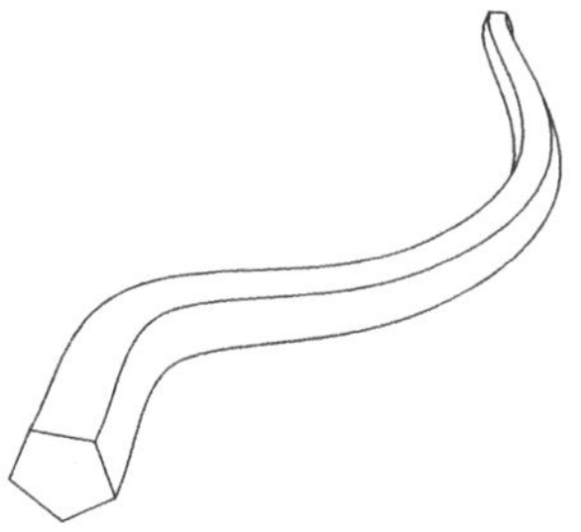

Figure 8-78 *Sweep with the **Scale** option*

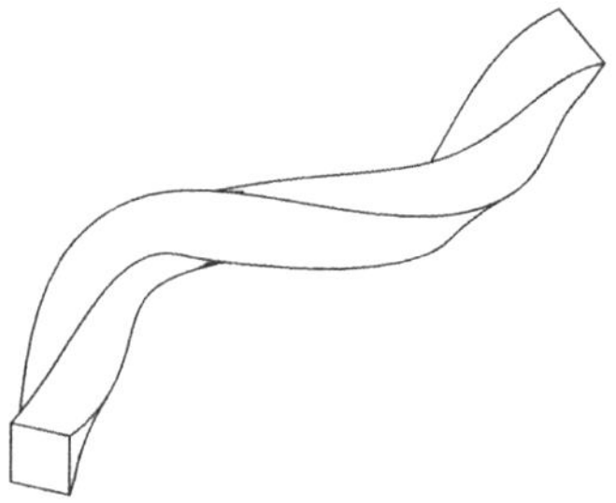

Figure 8-79 *Sweep with the **Twist** option*

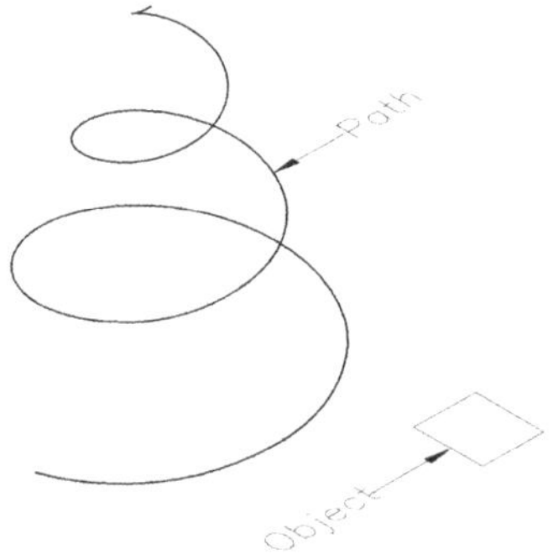

Figure 8-80 *Helical path and object to be swept*

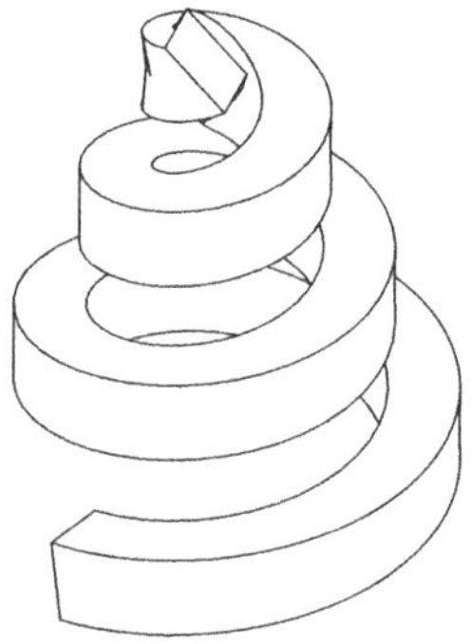

Figure 8-81 *Sweep feature with the helical path*

CREATING LOFTED SOLIDS

Ribbon: Home > Modeling > Solid Creation drop-down > Loft
Menu Bar: Draw > Modeling > Loft **Toolbar:** Modeling > Loft
Command: LOFT

The **Loft** tool is used to create a feature by blending two or more similar or dissimilar cross-sections together to get a free form shape. These similar or dissimilar cross-sections may or may not be parallel to each other. To create a loft feature, choose the **Loft** tool from the **Solid** panel, refer to Figure 8-82; the following prompt sequence will be displayed:

Figure 8-82 *Selecting the **Loft** tool from the **Sweep** drop-down in the **Solid** panel*

Select cross sections in lofting order or [POint/Join multiple edges/MOde]: _MO
Closed profiles creation mode [SOlid/SUrface] <Solid>: _SO
Select cross sections in lofting order or [POint/Join multiple edges/MOde]

Next, select at least two sections in a sequence in which you want to blend them. The prompt sequence that will be followed after choosing the **Loft** tool is given next.

> Select cross sections in lofting order or [POint/Join multiple edges/MOde]: 1 found
> Select cross sections in lofting order or [POint/Join multiple edges/MOde]: 1 found, 2 total Enter.
> Select cross sections in lofting order or [POint/Join multiple edges/MOde]: 2 cross sections selected
> Enter an option [Guides/Path/Cross sections only/Settings] <Cross sections only>: Enter.

Note

As you are prompted to select cross-sections while creating a loft, you can select open or closed sections. Note that if you select an open section first, all subsequent sections should be open. The model thus created will be a surface. Similarly, if you select a closed section, all subsequent sections should be closed. The model created using these sections can be solid/surface. By default, a loft model is solid. Therefore, if cross sections selected are closed profiles and you need a surface model, then first you need to change the mode by entering ***MO*** *at the* ***Select cross sections in lofting order or [POint/Join multiple edges/MOde]*** *prompt.*

After specifying the mode, you can select the cross sections, an imaginary point as the start point of the loft, or multiple edges on a solid model.

These options are discussed next.

POint

In AutoCAD, you can start a loft such that it begins from an imaginary point and passes through different sections. To do so, enter **PO** at the **Select cross sections in lofting order or [POint/Join multiple edges/MOde]** prompt and specify the start point of the loft, as shown in Figure 8-83. Next, select the cross sections in succession and press Enter after selecting all cross sections; the preview of the loft feature will be displayed. Also, a Look up grip near the last cross section and the **Enter an option [Guides/Path/Cross sections only/Settings/COntinuity/Bulge magnitude] <Cross sections only>** prompt will be displayed. Select the **Cross sections only** option and press Enter; the loft will be created, as shown in Figure 8-84.

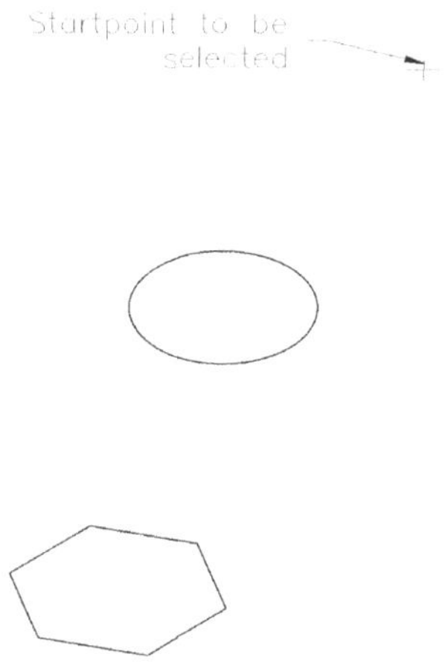

Figure 8-83 Sections and the imaginary start point to be selected

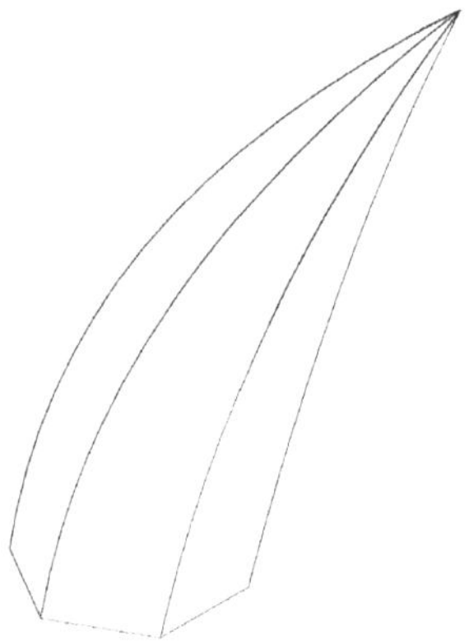

*Figure 8-84 Loft feature created by using the **PO** option*

Join multiple edges

In AutoCAD, you can create a loft feature between the edges of a solid model and a profile. To do so, enter **J** at the **Select cross sections in lofting order or [POint/Join multiple edges/MOde]** prompt; the cursor will have the symbol of solid and you will be prompted to select edges that are to be joined to a single cross section. Select the edges in succession, and press Enter, refer to Figure 8-85. Then, select the cross sections and press Enter; the preview of the loft will be displayed. One look up grip at the start of the loft surface and other look up grip near the base of the model will be displayed. The Look up grip at the start of the loft will have the surface continuity symbol, and the other Look up grip will have the Loft symbol, refer to Figure 8-86. Click on the Look up grip that has the surface continuity symbol and select the required option from the flyout displayed. The options in the other look up grip will be discussed later.

Given below is the prompt sequence to select the edges on the top face of the cuboid and a circle as the cross section.

Select cross sections in lofting order or [POint/Join multiple edges/MOde]: **J** Enter.
Select edges that are to be joined into a single cross section: (*Select the first edge*)1 found
Select edges that are to be joined into a single cross section: (*Select the second edge*) 1 found, 2 total
Select edges that are to be joined into a single cross section: (*Select the third edge*) 1 found, 3 total
Select edges that are to be joined into a single cross section: (*Select the fourth edge*) 1 found, 4 total
Select edges that are to be joined into a single cross section: Enter.
Select cross sections in lofting order or [POint/Join multiple edges/MOde]: 1 found

Select cross sections in lofting order or [POint/Join multiple edges/MOde]: Enter.
2 cross sections selected Enter.
Enter an option [Guides/Path/Cross sections only/Settings/COntinuity/Bulge magnitude] <Cross sections only>: Enter *(Preview of the loft will be displayed with grips, refer to Figure 8-86. Press Enter; the loft surface will be created, refer to Figure 8-87.*

After selecting all cross sections and on pressing Enter, the **Enter an option [Guides/Path/Cross sections only/Settings/COntinuity/Bulge magnitude] <Cross sections only>** prompt will be displayed. The **COntinuity** and **Bulge magnitude** options will be displayed in the Command prompt only if you have selected the edges of a model as one of the cross sections. Depending on requirement, you can invoke any one of those options. These options are discussed next.

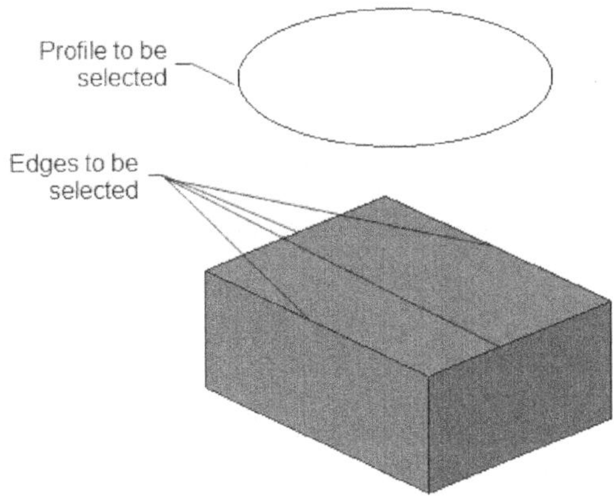

Figure 8-85 *Edges and the profile to be selected*

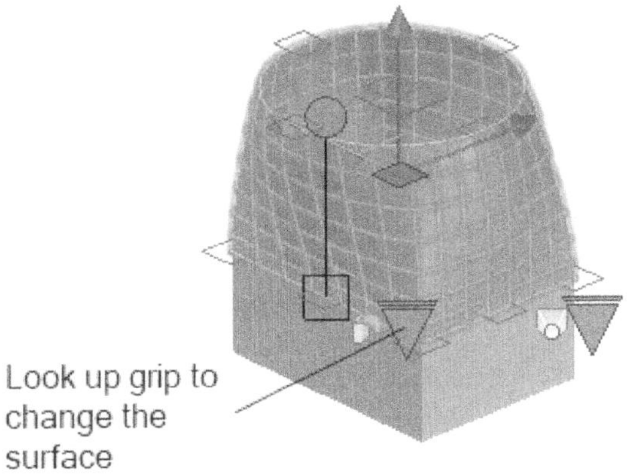

Figure 8-86 *Look up grips displayed*

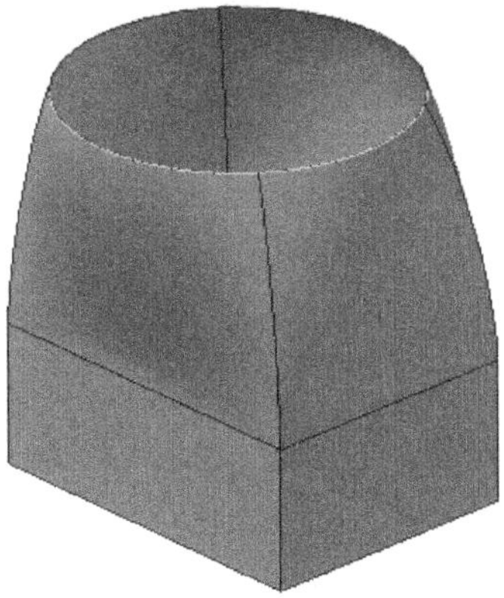

Figure 8-87 *Loft surface created*

Guide

AutoCAD enables you to select guide curves between the sections of the loft feature. These guide curves define the shape of the material addition between the selected sections for the loft feature. Guide curves also specify the points of different sections to be joined while adding material between them. This reduces the possibility of an unnecessary twist in the resulting feature. You can select as many guide curves as you require. But these guide curves should pass through or should touch each section that you selected for loft feature. Also the guides should start from the first section and terminate at the last section. Figure 8-88 shows three sections for the loft feature. Figure 8-89 shows the resulting loft feature. Figure 8-90 shows the sections to be lofted and the guide curves and Figure 8-91 shows the resulting model.

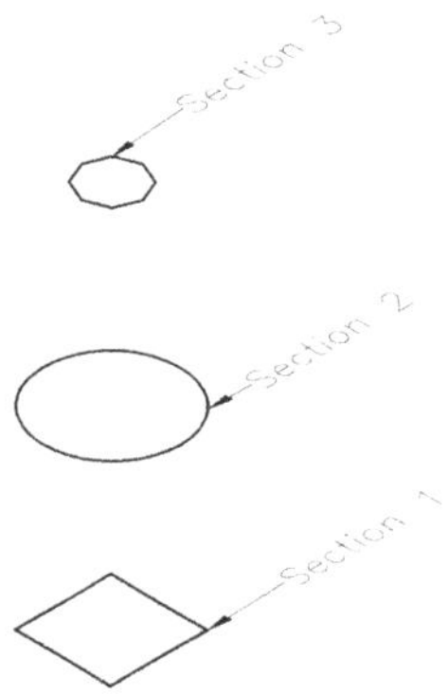

Figure 8-88 *Three section curves for the loft feature*

Figure 8-89 *Resulting loft feature*

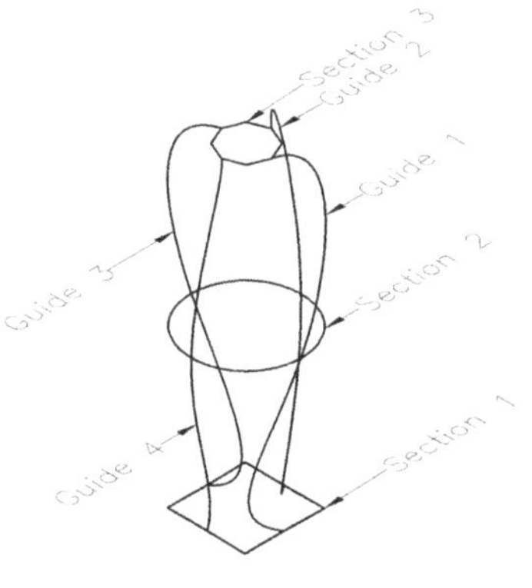

Figure 8-90 *Sections and guide curves for the loft feature*

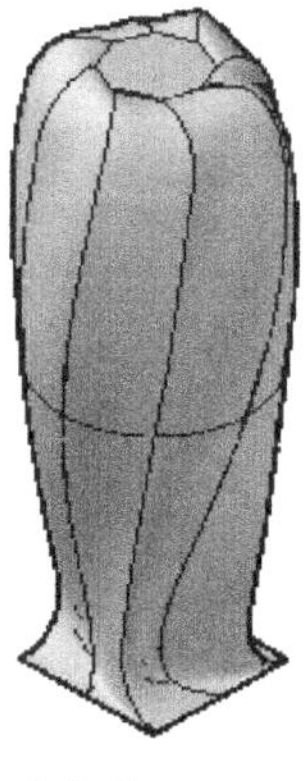

Figure 8-91 *The loft feature created by using the guide curve*

Path

The path option is used to create a loft feature by blending more than one section along the direction specified by the path curve. Note that you can select only one path curve. The selected path curve may or may not touch all sections, but it should pass through all sketching planes of the sections. Figure 8-92 shows the sections and the path along which the blending of material will propagate and Figure 8-93 shows the resulting loft feature.

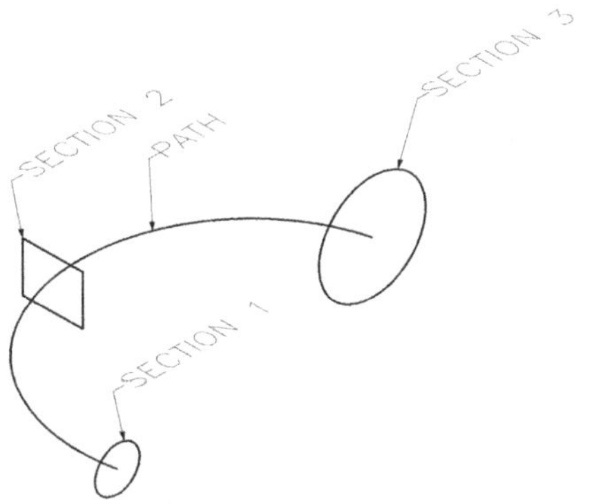

Figure 8-92 *Sections and path to be used for the **Loft** option*

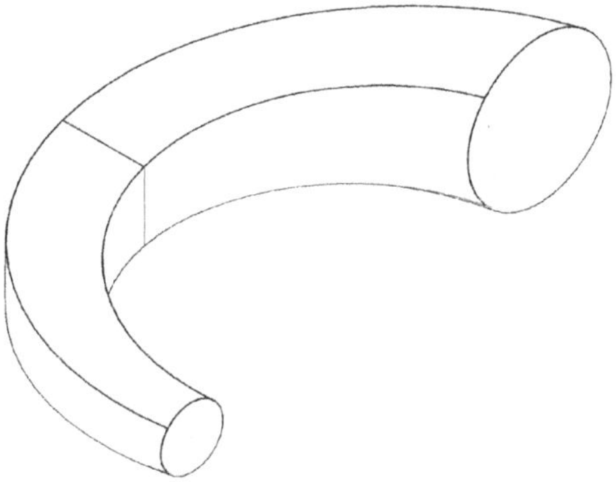

Figure 8-93 *Resulting loft feature after using the **Path** option*

Cross sections only

This is the default option displayed at the **Enter an option [Guides/Path/Cross sections only/ Settings/COntinuity/Bulge magnitude] <Cross sections only>** prompt. If you need to create a loft without a guide or path, press Enter; the loft feature will be created by using the cross sections only.

Settings

When you select **Settings**, the **Loft Settings** dialog box will be displayed, as shown in Figure 8-94. This dialog box is used to control the shape of the material addition between sections without specifying any guide curve or path. You can also select these options from the Look up grip displayed along with the preview. Various options in the **Loft Settings** dialog box are discussed next.

Ruled

If you select the **Ruled** radio button, a straight blend will be created by connecting different sections with straight lines. The loft feature created by this option will have sharp edges at the sections. Figure 8-95 shows the loft feature when the **Ruled** radio button is selected.

Smooth Fit

If you select the **Smooth Fit** radio button, a smooth loft will be created between sections. The loft feature created by this option will have smooth edges at the intermediate section. Figure 8-96 shows the loft feature when the **Smooth Fit** radio button is selected.

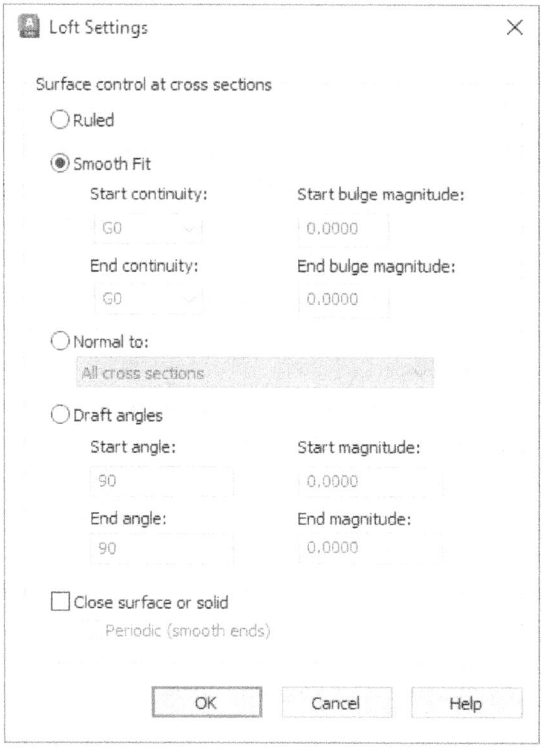

Figure 8-94 *The* ***Loft Settings*** *dialog box*

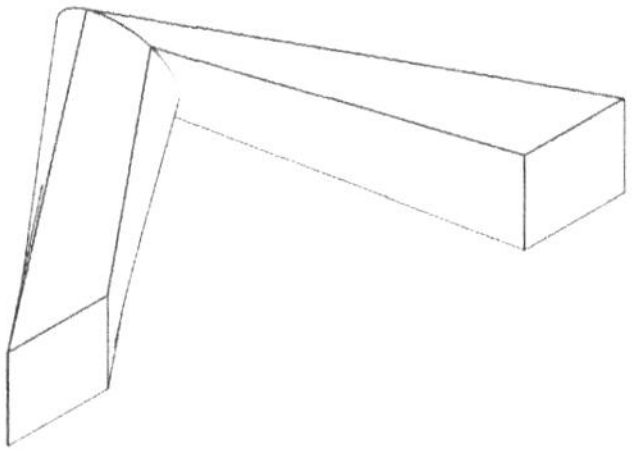

Figure 8-95 *Loft solid with the* ***Ruled*** *radio button selected*

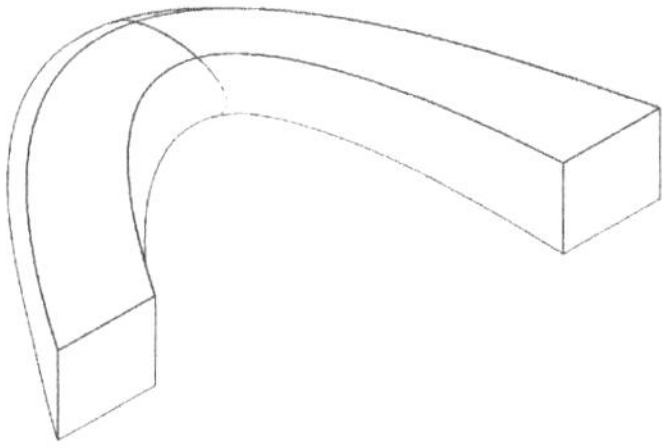

Figure 8-96 *Loft solid with the* ***Smooth Fit*** *radio button selected*

Normal to

This option controls the shape of the loft between the sections. When you select this radio button, the drop-down list will be enabled. The following options are available in this drop-down list:

Start cross section. In this option, the normal of the lofted feature is normal to the start section. The loft feature starts normal to the start section and follows a smooth polyline as it approaches the next section. Figure 8-97 shows the section selected to create the loft and Figure 8-98 shows the loft created by specifying the **Start cross section** option.

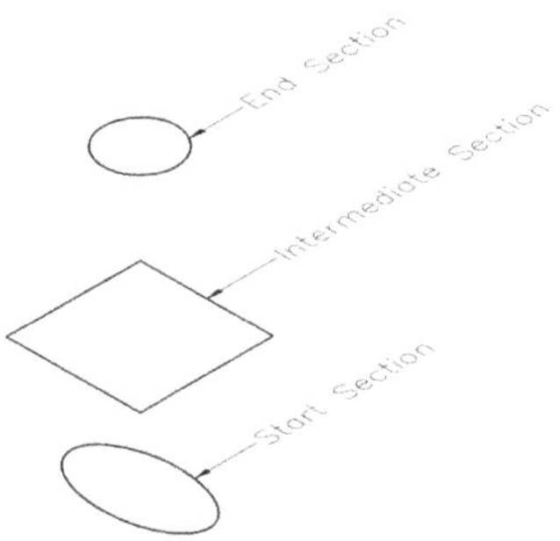

Figure 8-97 *Start and end sections to create loft*

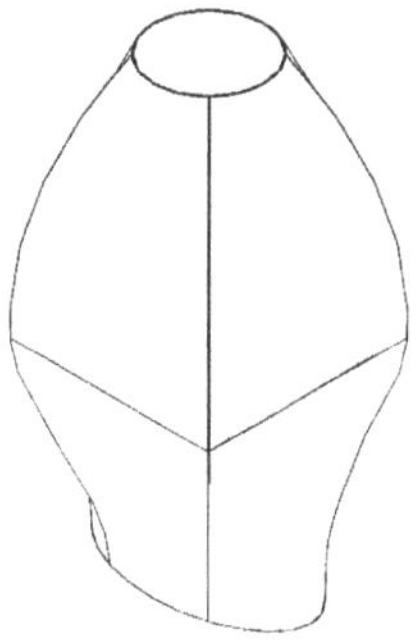

Figure 8-98 *Loft solid created by blending material normal to the start section*

End cross section. In this option, the normal to the blending material is normal to the end section. At the second last section, the blending material starts along a spline and while reaching up to end section, it becomes normal to it, as shown in Figure 8-99.

Start and End cross sections. In this option, the normal to the blending material is normal to both the start and end sections.

All cross sections. In this option, the normal to the blending material always remains normal to all cross-sections, as shown in Figure 8-100.

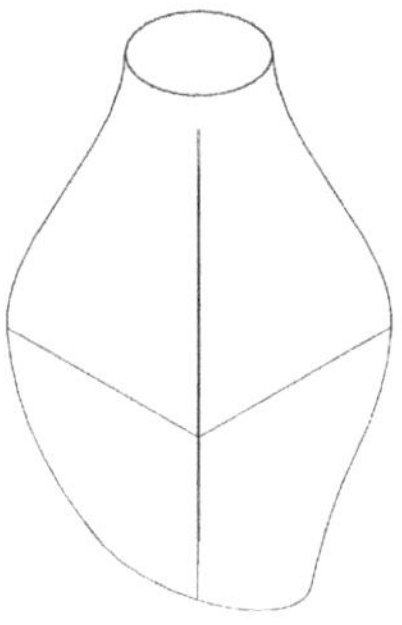

Figure 8-99 *Loft solid created by blending material normal to the end section*

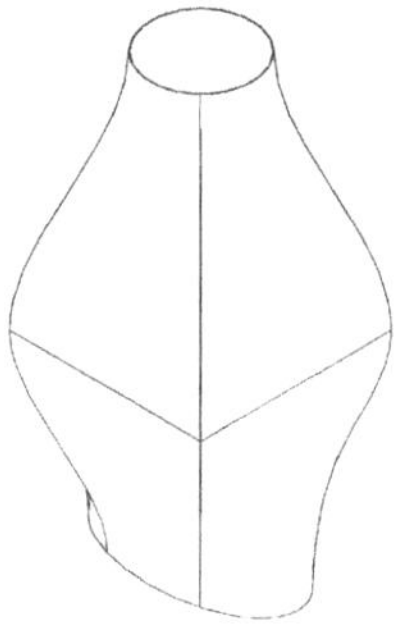

Figure 8-100 *Loft solid created by blending material normal to all sections*

Draft angles

In this option, you can define the angle at the start section and the end section of the loft. Remember that you cannot define an angle for the intermediate sketches. You can also specify the distance up to which the blending material will follow this draft angle before bending toward the intermediate sections. The various options for specifying the draft angle are discussed next.

Start angle. This edit box is used to specify the draft angle at the start section of the loft. Figure 8-101 shows the two sections to be blended and Figure 8-102 shows the loft with the start and end angles as 0-degree. Figures 8-103 and 8-104 show the loft feature with the start angle as 90-degree and 180-degree, respectively.

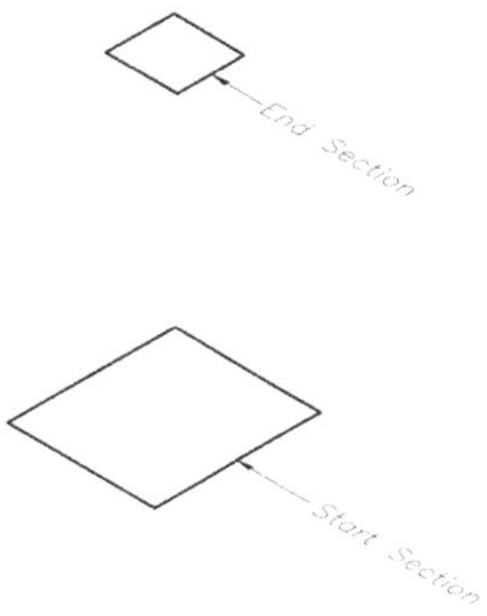

Figure 8-101 Start and end sections of the loft feature

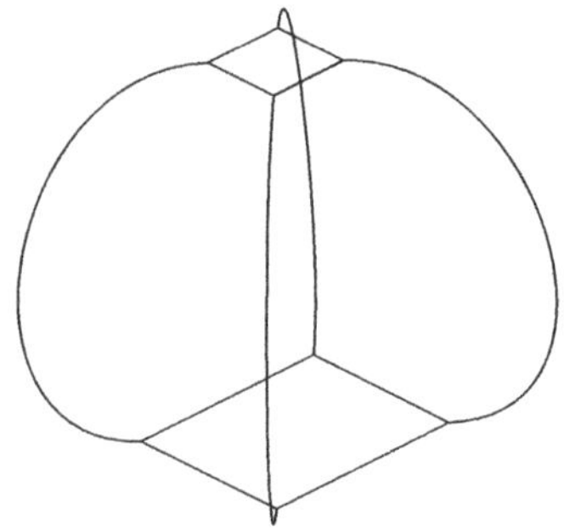

Figure 8-102 Loft feature with 0-degree start and end angles

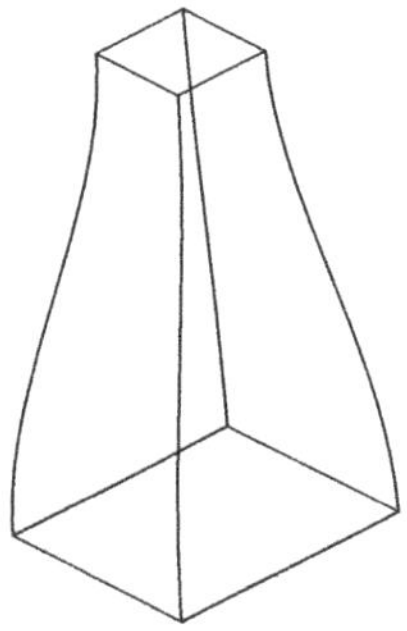

Figure 8-103 Loft feature with 90-degree start and end angles

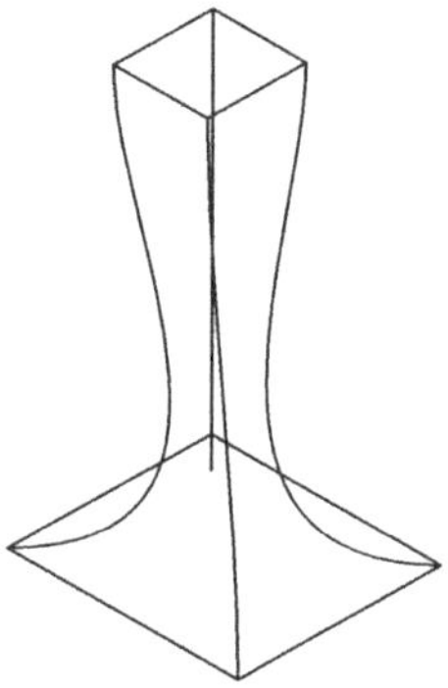

Figure 8-104 Loft feature with 180-degree start angle and 90-degree end angle

Start magnitude. The value specified in this region signifies the distance up to which the blending material will follow the start angle before bending toward the next section. Figure 8-105 shows a loft feature with 180-degree as the start and end angles, and 15 as the start magnitude. Figure 8-106 shows a loft feature with 180-degree as the start and end angles and 2 as the start magnitude. Notice the difference in the extent up to which the blended material follows the start angle in the two figures.

End angle. This edit box is used to specify the draft angle at the end section of the loft. Figure 8-101 shows two sections to be blended and Figure 8-102 shows the loft with the start and end angle as 0-degree. Figure 8-103 and Figure 8-104 show the loft feature with the end angle as 90-degree.

End magnitude. The value specified in this region signifies the distance up to which the blending material will follow the end angle before approaching the last section. Figure 8-105 shows a loft feature with 180-degree as the start and end angle, and 2 as the end magnitude. Figure 8-106 shows a loft feature with 180-degree as the start and end angle, and 10 as the end magnitude.

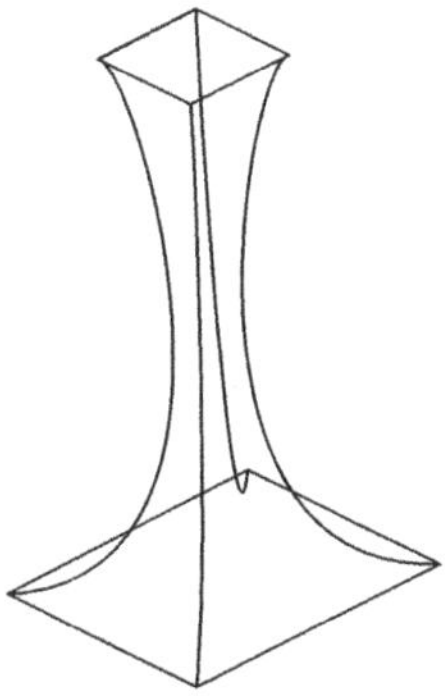

Figure 8-105 Loft feature with 180-degree as the start and end angle, 15 as the start magnitude, and 2 as the end magnitude

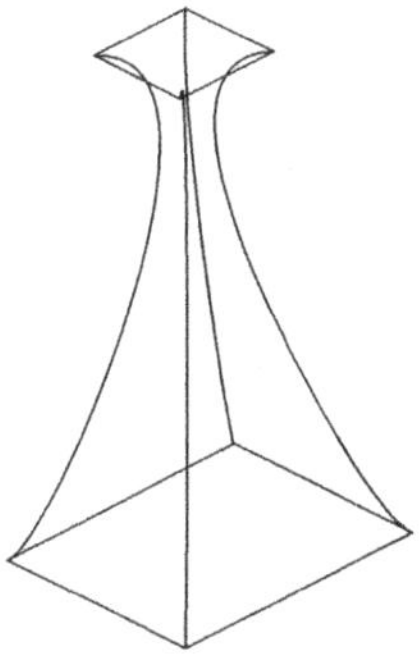

Figure 8-106 Loft feature with 180-degree as the start and end angle, 2 as the start magnitude, and 10 as the end magnitude

Notice the difference in the extent up to which the blended material follows the end angle in the two figures.

Close surface or solid

The **Close surface or solid** check box is selected to close a loft feature by joining the end section with the start section. Figure 8-107 shows a loft feature created with this check box cleared and Figure 8-108 shows the same sections lofted by this check box selected.

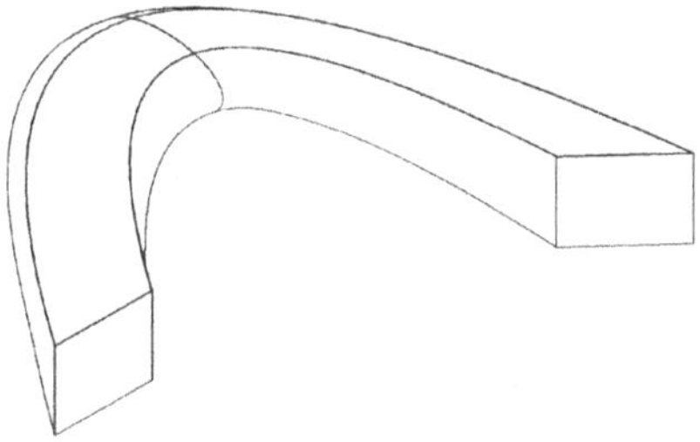

*Figure 8-107 Loft solid with the **Close surface or solid** check box cleared*

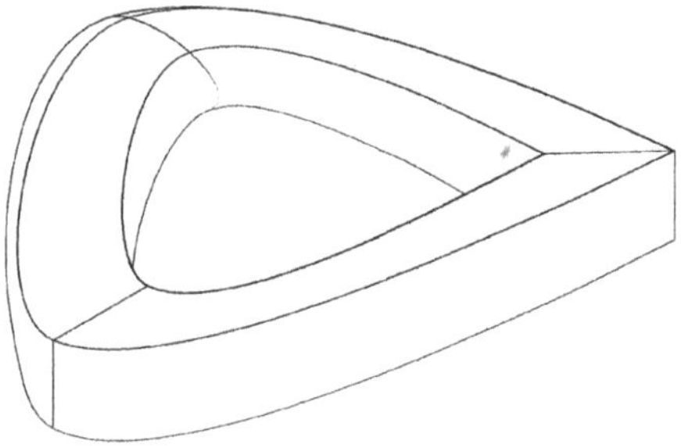

*Figure 8-108 Loft solid with the **Close surface or solid** check box selected*

Note

*To visualize the effect of the **Close surface or solid** option, the loft feature should contain at least three sections. If not so, the extra blending material will be added at the same location where the loft feature would have been created without selecting this check box, thereby resulting in no change.*

Periodic (smooth ends). If this check box is selected, the seam of the closed surface will not buckle, if you alter the shape of the surface.

Tip

You can also use a point as a section for the loft feature, but it should always be the start section or the end section of the loft feature.

Continuity

Continuity defines the smoothness of the loft surface between two cross sections, if one of the cross sections is an edge of a model. Continuity can be set to **G0** (position continuity), **G1** (tangency continuity), or **G2** (curvature continuity). **G0** maintains the position of the selected edges, **G1** maintains tangency of the loft surface where it meets edges, and **G2** maintains the same curvature. By default, the continuity is set to G0. To edit the continuity setting of a loft, enter **CO** at the **Enter an option [Guides/Path/Cross sections only/Settings/COntinuity/Bulge magnitude] <Cross sections only>** prompt and press Enter; you will be prompted to specify the continuity. Enter the required option and press Enter.

You can also set the surface continuity by using the Continuity grip.

Bulge magnitude

The bulge magnitude determines the roundness or the amount of bulge between two cross sections, if one of the cross sections is an edge of a model. By default, the bulge magnitude is set to 0.5. If you want to edit the bulge magnitude, enter **B** at the **Enter an option [Guides/Path/Cross sections only/Settings/COntinuity/Bulge magnitude] <Cross sections only>** prompt and press Enter; you will be prompted to enter the loft bulge magnitude at the start. Enter a value and press Enter. If there is only one solid edge as a cross section, then the bulge will be created. If there are two solid edges as cross sections (one at the start and the other at the end), then you will be prompted to enter the bulge magnitude at the start and end. Type a value and press Enter; the bulge will be created. If you need to change the bulge magnitude while creating, then click the Bulk magnitude Look up grip; a dot with a leader will be displayed. Drag the dot dynamically to change the bulk magnitude.

Figure 8-109 shows the edges on the top faces of two solids as well as the region which needs to be selected for creating a loft feature. Figure 8-110 shows the preview of the loft feature with grips. Figure 8-111 shows the loft feature with bulge magnitude added at the start and end.

Note

You can also set the surface continuity and the bulge continuity in the ***Loft Settings*** *dialog box.*

Figure 8-109 *Two solids and a region to create a loft*

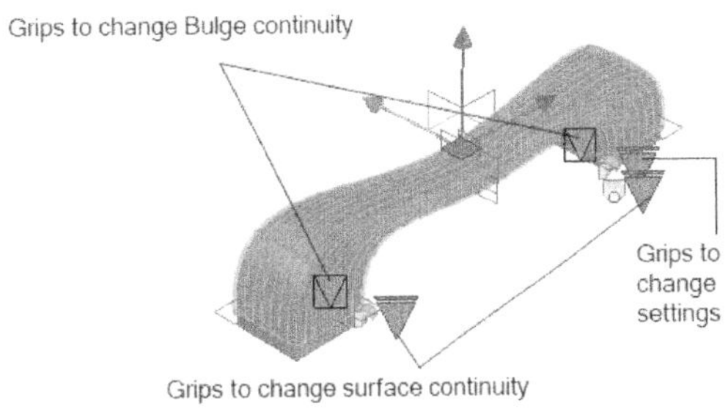

Figure 8-110 *Preview of the loft and the grips displayed*

Figure 8-111 *Loft surface created*

CREATING PRESSPULL SOLIDS

Ribbon: Home > Modeling > Presspull **Toolbar:** Modeling > Presspull
Command: PRESSPULL

The **Presspull** tool is used to remove or add material of any desired shape in a model. As the name presspull indicates, if you press a closed boundary inside an existing model, it will remove the material of the shape of the closed boundary. However, if you pull a closed boundary outside an existing model, it will add material to the model. To perform this operation, choose the **Presspull** tool from the **Modeling** panel. Next, click inside a closed boundary that you want to press or pull and then move the mouse in the desired direction. You can specify the desired height by entering a value or by clicking the mouse. Figure 8-112 shows the solid model with the closed area to be presspulled. Figure 8-113 shows the model created by pressing the closed region and Figure 8-114 shows the model created by pulling the closed area.

Given below is the prompt sequence displayed while creating the presspull feature.

Select object or bounded area : *Select any closed bounded area that you want to presspull*
Specify extrusion height or [Multiple] : *Click anywhere to specify the height of extrusion*
Select object or bounded area : Enter.

If the sketch that you select to press or pull has nested loops, as shown in Figure 8-115, the inner closed loops will be deleted from the outer loop, as shown in Figure 8-116. The closed area you select for the presspull should consist of lines, polylines, 3D face, edges, regions, and faces of a 3D solid. But all these entities should form a coplanar closed area.

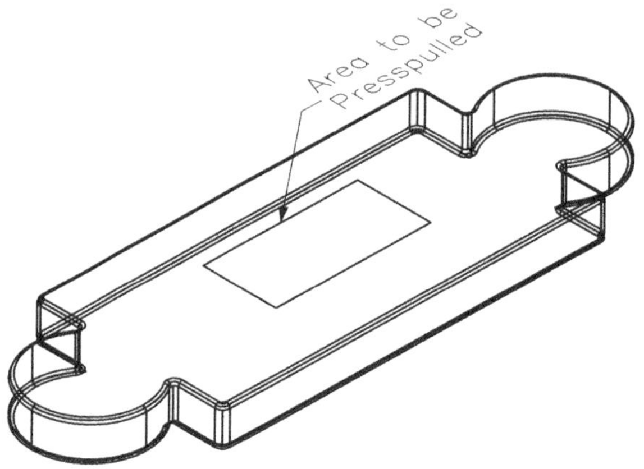

Figure 8-112 *Model with closed area to be presspulled*

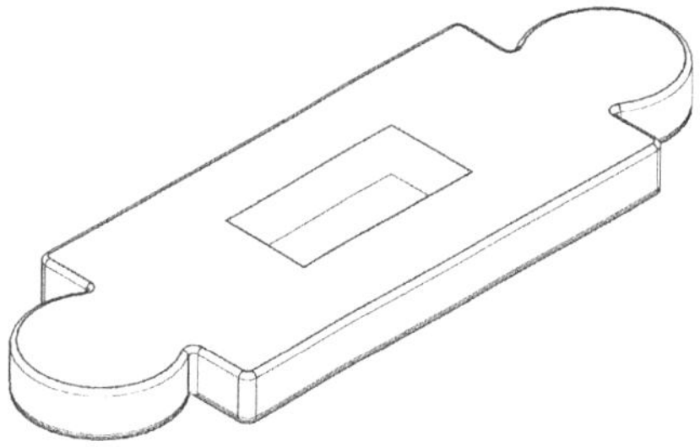

Figure 8-113 *Model with the closed area pressed*

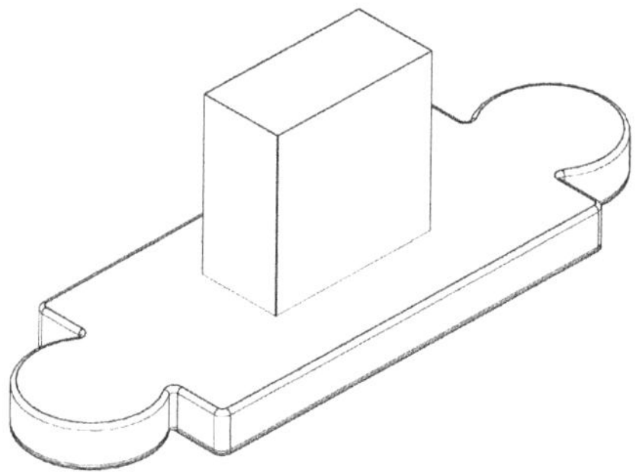

Figure 8-114 *Model with closed area pulled*

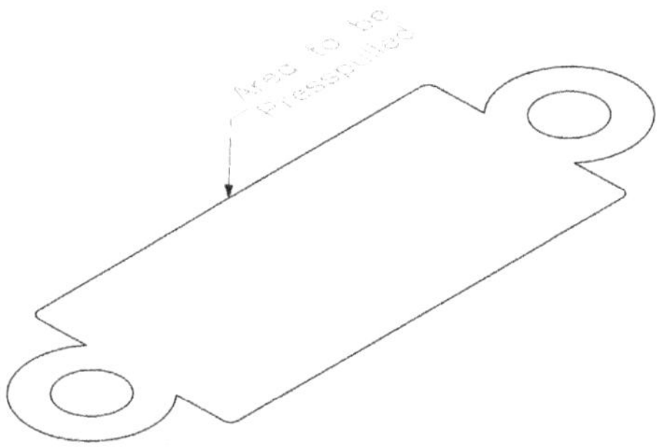

Figure 8-115 *Area to be presspulled with closed boundary inside it*

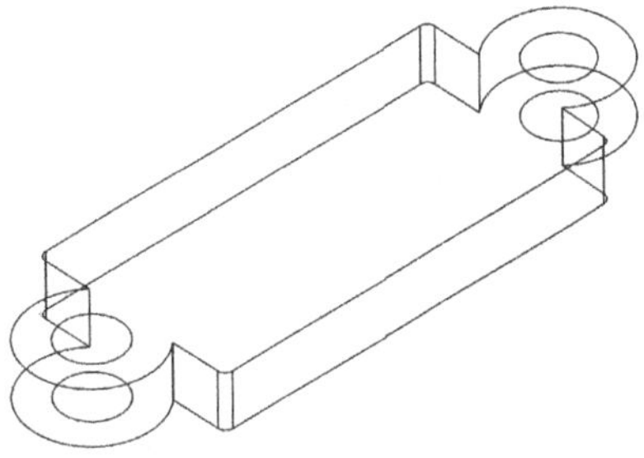

Figure 8-116 *The model after the presspull operation is performed*

Example 2

In this example, you will create the solid model shown in Figure 8-117.

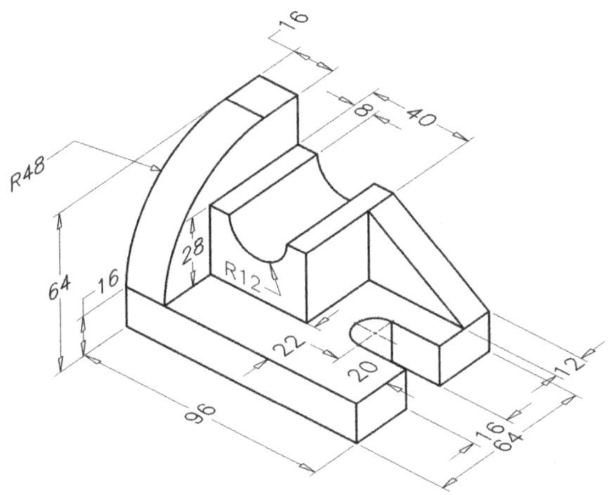

Figure 8-117 *Solid model for Example 2*

1. Start a new file using the *acad3D.dwt* template.

2. Set the drawing limits of the workspace to 120,120. Next, type ZOOM or Z at the command prompt and select **All** option from the options displayed.

3. Set the view to SE Isometric by using the ViewCube. Then, right-click on the ViewCube and choose the **Parallel** option.

4. Switch on the ortho mode. Using lines and arc, create the base of the model with the dimensions shown in Figure 8-118.

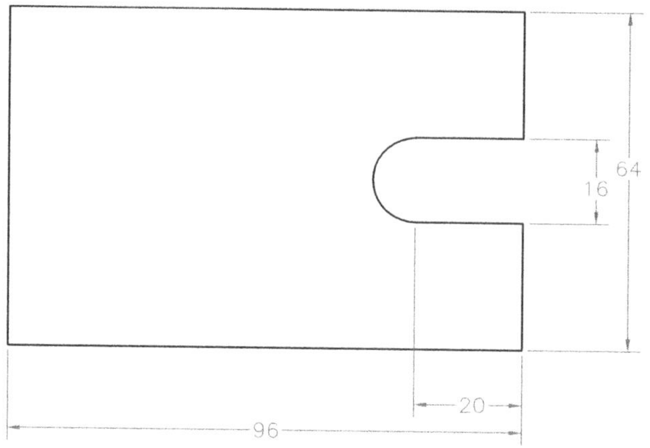

Figure 8-118 *Base for the solid model*

5. Choose the **Region** tool from the **Draw** panel in the **Home** tab and follow the prompt sequence given next to convert the sketch drawn into a region.

Select objects: *Select the complete base.*
Select objects: Enter.
1 loop extracted.
1 Region created.

Note

*You can also use the **Polyline** tool to create this sketch. In that case, you do not need to convert it into a region.*

6. Choose the **Extrude** tool from **Home > Modeling > Solid Creation** drop-down and follow the prompt sequence given next to extrude the region.

Current wire frame density: ISOLINES=4, Closed profiles creation mode = Solid
Select objects to extrude or [MOde]: _MO Closed profiles creation mode [SOlid/SUrface] <Solid>: _SO
Select objects to extrude or [MOde]: *Select the region* Enter.
1 found
Select objects to extrude or [MOde]: Enter.
Specify height of extrusion or [Direction/Path/Taper angle/Expression]: **16**

7. Change the visual style to Wireframe by choosing the **Wireframe** option from the **Visual Style Controls** drop-down list in the **In-canvas Viewport control**.

8. Choose the **Wedge** tool from **Home > Modeling > Solid Primitives** drop-down and follow the prompt sequence given next to create the next feature.

Specify first corner or [Center]: *Pick a point on the screen.*
Specify other corner or [Cube/Length]: **L**
Specify length: **40**
Specify width: **12**
Specify height or [2Point]: **28**

9. Move this wedge and align it with the base. Use the **Vertex** option of the **3D Object Snap** to snap the vertex. The model after applying the **Hidden** visual style is shown in Figure 8-119.

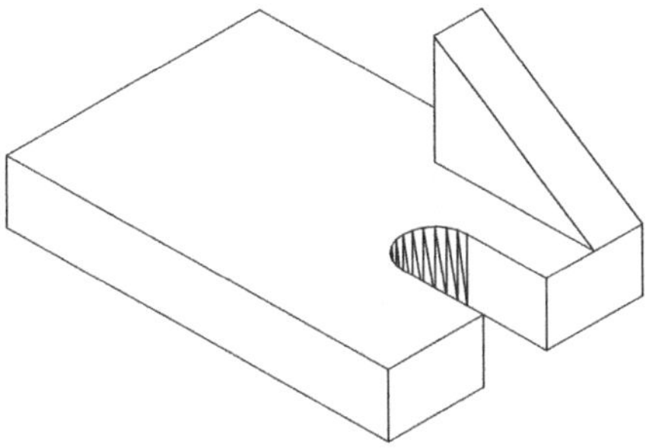

Figure 8-119 *Wedge aligned with the base*

10. Orient the view to **Front** by clicking on **Front** in the ViewCube and choose **WCS > New UCS** from the drop-down list below it; you are prompted to specify the origin.

11. Enter **V** at the **Specify origin of UCS or [Face/NAmed/OBject/Previous/View/World/X/Y/Z/ZAxis] <World>** prompt and press Enter.

12. Draw the profile shown in Figure 8-120 at any place in the drawing area and then convert it into a region.

13. Choose the **Extrude** tool from **Home > Modeling > Solid Creation** drop-down and extrude the region to a depth of 42 units.

14. Move this extrude feature and align it with the wedge feature. Use the **Vertex** option of the **3D Object Snap** to snap the vertex of the wedge feature.

The isometric view of the model after aligning the extrude feature is shown in Figure 8-121.

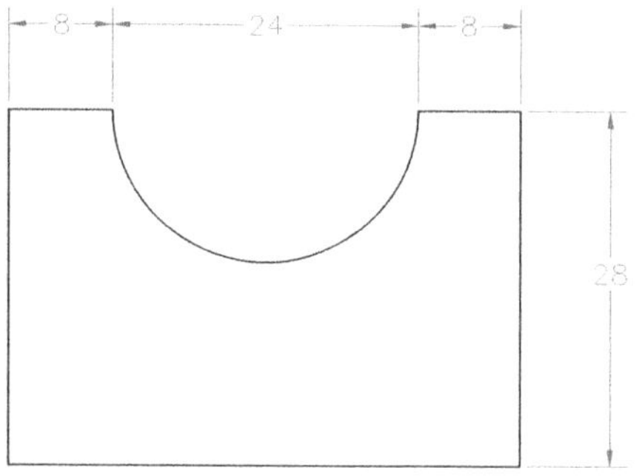

Figure 8-120 *The region to be extruded*

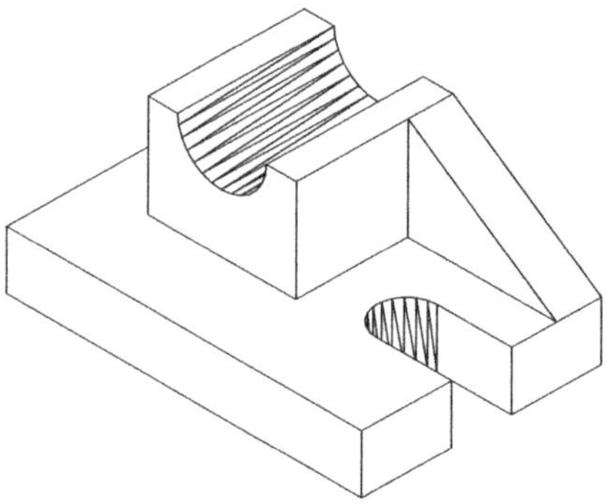

Figure 8-121 *Solid aligned with the base*

15. Orient the view to Right by clicking **Right** in the ViewCube and choose **WCS > New UCS** from the drop-down list below it; you are prompted to specify the origin.

16. Enter **V** at the **Specify origin of UCS or [Face/NAmed/OBject/Previous/View/World/X/Y/Z/ZAxis] <World>** prompt and press Enter.

17. Draw the profile shown in Figure 8-122 at any place in the drawing area and then convert it into a region.

18. Extrude the region to a depth of 16 units and then move it so that it is properly aligned with the base, refer to Figure 8-123.

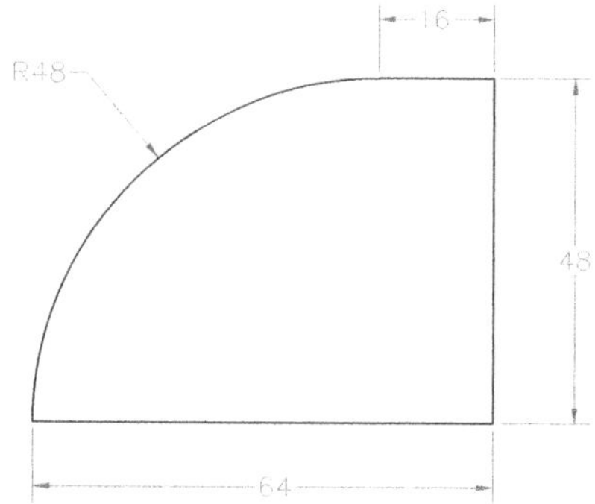

Figure 8-122 *The region before extrusion*

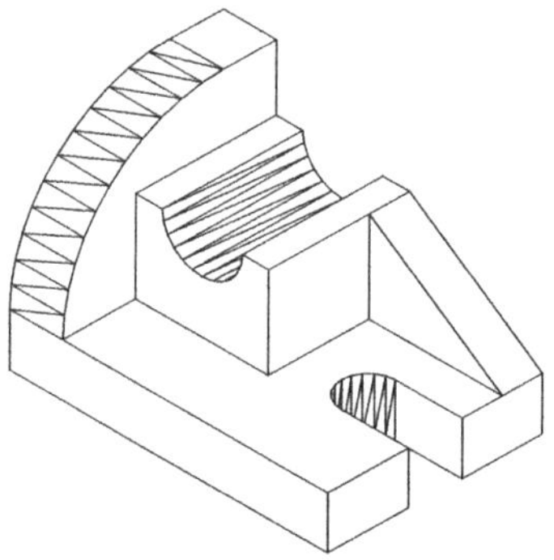

Figure 8-123 *Solid aligned with the base*

19. Choose the **Solid, Union** tool from the **Solid Editing** panel and follow the prompt sequence given next:

Select objects: *Select all objects.*
Select objects: Enter.

20. Change the visual style by selecting the **Shades of Gray** option from the **Visual Styles** drop-down list in the **In-canvas Viewport Controls**. The final solid model should look similar to the one shown in Figure 8-124.

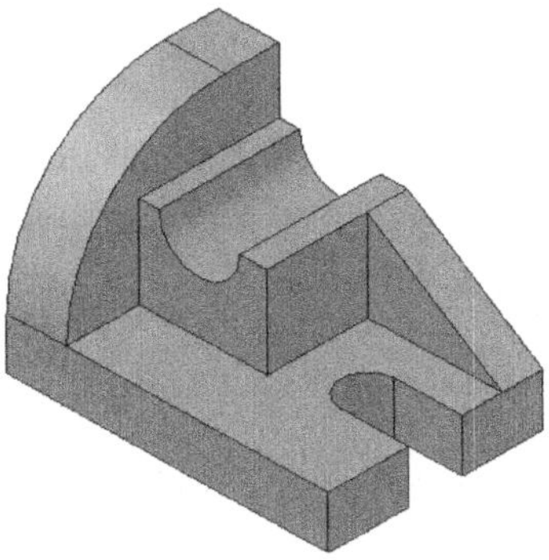

Figure 8-124 *Solid model for Example 2*

Example 3

In this example, you will create the solid model shown in Figure 8-125.

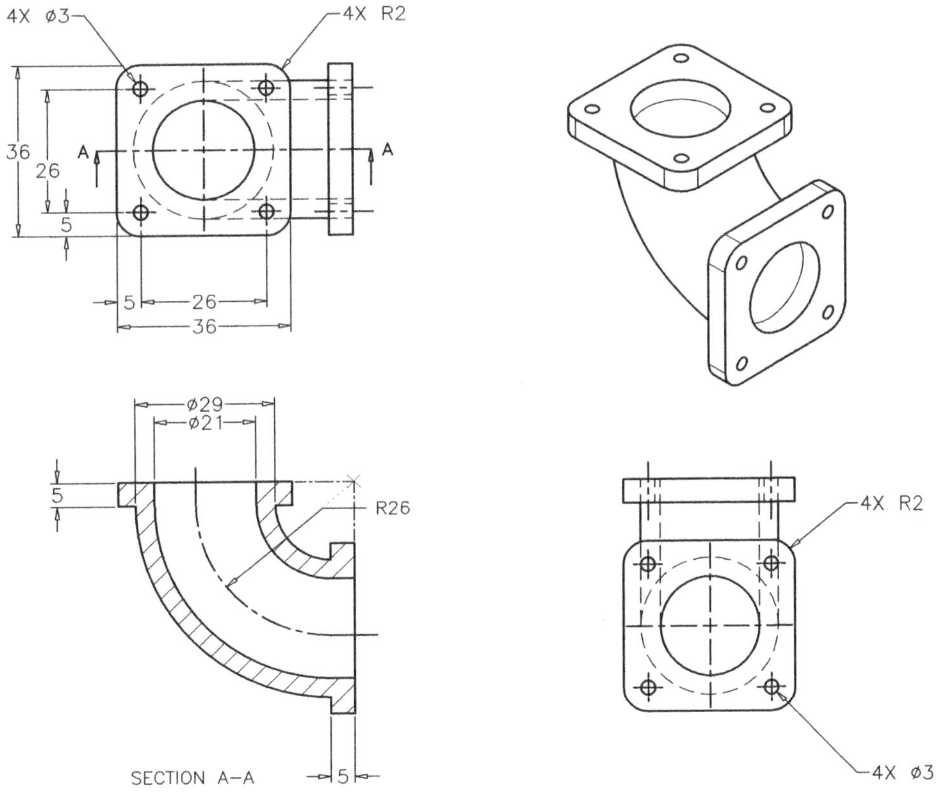

Figure 8-125 *Solid model for Example 3*

1. Start a new file using the *acad3D.dwt* template.

2. Set the drawing limits of the workspace to 75,75. Next, type ZOOM or Z at the command prompt and select the **All** option from the options displayed.

3. Orient the view to Left by choosing **Left** in the ViewCube and choose **WCS > New UCS** from the drop-down list below it; you are prompted to specify the origin.

4. Enter **V** at the **Specify origin of UCS or [Face/NAmed/OBject/Previous/View/World/X/Y/Z/ZAxis] <World>** prompt and press Enter.

5. Right-click on the ViewCube and choose the **Parallel** option.

6. Draw the cross section and path of the sweep feature, as shown in Figure 8-126.

7. Choose the **Region** tool from the **Draw** panel in the **Home** tab and follow the prompt sequence given next to convert the sketch into a region.

   Select objects: *Select both the circles.*
   Select objects: Enter.
   2 loops extracted.
   2 Regions created.

8. Choose the **Solid, Subtract** tool from the **Solid Editing** panel in the **Home** tab and follow the prompt sequence:

   Select objects: *Select the region of diameter 29.*
   Select objects: Enter.
   Select solids, surfaces, and regions to subtract.
   Select objects: *Select the region of diameter 21.*
   Select objects: Enter.

9. Change the visual style to Wireframe by selecting the **Wireframe** option from the **Visual Styles** drop-down list in the **View** panel.

10. Choose the **Sweep** tool from **Home > Modeling > Solid Creation** drop-down and follow the prompt sequence given next to sweep the region along the path.

    Current wire frame density: ISOLINES=4, Closed profiles creation mode = Solid
    Select objects to sweep or [MOde]: _MO Closed profiles creation mode [SOlid/SUrface] <Solid>: _SO
    Select objects to sweep or [MOde]: *Select the region created in Step 8*
    1 found
    Select objects to sweep or [MOde]: Enter.
    Select sweep path or [Alignment/Base point/Scale/Twist]: *Select the arc created in Step 6.*

11. Set the view to **SW Isometric** by choosing the appropriate hotspot in the ViewCube. Also, select the **Realistic** option in the **Visual Styles** drop-down list in the **View** panel. The resulting model should look similar to the one shown in Figure 8-127.

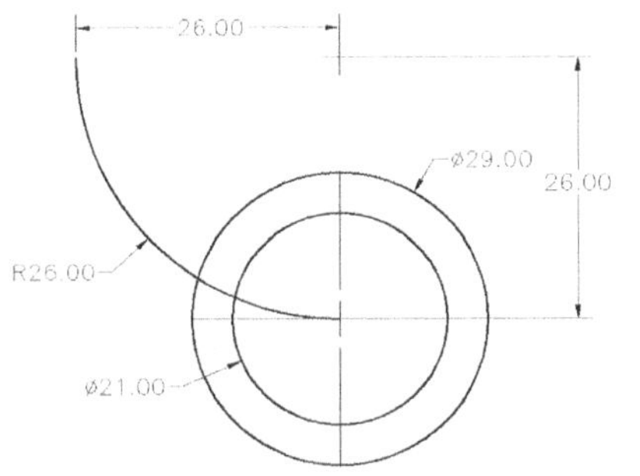

Figure 8-126 *Sketch for base pipe feature*

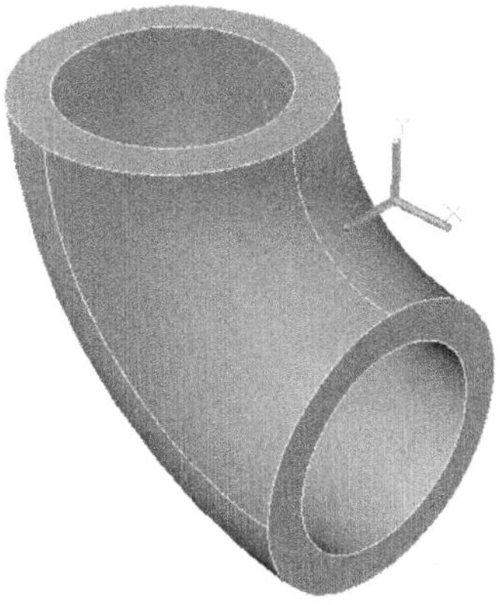

Figure 8-127 *Resulting sweep feature*

12. Choose the **Top** option from the **3D Navigation** drop-down in the **View** panel and draw the sketch with the dimensions shown in Figure 8-128.

13. Change the view to **SW Isometric**. The model after drawing the sketch and turning off the dimension is shown in Figure 8-129.

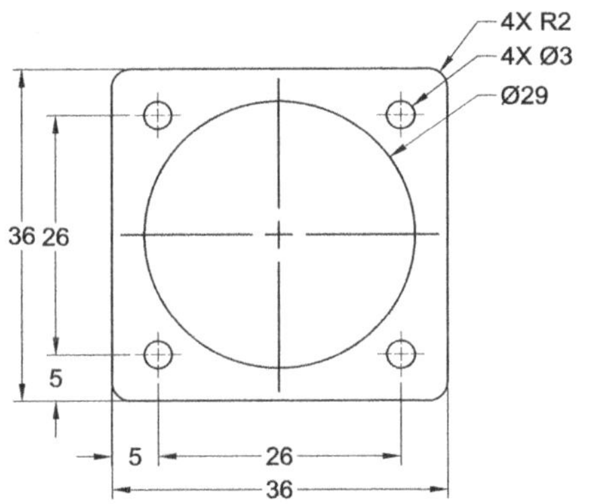

Figure 8-128 *Sketch for the area to Press/Pull*

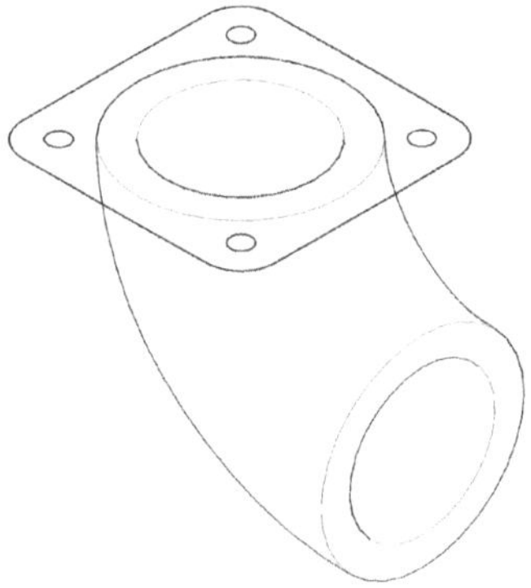

Figure 8-129 *Location of the sketch*

14. Using the **Region** and **Solid, Subtract** tools, create a region Area A, as shown in Figure 8-130.

15. Choose the **Extrude** tool from **Home > Modeling > Solid Creation** drop-down and select the region created in previous step and press Enter. Next, move the mouse in the upward direction, enter the value **5** at the Command prompt, and press Enter.

16. Choose the **Presspull** tool and pull the area shown as Area B in Figure 8-130 by the same value as specified in Step 15. The resulting model should look similar to the one shown in Figure 8-131.

17. Similarly, create the flange for the other face of the pipe. The resulting model should be similar to the one shown in Figure 8-132.

18. Choose the **Solid Union** tool from the **Solid Editing** panel in the **Home** tab and follow the prompt sequence given next.

    Select objects: *Select all objects.*
    Select objects: Enter.

The final solid model should look similar to the one shown in Figure 8-133.

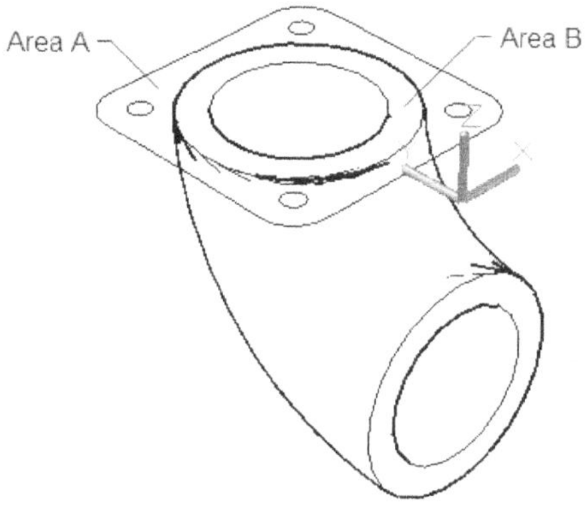

Figure 8-130 *Two areas to presspull*

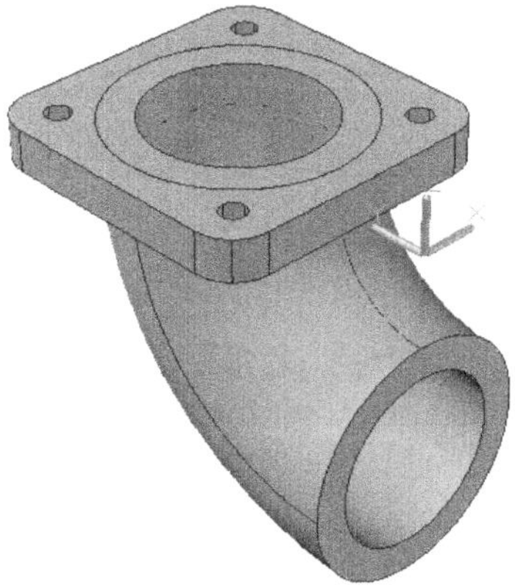

Figure 8-131 *Resulting model after Step 16*

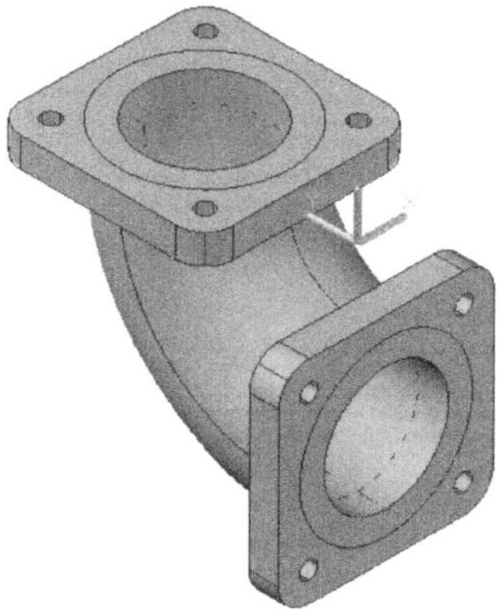

Figure 8-132 *Resulting model after Step 17*

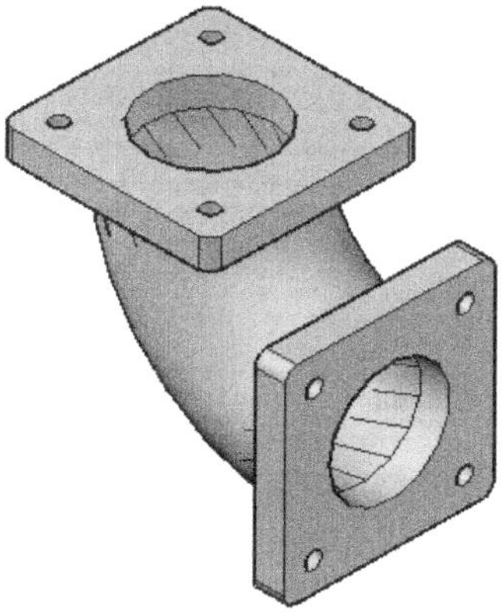

Figure 8-133 *Final model after Union*

Self-Evaluation Test

Answer the following questions and then compare them to those given at the end of this chapter:

1. The __________ tool can be used to add as well as remove material from a model.
2. The __________ tool is used to generate a helical curve.
3. The number of paths for a loft feature cannot be more than __________ .
4. At least __________ cross-sections are required to create a loft feature.
5. You can extrude the selected region about a path using the __________ option of the **Extrude** tool.
6. Open entities can be converted into regions. (T/F)
7. An ellipse can be converted into a polysolid. (T/F)
8. You can twist a cross-section while sweeping it. (T/F)
9. In AutoCAD, you can create a pyramid of maximum 42 sides. (T/F)
10. The **Cone** tool can be used to create a solid cone with a circular and an elliptical base. (T/F)

Review Questions

Answer the following questions:

1. Which of the following values for the taper angle is used to taper the extruded model from the base?

   (a) Positive (b) Negative
   (c) Zero (d) None of these

2. Which of the following tools is used to create a cube?

   (a) **Box** (b) **Cuboid**
   (c) **Polygon** (d) **Cylinder**

3. Which of the following commands is used to check the interference between selected solid models?

   (a) **INTERFERE** (b) **INTERSECT**
   (c) **INTERFERENCE** (d) **CHECK**

4. For which of the following functions is the **Presspull** tool used?

   (a) Add material (b) Remove material
   (c) Both add and remove material (d) Neither add nor remove material

5. The __________ direction is known as the extrusion direction.

6. The __________ tool is used to create an apple-like structure.

7. The __________ tool is used to create a revolved solid.

8. Guides for the **Loft** tool should always __________ the cross-section.

9. The __________ option of the **Revolve** tool is used to select a 2D entity as the revolution axis.

10. You can revolve an open entity. (T/F)

11. You cannot apply Boolean operations on regions. (T/F)

12. The entity to be revolved should lie completely on one side of the revolution axis. (T/F)

13. You cannot apply the **Presspull** tool on an open object. (T/F)

14. There cannot be more than one guide for the loft feature. (T/F)

15. A curve generated by the **Helix** tool can be used as a path for the swept solids. (T/F)

Exercise 2

In this exercise, you will create the solid model shown in Figure 8-134. Assume the missing dimensions.

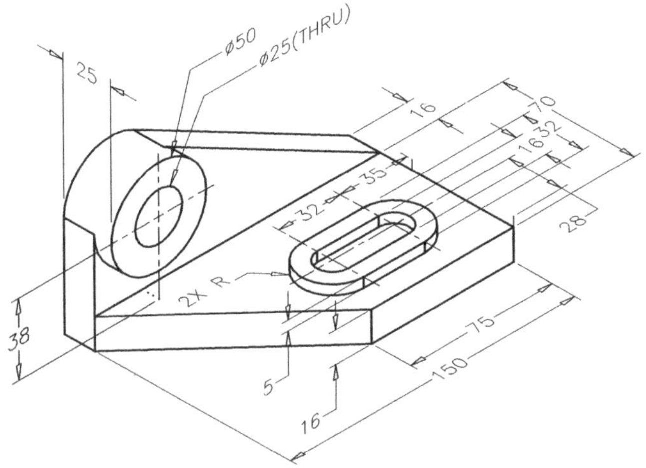

Figure 8-134 Model for Exercise 1

Problem-Solving Exercise 1

In this exercise, you will create the solid model with dimensions shown in Figure 8-135.

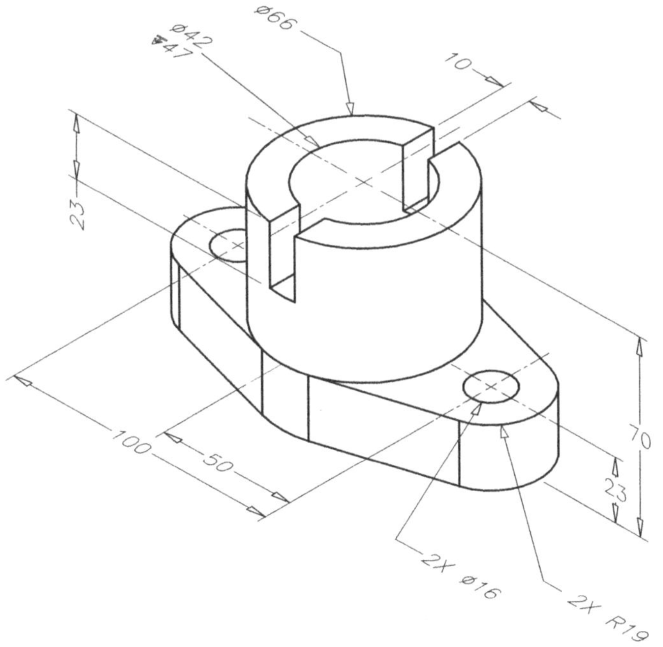

Figure 8-135 Solid model for Problem-Solving Exercise 1

Answers to Self-Evaluation Test

1. **Presspull**, 2. **Helix**, 3. one, 4. two, 5. **Path**, 6. F, 7. T, 8. T, 9. F, 10. T

Chapter 9

Editing 3D Objects-I

Learning Objectives

After completing this chapter, you will be able to:

- *Create fillets and chamfers in the solid models*
- *Rotate and mirror solid models in 3D space*
- *Create an array in 3D space*
- *Align the solid models*
- *Extract the edges of a solid model*
- *Slice the solid models and create cross-sections*
- *Convert objects to surfaces and solids*
- *Convert surfaces to solids*
- *Attaching the Point Cloud*

Key Terms

- *Fillet Edges*
- *Chamfer Edges*
- *Rotate 3D*
- *3D Mirror*
- *3D Move*
- *3DARRAY*
- *Align*
- *3D Align*
- *Extract Edges*
- *Convert to Surface*
- *Convert to Solid*
- *Thicken*
- *Slice*
- *SECTION*

FILLETING SOLID MODELS

Ribbon: Solid > Solid Editing > Fillet Edge drop-down > Fillet Edge
Menu Bar: Modify > Solid Editing > Fillet edges **Command:** FILLETEDGE

As the **Fillet** tool in the **Modify** panel is used to fillet the sharp corners in a sketch, the **Fillet Edge** tool in the **Fillet Edge** drop-down is used to round the edges of a model, refer to Figure 9-1. On invoking this tool, following prompt sequence will be displayed:

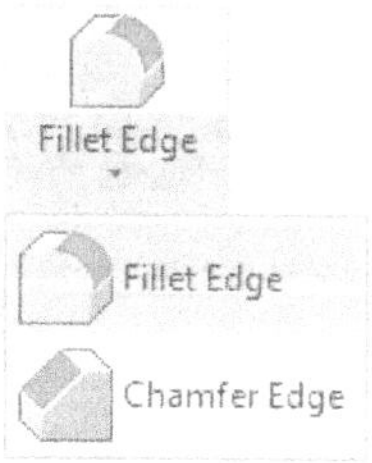

Figure 9-1 *Tools in the* ***Fillet Edge*** *drop-down*

Select an edge or [Chain/Loop/Radius]:

Select an edge; the preview of the fillet with default radius will be displayed and you will be prompted to select another edge. If you need to fillet multiple edges, select the edges in succession, refer to Figure 9-2. After selecting the edge or edges, press Enter to end the selection. On doing so, you will be prompted to press Enter again to accept the default radius or enter a new radius. Also, a grip will be displayed on the fillet. Enter **R** for a new radius; specify radius value and press Enter, or drag the grip to edit the fillet radius and press Enter; the fillet will be created, as shown in Figure 9-3.

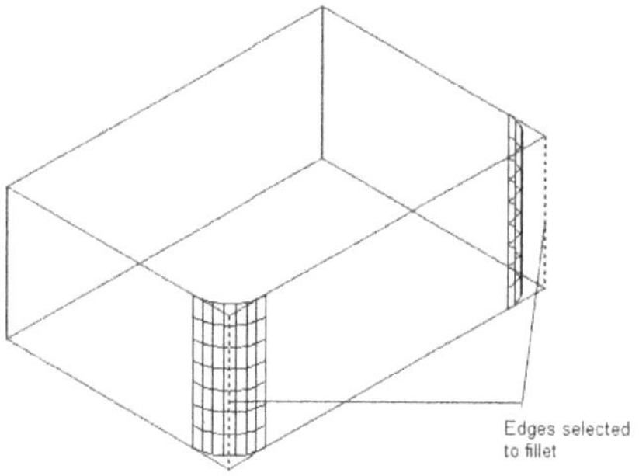

Figure 9-2 *The edges to be filleted*

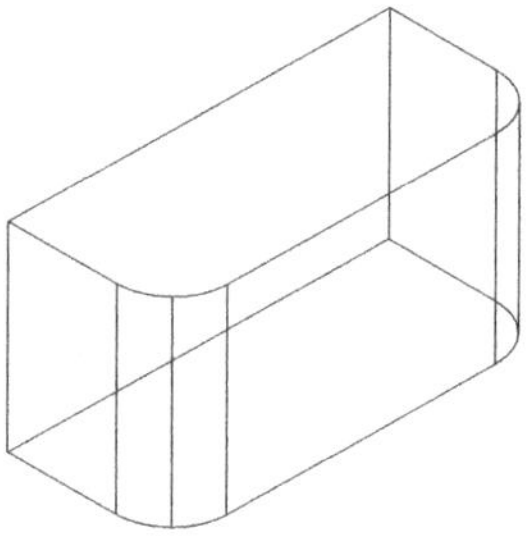

Figure 9-3 *Model after filleting the edges*

Other options in the Command prompt are discussed next.

Chain

On choosing this option, you can select all tangential edges on the face of a solid model in a single attempt, refer to Figure 9-4. Figure 9-5 shows the resulting fillet.

Loop

With this option, you can select any of the loops attached to the selected edge. On choosing this option, preview of the selected loop will be displayed and a contextual menu will open. In this menu, you can accept the loop displayed or select next to check the next possible loop.

Radius

This option is used to redefine the fillet radius. You can also define the radius using an expression.

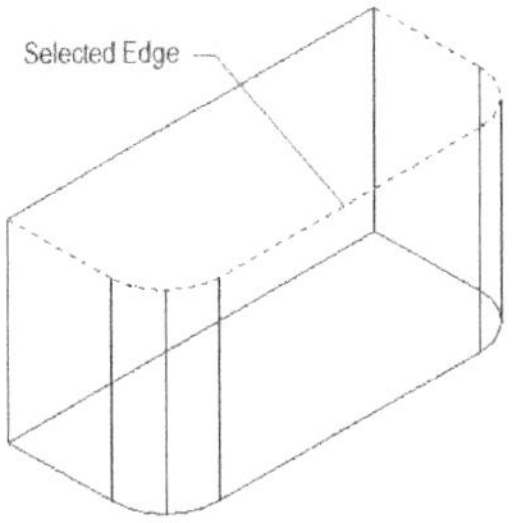

Figure 9-4 *Edge that will be selected using the **Chain** option*

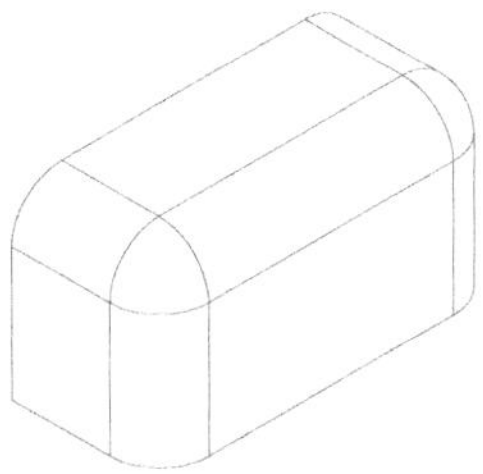

Figure 9-5 *The resulting fillet*

CHAMFERING SOLID MODELS

Ribbon: Solid > Solid Editing > Fillet Edge drop-down > Chamfer Edge
Menu Bar: Modify > Solid Editing > Chamfer edges **Command:** CHAMFEREDGE

The **Chamfer Edge** tool is used to bevel the edges of solid models. The working of this tool is similar to that of the **Fillet Edge** tool. To create a chamfer, invoke the **Chamfer Edge** tool from the **Solid Editing** panel, refer to Figure 9-1, and then select the edges of the same face in succession; the preview of the chamfer will be displayed. Press Enter to complete the selection; you will be prompted to specify a value for the new chamfer distance or press Enter to accept the default value. Also, two grips will be displayed at the edge selected to chamfer. You can enter the chamfer distances or drag the grips on each surface to change the chamfer distance. Then, press Enter to create the chamfer.

Figures 9-6 and 9-7 show the solid model before and after chamfering, respectively.

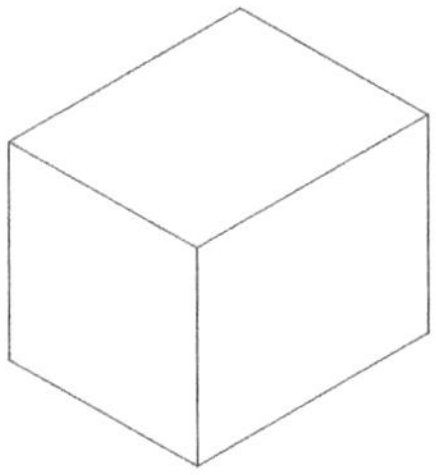

Figure 9-6 *Solid model before chamfering*

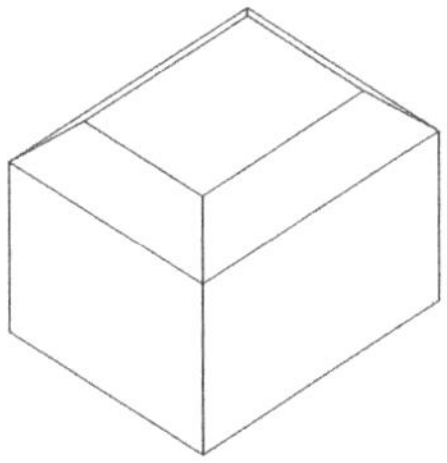

Figure 9-7 *Solid model after chamfering*

Loop

This option is used to select all edges that make a closed loop on the selected face of the solid model. To select edges using the loop option, enter **L** at the **Select an edge or [Loop/Distance]** prompt and select any one of the edges that forms the loop; all edges will be selected.

Distance

This option is used to define the chamfer distances. When the preview is displayed, you can also drag the grips displayed on the edge to be chamfered and change the chamfer distance.

Note

*You can also chamfer the edges by using the **Chamfer** tool in the **Modify** panel of the **Home** tab. On selecting an edge after invoking this tool, you will be prompted to specify the surface to be selected. Select the surface and press Enter to accept the surface selected, or select the next surface and press Enter; you will be prompted to specify the base surface chamfer distance and other surface chamfer distance. Enter suitable values and press Enter; you will be prompted to select an edge or loop. Select the edge or loop on which you want to create the chamfer and press Enter; chamfer will be created. In this case, the edit grips will not be displayed.*

ROTATING SOLID MODELS IN 3D SPACE

Command: ROTATE3D

The **ROTATE3D** command is used to rotate the selected solid model in the 3D space about a specified axis. The right-hand thumb rule will be used to determine the direction of rotation of the solid model in 3D space. The prompt sequence that will follow when you invoke this command is given next.

Current positive angle: ANGDIR=counterclockwise ANGBASE=0
Select objects: *Select the solid model.*
Select objects: Enter.
Specify first point on axis or define axis by
[Object/Last/View/Xaxis/Yaxis/Zaxis/2Points]: *Specify a point on the axis of rotation or select an option.*

2points

This is the default option for rotating solid models. This option allows you to rotate the solid model about an axis specified by two points. The direction of the axis will be from the first point to the second point. Using the direction of the axis, you can calculate the direction of rotation of the solid model by applying the right-hand thumb rule. The prompt sequence that will follow when you invoke this option is given next.

[Object/Last/View/Xaxis/Yaxis/Zaxis/2points]:2 Enter.
Specify first point on axis: *Specify the first point of the rotation axis, refer to Figure 9-8.*
Specify second point on axis: *Specify the second point of the rotation axis, refer to Figure 9-8.*
Specify rotation angle or [Reference]: *Specify the angle of rotation.*

Object

This option is used to rotate the solid model in the 3D space using a 2D entity. The 2D entities that can be used are line, circle, arc, or 2D polyline segment. If the selected entity is a line or a straight polyline segment, then it will be directly taken as the rotation axis. However, if the selected entity is an arc or a circle, then an imaginary axis will be drawn starting from the center and normal to the plane in which the arc or circle is drawn. The object will then be rotated about this imaginary axis. The prompt sequence that will follow when you invoke this option is given next.

[Object/Last/View/Xaxis/Yaxis/Zaxis/2points]: **O** Enter.
Select a line, circle, arc, or 2D-polyline segment: *Select the 2D entity, as shown in Figure 9-9.*
Specify rotation angle or [Reference]: *Specify the angle of rotation.*

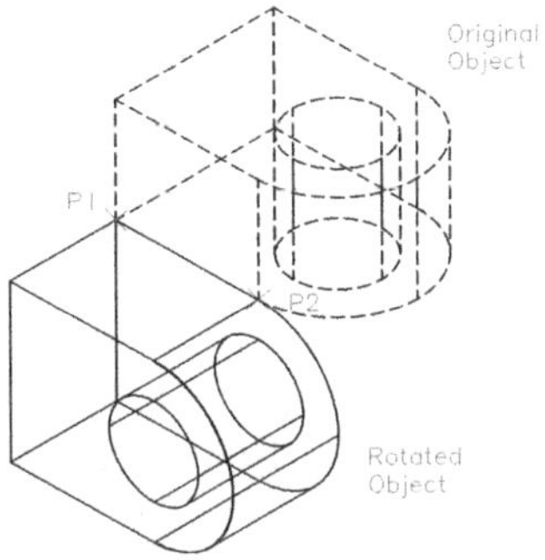

Figure 9-8 *Rotating the solid model using the* ***2points*** *option*

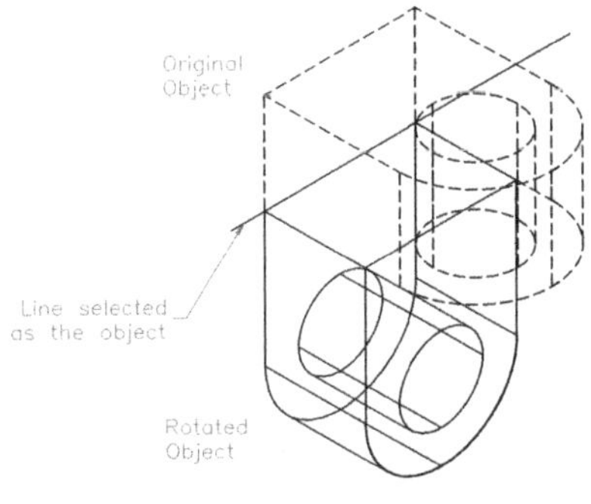

Figure 9-9 *Rotating the solid model using the* ***Object*** *option*

Last

This option uses the same axis that was last selected to rotate the solid model.

View

This option is used to rotate the solid model about the viewing plane. In this case, the viewing plane is the screen of the computer. This option draws an imaginary axis starting from the specified point which continues normal to the viewing plane. The model is then rotated about this axis. The prompt sequence that will follow when you invoke this option is given next.

Specify first point on axis or define axis by
[Object/Last/View/Xaxis/Yaxis/Zaxis/2points]: **V**
Specify a point on the view direction axis <0,0,0>: *Specify the point on the view plane, as shown in Figure 9-10.*
Specify rotation angle or [Reference]: *Specify the angle of rotation.*

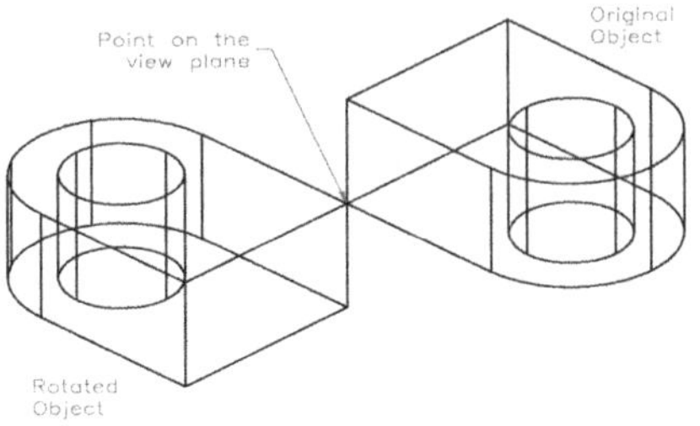

Figure 9-10 *Rotating the solid model using the* ***View*** *option through an angle of 180°*

Xaxis

This option is used to rotate the solid model about the positive X axis of the current UCS. On invoking this option, you will be prompted to select a point on the X axis. The prompt sequence that will follow when you invoke this command is given next.

Specify first point on axis or define axis by
[Object/Last/View/Xaxis/Yaxis/Zaxis/2points]: **X**
Specify a point on the X axis <0,0,0>: *Specify the point on the X axis.*
Specify rotation angle or [Reference]: *Specify the angle of rotation.*

Yaxis

This option is used to rotate the solid model about the positive Y axis of the current UCS. When you invoke this option, you will be prompted to select a point on the Y axis. The prompt sequence that will follow when you invoke this command is given next.

Specify first point on axis or define axis by
[Object/Last/View/Xaxis/Yaxis/Zaxis/2points]: **Y**
Specify a point on the Y axis <0,0,0>: *Specify the point on the Y axis.*
Specify rotation angle or [Reference]: *Specify the angle of rotation.*

Zaxis

This option is used to rotate the solid model about the positive Z axis of the current UCS. When you invoke this option, you will be prompted to select a point on the Z axis. The prompt sequence that will follow when you invoke this command is given next.

Specify first point on axis or define axis by
[Object/Last/View/Xaxis/Yaxis/Zaxis/2points]: **Z**
Specify a point on the Z axis <0,0,0>: *Specify the point on the Z axis.*
Specify rotation angle or [Reference]: *Specify the angle of rotation.*

ROTATING SOLID MODELS ABOUT AN AXIS

Ribbon: Home > Modify > 3D Rotate
Menu Bar: Modify > 3D Operations > 3D Rotate
Toolbar: Modeling > 3D Rotate **Command:** 3DROTATE

The **3D Rotate** tool is used to dynamically rotate an object or sub-objects such as edges and faces with respect to a specified base point and about a selected axis. To perform this operation, choose the **3D Rotate** tool from the **Modify** panel and select the object or subobject to be rotated. Then, press Enter; the Rotate Gizmo will be displayed at the center of the object, refer to Figure 9-11. Specify a base point which will be the center point of rotation about which you need to rotate the selected object. You need to select the axis about which you want to rotate the object. To do so, move the cursor close to the required axis handle; the axis gets highlighted and an axis passing through the center of the gizmo will be displayed, as shown in Figure 9-12. Click once and drag the cursor or enter a value at the Command prompt.

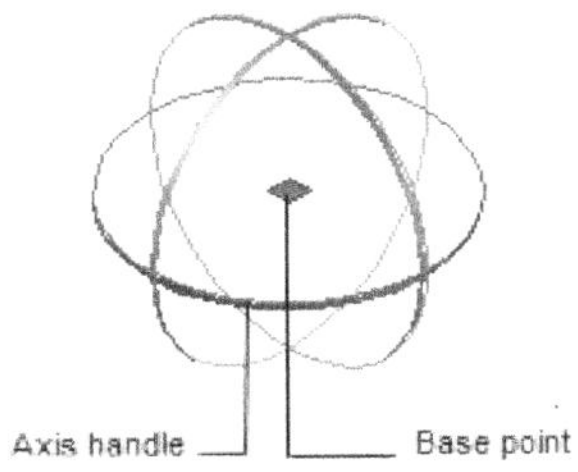

Figure 9-11 The **Rotate Gizmo**

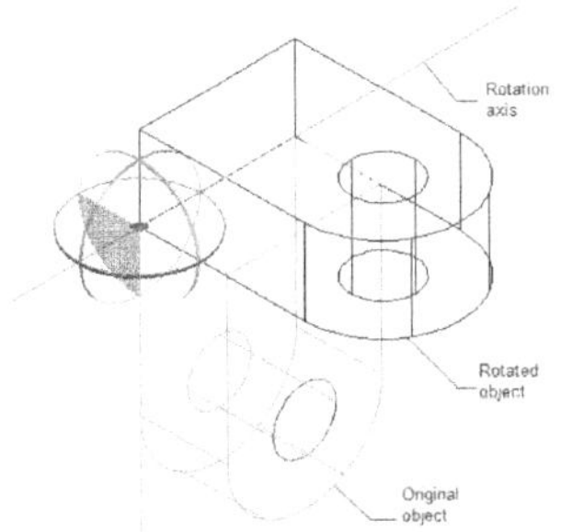

Figure 9-12 Model rotated by 90 degrees about the X axis

Tip

*If you select a model in **3D Modeling** workspace with 3D visual style, the Move Gizmo will be displayed on it. This is because the default gizmo displayed in the **Selection** panel of the **Home** tab is the Move Gizmo. If you choose the **Rotate Gizmo** tool from the **Gizmo** drop-down and select a model, the **Rotate Gizmo** will be displayed. Using this gizmo, you can directly rotate the model in 3D space.*

MIRRORING SOLID MODELS IN 3D SPACE

Ribbon: Home > Modify > 3D Mirror
Menu Bar: Modify > 3D Operations > 3D Mirror **Command:** MIRROR3D

The **3D Mirror** tool is used to mirror the solid models about a specified plane in the space. To mirror a solid model, choose the **3D Mirror** tool from the **Modify** panel and follow the prompt sequence given next.

Select objects: *Select the solid model to be mirrored.*
Select objects: Enter.
Specify first point of mirror plane (3 points) or
[Object/Last/Zaxis/View/XY/YZ/ZX/3points] <3points>: *Specify the first point on the mirror plane or select an option.*

The options in this prompt are discussed next.

3points

This is the default selected option for mirroring the solid models. As discussed earlier, a line can be defined by specifying two points through which the line will pass. Similarly, a plane can be defined by specifying three points through which it passes. This option allows you to specify the three points through which the mirroring plane passes. The prompt sequence that follows when you invoke this tool is given next.

Specify first point of mirror plane (3 points) or
[Object/Last/Zaxis/View/XY/YZ/ZX/3points] <3points>: Enter.
Specify first point on mirror plane: *Specify the first point on the plane, refer to Figure 9-13.*

Specify second point on mirror plane: *Specify the second point on the plane, refer to Figure 9-13.*
Specify third point on mirror plane: *Specify the third point on the plane, refer to Figure 9-13.*
Delete source objects? [Yes/No] <N>: Enter.

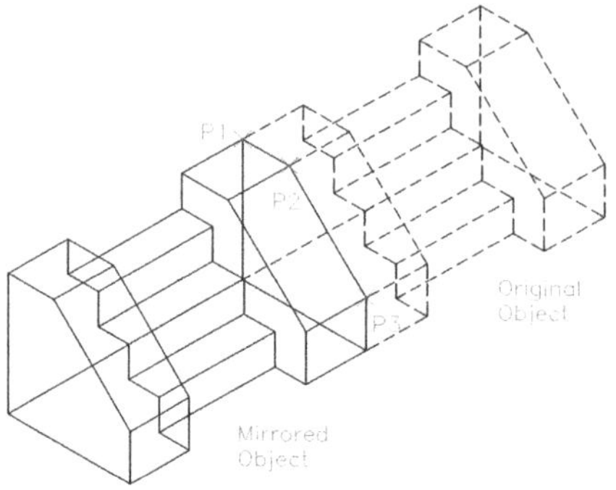

Figure 9-13 *Mirroring the solid model using the* ***3points*** *option*

Object

This option is used to mirror the solid model using a 2D entity, refer to Figure 9-14. The 2D entities that can be used to mirror the solids are circles, arcs, and 2D polyline segments. The prompt sequence that follows when you invoke this option is given next.

Specify first point of mirror plane (3 points) or
[Object/Last/Zaxis/View/XY/YZ/ZX/3points] <3points>: **O**
Select a circle, arc, or 2D-polyline segment: *Select the 2D entity, as shown in Figure 9-14.*
Delete source objects? [Yes/No] <N>: Enter.

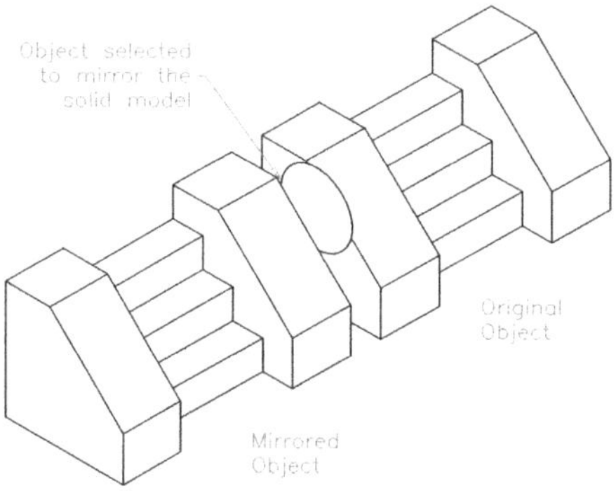

Figure 9-14 *Mirroring the solid model using the* ***Object*** *option*

Zaxis

This option allows you to define a mirroring plane using two points. The first point is the point on the mirroring plane and the second point is a point on the positive direction of the Z axis of that plane or normal to that plane. The prompt sequence that follows when you invoke this option is given next.

Specify first point of mirror plane (3 points) or
[Object/Last/Zaxis/View/XY/YZ/ZX/3points] <3points>: **Z**
Specify point on mirror plane: *Specify the point on the plane, as shown in Figure 9-15.*
Specify point on Z-axis (normal) of mirror plane: *Specify the point on the Z direction of the plane, refer to Figure 9-15.*
Delete source objects? [Yes/No] <N>: Enter.

View

This is one of the interesting options provided for mirroring solid models. This option is used to mirror the selected solid model about the viewing plane. The viewing plane, in this case, is the screen of the monitor, refer to Figure 9-16. The prompt sequence that follows when you invoke this tool is given next.

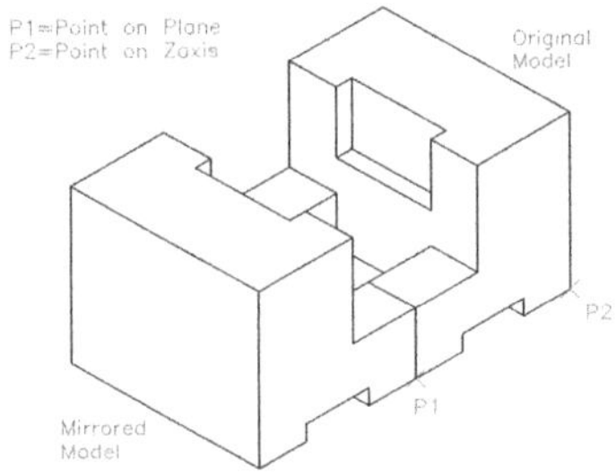

Figure 9-15 *Mirroring the solid model using the* ***Zaxis*** *option*

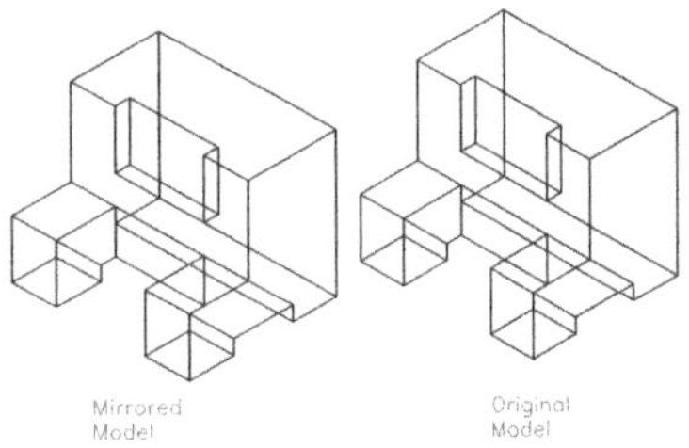

Figure 9-16 *A solid model mirrored using the* ***View*** *option and then moved*

Specify first point of mirror plane (3 points) or
[Object/Last/Zaxis/View/XY/YZ/ZX/3points] <3points>: **V**
Specify point on view plane <0,0,0>: *Specify the point on the view plane.*
Delete source objects? [Yes/No] <N>: Enter.

Tip

As the model is mirrored about the view plane, the new model will be placed over the original model when you view it from the current viewpoint. The best option to view the mirrored model is to hide the hidden lines using the ***Hide*** *tool. You can also move the new model away from the last model using the* ***Move*** *tool or change the viewpoint for viewing both the models simultaneously.*

XY/YZ/ZX

These options are used to mirror the solid model about the XY, YZ, or ZX plane of the current UCS.

Tip

All these planes will be considered with reference to the current orientation of the UCS and not with its world position. This means that when you select the ***XY*** *option to mirror the solid model, then the XY plane of the current UCS will be considered to mirror the model and not the XY plane of the world UCS.*

Example 1

In this example, you will create the solid model shown in Figure 9-17. Assume the missing dimensions.

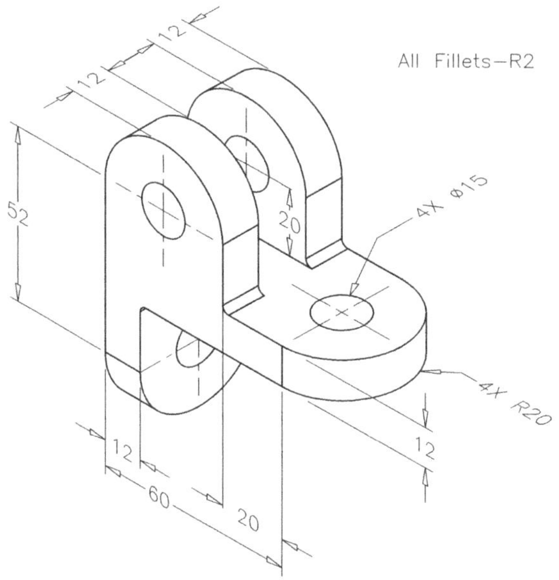

Figure 9-17 Solid model for Example 1

1. Start a new 3D template drawing file in **3D Modeling** workspace. Set the drawing limits of the workspace to 100,100.

2. Orient the view to top by choosing **Top** in the ViewCube. Next, choose **WCS > New UCS** from the **WCS** drop-down list below the ViewCube; you will be prompted to specify the origin. Enter **V** at the **Specify origin of UCS or [Face/NAmed/OBject/Previous/View/World/X/Y/Z/ZAxis] <World>** prompt and press Enter.

3. Create the base of the model and then change the view to the **SE Isometric** using the ViewCube, refer to Figure 9-18.

4. Next, orient the view to front by choosing **Front** in the ViewCube. Next, choose **WCS > New UCS** from the **WCS** drop-down list below the ViewCube; you will be prompted to specify the origin. Enter **V** at the **Specify origin of UCS or [Face/NAmed/OBject/Previous/View/World/X/Y/Z/ZAxis] <World>** prompt and press Enter.

5. Draw the sketch for the next object using the **Rectangle** tool. Convert one side of the rectangle to an arc by using the shortcut menu that is displayed when you hover the cursor on the middle grip. Then, create the object by using the **Region**, **Extrude**, and **Subtract** tools. The resulting object is shown in Figure 9-19.

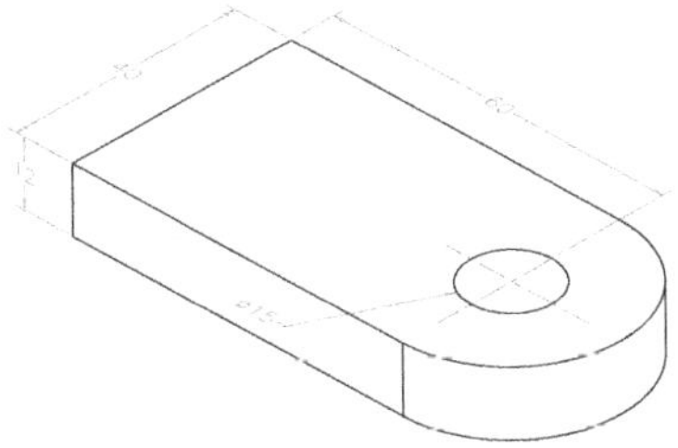

Figure 9-18 *Base of the model*

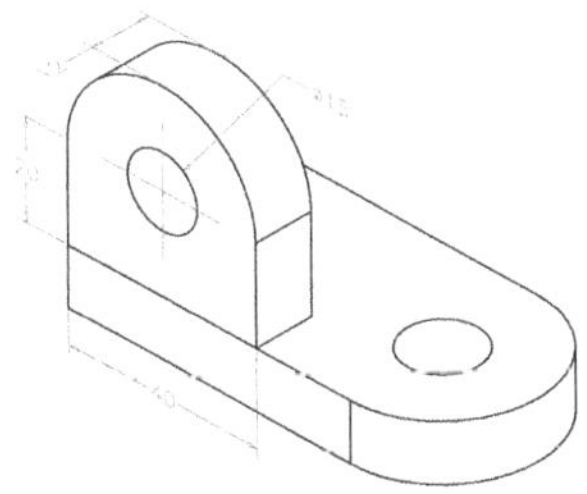

Figure 9-19 *Model after creating the next object*

6. Invoke the **3D Mirror** tool from the **Modify** panel and follow the prompt sequence given next.

   Select objects: *Select the last object.*
   Select objects: Enter.
   Specify first point of mirror plane (3 points) or
   [Object/Last/Zaxis/View/XY/YZ/ZX/3points] <3points>: **Z**
   Specify point on mirror plane: *Select P1, as shown in Figure 9-20.*

   Specify point on Z-axis (normal) of mirror plane: *Select P2, as shown in Figure 9-20.*
   Delete source objects? [Yes/No] <N>: Enter.

7. The object after mirroring and hiding the hidden lines should look similar to the model shown in Figure 9-21.

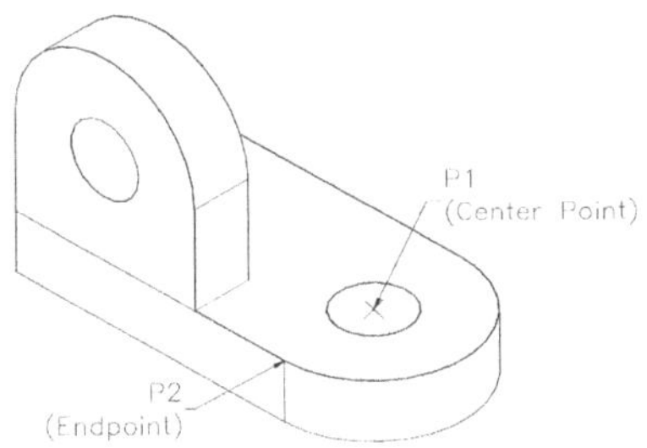

Figure 9-20 *Selecting the points to be mirrored*

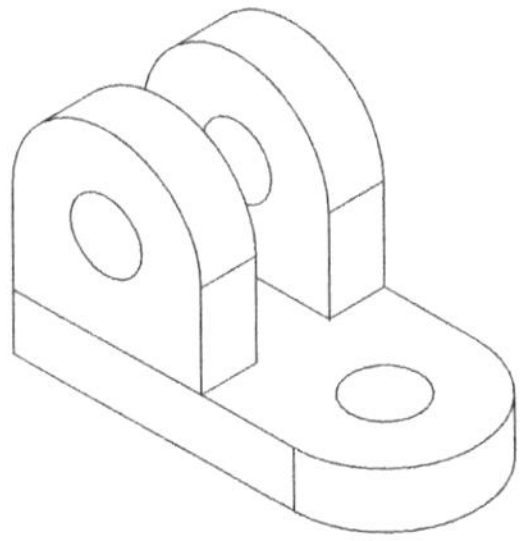

Figure 9-21 *Model after mirroring*

8. Set the UCS in the **Left** view and create the feature at the bottom, as shown in Figure 9-22.

9. Choose the **Solid, Union** tool from the **Solid Editing** panel and then unite all objects, refer to Figure 9-23.

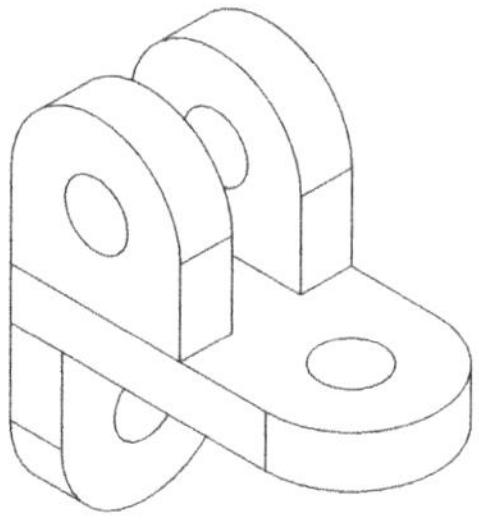

Figure 9-22 *Model after creating the next object at the bottom*

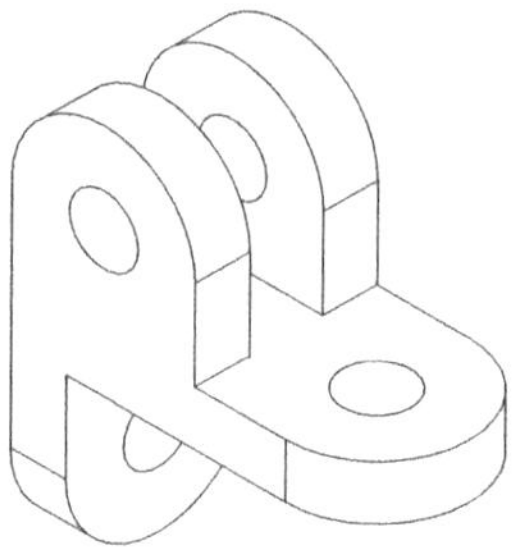

Figure 9-23 *Model after creating the union*

10. Choose the **Fillet Edge** tool from **Solid > Solid Editing > Fillet Edge** drop-down and follow the prompt sequence given below.

    Select an edge or [Chain/Loop/Radius]: *Select first edge, as shown in Figure 9-24.*
    Select an edge or [Chain/Loop/Radius]: *Select the second edge, as shown in Figure 9-24.*
    Select an edge or [Chain/Loop/Radius]: *Select the third edge, as shown in Figure 9-24.*
    Select an edge or [Chain/Loop/Radius]: Enter.
    3 edge(s) selected for fillet
    Press Enter to accept the fillet or [Radius]: **R**
    Specify Radius or [Expression]<1.0000>: **2** Enter.
    Press Enter to accept the fillet or [Radius]: Enter.

11. The final model for Example 1 should look similar to the model shown in Figure 9-25.

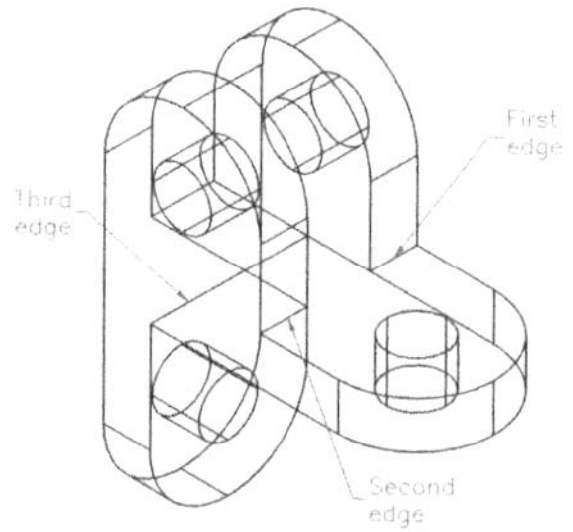

Figure 9-24 *Selecting the edges for filleting*

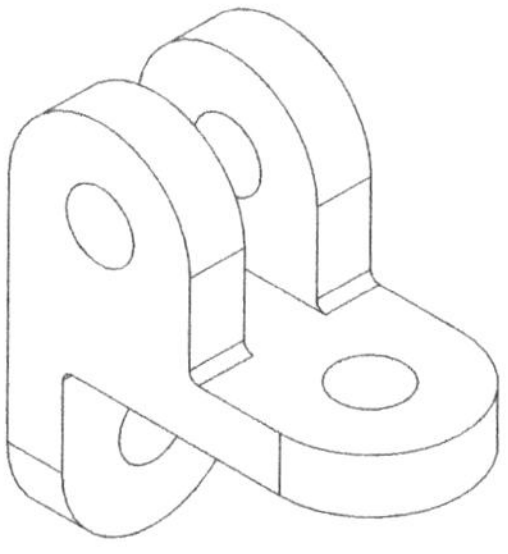

Figure 9-25 *The final model for Example 1*

MOVING MODELS IN 3D SPACE

Ribbon: Home > Modify > 3D Move
Menu Bar: Modify > 3D Operations > 3D Move **Toolbar:** Modeling > 3D Move
Command: 3DMOVE

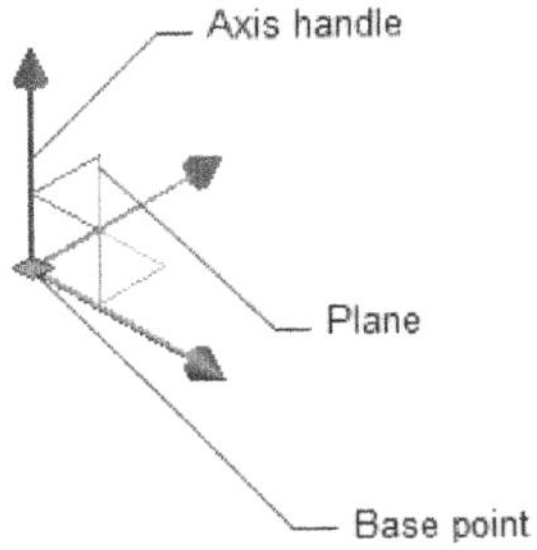

*Figure 9-26 The **Move Gizmo***

Sometimes, you need to move objects such as edges or faces of a solid model or the entire solid in 3D space. In such cases, you can use the **3D Move** tool to translate them to the desired location. You can move the selected object or subobject at an orientation parallel to a plane or along an axial direction. To perform this operation choose the **3D Move** tool from the **Modify** panel and select the object or subobject to be moved and press Enter; the **Move Gizmo** will be displayed on the selected object, refer to Figure 9-26. To move the object in 3D space with respect to a base point other than the default one, click in the drawing area; the new base point will be specified. Then, specify the displacement or drag the cursor and place the component.

To move an object along a particular direction, move the cursor near the axis handle corresponding to that direction; a line of the same color as the selected axis will be displayed. Click when the axis is highlighted and drag the cursor to move the object along that direction. To move a face or an edge of a solid model in a particular plane, invoke the **3D Move** tool, press the Ctrl key, select a face or an edge, and press Enter; the move gizmo will be displayed on the selected object. Next, move the cursor near the desired plane in the **Move Gizmo**; the plane, including the corresponding axis handle, will turn golden in color. Press and hold the left mouse button when the plane is highlighted and then drag; the selected object will move only parallel to the selected plane.

Tip
*By default, the **Move Gizmo** option is selected in the **Default Gizmo** drop-down available in the **Selection** panel. Therefore, on selecting an object, the **Move Gizmo** will be displayed on the object and you can translate the selected object. Also, by default, the **No Filter** option is selected in the **Filter** drop-down list. As a result, you can select a face, an edge, or a vertex of a model. However, if any other option is selected in the **Filter** drop-down list, then only the corresponding entity can be selected.*

CREATING ARRAYS IN 3D SPACE

Menu Bar: Modify > 3D Operations > 3D Array **Toolbar:** Modeling > 3D Array
Command: 3DARRAY

As mentioned earlier, the arrays are defined as the method of creating multiple copies of the selected object in a rectangular or a polar fashion. The 3D arrays can also be created similar to the 2D arrays. The only difference is that in a 3D array, another factor called the Z axis is also taken into consideration. There are two types of 3D arrays and these are discussed next.

3D Rectangular Array

Menu Bar: Modify > 3D Operations > 3D Array
Command: 3DARRAY

This is the method of arranging the solid model along the edges of a box. In this type of array, you need to specify three parameters. They are the rows (along the Y axis), the columns (along the X axis), and the levels (along the Z axis). You will also have to specify the distances between the rows, columns, and levels. The 3D rectangular array can be easily understood by taking an example shown in Figure 9-27. This figure shows two floors of a building. Initially, only one chair is placed on the ground floor. Now, if you create a 2D rectangular array, the chairs will be arranged only on the ground floor. However, when you create the 3D rectangular array, then the chairs will be arranged on the first floor (along the Z axis) as well as the ground floor, refer to Figure 9-28. In this example, the number of rows is three, columns is four, and levels is two.

The prompt sequence that will follow when you choose this tool is given next.

Select objects: *Select the object to array.*
Select objects: Enter.
Enter the type of array [Rectangular/Polar] <R>: Enter.
Enter the number of rows (---) <1>: *Specify the number of rows along the Y axis.*
Enter the number of columns (|||) <1>: *Specify the number of columns along the X axis.*
Enter the number of levels (...) <1>: *Specify the number of levels along the Z axis.*
Specify the distance between rows (---): *Specify the distance between the rows.*
Specify the distance between columns (|||): *Specify the distance between the columns.*
Specify the distance between levels (...): *Specify the distance between the levels.*

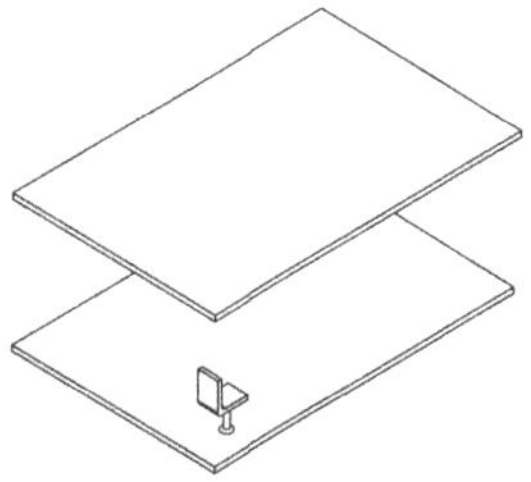

Figure 9-27 *The model before creating the rectangular array*

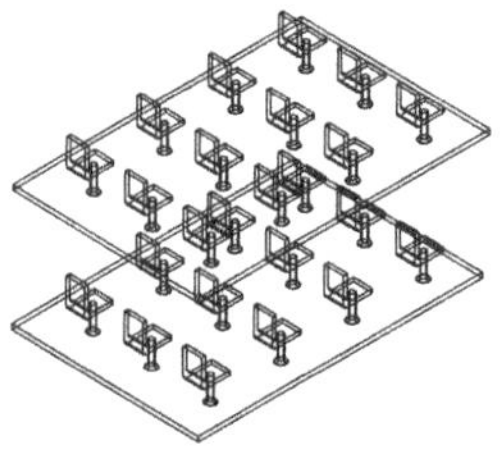

Figure 9-28 *The model after creating the array in 3D space*

3D Polar Array

Menu Bar: Modify > 3D Operations > 3D Array
Command: 3DARRAY

The 3D polar arrays are similar to the 2D polar arrays. The only difference between them is that in 3D, you will have to specify an axis about which the solid models will be arranged. For example, consider the solid models shown in Figure 9-29. This figure shows a circular plate that has four holes. Now, to place the bolts in this plate, you can use the 3D polar array, as shown in Figure 9-30. The axis for an array is defined using the centers at the top and the bottom faces of the circular plate. The prompt sequence that will follow is given next.

Select objects: *Select the object to array.*
Select objects: Enter.
Enter the type of array [Rectangular/Polar] <R>: **P**
Enter the number of items in the array: *Specify the number of items.*
Specify the angle to fill (+=ccw, -=cw) <360>: Enter.
Rotate arrayed objects? [Yes/No] <Y>: Enter.
Specify center point of array: *Specify the first point on the axis.*
Specify second point on axis of rotation: *Specify the second point on the axis.*

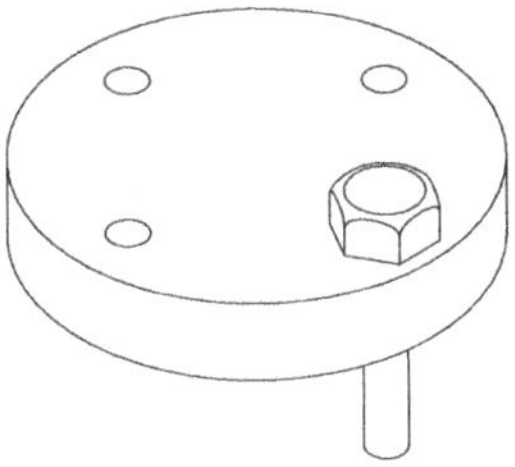

Figure 9-29 *Model before creating an array*

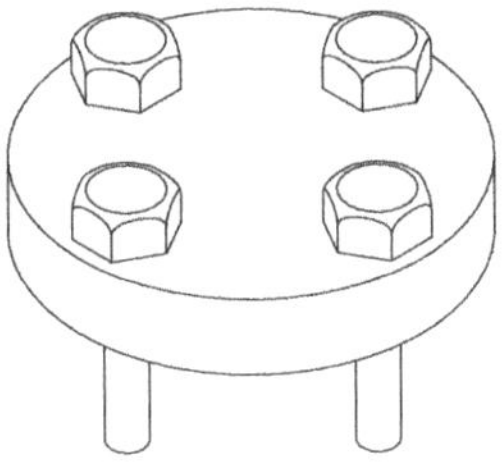

Figure 9-30 *Model after creating an array*

ALIGNING SOLID MODELS

Ribbon: Home > Modify > Align
Menu Bar: Modify > 3D Operations > Align **Command:** ALIGN

The **Align** tool is extensively used in solid modeling. As the name suggests, this tool is used to align the selected solid model with another solid model. It can also be used to translate, rotate, and scale the selected solid model. This tool uses pairs of source and destination points to align the solid model. The source point is a point with which you want to align the object. The destination point is a point on the destination object at which you want to place the source object. You can specify one, two, or three pairs of points to align the objects. However, the working of this tool will be different in all the three cases. All these three cases are discussed next.

Aligning the Objects Using One Pair of Points

When you align the object using just one pair of points, the working of this tool will be similar to the **Move** tool. This means that the source object will be moved as it is from its original location and will be placed on the destination object. Here, the source point will work as the first point of displacement and the destination point will work as the second point of displacement. Also, a reference line will be drawn between the source and the destination points. This line will disappear once you exit the tool. The prompt sequence is as follows:

Select objects: *Select the object to align.*
Select objects: Enter.
Specify first source point: *Select S1, as shown in Figure 9-31.*
Specify first destination point: *Select D1, as shown in Figure 9-31.*
Specify second source point: Enter.

Figure 9-32 shows the models after aligning.

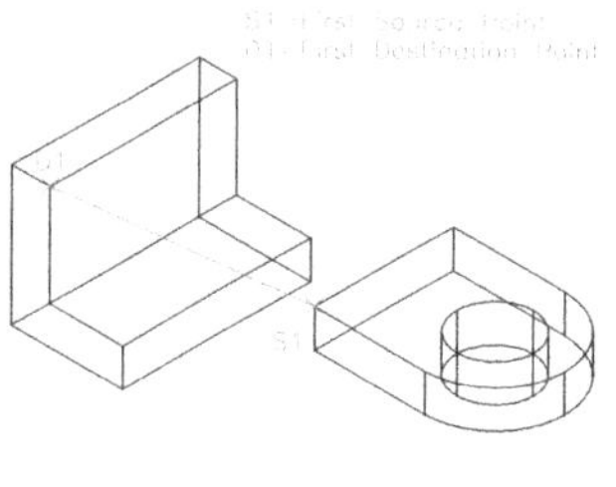

Figure 9-31 *Models before aligning*

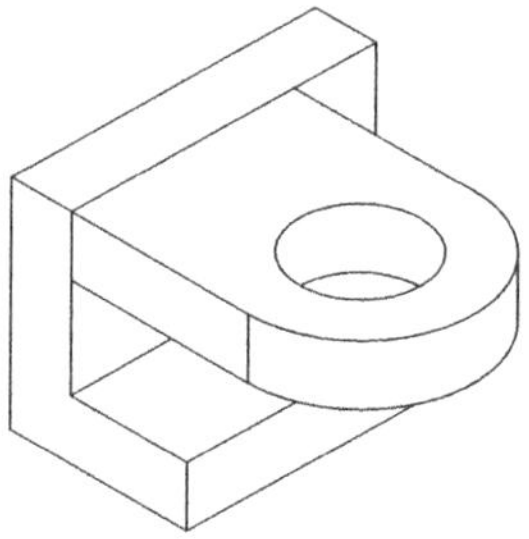

Figure 9-32 *Models after aligning*

Aligning the Objects Using Two Pairs of Points

The second case is to align the objects using two pairs of source and destination points. This method of aligning the objects forces the selected object to translate and rotate once. You are also provided with an option of scaling the source object to align with the destination object. The prompt sequence that follows is given next.

Select objects: *Select the object to align.*
Select objects: Enter.
Specify first source point: *Select S1, as shown in Figure 9-33.*
Specify first destination point: *Select D1, as shown in Figure 9-33.*
Specify second source point: *Select S2, as shown in Figure 9-33.*
Specify second destination point: *Select D2, as shown in Figure 9-33.*
Specify third source point or <continue>: Enter.
Scale objects based on alignment points? [Yes/No] <N>: **Y** *(You can also enter **N** at this prompt, if you do not want to scale the object).*

Figure 9-34 shows the objects after aligning and scaling.

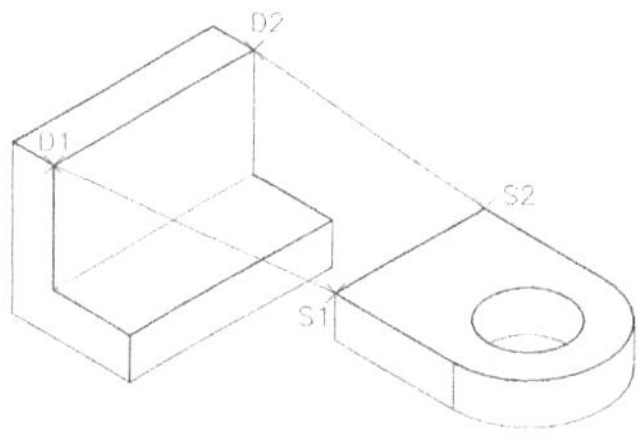

Figure 9-33 *Objects before aligning*

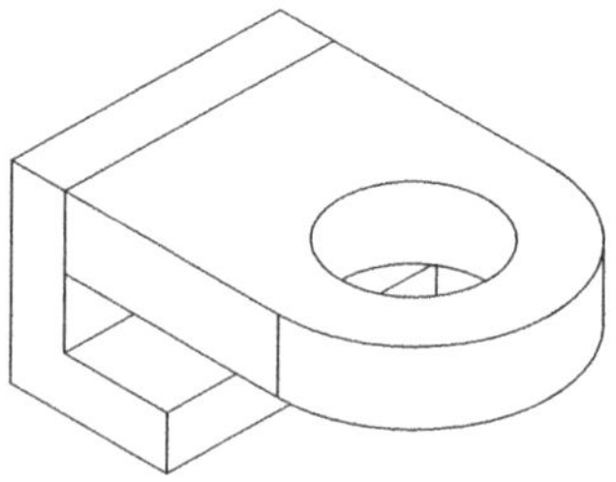

Figure 9-34 *Objects after aligning and scaling*

Aligning the Objects Using Three Pairs of Points

The third case is to align the objects using three pairs of points. This option forces the selected object to rotate and then translate, refer to Figures 9-35 and 9-36. The first pair of source and destination points is used to specify the base point of alignment, the second pair of source and destination points is used to specify the first rotation angle, and the third pair of source and destination points is used to specify the second rotation angle. In this case, you will not be allowed to scale the object. The prompt sequence that follows is given next.

Select objects: *Select the object to align.*
Select objects: Enter.
Specify first source point: *Select S1, as shown in Figure 9-35.*
Specify first destination point: *Select D1, as shown in Figure 9-35.*
Specify second source point: *Select S2, as shown in Figure 9-35.*
Specify second destination point: *Select D2, as shown in Figure 9-35.*
Specify third source point or <continue>: *Select S3, as shown in Figure 9-35.*
Specify third destination point: *Select D3, as shown in Figure 9-35.*

Figure 9-36 shows the objects after aligning and rotating.

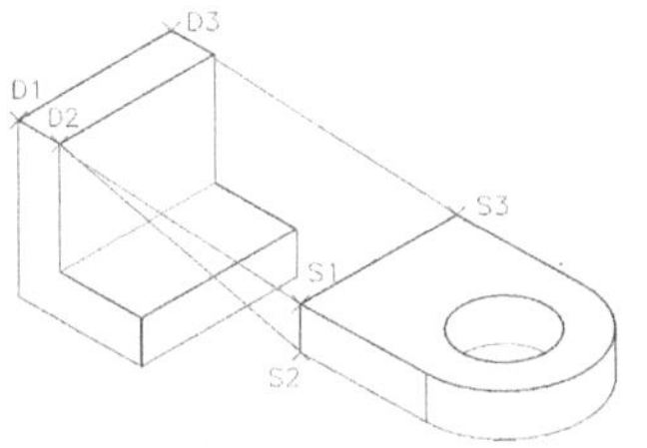

Figure 9-35 *Objects before aligning*

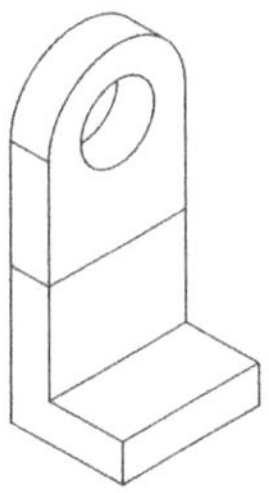

Figure 9-36 *Objects after aligning and rotating*

ALIGNING SOLIDS BY DEFINING AN ALIGNMENT PLANE

Ribbon: Home > Modify > 3D Align
Menu Bar: Modify > 3D Operations > 3D Align
Toolbar: Modeling > 3D Align
Command: 3DALIGN

The **3D Align** tool is used to align the selected solids or the copy of those solids with another solid object. To do so, define a plane for the source and destination objects that are to be aligned to each other. In this tool, you are prompted to specify the first, second, and third points continuously on the source to define a plane for the source. Then, you will be prompted to specify the first, second, and third points on the destination object to define a plane for the destination. As a result, these planes will be automatically aligned to each other. While specifying the points on the destination object, you get a dynamic preview for the placement of the source object. The following is the significance of each point that you specify on the source and destination objects.

First point on source. This is the base point on the source object that later coincides with the first point of the destination object.

Second point on source. This point defines the direction of the X axis on the new XY plane that will be created on the source object.

Third point on source. This point is specified on the new XY plane to define the direction of the Y axis. This completely defines the new XY plane of the source. After specifying this point, the source object is rotated to make this new XY plane parallel to the XY plane of the current UCS.

First point on destination. This is the base point of the destination. The base point of the source will coincide with this point.

Second point on destination. This point defines the direction of the X axis on the new XY plane of the destination object. The X axis of the source will get aligned to the X axis of the destination object.

Third point on destination. This point is specified on the new XY plane to define the direction of the Y axis. This completely defines the new XY plane of the destination.

The prompt sequence that will be followed when you choose the **3D Align** tool from the **Modeling** toolbar is given next.

Select objects: *Select the object to align.*
Select objects: Enter.
Specify source plane and orientation ...
Specify base point or [Copy]: *Select S1, as shown in Figure 9-37, or enter C to align the copy of the selected object and leave the original one as it is.*
Specify second point or [Continue] <C>: *Select S2, as shown in Figure 9-37.*
Specify third point or [Continue] <C>: *Select S3, as shown in Figure 9-37.*
Specify destination plane and orientation ...
Specify first destination point: *Select D1, as shown in Figure 9-37.*
Specify second destination point or [eXit] <X>: *Select D2, as shown in Figure 9-37.*
Specify third destination point or [eXit] <X>: *Select D3, as shown in Figure 9-37.*

Figure 9-38 shows the model after aligning.

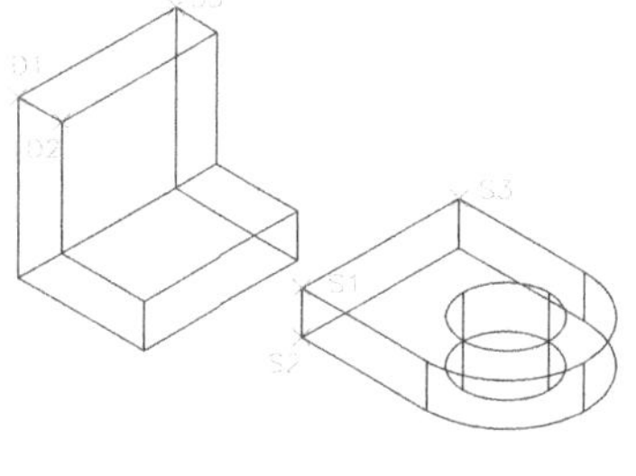

Figure 9-37 *Objects before aligning*

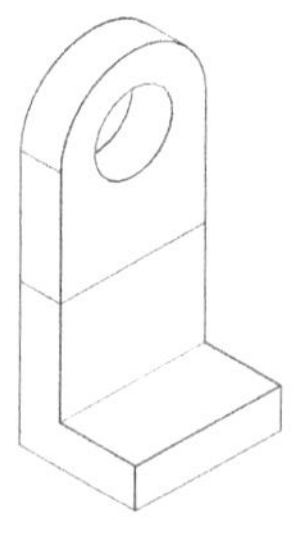

Figure 9-38 *Objects after aligning*

If you press the Enter key at the **Specify second point or [Continue] <C>** prompt, then AutoCAD assumes the X and Y axes of the new plane to be parallel and in same direction of the XY plane of the current UCS. Also, you will be prompted to select the first destination point.

If you press the Enter key at the **Specify second destination point or [eXit] <X>** prompt, then AutoCAD assumes the X and Y axes of the new plane for the destination to be parallel and in the same direction as the XY plane of the current UCS. Also, the XY plane of the source object will get aligned to this plane.

EXTRACTING EDGES OF A SOLID MODEL

Ribbon: Home > Solid Editing > Edge Editing drop-down > Extract Edges
Menu Bar: Modify > 3D Operations > Extract Edges **Command:** XEDGES

The **Extract Edges** tool is used to automatically generate the wireframe from a previously created solid model. The wireframe will be generated at the same location and with the same orientation where the parent model was located. The prompt sequence that will follow when you choose the **Extract Edges** tool from the **Solid Editing** panel is given next, refer to Figure 9-39 .

Select objects: *Select object from which you want to extract the edges.*
Select objects: *Select more objects or press* Enter.

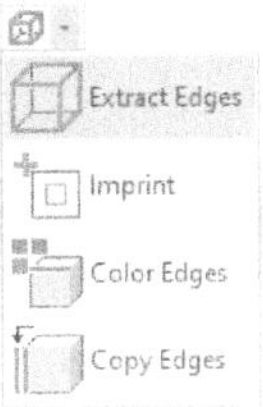

Figure 9-39 *The* ***Extract Edges*** *tool in the* ***Edge Editing*** *drop-down*

Figure 9-40 shows a model from which the edges are to be extracted and the wireframe extracted from that model after moving it to another location.

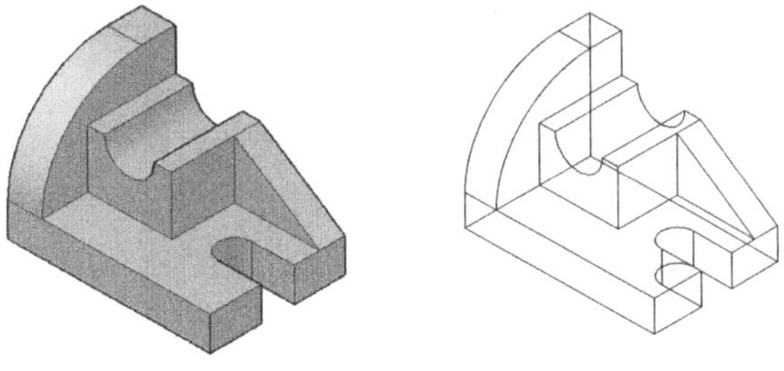

Figure 9-40 *Model and the resulting edges after extraction*

Note
The ***Extract Edges*** *tool can only be applied to regions, surfaces, and solids.*

Tip
To extract edges from a particular edge or face of the model, press and hold the Ctrl key during the selection of the objects.

CONVERTING OBJECTS TO SURFACES

Ribbon: Home > Solid Editing > Convert to Surface
Menu Bar: Modify > 3D Operations > Convert to Surface **Command:** CONVTOSURFACE

The **Convert to Surface** tool is used to convert objects into surfaces. The objects that can be converted to surfaces are arcs and lines with nonzero thickness, open zero width polyline having a nonzero thickness, 2D solids, donuts, boundary, regions, and 3D faces created on a plane.

To convert objects to surfaces, choose the **Convert to Surface** tool from the **Solid Editing** panel and then select the objects to be converted into a surface. Figure 9-41 shows a boundary to be converted into a surface and Figure 9-42 shows the resulting surface.

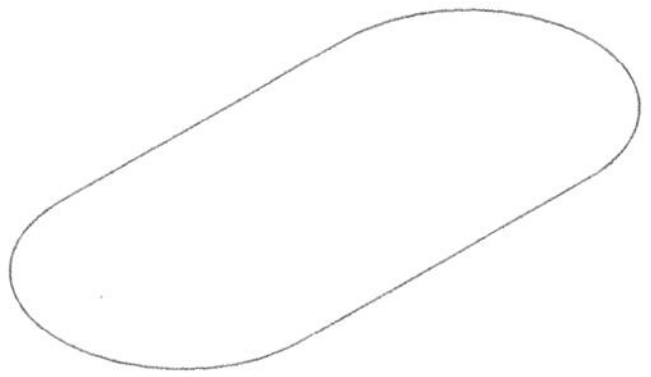

Figure 9-41 *The boundary to be converted into a surface*

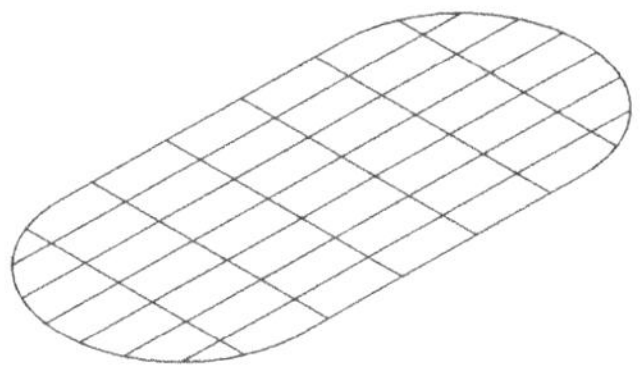

Figure 9-42 *The resulting surface*

Tip
*You can convert 3D solids with curved faces to surfaces by using the **Explode** tool. On invoking this tool, the curved faces of the solid will be converted into surfaces and the planar faces will be converted into regions.*

CONVERTING OBJECTS TO SOLIDS

Ribbon: Home > Solid Editing > Convert to Solid
Menu Bar: Modify > 3D Operations > Convert to Solid **Command:** CONVTOSOLID

The **Convert to Solid** tool is used to convert objects with some thickness into solid models. The solid generated by using this option will be similar to an extruded solid having height equal to the thickness of the object. The objects that can be converted into solids are open polylines with nonzero uniform width and thickness, closed polylines with thickness, and circles with thickness.

To convert objects into solids, choose the **Convert to Solid** tool from the **Solid Editing** panel and then select the objects to be converted into solids. Figure 9-43 shows a closed zero width polyline having a nonzero thickness and Figure 9-44 shows the resulting solid.

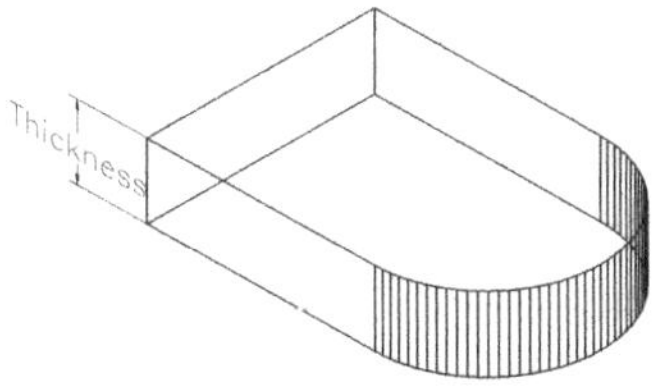

Figure 9-43 Polyline with thickness

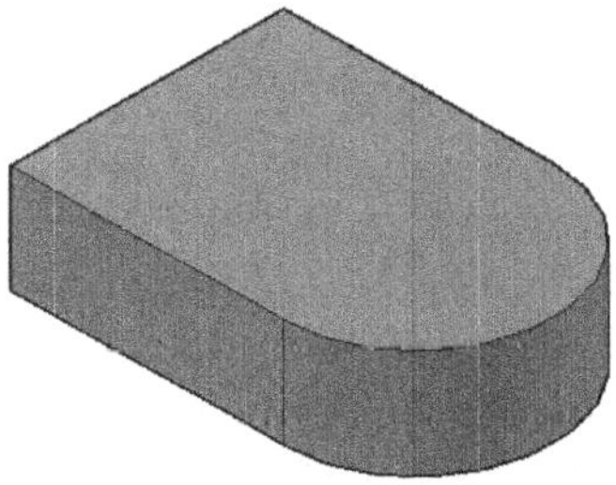

Figure 9-44 Resulting solid

CONVERTING SURFACES TO SOLIDS

Ribbon: Home > Solid Editing > Thicken
Menu Bar: Modify > 3D Operations > Thicken **Command:** THICKEN

The **Thicken** tool is used to convert any surface into a solid by adding material of a specified thickness to the surface. The material addition takes place in the direction normal to the surface. To convert surfaces into solids, choose the **Thicken** tool from the **Solid Editing** panel. Next, select the surface to thicken and then specify the thickness of the material to be added to the surface. Figure 9-45 shows the surface to be thickened and Figure 9-46 shows the resulting solid after thickening.

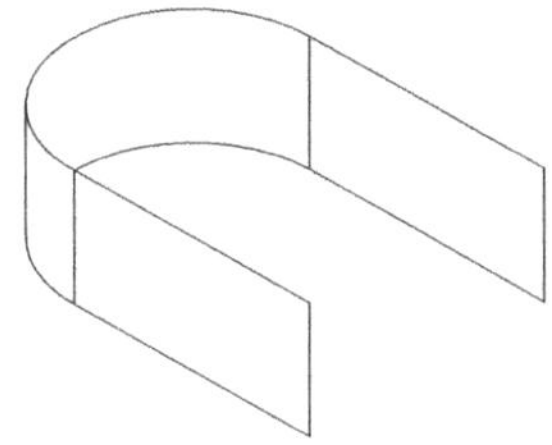

Figure 9-45 Surface to be thickened

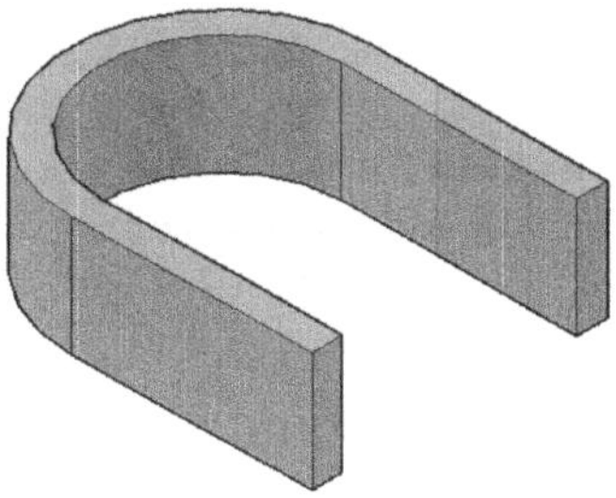

Figure 9-46 The solid after thickening

POINT CLOUD

The point cloud is a 3D scanned image consisting of a number of points having different x, y, and z coordinates. This image depicts the shape of the model. It is usually used as a guideline for drawing a model. After inserting point cloud in working environment, you can modify its properties like density, rotation, scale, color mapping, clipping boundaries, and so on. You can create or attach the point cloud file to the drawing file.

Attaching the Point Cloud

Ribbon: Insert > Reference > Attach **Command:** POINTCLOUDATTACH

To attach a point cloud to drawing, choose the **Attach** tool from the **Reference** panel of the **Insert** tab; the **Select Reference File** dialog box will be displayed. Now, browse to the location where the point cloud file is saved and then select it. Note that you can select the files having the *.rcp* and *.rcs* file formats only. After selecting the required file, choose the **Open** button; the **Attach Point Cloud** dialog box will be displayed, as shown in Figure 9-47. Some of the options available in the dialog box are discussed next.

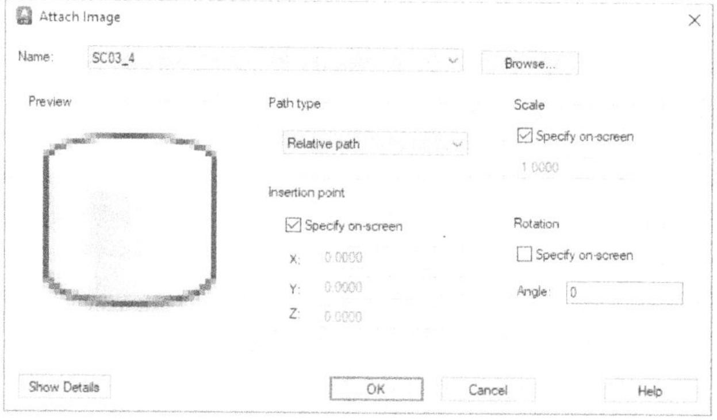

***Figure 9-47** The **Attach Image** dialog box*

Name

This edit box displays the name of the selected point cloud file. You can browse the file by choosing the **Browse** button located on the right of the **Name** drop-down list. On choosing the **Browse** button, the **Select Reference File** dialog box will be displayed. Now, you can select the required file.

Preview Area

This area is used to show the preview of the point cloud file that is to be attached in the drawing file.

Insertion Point

In this area, you can specify the position of the point cloud in the drawing area. You can specify the position by entering values in the **X**, **Y,** and **Z** edit boxes. If you select the **Specify on-screen** check box, you need to specify the insertion point on the screen.

Scale Area

In this area, you can specify the scaling value of the point cloud. If you select the **Specify on-screen** check box, you need to specify the scale in the drawing area.

Rotation Area

In this area, you can specify the rotation value of the point cloud.

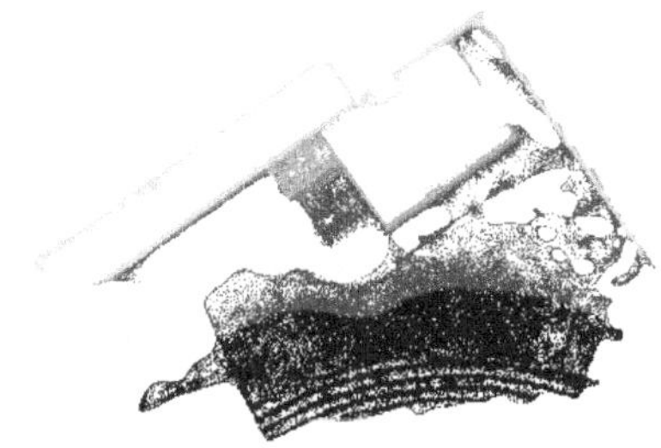

Figure 9-48 *The point cloud inserted*

After specifying all the parameters in the **Attach Image** dialog box, choose the **OK** button; you will be prompted to specify the insertion point. Specify the insertion point; the point cloud will be inserted, refer to Figure 9-48.

You can also change the properties of point cloud such as density and clipping boundary by selecting the suitable options from the **Point Cloud** contextual tab, which is displayed after selecting the point cloud in the drawing area, as shown in Figure 9-49.

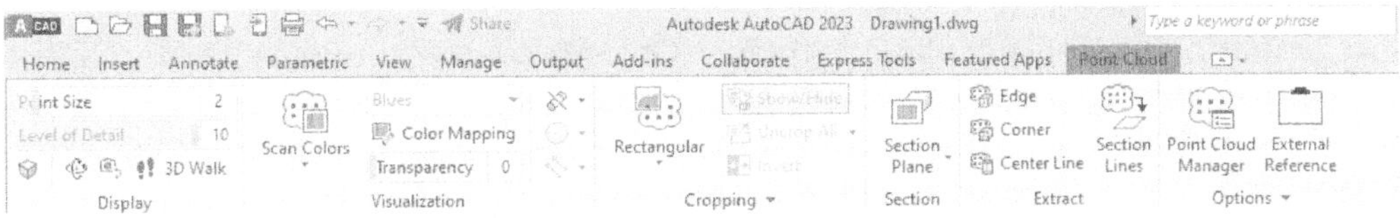

Figure 9-49 *The* ***Point Cloud*** *contextual tab*

In AutoCAD, you can change the color style of the point cloud by using the options in the **Visualization** panel. In this panel, the **Scan Colors** option is used to assign the original colors of the scanned file to the point cloud. The **Object Color** option is used to assign the current object color to the point cloud. The **Normal** option is used to assign the colors based on the normal direction of the points in a point cloud. The **Intensity** option is used to assign colors based on the intensity of the point cloud. Moreover, there are additional options available in the **Cropping** panel to specify the clipping boundary of the point cloud. You can specify the rectangular, polygonal, or circular boundary using the **Rectangular**, **Polygonal**, and **Circular** tools available in the **Crop** drop-down of the **Cropping** panel to specify the clipping boundary.

Figures 9-50 and 9-51 show the point cloud after decreasing the density and changing the clipping boundary, respectively.

Figure 9-50 *The point cloud after decreasing density*

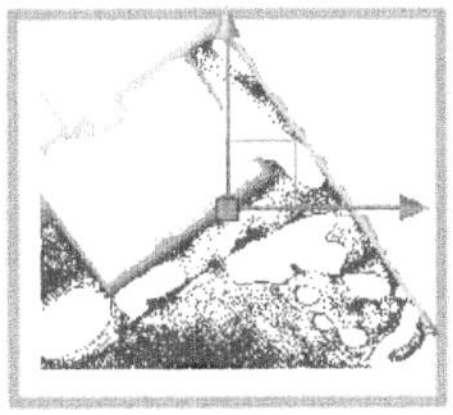

Figure 9-51 *The point cloud after clipping the boundary*

SLICING SOLID MODELS

Ribbon: Home > Solid Editing > Slice
Menu Bar: Modify > 3D Operations > Slice **Command:** SLICE

As the name suggests, the **Slice** tool is used to slice the selected solid with the help of a specified plane. You will be given an option to select the portion of the sliced solid that has to be retained. You can also retain both the portions of the sliced solids.

The prompt sequence that follows is given next.

Select objects to slice: *Select the object to slice.*
Select objects to slice: Enter.
Specify start point of slicing plane or [planar Object/Surface/Zaxis/View/XY/YZ/ZX/3points] <3points>: *Specify a point on the slicing plane or select an option.*

3points

This option is used to slice a solid by using a plane defined by three points, refer to Figures 9-52 and 9-53. The prompt sequence that follows is given next.

Select objects to slice: *Select the object to be sliced.*
Select objects to slice: Enter.
Specify start point of slicing plane or [planar Object/Surface/Zaxis/View/XY/YZ/ZX/3points] <3points>: Enter.
Specify first point on plane: *Specify the point P1 on the slicing plane, as shown in Figure 9-52.*
Specify second point on plane: *Specify the point P2 on the slicing plane, as shown in Figure 9-52.*
Specify third point on plane: *Specify the point P3 on the slicing plane, as shown in Figure 9-52.*
Specify a point on desired side or [keep Both sides] <Both>: *Select the portion of the solid to retain or enter B to retain both the portions of the sliced solid.*

The model after slicing is shown in Figure 9-53.

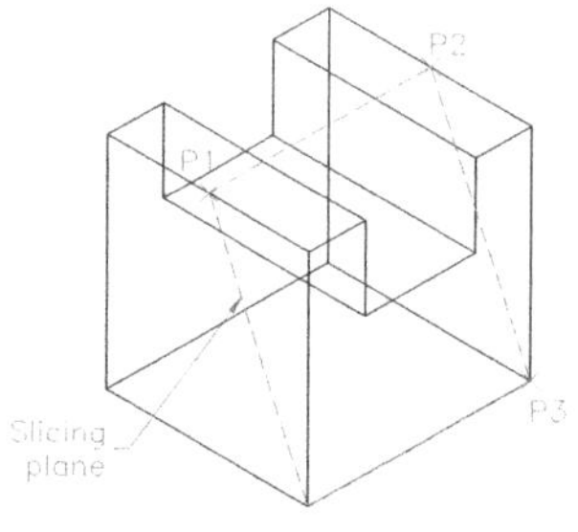

Figure 9-52 *Defining the slicing plane*

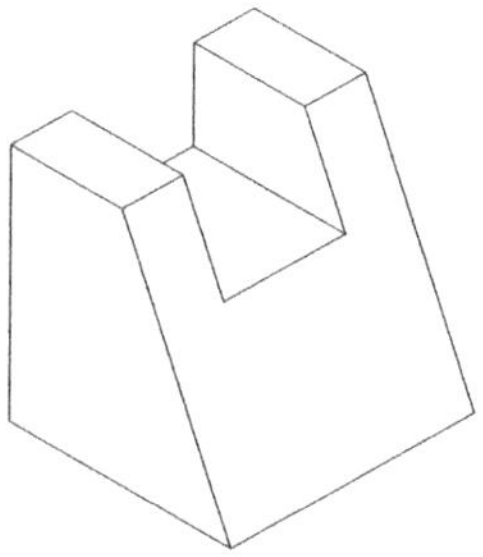

Figure 9-53 *Model after slicing*

planar Object

This option is used to slice the solid model using an object. The objects that can be used to slice the solid model include arcs, circles, ellipses, 2D polylines, and splines. The prompt sequence that will follow is given next.

Select objects to slice: *Select the object to slice.*
Select objects to slice: Enter.
Specify start point of slicing plane or [planar Object/ Surface/Zaxis/View/XY/YZ/ZX/3points] <3points>: **O**
Select a circle, ellipse, arc, 2D-spline, 2D-polyline to define the slicing plane: *Select the object to slice the solid.*
Specify a point on desired side or [keep Both sides]: *Specify the portion of the solid to retain.*

Surface

This option is used to slice the solid model using a surface. Note that the ruled, tabulated, revolved, or edge surfaces cannot be used for slicing the solids. Figure 9-54 shows the object to be sliced and the slicing surface and Figure 9-55 shows the model after slicing. The prompt sequence that will follow is given next.

Select objects to slice: *Select the object to slice.*
Select objects to slice: Enter.
Specify start point of slicing plane or [planar Object/Surface/Zaxis/View/XY/YZ/ZX/3points] <3points>: **S**
Select a surface: *Select the surface to slice the solid.*
Select sliced object to keep or [keep Both sides] <Both>: *Specify the portion of the solid to retain.*

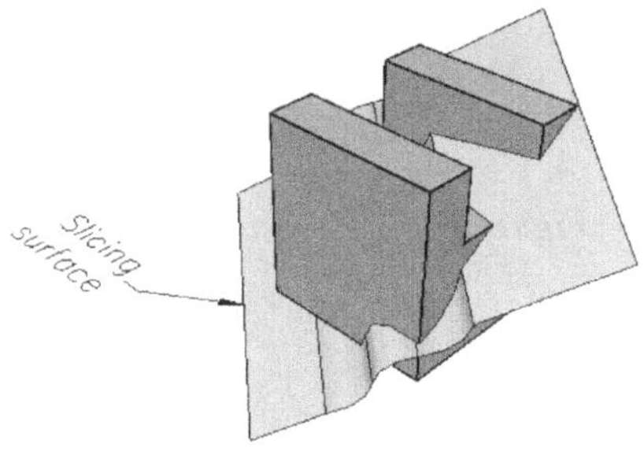

Figure 9-54 *Model with slicing surface*

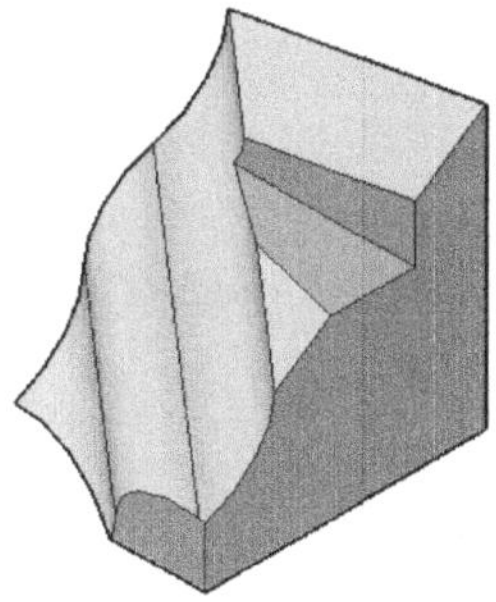

Figure 9-55 *Model after slicing*

Zaxis

This option is used to slice the solid using a plane defined by two points. The first point is the point on the section plane and the second point is the point in the direction of the Z axis of the plane. The prompt sequence that follows is given next.

Select objects to slice: *Select the object to slice.*
Select objects to slice: Enter.
Specify start point of slicing plane or [planar Object/Surface/Zaxis/View/XY/YZ/

ZX/3points] <3points>: **Z**
Specify a point on the section plane: *Specify the point on the section plane.*
Specify a point on the Z-axis (normal) of the plane: *Specify the point in the direction of the Z axis of the section plane.*
Specify a point on desired side or [keep Both sides] <Both>: *Select the portion to retain.*

View

This option is used to slice the selected solid about the viewing plane, refer to Figures 9-56 and 9-57. The viewing plane in this case will be the screen of the monitor. On selecting this option, you will be prompted to specify a point on the solid model through which the viewing plane will pass. The prompt sequence that will follow is given next.

Select objects to slice: *Select the object to slice.*
Select objects to slice: Enter.
Specify start point of slicing plane or [planar Object/Surface/Zaxis/View/XY/YZ/ZX/3points] <3points>: **V**
Specify a point on the current view plane <0,0,0>: *Specify the point P1, as shown in Figure 9-56.*
Specify a point on the desired side or [keep Both sides] <Both>: *Specify the portion of the solid to retain.*

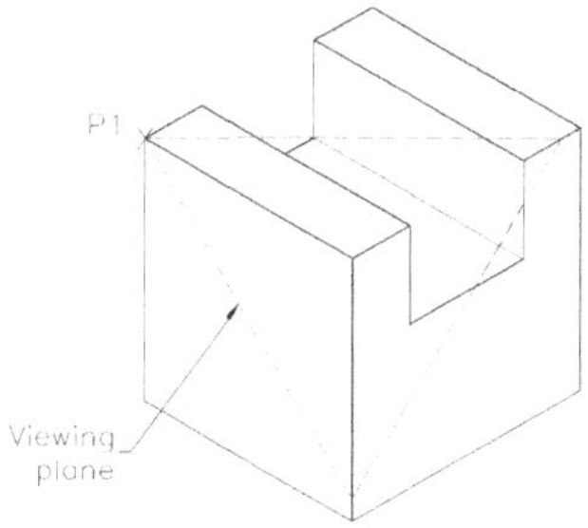

Figure 9-56 *Defining the slicing plane*

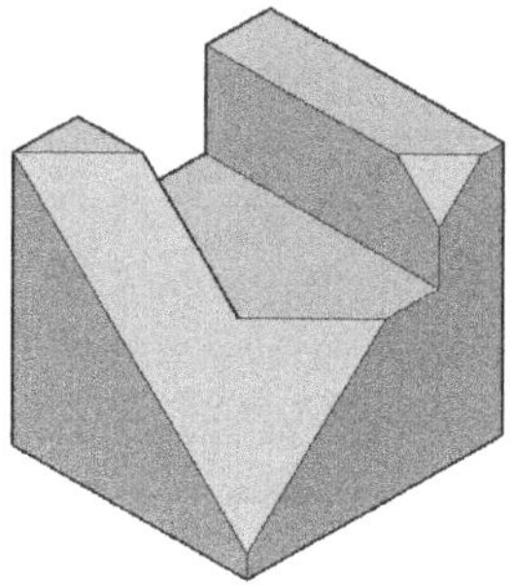

Figure 9-57 *Model after slicing*

XY/YZ/ZX

These options are used to slice the selected solid about the XY, YZ, or the ZX plane respectively. When you invoke this option, you will be prompted to select the point on the plane. The prompt sequence that will follow is given next.

Select objects to slice: *Select the object to slice.*
Select objects to slice: Enter.
Specify start point of slicing plane or [planar Object/ Surface/Zaxis/View/XY/YZ/ZX/3points] <3points>: *Select the XY, YZ, or the ZX plane.*
Specify a point on the XY-plane <0,0,0>: *Specify the point on the slicing plane.*
Specify a point on desired side or [keep Both sides] <Both>: *Specify the portion to retain.*

CREATING THE CROSS-SECTIONS OF SOLIDS

Command: SEC(SECTION)

The **SECTION** command works similar to the **Slice** tool. The only difference between these two is that this command does not chop the solid. Instead, it creates a cross-section along the selected section plane. The cross-section thus created is a region. You need to move the region created to view the cross section. If needed, you can hatch the region. Note that the regions are created in the current layer and not in the layer in which the sectioned solid is stored. The prompt sequence that follows when you enter the **SECTION** command is given next.

Select objects: *Select the object to section.*
Select objects: Enter.
Specify first point on section plane by [Object/Zaxis/View/XY/YZ/ZX/3points] <3points>:

3points

This option is used to define the section plane using three points.

Object

This option is used to specify the section plane using a planar object. The objects that can be used to create the sections are arcs, circles, ellipses, splines, or 2D polylines.

View

This option uses the current viewing plane to define the section plane. You will be prompted to specify the point on the current view plane. It will then automatically create a cross-section parallel to the current viewing plane and passing through the specified point.

XY/YZ/ZX

These options are used to define the section planes that are parallel to the XY, YZ, or the ZX planes, respectively. On invoking this option, you will be prompted to specify the points through which the selected plane will pass. Figure 9-58 displays the YZ plane which is being used to create the cross-section and Figure 9-59 displays the created section along the YZ plane, which is first isolated and then hatched for clarity purposes.

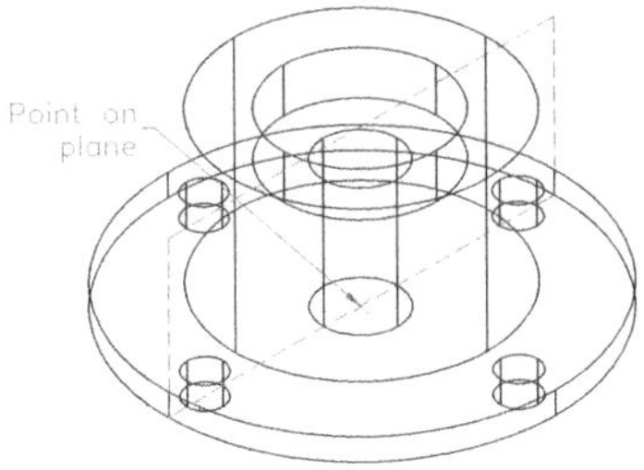

Figure 9-58 *Creating the cross-section along the YZ plane*

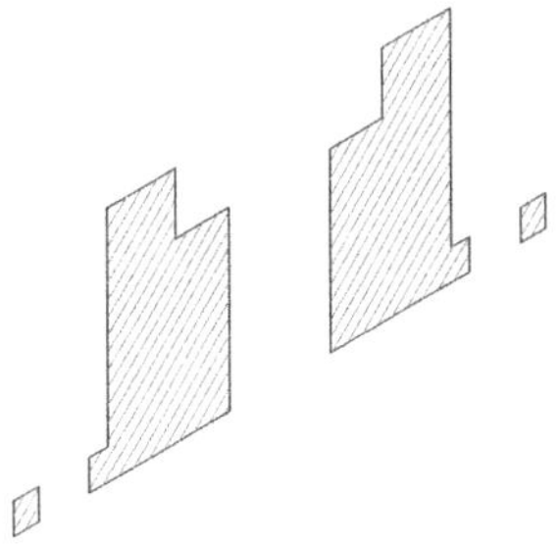

Figure 9-59 *Cross-section created, isolated, and hatched for clarity*

Tip

1. The number of regions created as cross-sections will be equal to the number of solids selected to create the cross-section.

2. You can also hatch the cross-section created using the ***SECTION*** *command. To do so, you need to select the entire region as the object for hatching. You may also have to define a new UCS based on the section to hatch it.*

Example 2

In this example, you will draw the solid model shown in Figure 9-60. The dimensions of the model are shown in Figure 9-61. After creating it, slice it as shown in Figure 9-62.

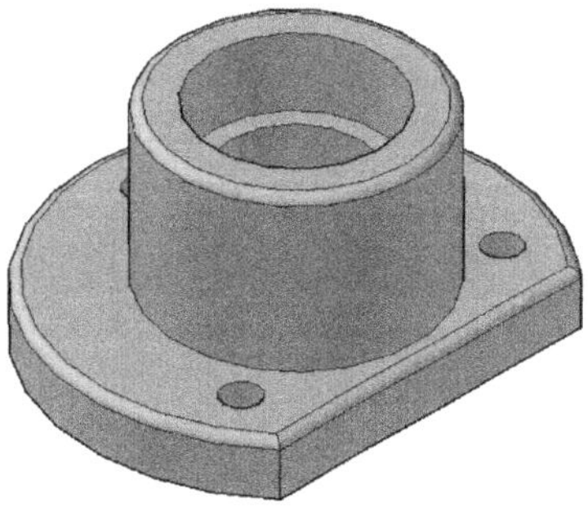

Figure 9-60 *Model for Example 2*

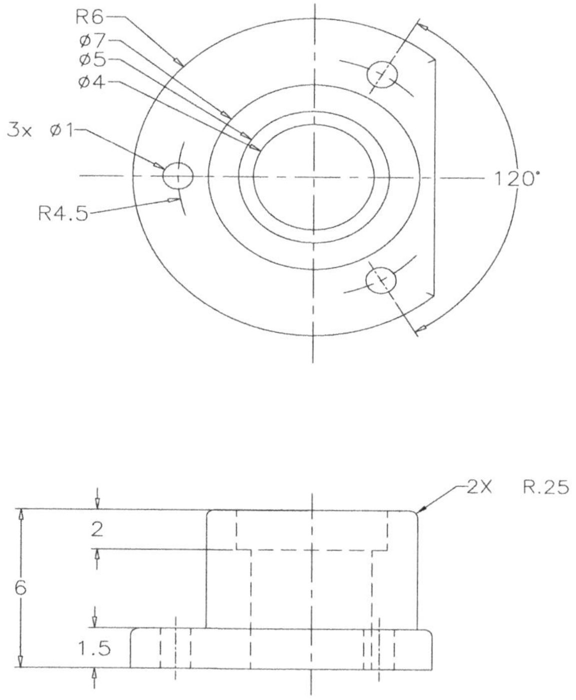

Figure 9-61 *Orthographic views of the solid model*

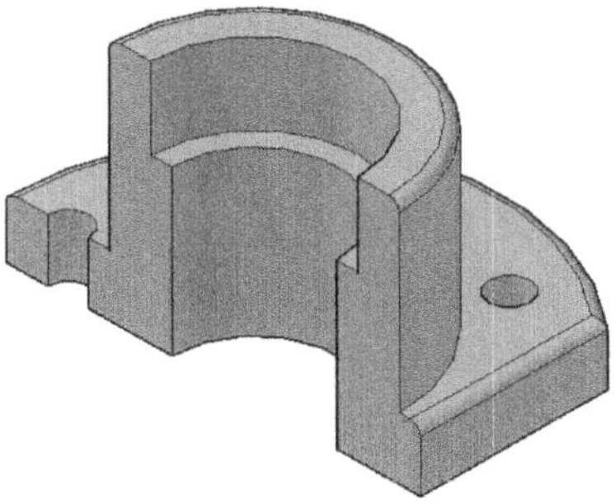

Figure 9-62 *The sliced solid*

1. Start a new 3D template drawing file and then draw the sketch for the base of the model in the Top view, as shown in Figure 9-63. Choose the **Region** tool from the **Draw** panel in the **Home** tab and convert the sketch to a region.

2. Choose the **Extrude** tool from **Home > Modeling > Solid Creation** drop-down and extrude the region to a distance of 1.5.

3. Set the view to **SW Isometric** by using the ViewCube. The model will look similar to the model shown in Figure 9-64.

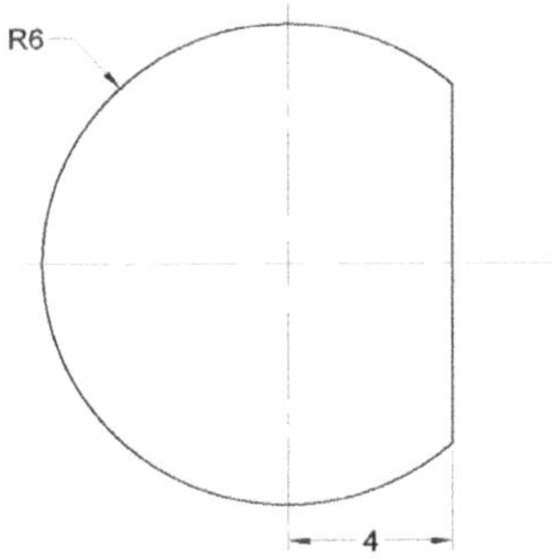

Figure 9-63 *Sketch for the base of the model*

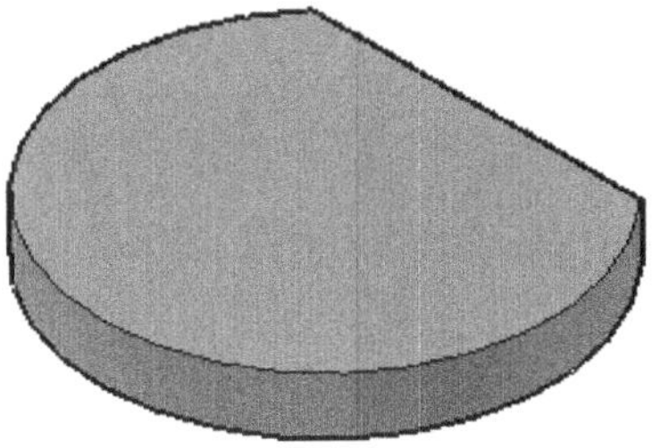

Figure 9-64 *Base of the model*

4. Set the view to **Front** and set the **UCS** aligned to this view. Draw the sketch for the next feature anywhere in the drawing area and convert it into a region, refer to Figure 9-65.

5. Choose the **Revolve** tool from **Home > Modeling > Solid Creation** drop-down and then revolve the sketch to an angle of 360 degrees.

6. Right-click on the **3D Object Snap** button in the Status Bar and select the **Center of face** option. Also, clear the other snap options.

7. Ensure that the **3D Object Snap** is on and **Object Snap** is off. Move the revolved feature by snapping the center point of the lower face and place it at the center of the upper face of the base of the model.

8. Choose the **Solid, Union** tool from the **Solid Editing** panel in the **Home** tab and then unite both the objects, refer to Figure 9-66.

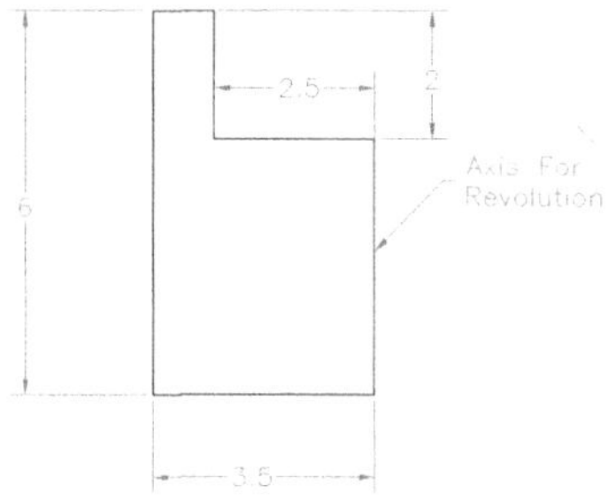

Figure 9-65 *Sketch for the nex feature*

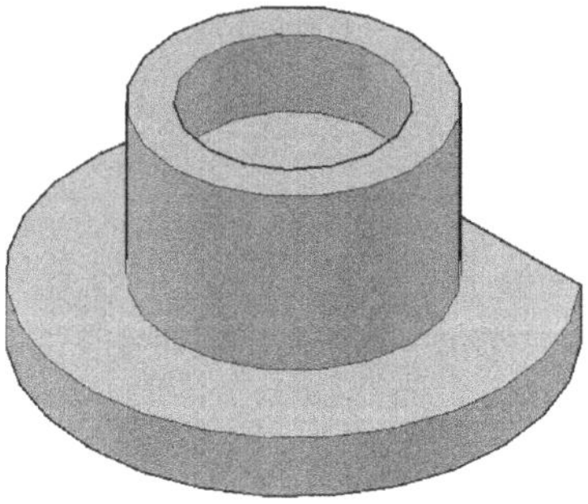

Figure 9-66 *Model after union*

9. Create a new cylinder of diameter 1 unit of the same height as that of the base.

10. Draw a circle of radius 4.5 units on the top face of the base.

11. Move the cylinder by snapping the center of the top face and place it on the quadrant point along the X-axis of the circle.

12. Choose **Modify > 3D Operations > 3D Array** from the Menu bar. The prompt sequence that follows is given next:

Initializing... 3DARRAY loaded.
Select objects: *Select the cylinder.*
Select objects: Enter.
Enter the type of array [Rectangular/Polar] <R>: **P**
Enter the number of items in the array: **3**
Specify the angle to fill (+=ccw, -=cw) <360>: Enter.
Rotate arrayed objects? [Yes/No] <Y>: Enter.
Specify center point of array: *Select the center of the base of the model.*
Specify second point on axis of rotation: *Select the center of the top face of the model.*

13. Subtract all three cylinders from the model by choosing the **Solid, Subtract** tool from the **Solid Editing** panel.

14. Create a cylinder of diameter 4 units and height 6 units and subtract it from the model to create the central hole.

15. Choose the **Fillet Edge** tool from **Solid > Solid Editing > Fillet Edge** drop-down; you are prompted to select the edges to be filleted.

16. Select the edges to fillet and press Enter; you are prompted to enter the radius. Specify the fillet radius as 0.25 units. The model after making the changes will look similar to the model shown in Figure 9-67, when you set the view to **SE Isometric** by using the ViewCube.

17. Relocate the UCS at the WCS.

18. Choose the **Slice** tool from the **Solid Editing** panel to cut the solid model to half. The prompt sequence is as follows:

    Select objects to slice: *Select the model.*
    Select objects to slice: [Enter].
    Specify start point of slicing plane or [planar Object/Surface/Zaxis/View/XY/YZ/ZX/3points] <3points>: **ZX**
    Specify a point on the ZX-plane <0,0,0>: *Select the center of the top face of the model.*
    Specify a point on desired side or [keep Both sides]: *Specify a point on the back side of the model to retain it.*

The final model for Example 2 will look similar to the model shown in Figure 9-68.

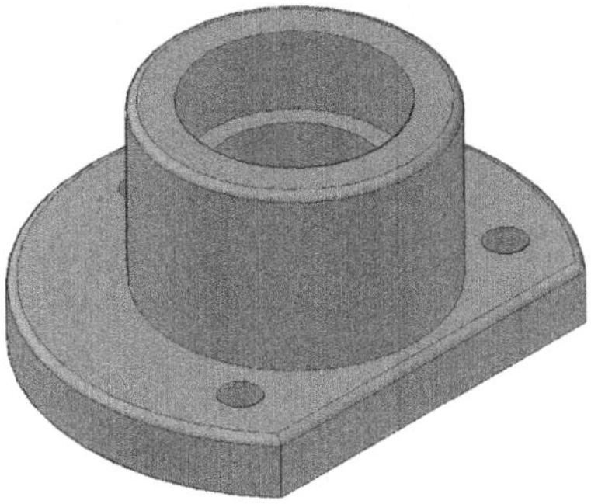

Figure 9-67 *Model after creating the fillet*

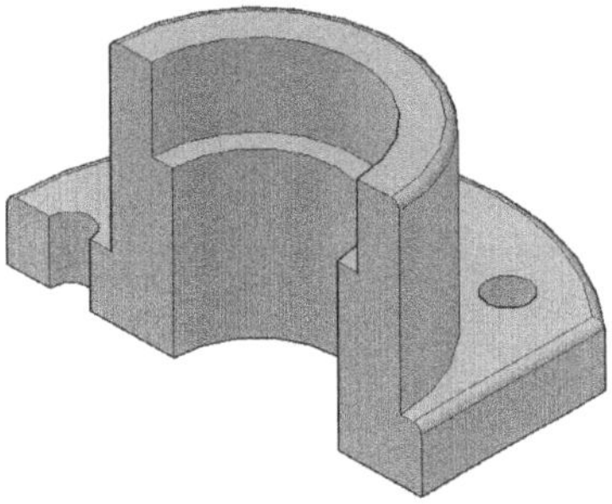

Figure 9-68 *Final model after slicing*

Self-Evaluation Test

Answer the following questions and then compare them to those given at the end of this chapter:

1. The __________ rule is used to determine the direction of rotation of the solid model in 3D space.

2. The __________ tool is used to extract edges from a solid model.

3. The __________ tool is used to move, rotate, and scale the solid model in a single attempt.

4. The **SECTION** command is used to create a __________ along the plane of a section.

5. The __________ tool is used to align solids by defining an alignment plane.

6. A model can be dynamically moved using the **3D Move** tool. (T/F)

7. The edges of a solid model can be filleted using the **3D Fillet** tool. (T/F)

8. You can select an ellipse as an object to rotate the solid model using the **Rotate 3D** tool. (T/F)

9. The **Convert to Surface** tool can be used to convert an open zero-width polyline having a nonzero thickness into a surface. (T/F)

10. The **SECTION** command is used to create a cross-section and also slice a model. (T/F)

Review Questions

Answer the following questions:

1. Which of the following options of the **ROTATE3D** command is used to select a 2D entity as an object for rotating the solid models?

   (a) **2D** (b) **Last**
   (c) **Object** (d) **Entity**

2. Which of the following commands is used to convert a surface to a solid?

   (a) **CONVTOSOLID** (b) **CONVQUILT**
   (c) **CONVTOSURFACE** (d) **THICKEN**

3. Which of the following objects can be converted into a solid using the **Convert to Solid** tool?

   (a) Rectangle (b) Circle
   (c) Ellipse (d) None of these

4. Which of the following options of the **3D Mirror** tool is used to mirror the object about the view plane?

   (a) **Object** (b) **Last**
   (c) **View** (d) **Zaxis**

5. What is the least number of points that you have to define on the source object to align it using the **3D Align** tool?

   (a) One (b) Two
   (c) Three (d) Four

6. The __________ command gives a dynamic preview while aligning the solid model.

7. The __________ option of the **3D Rotate** tool is used to select the same axis that was last selected to rotate the solid model.

8. While creating a 3D array using the **3D Array** tool, the levels are arranged along the __________ axis.

9. The object having some __________ can be converted into a solid using the **Convert to Solid** tool.

10. The __________ option is used to slice a model by using a sketched entity.

11. A surface can be used to slice a model using the **Slice** tool. (T/F)

12. The **Convert to Solid** tool is used to convert objects with a zero thickness into a solid. (T/F)

13. You can also extract an individual edge of a solid model using the **Extract Edges** tool. (T/F)

14. You can select all tangential edges of the selected solid model for filleting using the **Chain** option of the **Fillet Edges** tool. (T/F)

15. Regions can be converted to surfaces by using the **Convert to Surface** tool. (T/F)

Exercise 1

In this exercise, you will create a solid model shown in Figure 9-69. The dimensions of the model are shown in Figures 9-70. After creating it, slice it to get the model shown in Figure 9-71.

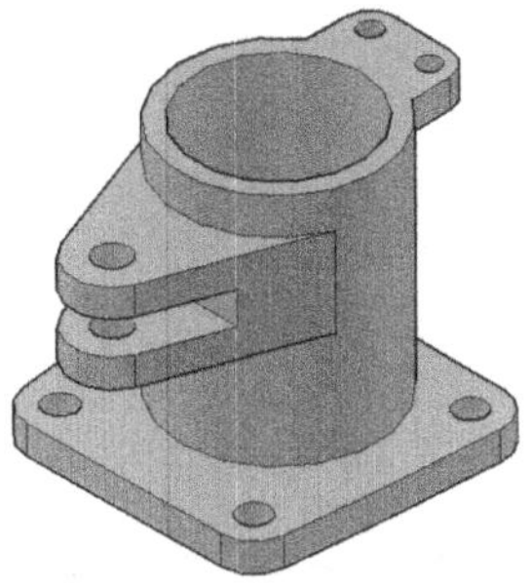

Figure 9-69 Model for Exercise 1

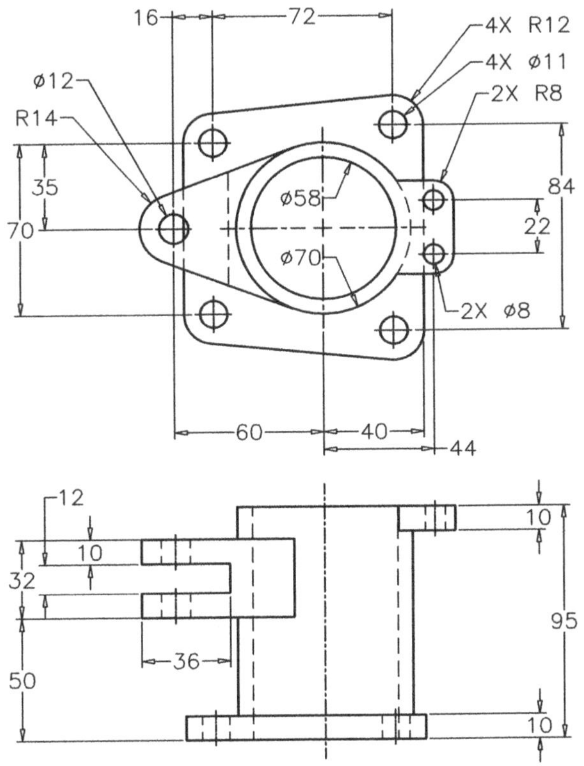

Figure 9-70 Orthographic views of the model

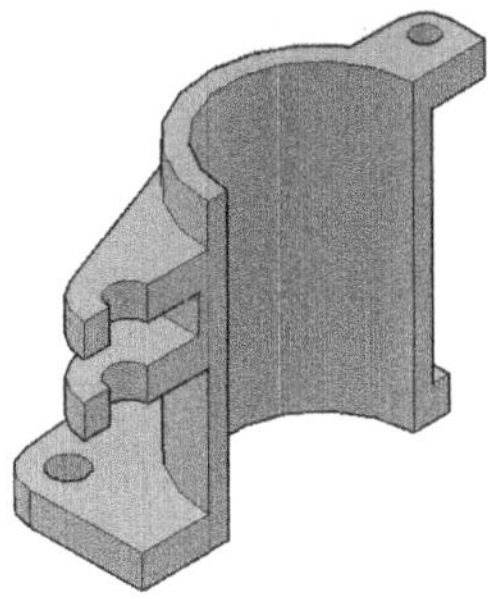

Figure 9-71 Model after slicing

Exercise 2

In this exercise, you will create the solid model shown in Figure 9-72. The dimensions of the model are given in the drawing shown in the same figure.

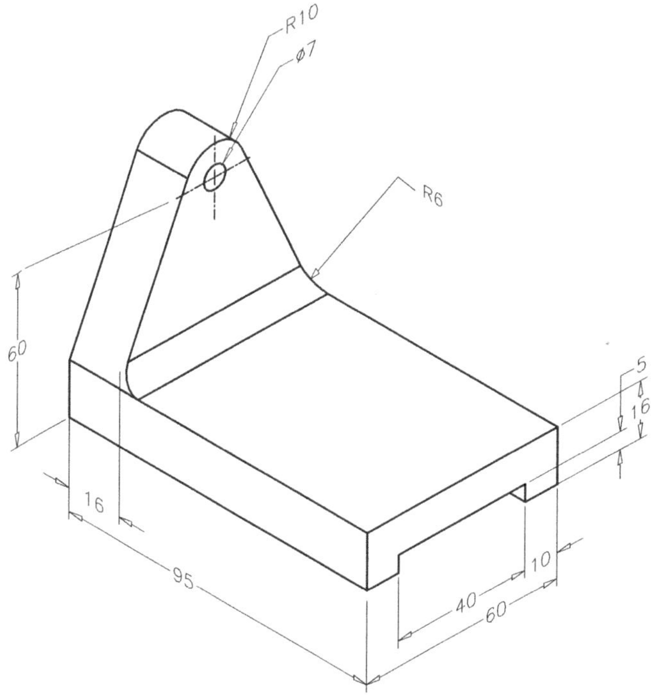

Figure 9-72 *Solid model for Exercise 2*

Exercise 3

In this exercise, you will create the solid model shown in Figure 9-73. The dimensions for the model are given in the same figure. The fillet radius is 0.13 units.

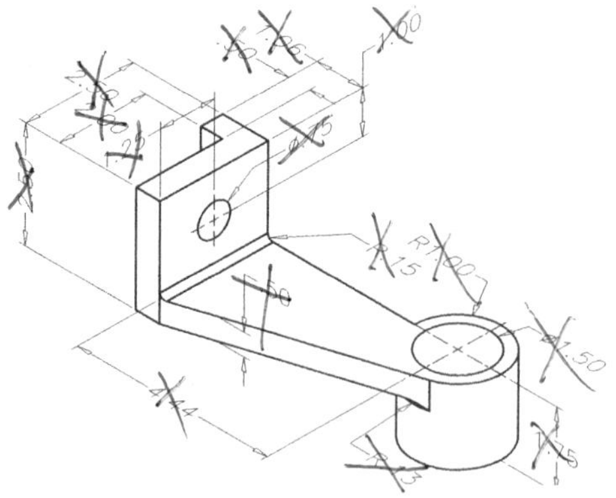

Figure 9-73 *Solid model for Exercise 3*

Exercise 4

In this exercise, you will create the solid model shown in Figure 9-74. The dimensions for the model are given in the same figure. Assume the missing dimensions.

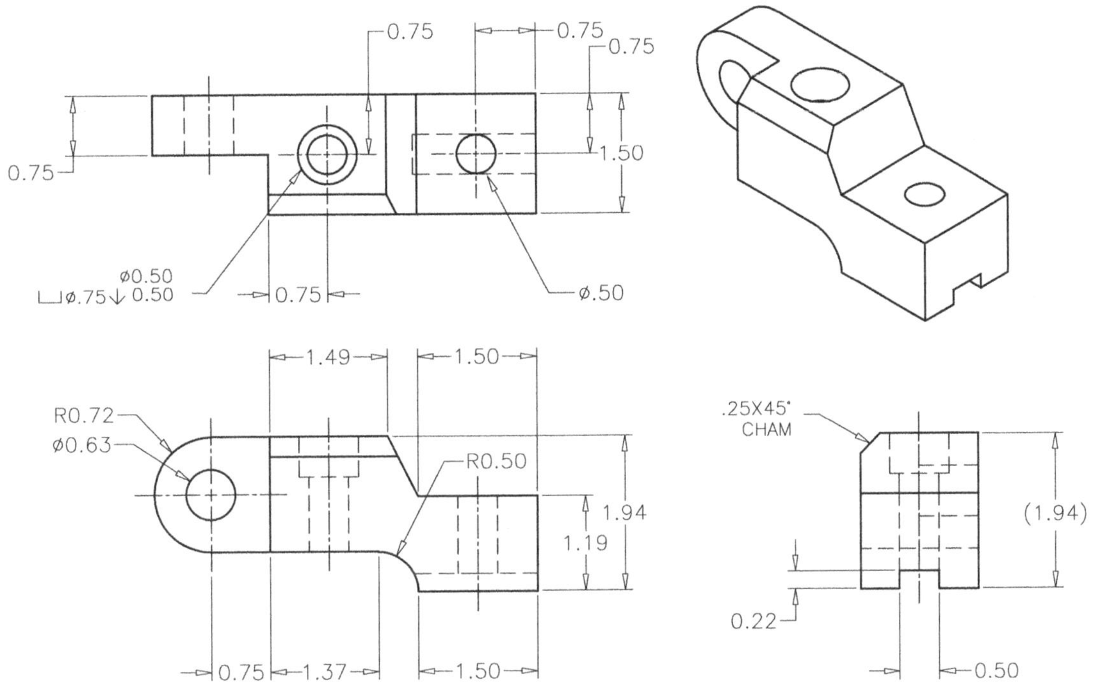

Figure 9-74 *Solid model and its orthographic views*

Problem-Solving Exercise 1

Create the model shown in Figure 9-75. The dimensions of the model are given in same figure.

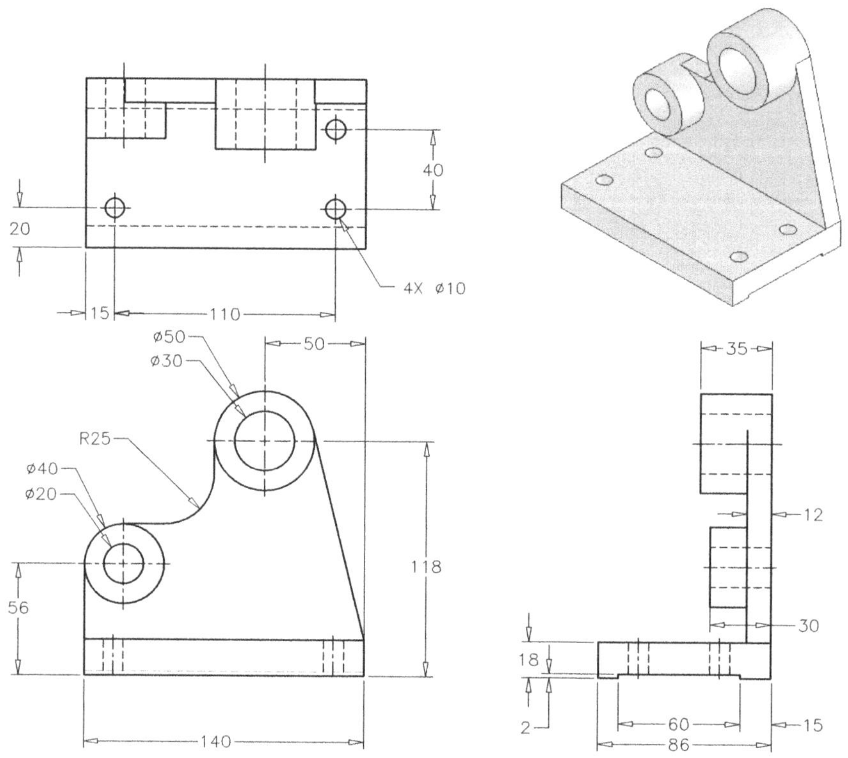

Figure 9-75 *Solid model for Problem-Solving Exercise 1*

Problem-Solving Exercise 2

Create the model shown in Figure 9-76. The dimensions of the model are given in Figure 9-77.

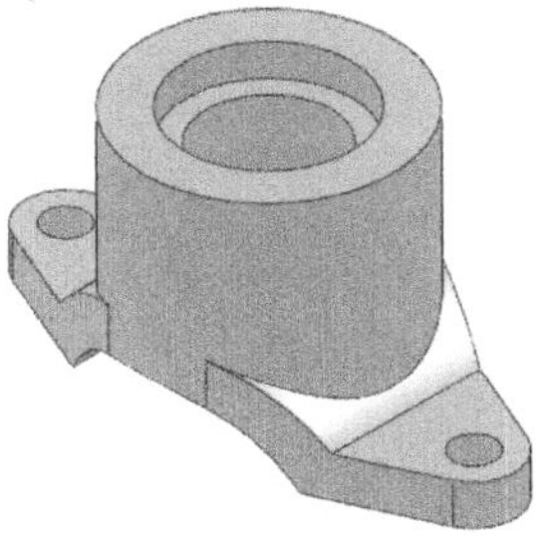

Figure 9-76 Solid model for Problem-Solving Exercise 2

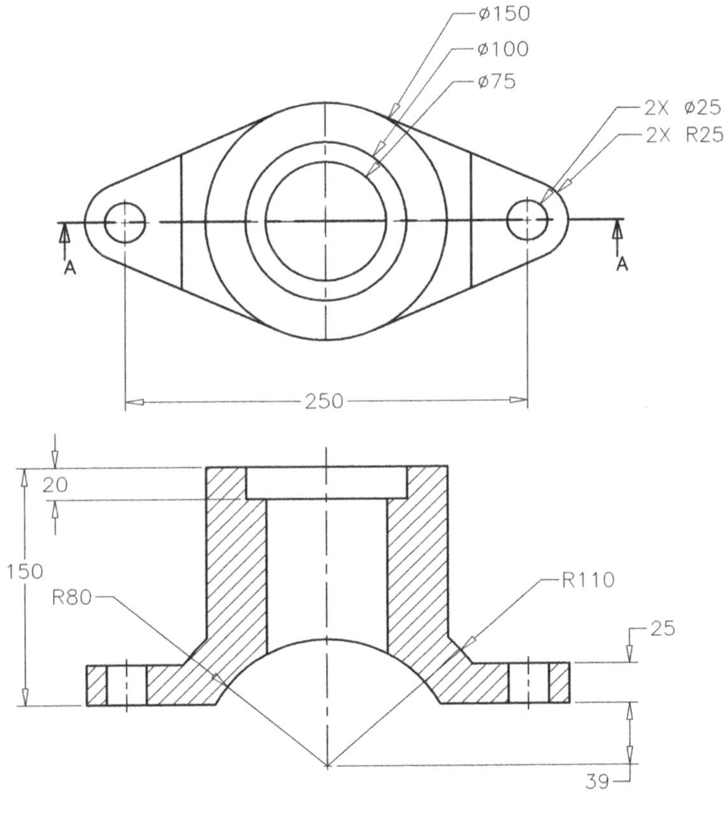

Figure 9-77 Dimensions for the solid model

Problem-Solving Exercise 3

Create the model shown in Figure 9-78. The sectioned view and dimensions of the model are given in Figure 9-79.

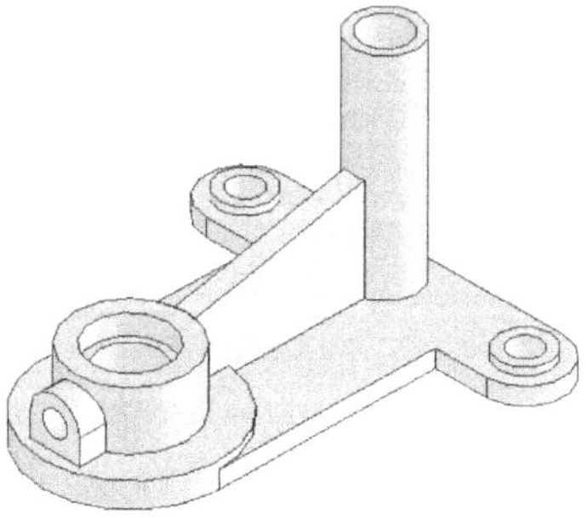

Figure 9-78 Solid model for Problem-Solving Exercise 3

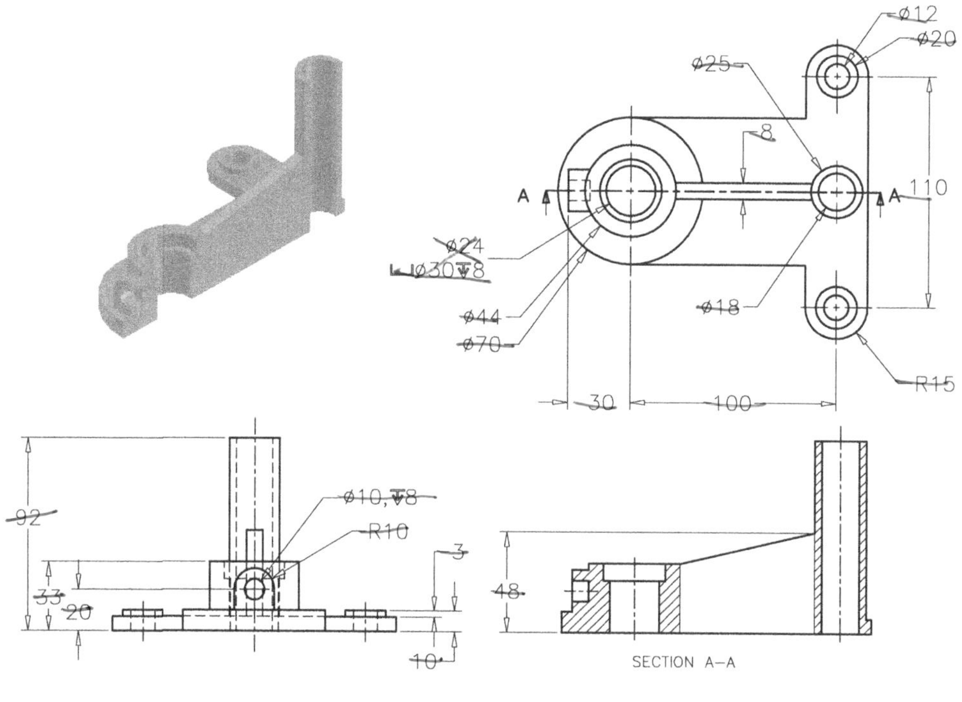

Figure 9-79 Sectioned view and dimensions for the solid model

Problem-Solving Exercise 4

Create the model shown in Figure 9-80. The sectioned view and dimensions of the model are given in Figure 9-81.

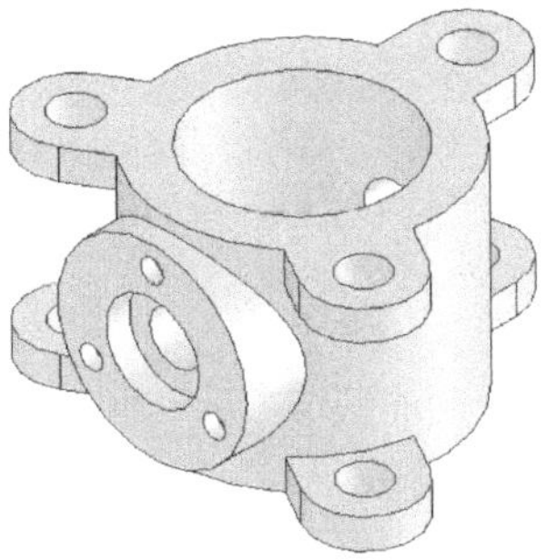

Figure 9-80 Solid model for Problem-Solving Exercise 4

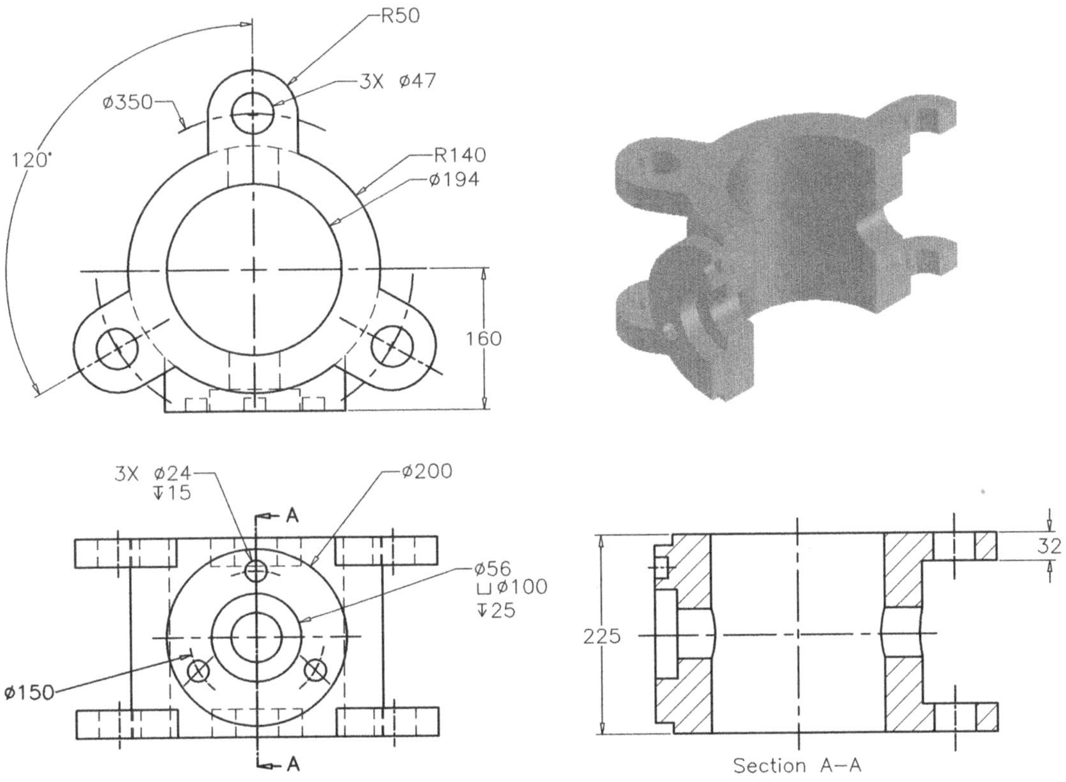

Figure 9-81 Sectioned view and dimensions of the solid model

Answers to Self-Evaluation Test

1. right-hand thumb, **2. Extract Edges**, **3. Align**, **4.** Cross-section, **5. 3D Align**, **6.** T, **7.** F, **8.** F, **9.** T, **10.** F

Chapter 10

Editing 3D Objects-II

Learning Objectives

After completing this chapter, you will be able to:

- *Edit solid models using the SOLIDEDIT command*
- *Generate sections of a model*
- *Modify a composite solid using the Solid History tool*
- *Generate drawing views of a solid model using the SOLVIEW command*
- *Generate profiles and sections in drawing views using the SOLDRAW command*
- *Create the profile images of a solid model using the SOLPROF command*
- *Calculate the mass properties of the solid models using the MASSPROP command*
- *Use the Action Recorder*
- *Use the ShowMotion tool for presentation*
- *Generate drawing views*

Key Terms

- *Extrude Faces*
- *Taper Faces*
- *Move Faces*
- *Copy Faces*
- *Offset Faces*
- *Delete Faces*
- *Rotate Faces*
- *Color Faces*
- *Extract Edges*
- *Color Edges*
- *Imprint*
- *Copy Edges*
- *Offset Edge*
- *Section Plane*
- *Live Section*
- *Solid History*
- *SOLVIEW*
- *SOLPROF*
- *Drawing Views*
- *Mass Properties*
- *Record*
- *ShowMotion*
- *Section Views*

EDITING SOLID MODELS

Ribbon: Home > Solid Editing **Menu Bar:** Modify > Solid Editing
Toolbar: Solid Editing **Command:** SOLIDEDIT

One of the major enhancements in the recent releases of AutoCAD is the editing of the solid models. The editing of the solid models has made solid modeling very user-friendly. It is done using the tools available in the **Solid Editing** panel. These tools can be used to edit selected faces, selected edges, or entire body of a solid model. Various editing processes and the tools used to perform them are discussed next.

Editing Faces of a Solid Model

You can edit the faces of the solid models by using the tools in the **Face Editing** drop-down of the **Solid Editing** panel, refer to Figure 10-1. The tools available in this drop-down are **Extrude Faces**, **Taper Faces**, **Move Faces**, **Copy Faces**, **Offset Faces**, **Delete Faces**, **Rotate Faces**, and **Color Faces**. These editing tools are discussed next.

Extrude Faces

The **Extrude Faces** tool is used to extrude the selected faces of a solid model to a specific height or along a selected path, refer to Figure 10-2. To extrude faces, choose the **Extrude Faces** tool from the **Face Editing** drop-down of the **Solid Editing** panel in the **Home** tab. The prompt sequence that will follow when you invoke this tool is given next.

Select faces or [Undo/Remove]: *Select faces to extrude or enter an option.*
Select faces or [Undo/Remove/ALL]: *Select another face, an option, or* Enter.

The **Undo** option cancels the selection of the most recently selected face. The **Remove** option allows you to remove a previously selected face from the selection set for extrusion. The **ALL** option selects all the faces of the specified solid. After you have selected a face for extrusion, the next prompt is given below:

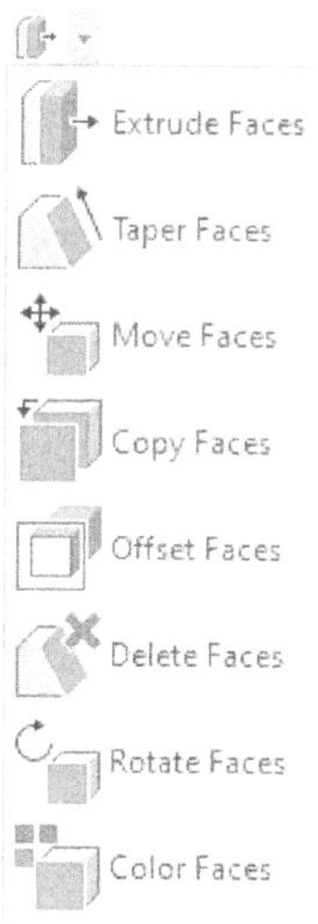

*Figure 10-1 The **Face Editing** drop-down*

Specify height of extrusion or [Path]: *Enter a height value or enter **P** to select a path.*

The **Path** option allows you to select a path for extrusion based on a specified line or curve. At the **Select extrusion path** prompt, select the line, circle, arc, ellipse, elliptical arc, polyline, or spline to be specified as the extrusion path. Note that this path should not lie on the same plane as the selected face and should not have areas of high curvature.

A positive value for the height of extrusion extrudes the selected face outwards, whereas a negative value extrudes the selected face inwards. After specifying the height of extrusion, the prompt sequence followed is given next.

Specify angle of taper for extrusion <0>: *Specify a value between -90 and +90 degree or press Enter to accept the default value.*

A positive angle value tapers the selected face inwards, refer to Figure 10-2 and a negative value tapers the selected face outwards.

Move Faces

The **Move Faces** tool is used to move the selected faces from one location to the other without changing the orientation of the solid, refer to Figure 10-3. For example, you can move holes from one location to the other without actually modifying the solid model. To move faces, choose the **Move Faces** tool from the **Face Editing** drop-down of the **Solid Editing** panel. The prompt sequence that will follow when you invoke this tool is given next.

Select faces or [Undo/Remove]: *Select one or more faces or enter an option.*
Select faces or [Undo/Remove/ALL]: *Select one or more faces, enter an option, or* Enter.
Specify a base point or displacement: *Specify a base point.*
Specify a second point of displacement: *Specify a point or* Enter.

The face moves to the specified location.

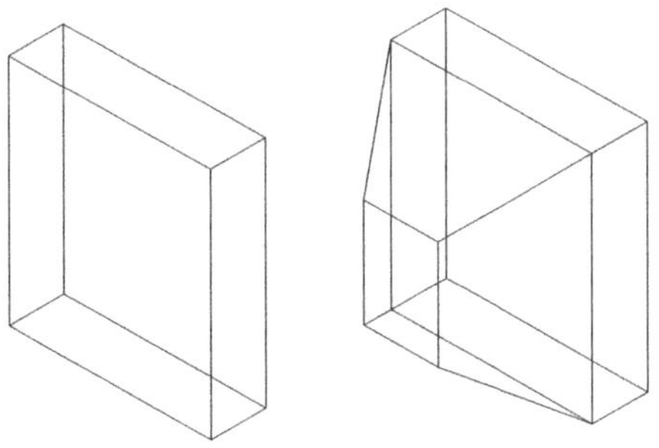

Figure 10-2 *Using the* ***Extrude Faces*** *tool to extrude a solid face with a positive taper angle*

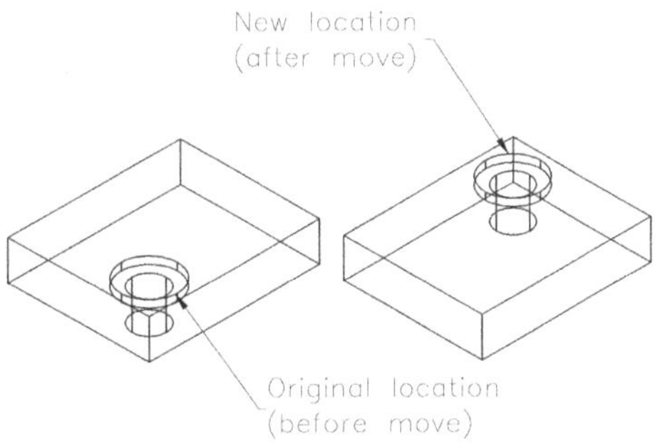

Figure 10-3 *Using the* ***Move Faces*** *tool to move the hole from the original position*

Tip
If the feature you want to move consists of more than one face, then you must select all the faces to move the entire feature.

Offset Faces

The **Offset Faces** tool is used to offset the selected faces of a solid model uniformly through a specified distance on the model. Offsetting takes place in the direction of the positive side of the face. For example, you can offset holes to a larger or smaller size in a 3D solid through a specified distance. In Figure 10-4, the hole on the solid has been offset to a larger size. To offset faces, choose the **Offset Faces** tool from the **Face Editing** drop-down of the **Solid Editing** panel. The prompt sequence that will follow when you choose this tool is given next.

Select faces or [Undo/Remove]: *Select one or more faces or enter an option.*
Select faces or [Undo/Remove/ALL]: *Select one or more faces, enter an option, or* Enter.
Specify the offset distance: *Specify the offset distance.*

The direction of offset can be controlled by entering positive or negative values of offset distance.

Rotate Faces

The **Rotate Faces** tool is used to rotate the selected faces of a solid model through a specified angle. For example, you can rotate cuts or slots around a base point through an absolute or relative angle, refer to Figure 10-5. The direction in which the rotation takes place is determined by the right-hand thumb rule. To rotate faces, choose the **Rotate Faces** tool from the **Face Editing** drop-down of the **Solid Editing** panel. The prompt sequence that will follow when you choose this tool is given next.

Select faces or [Undo/Remove]: *Select face(s) or enter an option.*
Select faces or [Undo/Remove/ALL]: *Select face(s), or enter an option, or* Enter.
Specify an axis point or [Axis by object/View/Xaxis/Yaxis/Zaxis] <2points>: *Select a point, enter an option, or* Enter.

If you press Enter to use the **2points** option, you will be prompted to select the two points that will define the axis of rotation. The prompt sequence is given next.

Specify the first point on the rotation axis: *Specify the first point.*
Specify the second point on the rotation axis: *Specify the second point.*
Specify a rotation angle or [Reference]: *Specify the angle of rotation or enter* ***R*** *to use the reference option.*

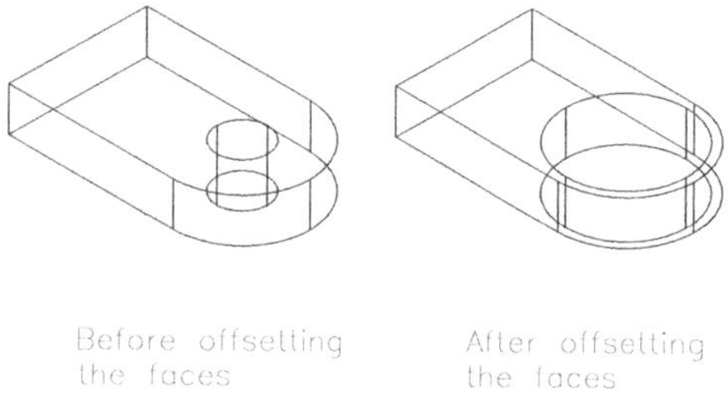

Figure 10-4 *Using the* ***Offset Faces*** *tool to offset a solid face with a positive taper angle*

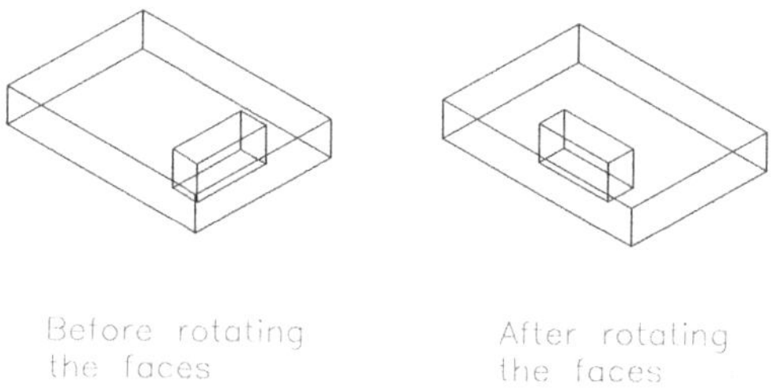

Figure 10-5 *Using the* ***Rotate Faces*** *tool to rotate the faces from the original position*

The **Axis by object** option is used to select an object to define the axis of rotation. The axis of rotation is aligned with the selected object; for example, if you select a circle, the axis of rotation will be aligned along the axis that passes through the center of the circle and will be normal to the plane of the circle. The selected object can also be a line, ellipse, arc, 2D polyline, 3D polyline, or even a spline. The prompt sequence is given next.

Select a curve to be used for the axis: *Select the object to be used to define the axis of rotation.*
Specify a rotation angle or [Reference]: *Specify rotation angle or use the reference angle option.*

The **Xaxis**, **Yaxis**, and **Zaxis** options align the axis of rotation with the axis that passes through the specified point. The prompt sequence is given next:

Specify the origin of rotation <0,0,0>: *Select a point through which the axis of rotation will pass.*
Specify a rotation angle or [Reference]: *Specify the rotation angle or use the reference angle option.*

Taper Faces

The **Taper Faces** tool is used to taper the selected face(s) through a specified angle, refer to Figure 10-6. Tapering takes place depending on the selection sequence of the base point and the second point along the selected face. It also depends on whether the taper angle is positive or negative. A positive value tapers the face inwards and a negative value tapers the face outwards. You can enter any value between -90-degree and +90-degree. The default value 0-degree extrudes the face along the axis that is perpendicular to the selected face. If you have selected more than one face, they will be tapered through the same angle. To create taper faces, choose the **Taper Faces** tool from the **Face Editing** drop-down of the **Solid Editing** panel. The prompt sequence that will follow when you choose this tool is given next.

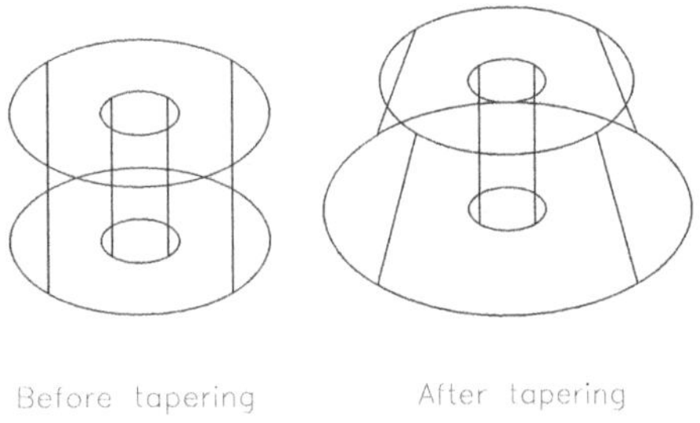

Figure 10-6 *Tapering the faces using the* ***Taper Faces*** *tool*

Select faces or [Undo/Remove]: *Select face(s) or enter an option.*
Select faces or [Undo/Remove/ALL]: *Select one or more faces, enter an option, or* Enter.
Specify the base point: *Specify a base point.*
Specify another point along the axis of tapering: *Specify a point.*
Specify the taper angle: *Specify an angle between –90 and +90-degree.*

Delete Faces

The **Delete Faces** tool is used to remove the selected face(s) from the specific 3D solid. It also removes chamfers and fillets, refer to Figure 10-7. To remove faces, choose the **Delete Faces** tool from the **Face Editing** drop-down of the **Solid Editing** panel. The prompt sequence that will follow when you choose this tool is given next.

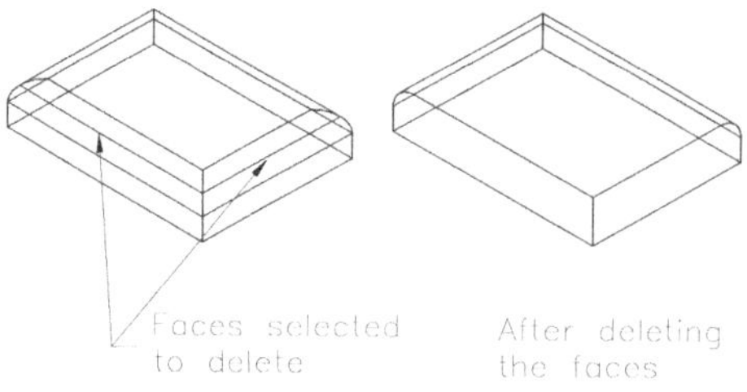

Figure 10-7 *Deleting the faces using the* ***Delete Faces*** *tool*

Enter a solids editing option [Face/Edge/Body/Undo/eXit] <eXit>: F
Enter a face editing option.
[Extrude/Move/Rotate/Offset/Taper/Delete/Copy/coLor/mAterial/Undo/eXit] <eXit>: D
Select faces or [Undo/Remove]: *Select the face to remove.*
Select faces or [Undo/Remove/ALL]: *Select one or more faces, enter an option, or* Enter.
Solid validation started.
Solid validation completed.

Copy Faces

The **Copy Faces** tool is used to copy a face as a body or a region, refer to Figure 10-8. To copy faces, choose the **Copy Faces** tool from the **Face Editing** drop-down of the **Solid Editing** panel. The prompt sequence that will follow when you choose this tool is given next.

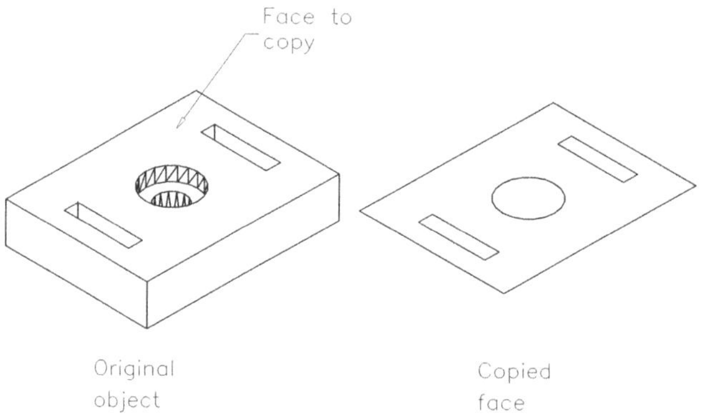

Figure 10-8 *Copying the face using the* ***Copy Faces*** *tool*

Select faces or [Undo/Remove]: *Select the faces to copy.*
Select faces or [Undo/Remove/ALL]: *Select one or more faces, enter an option, or* Enter.
Specify a base point or displacement: *Specify a base point.*
Specify a second point of displacement: *Specify the second point.*

Color Faces

The **Color Faces** tool is used to change the color of the selected face. To do so, choose the **Color Faces** tool from the **Face Editing** drop-down of the **Solid Editing** panel. The prompt sequence that will follow when you choose this tool is given next.

Select faces or [Undo/Remove]: *Select one or more faces, enter an option, or* Enter.
Select faces or [Undo/Remove/ALL]: *Select more faces, enter an option, or* Enter.

When you press Enter at the previous prompt, the **Select Color** dialog box will be displayed. You can assign the color to the selected face using this dialog box.

The above-mentioned face editing tools can also be assessed using the **Face** option of the **SOLIDEDIT** command. The other options available through this command are **mAterial**, **Undo** and **eXit**. These options are discussed next.

mAterial

This option is used to apply material to a selected face and is invoked using the **SOLIDEDIT** command. The prompt sequence that will follow is given next.

Command: **SOLIDEDIT**
Solids editing automatic checking: SOLIDCHECK=1
Enter a solids editing option [Face/Edge/Body/Undo/eXit] <eXit>: *Enter **F***
Enter a face editing option.
[Extrude/Move/Rotate/Offset/Taper/Delete/Copy/coLor/mAterial/Undo/eXit] <eXit>: *Enter **A***
Select faces or [Undo/Remove]: *Select one or more faces to apply the material.*
Select faces or [Undo/Remove/ALL]: *Select one or more faces, enter an option, or* Enter.
Enter new Material name <ByLayer>: *Enter the name of the material or* Enter.

Undo

This option is used to cancel the changes made to the faces of a solid model. This option will be available only when you invoke the **SOLIDEDIT** command by using the Command prompt.

eXit

This option is used to exit the face editing operations. This option will be available only when you invoke the **SOLIDEDIT** command using the Command prompt.

Tip
*You can select a face, edge, or solid and perform the editing operation. To select an entity with ease, set the appropriate option from the **Filter** drop-down in the **Selection** panel.*

Editing Edges of a Solid Model

To modify the properties of the edges of a solid, you can use the tools available in the **Edge Editing** drop-down of the **Solid Editing** panel, refer to Figure 10-9. The edge editing tools available in this drop-down are: **Extract Edges**, **Imprint**, **Color Edges**, and **Copy Edges**. Also you can use the **Offset Edge** tool to offset the edges of the model. These editing tools are discussed next.

Extract Edges

The **Extract Edges** tool is used to extract all the edges of a solid, a surface, or a mesh. The edges are copied as lines, polylines, arcs, circles, ellipses, or splines depending upon the model selected. To extract the edges, choose the **Extract Edges** tool from the **Edge Editing** drop-down of the **Solid Editing** panel. The prompt sequence that will follow when you choose this tool is given next.

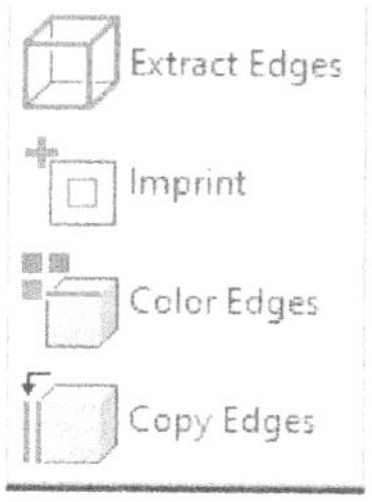

Figure 10-9 The ***Edge Editing*** *drop-down*

Select objects: *Select the solid from which edges are to be extracted.*
Select objects: 1 found.
Select objects: Enter.

All the edges of the solid will be extracted and you can select these edges individually.

Imprint

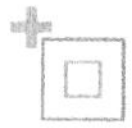

The **Imprint** tool is used to imprint an object on a 3D solid object. Remember that the object to be imprinted should intersect one or more faces of a solid object. The objects that can be imprinted are arcs, circles, lines, 2D and 3D polylines, ellipses, splines, regions, bodies, and 3D solids. To invoke this tool, choose the **Imprint** tool from the **Edge Editing** drop-down of the **Solid Editing** panel. The prompt sequence that will follow when you choose this tool is given next.

Select a 3D solid or surface: *Select an object.*
Select an object to imprint: *Select an object to be imprinted.*
Delete the source object [Yes/No] <N>: *Select an option or* Enter.
Select an object to imprint: *Select a new object or* Enter.

The above-mentioned body editing tools can also be accessed using the **Body** option of the **SOLIDEDIT** command. Other body editing options available for this command are **Undo** and **eXit**. The **Undo** option cancels the modifications made during the **Body** option of the **SOLIDEDIT** command, and **eXit** option is used to exit the **Body** option of this command.

Copy Edges

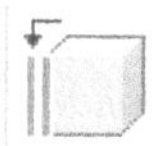

The **Copy Edges** tool is used to copy the individual edges of a solid model. The edges are copied as lines, arcs, circles, ellipses, or splines. To invoke this tool, choose the **Copy Edges** tool from the **Edge Editing** drop-down of the **Solid Editing** panel. The prompt sequence that will follow when you choose this tool is given next.

Select edges or [Undo/Remove]: *Select the edges to be copied.*
Select edges or [Undo/Remove]: Enter.
Specify a base point or displacement: *Specify the first point of displacement.*
Specify a second point of displacement: *Specify the second point of displacement.*

Color Edges

The **Color Edges** tool is used to change the color of a selected edge of a 3D solid. To invoke this tool, choose the **Color Edges** tool from the **Edge Editing** drop-down of the **Solid Editing** panel. The prompt sequence that will follow when you choose this tool is given next.

Select edges or [Undo/Remove]: *Select one or more edges or enter an option.*
Select edges or [Undo/Remove]: Enter.

After you select edges and press Enter, the **Select Color** dialog box will be displayed. You can assign the color to the selected edges using this dialog box. You can also assign color by entering their names or numbers. Individual edges can be assigned individual colors.

The discussed edge editing tools can also be assessed using the **Edge** option of the **SOLIDEDIT** command. The other edge editing options available for this command are **Undo** and **eXit**. The **Undo** option cancels the modifications made during the **Edge** editing of the **SOLIDEDIT** command, and the **eXit** option is used to exit the **Edge** editing of this command.

Offset Edge

The **Offset Edge** tool is used to offset the boundary edges of a planar solid face or a surface. You can offset the edges either dynamically or by setting the offset distance. Note that all the edges should lie on the same plane. Depending upon the position of the cursor, the selected edges will offset inwards or outwards. During the operation, you can choose the **Corner** option to make the corners of the offset edges sharp or rounded. To offset the boundary edges, choose the **Offset Edge** tool from the **Solid Editing** panel of the **Solid** tab. The prompt sequence for the **Offset Edge** tool is given next.

Corner = Sharp
Select face: *Select the face whose edges are to be offset.*
Specify through point or [Distance/Corner]: *Specify the point or [distance].*
Select face: Enter.

If you enter **Corner** at the **Specify through point or [Distance/Corner]** prompt, then the resulting offset profile will have filleted corners.

If you enter **Distance** at the **Specify through point or [Distance/Corner]** prompt, then you can specify the distance at which the offset edges will be created.

Editing Entire Body of a Solid Model

To edit the entire body of a solid model, you can use the tools available in the **Body Editing** drop-down of the **Solid Editing** panel, refer to Figure 10-10. The tools available in this drop-down are: **Separate**, **Clean**, **Shell**, and **Check**. Besides these tools, the **Imprint** tool available in the **Edge Editing** drop-down of the **Solid Editing** panel can also be used for editing a solid body, refer to Figure 10-9. The body editing tools are discussed next.

Separate

The **Separate** tool is used to separate 3D solids with disjointed volumes into separate 3D solids. Solids with disjointed volumes are created by the union of two solids that are not in contact with each other. Note that the composite solids created by performing the Boolean operations and share the same volume cannot be separated using this option. To invoke this tool, choose the **Separate** tool from the **Body Editing** drop-down of the **Solid Editing** panel. The prompt sequence that will follow when you choose this tool is given next.

Figure 10-10 *The* ***Body Editing*** *drop-down*

Select a 3D solid: *Select a solid object with multiple lumps.*

Shell

The **Shell** tool is one of the most extensively used tools for body editing. This tool is used to create a shell of a specified 3D solid model. Shelling is defined as a process of scooping out material from a solid model in such a manner that the walls with some thickness are left. One 3D object can have only one shell. You can exclude certain faces before scooping out the material. This means the selected face will not be included during the shelling, refer to Figure 10-11. To invoke this tool, choose the **Shell** tool from the **Body Editing** drop-down of the **Solid Editing** panel. The prompt sequence that will follow when you choose this tool is given next.

Select a 3D solid: *Select an object.*
Remove faces or [Undo/Add/ALL]: *Select one or more faces or enter an option.*
Remove faces or [Undo/Add/ALL]: *Select a face, enter an option, or* Enter.
Enter the shell offset distance: *Specify the wall thickness.*

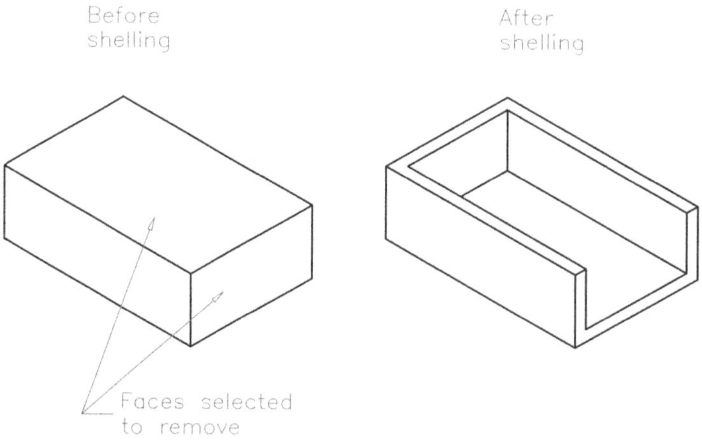

Figure 10-11 *Creating a shell in the solid model*

Tip

If you have specified a positive distance, the shell will be created on the inside perimeter of a solid and if it is negative, the shell will be created on the outside perimeter of the 3D solid.

Clean

The **Clean** tool is used to remove the shared edges or vertices sharing the same surface or curve definition on either side of the edge or vertex. It removes all redundant edges and vertices, imprinted as well as unused geometry. It also merges faces that share the same surface. To do so, choose the **Clean** tool from the **Body Editing** drop-down of the **Solid Editing** panel. The prompt sequence that will follow when you choose this tool is given next.

Select a 3D solid: *Select the solid model to clean.*

Check

The **Check** tool can be used to check if a solid object created is a valid 3D solid object. This option is independent of the settings of the **SOLIDCHECK** variable. The **SOLIDCHECK** variable turns on or off the solid validation for the current drawing session. The solid validation is turned on when the value of the **SOLIDCHECK** variable is set to 1, which is the default value. If a solid object is a valid 3D solid object, you can use solid editing options to modify it without AutoCAD displaying ACIS error messages. Solid editing can take place only on valid 3D solids. To invoke this tool, choose the **Check** tool from the **Body Editing** drop-down of the **Solid Editing** panel. The prompt sequence that will follow when you choose this tool is given next.

Select a 3D solid: *Select the solid you want to check.*
This object is a valid ShapeManager solid.

Example 1 — Solid Editing

In this example, you will create the solid model shown in Figure 10-12. After creating the model, modify it, as shown in Figure 10-13, using the tools in the **Solid Editing** panel.

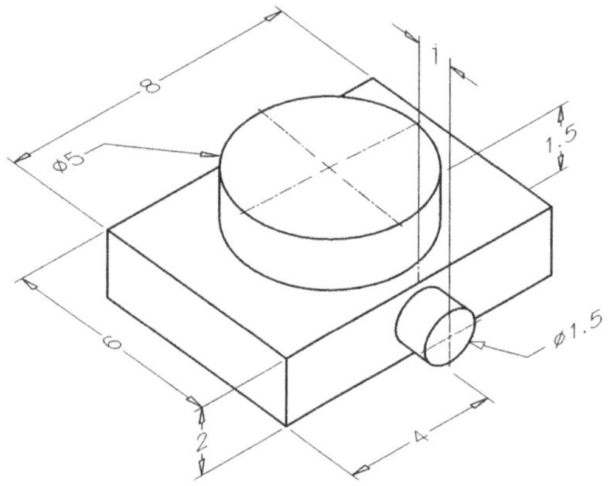

Figure 10-12 *Model for Example 1*

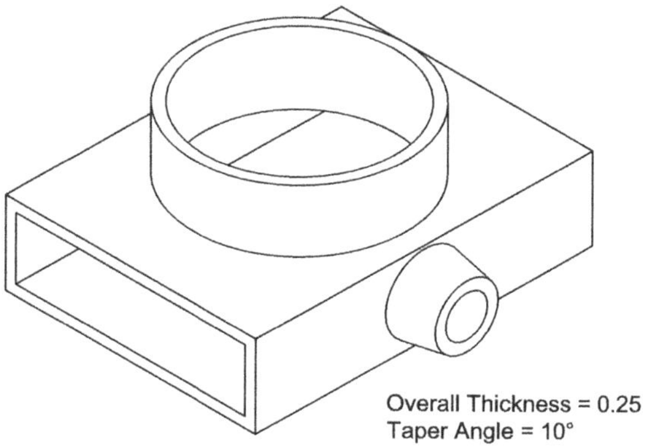

Figure 10-13 *Model after modification*

1. Create a box and two cylinders at appropriate position, refer to Figure 10-12.

2. Combine all the objects to make them a solid model.

3. Choose the **Shell** tool from **Home > Solid Editing > Body Editing** drop-down and follow the prompt sequence given below:

   Select a 3D solid: *Select the solid.*
   Remove faces or [Undo/Add/ALL]: *Click on the top face of the bigger cylinder.*
   Remove faces or [Undo/Add/ALL]: *Click on the front face of the smaller cylinder.*
   Remove faces or [Undo/Add/ALL]: *Click on the left face of the box.*
   Remove faces or [Undo/Add/ALL]: Enter.
   Enter the shell offset distance: **0.25** Enter.
   Solid validation started.
   Solid validation completed.
   Enter a body editing option.
   [Imprint/seParate solids/Shell/cLean/Check/Undo/eXit] <eXit>: Enter.
   Enter a solids editing option [Face/Edge/Body/Undo/eXit] <eXit>: *Press Esc.*

4. Choose the **Taper Faces** tool from **Home > Solid Editing > Face Editing** drop-down and follow the prompt sequence given below:

   Select faces or [Undo/Remove]: *Click on the cylindrical face of the smaller cylinder.*
   Select faces or [Undo/Remove/ALL]: Enter.
   Specify the base point: *Select the center of the front face of the smaller cylinder.*
   Specify another point along the axis of tapering: *Select the center at the back face of the smaller cylinder.*

Specify the taper angle: **-10** Enter.
Solid validation started.
Solid validation completed.
Enter a face editing option.
[Extrude/Move/Rotate/Offset/Taper/Delete/Copy/coLor/mAterial/Undo/eXit] <eXit>: Enter.
Enter a solids editing option [Face/Edge/Body/Undo/eXit] <eXit>: *Press Esc.*

The final model should look similar to the model shown in Figure 10-13.

GENERATING A SECTION BY DEFINING A SECTION PLANE

Ribbon: Home > Section > Section Plane
Menu Bar: Draw > Modeling > Section Plane **Command:** SECTIONPLANE

Section Plane

The **Section Plane** tool is used to create a sectioned object by defining a sectioning plane. By default, the section plane cuts all the 3D objects, surfaces, and regions lying in the line of this plane even if the section plane does not actually pass through them. Various methods of defining the section plane are discussed next.

Defining a Section Plane by Selecting a Face

In this method, the section plane will be aligned to the plane of the selected face of the 3D solid. Choose the **Section Plane** tool from the **Section** panel and select the desired face on the solid object; a section plane aligned with the selected face will be displayed, as shown in Figure 10-14. The prompt sequence is given next.

Select face or any point to locate section line or [Draw section/Orthographic/Type]: *Select a face on the 3D solid where you want to align the section plane.*

Now, you can move the section plane along normal direction to place it at the intended location. To do so, select a section line visible on that section plane, the **Move Gizmo** will be displayed at the center of the section line. Use the **Move Gizmo** to move the plane in any desired direction. Even if the display of gizmo is turned off, you can move the section plane along normal direction by using the triangular arrow grip displayed at the midpoint of the section line, refer to Figure 10-15. After moving the section plane at the desired location, click once to place the plane; the preview of the remaining section of the model will be displayed. Figure 10-16 shows the remaining section of the solid model after moving the section plane shown in Figure 10-14, to the center of the model.

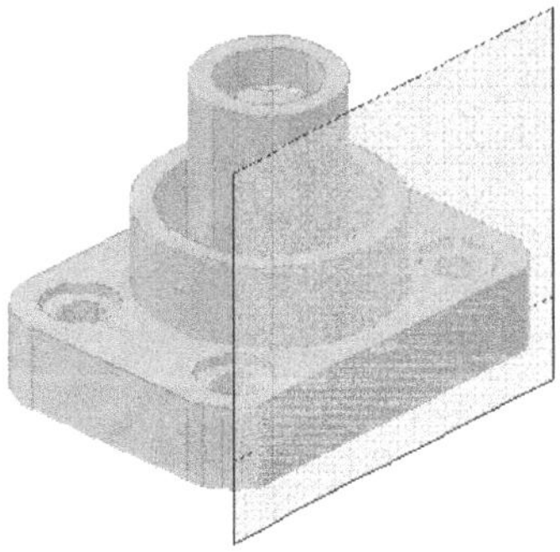

Figure 10-14 *Model with a section plane*

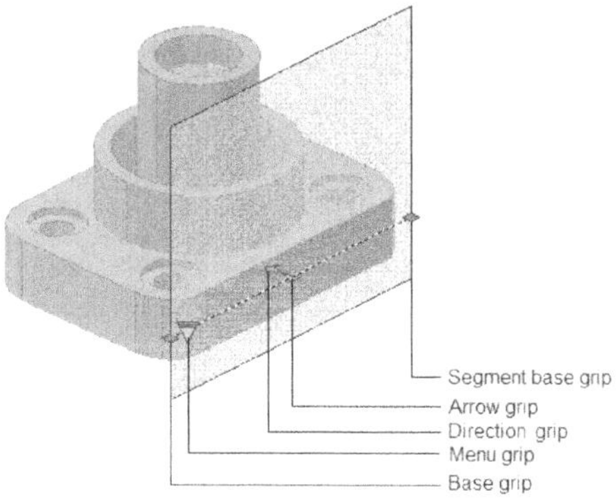

Figure 10-15 *Various grip visible on the section line*

You can also flip the direction of the sectioned portion of the model. To do this, click on the section line and then click on the direction grip, refer to Figure 10-17. To rotate the section plane, select the selection line and right click on it and then choose the **Rotate** option from the shortcut menu. Next, select the base point about which you want to rotate the section plane and specify the rotation angle. Figure 10-18 shows the remaining section of the model after rotating the section plane by -90-degree about the midpoint of the section line.

Instead of displaying only the section plane, you can show the section boundary with the section plane. The section boundary displays a two dimensional rectangular sketch. Only the object lying within this boundary will be displayed as the remaining section. To create a section boundary, click on the menu grip and choose the **Boundary** option. You can also show the section volume with the section boundary and the section plane. The section volume displays a three dimensional box and only the object lying within this boundary will be displayed as the remaining section. To create a section volume, choose the **Volume** option from the menu grip. Figure 10-19 shows a model with a section plane, section boundary, and section volume. The size of the section boundary and the section plane can also be edited with the help of grips.

Figure 10-16 *Remaining section of the model after moving the section plane*

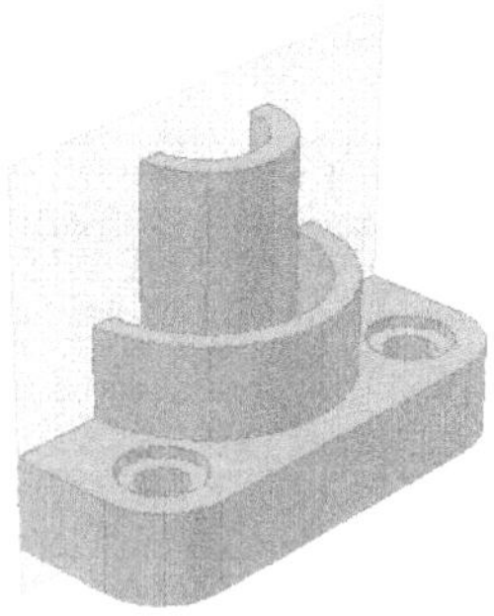

Figure 10-17 *Resulting model after flipping the direction of the section plane*

Generating a section by a section plane does not affect the original model. The original model is hidden and only the remaining section of the model is displayed. If you delete the section line from the drawing, the model will be redisplayed without any section.

AutoCAD also allows you to display both the sectioned and unsectioned portions of a 3D solid. To do so, choose the **Live Section** tool from the **Section** panel and select the section plane to activate or deactivate the live sectioning of the solid model. Alternatively, select the section line and right-click to display the shortcut menu. Clear the check mark displayed on the left of the **Activate live sectioning** option by choosing it from the shortcut menu.

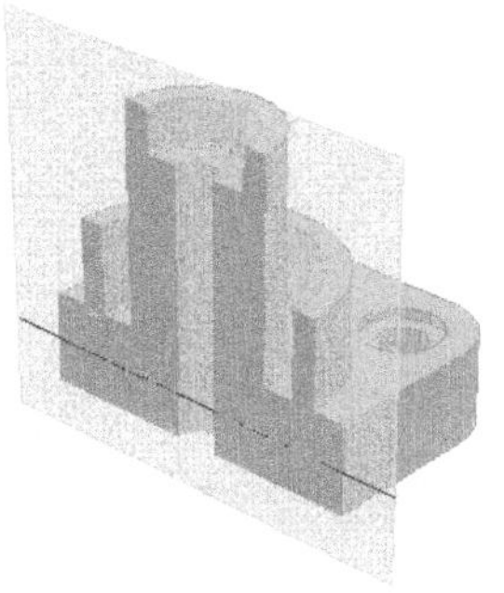

Figure 10-18 *Resulting model after rotating the section plane by -90°*

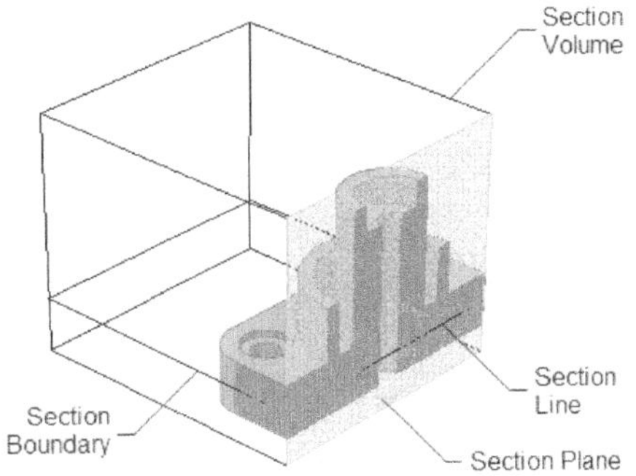

Figure 10-19 *Model after choosing the* ***Volume*** *option from the menu grip*

Even if the live sectioning is on, you can display the sectioned portion of the solid model. To do so, select the section line, invoke the shortcut menu, and choose the **Show cut-away geometry** option from it; a translucent and red colored sectioned model will be displayed.

You can add jogs to the section plane. A jog provides a 90-degree bend to the section plane for a certain distance and after that the section plane again continues in the original direction. To create a jog, choose the **Add Jog** tool from the **Section** panel; you will be prompted to select the section object. Select the section line from the drawing area. Next, you will be prompted to specify a point on the section line where you want to add the jog. Specify a location on the section line to create the jog. Alternatively, select the section line and choose **Add jog to section** from the shortcut menu to add a jog in the section line. After adding the jog, you can edit its length and location with the help of grips. You can add multiple jogs to the section plane.

Note

In all the methods to define a section plane, the procedure of modifying and adding jogs to a section plane, and of displaying the sectioned portion of the model is same.

Defining a Section Plane by Specifying Two Points

In this method, a section plane is generated such that it passes through the two points that are specified in the drawing area. If you select a face on the 3D object, it generates a section plane at the selected face, but if you specify the first point at any location in the drawing area or on the 3D object, this point acts as the base point about which the section plane can rotate.

Specifying the second point will fix the through point of the section plane. A section plane will be generated passing through these two points, refer to Figure 10-20. The prompt sequence for this option is given next.

Select face or any point to locate section line or [Draw section/Orthographic/Type]: *Specify a point on the screen or on the 3D object.*
Specify through point: *Specify the other point through which the section line will pass.*

Once you generate the section plane, you will not get a preview of the sectioned object. This is because the **Activate live sectioning** option is not active by default when you generate a section plane by specifying two points. To activate the live sectioning, choose the **Live Section** tool from the **Section** panel and select the section plane. Figure 10-20 displays a model sectioned by specifying two points with the live sectioning turned on. The prompt sequence for this tool is given next.

Select section object: *Select the section line on the section plane.*

Defining a Section Plane by Drawing the Section Line

In this method, you can draw a section line and generate a section plane that passes along it. You can section a 3D object in many planes by picking points through which the section plane will pass. To do so, choose the **Section Plane** tool from the **Section** panel. Next, right-click in the drawing area and choose the **Draw section** option from the shortcut menu. Now, specify the point from which the section line will start and then specify the points through which it will pass. After specifying all the points, press the Enter key and then specify the side of the object to be retained after sectioning. By default, the section plane in this case will be displayed as the section boundary with the live sectioning deactivated. Figure 10-21 shows the model sectioned by drawing a section line with the live sectioning activated.

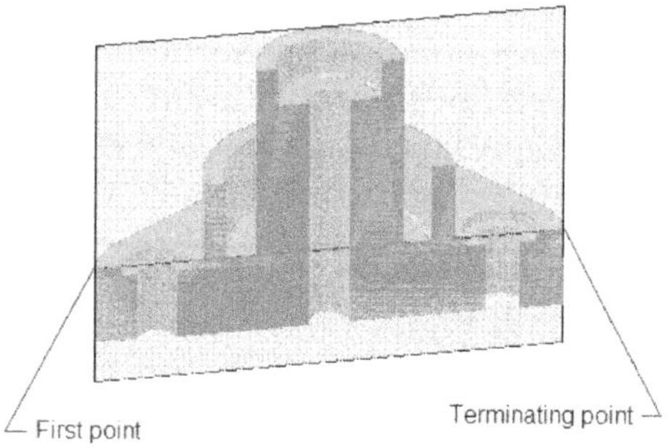

Figure 10-20 *Model sectioned by specifying two points*

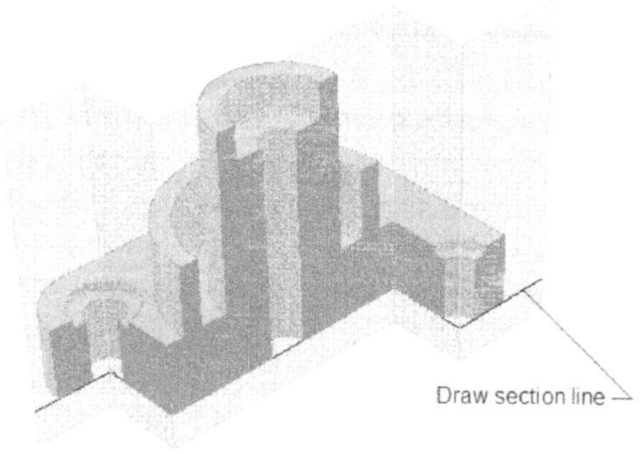

Figure 10-21 *Model sectioned by drawing the section line*

Note

A section line should be drawn only on one sketching plane. Otherwise, you will not be able to visualize the sectioned model after activating the live sectioning. Also, the drawn section line should not be self-intersecting.

Defining a Section Plane by Selecting a Preset Orthographic Plane

In this method, a section plane will be generated parallel to preset orthographic planes such as front, top, right so on, and passes through an imaginary center of a box. This box is calculated by enveloping all the solids, surfaces, and regions present in the drawing. Choose the **Section Plane** tool from the **Section** panel. Next, right-click in the drawing area and choose the **Orthographic** option from the shortcut menu; you will be prompted to select the predefined orthographic plane with which the generated section plane will be aligned. On selecting this, you get a sectioned solid whose material is chopped from the side you selected as the preset orthographic plane. In this option, you will instantaneously get the sectioned object because live sectioning is activated automatically.

Generating 2D and 3D Sections

As mentioned earlier, sectioning a model by generating a section plane does not affect the original model. The original model is hidden and only the remaining section of the sectioned model is displayed. On deleting the section plane, the sectioned object will get deleted. If you want to retain the generated section as a 2D or 3D section with the original model, you can use the **Generate Section** tool.

To generate a 2D or a 3D section, choose the **Generate Section** tool from the **Section** panel in the **Home** tab; the **Generate Section/Elevation** dialog box will be displayed. Alternatively, you can select a section plane to activate the **Section Plane** contextual tab and choose the **Generate Section Block** option from the **Generate** panel. You can also invoke this option from the shortcut menu by right clicking anywhere in the drawing area while the **Section Plane** contextual tab invoked and then choose the **2D/3D block** option from the **Generate Section** flyout to display the **Generate Section/Elevation** dialog box. Choose the **Show details** button to expand this dialog box, as shown in Figure 10-22. The options in this dialog box are discussed next.

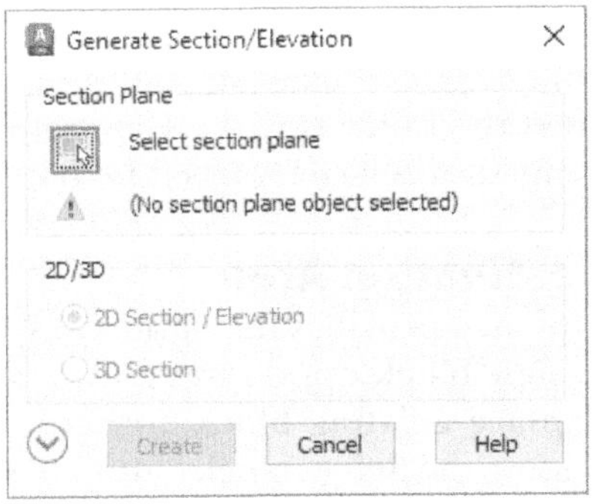

*Figure 10-22 The expanded **Generate Section/Elevation** dialog box*

Section Plane Area

Choose the **Select section plane** button from this area and select the section plane for which you need to create 2D/3D sections.

2D/3D Area

This area allows you to specify the type of section you want to generate. The **2D Section / Elevation** option is used to generate a two dimensional sketch of the sectioned object on the XY plane of the current UCS. The **3D Section** option generates a 3D sketch of the sectioned object on a plane parallel to the section plane. Figure 10-23 shows the model with its 2D section and Figure 10-24 shows the model with its 3D section.

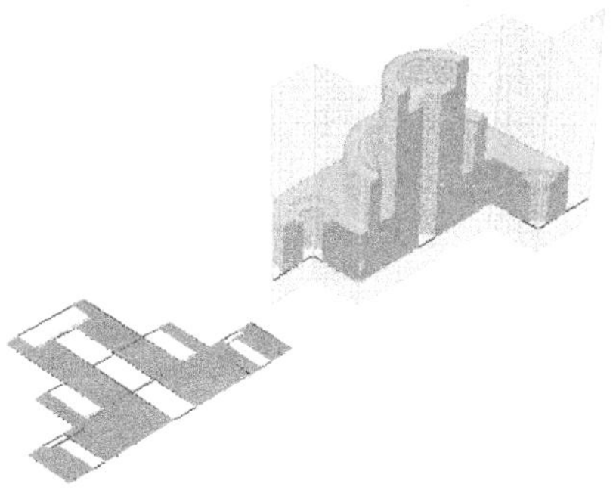

Figure 10-23 Model with its 2D section

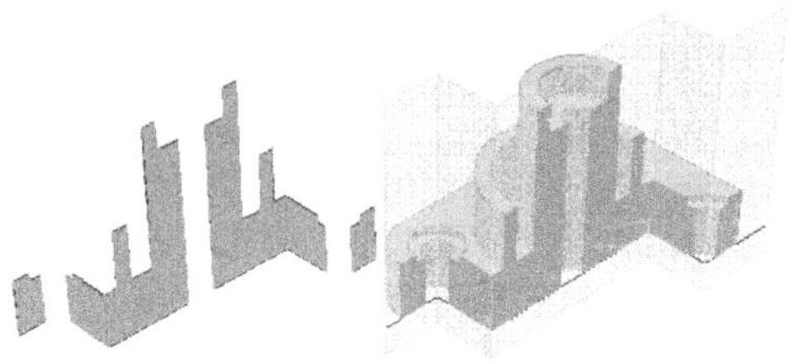

Figure 10-24 Model with its 3D section

Source Geometry Area

This area allows you to specify the objects of the drawing that you want to include while creating the 2D or 3D section. The **Include all objects** radio button, if selected, includes all the 3D objects, surfaces, and regions in the drawing. It also includes the external reference objects and blocks. The **Select objects to include** option allows you to select the objects to be included in the section generation. If you select the **Select objects to include** radio button and then choose the **Select objects** button, the **Generate Section/Elevation** dialog box will disappear allowing you to select the solids. After selecting the solids, surfaces, or regions, press the Enter key; the **Generate Section/Elevation** dialog box will reappear, displaying the number of selected objects below the **Select objects** button.

Destination Area

This area provides the option to specify how you want to use the generated section. The **Insert as new block** option inserts the generated section in the same drawing file as a block. The **Replace existing block** option inserts the generated section by replacing an existing block. Choose the **Select block** button to select the block to be replaced by the newly generated section block. The **Export to a file** option allows you to create a new drawing file with the generated section. To save it as a new file, choose the **Browse [...]** button to specify the location where you want to save the new drawing file.

Section Settings

This button is used to invoke the **Section Settings** dialog box, refer to Figure 10-25. You can also invoke this dialog box by clicking on the inclined arrow in the title bar of the **Section** panel. If you select the **2D Section/Elevation** option in the 2D/3D area, the **Section Settings** dialog box will be displayed with the **2D section / elevation block creation settings** radio button selected by default. Similarly, if you select the **3D section block creation settings** option in the 2D/3D area, the **Section Settings** dialog box will be displayed with the **3D section block creation settings** option selected by default. The **Section Settings** dialog box is used to modify the properties of the sections generated. These properties are displayed depending on the radio button selected.

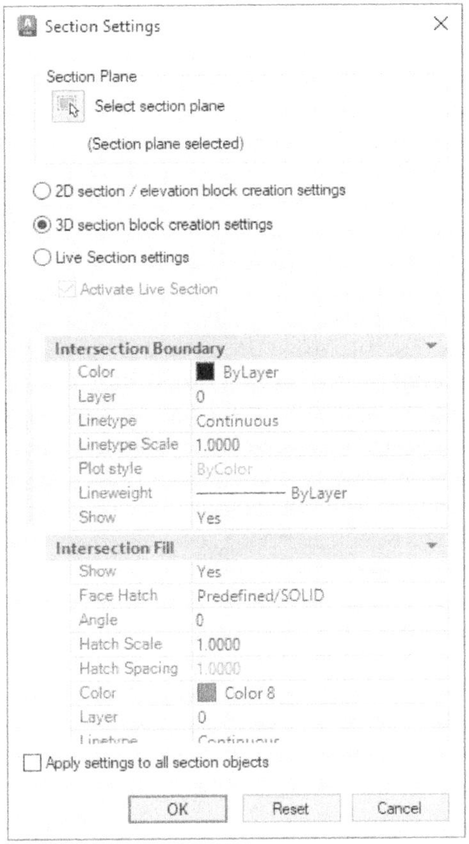

*Figure 10-25 The **Section Settings** dialog box*

Create

When you choose this button from the **Generate Section/Elevation** dialog box, the section generation process gets finished. If you insert the generated section as a new block, you will be prompted to specify the insertion point, scale factor, and the rotation angle for the new generated section to be inserted as a block. If you replace an existing block, the generated section will be inserted with the same values of insertion point, scale factor, and rotation angle as for the block selected to be replaced. If you choose to export the generated section to a new file, a new file will be created and the section will be created at the same location with the same scale and orientation as the model in the previous file.

Live Section settings

This option is used to control the dynamic display of a sectioned solid in the drawing. Select the section line and choose **Live Section settings** from the shortcut menu; the **Section Settings** dialog box will be displayed with the **Live Section settings** option selected by default. The options available to control the display of the live sectioning of the model are similar to the options discussed in the **Section Settings** dialog box. The **Face Transparency** and **Edge Transparency** options in the **Cut-away Geometry** area are only available for the live section settings. These two options control the transparency of the edge and the face of the cut-away solid for a better view of the section and the remaining portion of the model. The value of transparency signifies the amount of light that passes through the cut-away part.

SOLID HISTORY

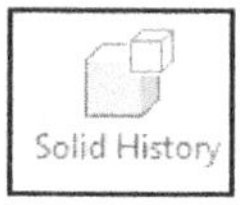

The **Solid History** button is available in the **Primitive** panel of the **Solid** tab. By default, this button is not chosen. As a result, you can directly edit faces, edges and vertices of a solid. If you choose the **Solid History** tool, the history of individual solid object is recorded. So, if a composite solid model is created by performing a Boolean operation, the features used to create solid will be saved with the composite solid. Therefore, you can modify the shape of the composite solid by modifying the original features.

Consider a case in which a composite solid is created by subtracting a wedge from the cylinder, as shown in Figures 10-26 and 10-27. To modify this composite solid, choose the **Solid History** option from **Solid > Selection > Subobject** drop-down; the solid history symbol will be attached to the cursor. Move the cursor near the composite solid and select the wedge when its preview is displayed, refer to Figure 10-28. You can also use the **Selection list** box to select the wedge. When the grips of the wedge are displayed, drag the grips and modify the shape of the wedge; the shape of the composite solid gets changed automatically, as shown in Figure 10-29.

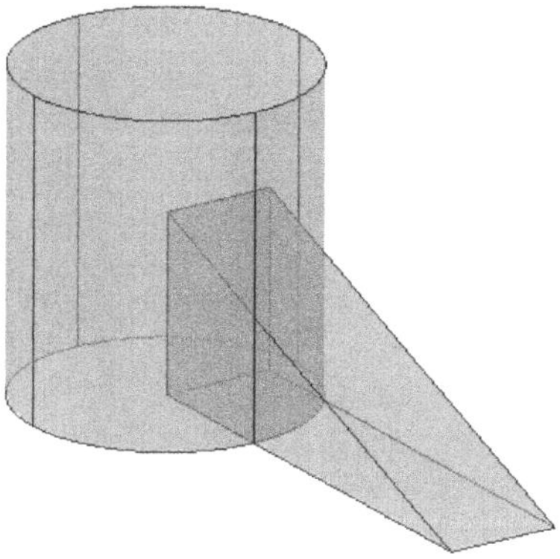

Figure 10-26 *A cylinder and a wedge as two separate solid bodies*

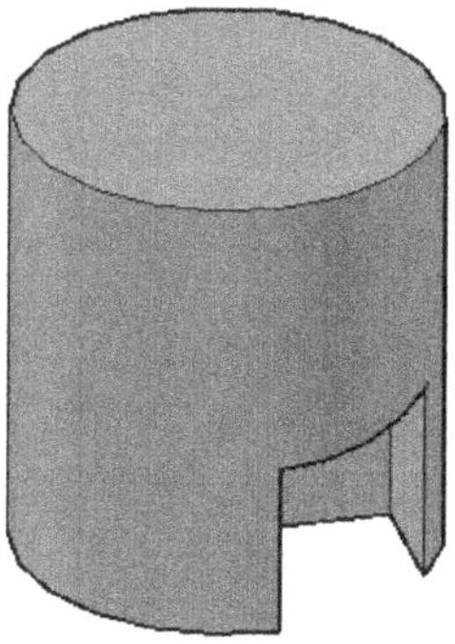

Figure 10-27 *Resulting composite solid model after subtracting the wedge from the cylinder*

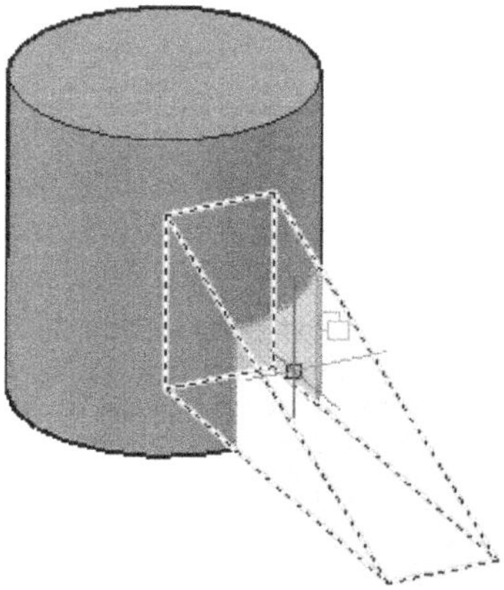

Figure 10-28 *Wedge with the preview displayed*

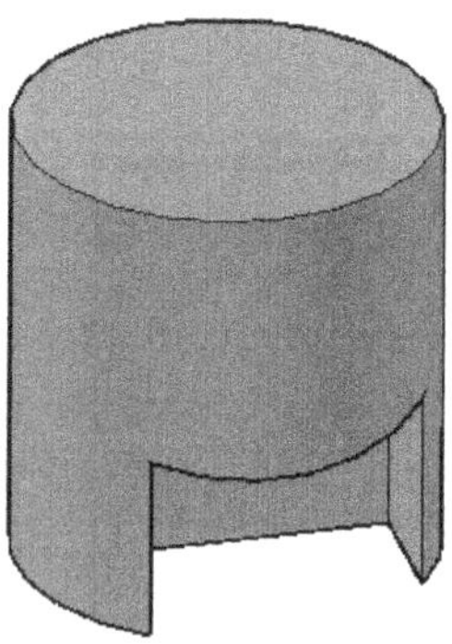

Figure 10-29 *Composite solid model after editing*

GENERATING DRAWING VIEWS OF A SOLID MODEL

As mentioned earlier, one of the major advantages of working with a solid model is that the drawing views of a solid model are automatically generated once you have the solid model with you. All you have to do is to specify the type of drawing view required. This is done using the **Solid View**, **Solid Drawing**, and **Solid Profile** tools. All these tools are discussed next.

Solid View

Ribbon: Home > Modeling > Solid View
Menu Bar: Draw > Modeling > Setup > View **Command:** SOLVIEW

The **Solid View** tool is an externally defined ARX application (*solids.arx*). This tool is used to create the documentation of the solid models in the form of the drawing views. This tool guides you through the process of creating orthographic or auxiliary views. The **Solid View** tool creates floating viewports using orthographic projections to layout sectional view and multiview drawings of solids, while you are in the **layout** tab.

For the ease of documentation, this tool automatically creates layers for visible lines, hidden lines, and section hatching for each view. This tool also creates layers for dimensioning that are visible in individual viewports. You can use these layers to draw dimensions in individual viewports. The following is the naming convention for layers.

Layer name	**Object type**
View name-VIS	Visible lines
View name-HID	Hidden lines
View name-DIM	Dimensions
View name-HAT	Hatch patterns (for sections)

The view name is the user-defined layer name given to the view when created.

Note
The information stored on these layers is deleted and updated when you use the ***Solid Drawing*** *tool. Therefore, do not place any permanent drawing information on these layers.*

To create the drawing views of a solid model, choose the **Solid View** tool from the **Modeling** panel. The prompt sequence that will be displayed is given next.

Enter an option [Ucs/Ortho/Auxiliary/Section]: *Select an option to generate the drawing view.*

These four options displayed in the Command prompt are discussed next.

Ucs Option

This option is used to create a profile view relative to a UCS. This is the first view that has to be generated. The reason for this is that the other options require existing viewports. The UCS can either be the current UCS or any other named UCS. The view generated using this option will be parallel to the *XY* plane of the current UCS. After selecting the **Ucs** option, the next prompt sequence is:

Enter an option [Named/World/?/Current] <Current>: *Enter an option or* Enter *to accept the current UCS.*

The **Named** option uses a named UCS to create the profile view. The prompt sequence is as follows:

Enter name of UCS to restore: *Enter the name of the UCS you want to use.*
Enter view scale <1.0>: *Enter a positive scale factor..*

This view scale value you enter is equivalent to zooming into your viewport by a factor relative to the paper space. The default ratio is 1:1. The next prompt sequence is as follows:

Specify view center: *Specify the location of the view.*
Specify view center <specify viewport>: Enter.

This point is based on the Model space extents. The next prompt sequence is as follows.

Specify the first corner of viewport: *Specify a point.*
Specify opposite corner of viewport: *Specify a point.*
Enter view name: *Enter a name for the view.*

The **World** option uses the *XY* plane of the WCS to create a profile view. The prompt sequences are the same as the **Named** option.

The **?** option lists all the named UCSs. The prompt sequence is given next.

Enter UCS names to list<*>: *Enter a name or press Enter to list all the named UCSs.*

The **Current** option uses the *XY* plane of the current UCS to generate the profile view. This is also the default option.

Ortho Option

An orthographic view is generated by projecting the lines on to a plane normal to an existing view. The **Ortho** option generates an orthographic view from the existing view. Keep in mind that the orthographic views created in AutoCAD are folded views and not the unfolded views. AutoCAD prompts you to specify the side of the viewport from where you want to project the view. The resultant view will depend on the side of the viewport selected. The prompt sequence is given next.

Specify side of viewport to project: *Select the edge of a viewport.*
Specify view center: *Specify the location of the orthographic view.*
Specify view center <specify viewport>: Enter.
Specify first corner of viewport: *Select the first point.*

Specify opposite corner of viewport: *Select the second point.*
Enter view name: *Specify the view name.*

Auxiliary Option

This option is used to create an auxiliary view from an existing view. An auxiliary view is the one that is generated by projecting the lines from an existing view on to a plane that is inclined at a certain angle. AutoCAD prompts you to define the inclined plane used for the auxiliary projection. The prompt sequence is as follows.

Specify first point of inclined plane: *Specify the first point on the inclined plane.*
Specify second point of inclined plane: *Specify the second point on the inclined plane.*
Specify side to view from: *Specify a point.*
Specify view center: *Specify the location of the view.*
Specify view center <specify viewport>: Enter.
Specify first corner of viewport: *Specify the first corner of the viewport.*
Specify opposite corner of viewport: *Specify the second corner of the viewport.*
Enter view name: *Enter the view name.*

Section Option

This option is used to create the section views of the solid model. The type of the section view depends on the alignment of the section plane and the side from which you view the model. Initially, the crosshatching is not displayed in the section view. To display the crosshatching, invoke the **Solid Drawing** tool. AutoCAD prompts you to define the cutting plane and the prompt sequence is as follows.

Specify first point of cutting plane: *Specify the first point on the cutting plane.*
Specify second point of cutting plane: *Specify the second point on the cutting plane.*

Once you have defined the cutting plane, you can specify the side to view from and the view scale relative to paper space. The prompt sequence is given next.

Specify side to view from: *Specify the point in the direction from which the section is viewed.*
Enter view scale <current>: *Enter a positive number.*
Specify view center: *Specify the location for the view.*
Specify view center <specify viewport>: Enter.
Specify first corner of viewport: *Specify the first corner of the viewport.*
Specify opposite corner of viewport: *Specify the second corner of the viewport.*
Enter view name: *Enter the view name.*

Solid Drawing

Ribbon: Home > Modeling > Solid Drawing
Menu Bar: Draw > Modeling > Setup > Drawing **Command:** SOLDRAW

The **Solid Drawing** tool generates profiles and sections in the viewports that were created with the **Solid View** tool. The basic function of this tool is to clean up the viewports created by the **Solid View** tool. It displays the visible and hidden lines that represent the silhouettes and edges of the solids in a viewport, and then projects them in a plane that is perpendicular to the viewing direction. When you use the **Solid Drawing** tool with the sectional view, a temporary copy of the solid is created.

This temporary copy is then chopped at the section plane defined by you. Then the **Solid Drawing** tool creates the visible half as the section and discards the copy of the solid model. The crosshatching is automatically created using the current hatch pattern (HPNAME), hatch angle (HPANG), and hatch scale (HPSCALE). In this case, the layer **View name- HID** is frozen. If there are any existing profiles and sections in the selected viewports, they are deleted and replaced with new ones. The prompt sequence is as follows.

Select viewports to draw...
Select objects: *Select viewports to be drawn.*

Solid Profile

Ribbon: Home > Modeling > Solid Profile
Menu Bar: Draw > Modeling > Setup > Profile **Command:** SOLPROF

The **Solid Profile** tool creates profile images of 3D solids by displaying only the edges and silhouettes of the curved surfaces of the solids in the current view. Note that before you invoke this tool, you must be in the temporary model space of the layout. This means that the value of the **TILEMODE** variable should be set to 0, but you should switch to the model space using the **MSPACE** command. The prompt sequence that follows when you invoke the **Solid Profile** tool is given next.

Select objects: *Select the object in the viewport.*
Select objects: Enter.
Display hidden profile lines on separate layer? [Yes/No] <Y>: *Specify an option.*
Project profile lines onto a plane? [Yes/No] <Y>: *Specify an option.*
Delete tangential edges? [Yes/No] <Y>: *Specify an option.*
One solid selected.

DRAWING VIEWS

In AutoCAD, drafting has become easier due to the introduction of a new tab called **Layout** tab in the **Ribbon**. Most of the tools available in this tab can be used only in the drafting space (Layouts). With the help of these tools, you can generate a base view, projected view, section view, and detail view of the solid or surface present in the model space. You can also generate views of a model created in **Autodesk Inventor**. The options available in the **Layout** tab are discussed next.

Base

The tools available in the **Base** drop-down are used to create the base view of a model opened in the Model Space or created in Autodesk Inventor. The tools available in this drop-down are discussed next.

From Model Space

Ribbon: Layout > Create View > Base > From Model Space **Command:** VIEWBASE

The **From Model Space** tool is used to create the base view of the model opened in the Model Space of the current session of AutoCAD. To use this tool, you need a solid model created or opened in AutoCAD. Note that only the visible entities can be imported in this process. If the model space is empty and you invoke this tool, then the **Select File** window will be displayed and you will be prompted to select an Autodesk Inventor model. Figure 10-30 shows a solid model and its drawing views. To create the base view of this model, you need to follow the procedure given next.

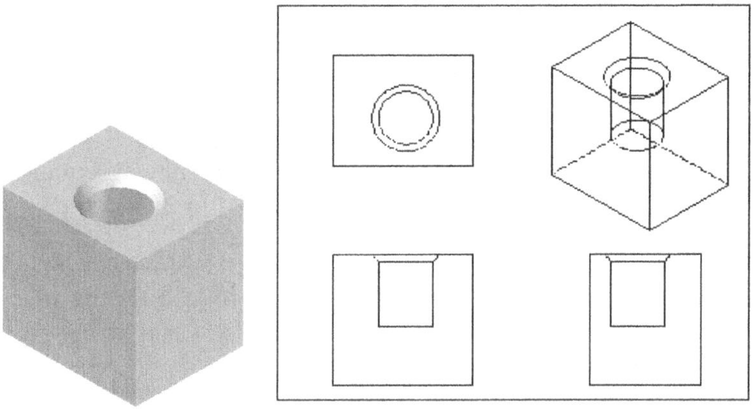

Figure 10-30 *Model and its drawing views*

Choose the Layout workspace and then delete the default viewport. Next, choose the **Base** tool from the **Create View** panel of the **Layout** tab; a flyout with the **From Model Space** and **From Inventor** tools will be displayed. Choose the **From Model Space** option from the flyout; a **Drawing View Creation** contextual tab will be displayed in the **Ribbon**, as shown in Figure 10-31. Select the desired orientation of the model for the drawing view from the **Orientation** list box. You can also choose the visual style of the base view from the **View Style** drop-down in the **Appearance** panel. You can specify the absolute scale of the object using the **Scale** drop-down list. You can control the visibility of the objects by selecting the check boxes provided in the **Edge Visibility** drop-down list. The check boxes available in the **Edge Visibility** drop-down list are discussed next.

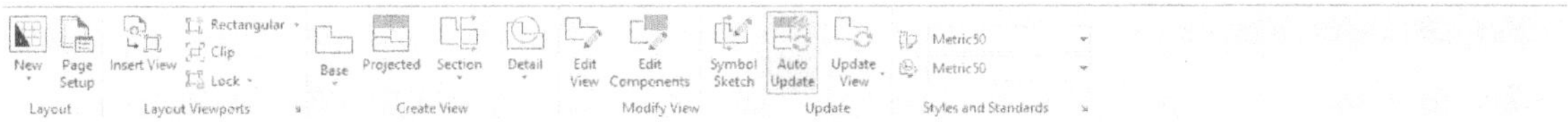

Figure 10-31 *The **Drawing View Creation** contextual tab*

Interference edges. This check box is used to toggle the visibility of both hidden and visible edges which are not displayed due to an intersection condition.

Tangent edges. This check box is used to toggle the visibility of the edges formed by tangential intersection of surfaces.

Tangent edges foreshortened. This check box is used to shorten the length of tangential edges to differentiate them from the visible edges.

Bend extents. This check box is used to toggle the display of the sheet metal extent lines. If there is a bend in the sheet metal part, then the **Bend extents** tool will be used to display the extent line of the sheet metal.

Thread features. This check box is used to toggle the display of thread lines on screws or tapped holes.

Presentation trails. This check box is used to display the lines that indicate the directions along which the components will move when assembled.

You can also specify the justification of a view by using the **View Options** in the **Appearance** panel. This dialog box can be invoked by clicking on the inclined arrow in the title bar of the **Appearance** panel. When you specify the scale of the view, the drawing view stretches or shrinks. If you select **Fixed** from the **View Justification** drop-down list, the alignment will remain unchanged. But if you select **Centered**, then the drawing view will be adjusted to the center position.

You can move the view to the required position by choosing the **Move** button in the **Modify** panel of the **Drawing View Creation** tab. This tab will become active only after placing the base view.

After specifying all the properties, click on the screen at the desired location; the base view will be created. Choose the **OK** button to place the base view; the **Drawing View Creation** tab will disappear and you will be prompted to specify the location of the projected view. The orientation of the projected view depends upon its location. Specify the location of projected view and exit by pressing Enter.

From Inventor

Ribbon: Layout > Create View > Base > From Inventor **Command:** VIEWBASE

The **From Inventor** tool is used to create the base view of the model created in Autodesk Inventor. On invoking this tool, the **Select File** window will be displayed and you will be prompted to select the **Autodesk Inventor** file to create the base view.

Projected View

Ribbon: Layout > Create View > Projected View **Command:** VIEWPROJ

The **Projected View** tool is used to create a projected view from the base view present in the layout workspace. By default, there are eight projected views, four orthogonal, and four isometric. You can create a projected view by using the procedure discussed next.

Choose the **Projected View** tool from the **Create View** panel of the **Layout** tab; you will be prompted to select the parent view. Select the existing view in the layout; the projected view will be attached to the cursor and you will be prompted to specify the location of the projected view. Specify the location; you will be prompted to specify the location of the projected view again. You can specify the location or you can exit by pressing Enter.

Edit View

Ribbon: Layout > Modify View > Edit View **Command:** VIEWEDIT

The **Edit View** tool is used to change the settings of a view such as representation, visibility, view style scale, and so on. After invoking this tool, you need to click on the drawing view; the **Drawing View Editor** contextual tab will be added to the **Ribbon**. Now, you can change the settings by selecting the required option from the **Drawing View Editor** tab. You can also move the view using the **Edit View** tool, but you cannot reorient it. Alternatively, you can invoke this tool by simply double-clicking on the drawing view.

Update View

Ribbon: Layout > Update > Update View **Command:** VIEWUPDATE

The **Update View** tool is used to update the layout. If you change the viewport, the drawing view will not be updated automatically. Therefore, you need to invoke the **Update View** tool to update the views. If you make changes to the model from which the views are derived, then the views in the layout will be displayed with a red mark on each corner. This red mark indicates that the model has been modified or removed. Also, a pop-up window is displayed at the bottom notifying that the model has been changed. You can update the views by choosing the **Update View** tool from the **Update** panel in the **Layout** tab. However, note that the **Update View** tool updates only the selected view. If you want to update all the views in the layout, then you have to choose the **Update all Views** tool from the **Update view** drop-down in the **Update** panel.

Auto Update

Ribbon: Layout > Update > Auto Update

The **Auto Update** tool is used to update the layout automatically when the source model is changed. By default, the **Auto Update** tool is activated in the **Update** panel. As a result, the layout views updates automatically, if any modification is made in the source model.

Drafting Standard

The **Drafting Standard** tool is used to set the default settings for drafting. These settings will be applied to the newly generated views. To invoke this tool, click on the inclined arrow located on the right of the **Styles and Standards** panel of the **Layout** tab; the **Drafting Standard** dialog box will be displayed, as shown in Figure 10-32. The three areas in this dialog box, **Projection type**, **Thread style**, and **Shading/Preview**, are discussed next.

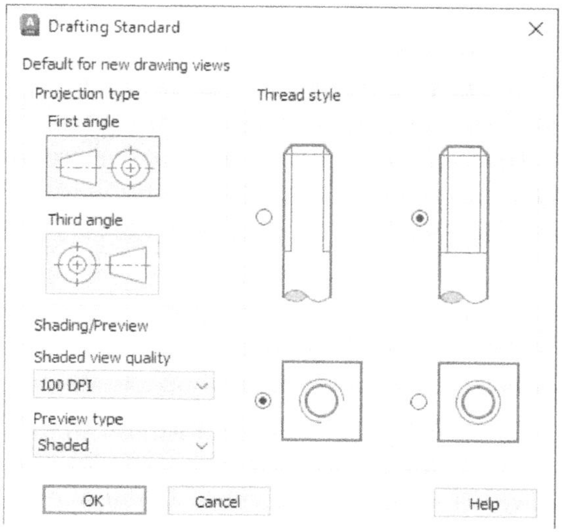

*Figure 10-32 The **Drafting Standard** dialog box*

Projection type. In this area, there are two buttons: **First angle** and **Third angle**. These buttons represent the first angle projection and the third angle projection, respectively. By default, **Third angle** is chosen.

Thread style. In this area, there are four radio buttons: **Partial section thread end**, **Full section thread end, Partial circular thread edge,** and **Full circular thread edge**. You can select the desired radio button to represent the threads.

Shading/Preview. In this area, there are two drop-down lists: **Shaded view quality** and **Preview type**. You can set the dot per inch quality of the shaded view in the drawing view by selecting the desired option from the **Shaded view quality** drop-down list. From the **Preview type** drop-down list, you can either select the **Shaded** preview or the **Bounding box** preview. If you select **Shaded**, the model is displayed shaded. If you select **Bounding box**, only the bounding box will be displayed in the preview, not the model.

Generating Section Views

In AutoCAD, you can generate the section views of the drawing view which are generated from a 3D model. The section views are generated by taking a portion of the existing view by using a cutting plane defined by the sketched line. The tools used for creating the section views are discussed next.

Full Section View

Ribbon: Layout > Create View > Section drop-down > Full **Command:** VIEWSECTION

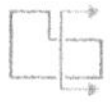

The **Full** tool is used to create the full section view of a model. This section view is created by cutting the model through its entire length. To do so, choose the **Full** tool from the **Section** drop-down in the **Create View** panel of the **Layout** tab and select the view of the model to be sectioned. Next, you will be prompted to specify the first point of the cutting section plane. Figure 10-33 shows the full section view created by using the **Full** tool. The prompt sequence for creating the full section view is given next.

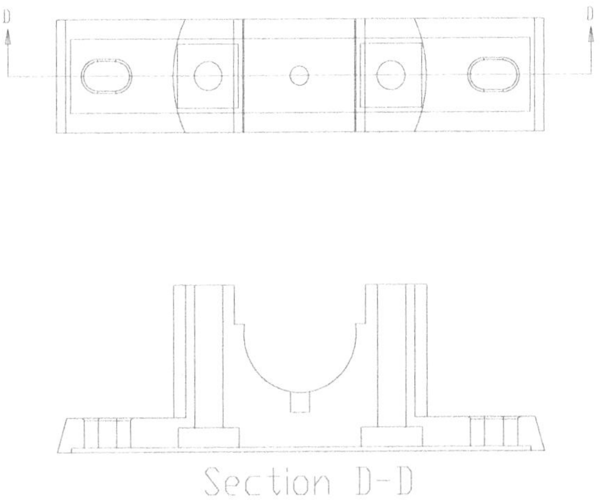

Figure 10-33 *Full section view created using the **Full** tool*

Select parent view: *Select a view.*
Specify start point: *Specify the start point to create the section plane defined by sketched line.*
Specify end point or undo : *Specify the end point which cuts the view through out the length.*
Specify location of the section view: *Specify the location of the view.*
Select option [Hidden lines/Scale/Visibility/Projection/Depth/Annotation/hatCh/Move/eXit] <eXit> : Enter.

Half Section View

Ribbon: Layout > Create View > Section drop-down > Half **Command:** VIEWSECTION

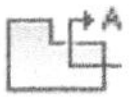

The **Half** tool is used to create the half section view of a model. The half section view is created by cutting the model through a portion of its length. To do so, choose the **Half** tool from the **Section** drop-down in the **Create View** panel of the **Layout** tab and select the view of the model to be sectioned. Create the cutting section plane which cuts the model through half of its length. Figure 10-34 shows the half section view created by using the **Half** tool. The prompt sequence for creating the half section view is given next.

Select parent view: *Select a view.*
Specify start point: *Specify the start point to create the section plane defined by sketched line.*
Specify next point or [Undo] : *Specify the next point.*
Specify end point or [Undo] : *Specify the end point.*
Specify location of the Section view or: *Specify the location of the view.*
Select option [Hidden lines/Scale/Visibility/Projection/Depth/Annotation/hatCh/Move/eXit] <eXit> : Enter.

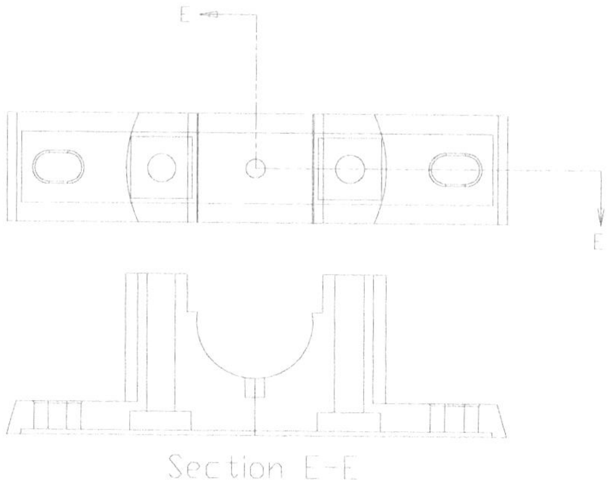

*Figure 10-34 Half section view created using the **Half** tool*

Offset Section View

Ribbon: Layout > Create View > Section drop-down > Offset **Command:** VIEWSECTION

The **Offset** tool is used to create the offset section view of a model. The offset section view is created by cutting the model at offset positions of the cutting plane. To create the offset section view, choose the **Offset** tool from the **Section** drop-down of the **Create View** panel in the **Layout** tab; you will be prompted to select the parent view. Select the model view and create the cutting section plane. Figure 10-35 shows the offset section view created by using the **Offset** tool. The prompt sequence for creating the offset section view is explained next.

Select parent view: *Select a view.*
Specify start point: *Specify the start point to create the section plane defined by sketched line.*
Specify next point or [Undo] : *Specify the next point.*
Specify next point or [Undo] : *Specify the next point and continue to specify the points.*
Specify next point or [Undo Done] <Done> : Enter.
Specify location of the Section view or: *Specify the location of the view .*
Select option [Hidden lines/Scale/Visibility/Projection/Depth/Annotation/hatCh/Move/eXit] <eXit> : Enter.

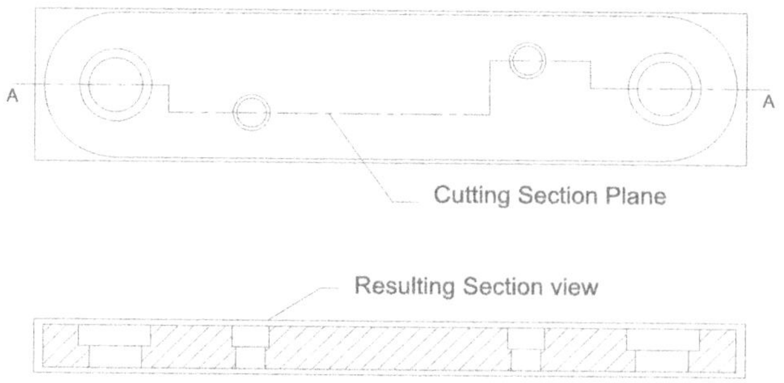

*Figure 10-35 Offset section view created using the **Offset** tool*

Aligned Section View

Ribbon: Layout > Create View > Section drop-down > Aligned **Command:** VIEWSECTION

The **Aligned** tool is used to create the aligned section view of a model. The aligned section view is created by cutting the model at different angles and lengths. To create the aligned section view, choose the **Aligned** tool from the **Section** drop-down of the **Create view** panel in the **Layout** tab; you will be prompted to select the section view. Next, create the cutting section axis which cuts the model at different angles and lengths. Figure 10-36 shows the aligned section view created using the **Aligned** tool. The prompt sequence for creating the aligned section view is given next.

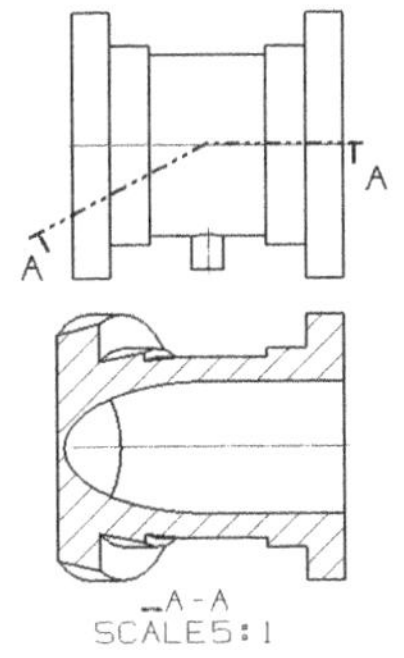

Figure 10-36 *Aligned Section view created using the **Aligned** tool*

Select parent view: *Select a view.*
Specify start point: *Specify the start point to create the section plane defined by sketched line.*
Specify next point or [Undo] : *Specify the next point.*
Specify next point or [Undo Done] <Done> : Enter.
Specify location of the Section view: *Specify the location of the view.*
Select option [Hidden lines/Scale/Visibility/Projection/Depth/Annotation/hatCh/Move/eXit] <eXit> : Enter.

From Object Section View

Ribbon: Layout > Create View > Section drop-down > From Object **Command:** VIEWSECTION

The **From Object** tool is used to create the object section view of a model. This object section view is created by cutting the model with an existing geometry line. To create object section view, draw a geometric line on the parent view through which you want to create the section view. Choose the **From Object** tool from the **Section** drop-down of the **Create View** panel in the **Layout** tab and select the parent view of the model. Figure 10-37 shows the section view created by using the **From Object** tool. The following prompt sequence for creating the object section view is explained next.

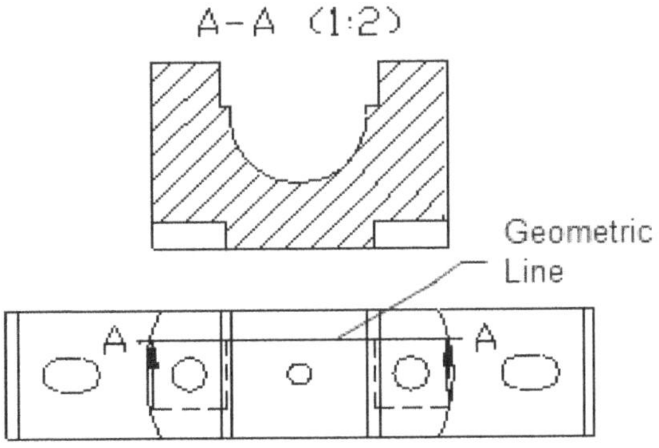

Figure 10-37 *Section view created using the **From Object** tool*

Select parent view: *Select a view.*
Select objects or [Done] : *Section the geometry to specify as a section line,* Enter.
Specify location of the Section view: *Specify the location of the view.*
Select option [Hidden lines/Scale/Visibility/Projection/Depth/Annotation/hatCh/Move/eXit] <eXit> : Enter.

The options available in the command prompt are discussed next.

Hidden Lines. This option is used to specify the line types displayed for the section view. When you select this option, you will be prompted to select the style of the hidden lines to be displayed. You can select any desired style to display the hidden lines by using the options in the command prompt.

Scale. This option is used to specify the scale of the section view. By default, the scale of the new section view is chosen from the base view. You can also specify the required scale for the section view.

Visibility. This option allows you to specify the type of visibility of the edges, features, and so on for the section view.

Projection. This option is used to specify the type of projection for the section view.

Depth. This option is used to specify the depth of the cut for the section view.

Annotation. This option is used to specify the type of annotations like the label and identifier of the section view.

Hatch. This option is used to turn on or off the display of the hatching for the section view.

CREATING FLATSHOT

Ribbon: Home > Section > Flatshot OR Solid > Section > Flatshot **Command:** FLATSHOT

The **Flatshot** tool creates a 2D sketch of a model by projecting the model in the current view on the XY plane of the current UCS. The created sketch is inserted in the drawing as a block. A flatshot can be created in any preset orthographic view or a view created in the parallel projection. If you create a flatshot in the perspective view, a 3D wireframe of the entire model will be created by projecting the model in the current view on the XY plane of the current UCS. Choose the **Flatshot** tool from the **Section** panel; the **Flatshot** dialog box will be displayed, refer to Figure 10-38. The options in this dialog box are discussed next.

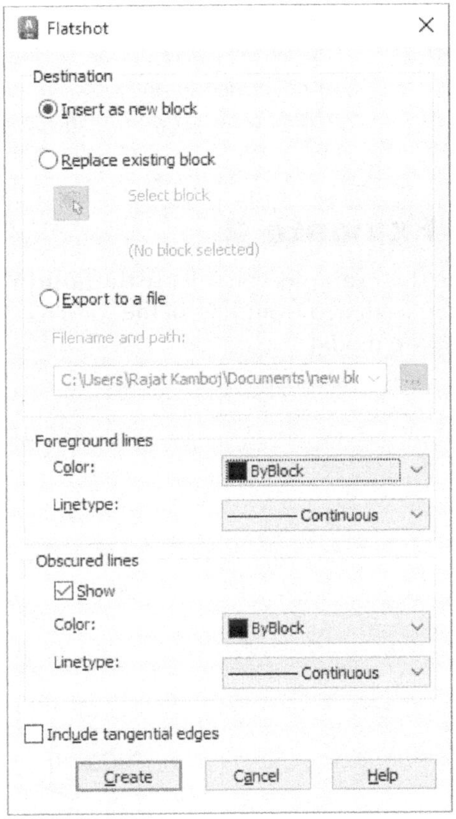

*Figure 10-38 The **Flatshot** dialog box*

Destination

By using the options in this area, you can specify how you want to use the generated flatshot. The **Insert as new block** radio button inserts the generated flatshot in the same drawing file as a block. The **Replace existing block** button inserts the generated flatshot by replacing an existing block. Choose the **Select block** button to select the block to be replaced by the newly generated block. The **Export to a file** radio button allows you to create a new drawing file with the generated flatshot. To save it as a new file, choose the **Browse [...]** button to specify the location where you want to save the new drawing file.

Foreground lines

The options in this area control the color and line type of the edges in the front at the time of the flatshot creation.

Obscured lines

The options in this area control the display, color, and line type of the hidden edges at the time of the flatshot creation.

Create

Choosing this button finishes the flatshot creation process.

Include tangential edges

Select this check box to include the tangential edges of the curved surface into the flatshot.

Note

The 3D objects that are sectioned by the section plane will be flatshot as if they are not sectioned.

Tip

All the 3D objects in the current drawing are included in the flatshot creation. If you do not want to include some objects in the flatshot creation, transfer them to a separate layer and freeze the layer before creating the flatshot.

Example 2 — Solid View & Solid Drawing

In this example, you will use the **Solid View** and **Solid Drawing** tools to generate the top view and the sectioned front view of the solid model shown in Figure 10-39. Assume the missing dimensions of the model.

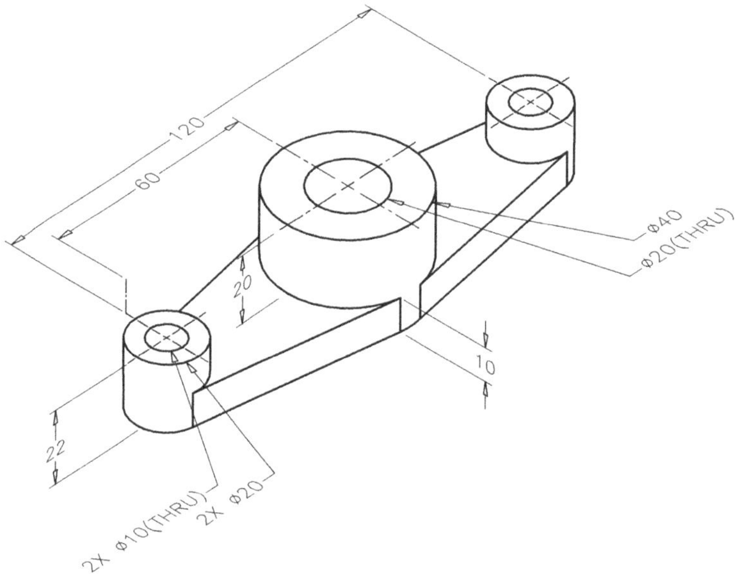

Figure 10-39 *Solid model to generate drawing views*

1. Create the solid model by assuming the dimensions.

2. Switch to **Layout1**; the default viewport is displayed.

3. Delete the default viewport. To do so, invoke the **Erase** tool, select the Viewport, and press Enter.

4. Choose the **Solid View** tool from the **Modeling** panel and follow the prompt sequence given below:

Enter an option [Ucs/Ortho/Auxiliary/Section]: **U**
Enter an option [Named/World/?/Current] <Current>: **W**
Enter view scale <1.0000>: Enter.
Specify view center: *Specify the view location close to the top left corner of the drawing window.*
Specify view center <specify viewport>: Enter.
Specify first corner of viewport: *Specify the point of the viewport, P1, refer to Figure 10-40.*
Specify opposite corner of viewport: *Specify the second point, P2, refer to Figure 10-40.*
Enter view name: **Top**
Enter an option [Ucs/Ortho/Auxiliary/Section]: Enter.

5. Double-click in the viewport to switch to the temporary model space. Zoom the drawing to the extents using the **Extents** option of the **ZOOM** command. Now, switch back to the paper space by choosing the **MODEL** button displayed in the Status Bar. The layout after generating the top view should look similar to the layout shown in Figure 10-41.

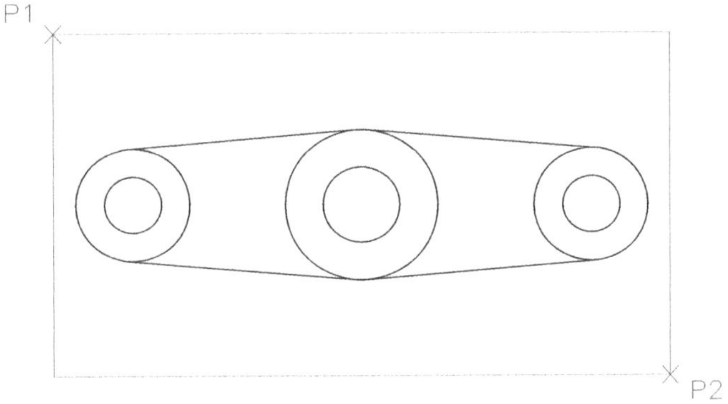

Figure 10-40 *Generating the top view*

6. Again, choose the **Solid View** tool from the **Modeling** panel and follow the prompt sequence given below:

Enter an option [Ucs/Ortho/Auxiliary/Section]: **S**
Specify first point of cutting plane: *Select the left quadrant of the left cylindrical portion in the top view.*
Specify second point of cutting plane: *Select the right quadrant of the right cylindrical portion in the top view.*
Specify side to view from: *Select a point below the top view in the viewport.*
Enter view scale <current>: Enter.
Specify view center: *Specify the location of the view below the top view.*
Specify view center <specify viewport>: Enter.
Specify first corner of viewport: *Select first corner of the viewport.*
Specify opposite corner of viewport: *Select the second corner of the viewport.*
Enter view name: **FRONT**
Enter an option [Ucs/Ortho/Auxiliary/Section]: Enter.

7. Choose the **Solid Drawing** tool from the **Modeling** panel and follow the prompt sequence given next.
   Select viewports to draw.
   Select objects: *Select the first viewport.*
   Select objects: Enter.
   Select objects: Enter.

8. The drawing view should look similar to the layout shown in Figure 10-41.

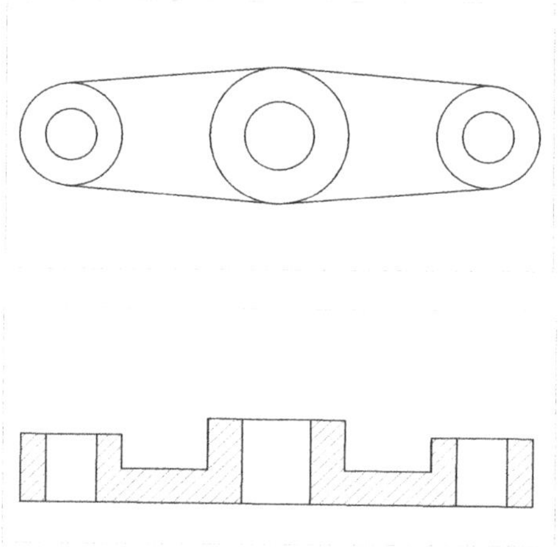

Figure 10-41 *Layout after generating the drawing views*

Tip
*You can change the scale and the type of hatch pattern using the **Properties** palette. You can also set different linetypes and colors to different lines in the views by selecting their respective layers using the **Layer Properties** tool.*

CALCULATING THE MASS PROPERTIES OF SOLID MODELS

Menu Bar: Tools > Inquiry > Region/Mass Properties
Toolbar: Inquiry > Region/Mass Properties **Command:** MASSPROP

The mass properties of the solids or the regions can be automatically calculated using the **Region/Mass Properties** tool. Various mass properties are displayed in the AutoCAD Text Window. You can also write these properties to a file. This file will be in the *.mpr* format. The properties thus calculated can be used in analyzing the solid models. Note that the mass properties are calculated by taking the density of the material of the solid model as one unit.

It is very important for you to first understand the various properties that will be calculated using this tool. The properties are:

Mass. This property provides the measure of mass of a solid. This property will not be available for the regions.

Area. This property provides the measure of area of the region. This property will be available only for the regions.

Volume. This property tells you the measure of the space occupied by the solid. Since AutoCAD assigns a density of 1 to solids, the mass and volume of a solid are equal. This property will be available only for the solids.

Perimeter. This property, providing the measure of the perimeter of the region, will be available only for the regions.

Bounding Box. If the solid were to be enclosed in a 3D box, the coordinates of the diagonally opposite corners would be provided by this property. Similarly, for regions, the *X* and the *Y* coordinates of the bounding box are displayed.

Centroid. This property provides the coordinates of the center of mass for the selected solid. The density of a solid is assumed to be unvarying.

Moments of Inertia. This property provides the mass moments of inertia of a solid about the three axes. The equation used to calculate this value is given next.

$$\text{mass\_moments\_of\_inertia} = \text{object\_mass} * (\text{radius of axis})^2$$

The radius of axis is nothing but the radius of gyration. The values obtained are used to calculate the force required to rotate an object about the three axes.

Products of Inertia. The value obtained with this property helps you to determine the force resulting in the motion of the object. The equation used to calculate this value is:

$$\text{product \_of\_inertia YX, XZ} = \text{mass} * \text{dist centroid\_to\_YZ} * \text{dist centroid\_to\_XZ}$$

Radii of Gyration. The equation used to calculate this value is given next.

$$\text{gyration\_radii} = (\text{moments\_of\_inertia/body\_mass})^{1/2}$$

Principal moments and X-Y-Z directions about centroid. This property provides you with the highest, lowest, and middle value for the moment of inertia about an axis passing through the centroid of the object.

The prompt sequence that follows when you invoke the **Region/Mass Properties** tool is given next.

Select objects: *Select the solid model.*
Select objects: ENTER.

```
---------------- SOLIDS ----------------

Mass:                     67278.5917
Volume:                   67278.5917
Bounding box:             X: 1.4012 -- 151.4012
                          Y: 118.6406    -- 158.6406
                          Z: 0.0000      -- 25.0000
Centroid:                 X: 76.4012
                          Y: 138.6406
                          Z: 9.2026

Moments of inertia:       X: 1308864825.5181
                          Y: 507244127.3062
                          Z: 1799135898.4724
Products of inertia:      XY: 712635884.7490
                          YZ: 85837337.1138
                          ZX: 47302745.3493
Radii of gyration:        X: 139.4790
                          Y: 86.8301
                          Z: 163.5285
Principal moments and X-Y-Z directions about centroid:
Press Enter to continue: Enter.
                          I: 9991363.2928 along [1.0000 0.0000 0.0000]
                          J: 108831209.8607 along [0.0000 1.0000 0.0000]
                          K: 113244795.9294 along [0.0000 0.0000 1.0000]

Write analysis to a file? [Yes/No] <N>: Specify an option.
```

If you enter **Y** at the last prompt, the **Create Mass and Area Properties File** dialog box will be displayed. This dialog box is used to specify the name of the *.mpr* file. The mass properties will then be written in this file.

RECORDING THE DRAWING STEPS BY USING THE ACTION RECORDER

Ribbon: Manage > Action Recorder > Record
Menu Bar: Tools > Action Recorder > Record   **Command:** ACTRECORD

The **Record** tool helps you to record the drawing steps quickly and easily. These steps are called actions. These actions are saved to a named macro for repeated use. To record an action, choose the **Record** tool from the **Action Recorder** panel of the **Manage** tab. On invoking this tool, a red circle appears near the cursor, indicating that the actions are recorded. Now, if you perform any action, it will be recorded. Also, the **Action Tree** will be expanded and the actions you perform will get updated simultaneously, as shown in Figure 10-42. If you need any message to be displayed during playback, choose the **Insert Message** tool from the **Action Recorder** panel; the **Insert User Message** dialog box will be displayed. Enter the message and choose the **OK** button; the message will be added to the **Action Tree**. This message will be displayed during playback. Similarly, if you want the user to input any values while playback, you can choose the **Pause for User Input** tool from the **Action Recorder** panel and continue recording the action. After recording the actions, choose the **Stop** button in the **Action Recorder** panel to stop the recording; the **Action Macro** dialog box will be displayed, as shown in Figure 10-43. Specify a name for the action macro in the **Action Macro Command Name** edit box. If you want to give any description of the action, enter it in the **Description** edit box. The check boxes in the **Restore pre-playback view** area are used to invoke the playback message box when you play the action macro. If you select the **Check for inconsistencies when playback begins** check box and if there is inconsistency in the workspace, template, or any other while you playback the action macro, then a warning box will be displayed. Remember that if you invoke any dialog boxes such as **Hatch and Gradient** or **OSnap** and change any settings during recording, then those settings will not be recorded. As a result, during the playback, the corresponding dialog box will be displayed again and you need to set the parameters again in it.

The **Folder Path** display box in the **Action Macro** dialog box displays the default path where the action macro is saved.

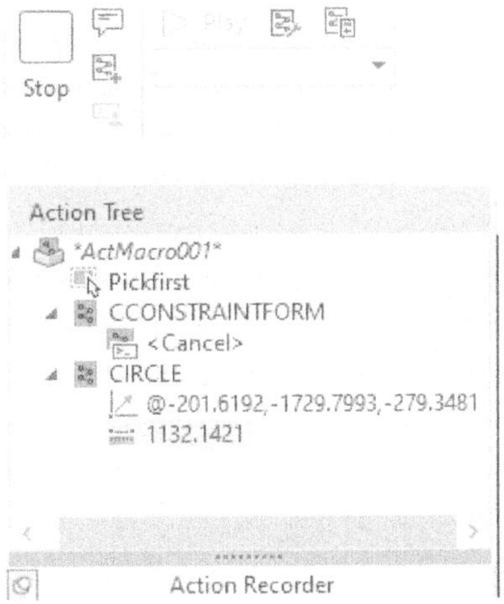

*Figure 10-42 The **Action Recorder** panel recording the actions performed*

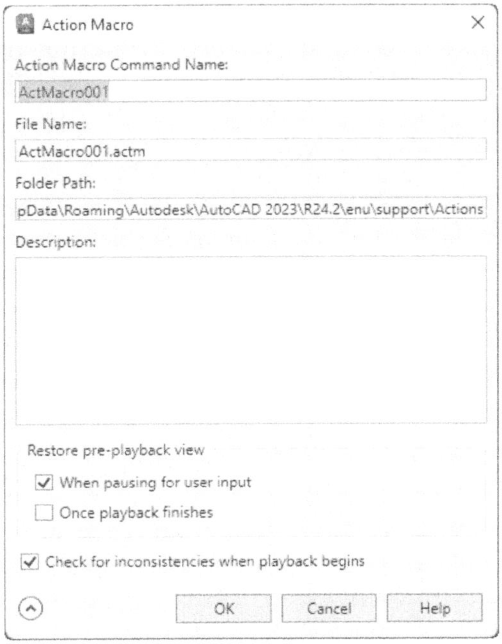

*Figure 10-43 The **Action Macro** dialog box*

The **ACTRECPATH** command is used to change the path where the action macro is stored, by default. On entering this command, the following prompt sequence will be displayed:

Command: **ACTRECPATH**
Enter new value for ACTRECPATH, or . for none <*"C:\Users\CADCIM Technologies\AppData\Roaming\Autodesk\AutoCAD 2023\R24.2\enu\support\Actions"*>: *Enter the new location within the quotes (" ")*

To playback the recorded action macro, select the action macro from the **Available Action Macro** drop-down list in the **Action Recorder** panel and choose the **Play** button; the action macro will start playing. You can use an existing action macro in a new drawing. To do so, open a new drawing file in the same template as used for the action macro. Next, choose the **Play** button from the **Action Recorder** panel.

USING SHOWMOTION FOR PRESENTATION

Menu Bar: View > ShowMotion **Navigation Bar:** ShowMotion **Command:** NAVSMOTION

The **ShowMotion** tool is used to create the animated views of the current drawing. This can be used to quickly step through different named views in the drawing, enabling you to play the animated views for presentations or to review the drawings.

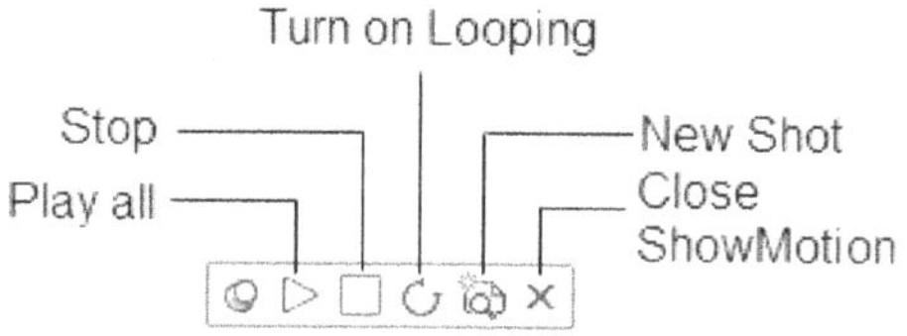

Figure 10-44 *The* ***ShowMotion*** *control panel*

On invoking this tool, a control panel for **ShowMotion** with six buttons will be displayed above the **Status Bar**, refer to Figure 10-44. The **Play all** button is used to play all the saved animations, which include shots and view categories, in a sequence. While playing the animations, the **Play all** button automatically gets converted into the **Pause** button, enabling you to pause the playback and vice-versa. The **Stop** button stops playing the animation. The **Turn on Looping** button of the **ShowMotion** allows the animation to continue playing until you choose the **Stop** button or press the Esc key. A new animated view or a shot is created by choosing the **New Shot** button. On choosing this button, the **New View / Shot Properties** dialog box will be displayed, refer to Figure 10-45. The options in this dialog box are discussed next.

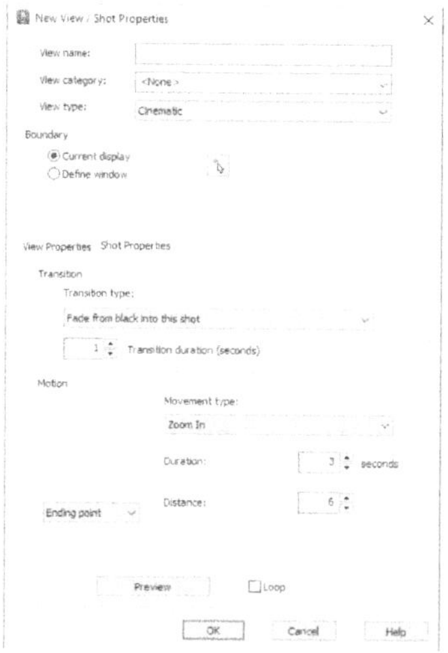

Figure 10-45 *The* ***New View/Shot Properties*** *dialog box*

View name. You can specify the name for the shot in the **View name** edit box. These names will be displayed below the respective shot thumbnails.

View category. You can enter the name of the category in this edit box. You can also group a sequence of shots of the same view categories. The different view categories are displayed as a series of thumbnails at the bottom of the drawing area.

View type. You can take three different types of shots using this drop-down list. These are **Still, Cinematic** and **Recorded Walk**. You can give transition effects between two shots, and the length or duration of the effects can be specified in the **Transition** area. Select an option in the **Transition type** drop-down list to specify the transition effects between two shots. You can see the preview of any view type in the preview box available in the **Motion** area of the **Shot Properties** tab of the dialog box.

If you select the **Still** option from the **View type** drop-down list, the position of camera will be fixed and you can set the duration of the shot in the **Motion** area of the dialog box.

If you select the **Cinematic** option from the **View type** drop-down list, you can move the camera position and set the duration of the recording. Select the type of movement in the **Movement type** drop-down list and specify the duration and distance in the respective spinners. On selecting the **Crane up** or **Crane down** option in the **Movement type** drop-down list, the **Shift left** check box becomes available. Consequently, you can specify the amount by which the camera shifts to left or right during the movement. On selecting the **Always look at camera pivot point** check box, the view is always focused at the camera.

If you select the **Recorded Walk** option from the **View type** drop-down list, you can create an animated view. To do so, choose the **Start Recording** button available in the **Motion** area of the **Shot Properties** tab. The dialog box disappears and a navigation tool is attached to the cursor. Next, press and hold the left mouse button and move the cursor. Once you release the left mouse button, the dialog box reappears. Choose the **OK** button to exit the dialog box.

Playing the Animation

Each **View Category** and its shots are displayed as thumbnails at the bottom of the drawing area. Each **View Category** thumbnail contains its corresponding name at its bottom. The series of shots under each category are displayed as smaller thumbnails above the **View Category** thumbnails, as shown in Figure 10-46. However, the thumbnails are enlarged when the cursor moves over them. Each thumbnail contains two buttons, **Play** and **Go**. Choosing the **Play** button on the shot thumbnail plays that particular animated shot whereas choosing the **Play** button on the **View Category** thumbnail plays the sequence of shots under that particular category. On choosing the **Go** button available on the right side of the thumbnails, you can move the camera to the camera position of the first shot. To play all the shots, choose the **Play all** button from the control panel.

You can rename, delete, recapture, or update a shot using the shortcut menu displayed on right-clicking on a thumbnail. You can also re-order the sequence of shots by moving them to the left or right using the options in the shortcut menu. To create a new shot, choose the **New View / Shot** option from the shortcut menu. To modify the shots, choose the **Properties** option from the shortcut menu; you will be prompted to enter the name of the view you want to edit.

Type the name of the view and press Enter; the **New View / Shot Properties** dialog box will be displayed. Now, you can change the required properties in this dialog box.

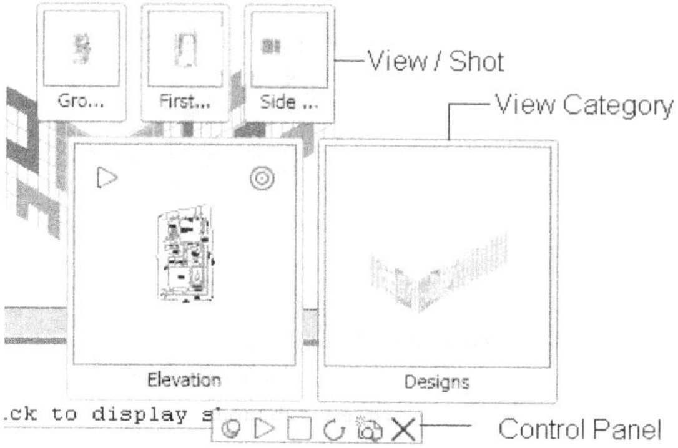

***Figure 10-46** The **ShowMotion** control panel and the **View Category** thumbnails*

Self-Evaluation Test

Answer the following questions and then compare them to those given at the end of this chapter:

1. The __________ tool is used to generate the drawing views of a solid model.

2. The mass properties of a selected solid model can be written into a file of __________ format.

3. The __________ tool creates a 2D sketch of a model by projecting the model in the current view on the XY plane of the current UCS.

4. Choose the __________ tool to separate 3D solids from the 3D solids with disjointed volumes.

5. The impression on a solid model can be removed using the __________ tool.

6. Solid models can be edited using the **EDITSOLID** command. (T/F)

7. You can create a shell in a solid model using the **Shell** tool. (T/F)

8. A section plane cuts all 3D objects, surfaces, and regions only if the section plane actually passes through them. (T/F)

9. The **Record** tool in the **Action Recorder** panel is used to create the animated views of the current drawing. (T/F)

10. The history of a composite solid created by performing the Boolean operation is saved along with the composite solid. (T/F)

Review Questions

Answer the following questions:

1. Which of the following tools is used to generate the profiles and sections in the viewports created using the **Solid View** tool?

   (a) **Solid Draw** (b) **Solid Profile**
   (c) **Solid Edit** (d) None of these

2. Which of the following methods is used to create a section plane?

   (a) by Specifying Two Points (b) by Selecting a Preset Orthographic Plane
   (c) by Drawing the Section Line (d) All of the above

3. Which option of the **SOLIDEDIT** command is used to edit the faces of a solid model?

   (a) **Body** (b) **Face**
   (c) **Solid** (d) None of these

4. Which of the following options of the **Solid View** tool is used to generate the drawing view relative to the current UCS?

   (a) **New** (b) **Section**
   (c) **UCS** (d) **Ortho**

5. Which of the following commands is used to calculate mass properties of the solid model?

   (a) **PROPERTIES** (b) **MASSPROP**
   (c) **CALCULATE** (d) **MASSPROPERTIES**

6. You can edit a wireframe model by using the **SOLIDEDIT** command. (T/F)

7. You can move a selected face of a solid model from one location to the other. (T/F)

8. You can assign different colors to different faces of a solid model. (T/F)

9. After adding a jog, you can edit its length and location with the help of grips. (T/F)

10. The sketch created using the **Flatshot** tool is inserted into a drawing as a block. (T/F)

Exercise 1

In this exercise, you will create the solid model shown in Figure 10-47. After creating the model, generate its top and sectioned front views and then shade the model by using the Shaded with Visible Lines option.

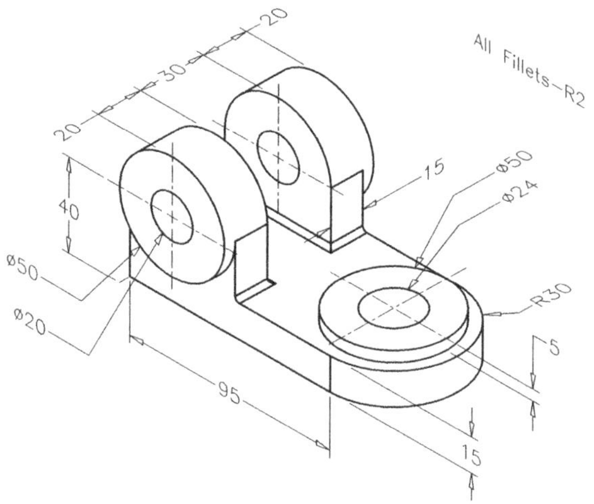

Figure 10-47 *Solid model for Exercise 1*

Exercise 2

In this exercise, you will create the solid model shown in Figure 10-48. After creating the model, shade and rotate it in the 3D space using the **Orbit** tool. Assume the missing dimensions.

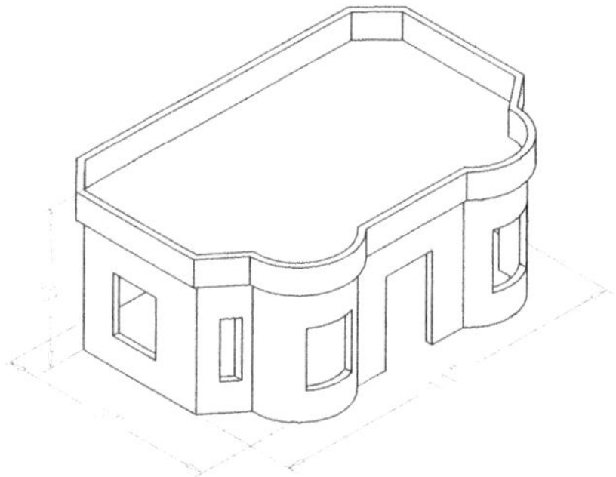

Figure 10-48 *Solid model for Exercise 2*

Problem-Solving Exercise 1

Draw the Piece part drawings shown in Figure 10-49. Then assemble them and create the Bill of Materials, as shown in Figure 10-50. The solid model of the assembled Tool Organizer is shown in Figure 10-51.

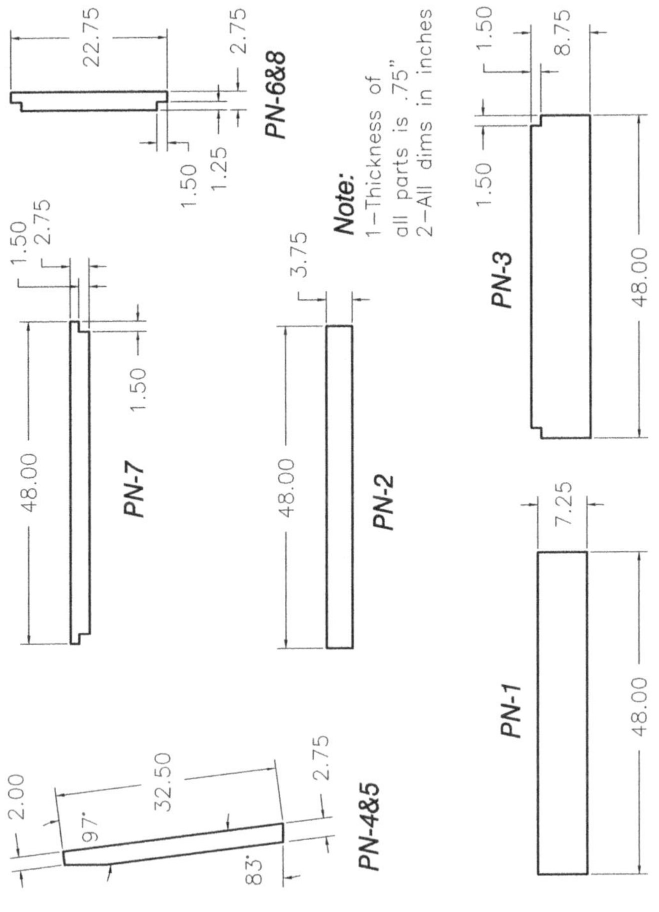

***Figure 10-49** Piece part drawing of the Tool Organizer*

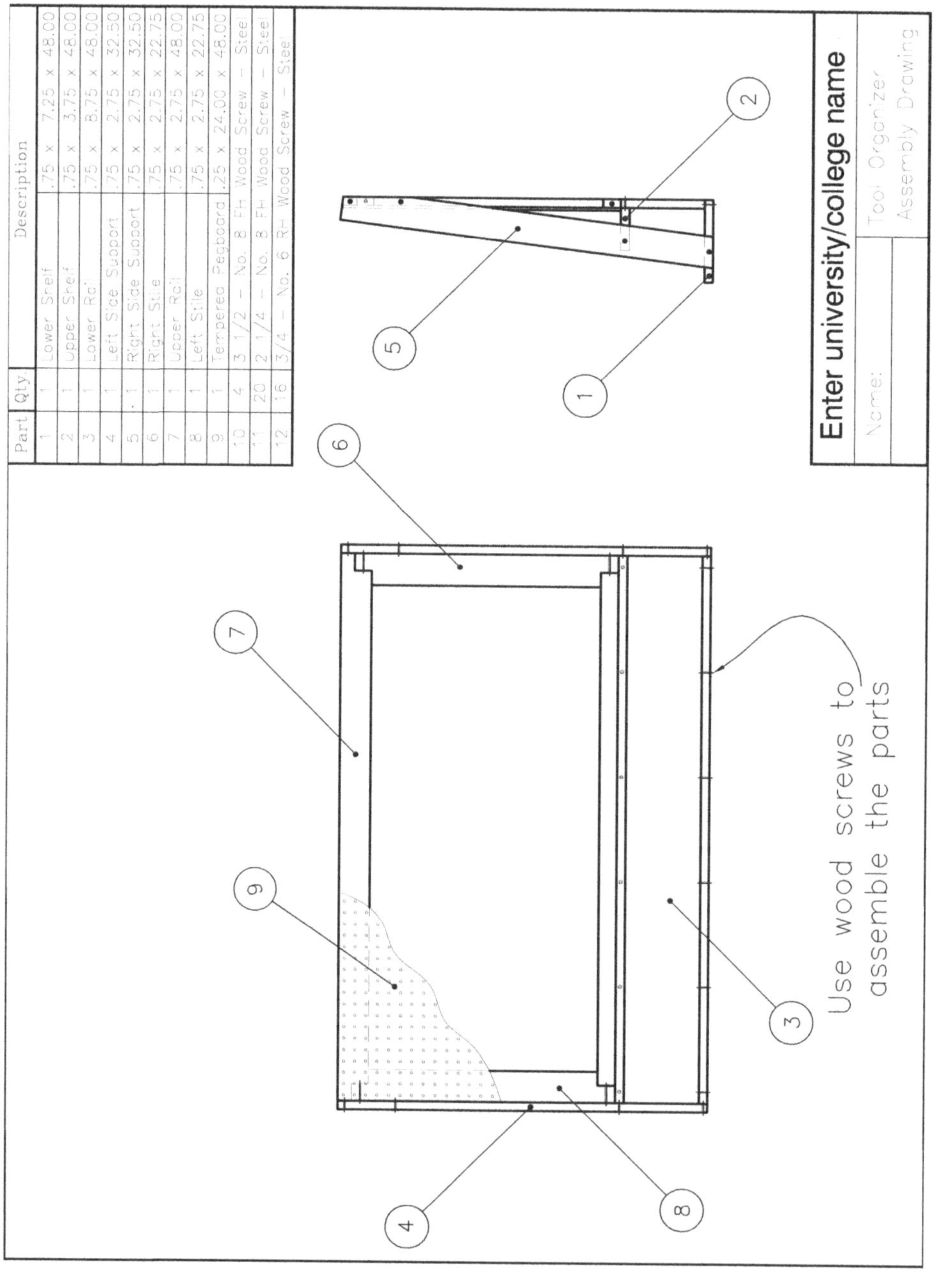

***Figure 10-50** Assembly drawing and BOM of the Tool Organizer*

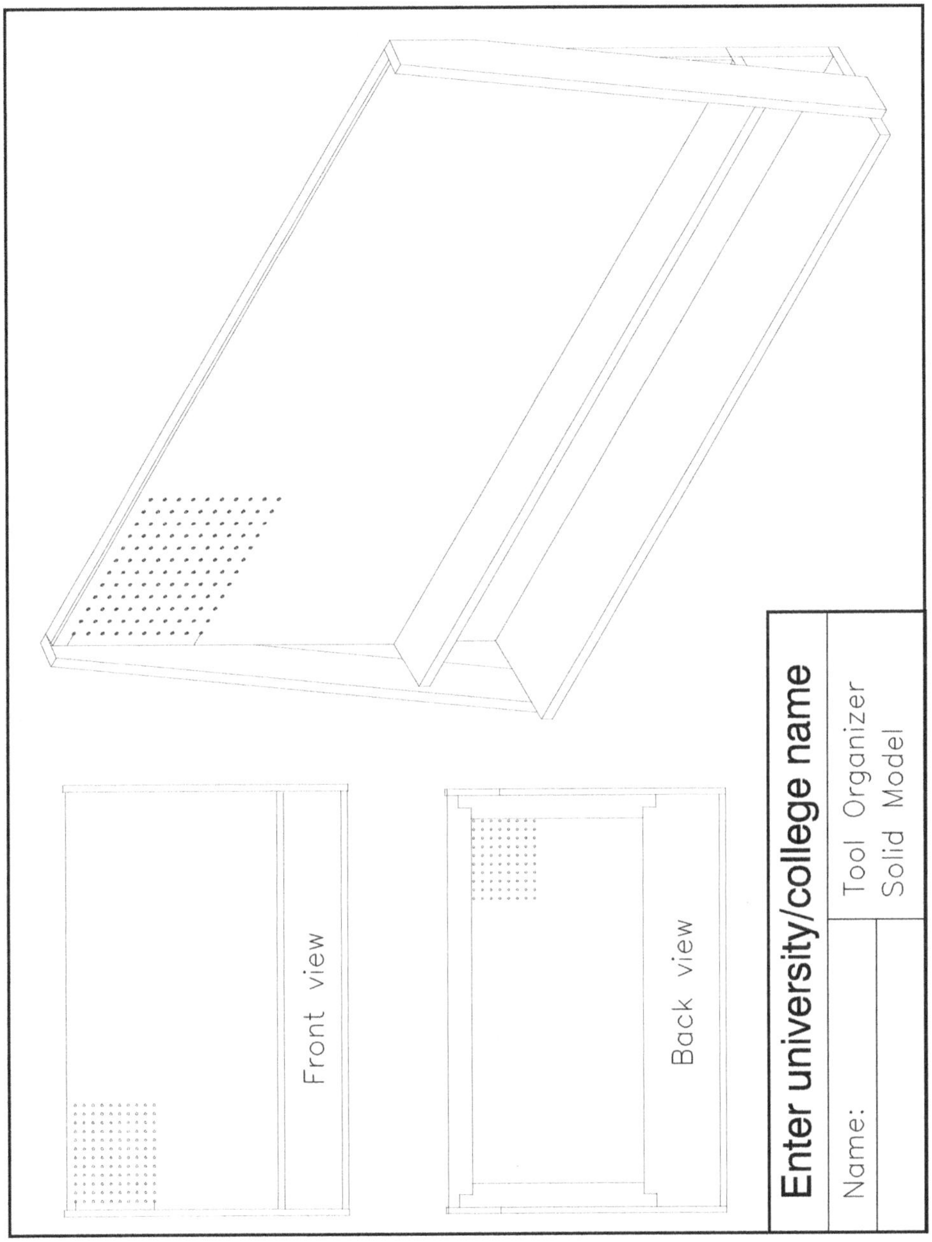

Figure 10-51 *Solid model of the Tool Organizer*

Problem-Solving Exercise 2

Draw the Piece part drawings shown in Figure 10-52. Then assemble them and create the Bill of Materials, as shown in Figure 10-53. The solid model of the assembled Work Bench is shown in Figure 10-54.

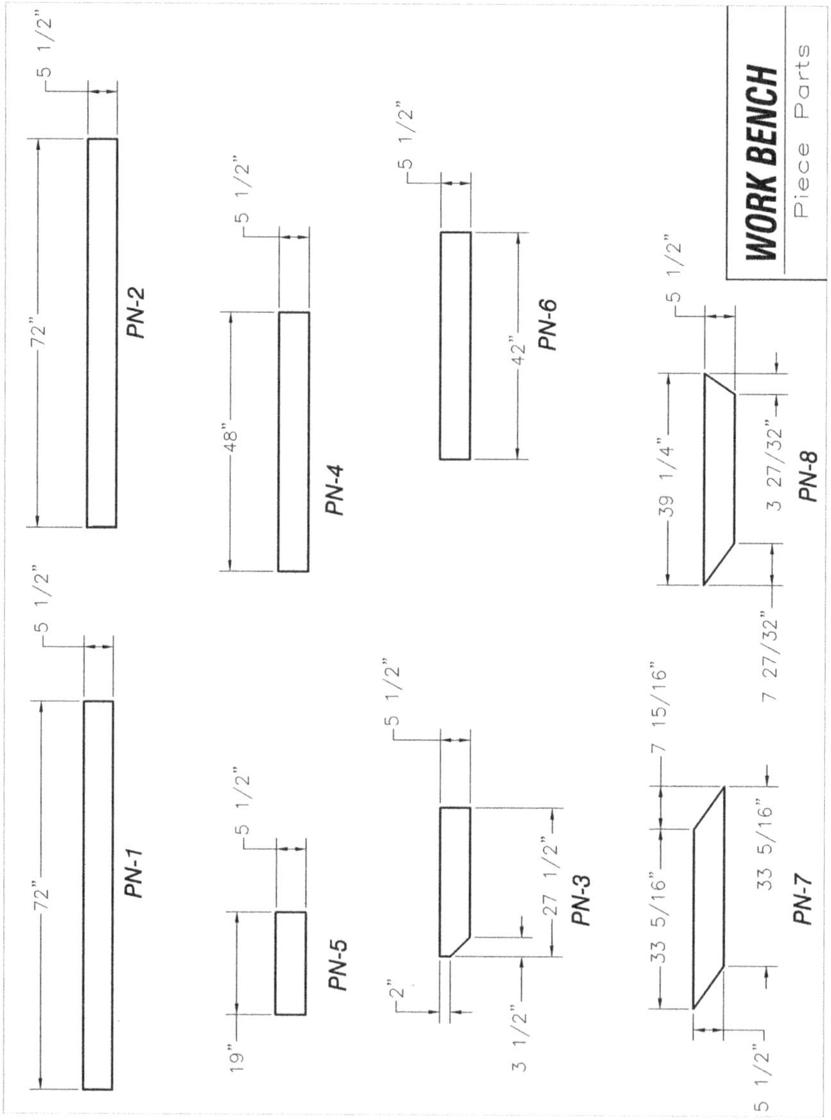

Figure 10-52 Piece part drawings of the Work Bench

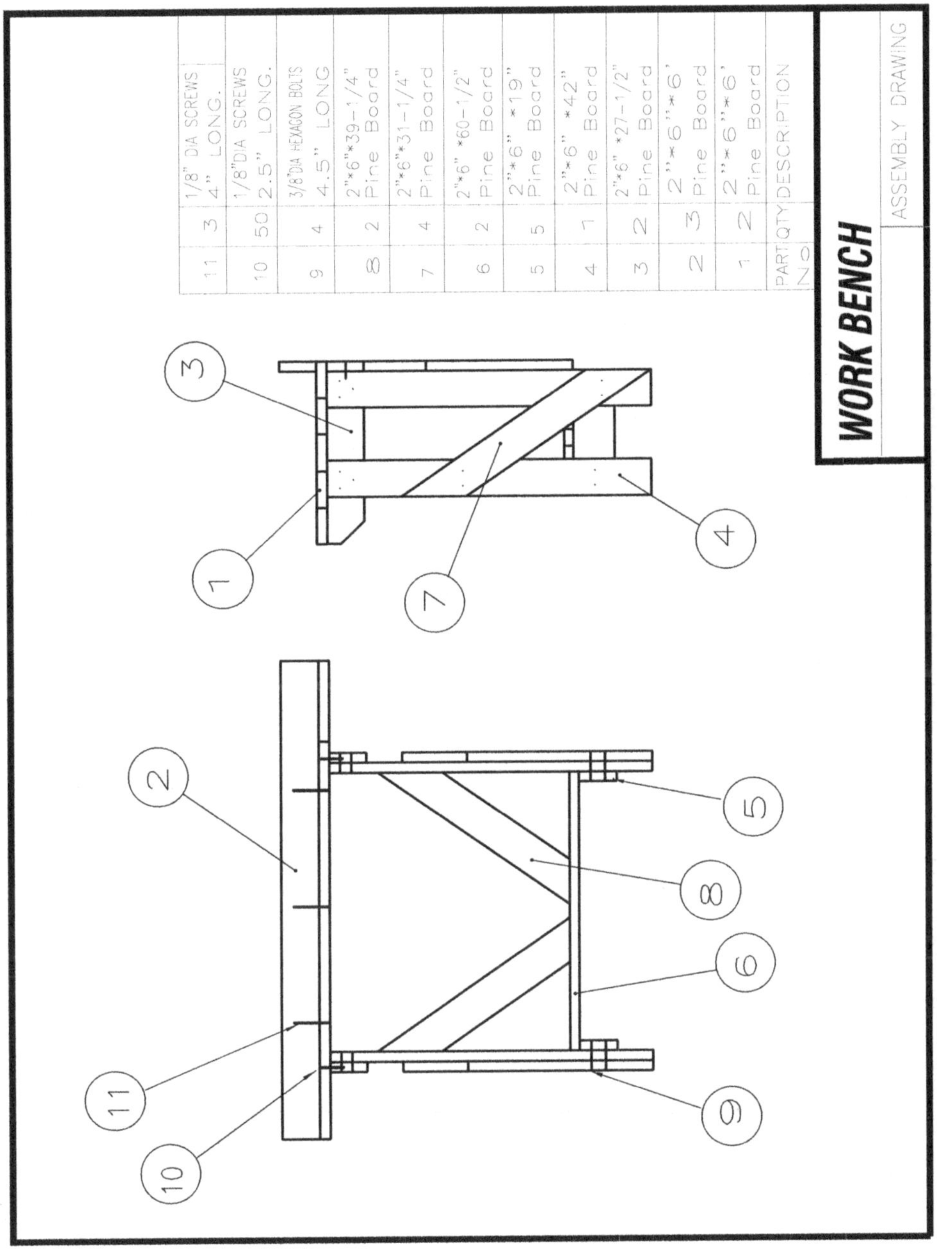

PART No	QTY	DESCRIPTION
11	3	1/8" DIA SCREWS 4" LONG.
10	50	1/8"DIA SCREWS 2.5" LONG.
9	4	3/8"DIA HEXAGON BOLTS 4.5" LONG
8	2	2"*6"*39-1/4" Pine Board
7	4	2"*6"*31-1/4" Pine Board
6	2	2"*6" *60-1/2" Pine Board
5	5	2"*6" *19" Pine Board
4	1	2"*6" *42" Pine Board
3	2	2"*6" *27-1/2" Pine Board
2	3	2"*6"*6' Pine Board
1	2	2"*6"*6' Pine Board

***Figure 10-53** Assembly drawing and BOM of the Work Bench*

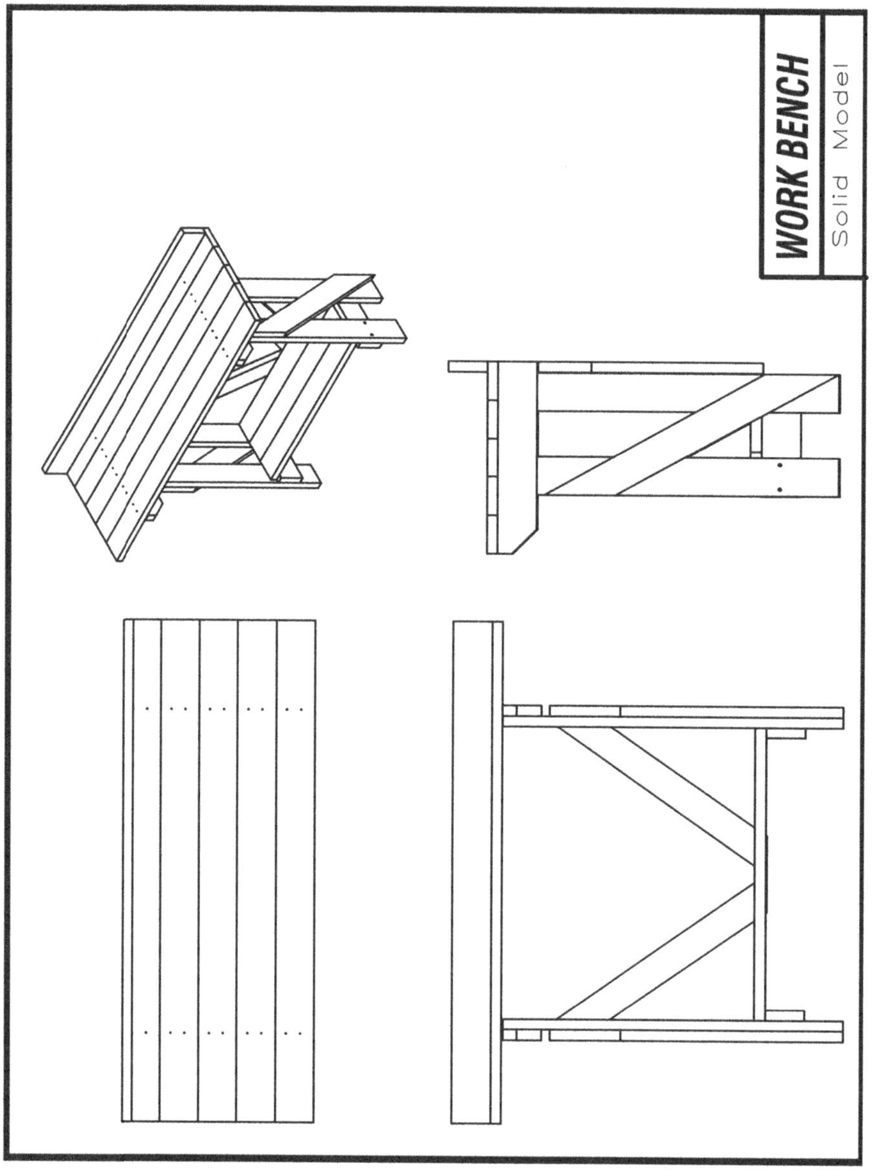

Figure 10-54 *Solid model of the Work Bench*

Problem-Solving Exercise 3

Create the model shown in Figure 10-55. Also, create the section view of the model as shown in Figure 10-56. The dimensions of the model are given in Figure 10-57.

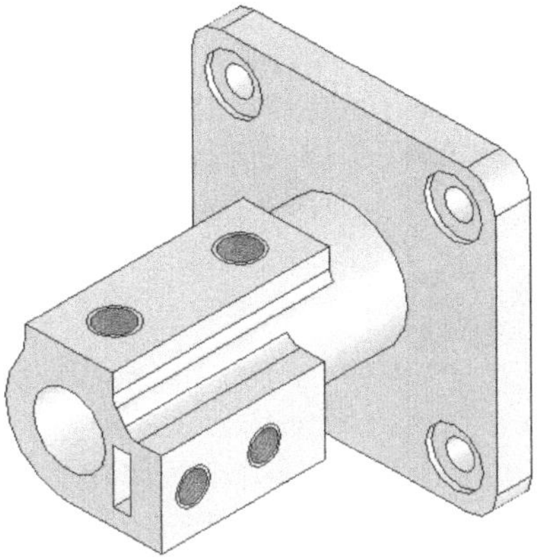

Figure 10-55 *Solid model*

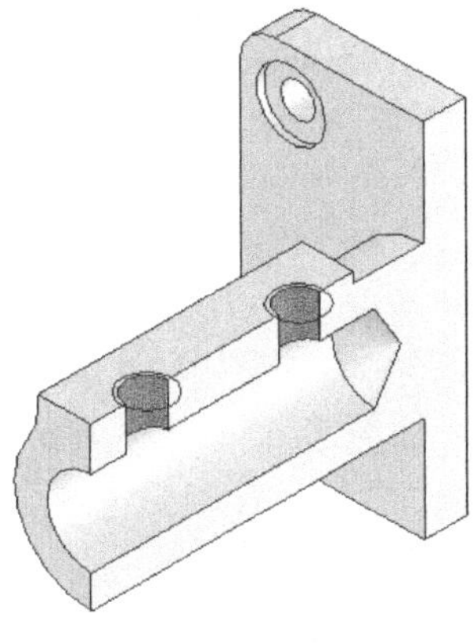

Figure 10-56 *Section view of the model*

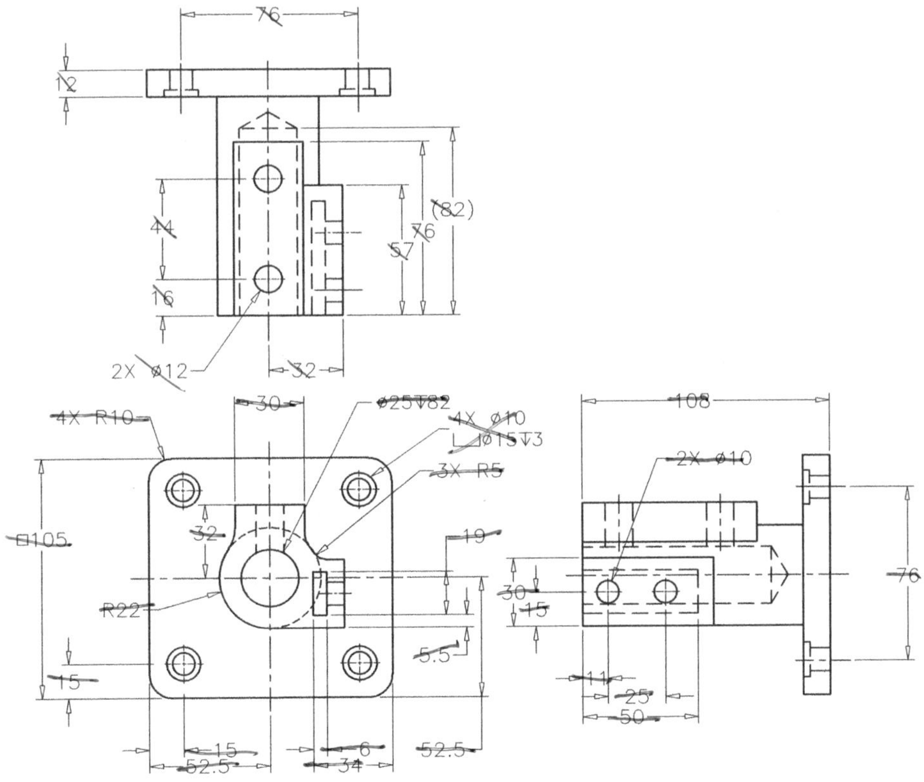

Figure 10-57 *Dimensions of the model for Problem-Solving Exercise 3*

Problem-Solving Exercise 4

Create various components of the Pipe Vice assembly and then assemble them by moving, rotating, and aligning. The Pipe Vice assembly is shown in Figure 10-58. For your reference, the exploded view of the assembly is shown in Figure 10-59. The dimensions of the individual components are shown in Figures 10-60 and 10-61.

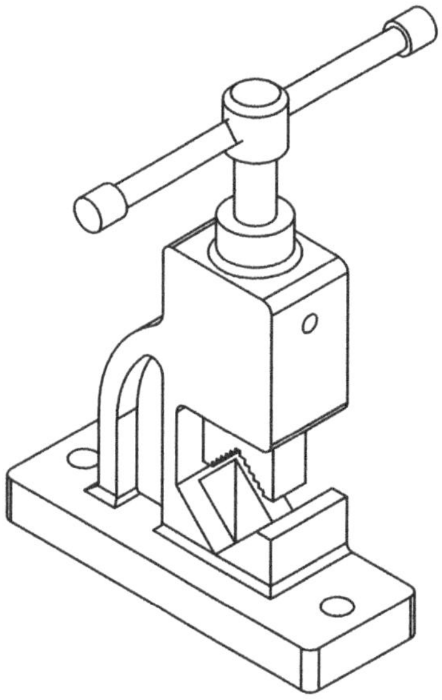

***Figure 10-58** The Pipe Vice assembly*

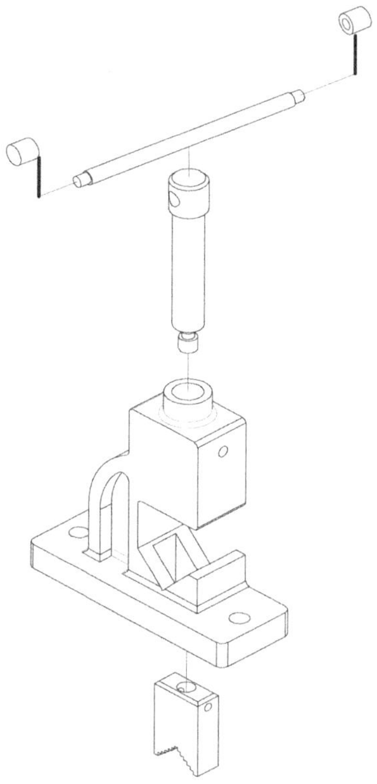

***Figure 10-59** Exploded view of the Pipe Vice assembly*

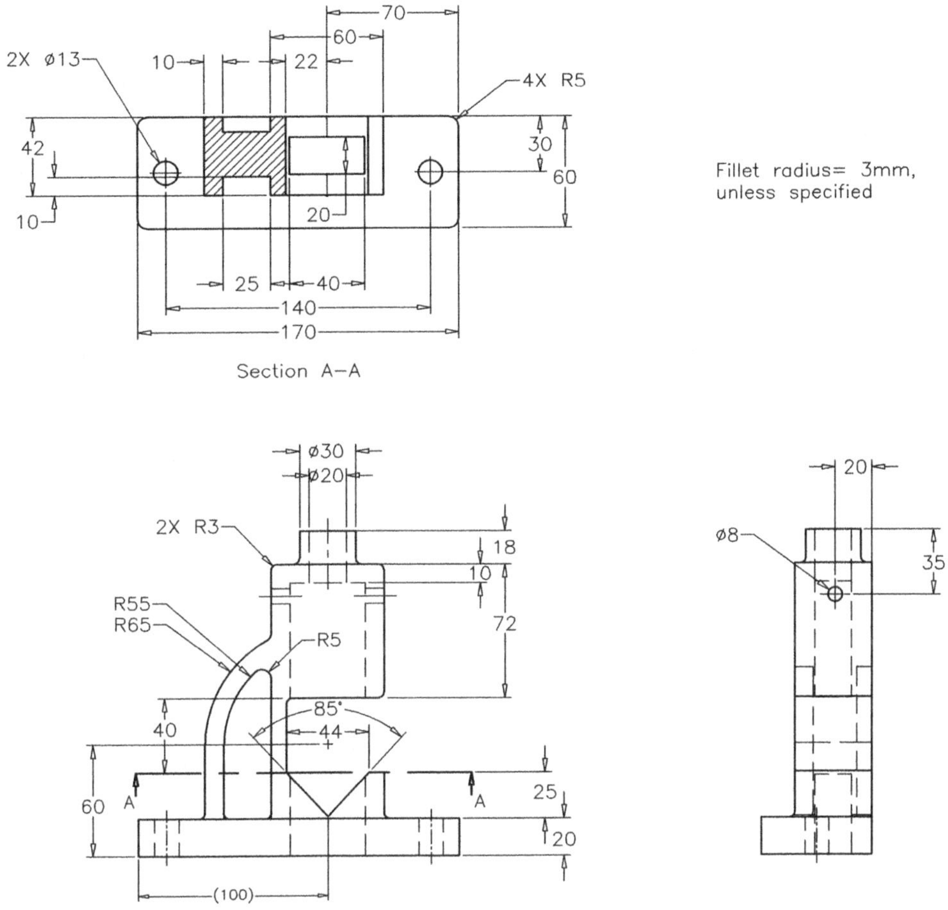

***Figure 10-60** Dimensions of the Base*

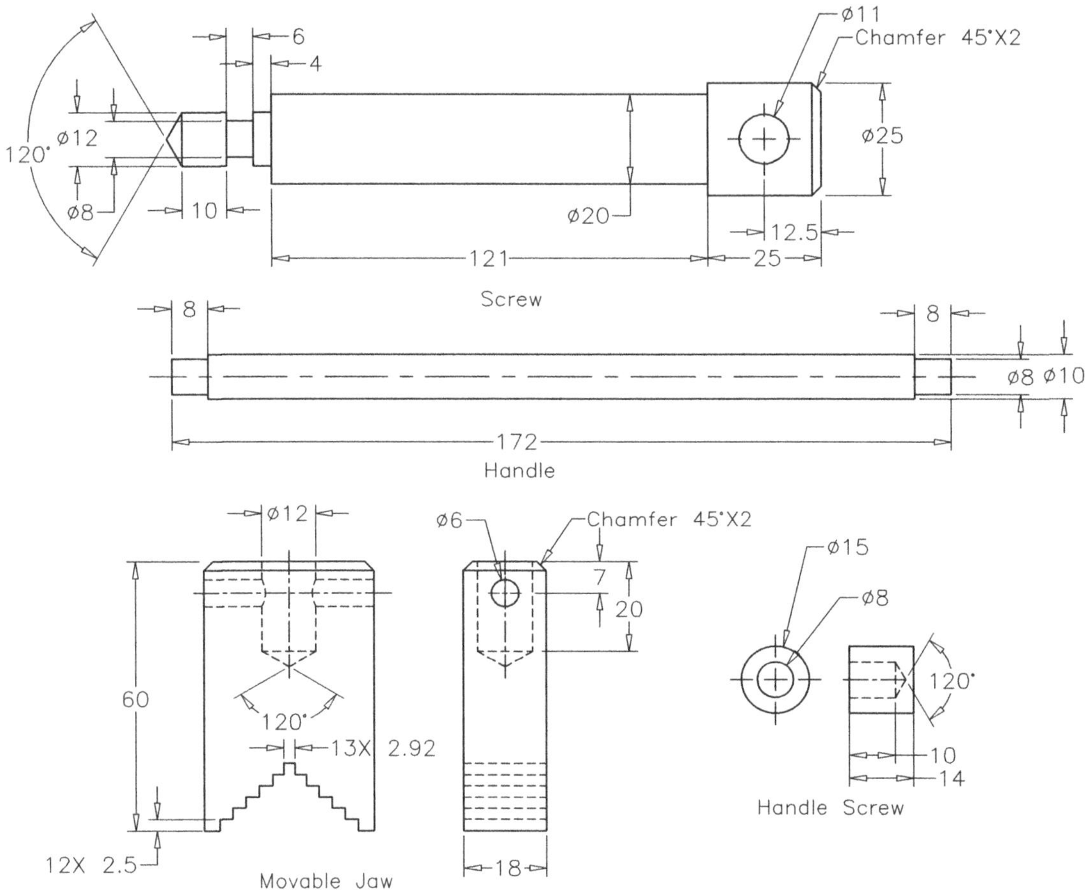

Figure 10-61 *Dimensions of the Screw, Handle, Movable Jaw, and Handle Stop*

Answers to Self-Evaluation Test

1. **Solid View**, **2.** *.mpr*, **3.** **Flatshot**, **4.** **Separate**, **5.** **Clean** **6.** F, **7.** T, **8.** F, **9.** F, **10.** T

Chapter 11

Surface Modeling

Learning Objectives

After completing this chapter, you will be able to:

- *Create wireframe elements*
- *Create extruded, revolved, and loft surfaces*
- *Create planar and network surfaces*
- *Create blend, patch, and offset surfaces*
- *Fillet, trim, untrim, extend, and sculpt surfaces*
- *Edit, add, remove, and rebuild the CVs of a NURBS surface*
- *Project geometries onto a surface*
- *Perform the zebra, curvature, and draft angle analysis on the surfaces*

Key Terms

- *SPLINE*
- *Spline Freehand*
- *PLANESURF*
- *SURFNETWORK*
- *Surface Associativity*
- *NURBS Creation*
- *Continuity*
- *Bulge magnitude*
- *SURFPATCH*
- *Constraining Geometry*
- *Solid*
- *Connect*
- *Surffillet*
- *Extend*
- *Projection Direction*
- *Untrim*
- *Sculpt*
- *Convert to NURBS*
- *CV Edit Bar*
- *Insert Knots*
- *Rebuild*
- *AutoTRIM*
- *Project to UCS*
- *Project to View*
- *Project to 2 Points*
- *Zebra Analysis*
- *Curvature Analysis*
- *Draft Analysis*
- *Isolines curves*

SURFACE MODELING

Surface models are three-dimensional (3D) models of zero thickness. Surface modeling is a technique that is used for creating planar or non-planar geometries of zero thickness.

Most of the real world models are solid models. However, some models are complex, therefore, first you need to create surfaces to get the desired complex shapes. After creating the required shape of a model using surfaces, you can convert it into a solid model. The technique of creating a surface using the surface modeling tools is discussed in this chapter. If you are familiar with the concept of solid modeling, it will be easier for you to learn surface modeling.

Surface modeling is used to create procedural as well as NURBS surfaces. These surfaces are discussed later in this chapter. In AutoCAD, the **Surface** tab contains all tools for creating and editing surfaces. In this chapter, you will learn to use all these tools.

CREATING WIREFRAME ELEMENTS

Wireframe elements help in creating surfaces. These elements can be used as profiles, guide curves, paths, and so on. The tools for constructing these wireframe elements are available in the **Curves** panel of the **Surface** tab. These tools include **Spline CV**, **Spline Fit**, **3D/2D Polyline**, **Line**, and so on. The **Spline** tools are grouped in the **Spline** drop-down. These tools have the compatible options for creating NURBS surfaces. The tools in the **Spline** drop-down are discussed next.

Spline CV

Ribbon: Surface > Curves > Spline drop-down > Spline CV **Command:** SPLINE

The **Spline CV** tool is used to draw a 3D spline by defining specific points that do not lie on that curve. These points act as control vertices for the curve, refer to Figure 11-1. You can modify the position of any control vertex. When you do so, only the part of the curve that is corresponding to CV point will be affected. You can also add, remove, or refine control points. These processes are discussed later in this chapter. To create a spline CV, choose the **Spline CV** tool from the **Spline** drop-down, refer to Figure 11-2; the **Specify first point or [Method/Degree/Object]:** prompt will be displayed. Now, you can specify the location of CV in a sequence for creation of curve. You can also specify the method of spline creation, set the degree of curve, or select a polyline object to convert it into a CV spline.

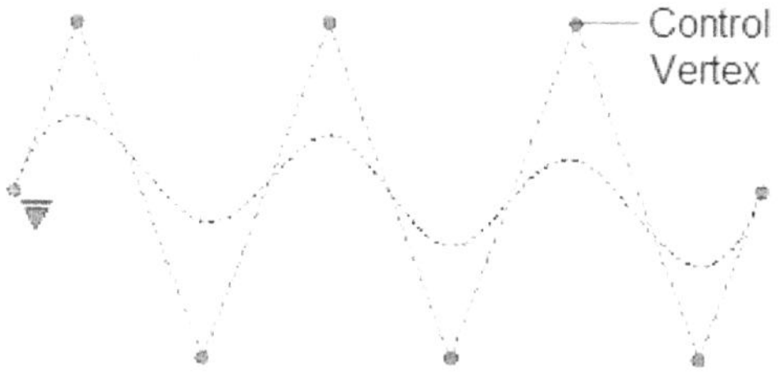

Figure 11-1 *The Spline CV curve*

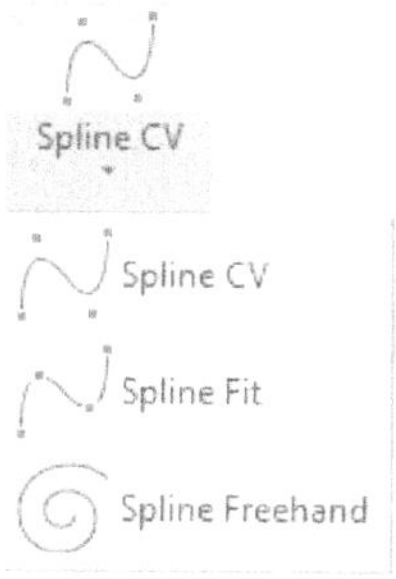

Figure 11-2 *The **Spline** drop-down*

Spline Fit

Ribbon: Surface > Curves > Spline drop-down > Spline Fit **Command:** SPLINE

The **Spline Fit** tool is used to draw a 3D spline by defining specific points that lie on that curve. These points are called knots or fit points. You can edit a curve directly by using these points, refer to Figure 11-3.

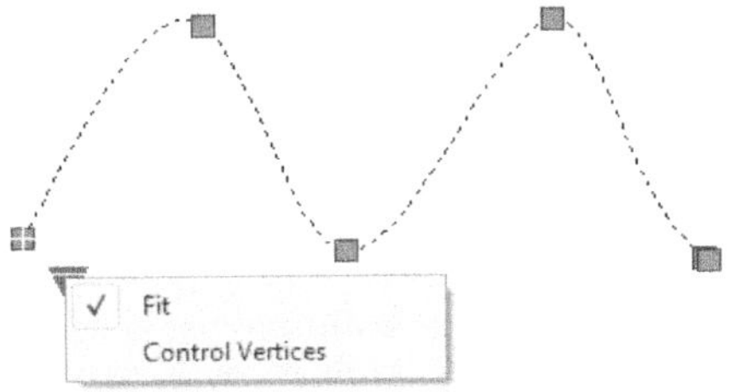

Figure 11-3 *Spline with fit points*

Spline Freehand

Ribbon: Surface > Curves > Spline drop-down > Spline Freehand **Command:** SKETCH

The **Spline Freehand** tool is used to create a spline by dragging the mouse in the drawing area. After the desired shape of curve is displayed on the screen, release the mouse button and press Enter; a spline will be created and also the CV or fit points will be created automatically on it. You can switch between CV's and fit points as per your requirement.

Note

After drawing a spline, if you select it, a menu grip will be displayed, refer to Figure 11-3. You can click on the grip and switch between control vertices and fit points. When you switch from ***Control Vertices*** *to* ***Fit****, the curve shown in Figure 11-3 will be displayed.*

Extract Isoline Curves

Ribbon: Surface > Curves > Extract Isolines **Toolbar:** Surface Editing
Menu Bar: Modify > 3D Operations > Extract Isolines **Command:** SURFEXTRACTCURVE

You can create isoline curves from the existing curves or edges of the surfaces or faces of 3D model, refer to Figure 11-4. To create an isoline curve, invoke the **Extract Isolines** tool from the **Curves** panel of the **Surface** tab; you will be prompted to select the surface, solid model or face of the solid model. Select the surface of the model; an isoline will be displayed on the selected surface. This isoline will move as you move the cursor on the selected surface. Move the cursor till the point where you want to specify the isoline curve and then left-click; the curve will be created. Similarly, you can specify the directions and splines on the surfaces.

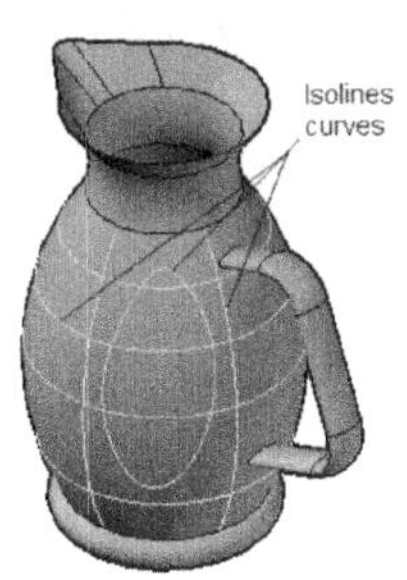

Figure 11-4 *A surface with isolines*

CREATING SURFACES BY USING PROFILES

The profile used to create surfaces can be open/close geometries, planar/non-planar geometries, or edges of an existing solid or surface. Open geometries always result in a surface, whereas closed geometries result in a solid or a surface, depending on the tool selected in the **Solid** or **Surface** tab. You can also create a surface when the **Solid** tab is active by changing the mode of creation. The profile surfaces include extruded surface, revolved surface, lofted surface, and swept surface. The functions of the tools in the **Surface** tab are similar to that of the solid modeling tools discussed in Chapter 8.

Creating an Extruded Surface

Ribbon: Surface > Create > Extrude **Command:** EXTRUDE

The **Extrude** tool is used to create solids as well as surfaces. Extruded surfaces are similar to extruded solids and are created by extending a profile in 3D space. As discussed earlier, if the profile drawn is an open curve, the resultant extruded model will be a surface only. But if the profile is a closed curve, the resultant model will be a surface, if this tool is selected from the **Surface** tab. To create an extruded surface, choose the **Extrude** tool from the **Create** panel. The command sequence that will follow when you choose this tool is given next.

Select objects to extrude or [MOde]: *Select an object to extrude.*
Select objects to extrude or [MOde]: *Select other object to extrude or* Enter.
Specify height of extrusion or [Direction/Path/Taper angle/Expression] <Current>:

Specify the height of extrusion and then, press Enter. You can also specify the direction, path, or taper angle of extrusion. These options have already been discussed in Chapter 8.

Note

*If you want to create a surface model by using the **Extrude** tool in the **Solid** tab, enter **MO** at the **Select objects to extrude or [MODE]** prompt; two options, **Solid** and **Surface**, will be displayed. Choose **Surface** to create the surface model. Next, select the required entities and press Enter; you will be prompted to define the height of extrusion.*

Figure 11-5 shows the open profile to be extruded and Figure 11-6 shows the resulting extruded surface. Figure 11-7 shows the closed profile to be extruded and Figure 11-8 shows the resulting extruded surface.

Figure 11-5 *Open profile to be extruded*

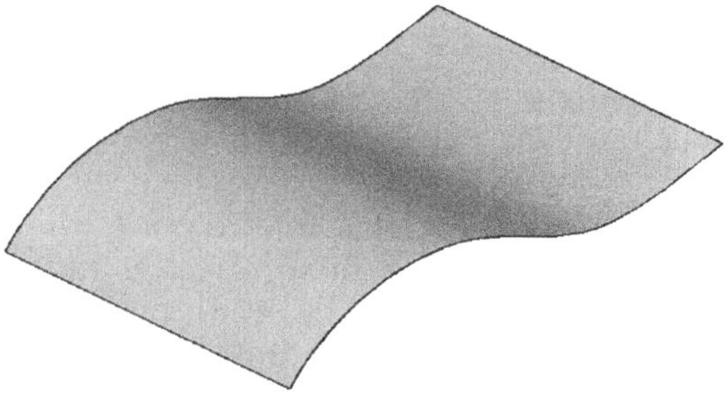

Figure 11-6 *The resulting extruded surface*

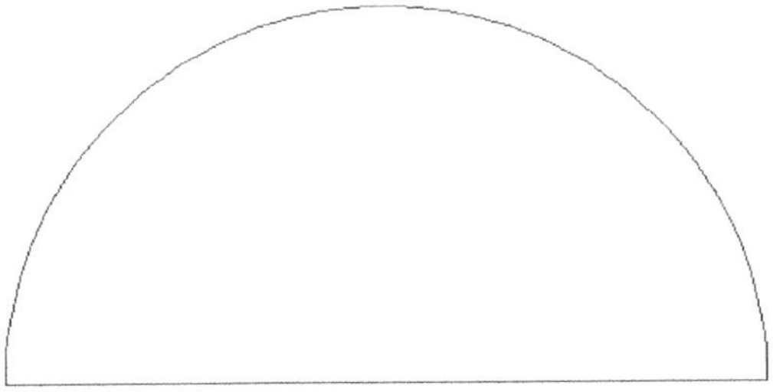

Figure 11-7 *Closed profile to be extruded*

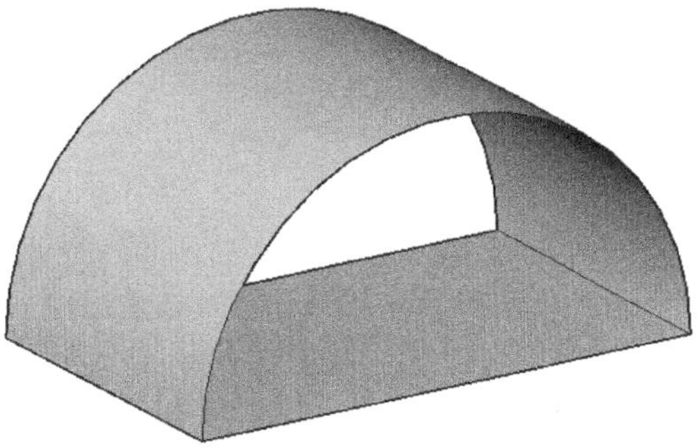

Figure 11-8 *The resulting extruded surface*

Select the extruded surface created; the grips will be displayed on it. You can drag the grip that is along the direction of extrusion to increase the extrusion depth. And, you can drag the grip that is normal to the direction of extrusion to provide a draft to the extruded surface. Figure 11-9 shows how to change distance by dragging one of the grips and Figure 11-10 shows how to change the angle by dragging another grip. Apart from these two grips, other grips will be displayed at the base and they are used to change the shape of the surface.

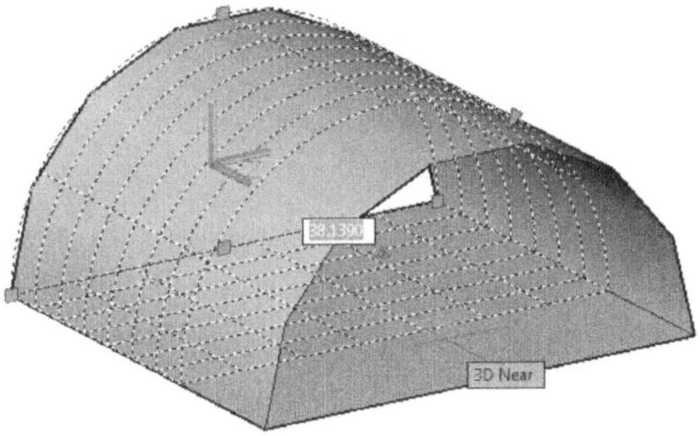

Figure 11-9 *Changing the distance*

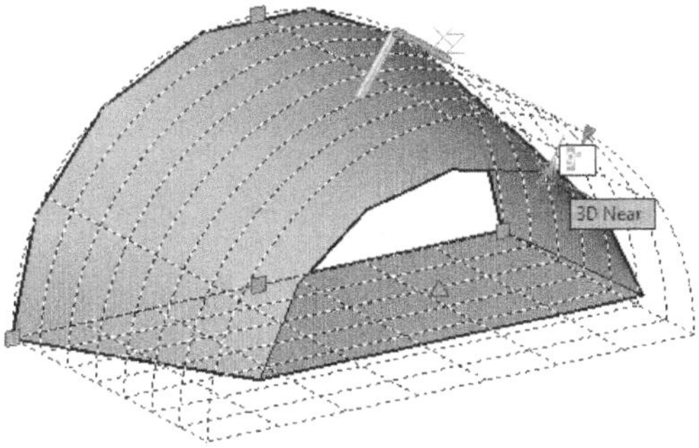

Figure 11-10 *Changing the angle*

Creating a Revolved Surface

Ribbon: Surface > Create > Revolve **Command:** REVOLVE / REV

You can create revolved surfaces by revolving a profile curve around an axis. To create a revolved surface, first draw the profile and then choose the **Revolve** tool from the **Create** panel. Next, select the objects to be revolved and then press Enter; the **Specify axis start point or define axis by [Object X Y Z] <Object> :** prompt will be displayed. Specify the axis start and end points or the object about which you want to revolve your object; the **Specify angle of revolution or [STart angle Reverse EXpression] <360>** : prompt will be displayed. Now, using the options available in this prompt, you can specify the angle of revolution, specify the start angle of the revolution, and reverse the direction of revolution.

Figure 11-11 shows a profile and an axis of revolution to create a revolved surface. Figure 11-12 shows the surface created by revolving the profile through an angle of 180 degrees.

Figure 11-11 *The profile and the axis of revolution*

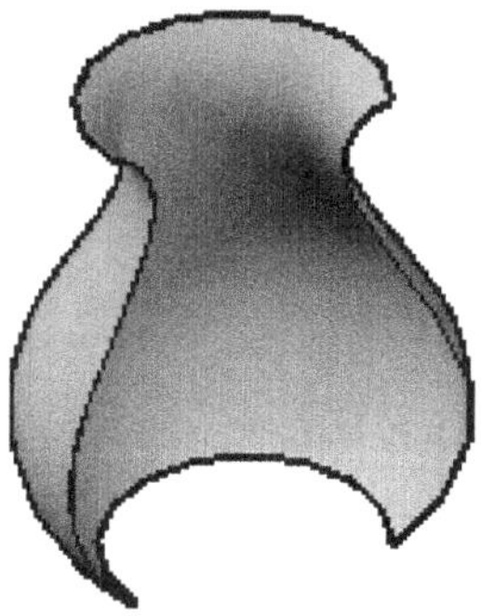

Figure 11-12 *Surface revolved through an angle of 180 degrees*

Creating a Loft Surface

Ribbon: Surface > Create > Loft **Command:** LOFT

You can blend more than one cross-section together to form a loft surface. These cross-sections can be open profiles, closed profiles, or edge subobjects. Also, the cross-sections may or may not be parallel to each other. The procedure to create a loft surface is the same as that of a loft solid, which has already been discussed in Chapter 8.

Creating a Sweep Surface

Ribbon: Surface > Create > Sweep **Command:** SWEEP

The procedure to create sweep surfaces is similar to that of sweep solids, which has been discussed in Chapter 8.

Creating a Planar Surface

Ribbon: Surface > Create > Planar **Toolbar:** Modeling > Planar Surface
Menu Bar: Draw > Modeling > Surfaces > Planar **Command:** PLANESURF

The **Planar** tool is used to generate 2D surfaces by specifying two diagonally opposite points. These two points specify the rectangular area to be covered by this planar surface, refer to Figure 11-13. The prompt sequence for this tool is discussed next.

Specify first corner or [Object] <Object>: *Specify the first corner point of the planar surface.*
Specify other corner: *Specify the diagonally opposite point of the planar surface.*

You can also convert an existing object into a surface by entering **O** at the **Specify first corner or [Object] <Object>** prompt. While selecting the object, you can directly select a region or a number of individual objects that result in a closed boundary, refer to Figure 11-14. The number of lines displayed on the surface is controlled by the **SURFU** and **SURFV** system variables.

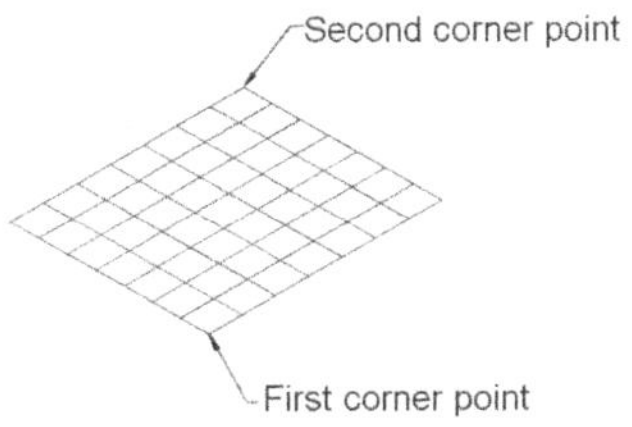

Figure 11-13 Planar surface created by specifying corner points

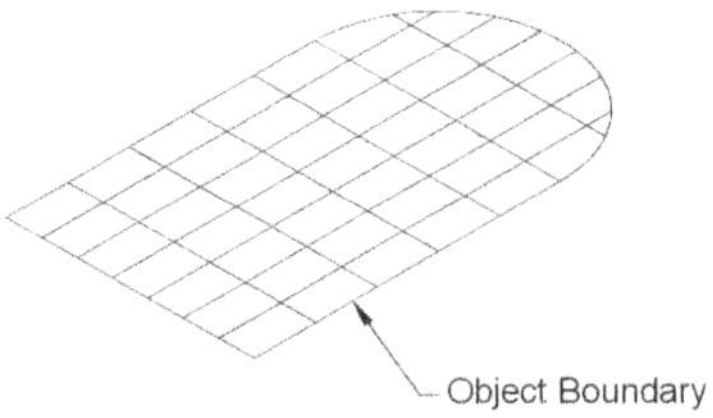

Figure 11-14 Planar surface created by selecting an object

Creating a Network Surface

Ribbon: Surface > Create > Network
Menu Bar: Draw > Modeling > Surfaces > Network **Command:** SURFNETWORK

The **Network** tool is used to create a surface between a number of boundary elements. These boundary elements can be 2D curves or existing edges of surfaces, solids, or regions. However, while creating a surface, there should not be any gap between the consecutive elements. Before creating a Network surface, you need to draw the boundary elements. After drawing them, choose the **Network** tool from the **Create** panel; you will be prompted to select curves or surface edges in the first direction. Select objects in the U or V direction and then press Enter; you will be prompted to select curves or surface edges in the second direction. Select objects in the other direction and press Enter again, network surface will be created. Figure 11-15 shows the elements to be selected. Here, Curve 1 and Curve 2 are selected in the first direction and Curve 3 and Curve 4 are selected in the second direction. Figure 11-16 shows the resulting network surface.

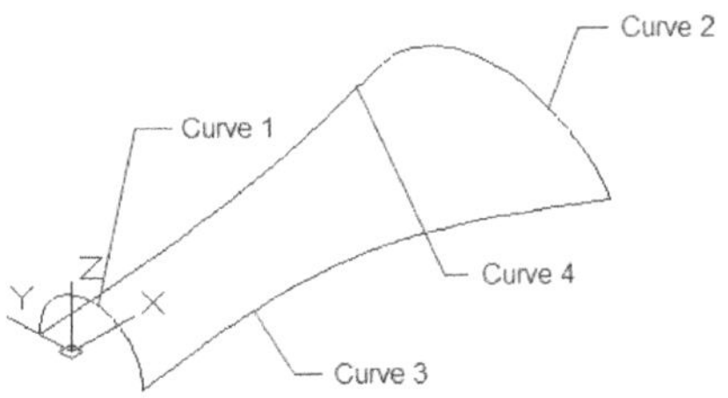

Figure 11-15 Curves to be selected

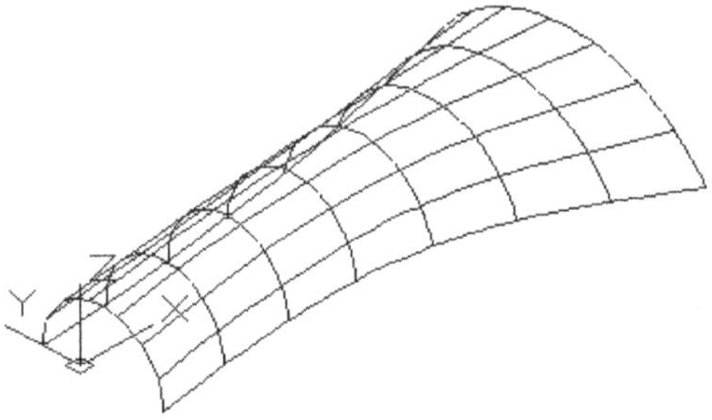

Figure 11-16 Network surface created

CREATING SURFACES FROM OTHER SURFACES

The tools discussed till now are used to create simple surfaces. But, most of the time, the product and industrial designers come up with some unique designs to make the products more attractive and presentable. In order to create such designs, you need some advanced tools. AutoCAD has some advanced tools like **Blend**, **Patch**, and **Offset** to create new surfaces by using the subobjects of other surfaces. These tools are discussed next.

Before you learn the usage of these tools, you need to learn about the procedural and NURBS surfaces in AutoCAD. The procedural surfaces are the surfaces that maintain relationship with other surfaces, even after getting edited. These surfaces are associative and get modified as a group. Therefore, the procedural surfaces are mostly used, when associativity is required to be maintained. To create a procedural surface, choose the **Surface Associativity** button in the **Create** panel and then invoke any surface creation tool; a procedural surface will be created. By default, this button is active and you need to choose it again to turn off associativity.

A NURBS surface is created when the shape of the surface needs to be modified. These surfaces are mostly used in ship building industries. These surfaces are parametric in nature and have multiple knots. These knots can be adjusted to modify the shape of the surface. To create a NURBS surface, choose the **NURBS Creation** button in the **Create** panel and then create a surface; the surface thus created will be a NURBS surface. You need to choose this button again to turn off the NURBS creation. Note that you can keep both the buttons, **Surface Associativity** and **NURBS Creation** on or off at the same time.

In the next section, you will learn about the tools that are used to create surfaces from other surfaces.

Creating a Blend Surface

Ribbon: Surface > Create > Blend **Command:** SURFBLEND

The **Blend** tool is used to create a new surface between two existing surfaces, solids, or regions. To create a blend surface, invoke the **Blend** tool from the **Create** panel; you will be prompted to select the first surface edge or edge chain to blend. Select the surface edge/s and press Enter; you will be prompted to select the second surface edge or edge chain to blend. Select it and press Enter again; preview of the blend surface will be displayed with the default settings. Figure 11-17 shows the entities selected to blend and Figure 11-18 shows preview of the blend surface. The default settings include the surface continuity and magnitude of bulge at both ends. Next, press Enter if the preview seems to be fine, else edit the continuity setting or the bulge magnitude. After adjusting the settings according to your requirement, press Enter to create the blend surface. The method to edit the continuity setting and the bulge magnitude is discussed next.

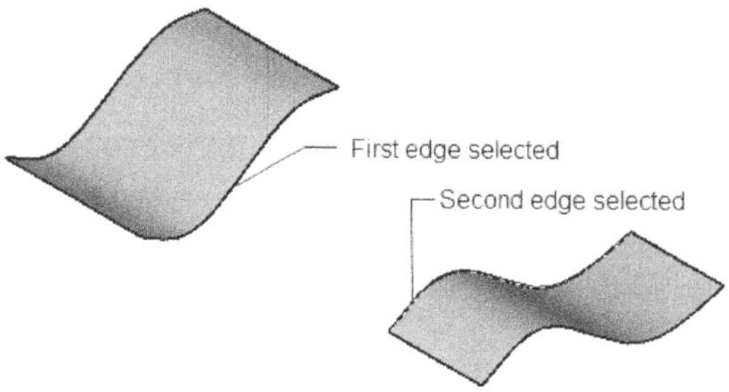

Figure 11-17 *The edges selected*

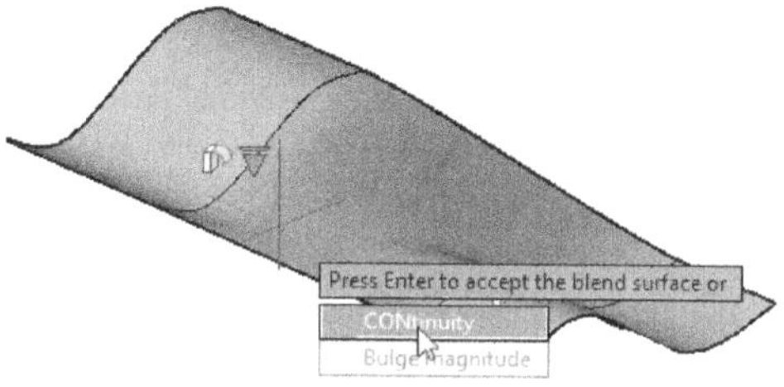

Figure 11-18 *Preview of the resulting blend surface*

Continuity

Continuity defines the smoothness of a blend surface at a point where it meets the other surface. Continuity can be set to **G0** (position), **G1** (Tangency), or **G2** (continuity). **G0** maintains the position of the selected edges, **G1** maintains the tangency of the blend surface where it meets the edges at both ends, and **G2** maintains the same curvature.

On selecting the **CONtinuity** option from the preview displayed in Figure 11-18, the continuity options for the first edge will be displayed. Choose the required option; you will be prompted to set the continuity of the second edge. Choose the required option; the preview of the blend surface will be updated. Also, you will be prompted to press Enter to accept or edit the settings. Edit or accept the settings to create the blend surface.

You can also edit the continuity of a blend surface after it is created. To do so, select the blend surface; grips will be displayed on both the edges of the surface. Now, if you choose a grip displayed on the surface, a flyout with the continuity options will be displayed, refer to Figure 11-19. By default, **G1** is chosen in this flyout. You can select any other option from the flyout to set continuity as per your requirement. Similarly, you can set the continuity of the other edge by clicking on it.

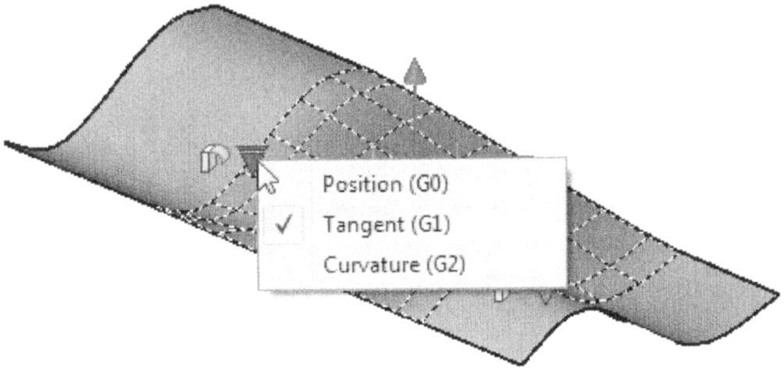

***Figure 11-19** Continuity options displayed on clicking a grip*

Bulge Magnitude

Bulge magnitude defines the roundness or the amount of bulge between the blend surface and the existing surface. In other words, it is the amount of curvature where two surfaces meet. This magnitude can only be applied to the surfaces that have the G1 or G2 continuity.

By default, the bulge magnitude is set to 0.5. If you want to edit the bulge magnitude, choose the respective option from the preview displayed or enter **B** at the **Press Enter to accept the blend surface or [CONtinuity/Bulge magnitude]:** Command prompt; you will be prompted to define the bulge magnitude for the first edge. Define the value of bulge for the first edge and then the value of bulge at the second edge. On entering 0 value, the surface will get flattened and on entering a value greater or equal to 1, the surface curvature will increase. The bulge magnitude has already been discussed in detail in Chapter 8.

You can modify a blend surface after it is created. To do so, select the blend surface and right-click; a shortcut menu will be displayed. Choose the **Properties** option from the shortcut menu; the **Properties** palette with the settings of the blend surface will be displayed. Using this palette, you can modify the continuity setting and the bulge magnitude of the surface at each edge, the appearance of the surface, and so on.

Creating a Patch Surface

Ribbon: Surface > Create > Patch **Command:** SURFPATCH

Using the **Patch** tool, you can close the open edges of an existing surface. To create a patch surface, invoke the **Patch** tool from the **Create** panel; you will be prompted to select the edges to create a patch. Select the edges one by one and then press Enter; the preview of the patch with the default settings will be displayed. Also, you will be prompted to either accept the preview, or change the settings for continuity between the patch surface and the edges selected, define the bulge magnitude, or define the geometry to be constrained. Figure 11-20 shows the model with open edge and Figure 11-21 shows the patch created on the open edge.

By default, the continuity is set to G0 and the bulge magnitude is set to 0.5. Continuity and bulge magnitude have already been discussed in the previous topic, and the method to specify the geometry to be constrained is discussed next.

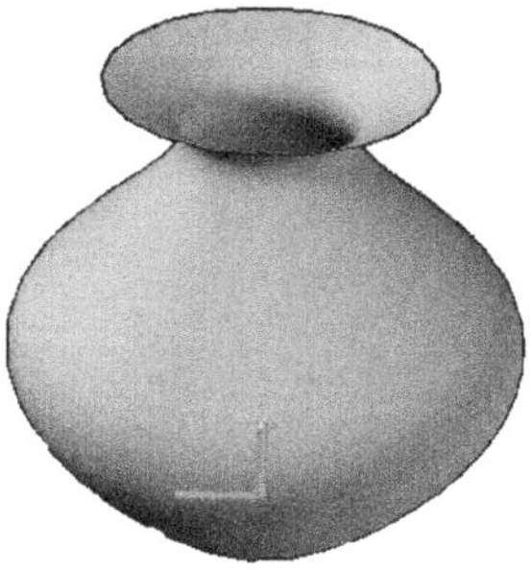

Figure 11-20 *Model before creating the patch*

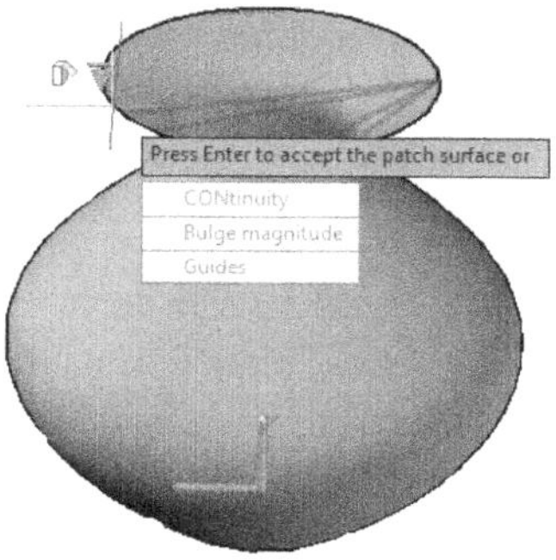

Figure 11-21 *Model after creating the patch*

Guides

You can use some additional curves as guide curves to create the patch. Guide curves are used to guide the shape of the patch as per the geometry of the guide curve. Note that you need to draw the guide curve first and then invoke the **Patch** tool. Choose this option when the **Press Enter to accept the patch surface or [CONtinuity/Bulge magnitude/Guides]:** prompt is displayed. Next, select the guide curve and press EnterS; a patch will be created. If you select the patch surface after it is created, a grip will be displayed. On clicking the grip, the options for continuity will be displayed. You can choose an option to specify the required continuity. Figure 11-22 shows the guide curve created for constraining the geometry and Figure 11-23 shows the patch created using the guide curve.

You can modify a patch surface by using the **Properties** palette. Invoke the **Properties** palette; the patch settings will be displayed in the **Geometry** area. You can modify the continuity option, the bulge magnitude, the number of isolines in the U and V directions, and so on using this palette.

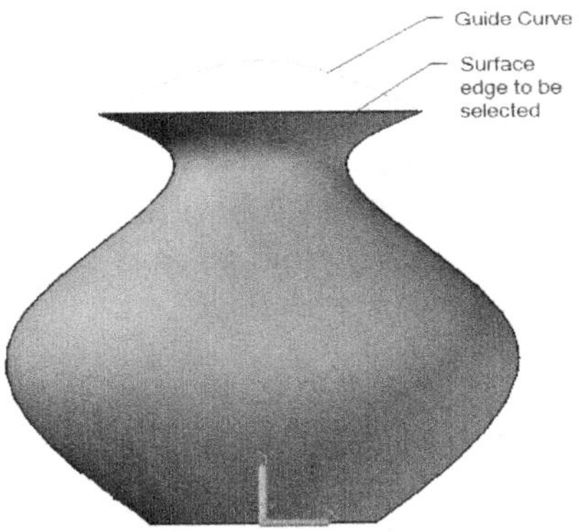

Figure 11-22 *Model before creating the patch*

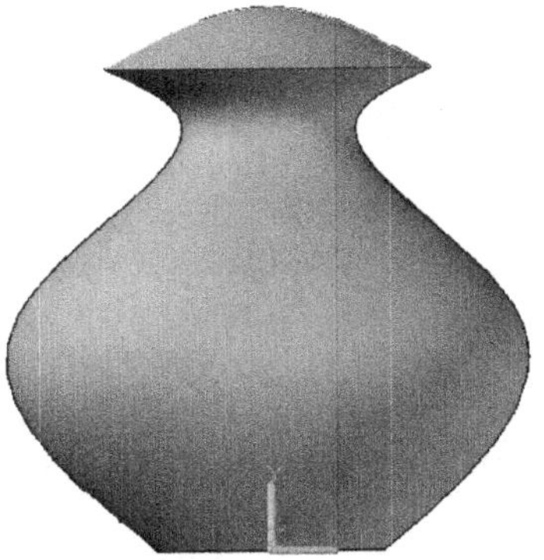

Figure 11-23 *Model after creating the patch*

Creating an Offset Surface

Ribbon: Surface > Create > Offset **Command:** SURFOFFSET

The **Offset** tool is used to create a surface at an offset distance from an existing surface. To do so, choose the **Offset** tool from the **Create** panel; you will be prompted to select surfaces or regions to offset. Select a surface and press Enter; the direction arrows will indicate the direction of the offset and the **Specify offset distance or [Flip direction/Both sides/Solid/Connect/Expression] <Current>:** prompt will be displayed. The options displayed in this prompt are discussed next.

Specify offset distance

If the direction of offset is as you want, then specify the required offset distance and press Enter; an offset surface will be created. Figure 11-24 shows the original surface and the offset surface.

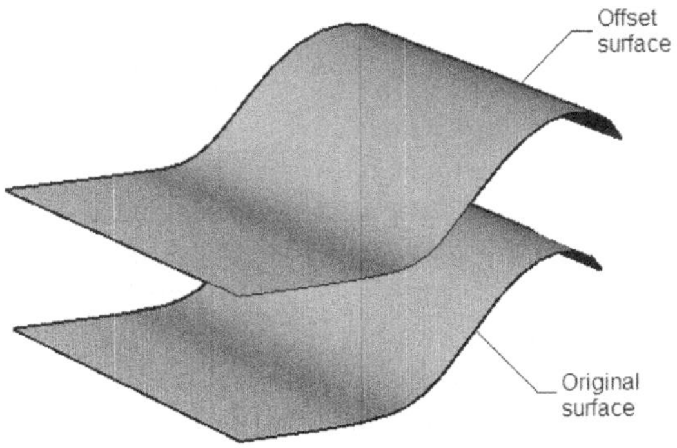

Figure 11-24 *The original and offset surfaces*

Flip direction

If you want to change the direction of offset surface creation, choose the **Flip direction** option in the prompt; the direction will be changed. Next, you can specify the offset distance.

Both sides

To create offset surfaces on both sides of the selected surface, choose the **Both sides** option. On doing so, you will notice that the direction arrows are displayed on both sides of the selected surface. Specify the offset distance.

Solid

The **Solid** option is used to create a solid by offsetting an existing surface. After selecting the surface, choose the **Solid** option; you will be prompted to specify the offset distance. Specify the value of the offset distance and press Enter; the resulting entity will be a solid.

Connect

The **Connect** option is used when you select multiple connected surfaces to offset and you need the offset surfaces to be connected to each other. Select the existing connected surfaces, choose the **Connect** option and specify the offset distance; the offset surfaces will be connected to each other. If you select an offset surface, a grip will be displayed on it. You can click on the grip and drag it to adjust the offset distance as per your need. An edit box is also displayed while dragging the grip. You can enter the required offset distance in this edit box and press Enter. On doing so, the offset surface will move to the specified distance.

You can control the display of the offset surface using the **Properties** palette. Invoke the **Properties** palette to set the number of isolines of the offset surface along the U and V directions.

Expression

The **Expression** option is used to relate the dimensional constraint applied in the drawing to the offset value. Also, you can setup an equation for calculating the offset value using different dimensional constraints.

EDITING SURFACES

After creating the surfaces, you may need to modify them. AutoCAD provides you with the surface operation tools to modify surfaces. The surface operation tools are used regularly while creating surface models. These tools are used to enhance the surfaces and help in creating complex geometries. They save a lot of modeling time as well. Various surface editing operations are discussed next.

Creating Fillets

Ribbon: Surface > Edit > Fillet	**Command:** SURFFILLET

The **Fillet** tool is used to create a rounded surface between two existing surfaces. To create a fillet surface, invoke the **Fillet** tool from the **Edit** panel; you will be prompted to select the surfaces between which you want the fillet to be created. Select the surfaces one by one and press Enter; a fillet will be created with the default settings. Also, you will be prompted to press Enter to accept the fillet created, or set the new fillet radius, or set the trim surface option. Press Enter to accept the fillet or choose the **Radius** option to enter the new radius for the fillet. You can also specify whether or not to trim the surfaces after creating the fillet by choosing the **Trim surface** option. If you select the fillet surface after creating it, a grip will be displayed. Click on the grip and drag it to modify the fillet radius dynamically. Figure 11-25 shows the model before creating the fillet and Figure 11-26 shows the model after creating the fillet.

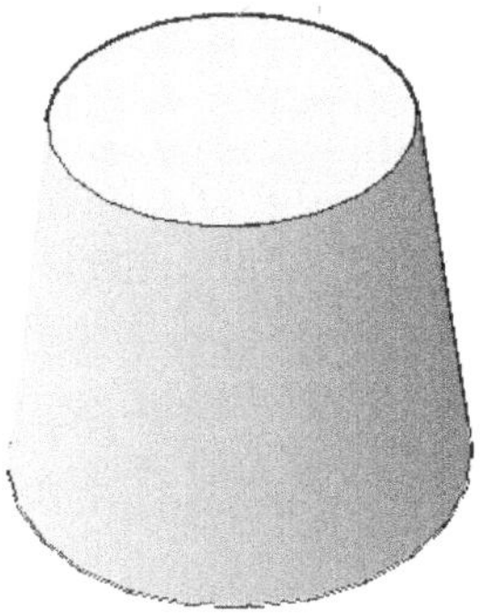

Figure 11-25 *Model before creating the fillet*

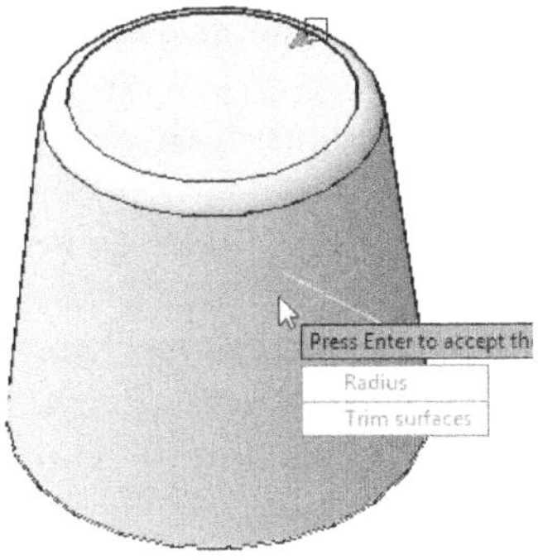

Figure 11-26 *Model after creating the fillet*

Trimming Surfaces

Ribbon: Surface > Edit > Trim	**Toolbar:** Surface Editing > Surface Trim
Menu Bar: Modify > Surface Editing > Trim	**Command:** SURFTRIM

The **Trim** tool is used to trim a portion of a surface or a region by using an intersecting object. The lines, arcs, ellipses, polylines, splines, curves, 3D polylines, 3D splines, helix, regions, and surfaces can be used as intersecting objects. You can invoke the **Trim** tool from the **Edit** panel. But before invoking this tool, you need to have the object to be trimmed and the object to be used as the cutting element. On invoking this tool, you will be prompted to select the objects to be trimmed. Select the object/s to be trimmed and press Enter; you will be prompted to select the cutting element to be used for trimming. Select the cutting element/s; you will be prompted to click on the portion to be removed. Click on the portion/s of the object to be trimmed; the selected object will be trimmed with the default settings. You can also specify the extension type and the projection direction. Figure 11-27 shows the surface before trimming and Figure 11-28 shows the surface after trimming.

Figure 11-27 *The untrimmed surface*

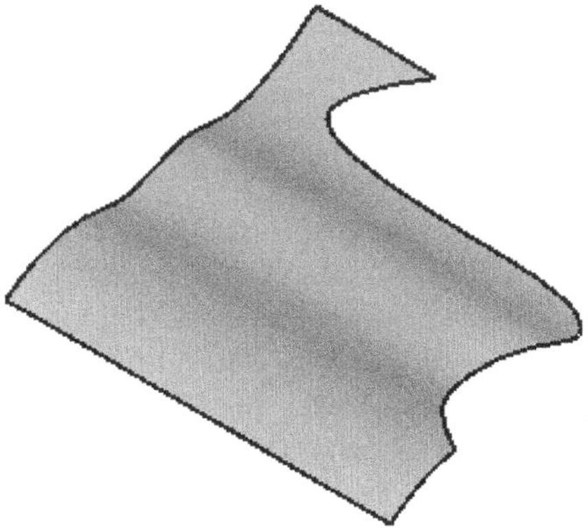

Figure 11-28 *The trimmed surface*

Select a trimmed surface and then right-click on it; a shortcut menu will be displayed. Choose the **Properties** option from this shortcut menu; the **Properties** palette will be displayed. Expand the **Trims** rollout in this window; various parameters in this rollout will be displayed. These parameters are discussed next.

- **Trimmed surface**. It displays **Yes** if the surface is trimmed.
- **Trimming edges**. It displays the number of trimming edges.
- **Edge**. It displays the edge number for which the associativity is being checked.
- **Associative Trim**. It indicates if the current edge is Associative or not.

The options displayed in the Command prompt on invoking the **Trim** tool are discussed next.

Extend

This option is used when the cutting element is a surface and it does not intersect the surface to be trimmed. If you set the **Extend** option to **Yes** at the Command prompt displayed on invoking the **Trim** tool, the selected surface gets trimmed at the imaginary intersection of the cutting element. But if it is set to **No**, the selected surface does not get trimmed as the surface does not intersect the cutting element. Figure 11-29 shows the surface to be trimmed and the cutting surface that is not intersecting the surface to be trimmed. Figure 11-30 shows the surface trimmed with the **Extend** option set to **Yes**.

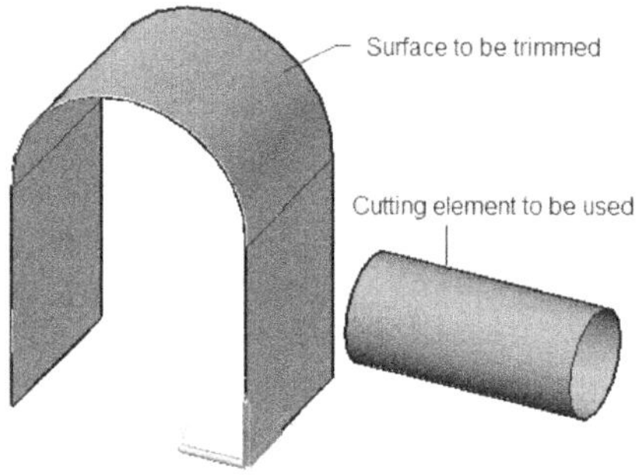

Figure 11-29 *Surfaces to be selected*

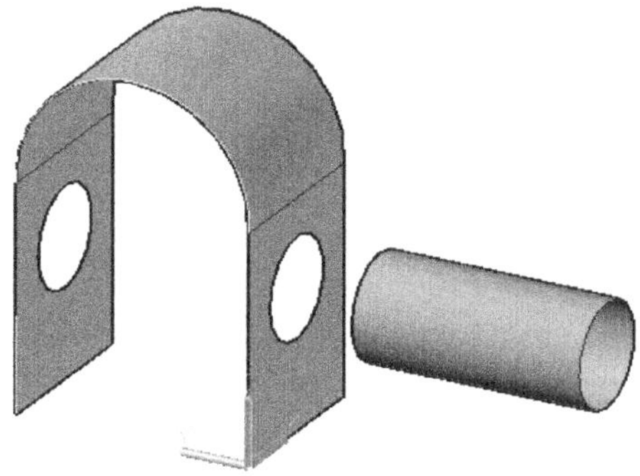

Figure 11-30 *Surface after trimming*

Projection direction

This option controls the direction of projection of the cutting element on the element to be trimmed. By default, the **Automatic** option is set. As a result, the direction of projection is set automatically depending on the view at which the trimming takes place. The other options in the projection direction are **View**, **UCS**, and **None**. If you choose the **View** option, the cutting geometry gets projected on the element to be trimmed along the current view direction. If you choose the **UCS** option, the geometry is projected in the +/- Z direction of the current UCS. But if you choose the **None** option, the geometry will not be projected and the trimming will take place only when the geometry will lie on the surface.

Note

If you select the objects after performing the trimming operation, grips will be displayed on both the trimmed object and as well as the trimming object. Click on the grip and drag; the trimmed object will move and the trim location will be updated automatically. Similarly, you can drag the grip of the cutting element to resize it. Figure 11-31 shows the model after moving the cutting element to its bottom and Figure 11-32 shows the model after resizing the cutting element.

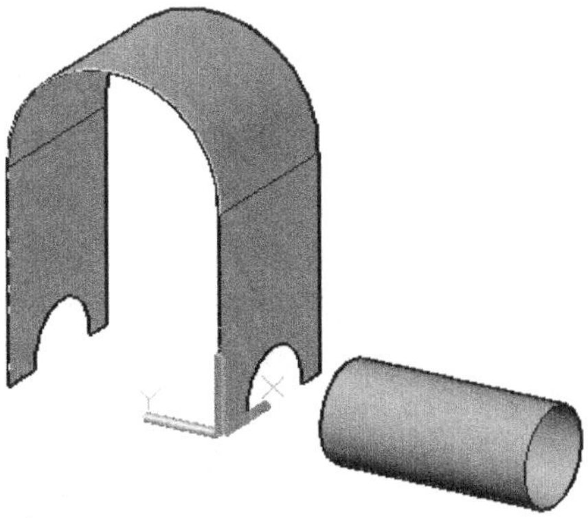

Figure 11-31 Model after moving the cutting element

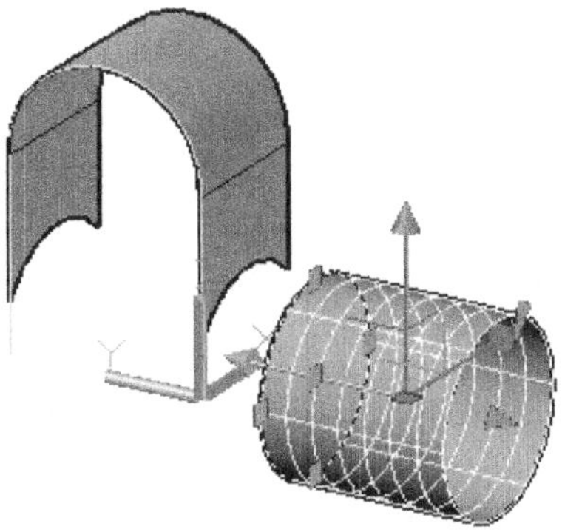

Figure 11-32 Model after resizing the cutting element

Untrimming Surfaces

Ribbon: Surface > Edit > Untrim
Toolbar: Surface Editing > Surface Untrim
Menu Bar: Modify > Surface Editing > Untrim
Command: SURFUNTRIM

The **Untrim** tool is used to untrim the trimmed edges or surfaces. To untrim a trimmed object, invoke the **Untrim** tool from the **Edit** panel; you will be prompted to select the trimmed edges or the trimmed surface. If you select the trimmed edges, only the portion removed at the selected edges will be regained. However, if you choose the **SURface** option from the Command prompt, then the portions removed from the selected surface will be regained. Figure 11-33 shows the edge selected from the surface to be untrimmed and Figure 11-34 shows the resultant untrimmed surface.

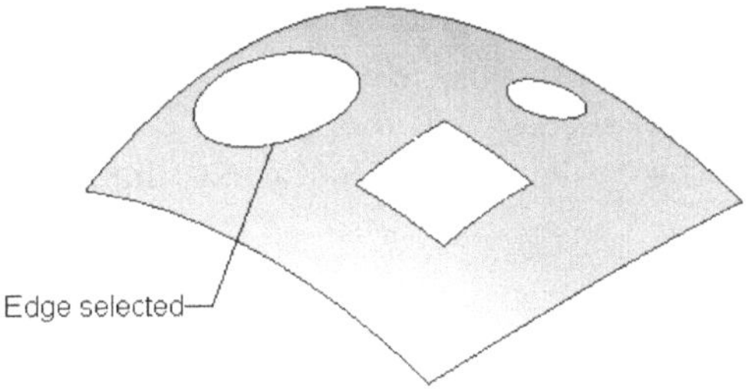

Figure 11-33 Edge selected to be untrimmed

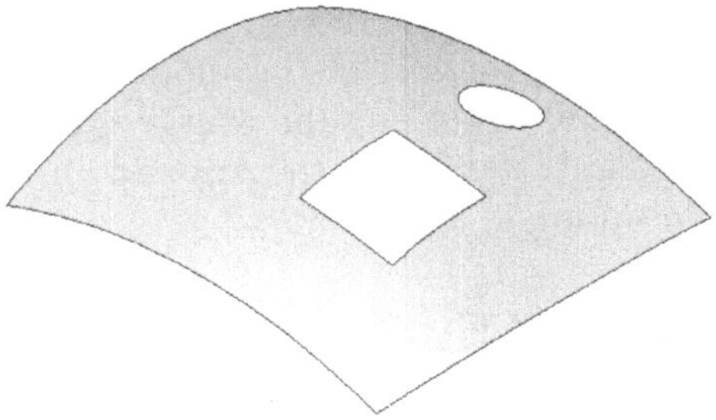

Figure 11-34 Resultant untrimmed surface

Extending Surfaces

Ribbon: Surface > Edit > Extend
Toolbar: Surface Editing > Surface Extend
Menu Bar: Modify > Surface Editing > Extend
Command: SURFEXTEND

You can extend or lengthen the edge/s of one or more surfaces to a certain distance. To extend a surface, invoke the **Extend** tool from the **Edit** panel; you will be prompted to select the edges of the surfaces to extend. Select the edges to extend and press Enter; you will be prompted to enter a distance value or specify the mode of extension. The options displayed in the prompt on invoking the **Extend** tool are discussed next.

Specify extend distance

Enter a value to specify the length of extension and press Enter; the surface will extend.

Expression

You can enter a formula or an equation at the Command prompt to control the geometry of extension.

Modes

You can specify the mode of extension by using the **Modes** option. On choosing the **Modes** option, you will be prompted to specify either the **Extend** or the **Stretch** extension type. If you choose the **Extend** option, the extended surface will resemble the shape of the original surface. However, if you choose the **Stretch** option, then the extended surface will not resemble the original surface. Figure 11-35 shows the surface extended using the **Extend** option and Figure 11-36 shows the surface extended using the **Stretch** option.

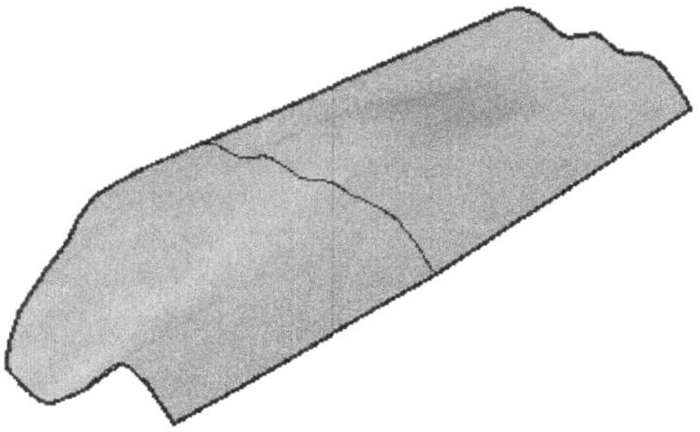

Figure 11-35 *Surface extended using the **Extend** option*

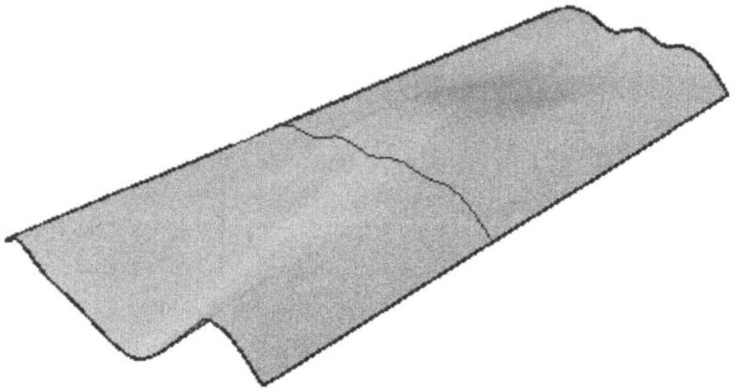

Figure 11-36 *Surface extended using the **Stretch** option*

Creation type

After you choose any of the modes and press Enter, two options, **Merge** and **Append**, are displayed. On choosing the **Merge** option, the extended surface will merge with the existing surface, and on choosing the **Append** option, a new surface will be added to the existing surface, thus resulting in two surfaces.

Sculpting Surfaces

Ribbon: Surface > Edit > Sculpt **Toolbar:** Surface Editing > Surface Sculpt
Menu Bar: Modify > Surface Editing > Sculpt **Command:** SURFSCULPT

The **Sculpt** tool is used to create a 3D solid by combining and trimming the surfaces that form a closed volume. To sculpt surfaces, invoke the **Sculpt** tool from the **Edit** panel; you will be prompted to select the continuous surfaces. Select the surfaces forming a sealed area and press Enter; the surfaces will get trimmed and a 3D solid will be formed. Figure 11-37 shows the surfaces enclosing a volume and Figure 11-38 shows the 3D solid created after sculpting the surfaces.

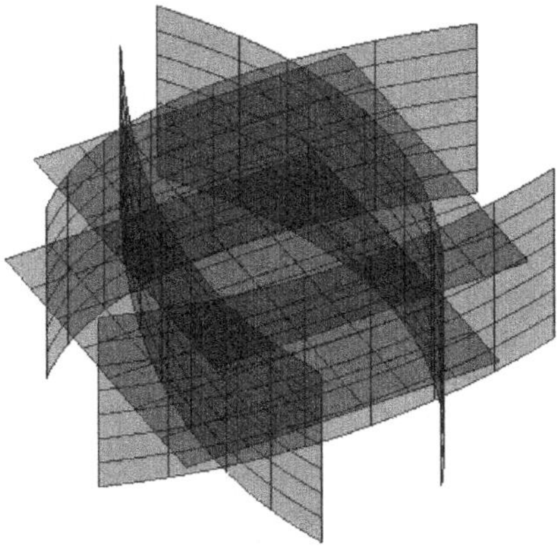

Figure 11-37 Surfaces enclosing a volume

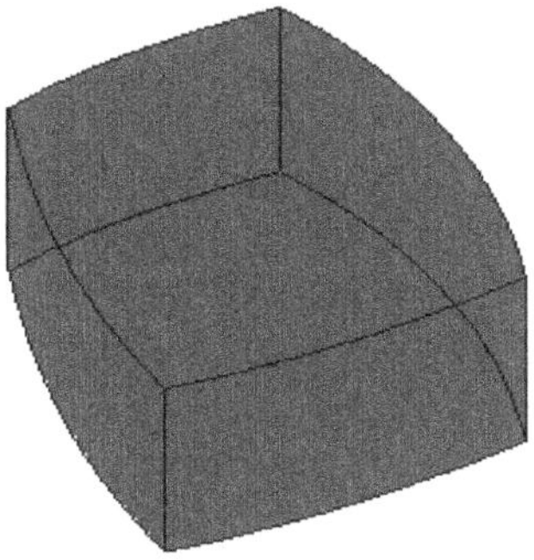

Figure 11-38 3D solid created after sculpting

Extracting Intersections

Ribbon: Surface > Edit > Extract Intersections
Menu Bar: Modify > 3D Oprerations > Interference Checking **Command:** INTERFERE

The **Extract Intersections** tool is used to create a solid, surface, or spline by extracting the intersections of two solids, a solid and a surface, or two surfaces, respectively. To extract intersection of two surfaces, invoke the **Extract Intersections** tool from the **Edit** panel of the **Surface** tab. You will be prompted to select two objects. Select two intersecting surfaces and press Enter; you will be asked if you want to create an intersecting object or not. Select **Yes** or type **Y** and press Enter; the spline will be created. Figure 11-39 shows two intersecting surfaces and Figure 11-40 shows the spline generated.

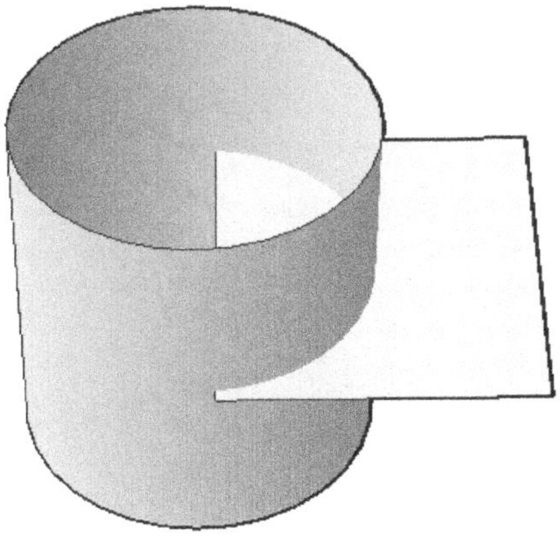

Figure 11-39 Two intersecting surfaces

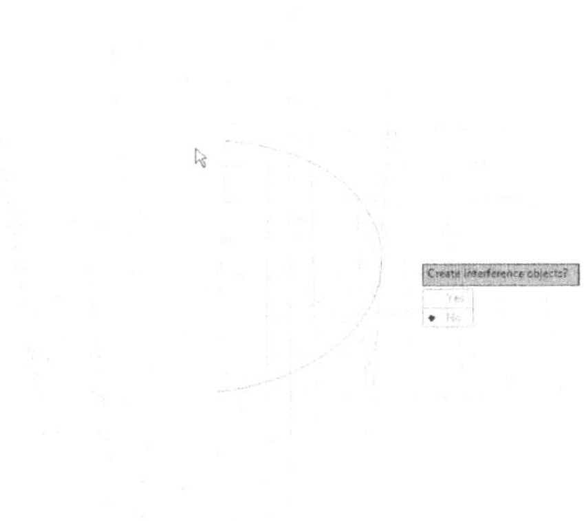

Figure 11-40 Interference spline

Example 1 Surface Creation

In this example, you will create the model shown in Figure 11-41. Its views and dimensions are shown in Figure 11-42. The dimensions are given for your reference only. You can use your own dimensions.

Figure 11-41 The isometric view of the model

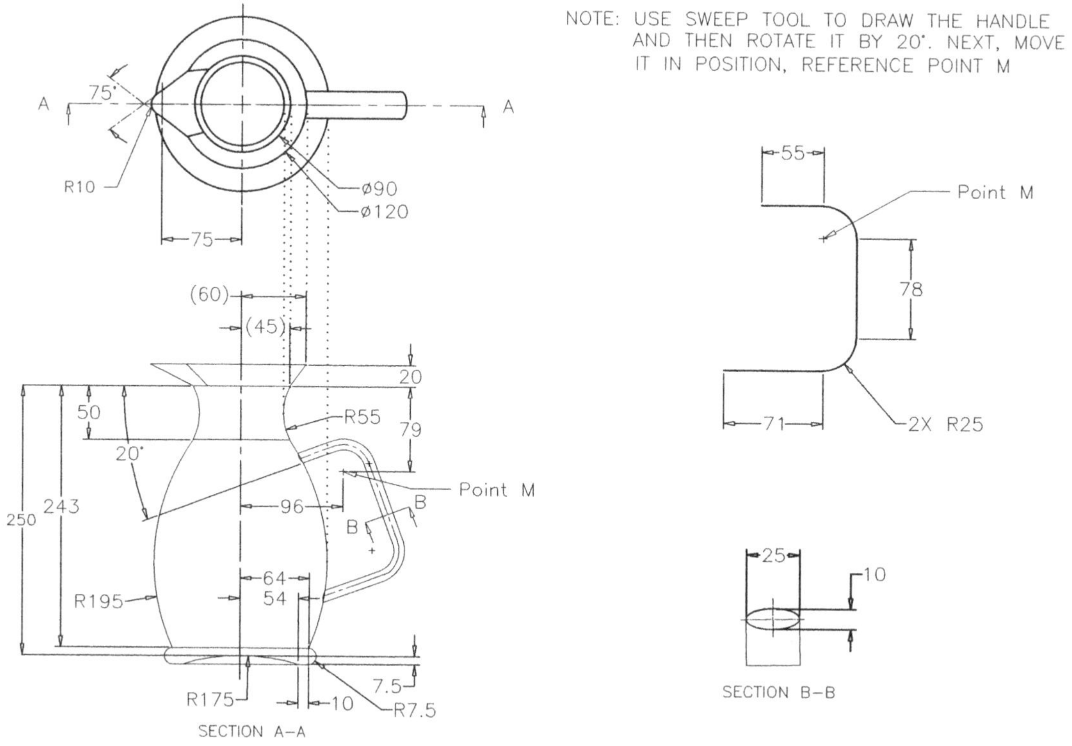

Figure 11-42 Orthographic views and dimensions of the model

1. Start a new drawing with **acad3D.dwt** template and draw the sketch of a circle with its center at the origin and diameter 90. This sketch is the first cross-section for the loft.

2. Draw another sketch for the second cross-section, as shown in Figure 11-43. Then, convert the sketch to a polyline by using the **Edit Polyline** tool.

3. Move the second sketch to a distance of 20 units along the Z axis.

4. Choose the **Loft** tool from the **Create** panel in the **Surface** tab; you are prompted to select the cross-sections that you want to loft. Select the two sketches one by one and press Enter; the preview of the loft surface is displayed.

5. Press Enter to create the loft surface, as shown in Figure 11-44.

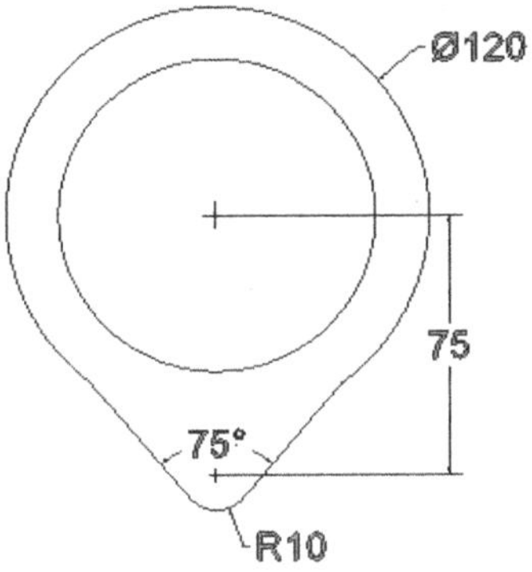

Figure 11-43 *The sketch for the second cross-section*

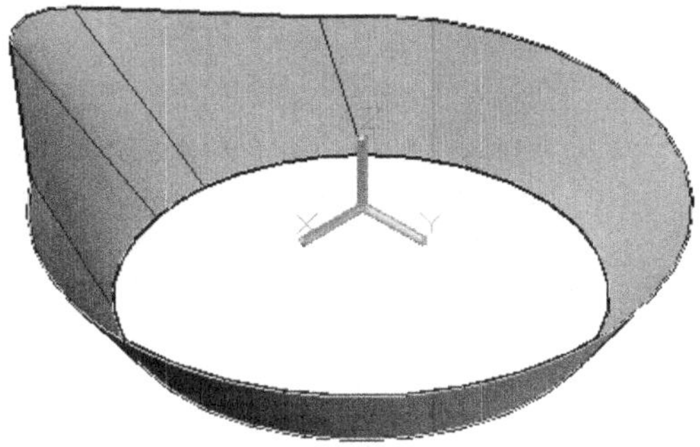

Figure 11-44 *The resulting loft surface*

Next, you need to create the revolved surface.

6. Switch to **Front** view.

7. Draw the sketch for the revolved feature, as shown in Figure 11-45, using the lines and arcs in the front view. Refer to Figure 11-42 for the missing dimensions. However, the profile may not be of exact dimensions.

8. Convert the profile into a polyline by using the **Join** tool.

9. Choose the **Revolve** tool from the **Create** panel in the **Surface** tab; you are prompted to select the profile to be revolved.

10. Select the sketch and press Enter; you are prompted to select the axis of revolution. You can select the axis of co-ordinate system in this case or draw a vertical line at the center for axis of revolution. Select the axis of revolution and press Enter; the revolved surface is created, as shown in Figure 11-46.

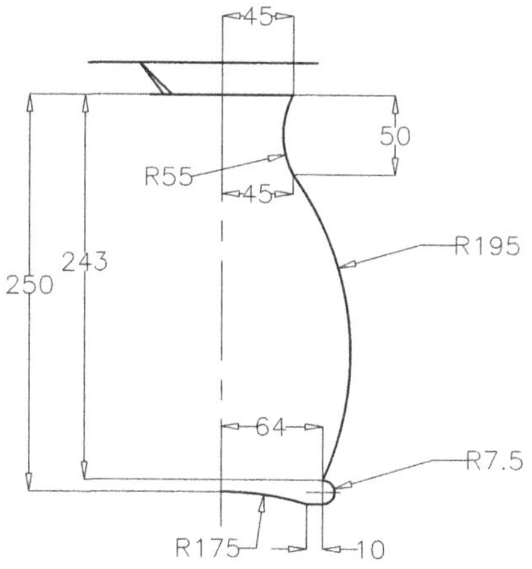

Figure 11-45 *The sketch for creating the revolved surface*

Figure 11-46 *The model after creating the revolved surface*

Next, you need to create the handle of the jug by sweeping a profile along a guide curve.

11. Draw the path for the sweep surface in the front view by using the **Polyline** tool, as shown in Figure 11-47. Note that the profile is rotated by 20 degrees.

12. Draw the profile of an ellipse, as shown in Figure 11-48, for creating the sweep surface. This profile can be drawn anywhere in the drawing area.

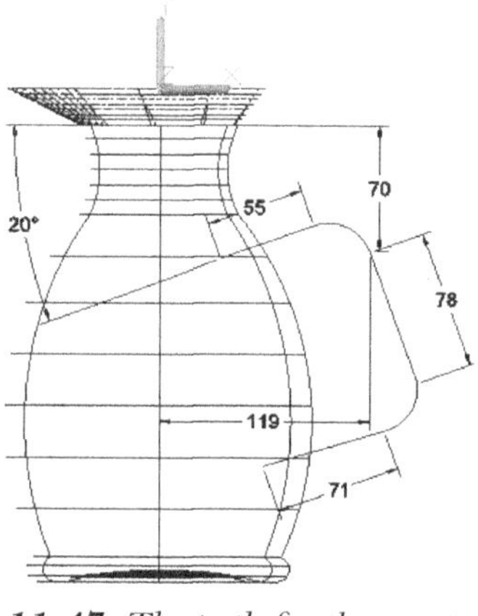

Figure 11-47 *The path for the sweep surface*

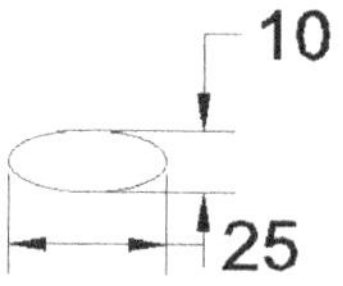

Figure 11-48 *The profile for the sweep surface*

13. Choose the **Sweep** tool from the **Create** panel in the **Surface** tab; you are prompted to select the profile to be swept.

14. Select the ellipse and press Enter; you are prompted to select the sweep path.

15. Select the sweep path created in Step 11 and press Enter; the sweep surface is created.

16. Create a new layer for profiles, move profiles to the new layer, and then freeze the layer so that the profiles are not displayed on the model. Next, the handle of the jug needs to be trimmed so that it does not penetrate the model.

17. Choose the **Trim** tool from the **Edit** panel in the **Surface** tab; you are prompted to select the surfaces to trim.

18. Select the sweep surface of the handle and press Enter; you are prompted to select the cutting elements.

19. Select the revolved surface of the jug and press Enter; you are prompted to select the area to be trimmed.

20. Rotate the model, select the inner portion of the sweep surface, and press Enter; the sweep surface penetrating the revolved surface is trimmed and the final model of the jug is created.

Exercise 1 — Surface Creation

In this exercise, you will create the model shown in Figure 11-49. Its drawing views and dimensions are shown in Figure 11-50.

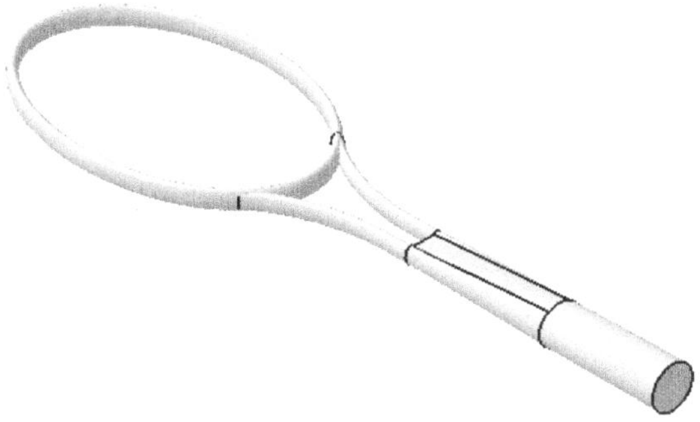

Figure 11-49 *The isometric view of the model*

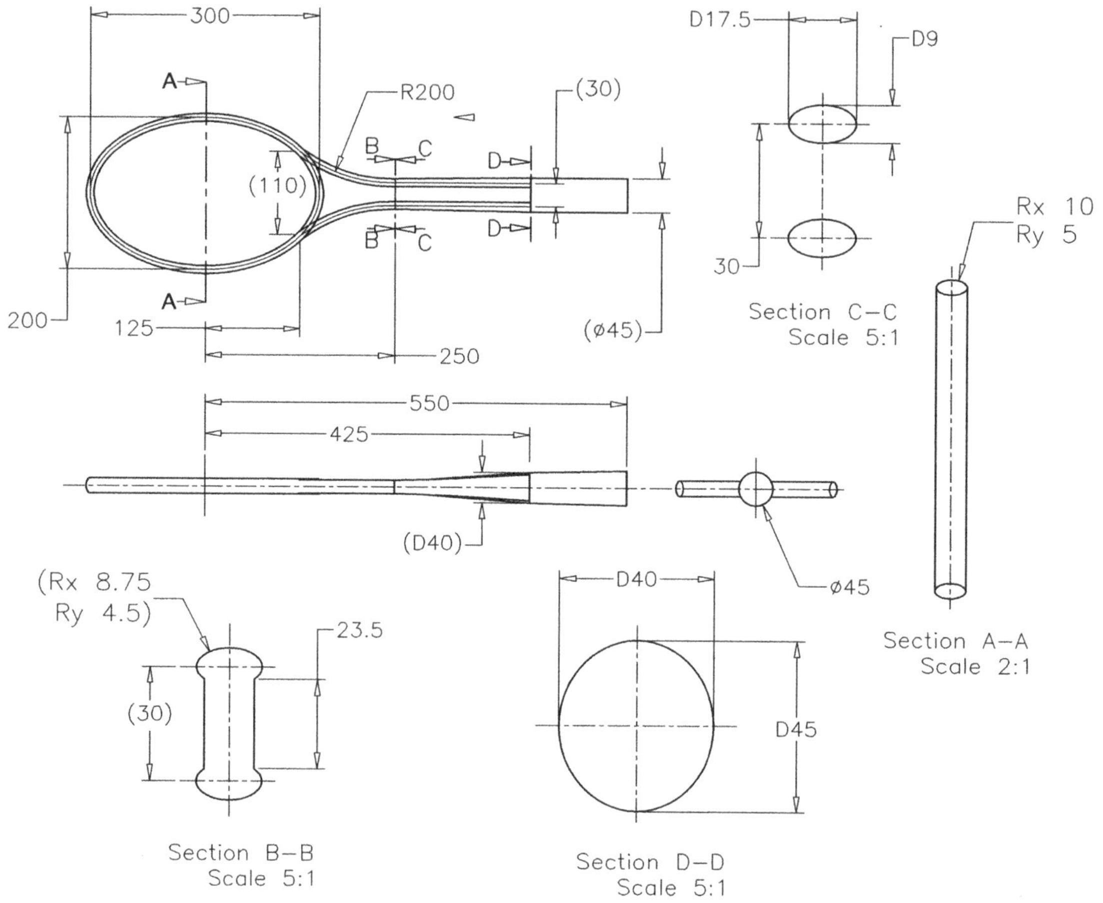

Figure 11-50 *The views and dimensions of the model*

Example 2 ***Surface Editing***

In this example, you will create the model of the back cover of a toy monitor, as shown in Figure 11-51. You will create this model using the editing tools. After creating the surface model, you need to convert it into a solid body. The orthographic views and dimensions of the model are shown in Figure 11-52.

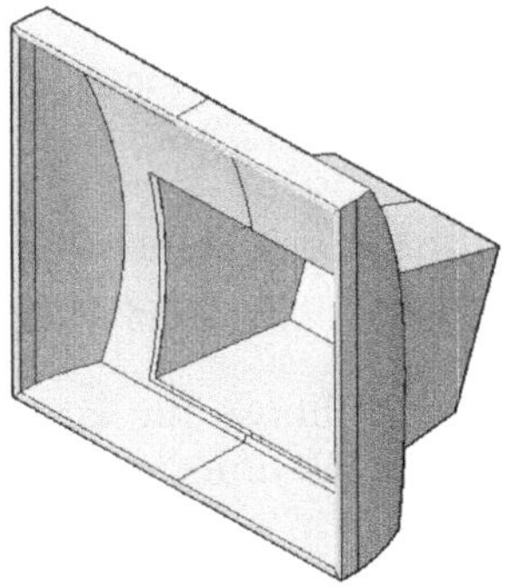

Figure 11-51 *Back cover of the toy monitor*

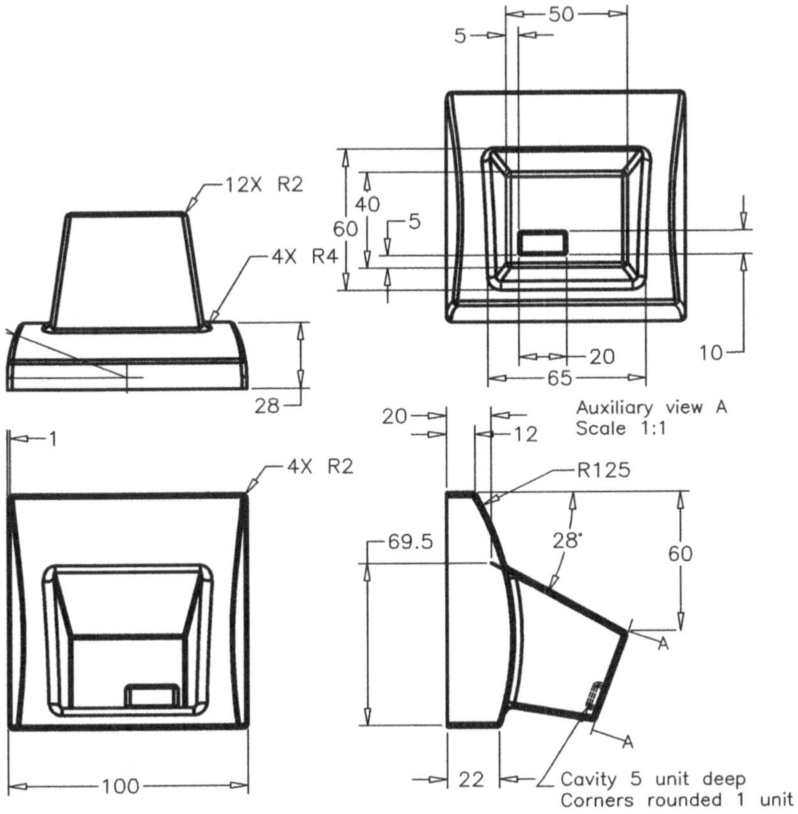

Figure 11-52 *Orthographic views and dimensions of the model for Example 2*

1. Start a new drawing file with **acad3D.dwt** template and switch to **Right** view.

2. Draw the sketch of the monitor, as shown in Figure 11-53, using the **Line** and **Arc** tools. Next, convert it into a polyline by using the **Join** tool.

3. Choose the **Extrude** tool from the **Create** panel of the **Surface** tab and extrude the sketch to a distance of 50 units; an extruded surface is created.

4. Change the view to **SW Isometric**. Choose the **Extend** tool from the **Edit** panel of the **Surface** tab and extend the surface to 50 units in the opposite direction; the base surface is created, as shown in Figure 11-54.

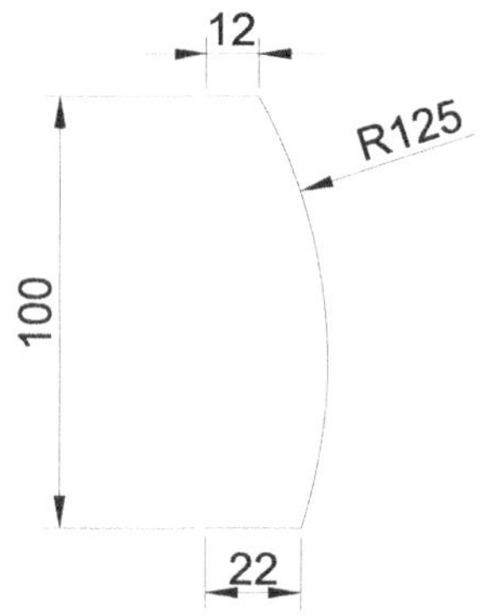

Figure 11-53 *Sketch of the base surface*

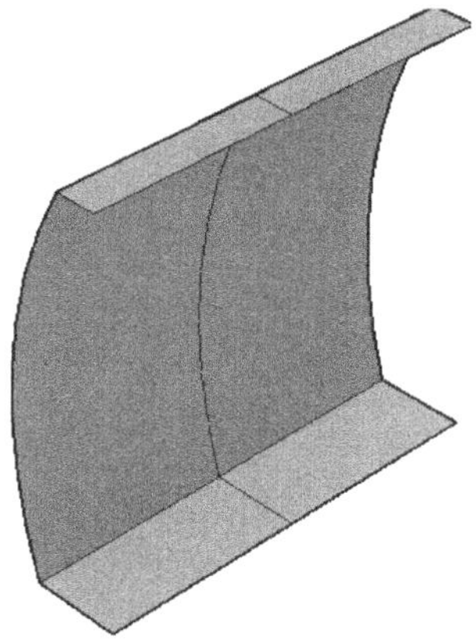

Figure 11-54 *Resulting base surface*

Next, you will create the loft surface. Therefore, you need to create the path and cross-sections for the loft.

5. Draw the sketch to create the path of the loft in the Right view, as shown in Figure 11-55.

6. Tilt the UCS using the **ZAxis** option of UCS command such that the cross-sections are aligned to the path created.

Note
You can also tilt the UCS dynamically as discussed in Chapter 6.

7. Draw two rectangular cross-sections, refer to Figure 11-56. For the dimensions, refer to Figure 11-52. Next, snap the midpoint of the top edge of the bigger rectangle to the left endpoint of the path, and midpoint of the top edge of the smaller rectangle to the right endpoint of the path.

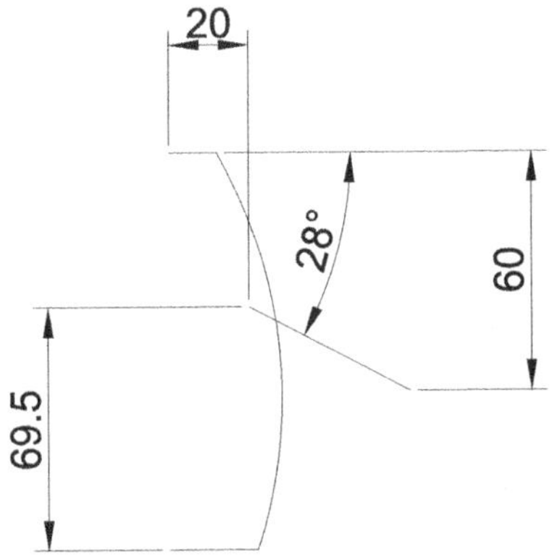

Figure 11-55 Path of the loft

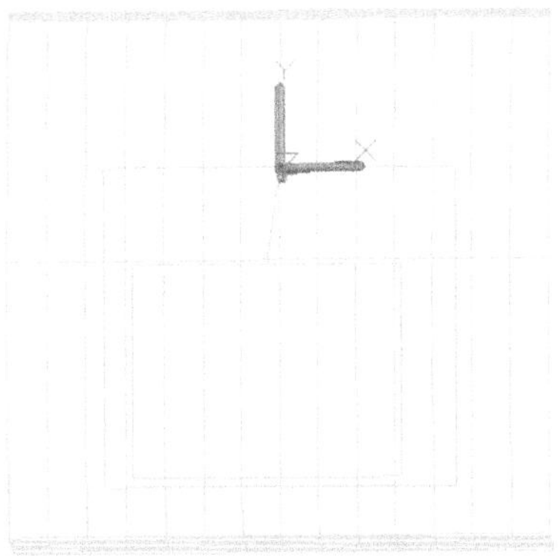

Figure 11-56 Cross-sections for the loft

8. Choose the **Loft** tool from the **Create** panel in the **Surface** tab; you are prompted to select the cross-sections.

9. Select the cross-sections one by one and press Enter; the preview of the loft is displayed and you are prompted to press Enter to accept or select a guide curve or a path.

10. Choose the **Path** option and select the line segment; the loft is created, as shown in Figure 11-57. Next, press Enter.

11. Draw the sketch on both sides on the top face of the base surface, as shown in Figure 11-58.

12. Choose the **Extrude** tool and extrude the sketch to coincide it with the bottom part of the first surface, refer to Figure 11-59. Use the 3D object snap to snap the extrusion height.

    Next, you need to trim the unwanted portions of the surfaces.

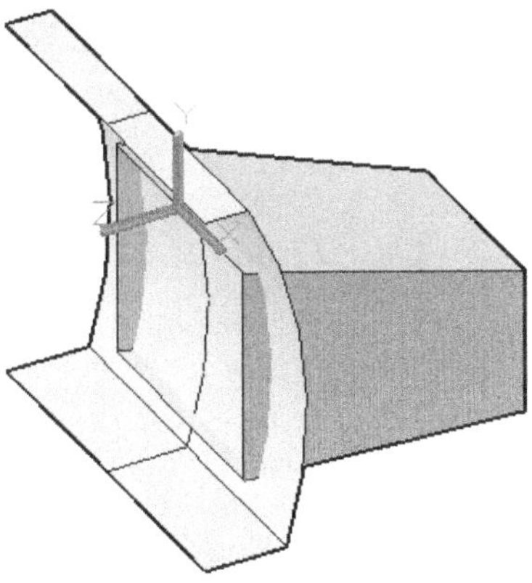

Figure 11-57 Resulting loft surface

13. Choose the **Trim** tool from the **Edit** panel of the **Surface** tab; you are prompted to select the surfaces to be trimmed.

14. Select the back face of the base surface and press Enter; you are prompted to select the surfaces used to trim. Select the left and right extruded surfaces, refer to Figure 11-60, and press Enter; you are prompted to select the portions to trim.

15. Select the part of the base surface that is projecting outward; the base surface gets trimmed.

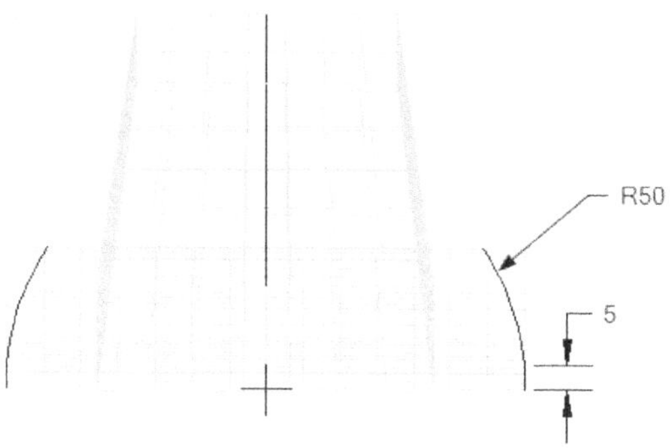

Figure 11-58 Sketch to be drawn

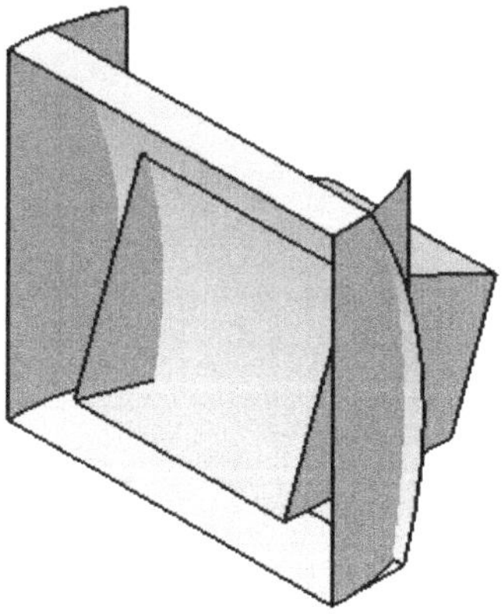

Figure 11-59 Resulting extruded surface

16. Similarly, trim all unwanted portions of the surfaces, as shown in Figure 11-61.

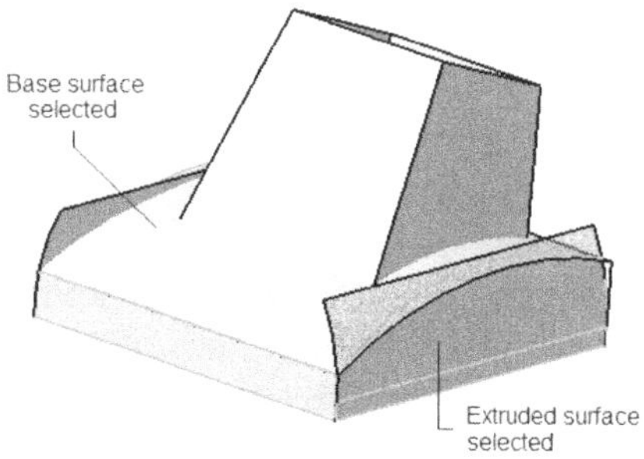

Figure 11-60 Surfaces selected for trimming

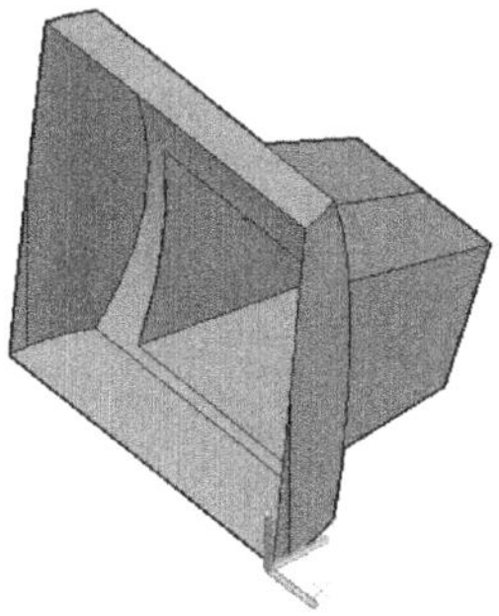

Figure 11-61 The model after trimming the surfaces

17. Create a new layer for the profiles, move all profiles to the new layer, and then freeze the layer so that the profiles are not displayed on the model.

    Next, you need to close the back face of the loft.

18. Invoke the **Patch** tool from the **Create** panel of the **Surface** tab; you are prompted to select the edges of the surfaces to patch.

19. Choose the **CHain** option and select all the four edges of the back face of the lofted surface and press Enter; the preview of the patch surface is displayed. Press Enter to accept it.

    Next, you need to create the frame of the monitor.

20. Now, create the cavity on the back face of the lofted surface, refer to Figure 11-52 for dimensions.

21. Choose the **Offset Surface** tool from the **Create** panel of the **Surface** tab. Select the extruded and extended surface and press Enter; the direction arrows are displayed. If the direction arrows are pointing outward, flip them. When the arrows point inward, set the offset value to 1.

22. Similarly, offset the other two sides inward to a distance of 1 units, refer to Figure 11-62.

23. Trim the four surfaces to form corners, refer to Figure 11-62.

    Next, you need to create a panel by closing the offset faces and the original faces.

24. Invoke the **Blend** tool from the **Create** panel in the **Surface** tab; you are prompted to select the first surface edge to blend.

25. Select the top edge of the extruded and extended surface, and then press Enter; you are prompted to select the second surface edge to blend.

26. Select the offset surface below the top edges and press Enter; the preview of the blend surface is created.

27. Press Enter to accept the settings of the blend surface. Similarly, blend all surfaces. The final model of the toy monitor after blending all surfaces is shown in Figure 11-63.

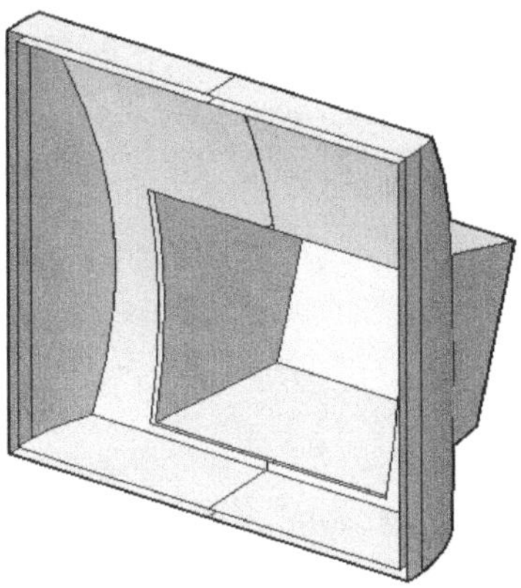

Figure 11-62 *Model after offsetting and trimming surfaces*

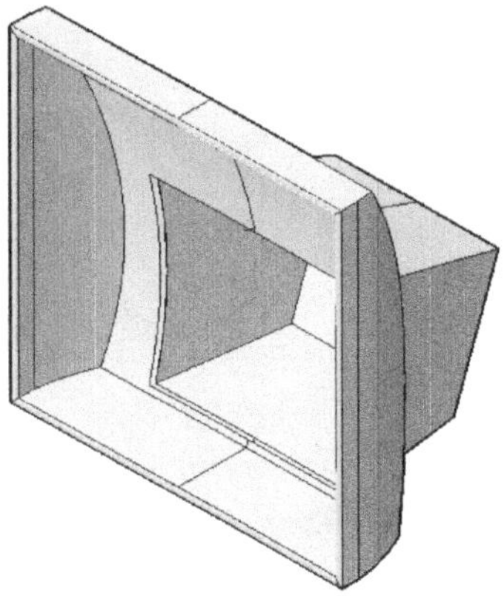

Figure 11-63 *Back cover of the toy monitor*

NURBS Surfaces

Ribbon: Surface > Control Vertices > Convert to NURBS
Menu Bar: Modify > Surface Editing > Convert to NURBS
Command: CONVTONURBS

NURBS is an acronym for 'Non-Uniform Rational B-Splines' and encompasses all characteristics of bezier curves or splines. However, in AutoCAD, splines are optimized to create NURBS. You can adjust the control points, fit points, and degree of a spline to control its shape, thereby controlling the NURBS surface. NURBS surface consists of control vertices and fit points, which can be used to modify the overall shape of a surface. While creating any surface, if you choose the **NURBS Creation** button, the NURBS surface will be created.

You can also convert an existing surface into a NURBS surface. To do so, choose the **Convert to NURBS** tool from the **Control Vertices** panel; you will be prompted to select the object to be converted into a NURBS surface. Select the surface and press Enter; the selected surface will be converted into a NURBS surface. Figure 11-64 shows a NURBS surface with its control vertices. If the CVs are not displayed on the NURBS surface, you need to invoke the **Show CV** tool. This tool is discussed next.

Displaying CVs

Ribbon: Surface > Control Vertices > Show CV/Hide CV
Menu Bar: Modify > Surface Editing > NURBS Surface Editing > Show CV/Hide CV
Command: CVSHOW/CVHIDE

You can edit the shape of a NURBS surface by dragging its control vertices or fit points. By default, control vertices are not displayed on the NURBS surface. To view the control vertices on the surface, choose the **Show CV** tool from the **Control Vertices** panel; the CVs will be displayed on the surface. You can drag these control vertices to new locations to edit the surface, refer to Figure 11-65. After editing the surface, if you want to hide the CVs from the NURBS surface, choose the **Hide CV** tool.

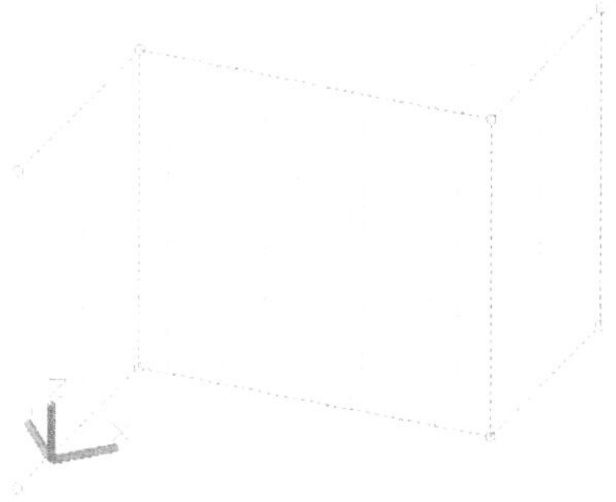

Figure 11-64 *NURBS surface*

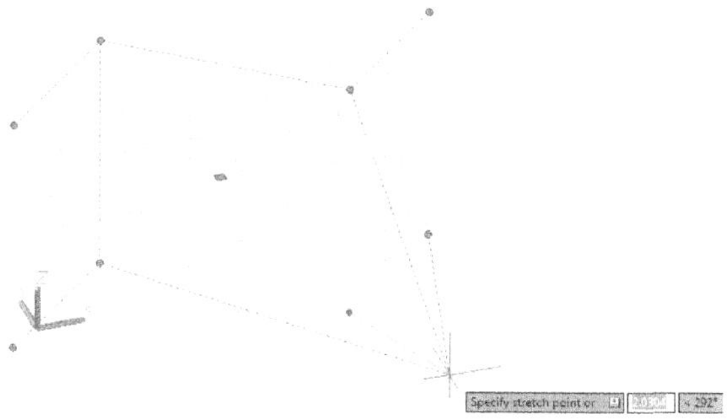

Figure 11-65 *Editing NURBS surface*

Editing CVs

Ribbon: Surface > Control Vertices > CV Edit Bar **Command:** 3DEDITBAR

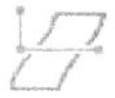
CV Edit Bar

While converting an existing surface into a NURBS surface, the CVs are formed at the corners of the NURBS surface. However, you can specify a point on the NURBS surface to create a CV at that particular point. To do so, choose the **CV Edit Bar** tool from the **Control Vertices** panel; you will be prompted to select a surface. Select the NURBS surface; the cursor will turn red. Now, you can specify the direction of creation of the CV on the surface. After specifying a point, a move gizmo along with two handles will be displayed on the specified point, refer to Figure 11-66. Using these handles, you can edit the shape of the NURBS surface. The horizontal triangular handle is used to specify the magnitude of drag and the square handle is used to move the selected point to a new place.

You can set the tangency conditions and position of a control vertex using the triangular grip displayed on the gizmo, refer to Figure 11-66. Right-click on the triangular grip; a shortcut menu will be displayed, as shown in Figure 11-67. The options in the shortcut menu are discussed next.

By default, the **Move Point Location** option is chosen in this shortcut menu. As a result, the NURBS surface will be modified with respect to the point but the tangency will not be modified. If you select the **Move Tangent Direction** option, the tangency of the curve will be modified. If you select the **U Tangent Direction** or **V Tangent Direction** option, the tangency will be modified only in the U-direction or V-direction, respectively. The **Normal Tangent Direction** option is used to edit the tangency of the curve normal to the current UCS. You can also constrain the change in tangency or point location to a particular axis using the **Set Constraint** option. You can also relocate the base point or realign the gizmo using the **Relocate Base Point** and **Align Gizmo With** options, respectively in this shortcut menu.

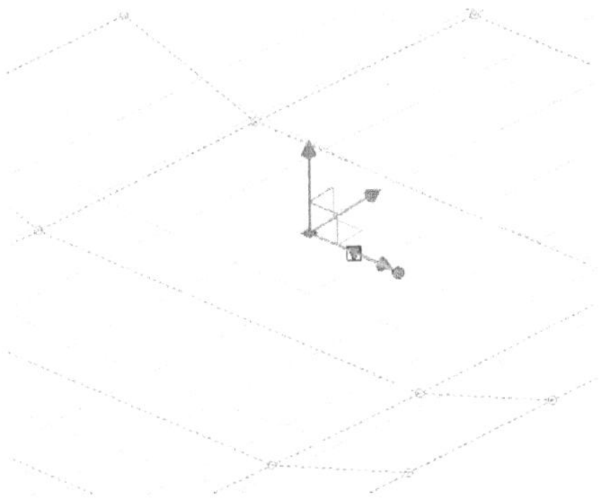

Figure 11-66 *Editing CVs*

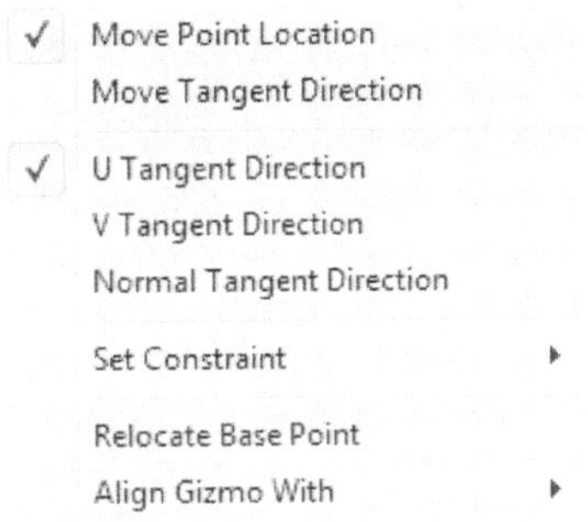

Figure 11-67 *Shortcut menu displayed at the triangular grip*

Adding CVs

Ribbon: Surface > Control Vertices > Add
Menu Bar: Modify > Surface Editing > NURBS Surface Editing > Add CV
Command: CVADD

When you create a NURBS surface, some CVs are displayed on it by default. However, you can add more CVs to it if you need. To add CVs, choose the **Add** tool from the **Control Vertices** panel; you will be prompted to select a NURBS surface or curve where you want to add CVs. Select the NURBS surface; preview of the CVs will be attached to the cursor, refer to Figure 11-68. By default, the CVs get added in the U-direction. If you want to add CVs in the V-direction, choose the **Direction** option from the Command prompt; the CVs will be added in the V-direction.

Figure 11-68 *Preview of CVs*

If you want to create knots on the surface, choose the **insert Knots** option from the Command prompt; knots or fit points will be created on the surface instead of CVs.

Rebuilding a NURBS Surface

Ribbon: Surface > Control Vertices > Rebuild **Command:** CVREBUILD
Menu Bar: Modify > Surface Editing > NURBS Surface Editing > Rebuild

You can reconstruct a NURBS surface by defining the number of CVs created on it and the degree of the CV curve. For example, the surfaces created by line, arc, or circle are of less than 3 degrees. You may need to change the degree of these surfaces. You can do so by invoking the **Rebuild** tool from the **Control Vertices** panel. On doing so, you will be prompted to select the surface to be rebuilt. Select the required surface; the **Rebuild Surface** dialog box will be displayed, as shown in Figure 11-69.

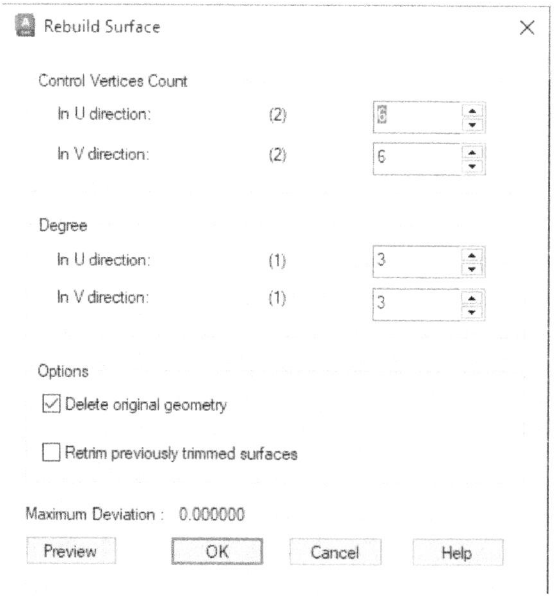

Figure 11-69 *The* ***Rebuild Surface*** *dialog box*

The areas in the dialog box are discussed next.

Control Vertices Count

In this area, you can specify the number of CVs to be created on the surface in the U and V directions.

Degree

In this area, you can specify the degree of a CV curve along the U and V directions.

Options

In this area, you can specify whether to delete the original geometry of a CV curve or retrim a surface that has already been trimmed.

Preview Button

You can preview the CVs created on a surface. To do so, first set the required values in the **Rebuild Surface** dialog box and then choose the **Preview** button; the preview of the CVs created will be displayed. If the preview of the CVs created is satisfactory, press Enter. If you want to change the values, press the Esc key.

Removing CVs

Ribbon: Surface > Control Vertices > Remove
Menu Bar: Modify > Surface Editing > NURBS Surface Editing > Remove CV
Command: CVREMOVE

You can remove the unwanted CVs from a NURBS surface. To do so, choose the **Remove** tool from the **Control Vertices** panel; you will be prompted to select a NURBS surface to remove the CVs. Select a NURBS surface and press Enter; you will be prompted to select a point on the surface to remove vertices in the U-direction. Select a point on the surface near the CV that you want to remove. If you want to change the direction of removal of CVs, use the **Direction** option; the CVs will be set to remove from the V-direction. Remember that the minimum number of CVs in each direction is 2.

Projecting Geometries

The Projection tools are used to project one or more elements on a surface. These tools are available in the **Project Geometry** panel of the **Surface** tab. You can project curves, lines, points, 2D polyline, 3D polyline, or helix onto a solid or a surface. When you project a curve, a duplicate of that curve is created. You can move, modify, change, delete this curve without affecting the original curve. You can also trim the surface onto which the curve has been projected. This can be done by using the **Auto Trim** button. When this button is active, the surface will be trimmed automatically on projecting the curve onto the surface. The projection of curves can be normal to the surface along a specified direction, normal to the current view, or along a specified path. These projection tools are discussed next.

Project to UCS

Using this tool, you can project a curve on a surface along the +z or -z axis of the current UCS.

Project to View

This tool enables you to project a curve on a surface based on the current view.

Project to 2 Points

Using this tool, you can project a curve along a path defined by two points. Figure 11-70 shows a surface and the curve to be projected. Figure 11-71 shows the curve projected using the **Project to UCS** tool with the **Auto Trim** button chosen and Figure 11-72 shows the curve projected using the **Project to View** tool with the **Auto Trim** button chosen. Figure 11-73 shows the curve projected on the surface by specifying the 2 endpoints of the line segment as the direction of projection with the **Auto Trim** button deactivated.

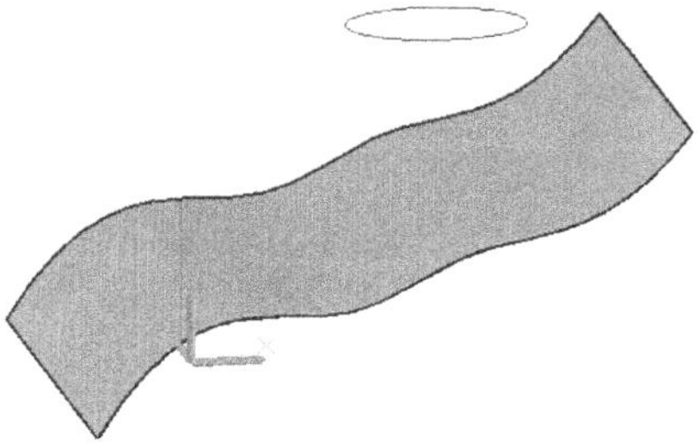

Figure 11-70 *Surface and curve to be projected*

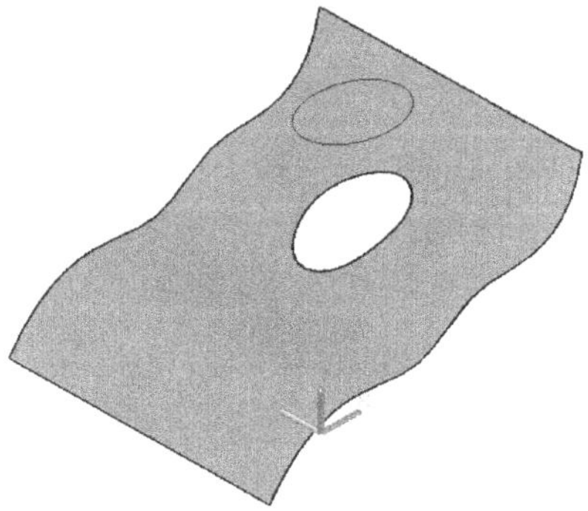

Figure 11-71 *Curve projected using the* ***Project to UCS*** *tool*

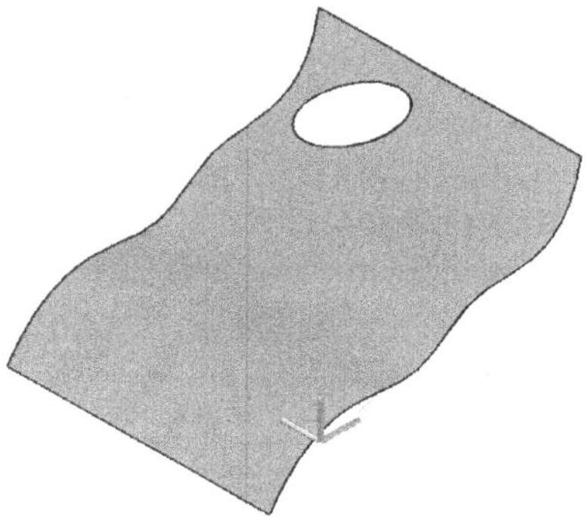

Figure 11-72 *Curve projected using the* ***Project to View*** *tool*

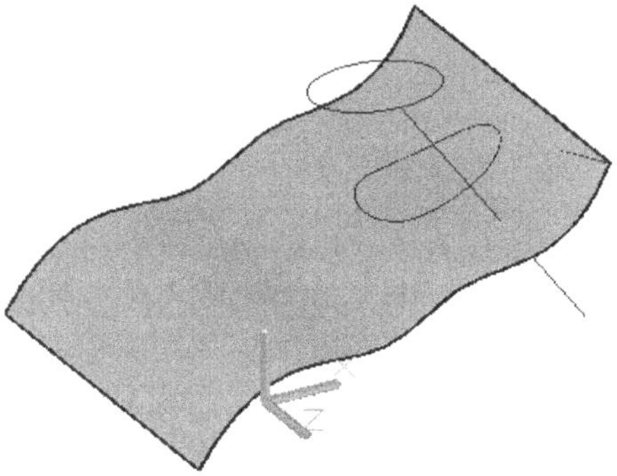

Figure 11-73 *Curve projected using the* ***Project to 2 Points*** *tool*

Example 3 — *Editing Tools*

In this example, you will create the model of eyeglasses, as shown in Figure 11-74. The dimensions of the model are shown in Figures 11-74(a) through 11-74(g). Assume the missing dimensions.

Figure 11-74 *Final model of the eyeglasses*

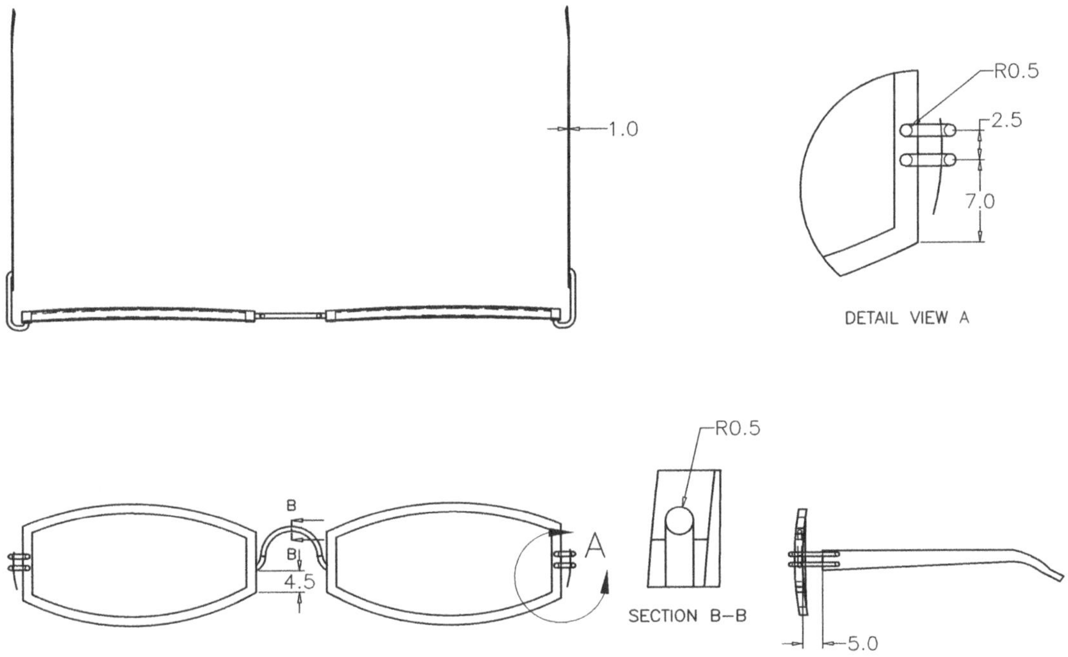

Figure 11-74(a) *Orthographic views of the model for Example 3*

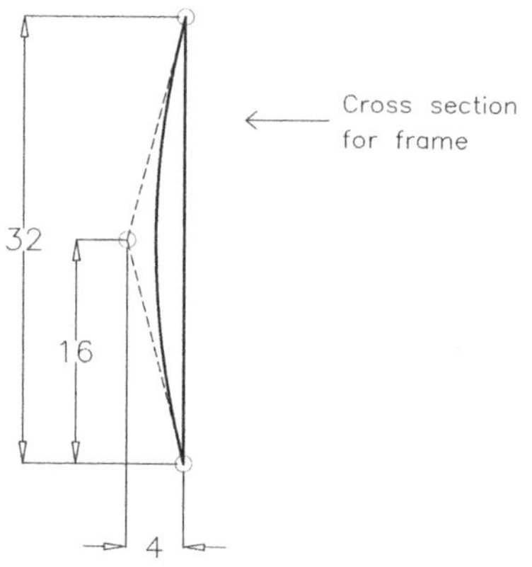

Figure 11-74(b) *Cross section for frame*

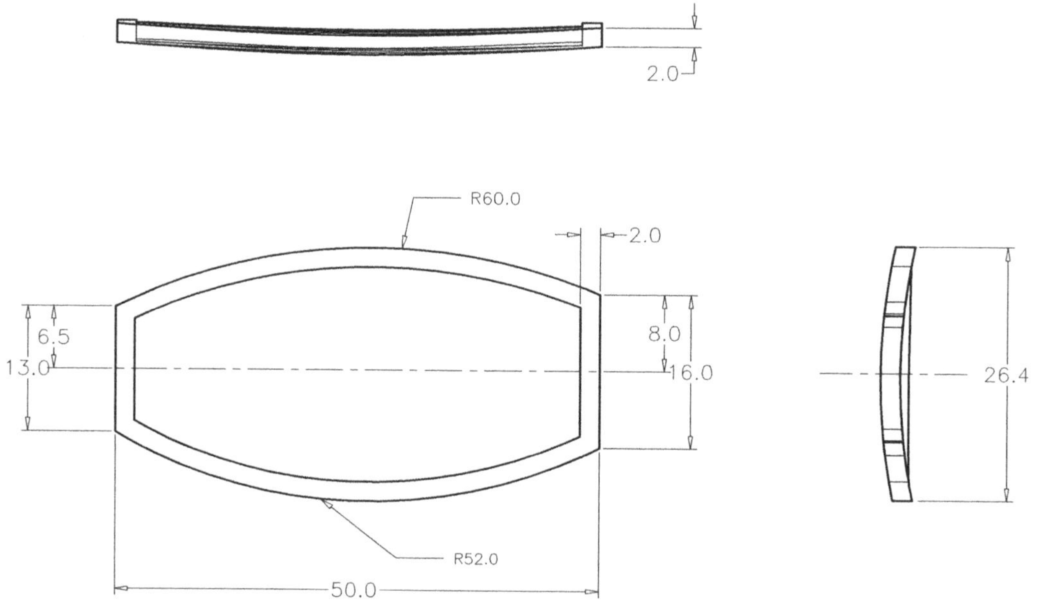

Figure 11-74(c) *Orthographic views of the lenses*

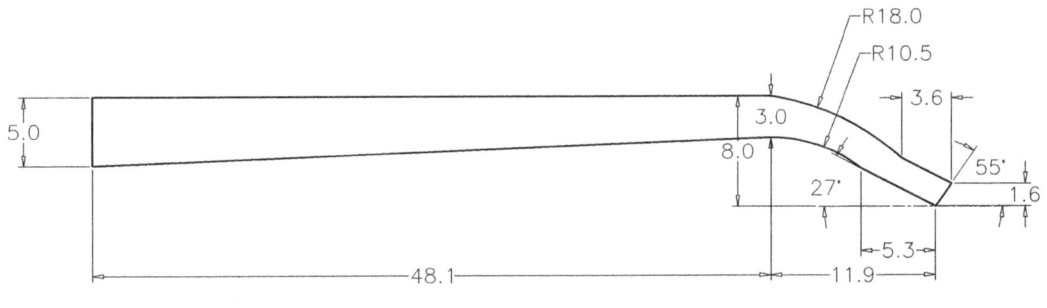

Figure 11-74(d) *Profile for the Temples*

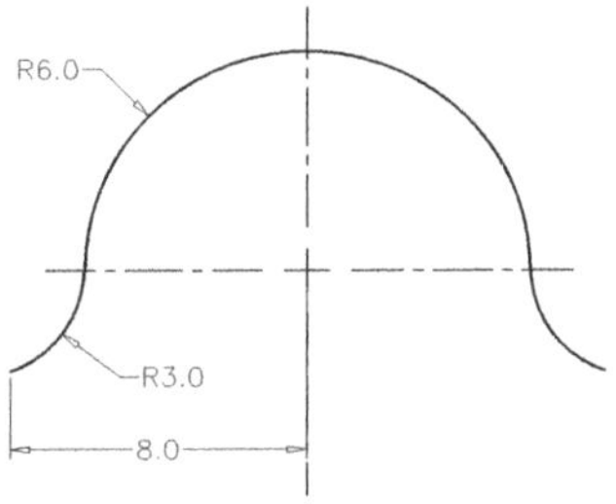

Figure 11-74(e) *Profile for the Bridge*

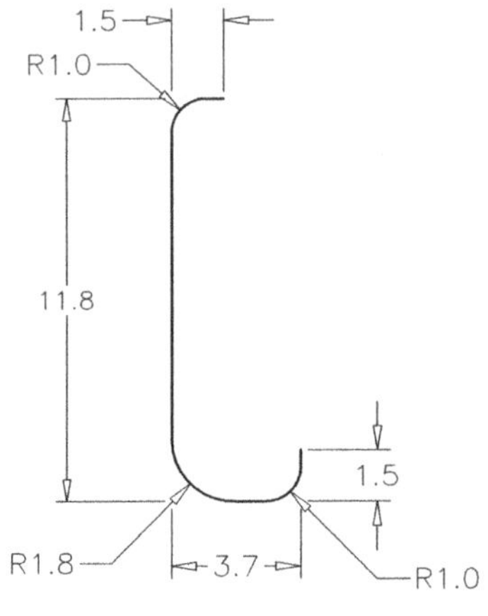

Figure 11-74(f) *Profile for the End Piece*

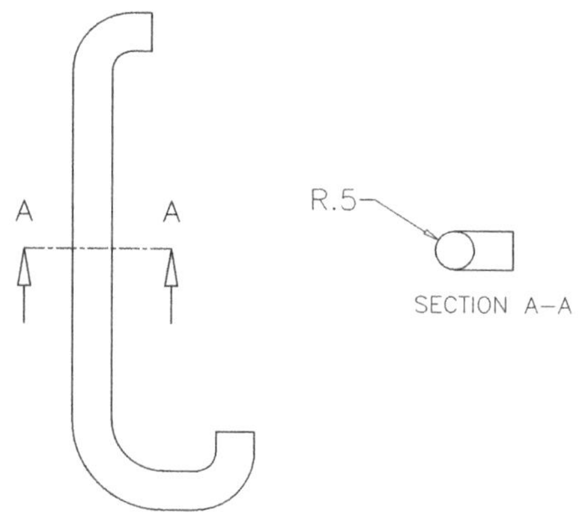

Figure 11-74(g) *Sectioned view of the End Piece*

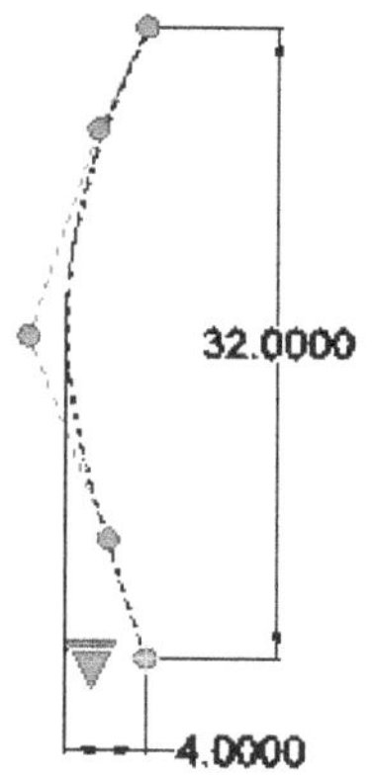

Figure 11-75 *Cross-section for frame*

1. Start a new drawing file using the **acad3D.dwt** template.
2. Switch to **Right** view.
3. Select the **Parallel** projection option from the **In-canvas Viewport Controls**.
4. Draw the spline using the **Spline CV** tool, as shown in Figure 11-75.
5. You need to array this spline along the Z-axis. To do so, invoke the **Copy** tool and create two more instances of spline by using the prompt sequence given next.

   Select objects: *Select the spline.*
   Select objects: Enter.
   Current settings: Copy mode = Multiple
   Specify base point or [Displacement/mOde] <Displacement>:*Select any point on the spline.*
   Specify second point or [Array] <use first point as displacement>: **ARRAY** Enter.
   Enter number of items to array: **3** Enter.
   Specify second point or [Fit]: **@0,0,60** Enter.
   Specify second point or [Array/Exit/Undo] <Exit>: Enter.

Next, you need to create guide curves.

6. Change the current viewport to **Front** and draw guide curves, as shown in Figure 11-76.

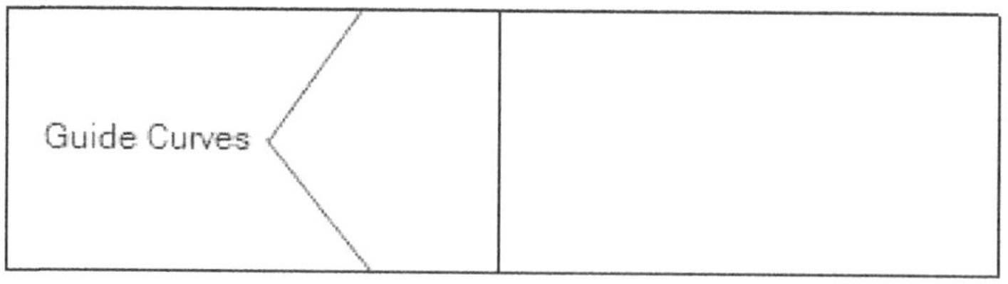

Figure 11-76 *Guide curves for frame*

7. Invoke the **Network** tool from the **Create** panel of the **Surface** tab; you are prompted to select the curves in the first direction.

8. Select the three splines created earlier and press Enter; you are prompted to select the curves in the second direction.

9. Select the two joining guide curves drawn previously and press Enter; the network surface is created. Change the current viewport to **SE Isometric** and then change the visual style; the surface will be displayed, as shown in Figure 11-77.

   Next, you need to draw the shape of the frame and then trim the unwanted portion.

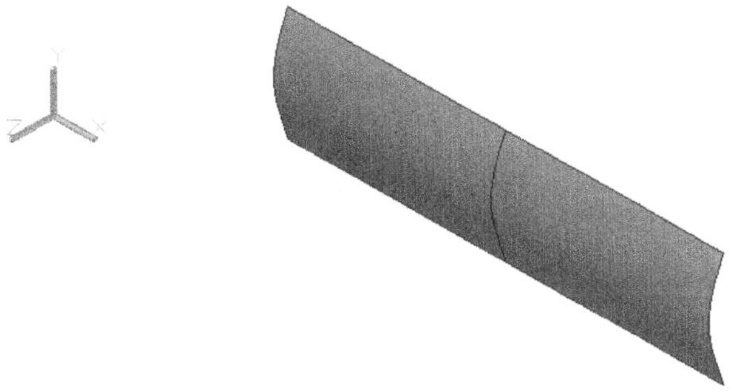

Figure 11-77 *Network surface created*

10. Align the UCS on the network surface and draw the sketch using the **Line** and **Arc** tools in the **Front** view, as shown in Figure 11-78. Refer to Figure 11-79 for dimensions.

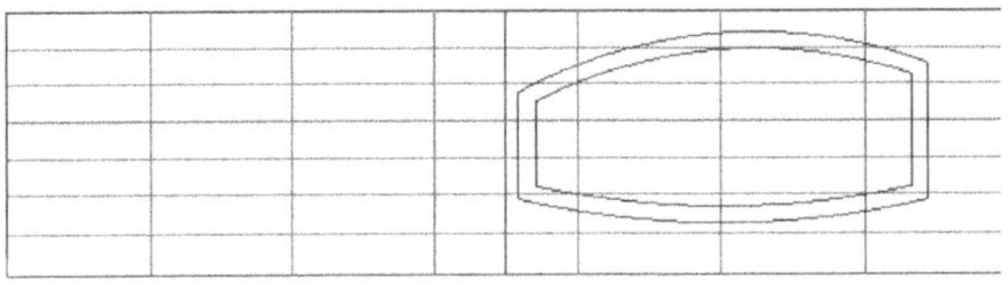

Figure 11-78 *Sketch to be drawn*

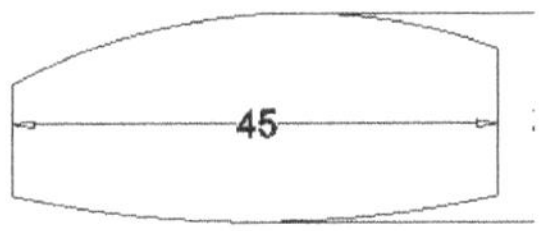

Figure 11-79 *Dimensions for sketch*

Note
The sketch created should be joined using the ***Join*** *tool.*

11. Invoke the **Trim** tool from the **Edit** panel in the **Surface** tab; you are prompted to select the objects to trim.

12. Select the network surface and press Enter; you are prompted to select the cutting curves.

13. Select the two joined curves and press Enter; you are prompted to select the area to be trimmed.

14. Select the innermost and outermost areas of the curves and press Enter; the surface is created and displayed, as shown in Figure 11-80.

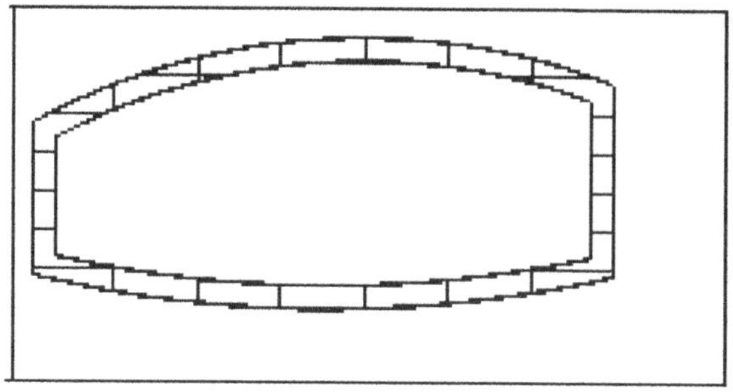

Figure 11-80 Partial view of glass frame

15. Create a new layer, move all profiles to the new layer, and then freeze the layer so that the profiles are not displayed on the model.

16. Change the current viewport to **SE Isometric**.

17. Invoke the **Extrude** tool, select the surface, and then extrude it by 2 units.

    Next, you need to create a surface for glasses.

18. Invoke the **Patch** tool from the **Create** panel of the **Surface** tab; you are prompted to select the surface edges. Select the innermost edge of the frame and press Enter twice; the surface will be created, as shown in Figure 11-81.

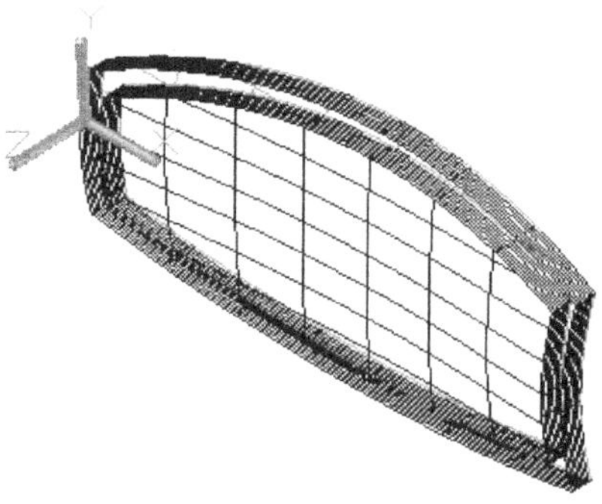

Figure 11-81 The patch surface created

Next, you need to create the side arm.

19. Change the current view to **Front** using the **In-canvas Viewport Controls** and then create a spline by using the **CV** method, refer to Figure 11-82.

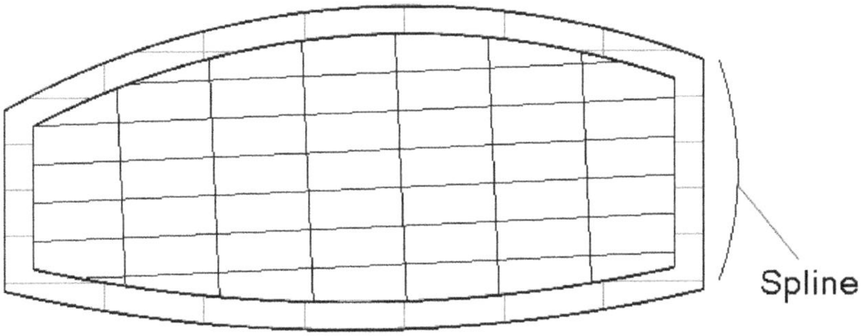

Figure 11-82 Spline created for arm

20. Invoke the **Extrude** tool and then extrude this spline to 100 units along negative Z-axis.

21. Change the current viewport to **Right** and align the UCS to the extruded surface created in Step 19.

22. Create a profile for side arm and join it using the **Join** tool, as shown in Figure 11-83.

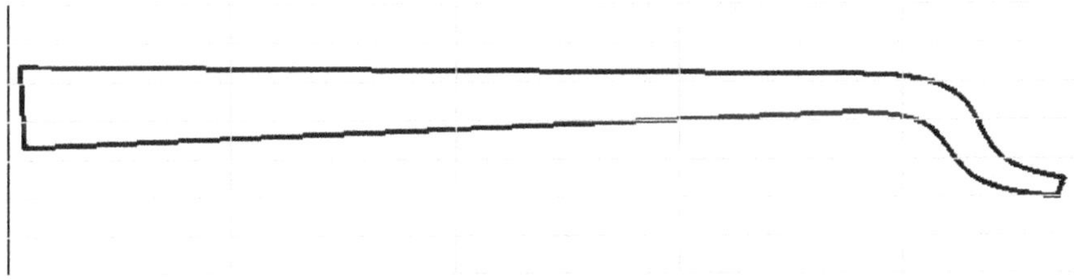

Figure 11-83 Profile for arm

23. Invoke the **Trim** tool from the **Edit** panel in the **Surface** tab; you are prompted to select the objects to trim.

24. Select the extruded surface and press Enter; you are prompted to select the curves for trimming the object.

25. Select the profile created for the arm and press Enter; you are prompted to select the area to be trimmed.

26. Select the outer area of the profile and press Enter; the surface is created.

27. Move the profiles to the frozen layer.

28. Select the newly created surface and extrude it to 1 unit along negative Z-axis.

29. Change the current viewport to **Front** and align the UCS to the front face of the frame.

30. Create two circles of radius 0.45 each and a spline, as shown in the Figure 11-84.

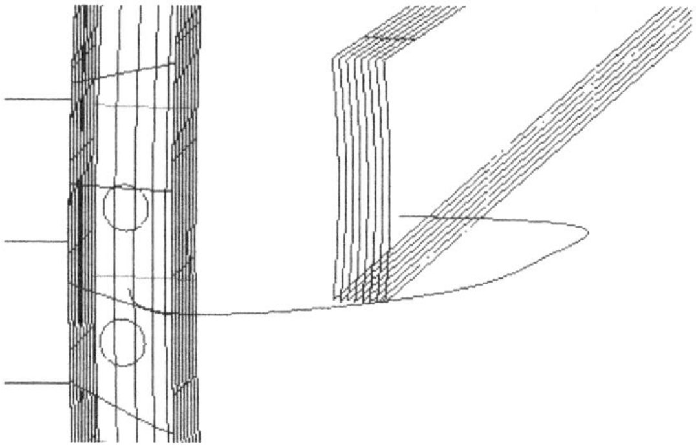

Figure 11-84 *Section and path for sweep feature*

31. Invoke the **Sweep** tool, select the two circles, and press Enter; you are prompted to select the sweep path.

32. Select the spline curve; the sweep feature is created. Move the profiles to the frozen layer.

33. Change the current viewport to **Front** and mirror all the features using the **Mirror** tool about a line drawn at a distance of 7.5 units from the edge opposite to the edge joined with the arm.

    Next, you need to link the mirrored feature with the original feature.

34. Align the UCS to the side face of the frame, as shown in the Figure 11-85, and create a circle of radius 0.5 at **0,0** co-ordinate.

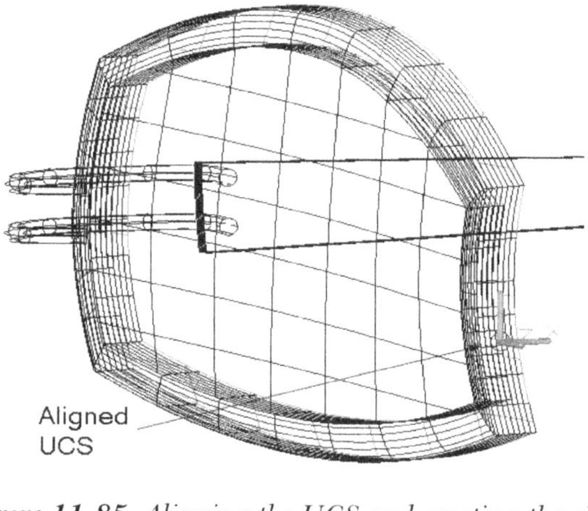

Figure 11-85 *Aligning the UCS and creating the circle*

35. Set the UCS to WCS, change the viewport to **Front**, and create a profile for the joint, as shown in Figure 11-86.

36. Move the profile to the center of the circle created in Step 34.

37. Sweep the circle on the profile drawn for creating the joint.

The final model of the eyeglasses after applying the desired materials is shown in shaded view in Figure 11-87.

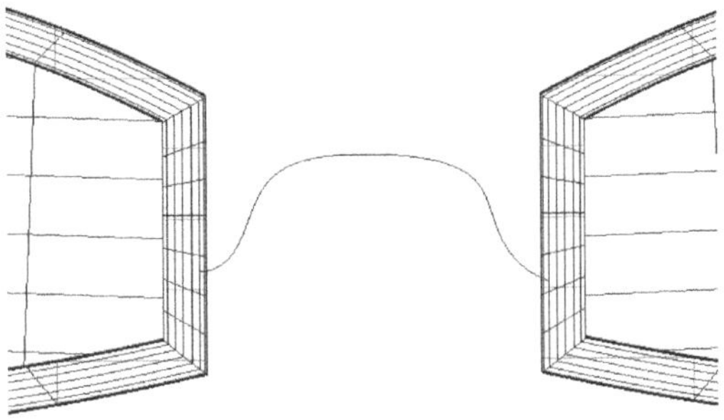

Figure 11-86 *Profile for joint*

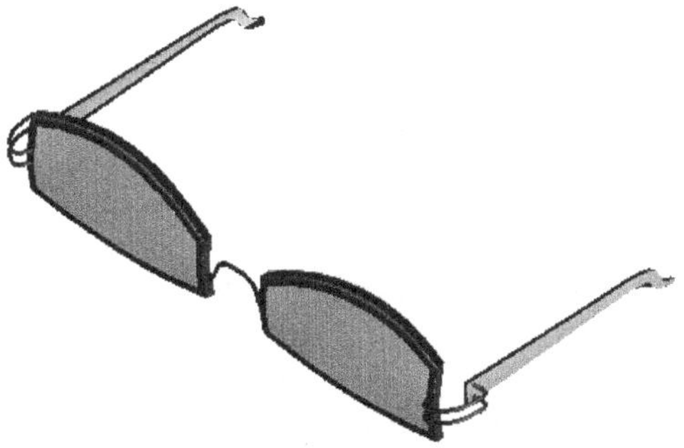

Figure 11-87 *Final model of the eyeglasses*

Note

You will learn about applying materials in Chapter 13.

PERFORMING SURFACE ANALYSIS

AutoCAD allows you to analyze the surface continuity, curvature, and draft angles of surfaces using the surface analysis tools. You can also validate surfaces and curves before manufacturing using these tools. There are three types of surface analysis tools: **Zebra**, **Curvature**, and **Draft**. Note that these tools work only in 3D visual styles. These tools are discussed in detail in the next section.

Zebra

Ribbon: Surface > Analysis > Analysis Zebra **Command:** ANALYSISZEBRA

The **Zebra** tool projects the zebra stripes on the selected model. This tool is used to visualize the curvature of surfaces and to determine if there are any surface discontinuities and inflections. To perform the **Zebra** analysis, invoke the **Zebra** tool from the **Analysis** panel of the **Surface** tab; you will be prompted to select the solid or surface on which you want to perform the analysis. Select the required surface and press Enter; zebra strips will be displayed on the selected model. Figure 11-88 shows the zebra analysis performed on a binocular. The way these strips are aligned or curved on the model allows you to interpret the smoothness of the surfaces. This type of analysis is mostly used where one surface joins with the other surface.

You can also change the settings of zebra stripes as per your requirements. To do so, choose the **Analysis Options** button from the **Analysis** panel; the **Analysis Options** dialog box will be displayed, as shown in Figure 11-89. By default, the **Zebra** tab is chosen in the dialog box.

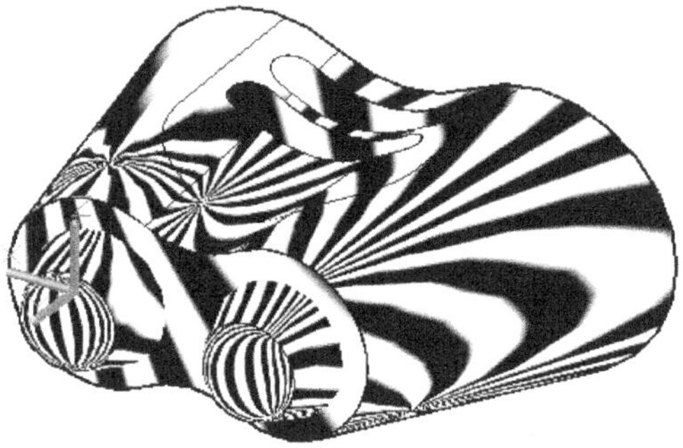

Figure 11-88 Zebra analysis performed

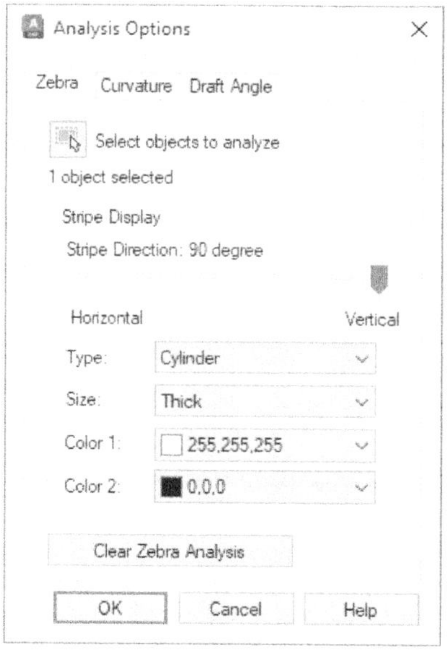

***Figure 11-89** The **Analysis Options** dialog box*

You can set the angle of stripes by using the slider available in the **Stripe Display** area of this dialog box. The value in the slider varies from 0 to 90. On setting 0, horizontal stripes are displayed on the model, whereas on setting 90, vertical stripes are displayed on the model. As you change the value on the slider bar, the zebra stripes will also change dynamically on screen. You can also set the type, color, and thickness of zebra strips in the **Stripe Display** area. Choose the **Clear Zebra Analysis** button in this dialog box to clear the zebra analysis. If you want to select objects for analysis, choose the **Select objects to analyze** button; the dialog box will disappear for a while, allowing you to select the objects from the screen.

Analysis Curvature

Ribbon: Surface > Analysis > Analysis Curvature **Command:** ANALYSISCURVATURE

The **Analysis Curvature** tool is used to display a color gradient or contours on the selected model. This color contour allows you to graphically visualize the radius of curvature of a model and evaluate the high and low areas of curvature. The contour also allows you to ensure that the model is within a certain range. The areas of high curvature or positive Gaussian value are displayed in red and the areas of low curvature or negative Gaussian value are displayed in blue. The mean curvature or a zero Gaussian value is displayed in red, which indicates a flat surface.

To perform the curvature analysis, choose the **Curvature** tool from the **Analysis** panel; you will be prompted to select the solid or surface on which you want to perform the analysis. Select the required objects and press Enter; the color gradient will be displayed on the model. Figure 11-90 shows the curvature analysis performed on the binocular. You can change the settings for the curvature analysis by choosing the **Curvature** tab in the **Analysis Options** dialog box. Figure 11-91 shows the **Analysis Options** dialog box with the **Curvature** tab chosen. You can set the display style of curvature to **Gaussian**, **Mean**, **Max radius**, or **Min radius** using the **Display style** drop-down list in this dialog box. You can also set the minimum and maximum range in the corresponding edit boxes in the **Color Mapping** area of the dialog box.

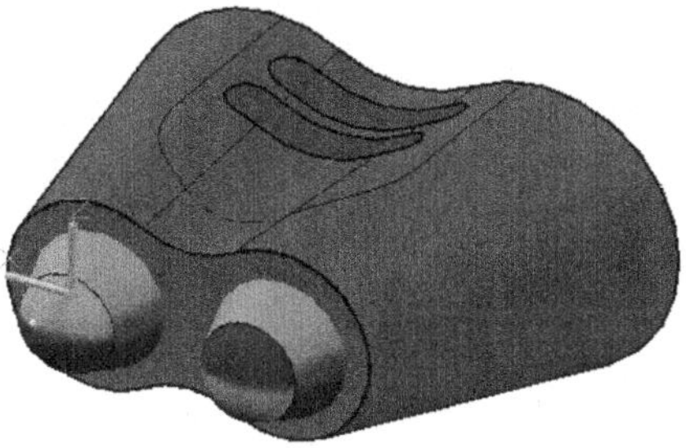

Figure 11-90 Curvature analysis performed

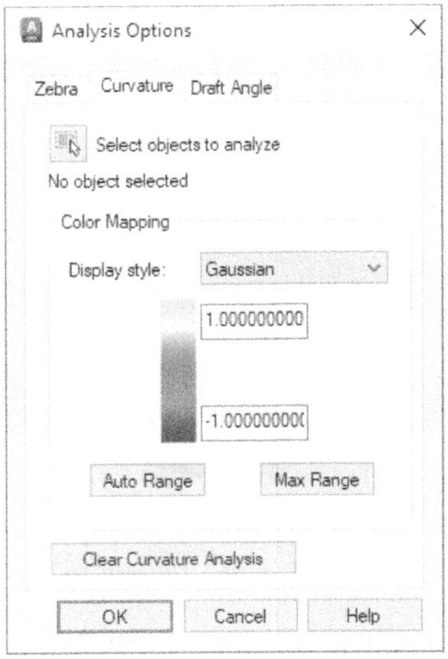

*Figure 11-91 The **Analysis Options** dialog box with the **Curvature** tab chosen*

To clear the curvature analysis, choose the **Clear Curvature Analysis** button in the **Analysis Options** dialog box.

Analysis Draft

Ribbon: Surface > Analysis > Analysis Draft **Command:** ANALYSISDRAFT

The **Analysis Draft** tool is used to visualize the draft applied on the selected model. If you are designing a model that can be cast, then this tool is used to check whether a part can be removed from a mold or die. Then, it calculates whether there is sufficient draft between the part and the mold, based on the pull direction. To perform the draft analysis, choose the **Draft** tool from the **Analysis** panel; you will be prompted to select the object on which you want to perform the analysis. Select the object and press Enter; the draft analysis will be performed on the object. Figure 11-92 shows the draft analysis performed on the binocular.

Surface angles are defined with respect to the draft plane. The colors displayed on the model after performing the draft analysis will depend on the angles defined. You can set these colors by using the **Draft Angle** tab of the **Analysis Options** dialog box, refer to Figure 11-93. Choose the **Clear Draft Angle Analysis** button to clear the draft angle analysis.

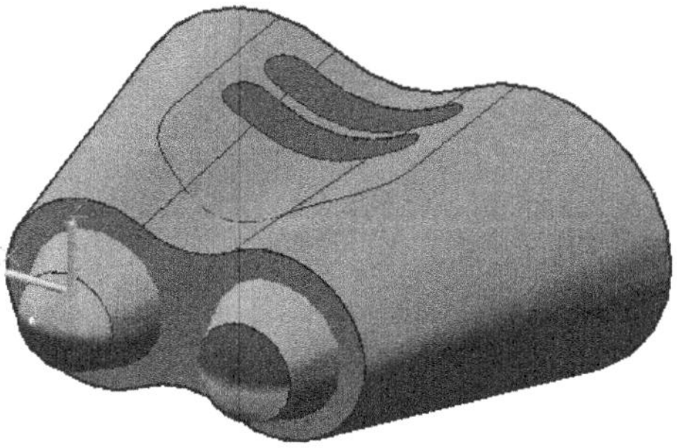

Figure 11-92 Draft analysis performed

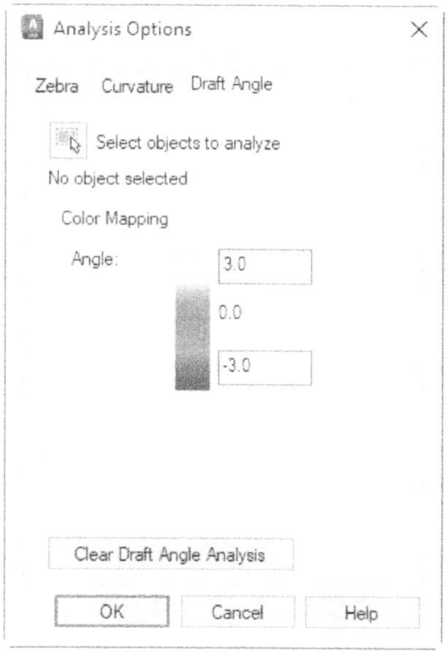

*Figure 11-93 The **Analysis Options** dialog box with the **Draft Angle** tab chosen*

Self-Evaluation Test

Answer the following questions and then compare them to those given at the end of this chapter:

1. Which of the following tools can be used to edit a surface?

   (a) **Fillet** (b) **Trim**
   (c) **Extend** (d) All of these

2. You can control the number of lines displayed in a Planar surface by using the __________ and __________ system variables.

3. To create procedural surfaces, the __________ button must be turned on.

4. Continuity can be set to __________, __________, or __________.

5. The __________ tool is used to fill the area formed between the open edges of a surface.

6. The __________ tool is used to create a 3D solid from a closed volume.

7. The __________ button is used to trim a surface when a geometry is projected on that surface.

8. You can create CVs and knots in curves using the **Spline** tool. (T/F)

9. You can create solids as well as surfaces using the **Extrude** tool. (T/F)

10. You can create a solid by offsetting a surface. (T/F)

Review Questions

Answer the following questions:

1. Which of the following tools can be used to project geometries on a surface?

   (a) **Project to UCS** (b) **Project to View**
   (c) **Project to 2 Points** (d) All of these

2. Which of the following analyses can be performed on a surface?

   (a) **Zebra** (b) **Curvature**
   (c) **Draft** (d) All of these

3. The __________ tool is used to create a surface between the elements forming a closed boundary.

4. To create a NURBS surface, the __________ button must be turned on.

5. The __________ defines the smoothness of the blend surface where it meets the other surfaces.

6. The bulge magnitude varies between __________ and __________.

7. In the **Extend** tool, the __________ and __________ options are available.

8. You can convert an existing surface into a NURBS surface using the __________ tool.

9. The __________ dialog box can be used to reconstruct the shape of a NURBS surface.

10. You can add, remove, or rebuild the CVs of the surfaces. (T/F)

Exercise 2 — Web Camera

In this exercise, you will create the model of a web camera, as shown in Figure 11-94. The reference dimensions for the model are given in Figure 11-95. Assume the missing dimensions.

Figure 11-94 *Model of a web camera*

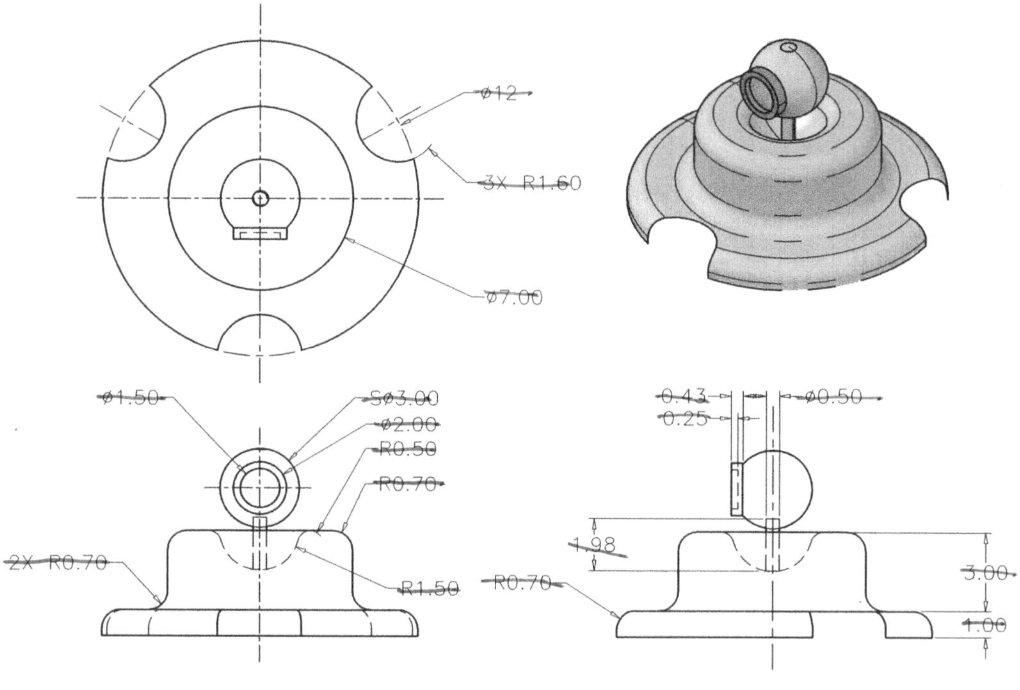

Figure 11-95 *Orthographic views of the model for Exercise 2*

Exercise 3 Surface Tools

In this exercise, you will create the model of a ship, as shown in Figure 11-96. The other views of the ship are shown in Figure 11-97. Assume the dimensions.

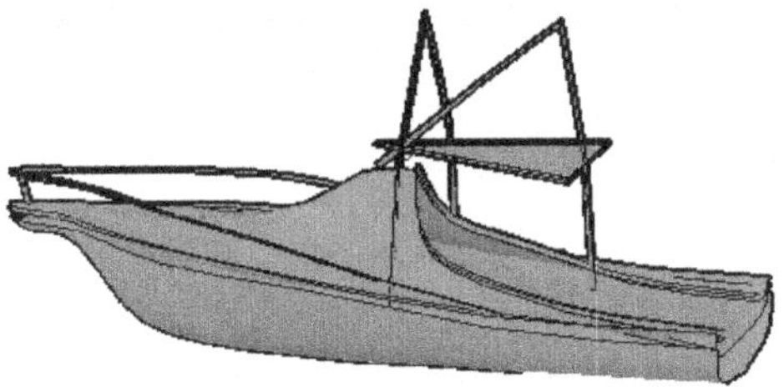

Figure 11-96 *Model of a ship*

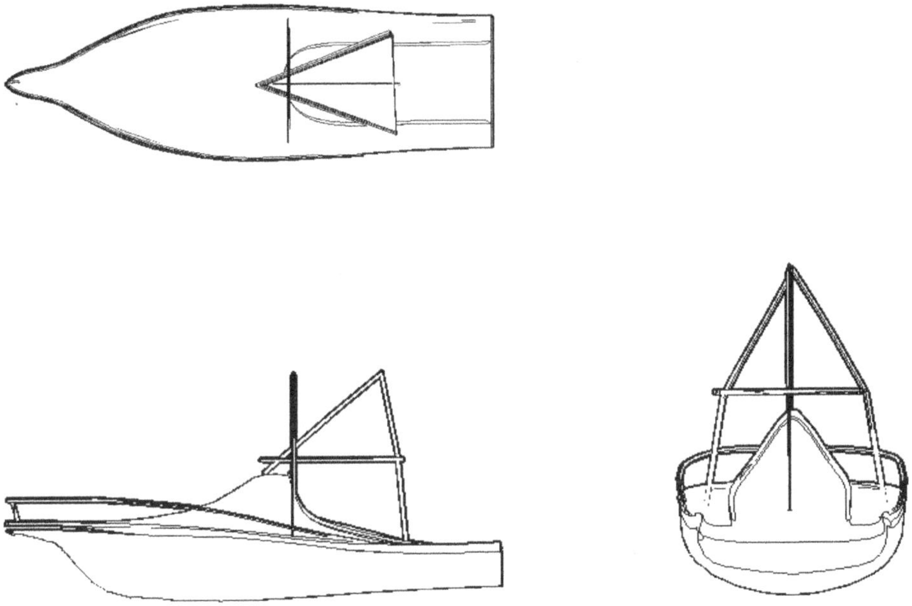

Figure 11-97 *Other views of the ship*

Answers to Self-Evaluation Test

1.d, **2. SURFU**, **SURFV**, **3. Surface Associativity**, **4.** G0, G1, G2, **5. Patch**, **6. Sculpt**, **7. Auto Trim**, **8.** T, **9.** T, **10.** T

Chapter 12

Mesh Modeling

Learning Objectives

After completing this chapter, you will be able to:

- *Create standard mesh primitives*
- *Create mesh surfaces*
- *Smoothen, refine, and crease mesh objects*
- *Edit mesh faces*
- *Convert mesh objects to solids and surfaces*
- *Work with gizmos*

Key Terms

- *MESH*
- *REVSURF*
- *EDGESURF*
- *RULESURF*
- *TABSURF*
- *Smooth Object*
- *Refine Mesh*
- *MESHCREASE*
- *Split Face*
- *MESHEXTRUDE*
- *Merge Face tool*
- *MESHCAP tool`*
- *MESHCOLLAPSE*
- *Spin Triangle Face*
- *CONVTOSOLID*
- *CONVTOSURFACE*
- *Move Gizmo*
- *Rotate Gizmo*
- *Scale Gizmo*

INTRODUCTION

A mesh model is similar to a solid model without mass and volume properties. The mesh modeling tools are available in the **3D Modeling** workspace. You can create mesh primitives as you create solid primitives and then create freeform designs from these mesh primitives. The mesh models are easily editable and can be smoothened to give a rounded effect. You can refine the meshes at required areas for precision. You can perform editing operations such as gizmo editing, extrusion on the mesh model, and so on to create freeform designs. Some of the important features of mesh modeling are that you can deform a mesh model using gizmos, add creases to sharpen the mesh model, split mesh faces to segment the meshes as required, and extrude mesh faces. You will learn all these techniques later in this chapter.

CREATING MESH PRIMITIVES

Mesh primitives are standard shapes that help you create complex models. These standard shapes include box, cone, cylinder, pyramid, sphere, wedge, and torus. You can create mesh primitives as you create solid models. By default, mesh primitives are not smooth. However, you can make these primitives smooth by adding smoothness to them. Note that as you smoothen the mesh, the model becomes complex and the system performance gets low. Therefore, you must perform the editing operations first and then smoothen the mesh to reduce the complexity of the model. The procedure for creating mesh primitives is given next.

Creating a Mesh Box

Ribbon: Mesh > Primitives > Mesh Primitives drop-down > Mesh Box
Command: Mesh

You can create a 3D mesh box similar to a solid or surface box. To do so, invoke the **Mesh Box** tool from the **Primitives** panel and follow the command sequence given next.

Specify first corner or [Center]: *Specify the first corner*
Specify other corner or [Cube/Length]: *Specify the diagonally opposite corner.*
Specify height or [2Point] : *Specify the height of the mesh box.*

After you specify the height of the mesh box, it will be created in the drawing area. Figure 12-1 shows the mesh box created.

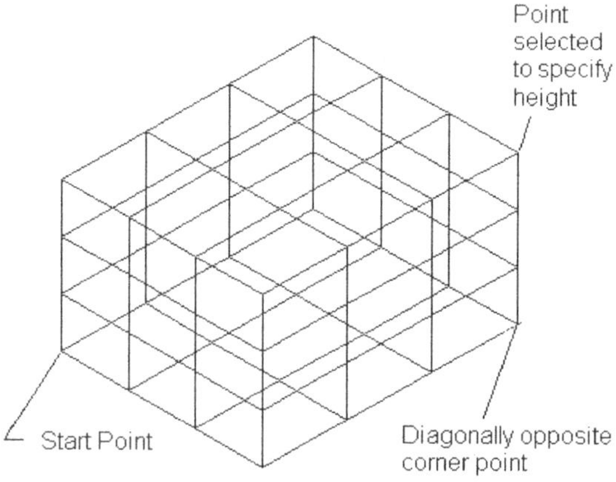

Figure 12-1 The mesh box created

You can create a mesh box in five ways using the above prompt. These ways are listed below:

1. Dynamically.
2. By first specifying the two corners of the rectangular base and then, the height of the box.
3. By first specifying the center, a corner of the box and then, the height of the box.
4. By specifying a corner and the length of the edge of cube.
5. By specifying the length, width, and height of the box.

The number of faces/divisions in a mesh box depend upon the values specified in the **Mesh Primitive Options** dialog box, refer to Figure 12-2. This dialog box can be invoked by clicking on the inclined arrow available in the **Primitives** panel of the **Mesh** tab. Specify the required values in the **Tessellation Divisions** rollout of this dialog box. Next, if you invoke the **Mesh Box** tool to create a new mesh, the model will be created based on the newly specified values. You can also change the appearance of the mesh by changing the level of smoothness of the model. Various areas of the **Mesh Primitive Options** dialog box are discussed next.

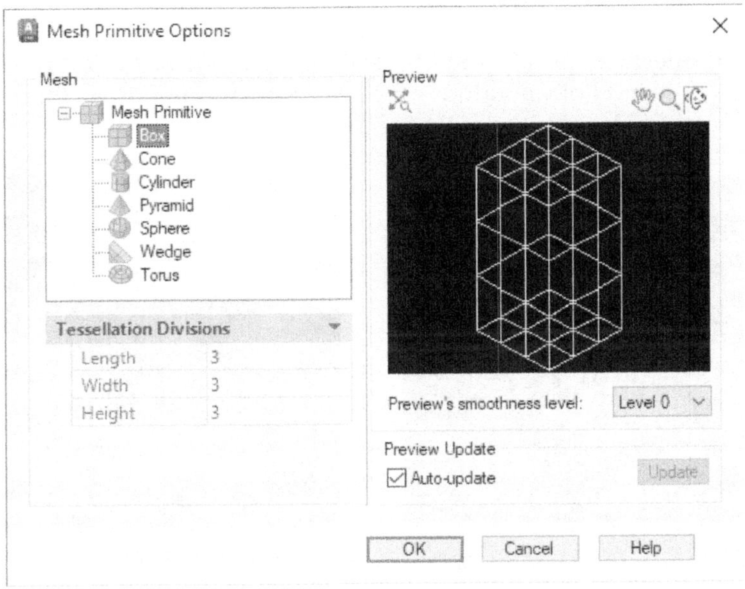

***Figure 12-2** The **Mesh Primitive Options** dialog box*

The Mesh Area

The **Mesh** area displays a list of mesh primitives and its corresponding parameters. You can select the required primitive from the **Mesh Primitive** list to control its appearance. The **Tessellation Divisions** rollout in this area displays the parameters of the selected primitive. You can edit the corresponding parameters to set the number of divisions on it. For example, if you choose **Cylinder** from the **Mesh Primitive** node in the **Mesh** area, the **Axis**, **Height**, and **Base** parameters will be available in the **Tessellation Divisions** rollout. Now, you can edit the number of faces along the axis, height, and base. Note that to create a mesh primitive with desired settings, first you need to set the values of the parameters and then create the mesh primitive.

The Preview Area

The **Preview** area displays the preview of the selected meshed primitive. The buttons in the **Preview** area are used to pan, zoom, or rotate the mesh primitive. To perform any of these operations, choose the respective button from the **Preview** area and then click on the preview screen. If you want the preview to be automatically updated according to the settings specified in the **Tessellation Divisions** rollout, select the **Auto-update** check box in the **Preview Update** area. Otherwise, choose the **Update** button to update the preview manually.

Note

To change the visual style of the model in the ***Preview*** *area, right-click and choose the required option from the* ***Visual Styles*** *menu.*

The **Preview's smoothness level** drop-down list in the **Preview** area is used to specify the level of smoothness of the mesh primitive. By default, **Level 0** is set in the drop-down list, which means, the mesh primitives created will not be smooth by default. Figures 12-3 to 12-5 show a mesh box with different levels of smoothness. You can set the level of smoothness even after the primitive has been created. To do so, select the required primitive and right-click in the display area. Next, select the **Quick Properties** option from the shortcut menu, the **Quick Properties** panel will be displayed. Select the level of smoothness from the **Smoothness** drop-down list in the **Quick Properties** panel; the mesh primitive will be smoothened.

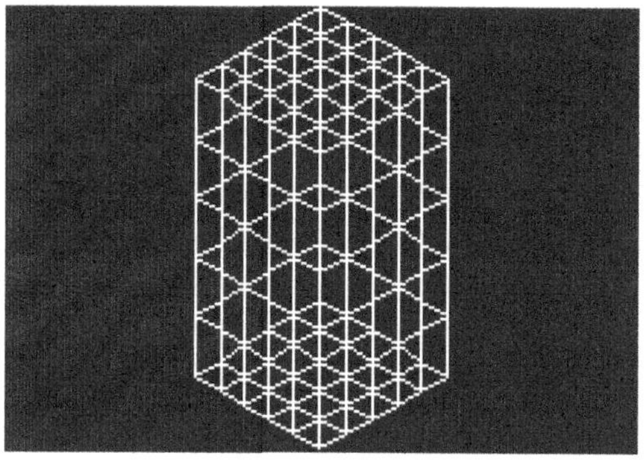

Figure 12-3 *Mesh box with smoothness level=0*

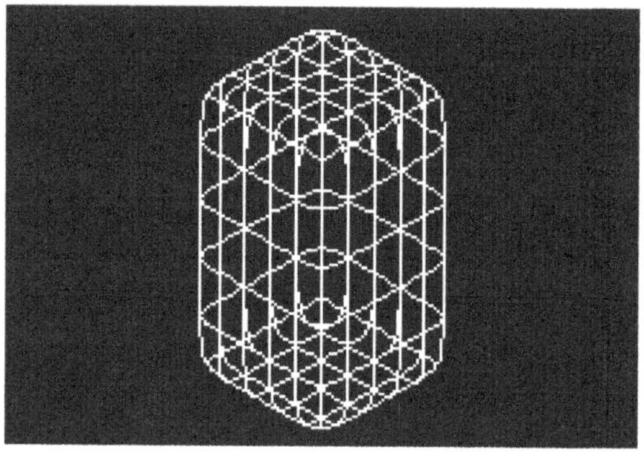

Figure 12-4 *Mesh box with smoothness level=2*

Like mesh box, the **MESH** command can also be used to create pointed or frustum mesh cones with circular or elliptical base, mesh cylinders with circular or elliptical base, mesh pyramids, mesh spheres, mesh wedges, and mesh torus. You can set the corresponding parameters of the mesh primitive in the **Mesh Primitive Options** dialog box. The procedure to create primitives is the same as that of solids.

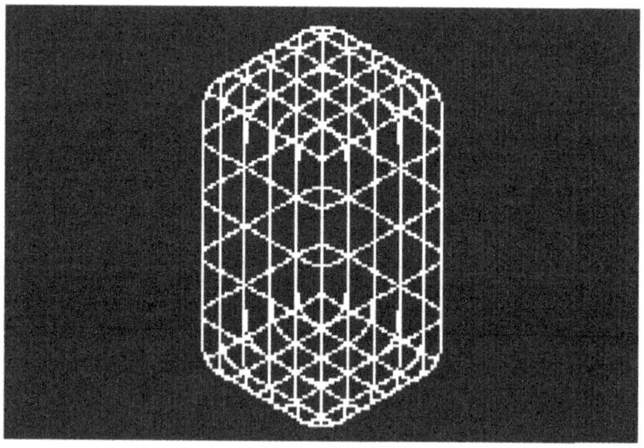

Figure 12-5 *Mesh box with smoothness level=4*

Note

By default, the ***Realistic*** *visual style is selected in the* ***Visual Styles*** *drop-down list of the* ***Visual Styles*** *panel in the Visualize tab. For clarity of printing, the visual style is set to* ***Wireframe****.*

CREATING SURFACE MESHES

Apart from creating basic mesh primitives, you can create various types of surface meshes. Surface meshes are created by filling the space between objects consisting of straight or curved edges. There are various types of surface meshes such as revolved surface, edge surface, ruled surface, and tabulated surface mesh. These surface meshes as well as the tools used to create them are discussed next.

Creating Revolved Surface Meshes

Ribbon: Mesh > Primitives > Modeling, Meshes, Revolved Surface
Command: REVSURF

In AutoCAD, you can create a revolved surface by choosing the **Modeling, Meshes, Revolved Surface** tool from the **Primitives** panel. A revolved surface is formed by revolving a path curve about the axis of rotation. You can select an open or a closed entity as the path curve. The direction of the revolution depends upon the side from which you select the revolution axis. Since it is not possible to define the clockwise and counterclockwise directions in 3D space, therefore, AutoCAD uses the right-hand thumb rule (refer to Chapter, Getting Started with 3D) to determine the direction of revolution. To create a revolved surface mesh, choose the **Modeling, Meshes, Revolved Surface** tool from the **Primitives** panel and follow the prompt sequence given next:

Select object to revolve: *Select the object to revolve around the axis.*
Select object that defines the axis of revolution: *Select the axis of revolution.*
Specify start angle <0>: *Specify the start angle to start the mesh at an offset from the profile curve.*
Specify included angle (+=ccw, -=cw) <360>: *Specify the included angle that indicates the distance through which the profile curve will be swept.*

Figure 12-6 shows a path curve and a revolution axis and Figure 12-7 shows the resultant revolved surface. You can specify the start angle and the included angle for the revolved surface as per your requirement, refer to Figures 12-8 and 12-9.

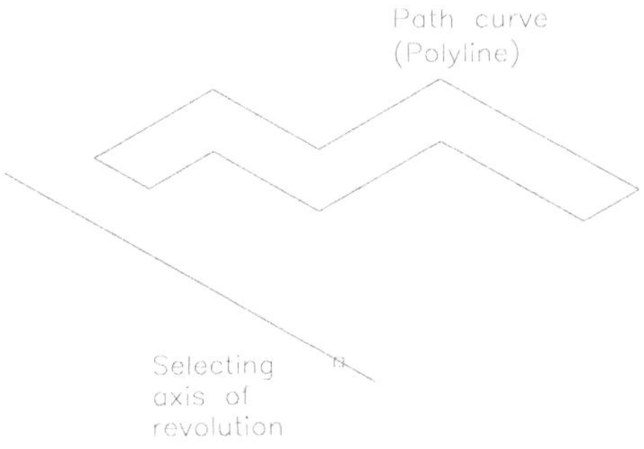

Figure 12-6 *The path curve and revolution axis*

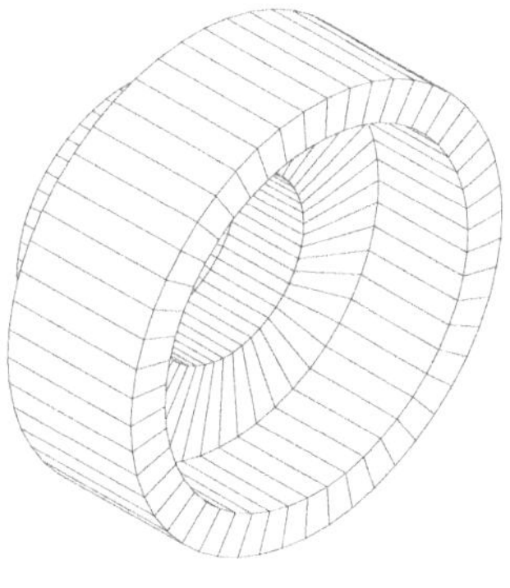

Figure 12-7 *The resultant revolved surface*

The smoothness of the revolved surface and the total number of lines that AutoCAD window will draw depend upon the value of the **SURFTAB1** system variable. AutoCAD draws tabulated lines in the direction of revolution. The number of tabulated lines is defined by the value of the **SURFTAB2** system variable, refer to Figure 12-10.

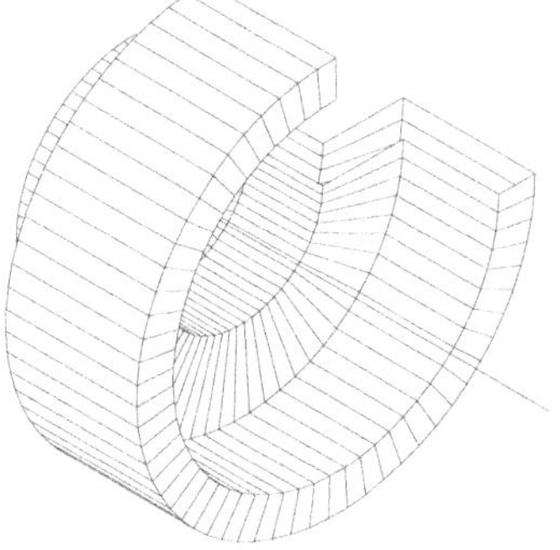

Figure 12-8** Revolved surface created with the start angle **0** and included angle **270

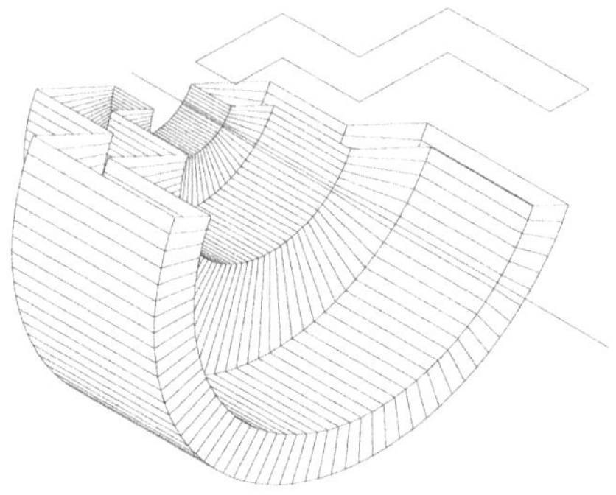

Figure 12-9** Revolved surface created with the start angle **25** and included angle **180

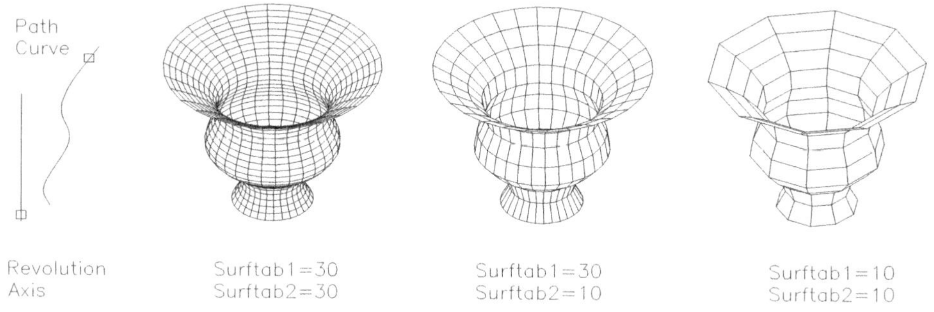

***Figure 12-10** Revolved surface created with different values of the **SURFTAB1** and **SURFTAB2** system variables*

Creating Edge Surface Meshes

Ribbon: Mesh > Primitives > Modeling, Meshes, Edge Surface **Command:** EDGESURF

The **Modeling, Meshes, Edge Surface** tool is used to create a 3D polygon mesh from the four adjoining edges that form a topologically closed loop. The entities that you select as edges can be lines, arcs, splines, open 2D polylines, or open 3D polylines. While creating an edge surface mesh, you can select the edges of the closed loop in any sequence. The **SURFTAB1** and **SURFTAB2** system variables control the appearance of the mesh and can be used to set the wireframe density. The edge that is selected first will define the M-direction (**SURFTAB1** direction). The other two edges that start from the endpoints of the first edge will define the N-direction (**SURFTAB2** direction), refer to Figures 12-11 and 12-12.

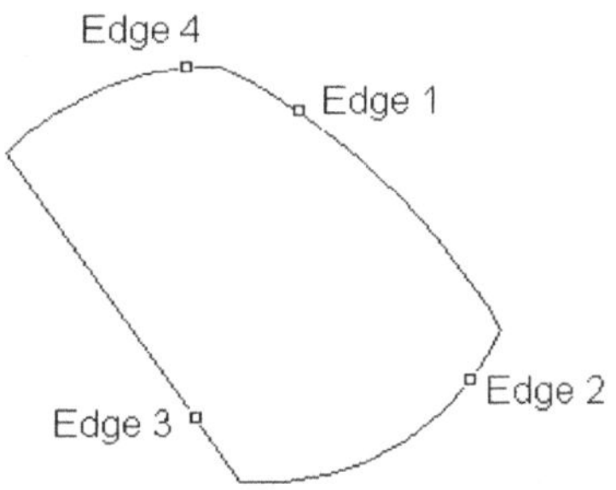

Figure 12-11 *Edges to be selected*

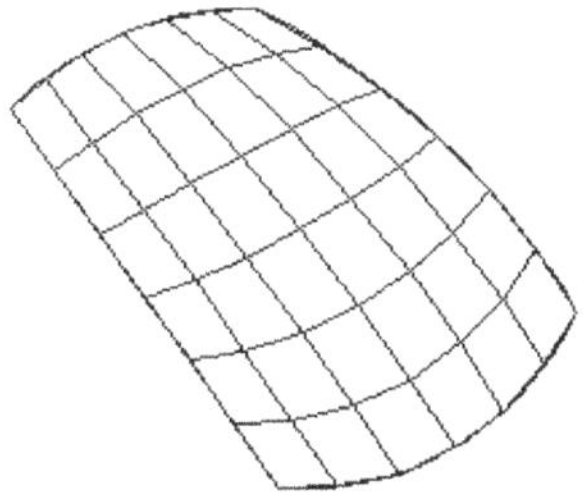

Figure 12-12 *An edge surface mesh created*

Creating Ruled Surface Meshes

Ribbon: Mesh > Primitives > Modeling, Meshes, Ruled Surface **Command:** RULESURF

You can create a ruled surface between two defined entities by choosing the **Modeling, Meshes, Ruled Surface** tool from the **Primitives** panel. The defined entities can be lines, circles, ellipses, arcs, polylines, curves, or splines. You can create a ruled surface mesh between two closed entities, two open entities, a point and a closed entity, and a point and an open entity. However, you cannot create a ruled surface between a closed and an open entity. Also, two points do not define a surface and therefore, a ruled surface cannot be created between them.

If the two defining entities are closed, the selection point does not make any difference in the resultant surface. In case of circles, the start point of the surface is determined by the combination of direction of the *X* axis and the current value of the **SNAPANG** system variable. In case of closed polylines, the ruled surface starts from the last vertex of the polyline and proceeds backward along the polyline segment.

If the two defined entities are open, the selection points do make a difference in the resultant surface. If you select open entities at the same end, a straight polygon mesh is created. If you select open entities at opposite ends, a self-intersecting polygon mesh is created, refer to Figures 12-13 and 12-14.

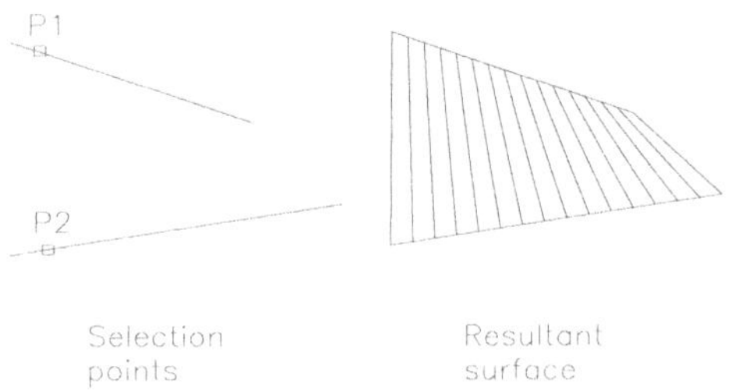

Figure 12-13 *Selecting objects at same ends and the resultant surface*

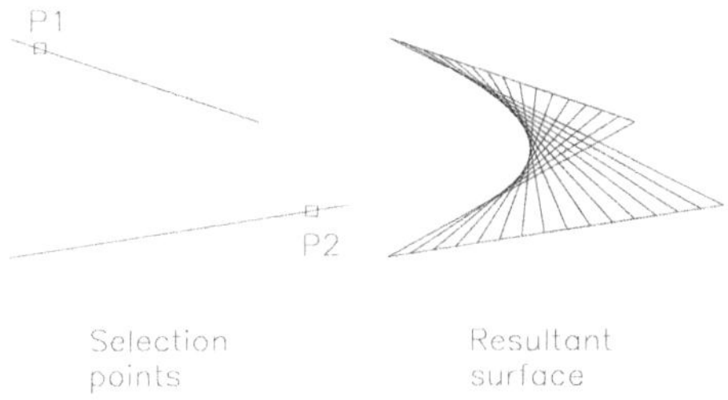

Figure 12-14 *Selecting objects at opposite ends and the resultant surface*

The smoothness of the ruled surface can be increased using the **SURFTAB1** system variable, refer to Figures 12-15 and 12-16. The default value of this system variable is 6, but it can accept any integer between 2 and 32766 as its value. Note that this value must be increased before creating the surface.

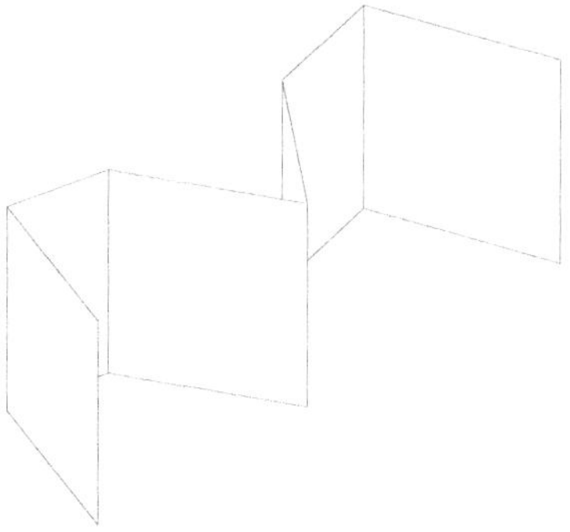

Figure 12-15 *The ruled surface created with* ***6*** *as the value of the* ***SURFTAB1*** *system variable*

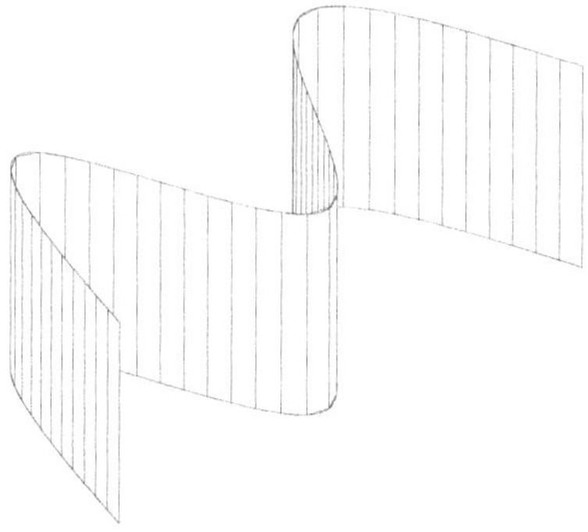

Figure 12-16 *The ruled surface created with* ***50*** *as the value of the* ***SURFTAB1*** *system variable*

Creating Tabulated Surface Meshes

Ribbon: Mesh > Primitives > Modeling, Meshes, Tabulated Surface **Command:** TABSURF

You can create a tabulated surface mesh by choosing **Modeling, Meshes, Tabulated Surface** from the **Primitives** panel. The tabulated surface mesh is formed when a profile is swept along the direction defined by the direction vector. The profile curves can be lines, circles, arcs, splines, 2D polylines, 3D polylines, or ellipses. The length of the tabulated surface will be equal to the length of the direction vector which in turn will be determined by the point selected for the direction vector, refer to Figures 12-17 and 12-18.

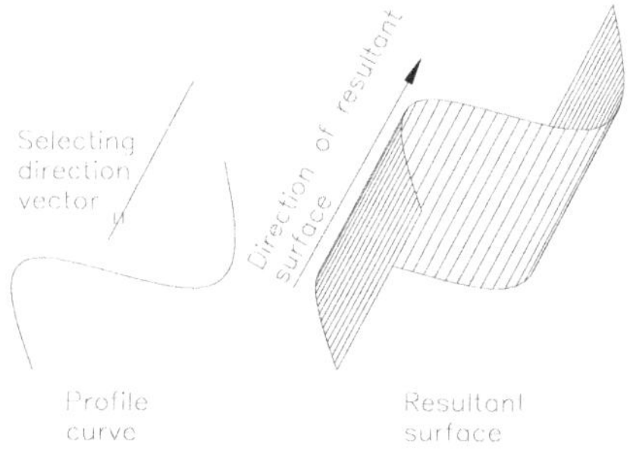

Figure 12-17 *Direction of the tabulated surface is upward*

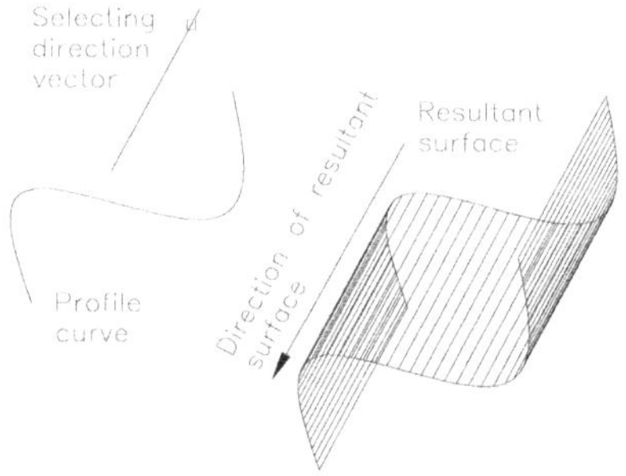

Figure 12-18 *Direction of the tabulated surface is downward*

If there are more than one direction vectors, all intermediate points will be ignored and an imaginary vector will be drawn between the first and last points on the polyline. The imaginary vector will be considered as the direction vector and the tabulated surface will be created along it, as shown in Figure 12-19.

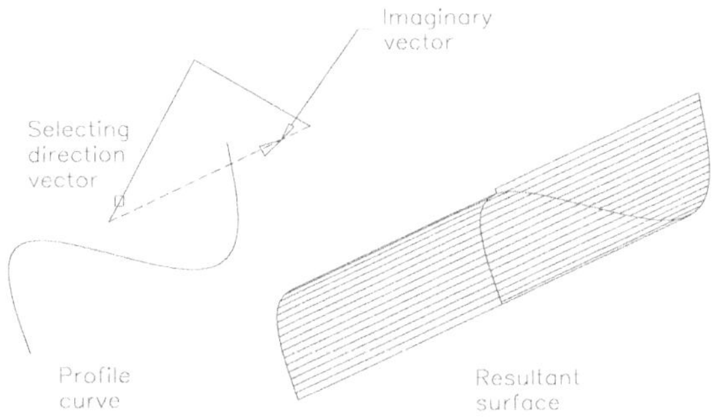

Figure 12-19 *Tabulated surface created along the imaginary vector*

Note

1. You cannot select a curved entity as the direction vector for defining the direction of the tabulated surface.

2. You can increase the smoothness of the tabulated surface by increasing the value of the ***SURFTAB1*** *system variable.*

3. Apart from surface meshes, the ***Modeling, Meshes, Revolved Surface, Edge Surface, Ruled Surface****, and* ***Tabulated Surface*** *commands can also be used to create surface models.*

Exercise 1 — Surfaces

In this exercise, you will create the model of a table, as shown in Figure 12-20, by using different types of surfaces. Assume the dimensions of the table.

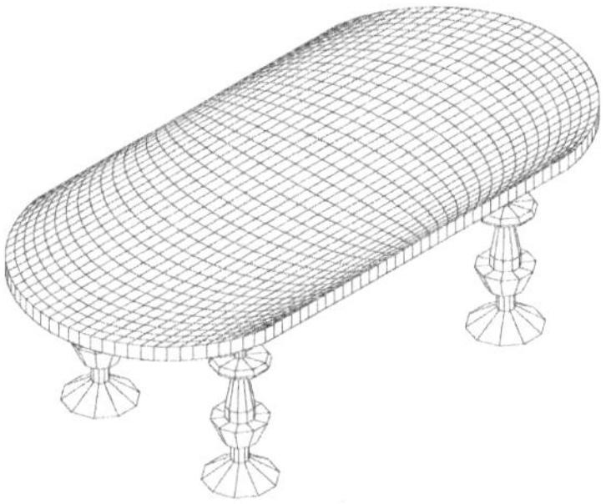

Figure 12-20 *Model for Exercise 1*

MODIFYING MESH OBJECTS

Mesh models can be modified to create freeform designs. This can be done by changing their smoothing levels, refining specific areas, adding creases to sharpen the edges, and so on. Various types of modifications that can be applied on meshes are discussed next.

Adding Smoothness to Meshes

Ribbon: Mesh > Mesh > Smooth Object
Menu Bar: Modify > Mesh Editing > Smooth More/Less **Toolbar:** Smooth Mesh
Command: MESHSMOOTH

Adding smoothness to a mesh results in roundness of the sharp edges of the meshed model. To change the level of smoothness of a mesh, select it; the **Quick Properties** panel will be displayed. In this panel, select the required level of smoothness from the **Smoothness** drop-down list; the selected smoothness level will be applied to the mesh. Note that **Level 0** indicates minimum smoothness, whereas **Level 4** indicates maximum smoothness. You can switch between different levels of smoothness with the help of the **Quick Properties** panel. Remember that the higher level of smoothness makes the mesh complex and thus, decreases the system performance. Figure 12-21 shows a mesh with different levels of smoothness applied to it. It is recommended that you first perform the required editing of the mesh and then apply smoothness to it.

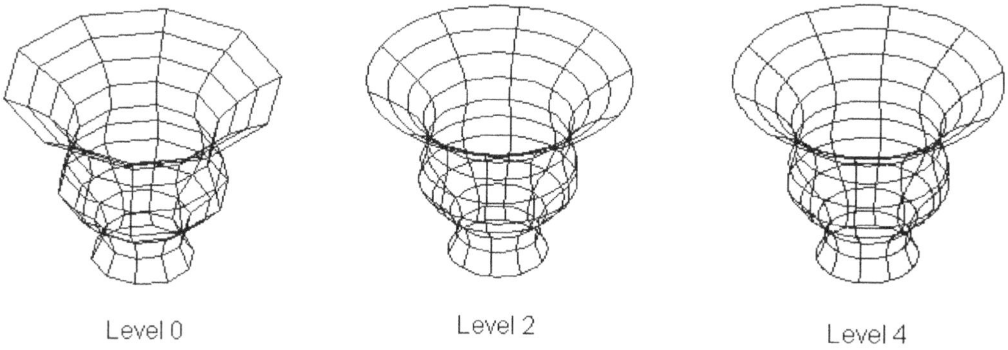

Figure 12-21 *Mesh with different levels of smoothness*

Note

You can also set the level of smoothness of the mesh from the ***Properties*** *palette. Also, on selecting an object, the* ***Quick Properties*** *panel will be displayed only if the* ***Quick Properties*** *button is enabled in the status bar.*

If you need to apply smoothness to objects other than the mesh objects, first convert the objects into mesh models. The objects that can be converted into mesh models include 3D solids, 3D surfaces, 3D faces, polygon meshes, regions, and closed polylines.

To convert an object into a mesh object, choose the **Smooth Object** tool from the **Mesh** panel; you will be prompted to select the object to convert. Select an object and press Enter; the 3D object will be converted into a mesh object. Now, you can perform the editing operations such as smoothening, refining, splitting, and so on. Note that the smoothening operation works best for primitive solids. But if you select objects other than the primitive solids, a message box will be displayed, as shown in Figure 12-22. Choose **Create mesh** from the message box; the selected objects will be converted into mesh models with default parameters.

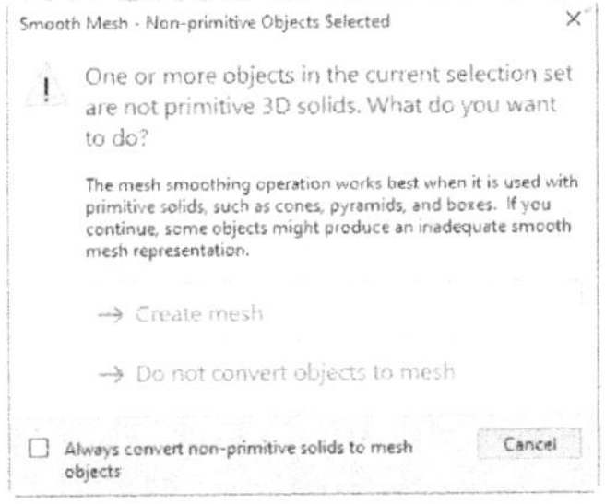

*Figure 12-22 The **Smooth Mesh - Non-primitive Objects Selected** message box*

However, you can modify the default parameters as per your requirement by invoking the **Mesh Tessellation Options** dialog box. To invoke this dialog box, click on the inclined arrow in the **Mesh** panel; the **Mesh Tessellation Options** dialog box will be displayed, as shown in Figure 12-23.

The options in this dialog box are discussed next.

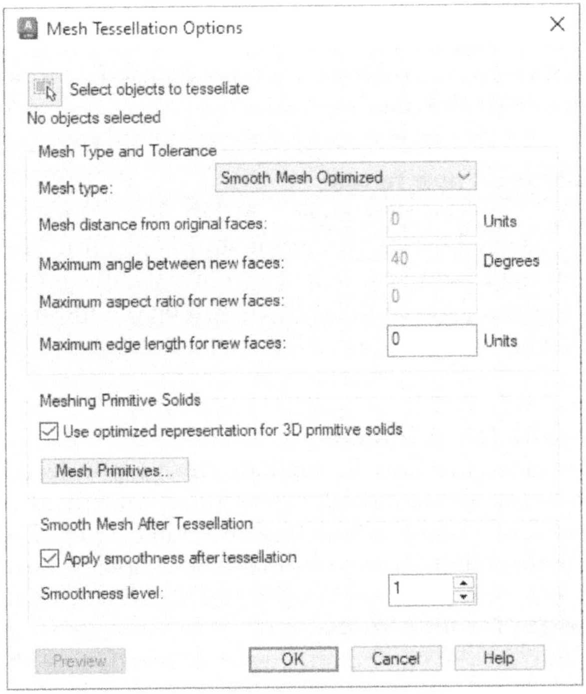

*Figure 12-23 The **Mesh Tessellation Options** dialog box*

Select objects to tessellate

This button enables you to select objects to tessellate while the **MESHOPTIONS** command is active. On choosing this button, the **Mesh Tessellation Options** dialog box will disappear allowing you to select objects. Select the required objects from the drawing area and press Enter; the dialog box will reappear and the number of objects selected will be displayed below the

Select objects to tessellate button. Now, you can specify the required parameters in the **Mesh Tessellation Options** dialog box.

Mesh Type and Tolerance Area

The options in this area are discussed next.

Mesh type

This drop-down list is used to specify the mesh type that you want to create. This drop-down list has three options: **Smooth Mesh Optimized**, **Mostly Quads**, and **Triangle**. By default, the **Smooth Mesh Optimized** option is selected and therefore, the shape of the mesh face will be the optimized mesh shape that can adapt to the shape of the mesh object. If you select the **Mostly Quads** option, the shape of the mesh face will be quadrilateral to its maximum possible, and if you select the **Triangle** option, the shape of the mesh face will be triangular to its maximum possible.

Mesh distance from original faces

This edit box helps you specify how closely the converted mesh object will adhere to the original shape of solid or surface. Smaller the values specified in this edit box, lesser the deviation from the original faces, and therefore, greater the number of faces created in the mesh. This means small value results in more accurate mesh objects but with slower performance of system. However, this edit box is not enabled if the **Smooth Mesh Optimized** option is selected in the **Mesh type** drop-down list.

Maximum angle between new faces

The **Maximum angle between new faces** edit box is not enabled if the **Smooth Mesh Optimized** option is selected in the **Mesh type** drop-down list. This edit box allows you to specify the maximum angle between the surface normal and continuous mesh faces. Larger the value specified in this edit box, more dense will be the mesh at higher curvatures and less dense at flat areas. This setting is used to refine the appearance of the curved features like holes or fillets.

Maximum aspect ratio for new faces

This edit box is not enabled in case the **Smooth Mesh Optimized** option is selected. This edit box allows you to set the maximum aspect ratio, which is, height/width ratio of new faces. This option is mostly used to avoid long and thin cylindrical faces. Note that smaller the value specified in this edit box, better will be the shape of the mesh.

Maximum edge length for new faces

This edit box is used to set the maximum length of the edges of the mesh objects that are created by converting solids and surfaces. Smaller the value specified in this edit box, better will be the shape/appearance of the mesh.

Meshing Primitive Solids

The options in this area are discussed next.

Use optimized representation for 3D primitive solids

Select this check box to apply the mesh settings specified in the **Mesh Primitive Options** dialog box and clear this check box to apply the settings specified in the **Mesh Tessellation Options** dialog box.

Mesh Primitives

The **Mesh Primitives** button will be enabled only when the **Use optimized representation for 3D primitive solids** check box is selected. On choosing the **Mesh Primitives** button, the **Mesh Primitive Options** dialog box will be displayed where you can specify the required settings for the mesh object.

Smooth Mesh After Tessellation

This area will be active only when the **Smooth Mesh Optimized** option is selected in the **Mesh type** drop-down list. This is because the mesh objects converted on selecting any of the other two options from the drop-down list do not have any smoothness. The options in this area are discussed next.

Apply smoothness after tessellation

Select this check box to apply smoothness to newly created mesh objects.

Smoothness level

This spinner will be available only when the **Apply smoothness after tessellation** check box is selected and you can set the level of smoothness of the mesh object in it.

Preview

This button is available when the objects required to be converted into meshes are selected. You can choose this button to preview the effect of the current settings in the drawing area. To go back to the dialog box, press Esc or press Enter to accept the mesh tessellation options.

Note

To increase the smoothness of mesh by one level, choose the ***Smooth More*** *button from the* ***Mesh*** *panel; the mesh will become more smooth (rounded). Similarly, if you choose the* ***Smooth Less*** *button, the smoothness of the mesh will be decreased by one level.*

Refining the Meshes

Ribbon: Mesh > Mesh > Refine Mesh
Menu Bar: Modify > Mesh Editing > Refine Mesh **Toolbar:** Smooth Mesh
Command: MESHREFINE

Refining the mesh means increasing the number of divisions in the mesh of an object, resulting in a dense mesh. You can refine the complete mesh object or a particular face of an object. Refining is mostly used for finer and detailed models, in which modification of small or refined divisions of the mesh is required. But remember that, denser the mesh, slower will be the performance of the system. To refine the mesh, choose the **Refine Mesh** tool from the **Mesh** panel; you will be prompted to select the mesh object or faces of the mesh object to refine. Select the entity and press Enter; the selected entity will get refined. Note that the **Refine Mesh** tool works only when the smoothness option of the selected mesh object is set to Level 1 or higher. Also note that, as you refine the object, its level of smoothness becomes zero.

To refine it again, you need to set the smoothness level to 1 or higher, and then follow the same procedure of refining. Figure 12-24 shows the mesh object before and after refinement.

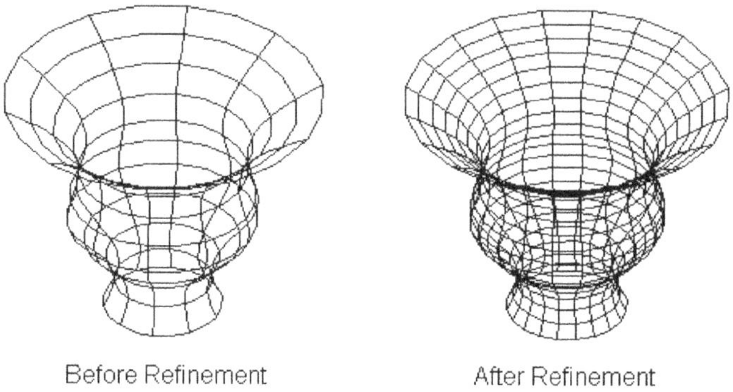

Figure 12-24 *Object before and after refinement*

To refine the faces of the selected mesh object, first you need to set the criteria for selecting faces. To do so, right-click anywhere on the screen, and then choose **Subobject Selection Filter > Face** from the menu displayed. Alternatively, choose **Face** from the **Subobject Selection filter** drop-down in the **Selection** panel of the **Solid** tab. After the selection criteria have been set, invoke the **Refine Mesh** tool. Next, you need to select a face of the mesh object. To do so, press CTRL and click on the required mesh face, and then press Enter; the specified face will be subdivided into four faces, as shown in Figure 12-25.

Note that refining an object resets the smoothness level to 0, whereas refining face/s does not affect the smoothness level.

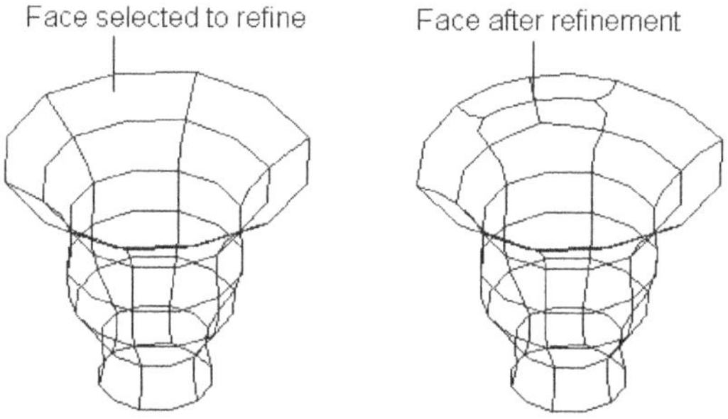

Figure 12-25 *Face before and after refinement*

Adding Crease to Meshes

Ribbon:	Mesh > Mesh > Add Crease	**Menu Bar:**	Modify > Mesh Editing > Crease
Toolbar:	Smooth Mesh	**Command:**	MESHCREASE

You can also modify a mesh object by adding creases to it. Creases are added to an object in order to sharpen the mesh sub-objects, thereby deforming the mesh object. You can sharpen the faces, edges, or vertices of a mesh object. To add crease to the selected mesh object, choose the **Add Crease** tool from the **Mesh** panel; you will be prompted to select the required mesh sub-objects. Select the mesh sub-objects and press Enter; the **Specify crease value [Always] <Always>:** prompt will be displayed. By default, the crease is set to **Always** which means the crease will retain its sharpness even if you smoothen or refine the mesh object. You can also specify a crease value at which the crease will start losing its sharpness. The crease value set to **-1** is the same as the crease value set to **Always**. If you specify **0** as the crease value, the existing crease will be removed. On sharpening a sub-object, the edges adjoining the selected sub-object are updated according to the modified model. Figures 12-26 through 12-31 show the effect of adding crease on various sub-objects.

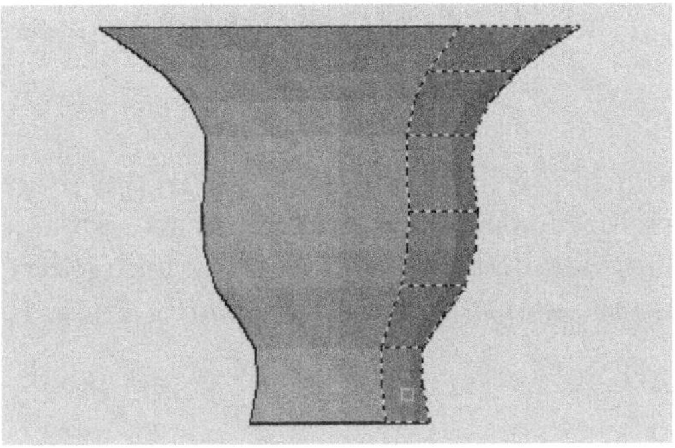

Figure 12-26 *Faces selected to be creased*

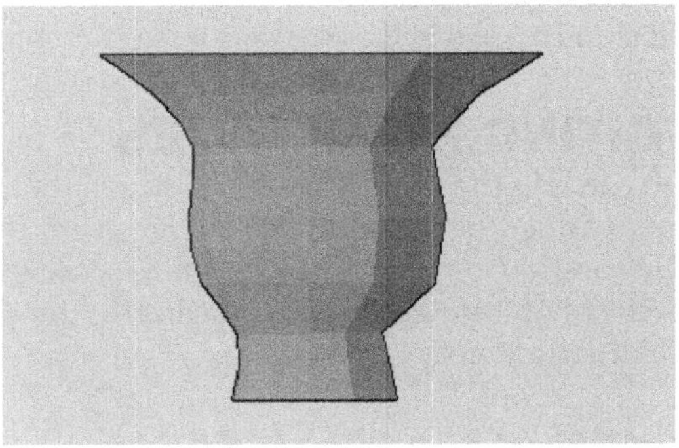

Figure 12-27 *Faces after adding crease*

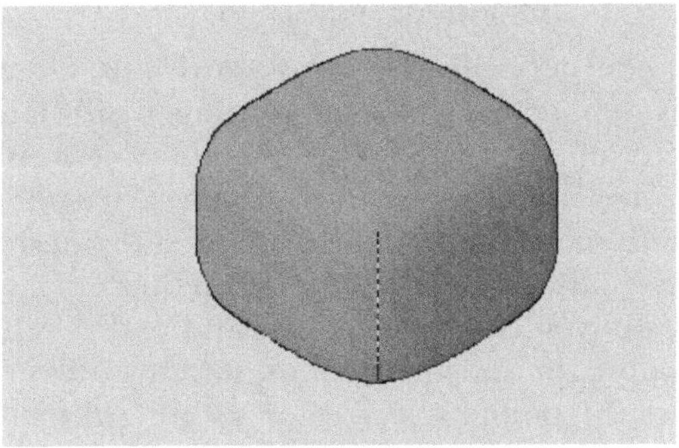

Figure 12-28 *Edge selected to be creased*

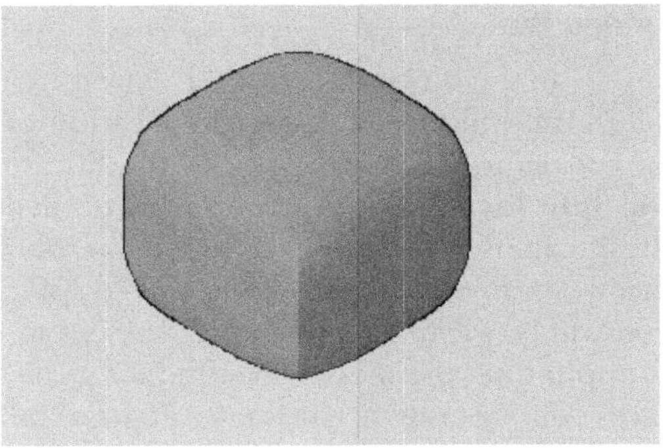

Figure 12-29 *Edge after adding crease*

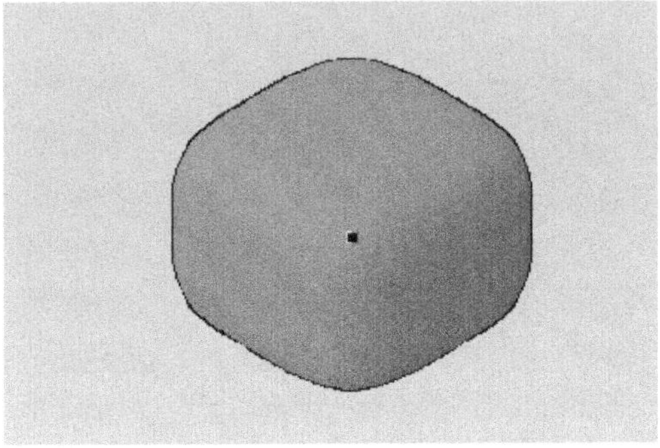

Figure 12-30 *Vertex selected to be creased*

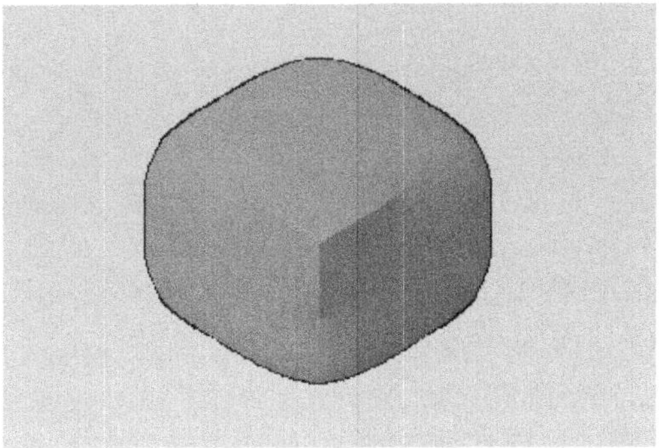

Figure 12-31 *Vertex after adding crease*

Note

*1. To select specific entities, right-click in the drawing area; a shortcut menu is displayed. Choose the desired sub-option of the **Subobject Selection Filter** option from this shortcut menu.*

2. The crease will not be visible when the level of smoothness is 0. So, increase the smoothness level to make it visible.

You can also remove the crease added to an object. To do so, choose the **Remove Crease** tool from the **Mesh** panel. Next, select the crease that you want to remove and press Enter; the selected crease will be removed from the object and the corresponding faces will be updated.

EDITING MESH FACES

You can edit the faces of a mesh object either by splitting or extruding its faces. In this process, the extruded or the split part merges with the original mesh object and act as a single entity. The splitting and extruding operations are useful for detailed and advanced modeling. To edit the faces of a mesh object, you can use the editing tools in the **Mesh Edit** panel. These tools are discussed next.

Splitting the Mesh Faces

Ribbon: Mesh > Mesh Edit > Split Face
Menu Bar: Modify > Mesh Editing > Split Face **Command:** MESHSPLIT

In the process of refining, the entire mesh model gets split into various divisions, whereas in Splitting, a particular location of split is defined. As a result, splitting avoids larger deformations for smaller modifications. You can edit a mesh object by splitting it using the **Split Face** tool. This tool is used to divide the selected mesh face into two parts. To split the mesh, choose the **Split Face** tool from the **Mesh Edit** panel; you will be prompted to select the face of mesh to split. Select the face to split; a knife symbol will be displayed with the cursor and you will be prompted to specify the cut in the mesh. Now, specify the start and end points of the split line; the mesh will split along the line joining the specified points, and the adjoining faces will separate accordingly. Figure 12-32 shows the points selected for splitting the mesh face.

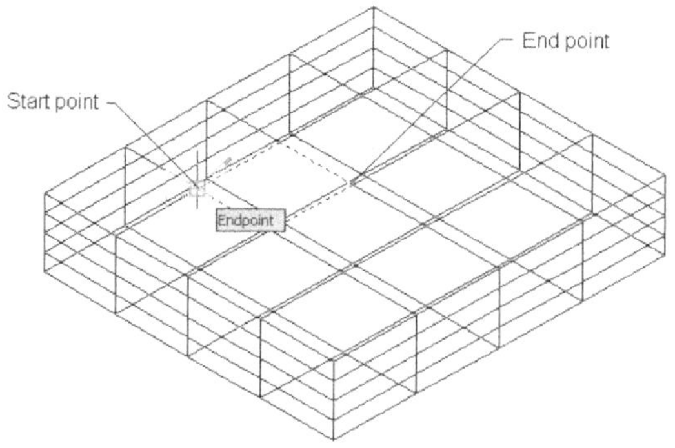

Figure 12-32 *Points selected for splitting the mesh*

Tip

In case of detailed modeling, it is advisable to first split the mesh faces and then refine the mesh model.

Extruding the Mesh Faces

Ribbon: Mesh > Mesh Edit > Extrude Face
Menu Bar: Modify > Mesh Editing > Extrude Face **Command:** MESHEXTRUDE

Extruding the mesh models is similar to extruding the 3D models. The only difference between the two processes is that in 3D modeling, the extruded part is created as a separate entity, whereas in mesh modeling, the extruded part merges with the mesh object and acts as a single entity. To extrude the mesh faces, choose the **Extrude Face** tool from the **Mesh Edit** panel; the Command sequence that will be displayed is given next.

Command: **MESHEXTRUDE**
Adjacent extruded faces set to: Join
Select mesh face(s) to extrude or [Setting]: *Select one or more faces to extrude.*
Specify height of extrusion or [Direction/Path/Taper angle] <100>: *Specify the height of extrusion.*

You can control the extrusion style of multiple adjacent mesh faces. To do so, set the adjacent mesh faces to be extruded as a single unit or select each face separately. By default, the setting is **Join**. As a result, the adjacent faces are extruded as a single unit. If you want to change the setting to **Unjoin**, then press **S** when **Select mesh face(s) to extrude or [Setting]** prompt is displayed; you will be prompted to specify whether to join the adjacent mesh faces or not. Choose **No**; the extrusion style is set to **Unjoin**.

You can extrude the mesh faces dynamically. Alternatively, you can do so by specifying height, by specifying the direction of extrusion, by specifying the path of extrusion, or by specifying an angle of taper for extrusion. All these options work in the same way as in the 3D modeling. Figure 12-33 shows a mesh model after splitting and Figure 12-34 shows a mesh box with extruded split faces. The splitting and extruding operations on mesh models result in creation of new designs.

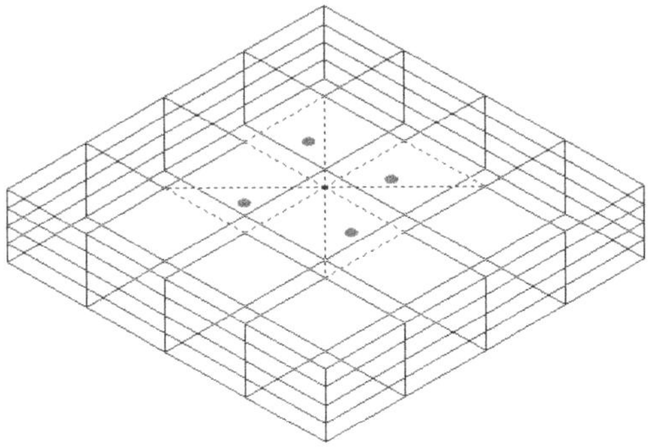

Figure 12-33 *Mesh model after splitting*

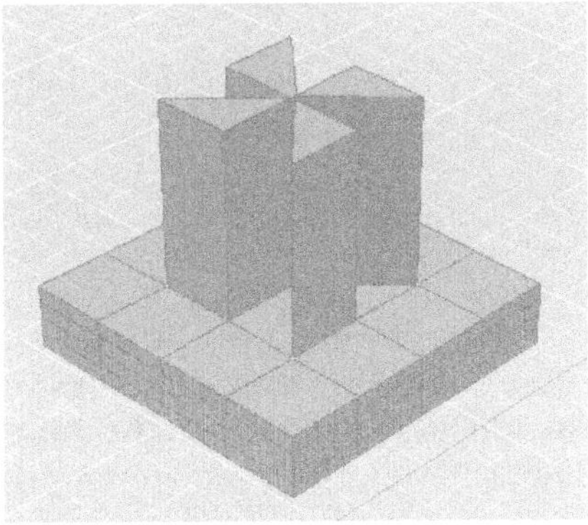

Figure 12-34 *Mesh model with extruded split faces*

Tip

To select the faces that you want to extrude, click on the required faces of the mesh object. Continue till the selection is completed. To remove a face from the selection, press Shift + Ctrl and click on the face to be deselected.

Merging the Mesh Faces

Ribbon: Mesh > Mesh Edit > Merge Face
Menu Bar: Modify > Mesh Editing > Merge Face **Command:** MESHMERGE

Using the **Merge Face** tool, you can merge one or more faces adjacent to a face into a single face. To merge the faces, invoke the **Merge Face** tool from the **Mesh Edit** panel; you will be prompted to select the adjacent faces of the specified face. Select the required number of faces and press Enter; the selected faces will be merged.

Closing the Gaps

Ribbon: Mesh > Mesh Edit > Close Hole
Menu Bar: Modify > Mesh Editing > Close Hole **Command:** MESHCAP

Sometimes, some gaps or holes are created due to open edges on the mesh object. You can fill these holes or gaps by selecting the edges surrounding the hole by using the **Close Hole** tool. To do so, invoke the **Close Hole** tool from the **Mesh Edit** panel; you will be prompted to select the connecting edges to form a mesh face. Select the edges and press Enter; a new mesh face will be formed between the connecting edges. Figure 12-35 shows the edges connecting the hole and Figure 12-36 shows a cap created on the hole.

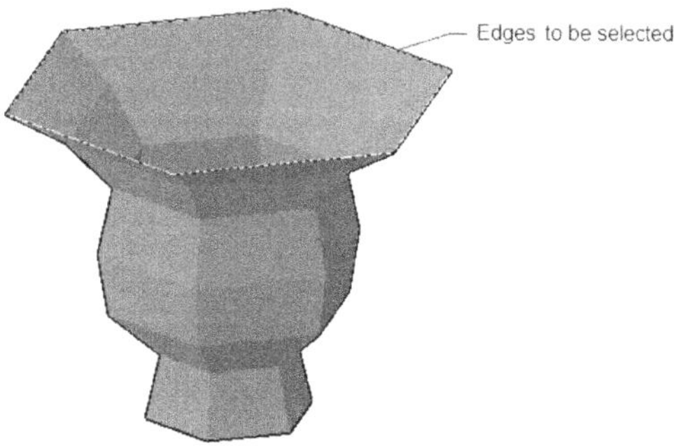

Figure 12-35 *Edges connecting the hole*

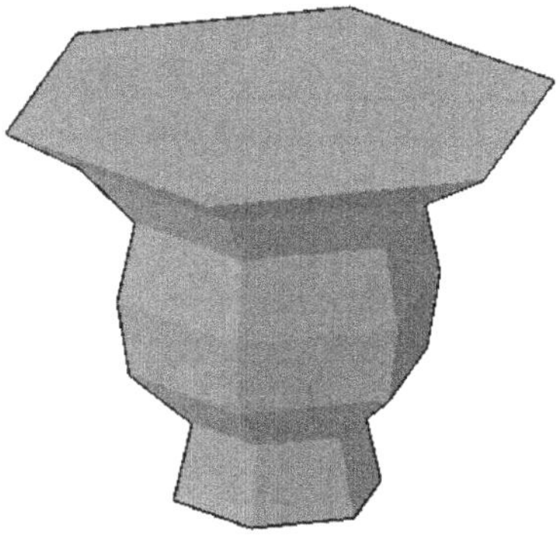

Figure 12-36 *Cap created*

You can also form gaps in the mesh objects. To do so, you can remove the faces, edges, or vertices of the mesh object by pressing the Delete key from the keyboard. You can also use the **Erase** tool to delete faces and form gaps. Note that on removing a face, only the selected face will be removed. However, on removing an edge, the adjacent face will also be removed and on removing a vertex, all the faces shared by the vertex will also be removed.

Collapsing the Mesh Vertices

Ribbon: Mesh > Mesh Edit > Collapse Face or Edge
Menu Bar: Modify > Mesh Editing > Collapse Face or Edge **Command:** MESHCOLLAPSE

The **Collapse Face or Edge** tool is used to converge the vertices of surrounding mesh faces to the center of the selected edge or face. To do so, invoke this tool from the **Mesh Edit** panel; you will be prompted to select the mesh face or edge to collapse. Select a mesh face or an edge; the vertices of the selected mesh face will be merged. Also, the adjacent faces will be updated based on the removed vertices. Figure 12-37 shows the model after collapsing the top face of the model shown in Figure 12-36.

Figure 12-37 *The top face collapsed*

Spinning the Edges of Triangular Faces

Ribbon: Mesh > Mesh Edit > Spin Triangle Face
Menu Bar: Modify > Mesh Editing > Spin Triangle Face **Command:** MESHSPIN

You can rotate the edge that is shared by two triangular mesh faces. To do so, invoke the Spin Triangle Face tool from the Mesh Edit panel; you will be prompted to select the triangular mesh faces adjacent to each other. Select the mesh faces; the edge shared by the two triangular mesh faces spins to connect the opposite vertices. For example, Figure 12-38 shows the model after spinning the triangular faces of the model.

Sometimes, while selecting the subobjects of a meshmodel, the hidden subobjects also get selected. You can control the selection of the subobjects hidden in the view by using the **Culling Object** button. This button is available in the **Selection** panel of the **Mesh** tab. When this button is active, only those subobjects that are normal to the view are selected or highlighted on rolling the mouse over them. However, if this button is not active, all subobjects including the hidden ones will be selected or highlighted when the mouse is rolled over them.

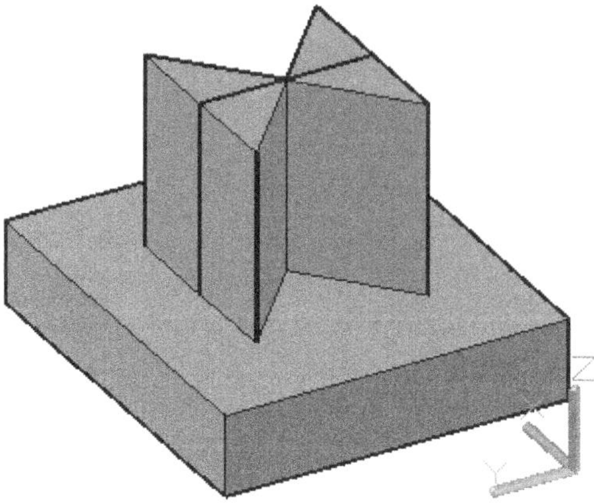

Figure 12-38 *Model after spinning*

Example 1 — *Mesh Edit Tools*

In this example, you will create a flash drive having dimensions = 50 X 18 X 8, as shown in Figure 12-39. The dimensions of the model are shown in Figure 12-39(a).

Figure 12-39 *Flash drive*

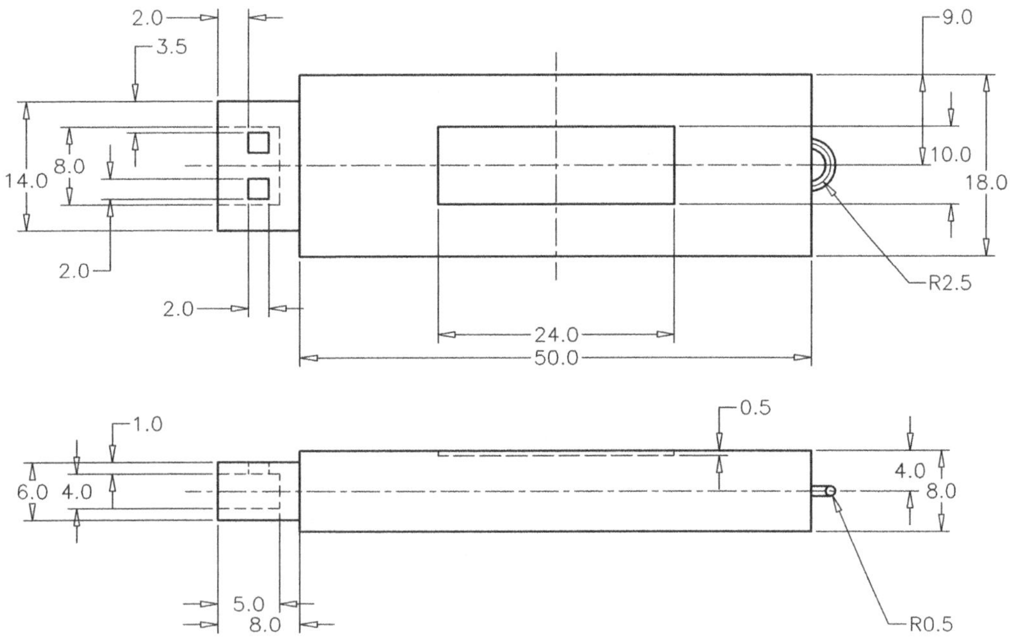

Figure 12-39(a) Orthographic views and dimensions of the Flash drive

Creating a Mesh Box

To create a mesh box, first you need to specify the parameters of the tessellation divisions on the mesh box.

1. Start a new *acad3D.dwt* file in the **3D Modeling** workspace.

2. Invoke the **Mesh Primitive Options** dialog box by clicking on the inclined arrow displayed at the lower right corner of the **Primitives** panel in the **Mesh** tab.

3. Select the **Box** option from the **Mesh Primitive** list box and set the following tessellation divisions: Length: **7**, Width: **7**, and Height: **7**. Choose the **OK** button from the **Mesh Primitive Options** dialog box to accept the settings and close the dialog box.

4. Choose the **Mesh Box** tool from **Mesh > Primitives > Mesh Primitives** drop-down; you are prompted to specify the first corner point.

5. Turn on the Ortho mode and specify the start point of the mesh box by clicking at the desired location in the drawing area; the **Specify other corner or [Cube/Length]** prompt is displayed.

6. Enter **L** at the Command prompt and specify the following dimensions to create a mesh box:

   Length: **50**, Width: **18**, and Height: **8**

7. Click on the **Visual Style Controls** on the top left corner of drawing area and then change the visual style to Wireframe. The mesh box is created, as shown in Figure 12-40.

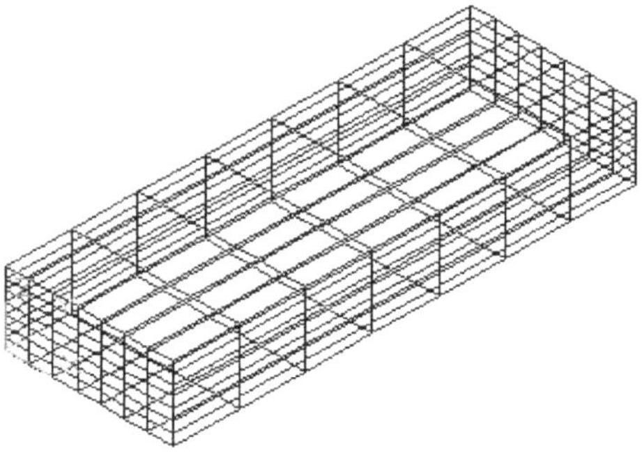

Figure 12-40 *The mesh box created*

Extruding the Selected Faces

Now, you need to extrude the inner faces at the left of the mesh box to create the port of the flash drive.

1. Press Ctrl and select the inner faces at the left of the mesh box, as shown in Figure 12-41.
2. Choose the **Extrude Face** tool from the **Mesh Edit** panel of the **Mesh** tab; you are prompted to specify the height of extrusion.
3. Enter **8** as the value of extrusion in the **Dynamic Input**; the selected faces are extruded.

   The final extruded model after changing the visual style is shown in Figure 12-42.

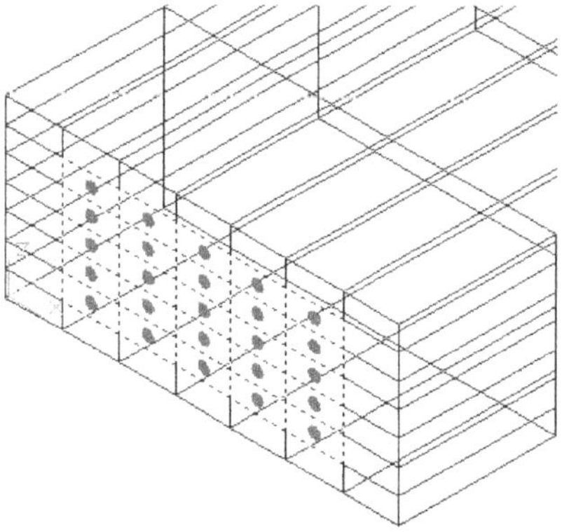

Figure 12-41 *Faces selected to extrude*

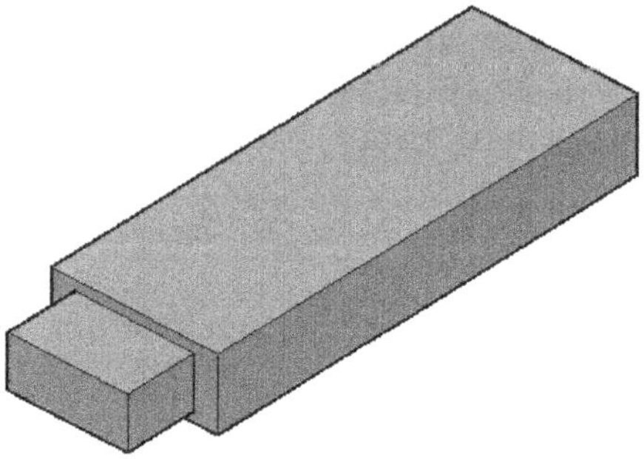

Figure 12-42 *The model after extruding*

Creating a Cut in the Port

To create a cut in the port, you need to extrude the inner faces of the port in negative direction.

1. Choose the **Extrude Face** tool from the **Mesh Edit** panel and then select the inner faces on the left of the port to create a cut, as shown in Figure 12-43.
2. Enter **-5** in the edit box displayed in the drawing area to specify the height of extrusion. Note that the negative value will extrude the inner faces inward, thereby creating a cut.

Next, you need to create a cut on the top of the port. But before creating the cut, you need to split the top mesh faces to the size of the cut.

3. Choose the **Split Face** tool from the **Mesh Edit** panel and select the second mesh face on the top of the port; you are prompted to select the first split point on the selected face.

4. Specify the first split point on the mesh face at a distance of 2 units from the outer end by using the **From** snap. Then, specify the second split point using the **Perpendicular** snap; one split line is created on it.

5. Create the other split line at a distance of 2 units from the first split line, refer to Figure 12-44.

6. Create another split on the fourth face at the top of the port, refer to Figure 12-44.

Figure 12-43 *Mesh faces selected to create a cut*

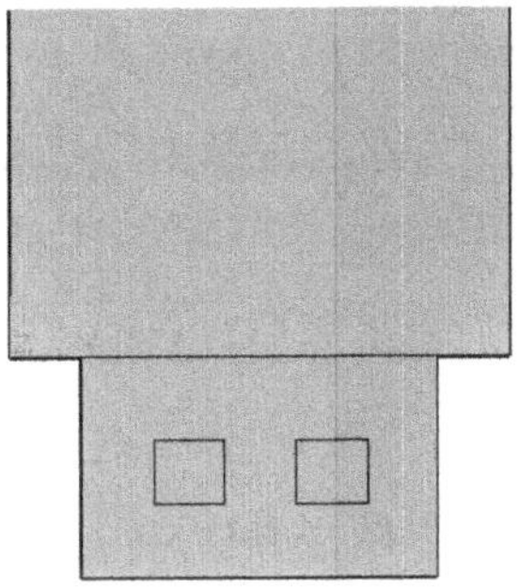

Figure 12-44 *Model after splitting faces*

7. Next, you need to create a cut at the top. Select the new mesh faces created by splitting and extrude them downward upto the inner face so that the model looks like Figure 12-45.

Creating a Loop

Next, you need to create a loop of torus shape which can be used for hanging the flash drive.

1. Invoke the **Mesh Primitive Options** dialog box and change the tessellation division of torus as follows:

   Radius: **30** Sweep path: **30**

2. To create a loop, you need to create a torus of radius 2.50 and tube radius 0.5.

3. Place the torus at the end of the flash drive, as shown in Figure 12-46.

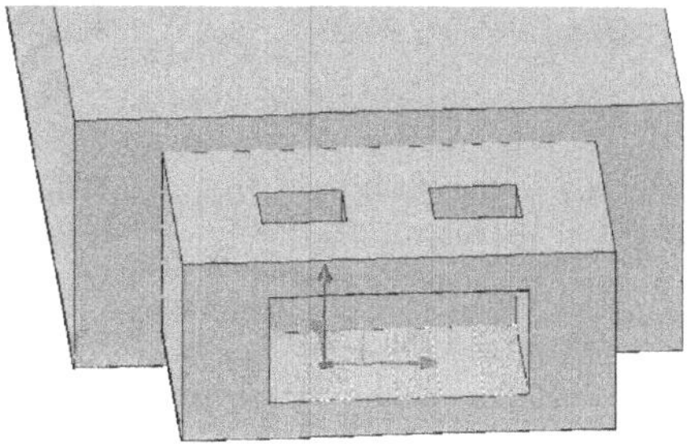

Figure 12-45 *Mesh faces selected to create a cut*

Figure 12-46 *Model after adding a loop*

Merging Faces

Next, you need to merge faces and then create a cut on it to place the text.

1. Choose the **Merge Face** tool from the **Mesh Edit** panel of the **Mesh** tab; you are prompted to select the adjacent mesh faces on the model.

2. Select the inner faces of the mesh, as shown in Figure 12-47, and press Enter; the selected faces are merged.

3. Select the merged face and extrude it to 0.5 unit along negative direction to create a cut, refer to Figure 12-48.

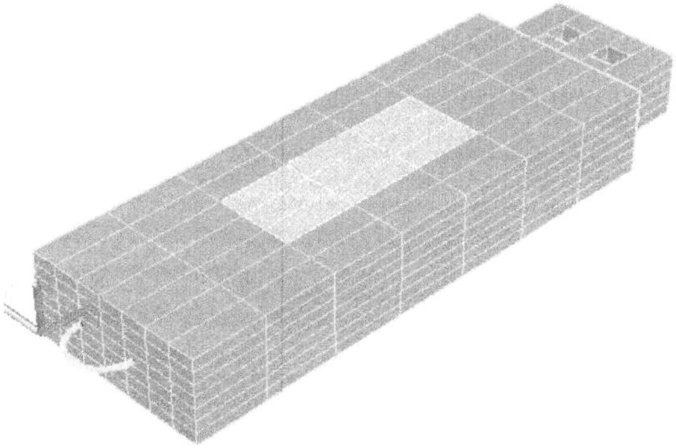

Figure 12-47 *Faces selected to be merged*

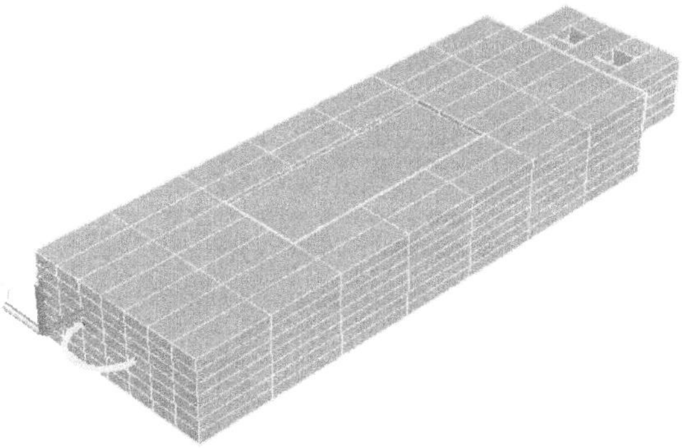

Figure 12-48 *Model after extruding the merged face*

4. Choose **Smooth More** from the **Mesh** panel of the **Mesh** tab; you are prompted to select the objects to be smoothened.

5. Select the mesh object and press Enter; the entire model gets smoothened.

As the port and the cut created cannot be smoothened, therefore, you need to sharpen them.

6. Choose the **Add Crease** tool from the **Mesh** panel; you are prompted to select the mesh subobjects to add crease.

7. Select the mesh objects, as shown in Figure 12-49, and press Enter; you are prompted to specify the crease value. Press Enter to retain the sharpness of the selected mesh object; the crease is applied to the selected edges, refer to Figure 12-50.

8. Similarly, select the subobjects to be sharpened such that the final model created looks similar to Figure 12-50.

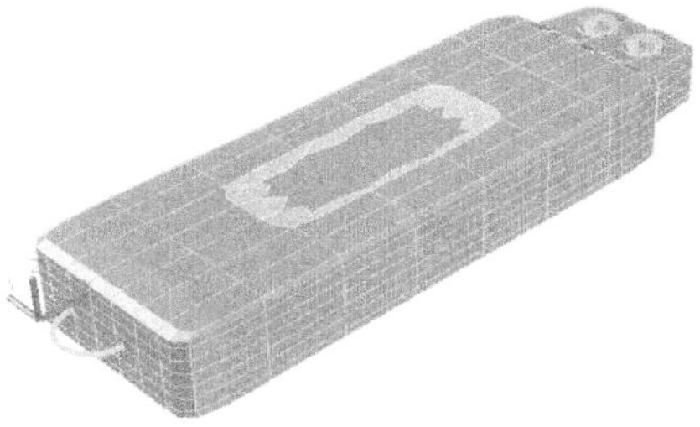

Figure 12-49 *Mesh faces selected to add crease*

Figure 12-50 *The final model after adding crease to the required entities*

CONVERTING MESH OBJECTS

You have already learned that 3D solids and surfaces can be converted into mesh objects using the **Smooth Object** tool so that they can be smoothened, refined, creased, and so on. Now, you will learn how to convert mesh objects into 3D solids or surfaces so that you can perform the solid modeling techniques such as union, subtraction, intersection, on them. Also, you can specify the settings such that the mesh objects converted into 3D solids or surfaces are smooth or faceted, or have merged faces.

Converting Mesh Objects into Solids

Ribbon: Mesh > Convert Mesh > Convert to Solid
Menu Bar: Modify > 3D Operations > Convert to Solid **Command:** CONVTOSOLID

To convert a mesh object into solid, choose the **Convert to Solid** tool from the **Convert Mesh** panel; you will be prompted to select a mesh object. Select the required mesh object and press Enter; the selected mesh object will be converted into a solid with default settings. To convert a mesh object into a solid with the user-defined settings, you need to specify the new settings before the conversion. You can also specify whether the converted solid will be smooth or faceted, or have merged faces.

Note

Other than the meshes, the closed polygons and circles with thickness, as well as the 3D surfaces can also be converted into solids. However, the objects like exploded solids, separate and continuous edges forming a surface, separate and continuous surfaces forming volumes, mesh with gaps between faces, and meshes with intersecting boundaries cannot be converted into solids.

To specify pre-defined settings for the solids that will be created from meshes, choose **Smooth, optimized** from the **Smooth Mesh Convert** drop-down, refer to Figure 12-51. The different tools in this drop-down are discussed next.

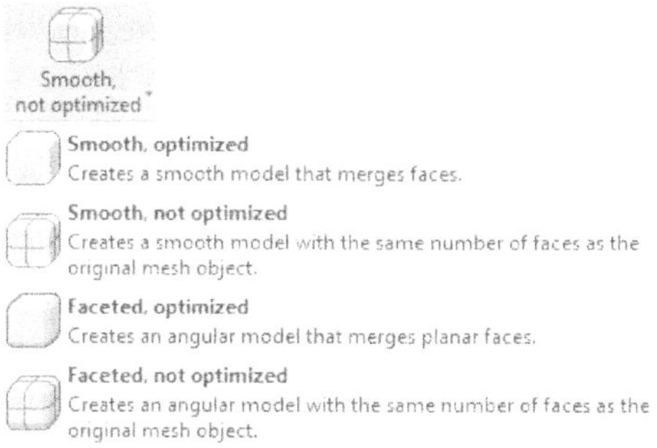

***Figure 12-51** The **Smooth Mesh Convert** drop-down*

Smooth, optimized

On choosing this tool, all tessellations of the mesh in the same plane will be merged into a single face in the solid. Also, the edges of the solid model will be rounded. Figure 12-52 shows a mesh box and Figure 12-53 shows the solid created from the mesh box on choosing the **Smooth, optimized** option.

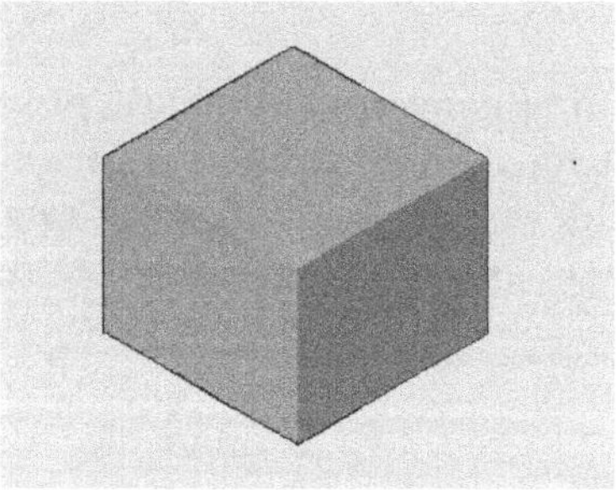

***Figure 12-52** A mesh box*

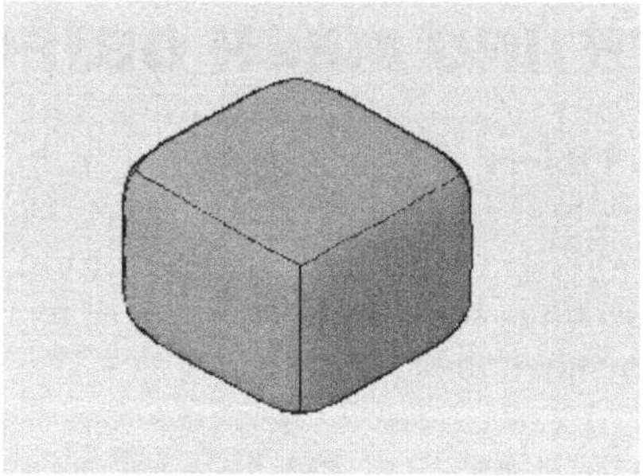

***Figure 12-53** The solid created on choosing the **Smooth, optimized** option*

Smooth, not optimized

On choosing this tool, the edges of the mesh will be rounded when the mesh is converted to solid, but the resulting faces will not be merged, and will remain the same as in the mesh object, as shown in Figure 12-54.

Faceted, optimized

On choosing this tool, all tessellations of the mesh in the same plane will be merged into a single face in the solid. Also, the edges in the resulting solid will not be rounded, but creased, as shown in Figure 12-55.

*Figure 12-54 The solid created on choosing the **Smooth, not optimized** tool*

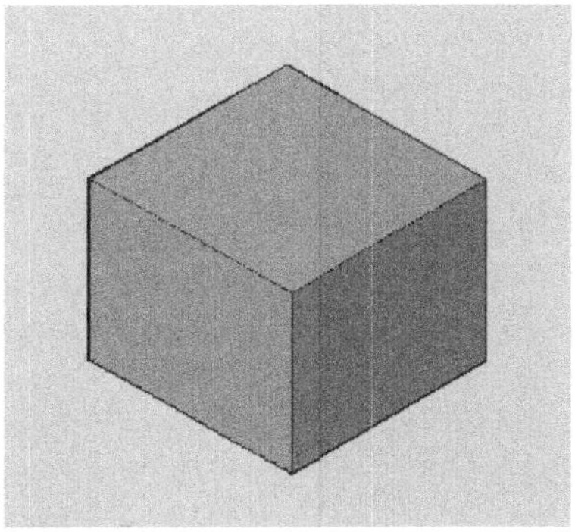

*Figure 12-55 The solid created on choosing the **Faceted, optimized** tool*

Faceted, not optimized

On choosing this tool, the faces of the converted solid will not be merged and the edges will not be rounded, as shown in Figure 12-56.

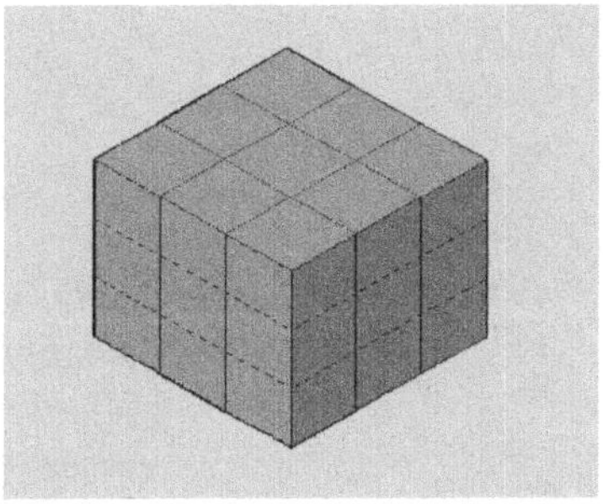

*Figure 12-56 The solid created on choosing the **Faceted, not optimized** tool*

Converting Mesh Objects into Surfaces

Ribbon: Mesh > Convert Mesh > Convert to Surface
Menu Bar: Modify > 3D Operations > Convert to Surface **Command:** CONVTOSURFACE

Like converting a mesh object into solid, you can also convert a mesh object into a surface. To do so, choose the **Convert to Surface** tool from the **Convert Mesh** panel; you will be prompted to select a mesh object. Select the required mesh object; the mesh object will be converted into a surface with default settings. You can change the default settings of the surface created as you did with solids. Figure 12-57 shows a mesh object and Figures 12-58 through Figure 12-61 show the surfaces created on applying different settings on this object.

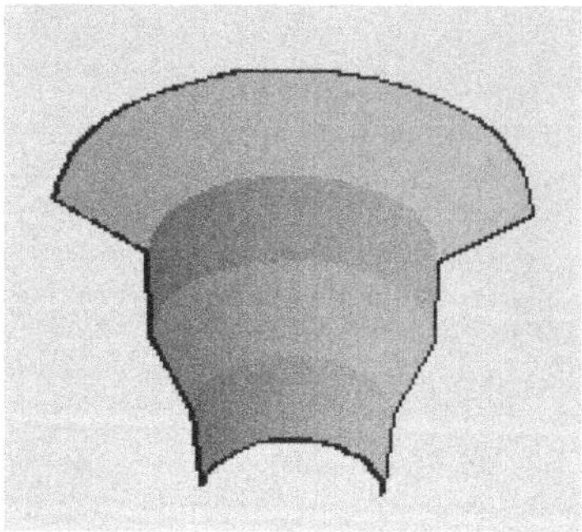

Figure 12-57 *A mesh object*

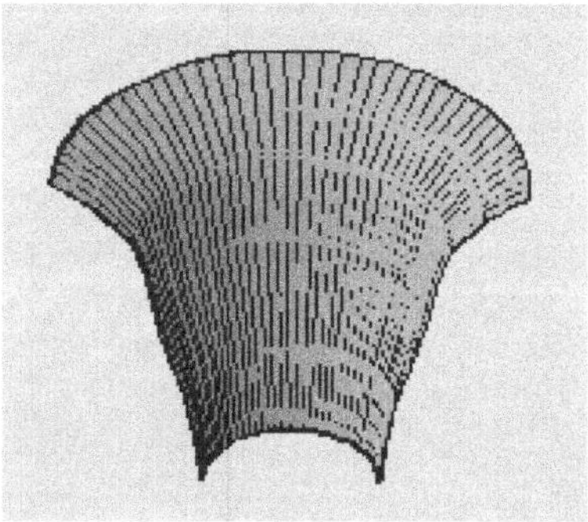

Figure 12-58 *The surface created on choosing the* ***Smooth, optimized*** *tool*

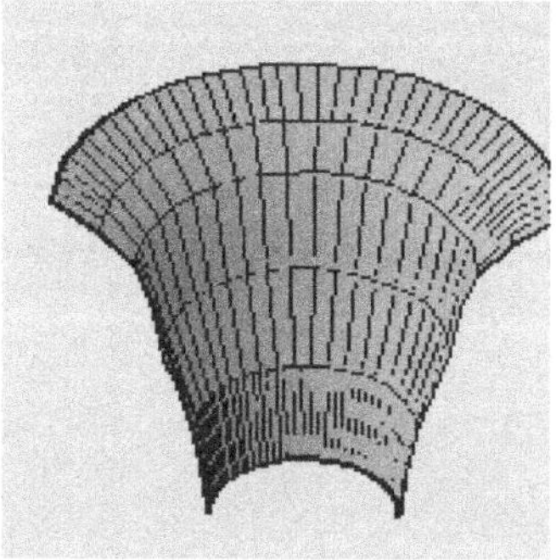

Figure 12-59 *The surface created on choosing the* ***Smooth, not optimized*** *tool*

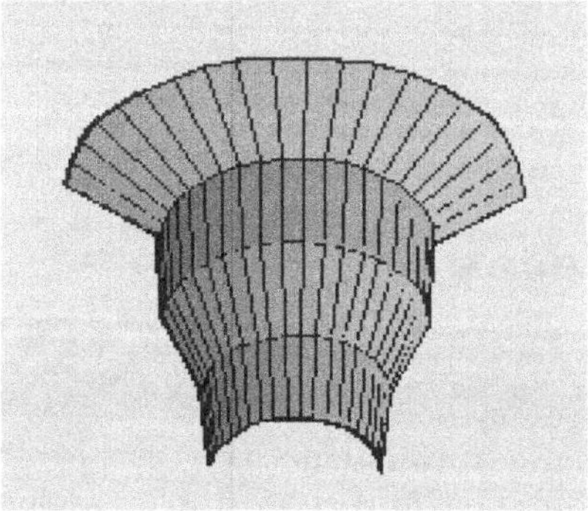

Figure 12-60 *The surface created on choosing the* ***Faceted, optimized*** *tool*

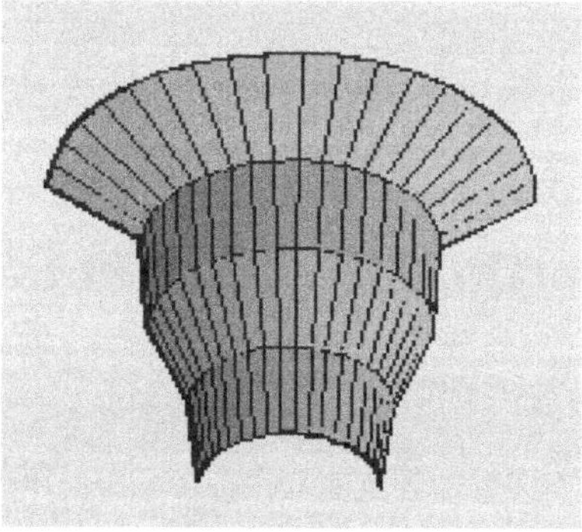

Figure 12-61 *The surface created on choosing the* ***Faceted, not optimized*** *tool*

Note

Other than meshes, regions, lines and arcs with some thickness, the planar 3D faces and 2D closed regions can also be converted into surfaces. Refer to Chapter 9 for details.

Tip

*You can create section views of the meshed models as you did for solid models in Chapter 8. The tools for creating section views are available in the **Section** panel of the **Home** tab or the **Mesh** tab.*

WORKING WITH GIZMOS

Ribbon: Mesh > Selection > Gizmo drop-down

Gizmo is a tool that helps you move, rotate, or scale 3D objects or their sub-objects along a specified axis or plane. When you select objects or subobjects in any 3D visual style, a gizmo is displayed. A gizmo is of three types: move, rotate, and scale, as shown in Figure 12-62. To set the gizmo that you want to be displayed by default, choose the required gizmo from the **Selection** panel. Also, if you do not want any gizmo to be displayed, specify it in the Selection panel. Various types of gizmos are discussed next.

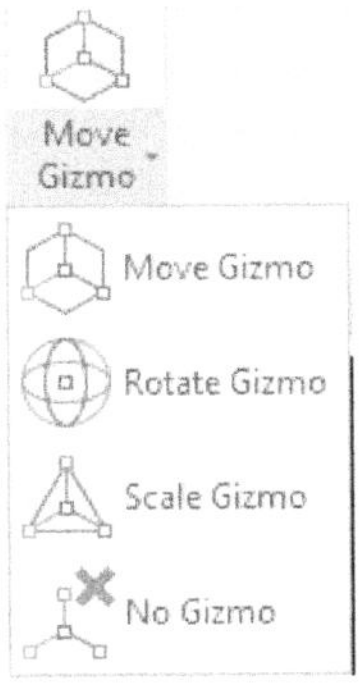

Figure 12-62 *The **Gizmo** drop-down*

Move Gizmo

When **Move Gizmo** is chosen from the **Selection** panel, the move gizmo is displayed on the first selected object or sub-object, refer to Figure 12-63. Move gizmo tool has three axis handles, three planes, and a base point. Using this gizmo, you can move the selected faces or edges of objects along any axis or plane, and thus, create freeform designs as per your requirement.

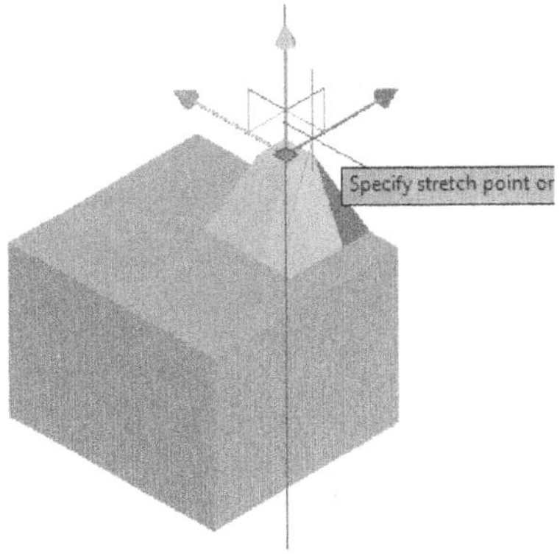

Figure 12-63 ***Move Gizmo*** *on the mesh object*

To move the selected object along any particular axis, click on the axis handle of the gizmo and drag along the axis; the selected object will move accordingly. To move the selected object anywhere along a plane, click on the rectangle formed in between the axes handles; the object will move along the specified plane. To relocate the base point of the gizmo, right-click on the gizmo, and then choose **Relocate Gizmo** from the shortcut menu displayed. You can also switch between various gizmos using this shortcut menu.

Rotate Gizmo

The rotate gizmo is displayed on the mesh object when **Rotate Gizmo** is chosen from the **Selection** panel. The rotate gizmo is displayed as a sphere with three axes and a base point on it. Figure 12-64 shows the rotate gizmo on the mesh model. The **Rotate Gizmo** tool is used to rotate the selected objects about a particular axis. By default, the gizmo is displayed at the center of the selected object. As you move the cursor over the rotate gizmo, the nearest axis of the gizmo will be highlighted. Click when the required axis gets highlighted and specify the rotation angle. You can relocate the gizmo as well as switch between various gizmos using the shortcut menu that is displayed on right-clicking on the gizmo.

Scale Gizmo

The scale gizmo is displayed when **Scale Gizmo** is chosen from the **Selection** panel. This tool is used to scale the selected objects uniformly along an axis or a plane. As you move the cursor toward the gizmo, the axis of scale will be displayed. Click and drag the axis to scale the object in that direction. To scale the object uniformly, click on the triangle that is formed between the axes. Figure 12-65 shows the scale gizmo on the mesh model.

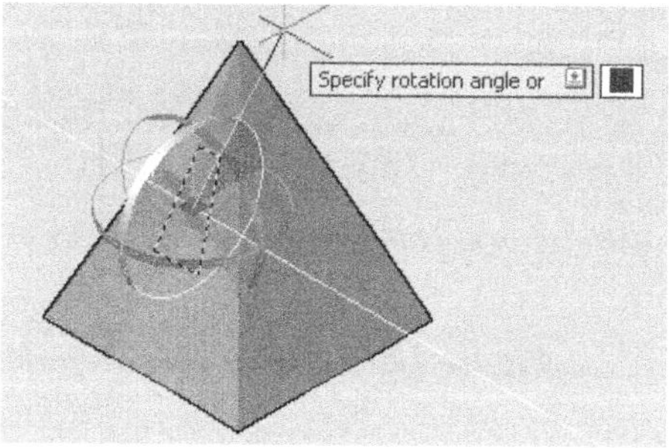

Figure 12-64 *The rotate gizmo on the mesh object*

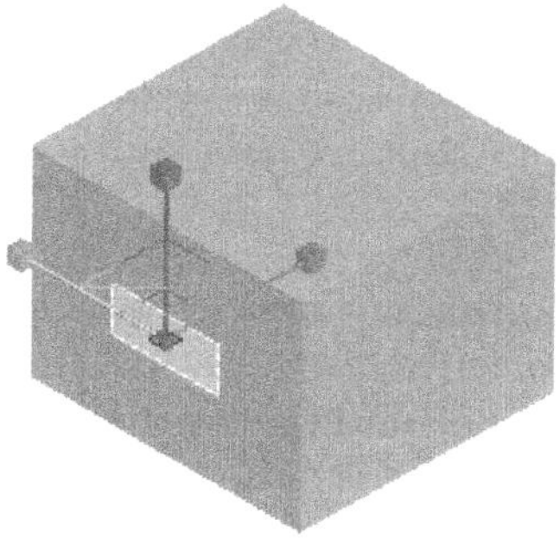

Figure 12-65 *The scale gizmo on the mesh object*

To summarize, in this section, you learned that all the three gizmos can be used to create freeform designs from primitive meshes. The next example illustrates the use of these gizmos.

Note

You can choose the ***No Gizmo*** *option from the* ***Selection*** *panel, if you do not want any gizmo to be displayed on selecting the objects in the 3D visual style.*

Example 2 — *Gizmos*

In this example, first you will create an elliptical mesh cylinder with the following dimensions: major axis = 55, minor axis = 15, and height = 100. Then, you will modify it using various gizmos. The final model should look similar to Figure 12-66.

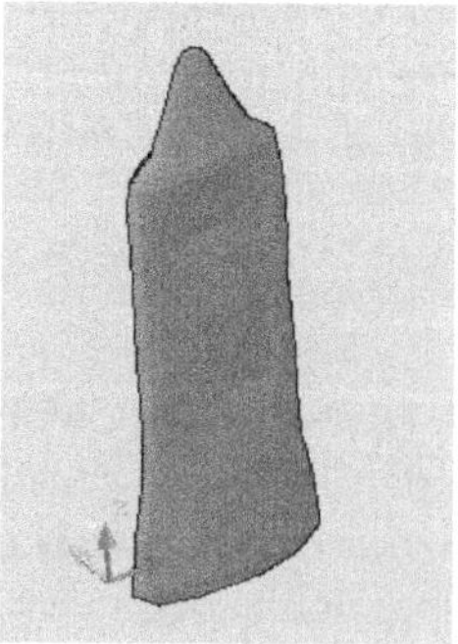

Figure 12-66 *The final model of an elliptical mesh cylinder*

Creating an Elliptical Cylinder

First, you need to start a new drawing file, specify the settings for the number of faces in the cylinder, and then create the cylinder.

1. Start a new *acad3D.dwt* file in the **3D Modeling** workspace.

2. Choose the inclined down-arrow displayed at the lower right corner of the **Primitives** panel of the **Mesh** tab; the **Mesh Primitive Options** dialog box is displayed.

3. In this dialog box, select **Cylinder** from the **Mesh Primitive** area and set the following parameters in the **Tessellation Divisions** rollout:

   Axis: **10** Height: **5** Base: **3**

4. Choose **OK** to accept the settings specified in the rollout and exit the dialog box.

5. Turn on the **Ortho Mode** and invoke the **Mesh Cylinder** tool from **Mesh > Primitives > Primitives** drop-down. Then, follow the Command sequence given next to create the mesh cylinder.

   Specify center point of base or [3P/2P/Ttr/Elliptical]: *Enter* ***E*** *to create elliptical base.*
   Specify endpoint of first axis or [Center]: *Enter* ***C*** *to specify the center of base.*
   Specify center point: *Specify the center point for the base of the cylinder.*
   Specify distance to first axis: *Drag the cursor along X axis and enter* ***55*** *in the Dynamic Input to specify a point on the first axis.*
   Specify endpoint of second axis: *Drag the cursor along Y axis and enter* ***15*** *in the Dynamic Input to specify a point on the second axis.*
   Specify height or [2Point/Axis endpoint]: *Enter* ***100*** *to specify the height of the cylinder.*

6. Change the view to **SW Isometric** and the visual style to **Wireframe**. Figure 12-67 shows the mesh model.

Moving the Edges

To move the edges, you first need to select the Edge selection filter and then move them.

1. To filter the selection, choose the **Edge** tool from **Mesh > Selection > Subobject Selection Filter** drop-down.

2. Change the visual style to **Realistic** from the **In-Canvas Visual Style Controls** at the top-left of the drawing area.

3. Press Ctrl and then select the required edge, as shown in Figure 12-68; the move gizmo is displayed by default.

Note

If move gizmo is not displayed by default, choose the ***Move Gizmo*** *tool from the* ***Default Gizmo*** *drop-down list in the* ***Selection*** *panel.*

4. Click on the X handle of the move gizmo such that the base of the cylinder is elongated; the preview of the moved edge is displayed. Next, click on the screen at the required distance (here, it is **20**). Similarly, move the edge on the other side to the same distance.

5. Now, you need to smoothen the mesh model. To do so, select it; the **Quick Properties** panel is displayed (if it does not appear, choose the **Quick Properties** button from the Status Bar). In this panel, select **Level 1** from the **Smoothness** drop-down list.

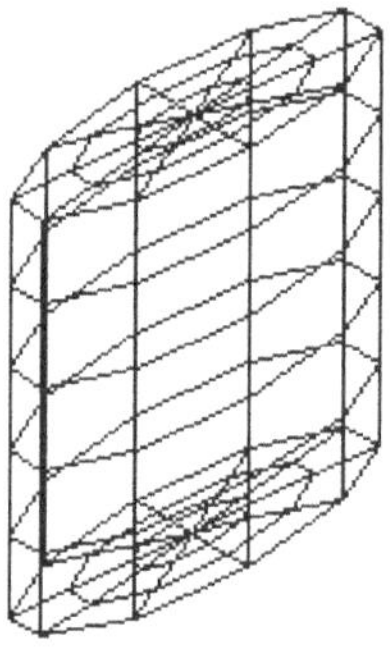

Figure 12-67 *The mesh model created*

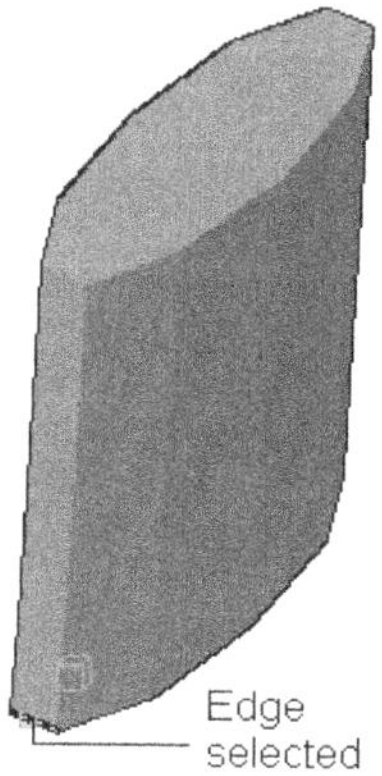

Figure 12-68 *Edge selected to be moved*

Rotating the Edges

You need to rotate the edges. Make sure the **Edge** option is selected in the **Subobject Selection Filter** drop-down list.

1. To invoke the rotate gizmo, choose the **Rotate Gizmo** tool (if the tool is not displayed then use 3DROTATE) from **Mesh > Selection > Gizmo** drop-down.

2. Select the required edges from the mesh model, as shown in Figure 12-69; the rotate gizmo is displayed on the first selected edge.

3. Click on the red handle of the rotate gizmo such that the adjoining faces are rotated inward; the preview of rotation is displayed. Click when the desired rotation is achieved (here, it is 60 degrees).

   Similarly, select the third set of edges in the same face and rotate the face. The final model, after rotating the edges, is shown in Figure 12-70.

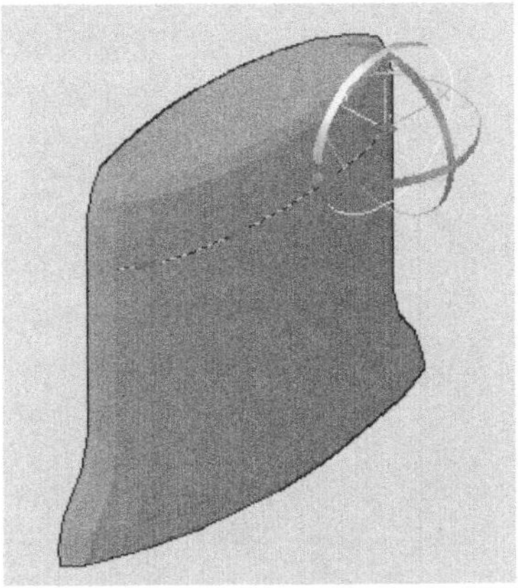

Figure 12-69 Edges selected to be rotated

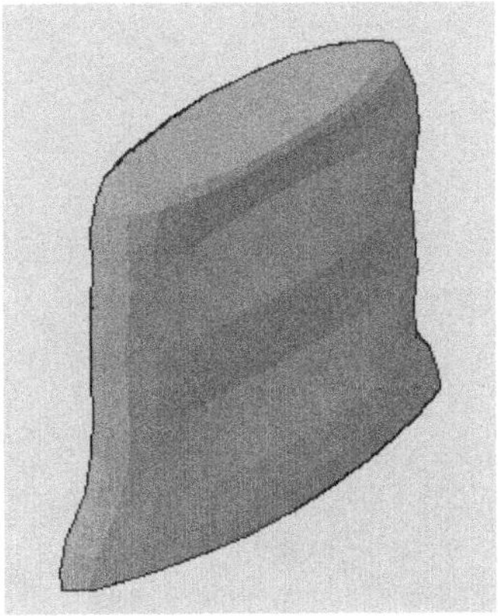

Figure 12-70 Final model after rotating the edges

Moving the Inner Faces of the Model

Now, you need to change the selection filter from edges to faces and then move faces.

1. To select faces, choose **Face** from **Mesh > Selection > Subobject Selection Filter** drop-down.
2. Choose the **Move Gizmo** tool (if the tool is not active then use **3DMove**) from **Mesh > Selection > Gizmo** drop-down.
3. Select the faces in the inner circular region at the top of the mesh model; the move gizmo is displayed on the selected faces.
4. Click on the Z handle of the gizmo and drag it; the selected faces are elongated. Click when the desired height is achieved.

Scaling the Entire Model

Now, you can elongate the model using the scale gizmo.

1. Choose the **Scale Gizmo** tool (if the tool is not active then use **3DSCALE**) from **Mesh > Selection > Gizmo** drop-down.
2. Select the model; the scale gizmo is displayed, as shown in Figure 12-71.
3. Click on the Z handle; the model is elongated in the Z-direction. Click in the drawing area at the required distance. The final model is created, as shown in Figure 12-72.

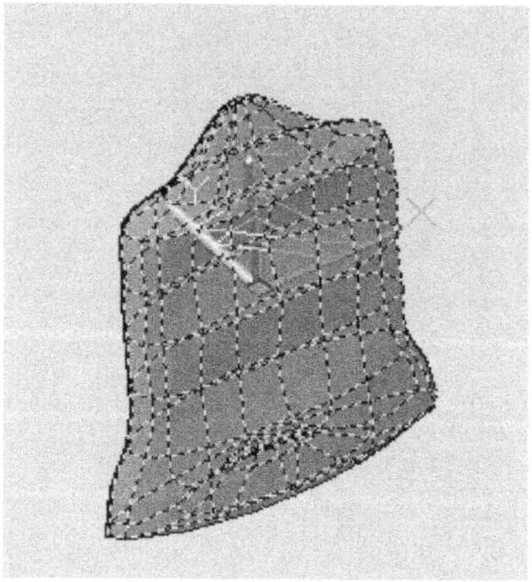

Figure 12-71 The scale gizmo displayed

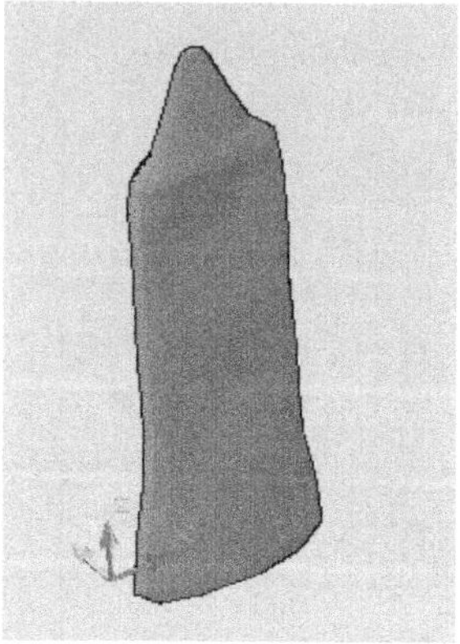

Figure 12-72 The final model

Example 3 — Mesh Tools

In this example, you will create a toy plane, refer to Figure 12-73 using various mesh tools.

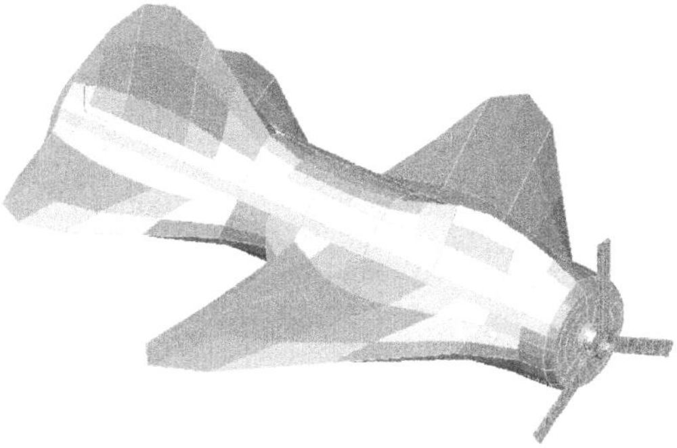

Figure 12-73 Final model of the toy plane

Creating the Cylinder

First, you need to create a cylinder facing the right view.

1. Start a new *acad3D.dwt* file in the **3D Modeling** workspace.

2. Set UCS to WCS and switch to the **Right** viewport. Rotate the WCS around the Y-axis by -90 degrees.

3. Select the **Wireframe** view style from the **In-Canvas View Controls**.

4. Invoke the **Mesh Primitive Options** dialog box and then choose **Cylinder** from the **Mesh Primitive** list.

5. Enter the following data in the **Tessellation Divisions** rollout:

   Axis = **16** Height = **8** Base = **5**

6. Choose **OK** to exit the dialog box.

7. Choose the **Mesh Cylinder** tool from **Mesh > Primitives > Mesh Primitives** drop-down; you are prompted to specify a centerpoint for the base of the cylinder.

8. Enter **0**; you are prompted to specify the base radius.

9. Enter **4** as radius; you are prompted to specify the height of the cylinder.

10. Enter **40** as the height; the cylinder is created.

    Now, you need to change the **UCS** to **WCS** and change the view to **SE Isometric**.

11. Choose the **WCS** option from the **WCS** drop-down below the ViewCube in the drawing area and click on the **SE-Isometric** hotspot in the ViewCube. The mesh cylinder will look similar to the model shown in Figure 12-74.

Extruding the Faces of the Cylinder

Now, you need to extrude the faces of the cylinder.

1. Select the inner faces on the right side of the cylinder, as shown in Figure 12-75.

2. Click on the red handle of the move gizmo to extrude; an edit box is displayed.

3. Enter **2** in the edit box; the faces are extruded.

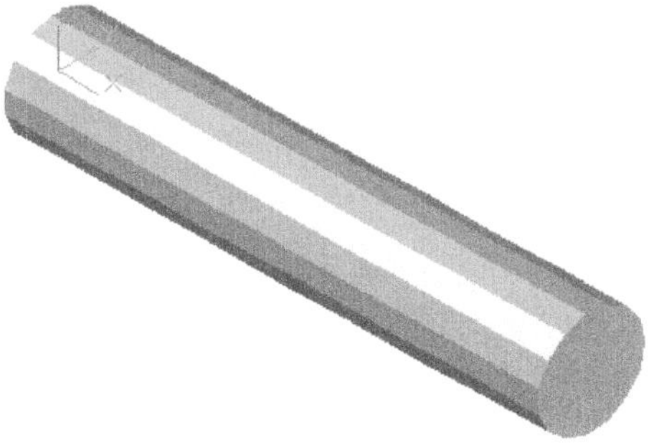

Figure 12-74 *Mesh cylinder created*

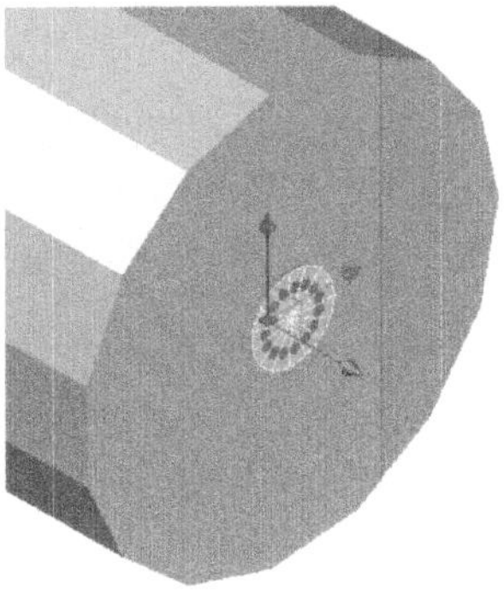

Figure 12-75 *Faces selected to be extruded*

Creating the Blades

To create blades, you need to create a thin and long mesh box. Before creating the mesh box, you need to change the UCS to Right.

1. Set UCS to WCS and switch to the **Right** viewport. Rotate the WCS around the Y-axis by -90°.

2. Choose the **Mesh Box** tool from **Mesh > Primitives > Mesh Primitives** drop-down; you are prompted to specify the first point of the mesh box.

3. Specify the point anywhere in the drawing, but not on the mesh model and create a mesh box of dimensions = 1 x 7 x 0.1.

4. Move the blade to the point on the circumference of extruded face of the cylinder, refer to Figure 12-76.

5. Now, you need to create a polar array of the blade. To do so, select the blade and invoke the **Array** tool; you are prompted to select the array type.

6. Choose the **POlar** option from the dynamic input box and specify the center point of the cylinder as the center point of the array. You can also enter **0,0** as the coordinates of the centerpoint.

7. Enter **3** in the number of items to fill; you are now prompted to specify the angle to fill.

8. Press **Enter** to accept the default angle which is 360 degrees; the preview of the array is displayed and you are prompted to accept or modify the settings.

   The model after creating the blades is shown in Figure 12-76.

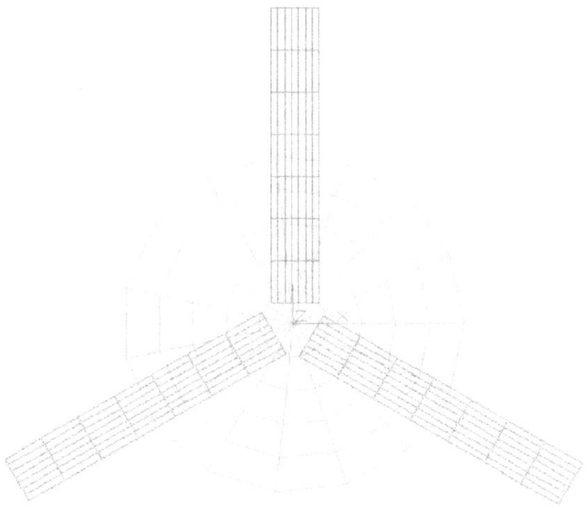

Figure 12-76 *Model created by combining various features*

Creating a Torus

You need to create a torus around the blades.

1. Choose the **Mesh Torus** tool from **Mesh > Primitives > Mesh Primitives** drop-down; you are prompted to specify a center point for the torus.
2. Specify the center point of the cylinder as thecenter point of torus and create the torus covering the start points of the blades.

The model after creating the torus is shown in Figure 12-77.

Figure 12-77 Model after creating the torus

Using Transform Gizmos and Stretching the Edge to Create a Plane

Now, you need to use various gizmos to get the shape of the plane. Before doing so, you need to set UCS to WCS and then switch to the **NE Isometric** view from the ViewCube.

1. Select the **Edge** option from the **Subobject Selection Filter** drop-down list and the **Move Gizmo** from the **Default Gizmo** drop-down list in the **Selection** panel.
2. Select the edge that is fourth on the right and third from the starting point of the mesh cylinder, as shown in Figure 12-78, to transform.
3. Now, click on the green handle; an edit box is displayed. Enter **20** in it.
4. Next, click on the red handle, move the handle backward, and enter **10** in the edit box displayed.

The model after stretching the edge on the right is shown in Figure 12-79.

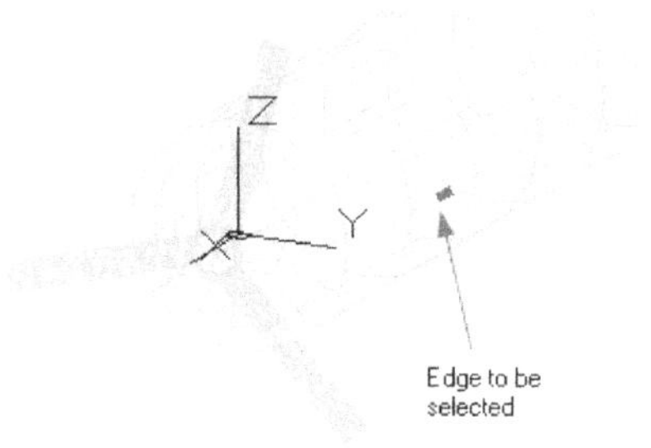

Figure 12-78 *Model created by combining various features*

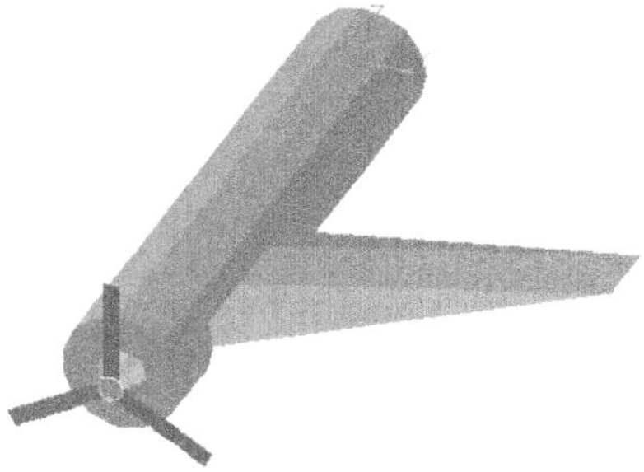

Figure 12-79 *Model after stretching the edge*

5. Similarly, stretch the edge on the other side of the model. The top view of the model after stretching edges at both sides is shown in Figure 12-80.

   Now, you need to stretch the edges on the bottom right side of the model.

6. Select the edge that is second from the bottom right end, as shown in Figure 12-81. For easy identification of the edge, you can use the **Back** viewport.
7. Drag the green handle and enter **10** in the edit box displayed.
8. Drag the red handle backward and enter **5** in the edit box displayed.

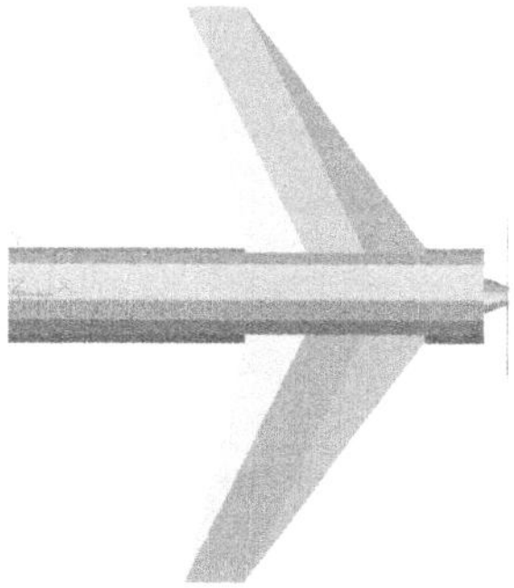

Figure 12-80 *Model after stretching the edge on the other side*

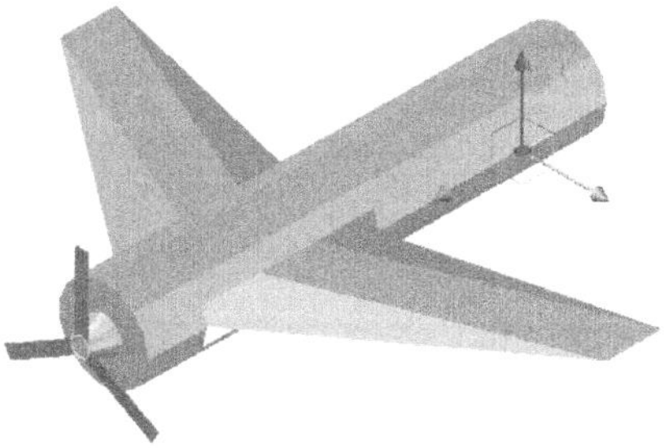

Figure 12-81 *Edge selected*

9. Similarly, modify the edge on the other side. The model after stretching the edges on both sides is shown in Figure 12-82.

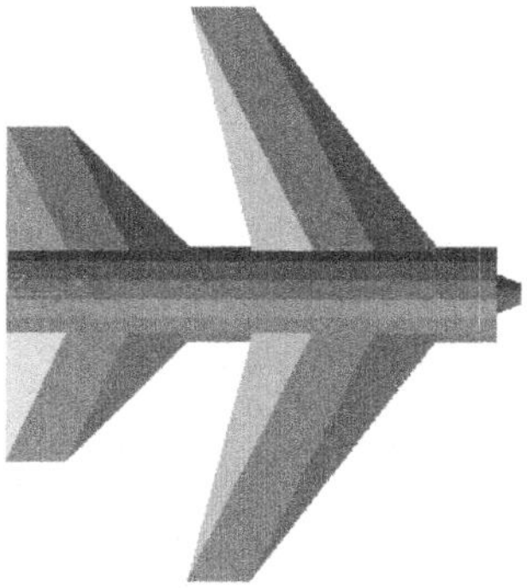

Figure 12-82 Model after stretching all the edges

Now, you will create a bulge at the top of the toy plane.

10. Select the second edge on the top of the plane, as shown in Figure 12-83.
11. Drag the blue handle and specify **2** as the distance of bulge.

    Now, you need to create a bulge on the top at the end of the model.

12. Select the edge second from the end and drag it toward the top to create the bulge, as shown in Figure 12-84.

Figure 12-83 Selecting an edge to create the bulge

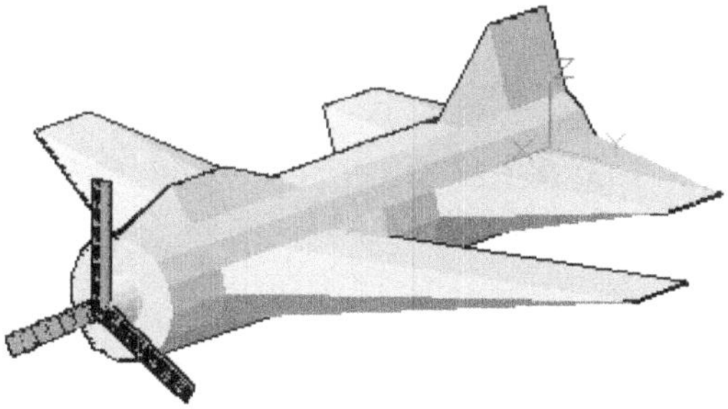

Figure 12-84 Model after creating both bulges

Smoothening the Mesh

1. Select the mesh model and choose the **Smooth More** tool from the **Mesh** panel of the **Mesh** tab.

   The final model of the toy plane after smoothening is shown in Figure 12-85.

Figure 12-85 *Final model of the toy plane*

Self-Evaluation Test

Answer the following questions and then compare them to those given at the end of this chapter:

1. Which of the following objects can be converted into mesh objects?

   (a) 3D objects (b) Closed Polygons
   (c) Regions (d) All the above

2. Which of the following options is used to convert 3D objects into meshed objects?

   (a) **Refine Mesh** (b) **Smooth More**
   (c) **Smooth Object** (d) None of these

3. Which of the following options is used to specify the default settings for the solid created from the meshed object?

   (a) **Smooth, optimized** (b) **Smooth, not optimized**
   (c) **Faceted, optimized** (d) All the above

4. You can specify values for the number of faces in the primitive mesh in the __________ dialog box.

5. The __________ command is used to create mesh primitives.

6. The __________ tool is used to create a mesh by adjoining four continuous edges or curves.

7. The mesh editing tools are available in the __________ panel of the **Mesh** tab of the **Ribbon**.

8. To retain the sharpness of the crease even when you smoothen or refine the mesh, you need to set the crease to __________.

9. You can invoke the ________ tool to sharpen faces, edges, or vertices of mesh objects.

10. A mesh model is similar to a solid model without mass and volume properties. (T/F)

Review Questions

Answer the following questions:

1. Which of the following is used to relocate a gizmo?

   (a) Mouse (b) shortcut menu
   (c) **Ribbon** (d) All the above

2. The ___________ and ____________ commands are used to set the wireframe density of primitives.

3. To create mesh cones with frustum, you need to choose the _________ option of the **Mesh Cone** tool.

4. The **Mesh Tessellation Options** dialog box will be displayed on entering __________ at the Command prompt.

5. To remove creases from the model, you need to enter _________ at the Command prompt.

6. In smoothening, the complexity of a model is decreased. (T/F)

7. You can set the level of smoothness of mesh objects using the **Properties** palette. (T/F)

8. The curves used to create ruled surfaces can be lines, arcs, polylines, curves, and splines. (T/F)

9. The **Refine Mesh** tool works only when the smoothening of the mesh object is set to **Level 1** or higher. (T/F)

10. Refining an object resets the smoothening level to 0, whereas refining a face does not reset the smoothing level. (T/F)

Exercise 2 — Mesh Surface

Create the 3D model of a globe shown in Figure 12-86 arbitrarily using the mesh modeling tools. The dimensions of the model are shown in Figure 12-86(a).

Figure 12-86 *Model of a globe*

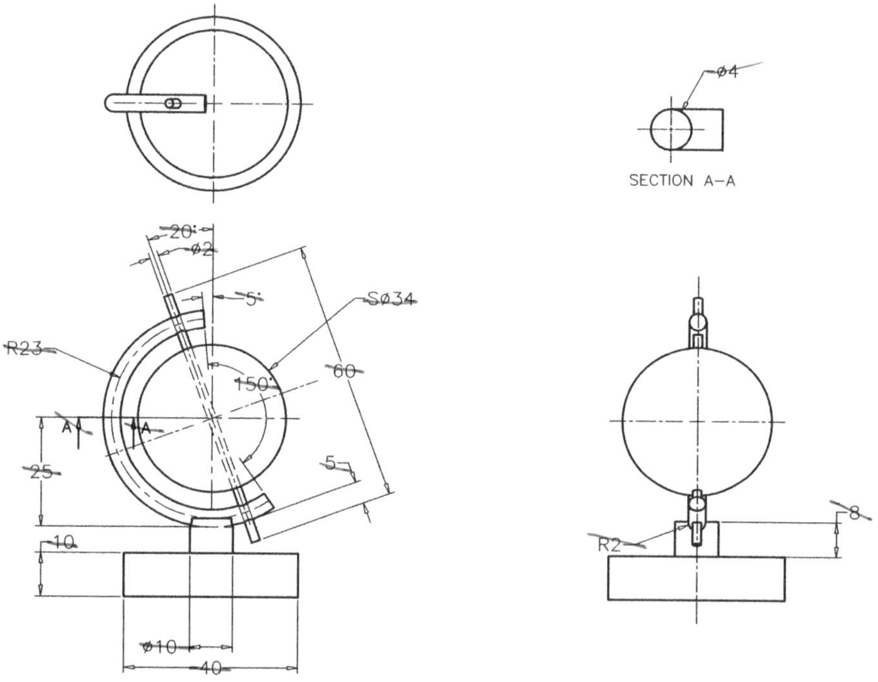

Figure 12-86(a) *Orthographic views and dimensions of the Model*

Exercise 3 Mesh Surface

Create the drawing shown in Figure 12-87. First, create the base unit (transition) and then the dish and cone.

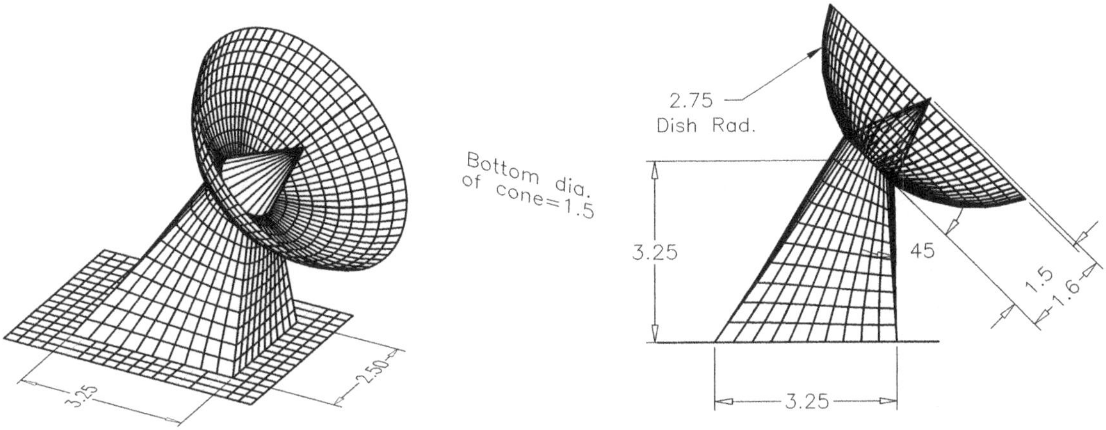

Figure 12-87 Dimensions for the mesh model

Exercise 4 Mesh Surface

Create the drawing shown in Figure 12-88. First, create one of the segments of the base and then use the **Rectangular Array** tool to complete it.

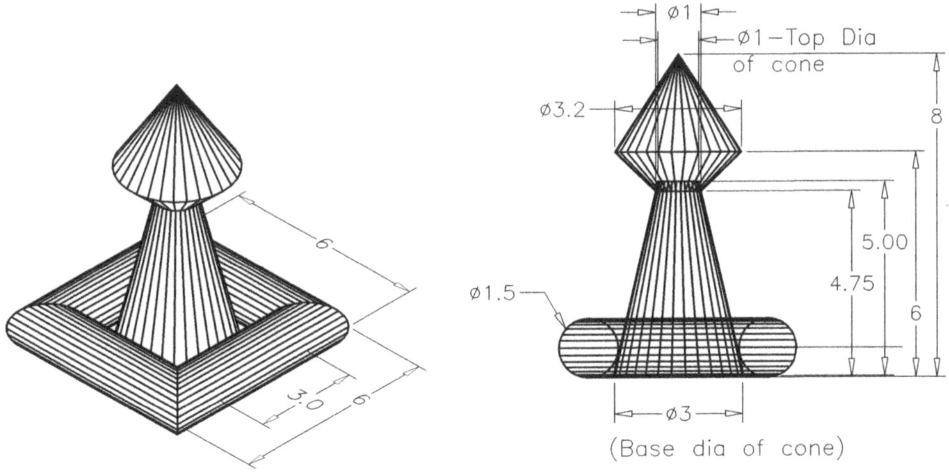

Figure 12-88 Dimensions for the mesh model

Answers to Self-Evaluation Test

1. d, **2.** c, **3.** d, **4. Mesh Primitive Options**, **5. MESH**, **6. Edge Surface**, **7. Mesh Edit**, **8.** Always, **9. Add Crease**, **10.** T

Chapter 13

Rendering and Animating Designs

Learning Objectives

After completing this chapter, you will be able to:

- *Render objects*
- *Browse and manage material libraries*
- *Assign materials to the drawing objects*
- *Create new materials as well as edit existing materials*
- *Map materials on objects*
- *Convert old materials into new materials*
- *Insert and modify light sources*
- *Convert old lights into new lights*
- *Select rendering types and render objects*
- *Define and modify rendering settings*
- *Replay and print renderings*
- *Define and apply background*
- *Save the rendering objects*
- *Configure, load, and unload AutoCAD Render*
- *Work with cameras*
- *Create animations*

Key Terms

- *Materials Browser*
- *Libraries*
- *Attach By Layer*
- *Materials Editor*
- *RENDER*
- *Material types*
- *Material properties*
- *Material Mapping*
- *Texture Editor*
- *Default Light*
- *Point Light*
- *Spot Light*
- *Distant Light*
- *Web Light*
- *Sun Light*
- *Set Location*
- *Render Presets*
- *History pane*
- *Shade plot*
- *CAMERA*
- *Set Camera View*
- *Animation Settings*
- *Motion Path*

UNDERSTANDING THE CONCEPT OF RENDERING

A rendered image makes it easier to visualize the shape and size of a 3D object as compared to a wireframe image or a shaded image. A rendered object also makes it easier to express your design ideas to other people. For example, to make a presentation of your project or design, you do not need to build a prototype. You can use a rendered image to explain your design more clearly because you have a complete control over the shape, size, color, surface material, and lighting of the rendered image.

Additionally, any required changes can be incorporated into the object, and it can be rendered to check or demonstrate the effect of these changes. Thus, rendering is a very effective tool for communicating ideas and demonstrating the shape of an object.

Generally, the process of adding a realistic effect to models (rendering) can be divided into the following four steps:

1. Selecting the material to be assigned to the design.
2. Assigning materials and textures to the design.
3. Applying additional effects to the model by assigning lights at different locations.
4. Using the **Render** tool to render the objects.

ASSIGNING MATERIALS

After creating a model, you need to assign materials to the objects in it to give it a realistic appearance. These materials create three types of effects. These effects are discussed next.

In the first type of material effect, the object is rendered without actually displaying the effect of the material applied. A global material is assigned to all objects. On rendering, the color of the rendered image depends on the color of the object. Rendering by using this type of material effect does not give a realistic effect to the model, refer to Figure 13-1.

In the second type of material effect, a material is assigned to the object. AutoCAD provides you with a number of predefined materials and material libraries from which you can select a material and apply to the model. The material libraries contain thousands of materials and you can browse them using the **Materials Browser**. The **Materials Browser** is discussed next. Once you have selected the material, you can assign it directly to the object, individual faces, blocks, or layers, and render the model. Figure 13-2 shows a model to which a material has been applied and then rendered.

The third type of material effect is photorealistic. In this type, additional parameters such as the mirror effect, reflection, and refraction can be defined for the material, refer to Figure 13-3. You can set these parameters in the **MATERIALS EDITOR**.

Figure 13-1 *Model rendered after applying the default global material*

Figure 13-2 *Model rendered after applying the material*

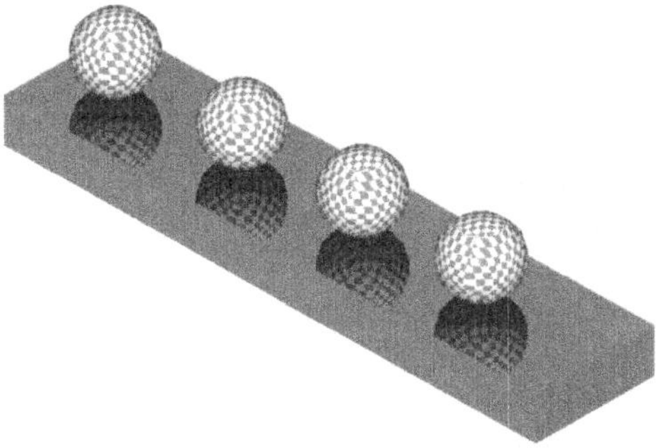

Figure 13-3 *Model rendered by adding effects such as the mirror effect*

Materials Browser

Ribbon: Visualize > Materials > Materials Browser
Menu Bar: View > Render > Materials Browser
Toolbar: Render **Command:** MAT or MATBROWSEROPEN

You can browse materials, manage material libraries, and apply the selected material to the drawing objects using the **Materials Browser** tool. You can download the Autodesk materials library available on the internet and install it, whenever required. When you choose the library to install, the library automatically gets installed in *Program Files (x86)\Common Files\Autodesk Shared\Materials\2023* folder. Also, the materials get automatically arranged into sub-folders. To apply material, choose the **Materials Browser** tool from the **Materials** panel of the **Visualize** tab. The **MATERIALS BROWSER** window will be displayed, as shown in Figure 13-4. For better utilization of the materials library, materials are arranged in nested categories. The different options of the **MATERIALS BROWSER** are discussed next.

Search

You can search a material from all the available material libraries by entering its name or keyword in the **Search** edit box.

Create Material

You can create your own materials using the **Create Material** option available at the bottom of the browser. When you select this option, a drop-down list is displayed with a list of material types. You can select a material type from the drop-down list. On doing so, the **MATERIALS EDITOR** is displayed with the predefined settings of the selected type. Using the **MATERIALS EDITOR**, you can change the settings of the material to modify the material as per your requirement. The **MATERIALS EDITOR** is discussed later in this chapter.

Document Materials

The **Document Materials** drop-down list acts as a filter to the materials used in the current drawing. The options in this drop-down list are **Show All**, **Show Applied**, **Show Selected**, **Show Unused**, and **Purge All Unused**. You can filter materials display in the **MATERIALS BROWSER** to display either all materials in the browser, only the materials applied to the drawing, only the materials of the selected entities, or only the materials that are not used in the drawing by selecting the respective option from the **Document Materials** drop-down list. You can also purge or delete the unused materials in the drawing.

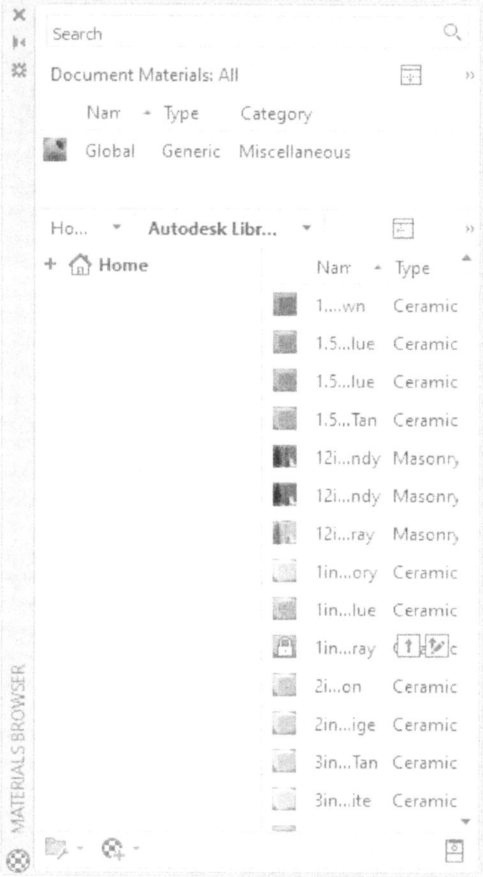

*Figure 13-4 The **MATERIALS BROWSER***

Autodesk Library

In this area, the Autodesk library with its pre-defined materials as well as other libraries with their user-defined materials are displayed. You can sort these materials by name, category, type, or material color using the drop-down list available on the extreme right of the Autodesk library drop-down above the **Preview** area. In this area, the preview swatches of the materials for the selected category/library are displayed. You can set the size of the preview swatches using the **Thumbnail Size** options available at the bottom of the drop-down list. You can set the display of swatches to icons, list, or text. After browsing to the required material, select the required material by clicking on it; the selected material will be added to the **Document Materials** list area. This material can now be applied to the drawing objects.

Manage

You can add, remove, or edit a library, or create or delete a category using the **Manage** drop-down list. The options in the **Manage** drop-down list are discussed next.

Open Existing Library

On selecting this option, the **Add Library** dialog box will be displayed. Using this dialog box, you can open an existing library.

Create New Library
On selecting this option, the **Create Library** dialog box will be displayed. Using this dialog box, you can save the newly created library.

Remove Library
You can remove the selected library using this option.

Create Category
You can create a new category of materials in the library by using the **Create Category** option. You can add materials under a new category by dragging and dropping.

Delete Category
You can delete the selected category by using the **Delete Category** option.

Rename
You can rename the selected category by using the **Rename** option.

Assigning Selected Materials to Objects
Once you have selected the materials to be applied to the object, you need to assign them to the objects in the current drawing. To do so, first invoke the **MATERIALS BROWSER** by choosing the **Materials Browser** button from the **Materials** panel of the **Visualize** tab and then browse to the required material from the library. After selecting the required material, drag and drop it on the drawing object on which you want to apply the selected material. If the visual style is set to Realistic, the material will be displayed instantaneously on the objects you select. Note that if a material is already applied to an object and you apply a new material on it again, then the new material will be updated on the object automatically.

Apart from dragging and dropping, you can also assign materials to the selected entities. To do so, select the object and then hover the cursor over the desired material in the **MATERIALS BROWSER**; the **Adds material to document** button will be displayed in the category column. Choose the button; the material will be applied to the selected object. Also, the material will be added to the **Document Materials** list automatically. Alternatively, select the entities, right-click on the selected material in the Browser, and then choose **Assign to Selection** from the shortcut menu displayed.

If you need to reuse certain materials again and again, then you can add those materials to the **My Materials** list, to the current drawing list, or to the active **Tool Palette**. To do so, right-click on the desired material; a shortcut menu will be displayed. Choose **Add to** from the shortcut menu; the **Document Materials**, **Favorites**, and **Active Tool Palette** sub-options are displayed. Using these sub-options, you can add the selected material to the required place.

Removing Materials from Selected Objects
To detach a material that has been applied to an object, invoke the **Remove Materials** tool from the **Materials** panel; the cursor will change into a paintbrush and you will be prompted to select the object from which you want to detach the material. Select the object; the material will be removed from it. By default, the global material will again be assigned to the object from which you have detached the material.

Attaching Material by Layers

Ribbon: Visualize > Materials > Attach By Layer **Command:** MATERIALATTACH

You can assign a particular material to a layer by choosing the **Attach By Layer** tool from the **Materials** panel. This means that you can apply a specified material to all the objects that are placed on a layer. When you choose this tool, the **Material Attachment Options** dialog box will be displayed. In this dialog box, all materials in the current drawing are placed under the **Material Name** column, the layers are placed in the **Layer** column, and the material attached to this layer is placed under the **Material** column, refer to Figure 13-5. To assign a material to a layer, select the material from the **Material Name** column and drag it to the desired layer in the **Layer** column. All objects placed in the selected layer will now be assigned with the specified material. After attaching the material to a layer, the **Detach** button is automatically added on the right of the **Material** column. You can detach the material from the selected layer by choosing the **Detach** button.

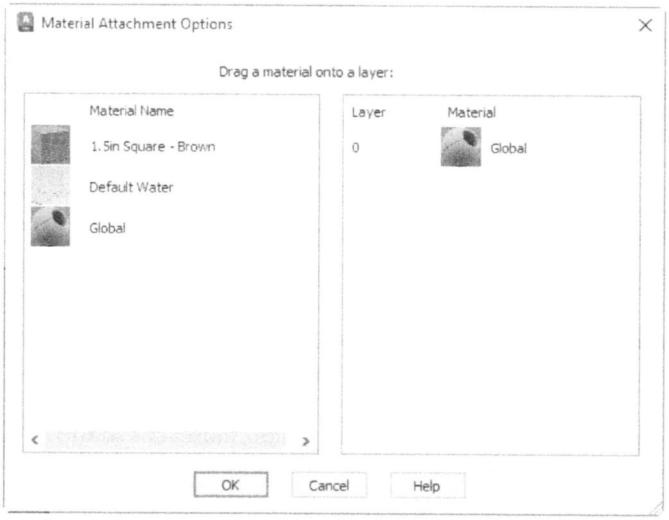

*Figure 13-5 The **Material Attachment Options** dialog box*

Creating and Editing Materials

Ribbon: Visualize > Materials > Materials Editor (Inclined arrow)
Menu Bar: View > Render > Materials Editor **Toolbar:** Render

In AutoCAD, you can create a new material or edit an existing material according to your requirements. This is done using the **MATERIALS EDITOR**. To edit an existing material, double-click on it in the **MATERIALS BROWSER**; the **MATERIALS EDITOR** will be displayed, as shown in Figure 13-6. Using the **MATERIALS EDITOR**, you can change the color, adjust material properties, and add textures to the selected material. The **MATERIALS EDITOR** has 2 tabs: **Appearance** and **Information** and these tabs are discussed next.

Note

*The **MATERIALS EDITOR** is also used to create new materials. In this case, you need not double-click on any material to invoke it. You can invoke it directly by choosing the inclined arrow on the title bar of the **Materials** panel of the **Visualize** tab. The procedure to create new materials is discussed later.*

Appearance Tab

In the **Appearance** tab, all the properties of a material are defined. These properties include glossiness, reflectivity, transparency, luminosity and so on. You can also add textures to the material, if required. Various areas in this tab are discussed next.

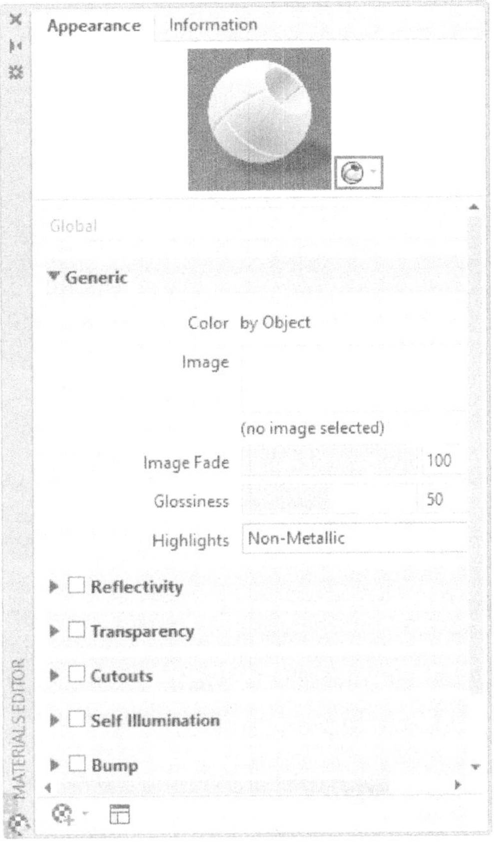

*Figure 13-6 The **MATERIALS EDITOR***

Preview

The preview area at the top of the **Appearance** tab displays the preview of the material. When you modify the material properties, the preview of the material also gets updated automatically. This helps you preview the materials with desired properties before you finally set the properties of the material and apply them to the model.

You can also select the shape of the thumbnail and render quality of the preview for better visualization of the material. To do so, choose the down arrow available in the lower right corner of the preview area; a list containing **Scene**, **Environment** and **Render Settings** is displayed. The Scene types include **Sphere**, **Cube**, **Cylinder**, **Canvas**, **Plane**, **Object**, **Vase**, **Draped Fabric**, **Glass Curtain Wall**, **Walls**, **Pool of liquid**, **Utility** and **Torus**. Select the required scene thumbnail. **The Render Settings** include **Quick**, **Draft**, and **Production** Qualities. Select the required render quality of the preview of the material. Note that higher the quality, slower the process of updating the materials.

Information Tab

In this tab, you can view the file properties as well as specify the description and keywords for the material created. The **MATERIALS EDITOR** with the **Information** tab chosen is shown in Figure 13-7.

Information

You can specify a name for the existing/new material by entering a new name in the **Name** edit box in the **Information** area of the **Information** tab. On entering a new name, the name will be updated in the **MATERIALS BROWSER** also. In the **Description** edit box, enter the material category. For easy indexing in the **Search** option, enter the keywords in the **Keywords** edit box.

About
This area displays the type and version of material.

Texture Paths
This area displays the path of the edited material in the selected storage media.

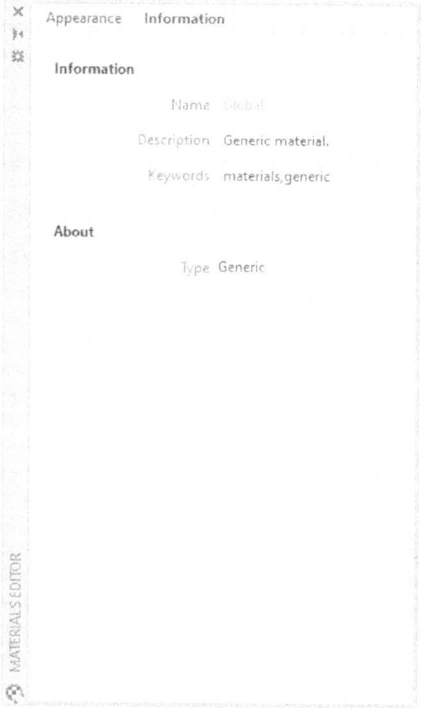

***Figure 13-7** The **MATERIALS EDITOR** with the **Information** tab chosen*

Note
*You cannot rename the **Global** material.*

Displays the MATERIALS BROWSER
This button is available at bottom left of the **MATERIALS EDITOR**. This is a toggle button and is used to display and hide the **MATERIALS BROWSER**.

The process of creating materials and adding texture maps is discussed later in this chapter.

BASIC RENDERING

Ribbon: Visualize > Render > Render to size drop-down	**Toolbar:** Render
Menu Bar: View > Render	**Command:** RENDER

In this section, you will learn about elementary or basic rendering. When you invoke the **Render** tool, the **Render** window will be displayed and the rendering process will be carried out. After the rendering has been completed, the rendered image will be displayed in the **Render** window, refer to Figure 13-8.

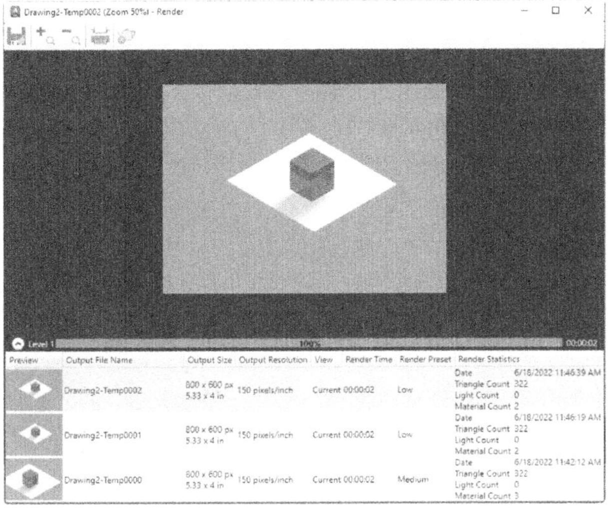

Figure 13-8 *The* ***Render*** *window*

Example 1

In this example, you will download the drawing file of the staircase shown in Figure 13-9 from *https://www.cadcim.com*. The path of the file is as follows: *Textbooks > CAD/CAM > AutoCAD Advanced > Advanced AutoCAD 2023: A Problem-Solving Approach, 3D and Advanced> Input Files*. Next, you will assign materials to the model and then render it. The materials that you need to assign to the model are given next.

Stairs	Flooring - Wood - Parquet - Brown
Balusters and Handrail	Metal Fabricated - Handrails and Railings - Painted White

1. Download the drawing file of the staircase shown in Figure 13-9 using the path mentioned above.

2. Invoke **MATERIALS BROWSER** from the **Materials** panel of the **Visualize** tab.

3. Select the **Flooring - Wood** category from the **Autodesk Library** list; all materials in the category are displayed in the preview list. Browse to the **Parquet - Brown**, select it, and then drag and drop it on stairs; the material is applied to the stairs.

4. As explained in Step 3, select the **Metal - Fabricated** category from the **Autodesk Library** list. Next, select **Handrails and Railings - Painted White** from the materials displayed and apply it to the balusters and handrails.

Note

*You will notice that the materials selected in Step 3 and Step 4 are automatically attached to the current drawing and displayed in the **Document Materials** list in the **MATERIALS BROWSER**.*

5. Choose the **Render to Size** tool from the **Render** panel; the rendering process starts and the rendered image is displayed in the **Render** window. The rendered image should look similar to the one shown in Figure 13-10. The background of the image is black by default. However, in this figure, the background has been changed to white for the clarity in print.

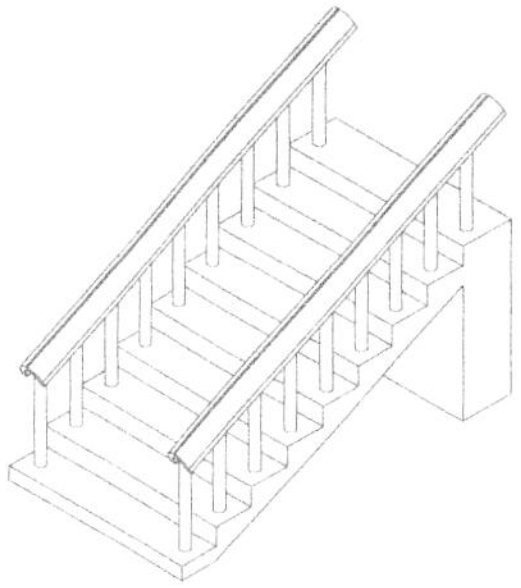

Figure 13-9 *Model for Example 1*

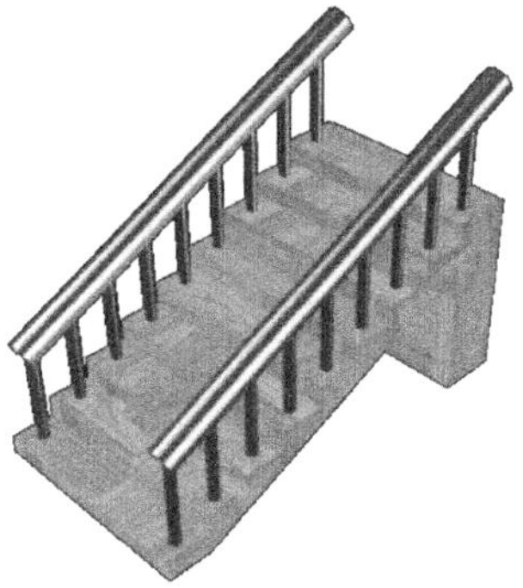

Figure 13-10 *Rendered image of staircase*

CREATING NEW MATERIALS

In AutoCAD, you can create new materials according to your requirement. To create a new material, click on the **Create Material** drop-down at the bottom of the **MATERIALS BROWSER**; a drop-down list with various material types will be displayed. Select the required material type; the **MATERIALS EDITOR** with the properties of the sample material type will be displayed, refer to Figure 13-6.

You can also create a new material directly from the **Materials Editor**. To do so, choose the **Create Material** button in the **MATERIALS EDITOR**; a drop-down list will be displayed, refer to Figure 13-11. Select the required material type from the drop-down list; all material properties based on the selected material type will be grouped together. For example, if you select metal, then the properties such as relief pattern, cutouts, and so on will be displayed. Whereas, if you select the **Wood** material, the properties displayed will be different. The preview of the selected material is displayed in the preview area. In the **Information** tab, you can rename the new material in the **Name** edit box. Also, you can give its description as well as specify the keywords to be used for searching it. This material will be automatically added in the **MATERIALS BROWSER**. Now, you can define the properties of the new material in the **MATERIALS EDITOR** by modifying the properties of the old material.

Figure 13-11 *The Create Material drop-down list*

Generic

In the **Generic** material type, almost all material properties are displayed. These properties are discussed next.

Color

By default, the **Color** option is selected in this area and therefore, the color of the object is assigned to the material. To assign any other color to the material, click on the arrow displayed on the right of the **Color** option; a drop-down list will be displayed, as shown in Figure 13-12. Select the **Color** option from the drop-down list; a color swatch will be displayed. Click on the swatch; the **Select Color** dialog box will be displayed. Select the required color from the dialog box; the selected color will be assigned to the material.

Image

You can assign textures to the color of the material. To do so, choose the arrow on the right in the **Image** area; a drop-down list will be displayed with a list of texture maps, refer to Figure 13-13. There are nine types of texture maps: **Image**, **Checker**, **Gradient**, **Marble**, **Noise**, **Speckle**, **Tiles**, **Waves**, and **Wood**.

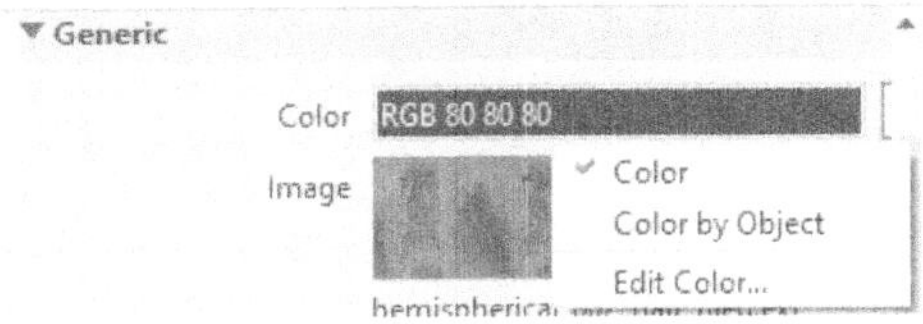

Figure 13-12 The ***Color*** *drop-down list*

If you select the **Image** option, the **Material Editor Open File** dialog box will be displayed, as shown in Figure 13-14. Browse to the required image and choose the **Open** button from the dialog box; the respective image will be displayed in the image area. Next, click on the displayed image; the **Texture Editor** window will be displayed. The **Texture Editor** displays the link for the texture image used, a slider to adjust the brightness of the image, a **Transforms** node that enables you to set the position, scale, and repetition of the image. Similarly, you can select other texture maps such as checker or gradient and then edit the appearance properties of the image and transform it according to your requirement.

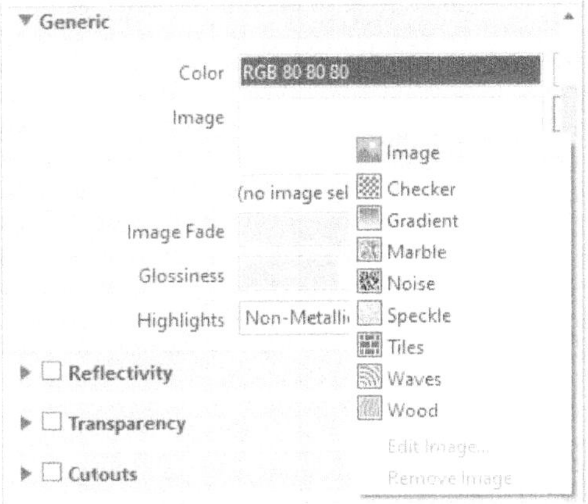

Figure 13-13 The ***Image*** *drop-down list*

If you select the **Marble** option from the drop-down list, the material will be mapped to the image of the marble and the properties of the marble will be displayed in the **Texture Editor**, refer to Figure 13-15. Click on the **Stone Color** swatch to change the color of the base stone and the **Vein Color** swatch to change the color of the veins displayed on the base stone. To interchange the color of the stone and vein, click on the down arrow next to the **Stone Color** swatch and choose the **Swap Colors** option. The **Vein Spacing** and **Vein Width** edit boxes are used to control the relative spacing between the veins and the relative size of the width of the vein, respectively.

If you select the **Wood** option from the drop-down list, the material will be mapped to the image of the wood. Also, the **Texture Editor** will be displayed. You can edit the image of an existing wood structure applied on the material. To do so, click in the preview swatch; the **Texture Editor** will be displayed with the properties of **Wood**, refer to Figure 13-16. Click on the required color buttons to change the color of the wood base and the pattern. Choose the **Swap Colors** option that is displayed on right-clicking on the color swatch to interchange the wood base and pattern colors. The **Radial Noise** and the **Axial Noise** options are used to decide the relative occurrence of patches of the wood in the radial and axial directions, respectively. The **Grain Thickness** option is used to specify the relative size of the grain patches in the material. All the values specified in this edit box are relative to the size of the object on which it will be applied.

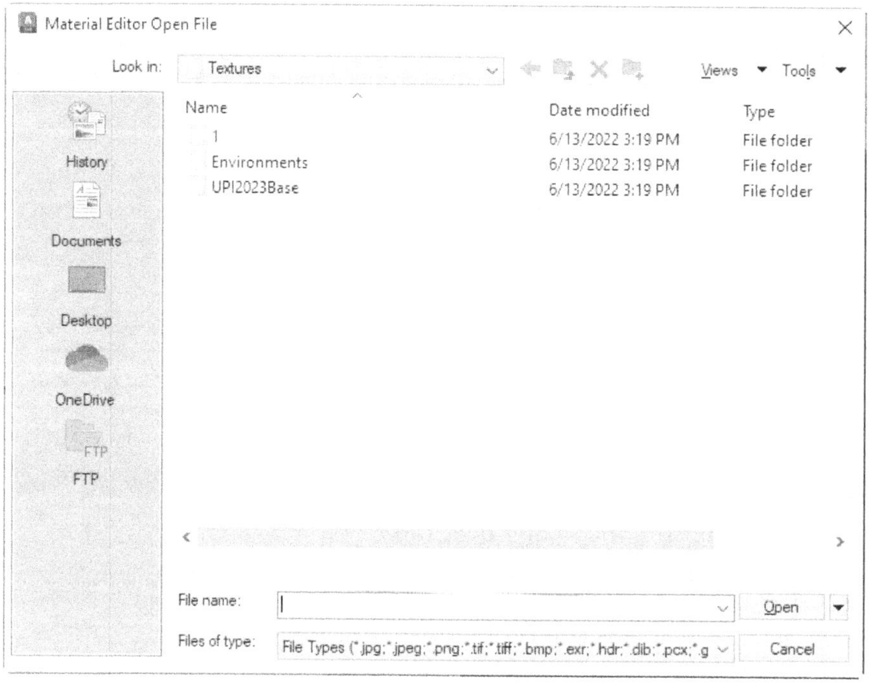

*Figure 13-14 The **Material Editor Open File** dialog box*

*Figure 13-15 Material properties for **Marble***

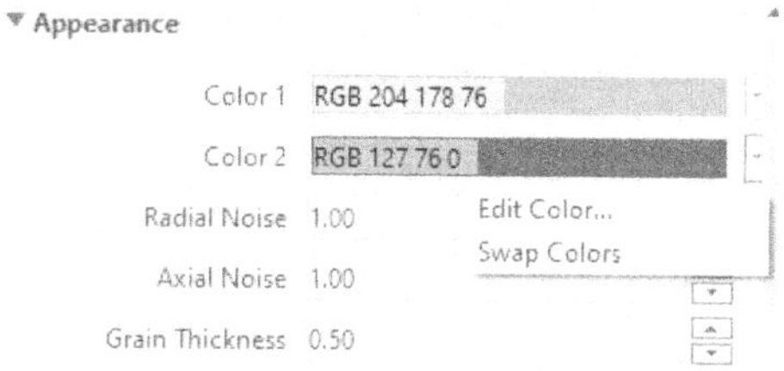

Figure 13-16 Material properties for Wood

Image Fade

Use this slider bar to specify the extents of the effect of the texture map on the material. Figure 13-17 shows the **Image Fade** slider. At 0 value, there will be no effect of the texture map and only the material will be displayed. Also, as this value increases, the effect of the texture map becomes more dominant on the material and at the value of 100, only the texture map will be displayed on the object.

*Figure 13-17 The **Image Fade** slider*

Glossiness

This property is used to set the shininess of the texture. It is actually the ability of a surface to reflect the light. If the material is more glossy, it will reflect more light and the color of the portion of the object hit by the light will become whitish because white is the default color assigned to glossiness. However, you can assign any other color to it. You can set the shininess value as well as apply an image or texture to the gloss.

Highlights

This property is used to disperse light non-uniformly from the material. You can set metallic or non-metallic highlight for the texture. The **Metallic** option is used to highlight the color of the material and the **Non-Metallic** option is used to highlight the color of the light hitting the material.

Apart from the general properties discussed above, there are some other properties that are used to add extra effects to the material. These properties are discussed next.

Reflectivity

Reflectivity is the reflective property of the material. A hundred percent reflective material displays the surrounding objects on its surface. The **Reflectivity** area is used to specify the environment reflecting qualities of a material. Select the **Reflectivity** check box on the left of the node to apply the reflection effect. By default, sliders are displayed for both the **Direct** and **Oblique** options. To apply a reflection map to an object, click on the black arrow at the right of the **Direct/Oblique** slider; a list of options will be displayed, refer to Figure 13-18.

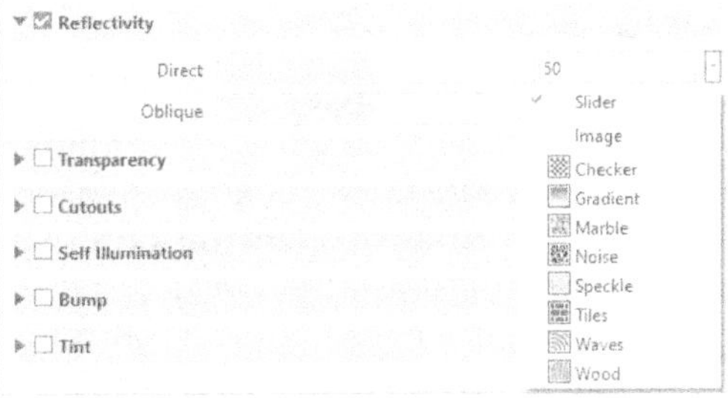

*Figure 13-18 Options available in the **Reflectivity** node*

Choose the required option from it. You can set an image file or some predefined textures to be reflected from the object as if the surrounding of the material is composed of this image/texture file. If you choose the **Image** option, the **Material Editor Open File** dialog box will be displayed. In this dialog box, you can select an image file to be reflected from the object. Similarly, you can select some predefined reflection maps from the drop-down list such as **Checker**, **Marble**, **Noise**, and so on. After selecting the map type, the **Texture Editor** will be displayed. Use the slider bar to set the brightness of the reflection map. The name of the texture file is displayed below the preview swatch and you can click on it to change the attached texture file. You can select or clear the **Reflectivity** check box to turn its effect on or off.

Transparency

Transparency controls the opaqueness of the material. The material with no transparency is opaque. The **Transparency** area is used to define an imaginary transparency or opacity effect of the material. Select the **Transparency** check box to apply the transparency settings on the object. You can specify the extent of transparency on the material by using the **Amount** slider. At 0 value, the material appears to be totally opaque and as this value increases, the transparency of the object also increases. You can set the image or texture for the transparency and adjust its color as discussed earlier. You can turn on or off the transparency effect by selecting or clearing this check box.

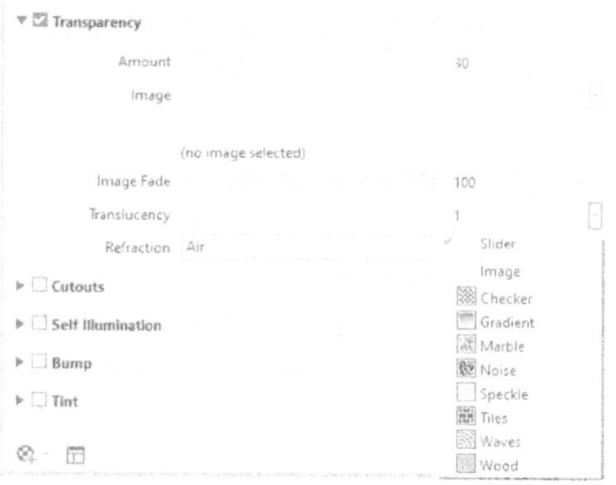

Figure 13-19 *The opacity map settings available for the* ***Translucency*** *option in the* ***Transparency*** *node*

Translucency controls the amount of light transmittedand scattered within an object. At 0 translucency, all the light will be transmitted through the material without scattering. As the value of translucency increases, the amount of light scattered within the material also increases. You can set the image or texture for the transparency, refer to Figure 13-19 and adjust its color as discussed earlier. Refractive index defines the extent by which the view of an object will distort if it is placed behind a translucent object. For a refractive index of 1 (Air), the view of the object will not distort at all. If this value is increased (1.5 for glass, 2.3 for diamond, and so on), the extent of distortion will also increase. The maximum value of refractive index is 5.

Cutouts

Cutouts are used to create a perforation effect on the material and make the material partially transparent. When you select the **Cutouts** check box in the **MATERIALS EDITOR**, the **Material Editor Open File** dialog box is displayed. In this dialog box, you can select cutout maps. After selecting the texture to open, the **TEXTURE EDITOR** is displayed. In the **TEXTURE EDITOR**, you can set the brightness, scale, and size of the cutout map. Note that light colors appear opaque and dark colors appear transparent. Figure 13-20 shows a checker map without cutout effect and Figure 13-21 shows a checker map with cutout effect.

Figure 13-20 *Checker map without cutout effect*

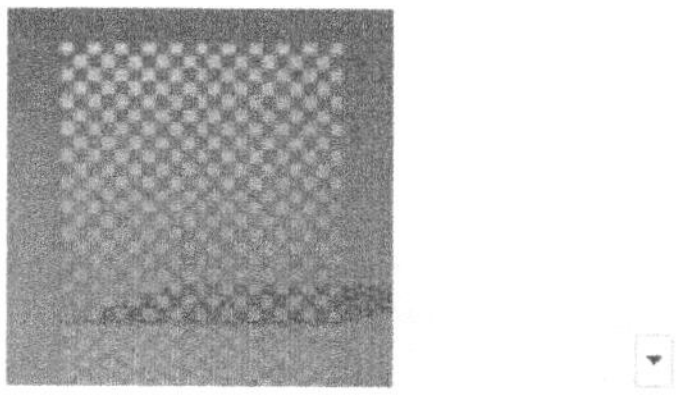

Figure 13-21 *Checker map with cutout effect*

Self-Illumination

Self-illumination makes the material appear as if the light is coming from the material itself. To apply this effect, select the **Self-Illumination** check box. You can control the **Filter Color**, **Luminance**, and **Color Temperature** by using the options activated upon selecting this check box. The **Filter Color** is used to define a color on the illuminated material. Luminance controls the amount of light reflected from a surface. It is a measure of how bright or dark a surface will appear. By default, the **Dim Glow** option is set in this option. The other options in the

Luminance drop-down list are shown in Figure 13-22. You can specify the value of luminance in the edit box in terms of candelas/meter^2. You can also define the color of the illumination using the **Color Temperature** option. The options displayed in the **Color Temperature** drop-down list are shown in Figure 13-23.

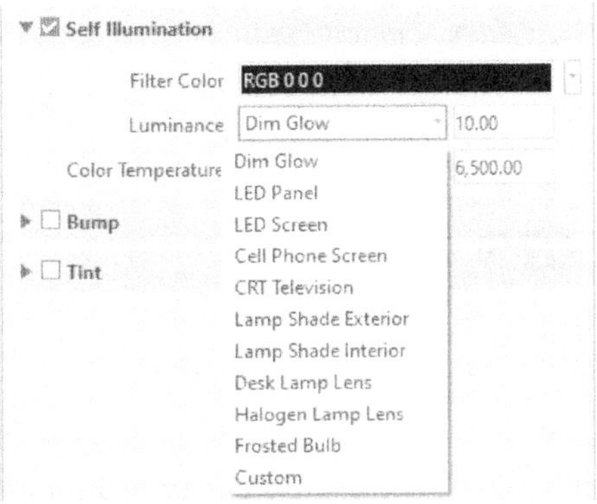

***Figure 13-22** The **Luminance** options*

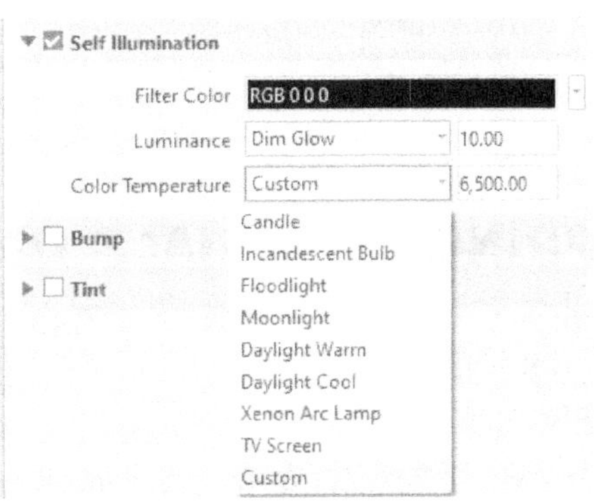

***Figure 13-23** The **Color Temperature** options*

Bump

The **Bump** area is used to add a bumpy or irregular effect to the surface of the material. Select the **Bump** check box to apply the reflection map settings on the object. On doing so, the **Material Editor Open File** dialog box will be displayed. You can use this dialog box to attach the required bump map. The attached map type in this area will appear to be engraved on the surface of the material. The light colors in this area will be projected outward or inward and the dark colors will remain as they are. Use the slider bar to adjust the extent of the bump. The value of the bump ranges from -1000 to 1000. For negative values, the brighter colors will appear to be projected inwards and for positive values, the brighter colors will appear to be projected outwards.

Note that the depth effect of a bump map is limited because it does not affect the profile of the object and cannot be self-shadowing. If you want extreme depth in a surface, you should use modeling techniques instead.

Note

1. The additional effects add realism to the object but at the same time increase the rendering time significantly.

*2. You can control the display of materials and textures from the **Materials/Textures** drop-down list in the **Materials** panel of the **Visualize** tab in the **Ribbon**. You can select the **Materials/Textures Off** or **Materials On/Textures Off**, or **Materials/Textures On** option from the **Material/Texture** drop-down list. On doing so, you can control the rendering time as well.*

*3. You can create a material similar to the original AutoCAD material. To do so, select the original material from the **MATERIALS BROWSER** and double-click to invoke the **MATERIALS EDITOR**. Next, click on the **Creates or duplicates a material** drop-down list and select the **Duplicate** option; the duplicate of the selected material will be created.*

4. The other options in the Materials window, the concept of mapping materials on an object, and the procedure of adjusting and modifying the maps will be discussed in later topics of this chapter.

Tip
The bitmap images in AutoCAD are stored in C:\Program Files (x86)\Common Files\Autodesk Shared\Materials\2023\assetlibrary_base.fbm\Mats folder. These bitmap images are in the .png format.

MAPPING MATERIALS ON OBJECTS

Ribbon: Visualize > Materials > MATERIALMAP drop-down
Menu Bar: View > Render > Mapping **Toolbar:** Mapping or Render > Mapping
Command: MATERIALMAP or SETUV

In AutoCAD, mapping is defined as the method used for adjusting the coordinates and the bitmap of the pattern of the material attached to a solid model. Mapping is required when the pattern of the material is not properly displayed on the object after rendering. Therefore, to display the material properly, you need to adjust the coordinates and the bitmap of the material properly.

To perform mapping on a model, choose the **Material Mapping** drop-down from the **Materials** panel; different types of mapping will be displayed, as shown in Figure 13-24. Choose the mapping type that you want to use on the object. The different types of tools available for mapping are: **Planar**, **Box**, **Cylindrical**, and **Spherical**. First, select an object; a material mapper grip tool will be displayed on the object. Use the grip tools on the object to adjust the display of the image on the model or on the face of the model. You can move or rotate the mapping about an axis by selecting the axis and right-clicking. Figure 13-25 shows a model with the **Planar** mapping and Figure 13-26 shows a model with the **Cylindrical** mapping.

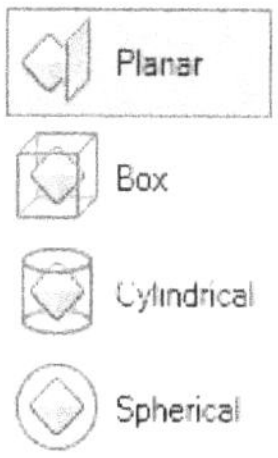

***Figure 13-24** The **Material Mapping** drop-down*

You can invoke the following options depending on your requirements.

Box

This tool is used to map an image on a box such that the image is repeated on each side of the object. The prompt sequence that will be followed on choosing the **Box** tool from the **Material Mapping** drop-down is given next.

Select an option [Box/Planar/Spherical/Cylindrical/copY mapping to/Reset mapping]<Box>: **_B**
Select faces or objects: *Select a face or object on which the image will be mapped by using the arrows .*
Select faces or objects: *Select more faces or objects on which the image will be mapped or* Enter.
Accept the mapping or [Move/Rotate/reseT/sWitch mapping mode]: *Accept the mapping as it is or select an option to modify it.*

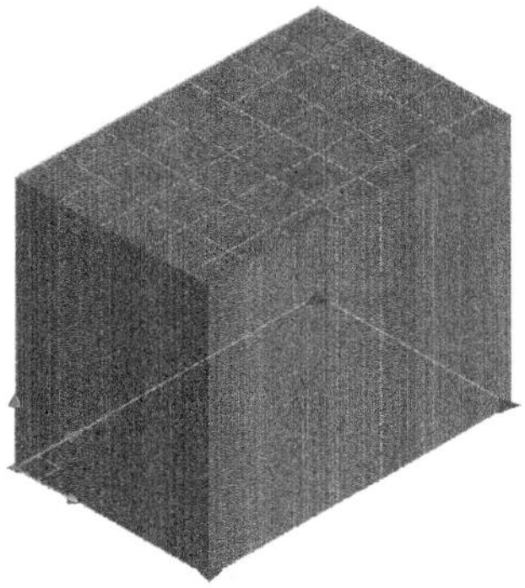

Figure 13-25 Model with the ***Planar*** *mapping*

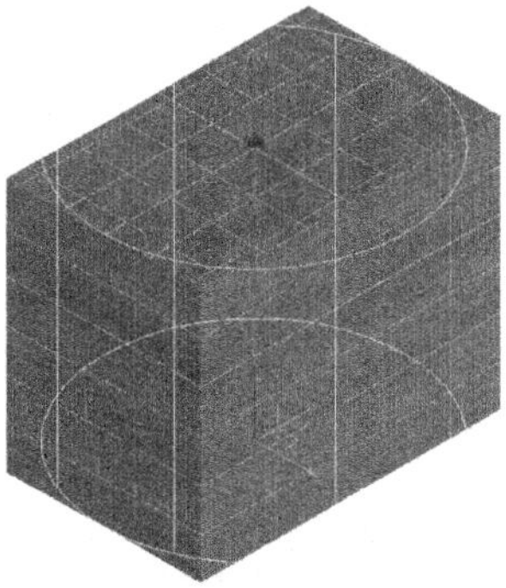

Figure 13-26 Model with the ***Cylindrical*** *mapping*

The sub-options that you can select at this prompt are given next.

Move
On selecting this sub-option, the move gizmo will be displayed on the object. You can move and adjust the mapped image along any selected axis handle. Dynamic grips are also displayed on the mapping box, which can be dragged to resize the map.

Rotate
On selecting this sub-option, the rotate gizmo will be displayed on the object. You can rotate and adjust the mapped image along any selected axis handle. Dynamic grips are also displayed on the mapping box, which can be dragged to resize the map.

reseT
This sub-option is used to reset all adjustments made in the mapping coordinate to the default one.

sWitch mapping mode
This sub-option is used to redisplay the main prompt sequence on the screen to change the type of mapping.

Planar
This tool is used to map the image on an object such that it seems to be projected on that object. The projected image is scaled automatically according to the size of the object. The prompt sequence that will follow on choosing the **Planar** tool from the **Material Mapping** drop-down is given next.

Select an option [Box/Planar/Spherical/Cylindrical/copY mapping to/Reset mapping]<Box>: **P**
Select faces or objects: *Select a face or object on which the image will be mapped.*
Select faces or objects: *Select more faces or objects on which the image will be mapped or* Enter.
Accept the mapping or [Move/Rotate/reseT/sWitch mapping mode]: *Accept the mapping as it is or select an option to modify it.*

The sub-options available at this prompt are similar to the ones discussed in the **Box** tool.

Spherical

This tool is used to map the image by warping the image horizontally and vertically. In this type of mapping, the top edge of the image converges at the north pole of the object and the bottom edge converges at the south pole. The prompt sequence for this tool is similar to that discussed in the **Box** tool.

Cylindrical

This tool is used to map the image by wrapping the image on a cylinder. The height of the image is scaled along the cylinder axis. The prompt sequence for this tool is similar to that discussed in the **Box** tool.

copY mapping to

You can also acquire the mapping from an existing object and copy it on the selected object. You can do so by choosing the **Copy Mapping Coordinates** tool from the expanded options of the **Materials** panel in the **Visualize** tab. The prompt sequence for this option is given next.

Select an option [Box/Planar/Spherical/Cylindrical/copY mapping to/Reset mapping]<Box>: **Y**
Select faces or objects: *Select the source object to copy the mapping information.*
Select the objects to copy the mapping to: *Select the object to apply the copied mapping information.*
Select faces or objects: *Select more objects or* Enter.

Reset mapping

This option is used to reset all the adjustments made in the mapping coordinates of the selected object to the default one produced by AutoCAD. To invoke this option, choose the **Reset Mapping Coordinates** tool from the expanded options of the **Materials** panel in the **Visualise** tab.

Adjusting the Bitmap Image on a Model

You can control the scale, tiling, and offset properties of a mapped image through the **Transforms** node of the **TEXTURE EDITOR**.

Figure 13-27 shows the **TEXTURE EDITOR** displayed on clicking on the **Checker** map applied to the color of the object in the **Generic** node.

In the **Appearance** area, you can modify the color of the selected texture map. The options displayed depend on the material selected. When you expand the **Transforms** node in the **Texture Editor**, the **Position**, **Scale**, and **Repeat** sub-nodes are displayed to enable you to transform the map, refer to Figure 13-28. Note that these sub-nodes are available only for the **Image**, **Checker**, **Gradient**, and **Tiles** map types.

In the **Position** sub-nodes, you can set the offset properties of the texture map. You can specify the start point of the map along the X and Y coordinates as well as rotate the map in this area. In the **Scale** area, you can specify the scale factor of the texture map in horizontal and vertical directions. You can also specify the method to be followed to create a pattern of the image. The options available in the **Repeat** area are used to set whether to tile the map in the Horizontal/ Vertical directions or not.

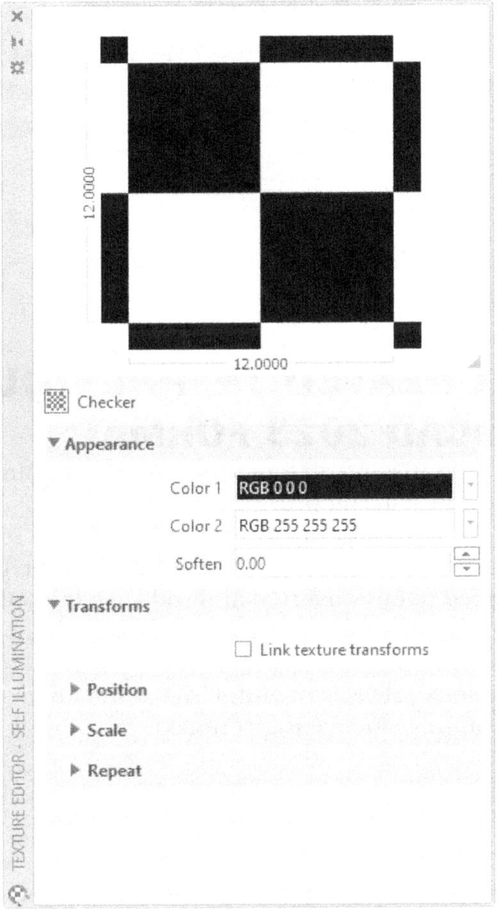

Figure 13-27 The ***TEXTURE EDITOR***

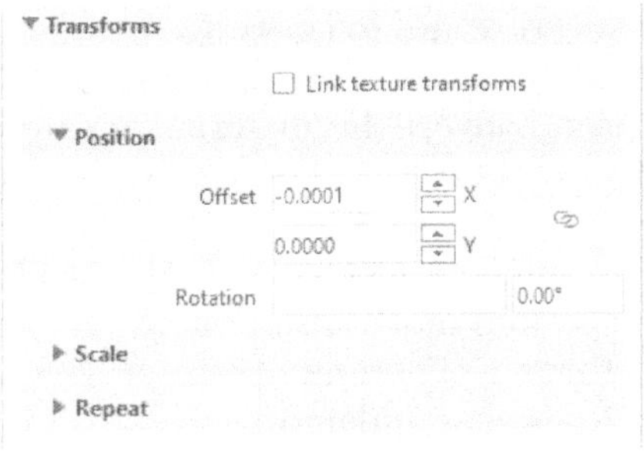

Figure 13-28 The ***Transforms*** *area of the* ***TEXTURE EDITOR***

Figures 13-29 and 13-30 show the models rendered with different width and height specified in the respective edit boxes in the **Scale** area of the **TEXTURE EDITOR**.

Figure 13-29 *Model rendered with* ***Width*** *= 8,* ***Height*** *= 2*

Figure 13-30 *Model rendered with* ***Width*** *= 4,* ***Height*** *= 1*

CONVERTING MATERIALS CREATED IN PREVIOUS AutoCAD RELEASE INTO AutoCAD 2023 FORMAT

The **3DCONVERSIONMODE** system variable is used to control the settings for the automatic conversion of the materials and light definitions created in the previous releases of AutoCAD. If the variable is set to 0, no conversion of material and lightening will take place. If it is set to a value of 1, the conversion will take place automatically. If the value is set to 2, then the user will be prompted when materials and lightening need to be converted and will have the option to convert or not to convert.

You can convert the materials created in the previous releases of AutoCAD manually by the **CONVERTOLDMATERIALS** command. The prompt sequence is given next.

Command: **CONVERTOLDMATERIALS**
Loading materials...done.
4 material(s) created.
7 object(s) updated.

The prompt sequence indicates that the four materials applied to seven objects have been converted to the AutoCAD 2023 format. This prompt sequence also indicates the materials which are not converted to AutoCAD 2023 format, if there are any.

ADDING LIGHTS TO THE DESIGN

Ribbon: Visualize > Lights > Create Light drop-down
Menu Bar: View > Render > Light **Toolbar:** Lights or Render > New Point Light
Command: LIGHT

Lights are vital to rendering a realistic image of an object. Without proper lighting, the rendered image may not show the features the way you expect. The lights can be added to the design using the **Lights** tool.

AutoCAD supports two types of lighting arrangements: Standard workflow and photometric workflow. The Photometric workflow is the default workflow in AutoCAD. The photometric workflow provides more accurate control over lighting through the photometric properties. The photometric workflow supports two types of lighting units: International (for example lux), and American (for example foot-candles). You can select the lighting workflow and its unit from the **Units for specifying the intensity of lighting** drop-down list in the **Lighting** area of the **Drawing Units** dialog box. To invoke this dialog box, choose **Drawing Utilities > Units** from the **Application Menu**. Alternatively, expand the **Lights** panel in the **Visualize** tab and specify the units from the **Lighting Units** drop-down.

Note

*The Standard workflow is enabled if **Generic lighting units** is selected as a unit in the **Lights** panel. Similarly, the Photometric workflow is enabled if **American lighting units** or **International lighting units** is selected as a unit in the **Lights** panel.*

All types of light sources supported by AutoCAD are discussed next.

Default Light

The default light is the natural light source that equally illuminates all surfaces of the objects, refer to Figure 13-31. The default light consists of two distance lights that do not have a source, and therefore, no location or direction. It is the default light that is automatically applied to the design. However, you can modify the brightness, contrast, and mid tone settings of the environment light by using the respective slider from the **Lights** panel in the **Visualize** tab, refer to Figure 13-32.

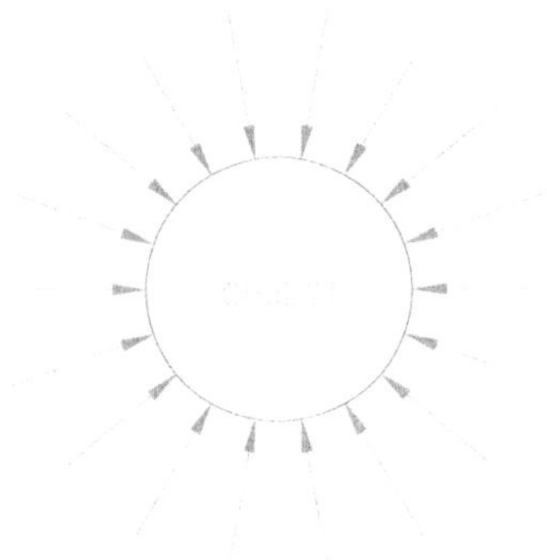

Figure 13-31 *Default light emitting constant illumination*

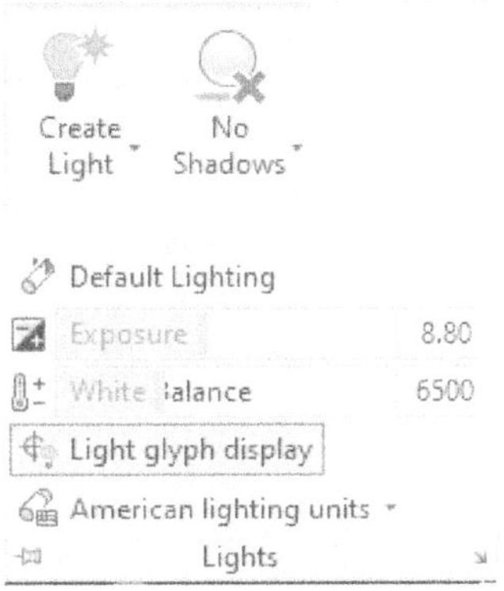

Figure 13-32 *The expanded **Lights** panel of the **Visualize** tab*

The **Exposure** and **White Balance** slider bars can be used to increase or decrease the exposure and white balance of the default light. By default, the color of the **Default lighting** is white. Figures 13-33 and 13-34 show the same model rendered using different values of exposure and white balance of the default light.

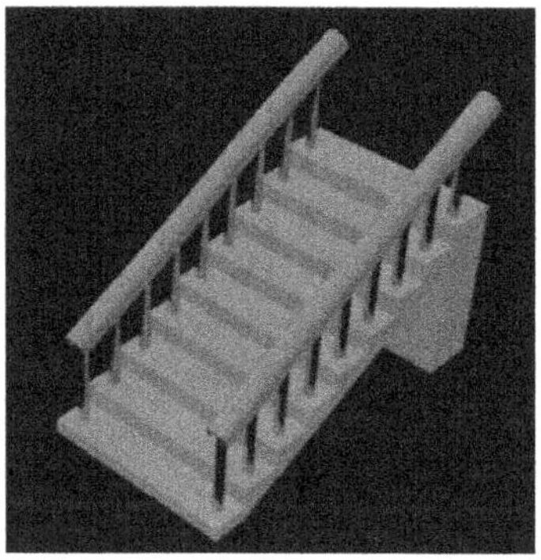

Figure 13-33 *Model rendered with high exposure and white balance value of ambient light*

Figure 13-34 *Model rendered with less exposure and white balance value of ambient light*

The **Exposure** option is used to set the value of light in the scene. You can move the exposure slider to make a scene light or dark. While the **White balance** option gives a cool or warm effect to the rendered image. When you invoke any new light to create user-defined lights, the **Lighting - Viewport Lighting Mode** message will be displayed on the screen, refer to Figure 13-35. If you want to render the model using the user-defined lights only, then choose the **Turn off the default lighting (recommended)** option. But if you want to render the model using both the default and user defined lights, then choose the **Keep the default lighting turned on** option. However, if you will keep the default lights turned on, the effects of the user-defined lights will not be displayed properly, so you need to turn off the default lighting manually. If you invoke the **Lights** tool again after turning off the default light, the **Lighting - Viewport Lighting Mode** message will not be displayed on the screen.

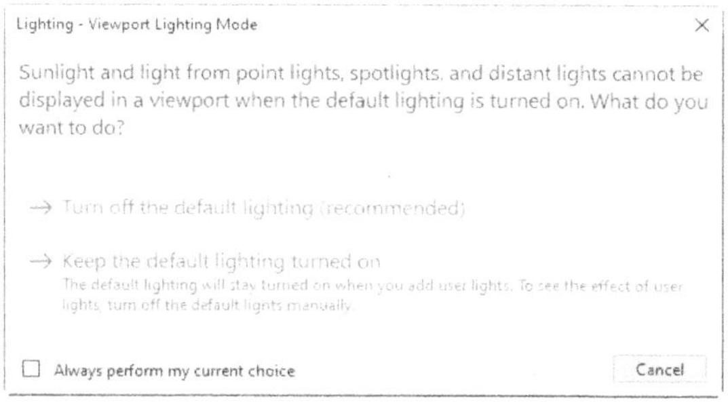

Figure 13-35 *The* ***Lighting - Viewport Lighting Mode*** *message box*

Point Light

Ribbon: Visualize > Lights > Create Light drop-down > Point
Menu Bar: View > Render > Light > New Point Light **Command:** POINTLIGHT

A point light source emits light in all directions and the intensity of the emitted light is uniform. You can visualize an electric bulb as a point light source. In AutoCAD render, if you select to add a point light, you can set the options of casting the shadow of the objects in the design. Figure 13-36 shows a point light source that radiates light uniformly in all directions.

As this is not the default light source, therefore, you will have to add it manually. This light source can be added by choosing the **Point** tool from the **Create Light** drop-down. The prompt sequence for the **Point** tool is given next.

Specify source location <0,0,0>: *Specify the location where you want to place the point light.*
Enter an option to change [Name/Intensity factor/Status/Photometry/shadoW/Attenuation/filterColor/eXit] <eXit>: *Specify an option or press* ENTER.

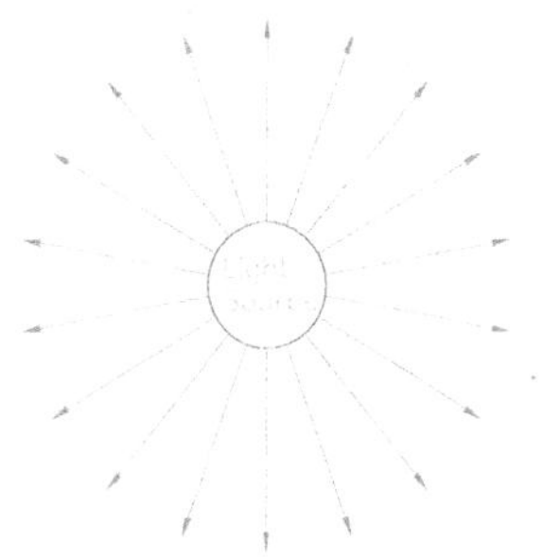

Figure 13-36 Point light source emitting light uniformly in all directions

The following options can be selected from this prompt:

Name

This option is used to specify the name of the point light. AutoCAD, by default, specifies a name to the newly created light. You can change the name by using this option.

Intensity factor

This option is used to specify the intensity of the point light. The prompt sequence that will be followed is given next.

Enter an option to change [Name/Intensity factor/Status/Photometry/shadoW/Attenuation/filterColor/eXit] <eXit>: **I** ENTER.
Enter intensity (0.00 - max float) <1.0000>: *Enter a value for the intensity of the light or press the* ENTER *key to accept the default value.*

Status

This option is used to turn the point light on and off.

Photometry

This property will be available only when you work in the photometric environment, which means the **American lighting units** or **International lighting units** is selected as a unit in the **Lights** panel. The **Photometry** option is used to control the intensity, unit of intensity, color, and type of point lights, so that you can define the lights accurately according to the real world requirement. Instead of specifying the photometric properties of the point light in the tool itself, you can also specify or modify all the photometric properties later in the **PROPERTIES** palette of the point light, refer to Figure 13-37. The options in the **Photometric properties** rollout are discussed next.

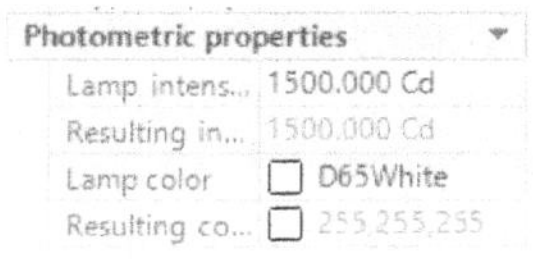

*Figure 13-37 The **Photometric properties** rollout of the **PROPERTIES** palette in the point light*

Lamp intensity. This property is used to specify the intensity, flux, or illuminance of the lamp. By default, the intensity of the light is specified in Candela. To change the properties, select the **Lamp intensity** edit box from the **PROPERTIES** palette and choose the swatch displayed on the right; the **Lamp Intensity** dialog box will be displayed, refer to Figure 13-38. Select the **Intensity (Candela)** radio button to specify the intensity of the point light in Candela. The **Flux (Lumen)** radio button is used to specify the flux of light in Lumen. The flux is the rate of total energy leaving the light source. The spinner on the right of the above mentioned radio button is used to change the value for both the intensity and flux depending on the radio button selected. The **Illuminance (Lux)** radio button is used to specify the amount of energy received per unit area by an object. In this case, you have to specify the distance at which the object is placed from the light source because the photometric lights are divergent by nature and their intensities will reduce with the increase of distance between the light source and the object. You can also increase or decrease the resulting intensity, flux, or illuminance of the light source by specifying a multiplying factor in the **Intensity factor** spinner of the **Resulting intensity** area. The resulting intensity will be the product of intensity input and the intensity factor.

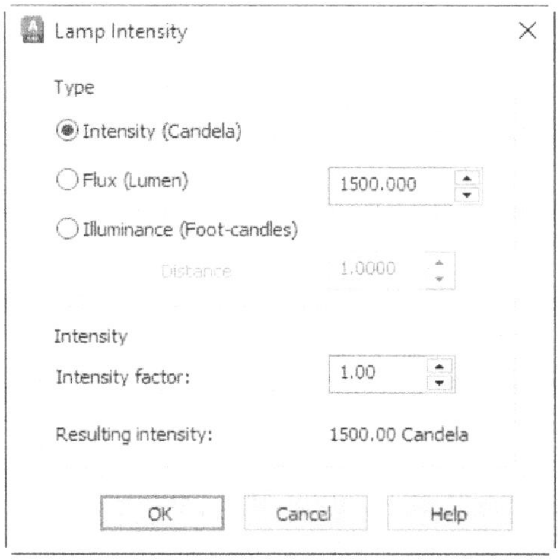

Figure 13-38 *The* ***Lamp Intensity*** *dialog box*

Resulting intensity. The **Resulting intensity** property displays the final intensity of the light source. This information is read-only.

Lamp color. This property is used to specify the lamp color of the light source. To specify or modify the lamp color, select the **Lamp color** edit box and choose the swatch displayed on the right; the **Lamp Color** dialog box will be displayed, refer to Figure 13-39. Select the **Standard colors** radio button and click on the down arrow; the **Standard colors** drop-down list will be displayed, refer to Figure 13-40. Select the standard predefined colored lights listed in this drop-down list. The preview of the selected light will be displayed in the color swatch on the right of the **Standard colors** drop-down list. An ideal black body emits a particular color at a particular temperature. To specify the lamp color with respect to temperature, select the **Kelvin colors** radio button. You can specify the temperature in Kelvin in the spinner just below the **Kelvin colors** radio button. The **Filter color** drop-down list in the **Resulting color** area is used to mix some colors with the lamp color. The final resulting color of the lamp will be a mixture of the lamp color and filter color. The preview of the resulting lamp color will be displayed in the color swatch in the **Resulting color** area.

Resulting color. The **Resulting color** property displays the resulting final color of the light source. This information is read-only.

shadoW

The sub-options provided under this option are used to control the display of the shadows of the objects after rendering. The sub-options are given next.

Off. This option is used to turn off the display of the shadow in rendering.

Sharp. This option is used to display the shadow of the objects with sharp edges.

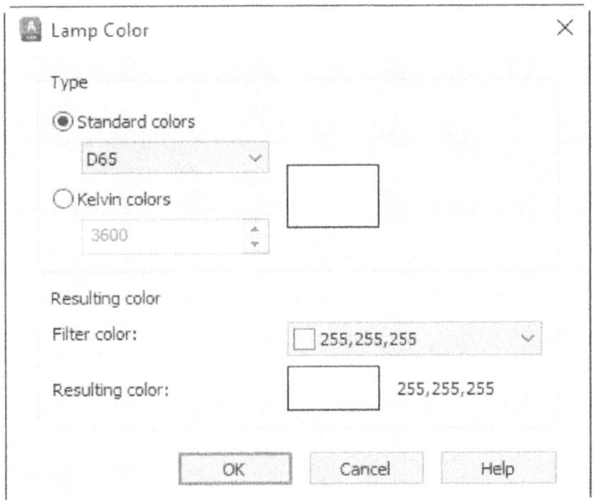

*Figure 13-39 The **Lamp Color** dialog box*

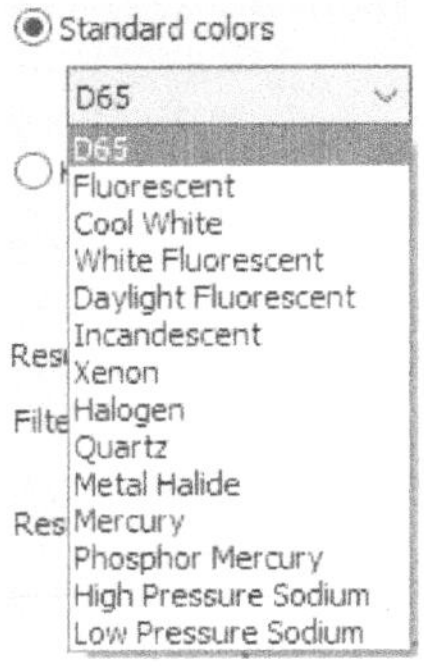

*Figure 13-40 The **Standard colors** drop-down list*

soFtmapped. This option is used to display the shadow with blurred edges. This gives a more realistic effect to the rendered image. If this sub-option is selected, you will have to specify the map size and softness of the shadow. The map size is calculated in terms of pixels. The greater the number of pixels, the better is the shadow. However, if the map size is large, the time taken to render the model will also increase. The shadow softness is used to specify the softness for the shadow. If the value of this option is increased, the shadow will be blurred. Figure 13-41 shows a model with a shadow map size=128 and softness=5, and Figure 13-42 shows a model with a shadow map size=1024 and softness=2.

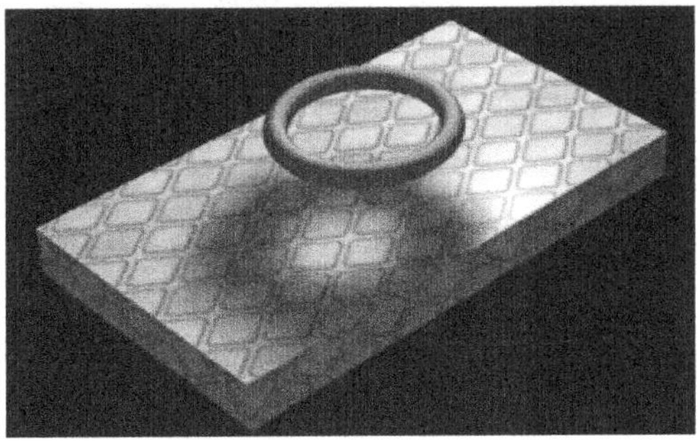

*Figure 13-41 Shadow map size =**128** and softness = **5***

*Figure 13-42 Shadow map size =**1024** and softness = **2***

Tip

You can view the best shadow effect by keeping the value of the shadow map size 512 or 1024 and the shadow softness between 3 and 4.

softsAmpled. This option is used to specify the shape of the point light lamp. The shadow of the object will be displayed depending upon the shape of the point light lamp. The prompt sequence for this option is given next.

Enter an option to change [Name/Intensity factor/Status/Photometry/shadoW/Attenuation/filterColor/eXit] <eXit>: **W** Enter.
Enter [Off/Sharp/soFtmapped/softsAmpled] <Sharp>: **A** Enter.
Enter an option to change [Shape/sAmples/Visible/eXit]<eXit>: **S** Enter.
Enter shape [Linear/ Disk/ Rect/ Sphere/ Cylinder] <Sphere>: *Enter an option to specify the shape of the slit from which the point light will pass through.*

After specifying the shape of the slit, you will be prompted to specify the dimensions of the shape. For example, you can specify the radius of the sphere or the length and width of a rectangle. The prompt sequence for the **Cylinder** option is given next.

Enter shape [Linear/Disk/Rect/Sphere/Cylinder] <Sphere>: **C** Enter.
Enter radius <0.0000>: *Specify the radius of the cylindrical slit.*
Enter Length <0.0000>: *Specify the height of the cylindrical slit.*
Enter an option to change [Shape/sAmples/Visible/eXit]<eXit>: *Specify an option or press* Enter.

The **sAmples** option in the above prompt is used to specify the size of the shadow samples for light. The default value of the shadow sample is 16. The **Visible** option is used to specify whether to display the shape of the lamp in rendering or not. Figure 13-43 displays the rendered image of a cylindrical shape point light without the visibility of the point light shape. Figure 13-44 displays the same rendered image with the point light shape visible.

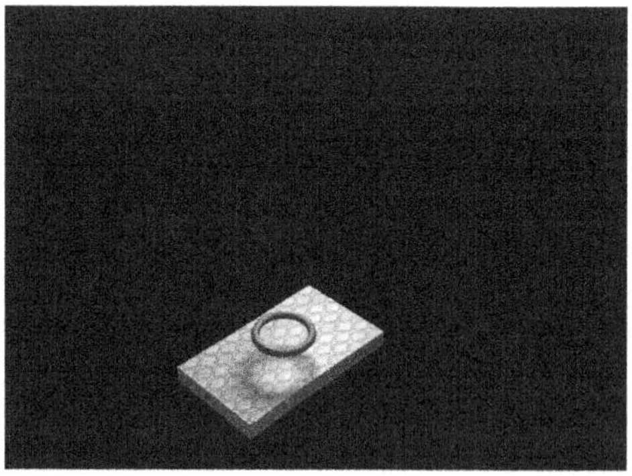

Figure 13-43 *Rendered image with the shape of cylindrical point light not visible*

Figure 13-44 *Rendered image with the shape of point light visible*

Note

The shape of the point light is also displayed in the drawing area close to the point light. When you move the cursor over the point light, the shape of the point light is highlighted in default color.

Attenuation

The light intensity is defined as the amount of light falling per unit of area. The intensity of light is inversely proportional to the distance between the light source and the object. Therefore, the intensity decreases as the distance increases. This phenomenon is called Attenuation. In AutoCAD, it occurs only with spotlights and a point light.

In Figure 13-45, light is emitted by a point source. Assume the amount of light incident on Area1 is I. Therefore, the intensity of light on Area1 = I/Area. As light travels farther from the source, it covers a larger area. The amount of light falling on Area2 is the same as on Area1 but the area is larger. Therefore, the intensity of light for Area2 is smaller (Intensity of light for Area2 = I/Area). Area1 will be brighter than Area2 because of a higher light intensity. The prompt sequence that will follow after selecting this option is given next.

Enter an option to change [attenuation Type/Use limits/attenuation start Limit/attenuation End limit/eXit] <eXit>:
Select a sub-option or press the ENTER *key.*

The sub-options that you can select at the above prompt are:

attenuation Type. AutoCAD render provides you with the following three types of attenuation.

None. If you select the **None** sub-option for the light falloff, the brightness of the objects will be independent of the distance. This means that the objects that are far away from the point light source will be as bright that are close to it.

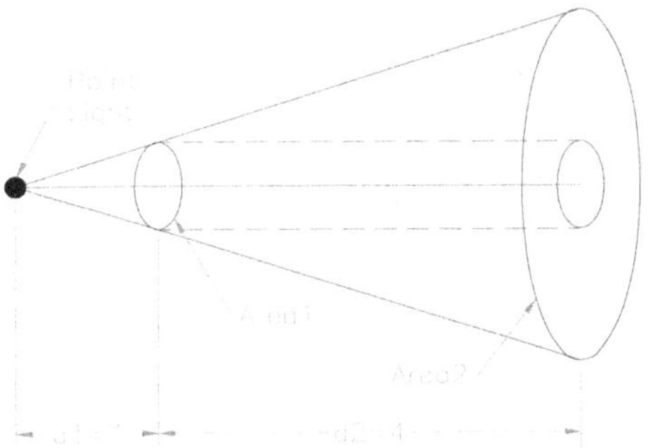

Figure 13-45 *Example of attenuation*

Inverse linear. In this sub-option, the light falling on the object (brightness) is inversely proportional to the distance of the object from the light source (Brightness = 1/Distance). As the distance increases, the brightness decreases. For example, assume that the intensity of the light source is I and the object is located at a distance of 2 units from the light source. Now, the brightness or intensity = I/2. If the distance is 8 units, the intensity (light falling on the object per unit area) = I/8. The brightness is a linear function of the distance of the object from the light source.

inverse Squared. In this sub-option, the light falling on the object (brightness) is inversely proportional to the square of the distance between the object and the light source (Brightness = $1/\text{Distance}^2$). For example, assume that the intensity of the light source is I and the object is located at a distance of 2 units from the light source. Now, the brightness or intensity = $I/(2)^2$ = I/4. If the distance is 8 units, the intensity (light falling on the object per unit area) = $I/(8)^2$ = I/64.

Use limits. This option is used to specify whether you want to use the sub-options of **attenuation start Limit and attenuation End limit**. The effect of these limits can only be visualized in rendering, if the sub-option of **Use limits** is turned on.

attenuation start Limit. This option is used to specify the distance from the centre of the light to the point where the light will start.

attenuation End limit. This option is used to specify the distance from the center of the light at which the light will finish. The objects beyond this limit will not be illuminated by this point light.

filterColor

This option is used to specify the color for the point light. You can define a custom color by using the RGB combination. You can select a color by choosing the **Index color** sub-option. Select the sub-option **Hsl** to define the color by Hue, Saturation, and Luminance. You can also specify the color of the point light from the color book by choosing the **colorBook** sub-option. Next, enter the name of the color book from which you want to choose the color.

eXit

This option is used to finish the process of defining the point light properties and to exit the **Point** tool.

Note

The lightings in the photometric workflow always follow the inverse squared attenuation type and the attenuation properties cannot be modified later on for photometric lights.

Tip

Instead of specifying all the above-mentioned properties of the point light in the tool itself, you can also specify or modify all the properties later on from the ***Properties*** *palette of the point light.*

Example 2

In this example, you will download the drawing file of the model shown in Figure 13-46 from *https://www.cadcim.com*. The path of the file is as follows: *Textbooks > CAD/CAM > AutoCAD Advanced > Advanced AutoCAD 2023: A Problem-Solving Approach, 3D and Advanced > Input Files*. Next, you will apply the point light at the lintel of the window and at the lintel of the door of the model, as shown in Figure 13-47. Choose your own materials to make the model look realistic and then render it.

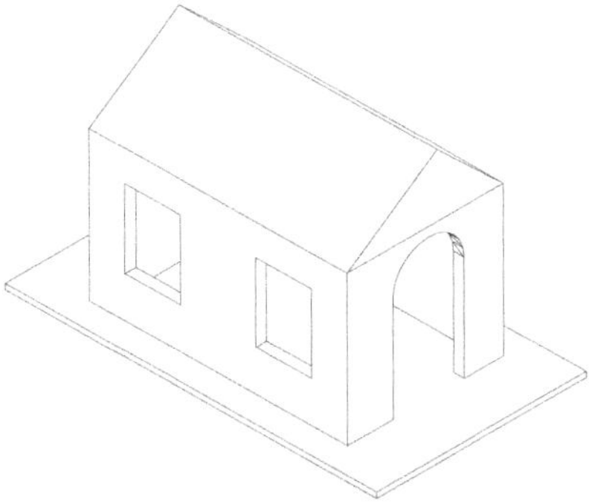

Figure 13-46 Model for Example 2

Figure 13-47 Model after rendering

1. Download the model shown in Figure 13-46 using the path mentioned above.

2. Choose materials from **Material Browser** and then attach them to the model as described in Example 1. (Recommended: Use **Masonry - Stone > Limestone - Ashlar Coursed** for Walls, **Ceramic - Tile > Mosaic Blue** for flooring, and **Flooring - Vinyl - Diamonds 1** for roof.)

3. Choose the **Point** tool from **Visualize > Lights > Create Light** drop-down to add a point light.

4. Choose the **Turn off the default lighting (recommended)** option from the **Lighting - Viewport Lighting Mode** message box. (This message box will be displayed when you create the light for the first time).

5. The prompt sequence of the **Point** light tool is given next.

   Specify source location <0,0,0>: *Specify the location of the point light at the lintel of the first window*
   Enter an option to change [Name/Intensity factor/Status/Photometry/shadoW/Attenuation/filterColor/eXit] <eXit>: **N** Enter.
   Enter light name <Pointlight>: **1** Enter.
   Enter an option to change [Name/Intensity factor/Status/Photometry/shadoW/Attenuation/filterColor/eXit] <eXit>: **C** Enter.
   Enter true color (R,G,B) or enter an option [Index color/Hsl/colorBook]<255,255,255>: **I** Enter.
   Enter color name or number (1-255): **Yellow** Enter.
   Enter an option to change [Name/Intensity factor/Status/Photometry/shadoW/Attenuation/filterColor/eXit] <eXit>: **I** Enter.
   Enter intensity (0.00 - max float) <1.0000>: *Specify the intensity based on the size of the objects in the drawing and press the* Enter key.
   Enter an option to change [Name/Intensity factor/Status/Photometry/shadoW/

Attenuation/filterColor/eXit] <eXit>: **S** Enter.
Enter status [oN/oFf] <On>: Enter.

6. Similarly, you can set the second light at the lintel of the door. Set the color of the light to green.

   Now, you need to set the background of the image from black to white. You can also set any image as the background image.

7. Invoke the **VIEW** command; the **View Manager** dialog box is displayed. Choose the **New** button from it; the **New View/Shot Properties** dialog box is displayed.

8. Select the **Solid** option from the **Background** drop-down list in the **Background** area in the **View Properties** tab of the dialog box; the **Background** dialog box is displayed.

9. Click on the **Color** swatch and select the white color as the background color and exit the dialog box.

10. Assign a name to the view in the **New View/ Shot Properties** dialog box and then exit it.

11. Select the view from the **Views** list and choose the **Apply** button.

12. Choose the **Render to size** tool in the **Render** panel; the **Render** window is displayed and the rendering process starts. The rendered image is displayed in the **Render** window. The rendered image looks similar to the image shown in Figure 13-48.

Figure 13-48 *Rendered model of a house*

Tip
*You can increase the smoothness of the rendered curved object by increasing the value of the **FACETRES** system variable. The default value of this variable is 0.5. Set this value close to **6**.*

Spotlight

Ribbon: Visualize > Lights > Create Light drop-down > Spot
Menu Bar: View > Render > Light > New Spotlight **Command:** SPOTLIGHT

A spotlight emits light in the defined direction with a cone-shaped light beam. This light has a focused beam that starts from a point and is targeted at another point. This type of light is generally used to illuminate a specific point, such as illuminating a person on a stage. The phenomenon of attenuation also applies to spotlights. This light source can be added by choosing the **Spot** light tool from the **Create Light** drop-down. When you choose this tool, you will be prompted to enter two values. As already mentioned, this type of light source has a start point and a target point. Therefore, you will first be prompted to specify the light location and then the light target. The prompt sequence displayed when the **Spot** light tool is invoked is given next.

Specify source location <0,0,0>: *Specify the point where you want to place the spotlight.*
Specify target location <0,0,-10>: *Specify the location on the object where you want to focus the spotlight.*
Enter an option to change [Name/Intensity factor/Status/Photometry/Hotspot/Falloff/shadoW/Attenuation/filterColor/eXit] <eXit>: *Specify an option or press* Enter.

Most of the options in the **Spot** light tool are similar to those in the **Point** tool. The options that are different are discussed next.

Hotspot/Falloff

As mentioned earlier, the spotlight has a focused beam of light that is targeted at a particular point. Therefore, there are two cones that comprise the spotlight.

The hotspot is the same as the cone that carries the highest intensity light beam. In this cone, the light beam is the most focused and is defined in terms of an angle, refer to Figures 13-49(a) and 13-49(b).

The prompt sequence for the **Hotspot** option is given next.

Enter an option to change [Name/Intensityfactor/Status/Photometry/Hotspot/Falloff/shadoW/Attenuation/filterColor/eXit]<eXit>: **H** Enter.
Enter hotspot angle (0.00-160.00) <45.0000>: *Specify the interior angle of the cone in which the intensity of light will be high or press the* Enter *key to accept the default value.*

The other cone is called a falloff and it specifies the full cone of light. It is the area around the hotspot where the intensity of the beam of light is not very high, as shown in Figures 13-49(a) and 13-49(b). It is defined in terms of an angle. The value of the hotspot and the falloff can vary from 0 to 160. The prompt sequence for the **Falloff** option is given next.

Enter an option to change [Name/Intensity factor/Status/Photometry/Hotspot/Falloff/shadoW/Attenuation/filterColor/eXit]<eXit>: **F** Enter.
Enter falloff angle (0.00-160.00) <current>: *Specify the interior angle of the cone in which the intensity of the light will be high or press the* Enter *key to accept the default value.*

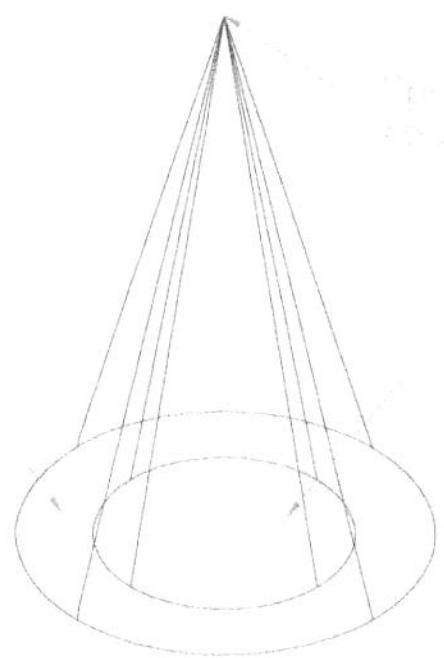

Figure 13-49(a) *The hotspot and falloff cones*

Figure 13-49(b) *The hotspot and falloff after rendering*

> **Tip**
> *The value of hotspot should always be less than the value of falloff. If you set the value of the hotspot more than the value of the falloff, then the value of the falloff will automatically change to one degree greater than the value of the hotspot.*

Distant Light

Ribbon: Visualize > Lights > Create Light drop-down > Distant
Toolbar: Lights > New Distant Light
Menu Bar: View > Render > Light > New Distant Light **Command:** DISTANTLIGHT

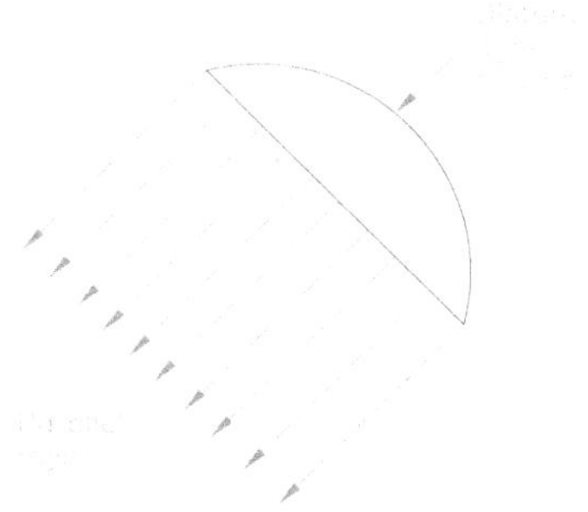

Figure 13-50 *Distant light source*

A distant light source emits a uniform parallel beam of light in a single direction only, refer to Figure 13-50. The intensity of the light beam does not decrease with the distance. It remains constant. For example, the sunrays can be assumed to be a distant light source because the light rays are parallel. When you use a distant light source in a drawing, the location of the light source does not matter; only the direction is critical. Distant light is mostly used to light objects or a backdrop uniformly and for getting the effect of the sunlight. The distant lights are inaccurate and their use in photometric workflow is not preferred. Therefore, the **Distant** light tool is not available for the use in the photometric workflow. However, to use the distant light in photometric workflow, choose the **Distant** tool from the **Create Light** drop-down of the **Lights** panel in the **Visualise** tab; the **Lighting - Viewport Lighting Mode** message box will be displayed on the screen. Choose the **Turn off the default lighting (recommended)** option so that the effect of the distant lights can be seen. On doing so, the **Lighting - Photometric Distant Lights** message box is displayed, refer to Figure 13-51. Choose the **Allow distant lights** button from this message box to invoke the **Distant** light tool. The prompt sequence displayed when the **Distant** light tool is invoked is given next.

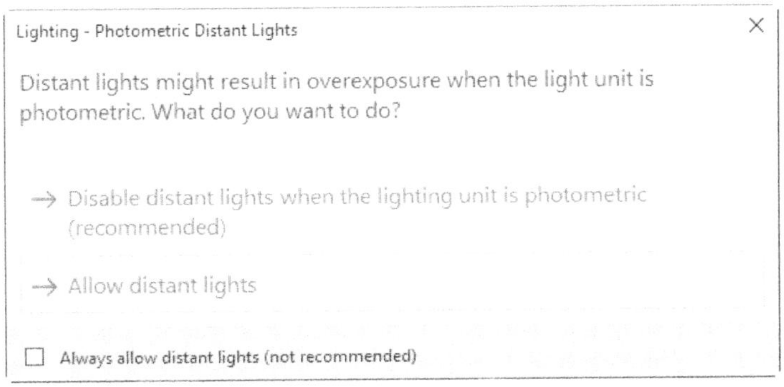

Figure 13-51 *The* ***Lighting - Photometric Distant Lights*** *message box*

Specify light direction FROM <0,0,0> or [Vector]: *Specify the start point to represent the viewing direction of the distant light or type* **V** *and press the Enter key.*
Specify light direction TO <1,1,1>: *Specify the endpoint to represent the viewing direction of the distant light.*
Enter an option to change [Name/Intensity factor/Status/Photometry/shadoW/filterColor/eXit] <eXit>: *Specify an option.*

If you select the **Vector** option at the **Specify light direction FROM <0,0,0> or [Vector]** prompt, then you will have to specify the vector direction in which the distant light will focus. The options in the **Distant** light tool are similar to those in the **Point** tool.

Web Light

Ribbon: Visualize > Lights > Create Light drop-down > Weblight
Command: WEBLIGHT

Web lights are used to create illuminated scenes that look more realistic than those created by using the spot or point lights. You can create a web light by invoking the **Weblight** tool from the **Lights** panel. On invoking this tool, you are prompted to specify the source and then the target point. Specify the source and then the target point. Next, specify the name, intensity, status, photometry, web file, shadows, etc to create the web light. The web lights offer a detailed 3D distribution of the intensity of a light in all directions. The distribution can be isotropic or anisotropic. The isotropic distribution represents a sphere-shaped web, and its effect will be the same as that of point light. However, the web light is generally used for anisotropic or non-uniform light distribution. The anisotropic distribution gives a unique washed effect on the surface it hits. The information regarding this light distribution is saved in an AutoCAD program file having extension *.ies*. These files are generally provided by manufacturers of lights and fixtures. You can load the manufacturers' *.ies* files in the **Photometric Web** panel of the **Properties** palette.To load the .ies files, go to the **PROPERTIES** palette; choose the swatch displayed on the right in the web file box; the **Select Web File** dialog box will be displayed, refer to Figure 13-52. In this palette, you can set the other properties such as intensity, as well.

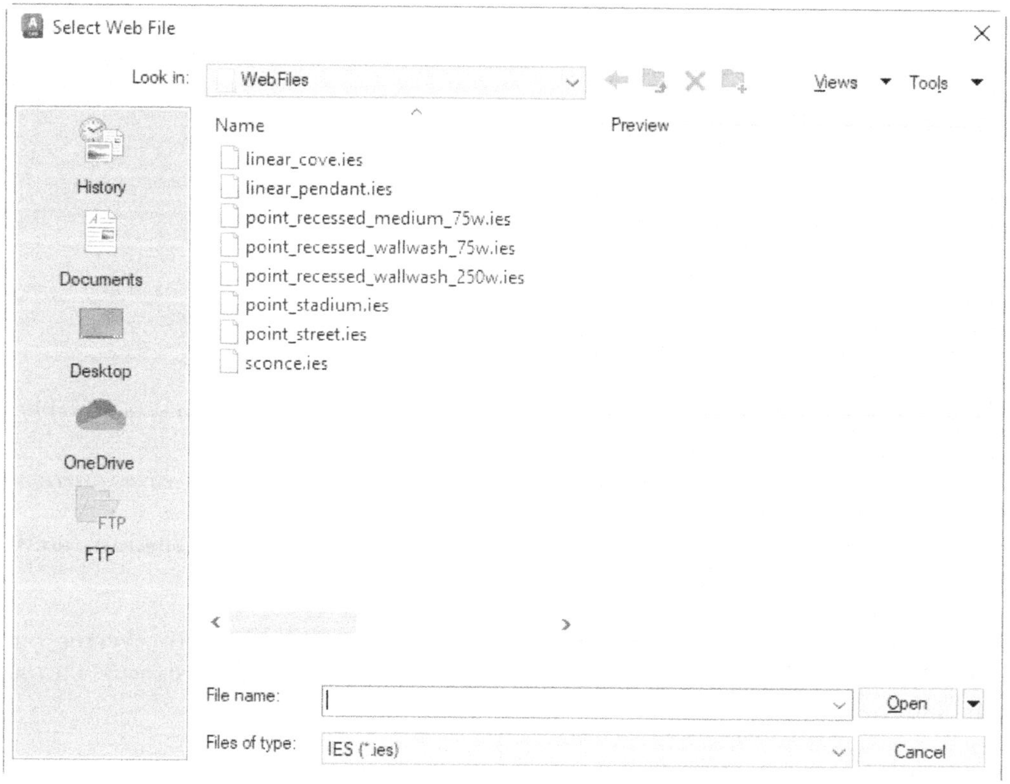

*Figure 13-52 The **Select Web File** dialog box*

Sun Light

Ribbon: Visualize > Sun & Location (Inclined Arrow)
Menu Bar: View > Render > Light > Sun Properties **Toolbar:** Lights > Sun Properties
Command: SUNPROPERTIES

This light is similar to the actual sun light in which the rays are parallel and have the same intensity at any distance. The angle subtended by rays on an object depends on the location, date, and time specified. You can also change the intensity and color of the sunlight. Unlike distant light, sunlight can only be one in number. In the photometric workflow, you can also control the illumination effect when the sky comes between the sunlight and the object. This helps in adding more realistic lighting caused by the interaction between the sun and the sky.

To use sunlight, click on the inclined arrow in the **Sun & Location** panel of the **Visualize** tab; the **SUN PROPERTIES** palette will be displayed, as shown in Figure 13-53. The options in this palette are discussed next.

General

In this area, you can switch on or off the sunlight and change its intensity and color.

Sky Properties

These properties are only available while working in the photometric workflow. You can use the sky in between the model and the sun for the illumination of the model. The options available in the **Status** drop-down list are **Sky Off**, **Sky Background**, and **Sky Background and Illumination**. These options are also available in the **Sky Status** drop-down list under **Sun & Location** panel of the **Visualize** tab. Note that these options are available in the Perspective view only.

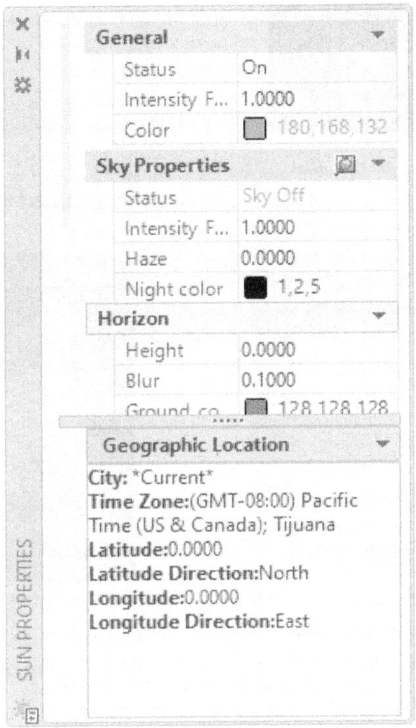

*Figure 13-53 The **SUN PROPERTIES** palette*

Figure 13-54 displays a model rendered by using the **Sky Off** option, Figure 13-55 displays a model rendered by using the **Sky Background** option, and Figure 13-56 displays the model rendered by using the **Sky Background and Illumination** option. The **Intensity Factor** edit box is used to magnify the brightness of the light reaching the object after passing through the sky. Figure 13-56 displays the rendered model by choosing the **Sky Background and Illumination** option and intensity factor set to **1** and Figure 13-57 displays the same model rendered by selecting the **Sky Background and Illumination** option and intensity factor set to **0.2**. The **Haze** edit box determines the amount of scattering in the atmosphere and the haze value can vary from 0 to 15. Figure 13-56 displays a rendered model with haze value set to **0** and Figure 13-58 displays the same model rendered with haze value set to **7**. The **Night Colour** edit box allows you to specify the colour of the night sky.

Figure 13-54 *Model rendered using the* ***Sky Off*** *option*

Figure 13-55 *Model rendered using the* ***Sky Background*** *option*

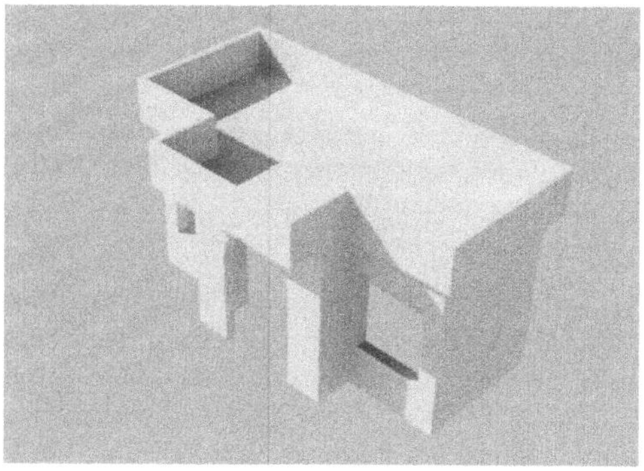

Figure 13-56 *Model rendered using the* ***Sky Background and Illumination*** *option with the intensity and haze values set to* ***1*** *and* ***0****, respectively*

Figure 13-57 *Model rendered using the* ***Sky Background and Illumination*** *option with the intensity value set to* ***0.2***

Horizon. The options in this area are used to control the location and appearance of the ground. Figure 13-59 displays a rendered model created by selecting the **Sun & Sky Background** option and setting that view as current. The ground color for the rendered image is set to **Cyan**.

Sun disk appearance. The properties under this rollout are used to control the appearance of the sun disk such as its size, intensity, and so on, when a view is saved with the **Sun & Sky Background**.

*Figure 13-58 Model rendered using the **Sky Background and Illumination** option with the intensity and haze values set to **1** and **7**, respectively*

*Figure 13-59 Model rendered with the view saved as **Sun & Sky Background** and ground color set to **Cyan***

Note

*You can also specify or modify the **Sky Properties** from the **Adjust Sun & Sky Background** dialog box which can be displayed by clicking on the swatch on the right side of the **Background** area in the **New View / Shot Properties** dialog box, refer to Figure 13-60.*

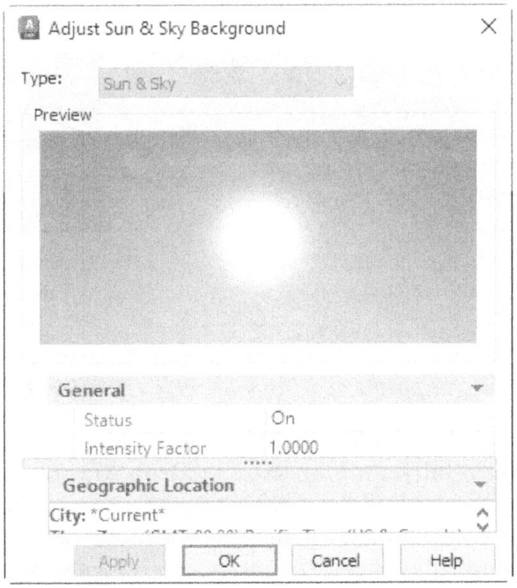

*Figure 13-60 The **Adjust Sun & Sky Background** dialog box*

Sun Angle Calculator

In this area, you can set the date and time in the **Date** and **Time** edit boxes, respectively. You can also switch on or off the effect of day light settings in the rendering. Apart from this, you can also view some read only information in this field such as the azimuth and altitude of the sun light direction. You can also view the default light source vector as the coordinates in the X, Y, and Z list boxes in the **Source Vector** area.

Geographic Location

This area displays information about the geographic location of the place where you want to view the light effect. You can edit this information by choosing the **From Map** tool from the **Set Location** drop-down of the **Sun & Location** panel of the **Visualize** tab; the **Geographic Location - Specify Location (Page 1 of 2)** window will be displayed with various options to define the location, refer to Figure 13-61. Note that you need to log into your Autodesk account to set the location from online maps. You can pick the location from this window. You can also define the location by importing the exact location data like longitude, latitude, and altitude from the *.kml* or *.kmz* files. To do so, choose the **From file** tool from the **Set Location** drop-down. The options in this dialog box are given next.

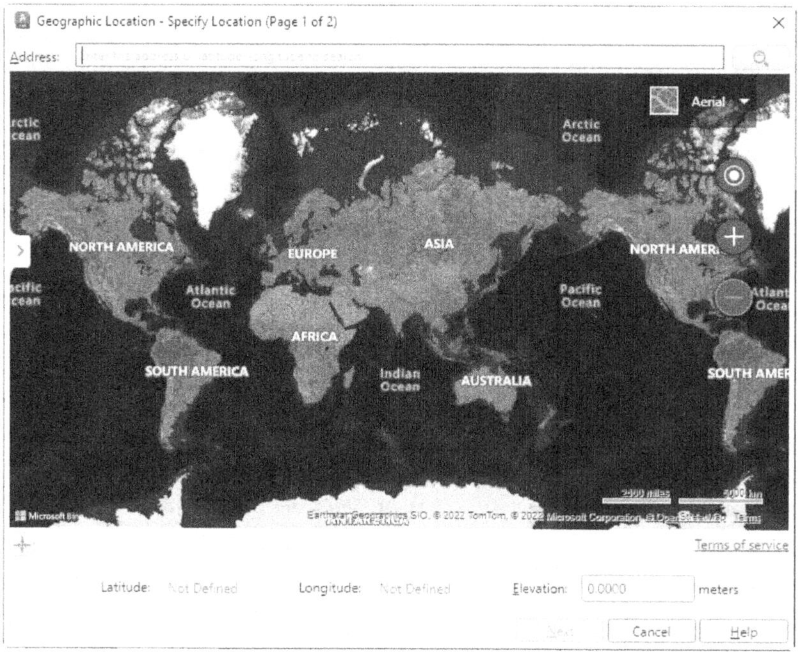

*Figure 13-61 The **Geographic Location - Specify Location (Page 1 of 2)** window*

You can select the location of drawing from the map available in this window. To do so, zoom to the required location, right-click and choose the **Drop Marker Here** option. On selecting the locations, a red colored cursor will be displayed on them. Alternatively, you can enter the location in the **Address** edit box available at the top of the dialog box. After entering the name of location, press Enter; the results related to the specified location will be displayed on the left side of the dialog box. Also, the **Drop Marker Here** button will be displayed on the selected result. Choose the button; the marker will be placed at the specified location.

You can also specify the values for GIS Coordinate System. To do so, choose the **Next** button from the **Geographic Location - Specify Location (Page 1 of 2)**; the **Geographic Location - Set Coordinate System (Page 2 of 2)** will be displayed, as shown in Figure 13-62. Also, a list of different coordinate systems will be displayed. Select the required coordinate system from the list. You can also specify different time zones and drawing units by selecting required options from the **Time Zone** and **Drawing Unit** drop-down lists. Next, choose the **Next** button from the dialog box; you will be prompted to specify a point for the location. Specify the point; you will be prompted to specify the north direction angle. Specify the direction; the geographic map will be displayed in the drawing area. Also, the **Geolocation** contextual tab will be added in the **Ribbon**, as shown in Figure 13-63.

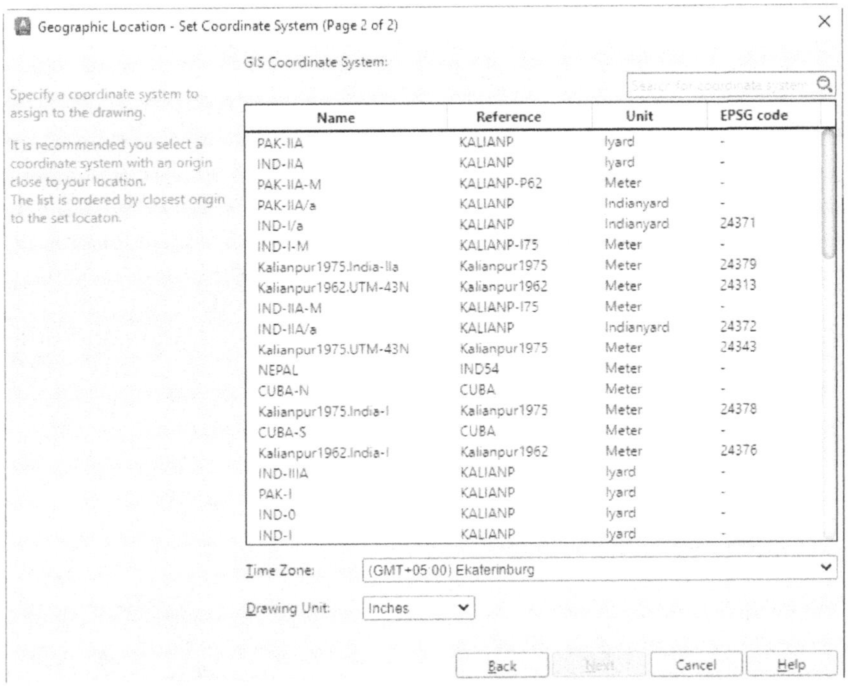

***Figure 13-62** The **Geographic Location - Specify Location (Page 2 of 2)** window*

You can use the options in this contextual tab to edit, reorient, remove, and map the locations. You can also capture area and viewport using the options in this tab.

***Figure 13-63** The **Geolocation** contextual tab*

Note

*1. If the **Sun Status** button is chosen in the **Sun & Location** panel, sunlight is turned on.*

2. Except for the geographic location, the rest of the settings for the sun and the sky are saved for a particular viewport and not for the entire drawing.

You can also switch the sun light on and off, set the sky background illumination, change the date and time, open and close the **Sun Properties** palette and the **Geographic Location** window directly from the **Visualize** tab of the **Ribbon**, refer to Figure 13-64.

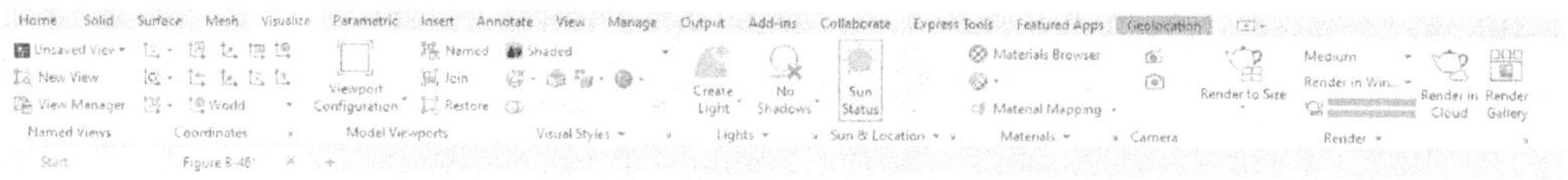

*Figure 13-64 The **Visualize** tab of the **Ribbon***

Example 3

In this example, you will download the drawing file of the model shown in Figure 13-65 from *https://www.cadcim.com*. The path of the file is as follows: *Textbooks > CAD/CAM > AutoCAD Advanced > Advanced AutoCAD 2023: A Problem-Solving Approach, 3D and Advanced > Input Files*. Next, you will apply materials of your choice to the downloaded model. Also, you will set the sun light using the geographic location and render it. The model after rendering should look similar to the model shown in Figure 13-66. The geographic location and other parameters are given next.

City: New York, Date: 15 April, 2023 Time: 04:00 pm

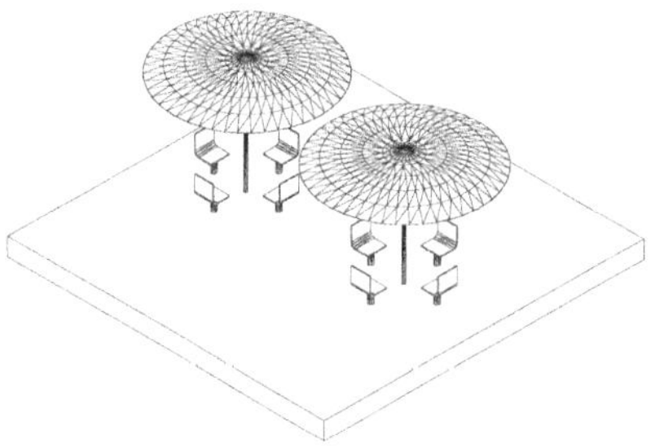

***Figure 13-65** Model for Example 3 before rendering*

***Figure 13-66** Model for Example 3 after rendering*

1. Download the model shown in Figure 13-65 using the path mentioned above.

2. Select the materials of your choice and apply them to the model, as explained earlier.

3. Choose the **Sky Background and Illumination** option from **Visualise > Sun & Location > Sky** drop-down.

4. Click on the inclined arrow in the **Sun & Location** panel of the **Visualize** tab to invoke the **SUN PROPERTIES** palette and set the **Intensity Factor** value to **2.0** under the **Sky Properties** rollout.

5. Specify a color of your choice for the ground in the **Ground color** edit box under the **Horizon** sub-rollout and then exit the **SUN PROPERTIES** palette.

6. Choose the **Set Location > From Map** tool from the **Sun & Location** panel of the **Visualize** tab; the **Geographic Location** window is displayed.

7. Enter **New York** in the search box located at the top of the **Geographic Location - Specify Location (Page 1 of 2)** window and choose the search button next to it; the search results are displayed on the left side of the window.

8. Place the cursor on **New York, NY** in the search results area and choose the **Drop Marker Here** button; a marker is placed in New York. Choose the **Next** Button; the **Geographic Location - Set Coordinate System (Page 2 of 2)** window will be displayed. The time zone is updated in the **Time Zone** drop-down list. Select any GIS coordinate system from the given list.

9. Choose the **Next** button from the dialog box; you are prompted to specify the location point in the drawing.

10. Select the point on the model, as shown in Figure 13-67; you are prompted to specify the north direction.

11. Move the cursor vertically and click to specify the north direction.

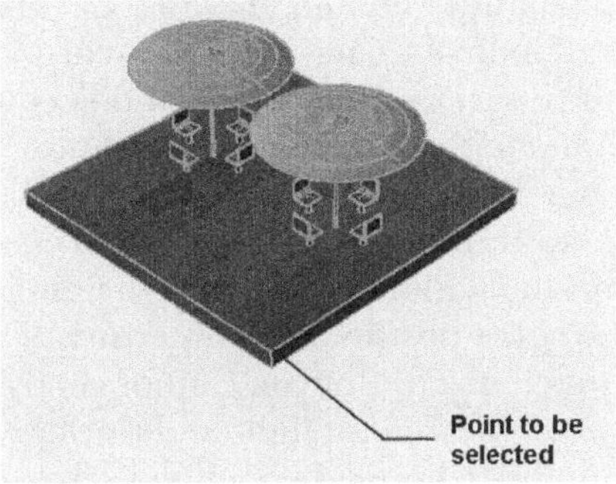

Figure 13-67 *Location point in the model*

12. Choose the **Sun Status** button from the **Sun & Location** panel of the **Visualize** tab; the **Lighting - Viewport Lighting Mode** message box is displayed. Choose the **Turn off the default lighting (recommended)** option.

13. Set the date and time as **4/15/2023** and **4:00 PM** in the **Date** and **Time** edit boxes, respectively in the **Sun & Location** panel of the **Visualize** tab.

14. Choose the **Render to size** tool from the **Visualize** tab to invoke the **Render** window. The rendering process will start and the rendered image will be displayed in the **Render** window.

CONVERTING LIGHTS CREATED IN AutoCAD'S PREVIOUS RELEASE INTO AUTOCAD 2023 FORMAT

For converting a model created in AutoCAD 2014 or earlier version of AutoCAD to AutoCAD 2023 format such that it supports both the standard workflow and the photometric workflow, set the value of **LIGHTINGUNITS** system variable to 1 or 2. The models and lights created prior to AutoCAD 2023 can be converted to the lights of AutoCAD 2023 by the **CONVERTOLDLIGHTS** command. The prompt sequence to do so is given next.

Command: **CONVERTOLDLIGHTS**
Loading materials...done.
2 light(s) converted

In the prompt sequence, only 2 lights have been converted for the current drawing. Therefore, the prompt sequence displays **2 light(s) converted**. The prompt sequence will display the number of lights converted and also the lights that are not converted. Note that after converting the lights, their effect is not always the same as in their original versions. Therefore, you have to modify some parameters such as intensity, color, and so on.

MODIFYING LIGHTS

As mentioned earlier, the lights and the lighting effects are important in rendering in order to create a realistic representation of an object. The sides of an object that face the light must appear brighter and the sides that are on the other side of the object must be darker. This smooth gradation of light produces a realistic image of the object. If the light intensity is uniform on the entire surface, the rendered object will not look realistic. For example, if you use the **SHADE** command to shade an object, it does not look realistic because the displayed model lacks any kind of gradation of light. Any number of lights can be added to the drawing. The color, location, and direction of all the lights can be specified individually. As mentioned earlier, you can specify an attenuation for the point lights and the spotlights. AutoCAD also allows you to change the color, position, and intensity of any light source. The point light and the spotlight can be interchanged. But you cannot change a distant light into a point light or a spotlight. All lights, except the default light and the sun light, attached to the current drawing are displayed in the light list. Choose the inclined arrow on the **Lights** panel of the **Visualize** tab of the **Ribbon**; the **LIGHTS IN MODEL** palette will be displayed, as shown in Figure 13-68. From this list box, select the light you want to modify, right-click, and then choose the **Properties** option from the shortcut menu displayed. Depending on the type of light selected, the **PROPERTIES** palette will be displayed. For example, if you select a distant light for modifications, the **PROPERTIES** palette with the distant light properties will be displayed. One such **PROPERTIES** palette is shown in Figure 13-69.

***Figure 13-68** The **LIGHTS IN MODEL** palette*

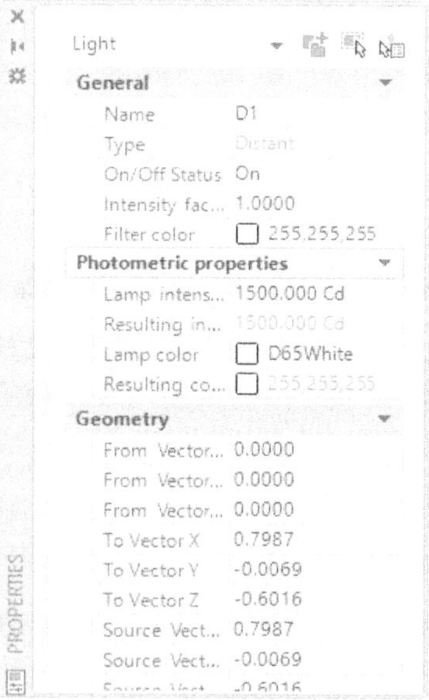

***Figure 13-69** The **PROPERTIES** palette for distant light*

All options in this window are similar to those under the **Point** tool. You can also modify the lights dynamically with the help of grips. This method provides a dynamic preview of the modifications made in lights. The symbols of the point light and the spot light can also be shown or hidden by choosing the **Light glyph display** button from the **Lights** panel of the **Visualize** tab.

UNDERSTANDING RENDERING PRESETS

As mentioned earlier, rendering allows you to control the appearance of the objects in the design. This is done by defining the surface material and the reflective quality of the surface and by adding lights to get the desired effects. The basic rendering has already been discussed earlier in this chapter.

You can also render the model using the **RENDER PRESETS MANAGER** window by choosing the **Render** button displayed at the upper right corner. To invoke the **RENDER PRESETS MANAGER** window, click on the inclined arrow in the **Render** panel of the **Visualize** tab. The options in this drop-down are discussed next.

Current Preset

The **current preset** drop-down list in the **RENDER PRESETS MANAGER** window contains six standard qualities of rendering as presets, refer to Figure 13-70. These are **Low**, **Medium**, **High**, **Coffee-Break Quality**, **Lunch Quality**, and **Overnight Quality**. The lowest quality of rendering is done in the **Low** preset. The quality of rendering goes on improving progressively on selecting different options, and it is the best when you select the **Overnight Quality** preset. However, you can also create your own render presets by creating copies of your current render settings, which will be explained in detail later in this chapter.

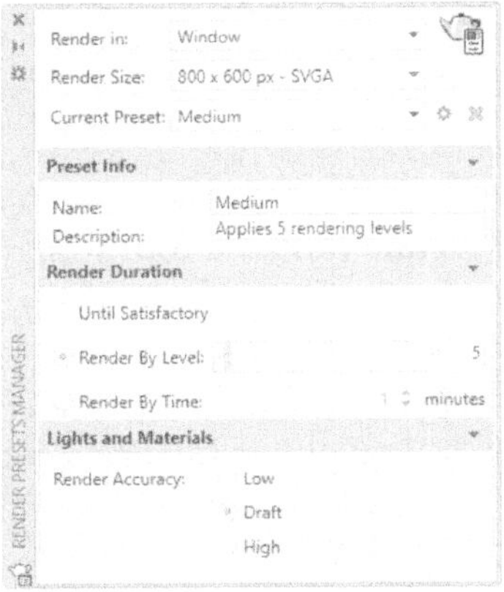

Figure 13-70 *The* ***RENDER PRESETS MANAGER*** *window*

Render Size

In this drop-down list, you can define custom output resolution of a rendered image. If you want to specify a user-defined resolution for output image, select **More Output Settings** from the drop-down list. On doing so, the **Render to Size Output Settings** window will be displayed. In this window, you can define settings for the custom resolution, as shown in Figure 13-71.

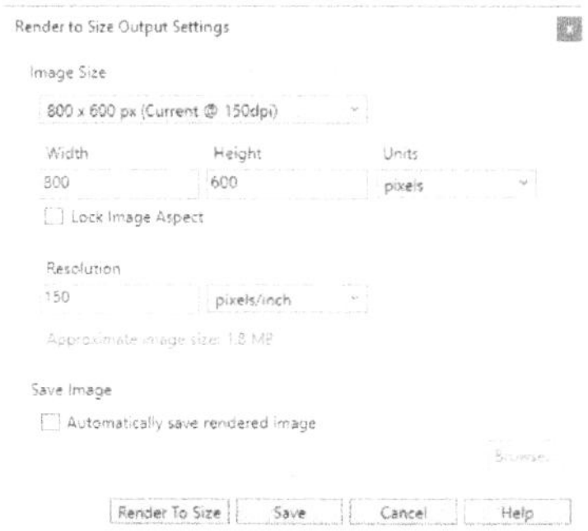

Figure 13-71 The ***Render to Size Output Settings*** *window*

Create Copy

This button is located on the right hand side of the **Current Preset** drop-down list and is used to create a copy of the selected render preset or a new render preset based on the selected render preset. Choose this button to create a copy of a render preset which will also be available in the custom section of the **Current Preset** drop-down list. Now, you can change the render properties of the newly created render preset according to your preferences.

Delete

This button is used to delete the selected custom render preset. You cannot delete the standard render preset.

Preset info

This rollout displays the information about the current preset. Here, you can edit the name and description of the custom render preset.

Render Duration

In this rollout, you can specify the duration of rendering. You can choose **Until Satisfactory, Render By Level**, and **Render By Time** radio buttons from this rollout.

Lights and Materials

In this rollout, you can specify rendering accuracy. You can choose **Low**, **Draft**, or **High** option to specify the desired level of material quality, colors, reflections, and shadows in the rendered image.

Note

Some of the options in the ***RENDER PRESETS MANAGER*** *window that are used for rendering a cropped region, selecting render presets, starting the rendering process, and specifying the resolution size of the rendered file can be directly changed from the* ***Render*** *panel in the* ***Visualize*** *tab, refer to Figure 13-72.*

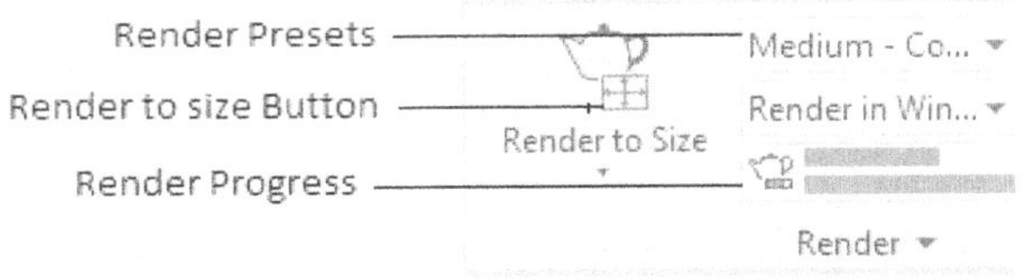

*Figure 13-72 The **Render** panel of the **Visualize** tab*

CONTROLLING THE RENDERING ENVIRONMENT

You can enhance the rendering by adding effects such as the surrounding environment of the model or by adding colors or images to the background of the model. The tools to do so are discussed next.

Rendering with a Background

You can render a model by changing its background. You can set a single color, combination of two colors, combination of three colors, an image, or sun and sky as the background of the model. To render the model with a background, you need to save a named view of the model with a background by using the **VIEW** command, as explained in the **View Manager** dialog box. Next, set the named view with a background as the current view and then render the model with the desired render settings. Figure 13-73 shows a rendered model with its named view saved with the gradient as the background, Figure 13-74 shows a rendered model with its named view saved with an image as the background, and Figure 13-75 shows a rendered model with its named view saved with the Sun and Sky as the background.

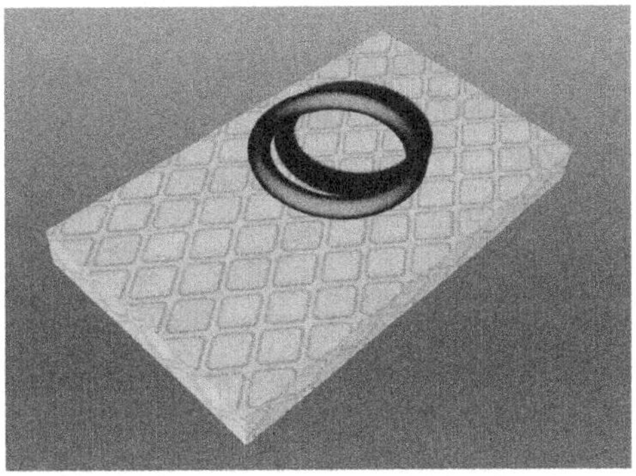

*Figure 13-73 The rendered model with the **Gradient** as the background*

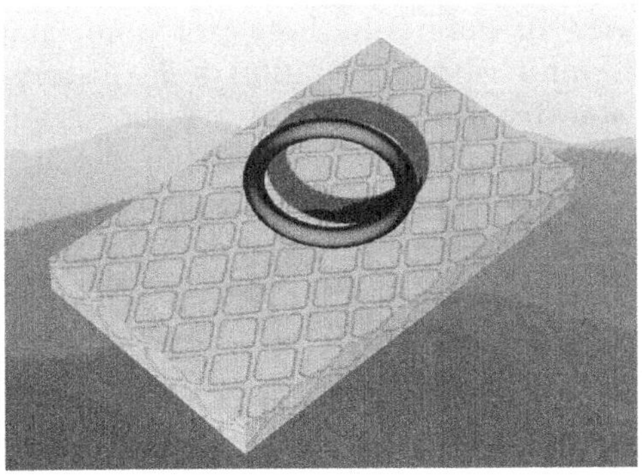

*Figure 13-74 The rendered model with **Image** as the background*

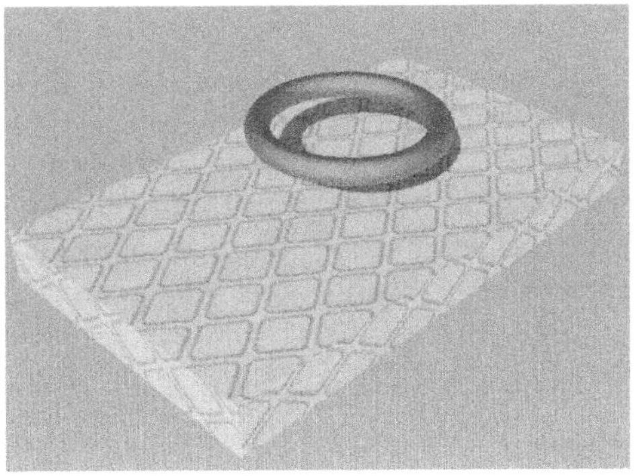

*Figure 13-75 The rendered model with the **Sun & Sky** as the background*

Adjusting the Lighting Exposure to Rendered Image

Ribbon: Visualize > Render > Render Environment and Exposure
Command: FOG / RENDEREXPOSURE / RENDERENVIRONMENT

The **Render Environment & Exposure** window is used to specify image-based lighting (IBL) settings such as image map, rotation, and background display, refer to Figure 13-76. You can use the toggle button in this dialog box to turn on and off the image based lighting when rendering. Using the **Image Based Lighting** drop-down list, you can specify different styles of image based lighting.

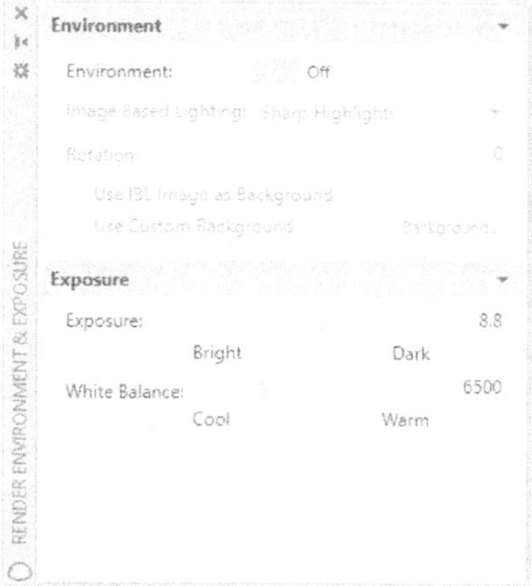

*Figure 13-76 The **RENDER ENVIRONMENT & EXPOSURE** dialog box*

RENDERING A MODEL WITH DIFFERENT RENDER SETTINGS

The rendering depends on the view that is current and the lights that are defined in the drawing. Sometimes, the current view or the lighting setup may not be enough to show all the features of an object. You might need different views with a certain light configuration to show different features of the object. But when you change the view or define the lights for rendering, the previous setup is lost. To bypass this, you can use the rendering information in the history pane of the **Render** window. In the lower portion of the **Render** window, the history pane is located. In this pane, you can get the recent history of the rendered images of the model in the drawing, refer to Figure 13-77. From this history pane, you can regain the previous rendering settings and can also save the rendered images. The data stored in the history pane includes: file name of the rendering, image size, view name (if no named view is used, the view is stored as current view), render time, and the name of the render preset used for the rendering.

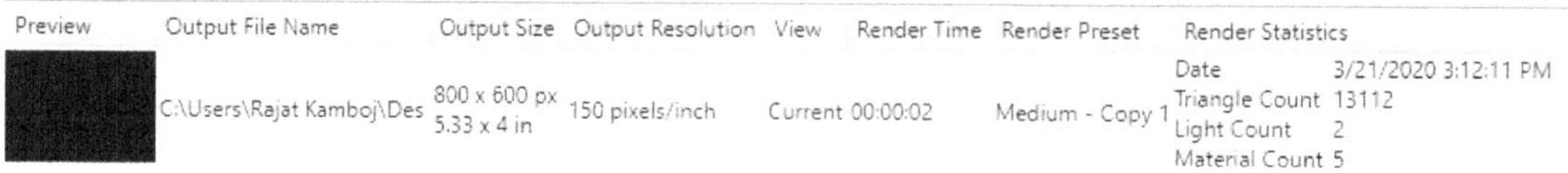

*Figure 13-77 The history pane in the **Render** window*

Right-clicking on a history entry displays a shortcut menu that contains the following options:

Render Again

This option restarts the renderer for the selected history entry with the same settings.

Save

This option displays the **Render Output File** dialog box where you can specify the name and format of the image file. After specifying the name and format of the image file, choose the **Save** button; the **BMP Image Options** dialog box will be displayed(if you choose BMP as the image format). You can choose the color quality of the image file from this dialog box, refer to Figure 13-78. Select the desired radio button and then choose the **OK** button to save the image file.

Save Copy

This option saves the image to a new location without affecting the location stored in the entry.

Make Render Settings Current

This option loads the render settings associated with the selected history entry, if multiple history entries are present with different render presets.

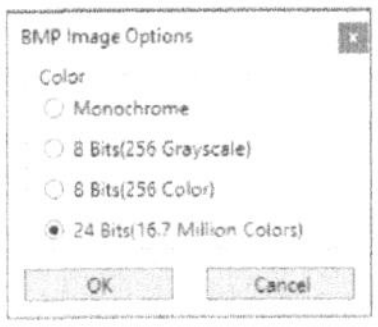

*Figure 13-78 The **BMP Image Options** dialog box*

Remove From The List

This option removes the entry from the history pane.

Delete Output File

This option removes the rendered image from the **Image** pane, but the entry remains in the history pane.

Note

Any entry that is not saved with the drawing exists only for the duration of the current drawing session. Once you close the file or exit the program, the unsaved history entries are lost.

Example 4

In this example, you will open the model used in Example 2 of this chapter and then create two rendered settings. Next, you will render the model with these settings and save the rendered image in a file. The first setting should display the effect of light 1 and the second setting should display the effect of light 2.

1. Open the drawing Example 2.

2. Choose the **Light glyph display** tool from the **Lights** panel of the **Visualize** tab.

3. Select light 2 from the **Lights in Model** palette and choose the **Properties** option from the shortcut menu; the **Properties** palette is displayed. In this palette, select the **Off** option from the **On/Off Status** drop-down list in the **General** rollout.

4. Choose the **Render to size** tool from the **Render** panel in the **Visualize** tab to perform rendering. The rendered model is displayed in the **Render** window with the effect of light 1 only, as shown in Figure 13-79.

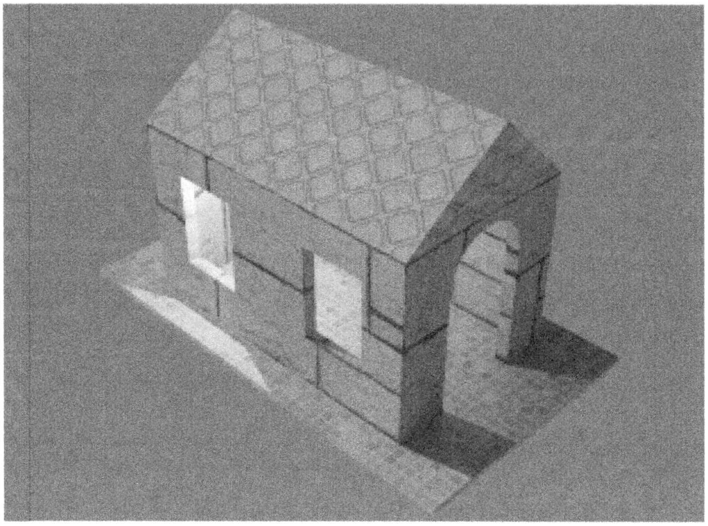

Figure 13-79 *Rendered model with the effect of light 1*

5. Next, switch off light 1 and switch on light 2, as explained in the previous steps, and then render the model. The rendered model is displayed in the **Render** window with the effect of light 2 only, as shown in Figure 13-80.

6. The history pane of the **Render** window displays both the render entries. Right click on one entry and choose the **Save** option from the shortcut menu. Now, specify the location, name, and format in which you want to save the image file in the **Render Output File** dialog box and choose the **Save** button.

7. Specify the **Color** and choose the **OK** button in the **BMP Image Options** dialog box.

8. Similarly, save the second history entry, as explained in Steps 6 and 7.

Note

You can render the model with the same rendered settings for all future references. To do so, select the history entry with that setting and choose the ***Make Render Settings Current*** *option from the shortcut menu.*

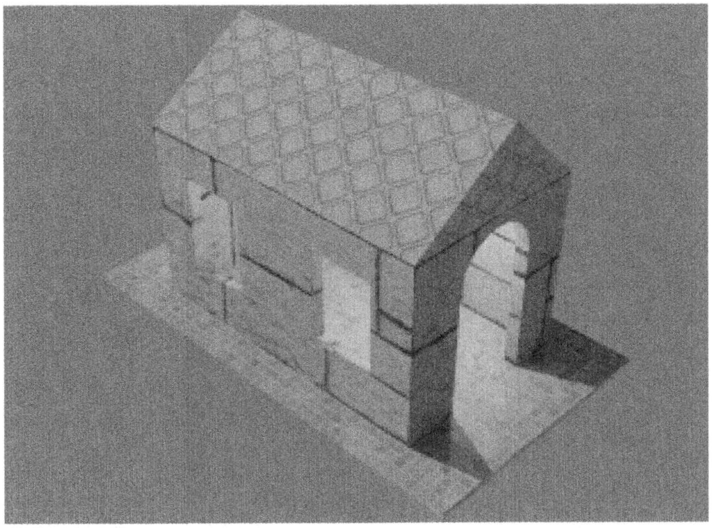

Figure 13-80 Rendered model with the effect of light 2

OBTAINING RENDERING INFORMATION

The bottom side area of the **Render** window is known as the statistics pane. This portion displays the details about the rendering and render settings in effect when the image was created. The information stated in the statistics pane is derived from the settings made in the **Render Presets Manager** window and the information that is generated at the time of the rendering.

SAVING A RENDERED IMAGE

A rendered image can be saved by rendering to a file or by rendering to the screen and then saving it. Redisplaying a saved rendering image requires very less time compared to the time involved in rendering. Various methods of saving the rendered image are discussed next.

Saving the Rendered Image to a File

You can save a rendered image directly to a file. One of the advantages of saving a rendered image to a file is that you can redisplay the rendered image in less time as compared to rendering the image again. Another advantage of saving a rendered image is that when you render a file in the viewport, the resolution of the image on rendering depends on the resolution of your current display. On the other hand, if you render the image to a file, you can specify a higher resolution. Later, you can display this rendered image that has a higher resolution. The rendered images can be saved in different formats, such as BMP, TGA, TIF, JPEG, and PNG. The following steps explain the procedure of saving a rendered image to a file.

1. Select the **More Output Settings** option from the **Render to Size** drop-down list in the **Render** panel of the **Visualize** tab.

2. Select the **Automatically save rendered image** check box and choose the **Browse** button; the **Render Output File** dialog box will be displayed.

3. Specify the file name and file type. Then, choose the **Save** button.

4. Choose the **Render to Size** tool from the **Render** panel of the **Visualize** tab. The rendered image is saved at the specified location.

Saving the Viewport Rendering

If you have selected the **Viewport** option from the **Render In** drop-down list, then the model will be rendered in the selected viewport. A rendered image in the viewport can be saved by using the **Save** option. To do so, choose the **Save** option from the **Tools > Display Image** in the menu bar; the **Render Output File** dialog box will be displayed. This dialog box is used to specify the file name and type. The valid output file formats are BMP, TGA, TIF, JPEG and PNG.

The steps given next explain the procedure of saving a viewport rendering.

1. Choose the **Save** option from **Tools > Display Image** in the menu bar to invoke the **Render Output File** dialog box.

2. Specify the file name and file type.Then, choose the **Save** button.

3. Specify the Color mode and choose the **OK** button in the **BMP Image Options** dialog box.

4. Choose the **Render to Size** tool from the **Render** panel in the **Visualize** tab; the rendered image is saved at the specified location.

Saving the Rendered Image from the Render Window

A rendered image in the **Render** window can be saved using the **Save** button of the **Render** window. In this case, the rendered image can be saved in any of these formats: BMP, TGA, TIF, JPEG, and PNG. The following steps explain the procedure for saving a render-window image:

1. Choose the **Render to Size** tool from the **Visualize** tab; the rendered image will be displayed in the **Render** window.

2. Choose the **Save** option from the shortcut menu displayed on right-clicking on the temporary image. Alternatively, use the **Save** button of the **Render** window to save the rendered image; the **Render Output File** dialog box is displayed.

3. Specify the file name and file type. Then, choose the **Save** button.

4. Specify the Color mode and choose the **OK** button in the **BMP Image Options** dialog box.

PLOTTING RENDERED IMAGES

To plot a rendered design, use the following steps:

1. Open the design to be plotted and then invoke the **Plot** dialog box. Remember that you do not need to first render the design and then invoke the **Plot** dialog box. You can also render the design while plotting. However, the render settings should be specified in advance.

2. Select the printer that supports rendered printing from the **Printer/plotter** area and select the other options.

3. Select the **Rendered** option from the **Shade plot** drop-down list in the **Shaded viewport options** area. If this area is not available by default, then choose **More Options** from the bottom right corner of the **Plot** dialog box.

4. Set the other options in this dialog box and then plot the design. The design will be first rendered and then plotted in the rendered form.

Note
If the ***Rendered*** *option is used for a highly complex set of objects, the hardcopy output might contain only the viewport border.*

UNLOADING AutoCAD RENDER

When you invoke any AutoCAD Render tool, AutoCAD Render is loaded automatically.

If you do not need AutoCAD Render, you can unload it by entering the **ARX** at the Command prompt. You can reload AutoCAD Render by invoking the **RENDER** command or any other command associated with rendering (such as **RENDERENVIRONMENT**, **LIGHT**, and so on).

Command: **ARX**
Enter an option [Files/Groups/Commands/CLasses/Services/Load/Unload]: **U**
Enter ARX/DBX file name to unload: **acrender**
acrender successfully unloaded.

WORKING WITH CAMERAS

Cameras are used to define the 3D perspective view of a model. In AutoCAD, you can place a camera, edit camera settings, turn on/off the camera, and save the perspective view. The options in the **Camera** panel are discussed next.

Create Camera

Ribbon: Visualize > Camera > Create Camera
Command: CAM(CAMERA)

To place a camera, choose the **Create Camera** tool from the **Camera** panel in the **Visualize** tab; you will be prompted to specify the camera location. Specify the camera position; the preview of the camera focus will be displayed and you will be prompted to specify the target location. Click in the drawing area to specify the required target location; the **Enter an option [?/Name/LOcation/Height/Target/LEns/Clipping/View/eXit]<eXit>:** prompt will be displayed. The options in the prompt are discussed next.

?

This option lists all cameras created in the current drawing.

Name

This option is used to specify a name for the camera.

LOcation

This option is used to change the location of the camera.

Height

This option is used to specify the height of the camera.

Target

This option is used to modify the target of the camera.

LEns

This option is used to define the magnification length or zoom factor of camera lens. Note that greater the lens length, narrower will be the view.

Clipping

Clipping planes define the boundaries for a view. On choosing this option, you can specify the location of the front and back clipping planes. On defining the front and back clipping planes, everything between the camera and front clipping plane and the target and back clipping plane will be hidden.

If you choose this option, a message prompting you to enable the front clipping plane will be displayed. If you choose **Yes**, then you will be prompted to specify the offset distance of the clipping plane from the target plane. Specify the required distance and press Enter; a message will be displayed prompting you to enable the back clipping plane. If you choose **Yes**, you will be prompted to specify the offset distance of the clipping plane from the target plane.

Figure 13-81 shows the model with the front and back clipping planes defined at 25 units from the target point. Figure13-82 shows the preview of the resultant model.

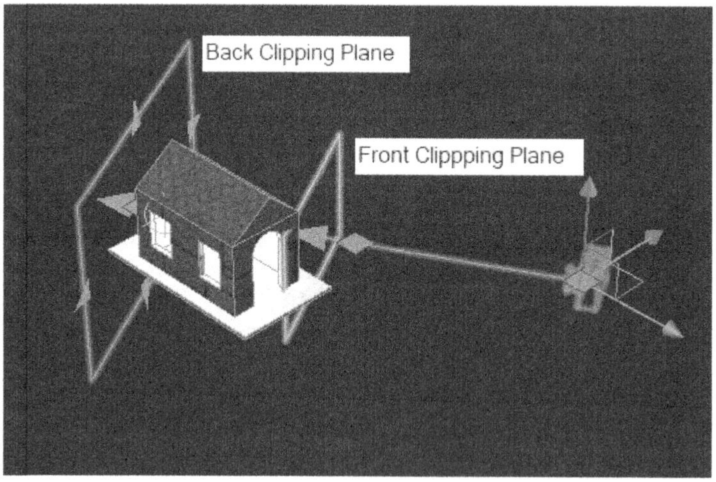

Figure 13-81 *The front and back clipping planes*

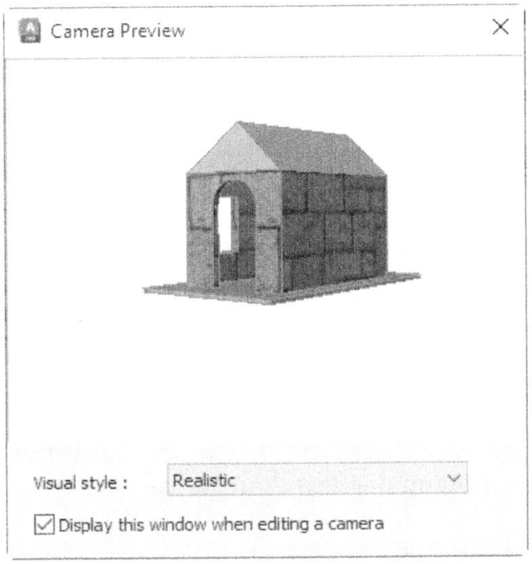

Figure 13-82 The preview of the model

You can turn off the display of front, back, or both clipping planes, display both the clipping planes, or adjust the offset values of the clipping planes using the **Properties** palette. To invoke the **Properties** palette, select the camera, right-click, and then choose the **Properties** option. You can also dynamically adjust the position of the clipping planes by using the grips displayed on selecting the camera.

View

This option is used to set the current view as the camera view.

eXit

This option is used to exit the tool.

Editing the Cameras

To edit a camera, select it from the drawing area; the **Camera Preview** window will be displayed, as shown in Figure 13-83. Also, the grips will be displayed on the length of the camera. You can adjust the focus of the camera by dragging these grips. The move gizmo will also be displayed when you move your cursor toward the source or target grip. You can use this gizmo to move the camera in the desired direction. The corresponding changes can also be viewed in the **Camera Preview** window. By default, the preview of the model will be displayed in the Wireframe mode, but we can change it to other visual styles. You can do so by using the **Visual style** drop-down in the **Camera Preview** window.

*Figure 13-83 The **Camera Preview** window*

Note

*The **Camera Preview** dialog box is displayed on selecting the camera because by default the **Display this window when editing a camera** check box is selected in the **Camera Preview** dialog box. If you do not want the dialog box to be displayed, you need to clear this check box. If you want to view it later, then select the camera, right-click, and then choose **View Camera Preview**; the **Camera Preview** dialog box will be displayed.*

Note that you can have more than one camera in one drawing. You can edit the camera properties by using the **Properties** palette. Using this palette, you can modify a camera's lens length, change its front and back clipping planes, and change the name of the camera.

You can set the camera view as the current view by selecting the camera from the **Views** drop-down list in the **Visualize** tab. Then, you can save the view by using the **View Manager** dialog box. You can also set the camera view by selecting the camera and then choosing the **Set Camera View** option from the shortcut menu displayed on right-clicking.

Note

*To toggle the display of camera glyph, choose the **Camera Display** button from the **Camera** panel of the **Visualize** tab.*

You can set the camera template from the **TOOL PALETTES**. To do so, invoke the **TOOL PALETTES** and right-click on its title bar; a shortcut menu will be displayed. Choose **Cameras** from the shortcut menu and then select the required option. The three camera options available in the menu are: **Normal Camera**, **Wide-angle Camera**, and **Extreme Wide-angle camera**.

CREATING ANIMATIONS

You can create a walk-through or fly-through animation by using the motion path animation. You can record and play back these presentations whenever required. This helps you communicate your design intent dynamically and with more impact. The tools to create an animation are not displayed in the **Ribbon** by default. To display them, choose the **Visualize** tab and right-click on any one of the buttons; a shortcut menu will be displayed. Choose **Show Panels > Animations** from the shortcut menu; the **Animations** panel will be added to the **Ribbon**. The methods of creating animations are discussed next.

Creating Animation of 3D Navigations

You can create, record, playback, and save animations of any of the 3D navigation modes, such as **Walk** and **Fly**. Before creating animations, you should specify the animation settings. To do so, choose the **Walk** or **Fly** button and right-click. Next, choose **Animation Settings** from the shortcut menu; the **Animation Settings** dialog box will be displayed, refer to Figure 13-84. In this dialog box, you can specify the visual style in which you want to view the model in animation, resolution of the frames, number of frames to be captured in one second, and the format (AVI, MPG, or WMV) in which you want to save the file while creating the animation of the 3D navigation.

Recording Animation

To create an animation, start any of the 3D navigation tool; the **Record Animation** button in the **Animations** panel in the **Visualize** tab will be enabled. Choose this button to start recording, refer to Figure 13-85. Navigate through the drawing model and all navigations will get recorded. You can also change the navigation mode while recording. To do so, choose the **Pause Animation** button from the **Animations** panel of the **Ribbon**. Next, right-click in the drawing area and choose an option from the **Other Navigation Modes**. Choose the **Record Animation** button again and the recording will start with the changed 3D navigation mode without any break in recording. If you are in the **Walk** or **Fly** navigation mode, you can also adjust the settings from the **POSITION LOCATOR** window, in the same way as explained above.

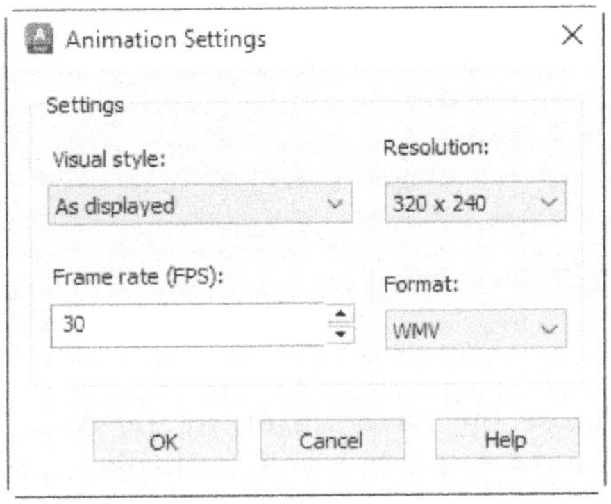

*Figure 13-84 The **Animation Settings** dialog box*

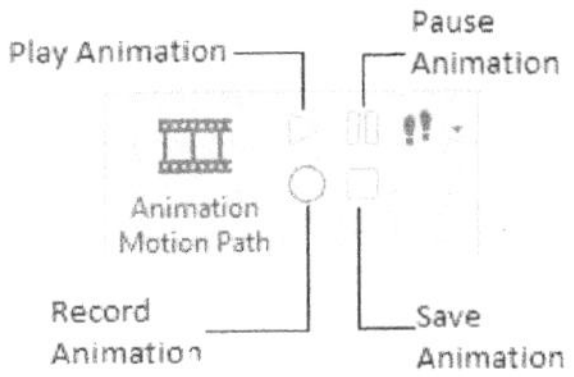

*Figure 13-85 The **Animations** panel in the **Visualize** tab*

Playing Animation

To preview a recorded animation, choose the **Play Animation** tool from the **Animations** panel in the **Visualize** tab; the recording will pause and the **Animation Preview** window will be displayed, refer to Figure 13-86. The **Animation Preview** window displays the animation. If you want to preview the animation in a different visual style, you can select another style from the drop-down list. The options in the **Visual Style** drop-down list are **Current**, **Hidden**, **Wireframe**, **Conceptual**, **Realistic**, **Shaded**, **Shaded with edges**, **Shades of Gray**, **Sketchy** and **X-Ray**. After playing the animation, you can also resume the recording by choosing the **Record** button displayed in red color in the **Animation Preview** window.

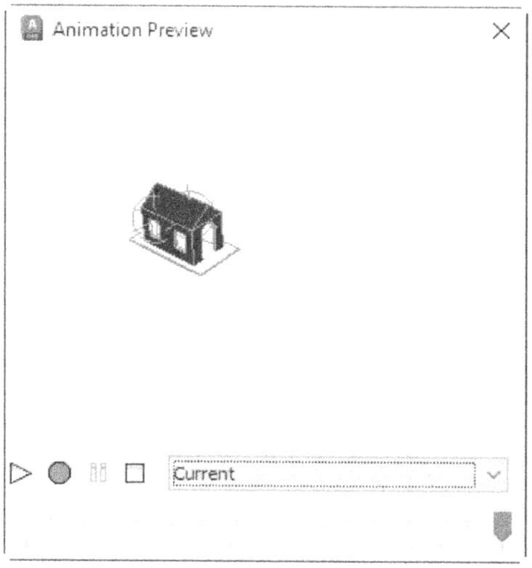

*Figure 13-86 The **Animation Preview** window*

Saving Animation

If you are satisfied with the animation playback, choose the **Save** button in the **Animation Preview** dialog box or the **Animations** panel; the **Save As** dialog box will be displayed on the screen. Select the file location, file name, type of file and then choose the **Save** button. In **Files of type** drop-down list of the **Save As** dialog box, you will get only the file type selected in the **Animation Settings** dialog box. To change the file type, choose the **Animation Settings** button from the **Save As** dialog box; the **Animation Settings** dialog box will be displayed. Select the desired file type from the **Format** drop-down list of the **Animation Settings** dialog box.

Creating Animation by Defining the Path of the Camera Movement

Ribbon: Visualize > Animations > Animation Motion Path
Menu Bar: View > Motion Path Animations **Command:** ANIPATH

In this method of creating an animation, you can control the camera motion by linking the camera movement and its target to a point or a path. If you want the camera or target to remain still while creating animation, link the camera or target to a point. However, if you want the camera or target to move along a path while creating animation, link the camera or target to a path. To create a motion path animation, choose the **Animation Motion Path** tool from the **Animations** panel in the **Visualize** tab; the **Motion Path Animation** dialog box will be displayed, refer to Figure 13-87. Using this dialog box, specify the settings for the camera motion path and create the animation file. The options in the **Motion Path Animation** dialog box are discussed next.

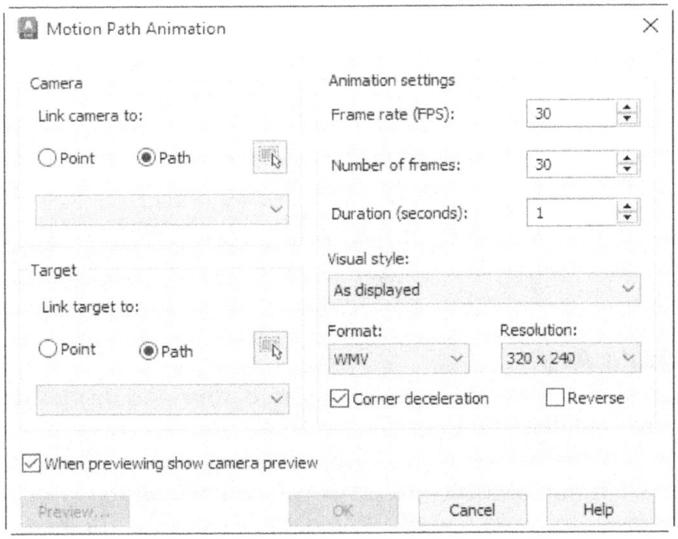

*Figure 13-87 The **Motion Path Animation** dialog box*

Camera Area

The options in this area are used to specify the camera movement. Select the **Point** or **Path** radio button, based on your requirement. Select the **Point** radio button, if you want the camera to remain stationary at the specified point in the drawing throughout the animation. Select the **Path** radio button, if you want the camera to move along the specified path in the drawing. Next, choose the **Pick Point** / **Select Path** button available next to the radio buttons to select the point/path in the drawing. Specify the point/path in the drawing; the **Point Name** or **Path Name** dialog box will be displayed, depending on whether the **Point** or **Path** radio button is selected as the camera link, respectively, refer to Figure 13-88. Specify a name for the point/path and choose the **OK** button. You can also select a previously created point/path from the drop-down list that displays the list of named points or paths.

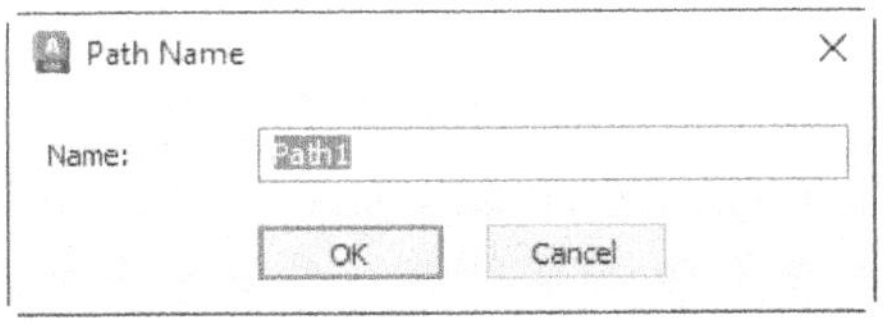

*Figure 13-88 The **Path Name** dialog box*

Target Area

The options in this area are used to specify the movement of the target with the movement of the camera. Select the **Point** or **Path** radio button, based on your requirement. To specify a target point, choose the **Pick Point** button and specify a point in the drawing. Enter a name for the point and choose the **OK** button in the **Point Name** dialog box. To specify a target path, choose the **Select Path** button and specify a path in the drawing. Enter a name for the path and choose the **OK** button in the **Path Name** dialog box. To specify an existing target point or path, select it from the drop-down list.

Note

1. You cannot link both the camera and the target to a point.

2. To create a path, you can link a camera to a line, arc, elliptical arc, circle, polyline, 3D polyline, or spline.

Tip

You must create the path object before you create the motion path animation. The path that you create will not be visible in the animation.

Animation settings Area

The options in this area are used to control the output quality and display of the animation file. The options in this area are discussed next.

Frame rate (FPS). The frames per second is the speed at which the animation will be played. The value of the FPS can vary from 1 to 60. The default value for the FPS is 30.

Number of frames. This option is used to specify the total number of frames to be created in the animation. This value divided by the FPS determines the duration of the animation file.

Duration (seconds). This option specifies the duration of the animation in seconds. Any change in the duration automatically resets the **Number of frames** value.

Visual style. This option displays a drop-down list of the visual styles and the render presets that can be applied to an animation file.

Note

You cannot create an animation of 3D navigation with a rendered model, however, you can create it by using a motion path.

Format. This drop-down list is used to specify the file format for the animation. You can save an animation to an **AVI**, **MPG**, and **WMV** file format.

Note

*The **MOV** format is available only if QuickTime Player is installed. The **WMV** format is available only if Microsoft Windows Media Player is installed. Otherwise, the **AVI** format is the default selection.*

Resolution. This drop-down list is used to specify the resolution of the resulting animation in terms of the width and height. The default value is 320 x 240.

Corner deceleration. This check box is used to specify the speed of the camera movement at the corners. If this check box is selected, the camera will move at a slower rate as it turns at a corner.

Reverse. This check box, if selected, will reverse the direction of the animation display.

When previewing show camera preview. This check box, if selected, will display the **Animation Preview** dialog box when you choose the **Preview** button so that you can preview the animation before you save it.

Preview. This button is used to get a preview of the animation in the **Animation Preview** dialog box, before saving it.

After you have finished adjusting the points, paths, and settings, choose **Preview** to view the animation, Next, choose the **OK** button to save the animation; the **Save As** dialog box will be displayed. Specify the location, file name, and file type of the animation to save and then choose the **Save** button.

Example 5

In this example, you will download the drawing file of the model shown in Figure 13-89 from *https://www.cadcim.com*. The path of the file is as follows: *Textbooks > CAD/CAM > AutoCAD Advanced > Advanced AutoCAD 2023: A Problem-Solving Approach, 3D and Advanced > Input Files*. Next, you will animate the downloaded model and then save this animation to a file.

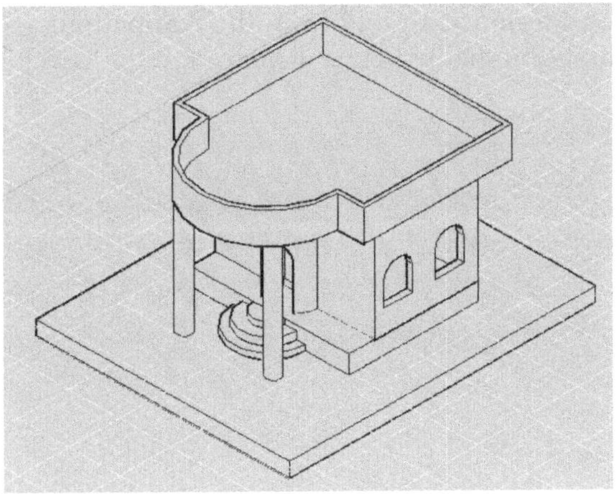

Figure 13-89 *Model for Example 5*

1. Download the model shown in Figure 13-89 using the path mentioned above.

2. Select the materials of your choice and attach them to the model, as described in Example 1. The rendered image of the model is shown in Figure 13-90.

3. Change the view of the model to the top view and create the path to attach the camera, refer to Figure 13-91.

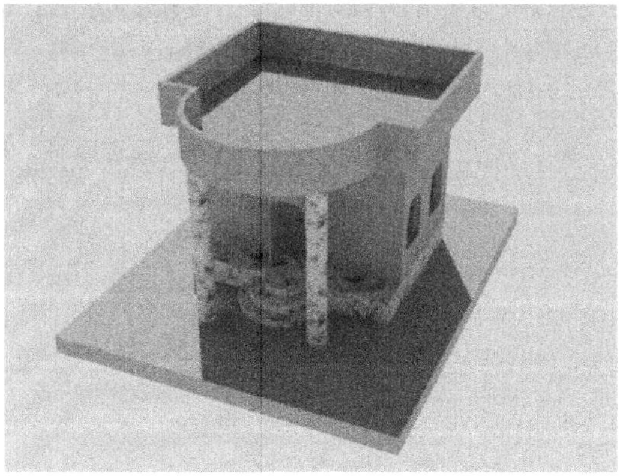

Figure 13-90 Rendered model for Example 5

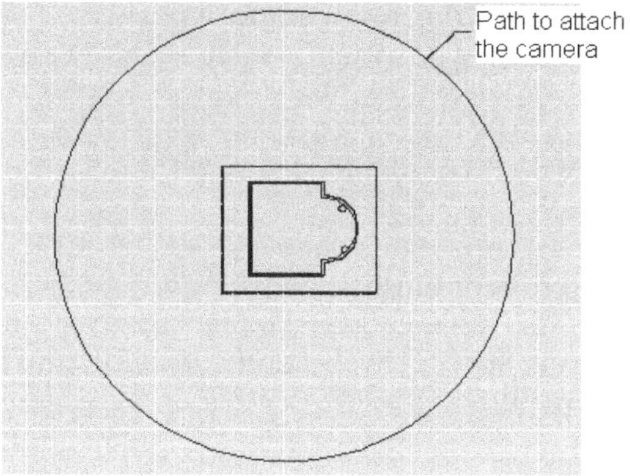

Figure 13-91 Top view of the model displaying the path to attach the camera

4. Move the path created in the previous step along the Z axis by a distance equal to half the height of the model.

5. Invoke the **Animation Motion Path** tool from the **Animations** panel in the **Visualize** tab; the **Motion Path Animation** dialog box is displayed, refer to Figure 13-92.

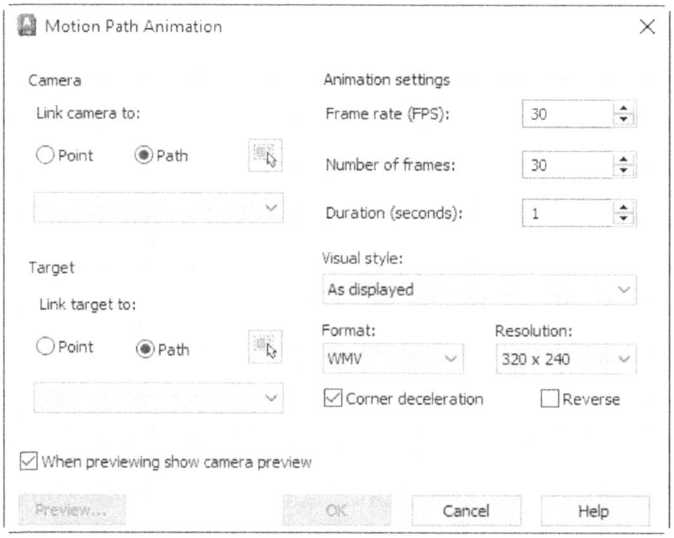

*Figure 13-92 The **Motion Path Animation** dialog box for Example 5*

6. Select the **Path** radio button and choose the **Select Path** button in the **Camera** area of the **Motion Path Animation** dialog box. Next, select the path created in the previous step; the **Path Name** dialog box is displayed. Enter the name of the path as **Path1**.

7. Select the **Point** radio button and choose the **Select Point** button in the **Target** area of the **Motion Path Animation** dialog box. Next, specify a point in the middle of the model, which

will act as the target of the camera. On doing so, the **Point Name** dialog box is displayed. In this dialog box, enter the name as **Point1**.

8. Change the values of the **Animation settings** area to the values shown in Figure 13-92.

9. Choose the **Preview** button to take a preview of the animation in the **Animation Preview** dialog box. Next, close the **Animation Preview** dialog box.

10. Choose the **OK** button to save the animation; the **Save As** dialog box is displayed. Specify the location, file name, and file type of the animation to save and then choose the **Save** button from the **Save As** dialog box.

Self-Evaluation Test

Answer the following questions and then compare them to those given at the end of this chapter:

1. The __________ tool is used to attach material to a layer in a drawing.

2. The __________ source emits a focused beam of light in the defined direction.

3. The __________ and __________ commands are used to adjust the coordinates and the bitmap of the pattern of the material attached to the solid model.

4. The __________ tool is used to set exposure in the rendered image.

5. A __________ light source emits light in all directions, and the intensity of the emitted light is uniform.

6. A rendered image makes it easier to visualize the shape and size of a 3D object. (T/F)

7. You can unload AutoCAD Render by invoking the **ARX** command. (T/F)

8. The falloff occurs with a distant source of light. (T/F)

9. You can change the color of the ambient light. (T/F)

10. You cannot take the printout of a model without rendering it. (T/F)

Review Questions

Answer the following questions:

1. Which of the following light does not have a source, and therefore, no location or direction?

   (a) **Default** (b) **Point**
   (c) **Spot** (d) **Distant**

2. The intensity of light decreases as the distance increases. This phenomenon is called:

   (a) **Attenuation** (b) **Frequency**
   (c) **Light Effect** (d) None of these

3. Which of the following lights allows you to define the geographic location?

   (a) **Sun** (b) **Point**
   (c) **Spot** (d) **Distant**

4. Which of the following commands can be used to define the background of an object while it is being rendered?

   (a) **RENDER** (b) **ARX**
   (c) **BACKGROUND** (d) **VIEW**

5. Which of the following commands is used to create a motion path animation?

   (a) **ANIMAP** (b) **ANITRAC**
   (c) **ANIPATH** (d) **ANIMATION**

6. In the __________ source, the brightness of the incident light on an object is inversely proportional to the distance of the object from the light source.

7. The __________ palette allows you to set the rendering preferences for the rendering.

8. A spotlight source emits a __________ beam of light in one direction only.

9. Redisplaying a saved rendered image takes __________ time as compared to the time involved in rendering.

10. The __________ command is used to render only the selected portion of a drawing.

11. Attenuation is defined as __________.

12. You can assign materials to an object using the AutoCAD Color Index. (T/F)

13. The phenomenon of attenuation occurs in case of direction lights. (T/F)

14. You can link both the camera and the target to a point. (T/F)

Exercise 1

In this exercise, you will download the drawing file of the model shown in Figure 13-93 from *https://www.cadcim.com*. The path of the file is as follows: *Textbooks > CAD/CAM > AutoCAD Advanced > Advanced AutoCAD 2023: A Problem-Solving Approach, 3D and Advanced > Input Files.* Next, render the drawing after applying materials and inserting lights at appropriate locations to get a realistic model.

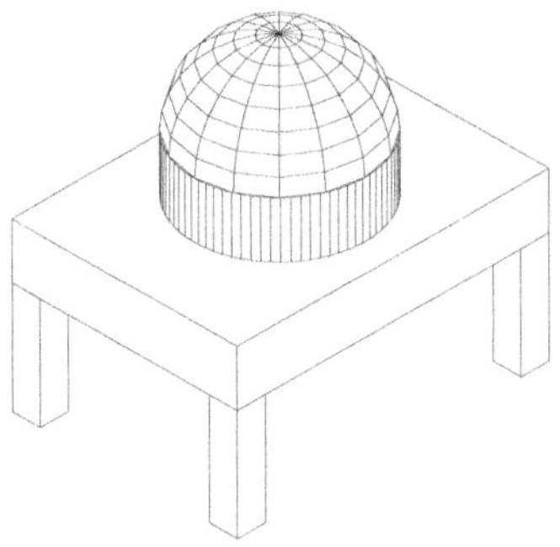

Figure 13-93 *Model for Exercise 1*

Exercise 2

In this exercise, you will download the drawing file of the model shown in Figure 13-94 from *https://www.cadcim.com*. The path of the file is as follows: *Textbooks > CAD/CAM > AutoCAD Advanced > Advanced AutoCAD 2023: A Problem-Solving Approach, 3D and Advanced > Input Files.* Next, you will apply materials of your choice to the downloaded model. Also, you will apply the Point light and the Spotlight at the sill of the window and at bottom of the door. Also, attach a background image to it and then render the model. If you want to create the model yourself, you can use the reference dimensions shown in Figure 13-94 (Assume the missing dimensions).

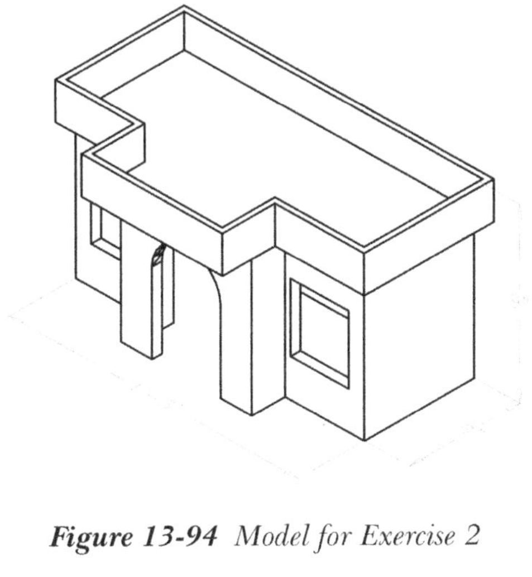

Figure 13-94 *Model for Exercise 2*

Exercise 3

Create the solid model shown in Figure 13-95. Also, assign brass material to the solid and render it.

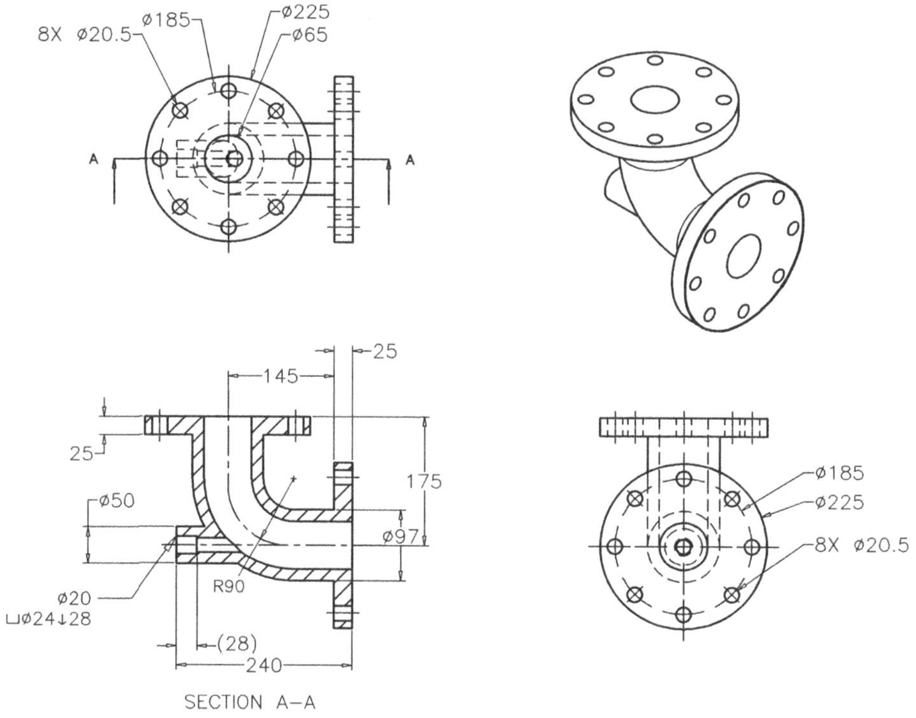

Figure 13-95 *Views and dimensions of the model for Exercise 3*

Exercise 4

In this exercise, you will download the drawing file of the model shown in Figure 13-96 from *https://www.cadcim.com*. The path of the file is as follows: *Textbooks > CAD/CAM > AutoCAD Advanced > Advanced AutoCAD 2023: A Problem-Solving Approach, 3D and Advanced > Input Files*. Also, you will assign materials and textures to different parts of the model and then render it.

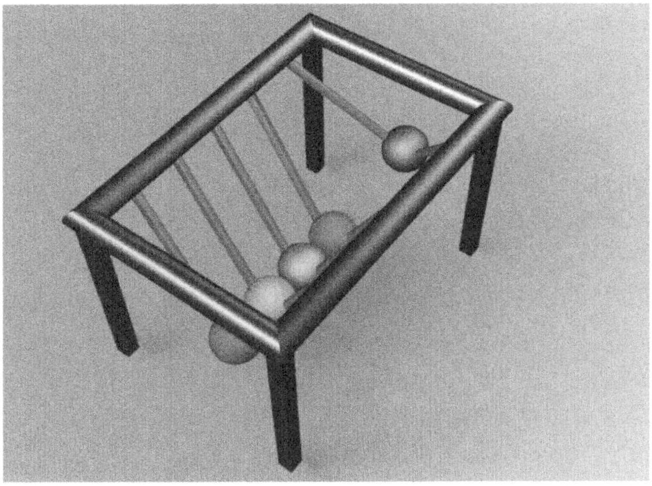

Figure 13-96 *Rendered image of the model*

Answers to Self-Evaluation Test

1. Attach By Layer, **2.** spotlight, **3. MATERIALMAP**, **SETUV**, **4. Environment**, **5.** distant, **6.** T, **7.** T, **8.** F, **9.** F, **10.** F

Chapter 14

Hyperlinks and 3D Printing

Learning Objectives

After completing this chapter, you will be able to:

- *Launch a Web browser from AutoCAD*
- *Place hyperlinks in a drawing*
- *Convert drawings into the DWF file format*
- *Share drawings on Autodesk account and on mobile*
- *Customize the synchronization settings*
- *Share and collaborate the DWG files*
- *3D Printing*

Key Terms

- *Browser*
- *URL*
- *Hyperlink*
- *i-Drop*
- *DWF*
- *Export to DWF*
- *3D Print*

INTRODUCTION

The Internet has become the most important and the fastest way to exchange information in the world. AutoCAD allows you to interact with the Internet in several ways. launch a web browser, and that can be opened using the web browser. For using the Internet features in AutoCAD 2023, some components of Microsoft Edge must be present in your computer. If Microsoft Edge is already installed, then you have these required components. If not, then the components are installed automatically during the installation of AutoCAD 2023 when you select: (1) the **Full Install**; or (2) the **Internet Tools** option during the **Custom** installation.

This chapter introduces the following Web-related commands:

BROWSER
Launches a Web browser from within AutoCAD.

HYPERLINK
Attaches and removes a uniform resource locator (URL) from an object or an area in the drawing.

HYPERLINKFWD
Moves to the next hyperlink (an undocumented command).

HYPERLINKBACK
Moves back to the previous hyperlink (an undocumented command).

HYPERLINKSTOP
Stops the hyperlink access action (an undocumented command).

PASTEASHYPERLINK
Attaches a URL to an object in the drawing from text stored in the Windows Clipboard (an undocumented command).

HYPERLINKBASE
A system variable for setting the path used for relative hyperlinks in the drawing.

INTERNET COMMANDS

The Internet related commands of AutoCAD are discussed next.

BROWSER: This command launches a Web browser from within AutoCAD. The default URL is now *https://www.autodesk.com*. However, you can type the URL without *http*. Also, you can specify the FTP location.

ATTACHURL: This command attaches a URL to an object or an area in the drawing. The **-HYPERLINK** command's **Insert** option supersedes this command.

GOTOURL: This command opens the URL attached to the selected object. Select an object that has a hyperlink; the file or web page that is associated with the hyperlink will open.

DETACHURL: This command removes the URL from an object. The **-HYPERLINK** command's **Remove** option supersedes this command.

DWFOUT: This command exports the drawing and embedded URLs as a DWF file. The **Plot** dialog box's **ePlot** option and the **Publish** tool supersedes this command. You can also choose the **DWF** tool from **Output > Export to DWF/PDF > Export** drop-down or **Export > DWF** from the **Application Menu** to export the drawing to DWF.

You are probably already familiar with the best-known uses of the Internet: e-mail and the www (stands for "World Wide Web"). E-mail allows the user to quickly exchange messages and data at very low cost. The Web brings together text, graphics, audio, and movies in an easy-to-use format. You can also use file transfer protocol (FTP) for effortless binary file transfer.

AutoCAD allows you to interact with the Internet in several ways. It can launch a Web browser from within AutoCAD with the **BROWSER** command. Hyperlinks can be inserted in drawings with the **HYPERLINK** command, which lets you link the drawing with the other documents on your computer and the Internet. With the **Plot** tool's ePlot option (short for "electronic plot), AutoCAD creates DWF files for viewing drawings in two-dimensional (2D) format on Web pages.

UNDERSTANDING URLS

The **Uniform Resource Locator**, known as URL, is the file naming system of the Internet. The URL system allows you to find any resource (a file) on the Internet. For example, resources include a text file, Web page, program file, an audio or movie clip, in short, anything you might also find on your own computer. The primary difference is that these resources are located on somebody else's computer. Various examples of URLs with their meanings are listed below:

Example of URL	Meaning
https://www.autodesk.com	Autodesk Primary Web site
news.autodesk.com	Autodesk Newsroom Web site

Note that the **https://** prefix is not required. Most of today's Web browsers automatically add it in the *routing* prefix, which saves you a few keystrokes.

URLs can access several different kinds of resources such as Web sites, e-mail, and news groups, but they always take the same general format as follows:

scheme://netloc

The scheme accesses the following specific resources on Internet:

Scheme	Meaning
file://	File is located on your computer's hard drive or local network
ftp://	File Transfer Protocol (used for downloading files)
http://	Hyper Text Transfer Protocol (the basis of Web sites)
mailto://	Electronic mail (e-mail)

news://	Usenet news (news groups)
telnet://	Telnet protocol
gopher://	Gopher protocol

The **://** characters indicate a network address. Autodesk recommends the following format for specifying URL-style file names with AutoCAD:

Resource	URL Format
Web Site	**http:**//*servername/pathname/filename*
FTP Site	**ftp:**//*servername/pathname/filename*
Local File	**file:**///*drive:/pathname/filename*
or	*drive:\pathname\filename*
or	**file:**///*drive* | */pathname/filename*
or	**file:**//*localPC\pathname\filename*
or	**file:**////*localPC/pathname/filename*
Network File	**file:**//*localhost/drive:/pathname/filename*
or	*localhost\drive:\pathname\filename*
or	**file:**//*localhost/drive* | */pathname/filename*

The terminology can be confusing. The following definitions will help you clarify these terms:

Term	Meaning
server name	The name or location of a computer on the Internet, for example: *www.autodesk.com*
path name	The same as a subdirectory or folder name
drive	The driver letter such as C: or D:
local pc	A file located on your computer
local host	The name of the network host computer

If you are not sure of the name of the network host computer, use Windows Explorer to check the Network Neighborhood for the network names of computers.

Launching a Web Browser

The **BROWSER** command lets you start a Web browser from within AutoCAD. The commonly used Web browsers are Microsoft Edge, Google Chrome, and Mozilla Firefox.

By default, the **BROWSER** command uses whatever brand of Web browser program is registered in your computer's Windows operating system. AutoCAD prompts you for the URL such as *https://www.autodesk.com*. The **BROWSER** command can be used in scripts, toolbars, or menu macros, and AutoLISP routines to automatically access the Internet.

Command: **BROWSER**
Enter Web location (URL) <http://www.autodesk.com>: *Enter a URL.*

The default URL is an HTML file added to your computer during AutoCAD's installation. After you type the URL and press Enter, AutoCAD launches the Web browser and contacts the Web site. Figure 14-1 shows the Microsoft Edge with the Autodesk's primary Web site.

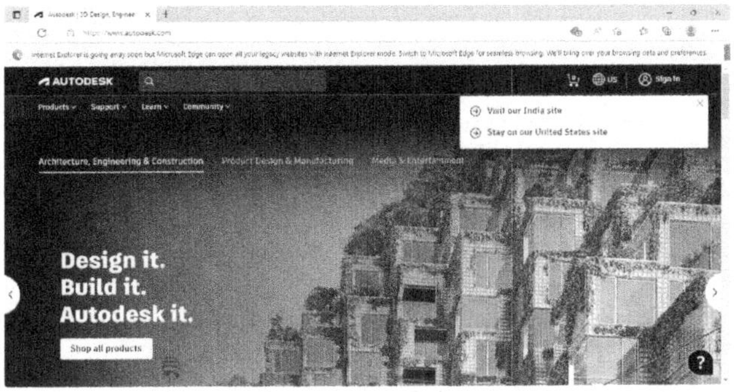

Figure 14-1 Microsoft Edge displaying the Autodesk website

Changing the Default Website

To change the default Web page that your browser starts from within AutoCAD, you need to change the setting in the **INETLOCATION** system variable. The variable stores the URL used by the last executed **BROWSER** command and the **Browse the Web** dialog box. Make the following change:

Command: **INETLOCATION**
Enter new value for INETLOCATION <"http://www.autodesk.com">: *Type URL.*

USING HYPERLINKS WITH AutoCAD

AutoCAD allows you to employ URLs in two ways:

1. Directly within an AutoCAD drawing.
2. Indirectly in DWF files displayed by a Web browser.

URLs are also known as hyperlinks. The term is used throughout this book. Hyperlinks are created, edited, and removed with the **HYPERLINK** command. You can also use the command line with the help of the **-HYPERLINK** command.

HYPERLINK Command

Ribbon: Insert > Data > Hyperlink **Menu Bar:** Insert > Hyperlink
Command: HYPERLINK

When you invoke this command, you will be prompted to select objects. Select the object(s) and press Enter; the **Insert Hyperlink** dialog box will be displayed, refer to Figure 14-2.

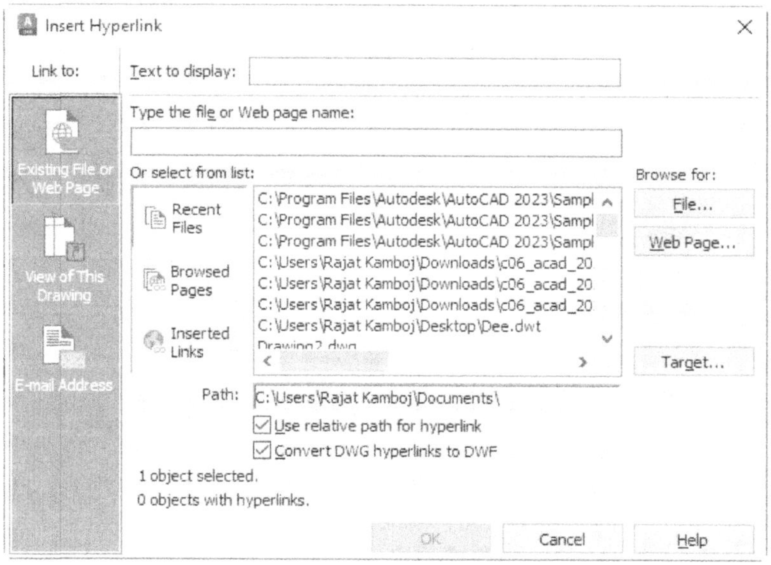

*Figure 14-2 The **Insert Hyperlink** dialog box*

If you select an object that has a hyperlink already attached to it, choose the swatch displayed on the right of the **Hyperlink** edit box from the **PROPERTIES** palette to display the **Edit Hyperlink** dialog box, as shown in Figure 14-3. The **Remove Link** button available in the dialog box is used to remove the hyperlink from an object.

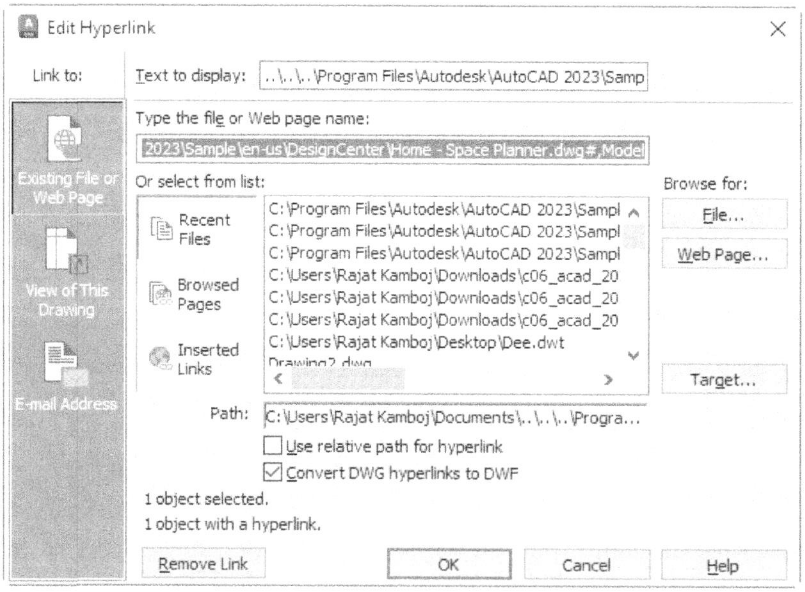

*Figure 14-3 The **Edit Hyperlink** dialog box*

If you use the Command line for inserting hyperlinks (**-HYPERLINK** command), you are also allowed to create hyperlink areas. A **h**yperlink area is a rectangular area that can be thought of as a 2D hyperlink (the dialog box-based **Hyperlink** command does not create hyperlink areas).

When you select the **Area** option from the Command line, a rectangular boundary object is placed automatically on the layer URLLAYER and it turns red, refer to Figure 14-4.

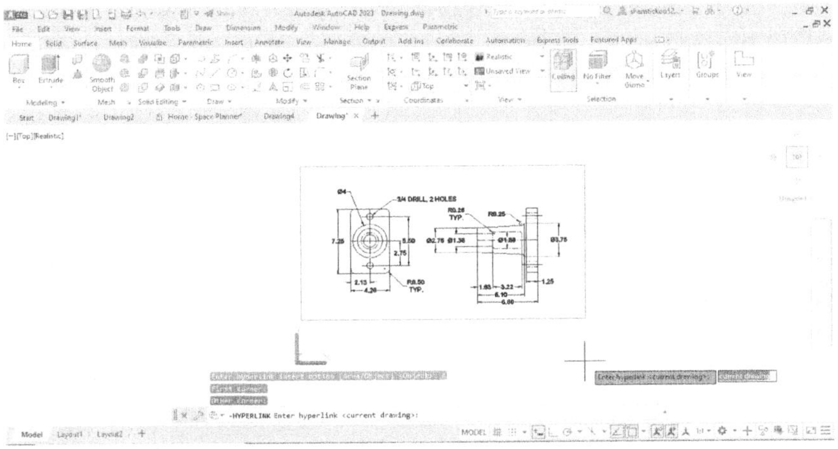

Figure 14-4 *The rectangular hyperlink area*

In the following sections, you will learn to apply and use hyperlinks in an AutoCAD drawing and in a Web browser through the dialog box-based **HYPERLINK** command.

Hyperlinks Inside AutoCAD

As mentioned earlier, AutoCAD allows you to add a hyperlink to any object in a drawing. An object is permitted just a single hyperlink. On the other hand, a single hyperlink may be applied to a selected set of objects.

You can determine whether an object has a hyperlink or not by moving the cursor over it. The cursor displays the tooltip describing the link, refer to Figure 14-5.

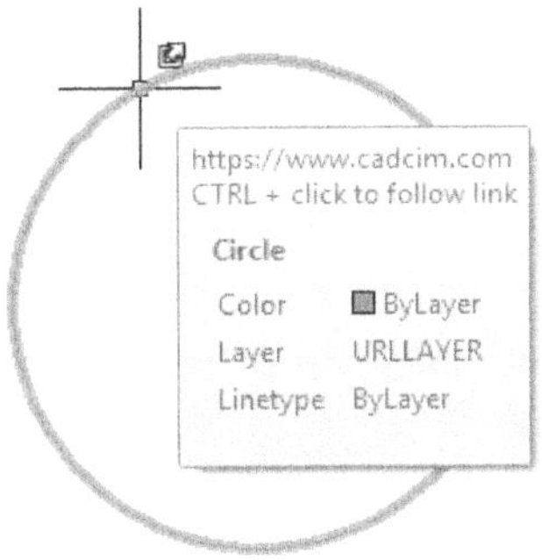

Figure 14-5 *The cursor displaying a hyperlink*

If, for some reason, you do not want to see the hyperlink cursor, you can turn it off. To do so, invoke the **Options** dialog box, choose the **User Preferences** tab from it. The **Display hyperlink cursor, tooltip, and shortcut menu** check box in the **Hyperlink** area toggles the display of the hyperlink cursor as well as the **Hyperlink** option in the shortcut menu. Select the check box as per your requirement.

Attaching Hyperlinks

The following example explains the method of attaching hyperlinks.

Example 2

In this example, you are given the drawing of a floor plan to which you will add hyperlinks of other AutoCAD drawing. They must be attached to objects. For this reason, you will place some text in the drawing and then attach hyperlinks to it.

1. Start the AutoCAD 2023 session.

2. Open the *Floor Plan Sample.dwg* file from the location *C:\Program Files\Autodesk\AutoCAD 2023\Sample\Database Connectivity*. The drawing will open as a **Read-Only** file.

3. Save this file with the name *Example2.dwg*.

4. Invoke the **Single Line** tool from **Annotate > Text > Text** drop-down and write the text as shown in Figure 14-6.

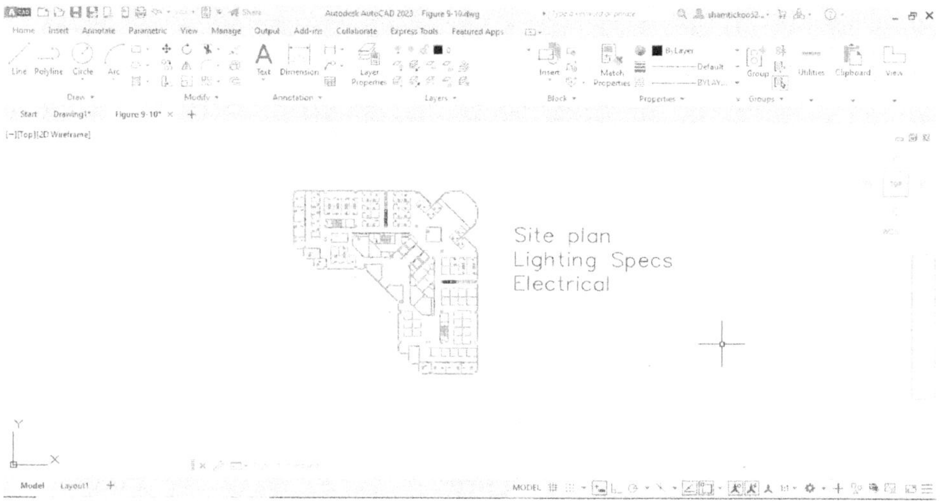

Figure 14-6 *Text placed in a drawing*

5. Choose the **Hyperlink** tool from the **Data** panel in the **Insert** tab; you are prompted to select objects. Select the text **Site Plan** and press Enter to display the **Insert Hyperlink** dialog box.

6. Choose the **File** button from the **Insert Hyperlink** dialog box to display the **Browse the Web – Select Hyperlink** dialog box. Browse to *C:\Program Files\Autodesk\AutoCAD 2023\Sample\en-us\DesignCenter* folder, if it is not already opened, and select the *Home - Space Planner.dwg* file, refer to Figure 14-7.

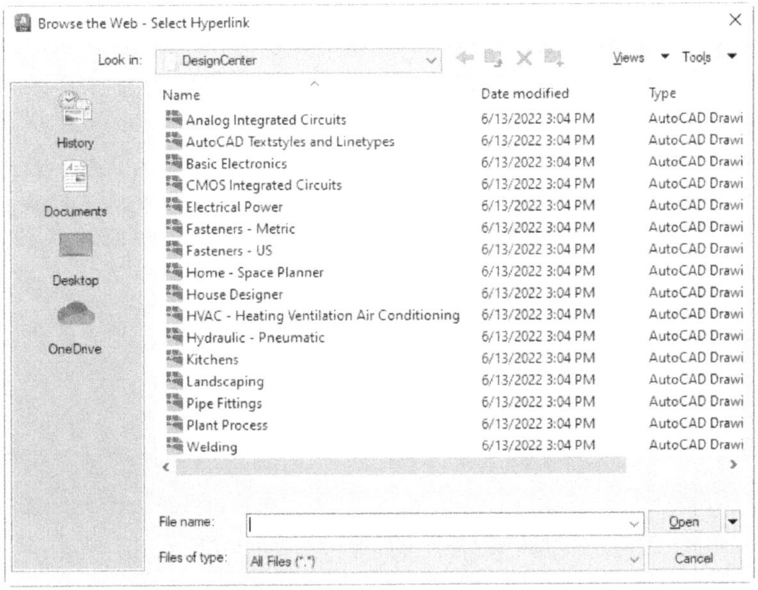

*Figure 14-7 The **Browse the Web - Select Hyperlink** dialog box*

7. Choose **Open** from the dialog box. AutoCAD does not open the drawing; rather, it copies the file's name to the **Insert Hyperlink** dialog box. The name of the drawing is displayed in the **Type the file or Web page name** edit box. The same name and path are also displayed in the **Text to display** edit box. Using this edit box, retain only the file name from the path and remove the rest.

8. Choose the **OK** button to close the dialog box. Move the cursor over the **Site Plan** text. A moment later, the tooltip displays the location of the drawing, refer to Figure 14-8.

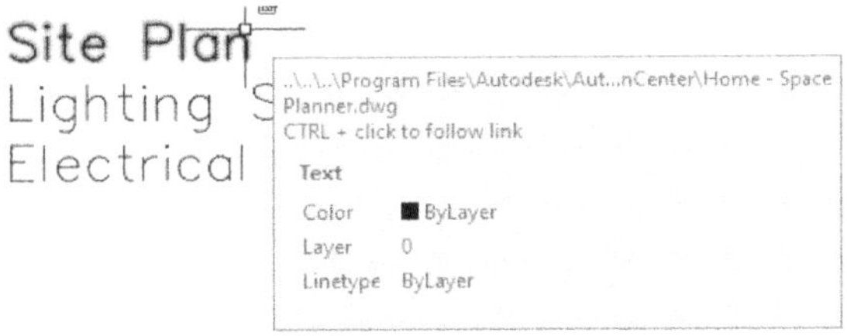

Figure 14-8 The Hyperlink cursor and tooltip

9. Connect to the Internet and then connect the URL *www.autodesk.com* to **Lighting Specs** using the **Web Page** button of the **Insert Hyperlink** dialog box.

10. You can directly open the file attached as hyperlink to the object by using the linked object. To do so, select the object to which the file is linked and then right-click to display the shortcut menu. In the shortcut menu, choose **Hyperlink > Open "file path'**. In this case, the file name is *Home - Space Planner.dwg*. Therefore, right-click and then choose **Hyperlink > Open "Home - Space Planner"** from the shortcut menu, refer to Figure 14-9.

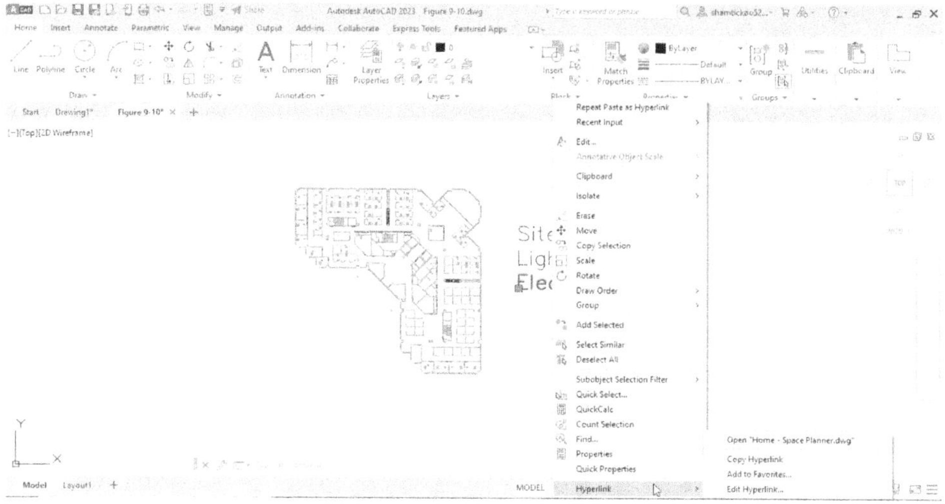

***Figure 14-9** Opening a hyperlink*

11. Choose the **Tile Vertically** button from the **Interface** panel in the **View** tab to view both the drawings together, refer to Figure 14-10.

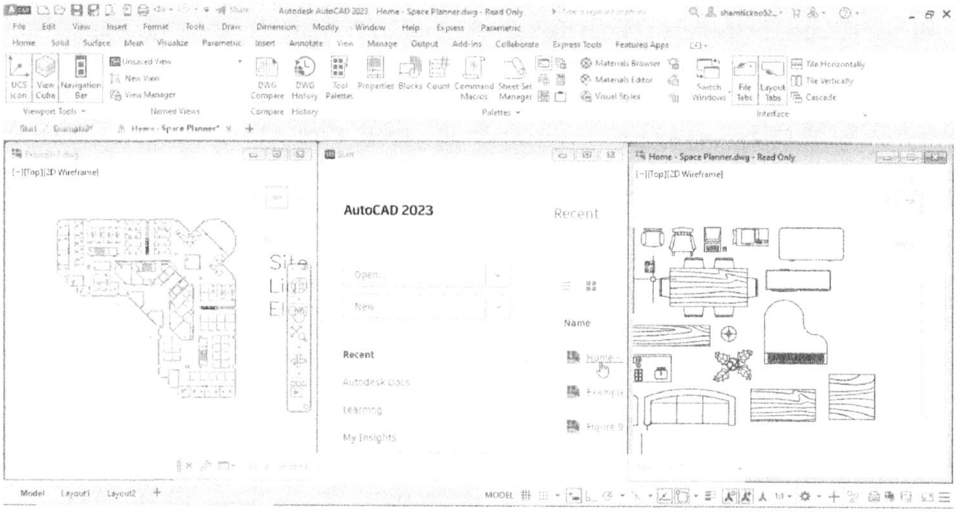

***Figure 14-10** Displaying both drawings in the drawing window*

12. Select the Lighting Specs text and then right-click on it. Choose *Hyperlink > Open "https://www.autodesk.com"* from the shortcut menu; the URL *www.autodesk.com* is launched in the web browser, refer to Figure 14-11. Make sure you are connected to the Internet before opening this URL.

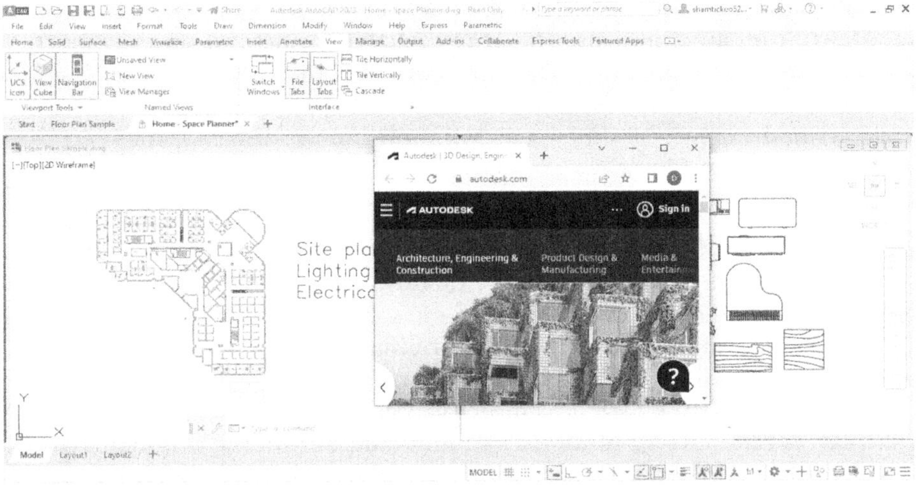

Figure 14-11 *Web browser opens the URL that was hyperlinked to the selected text*

13. Save the drawing.

PASTING AS HYPERLINK

AutoCAD has a shortcut method for pasting hyperlinks in the drawing. The hyperlink from one object can be copied and pasted on another object. This can be achieved by using the **PASTEASHYPERLINK** command.

1. In AutoCAD, select an object that has a hyperlink. Right-click to invoke the shortcut menu.
2. Choose **Hyperlink > Copy Hyperlink** from the shortcut menu.
3. Choose the **Paste as Hyperlink** tool from **Home > Clipboard > Paste** drop-down; you are prompted to select the object on which the hyperlink is to be pasted.
4. Select the object and press Enter. The hyperlink is pasted on the new object.

Note

*The **MATCHPROP** command does not copy the hyperlinks from the source objects to the destination objects.*

EDITING HYPERLINKS

AutoCAD allows you to edit the hyperlinks attached to an object. To do so, select the hyperlinked object and right-click. Choose **Hyperlink > Edit Hyperlink** from the shortcut menu; the **Edit Hyperlink** dialog box will be displayed, which looks identical to the **Insert Hyperlink** dialog box. Make the changes in the hyperlink and choose **OK**.

REMOVING HYPERLINKS FROM OBJECTS

To remove a URL from an object, use the **HYPERLINK** command on the object. When the **Edit Hyperlink** dialog box appears, choose the **Remove Link** button.

To remove a rectangular area hyperlink, you can simply use the **ERASE** tool; select the rectangle and AutoCAD erases the rectangle.

THE DRAWING WEB FORMAT

To display AutoCAD drawings on the Internet, Autodesk created a file format called Drawing Web format (DWF). The DWF file has several benefits and some drawbacks over DWG files. The DWF file is compressed eight times smaller than the original DWG drawing file. Therefore, it takes less time to transmit these files over the Internet, particularly with the relatively slow telephone modem connections. The DWF format is more secure as in this format the original drawing is not being displayed, therefore, another user cannot tamper with the original DWG file.

However, the DWF format has some drawbacks, which are mentioned below:

- You must go through the extra step of translating from DWG to DWF.
- DWF files cannot display rendered or shaded drawings.
- DWF is a flat 2D-file format; therefore, it does not preserve 3D data, although you can export a 3D view.
- AutoCAD itself cannot display DWF files.
- DWF files cannot be converted back to DWG format without using file translation software from a third-party vendor.
- Earlier versions of DWF did not handle paper space objects (version 2.x and earlier), or line widths, lineweights, and non-rectangular viewports (version 3.x and earlier).

To view a DWF file on the Internet, your Web browser needs to have a *plug-in* software extension called **Autodesk DWF Viewer**. This viewer is installed on your system with AutoCAD 2023 installation. **Autodesk DWF Viewer** allows Microsoft Edge (or later) to handle a variety of file formats. Autodesk makes this DWF Viewer plug-in freely available from its Web site at *https://www.autodesk.com*. It is a good idea to regularly check for updates of the DWF plug-in, which is updated frequently.

CREATING A DWF FILE

You can use two methods to create DWF files in AutoCAD. The first method is to use the **PLOT** command and the second method is to use the **PUBLISH** command.

Creating a DWF File Using the PLOT Command

The following steps explain the procedure to create a DWF file using the **PLOT** tool:

1. Open the file to be converted into a DWF file. Choose the **Plot** tool from the **Quick Access Toolbar**; the **Batch Plot** message box will be displayed, refer to Figure 14-12.

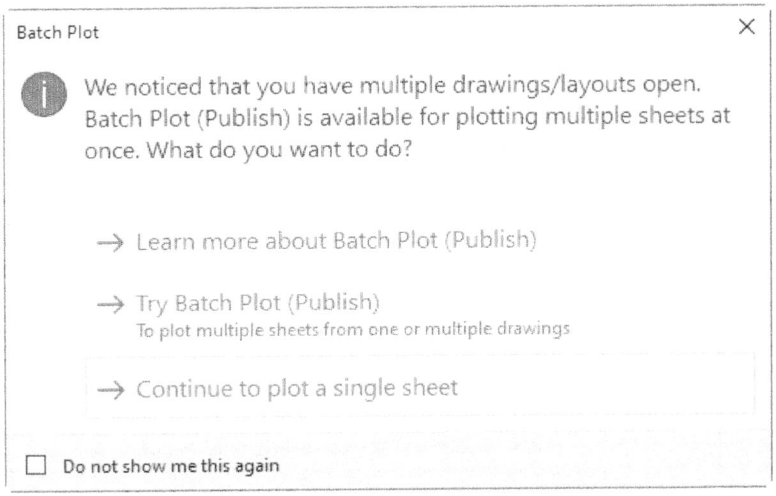

*Figure 14-12 The **Batch Plot** message box*

2. If you want to plot multiple sheets from one or multiple drawings, then choose the **Try Batch Plot (Publish)** option from the message box. Otherwise, choose **Continue to plot a single sheet** from the message box; the **Plot - Model** dialog box will be displayed, refer to Figure 14-13.

3. Select **DWF6 ePlot.pc3** from the **Name** drop-down list in the **Printer/plotter** area, refer to Figure 14-13.

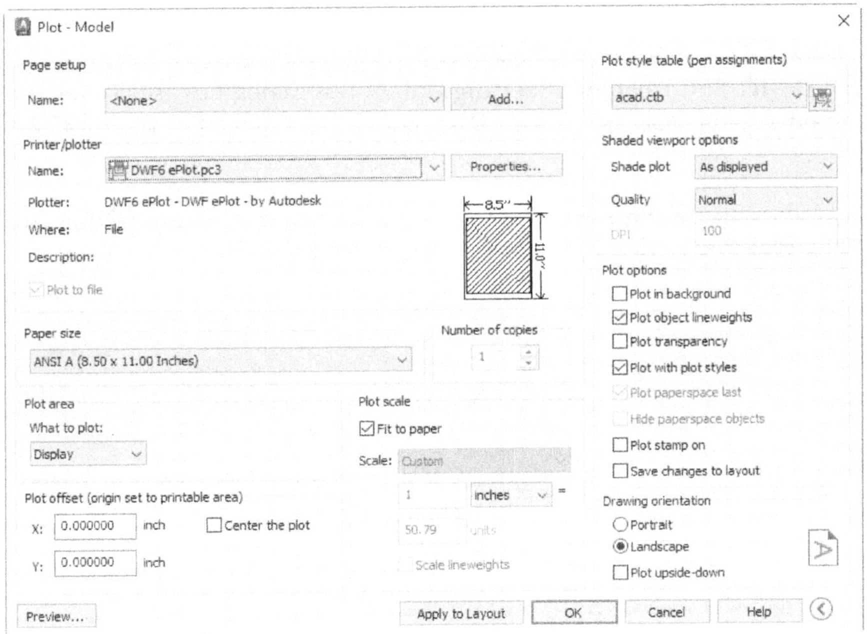

*Figure 14-13 The **Plot-Model** dialog box*

4. Choose the **Properties** button to display the **Plotter Configuration Editor** dialog box, refer to Figure 14-14.

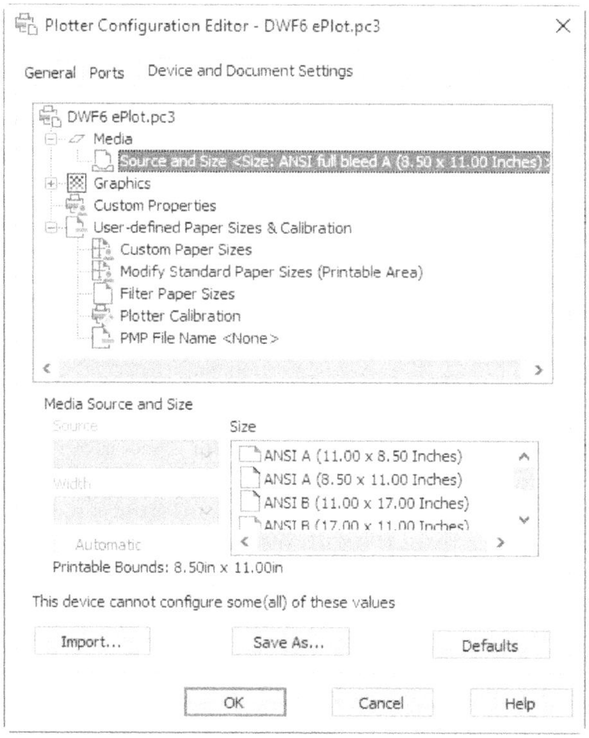

*Figure 14-14 The **Plotter Configuration Editor** dialog box*

5. In the **Device and Document Settings** tab of this dialog box, select **Custom Properties** in the tree view; the **Access Custom Dialog** area is displayed in the lower half of the dialog box.

6. Choose the **Custom Properties** button from the **Access Custom Dialog** area to display the **DWF6 ePlot Properties** dialog box, refer to Figure 14-15.

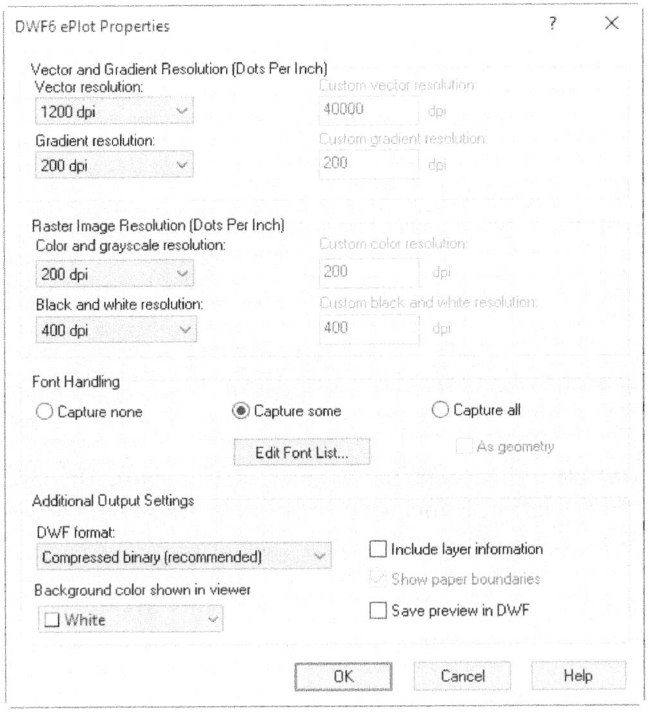

*Figure 14-15 The **DWF6 ePlot Properties** dialog box*

7. Set the required options in these dialog boxes and choose **OK** three times to return to the **Plot - Model** dialog box.

8. In the **Plot - Model** dialog box, use the required options to create the DWF file. Choose **OK** from the **Plot** dialog box; the **Browse for Plot File** dialog box will be displayed.

9. Specify the name of the DWF file in the **File name** edit box. If necessary, change the location where the file is to be stored.

DWF6 ePlot Properties Dialog Box Options

The options in this dialog box are discussed next.

Vector and Gradient Resolution (Dots Per Inch) Area

This area allows you to set the resolution for the vector information and gradients. Unlike AutoCAD DWG files that are based on real numbers, DWF files are saved using integer numbers. The higher the resolution, the better the quality of the DWF files. However, the size of the files also increases with the resolution.

Raster Image Resolution (Dots Per Inch) Area

This area allows you to set the resolution for the raster images in the DWF files.

Font Handling

This area of the **DWF6 ePlot Properties** dialog box is used to select the fonts that you need to include in the DWF file. You can choose the **Edit Font List** button from this area to display the list of the fonts. It should be noted that the fonts add to the size of the DWF file.

Additional Output Settings Area

The options available in this area are discussed next.

DWF format : This drop-down list provides the options for compressing or zipping while creating the DWF file.

Background color shown in viewer : This drop-down list is used to specify the background color of the resulting DWF file.

Include layer information : This check box is selected to include the layer information in the DWF file. If the layer information is included in the resulting DWF file, you can toggle layers off and on when the DWF file is being viewed.

Show paper boundaries : Selecting this check box results in a rectangular boundary at the drawing's extents, as displayed in the layouts.

Save preview in DWF : This check box allows you to save the preview in DWF file.

Creating a DWF File Using the PUBLISH Command

The following is the procedure to create a DWF file using the **PUBLISH** command:

Choose the **Batch Plot** tool from the **Plot** panel in the **Output** tab; the **Publish** dialog box will be displayed, refer to Figure 14-16. The options in this dialog box are discussed next.

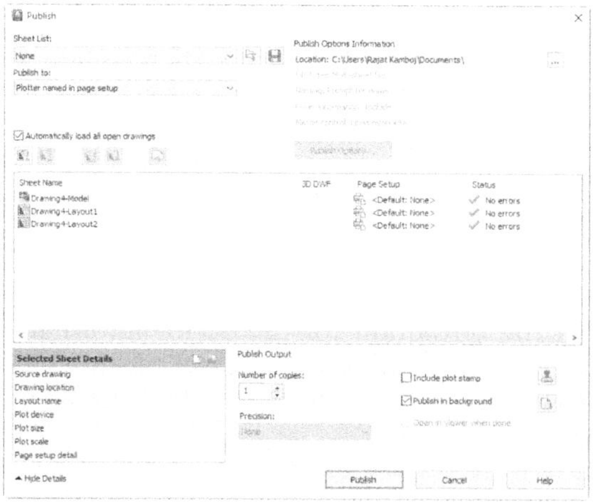

*Figure 14-16 The **Publish** dialog box*

The list box in the **Publish** dialog box lists the model and paper space layouts that will be included for publishing. Right-click on any of the sheets in the **Sheet Name** column to display a shortcut menu. The options in it can be used on the drawings listed in this area. You can change the page setup option of the sheets using the field in the **Page Setup/3D DWF** column. You can also import a page setup using the drop-down list that is displayed when you click on the field in this column. The remaining options in this area are discussed next.

Note

*If you have not saved the drawing before invoking the **PUBLISH** command, the sheet names in the list box will have prefix as **Unsaved**. Also, the status of the layouts that are not initialized will show **Layout not initialized**.*

Add Sheets. This button, when chosen, displays the **Select Drawings** dialog box. Using this dialog box, you can select the drawing files (*.dwg*). These files are then included in the creation of the DWF file.

Remove Sheets. This button is chosen to remove the sheet selected from the **Sheet Name** column.

Move Sheet Up. This button is chosen to move the selected sheet up by one position in the list.

Move Sheet Down. This button is chosen to move the selected sheet down by one position in the list.

Save Sheet List. This button, when chosen, displays the **Save List As** dialog box. This dialog box allows you to save the current list of drawing files as DSD files.

Load Sheet List. After saving a list, if you choose this button, the **Load List of Sheets** dialog box will be displayed with the saved list in the **Name** area of the **Load List of Sheets** dialog box. You can select the *.dsd* or *.bp3* file format from this dialog box and select the list to load. After selecting the list, you can proceed to publish the selected sheet list. But if you want to publish a different list, select the required list from the **Load List of Sheets** dialog box. On doing so, the **Publish - Load Sheet List** message box will be displayed. Choose the required option from this message box to continue with the publishing list.

Preview. This button is chosen to preview the sheet selected from the **Sheet Name** column.

Publish to

This drop-down list provides the options for specifying whether the output of the **PUBLISH** command should be plotted on a sheet using the printer mentioned in the page setup of the selected sheet or as a DWF or DWFx or PDF file.

Publish Output Area

This area provides the additional options while publishing the sheets. The **Number of copies** spinner is used to specify the number of copies to be published. Note that if you want the output in the form of a DWF file, the number of copies can only be one. The button below the **Plot Stamp Settings** button is used to reverse the default order of publishing the drawings listed in the list box. Select the **Include plot stamp** check box to include a plot stamp while publishing. The **Plot Stamp Settings** button is chosen to invoke the **Plot Stamp** dialog box for configuring the settings of the plot stamp. The **Publish in background** check box is used to publish the selected drawings in background, while you can continue working with AutoCAD. Select the **Open in viewer when done** check box to open the published file in a new window.

Publish Options

When you choose this button, the **DWF Publish Options** dialog box is displayed, as shown in Figure 14-17. It provides you with the options to publish the drawings. These options are discussed next.

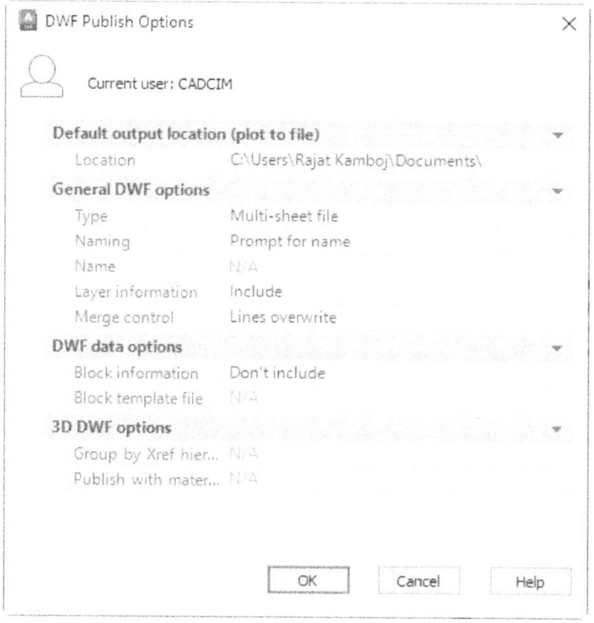

*Figure 14-17 The **DWF Publish Options** dialog box*

Default output location (plot-to-file) rollout. The options in this rollout are used to specify the location of the output of the **PUBLISH** command. By default, the sheets are published locally on the hard drive of your computer. You can modify the default location of the file using the edit box or the swatch button which is displayed when you click on the field that shows the name and location of the file.

General DWF options. The options in this rollout are used to specify DWF files. Click the particular field and specify the appropriate options.

DWF data options. The options in this area are used to specify the password protection. You can also specify whether the block information should be included in the resulting DWF file or not.

3D DWF options. The options in this area are used to specify the data that you can include in the 3D DWF publishing. When only 2D DWF files are listed for publishing, all of the **3D DWF options** are set to **N/A** and cannot be modified.

This completes the explanation of the options in the **DWF Publish Options** dialog box. The remaining options of the **Publish** dialog box are discussed next.

Show Details

When you choose this button, the **Publish** dialog box expands and shows the details related to the sheet selected from the **Sheet Name** list box.

Publish

This button is used to start the process of publishing or creating the DWF file.

Note

You may need to set the value of the ***BACKGROUNDPLOT*** *system variable to* ***0*** *if AutoCAD gives an error while publishing.*

Export to DWF Files

You can export a drawing to a DWF file by choosing the **DWF** tool from **Output > Export to DWF/PDF > Export** drop-down; the **Save As DWF** dialog box will be displayed, as shown in Figure 14-18. In this dialog box, the current settings for the DWF file will be displayed in the **Current Settings** area. To edit the current settings, choose the **Options** button; the **Export to DWF Options** dialog box will be displayed. In this dialog box, you can change the general information for the DWF file like file location, password protection, layer information, and so on. You can also invoke this dialog box by choosing the **Export to DWF Options** tool from the **Export to DWF/PDF** panel.

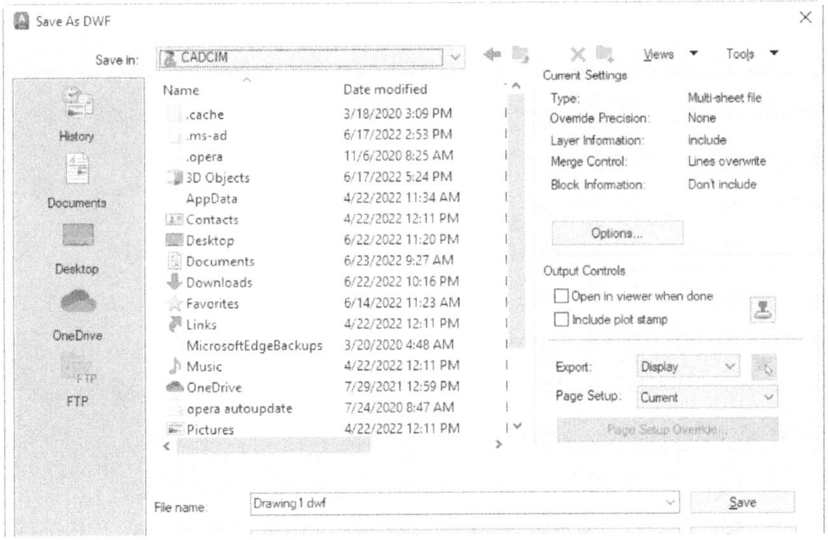

Figure 14-18 The ***Save As DWF*** *dialog box*

You can also select the portion of the drawing that is to be exported from the **Export** drop-down list in the **Save As DWF** dialog box. If you are in the **Model** tab, you can select the **Display** (objects currently displayed on the screen), **Extents** (drawing extents) or **Window** (selected area from the drawing) option and if you are in the **Layout** tab, you can select between the active layout or all layouts. These options are also available in the **What to Export** drop-down list of the **Export to DWF/PDF** panel in the **Output** tab of the **Ribbon**. You can also specify the page settings for the DWF file such as paper size, scale, and plot area. If you want to use the current settings of the **Page Setup Manager**, select the **Current** option from the **Page Setup** drop-down list in the **Save As DWF** dialog box or the **Export to DWF/PDF** panel. To override the current setting, choose the **Override** button. If you want to view the DWF in the Autodesk Design Review, select the **Open in viewer when done** check box. Select the **Include plot stamp** check box to include drawing name, paper size, date and time, and so on to the DWF file. After setting the parameters, choose **Save** from the **Save As DWF** dialog box; the drawing is exported.

Generating DWF Files for 3D Models

To create DWF files for 3D models, it is necessary to install 3D DWF Publish feature while installing AutoCAD 2023. Choose the **DWFx** tool from the **Export** drop-down of the **Export to DWF/PDF** panel in the **Output** tab to open the **Save As DWFx** dialog box, as shown in Figure 14-19. Browse to the location where you want to save the DWFx file, and then specify the name of the file. Next, choose the **Save** button to publish the drawing.

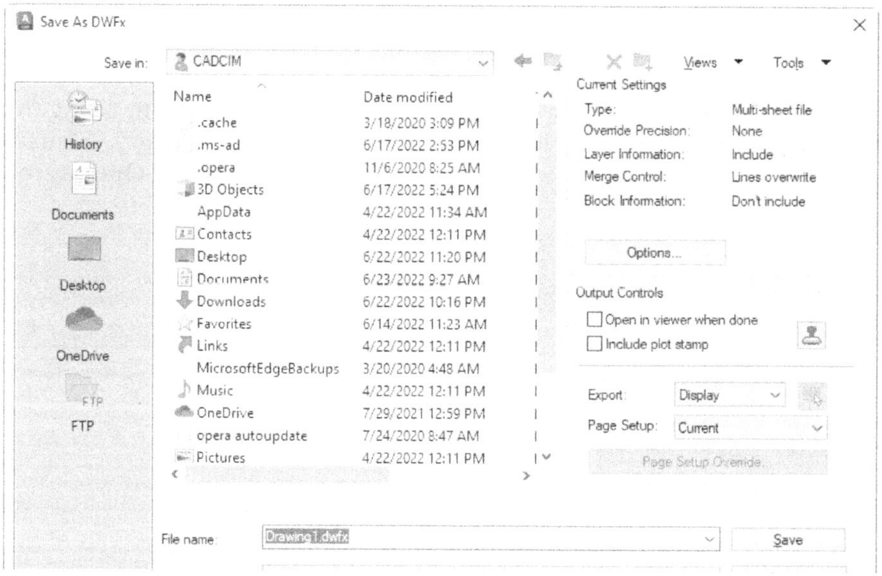

*Figure 14-19 The **Save As DWFx** dialog box*

Viewing DWF Files

Autodesk Design Review plug-in should be installed on your computer to view the DWF files. You can also use a Web browser with a special plug-in that allows the browser to correctly interpret the file for viewing the DWF files. Remember that you cannot view a DWF file with AutoCAD.

You can use various buttons provided in the Autodesk Design Review to manipulate the view of a DWF file. However, remember that the original objects of a DWF file cannot be modified. You can also right-click on the display screen to display a shortcut menu. The shortcut menu provides you with the options such as **Cut**, **Copy**, **Paste**, **Pan**, **Zoom**, **Steering Wheels**, and so on, refer to Figure 14-20. Choose an option from this shortcut menu to invoke the corresponding operation.

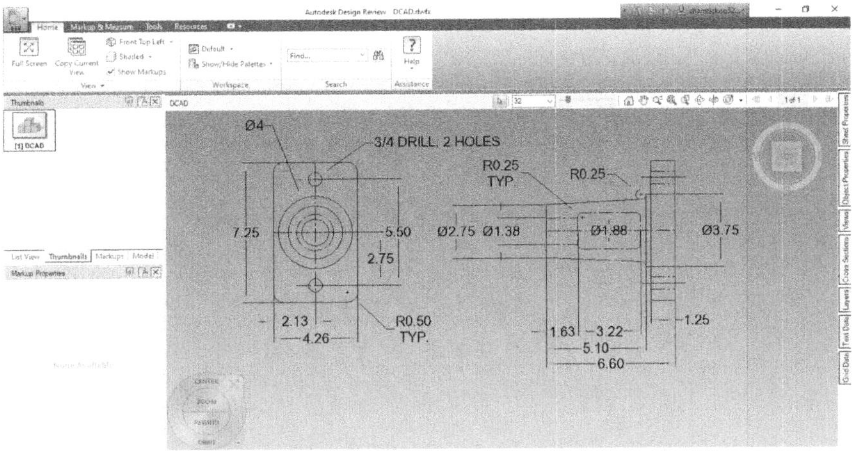

Figure 14-20 *The* ***Autodesk Design Review*** *with the shortcut menu*

Note

To publish a sheet, the ***DWF6 ePlot.pc3*** *plotter should be selected from the* ***Page Setup Manager*** *dialog box.*

3D PRINTING

3D printing or additive manufacturing is a process of making three dimensional solid objects from a digital file.

AutoCAD provides you the options to 3D print your digital files. 3D printing or additive manufacturing is a process of making three dimensional solid objects from a digital file. To 3D print a file in AutoCAD, click on the **Application menu** button to display Application menu, refer to Figure 14-21. You can use the **Publish** or **Print** option to print the 3D object.

To print an object using the **Publish** option, choose **Publish** from the Application Menu; a cascading menu will be displayed. Choose the **Send to 3D Print Service** from this menu; the **3D Printing - Prepare Model for Printing** message box is displayed, refer to Figure 14-22.

To print an object using the **Print** option, choose **3D Print** (if available) from the Application menu; a cascading menu will be displayed. Choose the **3D Print option** from this menu to display the **3D Printing - Prepare Model for Printing** message box, refer to Figure 14-22.

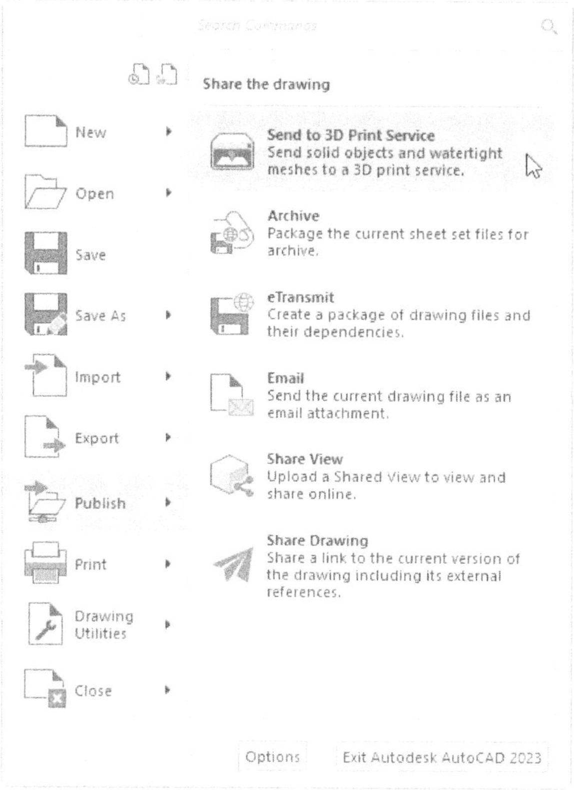

Figure 14-21 *The* ***Application Menu*** *tab*

The prompt sequuence to 3D print an object as follows:

3DPRINT Select solids or watertight meshes : *Select the solid(s) or watertight mesh(es) you want to send for 3D printing and press Enter.*

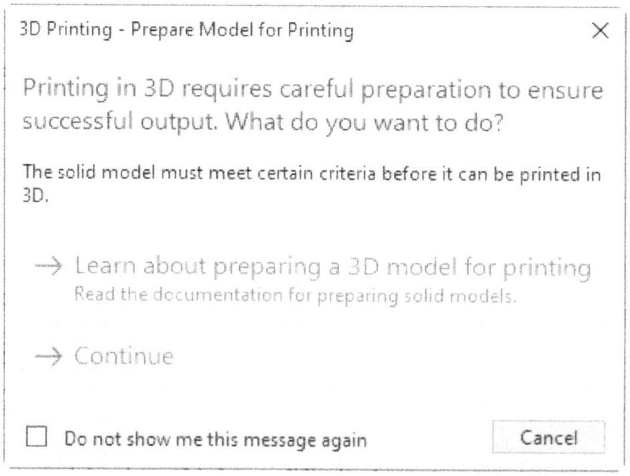

Figure 14-22 *The* ***3D Printing - Prepare Model for Printing*** *message box*

If you want to read the documentation for preparing a 3D model for printing, select **Learn about preparing a 3D model for printing** option from the message box. Otherwise, select **Continue** to proceed further. On selecting **Continue** from the message box, **3DPRINTSERVICE** command becomes active. The prompt sequence that will be followed is given next.

> **3DPRINTSERVICE** Select solids or watertight meshes : *Select the solid(s) or watertight mesh(es) you want to send for 3D printing and press Enter.*

On pressing Enter, the **3D Print Options** dialog box will be displayed, refer to Figure 14-23. In this dialog box, you can view and edit various settings including the output dimensions.

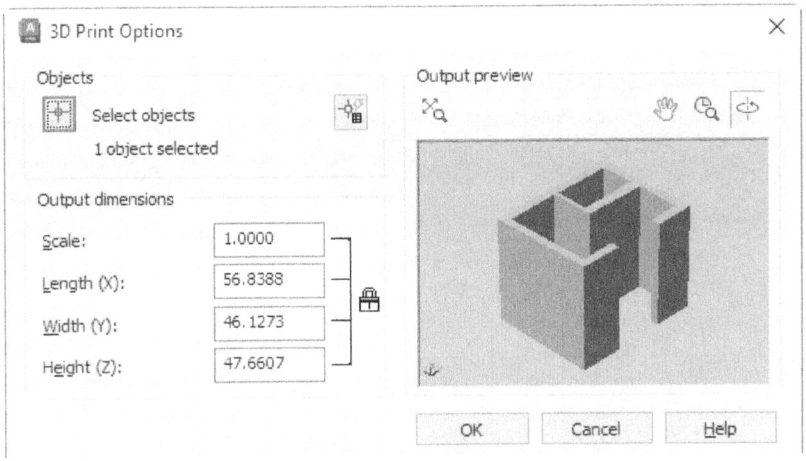

***Figure 14-23** The **3D Print Options** dialog box*

The options in the **3D Print Options** dialog box are discussed next.

Objects

The options in this area are discussed next.

Select objects

This button enables you to select the objects that you want to get 3D printed. When you choose the **Select objects** button, the **3D Print Options** dialog box disappears and allows you to select the objects. Once you select the objects and press Enter, the dialog box reappears with the selected objects displayed in the **Output preview** area.

Quick Select

On choosing this button, the **Quick Select** dialog box is invoked which enables you to create a new selection set that will either include or exclude all objects whose object type and property criteria match as specified for the selection set.

Output dimensions

In this area, you can set the scale, length, width, and height of the 3D model to be sent for 3D printing.

Output Preview

In this area, four buttons namely **Zoom Extents**, **Pan**, **Zoom**, and **Orbit** are available along with a preview pane for the display of selected objects.

Once you have made all the required settings, choose the **OK** button to exit the dialog box. On choosing the **OK** button, the **Create STL File** dialog box will be displayed, refer to Figure 14-24, and you will be prompted to save the output file to STL format. After saving the file in the STL format, you can send it to the 3D printer for printing.

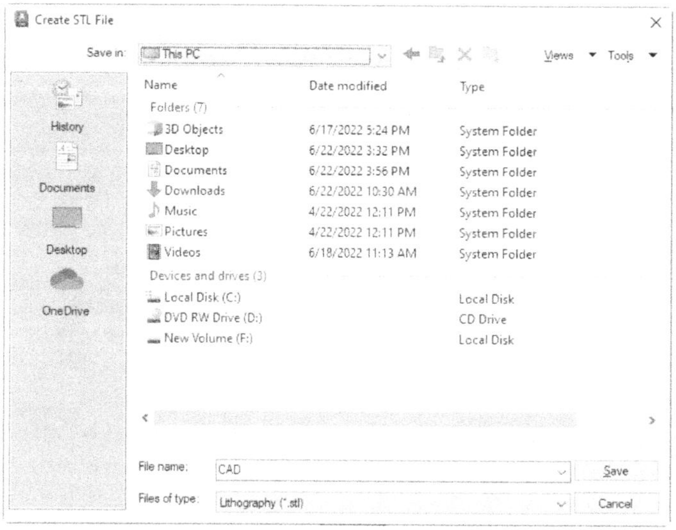

*Figure 14-24 The **Create STL File** dialog box*

Self-Evaluation Test

Answer the following questions and then compare them to those given at the end of this chapter:

1. Rectangular area hyperlinks are stored in the __________ layer.

2. To see the location of hyperlinks in a drawing, use the __________ command.

3. If you attach a hyperlink to a block, the hyperlink data is __________ when you scale the block unevenly, stretch the block, or explode it.

4. To access online resources, choose **Help > Additional Resources > Online Training Resources** from the menu bar. (T/F)

5. You cannot find out whether an object has a hyperlink or not. (T/F)

6. By default, the **Browse the Web** dialog box displays the contents of the URL stored in the **INETLOCATION** system variable. (T/F)

7. URLs are also known as hyperlinks. (T/F)

8. You can select text in an AutoCAD drawing which has hyperlink attached to it to paste it as a hyperlink. (T/F)

Review Questions

Answer the following questions:

1. Which of the following URLs are valid?

   (a) *www.autodesk.com* (b) *https://www.autodesk.com*
   (c) Both (a) and (b) (d) None of the above

2. You can launch a Web Browser within AutoCAD by using the ________ command.

3. DWF stands for ____________.

4. URL stands for ____________.

5. FTP stands for ____________.

6. Hyperlinks are created, edited, and removed with the ___________ command.

7. The purpose of URLs is to let you create __________ between files.

8. Hyperlinks are active in AutoCAD 2023. (T/F)

9. URL can be attached to any object. (T/F)

10. AutoCAD provides the tools to share the documents online. (T/F)

Answers to Self-Evaluation Test

1. URLLAYER, **2.** **HYPERLINK**, **3.** lost, **4.** T, **5.** F, **6.** T, **7.** T, **8.** T

Chapter 15

Script Files and Slide Shows

Learning Objectives

After completing this chapter, you will be able to:

- *Write script files and use the Run Script option to run script files*
- *Use the RSCRIPT and DELAY commands in script files*
- *Run script files while loading AutoCAD*
- *Create a slide show*
- *Preload slides while running a slide show*

Key Terms

- *Script Files*
- *RESUME*
- *Run Script*
- *Switches*
- *Preloading Slide*
- *Slide Library*
- *RSCRIPT*
- *Slides*
- *Delay Time*
- *Slide Show*

WHAT ARE SCRIPT FILES?

AutoCAD provides a facility called script files that allow you to combine different AutoCAD commands and execute them in a predetermined sequence. The commands can be written as a text file using any text editor like Notepad. These files, generally known as script files, have an extension *.scr* (example: *plot1.scr*). A script file is executed with the AutoCAD **Run Script** tool.

Script files can be used to generate a slide show, do the initial drawing setup, or plot a drawing to a predefined specification. They can also be used to automate certain command sequences that are used frequently in generating, editing, or viewing drawings. Remember that the script files cannot access dialog boxes or menus. When commands that open dialog boxes are issued from a script file, AutoCAD runs the command line version of the command instead of opening the dialog box.

Example 1 *Initial Setup of Drawing*

Write a script file that will perform the following initial setup for a drawing (file name *script1.scr*). It is assumed that the drawing will be plotted on 12x9 size paper (Scale factor for plotting = 4).

Ortho	On		Zoom	All
Grid	2.0		Text height	0.125
Snap	0.5		LTSCALE	4.0
Limits	0,0	48.0,36.0	DIMSCALE	4.0

Step 1: Understanding commands and prompt entries

Before writing a script file, you need to know the AutoCAD commands and the entries required in response to the Command prompts. To find out the sequence of the Command prompt entries, you can type the command and then respond to different Command prompts. The following is the list of AutoCAD commands and prompt entries for Example 1:

Command: **ORTHO**
Enter mode [ON/OFF] <OFF>: **ON**

Command: **GRID**
Specify grid spacing(X) or [ON/OFF/Snap/Major/aDaptive/Limits/Follow/Aspect]
<0.5000>: **2.0**

Command: **SNAP**
Specify snap spacing or [ON/OFF/Aspect/Legacy/Style/Type]<0.5000>: **0.5**

Command: **LIMITS**
Reset Model space limits:
Specify lower left corner or [ON/OFF] <0.0,0.0>: **0,0**
Specify upper right corner <12.0,9.0>: **48.0,36.0**

Command: **ZOOM**
Specify corner of window, enter a scale factor (nX or nXP), or
[All/Center/Dynamic/Extents/Previous/Scale/Window/Object] <real time>: **A**

Command: **TEXTSIZE**
Enter new value for TEXTSIZE <0.02>: **0.125**

Command: **LTSCALE**
Enter new linetype scale factor <1.0000>: **4.0**

Command: **DIMSCALE**
Enter new value for DIMSCALE <1.0000>: **4.0**

Step 2: Writing the script file

Once you know the commands and the required prompt entries, you can write a script file using any text editor such as the Notepad.

As you invoke the **NOTEPAD** command, AutoCAD prompts you to enter the file to be edited. Press Enter in response to the prompt to display the **Notepad** editor. Write the script file in the **Notepad** editor. Given below is the listing of the script file for Example 1:

```
ORTHO
ON
GRID
2.0
SNAP
0.5
LIMITS
0,0
48.0,36.0
ZOOM
ALL
TEXTSIZE
0.125
LTSCALE
4.0
DIMSCALE 4.0

```

(Blank line for Return.)

Note that the commands and the prompt entries in this file are in the same sequence as mentioned earlier. You can also combine several statements in one line, as shown in the following list:

```
;This is my first script file, SCRIPT1.SCR
ORTHO ON
GRID 2.0
SNAP 0.5
LIMITS 0,0 48.0,36.0
ZOOM
ALL
```

TEXTSIZE 0.125
LTSCALE 4.0
DIMSCALE 4.0
(Blank line for Return.)

Save the script file as *SCRIPT1.scr* and exit the text editor. Remember that if you do not save the file in the *.scr* format, it will not work as a script file. Notice the space between the commands and the prompt entries. For example, between the **ORTHO** command and the **ON** command, there is a space. Similarly, there is a space between **GRID** and **2.0**.

Note

1. In the script file, a space is used to terminate a command or a prompt entry. Therefore, spaces are very important in these files. Make sure there are no extra spaces, unless they are required.

2. After you change the limits, it is a good practice to use the ***ZOOM*** *tool with the* ***All*** *option to increase the drawing display area.*

3. Keyboard shortcuts are not allowed in the script files. Therefore, make sure not to use them in the script files.

Tip

AutoCAD ignores and does not process any lines that begin with a semicolon (;). This allows you to put comments in the related file or line.

RUNNING SCRIPT FILES

The **Run Script** tool allows you to run a script file while you are in the drawing editor. Choose the **Run Script** tool from the **Applications** panel of the **Manage** tab; the **Select Script File** dialog box will be invoked, refer to Figure 15-1. You can enter the name of the script file or you can accept the default file name. The default script file name is the same as the drawing name. If you want to enter a new file name, type the name of the script file without the file extension (**.SCR**). (The file extension is assumed and need not be included with the file name.)

Step 3: Running the script file

To run the script file of Example 1, invoke the **Run Script** tool, select the file **SCRIPT1**, and then choose the **Open** button in the **Select Script File** dialog box, refer to Figure 15-1. You will notice the changes taking place on the screen as the script file commands are executed.

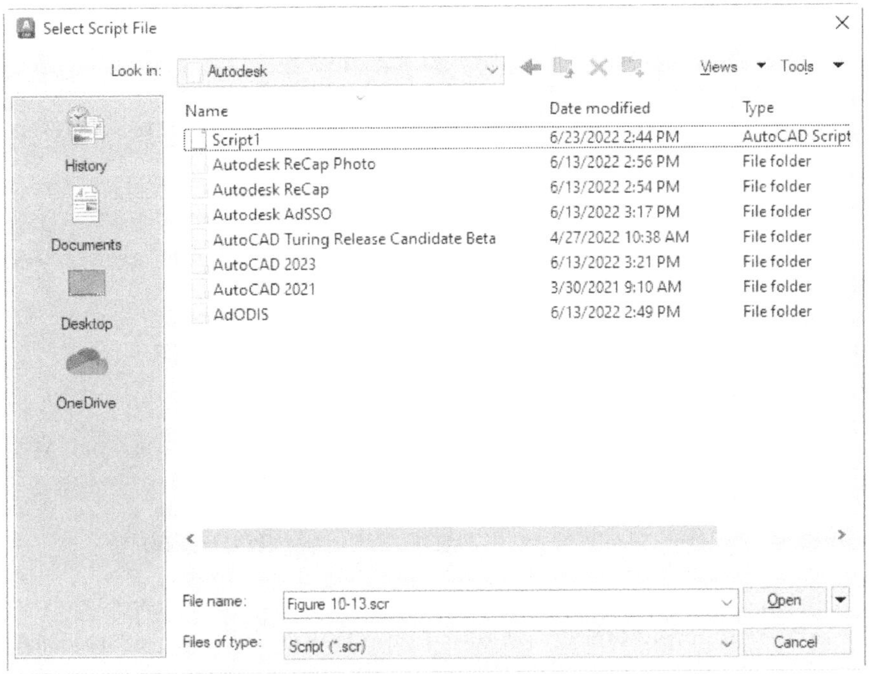

Figure 15-1 *The* ***Select Script File*** *dialog box*

You can also enter the name of the script file at the Command prompt by setting **FILEDIA**=0. The sequence for invoking the script using the Command line is given next.

Command: **FILEDIA**
Enter new value for FILEDIA <1>: **0**
Command: **SCRIPT**
Enter script file name <current>: *Specify the script file name.*

Example 2 — Layers

Write a script file that will set up the following layers with given colors and linetypes (file name *script2.scr*).

Layer Names	Color	Linetype	Line Weight
OBJECT	Red	Continuous	default
CENTER	Yellow	Center	default
HIDDEN	Blue	Hidden	default
DIMENSION	Green	Continuous	default
BORDER	Magenta	Continuous	default
HATCH	Cyan	Continuous	0.05

Step 1: Understanding commands and prompt entries

You need to know the AutoCAD commands and the required prompt entries before writing a script file. You need the following commands to create the layers with the given colors and linetypes.

Command: **-LAYER**
Enter an option
[?/Make/Set/New/Rename/ON/OFF/Color/Ltype/LWeight/TRansparency/MATerial/Plot/Freeze/Thaw/LOck/Unlock/stAte/Description/rEconcile]: **N**
Enter name list for new layer(s): **OBJECT,CENTER,HIDDEN,DIMENSION, BORDER, HATCH**

Enter an option
[?/Make/Set/New/Rename/ON/OFF/Color/Ltype/LWeight/TRansparency/MATerial/Plot/Freeze/Thaw/LOck/Unlock/stAte/Description/rEconcile]: **L**
Enter loaded linetype name or [?] <Continuous>: **CENTER**
Enter name list of layer(s) for linetype "CENTER" <0>: **CENTER**

Enter an option
[?/Make/Set/New/Rename/ON/OFF/Color/Ltype/LWeight/TRansparency/MATerial/Plot/Freeze/Thaw/LOck/Unlock/stAte/Description/rEconcile]: **L**
Enter loaded linetype name or [?] <Continuous>: **HIDDEN**
Enter name list of layer(s) for linetype "HIDDEN" <0>: **HIDDEN**

Enter an option
[?/Make/Set/New/Rename/ON/OFF/Color/Ltype/LWeight/TRansparency/MATerial/Plot/Freeze/Thaw/LOck/Unlock/stAte/Description/rEconcile]: **C**
New color [Truecolor/COlorbook]: **RED**
Enter name list of layer(s) for color 1 (red) <0>: **OBJECT**

Enter an option
[?/Make/Set/New/Rename/ON/OFF/Color/Ltype/LWeight/TRansparency/MATerial/Plot/Freeze/Thaw/LOck/Unlock/stAte/Description/rEconcile]: **C**
New color [Truecolor/COlorbook]: **YELLOW**
Enter name list of layer(s) for color 2 (yellow) <0>: **CENTER**

Enter an option
[?/Make/Set/New/Rename/ON/OFF/Color/Ltype/LWeight/TRansparency/MATerial/Plot/Freeze/Thaw/LOck/Unlock/stAte/Description/rEconcile]: **C**
New color [Truecolor/COlorbook]: **BLUE**
Enter name list of layer(s) for color 5 (blue)<0>: **HIDDEN**

Enter an option
[?/Make/Set/New/Rename/ON/OFF/Color/Ltype/LWeight/TRansparency/MATerial/Plot/Freeze/Thaw/LOck/Unlock/stAte/Description/rEconcile]: **C**
New color [Truecolor/COlorbook]: **GREEN**
Enter name list of layer(s) for color 3 (green)<0>: **DIMENSION**

Enter an option
[?/Make/Set/New/Rename/ON/OFF/Color/Ltype/LWeight/TRansparency/MATerial/Plot/Freeze/Thaw/LOck/Unlock/stAte/Description/rEconcile]: **C**
New color [Truecolor/COlorbook]: **MAGENTA**
Enter name list of layer(s) for color 6 (magenta)<0>: **BORDER**

Enter an option
[?/Make/Set/New/Rename/ON/OFF/Color/Ltype/LWeight/TRansparency/MATerial/Plot/Freeze/Thaw/LOck/Unlock/stAte/Description/rEconcile]: **C**
New color [Truecolor/COlorbook]: **CYAN**
Enter name list of layer(s) for color 4 (cyan)<0>: **HATCH**

Enter an option
[?/Make/Set/New/Rename/ON/OFF/Color/Ltype/LWeight/TRansparency/MATerial/Plot/Freeze/Thaw/LOck/Unlock/stAte/Description/rEconcile]: **LW**
Enter lineweight (0.0mm - 2.11mm): **0.05**
Enter name list of layers(s) for lineweight 0.05mm <0>: **HATCH**
[?/Make/Set/New/Rename/ON/OFF/Color/Ltype/LWeight/TRansparency/MATerial/Plot/Freeze/Thaw/LOck/Unlock/stAte/Description/rEconcile]: Enter.

Step 2: Writing the script file

The following file is a listing of the script file that creates different layers and assigns the given colors and linetypes to them:

```
;This script file will create new layers and
;assign different colors and linetypes to layers
LAYER
NEW
OBJECT,CENTER,HIDDEN,DIMENSION,BORDER,HATCH
L
CENTER
CENTER
L
HIDDEN
HIDDEN
C
RED
OBJECT
C
YELLOW
CENTER
C
BLUE
HIDDEN
C
GREEN
DIMENSION
C
MAGENTA
BORDER
C
CYAN
HATCH
```

*(This is a blank line to terminate the **LAYER** command. End of script file.)*
Save the script file as *script2.scr*.

Step 3: Running the script file

To run the script file of Example 2, choose the **Run Script** tool from the **Applications** panel of the **Manage** tab or enter **SCRIPT** at the Command prompt to invoke the **Select Script File** dialog box. Select **script2.scr** and then choose **Open**. You can also enter the **SCRIPT** command and the name of the script file at the Command prompt by setting **FILEDIA=0**.

Example 3 — *Rotating the Objects*

Write a script file that will rotate the line and the circle, as shown in Figure 15-2, around the lower endpoint of the line through 45 degree increments. The script file should be able to produce a continuous rotation of the given objects with a delay of two seconds after every 45 degree rotation (file name *script3.scr*). It is assumed that the line and circle are already drawn on the screen.

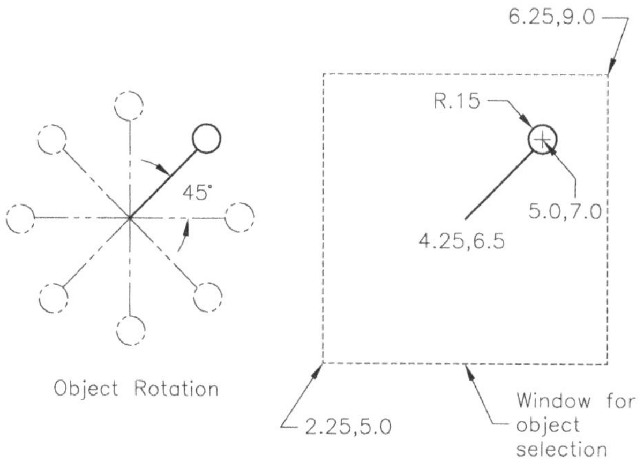

Figure 15-2 *Line and circle rotated through 45 degree increments*

Step 1: Understanding commands and prompt entries

Before writing the script file, enter the required commands and prompt entries. Write down the exact sequence of the entries in which they have been entered to perform the given operations. The following is the list of the AutoCAD command sequences needed to rotate the circle and the line around the lower endpoint of the line:

Command: **ROTATE**
Current positive angle in UCS: ANGDIR=counterclockwise ANGBASE=0
Select objects: **W** *(Window option to select object)*
Specify first corner: **2.25, 5.0**
Specify opposite corner: **6.25, 9.0**
Select objects: Enter.
Specify base point: **4.25,6.5**
Specify rotation angle or [Reference]: **45**

Step 2: Writing the script file

Once the AutoCAD commands, command options, and their sequences are known, you can write a script file. You can use any text editor to write a script file. The following is a listing of the script file that will create the required rotation of the circle and line of Example 3. The line numbers on the right and the text written as '(Blank line for Return)' are not a part of the file; they are shown here for reference only.

```
1 ROTATE
2 W
3 2.25,5.0
4 6.25,9.0
5                 (Blank line for Return.)
6 4.25,6.5
7 45
```

Line 1
ROTATE
In this line, **ROTATE** is an AutoCAD command that rotates the objects.

Line 2
W
In this line, **W** is the **Window** option for selecting the objects that need to be edited.

Line 3
2.25,5.0
In this line, 2.25 defines the *X* coordinate and 5.0 defines the *Y* coordinate of the lower left corner of the object selection window.

Line 4
6.25,9.0
In this line, 6.25 defines the *X* coordinate and 9.0 defines the *Y* coordinate of the upper right corner of the object selection window.

Line 5
Line 5 is a blank line that terminates the object selection process.

Line 6
4.25,6.5
In this line, 4.25 defines the *X* coordinate and 6.5 defines the *Y* coordinate of the base point for rotation.

Line 7
45
In this line, 45 is the incremental angle of rotation.

Note

One of the limitations of the script file is that all the information has to be contained within the same file. Such files do not let you enter any other information. For instance, in Example 3, if you want to use the ***Window*** *option to select the objects, the* ***Window*** *option (W) and the two points that define this window must be contained within the script file. The same is true for the base point and all other information that is entered in a script file. There is no way that a script file can prompt you to enter a particular piece of information and then resume the script file, unless you embed AutoLISP commands to prompt for user input.*

Step 3: Saving the script file

Save the script file with the name *script3.scr*.

Step 4: Running the script file

Choose **Tools > Run Script** from the menu bar, or choose the **Run Script** tool from the **Applications** panel of the **Manage** tab, or enter **SCRIPT** at the Command prompt to invoke the **Select Script File** dialog box. Select **script3.scr** and then choose **Open**. You will notice that the line and circle that were drawn on the screen are rotated once through an angle of 45 degrees. However, there will be no continuous rotation of the sketched entities. The next section (Repeating Script Files) explains how to continue the steps mentioned in the script file. You will also learn how to add a time delay between the continuous cycles in later sections of this chapter.

REPEATING SCRIPT FILES

The **RSCRIPT** command allows the user to execute the script file indefinitely until canceled. It is a very desirable feature when the user wants to run the same file continuously. For example, in the case of a slide show for a product demonstration, the **RSCRIPT** command can be used to run the script file repeatedly until it is terminated by pressing the Esc key. Similarly, in Example 3, the rotation command needs to be repeated indefinitely to create a continuous rotation of the objects. This can be accomplished by adding **RSCRIPT** at the end of the file, as shown in the following listing of the script file:

```
ROTATE
    W
    2.25,5.0
    6.25,9.0
                  (Blank line for Return.)
    4.25,6.5
    45
    RSCRIPT
```

The **RSCRIPT** command in line 8 will repeat the commands from line 1 to line 7, and thus set the script file in an indefinite loop. If you run the *script3.scr* file now, you will notice that there is a continuous rotation of the line and circle around the specified base point. However, the speed at which the entities rotate makes it difficult to view the objects. As a result, you need to add time delay between every repetition. The script file can be stopped by pressing the Esc or the Backspace key.

Note

You cannot provide conditional statements in a script file to terminate the file when a particular condition is satisfied unless you use the AutoLISP functions in the script file.

INTRODUCING TIME DELAY IN SCRIPT FILES

As mentioned earlier, some of the operations in the script files are performed very quickly thereby making it difficult to observe them on the screen. It might be necessary to intentionally introduce a pause between certain operations in a script file. For example, in a slide show for a product demonstration, there must be a time delay between different slides so that the audience have enough time to see each slide. This is accomplished by using the **DELAY** command, which introduces a delay before the next command is executed. The general format of the **DELAY** command is given next.

Command: **DELAY Time**
Where **Command** -----AutoCAD Command prompt
DELAY ---------**DELAY** command
Time ------------Time in milliseconds

The **DELAY** command is to be followed by the delay time in milliseconds. For example, a delay of 500 milliseconds means that AutoCAD will pause for approximately half a second before executing the next command. It is approximately half a second because computer processing speeds vary. The maximum time delay you can enter is 32,767 milliseconds (about 33 seconds). In Example 3, half a second delay can be introduced by inserting a **DELAY** command line between line 7 and line 8, as in the following file listing:

ROTATE
W
2.25,5.0
6.25,9.0
(Blank line for Return.)
4.25,6.5
45
DELAY 500
RSCRIPT

The first seven lines of this file rotate the objects through a 45 degree angle. Before the **RSCRIPT** command on line 8 is executed, there is a delay of 500 milliseconds (about half a second). The **RSCRIPT** command will repeat the script file that rotates the objects through another 45 degree angle. Thus, a slide show is created with a time delay of half a second after every 45 degree increment.

RESUMING SCRIPT FILES

If you cancel a script file and then want to resume it, you can use the **RESUME** command.
Command: **RESUME**

The **RESUME** command can also be used if the script file has encountered an error that suspends its function. The **RESUME** command will skip the command that caused the error and continue with the rest of the script file. If the error occurs when the command is in progress, use a leading apostrophe with the **RESUME** command (**'RESUME**) to invoke the **RESUME** command in the transparent mode.

Command: **'RESUME**

COMMAND LINE SWITCHES

The command line switches can be used as arguments to the *acad.exe* file that launches AutoCAD. You can also use the **Options** dialog box to set the environment or by adding a set of environment variables in the *autoexec.bat* file. The command line switches and environment variables override the values set in the **Options** dialog box for the current session only. These switches do not alter the system registry. The following is the list of the command line switches:

Switch	**Function**
/c	Controls where AutoCAD stores and searches for the hardware configuration file. The default file is *acad 2023.cfg*
/s	Specifies which directories to search for support files if they are not in the current directory
/b	Designates a script to run after AutoCAD starts
/t	Specifies a template to use while creating a new drawing
/nologo	Starts AutoCAD without first displaying the logo screen
/v	Designates a particular view of the drawing to be displayed on start-up of AutoCAD
/r	Reconfigures AutoCAD with the default device configuration settings
/p	Specifies the profile to use on start-up

RUNNING A SCRIPT FILE WHILE LOADING AutoCAD

The script files can also be run while loading AutoCAD, before it is actually started. The following is the format of the command for running a script file while loading AutoCAD.

"Drive\Program Files\Autodesk\AutoCAD 2023\acad.exe" [existing-drawing] [/t template] [/v view] /b Script-file

In the following example, AutoCAD will open the existing drawing (MYdwg1) and then run the script file (Setup) through the **Run** dialog box, as shown in Figure 15-3.

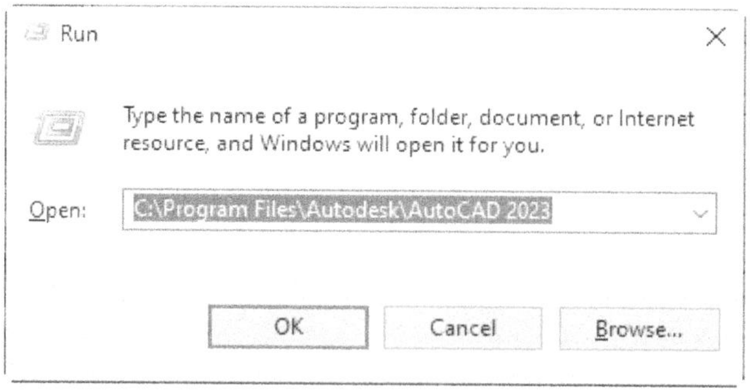

Figure 15-3 *Invoking the script file while loading AutoCAD using the* ***Run*** *dialog box*

Example:
"C:\Program Files\Autodesk\AutoCAD 2023\acad.exe" MYdwg1 /b Setup
Where, **AutoCAD** 2023 -------------AutoCAD 2023 subdirectory containing
---------------------AutoCAD system files
acad.exe --------ACAD command to start AutoCAD
MYDwg1 -------Existing drawing file name
Setup -----------Name of the script file

Note
Make sure that the drawing file that you want to open is saved in the C drive of your system. Also, you must have administrative privileges to save and open the drawing files from the C drive.

In the following example, AutoCAD will start a new drawing with the default name (Drawing), using the template file temp1, and then run the script file (Setup).

Example:
"C:\Program Files\Autodesk\AutoCAD 2023\acad.exe" /t temp1 /b Setup
Where **temp1** -----------Existing template file name
Setup -----------Name of the script file

or

"C:\ProgramFiles\Autodesk\AutoCAD 2023\acad.exe"/t temp1 "C:\MyFolder"/b Setup
Where **C:\Program Files\AutoCAD 2023\acad.exe** Path name for acad.exe
C:\MyFolder ---Path name for the Setup script file

In the following example, AutoCAD will start a new drawing with the default name (Drawing), and then run the script file (Setup).

Example:
"C:\Program Files\Autodesk\AutoCAD 2023\acad.exe" /b Setup
Where **Setup** ------------Name of the script file
Here, it is assumed that the AutoCAD system files are loaded in the AutoCAD 2023 directory.

Note
To invoke a script file while loading AutoCAD, the drawing file or the template file specified in the command must exist in the search path. You cannot start a new drawing with a given name. You can also use any template drawing file that is found in the template directory to run a script file through the ***Run*** *dialog box.*

Tip
You should avoid abbreviations to prevent any confusion. For example, C can be used as a close option when you are drawing lines. It can also be used as a command alias for drawing a circle. If you use both of them in a script file, it might be confusing.

Example 4 *Running a Script File while Loading AutoCAD*

Write a script file that can be invoked while loading AutoCAD and create a drawing with the following setup (filename *script4.scr*).

Grid	3.0
Snap	0.5
Limits	0,0
	36.0,24.0
Zoom	All
Text height	0.25
LTSCALE	3.0
DIMSCALE	3.0

Layers

Name	Color	Linetype
OBJ	Red	Continuous
CEN	Yellow	Center
HID	Blue	Hidden
DIM	Green	Continuous

Step 1: Writing the script file

Write a script file and save the file under the name *script4.scr*. The following is the listing of the script file that performs the initial setup for a drawing:

```
GRID 3.0
SNAP 0.5
LIMITS 0,0 36.0,24.0 ZOOM ALL
TEXTSIZE 0.25
LTSCALE 3
DIMSCALE 3.0
LAYER NEW
OBJ,CEN,HID,DIM
L CENTER CEN
L HIDDEN HID
C RED OBJ
C YELLOW CEN
C BLUE HID
C GREEN DIM
                    (Blank line for Enter.)
```

Step 2: Loading the script file through the Run dialog box

After you have written and saved the file, quit the text editor. To run the script file, *script4*, select **Start > Run** and then enter the following command line.

"C:\Program Files\Autodesk\AutoCAD 2023\acad.exe" /t EX4 /b script4

Where **acad.exe** --------ACAD to load AutoCAD

EX4 -------------Template file name
SCRIPT4 ------Name of the script file

Here, it is assumed that the template file (EX4) and the script file (script4) is on C drive. When you enter this line, AutoCAD is loaded and the file *ex4.dwt* is opened. The script file, script4, is then automatically loaded and the commands defined in the file are executed.

In the following example, AutoCAD will start a new drawing with the default name (Drawing), and then run the script file (script4), refer to Figure 15-4.

Example:
"C:\Program Files\Autodesk\AutoCAD 2023\acad.exe" /b script4
Where **script4** ----------Name of the script file

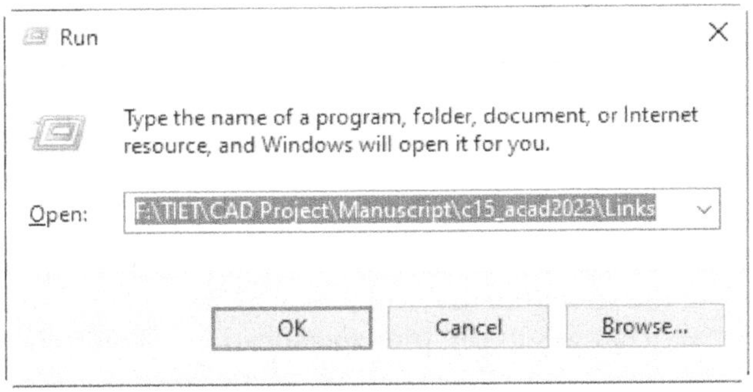

***Figure 15-4** Invoking the script file while loading AutoCAD using the **Run** dialog box*

Here, it is assumed that the AutoCAD system files are loaded in the AutoCAD 2023 directory.

Example 5 — *Plotting a Drawing*

Write a script file that will plot a 36" by 24" drawing to the maximum plot size on a 8.5" by 11" paper, using your system printer/plotter. Use the **Window** option to select the drawing to be plotted.

Step 1: Understanding commands and prompt entries

Before writing a script file to plot a drawing, find out the plotter specifications that must be entered in the script file to obtain the desired output. To determine the prompt entries and their sequence to set up the plotter specifications, enter the **-PLOT** command. Note the entries you make and their sequence (the entries for your printer or plotter will probably be different). The following is a listing of the plotter specifications with the new entries:

Command: **-PLOT**
Detailed plot configuration? [Yes/No] <No>: **Y**
Enter a layout name or [?] <Model>: Enter.
Enter an output device name or [?] <Default Printer name>: *Name of printer or plotter* Enter.
Enter paper size or [?] <Letter>: Enter.

Enter paper units [Inches/Millimeters] <Inches>: **I**
Enter drawing orientation [Portrait/Landscape] <Landscape>: **P**
Plot upside down? [Yes/No] <No>: **N**
Enter plot area [Display/Extents/Limits/View/Window] <Display>: **W**
Enter lower left corner of window <0.000000,0.000000>: **0,0**
Enter upper right corner of window <0.000000,0.000000>: **36,24**
Enter plot scale (Plotted Inches=Drawing Units) or [Fit] <Fit>: **F**
Enter plot offset (x,y) or [Center] <0.00,0.00>: **0,0**
Plot with plot styles? [Yes/No] <Yes>: **Yes**
Enter plot style table name or [?] (enter . for none) <>: **.**
Plot with lineweights? [Yes/No] <Yes>: **Y**
Enter shade plot setting [As displayed/Wireframe/Hidden/Visual styles/Rendered] <As displayed>: Enter.
Write the plot to a file [Yes/No] <N>: **N**
Save changes to page setup [Yes/No]? <N>: Enter.
Proceed with plot [Yes/No] <Y>: **Y**

Note that you need to have a printer installed on the system for successful execution of script.

Step 2: Writing the script file

Now you can write the script file by entering the responses of these prompts in the file. The following file is a listing of the script file that will plot a 36" by 24" drawing on 8.5" by 11" paper after making the necessary changes in the plot specifications. The comments on the right are not a part of the file.

```
PLOT
Y
                (Blank line for Enter, selects default layout.)
DWG TO PDF.pc3
                (Blank line for Enter, selects the default paper size.)
I
P
N
w
0,0
36,24
F
0,0
Y
.               (Enter . for none)
Y
A
N
N
Y
```

The method of saving and running the script file for this example is the same as that described in the previous examples. You can use a blank line to accept the default value for a prompt. A blank line in the script file will cause a Return. However, you must not accept the default plot specifications because the file may have been altered by another user or by another script file. Therefore, always enter the actual values in the file so that when you run a script file, it does not take the default values.

Example 6 — Animating a Clock

Write a script file to animate a clock with continuous rotation of the second hand (longer needle) through 5 degrees and the minutes hand (shorter needle) through 2 degrees clockwise around the center of the clock, refer to Figure 15-5.

Figure 15-5 *Drawing for Example 6*

The specifications are given next.

Specifications for the rim made of donut.

Color of Donut	Blue
Inner diameter of Donut	8.0
Outer diameter of Donut	8.4
Center point of Donut	5,5

Specifications for the digit mark made of polyline.

Color of the digit mark	Green
Start point of Pline	5,8.5
Initial width of Pline	0.25
Final width of Pline	0.25
Height of Pline	0.25

Specifications for second hand (long needle) made of polyline.

Color of the second hand	Red
Start point of Pline	5,5
Initial width of Pline	0.5
Final width of Pline	0.0
Length of Pline	3.5
Rotation of the second hand	5 degree clockwise

Specifications for minute hand (shorter needle) made of polyline.

Color of the minute hand	Cyan
Start point of Pline	5,5

Initial width of Pline	0.35
Final width of Pline	0.0
Length of Pline	3.0
Rotation of the minute hand	2 degree clockwise

Step 1: Understanding the commands and prompt entries for creation of the clock

For this example, you can create two script files and then link them. The first script file will demonstrate the creation of the clock on the screen. The next script file will demonstrate the rotation of the needles of the clock.

First write a script file to create the clock as follows and save the file under the name *clock.scr*. The following is the listing of this file:

Command: **-COLOR**

Enter default object color [Truecolor/COlorbook] <BYLAYER>: **Blue**

Command: **DONUT**

Specify inside diameter of donut<0.5>: **8.0**

Specify outside diameter of donut<0.5>: **8.4**

Specify center of donut or <exit>: **5,5**

Specify center of donut or <exit>: Enter.

Command: **-COLOR**

Enter default object color [Truecolor/COlorbook] <BYLAYER>: **Green**

Command: **PLINE**

Specify start point: **5,8.5**

Specify next point or [Arc/Halfwidth/Length/Undo/Width]: **Width**

Specify starting width<0.00>: **0.25**

Specify ending width<0.25>: **0.25**

Specify next point or [Arc/Halfwidth/Length/Undo/Width]: **@0.25<270**

Specify next point or [Arc/Halfwidth/Length/Undo/Width]: Enter.

Command: **-ARRAY**

Select objects: **Last**

Select objects: Enter.

Enter the type of array[Rectangular/PAth/Polar]<R>: **Polar**

Specify center point of array or [Base]: **5,5**

Enter the number of items in the array: **12**

Specify the angle to fill(+= ccw, -=cw)<360>: **360**

Rotate arrayed objects ? [Yes/No]<Y>: **Y**

Command: **-COLOR**

Enter default object color [Truecolor/COlorbook] <BYLAYER>: **RED**

Command: **PLINE**

Specify start point: **5,5**

Specify next point or [Arc/Close/Halfwidth/Length/Undo/Width]: **Width**

Specify starting width<.25>: **0.5**

Specify ending width<0.5>: **0**

Specify next point or [Arc/Halfwidth/Length/Undo/Width]: **@3.5<0**

Specify next point or [Arc/Close/Halfwidth/Length/Undo/Width]: Enter.

Command: **-COLOR**

Enter default object color [Truecolor/COlorbook] <BYLAYER>: **Cyan**

Command: **PLINE**
Specify start point: **5,5**
Specify next point or [Arc/Halfwidth/Length/Undo/Width]: **Width**
Specify starting width<0.0000>: **0.35**
Specify ending width<0.35>: **0**
Specify next point or [Arc/Halfwidth/Length/Undo/Width]: **@3<90**
Specify next point or [Arc/Close/Halfwidth/Length/Undo/Width]: [Enter].
Command: **SCRIPT**
ROTATE.SCR

Now you will write the script file by entering the responses to these prompts in the file *clock.scr*.

Next, you will write the script to rotate the clock hands and save the file with the name *ROTATE.scr*. Remember that while entering the commands in the script files, you do not need to add a hyphen (-) as a prefix to the command name to execute them from the command line. When a command is entered using the script file, the dialog box is not displayed and it is executed using the command line. For example, in this script file, the **COLOR** and **ARRAY** commands will be executed using the command line. Listing of the script file is given next.

```
Color
Blue
Donut
8.0
8.4
5,5
                    (Blank line for Enter.)
Color
Green
Pline
5,8.5
W
0.25
0.25
@0.25<270
                    (Blank line for Enter.)
Array
L
                    (Blank line for Enter.)
P
5,5
12
360
Y
Color
Red
Pline
5,5
W
```

0.5
0
@3.5<0
(Blank line for Enter.)
Color
Cyan
Pline
5,5
w
0.35
0
@3<90
(Blank line for Enter.)
Script
ROTATE.scr (Name of the script file that will cause rotation)
(Blank line for Enter.)

Save this file as *clock.scr* in a directory that is specified in the AutoCAD support file search path. It is recommended that the *ROTATE.scr* file should also be saved in the same directory. Remember that if the files are not saved in the directory that is specified in the AutoCAD support file search path using the **Options** dialog box, the linked script file (*ROTATE.scr*) may not run.

Step 2: Understanding the commands and sequences for rotation of the needles

The last line in the above script file is *ROTATE.scr*. This is the name of the script file that will rotate the clock hands. Before writing the script file, enter the **ROTATE** command and respond to the command prompts that will cause the desired rotation. The following is the listing of the AutoCAD command sequences needed to rotate the objects:

Command: **ROTATE**
Select objects: **L**
Select objects: Enter.
Specify base point: 5,5
Specify rotation angle or [Copy/Reference] <0>: -2
Command: **ROTATE**
Select objects: **C**
Specify first corner: 3,3
Specify other corner: 7,7
Select objects: **Remove**
Remove objects: **L**
Remove objects: Enter.
Specify base point: 5,5
Specify rotation angle or [Copy/Reference]: -5

Now you can write the script file by entering the responses to these prompts in the file *ROTATE.scr*. The following is the listing of the script file that will rotate the clock hands:

Rotate
L
(Blank line for Enter.)

```
5,5
-2
Rotate
c
3,3
7,7
R
L
                              (Blank line for Enter.)
5,5
-5
Rscript
                              (Blank line for Enter.)
```

Save the above script file as *ROTATE.scr*. Now, run the script file *clock.scr*. Since this file is linked with *ROTATE.scr*, it will automatically run *ROTATE.scr* after running *clock.scr*. Note that if the linked file is not saved in a directory specified in the AutoCAD support file search path, the last line of the *clock.scr* must include a fully-resolved path to *ROTATE.scr*, or AutoCAD would not be able to locate the file.

Exercise 1 — *Plotting a Drawing*

Write a script file that will plot a 288' by 192' drawing on a 36" x 24" sheet of paper. The drawing scale is 1/8" = 1'. (The filename is *script9.scr*. In this exercise, assume that AutoCAD is configured for the HPGL plotter and the plotter description is HPGL-Plotter.)

WHAT IS A SLIDE SHOW?

AutoCAD provides a facility of using script files to combine the slides in a text file and display them in a predetermined sequence. In this way, you can generate a slide show for a slide presentation. You can also introduce a time delay in the display so that the viewer has enough time to view each slide.

A drawing or parts of a drawing can also be displayed using the AutoCAD display commands. For example, you can use **ZOOM**, **PAN**, or other commands to display the details you want to show. If the drawing is very complicated, it takes time to display the desired information and it may not be possible to get the desired views in the right sequence. However, with slide shows you can arrange the slides in any order and present them in a definite sequence. In addition to saving time, this also helps to minimize the distraction that might be caused by constantly changing the drawing display. Also, some drawings are confidential in nature and you may not want to display some portions or views of them. You can send a slide show to a client without losing control of the drawings and the information that is contained in them.

WHAT ARE SLIDES?

A slide is the snapshot of a screen display; it is like taking a picture of a display with a camera. The slides do not contain any vector information like AutoCAD drawings, this means that the entities do not have any information associated with them. For example, the slides do not retain any information about the layers, colors, linetypes, start point, or endpoint of a line or viewpoint. Therefore, slides cannot be edited like drawings. If you want to make any changes in the slide, you need to edit the drawing and then make a new slide from the edited drawing.

CREATING SLIDES

In AutoCAD, slides are created using the **MSLIDE** command. If **FILEDIA** is set to 1, the **MSLIDE** command displays the **Create Slide File** dialog box, refer to Figure 15-6 on the screen. You can enter the slide file name in this dialog box. If **FILEDIA** is set to 0, the command will prompt you to enter the slide file name.

Command: **MSLIDE**
Enter name of slide file to create <Default>: *Slide file name.*

Example:
Command: **MSLIDE**
Slide File: <Drawing1> **SLIDE1**
Where **Drawing1** ------Default slide file name
SLIDE1 --------Slide file name

In this example, AutoCAD will save the slide file as *slide1.sld*.

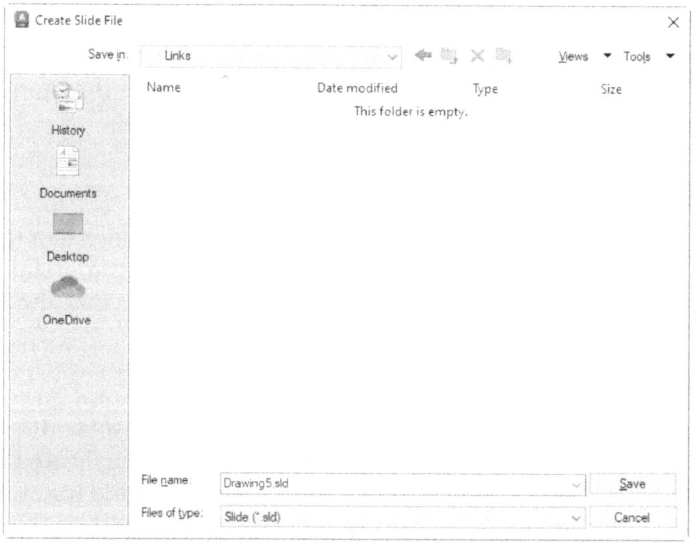

***Figure 15-6** The **Create Slide File** dialog box*

Note

*In model space, yuo can use the **MSLIDE** command to make a slide of the existing display in the current viewport. If you are in the paper space veiwport, you can make a slide of the display in the paper space that includes all floating viewports created in it. When the viewports are not active, the **MSLIDE** command will make a slide of the current screen display.*

VIEWING SLIDES

To view a slide, enter the **VSLIDE** command at the Command prompt; the **Select Slide File** dialog box will be displayed, as shown in Figure 15-7. Choose the file that you want to view and then click **Open** button to exit the dialog box. The corresponding slide will be displayed on the screen. If **FILEDIA** is 0, the slide that you want to view can be directly entered at the Command prompt.

Command: **VSLIDE**
Enter name of slide file to view<Default>: *Name*.

Example:
Command: **VSLIDE**
Slide file <Drawing1>: SLIDE1
Where **Drawing1** ------Default slide file name
SLIDE1 --------Name of slide file

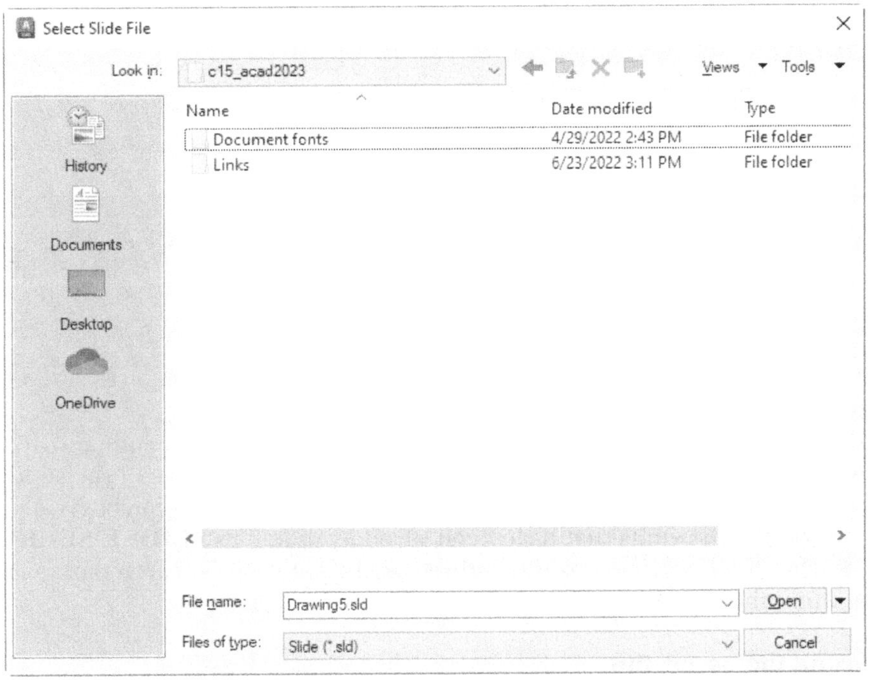

Figure 15-7 *The* ***Select Slide File*** *dialog box*

Note

*1. After viewing a slide, you can use the **REDRAW** command, roll the wheel, or pan with a mouse to remove the slide display and return to the existing drawing on the screen.*

*2. Any command that is automatically followed by the **REDRAW** command will also display the existing drawing. For example, AutoCAD **GRID**, **ZOOM ALL**, and **REGEN** commands will automatically return to the existing drawing on the screen.*

3. You can view the slides on a high-resolution or a low-resolution monitor. Depending on the resolution of the monitor, AutoCAD automatically adjusts the image. However, if you are using a high-resolution monitor, it is better to make the slides using the same monitor to take full advantage of that monitor.

Example 7 — *Slide Show*

Write a script file that will create a slide show of the following slide files, with a time delay of 15 seconds after every slide, refer to Figure 15-8.

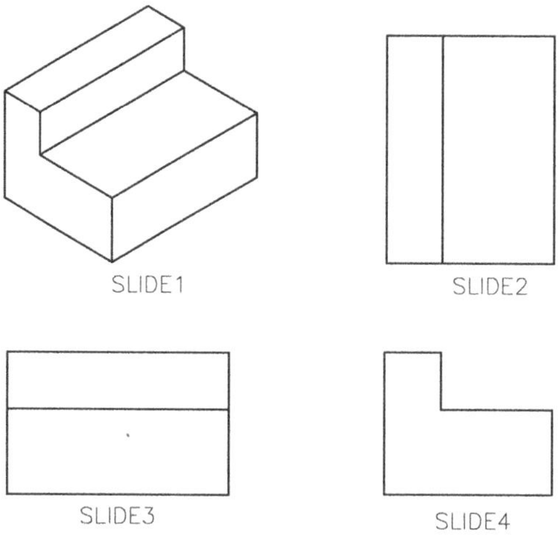

Figure 15-8 *Slides for slide show*

Step 1: Creating the slides

The first step in a slide show is to create the slides using the **MSLIDE** command. The **MSLIDE** command will invoke the **Create Slide File** dialog box. Enter the name of the slide as **SLIDE1** and choose the **Save** button to exit the dialog box. Similarly, other slides can be created and saved. Figure 15-8 shows the drawings that have been saved as slide files **SLIDE1**, **SLIDE2**, **SLIDE3**, and **SLIDE4**. The slides must be saved to a directory in AutoCAD's search path, otherwise, the script will not find the slides.

Step 2: Writing the script file

The second step is to find out the sequence, in which you want these slides to be displayed, with the necessary time delay, if any, between slides. Then you can use any text editor or the AutoCAD **EDIT** command (provided the *acad.pgp* file is present and **EDIT** is defined in the file) to write the script file with the extension *.scr*.

The following is the listing of the script file that will create a slide show of the slides in Figure 10-8. The name of the script file is **SLDSHOW1.scr**.

```
VSLIDE SLIDE1
DELAY 15000
```

```
VSLIDE SLIDE2
DELAY 15000
VSLIDE SLIDE3
DELAY 15000
VSLIDE SLIDE4
DELAY 15000
```

Step 3: Running the script file

To run this script file, choose the **Run Script** tool from **Manage > Applications** or enter **SCRIPT** at the Command prompt to invoke the **Select Script File** dialog box. Choose **SLDSHOW1** and then choose the **Open** button from the **Select Script File** dialog box. You can see the changes taking place on the screen.

PRELOADING SLIDES

In the script file of Example 7, VSLIDE SLIDE1 in line 1 loads the slide file, **SLIDE1**, and displays it on the screen. After a pause of 15,000 milliseconds, it starts loading the second slide file, **SLIDE2**. Depending on the computer and the disk access time, you will notice that it takes some time to load the second slide file. The same is true for the other slides. To avoid the delay in loading the slide files, AutoCAD has provided a facility to preload a slide while viewing the previous slide. This is accomplished by placing an asterisk (*) in front of the slide file name.

VSLIDE SLIDE1	*(View slide, SLIDE1.)*
VSLIDE *SLIDE2	*(Preload slide, SLIDE2.)*
DELAY 15000	*(Delay of 15 seconds.)*
VSLIDE	*(Display slide, SLIDE2.)*
VSLIDE *SLIDE3	*(Preload slide, SLIDE3.)*
DELAY 15000	*(Delay of 15 seconds.)*
VSLIDE	*(Display slide, SLIDE3.)*
VSLIDE *SLIDE4	
DELAY 15000	
VSLIDE	
DELAY 15000	
RSCRIPT	*(Restart the script file.)*

Example 8 — Preloading Slides

Write a script file to generate a continuous slide show of the SLD1, SLD2, and SLD3 slide files, with a time delay of two seconds between slides.

The slide files are located in different subdirectories, as shown in Figure 15-9.

C:

Program Files

Autodesk

AutoCAD 2023

SUBDIR1(SLD1)   SUBDIR2(SLD2)   SUBDIR3(SLD3)

Figure 15-9 *Subdirectories of the C drive*

Where
C: ---------------------*Root directory.*
Program Files -------------*Root directory.*
Autodesk -------------------*Root directory.*
AutoCAD 2023----------- *Subdirectory where the AutoCAD files are loaded.*
SUBDIR1------------------ *Drawing subdirectory.*
SUBDIR2 ----------------- *Drawing subdirectory.*
SUBDIR3 ----------------- *Drawing subdirectory.*
SLD1 --------------------- *Slide file in SUBDIR1 subdirectory.*
SLD2 ---------------------*Slide file in SUBDIR2 subdirectory.*
SLD3 ---------------------*Slide file in SUBDIR3 subdirectory.*

The following is the listing of the script files that will generate a slide show for the slides in Example 8:

```
1 VSLIDE "C:/Program Files/Autodesk/AutoCAD 2023/SUBDIR1/SLD1.SLD"
2 DELAY  2000
3 VSLIDE "C:/Program Files/Autodesk/AutoCAD 2023/SUBDIR2/SLD2.SLD"
4 DELAY 2000
5 VSLIDE "C:/Program Files/Autodesk/AutoCAD 2023/SUBDIR3/SLD3.SLD"
6 DELAY 2000
7 RSCRIPT
```

Line 1
VSLIDE "C:/Program Files/Autodesk/AutoCAD 2023/SUBDIR1/SLD1.SLD"
In this line, the AutoCAD command **VSLIDE** loads the slide file **SLD1**. The path name is mentioned along with the command **VSLIDE**. If the path name directory contains spaces, then the path name must be enclosed in quotes.

Line 2
DELAY 2000

This line uses the AutoCAD **DELAY** command to create a pause of approximately two seconds before the next slide is loaded.

Line 3
VSLIDE "C:/Program Files/Autodesk/AutoCAD 2023/SUBDIR2/SLD2.SLD"
In this line, the AutoCAD command **VSLIDE** loads the slide file **SLD2**, located in the subdirectory **SUBDIR2**. If the slide file is located in a different subdirectory, you need to define the path with the slide file.

Line 5
VSLIDE "C:/Program Files/Autodesk/AutoCAD 2023/SUBDIR3/SLD3.SLD"
In this line, the **VSLIDE** command loads the slide file SLD3, located in the subdirectory **SUBDIR3**.

Line 7
RSCRIPT
In this line, the **RSCRIPT** command executes the script file again and displays the slides on the screen. This process continues indefinitely until the script file is canceled by pressing the Esc key or the Backspace key.

SLIDE LIBRARIES

AutoCAD provides a utility, SLIDELIB, which constructs a library of the slide files. The format of the **SLIDELIB** utility command is as follows:

SLIDELIB (Library filename) <(Slide list filename)
Example:
SLIDELIB SLDLIB <SLDLIST
Where **SLIDELIB** -----AutoCAD's SLIDELIB utility
SLDLIB --------Slide library filename
SLDLIST ------List of slide filenames

The **SLIDELIB** utility is supplied with the AutoCAD software package. You can find this utility (SLIDELIB.EXE) in the *C:\Program Files\Autodesk\AutoCAD 2023* subdirectory. The slide file list is a list of the slide file names that you want in a slide show. It is a text file that can be written by using any text editor like Notepad.

C:

AutoCAD 2023

SUPPORT SLIDES

The slide file list can also be created by using the following command, if you have a DOS version 5.0 or above. You can use the make directory (md) or change directory (cd) commands in the DOS mode while making or changing directories.

C:\AutoCAD 2023\SLIDES>DIR *.SLD/B>SLDLIST

In this example, assume that the name of the slide file list is **SLDLIST** and all slide files are in the SLIDES subdirectory. To use this command to create a slide file list, all slide files must be in the same directory.

When you use the SLIDELIB utility, it reads the slide file names from the file that is specified in the slide list and the file is then written to the file specified by the library. In Example 9, the SLIDELIB utility reads the slide filenames from the file SLDLIST and writes them to the library file SLDSHOW1:

C:\AutoCAD 2023\SLIDES\ SLIDELIB SLDSHOW1 <SLDLIST

Note

1. You cannot edit a slide library file. If you want to change anything, you have to create a new list of the slide files and then use the SLIDELIB utility to create a new slide library.

*2. If you edit a slide while it is being displayed on the screen, the slide will not be edited. Instead, the current drawing that is behind the slide gets edited. Therefore, do not use any editing commands while you are viewing a slide. Use the **VSLIDE** and **DELAY** commands only while viewing a slide.*

3. The path name is not saved in the slide library. This is the reason if you have more than one slide with the same name, even though they are in different subdirectories, only one slide will be saved in the slide library.

Example 9 — Slide Library

Use AutoCAD's SLIDELIB utility to generate a continuous slide show of the following slide files with a time delay of 2.5 seconds between the slides. (The filenames are: SLDLIST for slide list file, SLDSHOW1 for slide library, SHOW1 for script file.)

front, top, rside, 3dview, isoview

The slide files are located in different subdirectories, as shown in Figure 15-10.

C

Dwg-Files

Proj-A	***Proj-B***	***Slide-Files***
front	*3dview*	*sldlist*
top	*isoview*	*slidelib.exe*
rside		

Figure 15-10 *Subdirectories to be created in C drive*

Where **C** ----------------- *(C drive.)*
Dwg-Files ---- *(Subdirectory where drawing files are located)*
Proj-A -------- *(Subdirectory where the slide files are located)*

Proj-B --------- *(Subdirectory where the slide files are located)*
Slide-Files --- *(Directory where Slidelib.exe and sldlist are copied)*

Step 1: Creating a list of the slide file names

The first step is to create a list of the slide file names with the drive and the directory information. Assume that you are in the **Slide-Files** subdirectory. You can use a text editor like Notepad to create a list of the slide files that you want to include in the slide show. After creating the list, save the text file and then remove its file extension. The following file is a listing of the file SLDLIST for Example 9:

```
c:\Dwg-Files\Proj-A\front
c:\Dwg-Files\Proj-A\top
c:\Dwg-Files\Proj-A\rside
c:\Dwg-Files\Proj-B\3dview
c:\Dwg-Files\Proj-B\isoview
```

Step 2: Copying the SLIDELIB utility

The **SLIDELIB** utility is supplied with the AutoCAD software package. You can find this utility (SLIDELIB.EXE) in the *C:\Program Files\Autodesk\AutoCAD 2023* subdirectory. Copy it to the **Slide-Files** folder.

Note
All related directories should be added in the AutoCAD's support files search path.

Step 3: Running the SLIDELIB utility

The third step is to use AutoCAD's SLIDELIB utility program to create the slide library. The name of the slide library is assumed to be **sldshow1** for this example. Before creating the slide library, copy the slide list file (SLDLIST) and the SLIDELIB utility from the support directory to the Slide-Files directory. This ensures that all the required files are in one directory. Enter the **SHELL** command at AutoCAD Command prompt and then press the Enter key at the OS Command prompt. The **AutoCAD Shell Active** Command window will be displayed on the screen, refer to Figure 15-11. You can also use Windows DOS box instead of **AutoCAD Shell Active** Command window by choosing **All Programs > Accessories > Command Prompt**. Make sure that the drawing file is saved before using the **SHELL** command.

Command: **SHELL**
OS Command: Enter.

Figure 15-11 *The* ***AutoCAD Shell Active*** *Command window*

Now, enter the following command in the Command window to run the SLIDELIB utility and create the slide library. Here it is assumed that **Slide-Files** directory is the current directory. Use the **cd** command in the Command window to change the directory.

C:\Dwg-Files\Slide-Files>SLIDELIB sldshow1 <sldlist

Where **SLIDELIB** -----AutoCAD's SLIDELIB utility
sldshow1 -------Slide library
sldlist -----------Slide file list

Step 4: Writing the script file

Now, you can write a script file for the slide show that will use the slides in the slide library. The name of the script file for this example is assumed to be SHOW1.

```
VSLIDE C:\Dwg-Files\Slide-Files\sldshow1(front)
DELAY 2500
VSLIDE C:\Dwg-Files\Slide-Files\sldshow1(top)
DELAY 2500
VSLIDE C:\Dwg-Files\Slide-Files\sldshow1(rside)
DELAY 2500
VSLIDE C:\Dwg-Files\Slide-Files\sldshow1(3dview)
DELAY 2500
VSLIDE C:\Dwg-Files\Slide-Files\sldshow1(isoview)
DELAY 2500
RSCRIPT
```

Step 5: Running the script file

Invoke the **Select Script File** dialog box, as shown in Figure 15-12, by choosing the **Run Script** tool from **Manage > Applications**. You can also enter the **SCRIPT** command at the Command prompt after setting the system variable FILEDIA to 0.

Command: **SCRIPT**
Enter script file name<default>: **SHOW1**

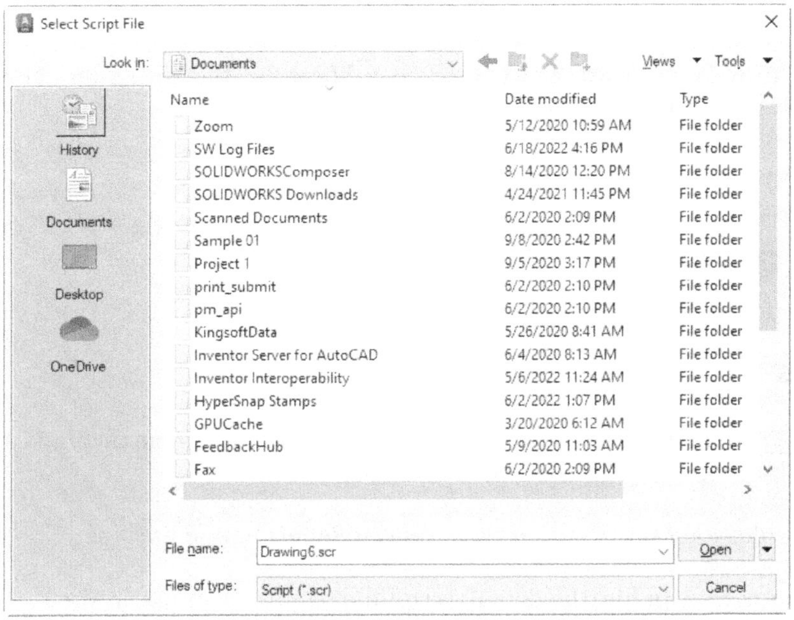

Figure 15-12 *Selecting the script file from the* ***Select Script File*** *dialog box*

Self-Evaluation Test

Answer the following questions and then compare them to those given at the end of this chapter:

SCRIPT FILES

1. In AutoCAD, you can use the __________ to combine different AutoCAD commands and execute them in a predetermined sequence.

2. Before writing a script file, you need to know the AutoCAD __________ and the __________ required in response to the command prompts.

3. In AutoCAD, the __________ command is used to run a script file.

4. In a script file, the __________ is used to terminate a command or a prompt entry.

5. The **DELAY** command is to be followed by __________ in milliseconds.

SLIDE SHOW

6. Slides do not contain any __________ information, which means that the entities do not have any information associated with them.

7. Slides can be created using the AutoCAD __________ command.

8. To view a slide, use the __________ command.

9. AutoCAD provides a utility that constructs a library of the slide files. This is done with AutoCAD's utility program called __________.

10. Slides cannot be edited like a drawing. (T/F)

Review Questions

Answer the following questions:

SCRIPT FILES

1. The __________ files can be used to generate a slide show, perform the initial drawing setup, or plot a drawing to a predefined specification.

2. In a script file, you can __________ several statements in one line.

3. When you run a script file, the default script file name is the same as the __________ name.

4. Type the name of the script file without the __________ file, when you run a script file.

5. One of the limitations of script files is that all the information has to be contained __________ the file.

6. The AutoCAD __________ command allows you to re-execute a script file indefinitely until the command is canceled.

7. You cannot provide a __________ statement in a script file to terminate the file when a particular condition is satisfied.

8. The AutoCAD __________ command schedules a delay before the next command is executed.

9. If the script file is canceled and you want to resume the script file, you need to use the ____________________ command.

SLIDE SHOW

10. A __________ can also be introduced in the script file so that the viewer has enough time to view a slide.

11. Slides are the __________ of a screen display.

12. In model space, you can use the __________ command to make a slide of the existing display in the current viewport.

13. If you want to make any changes in the slide, you need to __________ the drawing, then make a new slide from the edited drawing.

14. If the slide is in the slide library and you want to view it, the slide library name has to be __________ with the slide filename.

15. You cannot __________ a slide library file. If you want to change anything, you have to create a new list of the slide files and then use the __________ utility to create a new slide library.

16. If you are in paper space viewport, you can make a slide of the display in paper space that includes all floating viewports created in it. (T/F)

Exercise 2 — *Script Files*

Write a script file that will perform the following initial setup for a drawing.

Grid	2.0
Snap	0.5
Limits	0,0
	18.0,12.0
Zoom	All
Text height	0.25
LTSCALE	2.0
Overall dimension scale factor is 2	
Aligned dimension text with the dimension line	
Dimension text above the dimension line	
Size of the center mark is 0.75	

Exercise 3 — *Script Files*

Write a script file that will set up the following layers with the given colors and linetypes.

Layers **Name**	**Color**	**Linetype**
Contour	Red	Continuous
SPipes	Yellow	Center
WPipes	Blue	Hidden
Power	Green	Continuous
Manholes	Magenta	Continuous
Trees	Cyan	Continuous

Exercise 4 — *Script Files*

Write a script file that will perform the following initial setup for a new drawing.

Limits	0,0 24,18
Grid	1.0
Snap	0.25
Ortho	On

Snap	On
Zoom	All
Pline width	0.02
PLine	0,0 24,0 24,18 0,18 0,0
Ltscale	1.5
Units	Decimal units
	Precision 0.00
	Decimal degrees
	Precision 0
	Base angle East (0.00)
	Angle measured counterclockwise

Layers

Name	Color	Linetype
Obj	Red	Continuous
Cen	Yellow	Center
Hid	Blue	Hidden
Dim	Green	Continuous

Exercise 5 — *Script Files*

Write a script file that will plot a given drawing according to the following specifications. (Use the plotter for which your system is configured and adjust the values accordingly.)

Plot, using the Window option
Window size (0,0 24,18)
Do not write the plot to file
Size in inch units
Plot origin (0.0,0.0)
Maximum plot size (8.5,11 or the smallest size available on your printer/plotter)
90° plot rotation
No removal of hidden lines
Plotting scale (Fit)

Exercise 6 Script Files

Write a script file that will rotate a line continuously in 10 degrees increments around its midpoint, refer to Figure 15-13. The time delay between increments is one second.

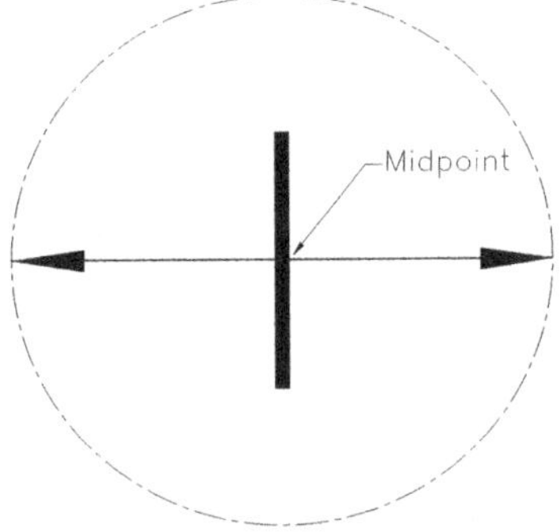

Figure 15-13 *Drawing for Exercise 6*

Exercise 7 Script Files

Write a script file that will continuously rotate the arrangement shown in Figure 15-14 as per the following instructions:

One set of two circles and one line should rotate clockwise, while the other set of two circles and the other line should rotate counterclockwise. Assume the rotation to be 5 degrees around the intersection of the lines for both sets of arrangements.

Specifications are given below:

Start point of the horizontal line	2,4
End point of the horizontal line	8,4
Center point of circle at the start point of horizontal line	2,4
Diameter of the circle	1.0
Center point of circle at the end point of horizontal line	8,4
Diameter of circle	1.0
Start point of the vertical line	5,1
End point of the vertical line	5,7
Center point of circle at the start point of the vertical line	5,1
Diameter of the circle	1.0
Center point of circle at the end point of the vertical line	5,7
Diameter of the circle	1.0

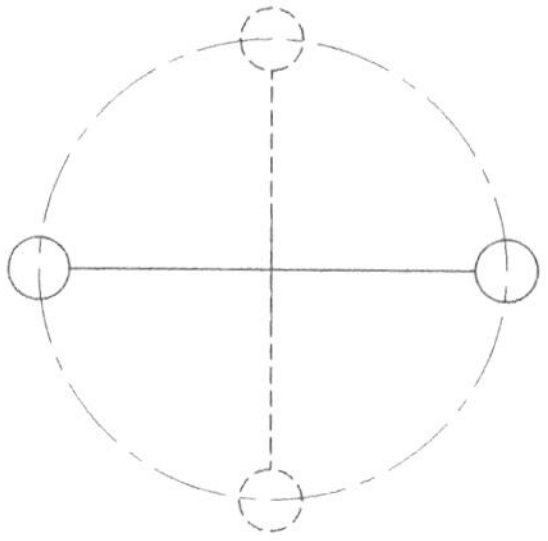

Figure 15-14 *Drawing for Exercise 7*

Hint: *Select one set of two circles and one line and then create one group. Similarly, select another set of two circles and one line and then create another group. Now, rotate one group clockwise and another group counterclockwise.*

Exercise 8 — *Slide Show*

Make the slides shown in Figure 15-15 and write a script file for a continuous slide show. Provide a time delay of 5 seconds after every slide. (You are not restricted to use only the slides shown in Figure 15-15; you can use any slides of your choice.)

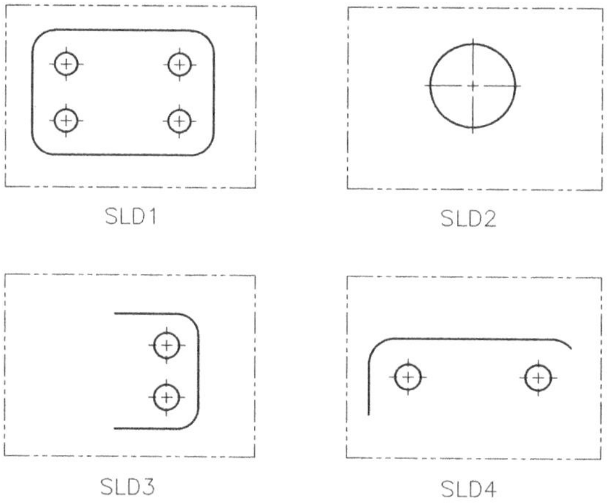

Figure 15-15 *Slides for slide show*

Exercise 9 *Slide Library*

List the slides used in Exercise 8 in a file SLDLIST2 and create a slide library file SLDLIB2. Then write a script file SHOW2 using the slide library with a time delay of 5 seconds after every slide.

Answers to Self-Evaluation Test

1. SCRIPT files, **2.** Commands, options, **3. SCRIPT**, **4.** blank space, **5.** time, **6.** vector, **7. MSLIDE**, **8. VSLIDE**, **9. SLIDELIB**, **10.** T

Chapter 16

Creating Linetypes and Hatch Patterns

Learning Objectives

After completing this chapter, you will be able to:
- *Write linetype definitions*
- *Create different linetypes*
- *Create linetype files*
- *Determine LTSCALE for plotting the drawing to given specifications*
- *Define alternate linetypes and modify existing linetypes*
- *Create string and shape complex linetypes*
- *Understand hatch pattern definition*
- *Create new hatch patterns*
- *Determine the effect of angle and scale factor on hatch*
- *Create hatch patterns with multiple descriptors*
- *Save hatch patterns in a separate file*
- *Customize hatch pattern file*

Key Terms

- *Linetype*
- **.lin Files*
- *Header Line*
- *Pattern Line*
- *LTSCALE*
- *CELTSCALE*
- *String Complex Linetypes*
- *Shape Complex Linetypes*
- *Hatch Descriptors*
- **.pat Files*

STANDARD LINETYPES

The AutoCAD software package comes with a library comprising 59 different standard linetypes, including ISO linetypes and seven complex linetypes. These linetypes are saved in the *acad.lin* and *acadiso.lin* file. You can modify existing linetypes or create new ones.

LINETYPE DEFINITIONS

All linetype definitions consist of two parts: **header line** and **pattern line**.

Header Line

The **header line** consists of an asterisk (*) followed by the name of the linetype and the linetype description. The name and the linetype description should be separated by a comma. If there is no description, the comma that separates the linetype name and the description is not required.

The format of the header line is:

*** Linetype Name, Description**

Example:
***HIDDEN,__ __ __ __ __ __**

Where * ------------------Asterisk sign
HIDDEN ------Linetype name
, -------------------Comma
__ __ __ __ -----Linetype description

All linetype definitions require a linetype name. When you load a linetype or assign a linetype to an object, AutoCAD recognizes the linetype by the name you have assigned to the linetype definition. The names of the linetype definition should be selected to help the user recognize the linetype by its name. For example, the linetype name LINEFCX does not give the user any idea about the type of line. However, a linetype name like DASHDOT gives a better idea about the type of line that a user can expect.

The linetype description is a textual representation of the line. This representation can be generated by using dashes, dots, and spaces at the keyboard. The graphic given in the code is used for displaying preview of the linetypes. The linetype description cannot exceed 47 characters.

Pattern Line

The **pattern line** contains the definition of the line pattern consisting of the alignment field specification and the linetype specification separated by a comma.

The format of the pattern line is:
Alignment Field Specification, Linetype Specification

Example:

A,.75,-.25,.75

Where **A** ----------------Alignment field specification
, ------------------Comma
.75,-.25,.75 ----Linetype specification

The letter used for alignment field specification is A. This is the only alignment field supported by AutoCAD; therefore, the pattern line will always start with the letter A. The linetype specification defines the configuration of the dash-dot pattern to generate a line. The maximum number for dash length specification in the linetype is 12, provided the linetype pattern definition fits on one 80-character line.

ELEMENTS OF LINETYPE SPECIFICATION

All linetypes are created by combining the basic elements in a desired configuration. There are three basic elements that can be used to define a linetype specification.

Dash	(Pen down)
Dot	(Pen down, 0 length)
Space	(Pen up)

Example:

_______ . _______ . _______ . _______

Where **.** ------------------Dot (pen down with 0 length)
Blank space ---------------Space (pen up)
_______ -----------------------------Dash (pen down with specified length)

The dashes are generated by defining a positive number. For example, .5 will generate a 0.5 units long dash. Similarly, spaces are generated by defining a negative number. For example, -.2 will generate a 0.2 units long space. The dot is generated by defining 0 length.

Example:

A,.5,-.2,0,-.2,.5

Where **0** ---------------Dot (zero length)
-.2 ---------------Length of space (pen up)
.5 ---------------Length of dash (pen down)

CREATING LINETYPES

Before creating a linetype, you need to decide the type of line that you want to generate. Draw the line on a piece of paper and measure the length of each element that constitutes the line. You need to define only one segment of the line because the pattern is repeated when you draw a line. Linetypes can be created or modified by any one of the following methods:

1. Using a text editor such as Notepad
2. Adding a new linetype in the *acad.lin* or *acadiso.lin* file
3. Using the **-LINETYPE** command

The following example explains how to create a new linetype using the three methods mentioned above.

Example 1 Linetype

Create a linetype DASH3DOT, refer to Figure 16-1 with the following specifications:

Length of the first dash 0.5
Blank space 0.125
Dot
Blank space 0.125
Dot
Blank space 0.125
Dot
Blank space 0.125

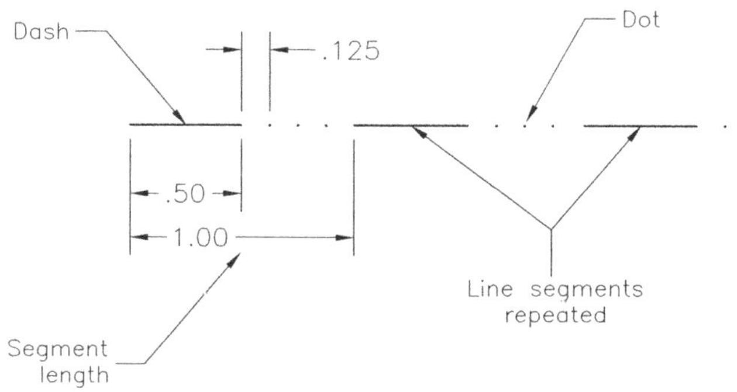

Figure 16-1 *Linetype specifications of DASH3DOT*

Using a Text Editor

Step 1: Writing Definition of Linetype

You can start a new linetype file and then add line definitions to this file. To do so, use any text editor such as Notepad to start a new file (*newlt.lin*) and then add the linetype definition of the DASH3DOT linetype. The name and the description must be separated by a comma (,). The description is optional. If you decide not to give one, omit the comma after the linetype name DASH3DOT.

***DASH3DOT,____ . . . ____ . . . ____**
A,.5,-.125,0,-.125,0,-.125,0,-.125

Save it as *newlt.lin* in AutoCAD's Support directory;
C:\Users\CADCIM\AppData\Roaming\Autodesk\AutoCAD 2023\ R24.2\enu\Support

Step 2: Loading the Linetype

To load this linetype, choose the **Other** option from **Properties > Linetype** drop-down list in the **Drafting & Annotation** workspace to display the **Linetype Manager** dialog box. Next, choose the **Load** button in the **Linetype Manager** dialog box to display the **Load or Reload Linetypes** dialog box. Choose the **File** button in the **Load or Reload Linetypes** dialog box to display the **Select Linetype File** dialog box, as shown in Figure 16-2. Select the *newlt.lin* file from the location where you have saved it and then choose **Open**. Again, the **Load or Reload Linetypes** dialog box will be displayed. Choose the **DASH3DOT** linetype in the **Available Linetypes** area and then choose **OK**; the **Linetype Manager** dialog box is displayed. Select the **DASH3DOT** linetype and then choose the **Current** button to make the selected linetype as the current linetype. Then, choose **OK**. Now, if you draw any object, then the new linetype will be used to draw that object.

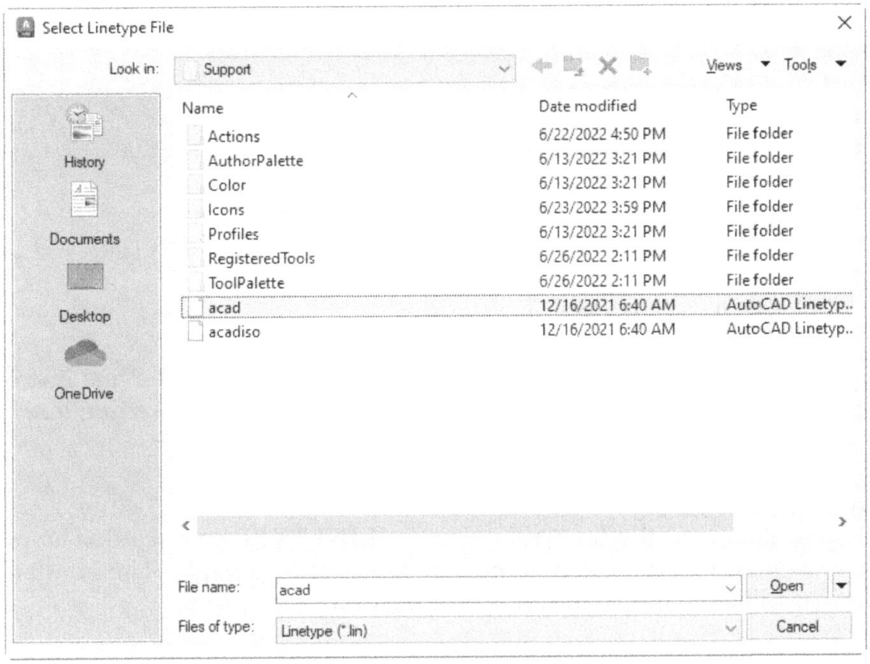

*Figure 16-2 The **Select Linetype File** dialog box*

Adding a New Linetype in the *acad.lin* File

Step 1: Adding a new linetype in the *acad.lin*

Browse to the *acad.lin* file and double-click on it; the *acad.lin* file opens in Notepad. In this text editor, you can insert the line definition that defines the new linetype. Given next is the partial listing of the *acad.lin* file after adding a new linetype to it:

```
*BORDER,Border __ __ . __ __ . __ __ . __ __ . __ __ .
A,.5,-.25,.5,-.25,0,-.25
*BORDER2,Border (.5x) __.__.__.__.__.__.__.__.__.__.__.
A,.25,-.125,.25,-.125,0,-.125
```

```
*BORDERX2,Border (2x) ____ ____ . ____ ____ . __
A,1.0,-.5,1.0,-.5,0,-.5
*CENTER,Center ____ _ ____ _ ____ _ ____ _ ____ _ ____
A,1.25,-.25,.25,-.25
*CENTER2,Center (.5x) ___ _ ___ _ ___ _ ___ _ ___ _ ___
A,.75,-.125,.125,-.125
*CENTERX2,Center (2x) ________ __ ________ __ _____
A,2.5,-.5,.5,-.5

*DASHDOT,Dash dot __ . __ . __ . __ . __ . __ . __ . __
A,.5,-.25,0,-.25
*DASHDOT2,Dash dot (.5x) _._._._._._._._._._._._._.
A,.25,-.125,0,-.125
*DASHDOTX2,Dash dot (2x) ____ . ____ . ____ . ___
A,1.0,-.50,-.5
|
|
*GAS_LINE,Gas line ----GAS----GAS----GAS----GAS----GAS----GAS--
A,.5,-.2,["GAS",STANDARD,S=.1,R=0.0,X=-0.1,Y=-.05],-.25
*ZIGZAG,Zig zag /\/\/\/\/\/\/\/\/\/\/\/\/\/\/\/\/\/\/\/\/\/\/\/\/\/\/\/\/\/\/\/\/\/\/\/\/\/\/\/\/\/\/\/\/\/\/\/\/\/\/\/
A,.0001,-.2,[ZIG,ltypeshp.shx,x=-.2,s=.2],-.4,[ZIG,ltypeshp.shx,r=180,x=.2,s=.2],-.2
*DASH3DOT,____ . . . ____ . . . ____
A,.5,-.125,0,-.125,0,-.125,0,-.125
```

The last two lines of this file define the new linetype, DASH3DOT. The first line contains the name DASH3DOT and the description of the line (___ . . .___). The second line contains the alignment and the pattern definition.

Step 2: Loading the linetype

Save the file and then load the linetype using the **LINETYPE** command. The procedure of loading the linetype is the same as described earlier in this example. The lines and polylines that this linetype will generate are shown in Figure 16-3.

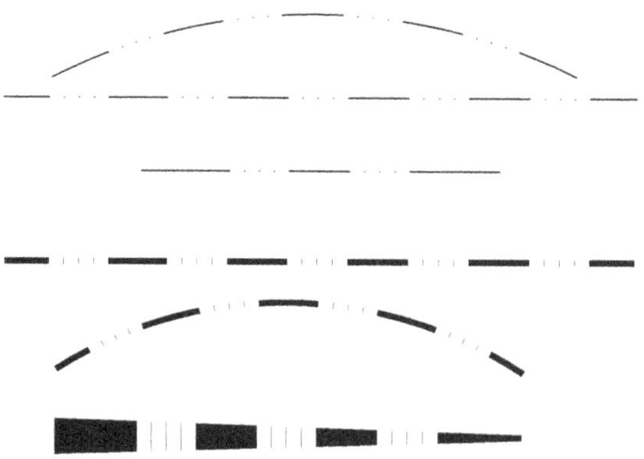

Figure 16-3 *Lines created by the linetype DASH3DOT*

Note

If you change the LTSCALE factor, all the lines in the drawing are affected by the new ratio.

Using the LINETYPE Command

Step 1: Creating a linetype

To create a linetype using the **LINETYPE** command, first make sure that you are in the drawing editor. Then enter the **-LINETYPE** command and choose the **Create** option to create a linetype.

Command: **-LINETYPE**
Enter an option [?/Create/Load/Set]: **C**

Enter the name of the linetype and the name of the library file in which you want to store the definition of the new linetype.

Enter name of linetype to create: **DASH3DOT**

If **FILEDIA**=1, the **Create or Append Linetype File** dialog box, refer to Figure 16-4, will appear on the screen. If **FILEDIA**=0, you are prompted to enter the name of the file.

Enter linetype file name for new linetype definition <default>: **Acad**

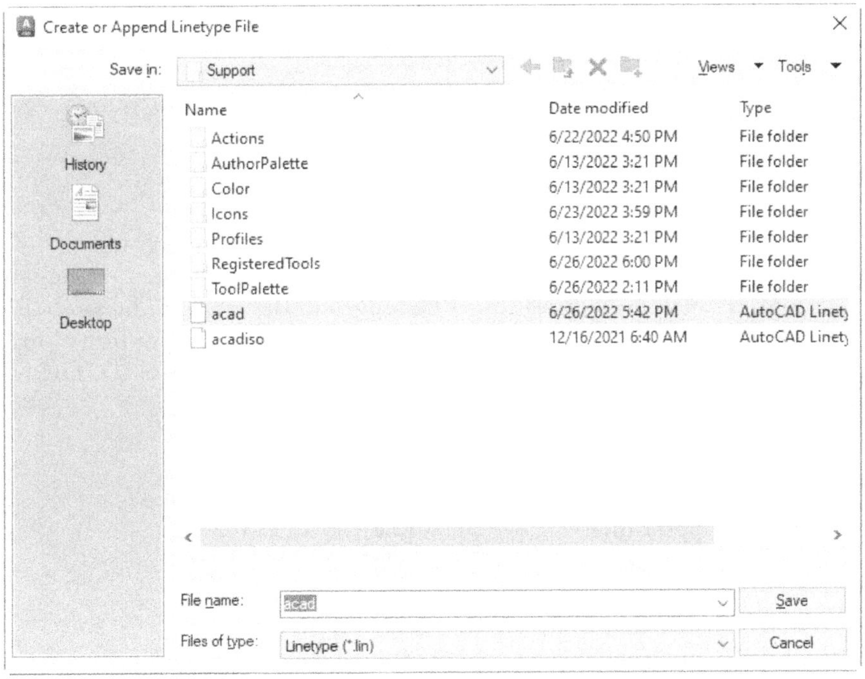

***Figure 16-4** The **Create or Append Linetype File** dialog box*

If the linetype already exists, the following message will be displayed on the screen:

Wait, checking if linetype already defined...
"Linetype" already exists in this file. Current definition is:
alignment, dash-1, dash-2, _____.
Overwrite?<N>

If you want to redefine the existing line style, enter **Y**. Otherwise, type **N** or press Enter to choose the default value of N. You can then repeat the process with a different linetype name. After entering the name of the linetype and the library file name, you are prompted to enter the descriptive text and the pattern of the line.

Descriptive text: ***DASH3DOT,____ . . . ____ . . . ____**
Enter linetype pattern (on next line):
A,.5,-.125,0,-.125,0,-.125,0,-.125

Descriptive Text

***DASH3DOT,____ . . . ____ . . . ____**

For the descriptive text, you have to type an asterisk (*) followed by the name of the linetype. For Example 1, the name of the linetype is DASH3DOT. The name *DASH3DOT can be followed by the description of the linetype; the length of this description cannot exceed 47 characters. In this example, the description is dashes and dots ____ . . . ____. It could be any text or alphanumeric string. The description is displayed on the screen when you list the linetypes.

Pattern

A,.5,-.125,0,-.125,0,-.125,0,-.125

The line pattern should start with an alignment definition. By default, AutoCAD supports only one type of alignment—A. Therefore, it is displayed on the screen when you execute the **LINETYP** command with the **Create** option. After entering **A** for the pattern alignment, define the pen position. A positive number (.5 or 0.5) indicates a "pen-down" position, and a negative number (-.25 or -0.25) indicates a "pen-up" position. The length of the dash or the space is designated by the magnitude of the number. For example, 0.5 will draw a dash 0.5 units long, and -0.25 will leave a blank space of 0.25 units. A dash length of 0 will draw a dot (.). The following are the pattern definition elements for Example 1:

.5	**pen down**	**0.5 units long dash**
-.125	**pen up**	**.125 units blank space**
0	**pen down**	**dot**
-.125	**pen up**	**.125 units blank space**
0	**pen down**	**dot**
-.125	**pen up**	**.125 units blank space**
0	**pen down**	**dot**
-.125	**pen up**	**.125 units blank space**

After you enter the pattern definition, the linetype (DASH3DOT) is automatically saved in the *acad.lin* file.

Step 2: Loading the linetype

Choose the **Other** option from **Home > Properties > Linetype** drop-down list to load the linetype or use the **LINETYPE** command. The linetype (DASH3DOT) can also be loaded using the **-LINETYPE** command and selecting the **Load** option.

ALIGNMENT SPECIFICATION

As the name suggests, the alignment specifies the pattern alignment at the start and the end of a line, circle, or arc. In other words, the line always starts and ends with the dash (___). The alignment definition "A" requires the first element to be a dash or dot (pen down), followed by a negative (pen up) segment. The minimum number of dash segments for alignment A is two. If the space is not enough for the line, a continuous line is drawn.

For example, in the linetype DASH3DOT of Example 1, the length of each line segment is 1.0 (.5 + .125 + .125 + .125 + .125 = 1.0). If the length of the line drawn is less than 1.00, a single line is drawn that looks like a continuous line, refer to Figure 16-5. If the length of the line is 1.00 or greater, the line will be drawn according to DASH3DOT linetype. AutoCAD automatically adjusts the length of the dashes and the line always starts and ends with a dash. The length of the starting and ending dashes is at least half the length of the dash as specified in the file. If the length of the dash as specified in the file is 0.5, the length of the starting and ending dashes is at least 0.25. To fit a line that starts and ends with a dash, the length of these dashes can also increase, as shown in Figure 16-5.

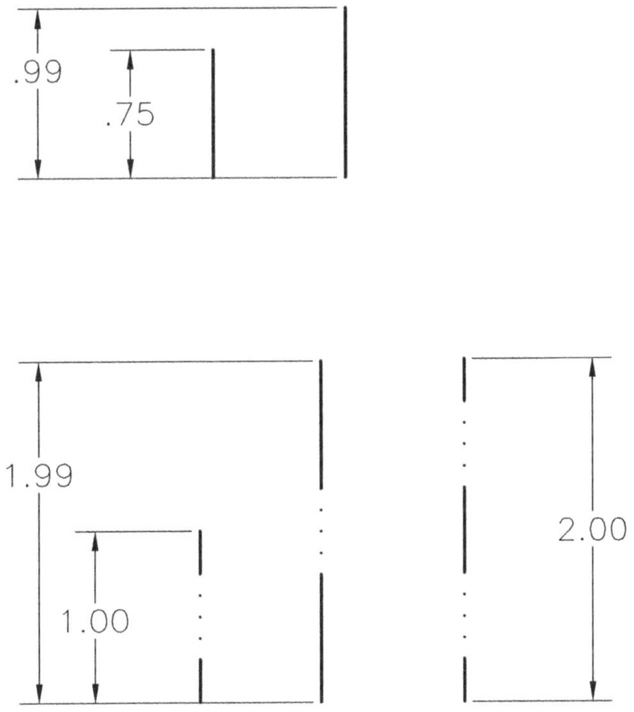

Figure 16-5 *Alignment of linetype DASH3DOT*

LTSCALE COMMAND

As mentioned earlier, the length of each line segment in the DASH3DOT linetype is 1.0 (.5 + .125 + .125 + .125 + .125 = 1.0). If you draw a line that is less than 1.0 unit long, a single dash is drawn that looks like a continuous line, refer to Figure 16-6. This problem can be rectified by changing the linetype scale factor variable **LTSCALE** to a smaller value. This can be accomplished using the **LTSCALE** command.

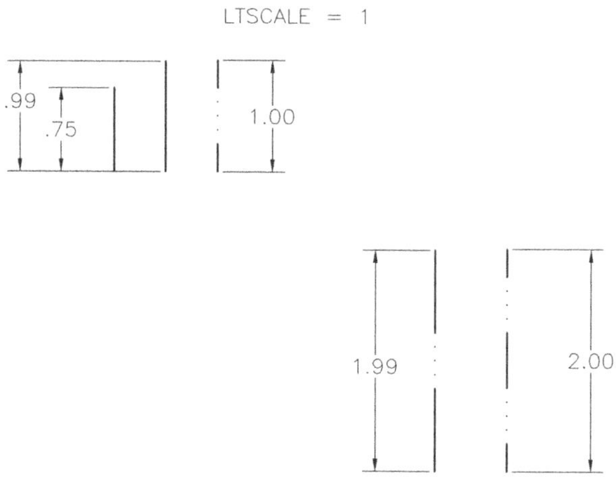

Figure 16-6 *Alignment when LTSCALE = 1*

Command: **LTSCALE**
Enter new linetype scale factor <default>: *New value.*

The default value of the **LTSCALE** variable is 1.0. If the LTSCALE is changed to 0.75, the length of each segment is reduced by 0.75 (1.0 x 0.75 = 0.75). Then, if you draw a line 0.75 unit or longer, it will be drawn according to the definition of DASH3DOT (___ . . . ____), refer to Figures 16-7 and 16-8.

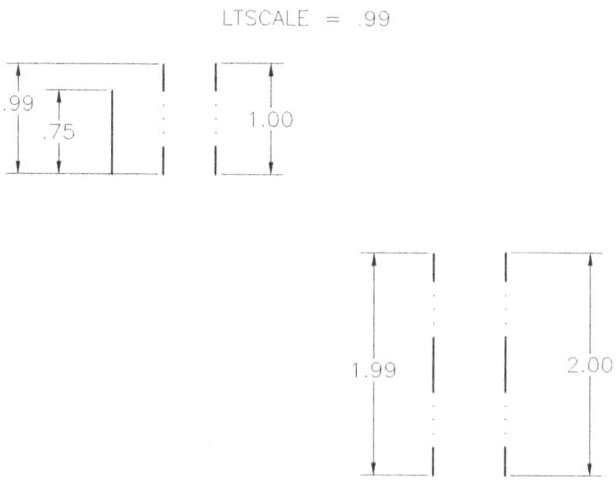

Figure 16-7 *Alignment when LTSCALE = 0.99*

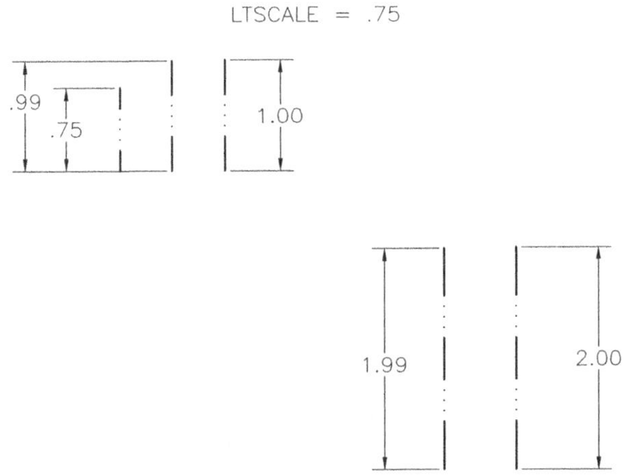

Figure 16-8 *Alignment when LTSCALE = 0.75*

The appearance of the lines is also affected by the limits of the drawing. Most of the AutoCAD linetypes work fine for drawings that have the limits 12,9. Figure 16-9 shows a line of linetype DASH3DOT that is four units long and the limits of the drawing are 12,9. If you increase the limits to 48,36 the lines will appear as continuous lines. If you want the line to appear the same as before on the screen, the LTSCALE needs to be changed. Since the limits of the drawing have increased four times, the LTSCALE should also be increased by the same proportion. If you change the scale factor to four, the line segments will also increase by a factor of four. As shown in Figure 16-9, the length of the starting and the ending dash has increased to one unit.

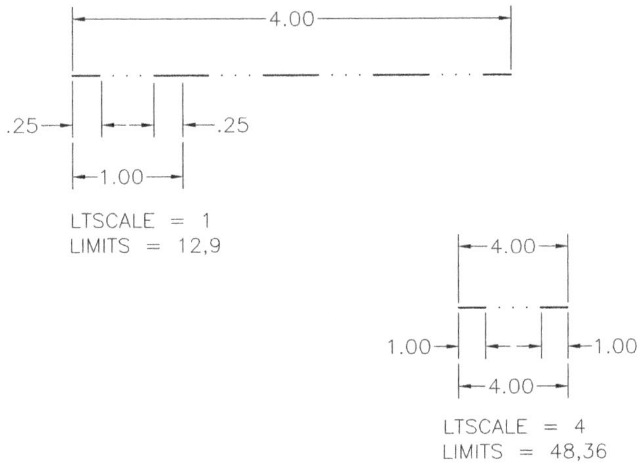

Figure 16-9 *Linetype DASH3DOT before and after changing the LTSCALE factor*

In general, the approximate LTSCALE factor for screen display can be obtained by dividing the X -limit of the drawing by the default X -limit (12.00). However, it is recommended that the linetype scale must be set according to plot scale discussed in the next section.

LTSCALE factor for SCREEN DISPLAY = X -limits of the drawing/12.00
Example:
Drawing limits are 48,36
LTSCALE factor for screen display= 48/12 = 4

Drawing sheet size is 36,24 and scale is 1/4" = 1'
LTSCALE factor for screen display = 12 x 4 x (36 / 12) = 144

LTSCALE FACTOR FOR PLOTTING

The LTSCALE factor for plotting depends on the size of the sheet used to plot the drawing. For example, if the limits are 48 by 36, the drawing scale is 1:1, and you want to plot the drawing on a 48" by 36" size sheet, the LTSCALE factor is 1. If you check the specification of a hidden line in the *acad.lin* file, the length of each dash is 0.25. Therefore, when you plot a drawing with 1:1 scale, the length of each dash in a hidden line is 0.25.

However, if the drawing scale is 1/8" = 1' and you want to plot the drawing on a 48" by 36" paper, the LTSCALE factor must be 96 (8 x 12 = 96). If you increase the LTSCALE factor to 96, the length of each dash in the hidden line will increase by a factor of 96. As a result, the length of each dash will be 24 units (0.25 x 96 = 24). At the time of plotting, the scale factor must be 1:96 to plot the 384' by 288' drawing on a 48" by 36" size paper. Each dash of the hidden line that was 24" long on the drawing will be 0.25 (24/96 = 0.25) inch long when plotted. Similarly, if the desired text size on the paper is 1/8", the text height in the drawing must be 12" (1/8 x 96 = 12").

Ltscale Factor for PLOTTING = Drawing Scale

Sometimes your plotter may not be able to plot a 48" by 36" drawing or you may like to decrease the size of the plot so that the drawing fits within the specified area. To get the correct dash lengths for hidden, center, or other lines, you must adjust the LTSCALE factor. For example, if you want to plot the previously mentioned drawing in a 45" by 34" area, the correction factor is:

Correction factor	= 48/45
	= 1.0666
New LTSCALE factor	= LTSCALE factor x Correction factor
	= 96 x 1.0666
	= 102.4

New LTSCALE Factor for PLOTTING = Drawing Scale x Correction Factor

Note
If you change the LTSCALE factor, all the lines in the drawing will be affected by the new ratio.

CURRENT LINETYPE SCALING (CELTSCALE)

Like **LTSCALE**, the **CELTSCALE** system variable controls the linetype scaling. The difference is that **CELTSCALE** determines the current linetype scaling. For example, if you set the **CELTSCALE** to 0.5, all the lines drawn after setting the new value for **CELTSCALE** will have the linetype scaling factor of 0.5. The value is retained in the **CELTSCALE** system variable. The first line (a) in Figure 16-10 is drawn with the **CELTSCALE** factor of 1 and the second line (b) is drawn with the **CELTSCALE** factor of 0.5. The length of the dashes is reduced by a factor of 0.5 when the **CELTSCALE** is 0.5.

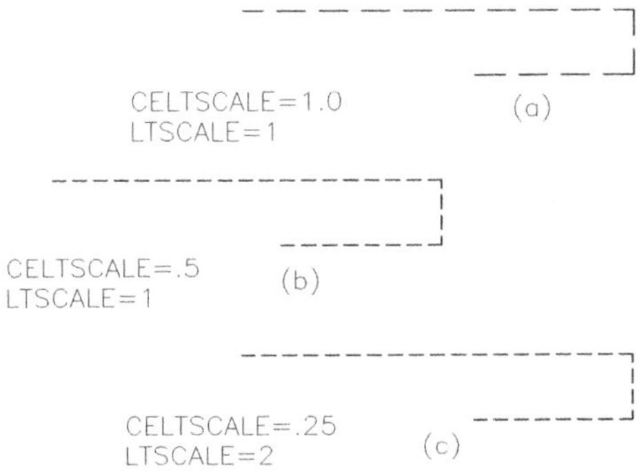

Figure 16-10 *Using **CELTSCALE** to control current linetype scaling*

The **LTSCALE** system variable controls the global scale factor. For example, if **LTSCALE** is set to 2, all the lines in the drawing will be affected by a factor of 2. The net scale factor is equal to the product of **CELTSCALE** and **LTSCALE**. Figure 16-10(c) shows a line that is drawn with **LTSCALE** of 2 and **CELTSCALE** of 0.25. The net scale factor is = **LTSCALE** x **CELTSCALE** = 2 x 0.25 = 0.5.

Note

*You can change the current linetype scale factor of a line by using the **Properties** palette that can be invoked by choosing the **Properties** tool from the **Quick Access** Toolbar (Customize to add).*

ALTERNATE LINETYPES

One of the problems with the LTSCALE factor is that it affects all the lines in a drawing. As shown in Figure 16-11(a), the length of each segment in all DASH3DOT type lines is approximately equal, no matter how long the lines are. You may want to have a small segment length if the lines are small and a longer segment length if the lines are long. You can accomplish this by using CELTSCALE (discussed later in this chapter) or by defining an alternate linetype with a different segment length. For example, you can define a linetype DASH3DOT and DASH3DOTX with different line pattern specifications.

```
*DASH3DOT,____ . . . ____ . . . ____ . . . ____
A,0.5,-.125,0,-.125,0,-.125,0,-.125
*DASH3DOTX,________ . . . __________
A,1.0,-.25,0,-.25,0,-.25,0,-.25
```

In the DASH3DOT linetype, the segment length is one unit; whereas, in the DASH3DOTX linetype the segment length is two units. You can have several alternate linetypes to produce the lines with different segment lengths. Figure 16-11(b) shows the lines generated by DASH3DOT and DASH3DOTX.

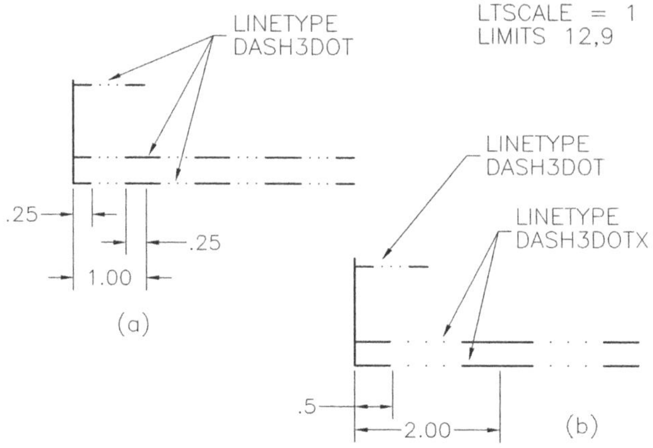

Figure 16-11 *Linetypes generated by DASH3DOT and DASH3DOTX*

Note

Although you may have used various linetypes with different segment lengths, the lines will be affected equally when you change the LTSCALE factor. For example, if the LTSCALE factor is 0.5, the segment length of DASH3DOT line will be 0.5 unit and the segment length of DASH3DOTX will be 1.0 unit.

MODIFYING LINETYPES

You can also modify the linetypes that are defined in the *acad.lin* or *acadiso.lin* file. You must save a copy of the original *acad.lin* or *acadiso.lin* file before making any changes to it. You need a text editor, such as Notepad, to modify the linetype. You can also use the **EDIT** function of DOS, or the **EDIT** command (provided the *acad.pgp* file is present and **EDIT** is defined in the file). For example, if you want to change the dash length of the border linetype from 0.5 to 0.75, load the file, and then edit the pattern line of the border linetype. The following file is a partial listing of the *acad.lin* file after changing the BORDER and CENTERX2 linetypes.

```
;; AutoCAD Linetype Definition file
;; Version 3.0

;; Copyright 2022 Autodesk, Inc.  All rights reserved.

*BORDER,Border __ __ . __ __ . __ __ . __ __ . __ __ .
A,.5,-.25,.5,-.25,0,-.25
*BORDER2,Border (.5x) __.__.__.__.__.__.__.__.__.__.__.
A,.25,-.125,.25,-.125,0,-.125
*BORDERX2,Border (2x) ____  ____  .  ____  ____  .  ___
A,1.0,-.5,1.0,-.5,0,-.5
```

```
*CENTER,Center ____ _ ____ _ ____ _ ____ _ ____ _ ____
A,1.25,-.25,.25,-.25
*CENTER2,Center (.5x) ___ _ ___ _ ___ _ ___ _ ___ _ ___
A,.75,-.125,.125,-.125
*CENTERX2,Center (2x) ________  __  ________  __  _____
A,2.5,-.5,.5,-.5

*DASHDOT,Dash dot __ . __ . __ . __ . __ . __ . __ . __
A,.5,-.25,0,-.25
*DASHDOT2,Dash dot (.5x) _._._._._._._._._._._._._.
A,.25,-.125,0,-.125
*DASHDOTX2,Dash dot (2x) ____  .  ____  .  ____  .  ___
A,1.0,-.5,0,-.5

*DASHED,Dashed __ __ __ __ __ __ __ __ __ __ __ __ __ _
A,.5,-.25
*DASHED2,Dashed (.5x) _ _ _ _ _ _ _ _ _ _ _ _ _ _ _ _ _ _
A,.25,-.125
*DASHEDX2,Dashed (2x) ____  ____  ____  ____  ____  ___
A,1.0,-.5

*DIVIDE,Divide ____ . . ____ . . ____ . . ____ . . ____
A,.5,-.25,0,-.25,0,-.25
*DIVIDE2,Divide (.5x) __..__..__..__..__..__..__..__.._
A,.25,-.125,0,-.125,0,-.125
*DIVIDEX2,Divide (2x) ________  .  .  ________  .  .  _
A,1.0,-.5,0,-.5,0,-.5

*DOT,Dot . . . . . . . . . . . . . . . . . . . . . . . .
A,0,-.25
*DOT2,Dot (.5x) ........................................
A,0,-.125
*DOTX2,Dot (2x) .  .  .  .  .  .  .  .  .  .  .  .  .  .
A,0,-.5

*HIDDEN,Hidden __ __ __ __ __ __ __ __ __ __ __ __ __ __
A,.25,-.125
*HIDDEN2,Hidden (.5x) _ _ _ _ _ _ _ _ _ _ _ _ _ _ _ _ _ _
A,.125,-.0625
*HIDDENX2,Hidden (2x) ____ ____ ____ ____ ____ ____ ____
A,.5,-.25

*PHANTOM,Phantom ______ __ __ ______ __ __ ______
A,1.25,-.25,.25,-.25,.25,-.25
*PHANTOM2,Phantom (.5x) ___ _ _ ___ _ _ ___ _ _ ___ _ _
A,.625,-.125,.125,-.125,.125,-.125
*PHANTOMX2,Phantom (2x) ____________   ____   ____   _
A,2.5,-.5,.5,-.5,.5,-.5
```

```
;;
;;  ISO 128 (ISO/DIS 12011) linetypes
;;
;;  The size of the line segments for each defined ISO line is
;;  defined for usage with a pen width of 1 mm. To use them with
;;  the other ISO predefined pen widths, the line has to be scaled
;;  with the appropriate value (e.g. pen width 0,5 mm -> ltscale 0.5).
;;
*ACAD_ISO02W100,ISO dash __ __ __ __ __ __ __ __ __ __ __ __ ___ __
A,12,-3
|
|
*ACAD_ISO15W100,ISO double-dash triple-dot __ __ . . . __ __ . .
A,12,-3,12,-3,0,-3,0,-3,0,-3

;;  Complex linetypes
;;  Complex linetypes have been added to this file.
;;  These linetypes were defined in LTYPESHP.LIN in
;;  Release 13, and are incorporated in ACAD.LIN in
;;  Release 14.
;;
;;  These linetype definitions use LTYPESHP.SHX.
;;
*FENCELINE1,Fenceline circle ----0-----0----0-----0----0-----0--
A,.25,-.1,[CIRC1,ltypeshp.shx,x=-.1,s=.1],-.1,1
*FENCELINE2,Fenceline square ----[]-----[]----[]-----[]----[]---
A,.25,-.1,[BOX,ltypeshp.shx,x=-.1,s=.1],-.1,1
*TRACKS,Tracks -|-|-|-|-|-|-|-|-|-|-|-|-|-|-|-|-|-|-|-|-|-|-|-
A,.15,[TRACK1,ltypeshp.shx,s=.25],.15
*BATTING,Batting SSSSSSSSSSSSSSSSSSSSSSSSSSSSSSSSSSSSSSSSSSSSSS
A,.0001,-.1,[BAT,ltypeshp.shx,x=-.1,s=.1],-.2,[BAT,ltypeshp.shx,r=180,x=.1,s=.1],-.1
*HOT_WATER_SUPPLY,Hot water supply ---- HW ---- HW ---- HW ----
A,.5,-.2,["HW",STANDARD,S=.1,R=0.0,X=-0.1,Y=-.05],-.2
*GAS_LINE,Gas line ----GAS----GAS----GAS----GAS----GAS----GAS--
A,.5,-.2,["GAS",STANDARD,S=.1,R=0.0,X=-0.1,Y=-.05],-.25
*ZIGZAG,Zig zag /\/\/\/\/\/\/\/\/\/\/\/\/\/\/\/\/\/\/\/\/
A,.0001,-.2,[ZIG,ltypeshp.shx,x=-.2,s=.2],-.4,[ZIG,ltypeshp.shx,r=180,x=.2,s=.2],-.2
```

Example 2 *Linetype*

Create a new file, *newlint.lin*, and define a linetype VARDASH with the following specifications:

Length of first dash 1.0
Blank space 0.25
Length of second dash 0.75
Blank space 0.25
Length of third dash 0.5

Blank space 0.25
Dot
Blank space 0.25
Length of next dash 0.5
Blank space 0.25
Length of next dash 0.75

Step 1: Writing definition of linetype

Use a text editor and insert the following lines to define the new linetype **VARDASH**.

***VARDASH,———— —— — . — —— ————**
A,1,-.25,.75,-.25,.5,-.25,0,-.25,.5,-.25,.75,-.25

Now, save this file with the name *newlint.lin*.

Step 2: Loading the linetype

You can use the **LINETYPE** command or choose **Home > Properties > Linetype > Other** from the **Ribbon** to load the linetype. The types of lines that this linetype will generate are shown in Figure 16-12.

Figure 16-12 *Lines generated by linetype VARDASH*

COMPLEX LINETYPES

In AutoCAD, you can create complex linetypes. The complex linetypes can be classified into two groups: string complex linetype and shape complex linetype. The difference between these line type is that the string complex linetype has a text string inserted in the line whereas the shape complex linetype has a shape inserted in the line. The facility of creating complex linetypes increases the functionality of lines. For example, if you want to draw a line around a building that indicates the fence line, you can do it by defining a complex linetype that will automatically give you the desired line with the text string (Fence). Similarly, you can define a complex linetype that will insert a shape (symbol) at predefined distances along the line.

CREATING A STRING COMPLEX LINETYPE

While writing the definition of a string complex linetype, the actual text and its attributes must be included in the linetype definition, refer to Figure 16-13.
The format of the string complex linetype is:

["String", Text Style, Text Height, Rotation, X-Offset, Y-Offset]

String. It is the actual text that you want to insert along the line. The text string must be enclosed in quotation marks (" ").

Text Style. This is the name of the text style file that you want to use for generating the text string. The text style must be predefined.

Text Height. This is the actual height of the text, if the text height defined in the text style is 0. Otherwise, it acts as a scale factor for the text height specified in the text style. In Figure 16-13, the height of the text is 0.1 units.

Rotation. The rotation can be specified as an absolute or relative angle. In the absolute rotation, the angle is always measured with respect to the positive *X* axis, no matter what AutoCAD's direction setting is. The absolute angle is represented by the letter "a".

In relative rotation, the angle is always measured with respect to orientation of dashes in the linetype. The relative angle is represented by the letter "r". The angle can be specified in radians (r), grads (g), or degrees (d). The default is degrees.

X-Offset. This is the distance of the lower left corner of the text string from the endpoint of the line segment measured along the line. If the line is horizontal, then the X-Offset distance is measured along the *X* axis. In Figure 16-13, the X-Offset distance is 0.05.

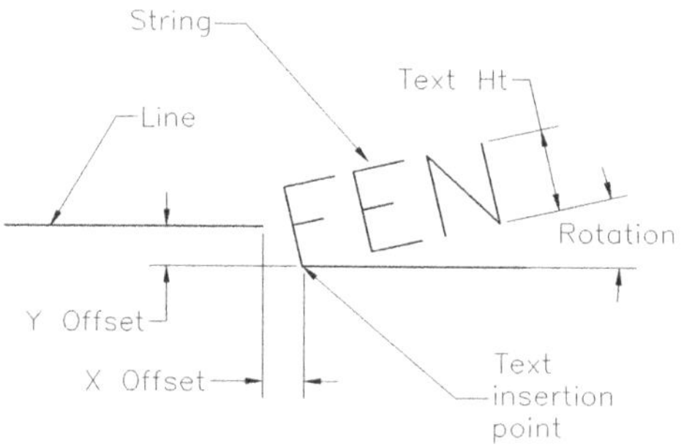

Figure 16-13 *Attributes of a string complex linetype*

Y-Offset. This is the distance of the lower left corner of the text string from the endpoint of the line segment measured perpendicular to the line. If the line is horizontal, then the Y-Offset distance is measured along the *Y* axis. In Figure 16-13, the Y-Offset distance is -0.05. The distance is negative because the start point of the text string is 0.05 units below the endpoint of the first line segment.

Example 3 String Complex Linetype

In this example, you will write definition of a string complex linetype that consists of the text string "Fence" and line segments. The length of each line segment is 0.75. The height of the text string is 0.1 units, and the space between the end of the text string and the following line segment is 0.05, refer to Figure 16-14.

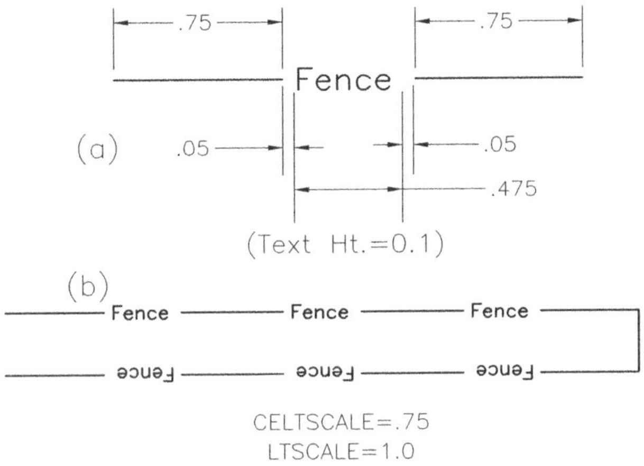

Figure 16-14 *The attributes of a string complex linetype and line specifications for Example 3*

Step 1: Determining the line specifications

Before writing the definition of a new linetype, it is important to determine the line specification. One of the ways to do this is to actually draw the lines and the text the way you want them to appear in the drawing. Once you have drawn the line and the text to your satisfaction, measure the distances needed to define the string complex linetype. The values are given as follows:

Text string	=Fence
Text style	=Standard
Text height	=0.1
Text rotation	=0
X-Offset	=0.05
Y-Offset	=-0.05
Length of the first line segment	=0.75
Distance between the line segments	=0.575

Step 2: Writing the definition of string complex linetype

Use a text editor to write the definition of the string complex linetype. You can add the definition to the *acad.lin* or *acadiso.lin* file or create a separate file. The extension of the file must be *.lin*. The following file is the listing of the *fence.lin* file for Example 3. The name of the linetype is NEWFence1.

```
*NEWFence1,New fence boundary line
A,.75,-.05,["Fence",STANDARD,S=.1,A=0.0,X=0,Y=-.05],-.575
```

Step 3: Loading the linetype

Choose the **Other** option from **Properties > Linetype** drop-down list to load the linetype or use the **LINETYPE** command. Now, draw a line or any object to check if the line is drawn as per given specifications, as shown in Figure 16-15. Notice that the text is always drawn along the *X* axis. Also, when you draw a line at an angle, polyline, circle, or spline, the text string does not align with the object, refer to Figure 16-15.

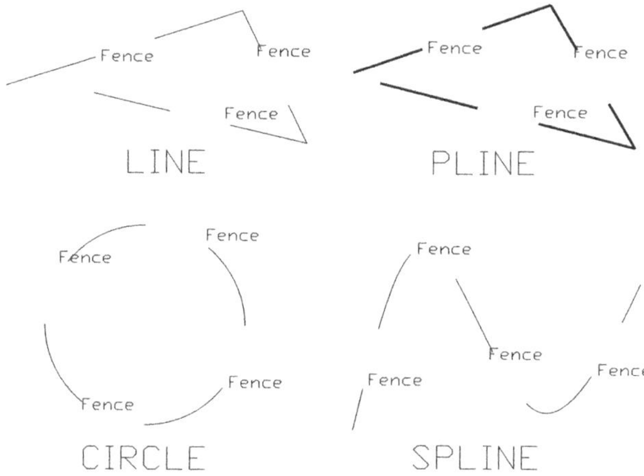

Figure 16-15 *Using string complex linetype with angle A=0*

Step 4: Aligning the text with the line

In the NEWFence linetype definition, the specified angle is 0° (Absolute angle A = 0). Therefore, when you use the NEWFence linetype to draw a line, circle, polyline, or spline, the text string (Fence) will be at zero degrees. If you want the text string (Fence) to align with the polyline, refer to Figure 16-16, spline, or circle, specify the angle as relative angle (R = 0) in the NEWFence linetype definition. The following is the linetype definition for NEWFence linetype with relative angle R = 0:

```
*NEWFence2,New fence boundary line
A,0.75,["Fence",Standard,S=0.1,R=0,X=0.05,Y=-0.05],-0.575
```

Note

You have to load the linetype again to get the changes updated.

Step 5: Aligning the midpoint of text with the line

In Figure 16-16, you will notice that the text string is not properly aligned with the circumference of the circle. This is because AutoCAD draws the text string in a direction that is tangent to the circle at the text insertion point.

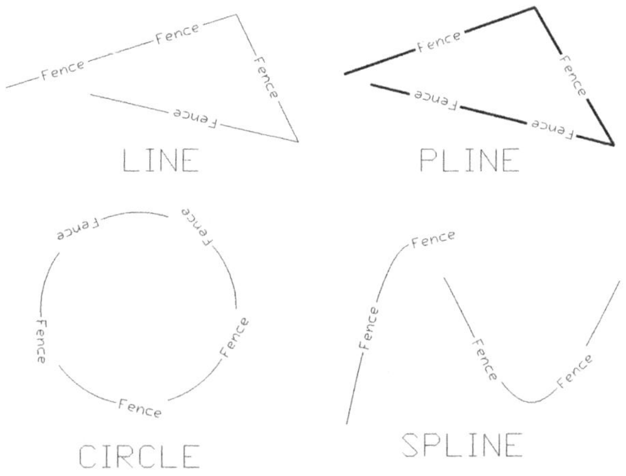

Figure 16-16 *Using a string complex linetype with angle R = 0*

To resolve this problem, you must define the mid point as the insertion point for the text string. Also, the line specifications should be assigned accordingly. Figure 16-17 shows the measurements of the NEWFence linetype with the mid point of the text as the insertion point and Figure 16-18 shows the entities sketched with the selected linetype.

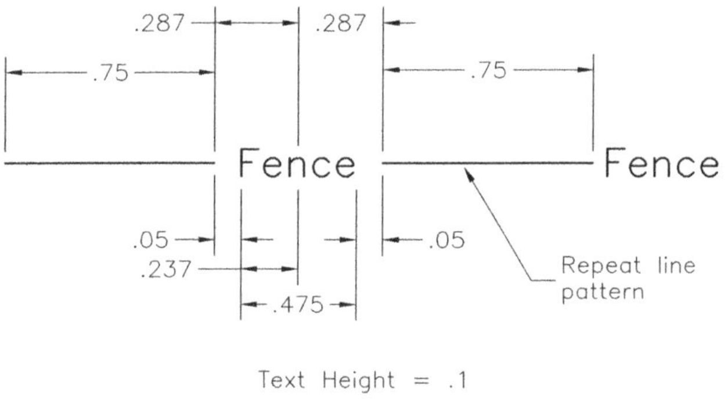

Figure 16-17 *Specifications of a string complex linetype with the middle point of the text string as the insertion point*

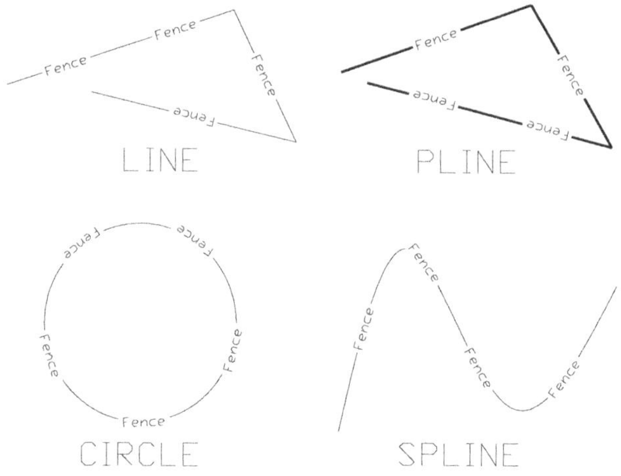

Figure 16-18 *Using a string complex linetype with the middle point of the text string as the text insertion point*

The following is the linetype definition for NEWFence linetype:

*NEWFence3,New fence boundary line
A,.75,-.287,["Fence",STANDARD,S=.1,X=-0.237,Y=.05],-.287

Note
If angle is not defined in the line definition, it acquires the default value of angle R = 0. But MID justification needs to be assigned to the text for proper alignment.

Creating a Shape Complex Linetype

As with the string complex linetype, when you write the definition of a shape complex linetype, the name of the shape, the name of the shape file, and other shape attributes such as rotation, scale, X-Offset, and Y-Offset, must be included in the linetype definition. The format of the shape complex linetype is:

[Shape Name, Shape File, Scale, Rotation, X-Offset, Y-Offset]

The following is the description of the attributes of Shape Complex Linetype, refer to Figure 16-19.

Shape Name. This is the name of the shape that you want to insert along the line. The shape name must exist; otherwise, no shape will be generated along the line.

Shape File. This is the name of the compiled shape file (*.shx*) that contains the definition of the shape being inserted in the line. The name of the subdirectory where the shape file is located must be in the AutoCAD search path. The shape files (*.shp*) must be compiled before using the **SHAPE** command to load the shape.

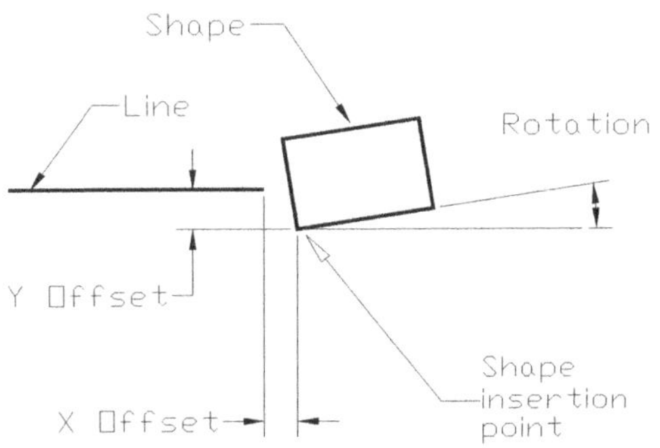

Figure 16-19 *The attributes of a shape complex linetype*

Scale. This is the scale factor by which the defined shape size is to be scaled. If the scale is 1, the size of the shape will be the same as defined in the shape definition (*.shp* file).

Rotation. The rotation can be specified as an absolute or relative angle. In absolute rotation, the angle is always measured with respect to the positive *X* axis, no matter what AutoCAD's direction setting. The absolute angle is represented by letter "a." In relative rotation, the angle is always measured with respect to the orientation of dashes in the linetype. The relative angle is represented by the letter "r." The angle can be specified in radians (r), grads (g), or degrees (d). The default is degrees.

X-Offset. This is the distance of the shape insertion point from the endpoint of the line segment measured along the line. If the line is horizontal, then the X-Offset distance is measured along the *X* axis.

Y-Offset. This is the distance of the shape insertion point from the endpoint of the line segment measured perpendicular to the line. If the line is horizontal, then the Y-Offset distance is measured along the *Y* axis.

Example 4 — *Shape Complex Linetype*

Write the definition of a shape complex linetype that consists of a shape (Manhole; the name of the shape is MH) and a line. The scale of the shape is 0.1, the length of each line segment is 0.75, and the space between line segments is 0.2.

Step 1: Determining the line specifications

Before writing the definition of a new linetype, it is important to determine the line specifications. One of the ways to do this is to actually draw the lines and the shape the way you want them to appear in the drawing, refer to Figure 16-20. Once you have drawn the line and the shape to your satisfaction, measure the distances needed to define the shape complex linetype. In this example, the values are as follows:

Shape name	=MH
Shape file name	=*mhole.shx* (Name of the compiled shape file.)

Scale	=0.1
Rotation	=0
X-Offset	=0.2
Y-Offset	=0
Length of the first line segment	= 0.75
Distance between the line segments	= 0.2

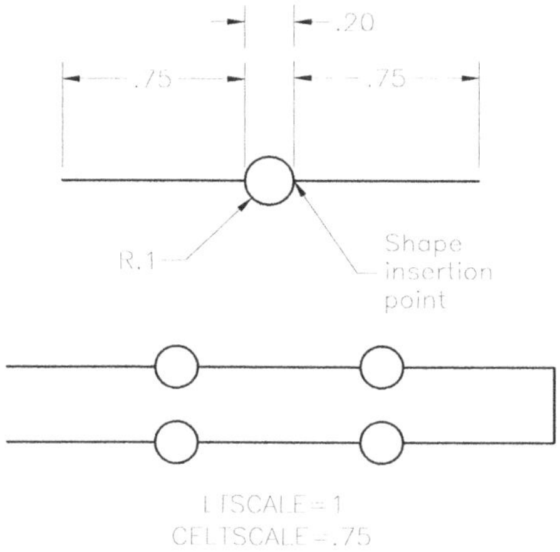

Figure 16-20 The attributes of the shape complex linetype and line specifications for Example 4

Step 2: Writing the definition of the shape

Use a text editor to write the definition of the shape file. The extension of the file must be *.shp*. The following file is the listing of the *mhole.shp* file for Example 4. The name of the shape is MH.

```
*215,9,MH
001,10,(1,007),
001,10,(1,071),0 Enter.
```

Step 3: Compiling the shape

Use the **COMPILE** command to compile the shape file (*.shp* file). Remember that the path of the folder in which you save the shape file should be specified in the AutoCAD support file search path. When you use this command, the **Select Shape or Font File** dialog box will be displayed, refer to Figure 16-21. If **FILEDIA** = 0, this command will be executed using the command line. The following is the command sequence for compiling the shape file:

Command: **COMPILE**
Enter shape (.SHP) or PostScript font (.PFB) file name: **MHOLE**

Step 4: Writing the definition of the shape complex linetype

Use a text editor to write the definition of the shape complex linetype. You can add the definition to the *acad.lin* file or create a separate file. The extension of the file must be *.lin*. The following file is the listing of the *mhole.lin* file for Example 4. The name of the linetype is MHOLE.

*MHOLE,Line with Manholes
A,0.75,[MH,MHOLE.SHX,S=0.10,X=0.2,Y=0],-0.2 Enter.

Step 5: Loading the linetype

To test the linetype, load the linetype using the **LINETYPE** command. Assign the linetype to a layer. Draw a line or any object to check if the line is drawn to the given specifications. The shape is drawn upside down when you draw a line from right to left. Figure 16-22 shows the execution of the linetype *mhole.lin* using line, pline, and spline. Figure 16-23 displays the region hatched using the string complex and shape complex line types, respectively.

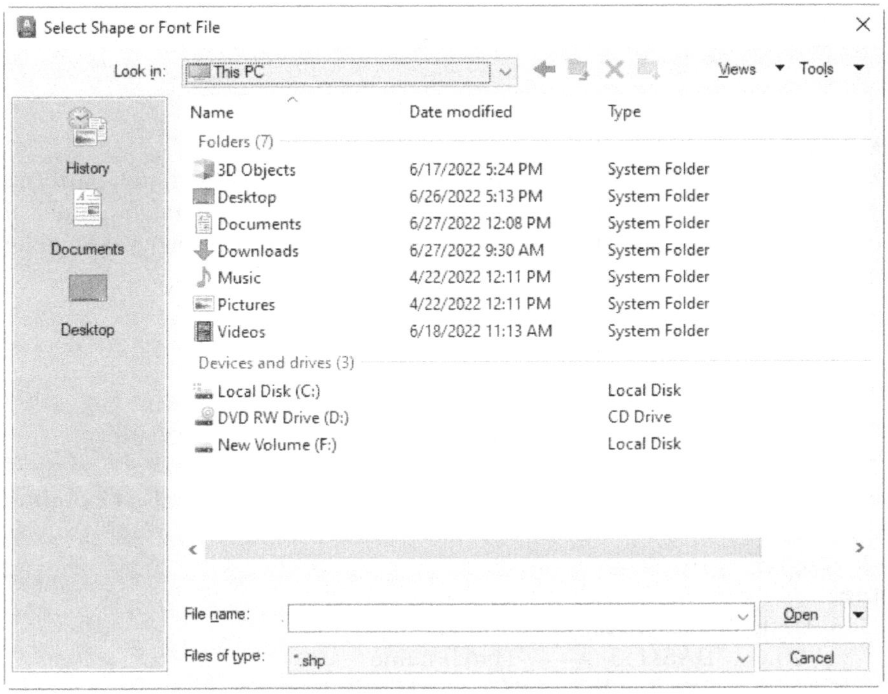

Figure 16-21 The ***Select Shape or Font File*** *dialog box*

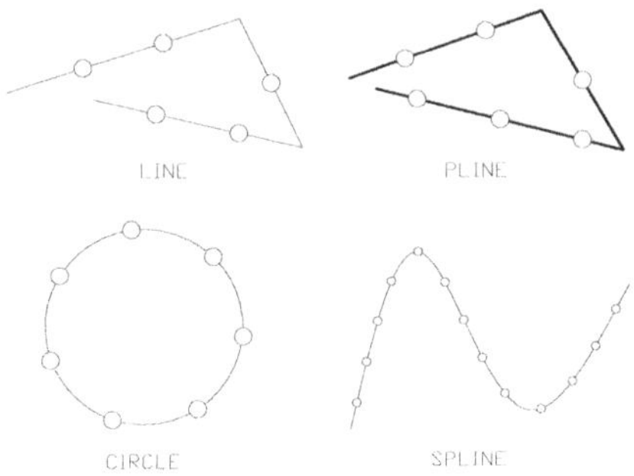

Figure 16-22 *Using a shape complex linetype*

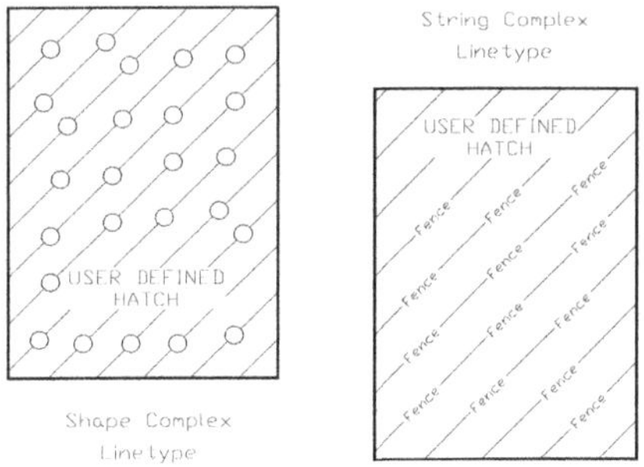

Figure 16-23 *Using shape and string complex linetypes to create custom hatch*

HATCH PATTERN DEFINITION

AutoCAD has a default hatch pattern library file, *acad.pat* and *acadiso.pat*, that contains 72 hatch patterns. Generally, you can hatch all the drawings using these default hatch patterns. However, if you need a different hatch pattern, AutoCAD allows you to create your own hatch patterns. There is no limit to the number of hatch patterns you can define.

The hatch patterns you define can be added to the hatch pattern library file, *acad.pat or acadiso.pat*. You can also create a new hatch pattern library file, provided the file contains only one hatch pattern definition, and the name of the hatch is the same as the name of the file.

The hatch pattern definition consists of the following two parts: Header Line and Hatch Descriptors.

Header Line

The header line consists of an asterisk (*) followed by the name of the hatch pattern. The hatch name is the name used in the hatch command to hatch an area. The hatch name is followed by the hatch description. Both are separated from each other by a comma (,). The general format of the header line is:

***HATCH Name, Hatch Description**

Where * ----------------------------Asterisk
HATCH Name -----------Name of hatch pattern
Hatch Description --Description of hatch pattern

The description can be any text that describes the hatch pattern. It can also be omitted, in which case, a comma should not follow the hatch pattern name.

Example:
***DASH45, Dashed lines at 45°**
Where **DASH45** --------Hatch name
Dashed lines at 45° --Hatch description

Hatch Descriptors

The hatch descriptors consist of one or more lines that contain the definition of the hatch lines. The general format of the hatch descriptor is:

Angle, X-origin, Y-origin, D1, D2 [,Dash Length.....]

Where **Angle** -----------Angle of hatch lines
X-origin --------*X* coordinate of hatch line
Y-origin --------*Y* coordinate of hatch line
D1 ---------------Displacement of second line (Delta-X)
D2 ---------------Distance between hatch lines (Delta-Y)
Length Length of dashes and spaces (Pattern line definition)

Example:

45,0,0,0,0.5,0.5,-0.125,0,-0.125

Where **45** ----------------Angle of hatch line
0 ------------------X-Origin
0 ------------------Y-Origin
0 ------------------Delta-X
0.5 ---------------Delta-Y
0.5 ---------------Dash (pen down)
-0.125 -----------Space (pen up)
0 ------------------Dot (pen down)
-0.125 -----------Space (pen up)
0.5,-0.125,0,-0.125 Pattern line definition

Hatch Angle

X-origin and Y-origin. The hatch angle is the angle that the hatch lines make with the positive *X* axis. The angle is positive if measured counterclockwise, refer to Figure 16-24, and negative if measured clockwise. When you draw a hatch pattern, the first hatch line starts from the point defined by X-origin and Y-origin.

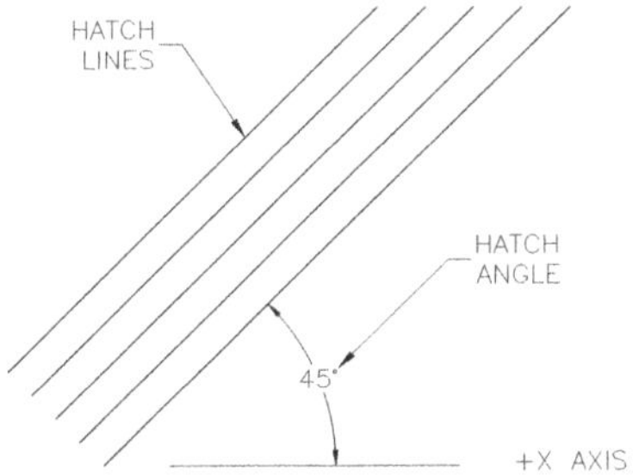

Figure 16-24 *Hatch angle*

The remaining lines are generated by offsetting the first hatch line by a distance specified by delta-X and delta-Y. In Figure 16-25(a), the first hatch line starts from the point with the coordinates X = 0 and Y = 0. In Figure 16-25(b), the first line of hatch starts from a point with the coordinates X = 0 and Y = 0.25.

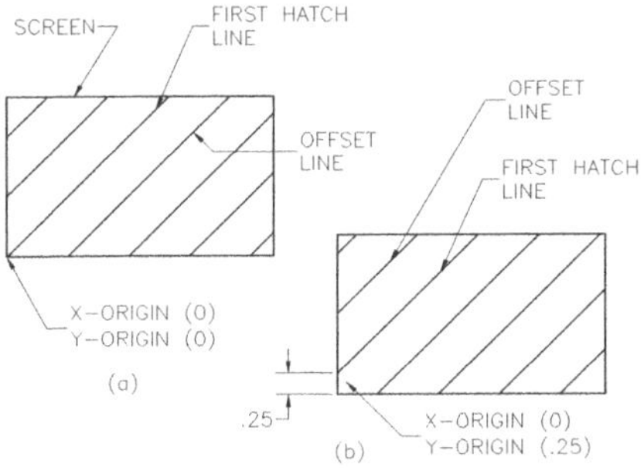

Figure 16-25 *X-origin and Y-origin of hatch lines*

Delta-X and Delta-Y. Delta-X is the displacement of the offset line in the direction in which the hatch lines are generated. For example, if the lines are drawn at a 0° angle and delta-X = 0.5, the offset line will be displaced by a distance delta-X (0.5) along the 0-angle direction. Similarly, if the hatch lines are drawn at a 45° angle, the offset line will be displaced by a distance delta-X (0.5) along a 45° direction, refer to Figure 16-26. Delta-Y is the displacement of the offset lines measured perpendicular to the hatch lines. For example, if delta-Y = 1.0, the space between any two hatch lines will be 1.0, refer to Figure 11-26.

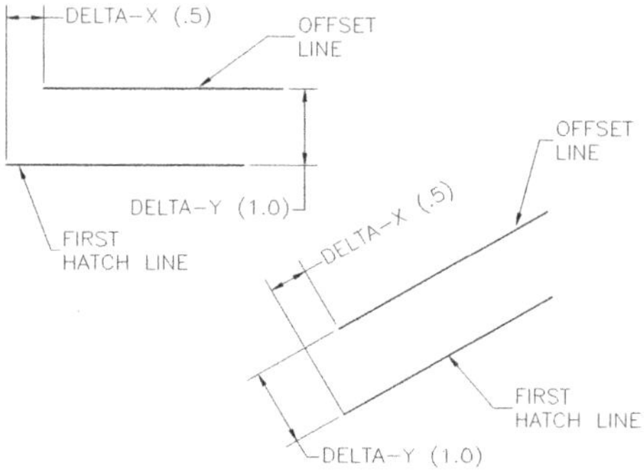

Figure 16-26 Delta-X and Delta-Y of hatch lines

HOW HATCH WORKS?

When you hatch an area, infinite number of hatch lines of infinite length is generated. The first hatch line always passes through the point specified by the X-origin and Y-origin. The remaining lines are generated by offsetting the first hatch line in both directions. The offset distance is determined by delta-X and delta-Y, refer to Figure 16-26. All selected entities that form the boundary of the hatch area are then checked for intersection with these lines. Any hatch lines found within the defined hatch boundaries are turned on, and the hatch lines outside the hatch boundary are turned off, as shown in Figure 16-27. Since the hatch lines are generated by offsetting, the hatch lines in all areas of drawing are automatically aligned relative to the drawing's snap origin. Figure 16-27(a) shows the hatch lines computed by AutoCAD. These lines are not drawn on the screen and are shown here for illustration only. Figure 16-27(b) shows the hatch lines generated in the circle that was defined as the hatch boundary.

Figure 16-27 Hatch lines outside the hatch boundary are turned off

SIMPLE HATCH PATTERN

It is a good practice to develop the hatch pattern specification before writing a hatch pattern definition. For simple hatch patterns, it may not be that important. However for more complicated hatch patterns, you should know the detailed specifications. Example 5 illustrates the procedure for developing a simple hatch pattern.

Example 5 — Hatch Pattern

Write a hatch pattern definition for the hatch pattern shown in Figure 16-28, with the following specifications:

Name of the hatch pattern	=HATCH1
X-Origin	=0
Y-Origin	=0
Distance between hatch lines	=0.5
Displacement of hatch lines	=0
Hatch line pattern	=Continuous

Step 1: Creating the hatch pattern file

This hatch pattern definition can be added to the existing *acad.pat* hatch file. You can use any text editor (like Notepad) to write the file. Load the *acad.pat* file that is located in the *C:\Users\CADCIM\AppData\Roaming\Autodesk\AutoCAD 2023\ R24.2\enu\Support* directory and insert the following two lines at the end of the file.

***HATCH1,Hatch Pattern for Example 5**
45,0,0,0,.5

Where **45** ----------------Hatch angle
0 ------------------X-origin
0 ------------------Y-origin
0 ------------------Displacement of second hatch line
.5 -----------------Distance between hatch lines

The first field of hatch descriptors contains the angle of the hatch lines and the value of this angle in this particular case with respect to the positive *X* axis is 45°. The second and third fields describe the *X* and *Y* coordinates of the first hatch line origin. The first line of the hatch pattern will pass through this point. If the values of the X-origin and Y-origin were 0.5 and 1.0, respectively, then the first line would pass through the point with the *X* coordinate of 0.5 and the *Y* coordinate of 1.0, with respect to the drawing origin 0,0. The remaining lines are generated by offsetting the first line, as shown in Figure 16-28.

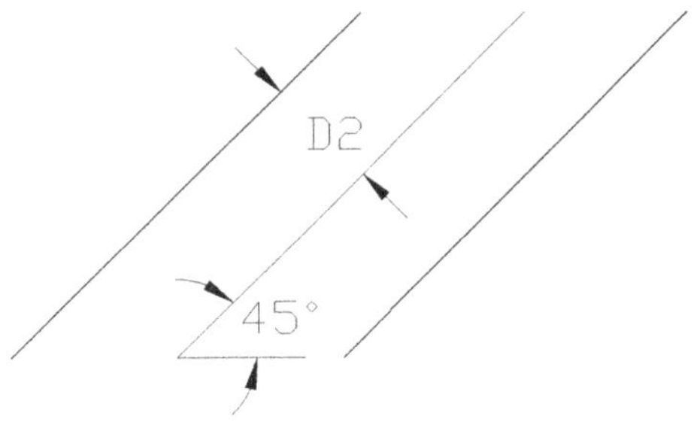

Figure 16-28 *Hatch pattern angle and offset distance*

Step 2: Applying the hatch pattern

Choose the **Hatch** tool from the **Draw** panel; the **Hatch Creation** context tab will get added to the **Ribbon**. Select the **HATCH1** pattern from **Pattern > Hatch Creation** context tab. If needed, change the **Scale** and **Angle** from the **Properties** panel of the **Hatch Creation** tab. Next, hatch a circle to test the hatch pattern.

EFFECT OF ANGLE AND SCALE FACTOR ON HATCH

When you hatch an area, to get the desired hatch spacing, you can alter the angle and displacement of hatch lines you have specified in the hatch pattern definition. You can do this by entering an appropriate value for angle and scale factor in the **HATCH** command.

To understand how the angle and the displacement can be changed, hatch an area with the hatch pattern HATCH1 in Example 5. You will notice that the hatch lines have been generated according to the definition of hatch pattern HATCH1. Notice the effect of hatch angle and scale factor on the hatch. Figure 16-29(a) shows a hatch with a 0° angle and a scale factor of 1.0. If the angle is 0, the hatch will be generated with the same angle as defined in the hatch pattern definition (45° in Example 5). Similarly, if the scale factor is 1.0, the distance between the hatch lines will be the same as defined in the hatch pattern definition. Figure 16-29(b) shows a hatch that is generated when the hatch scale factor is 0.5. If you measure the distance between the successive hatch lines, it will be 0.5 x 0.5 = 0.25. Figures 16-29(c) and (d) show the hatch when the angle is 45° and the scale factors are 1.0 and 0.5, respectively.

Scale and Angle can also be set by entering **-HATCH** at the Command prompt.

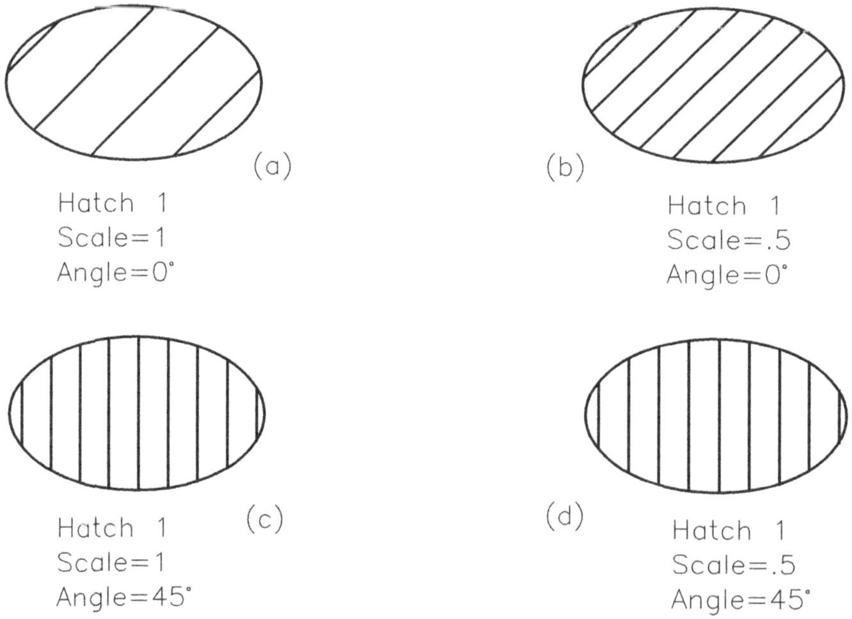

Figure 16-29 *Effect of angle and scale factor on hatch*

HATCH PATTERN WITH DASHES AND DOTS

The lines that you can use in a hatch pattern definition are not restricted to continuous lines. You can define any line pattern to generate a hatch pattern. The lines can be a combination of dashes, dots, and spaces in any configuration. However, the maximum number of dashes you can specify in the line pattern definition of a hatch pattern is six. Example 6 uses a dash-dot linetype to create a hatch pattern.

Example 6 — Hatch Pattern

Write a hatch pattern definition for the hatch pattern shown in Figure 16-30, with the following specifications. Define a new path such as *C:\Program Files\Hatch1* and save the hatch pattern in that path.

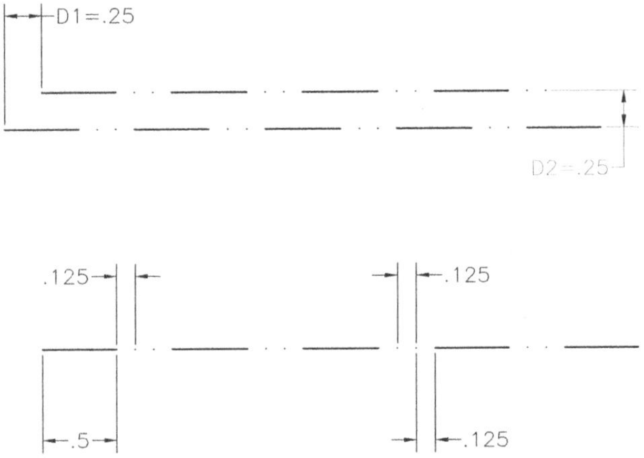

Figure 16-30 *Hatch lines made of dashes and dots*

Name of the hatch pattern =	HATCH2
Hatch angle =	0
X-origin =	0
Y-origin =	0
Displacement of lines (D1) =	0.25
Distance between lines (D2) =	0.25
Length of each dash =	0.5
Space between dashes and dots =	0.125
Space between dots =	0.125

Writing the definition of a hatch pattern

You can use any text editor (Notepad) to edit the *acad.pat* file. The general format of the header line and the hatch descriptors is:

***HATCH NAME, Hatch Description**
Angle, X-Origin, Y-Origin, D1, D2 [,Dash Length.....]

Substitute the values from Example 6 in the corresponding fields of the header line and field descriptor:

*HATCH2,Hatch with dashes and dots
0,0,0,0.25,0.25,0.5,-0.125,0,-0.125,0,-0.125
Where **0** ------------------Angle
0 -------------------X-origin
0 ------------------Y-origin
0.25 --------------Delta-X
0.25 --------------Delta-Y
0.5 ---------------Length of dash
-0.125 -----------Space (pen up)
0 ------------------Dot (pen down)
-0.125 -----------Space (pen up)
0 -------------------Dot
-0.125 Space

Specifying a New Path for Hatch Pattern Files

When you enter a hatch pattern name for hatching, AutoCAD looks for that file name in the **Support** directory or in the directory paths specified in the support file search path. You can specify a new path and directory to store your hatch files.

Create a new folder *Hatch1* in *C* drive under the *Program Files* folder. Save the *acad.pat* file with hatch pattern **HATCH2** definition in the same subdirectory, Hatch1. Right-click in the drawing area to activate the shortcut menu. Choose **Options** from the shortcut menu to display the **Options** dialog box. The **Options** dialog box can also be invoked by choosing the **Options** tool from the **Application Menu**. Choose the **Files** tab in the **Options** dialog box to display the **Search paths, file names and file locations** area. Click on the **+** sign of the **Support File Search Path** to display the different subdirectories of the **Support File Search Path**, as shown in Figure 16-31. Now, choose the **Add** button to display the space to add a new subdirectory. Enter the location of the new subdirectory, **C:\Program Files\Hatch1** or click on the **Browse** button to specify the path. Choose the **Apply** button and then choose **OK** to exit the **Options** dialog box. You have created a subdirectory and specified the search path for the hatch files.

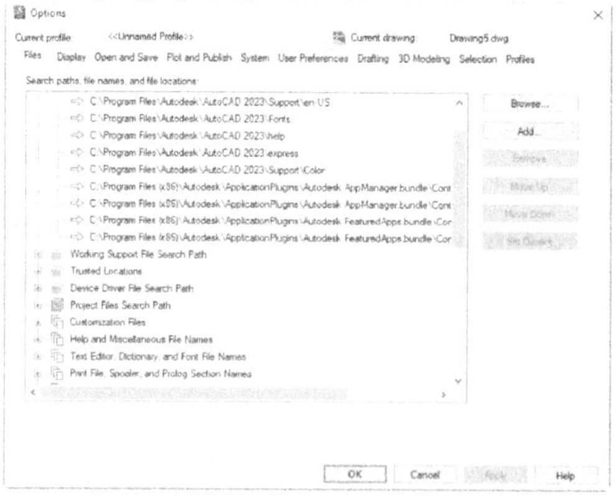

Figure 16-31 *The* ***Options*** *dialog box*

Follow the procedure as described in Example 5 to activate the hatch pattern. The hatch thus generated is shown in Figure 16-32. Figure 16-32(a) shows the hatch with a 0° angle and a scale factor of 1.0. Figure 16-32(b) shows the hatch with a 45° angle and a scale factor of 0.5.

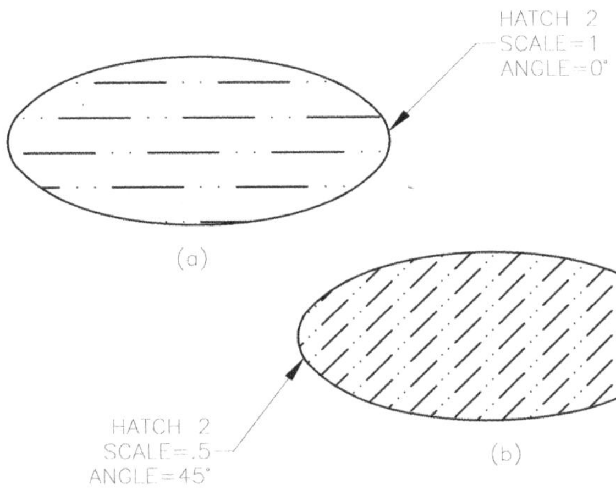

Figure 16-32 *Hatch pattern at different angles and scales*

HATCH WITH MULTIPLE DESCRIPTORS

Some hatch patterns require multiple lines to generate a shape. For example, if you want to create a hatch pattern of a brick wall, you need four hatch descriptors to generate rectangular shape. You can have any number of hatch descriptor lines in a hatch pattern definition. It is up to the user to combine them in any conceivable order. However, there are some shapes you can not generate. A shape that has a nonlinear element, such as an arc, cannot be generated by hatch pattern definition. However, you can simulate an arc by defining short line segments because you can use only straight lines to generate a hatch pattern. Example 7 uses three lines to define a triangular hatch pattern.

Example 7 — *Hatch Pattern*

Write a hatch pattern definition for the hatch pattern shown in Figure 16-33, with the following specifications:

Name of the hatch pattern	=HATCH3
Vertical height of the triangle	=0.5
Horizontal length of the triangle	=0.5
Vertical distance between the triangles	=0.5
Horizontal distance between the triangles	=0.5

Each triangle in this hatch pattern consists of the following three elements: a vertical line, a horizontal line, and a line inclined at 45°.

Step 1: Defining specifications for vertical line

For the vertical line, refer to Figure 16-34, the specifications are:

Hatch angle	=90°
X-origin	=0
Y-origin	=0
Delta-X (D1)	=0
Delta-Y (D2)	=1.0
Dash length	=0.5
Space	=0.5

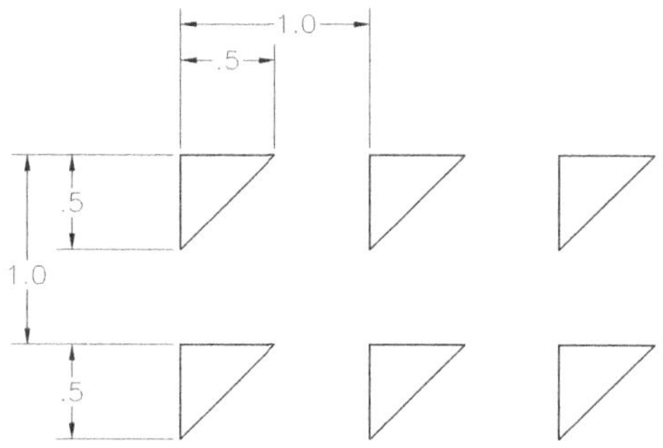

Figure 16-33 Triangle hatch pattern

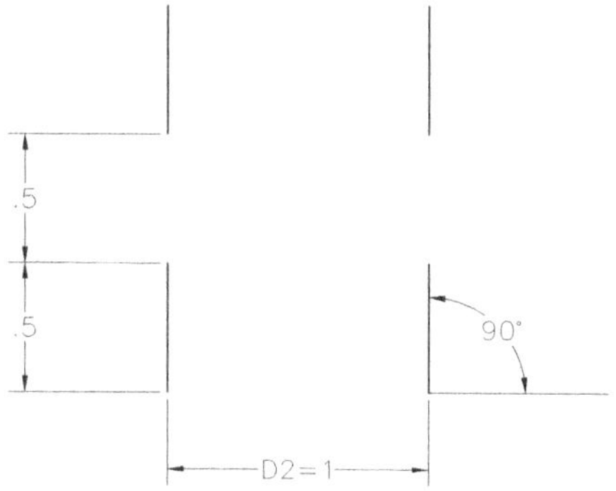

Figure 16-34 Vertical line

Substitute the values from the vertical line specification in various fields of the hatch descriptor to get the following line:

90,0,0,0,1,.5,-.5

Where **90** ----------------Hatch angle
0 ------------------X-origin
0 ------------------Y-origin
0 ------------------Delta-X
1 ------------------Delta-Y
.5 -----------------Dash (pen down)
-.5 ----------------Space (pen up)

Step 2: Defining specifications of horizontal line

For the horizontal line, refer to Figure 16-35, the specifications are:

Hatch angle	=0°
X-origin	=0
Y-origin	=0.5
Delta-X (D1)	=0
Delta-Y (D2)	=1.0
Dash length	=0.5
Space	=0.5

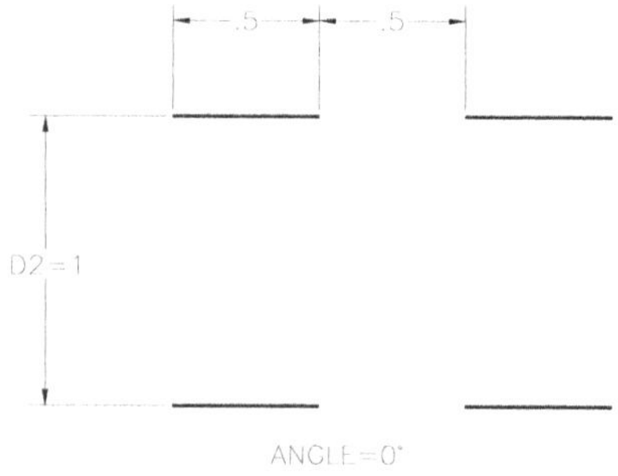

Figure 16-35 Horizontal line

The only difference between the vertical line and the horizontal line is the angle. For the horizontal line, the angle is 0°, whereas for the vertical line, the angle is 90°. Substitute the values from the vertical line specification to obtain the following line:

0,0,0.5,0,1,.5,-.5

Where **0** ------------------Hatch angle
0 ------------------X-origin
0.5 ---------------Y-origin
0 ------------------Delta-X
1 ------------------Delta-Y
.5 -----------------Dash (pen down)
-.5 ----------------Space (pen up)

Step 3: Defining specifications of the inclined line

This line is at an angle; therefore, you need to calculate the distances delta-X (D1) and delta-Y (D2), the length of the dashed line, and the length of the blank space. Figure 16-36 shows the calculations to find these values.

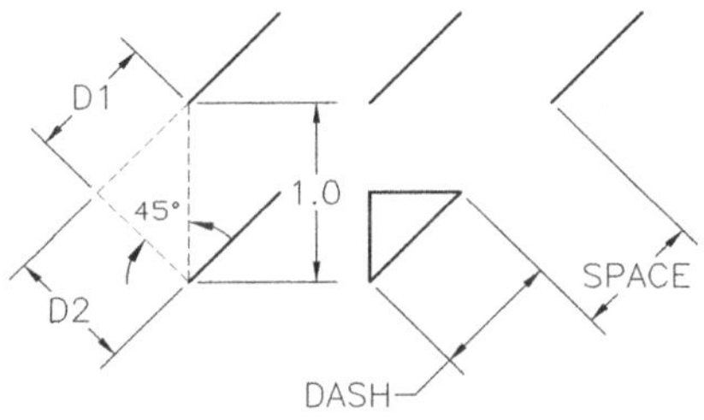

D1 = 1.0 x COS 45   D2 = 1.0 x SIN 45
D1 = .7071   D2 = .7071

DASH = SQRT(0.5^2 +0.5^2)
=.7071
SPACE = DASH =.7071

Figure 16-36 *Line inclined at 45°*

Hatch angle	=45°
X-Origin	=0
Y-Origin	=0
Delta-X (D1)	=0.7071
Delta-Y (D2)	=0.7071
Dash length	=0.7071
Space	=0.7071

After substituting the values in the general format of the hatch descriptor, you will obtain the following line:

45,0,0,.7071,.7071,.7071,-.7071

Where **45** ----------------Hatch angle
0 ------------------X-origin
0 ------------------Y-origin
.7071 ------------Delta-X
.7071 ------------Delta-Y
.7071 ------------Dash (pen down)
-.7071 -----------Space (pen up)

Step 4: Loading the hatch pattern

Now, you can combine three lines and insert them at the end of the *acad.pat* file or you can enter the values in a separate hatch file and save it. You can also use any text editor and insert the line definition.

The following file is a partial listing of the *acad.pat* file, after adding the hatch pattern definitions from Examples 5, 6, and 7.

```
*SOLID, Solid fill
45, 0,0, 0,.125
*Angle,Angle steel
0, 0,0, 0,.275, .2,-.075
90, 0,0, 0,.275, .2,-.075
*Ansi31,ANSI Iron, Brick, Stone masonry
45, 0,0, 0,.125
*Ansi32,ANSI Steel
45, 0,0, 0,.375
45, .176776695,0, 0,.375
*Ansi33,ANSI Bronze, Brass, Copper
45, 0,0, 0,.25
45, .176776695,0, 0,.25, .125,-.0625
*Ansi34,ANSI Plastic, Rubber
45, 0,0, 0,.75
45, .176776695,0, 0,.75
45, .353553391,0, 0,.75
45, .530330086,0, 0,.75
*Ansi35,ANSI Fire brick, Refractory material
45, 0,0, 0,.25
45, .176776695,0, 0,.25, .3125,-.0625,0,-.0625
*Ansi36,ANSI Marble, Slate, Glass
45, 0,0, .21875,.125, .3125,-.0625,0,-.0625

*Swamp,Swampy area
0, 0,0, .5,.866025403, .125,-.875
90, .0625,0, .866025403,.5, .0625,-1.669550806
90, .078125,0, .866025403,.5, .05,-1.682050806
90, .046875,0, .66025403,.5, .05,-1.682050806
|
|
```

```
0, 0,0, .125,.125, .125,-.125
90, .125,0, .125,.125, .125,-.125
*HATCH1,Hatch at 45 Degree Angle
45,0,0,0,.5
*HATCH2,Hatch with Dashes & Dots:
0,0,0,.25,.25,0.5,-.125,0,-.125,0,-.125
*HATCH3,Triangle Hatch:
90,0,0,0,1,.5,-.5
0,0,0.5,0,1,.5,-.5
45,0,0,.7071,.7071,.7071,-.7071
```

Load the hatch pattern as described in Example 5 and test the hatch. Figure 16-37 shows the hatch pattern that will be generated by this hatch pattern (HATCH3). In Figure 16-37(a) the hatch pattern is at a 0° angle and the scale factor is 0.5. In Figure 16-37(b) the hatch pattern is at a -45° angle and the scale factor is 0.5.

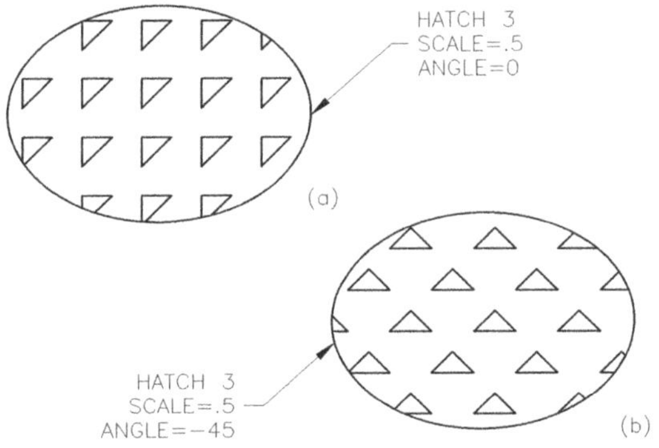

Figure 16-37 *Hatch generated by HATCH3 pattern*

SAVING HATCH PATTERNS IN A SEPARATE FILE

When you load a hatch pattern, AutoCAD looks for that definition in the *acad.pat* or *acadiso.pat* file. This is the reason the hatch pattern definitions must be in that file. However, you can add the new pattern definition to a different file and then copy that file to *acad.pat* or *acadiso.pat*. Be sure to make a copy of the original *acad.pat* or *acadiso.pat* file so that you can copy that file back when needed. Assume the name of the file that contains your custom hatch pattern definitions is *customh.pat*.

1. Copy *acad.pat* or *acadiso.pat* file to *acadorg.pat*
2. Copy *customh.pat* to *acad.pat* or *acadiso.pat*

If you want to use the original hatch pattern file, copy the *acadorg.pat* file to *acad.pat* or *acadiso.pat*.

CUSTOM HATCH PATTERN FILE

As mentioned earlier, you can add the new hatch pattern definitions to the *acad.pat* or *acadiso.pat* file. There is no limit to the number of hatch pattern definitions you can add to this file. However, if you have only one hatch pattern definition, you can define a separate file. It has the following requirements:

1. The name of the file has to be the same as the hatch pattern name.
2. The file can contain only one hatch pattern definition.
3. The hatch pattern name and the hatch file name should be unique.
4. If you use the hatch patterns saved on the removable drive quite often to hatch the drawings, you can add removable drive to the AutoCAD search path using the **Options** dialog box. AutoCAD will automatically search the file on the removable drive and will display it in the **Hatch Creation** tab of the **Ribbon**.

```
*HATCH3,Triangle Hatch:
90,0,0,0,1,.5,-.5
0,0,0.5,0,1,.5,-.5
45,0,0,.7071,.7071,.7071,-.7071
```

Note

1. The hatch lines can be edited after exploding the hatch with the ***EXPLODE*** *command. After exploding, each hatch line becomes a separate object. However, it is recommended not to explode a hatch because it increases the size of the drawing database. For example, if a hatch consists of 100 lines, save it as a single object. However, after you explode the hatch, every line becomes a separate object and you have 99 additional objects in the drawing.*

2. Keep the hatch lines in a separate layer to facilitate editing of the hatch lines.

3. Assign a unique color to hatch lines so that you can control the width of the hatch lines at the time of plotting.

Tip

1. The file or the subdirectory in which hatch patterns have been saved must be defined in the ***Support File Search Path*** *in the* ***Files*** *tab of the* ***Options*** *dialog box.*

2. The hatch patterns that you create automatically get added to AutoCAD's slide library as an integral part of AutoCAD and are displayed in the ***Preview Area*** *in the* ***Hatch Pattern Palette*** *dialog box under the* ***Hatch Creation*** *tab of the* ***Ribbon****. Hence, there is no need to create a slide library.*

Self-Evaluation Test

Answer the following questions and then compare them to those given at the end of this chapter:

1. The __________ command can be used to change the linetype scale factor.

2. The linetype description should not be more than __________ characters long.
3. A positive number denotes a pen __________ segment.
4. __________ segment length generates a dot.
5. A negative number denotes a pen __________ segment.
6. The __________ option of the **LINETYPE** command is used to generate a new linetype.
7. The description in the case of header line is __________.
8. The standard linetypes are stored in the __________ file.
9. The __________ determines the current linetype scaling.
10. The header line consists of an asterisk, the pattern name, and the __________.
11. The *acad.pat* or *acadiso.pat* file contains __________ number of hatch pattern definitions.
12. The standard hatch patterns are stored in the __________ file.
13. The first hatch line passes through a point whose coordinates are specified by __________ and __________.

Review Questions

Answer the following questions:

1. The __________ command can be used to create a new linetype.
2. The __________ command can be used to load a linetype.
3. In AutoCAD, the linetypes are saved in the __________ file.
4. AutoCAD supports only __________ alignment field specification.
5. A line pattern definition always starts with __________.
6. A header line definition always starts with __________.
7. The perpendicular distance between the hatch lines in a hatch pattern definition is specified by __________.
8. The displacement of the second hatch line in a hatch pattern definition is specified by __________.

9. The maximum number of dash lengths that can be specified in the line pattern definition of a hatch pattern is __________.

10. The hatch lines in different areas of the drawing will automatically __________ because the hatch lines are generated by offsetting.

11. The hatch angle as defined in the hatch pattern definition can be changed further when you use the __________ command.

12. When you load a hatch pattern, AutoCAD looks for that hatch pattern in the __________ file.

13. The hatch lines can be edited after __________ the hatch by using the __________ command.

Exercise 1 — Linetype

Using the **LINETYPE** command, create a new linetype "DASH3DASH" with the following specifications:

Length of the first dash 0.75
Blank space 0.125
Dash length 0.25
Blank space 0.125
Dash length 0.25
Blank space 0.125
Dash length 0.25
Blank space 0.125

Exercise 2 — Linetype

Use a text editor to create a new file, *newlt2.lin*, and a new linetype, DASH2DASH, with the following specifications:

Length of the first dash 0.5
Blank space 0.1
Dash length 0.2
Blank space 0.1
Dash length 0.2
Blank space 0.1

Exercise 3 — String Complex Linetype

a. Write the definition of a string complex linetype (hot water line), as shown in Figure 16-38(a). To determine the length of the HW text string, you should first draw the text (HW) using any text command and then measure its length.

b. Write the definition of a string complex linetype (gas line), as shown in Figure 16-38(b). Determine the length of the text string as mentioned in part a.

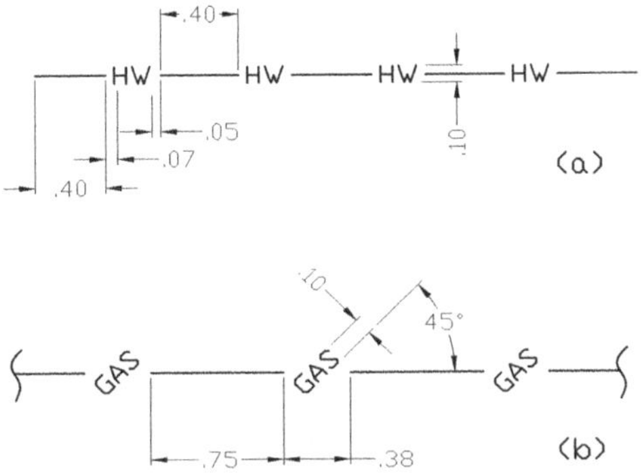

Figure 16-38 *Specifications for a string complex linetype*

Exercise 4 — Hatch Pattern

Determine the hatch pattern specifications and then write a hatch pattern definition for the hatch pattern shown in Figure 16-39.

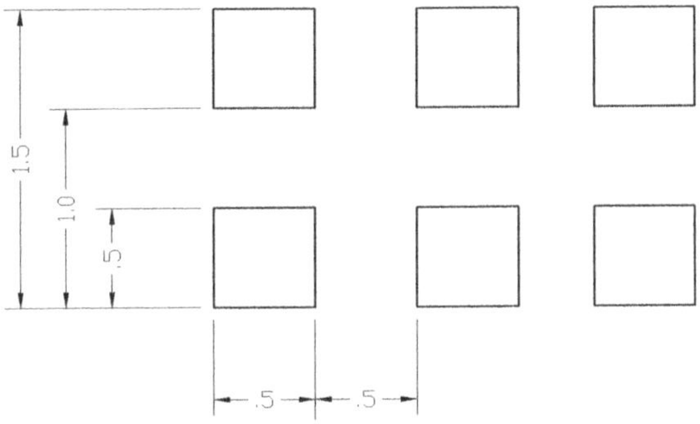

Figure 16-39 *Drawing for Exercise 4*

Exercise 5 — Hatch Pattern

Determine the hatch pattern specifications and then write a hatch pattern definition for the hatch pattern shown in Figure 16-40.

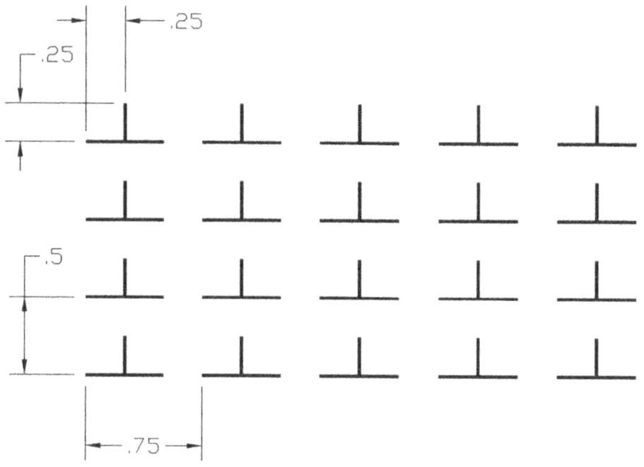

Figure 16-40 *Hatch pattern for Exercise 5*

Answers to Self-Evaluation Test

1. **LTSCALE**, **2.** 47, **3.** down, **4.** Zero, **5.** up, **6.** **Create**, **7.** optional, **8.** *acad.lin* or *acadiso.lin*, **9.** **CELTSCALE**, **10.** Pattern Description, **11.** 72, **12.** *acad.pat* or *acadiso.pat*, **13.** X-origin, Y-origin

Chapter 17

Customizing the acad.pgp File

Learning Objectives

After completing this chapter, you will be able to:
- *Customize the acad.pgp file*
- *Edit different sections of the acad.pgp file*
- *Abbreviate commands by defining command aliases*
- *Use the REINIT command to reinitialize the PGP file*

Key Terms

- *acad.pgp file*
- *Command Name*
- *OS Command Name*
- *Bit Flag*
- *Command Aliases*

WHAT IS THE acad.pgp FILE?

AutoCAD software comes with the program parameters file *acad.pgp*, which defines aliases for the operating system commands and some of the AutoCAD commands. When you install AutoCAD on a computer that runs on Windows 2000 or later versions, this file is automatically copied on to the *C:\Users\CADCIM\AppData\Roaming\Autodesk\AutoCAD 2023\R24.2\enu\Support* subdirectory of the hard drive. The *acad.pgp* file lets you access the commands of operating system from the drawing editor. For example, if you want to delete a file, all you need to do is enter **DEL** at the Command prompt (Command: **DEL**), and AutoCAD will prompt you to enter the name of the file that you want to delete.

The file also contains command aliases of some frequently used AutoCAD commands. For example, the command alias for the **LINE** command is L. This is the reason if you enter **L** at the Command prompt **(Command: L)**, AutoCAD will treat it as the **LINE** command. The *acad.pgp* file also contains comment lines that give you some information about different sections of the file. The *acad.pgp* file can be opened by choosing the **Edit Aliases** tool from the **Edit Aliases** drop-down of **Customization** panel in the **Manage** tab. You can also open the *acad.pgp* file by choosing the **Edit Program Parameters (acad.pgp)** tool from **Tools > Customize** in the menu bar. The following file shows the content of the standard *acad.pgp* file. Some of the lines have been deleted to make the file shorter.

```
;
;
; Program Parameters File For AutoCAD 2023
; External Command and Command Alias Definitions

; Copyright 2022 by Autodesk, Inc.  All Rights Reserved.
;
; Use of this software is subject to the terms of the Autodesk license
; agreement provided at the time of installation or download, or which
; otherwise accompanies this software in either electronic or hard copy form.

; Each time you open a new or existing drawing, AutoCAD searches
; the support path and reads the first acad.pgp file that it finds.

; -- External Commands --
; While AutoCAD is running, you can invoke other programs or utilities
; such Windows system commands, utilities, and applications.
; You define external commands by specifying a command name to be used
; from the AutoCAD command prompt and an executable command string
; that is passed to the operating system.

; -- Command Aliases --
; The Command Aliases section of this file provides default settings for
; AutoCAD command shortcuts.  Note: It is not recommended that you directly
; modify this section of the PGP file., as any changes you make to this section of the
; file will not migrate successfully if you upgrade your AutoCAD to a
```

```
; newer version. Instead, make changes to the new
; User Defined Command Aliases
; section towards the end of this file.

; -- User Defined Command Aliases --
; You can abbreviate frequently used AutoCAD commands by defining
; aliases for them in the User Defined Command Aliases section of acad.pgp.
; You can create a command alias for any AutoCAD command,
; device driver command, or external command.

; Recommendation: back up this file before editing it. To ensure that
; any changes you make to PGP settings can successfully be migrated
; when you upgrade to the next version of AutoCAD, it is suggested that
; you make any changes to the default settings in the User Defined Command
; Aliases section at the end of this file.

; External command format:
; <Command name>,[<Shell request>],<Bit flag>,[*]<Prompt>,

; The bits of the bit flag have the following meanings:
; Bit 1: if set, don't wait for the application to finish
; Bit 2: if set, run the application minimized
; Bit 4: if set, run the application "hidden"
; Bit 8: if set, put the argument string in quotes
;
; Fill the "bit flag" field with the sum of the desired bits.
; Bits 2 and 4 are mutually exclusive; if both are specified, only
; the 2 bit is used. The most useful values are likely to be 0
; (start the application and wait for it to finish), 1 (start the
; application and don't wait), 3 (minimize and don't wait), and 5
; (hide and don't wait). Values of 2 and 4 should normally be avoided,
; as they make AutoCAD unavailable until the application has completed.
;
; Bit 8 allows commands like DEL to work properly with filenames that
; have spaces such as "long filename.dwg". Note that this will interfere
; with passing space delimited lists of file names to these same commands.
; If you prefer multiplefile support to using long file names, turn off
; the "8" bit in those commands.

; Examples of external commands for command windows

DEL,      DEL,        8,File to delete: ,
DIR,      DIR,        8,File specification: ,
SH,       ,           1,*OS Command: ,
SHELL,    ,           1,*OS Command: ,
START,    START,      1,*Application to start: ,
TYPE,     TYPE,       8,File to list: ,
```

External commands area

```
; Examples of external commands for Windows
; See also the (STARTAPP) AutoLISP function for an alternative method.

EXPLORER,  START EXPLORER, 1,,
NOTEPAD,          START NOTEPAD,  1,*File to edit: ,
PBRUSH,           START PBRUSH,   1,,

; Command alias format:
;   <Alias>,*<Full command name>

;  The following are guidelines for creating new command aliases.
;  1. An alias should reduce a command by at least two characters.
;     Commands with a control key equivalent, status bar button,
;     or function key do not require a command alias.
;     Examples: Control N, O, P, and S for New, Open, Print, Save.
;  2. Try the first character of the command, then try the first two,
;     then the first three.
;  3. Once an alias is defined, add suffixes for related aliases:
;     Examples: R for Redraw, RA for Redrawall, L for Line, LT for
;     Linetype.
;  4. Use a hyphen to differentiate between command line and dialog
;     box commands.
;     Example: B for Block, -B for -Block.
;
; Exceptions to the rules include AA for Area, T for Mtext, X for Explode.

;  -- Sample aliases for AutoCAD commands --
;  These examples include most frequently used commands.  NOTE: It is recommended
;  that you not make any changes to this section of the PGP file to ensure the
;  proper migration of your customizations when you upgrade to the next version of
;  AutoCAD.  The aliases listed in this section are repeated in the User Custom
;  Settings section at the end of this file, which can safely be edited while
;  ensuring your changes will successfully migrate.

3A,                 *3DARRAY
3DMIRROR,           *MIRROR3D
3DNavigate,         *3DWALK
3DO,                *3DORBIT
3DP,                *3DPRINT
3DPLOT,             *3DPRINT
3DW,                *3DWALK
3F,                 *3DFACE
3M,                 *3DMOVE
3P,                 *3DPOLY
3R,                 *3DROTATE
3S,                 *3DSCALE
A,                  *ARC
AC,                 *BACTION
```

External commands

```
ADC,                    *ADCENTER
AECTOACAD,              *-ExportToAutoCAD
AA,                     *AREA
AL,                     *ALIGN
3AL,                    *3DALIGN
AP,                     *APPLOAD
APLAY,                  *ALLPLAY
AR,                     *ARRAY
-AR,                    *-ARRAY
ARR,                    *ACTRECORD
ARM,                    *ACTUSERMESSAGE
-ARM,                   *-ACTUSERMESSAGE
ARU,                    *ACTUSERINPUT
ARS,                    *ACTSTOP
-ARS,                   *-ACTSTOP
ATI,                    *ATTIPEDIT
ATT,                    *ATTDEF
-ATT,                   *-ATTDEF
ATE,                    *ATTEDIT
-ATE,                   *-ATTEDIT
ATTE,                   *-ATTEDIT
B,                      *BLOCK
|
|
|
HE,                     *HATCHEDIT
HB,                     *HATCHTOBACK
HI,                     *HIDE
I,                      *INSERT
-I,                     *-INSERT
IAD,                    *IMAGEADJUST
IAT,                    *IMAGEATTACH
ICL,                    *IMAGECLIP
IM,                     *IMAGE
-IM,                    *-IMAGE
IMP,                    *IMPORT
IN,                     *INTERSECT
INSERTCONTROLPOINT,     *CVADD
INF,                    *INTERFERE
IO,                     *INSERTOBJ
ISOLATE,                *ISOLATEOBJECTS
QVD,                    *QVDRAWING
QVDC,                   *QVDRAWINGCLOSE
QVL,                    *QVLAYOUT
QVLC,                   *QVLAYOUTCLOSE
J,                      *JOIN
L,                      *LINE
LA,                     *LAYER
```

```
-LA,                  *-LAYER
LAS,                  *LAYERSTATE
LE,                   *QLEADER
LEN,                  *LENGTHEN
LESS,                 *MESHSMOOTHLESS
LI,                   *LIST
LINEWEIGHT,           *LWEIGHT
LMAN,                 *LAYERSTATE
LO,                   *-LAYOUT
LS,                   *LIST
LT,                   *LINETYPE
-LT,                  *-LINETYPE
LTYPE,                *LINETYPE
-LTYPE,               *-LINETYPE
LTS,                  *LTSCALE
LW,                   *LWEIGHT
M,                    *MOVE
MA,                   *MATCHPROP
MAT,                  *MATERIALS
ME,                   *MEASURE
MEA,                  *MEASUREGEOM
MI,                   *MIRROR
ML,                   *MLINE
MLA,                  *MLEADERALIGN
MLC,                  *MLEADERCOLLECT
MLD,                  *MLEADER
|
|
|
R,                        *REDRAW
RA,                       *REDRAWALL
RC,                       *RENDERCROP
RE,                       *REGEN
REA,                      *REGENALL
REBUILD,                  *CVREBUILD
REC,                      *RECTANG
REFINE,                   *MESHREFINE
REG,                      *REGION
REMOVECONTROLPOINT,       *CVREMOVE
REN,                      *RENAME
-REN,                     *-RENAME
REV,                      *REVOLVE
RO,                       *ROTATE
|
|
|
; The following are alternative aliases and aliases as supplied
;  in AutoCAD Release 13.
```

```
AV,                    *DSVIEWER
CP,                    *COPY
DIMALI,                *DIMALIGNED
DIMANG,                *DIMANGULAR
DIMBASE,               *DIMBASELINE
DIMCONT,               *DIMCONTINUE
DIMDIA,                *DIMDIAMETER
DIMED,                 *DIMEDIT
DIMTED,                *DIMTEDIT
DIMLIN,                *DIMLINEAR
DIMORD,                *DIMORDINATE
DIMRAD,                *DIMRADIUS
DIMSTY,                *DIMSTYLE
DIMOVER,               *DIMOVERRIDE
LEAD,                  *LEADER
TM,                    *TILEMODE

; Aliases for Hyperlink/URL Release 14 compatibility
SAVEURL,               *SAVE
OPENURL,               *OPEN
INSERTURL,             *INSERT

; Aliases for commands discontinued in AutoCAD 2000:
AAD,                *DBCONNECT
AEX,                *DBCONNECT
ALI,                *DBCONNECT
ASQ,                *DBCONNECT
ARO,                *DBCONNECT
ASE,                *DBCONNECT
DDATTDEF,           *ATTDEF
DDATTEXT,           *ATTEXT
DDCHPROP,           *PROPERTIES
DDCOLOR,            *COLOR
DDLMODES,           *LAYER
DDLTYPE,            *LINETYPE
DDMODIFY,           *PROPERTIES
DDOSNAP,            *OSNAP
DDUCS,              *UCS

; Aliases for commands discontinued in AutoCAD 2004:
ACADBLOCKDIALOG,    *BLOCK
ACADWBLOCKDIALOG,   *WBLOCK
ADCENTER,           *ADCENTER
BMAKE,              *BLOCK
BMOD,               *BLOCK
BPOLY,              *BOUNDARY
|
|
```

```
|
PAINTER,                *MATCHPROP
PREFERENCES,            *OPTIONS
RECTANGLE,              *RECTANG
SHADE,                  *SHADEMODE
VIEWPORTS,              *VPORTS
|
|
|
; Aliases for commands discontinued in AutoCAD 2007:
RMAT,                   *MATBROWSEROPEN
FOG,                    *RENDERENVIRONMENT
FINISH,                 *MATERIALS
SETUV,                  *MATERIALMAP
SHOWMAT,                *LIST
RFILEOPT,               *RENDERPRESETS
RENDSCR,                *RENDERWIN

; Aliases for sysvars discontinued in AutoCAD 2013:
RASTERPREVIEW,          *THUMBSAVE
AUTOCOMPLETE,           *-INPUTSEARCHOPTIONS
AUTOCOMPLETEMODE,       *-INPUTSEARCHOPTIONS
AUTOCOMPLETEDELAY,      *INPUTSEARCHDELAY

; Aliases for commands discontinued in AutoCAD 2014:
3DCONFIG,          *GRAPHICSCONFIG
-3DCONFIG,         *-GRAPHICSCONFIG


;  -- User Defined Command Aliases --
;  Make any changes or additions to the default AutoCAD command aliases in
;  this section to ensure successful migration of these settings when you
;  upgrade to the next version of AutoCAD.  If a command alias appears more
;  than once in this file, items in the User Defined Command Alias take
;  precedence over duplicates that appear earlier in the file.
;  **********----------**********  ; No xlate ; DO NOT REMOVE
```

SECTIONS OF THE acad.pgp FILE

The contents of the AutoCAD program parameters file (*acad.pgp*) can be categorized into three sections based on the information that is defined in the *acad.pgp* file. They do not appear in any definite order in the file, and have no section headings. For example, the comment lines can be entered anywhere in the file and the same is true with external commands and AutoCAD command aliases. The *acad.pgp* file can be divided into three sections: comments, external commands, and command aliases.

Comments

The comments of *acad.pgp* file can contain any number of comment lines and can occur anywhere in the file. Every comment line must start with a semicolon (;) (This is a comment line). Any line that is preceded by a semicolon is ignored by AutoCAD. You should use the comment line to give some relevant information about the file that will help other AutoCAD users to understand, edit, or update the file.

External Command

In the external command section, you can define any valid external command that is supported by your system. The information must be entered in the following format:

<Command name>, [OS Command name],<Bit flag>, [*]<Command prompt>,

Command Name. This is the name you want to use to activate the external command from the AutoCAD drawing editor. For example, you can use **GOWORD** as a command name to load the Word program (Command: **GOWORD**). The command name must not be an AutoCAD command name or an AutoCAD system variable name. If the name is an AutoCAD command name, the command name in the **PGP** file will be ignored. Also, if the name is an AutoCAD system variable name, the system variable will be ignored. You should use the command names that reflect the expected result of the external commands. (For example, **HELLO** is not a good command name for a directory file.) The command names can be in uppercase or lowercase.

OS Command Name. The OS Command name is the name of a valid system command that is supported by an operating system. For example, in DOS, the command to delete files is DEL and therefore, the OS Command name used in the *acad.pgp* file must be DEL. The following is a list of the type of commands that can be used in the PGP file:

OS Commands (DEL, DIR, TYPE, COPY, RENAME, etc.)
Commands for starting a word processor, or a text editor (WORD, SHELL, etc.)
Name of the user-defined programs and batch files

Bit Flag. This field must contain a number, preferably 8 or 1. The following are the bit flag values and their meaning:

Bit flag set to	Meaning
0	Starts the application and waits for it to finish
1	Does not wait for the application to finish
2	Runs the application in minimized mode
4	Runs the application hidden
8	Puts the argument string in quotes

Command Prompt. The Command prompt field of the command line contains the prompt you want to display on the screen. It is an optional field that must be replaced by a comma if there is no prompt. If the operating system (OS) command that you want to use contains spaces, the prompt must be preceded by an asterisk (*). For example, the DOS command **EDIT NEW.PGP** contains a space between EDIT and NEW; therefore, the prompt used in this command line must be preceded by an asterisk. The command can be terminated by pressing Enter. If the OS command consists of a single word (DIR, DEL, TYPE), the preceding asterisk must be omitted. In this case, you can terminate the command by pressing the SPACEBAR or the Enter key.

Command Aliases

It is time-consuming to enter AutoCAD commands at the keyboard because it requires typing the complete command name before pressing Enter. AutoCAD provides a facility that can be used to abbreviate the commands by defining aliases for the commands. This is made possible by the AutoCAD program parameters file (*acad.pgp* file). Each command alias line consists of two fields **(L, *LINE)**. The first field **(L)** defines the alias of the command; the second field **(*LINE)** consists of the AutoCAD command. The command must be preceded by an asterisk for AutoCAD to recognize the command line as a command alias. The two fields must be separated by a comma. The blank lines and the spaces between the two fields are ignored. In addition to AutoCAD commands, you can also use aliases for AutoLISP command names, provided the programs that contain the definition of these commands are loaded.

REINITIALIZING THE acad.pgp FILE

When you make any changes in the *acad.pgp* file, there are two ways to reinitialize the *acad.pgp* file. One is to quit AutoCAD and then restart the AutoCAD program. When you start AutoCAD, the *acad.pgp* file is automatically loaded. You can also reinitialize the *acad.pgp* file by using the **REINIT** command. The **REINIT** command lets you reinitialize the I/O ports, digitizer, and AutoCAD program parameters file, *acad.pgp*. When you enter the **REINIT** command, AutoCAD will display the **Re-initialization** dialog box, refer to Figure 17-1. To reinitialize the *acad.pgp* file, select the corresponding check box, and then choose **OK**. AutoCAD will reinitialize the program parameters file (*acad.pgp*), and then you can use the command aliases defined in the file.

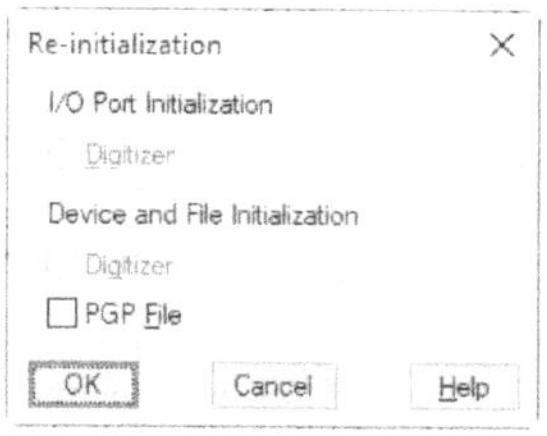

***Figure 17-1** The **Re-initialization** dialog box*

Tip

Copy and save the original acad.pgp file at some other location, so that after you have made changes in the acad.pgp file and used it, you could restore the default settings by copying and pasting the original acad.pgp file. This lets other users use the original, unedited file.

Example 1 — Adding New Command Aliases

Add the following external commands and AutoCAD command aliases to the AutoCAD program parameters file (*acad.pgp*).

External Commands

Abbreviation	Command Description
GOWORD	This command loads the word processor (Winword) program from *C:\Program Files\Winword*
RN	This command executes the rename command of DOS.
COP	This command executes the copy command of DOS.

Command Aliases Section

Abbreviation	Command	Abbreviation	Command
EL	Ellipse	T	Trim
CO	Copy	CH	Chamfer
O	Offset	ST	Stretch
S	Scale	MI	Mirror

The *acad.pgp* file is an ASCII text file. To edit this file, choose the **Edit Aliases** tool from the **Customization** panel in the **Manage** tab. You can also use text editor like notepad to edit the *acad.pgp* file. The following is a partial listing of the *acad.pgp* file after the insertion of the lines for the command aliases of Example 1. **The line numbers on the right are not a part of the file; they are given here for reference only.** The lines that have been added to the file are highlighted in bold face.

```
DEL,DEL,                8,File to delete: ,
DIR,DIR,                8,File specification ,
EDIT, START EDIT,       8,File to edit: ,
SH,                     1,*OS Command: ,
SHELL,                  1,*OS Command: ,
START,START,            1,Application to start: ,
TYPE,TYPE,              8,File to list: ,

GOWORD, START WINWORD,1,,
RN, RENAME,8,File to rename:,
COP,COPY,8,File to copy:,
DIMLIN          *DIMLINEAR
DIMORD,         *DIMORDINATE
DIMRAD,         *DIMRADIUS
DIMSTY,         *DIMSTYLE
DIMOVER,        *DIMOVERRIDE
LEAD,           *LEADER
TM,             *TILEMODE
EL,             *ELLIPSE
CO,             *COPY
O,              *OFFSET
S,              *SCALE
MI,             *MIRROR
ST,             *STRETCH
```

Explanation

Line 9

GOWORD, START WINWORD,1,,

In line 9, **GOWORD** loads the word processor program **(WINWORD)**. The **winword.exe** program is located in the winword directory under Program Files.

Lines 10 and 11

RN, RENAME,8,File to rename:,

COP,COPY,8,File to copy:,

Line 10 defines the alias for the DOS command **RENAME**, and the next line defines the alias for the DOS command **COPY**. The **8** is a bit flag, and the Command prompt **File to rename and File to copy** is automatically displayed to let you know the format and the type of information that is expected.

Lines 19 and 20

EL, *ELLIPSE

CO, *COPY

Line 19 defines the alias (**EL**) for the **ELLIPSE** command, and the next line defines the alias (**CO**) for the **COPY** command. The commands must be preceded by an asterisk. You can put any number of spaces between the alias abbreviation and the command.

To reinitialize these commands, use the **REINIT** command or quit and restart AutoCAD.

Note

*If a command alias definition duplicates an existing one then the one that is lower down in the file is given preference and is allowed to work. For example, in a standard file, if you add S, *SCALE to the end of the file then your definition works and the one higher up in the file is ignored.*

Self-Evaluation Test

Answer the following questions and then compare them to those given at the end of this chapter:

1. One way of reinitializing the *acad.pgp* file is to __________ AutoCAD and then __________it.

2. The command used to reinitialize the *acad.pgp* file is __________ .

3. In the command alias section, the AutoCAD command must be preceded by an __________ symbol.

4. Every comment line must start with a __________ .

5. The command alias and the AutoCAD command must be separated by a __________.

Review Questions

Answer the following questions.

1. The comment section can contain any number of lines. (T/F)
2. AutoCAD ignores any line that is preceded by a semicolon. (T/F)
3. The command alias must not be an AutoCAD command. (T/F)
4. The bit flag field must be set to 8. (T/F)
5. In the command alias section, the command alias must be preceded by a semicolon. (T/F)
6. You cannot use aliases for AutoLISP commands. (T/F)
7. The *acad.pgp* file does not come with AutoCAD software. (T/F)
8. The *acad.pgp* file is an ASCII file. (T/F)

Exercise 1 *Adding New Command Aliases*

Add the following external commands and AutoCAD command aliases to the AutoCAD program parameters file (*acad.pgp*):

External Command Section

Abbreviation	Command Description
MYWORDPAD	This command loads the WORDPAD program that resides in the **Program Files\Accessories** directory.
MYEXCEL	This command loads the EXCEL program that resides in the **Program Fies\Microsoft Office** directory.
CD	This command executes the CHKDSK command of DOS.
FORMAT	This command executes the FORMAT command of DOS.

Command Aliases Section

Abbreviation	Command	Abbreviation	Command
BL	**BLOCK**	LTS	**LTSCALE**
INS	**INSERT**	EXP	**EXPLODE**
DIS	**DISTANCE**	GR	**GRID**
TE	**TIME**		

Answers to Self-Evaluation Test

1. quit, restart, **2. REINIT**, **3.** asterisk, **4.** semicolon, **5.** comma

Chapter 18

Conventional Dimensioning and Projection Theory Using AutoCAD

Learning Objectives

After completing this chapter, you will be able to:

- *Understand the dimensioning units*
- *Understand about basic dimensioning rules*
- *Understand the dimensioning of cylindrical features, holes, rounds, fillets, chamfers, and repetitive features*
- *Understand reference dimensions*
- *Understand working drawings, detail drawings, and assembly drawings*
- *Understand the arrangement of projected views*
- *Understand about X, Y, and Z axes, XY, YZ and XZ planes, and parallel planes*
- *Draw orthographic projections and position views*
- *Dimension a drawing*
- *Draw sectional views using different types of sections*
- *Hatch sectioned surfaces*
- *Use and draw auxiliary views*

Key Terms

- *Dimensioning Rules*
- *Reference Dimensions*
- *Cylindrical Features*
- *Dimensioning fillets and chamfers*
- *Dimensioning Components*
- *Detail Drawing*
- *Assembly Drawing*
- *Bill of Materials*
- *Full Section*
- *Half Section*
- *Broken Section*
- *Revolved Section*
- *Offset Section*
- *Aligned Section*
- *Hatch Lines*
- *Auxiliary Views*

DIMENSIONING

Dimensioning is one of the most important elements in a drawing. When you dimension a drawing, you not only provide information of the size of a part, but also a series of instructions to a machinist, an engineer, or an architect. The way the part is positioned in a machine, the sequence of machining operations, and the location of different features of the part depend on how you dimension it. For example, the number of decimal places in a dimension (2.000) determines the type of machine to be used for the machining operation. The machining cost of such an operation is significantly higher than those that have dimension upto only one digit after the decimal (2.0). If you are using a computer numerical control (CNC) machine, then locating a feature may not be a problem, but the number of pieces that you can machine without changing the tool depends on the tolerance assigned to a dimension. A closer tolerance (+.0001, -.0005) will definitely increase the tooling cost and ultimately the cost of the product. Similarly, if a part is to be forged or cast, the radius of the edges and the tolerance you provide to these dimensions determine the cost of the product, the number of defective parts, and the number of parts you get from the die.

While dimensioning, you must consider the manufacturing process involved in making a part and the relationships that exist among different parts in an assembly. If you are not familiar with any operation, get help. You must not assume things when dimensioning or making a piece part drawing. The success of a product, to a large extent, depends on the way you dimension a part. Therefore, never underestimate the importance of dimensioning in a drawing.

DIMENSION UNITS

Generally, metric system of dimensioning is considered as the official standard of measurement for engineering drawings, but most of the drawings in North America are still dimensioned in decimal inches. So, you should be familiar with all dimensioning systems that are used in the interpretation of an engineering drawing. The dimensions used in this book are primarily decimal inch. However, metric dimensions are used very frequently. To make information more clear, engineering drawings should contain one of the following notes:

- Unless Otherwise Specified, All Dimensions Are in Millimeters
- Unless Otherwise Specified, All Dimensions Are in Inches

The Inch and Metric unit system is discussed next.

Inch Units

An inch is a unit of length in the imperial and United States customary systems of measurement. Historically, an inch was also used in a number of other systems of units. Traditional standards for the exact length of an inch have varied in the past, but since July 1959, when the international yard was defined as 0.9144 metres, the international inch has been exactly 25.4 mm. There are 12 inches in a foot and 36 inches in a yard.

The Decimal-Inch System

In the Decimal-Inch system, the parts are designed in basic decimal increments (preferably .02 inch) and the values are expressed as two numbers after the decimal, as shown in Figure 18-1. Using the .02 value as the increment the second value after the decimal will be an even number or zero. In some cases to meet the design requirements you can also use the values other than the increment of .02 inch, such as .25 inch or .29 inch. Whenever greater accuracy is required, the dimensions are expressed as values upto three or four decimal places, such as 1.6587 or 5.9876. In Decimal-Inch dimensioning system, the numbers to the right of the decimal point indicate the degree of precision. For the dimensions less than 1 there will not be a zero before the decimal point.

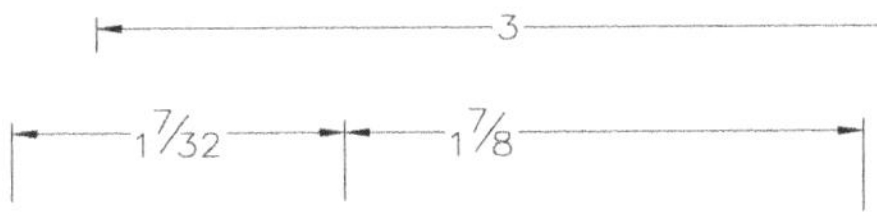

Figure 18-1 *Dimensions in the Fractional-Inch system*

The Fractional-Inch System

In the Fractional-Inch system, the parts are designed in common fractions, refer to Figure 18-2. The smallest fraction used is 1/256th of an inch. Sizes other than common fractions are expressed as decimals. This system of dimensioning was replaced by the Decimal-Inch dimensioning system of engineering drawings over 50 years ago. But you should be aware of this unit system because some tools like drills, reamers, and pipes are being manufactured using Fraction-Inch system.

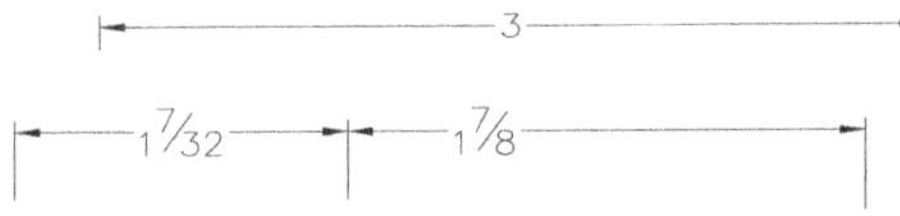

Figure 18-2 *Dimensions in the Fractional-Inch system*

SI (Metric) Units

The standard metric units used in an engineering drawing are the millimeters for linear measurements and the micrometers for surface roughness, refer to Figure 18-3. In the metric system of dimensioning, the numbers to the right of the decimal point indicate the degree of precision. Whole dimensions in a drawing do not require a zero to the right of the decimal point. For example, the dimension of 5 mm will be expressed as 5 not 5.0, unless and until the part to be manufactured requires that specific precision. For expressing large dimensions a space should be used to separate groups of three numbers in metric values, such as 54 487 or 4.524 47.

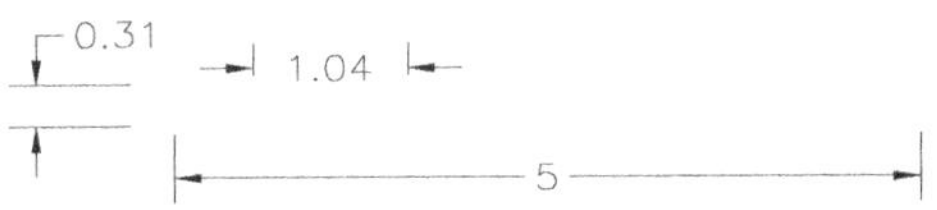

Figure 18-3 *Dimensions in the Metric (Millimeters) system*

DIMENSIONING COMPONENTS

A dimension consists of the following components, refer to Figure 18-4:

- Extension line
- Arrows or tick marks
- Dimension line
- Leader lines
- Dimension text

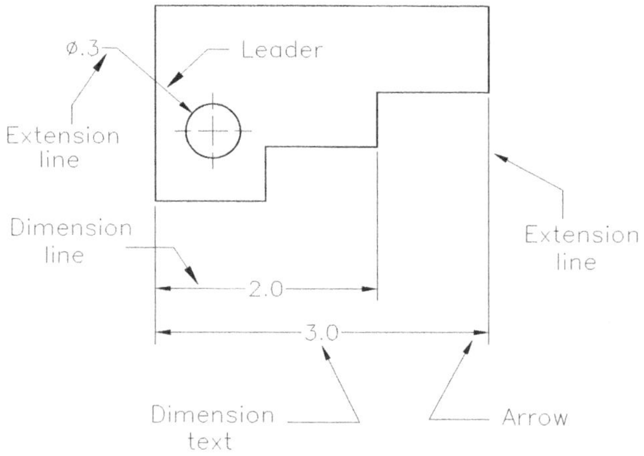

Figure 18-4 *Dimensioning components*

The extension lines are drawn to extend the points that are dimensioned. The length of the extension lines is determined by the number of dimensions and the placement of the dimension lines. These lines are generally drawn perpendicular to the surface. The dimension lines are drawn between the extension lines at a specified distance from the object lines. The dimension text is a numerical value that represents the distance between the points. The dimension text can also consist of a variable (A, B, X, Y, Z12,...). In such a case, the value assigned to it is defined in a separate table. The dimension text can be centered around or on the top of the dimension line. Arrows or tick marks are drawn at the end of the dimension line to indicate the start and end of the dimension. Leaders are used for dimensioning a circle, arc, or any nonlinear element of a drawing. They are also used to attach a note to a feature or to give the part numbers in an assembly drawing.

COMMON RULES FOR DIMENSIONING

1. Place dimensions in the view that best shows the shape of the object, refer to Figure 18-5. Sometimes dimensions can placed between views according to the availability of space between the views.

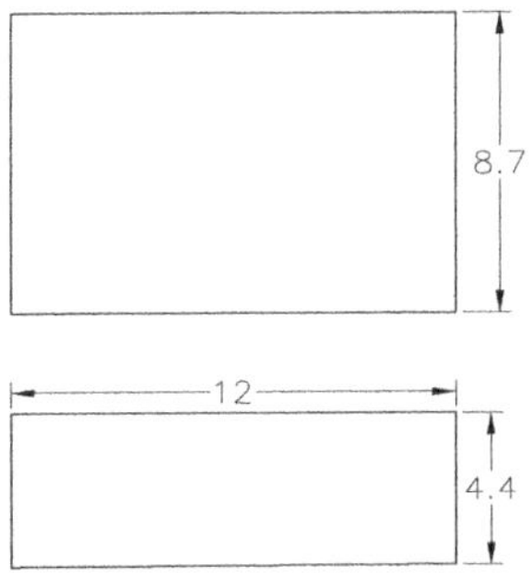

Figure 18-5 *Dimensions placed in appropriate views*

2. Place dimensions between the views when possible, refer to Figure 18-6.

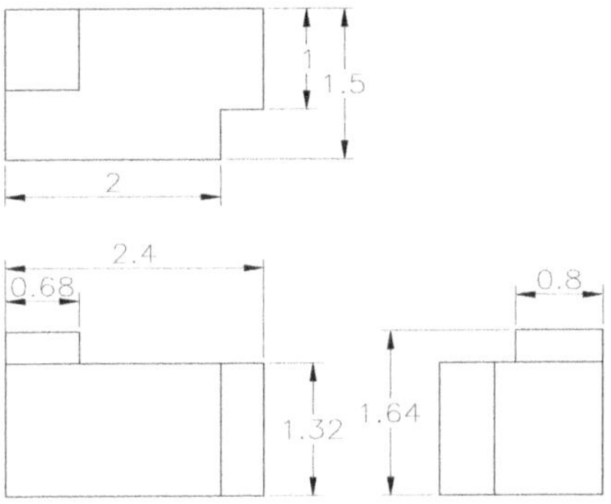

Figure 18-6 *Place dimensions between views*

3. You should make the dimensions in a separate layer/layers. This makes it easy to edit or control the display of dimensions (freeze, thaw, lock, and unlock). Also, the dimension layer/layers should be assigned a unique color so that at the time of plotting, you can assign the desired pen to plot the dimensions. This helps in controlling the line width and the contrast of dimensions at the time of plotting.

4. The distance of the first dimension line should be at least 0.375 units (10 units for metric drawing) from the object line. In CAD drawing, this distance may be 0.75 to 1.0 units (19 to 25 units for metric drawings). Once you decide on the spacing, it should be maintained throughout the drawing.

5. The distance between the first dimension line and the second dimension line must be at least 0.25 unit. In CAD drawings, this distance may be 0.25 to 0.5 unit (6 to 12 units for metric drawings). If there are more dimension lines (parallel dimensions), the distances between them must be the same (0.25 to 0.5 unit). Once you decide on the spacing (0.25 to 0.5), the same spacing should be maintained throughout the drawing. An appropriate snap setting is useful for maintaining this space. If you are using baseline dimensioning, you can use AutoCAD's **DIMDLI** variable to set the spacing. The dimensions must be placed in such a way so that they are not crowded, especially when there is not much space, refer to Figure 18-7.

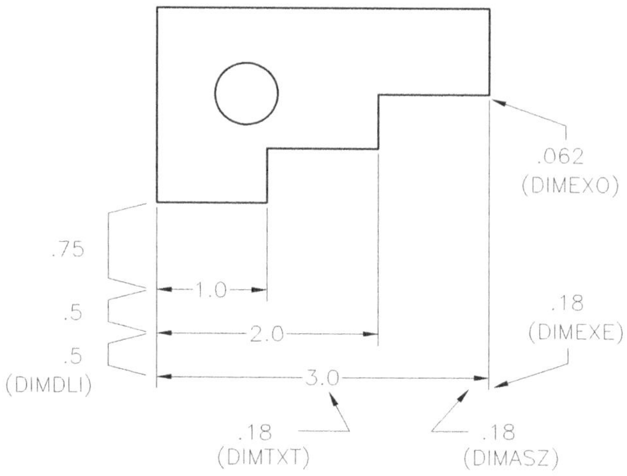

Figure 18-7 *Arrow size, text height, and spacing between dimension lines*

6. For parallel dimension lines, the dimension text can be staggered if there is not enough room between the dimension lines to place the dimension text. You can use the AutoCAD Object Grips feature or the **DIMTEDIT** command to stagger the dimension text, refer to Figure 18-8.

7. All dimensions should be given outside the view. However, the dimensions can be shown inside the view if they can be easily understood there and cause no confusion with the other dimensions or details, refer to Figure 18-9. In case of large drawings, dimensions can be placed on the view to improve clarity.

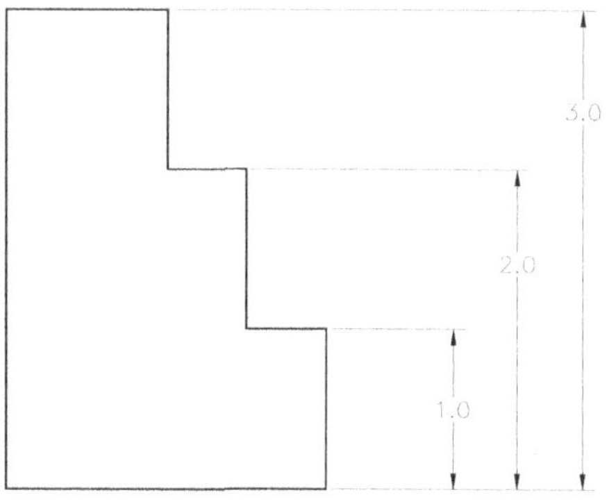

Figure 18-8 *Staggered dimensions*

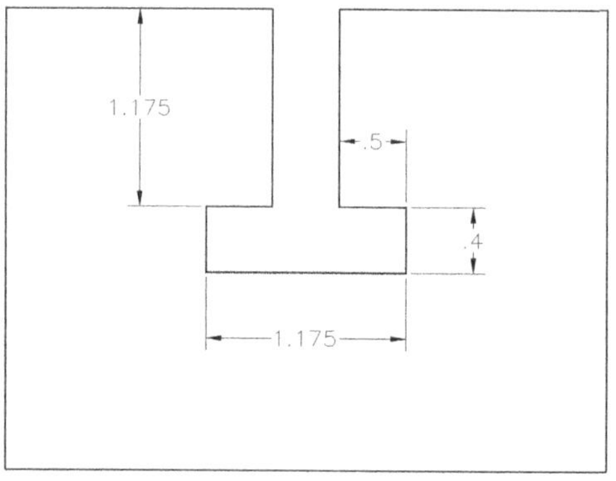

Figure 18-9 *Dimensions inside the view*

8. Dimension lines should not cross the extension lines, refer to Figure 18-10. You can accomplish this by giving the smallest dimension first and then the next largest dimension, refer to Figure 18-11.

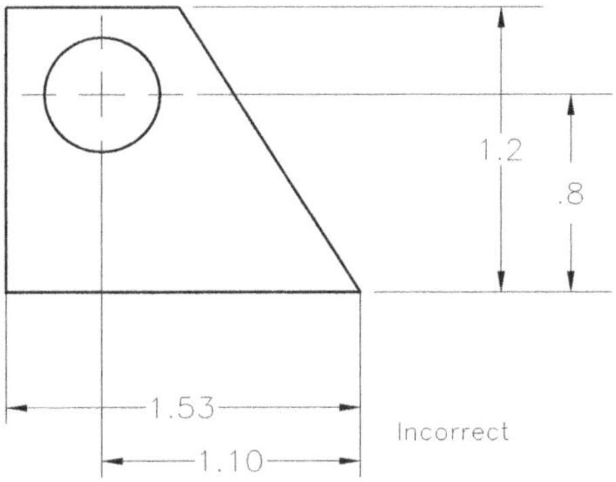

Figure 18-10 *Dimensions placed incorrectly*

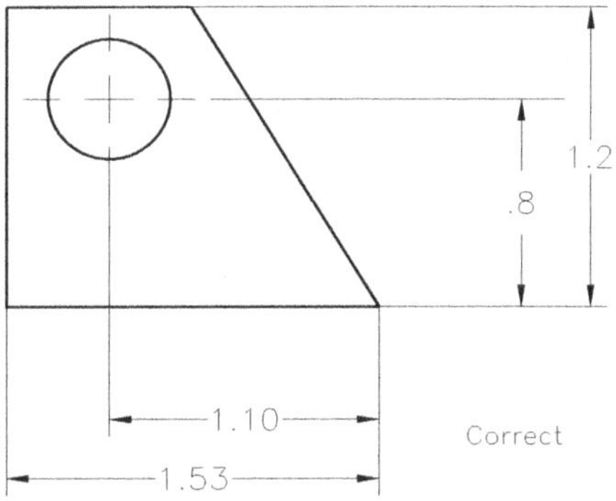

Figure 18-11 *Dimensions placed correctly*

9. If you decide to have the dimension text aligned with the dimension line, then the entire dimension text in the drawing must be aligned, refer to Figure 18-12. Similarly, if you decide to have the dimension text horizontal or above the dimension line, then to maintain uniformity in the drawing, the entire dimension text must be horizontal, refer to Figure 18-13 or above the dimension line, refer to Figure 18-14.

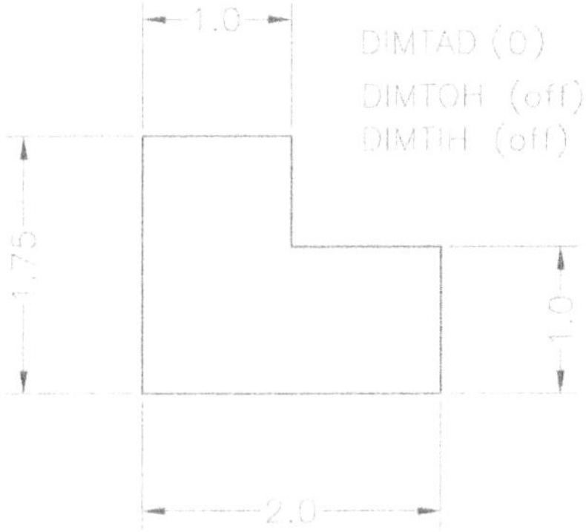

Figure 18-12 *Dimension text aligned with the dimension line*

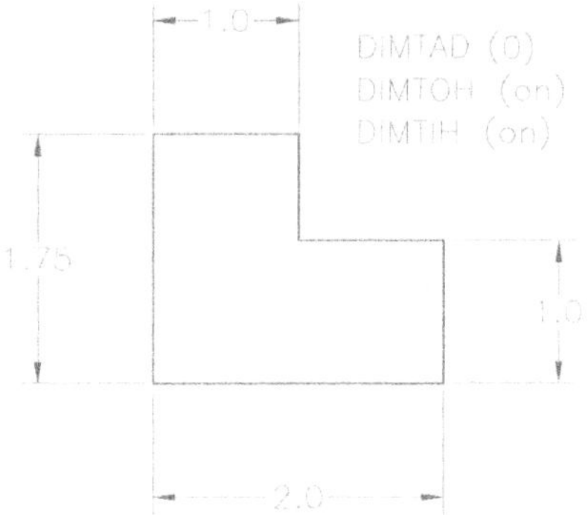

Figure 18-13 *Horizontal dimension text*

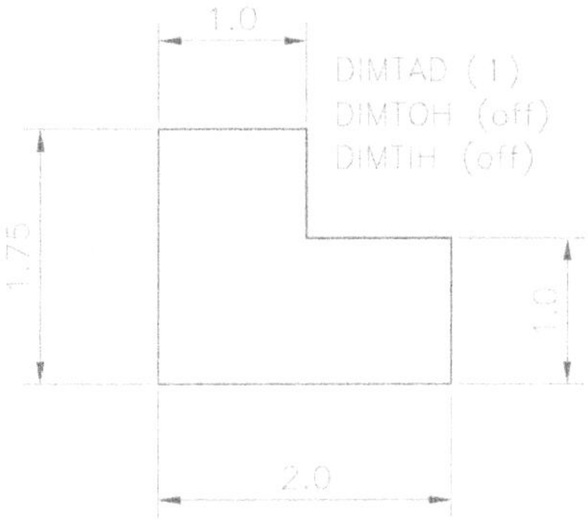

Figure 18-14 *Dimension text above the dimension line*

10. If you have a series of continuous dimensions, they should be placed in a continuous line, refer to Figure 18-15. Sometimes you may not be able to apply the dimensions in a continuous line even after adjusting the dimension variables. In that case, apply the dimensions that are parallel, refer to Figure 18-16.

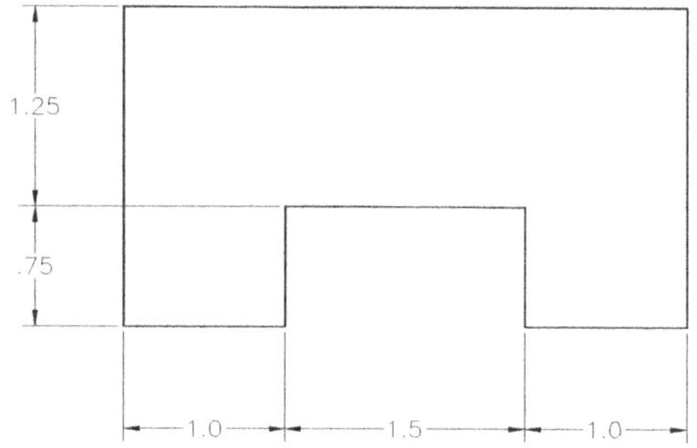

Figure 18-15 *Continuous dimensions*

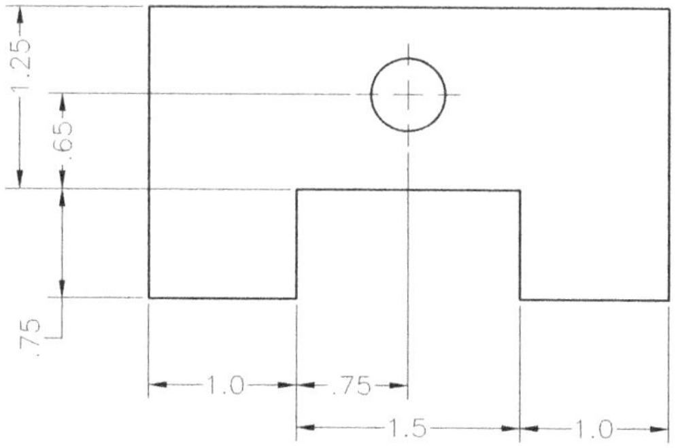

Figure 18-16 *Parallel dimensions*

11. You should not dimension with the hidden lines. The dimension should be given where the feature is visible, refer to Figure 18-17. However, in some complicated drawings, you might be justified to dimension a detail with a hidden line.

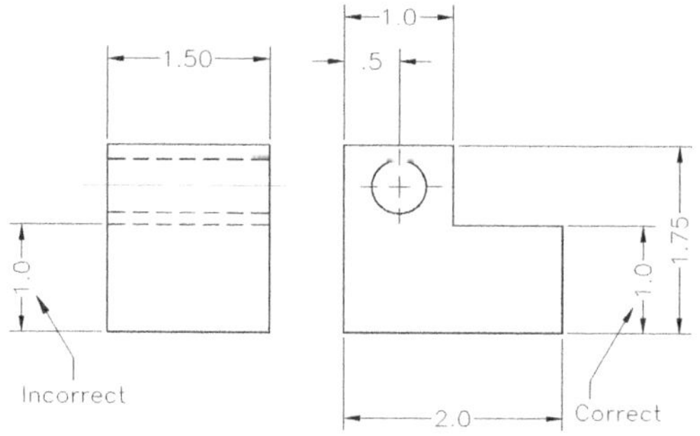

Figure 18-17 *Undimensioned hidden lines*

12. The dimensions must be given where the feature that you are dimensioning is obvious and shows the contour of the feature, refer to Figure 18-18.

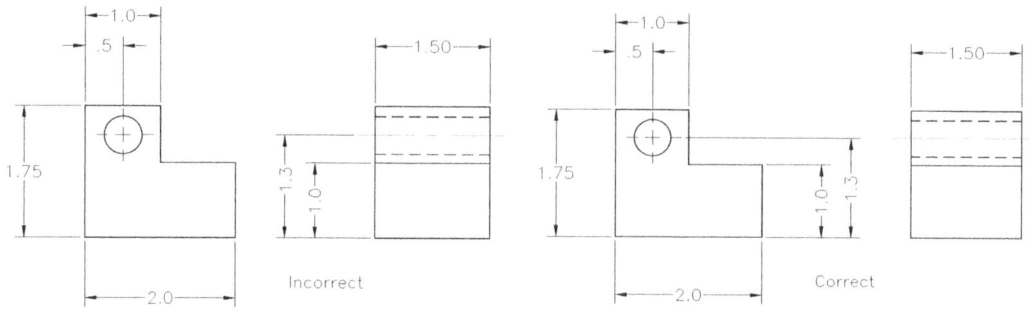

Figure 18-18 *Dimensions given where they are obvious*

13. The dimensions must not be repeated, as shown in Figure 18-19 as repeating dimensions makes difficult to update them.

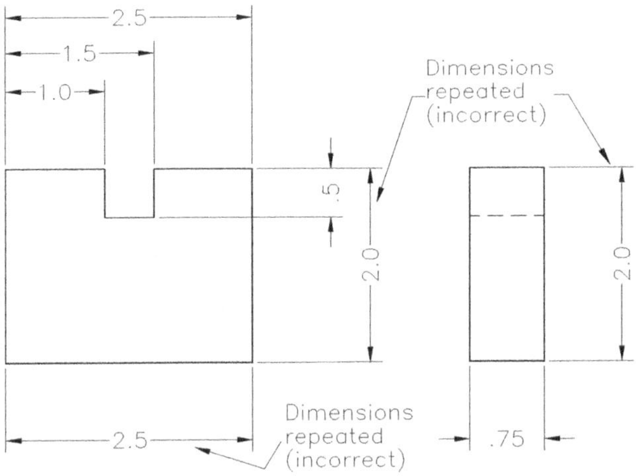

***Figure 18-19** Incorrect method of dimensioning*

14. The dimensions must be given depending on how the part will be machined, and also on the relationship that exists between the different features of the part, refer to Figure 18-20.

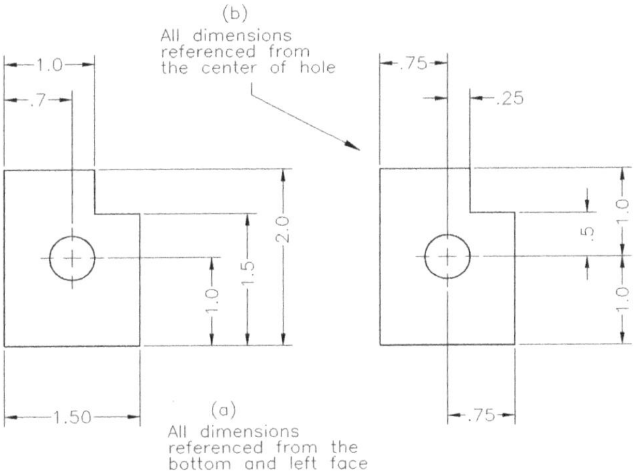

***Figure 18-20** Different dimensioning styles*

15. The dimensions enclosed in parenthesis can be identified as reference dimensions, refer to Figure 18-21. A reference dimension is placed on a drawing for information purpose only. Reference dimensions are not used for manufacturing of the part therefore it must be clearly labeled. Previously, reference dimensions were identified by placing the abbreviation REF after or below the dimension.

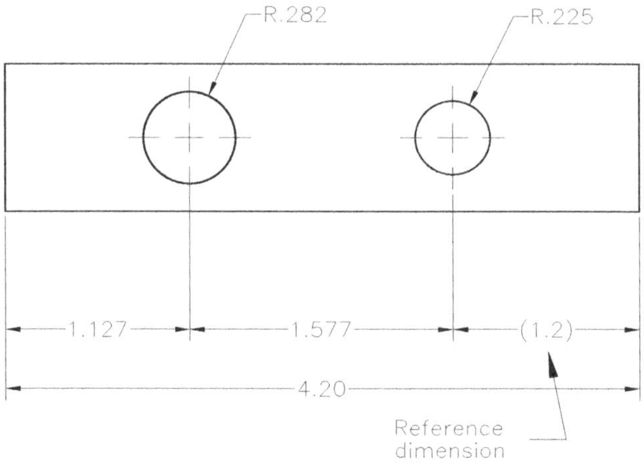

Figure 18-21 *Reference dimension marked in parenthesis*

16. If you give continuous (incremental) dimensions for dimensioning various features of a part, the overall dimension must be omitted or given as a reference dimension, refer to Figure 18-22. Similarly, if you give the overall dimension, one of the continuous (incremental) dimensions must be omitted or given as a reference dimension. Otherwise, there will be a conflict in tolerances. For example, the total positive tolerance on the three incremental dimensions shown in Figure 18-22 is 0.06. Therefore, the maximum size based on the incremental dimensions is (1 + 0.02) + (1 + 0.02) + (1 + 0.02) = 3.06. Also, the positive tolerance on the overall 3.0 dimension is 0.02. Based on this dimension, the overall size of the part must not exceed 3.02. This causes a conflict in tolerances with incremental dimensions because the total tolerance is 0.06, whereas with the overall dimension, the total tolerance is only 0.02.

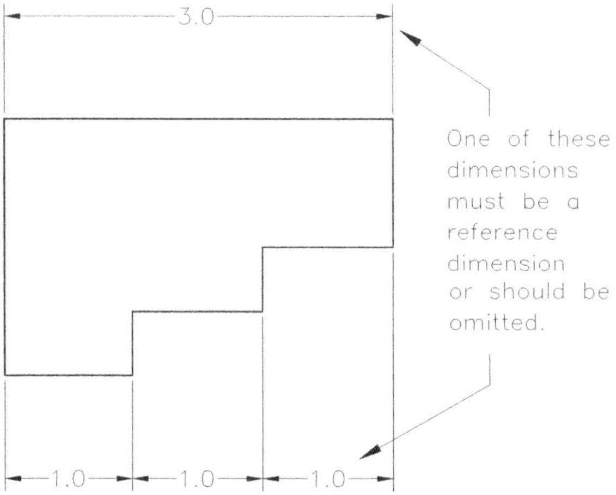

Figure 18-22 *Referencing or omitting a dimension*

17. If the dimension of a feature appears in a section view, you must not hatch the dimension text, refer to Figure 18-23. You can accomplish this task by selecting the dimension object while defining the hatch boundary. You can also accomplish this by drawing a rectangle around the dimension text and then hatching the area after excluding the rectangle from the hatch boundary.

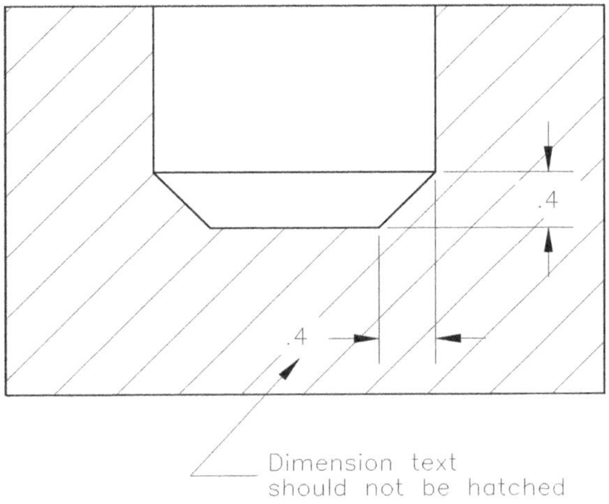

Figure 18-23 *Dimension text excluded from hatching*

18. While dimensioning a circle, the diameter should be preceded by the diameter symbol, refer to Figure 18-24. AutoCAD automatically puts the diameter symbol in front of the diameter value. However, if you override the default diameter value, you can use %%c followed by the value of the diameter (%%c1.00) to put the diameter symbol before the diameter dimension.

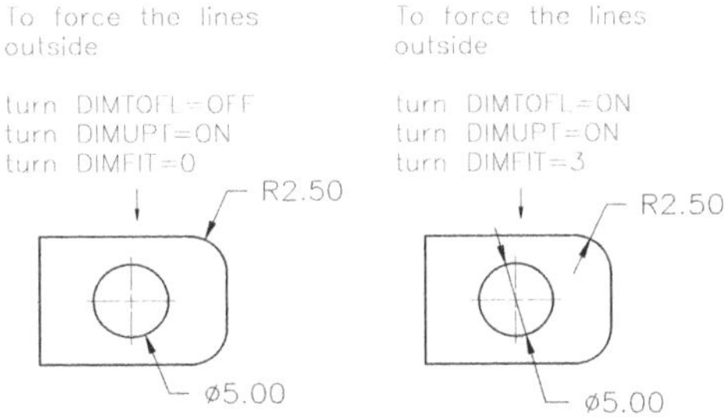

Figure 18-24 *Diameter should be preceded by the diameter symbol*

19. Cylindrical features should be dimensioned by the method shown in Figure 18-25. The circle must be dimensioned as a diameter, never as a radius. Where the diameters of a number of concentric cylinders are to be given, they must be shown on the end view, refer to Figure 18-26. For diameter dimensions, the diameter symbol Ø is used before the dimension.

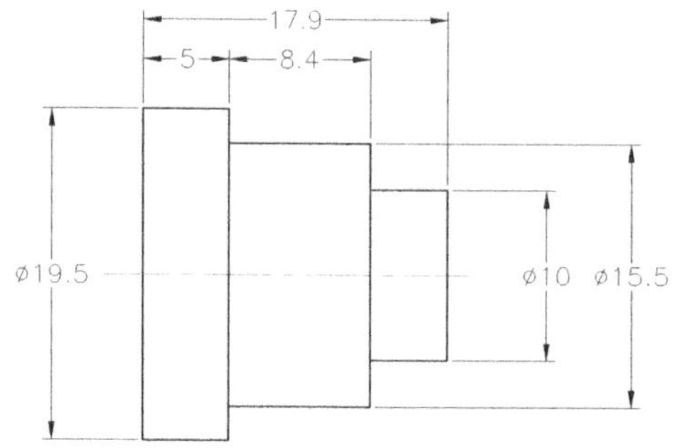

Figure 18-25 *Dimensioning of cylindrical features*

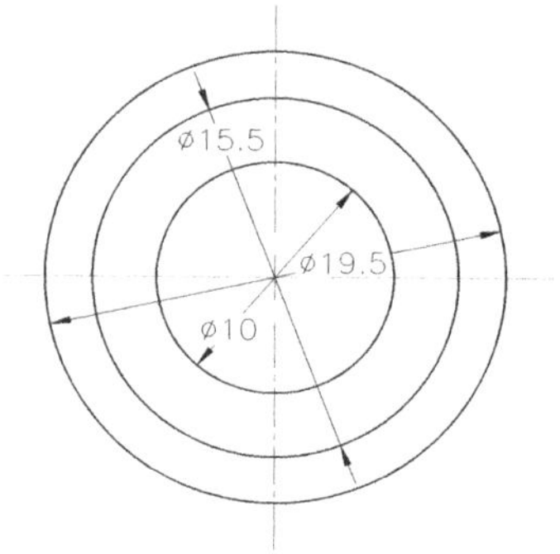

Figure 18-26 *Dimensioning diameters on end view*

20. For dimensioning a circular arc, letter R is added before the radius dimension, as shown in Figure 18-27. Also, the center of the arc should be indicated by a small cross. You can use the **DIMCEN** variable in AutoCAD to control the size of the cross. If the value of this variable is 0, AutoCAD does not draw the cross in the center when you dimension an arc or a circle.

21. The preferred method for designating the size of holes is shown in Figure 18–28. While dimensioning a hole feature a leader is used and the symbol Ø precedes the size of the hole. When two or more holes of the same size are required, the number of holes is specified. If a blind hole is required, the depth of the hole is specified by the depth symbol in the dimensioning note; otherwise, it is assumed that all holes shown are through holes. The degree of accuracy to which a hole is to be machined is specified on the drawing. The use of operational names such as *turn, bore, grind, ream, tap*, and *thread* with dimensions should be avoided.

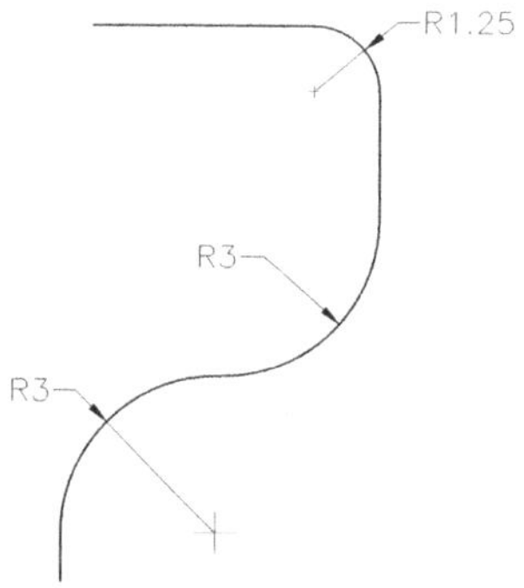

Figure 18-27 *Dimensioning of arcs*

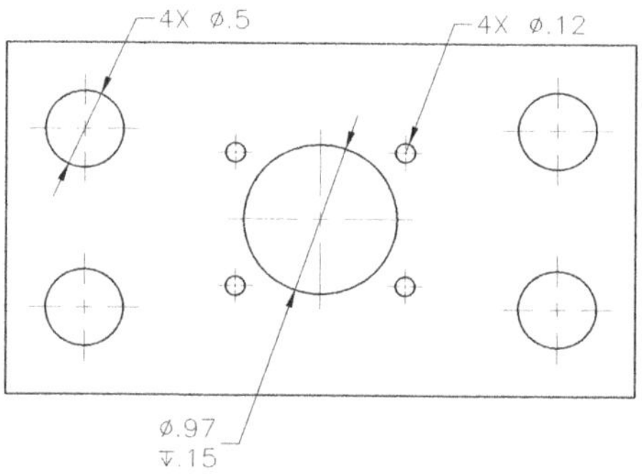

Figure 18-28 *Dimensioning of holes*

22. A dimension that is not to be scaled should be indicated by drawing a straight line under the dimension text, refer to Figure 18-29. This line can be drawn by using the **DDEDIT** command. If you invoke this command, AutoCAD will prompt you to select an annotative object. Select the object; the **Text Editor** will be displayed and a new **Text Editor** tab will be added to the **Ribbon**. Select the text (< >), and then choose the **U** button in the **Formatting** panel of the **Text Editor** tab to underline the text.

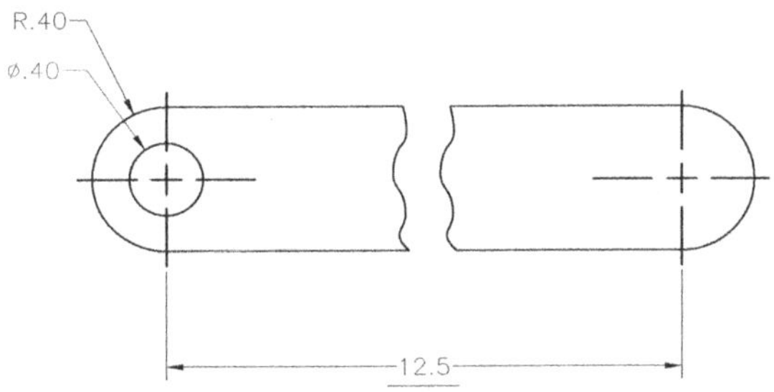

Figure 18-29 Specifying dimension that is not to be scaled

Dimensioning of Rounds and Fillets

A round, or radius, or chamfer is applied on the outer surface of a part to improve its appearance and to avoid formation of a sharp edge that might chip off under a sharp blow or cause interference. It is also a safety feature. In a fillet, additional material is allowed in the inner intersection of two surfaces, as shown in Figure 18-30. If all the fillets and rounds have equal dimension then a general note, such as ROUNDS AND FILLETS R10 or ROUNDS AND FILLETS R10 UNLESS OTHERWISE SPECIFIED, is normally used on the drawing instead of placing individual dimensions.

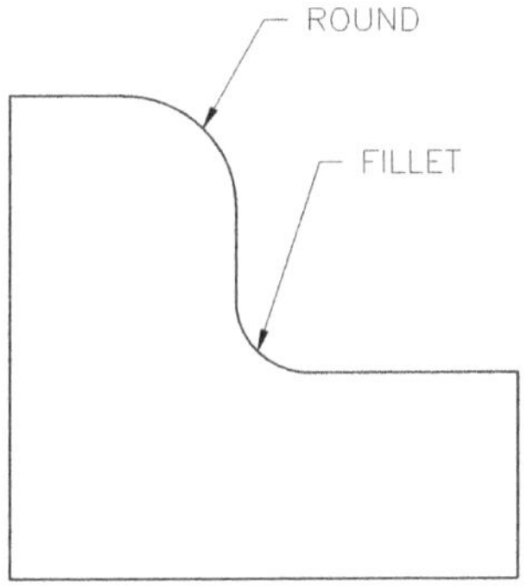

Figure 18-30 Fillets and rounds

A chamfer can be dimensioned by specifying the chamfer angle and the distance of the chamfer from the edge. It can also be dimensioned by specifying the distances, as shown in Figure 18-31.

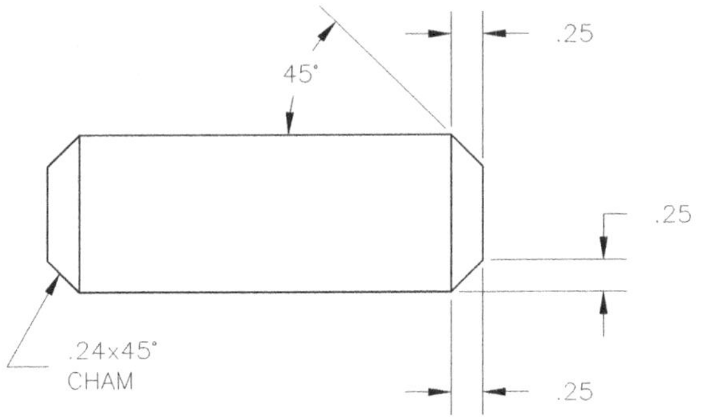

Figure 18-31 Different ways of specifying a chamfer

Dimensioning of Repetitive Features

Repetitive features and dimensions may be specified on a drawing by the use of an X preceded by the number to indicate the "number of times" or "places" for which they are required. A space is inserted between X and the specified dimension, as shown in Figure 18-32. If there are similar repetitive features of different sizes, some other form of indication may be required in order to ensure the legibility of drawing, as shown in Figure 18-33.

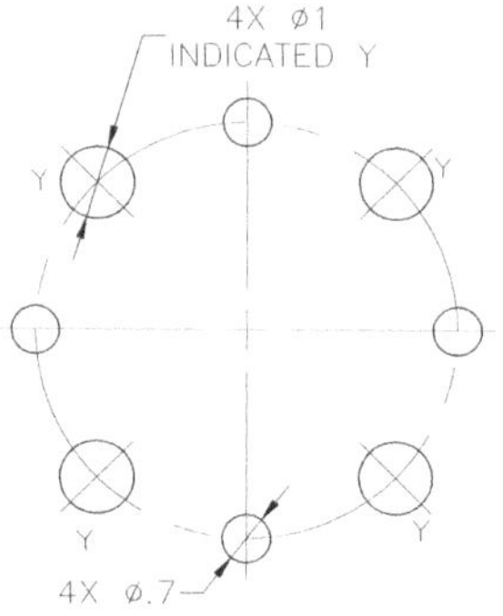

Figure 18-32 Dimensioning of repetitive features with different sizes

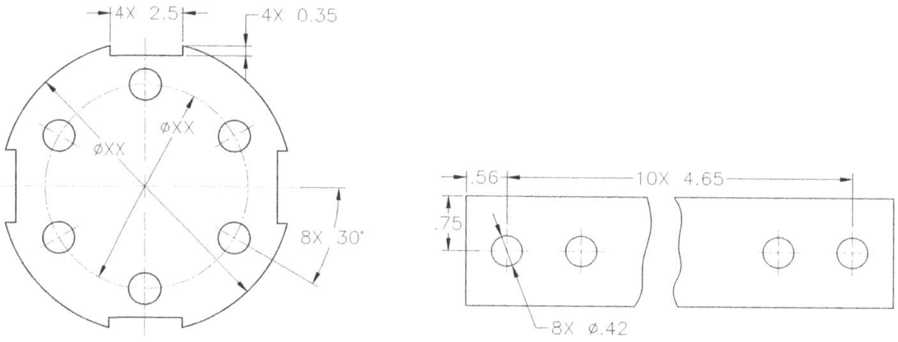

Figure 18-33 Dimensioning of repetitive features

WORKING DRAWINGS

A working drawing is a drawing that provides information and instructions for the manufacturing or construction of parts, machines, or structures. A working drawing is intended to provide the description about shape, dimensions or size, and specifications of the product. Because working drawings may be sent to another plant, another company, or even to another country to manufacture, construct, or assemble the final product, the drawing should qualify the drawing standards of the respective plant, company, or country.

Generally, working drawings are classified into two groups:

Detail Drawing

A detail drawing is the drawing of a single part that includes a complete and exact description of its form and shape. Detail drawings provide the necessary information for the manufacture of the parts for a specific product or structure, refer to Figure 18-34. Each detail drawing must be drawn and dimensioned to completely describe the size and shape of the part. It should also contain information that might be needed in manufacturing the part. The finished surfaces and all the necessary operations should be indicated by using symbols or notes on the drawing. The material of which the part is made and the number of parts that are required for the production of the assembled product must be given in the title block. Detail drawings should also contain part numbers. This information is used in the bill of materials and the assembly drawing. The part numbers make it easier to locate the drawing of a part. Regardless of the part's size, you should make a detail drawing of each part on a separate drawing. When required, these detail drawings can be inserted in the assembly drawing by using the **Attach** tool from the **Reference** panel of the **Insert** tab.

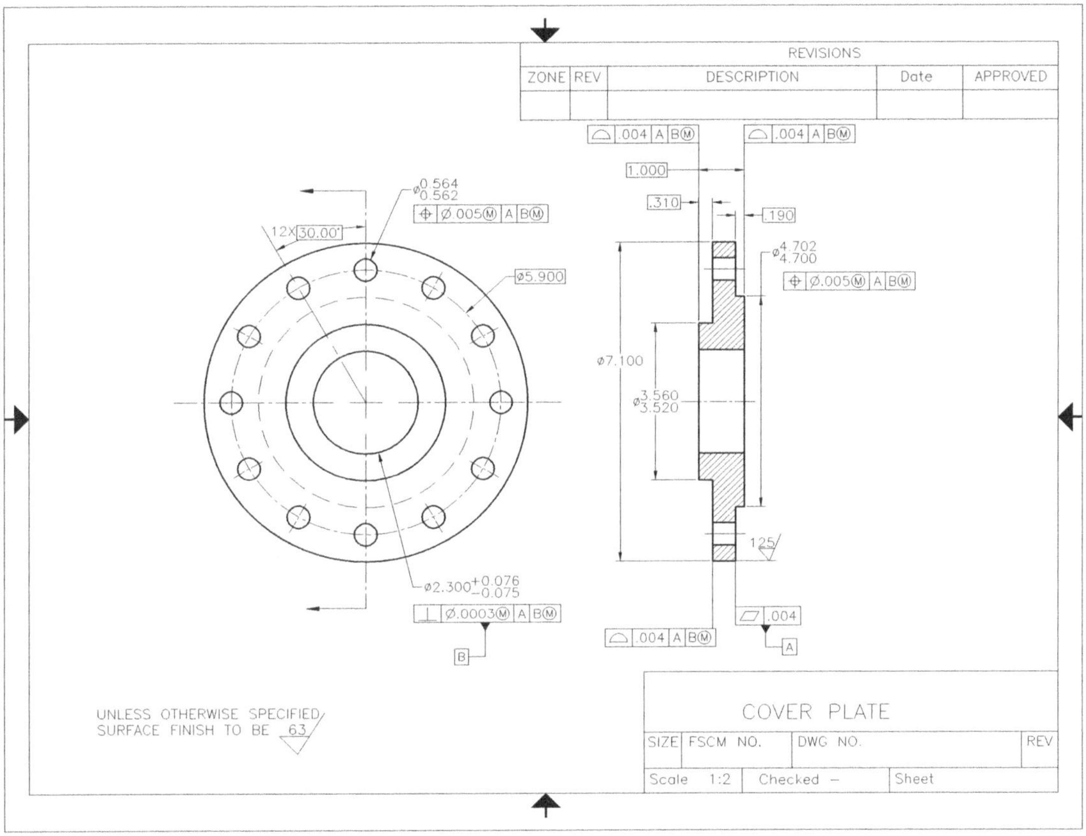

Figure 18-34 Detail drawing of Cover Plate

Assembly Drawing

An assembly drawing is the presentation of a product or structure put together, showing all parts in their operational positions. These drawings provide necessary information about the assembly of parts and structures, refer to Figure 18-35. Assembly drawings may include instructions, lists of component parts, reference numbers, references to detail drawings or shop drawings, and specifications. The main view may be drawn in full section so that the assembly drawing shows nearly all the individual parts and their locations. Additional views should be drawn only when some of the parts cannot be seen in the main view. The hidden lines, as far as possible, should be omitted from the assembly drawing because they clutter it and might cause confusion. However, a hidden line may be drawn if it helps to understand the product. Only assembly dimensions should be shown in the assembly drawing. Each part can be identified on the assembly drawing by the number used in the detail drawing and in the bill of materials. The part numbers should be given as shown in Figure 18-35. A part number consists of a text string for the detail number, a circle (balloon), a leader line, and an arrow or dot. The text should be made at least 0.2 inches (5 mm) high and enclosed in a 0.4 inch (10 mm) circle (balloon). The center of the circle must be located not less than 0.8 inches (20 mm) from the nearest line on the drawing. Also, the leader line should be radial with respect to the circle (balloon). The assembly drawing may also contain an exploded isometric or isometric view of the assembled unit.

BILL OF MATERIALS

A bill of materials is a list of parts placed on an assembly drawing just above the title block. The bill of materials contains the part number, part description, material, quantity required, and drawing numbers of the detail drawings, refer to Figure 18-35. If the bill of materials is placed above the title block, the parts should be listed in ascending order so that the first part is at the bottom of the table. The bill of materials may also be placed at the top of the drawing. In that case, the parts must be listed in descending order with the first part at the top of the table. This structure allows room for any additional items that may be added to the list.

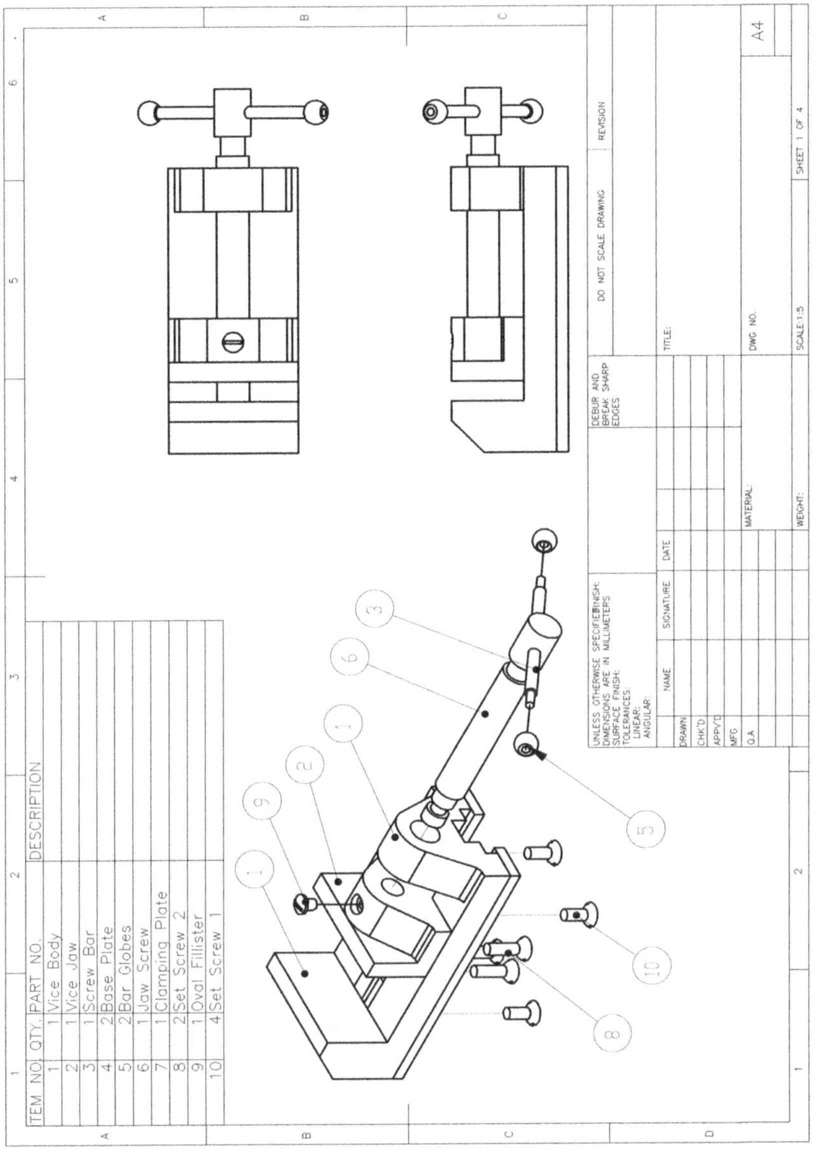

Figure 18-35 Assembly drawing with title block and bill of materials

MULTIVIEW DRAWINGS

When designers design a product, they visualize its shape in their minds. To represent that shape on paper or to communicate the idea to people, they must draw a picture of the product or its orthographic views. Pictorial drawings, such as isometric drawings, convey the shape of the object, but it is difficult to show all features and dimensions in an isometric drawing. Therefore, in industry, multiview drawings are the accepted standards for representing products. Multiview drawings are also known as orthographic projection drawings. To draw different views of an object, it is very important to visualize the shape of the product. The same is true when you look at different views of an object to determine its shape. To facilitate visualizing the shapes, you must picture the object in 3D space with reference to the *X*, *Y*, and *Z* axes. These reference axes can then be used to project the image into different planes. This process of visualizing objects with reference to different axes is, to some extent, natural in human beings. You might have noticed that sometimes, when looking at objects that are at an angle, people tilt their heads. This is a natural reaction, an effort to position the object with respect to an imaginary reference frame (*X*, *Y*, and *Z* axes).

UNDERSTANDING THE X, Y, AND Z AXES

To understand the *X*, *Y*, and *Z* axes, imagine a flat sheet of paper on the table. The horizontal edge represents the positive *X* axis, and the other edge along the width of the sheet, represents the positive *Y* axis. The point where these two axes intersect is the origin. Now, if you draw a line perpendicular to the sheet passing through the origin, the line defines the positive *Z* axis, refer to Figure 18-36. If you project the *X*, *Y*, and *Z* axes in the opposite direction beyond the origin, you will get the negative *X*, *Y*, and *Z* axes, refer to Figure 18-37.

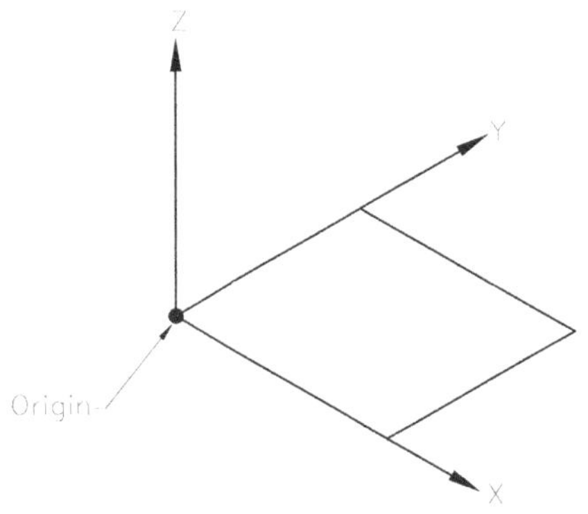

Figure 18-36 *X, Y, and Z axes*

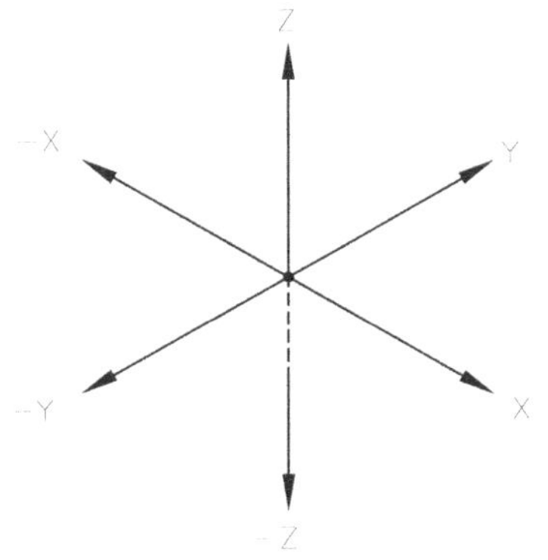

Figure 18-37 *Positive and negative axes*

The space between the *X* and *Y* axes is called the *XY* plane. Similarly, the space between the *Y* and *Z* axes is called the *YZ* plane, and the space between the *X* and *Z* axes is called the *XZ* plane, refer to Figure 18-38. A plane parallel to these planes is called a parallel plane, refer to Figure 18-39.

ORTHOGRAPHIC PROJECTIONS

The first step in drawing an orthographic projection is to position the object along the imaginary *X*, *Y*, and *Z* axes. For example, if you want to draw orthographic projections of the step block shown in Figure 18-40, position the block such that the far left corner coincides with the origin, and then align it with the *X*, *Y*, and *Z* axes.

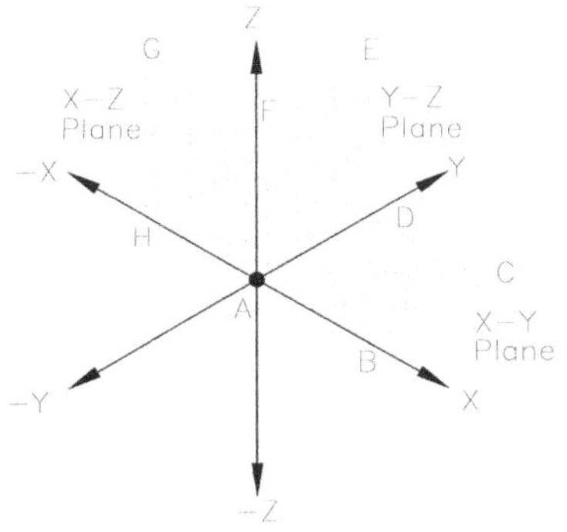

Figure 18-38 *XY, YZ, and XZ planes*

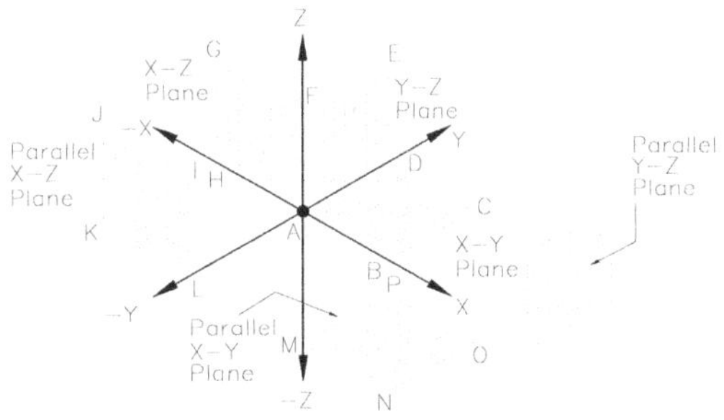

Figure 18-39 *Parallel planes*

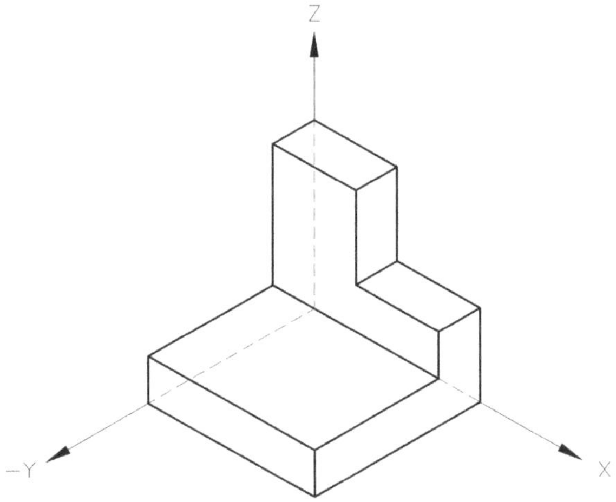

Figure 18-40 *Aligning the object with the X, Y, and Z axes*

Now, you can look at the object from different directions. Looking at the object along the negative *Y* axis and toward the origin is called the front view. Similarly, looking at it from the positive X direction is called the right side view. To get the top view, you can look at the object from the positive *Z* axis, refer to Figure 18-41.

To draw the front, side, and top views, project the points onto the parallel planes. For example, to draw the front view of the step block, imagine a plane parallel to the *XZ* plane located at a certain distance in front of the object. Now, project the points from the object onto the parallel plane, refer to Figure 18-42, and join them to complete the front view.

Repeat the same process for the side and top views. To represent these views on paper, position them, as shown in Figure 18-43.

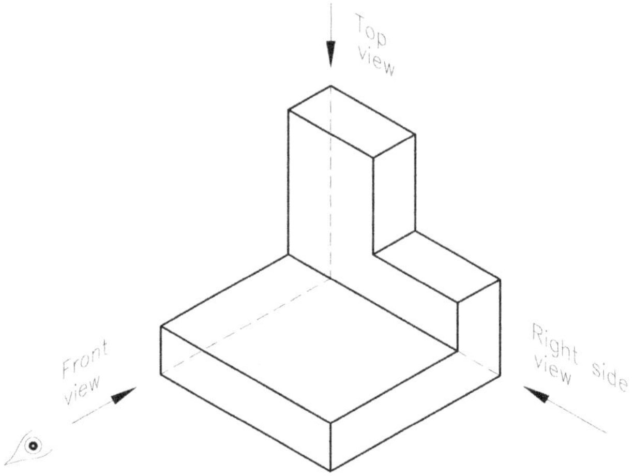

Figure 18-41 *Viewing directions for Front, Side, and Top views*

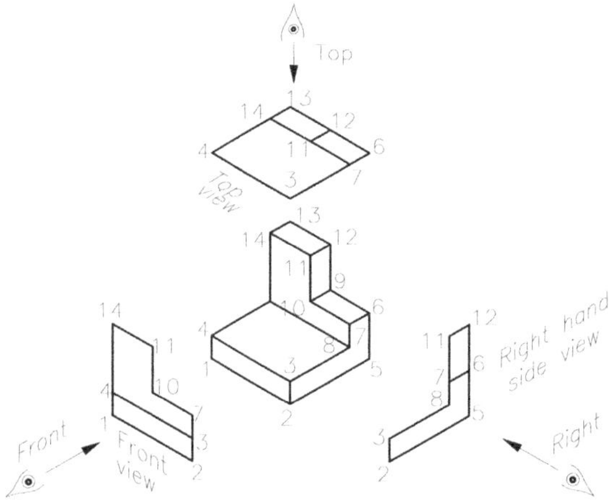

Figure 18-42 *Projecting points onto parallel planes*

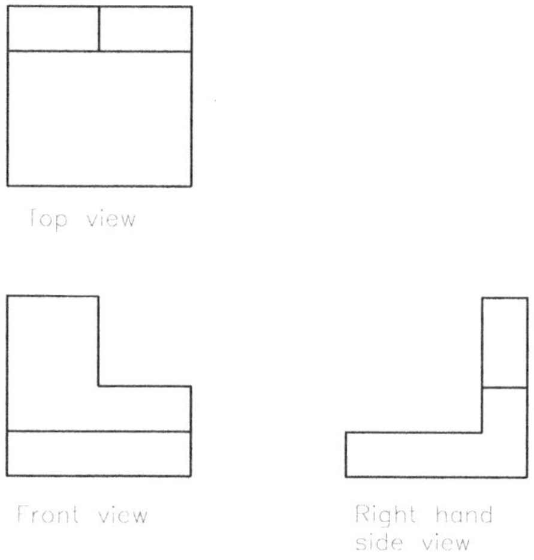

Figure 18-43 *Representing views on paper*

Another way of visualizing different views is to imagine the object enclosed in a glass box, refer to Figure 18-44.

Now, look at the object along the negative *Y* axis and draw the front view on the front glass panel. Repeat the process by looking along the positive *X* and *Z* axes, and draw the views on the right side and the top panel of the box, refer to Figure 18-45.

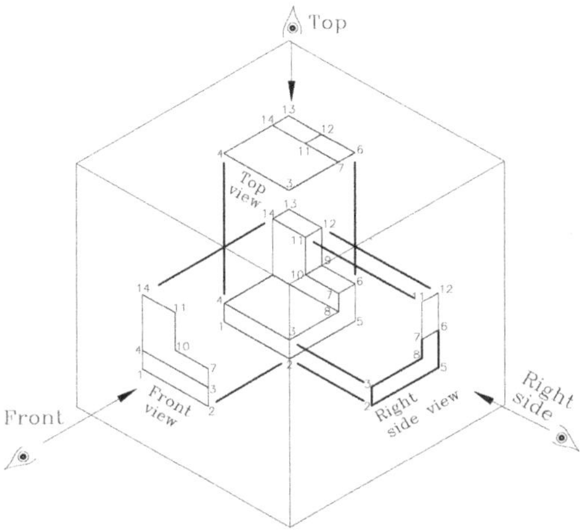

Figure 18-44 *Objects inside a glass box*

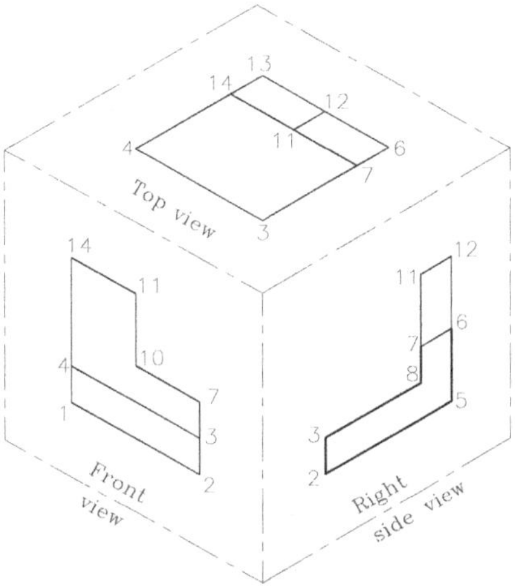

Figure 18-45 *Front, top, and side views*

To represent the front, side, and top views on paper, open the side and the top panels of the glass box, refer to Figure 18-46. The front panel is assumed to be stationary.

After opening the panels through 90 degree, the orthographic views will appear, as shown in Figure 18-47.

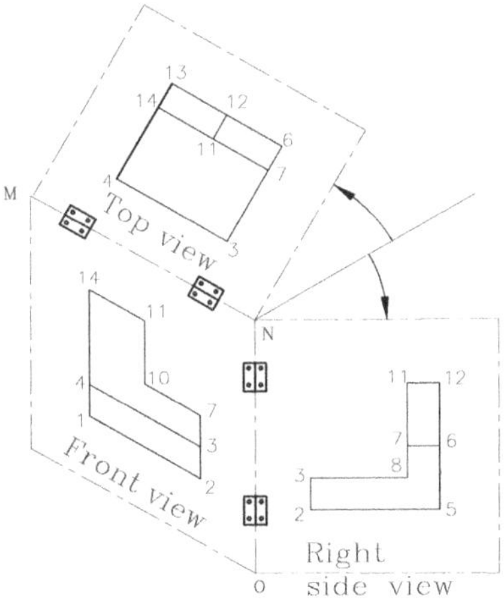

Figure 18-46 *Opening the side and top panels*

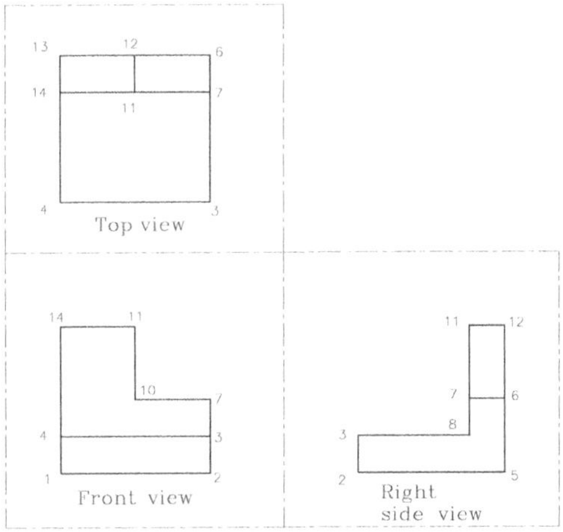

Figure 18-47 *Views after opening the panels*

POSITIONING ORTHOGRAPHIC VIEWS

Orthographic views must be positioned, as shown in Figure 18-48. The right side view must be positioned directly on the right side of the front view. Similarly, the top view must be directly above the front view. If the object requires additional views, they must be positioned, as shown in Figure 18-49.

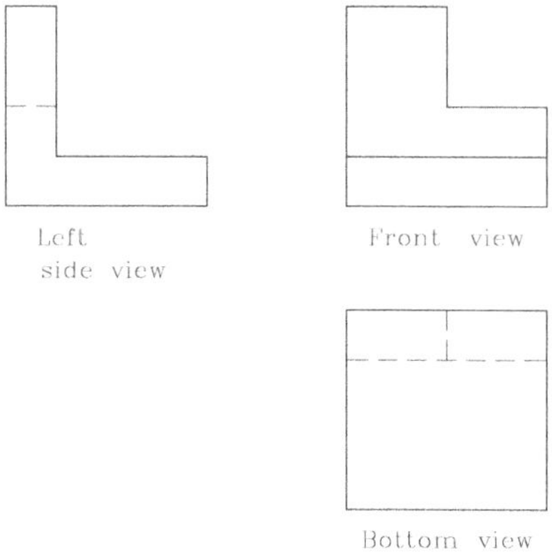

Figure 18-48 Positioning orthographic views

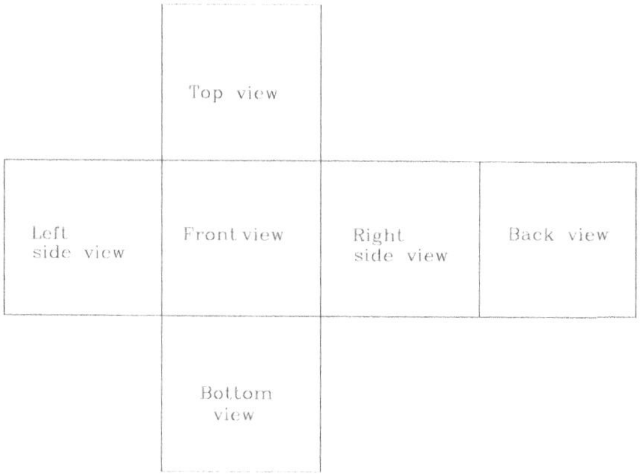

Figure 18-49 Standard placement of orthographic views

The different views of the step block are shown in Figure 18-50.

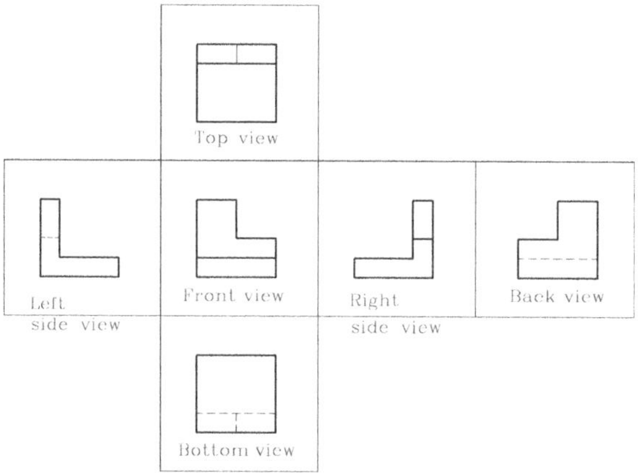

Figure 18-50 Different views of the step block

Example 1 Orthographic Views

In this example, you will draw the required orthographic views of the object shown in Figure 18-51. Assume the dimensions of the drawing.

Drawing the orthographic views of an object involves the following steps:

1. Look at the object and determine the number of views required to show all its features. For example, the object in Figure 18-51 requires three views only (front, side, and top).

2. Based on the shape of the object, select the side that you want to show as the front view. In this example, the front view, i.e. the view along -y axis, is the one that shows the maximum number of features or that gives a better idea about the shape of the object. Sometimes, the front view is determined by how the part will be positioned in an assembly.

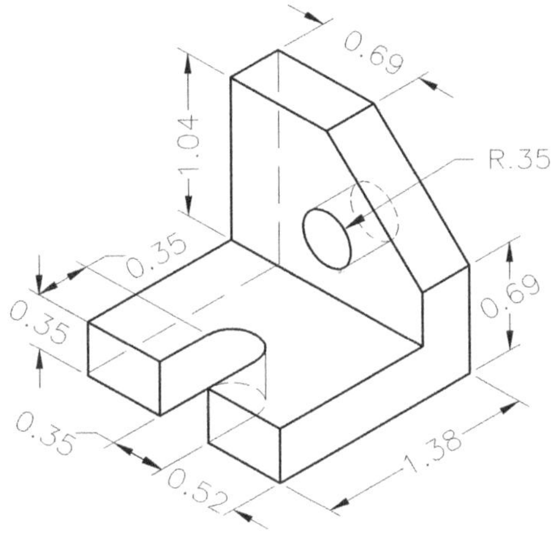

Figure 18-51 *Step block with hole and slot*

3. Picture the object in your mind and align it along the imaginary X, Y, and Z axes, refer to Figure 18-52.

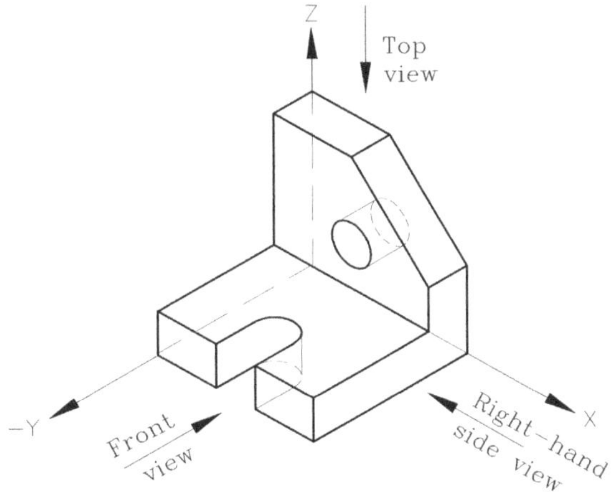

Figure 18-52 *Align the object with the imaginary X, Y, and Z axes*

4. Look at the object along the negative Y axis and project the image on the imaginary XZ parallel plane, refer to Figure 18-53.

5. Use the projection on imaginary XZ parallel plane to draw the front view of the object. If there are any hidden features, they must be drawn with hidden lines. The holes and slots must be shown with center lines.

6. To draw the right side view, look at the object along the positive *X* axis and project the image onto the imaginary YZ parallel plane.

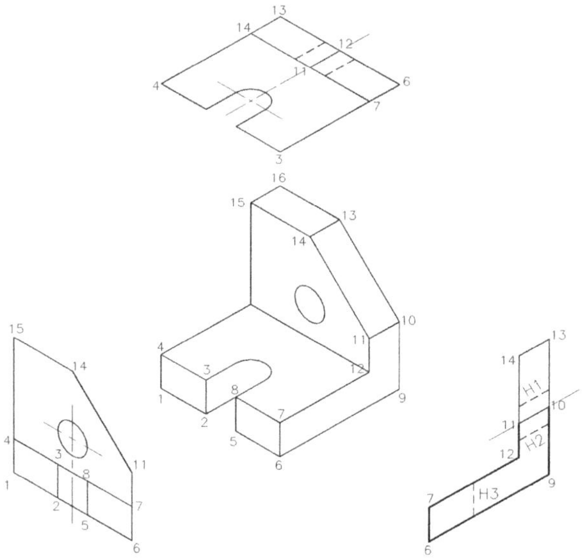

Figure 18-53 *Project the image onto the parallel planes*

7. Use the projection on imaginary YZ parallel plane to draw the right side view of the object. If there are any hidden features, they must be drawn with hidden lines. The holes and slots, when shown in the side view, must have one center line.

8. Similarly, draw the top view to complete the drawing. Figure 18-54 shows different views of the given object.

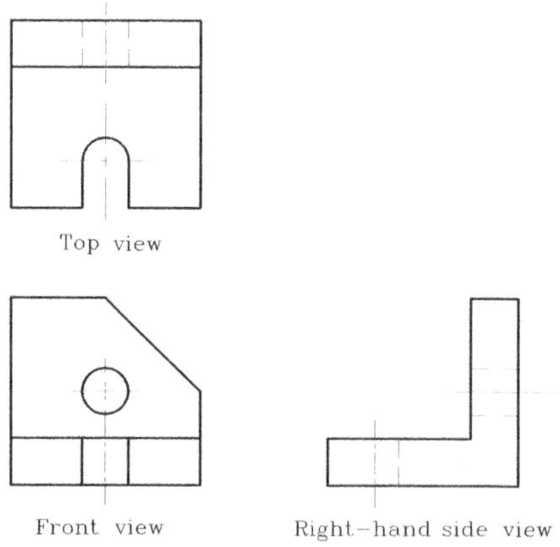

Figure 18-54 *Front, side, and top views*

Exercises 1 through 4 — Orthographic Views

Draw the required orthographic views of the objects shown in Figure 18-55 through Figure 18-58. The distance between the dotted lines is 1 unit.

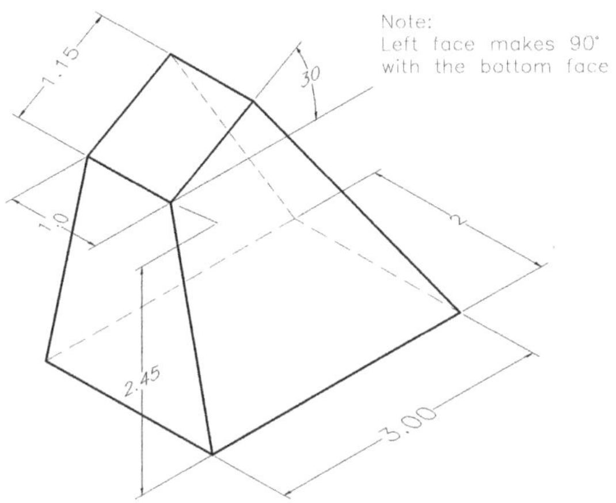

Figure 18-55 Drawing for Exercise 1 (the object is shown as a surface wireframe model)

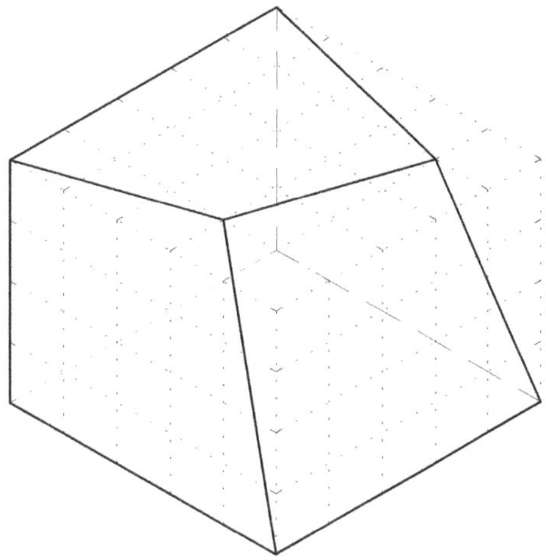

Figure 18-56 Drawing for Exercise 2

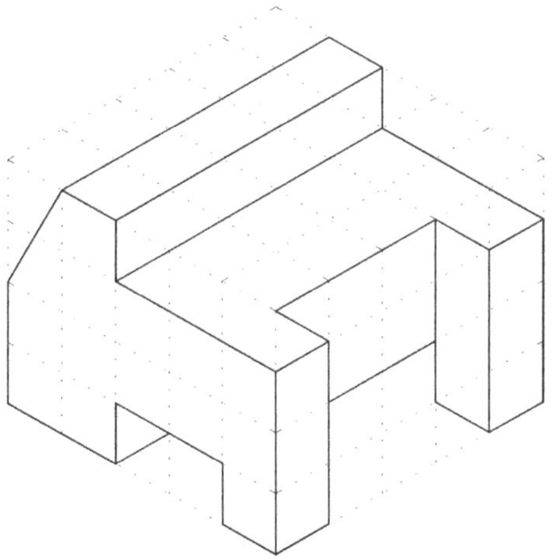

Figure 18-57 Drawing for Exercise 3

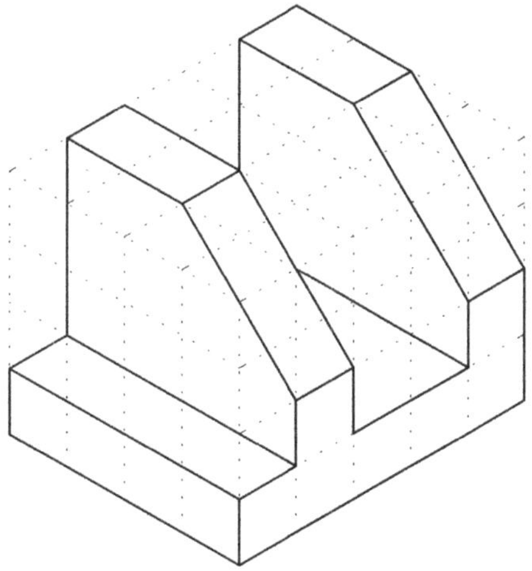

Figure 18-58 Drawing for Exercise 4

Exercises 5 through 10 *Orthographic Views*

Draw the required orthographic views of the following objects and then give the required dimensions, refer to Figures 18-59 through 18-64.

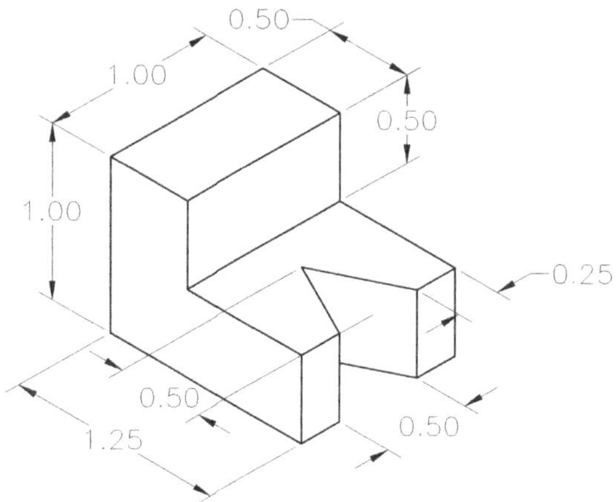

Figure 18-59 *Drawing for Exercise 6*

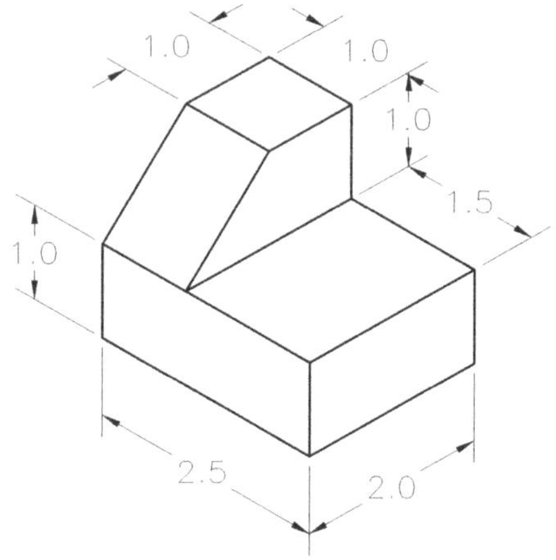

Figure 18-60 *Drawing for Exercise 5*

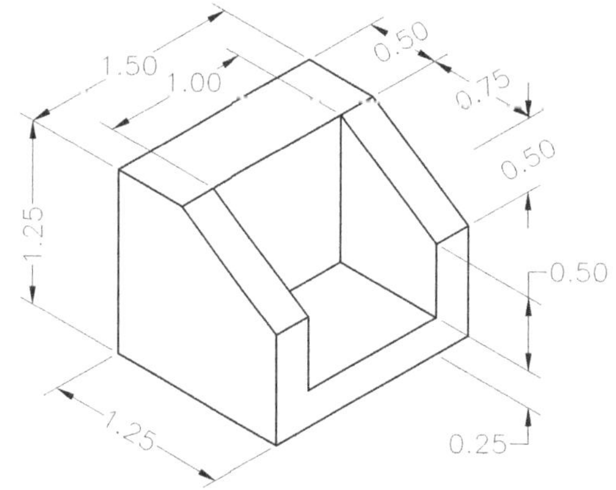

Figure 18-61 *Drawing for Exercise 7*

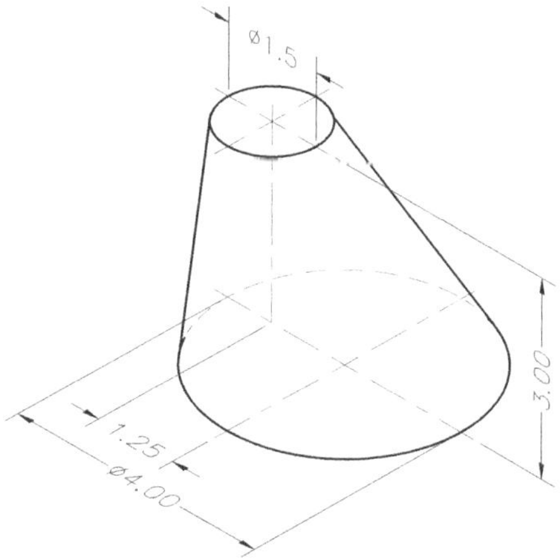

Figure 18-62 *Drawing for Exercise 8*

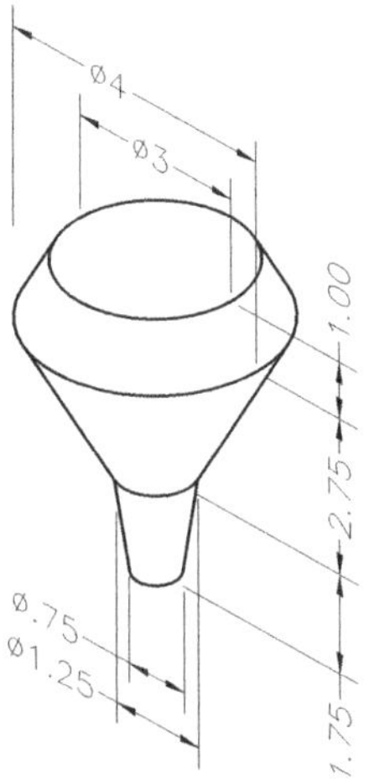

Figure 18-63 Drawing for Exercise 9

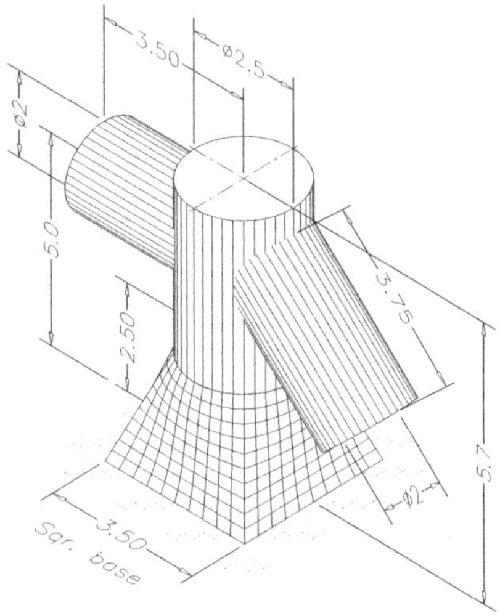

Figure 18-64 Drawing for Exercise 10
(assume the missing dimensions)

SECTIONAL VIEWS

In the principal orthographic views, the hidden features are generally shown by hidden lines. In some objects, the hidden lines may not be sufficient to represent the actual shape of the hidden feature. In such situations, sectional views can be used to show the features of the object that are not visible from outside. The location of the section and the direction of sight depend on the shape of the object and the features that need to be shown. Several ways to cut a section in the object are discussed next.

Full Section

Figure 18-65 shows an object that has a drilled counterbore hole, with taper. In the orthographic views, these features will be shown by the hidden lines, refer to Figure 18-66.

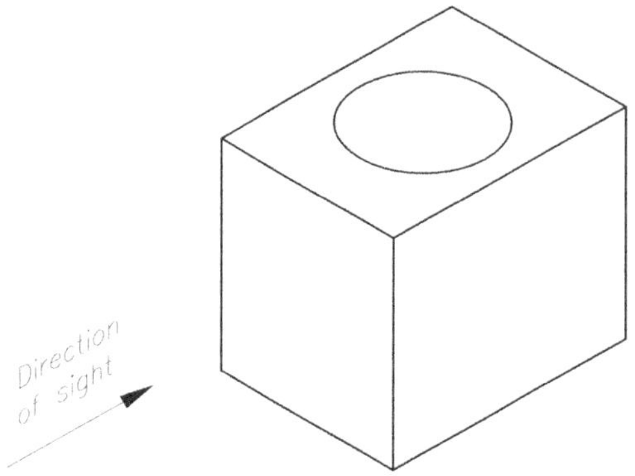

Figure 18-65 *Rectangular object with hole*

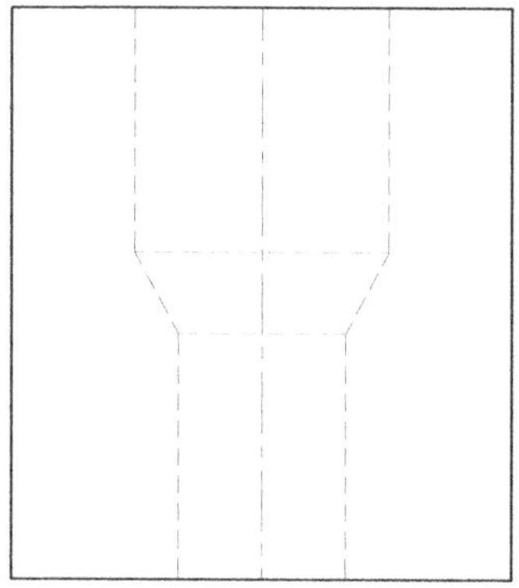

Figure 18-66 *Feature shown with hidden lines*

To better represent the hidden features, the object must be cut so that the hidden features are visible. In the full section, the object is cut along its entire length. To get a better idea of a full section, imagine that the object is cut into two halves along the centerline, as shown in Figure 18-67. Now, remove the left half and look at the right half in the direction that is perpendicular to the sectioned surface. The view you get after cutting the section is called a full section view, refer to Figure 18-68.

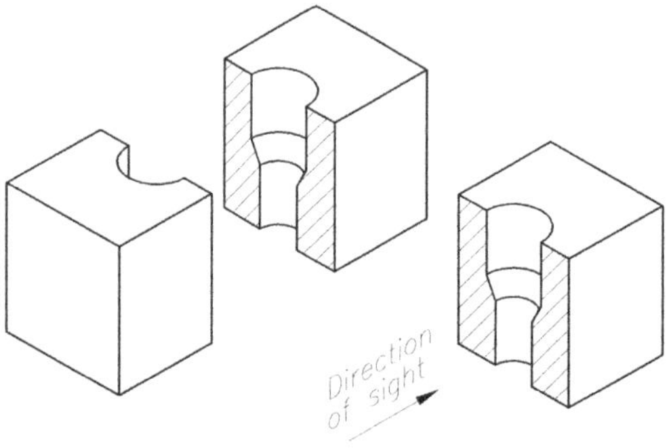

Figure 18-67 *One-half of the object removed*

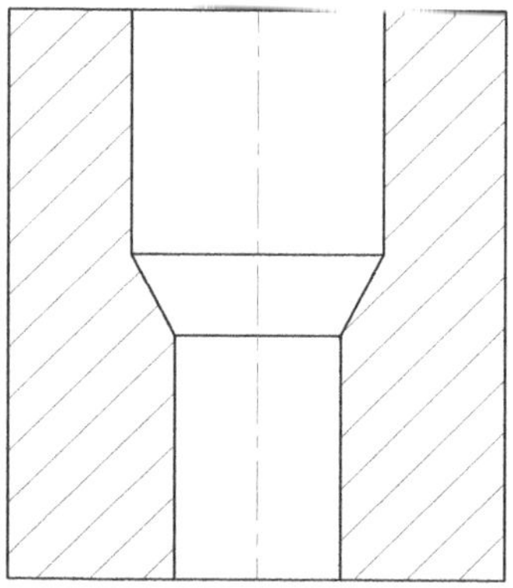

Figure 18-68 *Full section view*

In this section view, the features that would be hidden in a normal orthographic view are visible. Also, the part of the object where the material is actually cut is indicated by section lines. If the material is not cut, the section lines are not drawn. For example, if there is a hole, no material is cut when the part is sectioned, and so the section lines must not be drawn through that area of the section view.

Half Section

If the object is symmetrical, it is not necessary to draw a full section view. For example, in Figure 18-69, the object is symmetrical with respect to the centerline of the hole, so a full section is not required. But, in some objects it may help to understand and visualize the shape of the hidden details better to draw the view in half section. In half section, one-quarter of the object is removed, as shown in Figure 18-70. To draw a view in half section, imagine one-quarter of the object removed, and then look in the direction that is perpendicular to the sectioned surface.

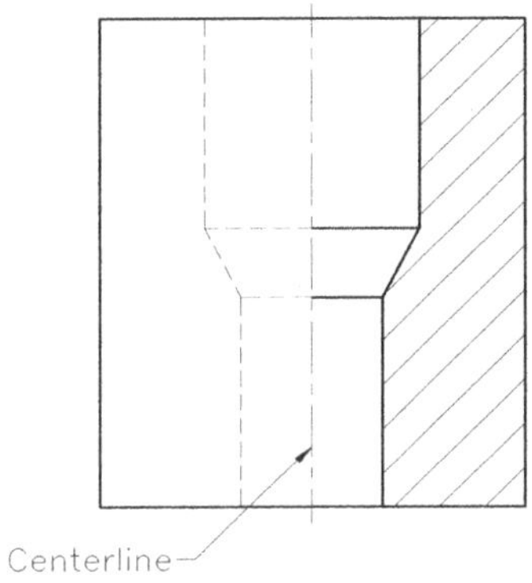

Figure 18-69 Front view in half section

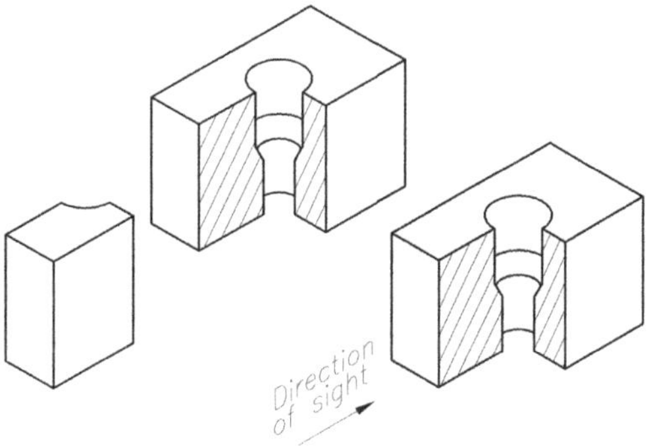

Figure 18-70 One-quarter of the object removed

You can also show the front view with a solid line in the middle, as shown in Figure 18-71. Sometimes the hidden lines, representing the remaining part of the hidden feature, are not drawn, refer to Figure 18-72.

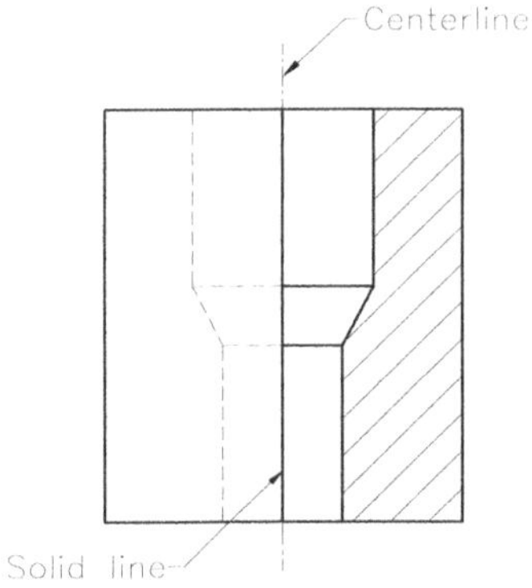

Figure 18-71 Front view in half section

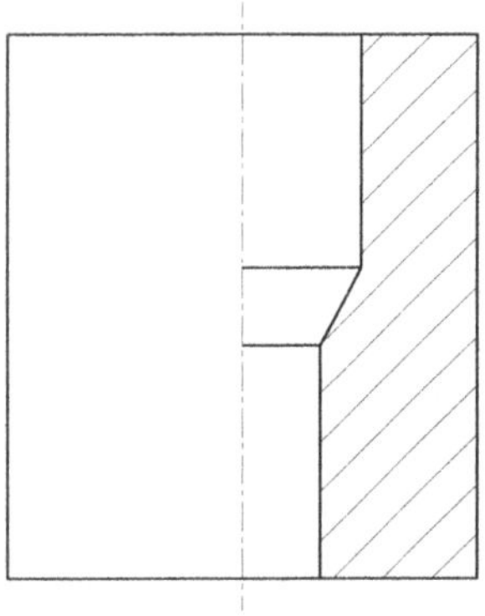

Figure 18-72 Front view in half section with the hidden features not drawn

Broken Section

In the broken section, only a small portion of the object is cut to expose the features that need to be drawn in the section. The broken section is designated by drawing a thick line in the section view, refer to Figure 18-73.

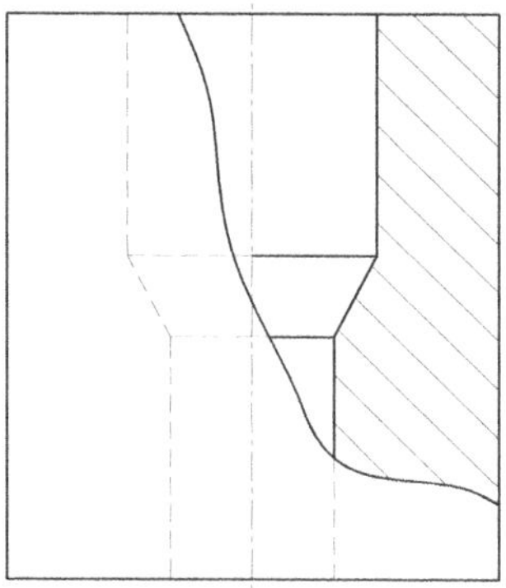

Figure 18-73 Front view with broken section

Revolved Section

The revolved section is used to show the true shape of the object at the point where the section is cut. The revolved section is used when it is not possible to show the features clearly in any principal view. For example, for the object shown in Figure 18-74, it is not possible to show the actual shape of the middle section in the front, side, or top view. Therefore, a revolved section is required to show the shape of the middle section.

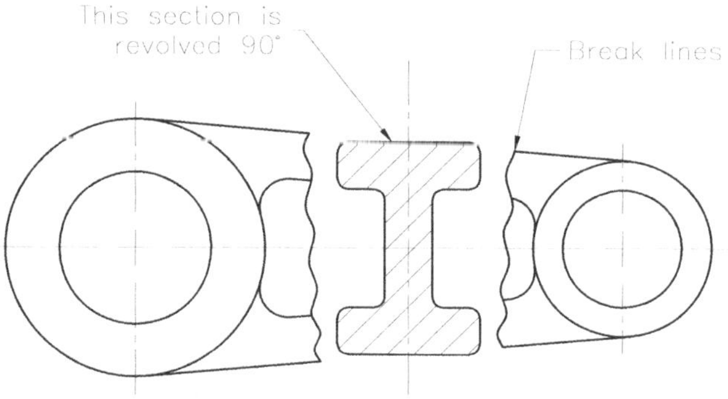

Figure 18-74 Front view with the revolved section

The revolved section involves cutting an imaginary section through the object and then looking at the sectioned surface in a direction that is perpendicular to it. To represent the shape, the view is revolved through 90 degrees and drawn in the plane of the paper, as shown in Figure 18-75. Depending on the shape of the object, and for clarity, it is recommended to provide a break in the object so that its lines do not interfere with the revolved section.

Removed Section

The removed section is similar to the revolved section, except that it is shown outside the object. The removed section is recommended when there is not enough space in the view to show it or if the scale of the section is different from the parent object. The removed section can be shown by drawing a line through the object at the point where the revolved section is required and then drawing the shape of the section, as shown in Figure 18-75.

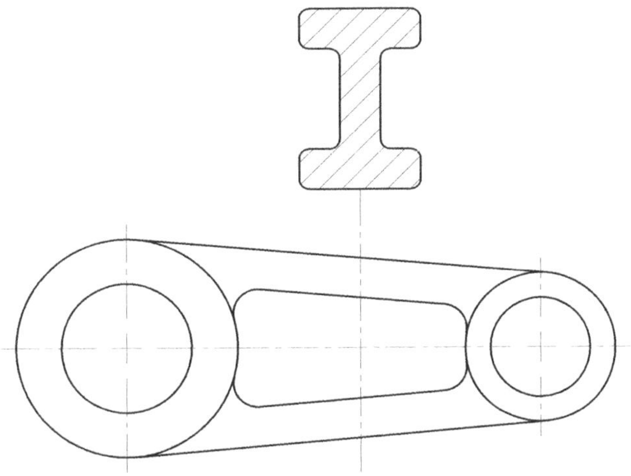

Figure 18-75 *Front view with the removed section*

The other way of showing a removed section is to draw a cutting plane line through the object where you want to cut the section. The arrows should point in the direction, in which you are looking at the sectioned surface. The section can then be drawn at a convenient place in the drawing. The removed section must be labeled, as shown in Figure 18-76. If the scale has been changed, it must be mentioned with the view description.

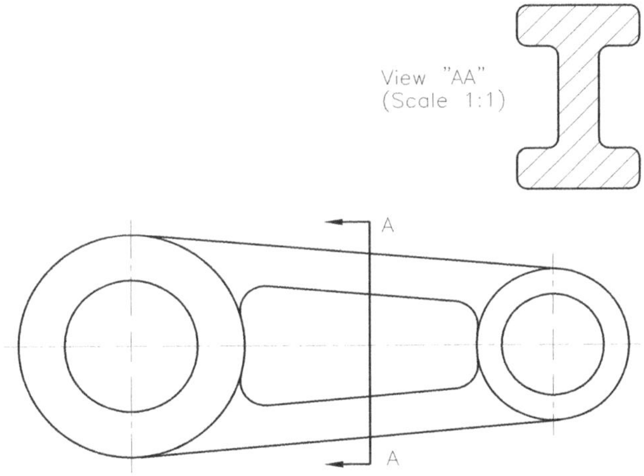

Figure 18-76 *Front view with the removed section drawn at a convenient place*

Offset Section

The offset section is used when the features of the object that you want to section are not in one plane. The offset section is designated by drawing a cutting plane line that is offset through the center of the features that need to be shown in the section, refer to Figure 18-77. The arrows indicate the direction in which the section is viewed.

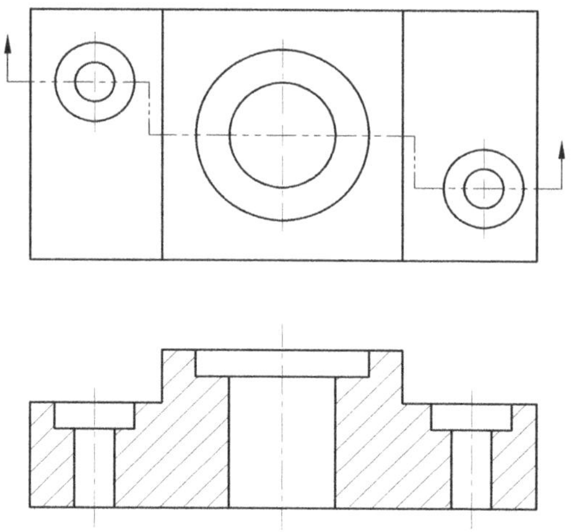

Figure 18-77 *Front view with offset section*

Aligned Section

In some objects, cutting a straight section might cause confusion in visualizing the shape of the section. Therefore, the aligned section is used to represent the shape along the cutting plane, refer to Figure 18-78. Such sections are widely used in circular objects that have spokes, ribs, or holes.

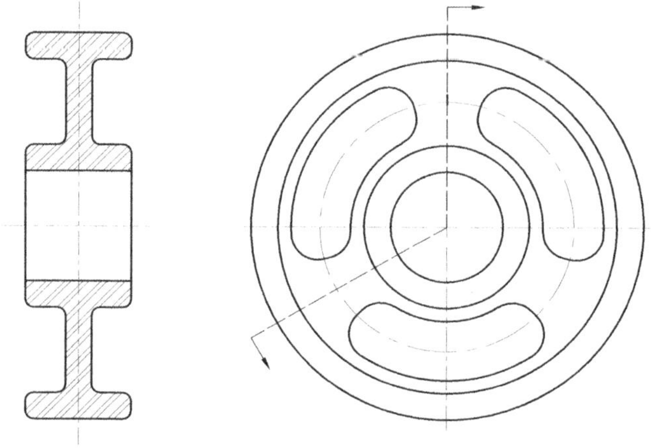

Figure 18-78 *Side view in section (aligned section)*

Cutting Plane Lines

Cutting plane lines are thicker than object lines, refer to Figure 18-79. You can use the **Polyline** tool to draw the polylines of the desired width, generally 0.005 to 0.01. However, for drawings that need to be plotted, you should assign a unique color to the cutting plane lines and then assign that color to the slot of the plotter that carries a pen of the required tip width.

In the industry, generally three types of lines are used to show the cutting plane for sectioning. The first line consists of a series of dashes 0.25 units long. The second type consists of a series of long dashes separated by two short dashes, refer to Figure 18-80. The length of the long dash can vary from 0.75 to 1.5 units, and the short dashes are about 0.12 units long. The space between the dashes should be about 0.03 units. Third, sometimes the cutting plane lines might clutter the drawing or cause confusion with other lines in the drawing. To avoid this problem, you can show the cutting plane by drawing a short line at the end of the section, refer to Figure 18-80 and Figure 18-81. The line should be about 0.5 units long.

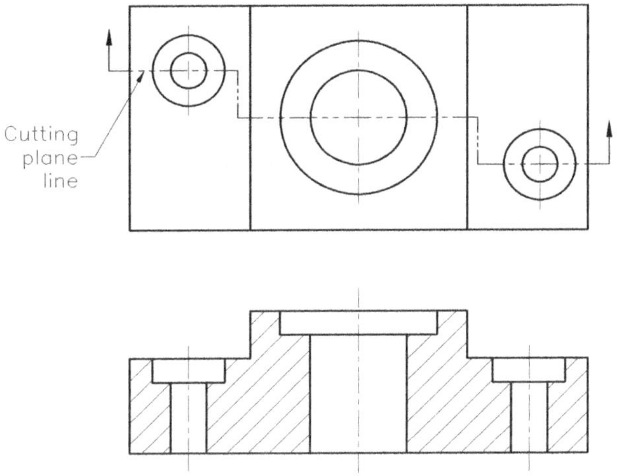

Figure 18-79 *Cutting plane lines*

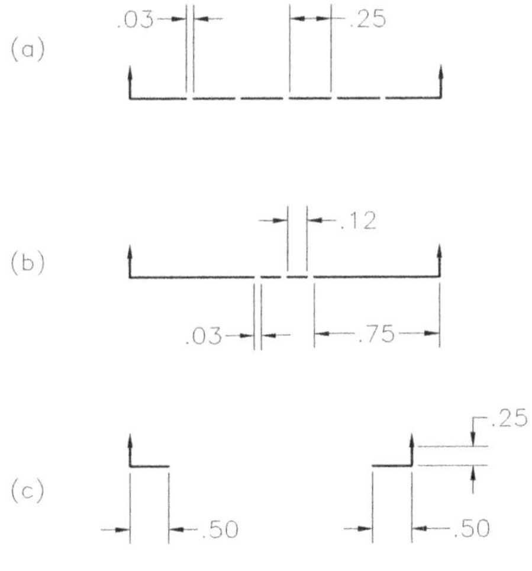

Figure 18-80 *Cutting plane lines*

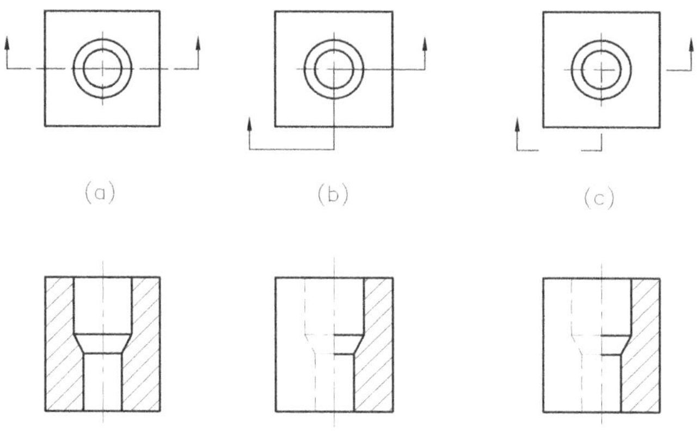

Figure 18-81 *Application of cutting plane lines*

Note

In AutoCAD, you can define a new linetype that you can use to draw cutting plane lines. Refer to Chapter 16 (Creating Linetypes and Hatch Patterns) for more information on defining linetypes. Add the following lines to the ***Aclt.lin*** *file, and then load the linetypes before assigning it to an object or a layer.*

```
*CPLANE1,___ ___ ___ ___
 A,0.25,-0.03
 *CPLANE2,___ ___ ___ ___
 A,1.0,-0.03,0.12,-0.03,0.12,-0.03
```

Spacing for Hatch Lines

The spacing between the hatch (section) lines is determined by the space that is being hatched, refer to Figure 18-82. If the hatch area is small, the spacing between the hatch lines should be smaller compared to a large hatch area.

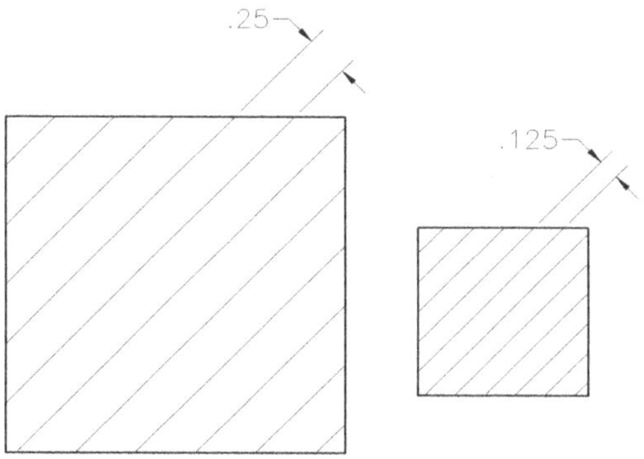

Figure 18-82 *Hatch line spacing*

In AutoCAD, you can control the spacing between the hatch lines by specifying the scale factor at the time of hatching. If the scale factor is 1, the spacing between the hatch lines is the same as defined in the hatch pattern file for that particular hatch. For example, in the following hatch pattern definition, the distance between the lines is 0.125.

***ANSI31, ANSI Iron, Brick, Stone masonry**
45, 0, 0, 0, .125

When the hatch scale factor is 1, the line spacing will be 0.125; if the scale factor is 2, the spacing between the lines will be 0.125 x 2 = 0.25.

Direction of Hatch Lines

The angle for the hatch lines should be 45 degrees. However, if there are two or more hatch areas next to one another representing different parts, the hatch angle must be changed so that the hatched areas look different, refer to Figure 18-83.

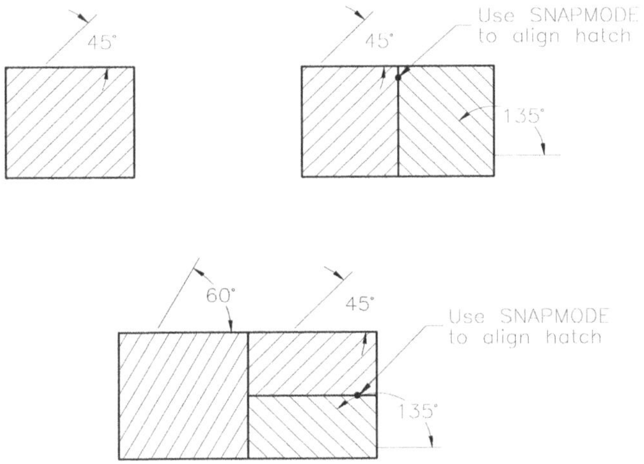

Figure 18-83 *Hatch angle for adjacent parts*

Also, if the hatch lines fall parallel to any edge of the hatch area, the hatch angle should be changed so that the lines are not parallel or perpendicular to any object line, refer to Figure 18-84.

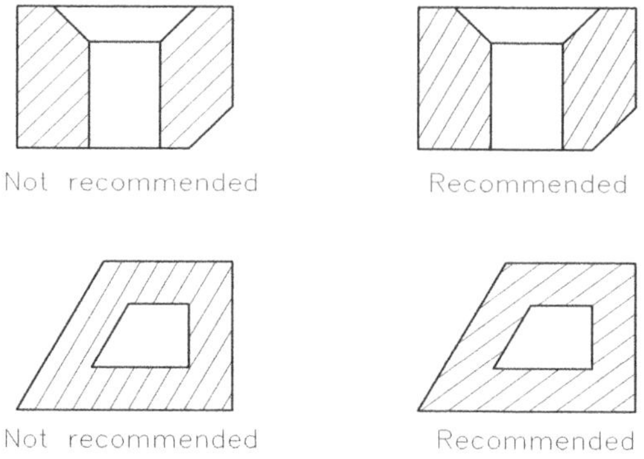

Figure 18-84 *Hatch angle*

Points to Remember

1. Some parts, such as bolts, nuts, shafts, ball bearings, fasteners, ribs, spokes, keys, and other similar items, if sectioned, should not be shown in the section. In case of ribs, if the cutting plane passes through the center plane of the feature, they should not be section-lined. If the cutting plane passes crosswise through ribs, they must be section-lined.

2. Hidden details should not be shown in the section view unless the hidden lines represent an important detail or help the viewer to understand the shape of the object.

3. The section lines (hatch lines) must be thinner than the object lines. You can accomplish this by assigning a unique color to the hatch lines and then assigning the color to that slot on the plotter that carries a pen with a thinner tip.

4. The section lines must be drawn on a separate layer for display and editing purposes.

Exercises 11 and 12 — *Section Views*

In the following drawings, refer to Figures 18-85 and 18-86, the views have been drawn without a section. Draw these views in the section as indicated by the cutting plane lines in each object.

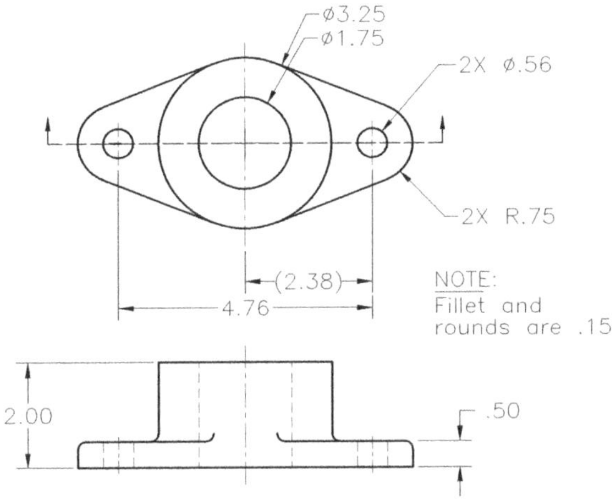

Figure 18-85 *Drawing for Exercise 11*

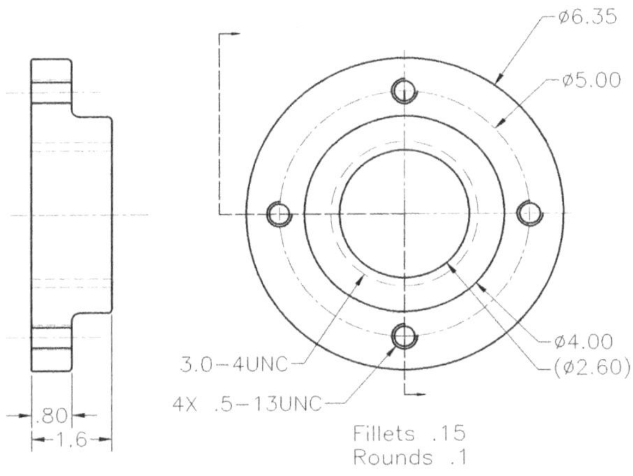

Figure 18-86 *Drawing for Exercise 12*

Exercises 13 and 14 — *Section Views*

Draw the orthographic views of the objects shown in Figures 18-87 and 18-88. The required view should be the front section view of the object such that the cutting plane passes through the holes. Also, draw the cutting plane lines in the top view.

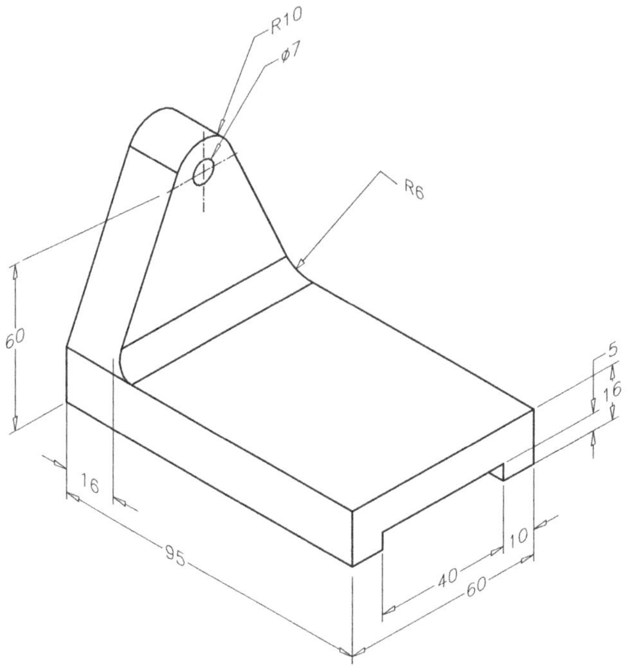

Figure 18-87 Drawing for Exercise 13

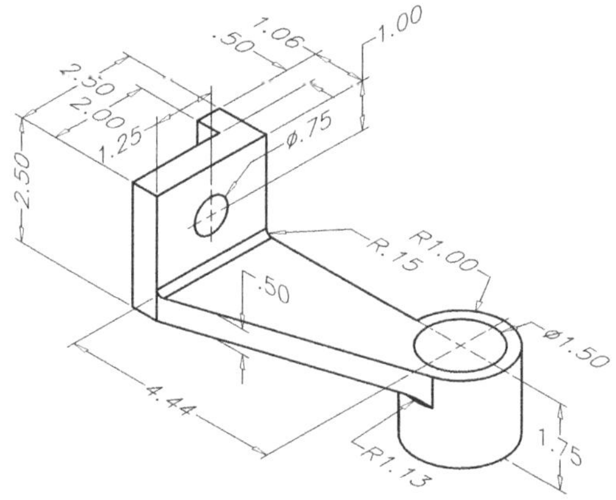

Figure 18-88 Drawing for Exercise 14

Exercise 15 Section View

Draw the required orthographic views of the object shown in Figures 18-89 and 18-90 with the front view in the section. Also, draw the cutting plane lines in the top view to show the cutting plane. The material thickness is 0.25 units. (The object has been drawn as a surfaced 3D wiremesh model.)

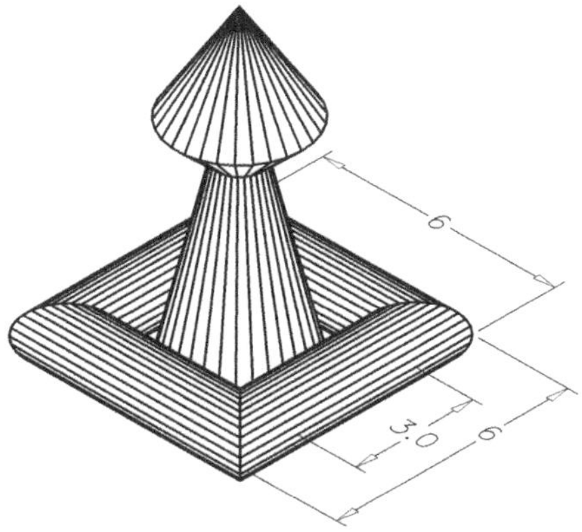

Figure 18-89 *Isometric view of the model*

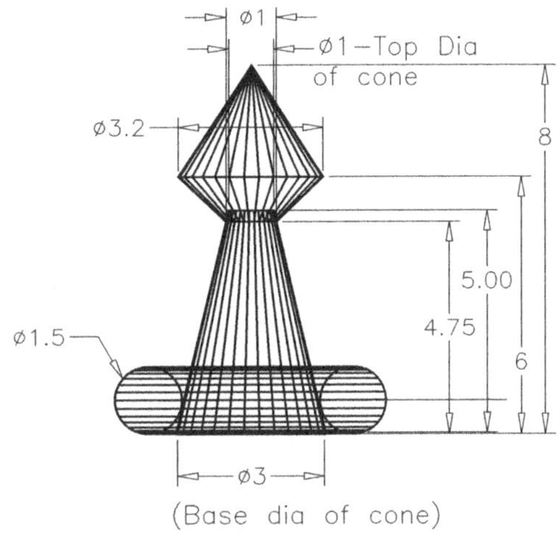

Figure 18-90 *Front view of the model*

AUXILIARY VIEWS

As discussed earlier, most objects generally require three principal views (front view, side view, and top view) to show all features of the object. Round objects may require just two views. Some objects have inclined surfaces. It may not be possible to show the actual shape of the inclined surface in one of the principal views. To get the true view of the inclined surface, you must look at the surface in a direction that is perpendicular to the inclined surface. Then you can project the points onto the imaginary auxiliary plane that is parallel to the inclined surface. The final view after projecting the points is called the auxiliary view, as shown in Figures 18-91 and 18-92.

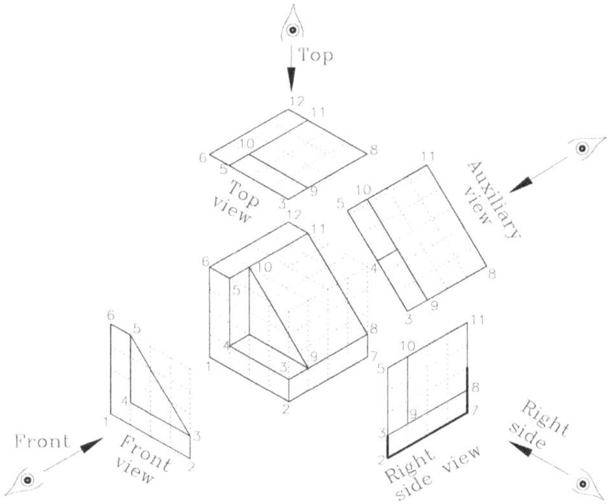

Figure 18-91 *Points projected on the auxiliary plane*

The auxiliary view in Figure 18-92 shows all the features of the object as seen from the auxiliary view direction. For example, the bottom left edge is shown as a hidden line. Similarly, the lower right and upper left edges are shown as continuous lines. Although these lines are technically correct, the purpose of the auxiliary view is to show the features of the inclined surface. Therefore, in the auxiliary plane, you should draw only those features that are on the inclined face, as shown in Figure 18-93. Other details that will help you to understand the shape of the object may also be included in the auxiliary view. The remaining lines should be ignored because they tend to cause confusion in visualizing the shape of the object.

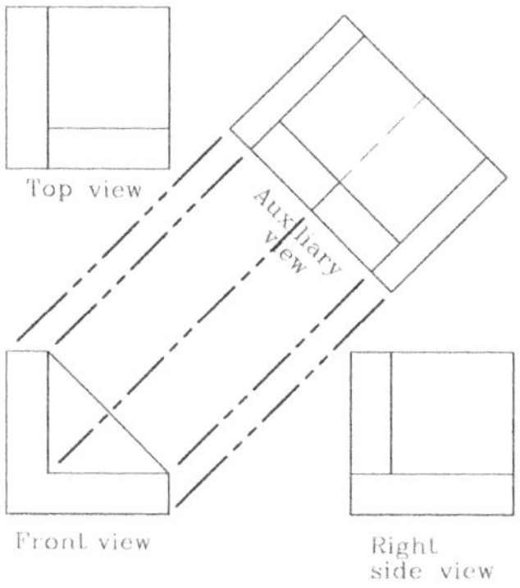

Figure 18-92 *Auxiliary, front, and side views*

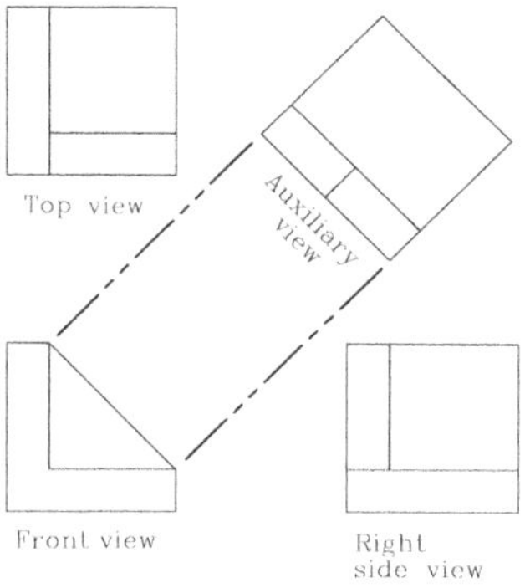

Figure 18-93 *Features on the inclined plane in an auxiliary view*

How to Draw Auxiliary Views

The following example illustrates how to use AutoCAD to generate an auxiliary view.

Draw the required views of the hollow triangular block that has a hole in the inclined face, as shown in Figure 18-94. (The block has been drawn as a solid model.)

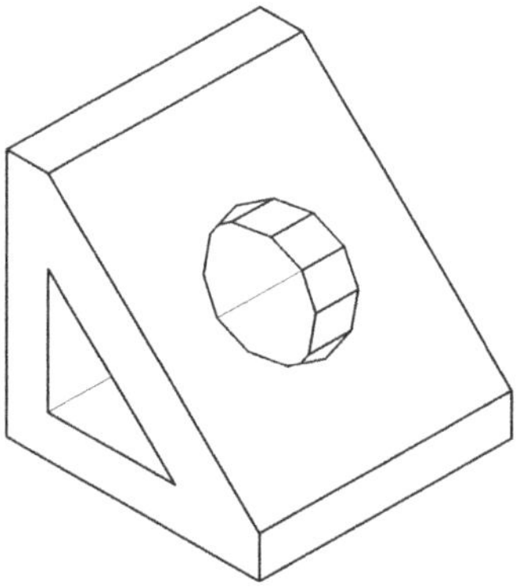

Figure 18-94 *Hollow triangular block*

The following steps are involved in drawing different views of this object.

1. Draw the required orthographic views: the front view, side view, and the top view as shown in Figure 18-95. The circles on the inclined surface appear like ellipses in the front and top views. These ellipses may not be shown in the orthographic views because they tend to clutter them, refer to Figure 18-96.

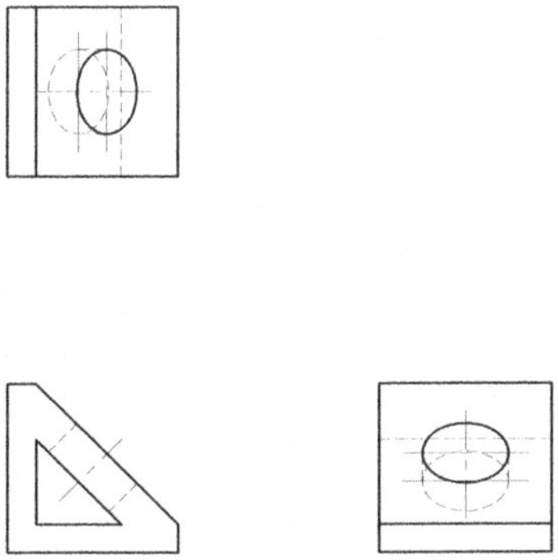

Figure 18-95 *Front, side, and top views*

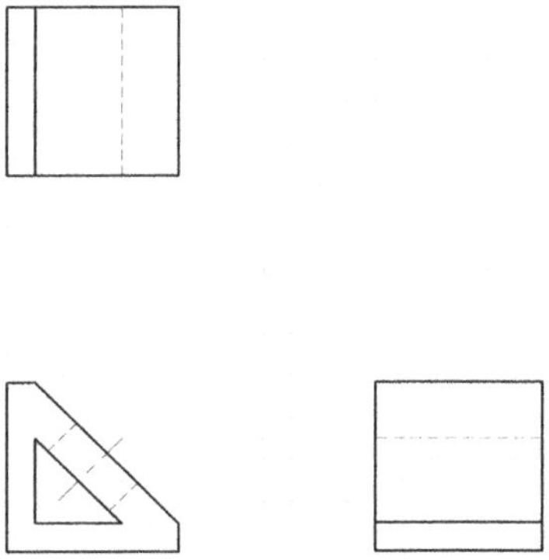

Figure 18-96 *The ellipses are not visible in the orthographic views*

2. Determine the angle of the inclined surface. In this example, the angle is 45 degrees. Use the **SNAP** command to rotate the snap by 45 degrees, refer to Figure 18-97 or rotate the UCS by 45 degrees around the *Z* axis.

Command: **SNAP** [Enter].
Specify snap spacing or [ON/OFF/Aspect/Style/Type] <0.5000>: **R** [Enter].
Specify base point <0.0000,0.0000>: *Select P1.*
Specify rotation angle <0>: **45** [Enter].

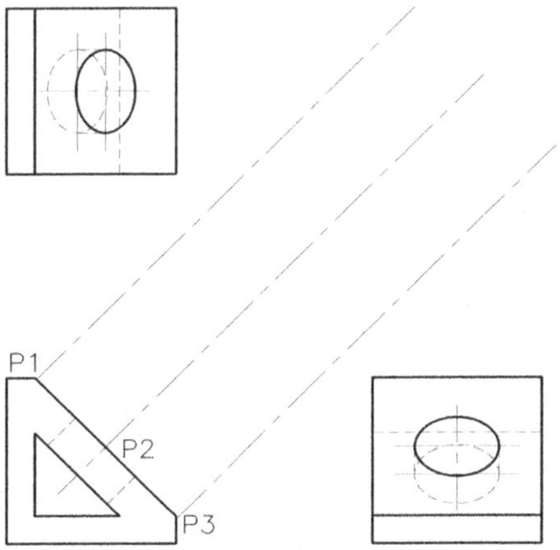

Figure 18-97 *Grid lines at 45-degree*

Using the rotate option, the snap will be rotated by 45 degrees and the grid lines will also be displayed at 45 degrees (if the **GRID** is on). Also, one of the grid lines will pass through point P1 because it was defined as the base point.

3. Turn **ORTHO** on, and project points P1, P2, and P3 from the front view onto the auxiliary plane. Now, you can complete the auxiliary view and give the dimensions. The projection lines can be erased after the auxiliary view is drawn, refer to Figure 18-98.

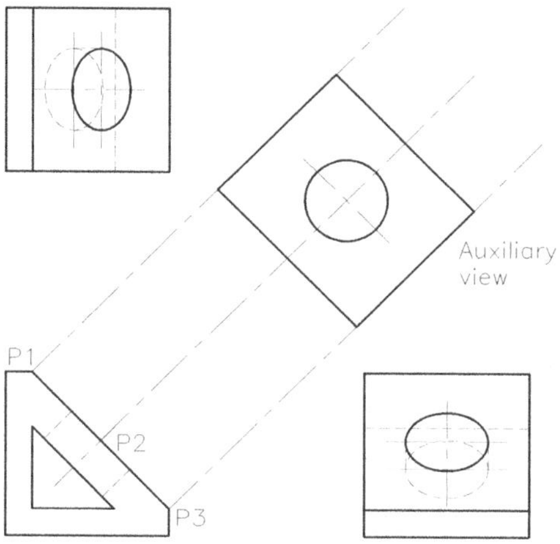

Figure 18-98 *Auxiliary, front, side, and top views*

Exercise 16 — Orthographic Views

Draw the orthographic and auxiliary views of the object shown in Figure 18-99. The object is drawn as a surfaced 3D wiremesh model.

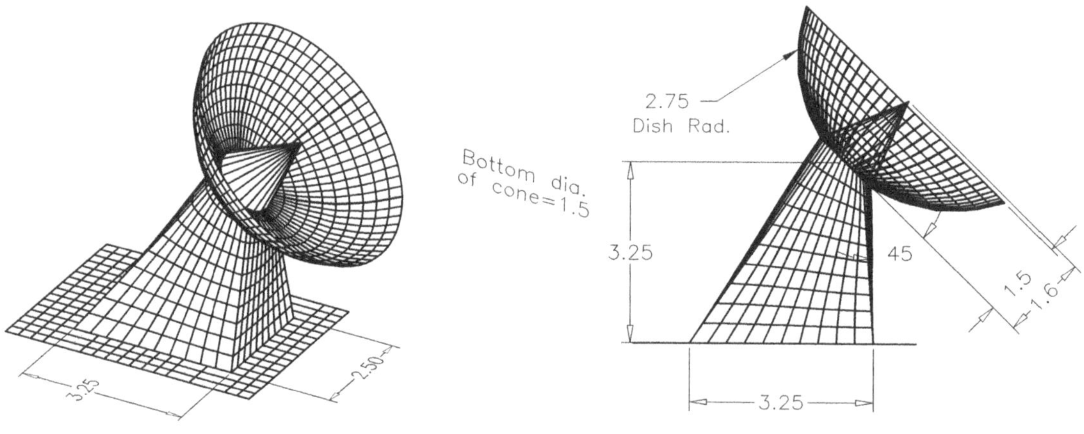

Figure 18-99 *Dimensions for the mesh model*

Exercises 17 and 18 *Orthographic Views*

Draw the orthographic and auxiliary views of the objects shown in Figure 18-100 and Figure 18-101. The objects are drawn as 3D solid models and are shown at different angles (viewpoints are different).

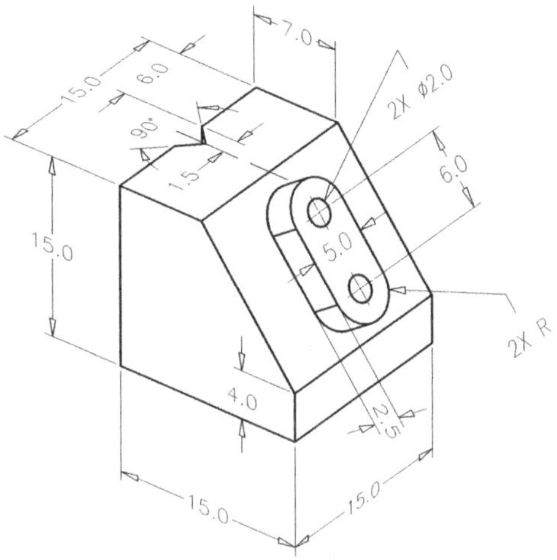

Figure 18-100 *Drawing for Exercise 17*

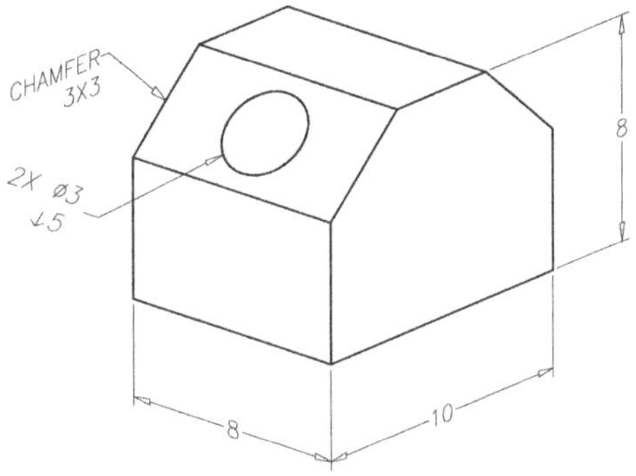

Figure 18-101 *Drawing for Exercise 18*

Self-Evaluation Test

Answer the following questions and then compare them to those given at the end of this chapter:

1. A line perpendicular to the *X* and *Y* axes defines the __________ axis.

2. The circle must be dimensioned as a __________, never as a radius.

3. If you give continuous (incremental) dimensioning for dimensioning various features of a part, the overall dimension must be omitted or given as a __________ dimension.

4. The removed section is similar to the __________section except that it is shown outside the object.

5. In AutoCAD, you can control the spacing between hatch lines by specifying the __________ at the time of hatching.

6. The distance between the first dimension line and the second dimension line must be __________ to __________units.

7. The reference dimension must be enclosed in __________.

8. The front view shows the maximum number of features or gives a better idea about the shape of the object. (T/F)

9. The number of decimal places in a dimension (for example, 2.000) determines the type of machine that will be used for performing the machining operation. (T/F)

10. The dimension layer/layers should be assigned a unique color so that at the time of plotting you can assign a desired pen to plot the dimensions. (T/F)

11. All dimensions should be placed inside the view. (T/F)

12. The dimensions can be placed inside the view if they can be easily understood and cause no confusion with the other object lines. (T/F)

13. If the object is symmetrical, it is not necessary to draw a full section view. (T/F)

14. When dimensioning, you must consider the manufacturing process involved in making a part and the relationship that exists between different parts in an assembly. (T/F)

15. A dimension must be given where the feature is visible. However, in some complicated drawings, you might be justified to dimension a detail with a hidden line. (T/F)

Review Questions

Answer the following questions:

1. Multiview drawings are also known as __________ drawings.

2. The distance of the first dimension line should be __________ to __________ units from the object line.

3. For parallel dimension lines, the dimension text can be __________ if there is not enough room between the dimension lines to place the dimension text.

4. When dimensioning a circle, the diameter should be preceded by the __________.

5. When dimensioning an arc or a circle, the dimension line (leader) must be __________.

6. A bolt circle should be dimensioned by specifying the __________of the bolt circle, the__________ of the holes, and the __________ of the holes in the bolt circle.

7. In the __________ section, the object is cut along the entire length.

8. The part of the object where the material is actually cut is indicated by drawing __________ lines.

9. The __________ section is used to show the true shape of the object at the point where the section is cut.

10. The __________section is used when the features of the object that you want to section are not in one plane.

11. The section lines must be drawn on a separate layer for __________ and __________purposes.

12. In a broken section, only a __________ of the object is cut to __________ the features that need to be drawn in section.

13. The assembly drawing is used to show the __________ and their __________ in an assembled product or a machine unit.

14. The space between the *X* and *Y* axes is called the *XY* plane. (T/F)

15. A plane that is parallel to the *XY* plane is called a parallel plane. (T/F)

16. If you look at the object along the negative *Y* axis and toward the origin, you will get the side view. (T/F)

17. The top view must be directly below the front view. (T/F)

18. Before drawing orthographic views, you must look at the object and determine the number of views required to show all features of the object. (T/F)

19. By dimensioning, you not only modify the size of a part, but also give a series of instructions to a machinist, an engineer, or an architect. (T/F)

20. You can change grid, snap or UCS origin, and snap increments to make it easier to place the dimensions. (T/F)

21. You should not dimension with hidden lines. (T/F)

22. A dimension that is not to be scaled should be indicated by drawing a straight line under the dimension text. (T/F)

23. Dimensions must be given where the feature that you are dimensioning is obvious and shows the contour of the feature. (T/F)

24. In radial dimensioning, you should place the dimension text vertically. (T/F)

25. If the dimension of a feature appears in a section view, you must hatch the dimension text. (T/F)

26. Dimensions must not be repeated as it makes their updation difficult. (T/F)

27. Cutting plane lines are thinner than object lines. You can use the **Polyline** tool to draw the polylines of the desired width. (T/F)

28. The spacing between the hatch (section) lines is determined by the space being hatched. (T/F)

29. The angle for the hatch lines should be 45-degree. However, if there are two or more hatch areas next to one another representing different parts, the hatch angle must be changed so that the hatched areas look different. (T/F)

30. Some parts, such as bolts, nuts, shafts, ball bearings, fasteners, ribs, spokes, keys, and other similar items that do not show any important feature, if sectioned, must be shown in section. (T/F)

31. Section lines (hatch lines) must be thicker than object lines. (T/F)

Exercises 19 through 24

Draw the required orthographic views of the following objects (the isometric view of each object is given in Figures 18-102 through 18-107). The dimensions can be determined by counting the number of grid lines. The distance between the isometric grid lines is assumed to be 0.5 units. Also, dimension the drawings.

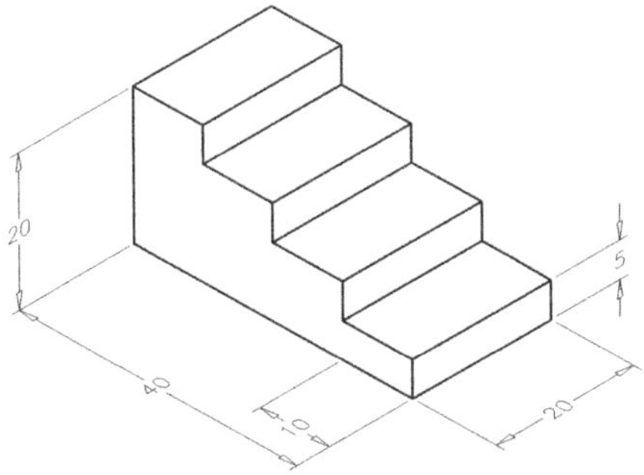

Figure 18-102 *Drawing for Exercise 19*

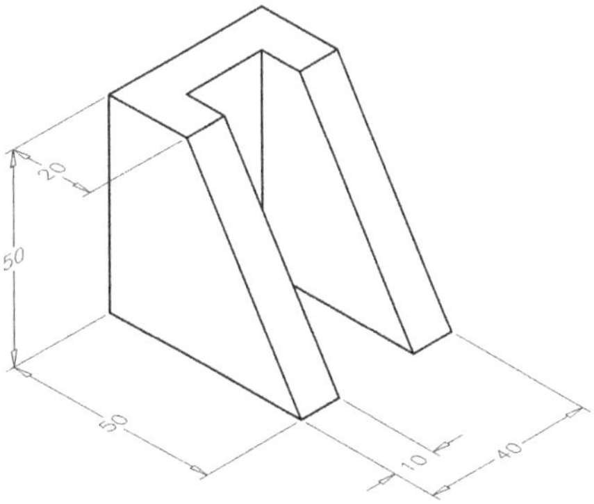

Figure 18-103 *Drawing for Exercise 20*

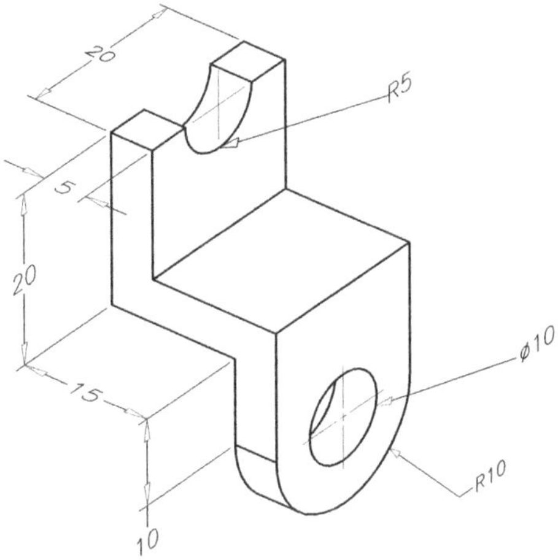

Figure 18-104 *Drawing for Exercise 21*

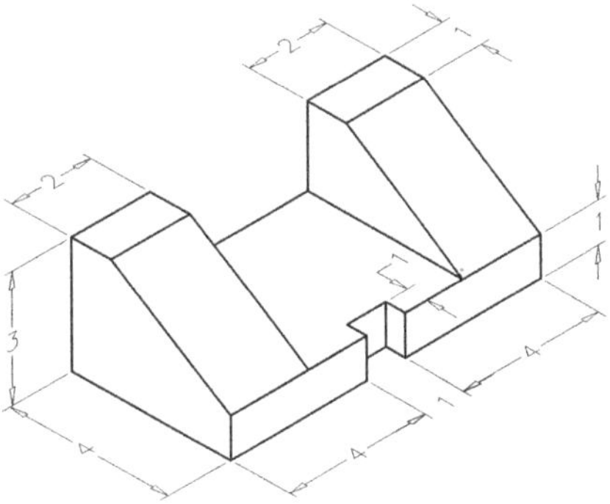

Figure 18-105 *Drawing for Exercise 22*

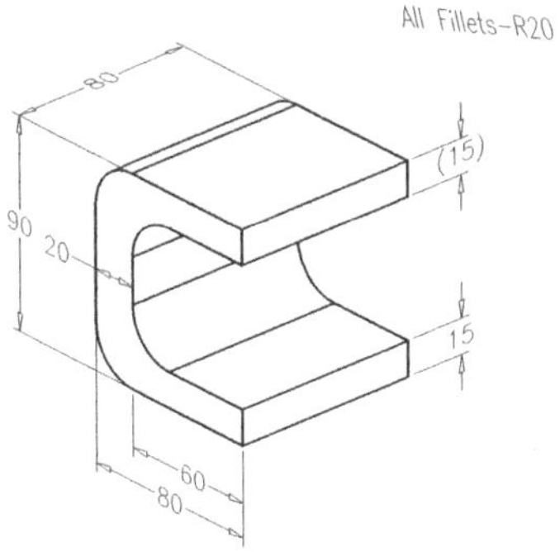

Figure 18-106 *Drawing for Exercise 23*

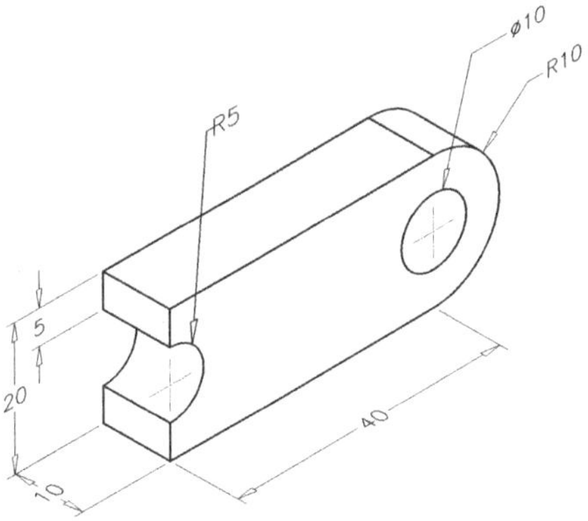

Figure 18-107 *Drawing for Exercise 24*

Answers to Self-Evaluation Test

1. Z, **2.** diameter, **3.** reference, **4.** revolved, **5.** scale factor, **6.** 0.25 to 0.5, **7.** parentheses, **8.** T, **9.** T, **10.** T, **11.** F, **12.** T, **13.** T, **14.** T, **15.**T

Chapter 19

Isometric Drawings

Learning Objectives

After completing this chapter, you will be able to:

- *Understand isometric drawings, isometric axes, and isometric planes*
- *Set isometric grid and snap*
- *Draw isometric circles in different isoplanes*
- *Dimension isometric objects*
- *Write text in isometric styles*

Key Terms

- *Isometric Planes*
- *Isometric Axes*
- *Isometric Snap*
- *Isometric Grid*
- *Iso Circles*
- *Isometric Text*

ISOMETRIC DRAWINGS

Isometric drawings are generally used to help visualize the shape of an object. For example, if you are given the orthographic views of an object, as shown in Figure 19-1, it takes time to put information together to visualize the shape. However, if an isometric drawing is given, as shown in Figure 19-2, it is easier to understand the shape of the object. Thus, isometric drawings are widely used in industry to help in understanding products and their features.

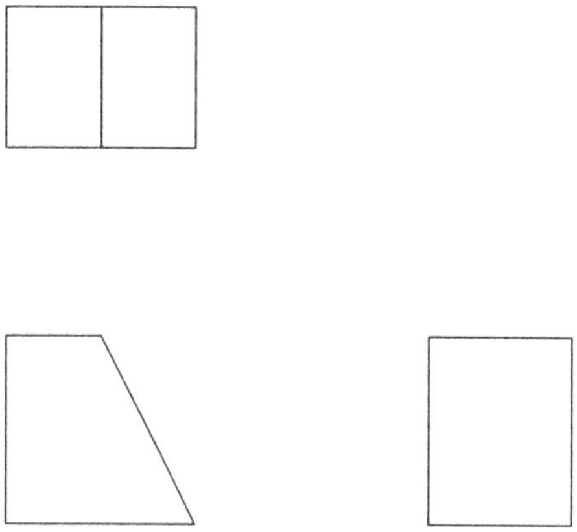

Figure 19-1 *Orthographic views of an object*

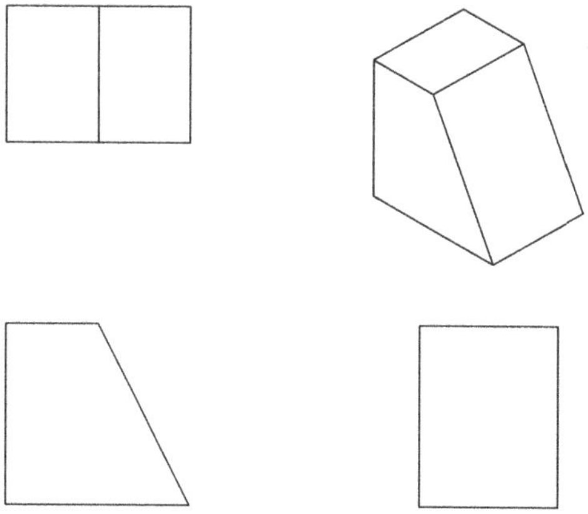

Figure 19-2 *Orthographic views with an isometric drawing*

An isometric drawing should not be confused with a three-dimensional (3D) drawing. An isometric drawing is just a two-dimensional (2D) representation of a 3D drawing on a 2D plane. A 3D drawing is the 3D model of an object on the X, Y, and Z axes. In other words, an isometric drawing is a 3D drawing on a 2D plane, whereas a 3D drawing is a true 3D model of the object. The model can be rotated and viewed from any direction. A 3D model can be a wireframe model, surface model, or solid model.

ISOMETRIC PROJECTIONS

The word "isometric" means equal measurement. The angle between any of the two principal axes of an isometric drawing is 120 degrees, refer to Figure 19-3. An isometric view is obtained by rotating the object by 45 degree angle around the imaginary vertical axis, and then tilting the object forward through a 35°16' angle. If you project the points and edges on the front plane, the projected length of the edges will be approximately 82 percent (isometric length/actual length = 9/11), which is shorter than the actual length of the edges. However, isometric drawings are always drawn to a full scale because their purpose is to help the user visualize the shape of the object. Isometric drawings are not meant to describe the actual size of the object. The actual dimensions, tolerances, and feature symbols must be shown in the orthographic views. Also, you should avoid showing any hidden lines

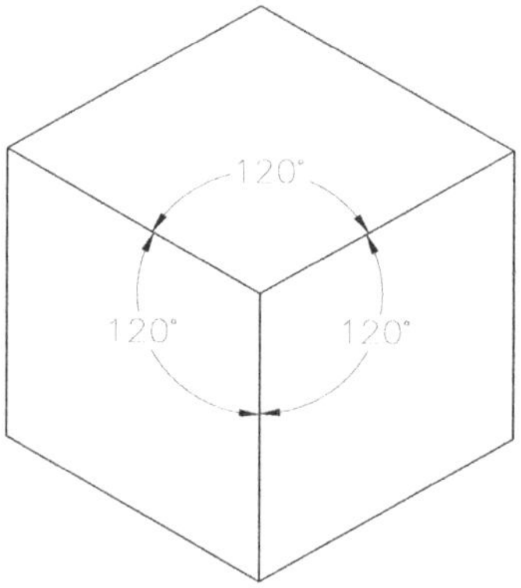

Figure 19-3 *Principal axes of an isometric drawing*

in the isometric drawings unless they show an important feature of the object or help in understanding its shape.

ISOMETRIC AXES AND PLANES

Isometric drawings have three axes: right horizontal axis (P0,P1), vertical axis (P0,P2), and left horizontal axis (P0,P3). The two horizontal axes are inclined at 30 degrees to the horizontal or X axis (X1,X2). The vertical axis is at 90 degrees, as shown in Figure 19-4.

When you draw an isometric drawing, the horizontal object lines are drawn along or parallel to the horizontal axis. Similarly, the vertical lines are drawn along or parallel to the vertical axis. For example, to make an isometric drawing of a rectangular block, the vertical edges of the block are drawn parallel to the vertical axis. The horizontal edges on the right side of the block are drawn parallel to the right horizontal axis (P0,P1), and the horizontal edges on the left side of the block are drawn parallel to the left horizontal axis (P0,P3). It is important to remember that the angles do not appear true in isometric drawings. Therefore, the edges or surfaces that are at an angle are drawn by locating their endpoints. The lines that are parallel to the isometric axes are called isometric lines. The lines that are not parallel to the isometric axes are called non isometric lines.

Similarly, the planes can be isometric planes or non isometric planes.

Isometric drawings have three principal planes, namely isoplane right, isoplane top, and isoplane left, as shown in Figure 19-5. The isoplane right (P0,P4,P10,P6) is defined by the vertical axis and the right horizontal axis. The isoplane top (P6,P10,P9,P7) is defined by the right and left horizontal axes. Similarly, the isoplane left (P0,P6,P7,P8) is defined by the vertical axis and the left horizontal axis.

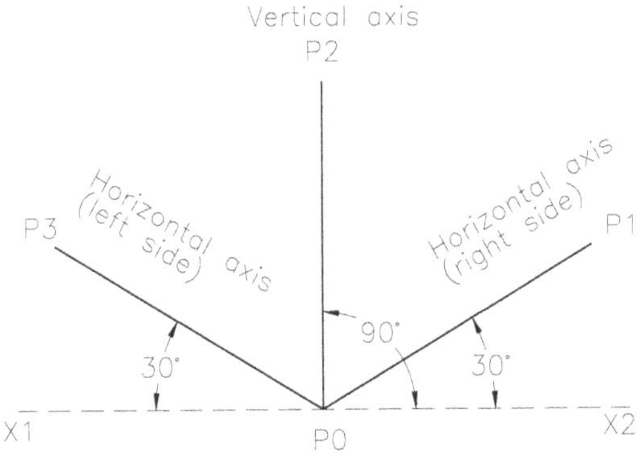

***Figure 19-4** Isometric axes*

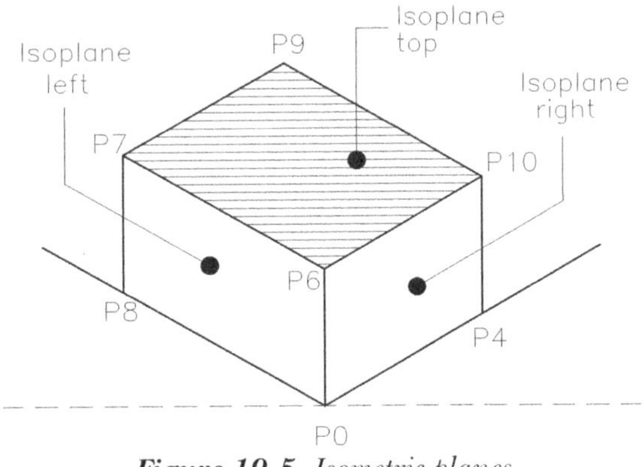

***Figure 19-5** Isometric planes*

SETTING THE ISOMETRIC GRID AND SNAP

You can use the **SNAP** command to set the isometric grid and snap. The isometric grid lines are displayed at 30 degree angle to the horizontal axis. Also, the distance between the grid lines is determined by the vertical spacing, which can be specified by using the **GRID** or **SNAP** command. The grid lines coincide with three isometric axes, which make it easier to create isometric drawings. The following command sequence and Figure 19-6 illustrate the use of the **SNAP** command to set the isometric grid and snap of 0.5 unit:

Command: **SNAP**
Specify snap spacing or [ON/OFF/Aspect/Legacy/Style/Type] <0.5000>: **S**
Enter snap grid style [Standard/Isometric] <S>: **I**
Specify vertical spacing <0.5000>: *Enter a new snap distance.*

Note

*1. When you use the **SNAP** command to set the isometric grid, the grid lines may not be displayed. To display the grid lines, turn the grid on by choosing the **Grid Display** button from the Status Bar or press F7.*

2. You cannot set the aspect ratio for the isometric grid. Therefore, the spacing between the isometric grid lines will be the same.

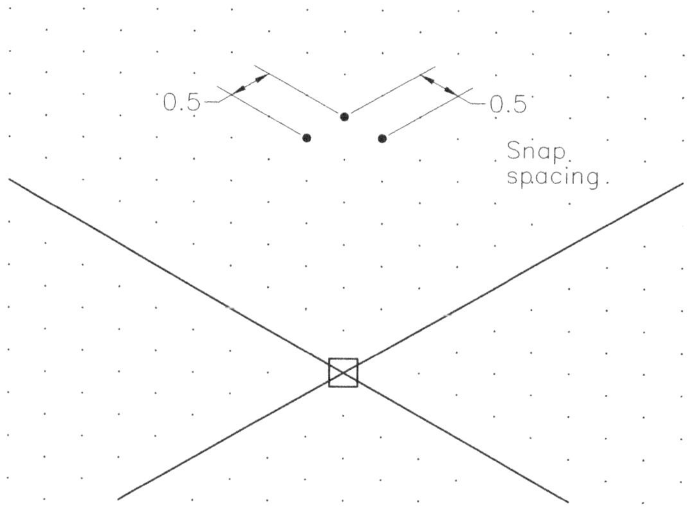

***Figure 19-6** Setting the isometric grid and snap in dotted grid*

You can also set the isometric grid and snap by using the **Drafting Settings** dialog box shown in Figure 19-7. You can invoke this dialog box by right-clicking on **SNAPMODE**, **GRIDMODE**, **Polar Tracking**, **Object Snap**, **3D Object Snap**, **Object Snap Tracking**, **Dynamic Input**, **Quick Properties**, or **Selection Cycling** button available in the Status Bar and then choosing **Settings** from the shortcut menu displayed. You can also invoke this dialog box by entering **DSETTINGS** at the Command prompt.

The isometric snap and grid functions can be turned on/off by choosing the **Grid On (F7)** check box located in the **Snap and Grid** tab of the **Drafting Settings** dialog box. The **Snap and Grid** tab also contains the radio buttons to set the snap type and style. To display the grid on the screen, make sure the grid is turned on.

When you set the isometric grid, the display of crosshairs also changes. The crosshairs are displayed at an isometric angle and their orientation depends on current isoplane. You can toggle between isoplane right, isoplane left, and isoplane top by pressing the Ctrl and E keys (Ctrl+E) simultaneously or by using the function key, F5. You can also toggle among different isoplanes by using the **Drafting Settings** dialog box or by entering the **ISOPLANE** command at the Command prompt:

Command: **ISOPLANE**
Enter isometric plane setting [Left/Top/Right] <Top>: **T**
Current Isoplane: **Top**

Figure 19-7 *The **Drafting Settings** dialog box*

The Ortho mode is useful when drawing in the Isometric mode. In the Isometric mode, Ortho aligns with the axes of the current isoplane.

Example 1 *Isometric Drawing*

In this example, you will create the isometric drawing shown in Figure 19-8.

1. Use the **SNAP** command to set the isometric grid and snap. The snap value is 0.5 unit.

   Command: **SNAP**
   Specify snap spacing or [ON/OFF/Aspect/Legacy/Style/Type] <0.5000>: **S**
   Enter snap grid style [Standard/Isometric] <S>: **I**
   Specify vertical spacing <0.5000>: **0.5** *(or press Enter.)*

2. Change the isoplane to the isoplane left by pressing the F5 key. Choose the **Line** tool and draw lines between the points P1, P2, P3, P4, and P1, as shown in Figure 19-9.

Tip

You can increase the size of the crosshairs using the ***Crosshair size*** *slider bar in the* ***Display*** *tab of the* ***Options*** *dialog box.*

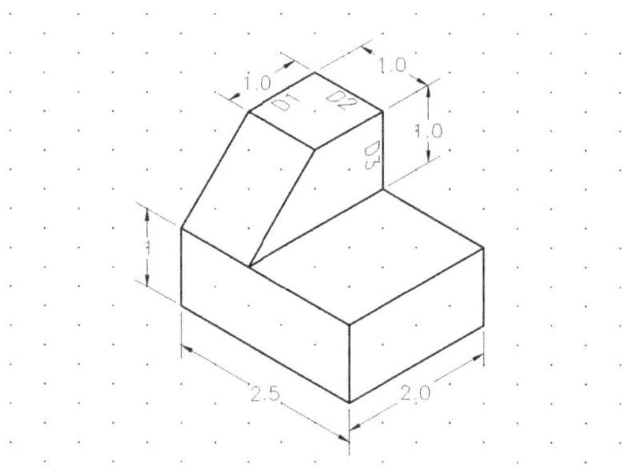

Figure 19-8 *Isometric drawing for Example 1*

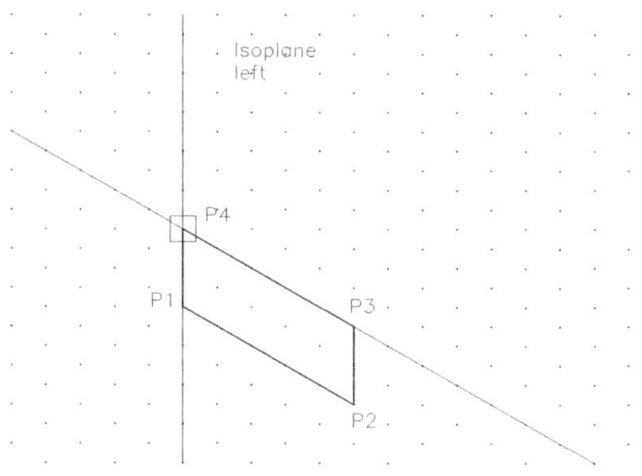

Figure 19-9 *Drawing the bottom left face*

3. Change the isoplane to the isoplane right by pressing the F5 key. Invoke the **Line** tool and draw the lines, as shown in Figure 19-10.

4. Change the isoplane to the isoplane top by pressing the F5 key. Invoke the **Line** tool and draw the lines, refer to Figure 19-11.

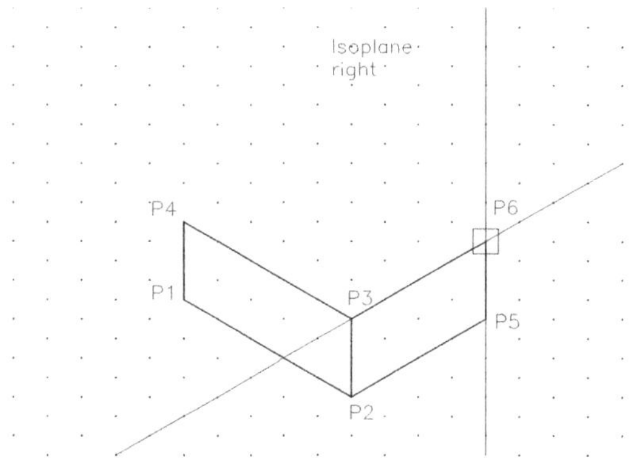

Figure 19-10 *Drawing the bottom right face*

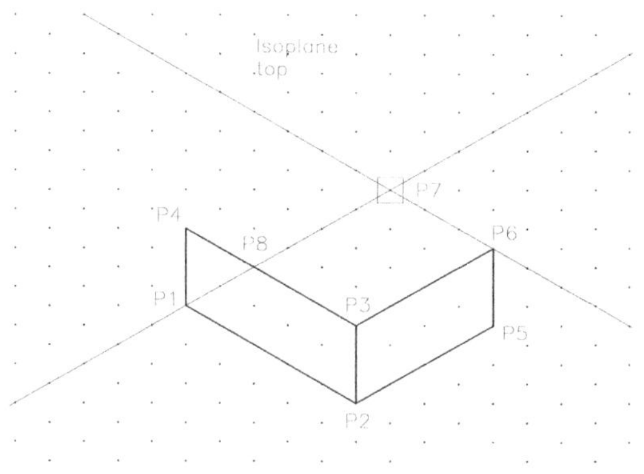

Figure 19-11 *Drawing the top face*

5. Similarly, draw the remaining lines, refer to Figure 19-12.

6. The front left end of the object is tapered at an angle. In isometric drawings, oblique surfaces (surfaces at an angle to the isometric axis) cannot be drawn like other lines. Make sure that the Endpoint Object Snap is on, and then locate the endpoints of the lines that define the oblique surface. Next, draw the lines between those points. To complete the drawing shown in Figure 19-8, draw a line from P10 to P8 and from P11 to P4, refer to Figure 19-13.

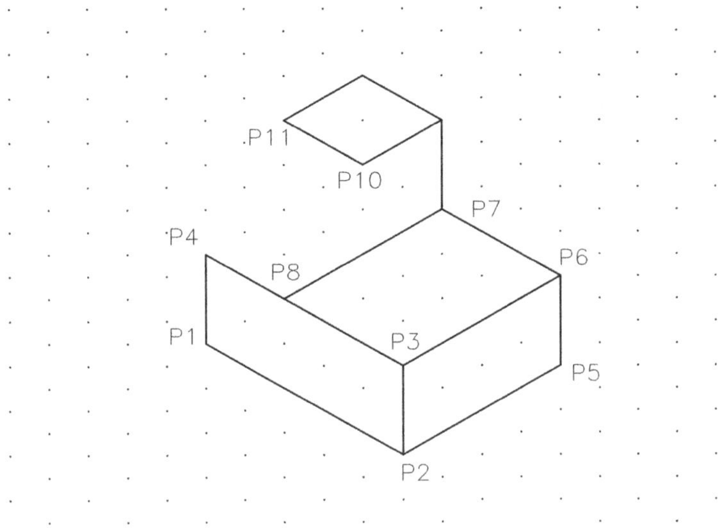

Figure 19-12 *Drawing the remaining lines*

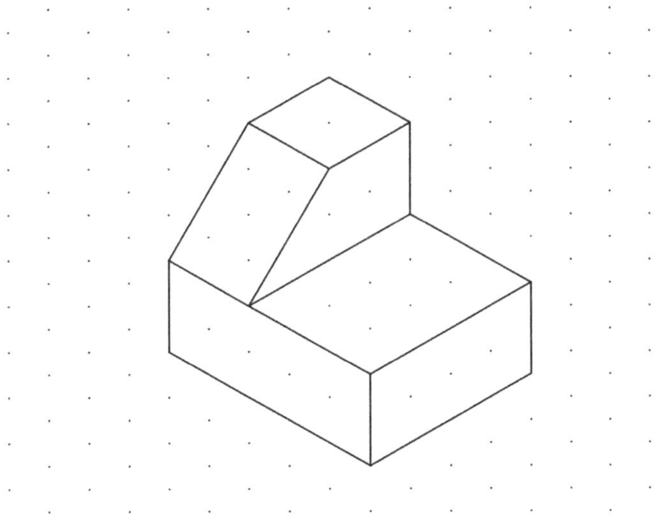

Figure 19-13 *Isometric drawing with the tapered face*

DRAWING ISOMETRIC CIRCLES

The isometric circles are drawn by using the tools available in the **Ellipse** drop-down and then selecting the **Isocircle** option. To draw an isometric circle, choose the **Axis**, **End,** or **Elliptical Arc** tool from the **Ellipse** drop-down. As soon as you select any of these options, the **Isocircle** option will be available in the Command prompt. Select the **Isocircle** option from the Command prompt; you will be prompted to specify the center of isocircle. Specify the center of the isocircle. Next, you will be prompted to specify the radius of the isocircle. Once you specify the radius and press enter, isocircle will be created.

Note that you must have the Isometric Snap on while using the Ellipse tools to display the **Isocircle** option. If the isometric snap is not ON, you cannot draw an isometric circle. Before entering the radius or diameter of the isometric circle, you must make sure that you are in the required isoplane.

For example, to draw a circle in the right isoplane, you must toggle through the isoplanes until the required isoplane (right isoplane) is displayed. You can also set the required isoplane as the current plane before choosing the **Ellipse** tool. The crosshairs and the shape of the isometric circle will automatically change as you toggle through different isoplanes. As you enter the radius or diameter of the circle, AutoCAD draws the isometric circle in the selected plane, refer to Figure 19-14.

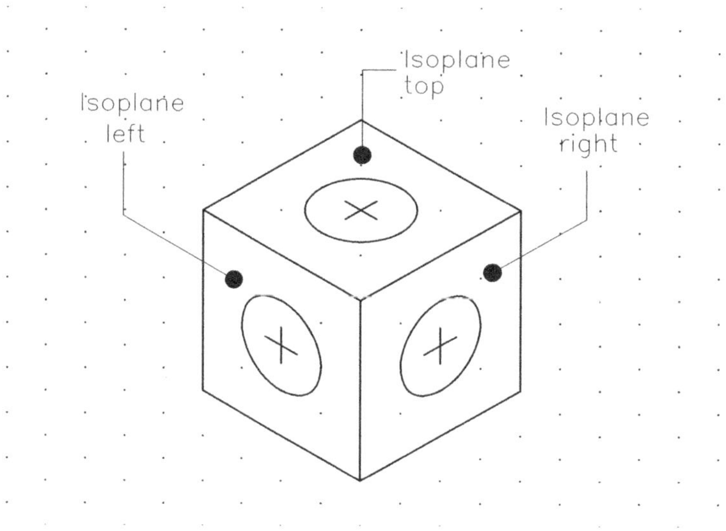

Figure 19-14 *Isometric circles drawn*

The prompt sequence used to draw an isometric circle after choosing the **Axis**, **End** tool from the **Ellipse** drop-down is as follows:

Specify axis endpoint of ellipse or [Arc/Center/Isocircle]: **I**
Specify center of isocircle: *Select a point.*
Specify radius of isocircle or [Diameter]: *Enter circle radius,* Enter.

Creating Fillets in Isometric Drawings

To create fillets in isometric drawings, you first need to create an isometric circle and then trim its unwanted portion. Remember that there is no other method to directly create an isometric fillet.

Dimensioning Isometric Objects

Isometric dimensioning involves two steps: (1) dimensioning the drawing using the standard dimensioning tools, (2) editing the dimensions to change them to oblique dimensions.

Example 2 — *Dimensioning*

The following example illustrates the process involved in dimensioning an isometric drawing. In this example, you will dimension the isometric drawing created in Example 1.

1. Dimension the drawing given in Example 1, as shown in Figure 19-15. You can use the aligned dimension to dimension the drawing. Remember that when you select the points, you must use the **Intersection** or **Endpoint** object snap to snap the endpoints of the object you are dimensioning. AutoCAD automatically leaves a gap between the object line and the extension line, as specified by the **DIMGAP** variable.

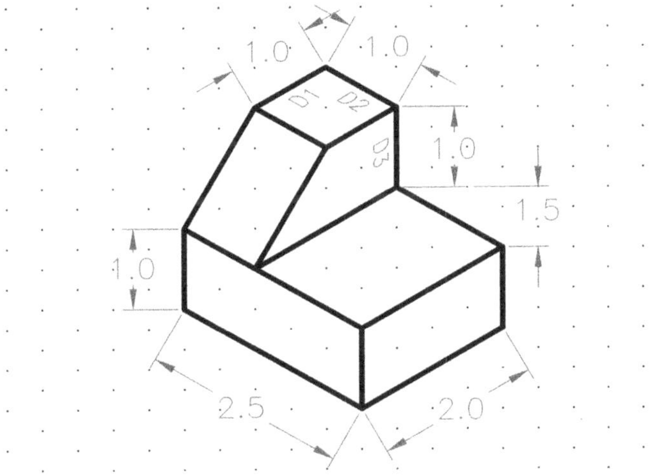

Figure 19-15 *The dimensioned isometric drawing before using the* ***Oblique*** *tool*

2. The next step is to edit the dimensions. You can choose the **Oblique** tool from the **Dimensions** panel of the **Annotate** tab. After selecting the dimension that you want to edit, you are prompted to enter the obliquing angle. The obliquing angle is determined by the angle that the extension line of the isometric dimension makes with the positive *X* axis. The following prompt sequence is displayed when you invoke this option from the **Ribbon**:

   Select objects: *Select the dimension (D1).*
   Select objects: *Press Enter.*
   Enter obliquing angle (Press Enter for none): **150**

For example, the extension line of the dimension labeled D1 makes a 150 degree angle with the positive X axis, refer to Figure 19-16(a), therefore, the oblique angle is 150 degrees. Similarly, the extension lines of the dimension labeled D2 and D3 make a 30 degree angle with the positive

X axis, refer to Figure 19-16 (b) and (c) , therefore, the oblique angle is 30 degrees. After you edit all dimensions, the drawing should appear as shown in Figure 19-17.

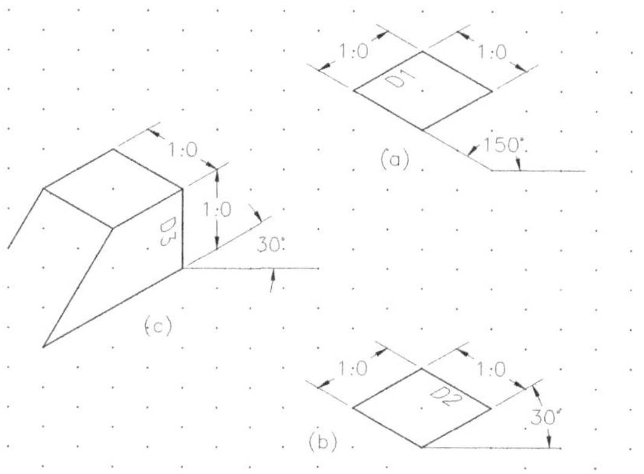

Figure 19-16 Determining the oblique angle

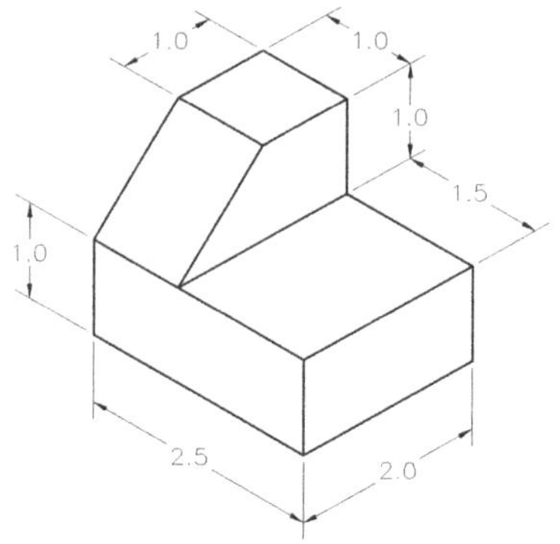

Figure 19-17 Object with isometric dimensions

ISOMETRIC TEXT

You cannot use regular text when placing the text in an isometric drawing because the text in an isometric drawing is obliqued at a positive or negative 30 degree angle. Therefore, you must create two text styles with oblique angles of positive 30 degrees and negative 30 degrees. You can use the **-STYLE** command or the **Text Style** dialog box to create a new text style. Figure 19-18 shows the **Text Style** dialog box with a new text style, **ISOTEXT1** and its corresponding values.

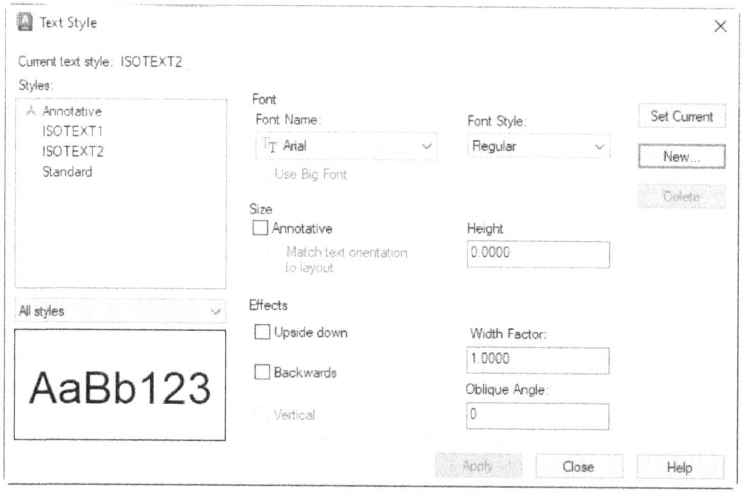

*Figure 19-18 The **Text Style** dialog box*

Similarly, you can create another text style, **ISOTEXT2**, with a negative 30 degrees oblique angle. When you place the text in an isometric drawing, you must also specify the rotation angle for the text. The text style and the text rotation angle depend on the placement of the text in the isometric drawing, as shown in Figure 19-19.

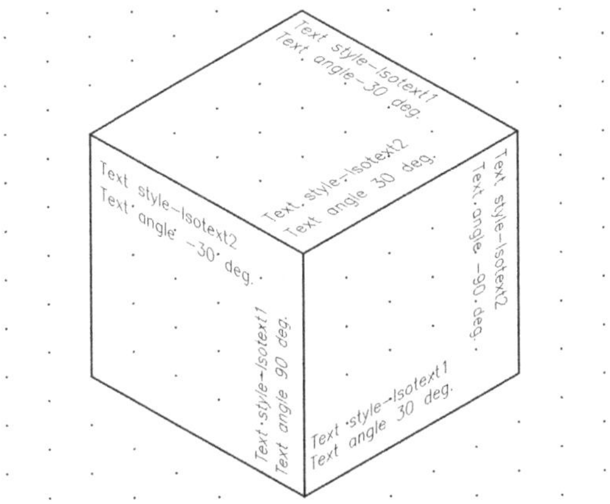

Figure 19-19 *Text style and rotation angle for isometric text*

Self-Evaluation Test

Answer the following questions and then compare them to those given at the end of this chapter:

1. The word "isometric" means __________. The three angles between the three principal axes of an isometric drawing measure __________ degree each.

2. The ratio of isometric length to the actual length in an isometric drawing is approximately __________.

3. The angle between the right isometric horizontal axis and the X axis is __________ degree.

4. Isometric drawings have three principal planes: isoplane right, isoplane top, and __________.

5. To toggle among isoplane right, isoplane left, and isoplane top, you can use __________ key combination or __________ function key.

6. The lines that are not parallel to the isometric axes are called __________.

7. You can only use the aligned dimension option to dimension an isometric drawing. (T/F)

8. The isometric snap must be turned on to display the **Isocircle** option while using the **Ellipse** tool. (T/F)

9. While placing text in an isometric drawing, you need to specify the rotation angles. (T/F)

10. You should avoid showing any hidden lines in isometric drawings. (T/F)

Review Questions

Answer the following questions:

1. Isometric drawings are generally used to help in __________ the shape of an object.
2. An isometric view is obtained by rotating an object by __________ degree around the imaginary vertical axis and then tilting the object forward through a __________ angle.
3. The isometric snap and grid can be turned on/off by selecting the __________ check box.
4. Isometric drawings have three axes: right horizontal axis, vertical axis, and __________.
5. The lines parallel to the isometric axis are called __________.
6. You can use the __________ command to set the isometric grid and snap.
7. Isometric grid lines are displayed at __________ degrees to the horizontal axis.
8. You can also set the isometric grid and snap by using the **Drafting Settings** dialog box, which can be invoked by entering __________ at the Command prompt.
9. Isometric circles are drawn by using the Ellipse tools and then selecting the __________ option.
10. To place text in an isometric drawing, you must create two text styles with oblique angles of __________ degree and __________ degree.
11. You should avoid showing hidden lines in isometric drawings unless they help in understanding its shape. (T/F)
12. Angles do not appear true in isometric drawings. (T/F)
13. You can set the aspect ratio for the isometric grid. (T/F)
14. You can draw an isometric circle without turning the isometric snap on. (T/F)
15. Only the aligned dimensions can be edited to change them to oblique dimensions. (T/F)

EXERCISES 1 through 4

Draw the following isometric drawings, refer to Figures 19-20 through 19-23. The dimensions can be determined by counting the number of grid lines. The distance between the isometric grid lines is assumed to be 0.5 unit. Dimension the drawing, as shown in Figure 19-23.

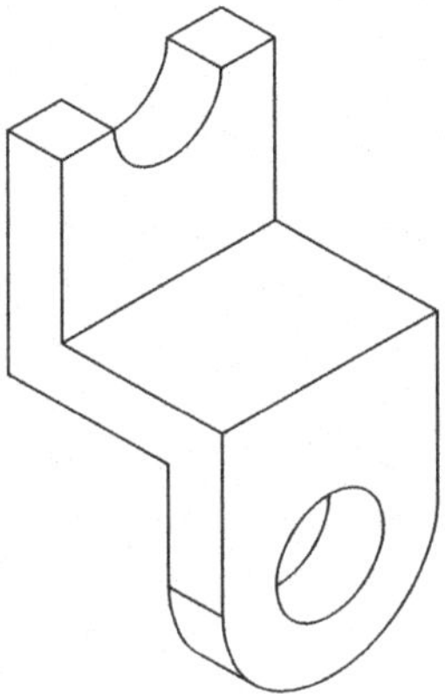

Figure 19-20 *Drawing for Exercise 1*

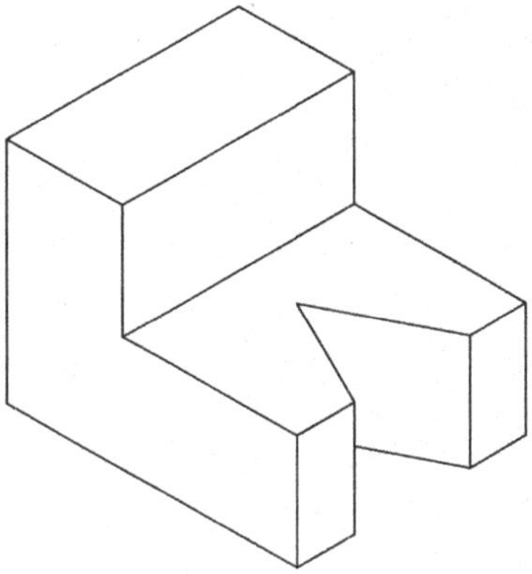

Figure 19-21 *Drawing for Exercise 2*

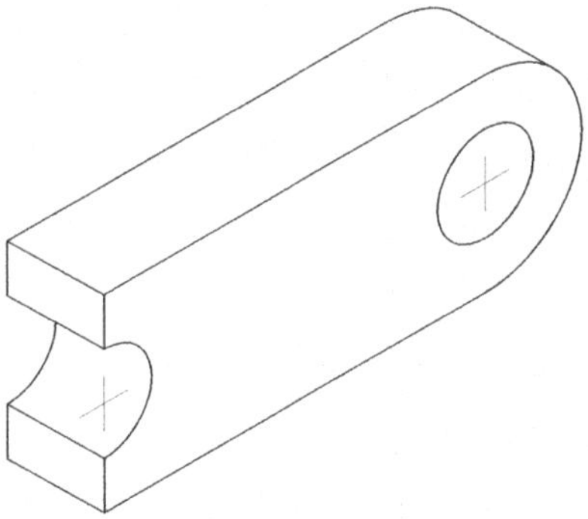

Figure 19-22 *Drawing for Exercise 3*

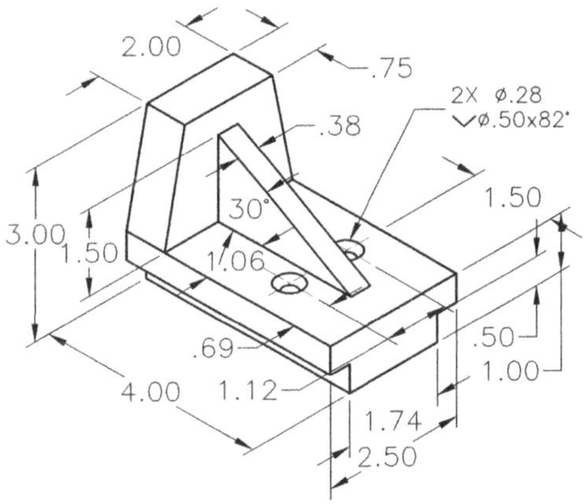

Figure 19-23 *Drawing for Exercise 4*

Answers to Self-Evaluation Test

1. equal measurement, 120, **2.** 9/11, **3.** 30, **4.** isoplane left, **5.** CTRL+E, F5, **6.** non isometric lines, **7.** T, **8.** T, **9.** F, **10.** T

Index

E

F

G

H

I

J

K

L

M

N

O

P

R

S

Other Publications by CADCIM Technologies

The following is the list of some of the publications by CADCIM Technologies. Please visit *www.cadcim.com* for the complete listing.

AutoCAD Textbooks

- AutoCAD 2023: A Problem-Solving Approach, Basic and Intermediate, 29th Edition
- AutoCAD 2022: A Problem-Solving Approach, Basic and Intermediate, 28th Edition
- AutoCAD 2021: A Problem-Solving Approach, Basic and Intermediate, 27th Edition
- AutoCAD 2020: A Problem-Solving Approach, Basic and Intermediate, 26th Edition
- AutoCAD 2019: A Problem-Solving Approach, Basic and Intermediate, 25th Edition
- AutoCAD 2018: A Problem-Solving Approach, Basic and Intermediate, 24th Edition
- Advanced AutoCAD 2021: A Problem-Solving Approach (3D and Advanced), 25th Edition

Autodesk Inventor Textbooks

- Autodesk Inventor Professional 2023 for Designers, 23rd Edition
- Autodesk Inventor Professional 2022 for Designers, 22nd Edition
- Autodesk Inventor Professional 2021 for Designers, 21st Edition

AutoCAD MEP Textbooks

- AutoCAD MEP 2020 for Designers, 5th Edition
- AutoCAD MEP 2018 for Designers, 4th Edition
- AutoCAD MEP 2016 for Designers, 3rd Edition

AutoCAD Plant 3D Textbooks

- AutoCAD Plant 3D 2023 for Designers, 7th Edition
- AutoCAD Plant 3D 2021 for Designers, 6th Edition
- AutoCAD Plant 3D 2020 for Designers, 5th Edition

Autodesk Fusion 360 Textbooks

- Autodesk Fusion 360: A Tutorial Approach, 3rd Edition
- Autodesk Fusion 360: A Tutorial Approach, 2nd Edition

Solid Edge Textbooks

- Solid Edge 2022 for Designers, 19th Edition
- Solid Edge 2021 for Designers, 18th Edition
- Solid Edge 2020 for Designers, 17th Edition

NX Textbooks

- Siemens NX 2022 for Designers,15th Edition
- Siemens NX 2021 for Designers,14th Edition
- Siemens NX 2020 for Designers,13th Edition

NX Mold Textbook

- Mold Design Using NX 11.0: A Tutorial Approach

NX Nastran Textbook
- NX Nastran 9.0 for Designers

SOLIDWORKS Textbooks
- SOLIDWORKS 2022 for Designers, 20th Edition
- SOLIDWORKS 2021 for Designers, 19th Edition
- SOLIDWORKS 2020 for Designers, 18th Edition
- Learning SOLIDWORKS 2019: A Project Based Approach

SOLIDWORKS Simulation Textbooks
- SOLIDWORKS Simulation 2018: A Tutorial Approach
- SOLIDWORKS Simulation 2016: A Tutorial Approach

CATIA Textbooks
- CATIA V5-6R2021 for Designers, 19th Edition
- CATIA V5-6R2020 for Designers, 18th Edition
- CATIA V5-6R2019 for Designers, 17th Edition

Creo Parametric Textbooks
- Creo Parametric 8.0 for Designers, 8th Edition
- Creo Parametric 7.0 for Designers, 7th Edition

ANSYS Textbooks
- ANSYS Workbench 2022 R1: A Tutorial Approach, 5th Edition
- ANSYS Workbench 2021 R2: A Tutorial Approach, 4th Edition

Creo Direct Textbook
- Creo Direct 2.0 and Beyond for Designers

Autodesk Alias Textbooks
- Learning Autodesk Alias Design 2016, 5th Edition
- Learning Autodesk Alias Design 2015, 4th Edition

AutoCAD LT Textbooks
- AutoCAD LT 2020 for Designers, 13th Edition
- AutoCAD LT 2017 for Designers, 12th Edition

EdgeCAM Textbooks
- EdgeCAM 11.0 for Manufacturers
- EdgeCAM 10.0 for Manufacturers

Autodesk Revit MEP Textbooks
- Exploring Autodesk Revit 2022 for MEP, 8th Edition
- Exploring Autodesk Revit 2021 for MEP, 7th Edition
- Exploring Autodesk Revit 2019 for MEP, 6th Edition

AutoCAD Civil 3D Textbooks
- Exploring AutoCAD Civil 3D 2023, 12th Edition
- Exploring AutoCAD Civil 3D 2022, 11th Edition
- Exploring AutoCAD Civil 3D 2020, 10th Edition

AutoCAD Map 3D Textbooks
- Exploring AutoCAD Map 3D 2022, 9th Edition
- Exploring AutoCAD Map 3D 2018, 8th Edition
- Exploring AutoCAD Map 3D 2017, 7th Edition

RISA-3D Textbook
- Exploring RISA-3D 14.0

Autodesk Navisworks Textbooks
- Exploring Autodesk Navisworks 2022, 9th Edition
- Exploring Autodesk Navisworks 2021, 8th Edition
- Exploring Autodesk Navisworks 2020, 7th Edition

AutoCAD Raster Design Textbooks
- Exploring AutoCAD Raster Design 2017
- Exploring AutoCAD Raster Design 2016

Bentley STAAD.Pro Textbooks
- Exploring Bentley STAAD.Pro CONNECT Edition, 5th Edition
- Exploring Bentley STAAD.Pro CONNECT Edition, 4th Edition
- Exploring Bentley STAAD.Pro (CONNECT) Edition

Autodesk 3ds Max Design Textbooks
- Autodesk 3ds Max Design 2015: A Tutorial Approach
- Autodesk 3ds Max Design 2014: A Tutorial Approach

Autodesk 3ds Max Textbooks
- Autodesk 3ds Max 2022 for Beginners: A Tutorial Approach, 22nd Edition
- Autodesk 3ds Max 2021: A Comprehensive Guide, 21st Edition
- Autodesk 3ds Max 2020: A Comprehensive Guide, 20th Edition

Autodesk Maya Textbooks
- Autodesk Maya 2023: A Comprehensive Guide, 14th Edition
- Autodesk Maya 2022: A Comprehensive Guide, 13th Edition
- Autodesk Maya 2020: A Comprehensive Guide, 12th Edition

Pixologic ZBrush Textbooks
- Pixologic ZBrush 2022: A Comprehensive Guide, 8th Edition
- Pixologic ZBrush 2021: A Comprehensive Guide, 7th Edition
- Pixologic ZBrush 2020: A Comprehensive Guide, 6th Edition

Fusion Textbooks
- Blackmagic Design Fusion 7 Studio: A Tutorial Approach, 3rd Edition
- The eyeon Fusion 6.3: A Tutorial Approach

Flash Textbooks
- Adobe Flash Professional CC 2015: A Tutorial Approach, 3rd Edition
- Adobe Flash Professional CC: A Tutorial Approach

Computer Programming Textbooks
- Introducing PHP 7/MySQL
- Introduction to C^{++} programming, 2nd Edition
- Learning Oracle 12c - A PL/SQL Approach
- Learning ASP.NET AJAX
- Introduction to Java Programming, 2nd Edition
- Learning Visual Basic.NET 2008

MAXON CINEMA 4D Textbooks
- MAXON CINEMA 4D S24 Studio: A Tutorial Approach, 8th Edition
- MAXON CINEMA 4D R20 Studio: A Tutorial Approach, 7th Edition
- MAXON CINEMA 4D R19 Studio: A Tutorial Approach, 6th Edition

Oracle Primavera Textbooks
- Exploring Oracle Primavera P6 Professional 18, 3rd Edition
- Exploring Oracle Primavera P6 v8.4

AutoCAD Textbooks Authored by Prof. Sham Tickoo and Published by Autodesk Press
- AutoCAD: A Problem-Solving Approach: 2013 and Beyond
- AutoCAD 2012: A Problem-Solving Approach
- AutoCAD 2011: A Problem-Solving Approach
- AutoCAD 2010: A Problem-Solving Approach
- Customizing AutoCAD 2010

Coming Soon from CADCIM Technologies
- Flow Simulation Using SOLIDWORKS 2021

Made in the USA
Monee, IL
22 February 2023

27927939R00437